THE POLITICAL WRITINGS

THE POLITICAL WRITINGS

Volume I. The Revolutions of 1848
Volume II. Surveys from Exile
Volume III. The First International

KARL MARX

Foreword by Tariq Ali
Introductions by David Fernbach

PUBLISHED IN ASSOCIATION WITH

new left *review*

VERSO
London • New York

Manifesto of the Communist Party first published in English 1850
This translation of the above first published 1888
This edition published by Verso 2019
Selection and notes © New Left Review 1974, 2019
Introductions © David Fernbach 1973, 2019
Foreword © Tariq Ali 2010, 2019

Translations: 'The Demands of the Communist Party in Germany' and the 'Minutes of the Central Committee Meeting of 15 September 1850' © Joris de Bres 1973, 2019; 'Articles from the *Neue Rheinische Zeitung*', *The Eighteenth Brumaire of Louis Bonaparte* © Ben Fowkes 1973, 2019; 'Addresses of the Central Committee to the Communist League' (March and June 1850), 'Articles on the North American Civil War', *The Class Struggles in France*, the German-language articles on Britain, 'Reviews from the *Neue Rheinische Zeitung Revue*', 'Speeches on Poland (29 November 1847)' © Paul Jackson 1973, 2019; 'Speeches on Poland (22 February 1848)' © Rosemary Sheed 1973, 2019

'Critique of the Gotha Programme' © Joris de Bres 1974, 2019; 'Conspectus of Bakunin's Statism and Anarchy', 'Introduction to the Programme of the French Workers' Party', and 'Letter to the Brunswick Committee of the SDAP' © David Fernbach 1974, 2019; 'Circular Letter to Bebel, Liebknecht, Bracke et al.', 'For Poland', the letters on Germany and on Ireland, 'The Prussian Military Question', and 'Speech on the Hague Congress' © Paul Jackson 1974, 2019; 'Political Indifferentism' © Geoffrey Nowell-Smith 1970, 2019 (reprinted here from the *Bulletin of the Society for the Study of Labour History*, no. 20, spring 1970); 'The Alleged Splits in the International' and 'The General Council to the Federal Council of French Switzerland' © Rosemary Sheed 1974, 2019

3 5 7 9 10 8 6 4 2

Verso
UK: 6 Meard Street, London W1F 0EG
US: 20 Jay Street, Suite 1010, Brooklyn, NY 11201
versobooks.com

Verso is the imprint of New Left Books

ISBN-13: 978-1-78873-686-2
ISBN-13: 978-1-78873-687-9 (UK EBK)
ISBN-13: 978-1-78873-688-6 (US EBK)

British Library Cataloguing in Publication Data
A catalogue record for this book is available from the British Library

Library of Congress Cataloging-in-Publication Data
A catalog record for this book is available from the Library of Congress

Typeset in Monotype Times by Hewer Text UK Ltd, Edinburgh
Printed and bound by CPI Group (UK) Ltd, Croydon, CR0 4YY

Contents

References to Marx and Engels's works in the most frequently quoted editions have been abbreviated as follows:

MECW 1–50   Marx and Engels, *Collected Works*, Lawrence & Wishart, 1975–2005.

MEW 1–39   *Marx-Engels-Werke*, Dietz Verlag, Berlin, 1956–64.

IWMA I–V   International Working Men's Association, *Documents of the First International*, Lawrence & Wishart, 1964–6.

Foreword

The recession caused by the capitalist crisis of 2008 triggered a revival of interest in Marx's *Capital* and his other writings on the specific dynamics of the capitalist mode of production. That this system was the central subject of his work is indisputable, but he never thought of the economy in isolation. Capitalism was, for him and Engels, above all a socio-economic or social formation. 'Politics', as one of Marx's more gifted followers from a subsequent generation wrote, 'is concentrated economics'. What was true, if only partially visible during the first few decades of the twentieth century, can now be seen in full-frontal view. In the traditional capitalist states, democracy is being hollowed out by a process – 'globalization' – that systematically subordinates politics to economics, reducing the basic differences between centre-left and centre-right so that there is virtually no difference between existing mainstream political parties. For all practical purposes, the West is in the grip of a political system that has both the incentive and the means to become increasingly despotic. Whether it does so will depend on the degree and nature of the opposition that it encounters from below.

It is this relegation of politics and its Siamese twins, history and philosophy, which makes the republication of Marx's political and historical writings all the more necessary at this time. We are living in a period of historical transition that began with the overwhelming triumph of capitalism in the last decade of the preceding century. As a result Marx's interventionist essays have suffered in recent years, but not, as is sometimes stated on the right, because their premises have been exploded. Marx's political writings have been a casualty of the downgrading and dumbing-down of politics, sociology and history as scholarly disciplines on both a secondary and tertiary level, especially, but not exclusively in English-speaking cultures.

Many of the new radicals of the present generation find it sexy to read *Capital* while ignoring the politics underlying the project. This would have angered Marx, who regarded his work as a unity, which is how it was read by some of his most astute opponents a century later. Joseph Schumpeter, to take one example, wrote in his classic work *Capitalism, Socialism and Democracy* that:

> We have seen how in the Marxian argument sociology and economics pervade each other. In intent and to some degree also in actual practice, they are one. All the major concepts and propositions are hence both economic and sociological and carry the same meaning on both planes.

In other words, it is difficult to grasp the essence of *Capital* without understanding Marx's revolutionary approach to politics and the understanding of history. How could it be otherwise? He belonged to a generation that came of age in the historical period that followed the French Revolution. The cyclical pattern of victory–defeat–restoration–new revolutions–new defeats, and so on, taught him that every historical epoch is a period of transition, of ebb and flow, of crash and renewal, of annihilation and resurgence. The socialism he favoured was based on a society of abundance; its political institutions a reflection of radical, popular sovereignty on every level; its culture transcending the confines of a single nation and creating a world-view. Most importantly, Marx visualized a state that, far from becoming huge, unwieldy and authoritarian, would be pushed to near oblivion. The contrast between this and what became the reality of 'actually existing socialisms' needs little commentary.

Cosmopolitan by nature, revolutions have no respect for borders and can never remain the exclusive property of the country in which they first occurred. This fact also shapes the counterrevolution. Marx observed that this was certainly the case for Europe and, possibly, North America, where the rise of capitalism, he thought, would produce midwives impatient to drag out new children from the womb of the system. As David Fernbach points out in his introductory text, it didn't quite turn out like that; the 'the rock of Soviet civilization' proved to be hollow. Still, the universality of the revolution, or its originality, was never in doubt. It leapt over the heartlands of capital and moved eastwards: first Russia, then China, later Vietnam and, last of all, the American hemisphere. Ignoring the mainland, it alighted on a small Caribbean island, which, at time of writing, remains the only space where capitalism has not yet been permitted to return.

The collapse of 'communism' resulted in passivity, a loss of hope and a new common sense of the age, according to which no alternatives to the new system were possible. Even the agency that

Marx had hoped would lead to revolutionary change in the West had been dismantled. Fordism lay dead, its founding factory in Detroit covered in cobwebs. Production moved east and China is today the workshop of the world, whose impact it is still far too early to predict.

In times like these, when reaction reigned supreme, Marx and Engels did not attempt to mask reality with false optimism. They had written the *Manifesto* while insurrections and civil war had erupted throughout continental Europe, but the 'spectre of communism' was defeated everywhere. The two authors now argued that the rise of a new revolutionary wave was impossible in the short to medium term and that communists should use the period of defeat to study, educate and work hard to develop theories that explained the mechanics of the world to future generations.

Engels retreated to Manchester to work for the family firm; Marx retired to the British Library to study economics. Their erstwhile comrades in the Communist League resorted to character assassination, denounced Marx and Engels as traitors and referred to them as 'counter-revolutionaries', 'hostile to the proletariat' and isolated 'literati'. Never one to ignore an insult, Marx responded in kind just as he had done earlier to Proudhon's intemperate assaults on Babeuf and his socialists. Like some latter-day unconscious mimics, Proudhon too believed that the world could be changed without taking power, a notion that won him the support of many a charlatan. The violent anti-communist language he used in *System of Economic Contradictions* found few defenders even in his own ranks. Marx responded that 'he (Proudhon) bursts into violent explosions of rage, vociferation and righteous wrath (*irae hominis probi*), foams at the mouth, curses, denounces, cries shame and murder, beats his breast and boasts before man and God that he is not defiled by socialist infamies.' Whatever else it was, the cut and thrust of political debate on the left was never a polite conversation, then or later. Nor were the results of this style of debate always positive.

Some of the writing contained in these volumes is the product of financial necessity. Compelled by poverty and the misery of everyday life in Soho to write regularly for the New York *Tribune*, Marx often cut corners and pronounced on subjects of which he could possess only limited information. This did not apply to his essays on Europe. The brilliant imagery contained in his texts on France remains striking to this day, and *The Eighteenth Brumaire of Louis Bonaparte* still inspires admiration from many non-Marxist writers. Unsurprisingly, he got things wrong, which is why his transformation into a secular icon after 1917 did Marx few favours. It was as if everything he wrote was scripture; memories of communist militants in different parts of the world repeating his phrases parrot-like still make one wince.

The idea of a new Marx Library, which originated on the Editorial Committee of *New Left Review* in 1968, was partly designed to challenge this doctrinal approach. It was a year before the magazine launched New Left Books (NLB), which was, in any case, intended to be a quality hardback publisher producing a limited number of books each year. The NLR was of the opinion that given the political and intellectual turbulence then sweeping the globe, a carefully selected and edited Marx Library with new translations from the German was best suited to a mass paperback imprint. Penguin Books and one of its more gifted publishers, Neil Middleton, appeared to be the perfect match at the time, and so it proved. The general editor of the series was Quintin Hoare, and his choices were happily vindicated by the sales figures. The fact that Penguin keeps most of the Library in print is a unique tribute in these times when commerce dominates all. Ernest Mandel introduced the three volumes of Marx's *Capital*, Lucio Colletti the *Early Writings*, and the *Grundrisse* was translated (for the first time in English) and introduced by the American scholar Martin Nicolaus. The political writings were edited and introduced by David Fernbach, who has helped to update this reissue.

The intellectual and commercial success of New Left Books led to the launch of its paperback imprint, Verso, in 1970. It is therefore only appropriate that as Verso marks its fortieth anniversary (and *New Left Review* its fiftieth), the political writings of the thinker who inspired the founders of both are made available once again. There is, of course, another reason. As the century moves forward it is likely that history will have a few pleasant surprises in store for Europe, Asia and Africa. Few predicted the turn of events in South America, where a combination of mass struggles produced social movements and a new-style social democracy that challenged the neo-liberal form of capitalism and reasserted the social responsibilities of the state. Future generations might thus be grateful to have these political texts available once again.

TARIQ ALI
MAY 2010

Volume I
The Revolutions of 1848

Introduction to Volume I

From Philosophy to Politics

Karl Marx was born in Trier, in the Prussian Rhineland, on 5 May 1818. His parents were of Jewish origin, but were baptized into the Prussian state church while Marx was still a small child. The ideology of the French Enlightenment had won a strong base in the Rhineland, which had been annexed to France from 1798 to 1815, and from his father and schoolteachers Marx acquired a liberal and humanist education.

The Germany in which Marx grew up was still a backward country by comparison with its western neighbours. It was overwhelmingly agricultural; urban production was still dominated by the guild system, and modern industry was making its first inroads only in the northern Rhineland. The German cities had grown little, if at all, since the sixteenth century, and the total urban population of Germany was only half as much again as the population of Paris. This economic backwardness was reflected in German political structures. Germany had not experienced any form of bourgeois revolution and was still divided between thirty-nine states, mainly absolutist, in a confederation underwritten by the Holy Alliance of Prussia, Austria and Russia.

However backward, German history was not static. The French Revolution had inspired a strong democratic sentiment among the artisans and intelligentsia in the German cities. This had not been entirely eradicated by the experience of Napoleonic domination and was still available to inspire a popular revolution. The 'War of Liberation' of 1813, although fought under Prussian leadership, aroused enthusiasm for German unification, which merged with the democratic current and led to the formation of secret societies known as the *Burschenschaften* (students' associations). Although confined to the universities, their demonstrations, particularly at the Wartburg festival of 1817, provided a focus for the national-democratic movement. In 1819 the repressive measures of the Karlsbad decrees, dictated by the Holy Alliance, were introduced to suppress this movement, which flared up again after the French July revolution of 1830 and received a new dose of repression.

Industrial development, both in textiles and heavy industry, got seriously under way in the 1830s and took advantage from the first of the technological advances made in England over the past sixty years. Railway building followed rapidly in the 1840s. The North German *Zollverein* (customs union) had been set up under Prussian auspices in 1834 to pre-empt bourgeois demands for national unification, but as capitalist development advanced, liberal pressure for a constitution built up in Prussia, particularly in the Rhineland, intensifying after the accession of Frederick William IV in 1840. The German population increased by 50 per cent between 1816 and 1846, despite a steady emigration to America, and this aggravated the pressure on the land, particularly in the eastern provinces of Prussia. The indebtedness of the peasantry in south and west Germany also intensified. In the 1840s an agrarian and trade depression began to cause rural and urban unrest. Economic, political and ideological factors were thus being formed which would fuse in the revolutionary conjuncture of 1848.

A paradoxical effect of German backwardness marked intellectual life, one sphere in which Germany was unquestionably advanced. From the time of the French Revolution onwards, German philosophy underwent a peculiar 'overdevelopment', producing the powerful idealist systems of Kant, Fichte, Schelling and Hegel. In the context of their national historical backwardness, German intellectuals were forced, as Marx put it, to 'think what others had done',[1] and this forced abstraction of their thought made the German philosophy of this period unequalled in the scope of its syntheses, culminating in Hegel's systematic integration of the natural sciences, logic and social theory.

In 1836 Marx began his university career at Bonn, but transferred the next year to Berlin. He had originally intended to read law, but his theoretical inclination soon drew him towards philosophy. In 1831 Hegel had died in office as Professor of Philosophy at Berlin, but by the middle of the decade his legacy was already in dispute, as the 'Left' or Young Hegelians fired their first shot at orthodoxy with the publication of David Strauss's *Life of Jesus*.[2]

1. Karl Marx, 'A Contribution to the Critique of Hegel's Philosophy of Right. Introduction', in Karl Marx, *Early Writings*, Harmondsworth, 1975.

2. English translation by Marian Evans (George Eliot) [1854], Bristol, 1998.

In the peculiar German circumstances of economic and political backwardness coupled with theoretical overdevelopment, the Hegelian philosophy, with its ambiguous political implications and internal tension between system and method, was for the next decade to provide a terrain for political battles that could not yet be fought out in the arena of open class struggle.

The 'Right' – i.e. orthodox – Hegelians fought for conservatism by defending Hegel's system, which under the dictum that 'the real is the rational' provided a legitimation for everything that existed, in particular the Christian religion and the Prussian monarchy. The 'Left' Hegelians used Hegel's dialectical method to criticize existing institutions as non-rational and therefore 'non-real', i.e. having outlived their historical moment and due to be changed. They thus re-fought, though in more sophisticated terms, the battles against religion and absolutism that the French Enlightenment had fought in the previous century. Rather than deny the truth of religion on its own ground, the Young Hegelians sought to explain religious dogma in terms of a different level of reality, which in the first instance was that of ethics. In 1841, Ludwig Feuerbach achieved what appeared to the Young Hegelians as a decisive 'abolition' of religion with his book *The Essence of Christianity*,[3] in which he transformed Hegel's idealism into a radical humanism by substituting for the abstract subject of Hegel's *Philosophy of Mind* the human species, and explaining religion as man's alienation of his own powers or essence and his subsequent domination by his own creations. In Prussia and the other absolutist states of Germany, religion was the natural starting point of rationalist criticism, as the state and the traditional social order still founded their legitimacy on a religious basis. Marx himself eagerly plunged into religious criticism, and his doctoral thesis, completed in 1841, was conceived as an anti-religious work.[4]

Marx approached politics under the aegis of his Young Hegelian colleague Bruno Bauer, who made the transition from religious to explicitly political criticism with his book *The Christian State*. In the summer of 1841 Marx joined Bauer in Bonn and worked with him for a while on an abortive plan for a journal, hoping also to obtain a place beside Bauer at the university. A few months later, however,

3. English translation by George Eliot [1853], Mineola, NY, 2008.
4. 'Difference between the Democritean and Epicurian Philosophy of Nature', in *MECW* 1, pp. 25–108.

Bauer's subversive activities led to his dismissal from Bonn, an event which simultaneously ditched Marx's own hopes of an academic career.

Marx's first political article was published in February 1842 in the Young Hegelian journal *Anekdota*. Commenting on the Prussian censorship, Marx exposed the inherent contradictions of the censorship system, and argued a liberal and rationalist defence of a free press and public opinion.[5]

During the course of 1842 Marx became increasingly involved with the recently founded *Rheinische Zeitung* (*Rhenish Gazette*), and was eventually appointed its editor. The *Rheinische Zeitung*, published in Cologne, represented a short-lived alliance between the Young Hegelian philosophers, already verging on radicalism, and the liberal Rhineland bourgeoisie who were restless with the failure of the new king to grant the long promised constitution. In the *Rheinische Zeitung* Marx dealt with current political questions within the limits of the liberal opposition, for he still believed possible and necessary the 'laborious task of winning freedom step by step'.[6] It was while working on the *Rheinische Zeitung* that Marx first came into contact with French socialist and communist ideas, which became current in Germany in 1842 with the propaganda of Moses Hess[7] and the publication of Lorenz von Stein's book *The Socialism and Communism of Contemporary France*. But Marx's attitude to French communism was still extremely cautious. When Hess came under attack for articles he had written in the *Rheinische Zeitung*, Marx wrote editorially, 'The *Rheinische Zeitung* ... cannot even concede theoretical reality to communistic ideas in their present form, and can even less wish to consider possible their practical realization.' However, he conceded that 'writings such as those by Leroux, Considérant, and above all Proudhon's penetrating work, can be criticized only after long and deep study'.[8]

5. 'Comments on the Latest Prussian Censorship Instruction', in *MECW* 1, pp. 109–31.

6. Marx to Oppenheim, 25 August 1842, in *MECW* 1, p. 392.

7. Moses Hess was at this time predominantly influenced by Fourier, the French utopian socialist, and was soon to be a founder of German 'true socialism'. He was later a member of the Communist League, although he never accepted Marx and Engels's scientific communism.

8. *MECW* 1, p. 220. Pierre Leroux was a Saint-Simonian, and Victor Considérant a Fourierist. On Saint-Simon, Fourier and Proudhon, see below, pp. 22–3.

It was more immediately important for Marx's development that as editor of the *Rheinische Zeitung* he was confronted practically with the 'social question'. Previously Marx had been concerned exclusively with religion and politics, in which fields he had been able to ascribe conflicts between men, in the idealist fashion, simply to the truth or falsity of their ideas. Now Marx came up against conflicts of material interest for the first time, in connection with the Rhineland Diet's[9] legislative encroachment on common timber rights and the destitution of the Mosel grape growers caused by the Zollverein. Marx criticized the Rhineland Diet for its class-biased legislation, but still believed that political reason could resolve such conflicts, the conditions for this being a free press and public debate.[10] As Marx later acknowledged, however, it was the problems presented by these issues that first led him away from the mainstream of Young Hegelian philosophical criticism and towards the theory of historical materialism.[11]

*

The suppression of the *Rheinische Zeitung* in March 1843 marked the end of the hope that Prussia could progress through constitutional monarchy to democratic freedom. The Young Hegelians now branched in different directions. Some, like Bruno and Edgar Bauer and Max Stirner, went on to develop increasingly radical theoretical positions, but kept safely away from all practical activity; others, particularly Arnold Ruge,[12] Moses Hess, Karl Marx and Frederick Engels, began to seek the means of turning the 'arm of criticism' into the 'criticism of arms'.[13] To that end Ruge and Marx left Germany in October 1843 for Paris, where

9. The Rhineland, as one of the eight provinces of the Prussian monarchy, had its own parliament. These Diets were, however, dominated by the aristocracy and had no more than advisory powers.

10. See 'Justification of the Correspondent from the Mosel', in *MECW* 1, pp. 332–58.

11. See Marx's brief and only account of his intellectual development in the 'Preface (to *A Contribution to the Critique of Political Economy*)', *Early Writings*, pp. 424–8.

12. Arnold Ruge, however, did not go with Marx as far as communism. In 1848 he sat with the Radical–Democratic party in the Frankfurt Assembly and later became a National Liberal.

13. 'A Contribution to the Critique of Hegel's Philosophy of Right. Introduction', in *Early Writings*, pp. 243–58.

Hess was already living, and where they planned to produce a journal, the *Deutsche-Französische Jahrbücher* (*Franco-German Yearbooks*). The move to Paris was not only necessitated by the Prussian censorship. As the title of their journal implied, Marx and his colleagues hoped to combine their philosophic results with the achievements of French political theory, and thus to arrive at the guiding principles of the radical revolution that they now believed necessary in Germany.

During the course of 1843 Marx had become an ardent follower of Feuerbach, who had developed his full position in that year with the publication of his *Provisional Theses for the Reform of Philosophy*. Feuerbach had already taught that the religious account of God as subject and Man as predicate had only to be inverted in order to reveal the true relationship. In the *Provisional Theses* he claimed that this 'transformative method' was the means to criticize all speculative philosophy (such as German idealism), since this was nothing more than religion in a secular guise. Feuerbach's key critical concept was that of *Gattungswesen*, or species-being, which he used to denote the sum of humanity's collective powers, and it is this that Marx sought to apply, first to the political state, then to the capitalist economy, in two major texts written in 1843 and 1844.

Marx wrote his *Critique of Hegel's Doctrine of the State* in the summer of 1843.[14] He had just married Jenny von Westphalen, to whom he had been engaged for seven years, and was shortly to move with her to Paris. In this text Marx attacked Hegel's presentation of the relation between the state and civil society (i.e. economic life) as a typical case of speculative philosophy. For Hegel, civil society was the sphere of material needs, while the state was the higher sphere of reason in which conflicts of material interest were resolved. Marx based himself on Feuerbach's humanism to assert that civil society, not the state, was the sphere of man's real life as a 'species-being', and that the 'reason' that governed the state presented man's real relations in an inverted form. Far from the state bureaucracy rationally mediating conflicts of material interest, it weighed on man's real existence as an oppressive force.

In this critique Marx already saw the resolution of the antagonism between state and civil society as requiring the dissolution of the

14. *Early Writings*, pp. 57–198.

former into the latter, a position he was later to integrate into his scientific communism. But at this stage in his development Marx had as yet only a vague conception of class antagonisms. He believed that universal suffrage would spell the dissolution of the oppressive state and the liberation of man's species-life, and did not yet recognize the abolition of private property – i.e. communism – as the essential condition of this liberation.

Feuerbach's doctrine of the species-being, however, easily led in the direction of communism, and Marx was rapidly to take this further step. Marx's conversion to communism came soon after his move to Paris, where he studied at first hand the French socialist and communist tendencies and engaged in discussion with the militants of the French workers' movement. In the class-conscious workers of Paris Marx found the solution to the problems he had analysed in the *Critique of Hegel's Doctrine of the State*, and his first mention of the proletariat is in the Introduction published in the *Deutsche-Französische Jahrbücher* to a projected edition of that manuscript. Here Marx argues that the only class that can make a radical revolution in Germany (i.e. one that would realize the goals of Feuerbach's humanist philosophy) is

a class with *radical chains*, a class in civil society which is not a class of civil society . . . a class which has a universal character because of its universal suffering and which lays claim to no *particular right* because the wrong it suffers it is not a *particular wrong* but *wrong in general* . . . This dissolution of society as a particular class is the proletariat.[15]

With his stay in Paris in 1843–4, Marx outgrew his early formation in German philosophy. He not only continued his study of French political theory, intending at one point to write a history of the French revolutionary Convention, but also, under the stimulus of his contacts with the proletarian movement, began to read the English economists who analysed the 'anatomy' of bourgeois society. Yet in the first text in which Marx dealt with the problems of economic theory and communism – the *Economic and Philosophical Manuscripts* of 1844 – he still attempted, for the first and last time, to integrate this new subject matter into the framework of Feuerbachian humanism.

In the 1844 Manuscripts Marx applied Feuerbach's 'transformative

15. 'A Contribution to the Critique of Hegel's Philosophy of Right. Introduction', in *Early Writings*, p. 256.

method' to political economy, criticizing the bourgeois economic system and its apologists for inverting the true relations of labour and capital. Instead of capital being the subject of the economic process and labour its predicate, in reality it is human labour, the natural activity of man's species-being, that is estranged or alienated and turned into the capital which oppresses the labourer. Communism is defined in these terms as the reappropriation of man's estranged productive powers, and thus as the form of society conforming to man's species-being.

These Manuscripts have often been considered the sign of Marx's arrival at the basic themes of his mature theory. It is certainly true that the notion of capital as 'estranged labour' presages Marx's later analysis of surplus-value, and that Marx for the first time here explicitly avows communism as the solution to social antagonisms. However the decisive break in Marx's theoretical development was still ahead. In the 1844 Manuscripts Marx did not take issue with the descriptive content of bourgeois economic theory, but criticized as inhuman the reality that it described and the ideologists who accepted and justified this reality. In *Capital*, however, Marx no longer criticized capitalist society simply on the basis of external humanistic criteria, but criticized bourgeois economic theory for its inadequate scientific comprehension of the capitalist economy and explained how the reality of the capitalist economy contains inherent contradictions that impel it into crisis. And although in 1844 Marx already accepted a communist solution to the antagonisms of capitalist society, he in fact criticized the communist tendencies of the day, represented by Blanqui and Cabet, on the grounds that their politics were based on the greed and envy that capitalism itself engendered, rather than transcending this 'selfish' motivation. Not long after, Marx was to accept that this 'selfish' class struggle was the motive force of history and would lead to communism, and criticize Cabet and Blanqui for quite different reasons.

The 1844 Manuscripts certainly foreshadow Marx's future concerns and contain important insights that Marx was to integrate into his theory of historical materialism. Yet rather than heralding the birth of the new theory, they represent in fact Marx's last staging-post within the realm of 'German ideology', as he was soon to call it, a desperate but untenable attempt to integrate the realities of political economy and communism into the philosophical humanism of Ludwig Feuerbach.

Historical Materialism and Scientific Communism

Before explaining the theoretical break that led Marx to elaborate the theory of historical materialism, it is necessary to introduce Frederick Engels, who, as Marx himself wrote, 'had by another road . . . arrived at the same result'.[16]

Engels was born in 1820 in Barmen, Westphalia, into a Calvinist mill-owning family. He did not undergo formal higher education, but made his mark as a literary figure while still extremely young with articles and pamphlets of religious criticism, often very satirical in character. From October 1841, shortly after Marx had left Berlin, Engels spent a year posted there on military service, and eagerly joined in the heady current of Young Hegelian philosophy. He became, like Marx, an ardent follower of Feuerbach. In November 1842 Engels travelled to England to work in Manchester for his family's cotton business, and there he came into first-hand contact with both working-class misery and the Chartist movement. In England, Engels gathered material for his book *The Condition of the Working Class in England in 1844*,[17] in which he presented, more clearly than Marx had yet done, the thesis that the movement of the industrial working class on the basis of its material conditions of life would be the agency of communist revolution. In September 1844 Engels travelled to Paris. He spent some weeks in discussion with Marx, and the two found themselves in close agreement on their basic theoretical positions. Their partnership continued unbroken from that time onwards.[18]

Marx and Engels's first joint venture was a book entitled *The Holy Family*,[19] a polemical work directed against the verbally radical, but idealist and apolitical, Young Hegelians, Bruno and Edgar Bauer and Max Stirner. This is very much a transitional work between Marx's early writings and the theory of historical materialism, and bears the marks of being written for hasty publication. Soon after finishing *The Holy Family* Marx moved to Brussels, being expelled from Paris at the request of the Prussian government for his activities among the German exiles (the newspaper *Vorwärts*). In spring 1845 Engels

16. 'Preface (to *A Contribution to the Critique of Political Economy*)', in *Early Writings*, pp. 426–7.
17. In *MECW* 4.
18. See below, p. 54.
19. In *MECW* 4.

visited Marx in Brussels, and the two began a period of intensive study, travelling to England together to do further research on political economy. The fruits of their work were the two volumes of *The German Ideology*, written in 1845–6, but published posthumously only in 1932.[20]

The German Ideology represents Marx and Engels's arrival at the theory of historical materialism that was to govern all their future work. It must be stressed that the materialist conception of history did not emerge fully fledged from the brains of its creators. In the two decades that lay between *The German Ideology* and *Capital*, Marx's general social theory was to be modified in certain important respects. In particular, *The German Ideology* is not free from a certain evolutionism, which presents the different modes of production which have characterized human history as a unilinear, if dialectical, series. Nevertheless, the basic framework of *The German Ideology*, for all its inadequacies, constitutes a radical rupture with Young Hegelian philosophy in general, and Feuerbachian humanism in particular. Whatever development the new theory was to undergo, its basis, like that of all new sciences, was laid in *The German Ideology* by an 'epistemological break'[21] that established an entirely new perspective for the understanding of history. *The German Ideology* is explicitly presented as a comprehensive critique of the same 'modern German philosophy'[22] which Marx and Engels had until recently accepted as their own theoretical framework. The fundamental theses of historical materialism are spelled out in the first chapter of the book, which is specifically devoted to the critique of Ludwig Feuerbach, the doyen of the Young Hegelians and Marx's own former mentor.

Marx opens *The German Ideology* by criticizing the Young Hegelian philosophers for seeking only to effect a change in consciousness, 'to interpret reality in another way'.[23] Young Hegelian philosophy, which started from the critique of religion, had criticized the dominant metaphysical, political, juridical and moral conceptions by exposing their religious basis, but it forgot that it was only counterposing its phrases to other phrases, and not

20. In *MECW* 5.

21. On this concept see Louis Althusser, *For Marx*, London, 1997, pp. 32–4.

22. The full subtitle of *The German Ideology* is 'Critique of Modern German Philosophy According to Its Representatives Feuerbach, Bruno Bauer and Stirner, and of German Socialism According to Its Various Prophets'.

23. *MECW* 5, p. 30.

combating the real existing world. In this respect the *Deutsche-Französische Jahrbücher* had certainly been less guilty than the 'critical critics' Bruno and Edgar Bauer, whom Marx had recently attacked in *The Holy Family*. But Marx goes on to criticize Feuerbach's equation of communism with humanism, and thus by implication his own position in the *Economic and Philosophical Manuscripts*. 'Feuerbach's whole deduction ... goes only so far as to prove that men need and have always needed each other', whereas communism 'in the real world means the follower of a definite revolutionary party'.[24]

Marx founds this distinction between philosophical and 'real' communism on a general sketch of historical development that situates communism as a 'definite revolutionary party', not in the world of ideas but as a determined product of social conditions. From this schema the basic concepts of historical materialism emerge. Marx presents his interpretation of history as radically different from that of German philosophy in that it proceeds 'from earth to heaven' instead of vice versa. It is the way in which men produce their material means of subsistence, how they 'work under definite material limits, presuppositions and conditions independent of their will', that determines 'the production of ideas, of conceptions, of consciousness'. 'Morality, religion, metaphysics, all the rest of ideology ... thus no longer retain the semblance of independence. They have no history, no development; but men, developing their material production and their material intercourse, alter, along with their real existence, their thinking and the products of their thinking'.[25]

The dynamic of historical development is provided by the development of the productive forces, and the changes in property relations that this requires. With the statement that 'the various stages of development in the division of labour are just so many different forms of ownership',[26] Marx introduces the historical periodization that is so crucial to his theory, positing tribal property, ancient (i.e. Graeco-Roman) 'communal and state property' and feudal property as the three major pre-bourgeois forms. Since consciousness has no independent development, then 'if this theory, theology, philosophy, ethics etc. come into contradiction with the existing relations, this can only occur because existing social relations have come into

24. Ibid., p. 57.
25. Ibid., pp. 36–7.
26. Ibid., p. 32.

contradiction with existing forces of production',[27] i.e. because the development of productive forces requires a new form of property that conflicts with that at present existing.

Each division of labour defines a number of social classes, which are mutually antagonistic from the time that private property first develops, involving as it does 'the *unequal* distribution, both quantitative and qualitative, of labour and its products'.[28] Ownership of property gives one class domination over others, and the political state becomes necessary in order to mediate the ensuing conflicts. 'All struggles within the state, the struggle between democracy, aristocracy and monarchy, the struggle for the franchise, etc., etc., are merely the illusory forms in which the real struggles of the different classes are fought out . . . Every class which is struggling for mastery . . . must first conquer for itself political power in order to represent its interest in turn as the general interest.'[29] The rule of the dominant class is always ideologically legitimated, since 'the class which has the means of material production at its disposal, has control at the same time over the means of mental production', and 'the ruling ideas are nothing more than the ideal expression of the dominant material relationships . . . the relationships which make one class the ruling one.'[30]

Within this interpretation of history Marx's conception of 'real' communism becomes intelligible. The ideas of communism are not the logical outcome of the history of philosophy, for philosophy has no independent history. Communist consciousness comes into being because the existing bourgeois relations of production can no longer contain the developing productive forces:

In the development of the productive forces there comes a stage when productive forces and means of intercourse are brought into being, which, under the existing relationships, only cause mischief, and are no longer productive but destructive forces (machinery and money); and connected with this a class is called forth, which has to bear all the burdens of society without enjoying its advantages, which, ousted from society, is forced into the most decided antagonism to all other classes; a class which forms the majority of all members of society, and from which emanates the consciousness of the necessity of a fundamental revolution.[31]

27. Ibid., p. 45.
28. Ibid., p. 46.
29. Ibid., p. 47.
30. Ibid., p. 59.
31. Ibid., p. 52.

In short, it is the material premises for communism that generate the communist consciousness that leads to social transformation. 'Communism is not for us a *state of affairs* which is to be established, an *ideal* to which reality (will) have to adjust itself. We call communism the real movement which abolishes the present state of things.'[32]

*

With *The German Ideology* Marx decisively rejected the concepts of Feuerbachian humanism which assumed an ideal human nature to which social institutions should be remoulded, in favour of objective scientific investigation of the real world, combined with political practice based on the class struggle to change it. Following the discovery of historical materialism, Engels later wrote:

Communism among the French and Germans, Chartism among the English, now no longer appeared as something accidental which could just as well not have occurred. These movements now presented themselves as a movement of the modern oppressed class, the proletariat, as the more or less developed forms of its historically necessary struggle against the ruling class, the bourgeoisie . . . And communism now no longer meant the concoction, by means of the imagination, of a social ideal as perfect as possible, but insight into the nature, the conditions and the consequent general aims of the struggle waged by the proletariat.[33]

Although Marx and Engels now realized that it was the actual workers' movement that had led them to communism, the ideology of this movement, even when it called itself communist and envisaged the abolition of private property, betrayed a quite inadequate conception of the society in which it had arisen, and of the possibilities and means of social transformation. Moreover, England was still the only country where industrial capitalism was unquestionably the dominant form of material production, where agriculture already involved less than half of the labouring population, and where earlier forms of urban production such as handicrafts and manufacture had been almost entirely squeezed out by machine industry. In the 1830s there had developed in England the first historic movement of a mass character that was based on the industrial proletariat: Chartism.

32. Ibid., p. 49.
33. 'On the History of the Communist League', in *MECW* 26, p. 381.

Recognizing this fact, Marx and Engels gave consistent support to the Chartists and were to work closely with the Chartist left wing led by Ernest Jones and Julian Harney.

(Ernest Jones, born into the minor aristocracy, became the most consistent representative of the revolutionary wing of the Chartist movement, and was the main surviving Chartist leader in the 1850s. For his part in the Chartist uprisings of 1848 he was imprisoned for two years in such conditions that two of his comrades imprisoned with him died of privation. Jones was the only British working-class leader of this period who understood Marx's theory of scientific communism. Although in 1858, with the final collapse of Chartism, Jones broke with Marx and collaborated with the bourgeois radicals, Engels nevertheless wrote to Marx on Jones's death in 1869 that he was 'the only *educated* Englishman ... who was, at bottom, entirely on our side'.[34] George Julian Harney, although influenced by Marx and Engels, was more of a revolutionary romantic. From 1843 to 1850 he was de facto editor of the main Chartist newspaper, Feargus O'Connor's *Northern Star*. Later, in his own newspaper, the short-lived *Red Republican*, he published in November 1850 the first English translation of the Communist Manifesto. In 1851, however, Harney broke with Marx and allied himself with the Schapper–Willich faction [see below, pp. 52–3]. The following year Harney's erratic and subjective politics led him to quarrel with Ernest Jones, and he soon after dropped out of the Chartist movement altogether.)

Chartism as such was by no means a communist or even a socialist movement, but was based simply on the programme of manhood suffrage. Communistic ideas, though not in the Marxist sense of the 'real movement', were represented in England by the followers of Robert Owen, who renounced the class struggle and hoped to lay the basis for their utopia by means of rational persuasion. When Engels arrived in England in October 1843, like Marx at the time a Feuerbachian humanist, his first political contacts were with the Owenists, and he frequently contributed to their paper the *New Moral World* for nearly two years before, in the light of the new theory, he switched his allegiance to the Chartist *Northern Star*.

In France, although capitalist development was considerably more backward than in England, political ideology was more sophisticated

34. 29 January 1869, in *MECW* 43, p. 210.

and complex, having developed in the hothouse of the Revolution of 1789 and its aftermath. Modern socialism had first originated in France with the utopian writings of Henri de Saint-Simon and Charles Fourier, who envisaged the planned direction of industrial technology in the general interest. However, the utopian socialists did not demand the abolition of all private property and did not see the industrial working class, still very undeveloped in early nineteenth-century France, as the agent of social transformation. By the 1840s the followers of Saint-Simon and Fourier only survived in the form of quasi-religious sects, but their writings continued to inspire all sorts of plans for solving the 'social question', i.e. the social upheaval caused by the beginnings of industrialization and the working-class unrest that accompanied it.

Among these socialist doctrines of the 1840s, two were not only particularly important in the history of socialist thought, but also won considerable support from the French workers. Louis Blanc pioneered modern 'democratic socialism' with his scheme for self-governing 'national workshops' set up by government action. Pierre-Joseph Proudhon, although he is sometimes classed rather as the founder of modern anarchism for his rejection of the state as an unnecessary evil, also had his socialist panacea. Proudhon counterposed the 'organization of credit' to Blanc's 'organization of labour', and held that exploitation would be abolished if associated groups of workers could produce and exchange on the basis of unlimited interest-free loans. Blanc believed that his workshops would eventually supersede the market economy, whereas Proudhon, in true petty-bourgeois spirit, equated the free market with freedom in general.[35]

The term 'communism' in the France of the 1840s denoted a very different phenomenon, an offshoot of the Jacobin tradition of the first French revolution. It was rather crude in its ideas, but – unlike the contemporary socialism – directly related to the historic struggles of the French masses. This communism went back to Gracchus Babeuf's Conspiracy of Equals of 1795, which aimed to install, by means of a conspiratorial coup, a dictatorship of 'true republicans' that would expropriate the rich, allocate work according to each individual's

35. During Marx's stay in Paris he maintained friendly relations with Proudhon and sought to influence him. In 1847, however, Marx's first published presentation of the theory of historical materialism took the form of a polemic against Proudhon, *The Poverty of Philosophy*. For a shorter critique of Proudhon, see Marx's letter to Schweitzer of 24 January 1865, in *MECW* 20, pp. 26–33.

capacity, and fix wages on the basis of strict equality. This egalitarian or 'crude' communism, as Marx called it, originated before the great development of machine industry. It appealed to the Paris *sans-culottes* – artisans, journeymen and unemployed – and potentially to the poor peasantry in the countryside. However, Babeuf's Conspiracy, as related by his disciple Buonarroti,[36] provided the model for revolutionary organizations formed under the July monarchy of 1830–48, and by this time both the class character of their social base and the objective possibilities of social transformation were rapidly changing with the development of machine industry. The idea of a communism of production based on machine industry was now popularized in Étienne Cabet's utopian novel, *Voyage en Icarie*, published in 1839.

The outstanding figure of French communism in the period before 1848 was Auguste Blanqui, whose Société des Saisons organized the revolutionary wing of the French workers' movement and carried out an attempt at insurrection in May 1839. Blanqui neither elaborated a utopia nor an economic doctrine. His economic writings are muddled, and he expressly censured Cabet and Proudhon for speculating on the details of the future social order. Blanqui believed it sufficient that the capitalist economy led to growing extremes of wealth and poverty, and must be replaced by some form of workers' cooperation, and focused rather on the problem of overthrowing the state that he correctly saw as the organized power of the propertied classes. Following Babeuf and Buonarroti, Blanqui argued his communism from the principle of equality. He saw France as divided between a small minority of the 'rich' and '30 million proletarians' (i.e. including the peasantry and urban artisans as well as the industrial working class), and counted on overthrowing the state power by means of a coup carried out by a secret society. On all those points Marx was to take issue with Blanqui. Yet Blanquism was unique among pre-Marxist socialism and communism in being a revolutionary proletarian movement, and in June 1848 the first real challenge to bourgeois class rule was to take place under Blanquist inspiration. It was Blanqui who coined the phrase 'dictatorship of the proletariat', and although Marx was to transform the concept of the proletariat, and to reject Blanqui's conspiratorial tactics, he retained Blanqui's

36. Philippe Buonarroti, *Buonarroti's History of Babeuf's Conspiracy of Equals*, London, 1836.

stress on the violent overthrow of the bourgeois state as the general precondition for communism.

We can now situate the basic principles of Marx's scientific communism in relation to the socialist and communist doctrines of the 1840s. Marx insisted, against the great utopians, Saint-Simon, Fourier and Owen, that the common goal of a rational reorganization of production could not be achieved simply by appeal to reason and, against the reformist schemes of Proudhon and Louis Blanc, that the working class could only be liberated by revolutionary political action to expropriate private property. Communism could only come about as a result of the antagonisms of capitalist society, by the victory of the working class over the bourgeoisie in class struggle. Yet while agreeing with Blanqui that the present ruling class had to be defeated politically, Marx rejected Blanqui's conception of the proletariat, i.e. the dispossessed social base of the revolution, as including all the labouring classes. For Marx, the new society was only possible on the basis of modern industry, and it was only the industrial working class, who did not own their means of production, that could be relied on to overthrow the capitalist order. But the obverse of Marx's restriction of the social base of the revolution was his extension of its political agency. Communist society could not be brought about, as Blanqui would have it, by a conspiratorial coup and the dictatorship of a political elite ruling on the proletariat's behalf, but only by the political organization of the industrial working class itself. Here Marx took his model from the English Chartists, the first mass organization of the modern working class. This political subject, the organized proletariat, was to expropriate the means of production and to exercise collective control over the productive process. With the abolition of antagonistic classes, political power would give way, as Saint-Simon had envisaged, to the mere administration of production.

The Communist League

At the beginning of 1846, having elaborated the basic principles of scientific communism, Marx and Engels moved to engage themselves practically in the proletarian movement. Yet the country to which they primarily directed their attention was not advanced England, but backward Germany. To some extent this choice was dictated to them. They already possessed a certain following among the German intelligentsia, while their capacity to intervene in English or French politics was severely limited. But besides this, Marx and Engels felt as Germans a special responsibility to their native land that they were to retain throughout their decades of exile, and in the late 1840s German absolutism was moving conspicuously and rapidly towards crisis. In the forthcoming German revolution, which Marx and Engels expected would overthrow the old regimes and transform German society along bourgeois lines, they saw a necessary step towards the final, communist revolution.

Germany in the 1840s still showed little sign of organized activity on the part of the industrial working class. Despite the economic development of the 1830s and 1840s, the proletariat, in the Marxian sense, was still a small minority of the population, concentrated particularly in the cotton mills of the northern Rhineland. The Silesian weavers' revolt of 1844 was not a movement of the modern proletariat, but one of traditional artisans starved out of production by the competition of machine industry. Among German skilled workers, however, there was already a significant political ferment, which, if it found little expression in Germany itself, where police conditions made this almost impossible, blossomed in the great centres of German emigration: Paris, Brussels, London, Geneva and New York. (In Paris alone, there were by 1843 some 85,000 emigrant German workers.)

The main organization of the German workers' movement of this time, which was also, in the circumstances of the emigration, 'the *first international workers' movement ever*',[37] was the League of the Just. This secret society, formed by German émigrés in Paris in 1836, had been closely connected with Blanqui's Société des Saisons and had suffered together with it in the defeated insurrection of 1839. In the 1840s, although the nominal centre of the League was still Paris, its real centre of gravity moved with the League's leading members to London, where the German Workers Educational Association was founded in 1840 as a public front for the League's activities.[38] In London in the 1840s the League

37. Engels, 'On the History of the Communist League', in *MECW* 26, p. 312.
38. The German Workers Educational Association, with its meeting hall in Great Windmill Street, Soho, served as the London centre of the German workers' movement for many years. It survived the dissolution of the Communist League in 1852 and was later associated with the German Social-Democratic Party, until in 1918 it was dissolved by the British government.

of the Just learned from the English Chartists the possibilities of mass working-class organization consequent on the development of modern industry. Though the League kept the structure of a conspiratorial organization, it began to distance itself from the tactics of Blanquism and sought alternative means to bring about its communist goal.

It was evidently towards the League of the Just that Marx and Engels had to orient themselves. Engels had already been in contact with the League circle in London, and both he and Marx respected the League for its militancy and recognized its importance as a workers' organization. At this time, however, the League was under the influence of the utopian communist Wilhelm Weitling,[39] and Marx and Engels were unwilling to join forces with it until it understood and accepted their scientific communism. They therefore decided, as an intermediate step, to set up a Communist Correspondence Committee based in Brussels, where Marx was still living, to conduct propaganda among the ranks of the German communists and win them over to their own theoretical position. The Communist Correspondence Committee was little more than a small group of Marx's personal followers, but it held meetings and exchanged letters with working-class militants in England, France and Germany, and in particular with the sections of the League of the Just, which it gradually succeeded in influencing. On 23 October 1846, for example, Engels could write to the Committee from Paris that, after several weeks of discussion, he had won the majority of the League circle to accept that, as communists, they pursued the interests of the proletariat in opposition to the bourgeoisie, aiming at the abolition of private property by means of a 'democratic revolution by force'.[40]

Early in 1847 the League had come close enough to Marx and Engels's theoretical position for them to be able to determine its future organization and tactics. In June 1847 a congress was held in London, attended by Engels and Wilhelm Wolff[41] on behalf of

---

39. Wilhelm Weitling was the first working-class publicist of communism in Germany. His *Guarantees of Harmony and Freedom* was inspired primarily by Fourier, and Marx had praised it highly in his Paris period.

40. *MECW* 38, p. 82.

41. Wilhelm Wolff, a journalist, remained a close comrade of Marx and Engels throughout the revolutionary period of 1848 and in exile in England. In 1867 Marx dedicated to Wolff the first volume of *Capital*, describing him as an 'intrepid, faithful, noble protagonist of the proletariat'.

the Communist Correspondence Committee, which transformed the League of the Just into the Communist League, reorganized its structure on democratic lines (though the League necessarily remained secret), and laid down, as the first article of its new rules, 'The aim of the League is the overthrow of the bourgeoisie, the rule of the proletariat, the abolition of the old, bourgeois society which rests on antagonism of classes and the foundation of a new society without classes and without private property.'[42] After the June Congress, Marx and his followers set up a public German Workers Association in Brussels, on the lines of the League's successful front organization in London, through which to influence the emigrant German workers. In November 1847 Marx and Engels travelled to London to attend the second congress of the Communist League, held secretly in the Great Windmill Street premises over a ten-day period. This congress discussed at length the principles of scientific communism presented by Marx and Engels, and at the end of the congress the two were mandated to draft a statement of principles for the League. Marx sent the *Manifesto of the Communist Party* to London at the end of January 1848, and it was published there in German just before revolution broke out in Paris on 21 February.[43]

The Communist Manifesto is justly Marx's most famous political text, formulating in polemical mode his general conception of the proletarian revolution, as this follows from the materialist concept of history. In the Manifesto, Marx did not merely set out to demonstrate the thesis that opens its first section, 'The history of all hitherto existing societies is the history of class struggles.'[44] Commenting on the Manifesto some four years later, Marx insisted:

Now as for myself, I do not claim to have discovered either the existence of classes in modern society or the struggle between them. Long before me, bourgeois historians had described the historical development of this struggle between the classes, as had bourgeois economists their economic anatomy. My own contribution was 1. to show that the *existence of classes* is merely bound up with *certain historical phases in the development of*

42. Quoted by Engels, 'On the History of the Communist League', in *MECW* 26, p. 321.

43. The Manifesto originally appeared without the names of its authors, and its title does not refer to the secret Communist League (Bund der Kommunisten). 'Party' (*Partei*) has here a meaning more like the modern 'movement'; it was a very loose word in mid nineteenth-century usage, both German and English.

44. See below, p. 61.

production; 2. that the class struggle necessarily leads to the *dictatorship of the proletariat*; 3. that this dictatorship itself only consitutes no more than a transition to the *abolition of all classes* and to a *classless society*.[45]

Marx's concern in the first section of the Manifesto is to explain in what way capitalist relations of production have become fetters on the development of the productive forces, and why the class that is exploited by capital, the industrial proletariat, is both capable of overthrowing this mode of production and indeed compelled by its position to do so. By way of comparison, Marx opens the Manifesto by outlining the transition from feudalism to capitalism, portraying the bourgeoisie in heroic guise as the representative of the new forces of production and exchange (manufacture, international trade) whose development was restricted by feudal social relations. To attain the free market it needed, the bourgeoisie had to overthrow the feudal organization of agriculture and industry, and the political superstructures built upon this, and it 'has at last, since the establishment of modern industry and of the world market, conquered for itself, in the modern representative state, exclusive political sway'.[46]

Just as the manufacturing system could not be contained within the feudal guilds, so bourgeois society is increasingly unable to control the means of production it has itself created, as evidenced by the periodic commercial and industrial crises caused by over-production – 'an epidemic that, in all earlier epochs, would have seemed an absurdity'.[47] In the Manifesto, Marx is content merely to indicate overproduction crises as the sign of the 'revolt of modern productive forces against modern conditions of production', and his theoretical explanation of this phenomenon and its implications was to wait until *Capital*. What must be stressed here, however, is the distinction that Marx makes between the constantly developing productive forces that are fettered by capitalist property relations, which Marx describes as 'weapons' that are 'turned against the bourgeoisie itself', and 'the men who are to wield these weapons – the proletarians'.[48] The industrial working class provides the political agency that will overthrow existing social relations, but it can only do so because the development of the productive forces places this task on the historical agenda.

45. Marx to Weydemeyer, 5 March 1852, in *MECW* 39, p. 62.
46. Below, p. 63.
47. Below, p. 67.
48. Ibid.

Marx proceeds to analyse the process by which the proletariat is organized into a class and onto the political arena by the very conditions of its social existence. What spurs its development from sporadic and inchoate rebellion, originally against the instruments of labour rather than the capitalists (e.g. Luddism), to sustained mass organization is the development of machine industry itself, which concentrates the workers together in great masses. In these conditions, combinations of workers, originally formed to bargain with the individual capitalist over wages, inevitably expand and develop, and in modern conditions the workers achieve a national union more quickly than did the burghers of the Middle Ages. As the union of the workers expands to include their whole class, their struggle becomes *ipso facto* a political one. Meanwhile, the development of capitalism causes intermediate classes that remain over from pre-capitalist modes of production (petty bourgeois, peasants, artisans, etc.) to disappear into the proletariat. Class antagonisms are thus simplified into the single antagonism between bourgeois and proletarians, and 'the proletarian movement is the self-conscious, independent movement of the immense majority, in the interests of the immense majority'. 'What the bourgeoisie, therefore, produces, above all, are its own grave-diggers. Its fall and the victory of the proletariat are equally inevitable.'[49]

In the second section of the Manifesto, Marx summarizes the goal of the proletarian revolution 'in the single sentence: Abolition of private property,' specifying, 'Modern bourgeois private property is the final and most complete expression of the system of producing and appropriating products that is based on class antagonisms, on the exploitation of the many by the few.' Since capital is already a 'social power', in the sense that 'only by the united action of all members of society, can it be set in motion',[50] and the vast majority of the population – i.e. the proletariat – is already devoid of private property, all that is necessary for the realization of a non-antagonistic, classless mode of production is to convert capital into common property, the property of society as a whole. And the agent of this transformation can only be the proletariat that is forming itself 'into a class, and consequently into a political party'[51] in the course of its struggle against its immediate exploiters. This is the point at which the distinctively Marxist synthesis of the social and the political

49. Below, pp. 72–3.
50. Below, pp. 74–80.
51. Below, p. 70.

revolution is made, and Marx goes on to specify that 'the proletariat will use its political supremacy to wrest, by degrees, all capital from the bourgeoisie, to centralize all instruments of production in the hands of the state, i.e. of the proletariat organized as the ruling class'.[52]

But the class struggle of the proletariat is itself only a necessary transitional stage towards the achieved communist society. Since 'political power . . . is merely the organized power of one class for oppressing another', when the proletariat

sweeps away by force the old conditions of production, it will, along with these conditions, have swept away the conditions for the existence of class antagonisms and of classes generally, and will thereby have abolished its own supremacy as a class . . . In place of the old bourgeois society, with its classes and class antagonisms, we shall have an association, in which the free development of each is the condition for the free development of all.[53]

In the third section of the Manifesto, Marx undertakes a fairly detailed critique of the various types and sub-types of contemporary socialist and communist literature. This polemic is directed against the whole welter of doctrines of social reform that flourished under the name of socialism and even communism in the 1840s, when the social conflicts generated by capitalist industrialization became an increasingly urgent problem for all classes in England, France and Germany. Although the particular doctrines and panaceas that Marx attacks here were specific to this period, Marx's critique still provides a paradigm of ideological analysis informed by the theory of historical materialism. The last sub-section 'Critical–Utopian Socialism and Communism' is particularly important as it presents an explanation of the development of socialist ideology from utopia to science and introduces the concept of sectarianism which Marx saw as the main obstacle in the way of the development of a revolutionary workers' movement.

As mentioned above, the idea of a rationally planned and collective mode of production, based on modern industry, was first formulated by Saint-Simon in opposition to the anarchic character of capitalist production and the extremes of wealth and poverty it produced, although Saint-Simon and the other utopians

52. Below, p. 80.
53. Below, p. 81.

were elitist and anti-democratic, and saw no connection between their own ideas and the workers' movement. Marx attributed this original distance between the critique of capitalism and the actual working-class movement to the still undeveloped stage of industrial capitalism, and consequently of the proletariat, in the early nineteenth century. Since the founders of the utopian systems saw the proletariat as 'a class without any historical initiative or any independent political movement',[54] they sought to realize their plans for social reconstruction by an appeal to society at large, especially to the educated and ruling classes. Although their writings 'attack[ed] every principle of existing society' and were therefore 'full of the most valuable materials for the enlightenment of the working class',[55] their ideas of the future society and the means to achieve it were inevitably characterized by all sorts of idiosyncracies. But as the struggle of the proletariat against the bourgeoisie developed, it became possible for the first time to conceive of communism as brought about not by the reconciliation of class antagonisms from outside, but by the victory of the proletariat over the bourgeoisie in class struggle. The subjective and arbitrary schemes of the utopians now acquired a reactionary significance, since they still endeavoured 'to deaden the class struggle and to reconcile the class antagonisms'.[56]

It is against this characterization of the utopian socialism and communism, which attempted to foist its subjective plans on the real proletarian movement, that Marx defines the tasks of the Communists in the second section of the Manifesto. As opposed to the utopians, 'the theoretical conclusions of the Communists . . . merely express, in general terms, actual relations springing from an existing class struggle, from an historical movement going on under our very eyes'. The Communists therefore 'do not form a separate party opposed to other working-class parties'[57] and 'do not set up any sectarian principles of their own, by which to shape and mould the proletarian movement'.[58] The particular task of the Communists, distinguished

54. Below, p. 89. In the first section of his 'Socialism: Utopian and Scientific', Engels expands on this analysis of the utopian socialists; see *MECW* 24, pp. 285–97.

55. Below, p. 90.

56. Ibid.

57. See above, p. 22, n. 43. The Communist League, if not a separate party in the contemporary sense of this term, was certainly separate from other working-class organizations, and indeed frequently opposed to them.

58. Below, pp. 73–4.

only by their theoretical insight into the historical process, is to struggle for the proletariat to recognize the revolutionary role that it is compelled to play by the objective dynamic of bourgeois society, to 'point out' to the proletariat as a whole its own international and long-term interests.

The Manifesto should not be regarded as the *summa* of Marx's political thought. It is certainly the most general formulation of the principles of scientific communism, and Marx himself was to refer to it as a touchstone throughout his life. However the Manifesto leaves many problems unresolved and gives inadequate solutions to others. The paramount problem is of course whether the 'historical movement going on under our very eyes' leads as straightforwardly to communism as Marx in 1848 believed, and we shall return to this in the Introduction to *The First International and After*. Other problems include those of how the working class organizes politically for the seizure of power, and how it confronts the state apparatus, as well as the problems of national antagonisms and intermediate classes, and these will be discussed as they arise in the context of Marx's political practice. The importance of the Manifesto is that it lays down the most general implications of the theory of historical materialism for the proletarian class struggle in a form that remains the corner-stone of Marx's distinctive political theory: the fetters that capitalist relations of production impose on the productive forces render inevitable the replacement of capitalism by communism; capitalist relations can only be abolished by the class struggles that they themselves engender; the proletariat can only transform capitalist into communist society by organizing itself as the ruling class and using its state power to expropriate the owners of capital; and the abolition of classes that is synonymous with the achievement of communism will lead to the withering away of the state itself.

The Problem of Tactics

In the Communist League Marx and Engels developed a working-class cadre that accepted their theory of scientific communism. But for this embryonic workers' party, as for every German opposition party at the time, a formulation of ultimate aims was not sufficient. It had been apparent since the beginning of the decade that the Prussian absolutist regime was moving into crisis. When in 1846 the liberal bourgeois opposition demanded the promulgation of a constitution before they would vote further taxation, the Communists, in common with all democrats,[59] began to expect the outbreak of revolution in the near future. The approach of revolution required the Communist League to define its tactical goals, which, given the infancy of German industrial capitalism, could not simply coincide with the strategic goal of the seizure of power by the working class.

The situation that the Communist League faced in the approaching German revolution seems at first sight inexplicable in terms of the historical schema presented in the Manifesto. The Manifesto was principally oriented to the development of the proletarian movement in the most advanced capitalist countries, which had long since experienced their bourgeois revolutions (e.g. England in the seventeenth and France in the eighteenth century), and where Marx expected the contradiction between the proletariat and the bourgeoisie to rapidly intensify and lead to communist revolution. But in Germany, which was so far behind the western countries in its economic and social development that the bourgeoisie had not yet taken power, how could there already be a proletarian movement directed against the bourgeoisie, and what should the German Communists do in such a situation?

The root cause of Germany's idiosyncratic political course is explained in Marxist theory by the concept of uneven development, which forms the object of many of Marx's analyses. In the historical process, societies originally separate from one another enter into relation with each other exhibiting different modes of production, and mutually affect each other's historical course by means of trade, war, the spread of technology, etc. It is this process of interaction that gives history its intricate complexity. And although Marx believed that capitalism was tending to level out national differences, it has itself generated new forms of uneven development. Only with world communism can we expect, at last, a single human history.

The survey of capitalist development that Marx presented in *The German Ideology* and the *Manifesto of the Communist Party* is a theoretical schema, not an empirical description. Marx was quite well aware that real history is more complicated, and he never

59. In this period, when the proletarian movement was only just beginning to distinguish itself from the movement of the petty bourgeoisie, the term 'democrat' was generally used in the wide sense to denote all who stood for rule by the people.

expected every country to follow an identical historical path. In the final section of the Manifesto, Marx himself alluded to the effects of uneven development with respect to Germany, although he did not explain its particular causes. With historical hindsight, these appear to be essentially of the following kind. Germany's previous history had left the country considerably behind its western neighbours in the transition from feudalism to capitalism (largely as a result of the Peasant War in the Reformation period and the Thirty Years War in the seventeenth century, which blocked the formation of a unified nation-state). Germany had not developed a strong commercial and financial bourgeoisie based on international trade, such as had overthrown the old regimes in England and France, but this did not prevent the rise of an industrial capitalist class in the nineteenth century, based on the new technology of machine industry, which had gradually been developed in the most advanced countries. Because of this, the German bourgeoisie did not confront 'its' revolution until it had already produced its *alter ego*, the industrial proletariat.[60] In the Manifesto, however, although Marx asserted that German history would take a different course from the 'classic' scenario of the English and French bourgeois revolutions, he presented this merely in terms of a condensed time-scale: the bourgeois revolution in Germany, 'to be carried out under more advanced conditions of European civilization, and with a much more developed proletariat, than that of England was in the seventeenth, and of France in the eighteenth century', would be 'the prelude to an immediately following proletarian revolution'.[61]

From early in 1846, when Marx and Engels began their systematic propaganda for scientific communism, they also put forward a specific tactic for the working class in the German revolution. Given that the coming revolution would bring the bourgeoisie to power in Germany, the proletariat should actively support the bourgeoisie in its struggle against absolutism and refrain from pursuing its own struggle against the bourgeoisie until the old regime had been decisively defeated. The first public statement of this position was in an article by Engels on 'The State of Germany',[62] published in the Chartist *Northern Star* (25 October 1845), where he wrote that the German workers' movement would subordinate itself to the

60. See below, pp. 40, 117.
61. See below, p. 92.
62. In *MECW* 6, p. 29.

bourgeoisie until the day that the bourgeoisie held full power, but that from that very day its struggle against the bourgeoisie would begin. A similar formulation is reproduced in Section IV of the Manifesto, with the proviso that the Communists 'never cease, for a single instant, to instil into the working class the clearest possible recognition of the hostile antagonism between bourgeoisie and proletariat',[63] so as to prepare the workers for the future battle against their present ally.

It is interesting to compare this new tactical position with that expressed by Marx before he developed his materialist conception of history. When Marx first committed himself to the proletariat, in 1844, it was as the class with 'radical chains', the agent of a revolution that had, by a '*salto mortale*' (mortal leap), to override both Germany's 'limitations' and those of the modern nations, because 'the development of the social conditions and the progress of political theory have demonstrated [the middle class's] point of view to be antiquated or at least problematical'.[64] By 1846, however, Marx's theory of historical materialism had led him to the conclusion that the German proletariat could not simply ignore the 'problematical' position of the bourgeoisie, and that, in the revolution now approaching, the working class must at first throw in its lot with its own immediate exploiter until feudalism and absolutism had been defeated. As we shall see, Marx was to insist on the need for this alliance with the bourgeoisie even at the expense of losing allies in the German working-class movement.[65]

In line with this tactic, Marx and Engels concentrated on attacking utopian ideas that held that communism was already possible in Germany, and in particular the ideas of 'true socialism' which dominated German socialist ideology at this time[66] and which used a critique of capitalism drawn from the French utopians to deflect the workers from participating in the growing democratic movement. At a discussion between the Communist Correspondence Committee and Weitling when the latter visited Brussels in March 1846, Marx denounced the 'fantastic hopes' of the utopians and argued his

63. Below, p. 92.

64. 'A Contribution to the Critique of Hegel's Philosophy of Right. Introduction', in *Early Writings*, pp. 252, 256.

65. Though rejected by Marx in 1846, the theory of the 'mortal leap' presaged the tactic of 'permanent revolution' which Marx developed in 1850, this time within the framework of scientific communism. See below, pp. 48–50.

66. See section III I.c. of the Communist Manifesto, below, pp. 84–7.

characteristic position that communism could not be achieved in Germany without the bourgeoisie first coming to power. On the basis of this position Marx and Engels could also work within the ranks of the general democratic exile of petty bourgeois and intellectuals, attempting to weld a solid alliance of Communists and democrats on a common programme of the overthrow of feudalism and absolutism, and the unification of Germany as a democratic republic. Marx therefore collaborated, from its foundation in the spring of 1847, with the *Deutsche-Brüsseller-Zeitung* (*Brussels German Gazette*), a German paper published in Brussels which was quite influential in the immediate pre-revolutionary period, and which towards the end of the year became the virtual organ of Marx and his followers. Marx represented German democracy in the Democratic Association for the Unification of All Countries, set up in November 1847, a Belgian organization in correspondence with the English Fraternal Democrats, which united workers and petty-bourgeois democrats and campaigned in solidarity with the nations and peoples of Europe oppressed by absolutism.[67]

Despite Marx's undoubtedly correct insistence on the primacy of the struggle against absolutism, his position on the relationship of the proletariat to the bourgeoisie in the bourgeois revolution was still rather ambivalent. According to the Manifesto, the communists were to 'instil into the working class the clearest possible recognition of the hostile antagonism between bourgeoisie and proletariat', while simultaneously mobilizing the proletariat to 'fight with the bourgeoisie whenever it acts in a revolutionary way'.[68] These two aims would seem in practice very difficult to reconcile, particularly as the German workers' movement was still at a very embryonic and spontaneous stage, and could not yet act as a disciplined unity. It is therefore not surprising that *The Demands of the Communist Party in Germany* which Marx and Engels drew up after the March revolutions in Germany as their basic programmatic document, and which summarizes in seventeen points the prerequisites of the radical-democratic overthrow of feudalism and absolutism, mentions not a word of the 'hostile antagonism between bourgeoisie and proletariat' that the Manifesto had promised to stress. Forced to choose between present and future needs, Marx now decided to sacrifice for

67. See p. 93, n. 1.
68. See below, p. 91.

time being the anti-capitalist education of the proletariat to the immediate struggle against the old regime.

As we shall see, Marx's tactic of a short-term alliance with the bourgeoisie proved untenable. In the context of Germany's uneven development, the very existence of a proletarian movement threatening it from behind seriously checked the revolutionary ardour of the bourgeoisie – a fact that Marx should perhaps have foreseen when he wrote that the German bourgeois revolution was 'the prelude to an immediately following proletarian revolution'. When the 1848 revolution broke out, however, Marx was still counting on the German bourgeoisie to take the initiative in the first stage of the revolution, as the French bourgeoisie had done in 1789. His policy was to spur on the bourgeoisie from an independent base on the left, organizing the plebeian classes separately from the bourgeoisie in order to strike together at the old regime, and to prepare this democratic bloc of proletariat, petty bourgeoisie and peasantry to step temporarily into the vanguard should the bourgeoisie show signs of cold feet, by analogy with the Jacobin government in France of 1793–4. (*The Demands of the Communist Party in Germany* was explicitly presented as representing the common interest of these three classes.) However, events were soon to show that the proletariat could not allay the fears it roused in the bourgeoisie merely by supporting it in the struggle against the old regime. Even if its political representatives refrained from mentioning the hostile antagonism between it and the bourgeoisie, the real existence of the communist 'spectre' could not be covered up, and the development of the revolution was to force Marx to abandon any hope that the bourgeoisie would move decisively against the old order.

The German Revolution

The February revolution in Paris, which overthrew the constitutional monarchy of Louis Philippe, rapidly detonated a revolutionary movement in Germany. On 13 March a popular uprising in Vienna crippled the Habsburg monarchy, and on 18 March the revolution spread to Berlin. Frederick William IV of Prussia was forced to allow free political activity and to promise not to stand in the way of democratic national unification.

Following the February revolution, Marx immediately left Brussels for Paris, where, by way of compensation for his expulsion three years earlier, the Provisional Government granted him honorary French citizenship. Marx had been authorized by the Communist League to set up a new Central Committee in Paris, which he formed out of his closest followers: Engels, Wilhelm Wolff from Brussels, and Bauer, Moll and Schapper from London.[69] The largest group of German exiles in Paris formed a 'legion' which optimistically aimed at spreading revolution to Germany by force of arms, but Marx and his friends spent their energies on sending several hundred Communist League members and supporters back clandestinely, until the March days in Berlin made open return possible. It was during their stay in Paris that Marx and Engels drew up *The Demands of the Communist Party in Germany*, which were distributed on a wide scale in Germany over the next few months.

Marx and Engels returned to Germany in April and decided to settle in Cologne. This choice was motivated by several considerations. Cologne was a Prussian city, from where they could confront one of the two German great powers. It was in the Rhineland province, economically the most advanced part of Germany, and which also retained the more liberal press laws of the Code Napoléon as a legacy from its French occupation. Cologne had been a centre of opposition activity throughout the 1840s and already possessed an active Communist League organization. Finally, Marx was himself remembered in Cologne from the days of the *Rheinische Zeitung* in 1842–3. This was particularly important given Marx's tactic of a bloc of all democratic forces, and on their return to Cologne Marx and Engels set out to obtain sufficient political and financial support from the Rhineland democrats to launch a daily paper. The *Neue Rheinische Zeitung* (*New Rhenish Gazette*) duly appeared on 1 June, subtitled '*Organ der Demokratie*'.

The twelve months that he spent in Germany in 1848–9 provide an unparalleled occasion to see Marx as a revolutionary militant, and we shall therefore examine his political practice in some detail. Throughout this period, Marx's base of operations was not

69. Joseph Moll, a watchmaker, and Karl Schapper, a compositor, were leading members of the League of the Just before its transformation into the Communist League. Both worked with Marx in Cologne during the 1848 revolution, and Moll was killed in 1849 during the Reich Constitution Campaign (see pp. 42–3). Schapper broke with Marx when the Communist League split in September 1850 (see below, pp. 51–3), though their differences were later reconciled. Heinrich Bauer, a shoemaker and also a leading member of the League of the Just, was not related to the Young Hegelian brothers Edgar and Bruno Bauer.

the Communist League but the *Neue Rheinische Zeitung*, a fact that requires some explanation. Engels was certainly justified in attributing this move to the fact that 'the League proved to be much too weak a lever by comparison with the popular mass movement that had now broken out'.[70] But there was more to it than that. Although Engels avoids mentioning it, there is every indication that Marx himself deliberately sabotaged the League, following the dispute that developed between him and Gottschalk.[71]

Andreas Gottschalk was the dominant figure in the Cologne district of the League and had used his position as a physician to build up a following among the workers and unemployed. After the March days he established an openly functioning Workers Society, which Marx and Engels made contact with when they returned to Cologne. Similar societies had been formed in many German towns, though not always with Communists in a leading position, and in Berlin the League member Stefan Born was attempting to unite these into a national association. Initially the Communist League hoped to control the open workers' societies through its secret 'communes', but by the end of April this hope had to be abandoned as illusory. The League was too thin on the ground numerically, its communications were poor, and – most crucially – the workers' societies were too strongly permeated by the old guild spirit and organized themselves along craft lines, reflecting their domination by artisans, and not workers in modern industry.

In the Cologne Workers Society, which rapidly acquired 5,000 members, Gottschalk pandered to the artisanal consciousness of the membership in a way that Marx considered intolerable. Not only did Gottschalk sanction the division of the society on craft lines, he supported its concentration on the particular problems of unemployment, etc. faced by the workers and compromised with politically backward elements on the crucial question of the republic, sticking at the demand for a federal constitutional monarchy. In April Gottschalk won the Workers Society, against Marx's counsel, for a boycott of the elections to the German National Assembly at Frankfurt, which were admittedly indirect and inegalitarian, and in May, more seriously, he actually opposed a demonstration against the return of the ultra-reactionary Prince William, who had fled to England at the

70. 'On the History of the Communist League', in *MECW* 26, p. 324.

71. This was first demonstrated by B. Nicolaevsky in 'Towards a History of the "Communist League" ', *International Review of Social History* vol. 1, no. 2, Amsterdam, 1956.

outbreak of revolution. Gottschalk's supporters formed a majority of the Communist League's Cologne district, although Marx controlled the Central Committee by virtue of the powers conferred on him from London. When Gottschalk refused League discipline, Marx appears to have decided that the League was, for the time being, more trouble than it was worth. He dissolved the Central Committee, thus leaving the League headless in the flux of the revolution, and worked from his base in the *Neue Rheinische Zeitung* with the handful of his closest supporters. Joseph Moll was sent to work in the Workers Society, where he conducted an educational campaign, dividing the meetings into small groups to discuss the League's demands. But Marx's supporters were far from controlling the Workers Society, and when the *Neue Rheinische Zeitung* showed that its main concerns were removed from the immediate economic problems of the working class, the Workers Society weekly paper began to attack the 'Organ of Democracy' for a 'callous' and 'exploitative' attitude towards the workers.[72]

By the time the *Neue Rheinische Zeitung* commenced publication, the revolutionary movement of March had forced democratic concessions in Prussia, Austria and the smaller German states; the all-German National Assembly had started its deliberations in Frankfurt, while a Prussian Assembly was sitting in Berlin. But in Germany, as in Europe as a whole, the first wave of the revolutionary movement, which had won extensive if fragile victories, had already spent its main force. In Italy, revolutionary Milan and Venice were on the defensive against the Austrian troops. In France the elections held in April with universal male suffrage had resulted in the defeat of the Provisional Government of 'red republicans' and socialists by an immense reactionary majority elected from the countryside. In Britain the 'monster' Chartist demonstration of 10 April had ended in a demobilizing shambles, and in Belgium the bourgeoisie had successfully contained the workers' movement by conceding reforms. In Germany itself, the Prussian and Austrian monarchies, though they had made concessions to the popular movement, were still secure in command of their armies and bureaucracies, and behind them loomed the power of tsarist Russia, their partner in the counter-revolutionary Holy Alliance.

In this political setting Marx was more than ever determined to concentrate single-mindedly on the struggle against the absolutist

72. Oscar J. Hammen, *The Red '48ers*, New York, 1969, p. 224.

regimes. Not only did the *Neue Rheinische Zeitung* avoid all talk of communism, but Marx was quite unmoved by the Workers Society's complaints that his paper ignored the workers' economic interests. As Engels later wrote, 'The political programme of the *Neue Rheinische Zeitung* consisted of two main points: a single, indivisible, democratic German republic, and war with Russia, which included the restoration of Poland.'[73] On the home front, Marx and Engels bent all their efforts to preparing and organizing the democratic forces for a decisive insurrection. And the importance that they attributed to offensive war against Russia was not only to pre-empt the threat of intervention and to restore Poland as a bastion of '20 million heroes' between Russia and the West.[74] War against Russia would also have demanded the marshalling of Germany's economic and military resources in an unprecedented manner, and thus more than anything else have required the centralization of power in a single national state and favoured the most decisive of the revolutionary parties in its bid for power. In this scenario as in so much else in the 1848 revolution, Marx had in mind the model of the first French Revolution, in this case the stimulus that foreign war had on its radicalization.

During the first weeks of the *Neue Rheinische Zeitung*'s existence, its chief concern was with the Frankfurt and Berlin Assemblies, belabouring them mercilessly for their 'parliamentary cretinism', i.e. their failure to recognize the crucial question of power.[75] In the columns of his paper Marx attempted to drive home to the Frankfurt Assembly the folly of its concern with constitution-making when it had no executive arm of its own and did not even sit in a city with a 'strong revolutionary movement' to defend it.[76] The *Neue Rheinische Zeitung* nicknamed the Berlin Assembly the '*Vereinbarungsversammlung*' ('assembly of agreement') for its passive acceptance of its royal mandate to draw up a constitution for Prussia 'by agreement with the Crown'. Despite the fact that the Berlin Assembly, unlike the Frankfurt, did have a 'strong revolutionary movement' behind it, it shared the illusion that history is made by parliamentary debate and not by the class struggle, whereas both assemblies owed their

73. 'Marx and the *Neue Rheinische Zeitung*', in *MECW* 26, pp. 120–8.

74. See Engels, 'Speech on Poland', below, pp. 99–102.

75. See 'Camphausen's Declaration in the Sitting of 30 May' and 'The 15 June Sitting of the "*Vereinbarungsversammlung*" ', below, pp. 108–12 and pp. 118–19.

76. See 'The Programmes of the Radical-Democratic Party and the Left in the Assembly', below, p. 115.

very existence to the barricade fighting of the March days. When the liberal Camphausen ministry in Prussia promised the abolition of feudal obligations, Marx wrote in heavy type beneath his report, 'But the Bastille has still not been stormed.'[77]

For the first three months of the German revolution, it appeared that the liberal bourgeoisie, though irresolute, might well be pushed by circumstances into decisive action, leading the plebeian classes in an offensive against the remaining institutions of the old regime. The *Neue Rheinische Zeitung* therefore sought to spur this class into action by appeal to its own interests. However, it soon became clear that this tactic was unviable. After the June insurrection in Paris, the showdown between the Constituent Assembly and the socialist workers who had made the February revolution, the Communists and the more consistent of their democratic allies could no longer hope to unite with the liberal bourgeoisie in a common front against the old regime. As Marx later wrote in *The Class Struggles in France*, the June days were 'the first great battle ... between the two great classes which divide modern society. It was a fight for the preservation or destruction of the bourgeois order.'[78] The significance of the June days was immediately apparent throughout Europe, and the spectre of proletarian revolution which, for the first time in history, had shown itself a practical possibility, consolidated all the exploiting classes in Germany on the side of reaction. Needless to say, the *Neue Rheinische Zeitung* came out unflinchingly on the side of the vanquished insurgents, exposing the brutal solidarity against the working class under the slogan of 'Order' that ran right through from the monarchists to the 'red republicans'.[79] But the timorous German bourgeoisie did not need Marx to spell out the lessons of the June days.

During the summer, and with the increasing stagnation of the Berlin and Frankfurt Assemblies, Marx and his comrades in Cologne concentrated their efforts on extending their organizational base so as to be prepared for any future contingencies. The arrest of Gottschalk, after the Workers Society held rallies in support of the Paris insurgents, provided a fortuitous occasion for Marx to augment his influence over the society. In July Moll and Schapper

77. See 'The 15 June Sitting of the "*Vereinbarungsversammlung*"', below, p. 119.
78. See below, pp. 392–3.
79. See 'The June Revolution', below, pp. 123–28.

were elected as its president and vice-president, and the society was reorganized with a smaller, directly elected executive committee to replace the old one elected on a guild basis and with fixed dues. The June days had caused severe tensions in the ranks of the democrats, but in the increasing climate of repression Marx, who was himself accused under the press laws, consolidated his support in the Cologne Democratic Society, where he now argued openly in favour of a revolutionary government brought about by new popular insurrection, which would represent all the 'heterogeneous elements' that made the revolution, i.e. not merely the bourgeoisie.[80] During the summer Marx and Engels pressed the Workers Society into starting agitation amongst the peasantry, and by September substantial Peasant Unions had been started up and down the Rhineland, as well as a peasant newspaper.

September 1848 saw a crisis in Prussia after the fiasco of the war against Denmark over the disputed territories of Schleswig-Holstein. The war had become a symbol of the movement for national unity and even an occasion for German chauvinism, and the Frankfurt Assembly, having no armed forces of its own, was forced to ask the Prussian monarchy to fight on behalf of the German nation. The Malmö armistice of 26 August, which Prussia accepted in deference to England and Russia, sparked off a wave of anger against the Prussian regime, leading to clashes between soldiers and citizens in Berlin, Cologne and other cities.[81]

On 16 September the crisis intensified, as the Frankfurt Assembly finally ratified the Malmö armistice. A popular insurrection broke out in Frankfurt, in which the peasantry played a major role, and the Frankfurt 'Reich ministry' called in Prussian, Austrian and Hessian troops to restore order. In Cologne, the Democratic and Workers Societies called a mass meeting to denounce the Frankfurt Assembly, and by 25 September, when a Rhineland Democratic Congress was scheduled to meet in Cologne, that city was also on the verge of insurrection. Marx, who had kept a low profile during the previous three weeks' agitation, and preferred where possible to work behind the scenes, realized that if the Democratic Congress met, a suicidal insurrection confined to Cologne was inevitable. While attempts by the police to arrest the most active leaders were delayed by popular action, Marx succeeded in getting the Congress cancelled and

---

80. Hammen, *The Red '48ers*, p. 266.
81. See 'The Crisis and the Counter-Revolution', below, pp. 150–58.

persuading the Workers and Democratic Societies not to be provoked into insurrection. Barricades were erected in Cologne in the evening, but the defenders quickly dispersed as the army advanced. Martial law was proclaimed with the support of the constitutionalist city council, the civic guard was disbanded, and the *Neue Rheinische Zeitung* and three other papers were banned. Engels, expecting imminent arrest for his role on the Committee of Public Safety formed to prepare for insurrection, fled to France, where he remained until the new year, and most of Marx's other chief supporters also either fled or were imprisoned.[82]

The *Neue Rheinische Zeitung* was allowed to reappear on 12 October, but took time to regain its former strength. On 17 October, in the absence of Moll and Schapper, Marx was himself elected president of the Workers Society, and a few weeks later delivered there his lectures on *Wage Labour and Capital*.[83]

Meanwhile, the German revolution came to its decisive stage. The high point of the revolution had been reached with the October events in Vienna, when the imminent departure of Habsburg troops against Hungary provoked a successful insurrection, and the city was liberated for three weeks. After heavy siege, the Vienna insurrection succumbed on 1 November, and the Prussian monarchy now also felt strong enough to move to the counter-offensive.[84] The king appointed an explicitly counter-revolutionary ministry under Count Brandenburg, and on 9 November, after the Prussian Assembly passed a vote of no confidence, signed a decree dissolving the Assembly, moved 10,000 troops into Berlin and declared martial law. The Assembly attempted to carry on its sessions, but reacted only passively to increasing harassment. Rather than take the opportunity to organize armed resistance, its members dispersed across the country to organize a campaign of tax refusal.[85]

At first the *Neue Rheinische Zeitung* participated in this campaign, as Marx hoped that the liberal bourgeoisie might once again rally to the side of the revolution. But when it became apparent that the bourgeois opposition would not go beyond peaceful protest, Marx

82. See 'The "Cologne Revolution" ', below, pp. 160–64.

83. In *MECW* 9, pp. 197–228.

84. See 'Revolution in Vienna' and 'The Victory of the Counter-Revolution in Vienna', below, pp. 158–60 and pp. 167–71.

85. See 'The Counter-Revolution in Berlin' and 'No More Taxes!!!', below, pp. 171–78.

made an attempt to turn passive into active resistance, and the *Neue Rheinische Zeitung* and the Workers Society called for the forcible deposition of government officials, the establishment of committees of public safety, and the formation of democratic troops of the military reserve into a people's militia. By 21 November the Cologne revolutionaries had their own armed forces, but two days later these collapsed without a struggle against the overwhelming force of the Prussian garrison. The Cologne city council refused to halt tax collection, and the Frankfurt Reich ministry declared a National Assembly motion to this end null and void. In December Frederick William, having used the red scare to entice the bourgeoisie back into the monarchist fold, consolidated his new reactionary bloc by granting a superficially liberal constitution and waited for the occasion when the forces of revolution could be decisively routed.

In December 1848, in the series of articles 'The Bourgeoisie and the Counter-Revolution', Marx analysed the Prussian bourgeoisie's backsliding into the camp of reaction. Whereas in the Manifesto Marx had predicted, from the fact that Germany was entering its bourgeois revolution with a more developed proletariat than had England and France at the corresponding stage of their development, that the German proletariat would seize power hard on the heels of the bourgeoisie, he was now forced to the realization that the effect of this uneven development was that the German bourgeoisie would not seize power at all:

The German bourgeoisie had developed so sluggishly, so pusillanimously and so slowly, that it saw itself threateningly confronted by the proletariat, and all those sections of the urban population related to the proletariat in interests and ideas, at the very moment of its own threatening confrontation with feudalism and absolutism . . . The Prussian bourgeoisie was not, like the French bourgeoisie of 1789, the class which represented the whole of modern society in face of the representatives of the old society, the monarchy and the nobility. It had sunk to the level of a type of estate . . . inclined from the outset to treachery against the people . . . because it itself already belonged to the old society.[86]

The bourgeois revolution in Germany could thus expect no help from the bourgeoisie itself – this was the paradoxical yet vitally important conclusion that Marx formulated for the first time in December 1848.

86. Below, pp. 187–8.

How then could the bourgeois revolution succeed, and what tactic should the proletariat follow? Marx had as yet no plan for this new contingency and was only to formulate one after the defeats of 1849. But if the bourgeoisie had decisively gone over to the counter-revolution, then there was no need for the proletariat to play down its antagonism to the bourgeoisie, and it was free to concentrate on building up its own independent organization, the better to prepare for the next round of the revolution. In the early part of 1849 Marx gradually moved to separate himself from the democrats and press for the construction of the independent workers' party which he had earlier blocked by dissolving the League's Central Committee. In the February elections under the new Prussian constitution, undemocratic as they were, Marx had still insisted on the Cologne Workers Society backing the democratic candidates, thereby incurring the vehement opposition of Gottschalk's faction, who charged Marx with 'asking the workers to endure the rule of capital'.[87] But on 18 February a new note crept into the columns of the *Neue Rheinische Zeitung*, when Marx referred to the paper as representing, not the democratic party, but 'the party of the people, which until now has existed only in elementary form'.[88] The *Neue Rheinische Zeitung* now turned decisively towards the working class, publishing Wilhelm Wolff's articles on the fraudulent 'emancipation' of the Silesian peasantry and Marx's lectures *Wage Labour and Capital*. On 14 April Marx and his group formally severed their ties with the democrats and declared that they would work instead 'for a closer union of workers' societies'.[89] Two days later the Cologne Workers Society called a regional congress of all workers' societies of Rhineland and Westphalia for 6 May and sent out reprints of *Wage Labour and Capital*, its own statutes and other documents by way of preparation.

In spring 1849 Marx and Engels counted on support from without as the only salvation for the German revolution. The Hungarian national army was successfully fending off Austrian invasion and was expected at one point to march on Vienna. In France the Constituent Assembly dissolved itself, and it looked as if a further advance of the revolution was possible there. Meanwhile, however, the ground was being prepared for the final battle of the German revolution

87. In *Freiheit, Arbeit*, the paper of the Workers Society, quoted in Hammen, *The Red '48ers*, p. 372.
88. 'Stein', in *MECW* 8, p. 390.
89. 'Statement', in *MECW* 9, p. 282.

in a way that Marx and Engels did not anticipate. On 4 March the Austrian government declared the Habsburg empire an indivisible monarchy, effacing for the first time all economic and military distinctions between the German and non-German provinces, and thus pre-empting the Frankfurt Assembly's claims for German unity. The Frankfurt Assembly had now completed its constitution-making and, abdicating its claims over German Austria, offered the crown of a 'little Germany' to Frederick William of Prussia, which on 12 April he refused. The previously impotent Assembly now acquired a last spurt of energy, and the Left found itself for the first time in the majority. The petty bourgeoisie, who had clung to the illusion of peaceful development until the last possible moment, decided, faced with the prospect of a return to unmediated absolutism, to engage in struggle behind the Frankfurt constitution and began an agitation that rapidly led to insurrection in Dresden, in the Prussian Rhineland and in Baden.

Marx and Engels were slow to respond to this Reich Constitution Campaign, since it did not aim at a unified democratic republic but only a constitutional monarchist federation. However, when the movement developed into insurrection, Marx and his followers placed their full weight behind it. In the Rhineland, the rising was rapidly defeated. The petty bourgeoisie, after taking the initiative in launching armed struggle, began to compromise once insurrection had broken out, and in Elberfeld, for instance, where Engels went to give military advice, the revolution was even disowned by its erstwhile leaders. On 16 May, Marx was served with an expulsion order, and the final issue of the *Neue Rheinische Zeitung* appeared on the 19th, printed in red, with the leading article 'To the Workers of Cologne'[90] advising against premature and isolated insurrection. Simultaneously, however, the *Neue Rheinische Zeitung* optimistically predicted that in 'a few weeks, perhaps even a few days', the revolutionary armies of France, Poland, Hungary and Germany would be in Berlin.[91]

Marx and Engels left Cologne for Frankfurt, where they vainly attempted to rouse the collapsing Assembly to give a decisive political leadership to the revolutionary forces. However, only in Baden and the Palatinate, where the entire state fell into the hands of the insurrection, did military operations last for more than a week.

90. Below, p. 258.
91. 'Hungary', in *MECW* 9, p. 466.

Engels joined the Baden army which resisted the Prussians until July, while Marx left for Paris and, soon expelled by the Cavaignac government, for London.

The National Question

The first of *The Demands of the Communist Party in Germany* was: 'The whole of Germany shall be declared a single and indivisible republic.'[92] In central and eastern Europe, dominated by the transnational empires of Austria and Russia, nationalism and democracy inevitably went hand in hand. The bourgeois revolution could only triumph if it broke up the Habsburg empire, fused together the petty German princedoms, and established a barrier against Russian intervention. Marx and Engels inherited from their bourgeois-democratic forebears the view of Russia as a barbarous Asiatic presence outside the pale of European civilization. In their later years they overcame this Eurocentrism, but they were at least justified at this time in their indiscriminate antipathy to all things Russian. In the 1848 period there was no possibility of support for the revolutionary movement from any class of Russian society, and since 1815 the tsarist regime had never hesitated, as the strongest partner in the Holy Alliance, to use its influence in Europe as the ultimate bulwark of reaction. It was generally believed that Russian military intervention against the French revolution of 1830 had only been prevented by the insurrection in Poland, and the tsar was to send Russian troops to put down the Hungarian revolution in 1849.

Poland had been completely partitioned between Prussia, Austria and Russia since 1795, and support for Polish independence was naturally common ground for all democrats. Next to German unification itself, Polish independence was the foundation stone on which Marx and Engels built their position on the national questions of central and eastern Europe. In their London speeches on Poland of 29 November 1847, a few weeks before the outbreak of the 1848 revolutions, Marx and Engels first began to integrate a national policy into their communist programme, a policy in which the restoration of Poland had a crucial place. Marx's own speech still betrays the rather idealistic euphoria that often characterized the early formulations of scientific communism from 1846 to the

92. Below, p. 101.

crucible of the 1848 revolution, in so far as he tended to reduce the struggle for Polish independence to an epiphenomenon of the universal proletarian revolution he believed impending. 'The victory of the proletariat over the bourgeoisie also signifies the emancipation of all downtrodden nations', and as 'of all countries it is England where the opposition between the proletariat and the bourgeoisie is most highly developed', 'Poland, therefore, must be freed, not in Poland, but in England'.[93] Engels, however, was already at this stage concerned with the tactical significance of the Polish movement to the German revolution. German democracy and Polish liberation were allied because 'the first condition for the freeing of both Germany and Poland is the overthrow of the present political regime in Germany . . . and the withdrawal of Russia to the Dniester and the Dvina'.[94]

During the 1848 revolution, as editors of the *Neue Rheinische Zeitung*, Marx and Engels had to develop their national policy at a more specific and detailed level. Given that the overthrow of absolutism required the establishment of strong national states, Engels, who generally acted as the pair's spokesman on national questions, put forward the theory of the 'great historic nations', Germany, Poland, Hungary and Italy, as the four peoples that could successfully create viable nation states in central and eastern Europe.

The reason why Engels was led to discriminate in this way between 'great historic nations' and lesser nationalities doomed to subordination was that the trans-national empires contained an intricate patchwork of overlapping populations at different stages of social development. Although the Communist Manifesto had asserted that 'national differences, and antagonisms between peoples, are daily more and more vanishing',[95] consequent on capitalist development, these antagonisms were at this very time bursting forth into open conflict in the eastern part of Europe and were as significant a factor in the revolutions of 1848 as were antagonisms of class. Given the overlap of national groups, antagonisms of this kind could never be solved according to principles of abstract justice, and Marx and Engels in any case rejected as idealist the so-called 'principle of nationalities', by which each national group was considered entitled to self-determination as an absolute right. The Germans, Poles,

93. Below, p. 94.
94. 'Speech of 22 February 1848', below, p, 102.
95. Below, p. 79.

Hungarians and Italians had long proved their viability in struggling for unity and independence, and Marx and Engels decided to hitch the proletarian wagon to these national stars. In the process, the claims of the smaller and less vocal nationalities – Czechs, Slovaks, Croats, Serbs, etc. – went by the board.

Marx and Engels had never been guilty of crude German chauvinism, as Engels could himself demonstrate by reference to their pre-1848 writings.[96] During the 1848 revolution itself, they struggled against the chauvinist degeneration of German nationalism when the Frankfurt National Assembly claimed for Germany a share of the Prussian and former Polish province of Posen (Poznán) which still had a Polish majority. Their error in 1848 was rather a general great-nation chauvinism, based on the major miscalculation that the smaller peoples of Europe were doomed by the logic of history and had irrevocably lost their autonomy.

The national policy of the *Neue Rheinische Zeitung* was premised on the assumption that the economic and cultural differences between the 'great historic nations' and the other nationalities were substantial enough to allow the former to divide up the map between them. But the gap between these two groups was simply not great enough to make this possible. The case of the Czechs is the most outstanding example of this error. The predominantly Czech provinces of Bohemia and Moravia had formed part of the old Holy Roman Empire, and it was on the grounds of this historic attachment to Germany, not simply because of their substantial German minorities, that the Frankfurt Assembly claimed them from Austria in the name of a united Germany. It was undoubtedly true that the Slavic nationalities were on the whole less advanced than the Germans, and that the cultural and economic development of the central and southern Slavs had owed a lot to their German neighbours. Yet it showed a substantial gap in Engels's historical knowledge, to say the least, to assert that the Czechs had 'never had a history'.[97] And, arguing against Bakunin's[98] programme of

96. See 'Democratic Pan-Slavism', below, p. 231.

97. Ibid., p. 226.

98. Michael Bakunin is chiefly remembered as the founder of revolutionary anarchism as a tendency in the working-class movement. For his disputes with Marx in this regard see the Introduction to *The First International and After*, pp. 727–37. In the mid 1840s Bakunin had been a member of the Young Hegelian circle in Germany and was close to Marx at the inception of the *Deutsch-Französische Jahrbücher*. Still a revolutionary democrat, Bakunin took an active part in the 1848 revolution. In May 1849 during the Reich Constitution Campaign he played a leading role in the

'democratic pan-Slavism', Engels went so far as to claim that 'apart from the Poles, the Russians, and at most the Slavs of Turkey, no Slav people has a future, for the simple reason that all the other Slavs lack the primary historical, geographical, political and industrial conditions for a viable independence'.[99] However, far from accepting their permanent incorporation into Germany, the Czechs were already in the sway of a cultural renaissance that blossomed in 1848 into a political movement for national independence. Slovaks, Croats, Serbs and others were later to follow in their wake.

The four 'great historic nations' were thus an insufficient base for Marx and Engels's national policy, and this untenable tactic itself contributed to the failure of the 1848 revolution. The opposition of all classes in Germany to Czech independence, which the *Neue Rheinische Zeitung* shared, helped to drive Czech nationalism onto a pro-Russian path, while the Magyar suppression of Croat nationalism, which the *Neue Rheinische Zeitung* actively encouraged, enabled the Habsburg monarchy to use the Croatian army against revolutionary Vienna. Bakunin's 1848 programme of a democratic pan-Slavist movement was certainly utopian, given the great diversity of conditions in the Slavic lands. And the 'principle of nationalities' which Bakunin accepted was both idealist and impossible to put into practice, as Engels argued. But Bakunin at least recognized the strength of the Slavic nationalisms and attempted to exploit their anti-tsarist potential. The Habsburg monarchy survived the 1848 revolution precisely because of its skill in playing off its subject nations against one another. Marx and Engels, however, completely failed to formulate a policy designed to counter this.

The Split in the Communist League

For the first year of his exile in England, Marx believed that the defeats of 1849 had been a temporary setback. He therefore applied his main energies to rebuilding the Communist League. Towards this end, he also worked in the German Workers Educational Association and the Social-Democratic Refugee Committee, and organized the publication, in Hamburg, of the monthly *Neue Rheinische Zeitung Revue*. The Central Committee of the League had been reconstituted

Dresden insurrection, was captured and handed over to the Russian government, and subsequently spent twelve years in prison before escaping.

99. 'Democratic Pan-Slavism', below, p. 225.

in London in autumn 1848 by the first of the new exiles who left Germany after the September crisis, though its links with Germany had so far remained fragile. Although Marx had himself dissolved the former Central Committee in May 1848, he recognized that a secret organization was again necessary, now that open political activity was once more impossible, and was unanimously voted onto the new Central Committee as soon as he arrived in London. Engels, who had taken refuge in Switzerland after the defeat of the Baden insurrection, joined Marx in London in October.

During this period Marx and Engels wrote two circular letters on behalf of the Central Committee, the *Addresses of the Central Committee to the Communist League of March and June 1850*. The March Address is the more important of these, and draws theoretical and tactical conclusions from the experience of 1848, to be applied in the next round of the German revolution which was expected shortly. Although written by Marx and Engels, it opens with a criticism of unnamed persons who are really none other than themselves. If 'a large number of members who were directly involved in the movement thought that the time for secret societies was over and that public action alone was sufficient', then the leaders of this tendency had unmistakably been Marx and Engels, and their allies on the *Neue Rheinische Zeitung*. And if 'the individual districts and communes allowed their connections with the Central Committee to weaken and gradually become dormant', the responsibility for this fell directly on Marx, who, entrusted with full executive power, had unilaterally dissolved the Central Committee and thus effectively prevented the League from functioning during the critical period of the revolution. As for the charge that, with the disorganization of the League, the workers' party had 'come under the complete domination and leadership of the petty-bourgeois democrats', again it was Marx and Engels who had deliberately blocked the Cologne Workers Society from putting up independent workers' candidates in the elections and had worked to subordinate the workers' movement to the broad democratic front right up to February 1849.[1]

The unexpected blow that had vitiated Marx's previous tactical position and led to this implicit self-criticism was the passage of the Prussian liberal bourgeoisie to the reactionary camp, analysed by Marx in 'The Bourgeoisie and the Counter-Revolution'. Marx had

1. See below, pp. 313–14.

held in the Communist Manifesto that the proletarian revolution in Germany would follow hard on the heels of the bourgeois revolution. Now that the bourgeois revolution had been deserted by its natural leader, the bourgeoisie, and the task of destroying feudalism and absolutism therefore fell to the plebeian classes alone, it seemed that the bourgeois revolution would directly merge into the first stages of the proletarian revolution. With this perspective, Marx developed in the March Address the tactic of 'permanent revolution'. Although the petty-bourgeois democrats are expected to take the initiative in the next revolutionary outbreak (carrying on the struggle they began with the Reich Constitution Campaign), Marx sets the German working class the task of inserting into the anti-feudal struggle its own leadership and carrying the revolution forward from the overthrow of absolutism to the overthrow of capital itself.

Marx stresses, therefore, that the workers, after they fought with the petty bourgeoisie against the existing governments, must not lay down their arms with the advent of the new regime, even if they themselves could not yet take and hold power. The workers must remain armed and organized so that, even if the petty-bourgeois democrats would seize power in the first instance, they could 'make it as difficult as possible for the petty bourgeoisie to use its power against the armed proletariat, and . . . dictate such conditions to them that the rule of the bourgeois democrats, from the very first, will carry within it the seeds of its own destruction, and its subsequent displacement by the proletariat will be made considerably easier'.[2] Although 'the German workers cannot come to power and achieve the realization of their class interests without passing through a protracted revolutionary development',[3] it is the exercise of their own independent political power that the workers must now be concerned with.

In this context, Marx develops two important points of revolutionary theory. Firstly, the state apparatus is not a mere machine that passes from the control of one class to another, so that the working class must prepare for taking power by building up its own state apparatus alongside and in opposition to that of the propertied classes. The workers will need their own armed and representative counter-state organizations, which Marx refers to as 'revolutionary local councils' or 'revolutionary workers' governments'. These were later to take

2. Below, p. 319.
3. Below, p. 324.

on a concrete historical existence in the form of the Paris Commune of 1871 and the Russian Soviets of 1905 and 1917. Secondly, the need for these counter-state organizations presented a new task for the Communists. Whereas in the Manifesto Marx had confined the Communists' specific task to propaganda work within the proletarian party, he now made it clear that it was the task, not just of the workers' party, but particularly of the organized Communists as its most advanced section, to ensure that this counter-state power was in fact set up.

The March Address marks a significant theoretical advance for the politics of scientific communism, but in practice, the tactic of permanent revolution was quite inapplicable in the circumstances of Germany in 1850. Marx and Engels had entered the revolutionary period of 1848 with a basically false assumption, that the impending revolutionary storm marked the beginning of the end for the bourgeois order. With the advantage of hindsight, it is clear that industrial capitalism was still in its early stages even in England, while on the Continent the new mode of production was only in its infancy. Throughout the 1848 period, Marx and Engels tended to read into the present what was still a long way in the future, an error of judgement which can be attributed to the novelty of the ideas of scientific communism and their birth so far ahead of their time.[4] We have already seen how the spectre of proletarian revolution led the German bourgeoisie to compromise its own goals and thus vitiated Marx and Engels's original tactic of alliance with the bourgeoisie in the bourgeois revolution. Once the bourgeoisie had passed over to the side of reaction, the assumption that socialism was on the historical agenda in Germany, and that only the class-conscious organization of the proletariat was necessary to overthrow capitalism, led Marx and Engels to a new tactical error. The tactic of permanent revolution could not have worked, as the weakness of the German working class at the time was due not simply to its political and ideological immaturity, but to the economic immaturity of German capitalism. There was not the slightest chance of the German proletariat, whatever the political circumstances, overthrowing capitalism and setting up a socialist economy.

4. See Engels's 1895 Introduction to *The Class Struggles in France*, in *MECW* 27, p. 512: 'History has proved us wrong, and all who thought like us. It has made clear that the state of economic development on the Continent at that time was not, by a long way, ripe for the elimination of capitalist production; it has proved this by the economic revolution which, since 1848, has seized the whole of the Continent . . .'

In the event, the revolutionary movement of 1848 had already been decisively defeated. Capitalism was to triumph in Germany without the revolutionary overthrow of the old regime, which would instead undertake its own 'modernization', and Germany was to be unified from above by Prussian arms. In the absence of a revolutionary situation, the tactics of the March Address were not put to the test, and the problem of the position of the proletariat in the bourgeois revolution disappeared from Marxist theory for half a century. Only in 1905 was Marxism finally to deal with the situation produced by the abdication of the bourgeoisie in the face of 'its own' revolution, when Lenin developed for the Russian revolution of that year a tactic that fully matched up to the torsions of this form of uneven development, that of the 'revolutionary-democratic dictatorship of the proletariat and the peasantry'. According to Lenin, the proletariat in this situation should struggle for leadership of the bourgeois revolution, even going so far as to temporarily seize state power with a provisional revolutionary government. The proletariat could thereby ensure what the petty bourgeoisie would not, the decisive defeat of all feudal and absolutist vestiges, and therefore the most favourable conditions for pursuing its own ultimate goals. It could do this without any illusions of the possibility of passing directly to socialism, and indeed it had to forgo the attempt to advance towards socialism at this stage, as it still needed the support of the peasantry as a whole (and not just the rural proletariat) in order to decisively defeat the old regime.[5]

The tactic of permanent revolution, although inapplicable in the Germany of 1850, remained as a valuable political legacy for the workers' movement. It was proposed by Trotsky for Russia in 1905, though Lenin still considered it premature to attempt to convert the bourgeois-democratic revolution into a proletarian one. In 1917, however, in the context of the all-European crisis brought about by the World War, Lenin and the Bolshevik party were able to apply successfully the tactic of permanent revolution, leading the Russian revolution of that year forward from the overthrow of tsarism to the overthrow of capital itself.

The June Address witnesses to the revival of the Communist League's organization in Germany, despite the difficult conditions created by the repression. It is noteworthy for its insistence on the

5. See 'Two Tactics of Social-Democracy in the Democratic Revolution', in Volume 1 of Lenin's *Selected Works*, online at www.marxists.org.

organizational unity of the Communists as the precondition for tactical action, and for the importance it attaches to the international alliances that the League had built with the left wing of the English Chartists, and with the exiled French Blanquists and Hungarian revolutionaries. In April 1850 the Central Committee of the League had founded, together with the Blanquists and left Chartists, a secret international organization confined to leading cadres, the 'Universal Society of Revolutionary Communists', based on the expectation of a new revolutionary outbreak and pledging mutual support. The first two articles of its constitution, signed by Adam and J. Vidil (Blanquists), G. Julian Harney (Chartist), and Marx, Engels and August Willich (Communist League), specified:

1. The aim of the association is the downfall of all privileged classes, the submission of those classes to the dictatorship of the proletariat by keeping the revolution in continual progress until the achievement of communism, which shall be the ultimate form of the constitution of the human family.
2. To contribute to the realization of this aim, the association will form ties of solidarity between all sections of the revolutionary communist party, causing national divisions to disappear according to the principle of republican fraternity.[6]

Soon after writing the June Address, however, Marx underwent a substantial change of perspective, perhaps the most important during his entire political work as a Communist. In the summer of 1850, he returned to the economic studies he had abandoned in 1848 and undertook a thorough analysis of the economic basis of the political upheavals of the past few years. The conclusion he came to was that the 1848 revolutions had been provoked by the trade crisis of the previous year, and that, with the economic recovery that was now in progress, 'there can be no question of a real revolution. Such a revolution is only possible at a time when *two factors* come into *conflict*: the *modern productive forces* and the *bourgeois forms of production* ... *A new revolution is only possible as a result of a new crisis; but it will come, just as surely as the crisis itself.*'[7]

6. *MECW* 10, p. 614.
7. 'Review: May–October 1850', below, p. 297, n. 47.

This analysis had substantial implications for Communist political practice, and a dispute arose between Marx's group and the 'Willich-Schapper faction'.[8] In the private context of this dispute Marx went further than in his Review and admitted that a successful proletarian revolution, in Germany at least, depended not simply on the next periodic trade crisis, but also on a considerable further development of the productive forces.

On 15 September 1850 the Central Committee of the League concluded its debate on 'the position of the German proletariat in the coming revolution'.[9] Schapper had argued to the Central Committee that the activities of the Communists only had meaning if the proletariat could come to power immediately with the next round of the revolution. Otherwise, they might as well give up political activity altogether. Arguing against Schapper, Marx subtly but decisively jettisoned the tactic of permanent revolution put forward in the March Address. While the Address had spoken of the working class having to undergo a 'protracted revolutionary development' before it could achieve its goal, Marx now mentioned 'fifteen, twenty or fifty years' of class struggle as the time-scale involved, ascribing this to the immaturity of economic conditions. Even if the workers' party did come to power now, it could only carry out petty-bourgeois measures (i.e. it could not socialize production, which was still predominantly small-scale).[10] Both sides agreed that this difference in perspective was too great to enable them to continue working together, and the League split in two.

Despite Willich and Schapper's fine revolutionary spirit, they had, as Marx claimed, renounced the scientific communism of the Manifesto. Unable to refute Marx's economic arguments, they ignored them and stressed 'the *will*, rather than the actual

8. August Willich, a former Prussian officer, joined with Karl Schapper in leading this 'left' opposition to Marx; in 1853 he emigrated to the USA and later fought for the North in the Civil War, like many other German communist émigrés.

9. See 'Minutes of the Central Committee Meeting of 15 September 1850', below, p. 335.

10. It might nevertheless be very important for the proletariat to come to power and carry out petty-bourgeois measures, as Lenin was to hold. Although Marx never developed the tactic of the 'revolutionary–democratic dictatorship', he had himself stressed in the March Address that the petty bourgeoisie would flinch from sufficiently radical measures to destroy all vestiges of feudalism, and this had already been shown in practice with the Reich Constitution Campaign. But in the light of Marx's thesis that 'there can be no question of a real revolution', the question had become, at least for the time being, an academic one.

conditions . . . as the chief factor in the revolution'.[11] This was in fact the position of the Blanquists, who held as a principle that only the activity of the vanguard was ever necessary in order to reopen the revolutionary process. When Marx rejected the possibility of a new revolution in the near future, there was no longer any occasion for his alliance with the Blanquists. After the split in the League, Marx, Engels and Harney wrote to the Blanquist leaders that they had 'long considered the association as *de facto* dissolved' (i.e. the Universal Society of Revolutionary Communists) and requested a meeting to burn the founding agreement.[12] Willich and Schapper, however, whose supporters formed the majority both in the Communist League's London district and in the German Workers Educational Association, slid from a tactical alliance with the Blanquists to a strategic one. Rather than 'work for the creation of an independent organization of the workers' party, both secret and open, alongside the official democrats',[13] which the March Address had laid down as the task of the Communist League in the immediate, pre-revolutionary period, they turned to conspiratorial activity precisely in harness with the petty-bourgeois democrats, who from the safety of exile in London were hatching all sorts of schemes that came to nothing. Marx's group, on the other hand, moved their Central Committee to Cologne, where it continued for a while to conduct propaganda work. In spring 1851, however, both groups' German organizations were totally destroyed by the Prussian police, and after the conviction of the accused in the Cologne Communist Trial of October 1852, Marx had his League formally wound up.

The first major phase of Marx's political practice as a scientific communist comes to an end with the close of the revolutionary period of 1848, and with Marx's recognition of this fact. The communist revolution had proved to be a much longer and harder struggle than Marx had originally anticipated. Marx had in fact seen the revolution of 1848 as an ultimate and general crisis of capitalism, when this was, like all crises, specific and particular. As the revolutionary tide ebbed, he began to stand back and take the measure of the events of the past few years. During the 1850s Marx returned to the economic studies that were to result in *Capital*

11. 'Minutes of the Central Committee Meeting of 15 September 1850,' below, p. 335.
12. *MECW* 10, p. 484.
13. Below, p. 318.

and sharpened his general theory of historical materialism, which was still very incomplete in the 1848 period. Politically, however, Marx was very isolated during the decade of reaction. After the Communist League was dissolved in 1852, he no longer belonged to any political organization, and he saw eye to eye with very few of his former comrades. Most of these had either followed Schapper and Willich, or abandoned political activity altogether. Between 1852 and 1864, Marx was to comment voluminously on developments in Europe and overseas, but he had resigned himself temporarily to the role of a spectator.

When the European workers' movements recovered from the defeats of 1848–50, Marx's overall perspective had substantially broadened. His horizon, originally simply European, was increasingly becoming a world one. And while Marx by no means abandoned his thesis of the necessity of violent revolution, he was to lay more stress on the gradual building of a mass workers' party as a necessary prerequisite for this. This process was set under way with the foundation, in 1864, of the International Working Men's Association – the First International – in which Marx himself played a leading role.

*

Besides several texts that Marx and Engels co-authored, a few articles written by Engels alone have been included in this volume where these are necessary to the understanding of Marx's own politics. Although Engels's positions sometimes diverged slightly from Marx's, the two did operate a very close division of labour from 1846 through to Marx's death, in which Marx generally left to Engels the fields of international politics and military affairs. Not only did Marx and Engels invariably consult together before publishing any significant political statement, but Engels often wrote pieces at Marx's express request. Although Engels's individual work, these are nevertheless an essential dimension of Marx and Engels's joint political practice. In the Introduction and Notes to this volume 'Marx' is sometimes used for 'Marx and Engels' in this sense, and when Marx alone is involved and it is necessary to avoid ambiguity, this is made explicit.

All texts written by Marx and Engels in German and French have been newly translated for this volume, with the exception of the Communist Manifesto, for which we have used the authorized

English translation by Samuel Moore, edited by Engels. Articles from the *Neue Rheinische Zeitung* and the Reviews from *Neue Rheinische Zeitung Revue* were annotated by Ben Fowkes.

DAVID FERNBACH
1973 AND 2010

Manifesto of the Communist Party

PREFACE TO THE ENGLISH EDITION OF 1888[1]

The Manifesto was published as the platform of the Communist League, a working men's association, first exclusively German, later on international, and, under the political conditions of the Continent before 1848, unavoidably a secret society. At a congress of the League, held in London in November 1847, Marx and Engels were commissioned to prepare for publication a complete theoretical and practical party programme. Drawn up in German, in January 1848, the manuscript was sent to the printer in London a few weeks before the French revolution of 24 February. A French translation was brought out in Paris shortly before the insurrection of June 1848. The first English translation, by Miss Helen Macfarlane, appeared in George Julian Harney's *Red Republican*, London, 1850. A Danish and a Polish edition had also been published.

The defeat of the Parisian insurrection of June 1848 – the first great battle between proletariat and bourgeoisie – drove again into the background, for a time, the social and political aspirations of the European working class. Thenceforth, the struggle for supremacy was again, as it had been before the revolution of February, solely between different sections of the propertied class; the working class was reduced to a fight for political elbow-room, and to the position of extreme wing of the middle-class radicals. Wherever independent proletarian movements continued to show signs of life, they were ruthlessly hunted down. Thus the Prussian police hunted out the Central Board[2] of the Communist League, then

---

1. This translation of the Communist Manifesto was made by Samuel Moore in 1888, and edited by Engels. His notes are identified in this edition by [Engels]. Besides printer's errors, inconsistent and old-fashioned punctuation and orthography, a very few linguistic archaisms have also been amended.

2. I.e. the Central Committee, as it is referred to elsewhere in this edition.

located in Cologne. The members were arrested, and, after eighteen months' imprisonment, they were tried in October 1852. This celebrated 'Cologne Communist Trial' lasted from 4 October till 12 November; seven of the prisoners were sentenced to terms of imprisonment in a fortress, varying from three to six years. Immediately after the sentence, the League was formally dissolved by the remaining members. As to the Manifesto, it seemed thenceforth to be doomed to oblivion.

When the European working class had recovered sufficient strength for another attack on the ruling classes, the International Working Men's Association sprang up.[3] But this association, formed with the express aim of welding into one body the whole militant proletariat of Europe and America, could not at once proclaim the principles laid down in the Manifesto. The International was bound to have a programme broad enough to be acceptable to the English trade unions, to the followers of Proudhon in France, Belgium, Italy and Spain, and to the Lassalleans[4] in Germany. Marx, who drew up this programme to the satisfaction of all parties, entirely trusted to the intellectual development of the working class, which was sure to result from combined action and mutual discussion. The very events and vicissitudes of the struggle against capital, the defeats even more than the victories, could not help bringing home to men's minds the insufficiency of their various favourite nostrums, and preparing the way for a more complete insight into the true conditions of working-class emancipation. And Marx was right. The International, on its breaking up in 1874,[5] left the workers quite different men from what it had found them in 1864. Proudhonism in France, Lassalleanism in Germany were dying out, and even the conservative English trade unions, though most of them had long since severed their connection with the International, were gradually advancing towards that point at which, last year at Swansea, their President could say in their name, 'Continental socialism has lost its terrors

3. On the International, see the Introduction to *The First International and After*.

4. Lassalle personally, to us, always acknowledged himself to be a disciple of Marx, and, as such, stood on the ground of the Manifesto. But in his public agitation, 1862–4, he did not go beyond demanding cooperative workshops supported by state credit [Engels].

5. In fact the International was not officially wound up until 1876, although it effectively ceased to function when the General Council was transferred to New York in 1872.

for us.'[6] In fact: the principles of the Manifesto had made considerable headway among the working men of all countries.

The Manifesto itself thus came to the front again. The German text had been, since 1850, reprinted several times in Switzerland, England and America. In 1872, it was translated into English in New York, where the translation was published in *Woodhull and Claflin's Weekly*.[7] From this English version, a French one was made in *Le Socialiste* of New York. Since then at least two more English translations, more or less mutilated, have been brought out in America, and one of them has been reprinted in England. The first Russian translation, made by Bakunin, was published at Herzen's *Kolokol*[8] office in Geneva, about 1863; a second one, by the heroic Vera Zasulich,[9] also in Geneva, 1882. A new Danish edition is to be found in *Socialdemokratisk Bibliothek*, Copenhagen, 1885; a fresh French translation in *Le Socialiste*, Paris, 1885. From this latter a Spanish version was prepared and published in Madrid, 1886. The German reprints are not to be counted, there have been twelve altogether at the least. An Armenian translation, which was to be published in Constantinople some months ago, did not see the light, I am told, because the publisher was afraid of bringing out a book with the name of Marx on it, while the translator declined to call it his own production. Of further translations into other languages I have heard, but have not seen them. Thus the history of the Manifesto reflects, to a great extent, the history of the modern working-class movement; at present it is undoubtedly the most widespread, the most international production of all socialist literature, the common platform acknowledged by millions of working men from Siberia to California.

Yet, when it was written, we could not have called it a 'Socialist'

6. W. Bevan, in his address to the TUC Congress, reported in the *Commonweal*, 17 September 1887.

7. This paper was published by two American feminists, Victoria Woodhull and her sister Tennessee Claflin, whose campaign Marx considered 'middle-class humbug' and who were eventually expelled from the International. (See *IWMA* V, pp. 323–32). It carried an abridged translation of the Manifesto on 30 December 1871.

8. Alexander Herzen was a Russian philosopher and revolutionary democrat. His paper *Kolokol* (The Bell) was the leading organ of the Russian emigration in the 1860s. Bakunin's translation of the Manifesto was in fact published in 1869.

9. Engels celebrates Vera Zasulich for her attempted assassination of the governor of St Petersburg, General Trepov, in 1878. The translation was in fact by George Plekhanov, the founder of Russian Marxism.

manifesto. By 'socialists', in 1847, were understood, on the one hand, the adherents of the various utopian systems: Owenites in England, Fourierists in France, both of them already reduced to the position of mere sects, and gradually dying out; on the other hand, the most multifarious social quacks, who, by all manners of tinkering, professed to redress, without any danger to capital and profit, all sorts of social grievances; in both cases men outside the working-class movement, and looking rather to the 'educated' classes for support. Whatever portion of the working class had become convinced of the insufficiency of mere political revolutions, and had proclaimed the necessity of a total social change, that portion then called itself communist. It was a crude, rough-hewn, purely instinctive sort of communism; still, it touched the cardinal point and was powerful enough amongst the working class to produce the utopian communism, in France, of Cabet, and in Germany, of Weitling. Thus, socialism was, in 1847, a middle-class movement, communism a working-class movement. Socialism was, on the Continent at least, 'respectable'; communism was the very opposite. And as our notion, from the very beginning, was that 'the emancipation of the working class must be the act of the working class itself', there could be no doubt as to which of the two names we must take. Moreover, we have, ever since, been far from repudiating it.

The Manifesto being our joint production, I consider myself bound to state that the fundamental proposition, which forms its nucleus, belongs to Marx. That proposition is: that in every historical epoch, the prevailing mode of economic production and exchange, and the social organization necessarily following from it, form the basis upon which is built up, and from which alone can be explained, the political and intellectual history of that epoch; that consequently the whole history of mankind (since the dissolution of primitive tribal society, holding land in common ownership) has been a history of class struggles, contests between exploiting and exploited, ruling and oppressed classes; that the history of these class struggles forms a series of evolutions in which, nowadays, a stage has been reached where the exploited and oppressed class – the proletariat – cannot attain its emancipation from the sway of the exploiting and ruling class – the bourgeoisie – without, at the same time, and once and for all, emancipating society at large from all exploitation, oppression, class distinctions and class struggles.

This proposition which, in my opinion, is destined to do for history what Darwin's theory has done for biology, we, both of us, had been gradually approaching for some years before 1845. How far I had independently progressed towards it is best shown by my *Condition of the Working Class in England*. But when I again met Marx at Brussels, in spring 1845, he had it ready worked out, and put it before me, in terms almost as clear as those in which I have stated it here.

From our joint preface to the German edition of 1872, I quote the following:

However much the state of things may have altered during the last twenty-five years, the general principles laid down in this Manifesto are, on the whole, as correct today as ever. Here and there some detail might be improved. The practical application of the principles will depend, as the Manifesto itself states, everywhere and at all times, on the historical conditions for the time being existing, and, for that reason, no special stress is laid on the revolutionary measures proposed at the end of section II. That passage would, in many respects, be very differently worded today. In view of the gigantic strides of modern industry since 1848, and of the accompanying improved and extended organization of the working class; in view of the practical experience gained, first in the February revolution, and then, still more, in the Paris Commune, where the proletariat for the first time held political power for two whole months, this programme has in some details become antiquated. One thing especially was proved by the Commune, viz., that 'the working class cannot simply lay hold of the ready-made state machinery, and wield it for its own purposes'. (See 'The Civil War in France', section III, where this point is further developed.) Further, it is self-evident that the criticism of socialist literature is deficient in relation to the present time, because it comes down only to 1847; also, that the remarks on the relation of the Communists to the various opposition parties (section IV), although in principle still correct, yet in practice are antiquated, because the political situation has been entirely changed, and the progress of history has swept from off the earth the greater portion of the political parties there enumerated.

But then, the Manifesto has become a historical document which we have no longer any right to alter.

The present translation is by Mr Samuel Moore, the translator of the greater portion of Marx's *Capital*. We have revised it in common, and I have added a few notes explanatory of historical allusions.

London, 30 January 1888   FREDERICK ENGELS

MANIFESTO OF THE COMMUNIST PARTY

A spectre is haunting Europe – the spectre of Communism. All the powers of old Europe have entered into a holy alliance to exorcize this spectre: Pope and Tsar, Metternich[10] and Guizot,[11] French radicals and German police spies.

Where is the party in opposition that has not been decried as communistic by its opponents in power? Where the opposition that has not hurled back the branding reproach of Communism, against the more advanced opposition parties, as well as against its reactionary adversaries?

Two things result from this fact.

1. Communism is already acknowledged by all European powers to be itself a power.

2. It is high time that Communists should openly, in the face of the whole world, publish their views, their aims, their tendencies, and meet this nursery tale of the Spectre of Communism with a manifesto of the party itself.

To this end, Communists of various nationalities have assembled in London, and sketched the following manifesto, to be published in the English, French, German, Italian, Flemish and Danish languages.

1. Bourgeois and Proletarians[12]

The history of all hitherto existing society[13] is the history of class struggles.

10. Clemens Lothar, prince Metternich, was the leading Austrian statesman from 1809 to 1848 and the architect of the counter-revolutionary Holy Alliance.

11. François Guizot was a French historian and *de facto* Prime Minister from 1840 to 1848 under the Orleanist 'July' monarchy of Louis Philippe.

12. By bourgeoisie is meant the class of modern capitalists, owners of the means of social production and employers of wage labour. By proletariat, the class of modern wage labourers who, having no means of production of their own, are reduced to selling their labour power in order to live [Engels].

13. That is, all *written* history. In 1847, the pre-history of society, the social organization existing previous to recorded history, was all but unknown. Since then, Haxthausen discovered common ownership of land in Russia, Maurer proved it to be the social foundation from which all Teutonic races started in history, and by and by village communities were found to be, or to have been the primitive form of society everywhere from India to Ireland. The inner organization of this primitive communistic society was laid bare, in its typical form, by Morgan's crowning discovery of the true nature of the

Freeman and slave, patrician and plebeian, lord and serf, guild-master[14] and journeyman, in a word, oppressor and oppressed, stood in constant opposition to one another, carried on an uninterrupted, now hidden, now open fight, a fight that each time ended, either in a revolutionary reconstitution of society at large, or in the common ruin of the contending classes.

In the earlier epochs of history, we find almost everywhere a complicated arrangement of society into various orders, a mani-fold gradation of social rank. In ancient Rome we have patricians, knights, plebeians, slaves; in the Middle Ages, feudal lords, vassals, guild-masters, journeymen, apprentices, serfs; in almost all of these classes, again, subordinate gradations.

The modern bourgeois society that has sprouted from the ruins of feudal society has not done away with class antagonisms. It has but established new classes, new conditions of oppression, new forms of struggle in place of the old ones.

Our epoch, the epoch of the bourgeoisie, possesses, however, this distinctive feature: it has simplified the class antagonisms. Society as a whole is more and more splitting up into two great hostile camps, into two great classes directly facing each other: bourgeoisie and proletariat.

From the serfs of the Middle Ages sprang the chartered burghers of the earliest towns. From these burgesses the first elements of the bourgeoisie were developed.

The discovery of America, the rounding of the Cape, opened up fresh ground for the rising bourgeoisie. The East Indian and Chinese markets, the colonization of America, trade with the colonies, the increase in the means of exchange and in commodities generally, gave to commerce, to navigation, to industry, an impulse never before known, and thereby, to the revolutionary element in the totter-ing feudal society, a rapid development.

The feudal system of industry, under which industrial produc-tion was monopolized by closed guilds, now no longer sufficed for the growing wants of the new markets. The manufacturing

---

gens and its relation to the *tribe*. With the dissolution of these primeval com-munities society begins to be differentiated into separate and finally antagonistic classes. I have attempted to retrace this process of dissolution in: *Der Ursprung der Familie, des Privateigenthums und des Staats* (*The Origin of the Family, Private Property and the State*) [Engels].

14. Guild-master, that is, a full member of a guild, a master within, not a head of a guild [Engels].

system took its place. The guild-masters were pushed on one side by the manufacturing middle class; division of labour between the different corporate guilds vanished in the face of division of labour in each single workshop.

Meantime the markets kept ever growing, the demand ever rising. Even manufacture no longer sufficed. Thereupon, steam and machinery revolutionized industrial production. The place of manufacture was taken by the giant, modern industry, the place of the industrial middle class, by industrial millionaires, the leaders of whole industrial armies, the modern bourgeois.

Modern industry has established the world market, for which the discovery of America paved the way. This market has given an immense development to commerce, to navigation, to communication by land. This development has, in its turn, reacted on the extension of industry; and in proportion as industry, commerce, navigation, railways extended, in the same proportion the bourgeoisie developed, increased its capital, and pushed into the background every class handed down from the Middle Ages.

We see, therefore, how the modern bourgeoisie is itself the product of a long course of development, of a series of revolutions in the modes of production and of exchange.

Each step in the development of the bourgeoisie was accompanied by a corresponding political advance of that class. An oppressed class under the sway of the feudal nobility, an armed and self-governing association in the medieval commune;[15] here independent urban republic (as in Italy and Germany), there taxable 'third estate' of the monarchy (as in France), afterwards, in the period of manufacture proper, serving either the semifeudal or the absolute monarchy as a counterpoise against the nobility, and, in fact, corner stone of the great monarchies in general, the bourgeoisie has at last, since the establishment of modern industry and of the world market, conquered for itself, in the modern representative state, exclusive political sway. The executive of the modern state is but a committee for managing the common affairs of the whole bourgeoisie.

15. 'Commune' was the name taken, in France, by the nascent towns even before they had conquered, from their feudal lords and masters, local self-government and political rights as the 'third estate'. Generally speaking, for the economic development of the bourgeoisie, England is here taken as the typical country; for its political development, France [Engels].

The bourgeoisie, historically, has played a most revolutionary part.

The bourgeoisie, wherever it has got the upper hand, has put an end to all feudal, patriarchal, idyllic relations. It has pitilessly torn asunder the motley feudal ties that bound man to his 'natural superiors', and has left remaining no other nexus between man and man than naked self-interest, than callous 'cash payment'. It has drowned the most heavenly ecstasies of religious fervour, of chivalrous enthusiasm, of philistine sentimentalism, in the icy water of egotistical calculation. It has resolved personal worth into exchange value, and in place of the numberless indefeasible chartered freedoms, has set up that single, unconscionable free- dom – free trade. In one word, for exploitation, veiled by religious and political illusions, it has substituted naked, shameless, direct, brutal exploitation.

The bourgeoisie has stripped of its halo every occupation hitherto honoured and looked up to with reverent awe. It has converted the physician, the lawyer, the priest, the poet, the man of science, into its paid wage labourers.

The bourgeoisie has torn away from the family its sentimental veil, and has reduced the family relation to a mere money relation.

The bourgeoisie has disclosed how it came to pass that the brutal display of vigour in the Middle Ages, which reactionists so much admire, found its fitting complement in the most slothful indolence. It has been the first to show what man's activity can bring about. It has accomplished wonders far surpassing Egyp- tian pyramids, Roman aqueducts, and Gothic cathedrals; it has conducted expeditions that put in the shade all former exoduses of nations and crusades.

The bourgeoisie cannot exist without constantly revolutionizing the instruments of production, and thereby the relations of produc- tion, and with them the whole relations of society. Conservation of the old modes of production in unaltered form, was, on the contrary, the first condition of existence for all earlier industrial classes. Constant revolutionizing of production, uninterrupted disturbance of all social conditions, everlasting uncertainty and agitation distinguish the bourgeois epoch from all earlier ones. All fixed, fast-frozen relations, with their train of ancient and vener- able prejudices and opinions, are swept away, all new-formed ones become antiquated before they can ossify. All that is solid melts into air, all that is holy is profaned, and man is at last compelled to face with sober senses, his real conditions of life, and his relations with his kind.

The need of a constantly expanding market for its products chases the bourgeoisie over the whole surface of the globe. It must nestle everywhere, settle everywhere, establish connections everywhere.

The bourgeoisie has through its exploitation of the world market given a cosmopolitan character to production and consumption in every country. To the great chagrin of reactionists, it has drawn from under the feet of industry the national ground on which it stood. All old-established national industries have been destroyed or are daily being destroyed. They are dislodged by new industries, whose introduction becomes a life and death question for all civilized nations, by industries that no longer work up indigenous raw material, but raw material drawn from the remotest zones; industries whose products are consumed, not only at home, but in every quarter of the globe. In place of the old wants, satisfied by the productions of the country, we find new wants, requiring for their satisfaction the products of distant lands and climes. In place of the old local and national seclusion and self-sufficiency, we have intercourse in every direction, universal interdependence of nations. And as in material, so also in intellectual production. The intellectual creations of individual nations become common property. National one-sidedness and narrow-mindedness become more and more impossible, and from the numerous national and local literatures, there arises a world literature.

The bourgeoisie, by the rapid improvement of all instruments of production, by the immensely facilitated means of communication, draws all, even the most barbarian, nations into civilization. The cheap prices of its commodities are the heavy artillery with which it batters down all Chinese walls, with which it forces the barbarians' intensely obstinate hatred of foreigners to capitulate. It compels all nations, on pain of extinction, to adopt the bourgeois mode of production; it compels them to introduce what it calls civilization into their midst, i.e., to become bourgeois themselves. In one word, it creates a world after its own image.

The bourgeoisie has subjected the country to the rule of the towns. It has created enormous cities, has greatly increased the urban population as compared with the rural, and has thus rescued a considerable part of the population from the idiocy of rural life.

Just as it has made the country dependent on the towns, so it has made barbarian and semi-barbarian countries dependent on the civilized ones, nations of peasants on nations of bourgeois, the East on the West.

The bourgeoisie keeps more and more doing away with the scattered state of the population, of the means of production, and of property. It has agglomerated population, centralized means of production, and has concentrated property in a few hands. The necessary consequence of this was political centralization. Independent, or but loosely connected provinces, with separate interests, laws, governments and systems of taxation, became lumped together into one nation, with one government, one code of laws, one national class interest, one frontier and one customs tariff.

The bourgeoisie, during its rule of scarce one hundred years, has created more massive and more colossal productive forces than have all preceding generations together. Subjection of nature's forces to man, machinery, application of chemistry to industry and agriculture, steam navigation, railways, electric telegraphs, clearing of whole continents for cultivation, canalization of rivers, whole populations conjured out of the ground – what earlier century had even a presentiment that such productive forces slumbered in the lap of social labour?

We see then: the means of production and of exchange, on whose foundation the bourgeoisie built itself up, were generated in feudal society. At a certain stage in the development of these means of production and of exchange, the conditions under which feudal society produced and exchanged, the feudal organization of agriculture and manufacturing industry, in one word, the feudal relations of property became no longer compatible with the already developed productive forces; they became so many fetters. They had to be burst asunder; they were burst asunder.

Into their place stepped free competition, accompanied by a social and political constitution adapted to it, and by the economical and political sway of the bourgeois class.

A similar movement is going on before our own eyes. Modern bourgeois society with its relations of production, of exchange and of property, a society that has conjured up such gigantic means of production and of exchange, is like the sorcerer, who is no longer able to control the powers of the nether world whom he has called up by his spells. For many a decade past, the history of industry and commerce is but the history of the revolt of modern productive forces against modern conditions of production, against the property relations that are the conditions for the existence of the bourgeoisie and of its rule. It is enough to mention the commercial crises that by their periodical return put on trial, each time more threateningly, the existence of the entire bourgeois society. In these crises a great part not only of the existing products, but also of the previously created productive forces, are periodically destroyed. In these crises there breaks out an epidemic that, in all earlier epochs, would have seemed an absurdity – the epidemic of overproduction. Society suddenly finds itself put back into a state of momentary barbarism; it appears as if a famine, a universal war of devastation had cut off the supply of every means of subsistence; industry and commerce seem to be destroyed; and why? Because there is too much civilization, too much means of subsistence, too much industry, too much commerce. The productive forces at the disposal of society no longer tend to further the development of the conditions of bourgeois property; on the contrary, they have become too powerful for these conditions, by which they are fettered, and so soon as they overcome these fetters, they bring disorder into the whole of bourgeois society, endanger the existence of bourgeois property. The conditions of bourgeois society are too narrow to comprise the wealth created by them. And how does the bourgeoisie get over these crises? On the one hand by enforced destruction of a mass of productive forces; on the other, by the conquest of new markets, and by the more thorough exploitation of the old ones. That is to say, by paving the way for more extensive and more destructive crises, and by diminishing the means whereby crises are prevented.

The weapons with which the bourgeoisie felled feudalism to the ground are now turned against the bourgeoisie itself.

But not only has the bourgeoisie forged the weapons that bring death to itself; it has also called into existence the men who are to wield those weapons – the modern working class – the proletarians.

In proportion as the bourgeoisie, i.e., capital, is developed, in the same proportion is the proletariat, the modern working class, developed – a class of labourers, who live only so long as they find work, and who find work only so long as their labour increases capital. These labourers, who must sell themselves piecemeal, are a commodity, like every other article of commerce, and are consequently exposed to all the vicissitudes of competition, to all the fluctuations of the market.

Owing to the extensive use of machinery and to division of labour, the work of the proletarians has lost all individual character, and, consequently, all charm for the workman. He becomes an appendage of the machine, and it is only the most simple, most monotonous, and most easily acquired knack, that is required of him. Hence, the cost of production of a workman is restricted, almost entirely, to the means of subsistence that he requires for his maintenance, and for the propagation of his race. But the price of a commodity, and therefore also of labour,[16] is equal to its cost of production. In proportion, therefore, as the repulsiveness of the work increases, the wage decreases. Nay more, in proportion as the use of machinery and division of labour increases, in the same proportion the burden of toil also increases, whether by prolongation of the working hours, by increase of the work exacted in a given time or by increased speed of the machinery, etc.

Modern industry has converted the little workshop of the patriarchal master into the great factory of the industrial capitalist. Masses of labourers, crowded into the factory, are organized like soldiers. As privates of the industrial army they are placed under the command of a perfect hierarchy of officers and sergeants. Not only are they slaves of the bourgeois class, and of the bourgeois state; they are daily and hourly enslaved by the machine, by the overseer, and, above all, by the individual bourgeois manufacturer himself. The more openly this despotism proclaims gain to be its end and aim, the more petty, the more hateful and the more embittering it is.

The less the skill and exertion of strength implied in manual labour, in other words, the more modern industry becomes developed, the more is the labour of men superseded by that of women. Differences of age and sex have no longer any distinctive social validity for the working class. All are instruments of labour, more or less expensive to use, according to their age and sex.

No sooner is the exploitation of the labourer by the manufacturer so far at an end that he receives his wages in cash, than he is set upon by the other portions of the bourgeoisie, the landlord, the shopkeeper, the pawnbroker, etc.

16. In Marx's later theory of surplus value, he concluded that it is the worker's *labour power*, not his labour, that is sold to the capitalist as a commodity. (See 'Value, Price and Profit', in *MECW* 20.)

The lower strata of the middle class – the small tradespeople, shopkeepers, and *rentiers*, the handicraftsmen and peasants – all these sink gradually into the proletariat, partly because their diminutive capital does not suffice for the scale on which modern industry is carried on, and is swamped in the competition with the large capitalists, partly because their specialized skill is rendered worthless by new methods of production. Thus the proletariat is recruited from all classes of the population.

The proletariat goes through various stages of development. With its birth begins its struggle with the bourgeoisie. At first the contest is carried on by individual labourers, then by the workpeople of a factory, then by the operatives of one trade, in one locality, against the individual bourgeois who directly exploits them. They direct their attacks not against the bourgeois conditions of production, but against the instruments of production themselves; they destroy imported wares that compete with their labour, they smash to pieces machinery, they set factories ablaze, they seek to restore by force the vanished status of the workman of the Middle Ages.

At this stage the labourers still form an incoherent mass scattered over the whole country, and broken up by their mutual competition. If anywhere they unite to form more compact bodies, this is not yet the consequence of their own active union, but of the union of the bourgeoisie, which class, in order to attain its own political ends, is compelled to set the whole proletariat in motion, and is moreover yet, for a time, able to do so. At this stage, therefore, the proletarians do not fight their enemies, but the enemies of their enemies, the remnants of absolute monarchy, the landowners, the non-industrial bourgeois, the petty bourgeoisie. Thus the whole historical movement is concentrated in the hands of the bourgeoisie; every victory so obtained is a victory for the bourgeoisie.

But with the development of industry the proletariat not only increases in number; it becomes concentrated in greater masses, its strength grows, and it feels that strength more. The various interests and conditions of life within the ranks of the proletariat are more and more equalized, in proportion as machinery obliterates all distinctions of labour, and nearly everywhere reduces wages to the same low level. The growing competition among the bourgeois, and the resulting commercial crises, make the wages of the workers ever more fluctuating. The unceasing improvement of machinery, ever more rapidly developing, makes their livelihood more and more precarious; the collisions between individual work-men and individual bourgeois take more and more the character of collisions between two classes. Thereupon the workers begin to form combinations (trade unions) against the bourgeois; they club together in order to keep up the rate of wages; they found permanent associations in order to make provision beforehand for these occasional revolts. Here and there the contest breaks out into riots.

Now and then the workers are victorious, but only for a time. The real fruit of their battles lies, not in the immediate result, but in the ever expanding union of the workers. This union is helped on by the improved means of communication that are created by modern industry, and that place the workers of different localities in contact with one another. It was just this contact that was needed to centralize the numerous local struggles, all of the same char-acter, into one national struggle between classes. But every class struggle is a political struggle. And that union, to attain which the burghers of the Middle Ages, with their miserable highways, required centuries, the modern proletarians, thanks to railways, achieve in a few years.

This organization of the proletarians into a class, and conse-quently into a political party, is continually being upset again by the competition between the workers themselves. But it ever rises up again, stronger, firmer, mightier. It compels legislative recogni-tion of particular interests of the workers, by taking advantage of the divisions among the bourgeoisie itself. Thus the Ten Hours Bill in England was carried.[17]

Altogether, collisions between the classes of the old society further, in many ways, the course of development of the proletariat. The bourgeoisie finds itself involved in a constant battle: at first with the aristocracy; later on, with those portions of the bourgeoisie itself, whose interests have become antagonistic to the progress of industry; at all times, with the bourgeoisie of foreign countries. In all these battles it sees itself compelled to appeal to the proletariat, to ask for its help, and thus to drag it into the political arena. The bourgeoi-sie itself, therefore, supplies the proletariat with its own elements of political and general education, in other words, it furnishes the proletariat with weapons for fighting the bourgeoisie.

17. In 1846. See Engels's article 'The English Ten Hours Bill', *MECW* 10, pp. 288–300.

Further, as we have already seen, entire sections of the ruling classes are, by the advance of industry, precipitated into the proletariat, or are at least threatened in their conditions of existence. These also supply the proletariat with fresh elements of enlightenment and progress.

Finally, in times when the class struggle nears the decisive hour, the process of dissolution going on within the ruling class, in fact within the whole range of old society, assumes such a violent, glaring character, that a small section of the ruling class cuts itself adrift, and joins the revolutionary class, the class that holds the future in its hands. Just as, therefore, at an earlier period, a section of the nobility went over to the bourgeoisie, so now a portion of the bourgeoisie goes over to the proletariat, and in particular, a portion of the bourgeois ideologists, who have raised themselves to the level of comprehending theoretically the historical movement as a whole.

Of all the classes that stand face to face with the bourgeoisie today, the proletariat alone is a really revolutionary class. The other classes decay and finally disappear in the face of modern industry; the proletariat is its special and essential product.

The lower middle class, the small manufacturer, the shopkeeper, the artisan, the peasant, all these fight against the bourgeoisie, to save from extinction their existence as fractions of the middle class. They are therefore not revolutionary, but conservative. Nay more, they are reactionary, for they try to roll back the wheel of history. If by chance they are revolutionary, they are so only in view of their impending transfer into the proletariat, they thus defend not their present, but their future interests, they desert their own standpoint to place themselves at that of the proletariat.

The 'dangerous class',[18] the social scum, that passively rotting mass thrown off by the lowest layers of old society, may, here and there, be swept into the movement by a proletarian revolution; its conditions of life, however, prepare it far more for the part of a bribed tool of reactionary intrigue.

In the conditions of the proletariat, those of old society at large are already virtually swamped. The proletarian is without property; his relation to his wife and children has no longer anything in common with the bourgeois family relations; modern industrial labour, modern subjection to capital, the same in England as in

18. I.e. the lumpenproletariat of casual labourers and unemployed, which was very extensive in the cities of nineteenth-century Europe.

France, in America as in Germany, has stripped him of every trace of national character. Law, morality, religion, are to him so many bourgeois prejudices, behind which lurk in ambush just as many bourgeois interests.

All the preceding classes that got the upper hand, sought to fortify their already acquired status by subjecting society at large to their conditions of appropriation. The proletarians cannot become masters of the productive forces of society, except by abolishing their own previous mode of appropriation, and thereby also every other previous mode of appropriation. They have nothing of their own to secure and to fortify; their mission is to destroy all previous securities for, and insurances of, individual property.

All previous historical movements were movements of minorities, or in the interest of minorities. The proletarian movement is the self-conscious, independent movement of the immense majority, in the interest of the immense majority. The proletariat, the lowest stratum of our present society, cannot stir, cannot raise itself up, without the whole superincumbent strata of official society being sprung into the air.

Though not in substance, yet in form, the struggle of the proletariat with the bourgeoisie is at first a national struggle. The proletariat of each country must, of course, first of all settle matters with its own bourgeoisie.

In depicting the most general phases of the development of the proletariat, we traced the more or less veiled civil war, raging within existing society, up to the point where that war breaks out into open revolution, and where the violent overthrow of the bourgeoisie lays the foundation for the sway of the proletariat.

Hitherto, every form of society has been based, as we have already seen, on the antagonism of oppressing and oppressed classes. But in order to oppress a class, certain conditions must be assured to it under which it can, at least, continue its slavish existence. The serf, in the period of serfdom, raised himself to membership in the commune, just as the petty bourgeois, under the yoke of feudal absolutism, managed to develop into a bourgeois. The modern labourer, on the contrary, instead of rising with the progress of industry, sinks deeper and deeper below the conditions of existence of his own class. He becomes a pauper, and pauperism develops more rapidly than population and wealth. And here it becomes evident that the bourgeoisie is unfit any longer to be the ruling class in society, and to impose its conditions of existence upon society as an overriding law. It is unfit to rule because it is incompetent to assure an existence to its slave within his slavery, because it cannot help letting him sink into such a state that it has to feed him, instead of being fed by him. Society can no longer live under this bourgeoisie, in other words, its existence is no longer compatible with society.

The essential condition for the existence, and for the sway of the bourgeois class, is the formation and augmentation of capital; the condition for capital is wage labour. Wage labour rests exclusively on competition between the labourers. The advance of industry, whose involuntary promoter is the bourgeoisie, replaces the isolation of the labourers, due to competition, by their revolutionary combination, due to association. The development of modern industry, therefore, cuts from under its feet the very foundation on which the bourgeoisie produces and appropriates products. What the bourgeoisie therefore produces, above all, are its own grave-diggers. Its fall and the victory of the proletariat are equally inevitable.

II. Proletarians and Communists

In what relation do the Communists stand to the proletarians as a whole?

The Communists do not form a separate party opposed to other working-class parties.

They have no interests separate and apart from those of the proletariat as a whole.

They do not set up any sectarian principles of their own, by which to shape and mould the proletarian movement.

The Communists are distinguished from the other working-class parties by this only:

1. In the national struggles of the proletarians of the different countries, they point out and bring to the front the common interests of the entire proletariat, independently of all nationality.

2. In the various stages of development which the struggle of the working class against the bourgeoisie has to pass through, they always and everywhere represent the interests of the movement as a whole.

The Communists, therefore, are on the one hand, practically, the most advanced and resolute section of the working-class parties of every country, that section which pushes forward all others; on the other hand, theoretically, they have over the great mass of the proletariat the advantage of clearly understanding the line of march, the conditions, and the ultimate general results of the proletarian movement.

The immediate aim of the Communists is the same as that of all the other proletarian parties: formation of the proletariat into a class, overthrow of the bourgeois supremacy, conquest of political power by the proletariat.

The theoretical conclusions of the Communists are in no way based on ideas or principles that have been invented, or discovered, by this or that would-be universal reformer.

They merely express, in general terms, actual relations springing from an existing class struggle, from a historical movement going on under our very eyes. The abolition of existing property relations is not at all a distinctive feature of communism.

All property relations in the past have continually been subject to historical change consequent upon the change in historical conditions.

The French Revolution, for example, abolished feudal property in favour of bourgeois property.

The distinguishing feature of communism is not the abolition of property generally, but the abolition of bourgeois property. But modern bourgeois private property is the final and most complete expression of the system of producing and appropriating products that is based on class antagonisms, on the exploitation of the many by the few.

In this sense, the theory of the Communists may be summed up in the single sentence: Abolition of private property.

We Communists have been reproached with the desire of abolishing the right of personally acquiring property as the fruit of a man's own labour, which property is alleged to be the ground work of all personal freedom, activity and independence.

Hard-won, self-acquired, self-earned property! Do you mean the property of the petty artisan and of the small peasant, a form of property that preceded the bourgeois form? There is no need to abolish that; the development of industry has to a great extent already destroyed it, and is still destroying it daily.

Or do you mean modern bourgeois private property?

But does wage labour create any property for the labourer? Not a bit. It creates capital, i.e., that kind of property which exploits wage labour, and which cannot increase except upon conditions of begetting a new supply of wage labour for fresh exploitation. Property, in its present form, is based on the antagonism of capital and wage labour. Let us examine both sides of this antagonism.

To be a capitalist, is to have not only a purely personal, but a social status in production. Capital is a collective product, and only by the united action of many members, nay, in the last resort, only by the united action of all members of society, can it be set in motion.

Capital is, therefore, not a personal, it is a social power.

When, therefore, capital is converted into common property, into the property of all members of society, personal property is not thereby transformed into social property. It is only the social character of the property that is changed. It loses its class character.

Let us now take wage labour.

The average price of wage labour is the minimum wage, i.e., that quantum of the means of subsistence which is absolutely requisite to keep the labourer in bare existence as a labourer. What, therefore, the wage labourer appropriates by means of his labour, merely suffices to prolong and reproduce a bare existence. We by no means intend to abolish this personal appropriation of the products of labour, an appropriation that is made for the maintenance and reproduction of human life, and that leaves no surplus wherewith to command the labour of others. All that we want to do away with, is the miserable character of this appropriation, under which the labourer lives merely to increase capital, and is allowed to live only in so far as the interest of the ruling class requires it.

In bourgeois society, living labour is but a means to increase accumulated labour. In communist society, accumulated labour is but a means to widen, to enrich, to promote the existence of the labourer.

In bourgeois society, therefore, the past dominates the present; in communist society, the present dominates the past. In bourgeois society capital is independent and has individuality, while the living person is dependent and has no individuality.

And the abolition of this state of things is called by the bourgeois, abolition of individuality and freedom! And rightly so. The abolition of bourgeois individuality, bourgeois independence, and bourgeois freedom is undoubtedly aimed at.

By freedom is meant, under the present bourgeois conditions of production, free trade, free selling and buying.

But if selling and buying disappears, free selling and buying disappears also. This talk about free selling and buying, and all the other 'brave words' of our bourgeoisie about freedom in general, have a meaning, if any, only in contrast with restricted selling and buying, with the fettered traders of the Middle Ages, but have no meaning when opposed to the communistic abolition of buying and selling, of the bourgeois conditions of production, and the bourgeoisie itself.

You are horrified at our intending to do away with private property. But in your existing society, private property is already done away with for nine tenths of the population; its existence for the few is solely due to its non-existence in the hands of those nine tenths. You reproach us, therefore, with intending to do away with a form of property, the necessary condition for whose existence is the non-existence of any property for the immense majority of society.

In one word, you reproach us with intending to do away with your property. Precisely so; that is just what we intend.

From the moment when labour can no longer be converted into capital, money, or rent, into a social power capable of being monopolized, i.e., from the moment when individual property can no longer be transformed into bourgeois property, into capital, from that moment, you say, individuality vanishes.

You must, therefore, confess that by 'individual' you mean no other person than the bourgeois, than the middle-class owner of property. This person must, indeed, be swept out of the way, and made impossible.

Communism deprives no man of the power to appropriate the products of society; all that it does is to deprive him of the power to subjugate the labour of others by means of such appropriation.

It has been objected that upon the abolition of private property all work will cease, and universal laziness will overtake us.

According to this, bourgeois society ought long ago to have gone to the dogs through sheer idleness; for those of its members who work, acquire nothing, and those who acquire anything, do not work. The whole of this objection is but another expression of the tautology that there can no longer be any wage labour when there is no longer any capital.

All objections urged against the communistic mode of producing and appropriating material products have, in the same way, been urged against the communistic mode of producing and appropriating intellectual products. Just as, to the bourgeois, the disappearance of class property is the disappearance of production itself, so the disappearance of class culture is to him identical with the disappearance of all culture.

That culture, the loss of which he laments, is, for the enormous majority, a mere training to act as a machine.

But don't wrangle with us so long as you apply, to our intended abolition of bourgeois property, the standard of your bourgeois notions of freedom, culture, law, etc. Your very ideas are but the outgrowth of the conditions of your bourgeois production and bourgeois property, just as your jurisprudence is but the will of your class made into a law for all, a will whose essential character and direction are determined by the economical conditions of existence of your class.

The selfish misconception that induces you to transform into eternal laws of nature and of reason the social forms springing from your present mode of production and form of property – historical relations that rise and disappear in the progress of production – this misconception you share with every ruling class that has preceded you. What you see clearly in the case of ancient property, what you admit in the case of feudal property, you are of course forbidden to admit in the case of your own bourgeois form of property.

Abolition of the family! Even the most radical flare up at this infamous proposal of the Communists.

On what foundation is the present family, the bourgeois family, based? On capital, on private gain. In its completely developed form this family exists only among the bourgeoisie. But this state of things finds its complement in the practical absence of the family among the proletarians, and in public prostitution.

The bourgeois family will vanish as a matter of course when its complement vanishes, and both will vanish with the vanishing of capital.

Do you charge us with wanting to stop the exploitation of children by their parents? To this crime we plead guilty.

But, you will say, we destroy the most hallowed of relations, when we replace home education by social.

And your education! Is not that also social, and determined by the social conditions under which you educate, by the intervention direct or indirect, of society, by means of schools, etc.? The Communists have not invented the intervention of society in education;

they do but seek to alter the character of that intervention, and to rescue education from the influence of the ruling class.

The bourgeois claptrap about the family and education, about the hallowed co-relation of parent and child, becomes all the more disgusting, the more, by the action of modern industry, all family ties among the proletarians are torn asunder, and their children transformed into simple articles of commerce and instruments of labour.

But you Communists would introduce community of women, screams the whole bourgeoisie in chorus.

The bourgeois sees in his wife a mere instrument of production. He hears that the instruments of production are to be exploited in common, and, naturally, can come to no other conclusion than that the lot of being common to all will likewise fall to the women.

He has not even a suspicion that the real point aimed at is to do away with the status of women as mere instruments of production.

For the rest, nothing is more ridiculous than the virtuous indignation of our bourgeois at the community of women which, they pretend, is to be openly and officially established by the Communists. The Communists have no need to introduce community of women; it has existed almost from time immemorial.

Our bourgeois, not content with having the wives and daughters of their proletarians at their disposal, not to speak of common prostitutes, take the greatest pleasure in seducing each other's wives.

Bourgeois marriage is in reality a system of wives in common, and thus, at the most, what the Communists might possibly be reproached with, is that they desire to introduce, in substitution for a hypocritically concealed, an openly legalized community of women. For the rest, it is self-evident that the abolition of the present system of production must bring with it the abolition of the community of women springing from that system, i.e., of prostitution both public and private.

The Communists are further reproached with desiring to abolish countries and nationality.

The working men have no country. We cannot take from them what they have not got. Since the proletariat must first of all acquire political supremacy, must rise to be the leading class of the nation, must constitute itself as the nation, it is, so far, itself national, though not in the bourgeois sense of the word.

National differences, and antagonisms between peoples, are daily more and more vanishing, owing to the development of the bourgeoisie, to freedom of commerce, to the world market, to uniformity in the mode of production and in the conditions of life corresponding thereto.

The supremacy of the proletariat will cause them to vanish still faster. United action, of the leading civilized countries at least, is one of the first conditions for the emancipation of the proletariat.

In proportion as the exploitation of one individual by another is put an end to, the exploitation of one nation by another will also be put an end to. In proportion as the antagonism between classes within the nation vanishes, the hostility of one nation to another will come to an end.

The charges against communism made from a religious, a philosophical, and, generally, from an ideological standpoint, are not deserving of serious examination.

Does it require deep intuition to comprehend that man's ideas, views and conceptions, in one word, man's consciousness, changes with every change in the conditions of his material existence, in his social relations and in his social life?

What else does the history of ideas prove, than that intellectual production changes its character in proportion as material production is changed? The ruling ideas of each age have ever been the ideas of its ruling class.

When people speak of ideas that revolutionize society, they do but express the fact that within the old society, the elements of a new one have been created, and that the dissolution of the old ideas keeps even pace with the dissolution of the old conditions of existence.

When the ancient world was in its last throes, the ancient religions were overcome by Christianity. When Christian ideas succumbed in the eighteenth century to rationalist ideas, feudal society fought its death battle with the then revolutionary bourgeoisie. The ideas of religious liberty and freedom of conscience merely gave expression to the sway of free competition within the domain of knowledge.

'Undoubtedly,' it will be said, 'religious, moral, philosophical and juridical ideas have been modified in the course of historical development. But religion, morality, philosophy, political science and law constantly survived this change.'

'There are, besides, eternal truths, such as freedom, justice, etc., that are common to all states of society. But communism abolishes eternal truths, it abolishes all religion and all morality, instead of constituting them on a new basis; it therefore acts in contradiction to all past historical experience.'

What does this accusation reduce itself to? The history of all past society has consisted in the development of class antagonisms, antagonisms that assumed different forms at different epochs.

But whatever form they may have taken, one fact is common to all past ages, viz., the exploitation of one part of society by the other. No wonder, then, that the social consciousness of past ages, despite all the multiplicity and variety it displays, moves within certain common forms, or general ideas, which cannot completely vanish except with the total disappearance of class antagonisms.

The communist revolution is the most radical rupture with traditional property relations; no wonder that its development involves the most radical rupture with traditional ideas.

But let us have done with the bourgeois objections to communism.

We have seen above, that the first step in the revolution by the working class is to raise the proletariat to the position of ruling class, to win the battle of democracy.

The proletariat will use its political supremacy to wrest, by degrees, all capital from the bourgeoisie, to centralize all instruments of production in the hands of the state, i.e., of the proletariat organized as the ruling class, and to increase the total of productive forces as rapidly as possible.

Of course, in the beginning, this cannot be effected except by means of despotic inroads on the rights of property, and on the conditions of bourgeois production; by means of measures, therefore, which appear economically insufficient and untenable, but which, in the course of the movement, outstrip themselves, necessitate further inroads upon the old social order, and are unavoidable as a means of entirely revolutionizing the mode of production.

These measures will of course be different in different countries.

Nevertheless, in the most advanced countries, the following will be pretty generally applicable.

1. Abolition of property in land and application of all rents of land to public purposes.

2. A heavy progressive or graduated income tax.

3. Abolition of all right of inheritance.

4. Confiscation of the property of all emigrants and rebels.

5. Centralization of credit in the hands of the state, by means of a national bank with state capital and an exclusive monopoly.

6. Centralization of the means of communication and transport in the hands of the state.

7. Extension of factories and instruments of production owned by the state; the bringing into cultivation of waste lands, and the improvement of the soil generally in accordance with a common plan.

8. Equal liability of all to labour. Establishment of industrial armies, especially for agriculture.

9. Combination of agriculture with manufacturing industries; gradual abolition of the distinction between town and country, by a more equable distribution of the population over the country.

10. Free education for all children in public schools. Abolition of children's factory labour in its present form. Combination of education with industrial production, etc.

When, in the course of development, class distinctions have disappeared, and all production has been concentrated in the hands of a vast association of the whole nation, the public power will lose its political character. Political power, properly so called, is merely the organized power of one class for oppressing another. If the proletariat during its contest with the bourgeoisie is compelled, by the force of circumstances, to organize itself as a class; if, by means of a revolution, it makes itself the ruling class, and, as such, sweeps away by force the old conditions of production, then it will, along with these conditions, have swept away the conditions for the existence of class antagonisms and of classes generally, and will thereby have abolished its own supremacy as a class.

In place of the old bourgeois society, with its classes and class antagonisms, we shall have an association, in which the free development of each is the condition for the free development of all.

III. Socialist and Communist Literature

1. Reactionary Socialism

a. Feudal Socialism. Owing to their historical position, it became the vocation of the aristocracies of France and England to write pamphlets against modern bourgeois society. In the French revolution of July 1830, and in the English Reform agitation,[19] these aristocracies again succumbed to the hateful upstart. Thenceforth, a serious political contest was altogether out of question. A literary battle alone remained possible. But even in the domain of literature the old cries of the Restoration period[20] had become impossible.

In order to arouse sympathy, the aristocracy were obliged to lose sight, apparently, of their own interests, and to formulate their indictment against the bourgeoisie in the interest of the exploited working class alone. Thus the aristocracy took their revenge by singing lampoons on their new master, and whispering in his ears sinister prophecies of coming catastrophe.

In this way arose feudal socialism: half lamentation, half lampoon; half echo of the past, half menace of the future; at times, by its bitter, witty and incisive criticism, striking the bourgeoisie to the very heart's core; but always ludicrous in its effect, through total incapacity to comprehend the march of modern history.

The aristocracy, in order to rally the people to them, waved the proletarian alms-bag in front for a banner. But the people, so often as it joined them, saw on their hindquarters the old feudal coats of arms, and deserted with loud and irreverent laughter.

One section of the French Legitimists,[21] and 'Young England',[22] exhibited this spectacle.

In pointing out that their mode of exploitation was different to that of the bourgeoisie, the feudalists forget that they exploited under circumstances and conditions that were quite different, and that are now antiquated. In showing that, under their rule, the modern proletariat never existed, they forget that the modern bourgeoisie is the necessary offspring of their own form of society.

For the rest, so little do they conceal the reactionary character of their criticism that their chief accusation against the bourgeoisie amounts to this, that under the bourgeois regime a class is being developed, which is destined to cut up root and branch the old order of society.

19. Of 1830–32.

20. Not the English Restoration 1660 to 1689, but the French Restoration 1814 to 1830 [Engels].

21. The supporters of the restored Bourbon monarchy of 1814–30, representing the landed aristocracy.

22. A literary circle attached to the Tory party. Benjamin Disraeli's *Sybil: or Two Nations*, and Thomas Carlyle's pamphlets, were among its typical expressions.

What they upbraid the bourgeoisie with is not so much that it creates a proletariat, as that it creates a *revolutionary* proletariat.

In political practice, therefore, they join in all coercive measures against the working class; and in ordinary life, despite their high-falutin phrases, they stoop to pick up the golden apples dropped from the tree of industry, and to barter truth, love, and honour for traffic in wool, beetroot-sugar, and potato spirits.[23]

As the parson has ever gone hand in hand with the landlord, so has clerical socialism with feudal socialism.

Nothing is easier than to give Christian asceticism a socialist tinge. Has not Christianity declaimed against private property, against marriage, against the state? Has it not preached in the place of these, charity and poverty, celibacy and mortification of the flesh, monastic life and Mother Church? Christian socialism is but the holy water with which the priest consecrates the heart-burnings of the aristocrat.

b. Petty-Bourgeois Socialism. The feudal aristocracy was not the only class that was ruined by the bourgeoisie, not the only class whose conditions of existence pined and perished in the atmosphere of modern bourgeois society. The medieval burgesses and the small peasant proprietors were the precursors of the modern bourgeoisie. In those countries which are but little developed, industrially and commercially, these two classes still vegetate side by side with the rising bourgeoisie.

In countries where modern civilization has become fully developed, a new class of petty bourgeois has been formed, fluctuating between proletariat and bourgeoisie and ever renewing itself as a supplementary part of bourgeois society. The individual members of this class, however, are being constantly hurled down into the proletariat by the action of competition, and, as modern industry develops, they even see the moment approaching when they will completely disappear as an independent section of modern society, to be replaced, in manufacture, agriculture and commerce, by overseers, bailiffs, and shop assistants.

23. This applies chiefly to Germany where the landed aristocracy and squirearchy have large portions of their estates cultivated for their own account by stewards, and are, moreover, extensive beetroot-sugar manufacturers and distillers of potato spirits. The wealthier British aristocracy are, as yet, rather above that; but they, too, know how to make up for declining rents by lending their names to floaters of more or less shady joint-stock companies [Engels].

In countries like France, where the peasants constitute far more than half of the population, it was natural that writers who sided with the proletariat against the bourgeoisie should use, in their criticism of the bourgeois regime, the standard of the peasant and petty bourgeois, and from the standpoint of these intermediate classes should take up the cudgels for the working class. Thus arose petty-bourgeois socialism. Sismondi[24] was the head of this school, not only in France but also in England.

This school of socialism dissected with great acuteness the contradictions in the conditions of modern production. It laid bare the hypocritical apologies of economists. It proved, incontrovertibly, the disastrous effects of machinery and division of labour; the concentration of capital and land in a few hands; overproduction and crises; it pointed out the inevitable ruin of the petty bourgeois and peasant, the misery of the proletariat, the anarchy in production, the crying inequalities in the distribution of wealth, the industrial war of extermination between nations, the dissolution of old moral bonds, of the old family relations, of the old nationalities.

In its positive aims, however, this form of socialism aspires either to restoring the old means of production and of exchange, and with them the old property relations and the old society, or to cramping the modern means of production and of exchange within the framework of the old property relations that have been, and were bound to be, exploded by those means. In either case, it is both reactionary and utopian.

Its last words are: corporate guilds for manufacture; patriarchal relations in agriculture.

Ultimately, when stubborn historical facts had dispersed all intoxicating effects of self-deception, this form of socialism ended in a miserable fit of the blues.

c. German or 'True' Socialism. The socialist and communist literature of France, a literature that originated under the pressure of a bourgeoisie in power, and that was the expression of the struggle against this power, was introduced into Germany at a time when the bourgeoisie, in that country, had just begun its contest with feudal absolutism.

German philosophers, would-be philosophers and *beaux esprits* eagerly seized on this literature, only forgetting that when these

24. Sismondi's *Principles of Political Economy* first appeared in 1803.

writings immigrated from France into Germany, French social conditions had not immigrated along with them. In contact with German social conditions, this French literature lost all its immediate practical significance, and assumed a purely literary aspect.[25] Thus, to the German philosophers of the eighteenth century, the demands of the first French revolution were nothing more than the demands of 'practical reason' in general, and the utterance of the will of the revolutionary French bourgeoisie signified in their eyes the laws of pure will, of will as it was bound to be, of true human will generally.

The work of the German *literati* consisted solely in bringing the new French ideas into harmony with their ancient philosophical conscience, or rather, in annexing the French ideas without deserting their own philosophic point of view.

This annexation took place in the same way in which a foreign language is appropriated, namely by translation.

It is well known how the monks wrote silly lives of Catholic saints *over* the manuscripts on which the classical works of ancient heathendom had been written. The German *literati* reversed this process with the profane French literature. They wrote their philosophical nonsense beneath the French original. For instance, beneath the French criticism of the economic functions of money, they wrote 'alienation of humanity', and beneath the French criticism of the bourgeois state they wrote, 'dethronement of the category of the general', and so forth.

The introduction of these philosophical phrases at the back of the French historical criticisms they dubbed 'philosophy of action', 'true socialism', 'German science of socialism', 'philosophical foundation of socialism', and so on.

The French socialist and communist literature was thus completely emasculated. And, since it ceased in the hands of the German to express the struggle of one class with the other, he felt conscious of having overcome 'French one-sidedness' and of representing, not true requirements, but the requirements of truth; not the interests of the proletariat, but the interests of human nature, of man in general, who belongs to no class, has no reality, who exists only in the misty realm of philosophical fantasy.

This German socialism, which took its schoolboy task so

25. In the German editions of the Manifesto there is an additional sentence here which reads (1872): 'It was bound to appear as idle speculation about the realization of the essence of man.'

seriously and solemnly, and extolled its poor stock-in-trade in such mountebank fashion, meanwhile gradually lost its pedantic innocence.

The fight of the German, and especially the Prussian bourgeoisie, against feudal aristocracy and absolute monarchy, in other words, the liberal movement, became more earnest.

By this, the long wished-for opportunity was offered to 'true' socialism of confronting the political movement with the socialist demands, of hurling the traditional anathemas against liberalism, against representative government, against bourgeois competition, bourgeois freedom of the press, bourgeois legislation, bourgeois liberty and equality, and of preaching to the masses that they had nothing to gain, and everything to lose, by this bourgeois movement. German socialism forgot, in the nick of time, that the French criticism, whose silly echo it was, presupposed the existence of modern bourgeois society, with its corresponding economic conditions of existence and the political constitution adapted thereto, the very things whose attainment was the object of the pending struggle in Germany.

To the absolute governments, with their following of parsons, professors, country squires and officials, it served as a welcome scarecrow against the threatening bourgeoisie.

It was a sweet finish after the bitter pills of floggings and bullets with which these same governments, just at that time, dosed the German working-class risings[26].

While this 'true' socialism thus served the governments as a weapon for fighting the German bourgeoisie, it, at the same time, directly represented a reactionary interest, the interest of the German philistines. In Germany the petty-bourgeois class, a relic of the sixteenth century, and since then constantly cropping up again under various forms, is the real social basis of the existing state of things.

To preserve this class is to preserve the existing state of things in Germany. The industrial and political supremacy of the bourgeoisie threatens it with certain destruction – on the one hand, from the concentration of capital; on the other, from the rise of a revolutionary proletariat. 'True' socialism appeared to kill these two birds with one stone. It spread like an epidemic.

The robe of speculative cobwebs, embroidered with flowers of rhetoric, steeped in the dew of sickly sentiment, this transcenden-

26. I.e. the Silesian weavers' revolt of 1844.

tal robe in which the German socialists wrapped their sorry 'eternal truths', all skin and bone, served to wonderfully increase the sale of their goods amongst such a public.

And on its part, German socialism recognized, more and more, its own calling as the bombastic representative of the petty-bourgeois philistine.

It proclaimed the German nation to be the model nation, and the German petty philistine to be the typical man. To every villainous meanness of this model man it gave a hidden, higher, socialistic interpretation, the exact contrary of its real character. It went to the extreme length of directly opposing the 'brutally destructive' tendency of communism, and of proclaiming its supreme and impartial contempt of all class struggles. With very few exceptions, all the so-called socialist and communist publications that now (1847) circulate in Germany belong to the domain of this foul and enervating literature.

2. *Conservative or Bourgeois Socialism*

A part of the bourgeoisie is desirous of redressing social grievances, in order to secure the continued existence of bourgeois society.

To this section belong economists, philanthropists, humanitarians, improvers of the condition of the working class, organizers of charity, members of societies for the prevention of cruelty to animals, temperance fanatics, hole-and-corner reformers of every imaginable kind. This form of socialism has, moreover, been worked out into complete systems.

We may cite Proudhon's *Philosophie de la Misère*[27] as an example of this form.

The socialistic bourgeois want all the advantages of modern social conditions without the struggles and dangers necessarily resulting therefrom. They desire the existing state of society minus its revolutionary and disintegrating elements. They wish for a bourgeoisie without a proletariat. The bourgeoisie naturally conceives the world in which it is supreme to be the best; and bourgeois socialism develops this comfortable conception into various more or less complete systems. In requiring the proletariat to carry out such a system, and thereby to march straightway into

27. It was in reply to Proudhon's *Philosophy of Poverty* (1846) that Marx wrote his *Poverty of Philosophy* (1847).

the social New Jerusalem, it but requires in reality that the proletariat should remain within the bounds of existing society, but should cast away all its hateful ideas concerning the bourgeoisie.

A second and more practical, but less systematic, form of this socialism sought to depreciate every revolutionary movement in the eyes of the working class, by showing that no mere political reform, but only a change in the material conditions of existence, in economical relations, could be of any advantage to them. By changes in the material conditions of existence, this form of socialism, however, by no means understands abolition of the bourgeois relations of production, an abolition that can be effected only by a revolution, but administrative reforms, based on the continued existence of these relations; reforms, therefore, that in no respect affect the relations between capital and labour, but, at the best, lessen the cost, and simplify the administrative work, of bourgeois government.

Bourgeois socialism attains adequate expression when, and only when, it becomes a mere figure of speech.

Free trade; for the benefit of the working class. Protective duties: for the benefit of the working class. Prison reform: for the benefit of the working class. This is the last word and the only seriously meant word of bourgeois socialism.

It is summed up in the phrase: the bourgeois is a bourgeois – for the benefit of the working class.

3. Critical-Utopian Socialism and Communism

We do not here refer to that literature which, in every great modern revolution, has always given voice to the demands of the proletariat, such as the writings of Babeuf and others.

The first direct attempts of the proletariat to attain its own ends, made in times of universal excitement, when feudal society was being overthrown, these attempts necessarily failed, owing to the then undeveloped state of the proletariat, as well as to the absence of the economic conditions for its emancipation, conditions that had yet to be produced, and could be produced by the impending bourgeois epoch alone. The revolutionary literature that accompanied these first movements of the proletariat had necessarily a reactionary character. It inculcated universal asceticism and social levelling in its crudest form.

The socialist and communist systems properly so called, those of Saint-Simon, Fourier, Owen and others, spring into existence in the early undeveloped period, described above, of the struggle between proletariat and bourgeoisie (see section I, 'Bourgeoisie and Proletariat').

The founders of these systems see, indeed, the class antagonisms, as well as the action of the decomposing elements in the prevailing form of society. But the proletariat, as yet in its infancy, offers to them the spectacle of a class without any historical initiative or any independent political movement.

Since the development of class antagonism keeps even pace with the development of industry, the economic situation, as they find it, does not as yet offer to them the material conditions for the emancipation of the proletariat. They therefore search after a new social science,[28] after new social laws, that are to create these conditions.

Historical action is to yield to their personal inventive action, historically created conditions of emancipation to fantastic ones, and the gradual, spontaneous class organization of the proletariat to an organization of society specially contrived by these inventors. Future history resolves itself, in their eyes, into the propaganda and the practical carrying out of their social plans.

In the formation of their plans they are conscious of caring chiefly for the interests of the working class, as being the most suffering class. Only from the point of view of being the most suffering class does the proletariat exist for them.

The undeveloped state of the class struggle, as well as their own surroundings, cause socialists of this kind to consider themselves far superior to all class antagonisms. They want to improve the condition of every member of society, even that of the most favoured. Hence, they habitually appeal to society at large, without distinction of class; nay, by preference, to the ruling class. For how can people, when once they understand their system, fail to see in it the best possible plan of the best possible state of society?

Hence, they reject all political, and especially all revolutionary, action; they wish to attain their ends by peaceful means, and

28. Here, as in other writings of the 1840s, Marx and Engels still used 'science' in a now archaic sense of the term, roughly equivalent to the modern 'doctrine'. Although the substance of their argument remained the same, the change in usage led them later to refer to their own theory as 'scientific', in contrast to the utopianism of their predecessors. See, for example, *Capital* (*MECW* 35), and Engel's Introduction to *Anti-Dühring* (*MECW* 25, pp. 16–27).

endeavour, by small experiments, necessarily doomed to failure, and by the force of example, to pave the way for the new social gospel.

Such fantastic pictures of future society, painted at a time when the proletariat is still in a very undeveloped state and has but a fantastic conception of its own position, correspond with the first instinctive yearnings of that class for a general reconstruction of society.

But these socialist and communist publications contain also a critical element. They attack every principle of existing society. Hence they are full of the most valuable materials for the enlightenment of the working class. The practical measures proposed in them – such as the abolition of the distinction between town and country, of the family, of the carrying on of industries for the account of private individuals, and of the wage system, the proclamation of social harmony, the conversion of the functions of the state into a mere superintendence of production – all these proposals point solely to the disappearance of class antagonisms which were, at the time, only just cropping up, and which, in these publications, are recognized under their earliest, indistinct and undefined forms only. These proposals, therefore, are of a purely utopian character.

The significance of critical-utopian socialism and communism bears an inverse relation to historical development. In proportion as the modern class struggle develops and takes definite shape, this fantastic standing apart from the contest, these fantastic attacks on it, lose all practical value and all theoretical justification. Therefore, although the originators of these systems were, in many respects, revolutionary, their disciples have, in every case, formed mere reactionary sects. They hold fast by the original views of their masters, in opposition to the progressive historical development of the proletariat. They therefore endeavour, and that consistently, to deaden the class struggle and to reconcile the class antagonisms. They still dream of experimental realization of their social utopias, of founding isolated '*phalanstères*', of establishing 'home colonies', of setting up a 'little Icaria'[29] – duodecimo editions of the New Jerusalem – and to realize all these castles in the air, they are compelled to appeal to the feelings and purses of the

29. *Phalanstères* were socialist colonies on the plan of Charles Fourier; Icaria was the name given by Cabet to his utopia and, later on, to his American communist colony [Engels].

bourgeois. By degrees they sink into the category of the reactionary conservative socialists depicted above, differing from these only by more systematic pedantry, and by their fanatical and superstitious belief in the miraculous effects of their social science.

They therefore violently oppose all political action on the part of the working class; such action, according to them, can only result from blind unbelief in the new gospel.

The Owenites in England, and the Fourierists in France, respectively oppose the Chartists and the Réformistes.

IV. Position of the Communists in Relation to the Various Existing Opposition Parties

Section II has made clear the relations of the Communists to the existing working-class parties, such as the Chartists in England and the agrarian reformers[30] in America.

The Communists fight for the attainment of the immediate aims, for the enforcement of the momentary interests of the working class; but in the movement of the present, they also represent and take care of the future of that movement. In France the Communists ally themselves with the Social-Democrats,[31] against the conservative and radical bourgeoisie, reserving, however, the right to take up a critical position in regard to phrases and illusions traditionally handed down from the great Revolution.

In Switzerland they support the Radicals, without losing sight of the fact that this party consists of antagonistic elements, partly of democratic socialists, in the French sense, partly of radical bourgeois.

In Poland they support the party that insists on an agrarian revolution as the prime condition for national emancipation, that party which fomented the insurrection of Cracow in 1846.[32]

In Germany they fight with the bourgeoisie whenever it acts in a revolutionary way, against the absolute monarchy, the feudal squirearchy, and the petty bourgeoisie.[33]

30. This seems to be a reference to the Free Soil movement, which demanded the free distribution of uncultivated land to small farmers.

31. The party then represented in parliament by Ledru-Rollin, in literature by Louis Blanc, in the daily press by *La Réforme*. The name 'Social-Democracy' signified, with these its inventors, a section of the democratic or republican party more or less tinged with socialism [Engels].

32. See below, p. 96 n. 1.

33. *Kleinbürgerei* in the original. 'Petty-bourgeois conditions' would be a more accurate translation.

But they never cease, for a single instant, to instil into the working class the clearest possible recognition of the hostile antagonism between bourgeoisie and proletariat, in order that the German workers may straightway use, as so many weapons against the bourgeoisie, the social and political conditions that the bourgeoisie must necessarily introduce along with its supremacy, and in order that, after the fall of the reactionary classes in Germany, the fight against the bourgeoisie itself may immediately begin.

The Communists turn their attention chiefly to Germany, because that country is on the eve of a bourgeois revolution that is bound to be carried out under more advanced conditions of European civilization, and with a much more developed proletariat, than that of England was in the seventeenth, and of France in the eighteenth century, and because the bourgeois revolution in Germany will be but the prelude to an immediately following proletarian revolution.

In short, the Communists everywhere support every revolutionary movement against the existing social and political order of things.

In all these movements they bring to the front, as the leading question in each, the property question, no matter what its degree of development at the time.

Finally, they labour everywhere for the union and agreement of the democratic parties of all countries.

The Communists disdain to conceal their views and aims. They openly declare that their ends can be attained only by the forcible overthrow of all existing conditions. Let the ruling classes tremble at a communistic revolution. The proletarians have nothing to lose but their chains. They have a world to win.

WORKING MEN OF ALL COUNTRIES, UNITE!

Speeches on Poland (29 November 1847)[1]

9 December 1847

SPEECH BY KARL MARX

The unification and brotherhood of nations is a phrase which is nowadays on the lips of all parties, particularly of the bourgeois free traders. A kind of brotherhood does indeed exist between the bourgeois classes of all nations. It is the brotherhood of the oppressors against the oppressed, of the exploiters against the exploited. Just as the bourgeois class of one country is united in brotherhood against the proletarians of that country, despite the competition and struggle of its members among themselves, so the bourgeoisie of all countries is united in brotherhood against the proletarians of all countries, despite their struggling and competing with each other on the world market. In order for peoples to become really united their interests must be common. For their interests to be common the existing property relations must be abolished, since the exploitation of one nation by another is caused by the existing property relations. And it is only in the interests of the working class to abolish the existing property relations; only

1. These speeches were delivered by Marx and Engels at a meeting in London commemorating the seventeenth anniversary of the Polish revolution of 1830. The meeting was organized by the Fraternal Democrats, an organization that served as the international department of the Chartists and campaigned in solidarity with the oppressed nations of Europe. Marx spoke as the representative of the Democratic Association in Brussels, of which he was in fact vice-president. The Democratic Association, like the Fraternal Democrats, included both petty-bourgeois democrats and Communists. The meeting coincided with the opening of the secret second congress of the Communist League, which was the real reason for Marx and Engels's journey to London. The speeches are translated here from the text of the *Deutsche-Brüsseler-Zeitung* (9 December 1847) a German democratic paper in Brussels in which Marx was editorially involved, as reproduced in *MEW* 4. The Polish uprising of November 1830 was led by the nobles and intellectuals of Russian Poland. A provisional government was set up in Warsaw, which attempted to bargain with the tsar for reforms. In February 1831 a Russian army invaded Poland, which took until the end of the year to restore 'order', and conducted vicious reprisals.

they have the means to achieve it. The victory of the proletariat over the bourgeoisie represents at the same time the victory over national and industrial conflicts, which at present create hostility between the different peoples. Therefore, the victory of the proletariat over the bourgeoisie also signifies the emancipation of all downtrodden nations.

The old Poland is certainly lost, and we should be the last to wish for its restoration. But not only is the old Poland lost. The old Germany, the old France, the old England, the old social order in general is lost. The loss of the old social order, however, is not a loss for those who have nothing to lose in the old society, and at the present time this is the case for the large majority of people in all countries. They have, in fact, everything to gain from the destruction of the old society, for it is a precondition for the formation of a new society no longer based on class antagonisms.

Of all countries it is England where the opposition between the proletariat and the bourgeoisie is most highly developed. Thus the victory of the English proletariat over the English bourgeoisie is of decisive importance for the victory of all oppressed peoples over their oppressors. Poland, therefore, must be freed, not in Poland, but in England. You Chartists should not express pious wishes for the liberation of nations. Defeat your own enemies at home and then you may be proudly conscious of having defeated the old social order in its entirety.

SPEECH BY FREDERICK ENGELS

My friends, allow me today to appear for once in my capacity as a German. For we Germans have a particular interest in the liberation of Poland. German princes have profited from the partition of Poland[2] and German soldiers are still exercising oppression in Galicia and Posen. It must be the concern of us Germans, above all, of us German democrats, to remove this stain from our nation. A nation cannot be free and at the same time continue to oppress other nations. Thus Germany cannot be liberated without the liberation of Poland from oppression by Germans. And for this reason Poland and Germany have a common interest, for

2. After the three partitions of Poland, in 1772, 1793 and 1795, the country was entirely divided between Austria, Prussia and Russia, with the nominally independent district of Cracow itself occupied by the three powers. Galicia was in Austrian hands, and Posen (now Poznań) in Prussian.

this reason Polish and German democrats can work together for the liberation of both nations.

I, too, am of the opinion that the first decisive blow from which the victory of democracy, the liberation of all European countries will ensue, will be delivered by the English Chartists; I have been in England for several years and during this time I have openly joined in the Chartist movement. The English Chartists will rise up first because it is precisely here that the struggle between bourgeoisie and proletariat is at its fiercest. And why is it at its fiercest? Because in England, as a result of modern industry and machines, all the oppressed classes have been thrown together into one huge class with common interests, the class of the proletariat; because, conversely, as a result of these developments all the oppressing classes have likewise been united into a single class, the bourgeoisie. Thus the struggle has been simplified; thus it will be resolved at one great decisive stroke. Is this not so? The aristocracy has no more power in England; the bourgeoisie alone rules and has taken the aristocracy in tow. The bourgeoisie, however, is faced by the great mass of the people, united in a terrible phalanx, whose victory over the ruling capitalists is drawing nearer and nearer. And this destruction of the divergent interests which earlier divided the different sections of the workers, this reduction of the lives of all workers to the same level you owe to machinery; without machinery there would be no Chartism, and even though your situation may be becoming worse at present as a result of machinery, it is, for this very reason, making our victory possible. But it has had this result not just in England but also in all other countries. In Belgium, in America, in France, in Germany it has reduced the conditions of all workers to the same level and it is making them increasingly similar day by day; in all these countries the workers have the same interest, that is, to overthrow the class which is oppressing them, the bourgeoisie. This levelling out of conditions, this international identity of interest of the workers' party is the result of machinery; machinery therefore, remains an enormous historical advance. What conclusions can be drawn from this? Because the position is the same for the workers of all countries, because their interests are the same and their enemies are the same, for this reason they must also fight together, they must oppose the brotherhood of the bourgeoisie of all nations with the brotherhood of the workers of all nations.

Speeches on Poland (22 February 1848)[1]

SPEECH BY KARL MARX

Gentlemen,

There are some striking analogies in history. The Jacobin of 1793 has become the communist of our own day. In 1793, when Russia, Austria and Prussia divided Poland, the three powers justified themselves by citing the constitution of 1791, which was condemned by general agreement on the grounds of its reputedly Jacobin principles.

And what had the Polish constitution of 1791 proclaimed? No more and no less than constitutional monarchy: legislation to be placed in the hands of the country's representatives, freedom of the press, freedom of conscience, judicial hearings to be made public, serfdom to be abolished, etc. And all this was at that time simply called Jacobinism! So, gentlemen, you see how history has progressed. The Jacobinism of that time has today become, in the form of liberalism, all that is most moderate.

The three powers have moved with the times. In 1846, when they took away the last vestiges of Polish nationality by incorporating Cracow into Austria, they referred to what they used to call Jacobinism as communism.

1. These speeches were delivered by Marx and Engels in Brussels at a meeting to commemorate the Cracow insurrection. They were published in the pamphlet *Célébration, à Bruxelles, du deuxième anniversaire de la Révolution Polonaise du 22 Février 1846*, Brussels, 1848, and are translated here from the texts reproduced by D. Ryazanov in *Archiv für die Geschichte des Sozialismus*, vol. VI, Leipzig, 1916.

The Polish uprising of 1846 was led by revolutionary democrats. It began on 22 February with an insurrection in the 'free state' of Cracow. The national government in Cracow proclaimed a radical programme that included the abolition of feudal dues, the redistribution of land, and 'social' workshops. However it failed, from insufficient organizational preparation, to ensure rapid enough support from the peasantry. Cracow was recaptured by the beginning of March, although sporadic resistance in the countryside continued for several weeks. In November 1846, Cracow was annexed to Austria.

But what was communist about the Cracow revolution? Was it communist to want to re-establish Polish nationality? One might equally say that the war of the European Coalition against Napoleon to save the various nationalities was a communist war, and that the Congress of Vienna was made up of communists with crowned heads. Or was the Cracow revolution communist for wanting to set up a democratic government? No one would accuse the millionaires of Berne or New York of communist tendencies.

Communism denies the need for classes to exist: it wants to get rid of all classes and all class distinctions. But the Cracow revolutionaries merely wanted to get rid of *political* distinctions between the classes; they wanted to give all classes equal rights.

Just what then was communist about that Cracow revolution?

Was it possibly that it was trying to break the chains of the feudal system, to liberate land subject to tribute and transform it into free, modern property?

If one were to say to French landowners: 'Do you realize what the Polish democrats want? They want to bring into their country the form of ownership already existing in your country'; then the French landowners would answer: 'They are doing the right thing'. But say, like M. Guizot, to the French landowners: 'The Poles want to get rid of landownership as established by you in the 1789 revolution, and as it still exists in your country.' 'Good God!' they would cry, 'then they are revolutionaries, communists! These evil men must be crushed.' The abolition of guild wardens and corporations, and the introduction of free competition, is now in Sweden called communism. The *Journal des Débats* goes further: abolishing the income which the two hundred thousand electors' right of corruption brings in – that means abolishing a source of revenue, destroying an existing property, communism.[2] Certainly the Cracow revolution also wanted to abolish a form of property. But what kind of property? A kind which can no more be destroyed anywhere else in Europe, than can the Sonderbund[3] in Switzerland, because it simply does not exist any more.

2. The *Journal des Débats* was the official newspaper of the July monarchy of 1830–48. Marx is alluding to the electoral corruption that the restricted franchise of this regime fostered.

3. The Swiss Sonderbund (separatist league) was formed by the reactionary Catholic 'founding cantons' in 1847, to resist the greater centralization that the federal government was mandated to carry out. The Sonderbund was defeated with a short military campaign in November 1847.

No one will deny that in Poland and political question is linked with a social question. The one is always inseparable from the other.

You can ask the reactionaries about that! Under the Restoration,[4] were they only struggling against political liberalism and its necessary corollary, Voltaireanism? One respected reactionary writer freely admitted that the highest metaphysic of a de Maistre and a de Bonald[5] came down ultimately to a question of money, and is not every question of money a social question? The men of the Restoration did not hide the fact that to return to sound politics, they had to bring back sound property, feudal property, moral property. Everyone knows that faithful royalism cannot manage without tithes and *corvée*.

Let us go back further: in 1789 the political question of human rights concealed the social question of free competition.

And what is happening in England? In all matters from the Reform Bill[6] to the repeal of the Corn Laws,[7] have the political parties fought for anything but changes of property, questions of property – social questions?

Here, in Belgium itself, is the battle between liberalism and Catholicism anything other than a battle between industrial capital and the large landowners?

And all the political questions that have been debated for the past seventeen years[8] – are they not all at bottom social questions?

So whatever point of view you may adopt, whether it be liberal, radical or even aristocratic, you can hardly still dare to blame the Cracow revolution for having attached a social question to a political one.

The men who led the revolutionary movement in Cracow were absolutely convinced that only a democratic Poland could be free, and that there could be no democratic Poland without the abolition of all feudal rights, and without an agrarian movement which would transform the peasants from landowners forced to pay tribute into free, modern landowners.

If the Russian autocrat were to be replaced by Polish aristo-

---

4. I.e. the restored Bourbon monarchy in France, 1814–30.

5. Joseph-Marie, comte de Maistre, and Louis-Gabriel-Ambroise, vicomte de Bonald, were both ideologists of the aristocratic and clerical reaction in the Restoration period.

6. 1832.

7. 1846.

8. I.e. since Belgium gained independence in 1831.

crats, then despotism would merely have taken out naturalization papers. Thus the Germans, in their battle against the foreigner, exchanged one Napoleon for thirty-six Metternichs.[9] Though the Polish lord would no longer have a Russian lord over him, the Polish peasant would still have a lord over him – only a lord who was free rather than one who was a slave. This particular political change involves no social change at all.

The Cracow revolution has given all of Europe a magnificent example by identifying the cause of nationhood with the cause of democracy and the liberation of the oppressed class.

Though that revolution has for the time been stifled by the blood-stained hands of paid assassins, it is rising again in glory and triumph in Switzerland and Italy.[10] It is finding its principles confirmed in Ireland, where the purely nationalist party has gone to the grave with O'Connell, and the new national party is above all reforming and democratic.[11]

It is still Poland that has taken the initiative – not the feudal Poland of the past, but democratic Poland – and from now on its liberation has become a point of honour for all the democrats in Europe.

SPEECH BY FREDERICK ENGELS

Gentlemen,

The rising whose anniversary we are celebrating today failed. After a few days of heroic resistance, Cracow was taken, and the bloody ghost of Poland, which had for a moment risen before the eyes of her assassins, returned to the tomb.

The Cracow revolution was a defeat, a most deplorable defeat. We must pay our last honours to the fallen heroes, lament their failure, and express our sympathies to the twenty million Poles whose chains have been drawn tighter by it.

9. Marx refers to the result of the 'War of Liberation' of 1813–14. See Introduction, p. 9.

10. The defeat of the Sonderbund in November 1847 was seen as a victory for the democratic revolution. Revolution broke out in Palermo on 12 January 1848.

11. The Irish Confederation was formed in June 1847 by radical democrats, mainly intellectuals from the Young Ireland group, who broke with the liberal bourgeois Repeal Association founded by Daniel O'Connell. In 1848 the left wing of the Irish Confederation attempted an insurrection on the basis of Thomas Meagher's Proclamation which linked national independence with democratic reforms. O'Connell died in 1847.

But, gentlemen, is that all we have to do? Is it enough to drop a tear on the tomb of an unhappy country, and swear implacable hatred towards its oppressors – implacable, but hitherto impotent?

No, gentlemen! The anniversary of Cracow is not only a day of mourning, but for us democrats it is also a day of rejoicing; for even in that defeat there is contained a victory, and the fruits of that victory are something that will live, whereas the results of the defeat will pass.

That victory is the victory of the young democratic Poland over the old aristocratic Poland.

Yes, Poland's last struggle against her foreign oppressors was preceded by a hidden, unseen but decisive struggle inside Poland herself; the struggle of the oppressed Poles against the oppressing Poles, of Polish democracy against Polish aristocracy.

Compare 1830 and 1846: compare Warsaw and Cracow. In 1830, the ruling class in Poland was as selfish, as limited, as cowardly in the legislature as it was dedicated, enthusiastic and brave on the battlefield. What did the Polish aristocracy want in 1830? To preserve its own entrenched rights as against the tsar. It restricted its rebellion to that little area which it pleased the Congress of Vienna to designate the Kingdom of Poland;[12] it restrained the fighting spirit of the other Polish provinces, and did nothing to mitigate the degrading slavery of the peasants or the iniquitous conditions of the Jews. Though, during the course of the rebellion, the aristocracy was forced to make concessions to the people, by the time they made them it was too late and the rebellion had already failed.

We may say categorically: the 1830 rebellion was neither a national revolution (it excluded three quarters of Poland), nor a social or political revolution; it did nothing to change the situation of the people inside the country; it was a conservative revolution.

But within that conservative revolution, actually within the national government, there was one man who forcefully attacked the narrow views of the ruling class. He proposed genuinely revolutionary measures which appalled the aristocrats in the Diet by their boldness. He wanted to make the national cause the cause of liberty, and to identify the interest of all peoples with that of the

12. The Grand Duchy of Warsaw created by Napoleon in 1807 as a satellite state was handed to Russia by the Congress of Vienna. Tsar Alexander I made this 'Congress Poland' into his 'Kingdom of Poland', granting it a minimal autonomy in the hope of staving off nationalist agitation.

Polish people, by calling all of what was formerly Poland to arms, and thus making the Polish war of independence a European war, by emancipating the Jews and the peasants, by giving the latter a share in land ownership, and by reconstructing Poland on a basis of democracy and equality. It seems hardly necessary to name the man whose genius conceived this plan at once so immense and so simple – it was Lelewel.[13]

In 1830, those proposals were repeatedly rejected, owing to the self-interested blindness of the majority of the aristocracy. But those principles, ripened and developed by the experience of fifteen years' slavery, are the principles we have since seen emblazoned on the flag of the Cracow revolution. In Cracow, as we saw, there was no one left with a lot to lose, there were no aristocrats, and every step that was taken bore the mark of that democratic, almost proletarian boldness which has nothing to lose but its poverty, and a country, indeed a whole world, to gain. There was no hanging back, no scruple, there: they attacked all three powers at once; they proclaimed freedom for the peasants, agrarian reform, emancipation of the Jews – and all this without a moment's anxiety as to whether it might go counter to this or that aristocratic interest.

The Cracow revolution sought neither to re-establish the Poland of the past, nor to preserve such of the old Polish institutions as the foreign governments had left in existence; it was not reactionary, nor was it conservative.

No, it was even more hostile to Poland herself than to her foreign oppressors; hostile to the Poland of the past, barbarous, feudal, aristocratic, founded on the slavery of the majority of the people. Far from re-establishing that old Poland, it sought to turn it entirely upside down, and to found upon what remained, with an entirely new class, with the majority of the people, a new, civilized, democratic, modern Poland, worthy of the nineteenth century, which would be a real advance post of civilization.

The difference between 1830 and 1846, the immense progress achieved inside even that unhappy, bleeding, shattered country; the Polish aristocracy completely separated from the people and thrown into the arms of their country's oppressors; the Polish people

13. Joachim Lelewel was a Polish historian, who after the defeat of the 1830–31 revolution became the leader of the democratic wing of the Polish refugees. At this time he lived in Brussels and was an executive member of the Democratic Association.

wholly won over to the cause of democracy; and finally the struggle of class against class, which is the prime mover of all social progress, established in Poland just as it is here – that is the victory of democracy achieved by the Cracow revolution, the result that will still bear fruit when the defeat of the rebels has long been avenged.

Yes, gentlemen, the Cracow rebellion has made the Polish cause, nationalist though it may be, the cause of all peoples; from being merely a matter for sympathy, it has become a matter of interest to all democrats. Until 1846 we had a crime to avenge; from now on, we have allies to support, and we shall support them.

It is especially our own Germany which can congratulate herself for that explosion of democratic feeling in Poland. We ourselves are on the point of having a democratic revolution; we shall have to fight the barbarian hordes of Austria and Russia. Before 1846, we had some hesitation as to which side Poland might support in a democratic revolution in Germany, but the Cracow revolution has resolved all our doubts. Henceforth the German and Polish peoples are forever allied. We have the same enemies, the same oppressors, for the Russian government weighs us down as heavily as the Poles. The first condition for the freeing of both Germany and Poland is the overthrow of the present political regime in Germany, the fall of Prussia and Austria, and the withdrawal of Russia to the Dniester and the Dvina.

Thus, the alliance of our two nations is far from being a beautiful dream, a delightful illusion; no, gentlemen, it is an inevitable necessity, given the common interests of the two countries, and it is the Cracow revolution that has made it a necessity. The German people who, up to now, have had little more than words to use on their own behalf, will have actions for their brothers in Poland. And just as we German democrats who are here today hold out our hand to the Polish democrats, so the entire German people will celebrate their alliance with the people of Poland on the battlefield on which we win our first victory together over our common oppressors.

The Demands of the Communist Party in Germany[1]

Karl Marx and Frederick Engels

Proletarians of all countries, unite!

1. The whole of Germany shall be declared a single and indivisible republic.

2. Every German over twenty-one years of age shall be able to vote and be elected, provided he has no criminal record.

3. Representatives of the people shall be paid, so that workers, too, will be able to sit in the parliament of the German people.

4. The whole population shall be armed. In future, the armed forces are to be forces of workers as well, so that the army will not merely be a consumer, as it was in the past, but will produce even more than the cost of its upkeep.

Furthermore, this will be a means of organizing labour.

5. The exercise of justice shall be free of charge.

6. All the feudal dues, tributes, duties, tithes, etc., which have oppressed the rural population until now, shall be abolished, with no compensation whatsoever.

7. The estates of princes and other feudal lords, and all mines and pits, etc., shall become state property. On these estates, large-scale agriculture is to be introduced for the benefit of all and using the most modern scientific aids.

8. Mortgages on peasant lands shall be declared state property. The peasants are to pay the interest on these mortgages to the state.

9. In those regions where there is a developed system of lease-holding, the ground rent or the 'lease shilling' shall be paid to the state as tax.

---

1. These Demands were drawn up by Marx and Engels on behalf of the Central Committee of the Communist League in Paris during the last week of March 1848. They were published there on 31 March as a leaflet, and at the beginning of April in various democratic German newspapers. In summer 1848 the Demands were reprinted in Cologne. They are translated here from the text of the Cologne leaflet, as printed in *MEW* 5.

All the measures listed in 6, 7, 8 and 9 are designed to reduce public and other burdens on peasants and small tenant farmers, without reducing the requisite means for paying the expenses of the state and without endangering production itself.

The real landowner, who is neither a peasant nor a tenant, has no part in production. His consumption is therefore nothing but misuse.

10. One state bank shall replace all the private banks, and its note issue shall be legal tender.

This measure will make it possible to regulate credit in the interests of the *whole* population and thus undermine the domination of the big money-men. The gradual replacement of gold and silver by paper money will reduce the cost of the indispensable instrument of bourgeois commerce, the universal means of exchange, and reserve gold and silver for effective use abroad. Finally, this measure is needed in order to bind the interests of the conservative bourgeois to the revolution.[2]

11. All means of transport: railways, canals, steamships, roads, stations, etc. shall be taken over by the state. They are to be transformed into state property and put at the free service of the needy.

12. All civil servants shall receive the same pay, without any distinction other than that those *with* a family, i.e. with more needs, will also receive a higher salary than the rest.

13. The complete separation of Church and State. Ministers of all confessions are to be paid only by their congregations.

14. Restriction of the right of inheritance.

15. The introduction of severely progressive taxation and the abolition of taxes on consumption.

16. The establishment of national workshops. The state is to guarantee all workers their existence and care for those unable to work.

17. Universal and free education for the people.

It is in the interests of the German proletariat, petty bourgeoisie and peasantry to work energetically for the implementation of the above measures. Through their realization alone can the millions

2. The original text of the tenth Demand, in place of '*an die Revolution zu knüpfen*' (to bind [the interests of the conservative bourgeois] to the revolution), read '*an die Regierungen zu fesseln*' (to chain [the interests of the conservative bourgeois] to the governments).

of German people, who have up till now been exploited by a small handful, and whom some will attempt to maintain in renewed oppression, get their rights, and the power that they are due as the producers of all wealth.

The Committee:

KARL MARX	F. ENGELS
KARL SCHAPPER	J. MOLL
H. BAUER	W. WOLFF

Articles from the *Neue Rheinische Zeitung*[1]

THE DEMOCRATIC PARTY[2]

N.Rh.Z., 2 June 1848

Cologne, 1 June

Any new organ of public opinion commonly has to fulfil certain requirements: enthusiastic support for the party whose principles it professes; unlimited confidence in its strength; constant readiness both to gloss over real weakness with the lustre of principle and to use real strength to make up for an absence of principle. However, we shall not comply with these demands. We shall not seek to gild the defeats that have been suffered with misleading illusions.

The democratic party has suffered defeats; the fundamental principles which it proclaimed at the moment of its triumph have been put in question, the terrain which it had actually won has been progressively converted back into debatable ground. It has already suffered heavy losses, and we shall soon have to ask what is still left to it.

What we are concerned about is that the democratic party should become aware of its situation. We may well be asked why we address ourselves to a party, why we do not instead simply keep in view the goal of democratic endeavour, the good of the people, the salvation of everyone without distinction.

This is our right and the normal practice of the struggle. The salvation of the new age can only grow from the *struggle* of parties, not from apparently clever compromises or a sham association of contradictory views, interests and aims.

1. These articles are selected from approximately two hundred and twenty that Marx and Engels wrote for the *Neue Rheinische Zeitung* between 1 June 1848 and 19 May 1849. They are translated here from the texts printed in *MEW* 5 and 6.

2. This article was based on a draft by Heinrich Bürgers, who was taken onto the editorial board of the *Neue Rheinische Zeitung* as a concession to the local Cologne Communists in return for their allowing Marx and Engels to determine the policy of the newspaper. Marx edited the article, making extensive alterations to one half of it, and striking out the other half.

The 'democratic party' of this article refers to the broad democratic movement, not to any particular organized group.

We demand that the democratic party become aware of its situation. This demand has arisen from the experiences of the last few months. The democratic party has abandoned itself far too much to the ecstatic celebration of its first victories. Drunk with joy at being permitted at last to declare its principles loudly and frankly, it imagined that it was only necessary to proclaim them to be certain of their immediate realization. After its first triumph and the concessions directly linked to this, the democratic party never did more than proclaim its principles. But while, in its generosity, it embraced as a brother anyone who did not venture immediately to contradict it, other people, who had either been left in power or just presented with it, were taking action. And the results of their activity are not to be despised. They kept their principles in the background, only allowing them to obtrude in so far as they were directed against the old situation overthrown by the revolution. Cautiously they restricted the movement, wherever the interest of the newly created legal framework or the establishment of external order could serve as an excuse. They made apparent concessions to the friends of the old order, to be the more certain of their support in carrying out their plans. Then they gradually introduced their own political system in its basic features, and finally succeeded in winning the middle ground between the democratic party and the absolutists. Looked at from one side they are moving forwards, from the other side they are pushing backwards. They are at once progressive – against absolutism, and reactionary – against democracy.

This is the party of the prudent, moderate bourgeoisie, by which the party of the people in its initial drunkenness allowed itself to be outsmarted, until finally its eyes were opened when it was contemptuously rejected, denounced as subversive, and had all possible reprehensible tendencies attributed to it. Then the democratic party realized that basically it had achieved no more than what the gentlemen of the bourgeoisie regarded as compatible with their own well-understood interests. Involved in self-contradiction by undemocratic electoral laws, and beaten in the elections, the democratic party now sees itself confronted with two representative bodies,[3] and the only disputable point about them in which one opposes the strongest resistance to its demands.

3. The two representative bodies were the German National Assembly, which met at Frankfurt on 18 May 1848, and the Prussian National Assembly, which met at Berlin on 22 May 1848.

With this, of course, its enthusiasm has cooled off, and given place to the sober recognition that a powerful reaction has attained power, and, peculiarly enough, before any action of a revolutionary kind has taken place.

Although all this is indubitable, it would be dangerous now if the democratic party allowed itself to be persuaded, by the bitterness of the first defeat, for which it is itself partly responsible, to return to that accursed idealism, unfortunately so dear to the German character, in virtue of which a principle which cannot immediately be put into practice is recommended for the remote future, but for the present left to the harmless elaborations of the 'thinkers'.

We must give a direct warning against those hypocritical friends who declare their agreement with the principle, but who are doubtful of its feasibility because the world is not yet ripe for it. They have no intention of bringing this ripeness about, but prefer rather to revert, in this depraved earthly existence, to man's general fate of depravity. If these are the crypto-republicans, so feared by Hofrat Gervinus,[4] we must agree with him whole-heartedly: such men are dangerous.

CAMPHAUSEN'S DECLARATION IN THE SITTING OF 30 MAY 1848

N.Rh.Z., 3 June 1848

Cologne, 2 June

Post hoc et non propter hoc. Herr Camphausen[5] did not become Prime Minister *on account of* the March revolution but merely *after* the March revolution. On 30 May 1848 he revealed the subsequent character of his cabinet in a solemn, highly declamatory manner, with that so to speak serious corporeality which conceals the lack of a soul,[6] to the Berlin Assembly agreed on between the

---

4. Georg Gottfried Gervinus was a historian, court councillor (Hofrat), and member of the Frankfurt National Assembly. As a supporter of the constitutional monarchist Right Centre, Gervinus opposed the 'crypto-republicans' of the Left Centre, referred to here by Marx.

5. Ludolf Camphausen was a Cologne banker, one of the leading Rhineland liberals before 1848, and Prime Minister of Prussia from March to June 1848.

6. A quotation from Book I, chapter 11 of Lawrence Sterne's novel *Tristram Shandy*.

indirect electors[7] and himself. 'The ministry of state which was formed on 29 March', says the *thinking friend of history*,[8] 'met together shortly *after* an occurrence the significance of which it has not failed to appreciate and will not fail to appreciate.'

The evidence for Herr Camphausen's assertion that he did *not* form a cabinet *before* 29 March will be found in the last few months' issues of the *Preussische Staats-Zeitung*.[9] And we may reliably assume that the date which forms at least the chronological starting-point for Herr Camphausen's ascension into heaven possesses a great 'significance' for him. What reassurance for the dead of the barricades, that their cold corpses should figure as a sign-post, a pointer towards the ministry of 29 March! What an honour!

To put it briefly: after the March revolution a Camphausen ministry was formed; that same Camphausen ministry recognizes the 'great significance' of the March revolution; at any rate it does not *fail to appreciate* it. The revolution itself is a mere bagatelle, but we are speaking of its *significance*. What it *signifies* is the Camphausen ministry, at any rate retrospectively. 'This occurrence' – the formation of the Camphausen ministry or the March revolution? – 'belongs among the most essential contributory causes of the reconstruction of our *internal* constitution.'

He apparently means that the March revolution was an 'essential contributory cause' of the formation of the ministry of 29 March, i.e. of Camphausen's ministry. Or is he merely saying: the Prussian March revolution has revolutionized Prussia? We might very well expect a solemn tautology of this nature from a 'thinking friend of history'. 'We stand at the entrance to the same' (namely the reconstruction of the internal relations of our state), 'and we have a long road ahead of us, as the government recognizes.'

In short, the Camphausen ministry recognizes that it still has a long road ahead of it, i.e. it expects to last a long time. Short is art, i.e., the revolution, and long is life, i.e. the subsequent ministry. What a superfluity of self-recognition! Or should Camphausen's words be interpreted in some other way? One would certainly not expect from the *thinking friend of history* the

7. The Prussian National Assembly was elected on a two-tier voting system which was intended to cancel out the effect of universal suffrage.

8. This is Marx's ironic description of Camphausen, and refers to the dedication of Karl von Rotteck's well-known *Allgemeine Geschichte* (Freiburg, 1834), which was compiled 'for thinking friends of history'.

9. The semi-official organ of the Prussian government from 1819 to April 1848.

trivial statement that peoples which stand on the threshold of a new historical epoch stand at its threshold, and that the road which every epoch has *ahead of it* is precisely as long as the *future*.

Thus far the *first* part of the laborious, serious, formal, upright and shrewd speech of Prime Minister Campahusen. It can be summed up in three phrases: *after* the March revolution the Camphausen ministry; great significance of the Camphausen ministry; long road *ahead* of the Camphausen ministry.

Now the *second* part. 'We have by no means', pontificates Herr Camphausen,

conceived the situation to be that this occurrence [he means the March revolution] has brought about a complete upheaval, that the entire constitution of our state has been overthrown, that what we see before us has ceased to exist in law, and that all our institutions require a new legal foundation. On the contrary. Immediately they had met together, the ministers agreed to view it as a matter of the ministry's very existence that the United Diet[10] called at that time should actually meet, despite the petitions handed in against it. We agreed that the passage from the existing constitution to the new constitution should take place through the legal means provided by the former, and without cutting off the bond which links the old to the new. We strictly maintained this unquestionably correct course. The electoral law was presented to the United Diet and issued with its concurrence. Later on the attempt was made to empower the government to alter the law out of the plenitude of its own power, namely to change the indirect into the direct electoral system. The government did not give way to this. The government has not exercised a dictatorship; it has not been able to, nor has it *wanted* to. The electoral law has in fact been brought into operation in the form in which it exists legally. The electors, the deputies, have been elected on the basis of this electoral law. They are here on the basis of this electoral law with full powers to agree jointly with the Crown upon a constitution for the future which it is hoped will be a lasting constitution.

A kingdom for a doctrine! A doctrine for a kingdom! First comes the 'occurrence', shamefaced title of the *revolution*. Then along comes the doctrine and swindles the 'occurrence'.

10. The first United Diet (Vereinigte Landtag) sat in Berlin from April to June 1847. It consisted of representatives of the eight Provincial Diets of Prussia, assembled in two Curias, or chambers, one for the nobility and the other for the three mock-medieval estates of knights, towns and rural districts. A second United Diet was called on the same basis after the March revolution, but only for the purpose of passing the electoral law for the forthcoming National Assembly and granting the loan refused by the first United Diet. It was dissolved on 10 April 1848.

The unlawful 'occurrence' makes Herr Camphausen a *responsible* Prime Minister, makes him a being both out of place and meaningless in the old regime, under the existing constitution. With a breathtaking leap we brush aside the old order and are fortunate enough to find a responsible minister. But the responsible minister is still luckier: he finds a doctrine. The absolute monarchy expired, perished, at the first breath of the *responsible Prime Minister*. The late lamented 'United Diet', that repulsive mixture of Gothic fantasy and modern falsehood,[11] was the first victim of the responsible ministry. The 'United Diet' was the 'faithful follower', the 'little donkey' of the absolute monarchy. The German republic can only celebrate its triumphal entry over the dead body of Herr Venedey,[12] the responsible ministry only over the dead body of the 'faithful follower'. The responsible minister now seeks out the missing corpse, or conjures up the *ghost* of the faithful 'United', which does indeed appear but dangles unhappily in the air, cutting the most peculiar capers since it no longer finds any *ground* beneath its feet, the old *legal and moral foundation* having been swallowed up by the earthquake of the 'occurrence'. The magician informs the ghost that he has called it up in order to liquidate its remains and to be able to behave as its loyal heir. This polite mode of action is beyond all praise, he says, for in ordinary life the dead are not permitted to draw up their wills posthumously. The highly flattered ghost nods like an oriental figurine to all the magician's commands, makes his obeisance on the way out, and vanishes. The law of indirect election is his posthumous testament.

This is the doctrinal sleight-of-hand by which Herr Camphausen makes the transition 'from the existing constitution to the new constitution, through the legal means provided by the former'. An illegal occurrence makes Herr Camphausen an *illegal* person in the sense of the 'existing constitution' of the 'old order'. It makes him a responsible Prime Minister, a *constitutional minister*. The constitutional minister illegally makes the *anti-constitutional*, *predemocratic*, faithful *United Diet* a *constituent* assembly. The faithful 'United' illegally establishes indirect suffrage. Indirect suffrage

11. Heinrich Heine, 'Germany: A Winter's Tale', English translation in F. Ewen (ed.), *The Poetry and Prose of Heinrich Heine*, Citadel, New York, 1948.
12. Jakob Venedey was a radical journalist, and sat in the Frankfurt National Assembly as a member of the Radical-Democratic party.

produces the Berlin Assembly, the Berlin Assembly produces the constitution, the constitution produces all subsequent assemblies and so on *ad infinitum*.

In this way the egg comes out of the goose, and the goose comes out of the egg. However the people soon realize, from the cackling that saved the Capitol, that someone has filched the golden eggs of Leda,[13] laid by the goose during the revolution. Even deputy Milde[14] does not seem to be the son of Leda, the ever-shining Castor.

THE CAMPHAUSEN MINISTRY

N.Rh.Z., 4 June 1848

Cologne, 3 June

It is well known that an Assembly of Notables preceded the French National Assembly of 1789, and that this assembly, like the Prussian United Diet, was composed of *estates*. In the decree in which minister Necker convoked the National Assembly, he referred to the wish the notables had expressed for the convocation of the Estates General. Necker therefore had a considerable advantage over Camphausen. He did not need to await the storming of the Bastille and the fall of the absolute monarchy in order to link the old and the new in doctrinaire fashion, so as to maintain with great effort the *appearance* that France had achieved its new Constituent Assembly by the lawful means provided by the old constitution. He had other advantages too. He was a minister of France and not of Alsace-Lorraine, whereas Herr Camphausen is not a minister of Germany but of Prussia. And with all these advantages, Necker did not succeed in making a quiet reform out of a revolutionary movement. The great sickness was not to be healed with attar of roses.[15] So much the less will Herr Camphausen change the character of the movement with an artificial theory which draws a straight line between his ministry and the previous situation in the Prussian monarchy. The March revolution, and the German revolutionary movement in general, will not

13. According to the Greek legend, the children of the Spartan queen Leda and the god Zeus came out of an egg.

14. Karl August Milde was a Silesian cotton manufacturer, a liberal monarchist, chairman of the Prussian National Assembly and Prussian Minister of Trade from June to September 1848.

15. Heine, 'Germany: A Winter's Tale.'

allow themselves to be transformed into *incidents* of greater or lesser importance by any kind of stratagem. Was Louis Philippe chosen king of the French *because* he was a Bourbon? Was he chosen *although* he was a Bourbon? Remember that this question divided the parties shortly after the July revolution. What did the question itself signify? That the revolution had been put in question, and that the interest of the revolution was not the interest of the class that had achieved mastery, nor of its political representatives.

This is also the meaning of Herr Camphausen's declaration that his ministry did not come into the world *on account of* the March revolution, but *after* it.

THE PROGRAMMES OF THE RADICAL-DEMOCRATIC PARTY AND THE LEFT IN THE FRANKFURT ASSEMBLY

N.Rh.Z., 7 June 1848

Cologne, 6 June

Yesterday we communicated to our readers the 'Reasoned Manifesto of the Radical-Democratic Party in the Constituent National Assembly at Frankfurt-am-Main'. Today, under the heading 'Frankfurt', you will find the manifesto of the Left.[16] The two manifestos appear at first sight to be scarcely distinguishable except in form, in that the Radical-Democratic party's writer is clumsy while the Left's is skilful. On closer inspection, however, there stand out certain essential points of difference. The Radical manifesto demands a National Assembly 'on the basis of *direct elections* without property qualifications'. The Left's manifesto calls for 'free election by everyone'. *Free election by everyone* excludes the property qualifications but by no means excludes the *indirect* method. And what indeed is the reason for this indefinite, ambiguous expression?

We are once again confronted with the greater scope and the flexibility of the demands of the Left, as opposed to the demands of the Radical party. The Left calls for 'an executive central authority, elected *by* the National Assembly for a specified period,

16. The left wing of the Frankfurt National Assembly split into two parts in May 1848. The larger and more moderate group was the Left proper, led by Robert Blum; the smaller, more extreme group was the Radical-Democratic party.

and responsible to it'. It leaves undecided whether this central authority is to emerge *from the ranks of the National Assembly*, as expressly
laid down by the Radical manifesto.

Finally, the manifesto of the Left demands that the fundamental
rights of the German people be immediately determined, proclaimed,
and protected against all possible attacks by the individual German
governments. The Radical manifesto does not content itself with this,
but declares: 'The Assembly already contains within itself the full
powers of the whole state; it must *immediately* put into operation its
various powers and the forms of political life it has been called to
decide, and deal with the internal and external policy of the whole
state'.

Both manifestos agree that they want to leave the 'establishment of the German constitution to the National Assembly alone',
excluding the participation of the governments. Both agree in leaving each individual state the choice of its constitution, whether it is
to be a constitutional monarchy or a republic, 'without prejudice to
the rights of the people, to be proclaimed by the National Assembly'. Finally, both agree that they want to transform Germany into a
confederation or federal state.

At least the Radical manifesto expresses the *revolutionary*
nature of the National Assembly. It enlists the aid of the revolutionary activities appropriate to it. The very existence of a
constituent National Assembly shows, does it not, that a constitution no longer *exists*. But if a constitution no longer exists, a
government no longer exists. If there is no longer a government,
the National Assembly itself must govern. Its first sign of life
ought to have been the six-word decree: 'The Federal Diet[17] is
permanently abolished.'

A constituent National Assembly should above all be an *active*
assembly, active in a revolutionary sense. The Assembly in Frankfurt
performs parliamentary exercises and lets the governments act. Even
assuming that this learned council succeeds in contriving the best
agenda and the best constitution, what use is the best agenda and the
best constitution when in the meantime the governments have placed
bayonets on the agenda?

The German National Assembly, leaving aside the fact that its
members were elected *indirectly*, suffers from a peculiarly Ger-

17. The Federal Diet (Bundestag) was the assembly of representatives of the thirty-nine German states in the German confederation (Deutscher Bund), formed in 1815
by the Congress of Vienna.

manic disease. Its seat is Frankfurt-am-Main, and Frankfurt is only an ideal centre, corresponding to the previously existing ideal, i.e. only imagined, unity of Germany. Moreover, Frankfurt-am-Main is not a big city with a strong revolutionary movement capable of standing behind the National Assembly, partly to protect it, partly to drive it forwards. For the first time in world history, the constituent assembly of a great nation has held its meetings in a small town. This was a result of Germany's previous development. Whereas the French and the English national assemblies stood on the volcanic soil of Paris and London, the German National Assembly was content to find a piece of *neutral* ground, where it could reflect on the best possible constitution and the best possible order of business without its peace of mind being disturbed. Despite this, the present situation in Germany offered the Assembly the opportunity of overcoming its unfortunate material position. It needed only to oppose the reactionary encroachments of the antiquated German governments in a dictatorial fashion, and it would have conquered a position in the public esteem impregnable to bayonets and rifle-butts. Instead, the Assembly knowingly left Mainz to the mercy of the soldiery, and delivered German-speaking foreigners to the chicaneries of the philistine citizens of Frankfurt. It bores the German people, instead of inspiring them or being itself inspired by them. It admits the existence of a *public*, which in the meantime still observes the comical antics of the resurrected spirit of the Holy Roman German Imperial Diet[18] with generous good humour, but not the existence of a *nation*, rediscovering its national life in and through the life of the Assembly. Far from being the central organ of the revolutionary movement, it has so far not even been its echo.

Even if the National Assembly should give birth to a central authority[19] we can expect little satisfaction from this provisional government, in view of the Assembly's present composition and its failure to grasp the most favourable moment for action. If no central authority is set up, however, the Assembly will have

18. Marx is alluding to the archaic nature of the German Federal Diet.
19. The question of a possible central authority (*Zentralgewalt*) occupied the centre of the discussions of the Frankfurt Assembly in June 1848, and was finally settled by the decision of 28 June 1848 to set up the Provisional Central Authority of Germany, consisting of a Reich regent (Reichsverweser) and a Reich ministry (Reichsministerium) appointed by him. Archduke John of Austria was chosen as the regent.

abdicated of its own accord, and will be scattered in all directions by the weakest puff of the revolutionary wind.

It is to the credit of both the Left and the Radical-Democrats that they have understood this necessity and included the central authority in their programmes. Both programmes also proclaim, with Heine:

> Considering how matters stand,
> We need no king at all.[20]

and the difficulty of deciding *who* shall be kaiser, as well as the fact that both the elective and the hereditary systems have good grounds in their favour, will also compel the conservative majority of the Assembly to cut the Gordian knot by choosing *no kaiser at all*.

What is incomprehensible is how the so-called Radical-Democratic party has been able to proclaim a *federation* of constitutional monarchies, principalities and mini-republics as the ultimate constitution for Germany. For the proposed central committee (an idea naturally accepted by the Left, but now also by the Radical party) is nothing more than a republican government at the head of a monarchical federation composed of the above heterogeneous elements.

There is no doubt about it. The German central government elected by the National Assembly must first emerge *alongside* the individual governments, which still exist *de facto*. But the struggle with the individual governments commences with its very existence, and in this struggle either the central government and with it the unity of Germany will go under, or the individual governments will, i.e. the constitutional princes and the obscure little republics.

We are not making here the utopian demand that a united, indivisible German republic be proclaimed here and now, but rather that the so-called Radical-Democratic party cease to confuse the starting-point of the struggle and the revolutionary movement with its final goal. German unity and a German constitution can only emerge as a result of a movement in which the internal conflicts as well as the war with the East[21] will reach their decision. The definitive constitution cannot be *decreed*; it coincides with the

20. *The Poetry and Prose of Heinrich Heine*, p. 215.
21. I.e. with Russia.

process we shall have to pass through. It is not a question of the realization of this or that opinion, of this or that political idea; it is a question of understanding the course of development. The task of the National Assembly is simply to take the immediately possible practical steps.

Despite his assertion that 'every man is happy to get rid of his confusions', there is nothing more confused than the idea put forward by the writer of the Radical-Democratic manifesto that the German constitution should take as its example the constitution of the *federal state in North America*!

The United States of America, apart from the fact that they all have similar constitutions, extend over an area as large as civilized Europe. An analogy could only be found in a *European* federation. And before Germany can federate with other countries it must itself first become a *single* country. In Germany, the struggle of centralization with federalism is the struggle between modern civilization and feudalism. Germany decayed into a bourgeoisified feudalism at the very moment when the great monarchies of western Europe were established, and it was excluded from the world market at the very moment when that market was opened to western Europe. Germany declined into poverty, whilst the others enriched themselves. Germany became ruralized, whilst the others became urbanized. Even if Russia were not at the gates, Germany's economic condition alone would compel the most rigid centralization. Even from a purely bourgeois standpoint, absolute unity is the first requirement for saving Germany from its previous misery and building up the national economy. Indeed, how could any modern social tasks be accomplished on the basis of a land divided into thirty-nine parts?

The writer of the Democratic programme did not in any case find it necessary to deal with the petty question of material economic relations. His justification remained at the level of the concept of federation. A *federation* is a *union of free and equal people*. *Therefore*, Germany must be a *federal state*. But couldn't the Germans also federate themselves into a *single* great state, without sinning against the concept of a union of free and equal people?

THE 15 JUNE SITTING OF THE
'VEREINBARUNGSVERSAMMLUNG'[22]

N.Rh.Z., 18 June 1848

Cologne, 17 June

We told you some days ago:[23] the existence of the revolution has been denied; it will demonstrate its existence by means of a second revolution.

The events of 14 June[24] are only the first flashes of lightning heralding this second revolution, and the Camphausen ministry has already disintegrated. The *Vereinbarungsversammlung* has given the people of Berlin a vote of confidence by placing itself under their protection.[25] This is a retrospective recognition of the March fighters. The Assembly has taken the constitution out of the ministers' hands and is endeavouring to 'make an agreement' with the people, by setting up a commission to examine all petitions and addresses relevant to the constitution. This is a retrospective rejection of its own declaration of incompetence.[26] The Assembly has promised to begin its work of constitution-making by the removal of the foundation-stone of the old building – the feudal relationships which burden the land. This is to promise a night of 4 August.[27]

In short: the Berlin Assembly denied its own past on 15 June,

22. '*Vereinbarungsversammlung*' (literally, 'assembly of agreement') was Marx's ironic term for the Prussian National Assembly, called on 22 May 1848 'to establish the future constitution of the state by agreement (*Vereinbarung*) with the Crown'. On the theory of *Vereinbarung*, see 'The Bourgeoisie and the Counter-Revolution', part III.

23. 'The Berlin Debate on the Revolution' (Engels, 14 June 1848), *MECW* 7, pp. 73–86.

24. On 14 June 1848 the people of Berlin carried out a series of spontaneous and unorganized actions (in particular the storming of the arsenal) in response to the National Assembly's refusal to declare that those who had fought in the March revolution 'had served the fatherland well'.

25. By the resolution of 15 June that the Assembly 'does not require the protection of the armed forces and has placed itself under the protection of the Berlin population'.

26. This refers to the resolution of 9 June that the Assembly's 'task was not to give judgements but to work out the constitution by agreement with the Crown'.

27. During the night of 4 August 1789 the French National Assembly proclaimed the abolition of a large number of feudal burdens.

just as it denied the past of the people on 9 June. It has undergone its own 21 March.[28]

But the Bastille has still not been stormed.

Meanwhile, an apostle of revolution is approaching from the East, unstoppable, irresistible. He already stands before the gates of Toruń.[29] He is the *tsar of Russia. The tsar will save the German revolution by forcing its centralization.*

THE PRAGUE RISING

N.Rh.Z., 18 June 1848   Frederick Engels
                                                                        Cologne, 17 June

A new Posen bloodbath[30] is being prepared in Bohemia. The Austrian soldiery has drowned the possibility of peaceful coexistence between Bohemia and Germany in Czech blood.

Prince Windischgrätz[31] was positioning his cannons against Prague on the Vyšehrad and the Hradčany.[32] Troop concentrations were being built up and a surprise attack was being prepared against the Slav Congress[33] and the Czechs.

The people learned of these military preparations. They swarmed around the prince's residence and demanded weapons. They met with a refusal. Excitement mounted, the armed and unarmed crowds grew in size. Then a shot was fired from an inn opposite the commander's palace; Princess Windischgrätz fell to the ground, mortally wounded. The order to attack was given on the spot; the infantry advanced and the people were pressed back. But every-

28. On 21 March 1848 Frederick William appeared to yield to popular demands he had previously resisted and promised that Prussia would be turned into a constitutional state and merged in a united Germany.

29. A fortress in Posen, on the frontier with the Russian empire.

30. This refers to the bloody suppression by Prussian troops of the Polish rising in the Grand Duchy of Posen and the fierce persecution of Polish revolutionaries which followed in May and June 1848.

31. Alfred, Fürst zu Windischgrätz was an Austrian field-marshal.

32. Vyšehrad and Hradčany are the respective names of the southern and the north-western districts of old Prague.

33. The Slav Congress met in Prague on 2 June 1848. Most of its supporters adopted the theory of Austro-Slavism, that the Austrian state must be maintained so as to preserve the small Slav nationalities (in particular the Czechs) from German domination. However, a strong minority upheld the democratic and revolutionary idea of the destruction of the Austrian state in alliance with the German and Hungarian democrats, and it was their agitation on the streets of Prague which led Windischgrätz to make the preparations mentioned here.

where barricades were set up, halting the advance of the troops. Cannons were moved up, and the barricades were destroyed with grape-shot. The blood flowed in streams. The struggle lasted throughout the night of the 12th–13th and into the next morning. Finally the soldiers managed to take the main streets and force the people back into the more confined parts of the town, where artillery cannot be used.

This is as far as our latest information goes. Moreover, many members of the Slav Congress have been expelled from the town under strong military escort. It would seem then that the military have secured at least a partial victory.

However the rising may end, a war of annihilation of the Germans against the Czechs is now the only possible solution.[34]

In making their revolution, the Germans had to be punished for the sins of their entire past. They were punished for them in Italy. In Posen they have once more been burdened with the curses of all Poland. And now there is Bohemia as well.

Even in places where the French came as enemies,[35] they were able to gain recognition and sympathy. The Germans, however, are recognized nowhere and find sympathy nowhere. Even where they come forward as the magnanimous apostles of liberty they are rejected with bitter sarcasm.

And rightly so. A nation which has allowed itself to be used throughout its history as an instrument for oppressing all other nations, a nation of this kind must first prove that it has really become revolutionary. It must prove this in some other way than through a few semi-revolutions, which have had no other result than to allow the old indecisiveness, weakness and disunity to continue in altered forms; revolutions during which a Radetzky[36] remains in Milan, a Colomb and a Steinäcker in Posen, a Windischgrätz in Prague and a Hüser in Mainz, just as if nothing had happened.[37]

---

34. This apparently opaque sentence can be explained as follows: Engels considered that with the defeat of the Prague rising the revolutionary and democratic minority among the Czechs had been crushed. The Czech people were therefore now solidly counter-revolutionary, under the control of Windischgrätz, and a revolutionary Germany would have to fight against them.

35. I.e. in the French revolutionary wars of 1792–1814.

36. Count Joseph Radetzky was an Austrian field-marshal, and supreme commander of the Austrian troops in Italy in 1848.

37. Colomb, Steinäcker and Hüser were all Prussian generals.

A revolutionized Germany would have to disown the whole of its past, especially in relation to the neighbouring peoples. It would have to proclaim the freedom of the peoples it had previously oppressed, at the same time as it proclaimed its own freedom.

And what *has* revolutionary Germany done? It has completely ratified the old oppression of Italy, Poland, and now Bohemia too, by the German soldiery. Kaunitz[38] and Metternich have received a complete justification.

After all this, are the Germans really asking the Czechs to trust them?

And are the Czechs at fault for their unwillingness to attach themselves to a nation which oppresses and ill-treats other nations while freeing itself?

Are they at fault for refusing to send representatives to an assembly like our miserable, half-hearted Frankfurt 'National Assembly', which trembles at the prospect of its own sovereignty?[39]

Are they at fault for disowning the impotent Austrian government, whose indecision and paralysis seems to serve neither to prevent nor to organize the dissolution of Austria, but only to confirm it? A government which is too weak to liberate Prague from the cannons and the soldiers of a Windischgrätz?

But it is the brave Czechs themselves who are to be pitied most of all. Whether they win or lose, their downfall is assured. They have been driven into the arms of the Russians by four hundred years of German oppression, of which the street battles in Prague are but a continuation. In the great struggle between the West and the East of Europe, which will break out in a very short time – perhaps in a few weeks – an unhappy destiny has placed the Czechs on the side of the Russians, on the side of despotism against the revolution. The revolution will win, and the Czechs will be the first to be crushed by it.

It is the Germans again who will bear the guilt for the downfall of the Czechs. It is the Germans who have betrayed them to Russia.

38. Wendel Anton, Fürst von Kauntiz, was an Austrian diplomat and protagonist of 'enlightened despotism'.

39. Most German liberals and radicals in 1848 claimed that Bohemia was a part of Germany, and that it should be represented in the Frankfurt National Assembly. However, the leader of the Czech national movement, Palacký, replied to an invitation to join in elections to the Assembly with an outright refusal (8 April), and he was followed in this by the Czech, though not by the German, inhabitants of Bohemia.

THE FALL OF THE CAMPHAUSEN MINISTRY

N.Rh.Z., 23 June 1848

Cologne, 22 June

Scheint die Sonne noch so schön
Einmal muss sie untergehn,[40]

and this applies even to the sun of 30 March, reddened with hot Polish blood.[41]

The Camphausen ministry was the liberal-bourgeois garment put on by the counter-revolution. Now the counter-revolution feels strong enough to cast off the burdensome disguise.

Some kind of temporary left-centre cabinet could perhaps follow the ministry of 30 March in a few days' time. However, its real successor will be the *ministry of the Prince of Prussia.*[42] Camphausen has thus had the honour of providing the party of feudal absolutism with its natural chief, and his ministry with this successor.

Was there any need to pamper the bourgeois guardians any longer? Do not the Russians stand at the eastern border, and Prussian troops in the west? Have the Poles not been won over to Russian propaganda by means of shrapnel and caustic? Have not all preparations been made to repeat the bombardment of Prague in almost all the towns of the Rhineland? Has the army not had plenty of time to revert into brutality in the Danish and Polish wars, and in the many small-scale conflicts between the military and the people? Is the bourgeoisie not tired of revolution? And has there not risen up in the middle of the sea the rock on which the counter-revolution will build its church, namely England?

The Camphausen ministry is still trying to grab a few penn'orths of popularity, still trying to arouse public sympathy, by ensuring that it withdraws from the stage as the *victim of deception*. It is in fact the deceiver deceived. In the service of the big bourgeoisie, it had to try to defraud the revolution of its democratic

40. 'However beautifully the sun shines, it must go down eventually.' From Raimund's play *Das Mädchen aus der Feenwelt oder der Bauer als Millionär* (*The Girl from Fairyland or The Peasant as Millionaire*), II, vi.

41. The Camphausen ministry took office on 30 March 1848, and its period of office coincided with the suppression of the Polish rising in Posen (April–May 1848). Camphausen's ministry came to an end on 20 June 1848.

42. See p. 140, n. 85.

achievements; in the struggle with democracy it had to make an alliance with the aristocratic party and become the instrument of its counter-revolutionary appetites. Now that party is strong enough to be able to throw its protector overboard. *Herr Camphausen sowed reaction in the interests of the big bourgeoisie; he has harvested it in the interests of the feudal party.* The former was his good intention, the latter his bad luck. A penn'orth of popularity for a disappointed man! A penn'orth of popularity!

> *Scheint die Sonne noch so schön*
> *Einmal muss sie untergehn!*

But in the East the sun is rising again.

THE JUNE REVOLUTION

N.Rh.Z., 29 June 1848

The Paris workers have been *overwhelmed* by superior forces; they have not *succumbed* to them. They have been *beaten*, but it is their enemies who have been *vanquished*. The momentary triumph of brutal violence has been purchased with the destruction of all the deceptions and illusions of the February revolution, with the dissolution of the whole of the old republican party, and with the fracturing of the French nation into two nations, the nation of the possessors and the nation of the workers. The tricolour republic now bears only *one colour*, the colour of the defeated, the *colour of blood*. It has become the *red republic*.

There was no republican group of repute on the side of the people, neither that of the *National* nor that of the *Réforme*.[43] Without leaders, without any means other than the insurrection itself, the people withstood the united bourgeoisie and soldiery longer than any French dynasty, with all its military apparatus, ever withstood a fraction of the bourgeoisie united with the people. In order that the people's last illusion should disappear, in order to allow a complete break with the past, it was necessary for the customary poetic accompaniment of a French rising, the enthusiastic youth of the bourgeoisie, the pupils of the École Polytechnique, the three-cornered hats, to take the side of the

43. The two main republican groups in France in 1848 were centred around the newspapers *Le National* and *La Réforme*, characterized elsewhere by Marx as the respective organs of bourgeois and petty-bourgeois republicanism.

oppressors. The pupils of the Faculty of Medicine had to deny the aid of science to the wounded plebeians, who have committed the unspeakable, infernal crime of hazarding their lives for their own existence for once, instead of for Louis Philippe or M. Marrast.[44]

The last official remnant of the February revolution, the Executive Commission,[45] has melted away like an apparition before the seriousness of events. Lamartine's[46] fireworks have turned into Cavaignac's[47] incendiary rockets. '*Fraternité*', the brotherhood of opposing classes, one of which exploits the other, this '*fraternité*' was proclaimed in February and written in capital letters on the brow of Paris, on every prison and every barracks. But its true, genuine, prosaic expression is *civil war* in its most terrible form, the war between labour and capital. This fraternity flamed in front of all the windows of Paris on the evening of 25 June. The Paris of the bourgeoisie was illuminated, while the Paris of the proletariat burned, bled and moaned in its death agony.

Fraternity lasted only as long as there was a fraternity of interests between bourgeoisie and proletariat. Pedants of the old revolutionary traditions of 1793; constructors of socialist systems, who went begging to the bourgeoisie on behalf of the people, and who were allowed to preach long sermons and to compromise themselves as long as the proletarian lion had to be lulled to sleep;[48] republicans, who wanted to keep the whole of the old bourgeois order, but remove the crowned head; supporters of the dynastic opposition,[49] upon whom chance had foisted the fall of a dynasty instead of a change of ministers; Legitimists, who

44. Armand Marrast was the leader of the moderate republicans in the 1840s, the editor of *Le National*, a member of the Provisional Government of February–May 1848, and the chairman of the Constituent National Assembly.

45. The Executive Commission set up by the Constituent Assembly replaced the Provisional Government on 10 May 1848, and lasted until 24 June.

46. Alphonse de Lamartine was a French poet and historian, a moderate republican in politics. He was Foreign Minister in the Provisional Government of 1848, at which time he issued his fiery declarations to the governments of Europe, hence 'fireworks'.

47. Louis-Eugène Cavaignac was a French general and a moderate republican. In May 1848 he was made Minister of War, and in June was given dictatorial powers to suppress the Paris insurrection.

48. See the Communist Manifesto, above, pp. 88–91.

49. The group led by Odilon Barrot before 1848, which supported a moderate reform of the electoral system and the removal of Guizot, hoping thereby not to overthrow the Orleans monarchy but to broaden its base of support.

wanted not to cast aside the livery but to change its cut; all these were the allies with whom the people made its February. What the people instinctively hated in Louis Philippe was not the man himself but the crowned rule of a class, capital on the throne. But, generous as ever, it imagined it had destroyed its enemy when it had only overthrown the enemy of its enemy, the *common* enemy.

The *February revolution* was the *beautiful* revolution, the revolution of universal sympathy, because the conflicts which erupted in the revolution against the monarchy slumbered harmoniously side by side, as yet *undeveloped*, because the social struggle which formed its background had only assumed an airy existence – it existed only as a phrase, only in words. The June revolution is the *ugly* revolution, the repulsive revolution, because realities have taken the place of words, because the republic has uncovered the head of the monster itself by striking aside the protective, concealing crown.

Order! was Guizot's battle cry. *Order!* screamed Sébastiani,[50] Guizot's follower, as Warsaw reverted to Russian rule. *Order!* screams Cavaignac, the brutal echo of the French National Assembly and the republican bourgeoisie.

Order! thundered his grape-shot, as it lacerated the body of the proletariat.

None of the innumerable revolutions of the French bourgeoisie since 1789 was an attack on *order*; for they perpetuated class rule, the slavery of the workers, *bourgeois order*, no matter how frequent the changes in the political form of this rule and this slavery. June has violated this *order*. Woe unto June!

Under the *Provisional Government* it was customary, indeed it was a *necessity*, combining politics and enthusiasm at once, to preach to the generous workers who (as could be read on thousands of official placards) had '*placed three months of misery at the disposal of the republic*', that the February revolution had been made *in their own interests*, and that the February revolution was concerned above all with the *interests of the workers*. But after the opening of the National Assembly everyone came down to earth. What was important now was *to bring back labour to its old*

50. Horace, comte Sébastiani was the French Minister of Foreign Affairs from 1830 to 1832. In 1831 he refused to protest against the tsar's suppression of the Polish revolution, and called for a return by both parties to the treaty settlement of 1815. By this the greater part of Poland formed part of the Russian empire, with the tsar as its king.

situation, as Minister Trélat[51] said. In other words, the workers had fought in February in order to be thrown into an industrial crisis.

The task of the National Assembly was to reverse the events of February, at least for the workers, and to throw them back into their old situation. But even that did not happen, because it is no more in the power of an assembly than that of a king to call a halt to an industrial crisis of a general character. The National Assembly, in its brutal eagerness to finish with the tiresome phrases of February, did not even adopt those measures which *were* possible on the basis of the old conditions. It either pressed the Paris workers between the ages of seventeen and twenty-five into the army, or it threw them onto the streets; non-Parisian workers were expelled from Paris and sent to the Sologne, without receiving even the money customarily provided on dismissal; finally, Parisians of full age were given alms, provisionally and in militarily organized factories, on condition that they did not take part in any public meetings, i.e. on condition that they ceased to be republicans. The sentimental post-February rhetoric proved inadequate. So also did the brutal legislation enacted after 15 May.[52] The decision had to be made in fact, in practice. Has the rabble made the February revolution for *itself* or for *us*? In June the bourgeoisie posed the question in such a way that it had to be answered – with grape-shot and barricades.

And yet, as one deputy said on 25 June,[53] the whole National Assembly was stupefied by the rising. As the question and its answer drowned the walls of Paris in blood, it was dazed with astonishment. Some were stunned because their illusions were vanishing in a cloud of gunsmoke; others because they could not understand how the people could dare to come forward *independently* on behalf of its *very own* interests. Russian gold, English gold, the Bonapartist eagle, the *fleur-de-lis*: talismans of all kinds had to be interposed between this remarkable occurrence and their understanding. However, *both sides* of the Assembly felt that they

51. Ulysse Trélat was a doctor and politician, on the editorial board of *Le National* and Minister of Public Works from May to June 1848.

52. On 15 May 1848 Blanqui and his party led their supporters to a number of key points in order to set up a new Provisional Government to replace the National Assembly and the Executive Commission. The latter replied with a number of measures directed against the political life of Paris and the national workshops.

53. Ducoux [Marx].

were separated from the people by an immeasurable chasm. No one dared to speak on behalf of the people.

As soon as the astonishment had passed, there followed an outbreak of rage, and the majority rightly hissed off the stage those miserable utopians and hypocrites who commited the anachronism of continuing to utter the word '*fraternité*'. It was now a matter of abolishing this word and the illusions hiding in its ambiguous bosom. When La Rochejaquelein,[54] the Legitimist, with his enthusiasm for chivalry, inveighed against the infamy of the declaration *Vae victis*,[55] the majority of the Assembly suffered an attack of St Vitus' dance, as if stung by an adder. The Assembly cries 'woe' over the workers in order to conceal that the 'vanquished' is none other than itself. Either it or the republic must now disappear. Hence its frantic howls of 'long live the republic'.

A deep abyss has opened before us. Should it mislead democrats, should it delude us into thinking that struggles over the form of the state are without content, illusory, null and void?

Only weak and cowardly temperaments can bring up this question. The confrontations which arise out of the very conditions of bourgeois society must be fought out, they cannot be imagined away. The best form of state is not that in which social antagonisms are blurred or forcibly shackled, that is to say artificially shackled, shackled only in appearance. It is rather that in which they can freely come into conflict, and thus be solved.

We shall be asked whether we have no tears, no sighs, no words for the victims of the people's rage, for the National Guard, the Mobile Guard, the Republican Guard, the troops of the line.[56]

54. Henri, marquis de La Rochejaquelein was a leading Legitimist, and a deputy in 1848 to the Constituent National Assembly. The reference here is to his speech of 25 June 1848 suggesting that the Assembly should declare an amnesty for insurgents who surrendered.

55. 'Woe to the vanquished.' The expression is supposed to have been used by the Roman Brennus in 390 B.C. on the occasion of the fall of Rome to the Gauls.

56. The National Guard had existed since 1789, with some interruptions. As reorganized by Louis Philippe in 1831 it was limited to property-owning citizens who would, it was thought, maintain the monarchy and the existing social order. In 1848, however, it abandoned the July monarchy and joined the republican forces. It was democratized in February 1848 by the admission of all (male) citizens between the ages of twenty and sixty. The Mobile Guard was set up on 25 February 1848 by the Provisional Government to maintain order in Paris (see 'The Class Struggles in France', below, pp. 386–7). The Republican Guard was founded in 1800 as the Guard of Paris, and

The reply is this: the state will look after their widows and orphans, decrees will glorify them, solemn funeral processions will inter their remains, the official press will declare them immortal, the European reaction from east to west will pay homage to them.

But the plebeians are tortured with hunger, reviled by the press, abandoned by doctors, abused by honest men as thieves, incendiaries, galley-slaves, their women and children thrown into still deeper misery, their best sons deported overseas: it is the *privilege*, it is the *right of the democratic press* to wind the laurels around their stern and threatening brows.

THE PRUSSIAN PRESS BILL

N.Rh.Z., 20 July 1848

Cologne, 19 July

We were thinking of amusing our readers once more with the debates of the *Vereinbarungsversammlung*, and in particular of presenting a brilliant speech by deputy Baumstark,[57] but events have prevented this.

Charity begins at home. When the existence of the press is threatened, even deputy Baumstark must be left aside.

Herr Hansemann[58] has laid an interim press law before the Assembly. His fatherly concern for the press demands our immediate consideration.

Before 1848, the Code Napoléon[59] was beautified by the addition of the most edifying sections of the Landrecht.[60] After the

---

continued to exist throughout the nineteenth century under various names. As the Municipal Guard of Paris under the July monarchy it put down a number of insurrections with ferocity, and was the object of particular hatred on the part of the people in February 1848. The Provisional Government at first intended to dissolve it, but a paramilitary force of this nature soon turned out to be necessary to suppress opposition from the left, and it was therefore kept in being and in May 1848 given the new name of Republican Guard of Paris (later simply Republican Guard).

57. Eduard Baumstark was a university professor and a Right deputy in the Berlin Assembly.

58. David Justus Hansemann was an industrialist from the Rhineland, and the leader of the liberal movement of the 1840s there; from March to September 1848 he was Prussian Minister of Finance.

59. The French civil law issued in 1807 and imposed on the occupied regions of western Germany. It remained in force in the Rhineland after 1815.

60. The Prussian legal code.

revolution, this has changed; now the Landrecht is enriched with the most fragrant blossoms of the Code and the September laws.[61] Duchâtel[62] is naturally no Bodelschwingh.[63]

We have already given the main details of this press bill.[64] We had only just had the opportunity to show that articles 367 and 368 of the Code Pénal[65] stood in the most glaring contradiction with the freedom of the press (by undergoing an investigation for libel),[66] when Herr Hansemann proposed not only to extend it to the whole of the kingdom, but also to make it three times more severe. In the new bill, we find everything we have grown to know and love through practical experience.

We find it prohibited, on pain of three months' to three years' imprisonment, to accuse anyone of an action which is punishable by law, or which merely 'puts him in public contempt'; we find it prohibited to assert the truth of a fact except on the basis of 'completely valid evidence'; in short, we rediscover the most classic characteristics of Napoleon's despotic rule over the press.

One might well say that Herr Hansemann has fulfilled his promise to give the old Prussian provinces a share in the advantages of the laws of the Rhineland!

These measures are crowned by paragraph 10 of the bill: if the libel was committed against *state officials* in relation to their official business, the normal punishment can be *increased by a half*.

Article 222 of the Code Pénal provides for a period of from one month up to two years' imprisonment when an official has received an insult in words (*outrage par parole*) during the performance of, or incidentally (*à l'occasion*) to, the performance of

61. These were laws sharpening the censorship of the press and restricting the application of the jury system, which were issued in France in September 1835.

62. Charles, comte Duchâtel was a member of De Broglie's ministry of 1834 to 1836 which introduced the September laws.

63. Ernst, Freiherr von Bodelschwingh, a Prussian official who, as Oberpräsident of the Rhine province (1834–42), endeavoured to introduce the Landrecht into the Rhineland. From 1845 to 1848 he was Minister of the Interior.

64. *Neue Rheinische Zeitung*, 17 July 1848 (not written by Marx or Engels).

65. The Napoleonic code of criminal law was extended to the occupied regions of western Germany, and remained in force in the Rhineland after 1815.

66. A libel investigation against the *Neue Rheinische Zeitung* had followed an article on 5 July reporting the arrest of Gottschalk and Anneke, and accusing the police of brutality ('Arrests', *MECW* 7, pp. 177–9). See also *MECW* 7, pp. 208–11.

his office. So far, and despite the benevolent endeavours of public prosecutors, this article did not apply to the press, and for good reasons. In order to remedy this abuse, Herr Hansemann transformed article 222 into the above-mentioned paragraph 10. Firstly, 'incidentally' was changed into the more convenient phrase 'in relation to their official business'; secondly, the tiresome 'in word' was changed into 'in writing'; thirdly, the punishment was increased threefold.

From the day when this law comes into force, the Prussian officials will be able to sleep soundly. If Herr Pfuel[67] burns the hands and ears of the Poles with caustic, and the press publishes this: four and a half months to four and a half years in prison! If citizens are thrown into prison by mistake, although it is known that they are not the guilty ones, and the press points this out: four and a half months to four and a half years in prison! If local officials become travelling salesmen of the reaction and collect signatures for royalist addresses, and the press unmasks those gentlemen; four and a half months to four and a half years in prison!

From the day when this law comes into force, the officials will be able, unpunished, to commit any arbitrary, tyrannical, or illegal action; they will be free to flog and order floggings, to arrest and imprison without trial; the only effective control, the press, will have been made ineffective. On the day when this law comes into force, the bureaucracy will be able to celebrate and rejoice: it will be more powerful, more unhindered, and stronger than before March.

Indeed, what is left of the freedom of the press when the press may no longer hold up to the contempt of the public that which *deserves* the contempt of the public?

According to the existing laws, the press could at least present the facts as proofs of its general assertions and accusations. This situation will now come to an end. The press will no longer *report*, it will only be permitted to engage in general phrase-making, so that right-thinking people, from Herr Hansemann down to the simple citizen drinking his pale ale will have the right to say, 'The press merely *grumbles*, it never *brings proof*.' It is precisely for that reason that the bringing of proof is being forbidden.

67. Ernst Heinrich von Pfuel was a Prussian general, in charge of the suppression of the Posen rising in April and May 1848.

By the way, we would recommend Herr Hansemann to make an addition to his generous bill. He should declare it a punishable offence to hold up the gentlemen of the bureaucracy, not just to public contempt, but also to public ridicule. This omission will otherwise be painfully felt.

We shall not deal with the paragraphs on obscenity, the regulations relating to confiscation, etc. in any detail. They outdo the cream of the press legislation of the July monarchy and the Restoration.[68] Just one specific point: by paragraph 21, the public prosecutor can demand the confiscation of both the finished publication and the *manuscript handed over for printing*, if the content constitutes a felony or a misdemeanour liable to official prosecution. What broad pastures this opens for philanthropic state prosecutors! What an enjoyable diversion, to go to a newspaper office whenever you wish and have the 'manuscript handed over for printing' presented to you for examination, as it is after all possible that it could constitute a felony or a misdemeanour.

How laughable is the solemn seriousness of that paragraph of the proposed constitution[69] and the 'fundamental rights of the German people' which states that '*the censorship can never be reestablished*', when placed beside this bill!

THE BILL FOR THE ABOLITION OF FEUDAL BURDENS[70]

N.Rh.Z., 30 July 1848

Cologne, 29 July

If any Rhinelander has forgotten what he owes to 'foreign domination' and the 'oppression of the Corsican tyrant', he should read the bill for the abolition of various burdens and dues without compensation which Herr Hansemann, in the year of grace 1848, has allowed the *Vereinbarungsversammlung* to see 'for clarification'. Fealty, enfranchisement-money, relief, heriot, protection-money, jurisdiction-tax, village court tax, wardship, sealing-money, cattle-tithe, bee-tithe, etc.[71] – how strange, how

68. The French constitutional monarchy of Louis Philippe (1830–48) and the restored Bourbon monarchy (1814–30).

69. The 'Draft of a Constitutional Law for the Prussian State', issued on 20 May 1848.

70. This bill was laid before the Prussian National Assembly on 11 July 1848, and introduced by Gierke on 18 July.

71. An attempt has been made to give the approximate English feudal equivalent to the German terms in the text. The German terms are, in order

barbaric, is the sound of these preposterous names to our ears which have been civilized by the Code Napoléon, by the French Revolution's destruction of feudal survivals! How incomprehensible to us is this whole jumble of semi-medieval services and dues, this natural history museum of the mouldiest plunder of antediluvian times!

But take off your shoes, German patriot, for you are standing on hallowed ground! These barbarisms are the remnants of the glory of Germanic Christendom, they are the final links of a chain which weaves its way through history and unites you with the majesty of your forefathers, right back to the Cheruskans in their woods. This stink of putrefaction, this feudal slime, found here in its classical purity, is the most genuine product of our fatherland, and he who is a true German must exclaim, with the poet:

> This is truly my native air!
> It touched my cheeks, and they glowed!
> And this is the muck of my fatherland:
> This mud of the country road![72]

When one reads this bill, it appears at first sight that our Minister of Agriculture, Herr Gierke,[73] is making a tremendous 'bold stroke'[74] on the instructions of Herr Hansemann, and abolishing a whole medieval situation with a stroke of the pen, and gratis too of course.

If, however, one looks at the *justification* given for the bill, one finds that it demonstrates right at the beginning that in fact *absolutely no* feudal burdens will be abolished without compensation, with a bold assertion which directly contradicts the 'bold stroke'.

The practical timidity of the honourable minister treads warily and cautiously between these two pieces of audacity. On the left

---

of appearance, *Lehnsherrlichkeit, Allodifikationszins, Sterbefall, Besthaupt, Kurmede* (both forms of heriot), *Schutzgeld, Jurisdiktionszins, Dreidinggelder, Zuchtgelder, Siegelgelder, Blutzehnt,* and *Bienenzehnt*.

72. Heine, 'Germany: A Winter's Tale', *The Poetry and Prose of Heinrich Heine*, p. 198.

73. Julius Gierke was the town syndic of Stettin, in 1848 a deputy in the Prussian National Assembly (Left Centre), and Prussian Minister of Agriculture from March to September.

74. An ironic reference to Heinrich von Gagern's famous speech of 24 June 1848 in the Frankfurt Assembly in which he proposed what he described as a 'bold stroke': the immediate creation of a provisional central authority for Germany by the Assembly itself.

we have 'the general welfare' and the 'requirements of the spirit of the age', on the right the 'established rights of the landed estates', and in the middle the 'praiseworthy idea of a freer development of relations on the land', embodied in the shame-faced embarrassment of Herr Gierke. What a triptych!

Enough of this. The minister fully recognizes that in general feudal burdens may only be abolished in return for compensation. With this, the most oppressive, widespread and important burdens *remain in existence*, or, in other words, in view of the fact that the peasants had already got rid of them, they *are restored*.

'But', says Herr Gierke,

if nevertheless certain relations, which lack internal justification or whose continued existence cannot be brought into consonance with the requirements of the spirit of the age and the general welfare, have been abolished *without compensation*, the people hit by this should not fail to realize that they are making some sacrifices, not only to the general good, but also in their own properly understood interest, in order to make the relation between those with rights and those with duties peaceful and friendly, and in this way to guarantee to landed property in general the position in the state which is due to it for the common good.

The revolution on the land consisted in the actual removal of all feudal burdens. The 'Ministry of the Deed',[75] which recognized the revolution, now recognizes it in the countryside by liquidating it on the quiet. The old *status quo* cannot be restored in its entirety; even Herr Gierke sees that the peasants would kill their feudal barons without further ado. A spectacular list of insignificant, regionally limited feudal burdens are therefore abolished, and the main feudal burden, summed up in the simple phrase *compulsory labour services*, is restored.

With the abolition of all the rights listed above, the nobility sacrifices less than 50,000 thalers a year, but thereby saves many millions. In this way the nobility will surely be able to reconcile itself with the peasants, as the minister hopes, and in the future even gain their votes at elections. This would indeed be a good bargain, if Herr Gierke has made no mistakes in his calculations.

The objections of the peasants would be removed, and so would those of the nobility, provided it correctly grasped the situation.

---

75. The usual designation of the Auerswald-Hansemann ministry, which lasted from 26 June to 21 September 1848, and opened with Hansemann's public 'recognition of the revolution' in an attempt to gain the support of the Left in the Assembly.

There remains the Assembly itself and its scruples, which arise from the rigid attachment to logic displayed by jurists and radicals. The distinction between burdens to be abolished and burdens to be retained, which is nothing other than a distinction between fairly valueless and very valuable burdens, must receive an apparent justification in law and economics for the sake of the Assembly. Herr Gierke must prove that the burdens to be abolished 1) lack an adequate inner justification, 2) go against the general welfare, 3) go against the requirements of the spirit of the age, and 4) can be abolished without injuring the rights of private property, without what would be called expropriation without compensation.

In order to demonstrate the insufficiency of the grounds for these dues and services, Herr Gierke immerses himself in the most shadowy regions of feudal law. He conjures up the whole of the 'originally very slow development of the Germanic states in the course of a millennium'. But what use is that to him? The deeper he goes, the more he stirs up the musty sediment of feudal law, the more does it demonstrate to him not the insufficient, but, from the feudal standpoint, the very solid basis of the burdens under consideration; and the unfortunate minister merely exposes himself to general mirth when he spares no pains to get feudal law to give forth oracular judgements appropriate to modern civil law, or to make the feudal baron of the twelfth century think and decide in the same way as the bourgeois of the nineteenth century.

Fortunately, Herr Gierke has inherited von Patow's principle:[76] everything which emanates from specifically feudal qualities and hereditary subjection is to be abolished without compensation, the remainder must be redeemed in cash. But does Herr Gierke believe it requires any great penetration to demonstrate that, on the contrary, all the burdens to be abolished are equally 'emanations of feudal qualities'?

We hardly need to add that, in the interests of overall consistency, Herr Gierke smuggles modern legal concepts in among the feudal legal distinctions, and always appeals to the former in time of need. However, since he measures some of the feudal burdens against the conceptions of modern law, one cannot see why this

76. Erasmus, Freiherr von Patow was a moderate liberal. In 1848 he sat in the Prussian National Assembly, from April to June 1848 he was Minister of Trade, and on 20 June he presented to the Assembly his memorandum on the redemption of feudal burdens, containing the principle mentioned in the text.

does not happen in all cases. But of course, the compulsory labour services would come off badly when measured against the modern freedom of the individual and of property.

It is still worse for Herr Gierke when he introduces the argument of 'the public welfare' and 'the requirements of the spirit of the age'. It is perfectly obvious that if these insignificant burdens are obstacles to the public welfare, and contradict the spirit of the age, then so do the labour services, the *corvées* and the *laudemia*,[77] only to a greater extent. Or does Herr Gierke find that the right to pluck the peasant's *geese* (paragraph 1, section 14) is outdated, while the right to fleece the *peasant* is appropriate to the times?

There follows the demonstration that the abolition in question does not injure the rights of property. This glaring untruth can only appear proven by pretending to the nobility that these rights are of no value to them. The minister now proceeds to enumerate with great enthusiasm all eighteen sections of the first paragraph, but he does not realize that the more worthless the relevant *burdens*, the more worthless the *bill*. Good for him! What a shame it is that we have to snatch him away from his sweet delusions and break into the Archimedean circle of feudalism which he has constructed!

But now one more difficulty! In previous monetary redemptions of the burdens now to be abolished, the peasants have been terribly cheated by corrupt commissions acting in favour of the nobility. Now they are demanding the revision of all redemption agreements concluded under the old government, and they are quite right to do so.

Herr Gierke, however, cannot permit this. 'Formal right and law' stand against this, as against any progress at all, since every new law abolishes an old 'formal right and law'.

The consequences of such an act can be stated with certainty. If, in order to bring advantages to the obligated (the peasants), action is taken in a manner contradicting basic legal principles (revolutions also contradict basic legal principles), untold harm must result for a very great part of the landed property in the state, and consequently (!) for the state itself.

And now Herr Gierke shows with shattering thoroughness that such a proceeding

77. A Roman Law term applied in the Middle Ages to the sum of money paid by the vassal to his lord for the latter's consent to the alienation of the fief.

would put in question the whole legal foundation of landed property, and thereby, in connection with innumerable trials and costs, afflict landed property, the main basis of national prosperity, with a wound only to be healed with difficulty.

He shows further that

it is an attack on the legal validity of contracts, an attack on the most indubitable contractual relationships, and would result in the destruction of all confidence in the stability of the civil law and therefore endanger the whole of commercial intercourse in the most threatening way.

Here too the minister sees an attack on the right of property, which would offend against legal principles. Why then is abolition of the burdens themselves without compensation not an attack on property? It involves not only the most indubitable contractual relationships but also services carried out without objection since time immemorial, whereas the contracts the peasants wanted to revise were by no means undisputed, since the bribes and the frauds were notorious and in many cases demonstrable.

It cannot be denied: insignificant as the suppressed burdens are, Herr Gierke has indeed 'brought advantages to the obligated in a manner contradicting basic legal principles', and 'formal right and law *are* directly opposed to this action'; he is destroying 'the whole legal foundation of landed property', and striking at the roots of the 'most indubitable rights'.

Was it worth it, to commit such terrible sins in order to achieve such miserable results?

Of course the minister is attacking property – that is undeniable – but it is feudal, not modern bourgeois property he is attacking. Bourgeois property, which raises itself on the ruins of feudal property, is *strengthened* by this attack on feudal property. The only reason for Herr Gierke's refusal to revise the redemption contracts is that those contracts have changed feudal property relations into *bourgeois* property relations, and that he cannot therefore revise them without at the same time formally injuring bourgeois property. And bourgeois property is naturally just as holy and untouchable as feudal property is assailable, and, depending on the level of the minister's need and courage, actually assailed.

What, then, is the short meaning of this long law?

It is the most conclusive proof that the German revolution of 1848 is only a parody of the French revolution of 1789.

The French people finished with the feudal burdens in *one day*, the fourth of August 1789, three weeks after the storming of the Bastille.

On 11 July 1848, four months after the March barricades, the feudal burdens finished with the German people, as testified by Gierke and Hansemann.

The French bourgeoisie of 1789 did not leave its allies the peasants in the lurch for one moment. It knew that the basis of its rule was the destruction of feudalism on the land and the establishment of a class of free peasant landowners.

The German bourgeoisie of 1848 does not hesitate to betray the peasants who are its *natural allies*, its own flesh and blood, and without the peasants this bourgeoisie is powerless against the nobility.

The continued existence of feudal rights, their sanctioning in the form of their (illusory) abolition, that then is the result of the German revolution of 1848. The mountain moved and lo! – a mouse emerged.

THE RUSSIAN NOTE

N.Rh.Z., 3 August 1848

Cologne, 1 August

Instead of falling upon Germany with an army, Russian diplomacy has provisionally made do with a note, in the form of a circular sent to all the Russian consulates in Germany. This note was first published in the official organ[78] of the regency in Frankfurt, and soon met with a friendly reception in other official and unofficial papers. It is unusual that Nesselrode, the Russian Minister of Foreign Affairs, should ply his craft in public in this way, and this activity therefore deserves a close examination.

In the happy days before 1848 the German censorship made sure that nothing the Russian government might dislike could be printed, even under the heading 'Greece', or 'Turkey'.

Since the terrible March days this convenient way out has unfortunately been barred. Nesselrode has therefore had to turn journalist.

---

78. The official organ of the Reichsverwesung was the *Frankfurter Oberpostamts-Zeitung*, and Nesselrode's circular, issued on 6 July, was published therein on 28 July. It is printed in full in *Nouveau Recueil Général de Traités*, vol. XI, Göttingen, 1853, pp. 461–7.

According to him it is the 'German press, whose hatred of Russia seemed to have ended momentarily', which has called forth 'the most unfounded speculations and commentaries' in relation to Russian 'security measures' on the border. After the gentle introduction, a stronger tone is adopted: 'Daily, the German press spreads the most tasteless rumours, the most hateful calumnies against us.' Nesselrode goes on to refer to 'raving declamations', 'madcaps' and 'perfidious malevolence'.

At the next press trial a German state prosecutor may well use the Russian note as a certified basis for his accusations.

And why must the German, and in particular the 'democratic' press be attacked, and if possible destroyed? Because it misunderstands the 'benevolent and disinterested sentiments', the 'open and peaceful intentions' of the Russian tsar.

'When has Germany had any reason to complain of us?' asks Nesselrode in the name of his lord and master. 'During the whole period of the oppressive rule of a conqueror on the Continent, Russia poured out her blood in order to *support Germany in maintaining her integrity and independence*. Although Russian land had already long been liberated, Russia continued to follow its German allies to all the battlefields of Europe and to stand by them.'

In spite of its many well-paid agents, Russia is involved in a serious self-deception if it imagines sympathies can be awakened in the year 1848 by the memory of the so-called wars of liberation. And did Russia really shed its blood for us Germans?

Quite apart from the fact that before 1812 Russia 'supported' Germany's 'integrity and independence' by means of an open alliance and secret negotiations with Napoleon, sufficient compensation for this so-called help was taken later, in the form of robbery and plunder. The tsar's help was given in fact to the princes allied with him, his support, despite the Proclamation of Kalisch,[79] was given to the representatives of absolutism 'by the grace of God' against a ruler who emerged from the French Revolution. The Holy Alliance and its unholy works, the bandit congresses of Karlsbad, Laibach, Verona, etc.,[80] the joint

79. This proclamation was issued by Alexander I and Frederick William III on 25 March 1813, offering freedom and independence to the German people if they would take part in the war against Napoleon.

80. The Russians only attended the Congresses of Troppau-Laibach (October 1820–May 1821) and Verona (October–November 1822). The Karlsbad meeting of August 1819 was limited to the chief member-states of the German Confederation, above all Austria and Prussia.

Russian-German persecution of any liberal utterance, in short the whole policy directed by Russia since 1815, have certainly given us a feeling of deep thankfulness. The house of Romanov and its diplomats need not worry: we shall never forget *this* debt. As far as Russian help in the years 1814 and 1815 is concerned, gratitude for this aid, paid for with English subsidies, is absolutely the last feeling to which we are susceptible.

The reasons for this are quite obvious to anyone with a little insight. If Napoleon had remained victorious in Germany, he would have removed at least three dozen well-loved princelings, adopting his customarily energetic procedure. French legislation and administration would have created a solid foundation for German unity and spared us thirty-three years of shame, as well as the tyranny of the Federal Diet, which Nesselrode naturally praises to the skies. A couple of Napoleonic decrees could have completely destroyed the whole medieval wilderness, those labour services and tithes, those exemptions and privileges, in short that economy of feudalism and patriarchalism with which we are now tortured in all the nooks and crannies of our 'fatherlands'. The rest of Germany would then have long stood at the level reached by the left bank of the Rhine soon after the first French revolution; we should have had neither grandees from Uckermark[81] nor a Pomeranian Vendée,[82] and there would have been no more need to inhale the stagnant air of the 'historic' and 'Teutonic-Christian' swamps.

But Russia is magnanimous. Even without receiving any thanks, the tsar retains his 'benevolent and disinterested attitude' towards us. Yes, 'despite insults and provocations', his 'opinions have undergone no change'.

For the moment, these attitudes are manifested in a 'passive and observational system' which Russia has undeniably brought to a pitch of great virtuosity. The tsar knows how to wait until the appropriate moment. Notwithstanding the immense troop movements which have taken place since March in Russia, Nesselrode is naive enough to pretend that all Russian troops have constantly

81. The northern part of the Mark of Brandenburg, like Pomerania a purely agricultural region of Prussia and a junker stronghold.

82. The counter-revolutionary insurrection led by the nobility and supported by the peasantry which took place in that region of western France in 1793. Marx uses the word in a general sense to cover all counter-revolutionary intrigues and plots.

remained 'motionless in their barracks'. In spite of the classic 'To horse, gentlemen!',[83] in spite of the confidential, frank and venomous outpourings of police chief Abramovicz in Warsaw against the German people, in spite, or rather because, of the success of the threatening notes from St Petersburg, the Russian government is and remains animated by feelings of 'peace and reconciliation'. Russia continues to be 'open, peaceful and defensive'. In Nesselrode's circular, Russia is patience itself and pure innocence, despite many insults and provocations.

Let us set out some of Germany's crimes against Russia, as listed in the note. First: a 'hostile attitude', and second: 'fever for change over the whole of Germany'. So much benevolence from the tsar as opposed to a 'hostile' attitude by Germany! How insulting to the fatherly heart of our dear brother-in-law![84] And this accursed sickness: 'fever for change'! That is actually the main atrocity, although listed here as the second. From time to time Russia presents us with a different illness; the cholera. Never mind! The 'fever for change' referred to here is not only infectious; it often takes on a virulently severe form, so that people of the highest rank are required to make a hurried departure for England.[85] Was the German 'fever for change' perhaps one of the grounds which spoke against Russian intervention in March and April? Germany's third crime: the pre-parliament[86] in Frankfurt presented war against Russia as a necessity of contemporary politics. The same thing occurred in clubs and newspapers, and was the more unforgivable in that according to the stipulations of the Holy Alliance and later treaties between Russia, Austria and Prussia, we Germans should pour out our blood only in the interests of the princes, and not in our own. The fourth: discussions took place in Germany about the restoration of the old

83. Nicholas I is said to have uttered this phrase on hearing of the proclamation of the republic in France in February 1848.

84. Tsar Nicholas I of Russia was the brother-in-law of Frederick William IV of Prussia.

85. William, prince of Prussia (later William I) was the person of the 'highest rank'. He was the leading supporter within the royal family of the clique of Prussian nobles and generals who opposed all concessions to the revolution. He was compelled to flee from Berlin in March 1848 and stayed in London until June.

86. The pre-parliament consisted of a group of notables who met in Frankfurt after the March revolutions and took it upon themselves to convene the German National Assembly.

Poland within its genuine 1772 boundaries. The knout for you Germans, followed by Siberia! But no, when Nesselrode wrote this circular he did not yet know the Frankfurt Assembly's vote on the question of the annexation of Posen.[87] The Assembly has expiated our guilt, and a mild, forgiving smile now appears on the lips of the tsar. Germany's fifth crime: 'its deplorable war against a Nordic monarchy'.[88] Germany presumably deserves a milder punishment than would otherwise be necessary for this, owing to the success of Russia's threatening note, the hurried retreat of the German army (ordered by Potsdam[89]), and the explanation given by the Prussian envoy in Copenhagen of the motive and the aim of the war.[90] Six: 'open advocacy of a defensive and offensive alliance between Germany and France'. Finally, seven: 'the reception given to the Polish refugees, their free journey on the railways, and the insurrection in the Posen district'.

If language did not serve diplomats and similar persons 'as a means of concealing their thoughts', Nesselrode and brother-in-law Nicholas would joyfully embrace us, and give fervent thanks that so many Poles from France, England, Belgium, etc. were enticed to Posen, and given travelling facilities, so that they might be shot down with grape-shot and shrapnel, branded with caustic, slaughtered, sent away with shorn heads and, if possible (as in Cracow[91]), completely wiped out by a treacherous bombardment.

Despite these seven deadly sins committed by Germany, is it true that Russia has remained on the defensive, taken no offensive steps? It is, and that is why the Russian diplomat invites the world to admire the love of peace and the moderation of his tsar.

87. On 27 July the Frankfurt Assembly voted to accept Pfuel's line of demarcation of 4 June between German and Polish Posen and to incorporate the German part into Germany, after a debate in which most speakers rejected the idea of a restoration of the old Poland of 1772. See below, p. 145.

88. The war of April-August 1848 over Schleswig-Holstein between Prussia (acting initially on the intructions of the German Confederation and later, as the Frankfurt Assembly thought, on its own instructions) and Denmark.

89. The seat of the Prussian monarchy, near Berlin.

90. The note of 8 April 1848 from Major Wildenbruch, emissary extraordinary of the king of Prussia, to the Danish Foreign Minister, in which it was pointed out that Prussia was waging war not to snatch the duchies from Denmark but to oppose and crush the 'radical and republican elements from Germany' which were stirring up trouble in the king of Denmark's dominions. Printed in *Nouveau Recueil*, vol. XI, pp. 507–8.

91. Cracow, the centre of the Polish national movement in Austria, was bombarded on 26 April by the Habsburg authorities.

According to Nesselrode, the Russian tsar's rule of procedure 'from which he has not deviated for one moment', is as follows:

Russia will in no way intervene in the internal affairs of those countries which want to change their organization, but will rather leave the peoples completely free, without any obstacle from the Russian side, to accomplish the political and social experiments they want to undertake, and not attack any power which has not itself attacked Russia; however, we are resolved to reject any enroachment on our own internal security, and to make sure that if the territorial equilibrium is destroyed or altered in some respect this will not happen at the expense of our rightful interests.

The sender of the Russian note has forgotten to add illustrative examples. After the July revolution, the tsar assembled an army on his western borders, in order to make a practical demonstration to the French, in alliance with his faithful German servants, of the way in which he intended 'to leave the peoples completely free to accomplish their political and social experiments.' It was not his fault, but that of the Polish revolution of 1830, that this rule of procedure could not be applied, and that his plans had to take another direction.[92] Soon afterwards, the same manoeuvre was seen in relation to Spain and Portugal. The proof is to be found in the tsar's open and secret support for Don Carlos and Dom Miguel.[93] When, at the end of 1842, the king of Prussia wanted to set up a kind of constitution, on the harmless 'historical' basis of the medieval estates, which played such an appropriate role in the Patents of 1847,[94] it was Nicholas, as is well known, who refused

92. Like most European democrats and revolutionaries of the time, Marx took the view that the revolutionary outbreak in Poland on 29 November 1830 prevented an impending Russian attack on France. It now seems more likely (from Nicholas's correspondence with Grand Duke Constantine) that the idea of intervention against France was dropped in August 1830 owing to the failure of the other reactionary powers to cooperate, and that the mobilization of the Russian army was meant to deter the Germans from following the French path and in general to provide backing for the tsar's diplomatic manoeuvres.

93. Don Carlos was the brother of the Spanish king, Ferdinand VII, and the clerical and conservative pretender to the Spanish throne in the early nineteenth century; he was at the centre of the Carlist War of 1833–40. Dom Miguel was similarly a clerical and conservative pretender, who usurped the Portuguese throne in 1828 and was defeated and deposed in 1834.

94. There was in fact only one Patent, issued on 3 February 1847, convoking the first United Diet. Alongside the Patent there were issued three ordinances on the same day, specifying the Diet's mode of organization and procedure.

to tolerate this and cheated us 'Christian Germans' out of many years of patented joy.[95] As Nesselrode says, he did this because Russia never intervenes in the internal organization of another country. We hardly need to mention Cracow. Let us consider merely the latest example of the tsar's 'rule of procedure'. The Wallachians overthrow their old government and provisionally replace it with a new one. They want to transform the whole of the old system and follow the example of civilized peoples. 'In order to allow them to accomplish their political and social experiments completely freely', a Russian army corps invades the country.[96]

After these examples, it should be possible for everyone to find the application of this 'rule of procedure' to Germany. However, the Russian note spares us the need to follow our own logic. It says:

As long as the Confederation, in whatever *new form* it may appear, leaves untouched the neighbouring states and does not seek forcibly to extend its territorial area or jurisdiction outside the *limits* provided for it by the *treaties*, the tsar will also respect its *internal* independence.

The second relevant passage speaks a clearer language:

When Germany really succeeds in solving the problem of its organization, without disadvantage for its internal order, and if the new forms imprinted with its nationality are not such as to endanger order in other states, we shall genuinely offer our congratulations, for the same reasons as those which led us to want a strong and united Germany in its previous political forms.

It is the following passage, however, which has the plainest and most indubitable ring. Here Nesselrode speaks of Russia's ceaseless endeavours to recommend and uphold harmony and unity in Germany:

We are not referring of course to that material unity dreamed of today by a levelling and megalomaniac democracy, which would sooner or later inevitably place Germany in a state of war with all the neighbouring

95. In the summer of 1842 Frederick William IV visited Nicholas in St Petersburg, and the tsar attempted to dissuade him from calling together representatives from the Provincial Diets to form a United Committee in Berlin. He failed, but his opposition, together with that of Metternich and the prince of Prussia, contributed to strengthening Frederick William's hesitations and no doubt delayed the calling of the United Diet.

96. On 10 July 1848 Russian troops invaded Wallachia (the central part of what is now Romania) in reply to the revolution in Bucharest and the formation of a liberal provisional government.

states if it could realize its ambitious theories as it conceives them; we are referring rather to the *moral unity*, the genuine agreement in views and intentions in all political questions which the German Confederation had to present to the external world. The aim of our policy is only to *maintain this unity*, the bond which attaches the German governments to each other. We still want now what we wanted at that time.

As can be seen from the foregoing, the Russian government is genuinely willing to allow us the *moral* unity of Germany. However, no *material* unity! No supersession of the previous administration of the Federal Diet by a central power based on popular sovereignty, a power real not apparent, a power which acts seriously and capably! What magnanimity!

'We still want now what we wanted then' (i.e. before February 1848). That is the sole phrase in the Russian note that no one will doubt. We would however point out to Herr Nesselrode that the wish and its accomplishment are and remain two separate things.

The Germans now know exactly what they can expect of Russia. As long as the old system lasts, painted over with new modern colours, or if the Germans return obediently to the Russian and 'historical' track deserted in 'momentary inebriation and exaltation', Russia will stand by 'openly and pacifically'.

The situation within Russia – the cholera epidemic, the partial rebellions in some districts, the revolution fomented in St Petersburg but prevented at the last minute, the plot in the Warsaw citadel, the volcanic soil of the Kingdom of Poland;[97] all these circumstances contributed towards the benevolent and 'disinterested attitude' of the tsar towards Germany.

But a much more powerful influence over the 'passive and observational system' of the Russian government was doubtless exercised by the course of events in Germany itself.

Could Nicholas himself have looked after his own interests any better, and fulfilled his intentions any quicker, than the rulers of Berlin-Potsdam, Innsbruck, Vienna, Prague, Frankfurt, Hanover and almost every other cosy corner of our fatherland, now once more replete with moral unity in the Russian style? Have not Pfuel (of the caustic[98]), Colomb and the shrapnel-general[99] in

97. See p. 100, n. 12.

98. General Pfuel gained the nickname 'Pfuel von Höllenstein' from his use of caustic (*Höllenstein*) to brand Polish prisoners in Posen.

99. Nickname of General Hirschfeld, Colomb's second in command in Posen.

Posen, Windischgrätz in Prague, all worked in such a way as to fill the tsar's heart with ecstasy? Did not Windischgrätz receive a dazzling letter of commendation from Nicholas, presented to him in Potsdam by the young Russian envoy, Meyendorf? Has Russia any reason to be dissatisfied with Hansemann, Milde and Schreckenstein in Berlin, and Radowitz, Schmerling and Lichnowsky[1] in Frankfurt? The gullibility of the Frankfurt Assembly must surely be a healing balm for some of the pains of the recent past. Under such conditions, Russian diplomacy has no need of an armed invasion of Germany. The 'passive and observational system' is quite sufficient – and the note we have just discussed.

THE DEBATE ON POLAND IN THE FRANKFURT ASSEMBLY[2]

N.Rh.Z., 20 August 1848   Frederick Engels
                                                                            Cologne, 19 August

We have made a detailed examination of Stenzel's[3] report, which was the basis of the debate. We have demonstrated how he falsifies the remote as well as the recent history of Poland and of the Germans in Poland, how he distorts the whole question, how the historian Stenzel has rendered himself guilty not only of intentional falsification but also of crude ignorance.[4]

Before we deal with the debate itself, we must glance once more at the Polish question.

Considered in isolation, the question of Posen is entirely lacking in meaning, and impossible to solve. It is a fragment of the Polish question, and can only be solved in conjunction with the latter. The boundary between Germany and Poland can only be determined when Poland again exists.

1. These six men had only a negative quality in common: they were not of the Left. Hansemann, Milde and Schreckenstein were Prussian ministers at the time, Radowitz and Lichnowsky were on the pro-Prussian Right of the Frankfurt Assembly, and Schmerling sat with the Right Centre there and worked for Austria rather than Prussia.
2. This is the third article in a series of nine.
3. Gustav Adolf Stenzel was a liberal historian and a deputy to the Frankfurt National Assembly in 1848, moving from the Left Centre to the Right Centre in the course of the year. He presented the report on the annexation of part of Posen to Germany on 24 July 1848 on behalf of the Assembly's committee on international law.
4. In the first two articles of this series, published on 9 and 12 August (*MECW* 7, pp. 337–50).

But can and will Poland exist again? This was denied in the debate.

A French historian has said: *Il y a des peuples nécessaires*; there are *necessary peoples*. The Polish people belongs unconditionally amongst these necessary peoples in the nineteenth century.

But the national existence of Poland is more necessary for us Germans than for any other people.

What has been the immediate basis of the power of reaction in Europe since 1815, in part, indeed, since the first French revolution? It is the Holy Alliance between Russia, Prussia and Austria. And what holds this Holy Alliance together? The *division of Poland*, which is advantageous to all three allies.

The line of cleavage which the three powers drew through Poland is the band which chains them together; a jointly committed crime has made each responsible for the other.

From the moment when the first rape of Poland was committed, Germany was a dependency of Russia. Russia ordered Prussia and Austria to remain absolute monarchies, and Prussia and Austria had to obey. The endeavours of the Prussian bourgeoisie to conquer power for itself, half-hearted and timid endeavours in any case, were completely shipwrecked on the impossibility of detaching Prussia from Russia, on the backing provided by Russia for the Prussian feudal and absolutist class.

A contributory factor to this situation was that, right from the first attempts made by the Holy Alliance to suppress Poland, the Poles were engaged not only in an insurrectional struggle for their independence but also, and simultaneously, in a revolutionary confrontation with their own internal social conditions.

The partition of Poland was a result of the alliance of the big feudal aristocracy in Poland with the three partitioning powers. It was not a progressive step, as asserted by the ex-poet Herr Jordan,[5] but rather the last remaining means for the big aristocracy to save itself from a revolution. It was completely and utterly reactionary.

Even the first partition resulted in an entirely natural alliance of the other classes, i.e. the gentry, the burghers of the towns and, in part, the peasants, against both the external oppressors of Poland

5. Wilhelm Jordan was a poet and journalist, and a member of the Left in the Frankfurt National Assembly until the Polish debate of July 1848, when his extreme nationalist and anti-Polish opinions led him to move to the Centre.

and the big aristocracy of the country itself. The constitution of 1791[6] shows how well the Poles of that time already understood that their independence *vis-à-vis* foreign powers was inseparable from the overthrow of the aristocracy and agrarian reform within the country.

The vast agricultural lands between the Baltic and the Black Sea can only be freed from patriarchal-feudal barbarism by an agrarian revolution which will transform the serfs and the peasants owing compulsory labour services into free landed proprietors, a revolution which will be identical with the French revolution of 1789 in the country districts. The Polish nation has the merit of having been the first of all the neighbouring agricultural peoples to proclaim this necessity. Their earliest attempt at reform was the constitution of 1791; during the rising of 1830 Lelewel described agrarian revolution as the sole means of saving the country, but his view was adopted too late by the Diet; finally, agrarian revolution was openly proclaimed in the insurrections of 1846 and 1848.

From the day when Poland's oppression began the Poles have played a revolutionary role and thereby riveted their oppressors even more firmly to the counter-revolution. They compelled their oppressors to maintain the patriarchal-feudal situation not just in Poland but in their other possessions. And particularly after the Cracow rising of 1846,[7] the struggle for Polish independence has at the same time been the struggle of *agrarian democracy* – the only kind possible in eastern Europe – against *patriarchal-feudal absolutism*.

As long as we help to oppress Poland, therefore, as long as we chain a part of Poland to Germany, just so long do we remain chained to Russia and Russia's policies, just so long do we remain unable to break thoroughly with our own indigenous patriarchal-

6. The Polish constitution of 3 May 1791 contained a number of important reforms, such as the abolition of the noble's right of veto and the establishment of ministerial responsibility to the Diet, and it made a slight breach in the system of serfdom by giving binding legal force to emancipation contracts between lord and peasant. The reaction of the conservative nobility to the constitution of 1791 was to call in the aid of Catherine II of Russia. After a short war (1792–3) the constitution was abolished and Poland partitioned a second time.

7. The democratic aspect of Polish nationalism, which first came to the fore in the Cracow uprising of 1846, was even stronger in the Posen rising of March–May 1848, which was joined by the Polish peasants and artisans, though still led by the lesser nobility.

feudal absolutism. The creation of a democratic Poland is the first condition for the creation of a democratic Germany.

But it is not simply that the creation of Poland and the regulation of its boundary with Germany is necessary; it is also by far the most soluble of all the political questions which have come to the surface since the revolution in eastern Europe. The independence struggles of the variegated jumble of nationalities to the south of the Carpathians are of an entirely different order of complexity from the Polish struggle for independence and the settling of the border between Germany and Poland, and they will cost far more blood, confusion and civil war.

It is obvious that the issue at stake here is the creation of a state on a viable basis, not the setting up of a sham Poland. Poland must have at least the boundaries of 1772; it must possess not only the regions around its great rivers but also their outlets to the sea, and at the very least an extensive stretch of coastline on the Baltic.

Germany could have guaranteed all this to Poland while still securing its own interests and honour if, after the revolution and in its own interests, it had had the courage to demand, arms in hands, that Russia give up Poland. In view of the German-Polish intermixture in the border regions and particularly on the coast, it was a matter of course that both sides would have had to make mutual concessions, that some Germans would have had to become Polish and vice versa; but this would not have created any difficulty.

After the German semi-revolution, however, no one had the courage to take such a decisive stand. To make spectacular speeches about the liberation of Poland; to receive Poles at railway stations on their way through Germany and offer them the warmest sympathy of the German people (to whom has that not been offered?): all this was perfectly acceptable. But to begin a war with Russia, to call into question the whole European balance of power and, above all, to give back a single fragment of the stolen territory? No, he who asks for this does not know his Germans!

And what was the significance of war with Russia? War with Russia meant the complete, open and real break with the whole of our shameful past, it meant the real liberation and unification of Germany, it meant the erection of democracy on the ruins of feudalism and the bourgeoisie's short dream of domination. War with Russia was the only possible way to save our honour and our interest *vis-à-vis* our Slav neighbours, and in particular the Poles.

But we were philistines, and we remain philistines. We made a couple of dozen large and small revolutions which we ourselves became terrified of even before they had been completed. After a lot of loud talk we did precisely nothing. All problems were dealt with in a spirit of the most faint-hearted, thick-headed, narrow-minded philistinism, and in this way our real interests were naturally again compromised. From the standpoint of this petty philistinism even the great question of the liberation of Poland was reduced to a trifling phrase about the reorganization of a part of the province of Posen, and our enthusiasm for the Poles changed into shrapnel and caustic.[8]

The sole possible solution, the only solution which would have preserved Germany's honour and Germany's interests was, we repeat, war with Russia. The risk of war was not taken, and there followed the unavoidable consequence: the soldiery of reaction, beaten in Berlin, raised their heads again in Posen. Under the cover of saving Germany's honour and nationality they took up the banner of the counter-revolution and suppressed the Polish revolutionaries, our allies. Germany, taken in by this, momentarily applauded its own victorious foes. The new partition of Poland was accomplished and all that was lacking was the sanction of the German National Assembly.

The Frankfurt Assembly had open to it one last way of making reparation: it could have excluded the whole of Posen from the German Confederation and declared the question of the boundary to be open until it was possible to negotiate over it on equal terms with a restored Poland.

But this would have been demanding too much of our Frankfurt professors, lawyers and clerics in the National Assembly! The temptation was too great; they, peaceful citizens who had never fired a gun, had the opportunity, by standing up and sitting down

8. Originally, in March 1848, there was great sympathy among German liberals for the Poles, and the Prussian government was compelled to promise that a commission would be set up to discuss the 'national reorganization of the Grand Duchy of Posen', which was to include the arming of Polish troops, the appointment of Poles to official positions, and the introduction of Polish as the official language. On 14 April, however, this 'reorganization' was limited to the eastern part of the province, and the area in question was further reduced in size by the decree of 26 April. Meanwhile, the Germans of Posen had come into conflict with the Polish National Committee on the spot, a situation which degenerated into a civil war in late April between the Poles and the Prussian troops. This time most German liberals took the Prussian army's side, under the influence of the strong agitation of the German minority there.

again, of conquering an area of five hundred square miles for Germany, of annexing eight hundred thousand *Netzbrüder*, German Poles,[9] Jews and Poles, even if at the cost of Germany's honour and her real, lasting interest. What a temptation! They have succumbed to it, they have confirmed the partition of Poland.

THE CRISIS AND THE COUNTER-REVOLUTION

I *N.Rh.Z.*, 12 September 1848

Cologne, 11 September

Read our reports from Berlin, and you will see whether we did not correctly predict the development of the ministerial crisis there.[10] The old ministers resign; the ministry's plan to maintain itself by dissolving the *Vereinbarungsversammlung*, by using cannons and martial law, does not appear to have met with the approval of the camarilla.[11] The junkers of Uckermark are burning with eagerness for a conflict with the people, for a repetition of the Paris June scenes in the streets of Berlin; however, they will fight only for the MINISTRY OF THE PRINCE OF PRUSSIA and never for the Hansemann ministry. They will call on Radowitz,[12] Vincke[13] and

9. *Netzbrüder*: German-speaking colonists introduced into the Netz district by Frederick II after the first partition of Poland (1772).

German Poles: German-speaking inhabitants of Poland, referred to as German Poles (*Deutschpolen*) by Engels to underline their lack of real historical ties with Germany and their long-standing connection with Poland in previous centuries.

10. The ministerial crisis in Prussia began with the resignation of the Auerswald-Hansemann ministry on 8 September and ended temporarily with the formation of the Pfuel ministry on 22 September. It was set off by the Prussian National Assembly's vote of 7 September in favour of a resolution introduced by deputy Stein calling on the Minister of War to order all officers to abstain from reactionary intrigues and to cooperate in setting up the constitutional state. The resolution was adopted with 219 votes in favour and 143 against. It had in fact already been passed once on 9 August (as the Stein-Schulze army order), but the Minister of War had failed to act on it, and the Assembly was therefore trying again.

11. The clique of reactionary Prussian nobles and officers, headed by Leopold von Gerlach, which gathered around Frederick William IV at Potsdam and had a determining influence on royal policy behind the scenes.

12. Joseph von Radowitz was a Prussian general and politician, one of Frederick William's closest associates. He was a leading member of the pro-Prussian Right in the Frankfurt Assembly.

13. Georg, Freiherr von Vincke was a liberal member of the Westphalian nobility, who sat in the United Diet of 1847 and on the Right in the Frankfurt Assembly in 1848.

reliable people of that type, who stand apart from the Berlin Assembly and are not obliged to it in any way. The cream of the Prussian and Westphalian nobility – associated on the face of it with certain bourgeois innocents of the extreme Right such as Beckerath[14] and his friends, who will take over the prosaic commercial business of the state – that is the Ministry of the prince of Prussia which they intend to bless us with. In the meantime they will throw out hundreds of rumours, possibly call on Waldeck[15] or Rodbertus[16] and mislead public opinion, while at the same time making their military preparations. Finally, when the time is ripe, they will come out openly.

We are approaching a decisive struggle. The counter-revolution is compelled to fight its last battle by the simultaneous crises in Frankfurt and Berlin, and by the latest decisions of the two Assemblies. If in Berlin they take the risk of trampling underfoot the constitutional principle of the rule of the majority, if they put against the 219 votes of the majority twice that number of cannons, if they take the risk of defying the majority both in Berlin and in Frankfurt with a ministry regarded as impossible by both Assemblies – **If in this way they provoke civil war between Prussia and Germany, Democrats will know what to do.**

II *N.Rh.Z.*, 13 September 1848

Cologne, 12 September

In Frankfurt a new Reich ministry is being formed, as we reported yesterday, and as has now been confirmed from other sources. We shall perhaps hear by midday today that it has been definitively constituted. In Berlin the ministerial crisis continues. This crisis is only susceptible of two solutions.

Either a Waldeck ministry, with the recognition of the authority

14. Hermann von Beckerath was a banker in Krefeld and a leading Rhenish liberal. In 1848 he sat with the Right Centre in the Frankfurt Assembly, and was Reich Minister of Finance from August to September 1848. It is not clear why Marx places Beckerath on the 'extreme Right'.

15. Benedict Francis Waldeck was a Prussian state official in Berlin. In 1848 he led the Left in the Berlin Assembly.

16. Johann Karl Rodbertus was a Prussian landowner and economist, who upheld a form of 'state socialism'. In 1848 he led the Left Centre in the Prussian Assembly and was Minister of Religious Affairs in the Auerswald-Hansemann cabinet.

of the German National Assembly, and of the sovereignty of the people.

Or a Radowitz-Vincke ministry, with the dissolution of the Berlin Assembly, the liquidation of the conquests of the revolution and sham constitutionalism, or indeed, the return of the United Diet.

Let us not hide this point from ourselves: the conflict which has broken out in Berlin is a conflict between the Assembly, which has asserted its *constituent* nature for the first time, and the Crown, not between the *Vereinbarer*[17] and the ministers.

Everything turns on whether they have the courage to dissolve the Assembly or not.

But has the Crown the right to dissolve the Assembly?

In constitutional states, of course, the Crown has the right, in case of a conflict, to dissolve legislative chambers called on the basis of the constitution, and to appeal to the people through new elections.

Is the Berlin Assembly a constitutional, legislative chamber?

No. It has been called 'to agree with the Crown on the constitution of the Prussian state', and is founded not on a constitution but on a *revolution*. It in no sense received its mandate from the Crown or its responsible ministers, but solely from its electors and from itself. The Assembly was sovereign as the legitimate expression of the revolution, and the mandate which Camphausen and the United Diet drew up for it, in the electoral law of 8 April, was nothing more than a *pious wish*, the fate of which was to be decided by the Assembly itself.

At the outset the Assembly more or less accepted the theory of *Vereinbarung*. Then it saw how it had been swindled by the ministers and the camarilla. Finally, it performed an act of sovereignty, it momentarily presented itself as a constituent assembly instead of a *Vereinbarungsversammlung*.

As the sovereign assembly for Prussia it had a full right to do this.

However, a sovereign assembly cannot be dissolved by anyone, it is subject to no one's orders.

Even as a mere *Vereinbarungsversammlung*, even according to Camphausen's own theory, it stands beside the Crown as an *equal partner*. Both parties *contract* a state treaty, both parties have an

---

17. The compromisers or 'agreers', i.e. the members of the *Vereinbarungsversammlung*.

equal share in sovereignty – that is the theory of 8 April, the Camphausen-Hansemann theory, and therefore the *official* theory, recognized by the Crown itself.

If the Assembly is the *equal* of the Crown, *the Crown has no right to dissolve the Assembly*. Otherwise, logically, the Assembly would have the *right to depose the king*.

The dissolution of the Assembly would therefore be a coup d'état. And the way to reply to a coup d'état has already been demonstrated, on 29 July 1830 and 24 February 1848.[18]

It will be said that the Crown could after all appeal again to the same electors. But everyone knows that *today* the electors would elect an entirely different Assembly, an Assembly which would make short work of the Crown.

It is clear that after the dissolution of this Assembly the only appeal possible is to *entirely different electors* from those of 8 April. No other elections are possible than elections held under the tyranny of the sabre.

Let us therefore have no illusions: if the Assembly is victorious, if it enforces a ministry of the Left, the power of the Crown *alongside* the Assembly will be broken, the king will simply be the paid servant of the people, we shall stand again in the morning light of 19 March[19] – provided always that the Waldeck ministry does not betray us as previous ministries have done.

If the Crown is victorious, if it enforces the Ministry of the prince of Prussia, the Assembly will be dissolved, the right of association will be suppressed, the press will be muzzled, an electoral law with property qualifications will be decreed, perhaps indeed the United Diet will be conjured up once again, and all this will occur under the protection of a military dictatorship, of cannons and bayonets.

Which of the two sides gains the victory will depend on the

18. On 26 July 1830 the government of Charles X of France issued four ordinances dissolving the Chamber of Deputies, prescribing new elections on a much narrower franchise, and introducing a stringent censorship. The reply to this royal coup d'état was the 1830 revolution, which culminated in the removal of the Bourbon monarchy on 29 July and its replacement by the Orleans monarchy. On 24 February 1848 the Orleans monarchy was in its turn overthrown.

19. On 19 March 1848, after the bloody street battles of the previous day in Berlin, Frederick William IV issued his proclamation 'To my dear Berliners' promising the withdrawal of the troops from Berlin if the rebels dismantled their barricades.

attitude of the people, and in particular on the attitude of the democratic party. The democrats must choose.

We stand on the threshold of 26 July.[20] Will the Crown take the risk of issuing the ordinances now being devised in Potsdam? Will it provoke the people into making the leap from 26 July to 24 February in *one* day?

The intention is there, certainly, but what is needed is the courage to act.

III *N.Rh.Z.*, 14 September 1848

Cologne, 13 September

The crisis in Berlin has gone a step further: the *conflict with the Crown*, which yesterday we could only describe as unavoidable, *has now really begun*.

Our readers will find the king's answer to the resignation of the ministers in another column.[21] By this letter the Crown itself has entered the foreground, taken sides with the ministers, and placed itself in opposition to the Assembly.

But it has gone further than this: it has formed an extra-parliamentary ministry, it has called on Beckerath, who sits with the extreme Right in Frankfurt and, as everyone knows in advance, will never be able to reckon on a majority in Berlin.

The king's answer is countersigned by Auerswald.[22] Auerswald is responsible for pushing the Crown forward in this way in order to cover his dishonourable retreat, and for his attempt simultaneously to hide behind the constitutional principle and to tread it underfoot, with the result that he has *compromised the Crown and formented republicanism*.

'The constitutional principle', scream the ministers. 'The constitutional principle', screams the Right. 'The constitutional principle', wheezes the *Kölnische Zeitung*[23] in an empty echo.

---

20. See p. 153, n. 18.

21. In his message of 10 September 1848 to the Assembly, Frederick William IV declared that its resolution of 7 September 1848 was a violation of the principles of constitutional monarchy, and that the Auerswald-Hansemann ministry had been right to resign in protest against it.

22. Rudolf von Auerswald was a liberal member of the Prussian nobility. He was Prime Minister and Foreign Minister from June to September 1848.

23. A daily newspaper which had appeared in Cologne since 1802. In the 1840s it was the main organ of the moderate Rhineland liberals, and had a standing feud with the *Neue Rheinische Zeitung* throughout the period of the revolution.

'The constitutional principle'! Are these gentlemen really so stupid as to believe that the German people can be led out of the storms of 1848, out of the daily more threatening collapse of all the institutions handed down by history, by means of the worm-eaten doctrine of the separation of powers as put forward by Montesquieu and Delolme,[24] by means of worn-out phrases and long-exploded fictions?

'The constitutional principle'! But these very gentlemen, who want to save the constitutional principle at any price, must first of all realize that in a provisional situation it can only be saved by energetic action.

'The constitutional principle'! But has it not already been shown, by the vote of the Berlin Assembly, by the conflicts between Potsdam and Frankfurt, by the disturbances, the attempts at reaction, and the provocations of the soldiery, that in spite of all phrases we still *stand on a revolutionary footing*, that the fiction that we are already in a situation of *constituted*, completed constitutional monarchy leads to nothing but conflicts, conflicts which have already brought the 'constitutional principle' to the edge of the abyss?

Every state which finds itself in a provisional situation after a revolution requires a dictator, an energetic dictator at that. We attacked Camphausen from the beginning for failing to act dictatorially, for failing to destroy and remove the remnants of the old institutions immediately. Thus, while Camphausen lulled himself to sleep with constitutional fairy-tales, the defeated party strengthened its positions in the bureaucracy and the army. Here and there, indeed, it even ventured on an open struggle. The Assembly was called in order to negotiate a constitution. It took its place beside the Crown as an equal partner. Two powers with equal rights in a provisional situation! Camphausen sought to 'save freedom' by means of the separation of powers. But precisely this separation of powers had to lead to conflicts in such a situation. Behind the Crown lay hidden the counter-revolutionary camarilla of the nobility, the military and the bureaucracy. Behind the majority of the Assembly stood the bourgeoisie. The

24. Montesquieu's doctrine, as expressed notably in *The Spirit of the Laws* (1748) was that the ideal form of state was a constitutional monarchy, in which the three powers, i.e. the legislature, executive and judiciary, were separate and independent of each other. This doctrine was further developed some fifty years later by the Swiss constitutional lawyer Delolme.

ministry endeavoured to mediate between them. Too weak to represent the interests of the bourgeoisie and the peasants in a decisive fashion, and to overthrow the power of the nobility, the bureaucracy and the army leaders at one stroke, too maladroit to avoid injuring the bourgeoisie on all sides by its financial measures, it achieved nothing apart from making itself impossible for all parties, and bringing about the very collision it wanted to prevent.

It is the *salut public*, public safety, which is of decisive significance in an unconstitutional situation, not this or that principle. The ministry could only avoid a conflict between the Assembly and the Crown by unilaterally recognizing the principle of public safety, even at the risk of a conflict between the ministry itself and the Crown. But it preferred to remain 'presentable' at Potsdam. It never hesitated to apply measures of public safety, i.e. dictatorial measures, against the democrats. What else can one call the application of the old laws regarding political crimes, at a time when Herr Märker[25] himself had already recognized that these paragraphs of the old Prussian Landrecht had to be removed? What else were the mass arrests which took place in all parts of the kingdom?

But the ministry has taken good care not to intervene against the counter-revolution on grounds of public safety!

Owing to this half-heartedness of the ministry when confronted with the daily more threatening counter-revolution, it became necessary for the Assembly *itself to dictate* measures of public safety. If the Crown, as represented by the ministers, was too weak, the Assembly itself had a duty to intervene. This it did by the resolution of 9 August,[26] but only in a very mild manner. The ministers were given a single warning, and they disregarded it.

But how could they possibly have accepted it? The resolution of 9 August tramples on the constitutional principle, it is an infringement by the legislature against the executive, it disturbs the separation of powers and their control by each other which is so necessary in the interests of freedom, it turns the *Vereinbarungsversammlung* into a National Convention.[27]

25. Friedrich August Märker sat with the Centre in the Prussian National Assembly, and from June to September 1848 he was Prussian Minister of Justice.
26. See p. 150, n. 10.
27. A reference to the revolutionary assembly of September 1792-November 1795 in France, which (until the Thermidor reaction of July 1794) exercised dictatorial powers in the interests of the revolution, executed the king, and played a part in initiating the Terror.

And there follows a flood of threats, a thunderous appeal to the fears of the petty bourgeoisie, and a long-term perspective of a terrorist regime with the guillotine, progressive taxation, confiscations and the red flag.

The Berlin Assembly a Convention! What irony!

But the gentlemen who predict this are not entirely mistaken. If the government continues on its present course, we shall have a Convention in the near future, a Convention not just for Prussia but for the whole of Germany, a Convention whose task will be to suppress the insurrection of our twenty Vendées, and to prosecute the unavoidable Russian war by all possible means. Now, of course, we only have a parody of the Constituent Assembly.[28]

But how has the constitutional principle been upheld by the ministerial gentlemen who appeal to it?

On 9 August they calmly allowed the Assembly to adjourn in the belief that the ministers would carry out the resolution. The latter had no intention of announcing their refusal to the Assembly; much less did they intend to lay down their offices.

After a whole month of reflection, and under the threat of numerous interpellations, they abruptly pointed out to the Assembly that there was no question of their carrying out the resolution.

When the Assembly replied by instructing the ministers to carry out the resolution in any case, they hid behind the Crown, produced a split between the Crown and the Assembly, and thereby provoked a tendency towards republicanism. And these gentlemen still speak of the constitutional principle!

Let us sum up. The inevitable conflict between two equal powers in a provisional situation has set in. The ministry did not carry on the business of government energetically enough, it omitted to take measures necessary for public safety. The Assembly was only doing its duty when it called on the ministry to fulfil its obligations. The ministry asserted that this was an attack on the Crown, and compromised the Crown at the very moment of its resignation. Crown and Assembly confront each other. *Vereinbarung* has led to division, to conflict. Perhaps the sword will decide.

He who is most courageous and consistent will gain the victory.

---

28. The French Constituent Assembly of June 1789-September 1791 laid the foundations of the constitutional monarchy.

IV *N.Rh.Z.*, 16 September 1848

Cologne, 15 September

The ministerial crisis has once more entered a new stage; not through the arrival and vain endeavours of the impossible Herr Beckerath, but through the *military revolt in Potsdam and Nauen*.[29] The conflict between democracy and aristocracy has broken out *in the very bosom of the Guard:* the soldiers see their liberation from the tyranny of the officers in the Assembly's resolution of 7 September; they are issuing addresses of thanks to the Assembly, they are giving it a hearty cheer.

With this the sword has been wrested from the hands of the counter-revolution. Now they are not likely to risk dissolving the Assembly, and if they do not take that step there will be nothing left but to give way, to carry out the resolution of the Assembly, and to call on Waldeck to form a ministry.

The revolt of the Potsdam soldiers has probably spared us the trouble of making a revolution.

REVOLUTION IN VIENNA

N.Rh.Z., 12 October 1848

Cologne, 11 October

In its *first* number (1 June) the *Neue Rheinische Zeitung* had a revolution to report from Vienna (that of 26 May[30]). Today, on the occasion of our *first* reappearance after the interruption brought about by the state of siege in Cologne, we bring news of the much more important Vienna revolution of 6 and 7 October.[31]

29. In Nauen, on 10 September, the Guards refused to obey an order to attack the citizens of the town; in Potsdam, on 13 September, the First and Second Guards Regiments rose in revolt against their officers. The main reason for this was the confiscation of an address of thanks the soldiers intended to send to deputy Stein and the Berlin Assembly for the resolution of 7 September. (See p. 150, n. 10.)

30. The revolutionary *journée* of 26 May in Vienna was the response of the students and workers to the Pillersdorf ministry's proclamation of 25 May dissolving the Academic Legion and closing the University.

31. The Vienna revolution of 6–7 October broke out under the impact of the news that the Habsburg government was about to attack Hungary (on 3 October a state of siege had been proclaimed over Hungary, the Budapest parliament had been dissolved, and Jellačić had been appointed as Supreme Commander).

The detailed reports on the Vienna events have compelled us to leave aside all discussion articles for today. We shall say just a few words, therefore, about the Vienna revolution itself. Our readers will observe from the reports of our correspondent in Vienna[32] that this revolution is in danger, if not of being wrecked, at least of being obstructed in its development, by the bourgeoisie's mistrust of the working class. Even so, its impact on Hungary, Italy and Germany has shattered the whole military strategy of the counter-revolution. The flight of the emperor and the Czech deputies from Vienna[33] compels the Viennese bourgeoisie to continue the struggle or to surrender unconditionally. The Frankfurt Assembly, which is at present engaged in giving us Germans

A NATIONAL HOUSE OF REFORM AND ONE GREAT
WHIP FOR US ALL[34]

is rudely awakened from its dreams by the Vienna events; the Berlin ministry realizes the mistake it is making in relying on the cure-all known as the *state of siege*. Like the revolution, the state of siege has made the grand tour of the world. The attempt was even made to apply the experiment on a large scale to a whole country, Hungary. This precipitated a revolution in Vienna instead of a counter-revolution in Hungary. The state of siege will not recover from this setback. The state of siege has been compromised for ever. It is an irony of fate that Cavaignac, the western hero of the state of siege, simultaneously with Jellačić, its eastern hero,[35] has become the target of attack of all the classes he saved in June with his grape-shot. He can only retain his position for a short while by going over resolutely to the revolution.

32. Eduard von Müller-Tellering. He survived the siege of Vienna and later lived in exile in London.

33. On 7 October the Austrian Emperor Ferdinand fled from Vienna to Olmütz (Olomouc); at the same time most of the Czech deputies to the Reichstag left Vienna for Prague.

34. 'Der Tannhäuser', *The Poetry and Prose of Heinrich Heine*, p. 215.

35. Josip Jellačić, count of Bužim was a Croat and an Austrian general, appointed Ban of Croatia in 1848 as a counterweight to the Hungarians. He took an active part in putting down the revolutions in Austria and in Hungary.

THE 'COLOGNE REVOLUTION'

N.Rh.Z., 13 October 1848

Cologne, 12 October

The *Kölnische Zeitung* tells us that the 'Cologne Revolution' of 25 September was a carnival jest, and the *Kölnische Zeitung* is right. On 26 September the commander of the Cologne garrison played Cavaignac. And the *Kölnische Zeitung* admires the commander for his wisdom and moderation. Which is the pathetic spectacle, however: the workers of 25 September, practising barricade-construction, or the Cavaignac of 26 September, who in all seriousness proclaimed a state of siege, suspended newspapers, disarmed the citizens' militia[36] and banned the societies?

Poor *Kölnische Zeitung*! The Cavaignac of the 'Cologne Revolution' cannot be an inch taller than the 'Cologne Revolution' itself. Poor *Kölnische Zeitung*! It has to take the 'revolution' as a joke and the 'Cavaignac' of this droll revolution in earnest. O tiresome, thankless, self-contradictory subject!

We shall not waste a word on the question of the justification of the Cologne commander's action. D'Ester[37] has exhausted this subject.[38] In any case, we view the Cologne military head-quarters as a subordinate instrument. The real authors of this curious tragedy were the 'loyal citizens', the Dumonts[39] and their allies. No wonder, then, that Dumont had his newspapers spread abroad the address against d'Ester, Borchardt and Kyll.[40] What

36. One of the many ways in which the German revolutions of March 1848 drew inspiration from the French example was the well-nigh universal demand for the setting up of a *Bürgerwehr* or citizens' militia on the model of the French National Guard (see p. 127, n. 56). These militias were often, as in Cologne, formed on a voluntary basis, but did not receive official recognition.

37. Karl Ludwig d'Ester was a Cologne doctor, a member of the Cologne branch of the League of Communists, and a leader of the Democratic party in the Prussian National Assembly. Following the breach between Marx and the Cologne district of the League, d'Ester took up a petty-bourgeois democratic position.

38. On 29 September 1848 in the Berlin Assembly d'Ester demanded the raising of the state of siege in Cologne and the disciplining of the Cologne military commander for his illegal actions.

39. Joseph Dumont was a moderate liberal, and the proprietor of the *Kölnische Zeitung*.

40. The Rhineland deputies Borchardt and Kyll had supported d'Ester's demand for the raising of the state of siege. Certain right-wing members of the Cologne bourgeoisie replied to this on 2 October with an address to the Prussian National Assembly attacking the three deputies for their attitude.

these 'loyal men' had to defend was their own action, not the Cologne commander's.

The occurrence at Cologne wandered through the Sahara desert of the German press in the form given to it by the Cologne version of the *Journal des Débats*.[41] This is sufficient reason to return to the question.

Moll, one of the best-loved leaders of the Workers Society, was about to be arrested. Schapper and Becker[42] had already been arrested. The authorities had chosen a Monday to carry out these measures, a day on which, as is well known, most of the workers have no employment. They must therefore have known beforehand that the arrests would call forth great unrest among the workers, and might even provoke violent resistance. Curious coincidence that these arrests took place precisely on a Monday. It was the easier to foresee the disturbance in that at any moment, after Stein's[43] army order, Wrangel's proclamation[44] and Pfuel's appointment as Prime Minister,[45] a decisive counter-revolutionary stroke, and therefore a revolution, was awaited from Berlin. The workers had therefore to regard the arrests as *political* rather than judicial measures. They saw the office of public prosecutor as simply a counter-revolutionary authority. They believed that the intention was to rob them of their leaders on the eve of important events. They decided to get Moll out of jail at any

41. A French daily newspaper founded in 1789, which was the organ of the Orléanists in the 1830s and 1840s. It opposed the revolution of 1848. The 'Cologne version' was presumably the *Kölnische Zeitung*.

42. Hermann Heinrich Becker was a Cologne journalist and judicial official. In 1848 he was a member of the Cologne Democratic Society, the Rhineland District Committee of Democrats, the Cologne Committee of Public Safety and the Workers Society.

43. Julius Stein was a Breslau headmaster and a democratic journalist. In 1848 he sat with the Left in the Prussian National Assembly, and acted as chairman of the Berlin Democratic Club. On the army order see p. 150, n. 10.

44. Friedrich Heinrich, Graf von Wrangel was a Prussian general and a member of the camarilla. In 1848 he was in command of the Third Army Corps in Berlin, and on 13 September was appointed to the newly created post of Commander of all Troops in the Marks (i.e. in the province of Brandenburg, in which Berlin was situated). In this capacity he issued a proclamation on 17 September, declaring that it was his task 'to uphold public order' and attacking 'elements which wanted to seduce the people into illegal actions'.

45. The Pfuel ministry was formed on 21 September, with Pfuel as Prime Minister, Eichmann as Minister of the Interior, and Graf von Dönhoff as Foreign Minister. It was a ministry of Prussian officials and soldiers, and lasted only until 31 October.

price. And they only left the field of battle when they had achieved
their aim. The first barricades were set up when the workers,
assembled on the Altenmarkt, were informed that the military
was advancing to the attack on all sides. They were not in fact
attacked; they therefore did not have to defend themselves. In
addition, it had become known to them that there was absolutely
no important news from Berlin. They therefore withdrew, after
they had vainly awaited the enemy for a great part of the night.

There is thus nothing more ridiculous than the accusation of
cowardice made against the Cologne workers.

But certain other accusations have been made against them
in order to justify the state of siege and to fashion the Cologne
events into a June insurrection on a small scale. The actual plan of
the workers, it is said, was to plunder the good town of Cologne.
This accusation rests on the rumoured plundering of *one* draper's
shop. As if every town did not have its contingent of thieves, who
naturally make use of days of public disturbance! Or is the plundering in question the plundering of arsenals? In that case, the
Cologne prosecutor should be sent to Berlin to draw up the act of
accusation against the March revolution. Without the plundering
of arsenals we should perhaps never have experienced the pleasure of seeing Herr Hansemann transformed into a bank director
and Herr Müller[46] into a state secretary.

We have said enough of the Cologne workers. Now we come to
the so-called democrats. What does the *Kölnische Zeitung* reproach
them with (along with the *Deutsche Zeitung*,[47] the *Augsburger Allgemeine Zeitung*,[48] and the other 'loyal' papers, whatever their names
may be)?

The heroic Brüggemanns,[49] Bassermanns,[50] etc. demanded

46. Friedrich Müller was the Cologne police director before 1848. In 1848 he
became a deputy in the Prussian National Assembly, sitting with the Right Centre, and
was appointed a junior minister in the Ministry of Justice.

47. A south German liberal newspaper, which favoured the unification of Germany as a constitutional monarchy under Prussian leadership. It appeared from 1847
to September 1848 in Heidelberg with the historian Gervinus as its editor.

48. A newspaper published in Augsburg from 1810 to 1882. It supported the
constitutional monarchist Right in the 1848 revolution.

49. Karl Heinrich Brüggemann was an economist and a liberal journalist. He
edited the *Kölnische Zeitung* from 1846 to 1855.

50. Friedrich Daniel Bassermann was a Mannheim bookseller and a moderate
liberal politician. In 1848 he represented the government of Baden at the Federal Diet,
and sat with the Right Centre in the Frankfurt National Assembly.

blood, and the soft-hearted democrats, owing to their *cowardice*, allowed no blood to flow.

The true facts are simply these: the democrats told the workers, in the inn Zum Kranz (on the Altenmarkt), in the Eiser Hall, and on the barricades, that under no circumstances did they want a putsch.[51] At that moment, indeed, when there was no great question impelling the whole population to take part in the struggle, with the result that any uprising was bound to fail, such an action would be senseless, they said, and, still worse, would exhaust the workers *before* the day of decision, since tremendous events were expected in the next few days. The day for the people to venture on revolution would come when the Berlin ministry ventured on counter-revolution. The judicial investigation will confirm our account. The gentlemen of the *Kölnische Zeitung* would have done better to harangue the deluded workers with their words of wisdom from the top of the barricades, instead of standing in front of them in the 'nocturnal gloom' with 'folded arms and stern looks' and 'reflecting on the future of their people'.[52] What use is wisdom after the event?

But the good press played its worst tune of all in connection with the situation of the citizens' militia. The militia refused to sink to the position of abject servant of the police; that was its duty. But it also delivered up its weapons voluntarily; this can only be excused for one reason: the liberal section of the militia knew that the illiberal section would joyfully seize the opportunity of stripping itself of its weapons. A partial resistance would have been pointless.

The 'Cologne revolution' has had *one* result. It has revealed the existence of a phalanx of more than two thousand saints, whose 'satisfied virtue and solvent morality'[53] can only lead a 'free life' in a state of siege. Perhaps there will be an opportunity one day to write an *Acta Sanctorum* – the biographies of these saints. Our readers will then discover how they obtained the 'treasures' which are resistant 'both to moths and to rust', they will learn how the economic background of the 'noble sentiments' was acquired.

51. The Cologne democrats referred to here included, in particular, Marx and his supporters. See Introduction, p. 44.

52. These are quotations from the article 'Die Barrikaden in Köln', published in the *Kölnische Zeitung*, 30 September 1848.

53. *Satte Tugend und zahlungsfähige Moral*, from Heine's poem 'Anno 1829'.

THE PROCLAMATION OF THE DEMOCRATIC CONGRESS
TO THE GERMAN PEOPLE

N.Rh.Z., 3 November 1848

Cologne, 2 November

We reproduce below the proclamation of the 'Democratic Congress';[54]

To the German People

Through long shame-filled years the German people has sighed beneath the yoke of tyranny. The bloody deeds of Vienna and Berlin gave justification to the hope that its freedom and unity would with a single stroke come true. The devilish arts of an accursed reaction opposed this development, in order to cheat the heroic people of the fruits of its magnificent uprising. Vienna, a central bastion of German freedom, stands at this very moment in the greatest peril. Sacrificed to the machinations of a still powerful camarilla,[55] it was to have been delivered over again to the bonds of tyranny. But its noble population rose up as one man, and now stands face to face with the armed hordes of its oppressors, defiant unto death. Vienna's cause is Germany's, it is the cause of freedom. With the fall of Vienna, the old despotism will raise its banner still higher; with the victory of Vienna, it will be annihilated. It is our duty, German brethren, not to allow Vienna's freedom to perish, not to abandon Vienna's freedom to the military victories of barbaric hordes. It is the holiest duty of the German governments to hurry to the aid of this hard-pressed sister-city with all their influence; but it is also the holiest duty of the German people at the same time to make any sacrifice to save Vienna, in the interests of its own freedom, in the interests of its self-preservation. Let the German people never be burdened with the shame of callous indifference where all is at stake. We therefore ask you, brethren, to contribute, each according to his own strength, towards saving Vienna from ruin. What we do for Vienna, we do for Germany. Help yourselves! The men you sent to Frankfurt to

54. The second Democratic Congress was held in Berlin from 26 to 30 October 1848. It was dominated by the conflict between the Cologne Workers Society and petty-bourgeois democrats such as d'Ester and Reichenbach over the programme to be adopted. As the bourgeois democrats were in the majority, the proclamation finally adopted and quoted here was not to the satisfaction of Marx and his followers, for the reasons he gives.

55. The Vienna camarilla, like its Berlin counterpart, was a group of reactionary generals and nobles who gathered around the reigning monarch. In the Austrian case, the camarilla was dominated by three men, Windischgrätz, Schwarzenberg, and Thun, and was in practice the ruling body, owing to the feeble-mindedness of Emperor Ferdinand.

establish liberty have rejected the call to help Vienna with scornful laughter. It is now up to you to act. Insist with a powerful and immutable will that your governments submit to the voice of your majority and save the German cause and the cause of freedom in Vienna. Hurry! You are the power, your will is law! Rise up! Rise up! you men of freedom, in all German lands and wherever else the ideas of freedom and humanity inspire noble hearts. Rise up before it is too late! Save Vienna's freedom, save Germany's freedom. The present will admire you, posterity will reward you with immortal renown!

29 October 1848   THE DEMOCRATIC CONGRESS IN BERLIN

This proclamation makes up for its lack of revolutionary energy with a snivelling pathos reminiscent of a sermon, behind which lies concealed the most utter poverty of thought and emotion.

Some examples!

The proclamation expected that with the Vienna and Berlin revolutions of March, 'the unity and freedom of the German people would *with a single stroke* come true'. In other words, the proclamation dreamed of a '*single stroke*' which would make the '*development*' of the German people towards 'unity and freedom' superfluous.

However, immediately afterwards, the absurd 'single stroke' which replaces the development itself turns into a '*development*' which the reaction *opposed*. A mere phrase, a phrase which cancels itself out!

We take no account of the monotonous repetition of the basic theme: Vienna is in danger, therefore Germany's freedom is in danger; help Vienna, and you will help yourself. This idea is never clothed in flesh and blood; instead the *one* phrase is turned around itself so often that it extends into an oration. We shall only remark that the artificial, untrue sentiment of the proclamation always succumbs to this clumsy rhetoric.

It is our duty, German brethren, not to allow Vienna's freedom to perish, not to abandon Vienna's freedom to the military victories of barbaric hordes.

And how are we to make a start on this task?

First of all, by appealing to the sense of duty of the German governments. This is simply incredible!

It is the holiest duty of the German governments to hurry to the aid of this hard-pressed sister-city with all their influence.

Should the Prussian government send Wrangel, Colomb or the prince of Prussia against Auersperg,[56] Jellačić and Windischgrätz? Was it permissible for the 'Democratic' Congress to adopt for one moment this childish and conservative attitude towards the German governments? Could it indeed for one moment separate the cause and the 'holiest interests' of the German governments from the cause and the interests of 'Croat order and freedom'?[57] The governments will smile in self-satisfaction at this innocent enthusiasm.

And the people?

The people are in general exhorted 'to make any sacrifice to save Vienna'. Well and good! But the 'people' expect specific demands from the Democratic Congress. He who demands everything demands nothing and receives nothing. The *specific* demand, i.e. the *point*, is this:

Insist with a powerful and immutable will that your governments submit to the voice of your majority and save the German cause and the cause of freedom in Vienna. Hurry! You are the power, your will is law! Rise up!

Let us assume that huge popular demonstrations succeed in persuading the governments to take public steps to save Vienna – we would simply be blessed with a second edition of Stein's army order. They want to use the present 'German governments' as 'saviours of freedom'! As if they were not accomplishing their true mission, their 'holiest duty' as the Gabriels of 'constitutional freedom' in executing the orders of the Reich ministry! The 'Democratic Congress' should either have kept quiet about the German governments, or mercilessly revealed their conspiracy with Olmütz[58] and St Petersburg.

Although the proclamation recommends 'haste', and there is in truth no time to lose, its humanistic phraseology snatches it away, beyond the boundaries of Germany, beyond all geographical

56. Karl, Graf von Auersperg was an Austrian general; he commanded the garrison of Vienna, and actively helped to defeat the October insurrection.

57. The phrase refers ironically to the support given by the Croats under Jellačić to the Austrian government in its attacks on the Hungarian and Viennese revolutions.

58. Olmütz, now Olomouc, was the town in Moravia which formed the temporary residence of the Austrian court during the siege of Vienna.

limits, into the cosmopolitan and misty land of the 'noble heart' in general:

Hurry! Rise up! you men of freedom, in all German lands and *wherever else* the ideas of freedom and humanity inspire noble hearts.

We do not doubt that such 'hearts' exist even in Lapland.

In Germany and *wherever else*! By fizzling out into this empty, indeterminate phrase, this 'proclamation' has managed to express its true nature.

It remains unforgivable that the 'Democratic Congress' should have approved such a document. For this 'the present' will not 'admire' it, nor will 'posterity reward it with immortal renown'.

Let us hope that, despite the 'Proclamation of the Democratic Congress', the people will awake from their lethargy and bring to the Viennese the only help they can still bring them at this moment – by defeating the counter-revolution which is on their own doorstep.

THE VICTORY OF THE COUNTER-REVOLUTION IN VIENNA[59]

N.Rh.Z., 7 November 1848

Cologne, 6 November

Croat freedom and order has conquered and celebrated its victory with arson, rape, plunder and indescribable atrocities. *Vienna is in the hands of Windischgrätz, Jellačić and Auersperg.* Whole hecatombs of human sacrifices have been flung into the grave of the aged traitor Latour.[60]

All the dismal prophecies of our Vienna correspondent have been confirmed, and he himself has perhaps already been slaughtered.[61]

We hoped at one time that Vienna's deliverance would come through the aid of the Hungarians, and we are still in the dark about the movements of the Hungarian army.

59. Vienna fell on 31 October 1848 to the combined armies of Windischgrätz, Jellačić and Auersperg.

60. Theodor, Graf Baillet von Latour, an Austrian general, was Minister of War from July to October 1848. In the course of the revolutionary *journée* of 6 October in Vienna he was put to the sword, after which his corpse was suspended from a lamp-post.

61. See p. 153, n. 32.

Treachery of all kinds has prepared the fall of Vienna. The whole of the history of the Reichstag[62] and the city council since 6 October is nothing but a continuous story of treachery. Who was represented in the Reichstag and the city council?

The *bourgeoisie*.

One part of the Vienna citizens' militia openly sided with the camarilla at the beginning of the October revolution. And at the end of the October revolution we find another part of the militia fighting against the proletariat and the Academic Legion,[63] in collusion with the imperial bandits. To whom do these sections of the citizens' militia belong?

To the *bourgeoisie*.

In France, however, the bourgeoisie took its place at the *head* of the counter-revolution only after it had levelled every barrier which stood in the way of its supremacy as a class. In Germany the bourgeoisie finds itself pressed into the *retinue* of absolute monarchy and feudalism before it has even made sure of the basic conditions for its own freedom and supremacy. In France it stepped forth as a despot, and made its own counter-revolution. In Germany it plays the role of a slave, and makes the counter-revolution required by the despots who rule it. In France it conquered in order to humble the people. In Germany it humbles itself in order to prevent the people from conquering. In the whole of history there is no more ignominious example of abjectness than that provided by the *German bourgeoisie*.

Who flocked out of Vienna and left the surveillance of its abandoned riches to the people's generosity, only to slander the people for standing guard during their flight, and to watch them being slaughtered on its return?

The *bourgeoisie*.

Whose innermost secrets are expressed by that thermometer which fell when the people of Vienna showed signs of life and rose in their death-agony? Who speaks in the Runic language of the stock market quotations?

The *bourgeoisie*.

62. The Constituent Assembly of the hereditary lands of the Austrian Empire (i.e. excluding Hungary), which was elected in July 1848. After the Vienna revolution of 6 October the Czechs withdrew from the Reichstag, and the remaining deputies elected a permanent committee which played the part of a revolutionary government, jointly with the city council, from 7 to 31 October.

63. This consisted of university students, and was the most radical of the military organizations engaged in the defence of Vienna at this time.

The 'German National Assembly' and its 'Central Authority' have betrayed Vienna. Whom do they represent?

First and foremost, the *bourgeoisie*.

The victory of 'Croat freedom and order' in Vienna was conditioned by the victory of the 'respectable' republic in Paris. Who was the victor of the June days?

After the victory of the bourgeoisie in Paris, the European counter-revolution could begin its orgies of celebration.

The power of arms was defeated everywhere in the February and March days. Why? Because it represented nothing but the *governments*. After the June days the power of arms has conquered everywhere, because everywhere the *bourgeoisie* is to be found in collusion with the governments, while, on the other side, it has control of the official leadership of the revolutionary movement, and puts into operation all those half-measures which have their natural outcome in an abortion.

The nationalist fanaticism of the Czechs was the most powerful instrument of the Vienna camarilla. *The allies are already at logger-heads*. Our readers will find printed in this issue the protest of the Prague deputation against the contemptuous rudeness with which they were greeted at Olmütz.[64]

This is *the first symptom of the war which will begin between the Slav party with its hero Jellačić and the party of the pure camarilla with its hero Windischgrätz, which is above all feelings of nationality*. The German country people of Austria are for their part as yet unpacified. Their voice will penetrate shrilly through the cater-wauling of the Austrian nationalities. And from a third side, as far as Budapest, there can be heard the voice of that friend of the peoples, the tsar; his executioners are waiting in the Danubian principalities for the decisive word.

Finally, the latest decision of the German National Assembly in Frankfurt, by which German Austria is incorporated into the German Reich,[65] ought itself to have led to a gigantic conflict, if

64. This is in fact a reference to the protest of the Czech deputation to Olmütz against the absolutist tone of the manifesto of 16 October entrusting Windischgrätz with dictatorial powers. The conflict Marx speaks of did not take place because the Court gave way, issuing instead the more conciliatory manifesto of 19 October which promised the immediate recall of the Reichstag.

65. On 27 October the Frankfurt Assembly adopted the 'greater German' solution of the German problem by including German Austria into the German Reich, but excluding the rest of Austria, and thereby calling for the

the German Central Authority and the German National Assembly did not find that their mission was accomplished simply by appearing on the stage, to be hissed off by the European public. Despite their pious resignation, the struggle in Austria will take on dimensions more colossal than any struggle world history has yet seen.

What has just been played in Vienna is the second act of a drama. Its first act was played in Paris under the title '*The June Days*'. In Paris the Mobile Guard, in Vienna the Croats – in both cases the *lazzaroni*, the armed and bought lumpenproletariat, fighting against the working and thinking proletariat. We shall soon experience the third act in Berlin.

If we assume that the counter-revolution lives throughout Europe through *weapons*, it will die throughout Europe through *money*. The fate that will annul the victory of the counter-revolution will be general European *bankruptcy*, the *bankruptcy of the state*. The points of bayonets will break like brittle firewood on the points of economics.

But the course of development will not wait for the payment-day of that promissory note drawn by the European states on European society. The devastating counter-blow to the June defeat will be struck in Paris. With the victory of the 'red republic' in Paris, the *armies* will be vomited forth from the *inside* of the other countries[66] and over the boundaries, and the *real power* of the contending parties will reveal itself in a pure form. Then we shall remember June and October, and we too shall call out: '*Vae victis!*'

The pointless massacres since the June and October days, the tedious sacrificial feast since February and March, the cannibalism of the counter-revolution itself, all these things will convince the peoples that there is only one way of *shortening*, simplifying and concentrating the murderous death-pangs of the old society, the bloody birth-pangs of the new, only *one way – revolutionary terrorism*.

---

dissolution of the Habsburg monarchy. (Article 3 of the Constitution: 'If a German land is under the same sovereign as a non-German land, the relations between the two lands can only be based on the principles of a personal union.')

66. I.e. the Holy Alliance countries.

THE COUNTER-REVOLUTION IN BERLIN

I *N.Rh.Z.*, 12 November 1848

Cologne, 11 November

The *Pfuel ministry* was a 'misunderstanding'; its real meaning is the *Brandenburg ministry*.[67] The Pfuel ministry was an *announcement of the content*, the Brandenburg ministry *is* the content.

Brandenburg in the Assembly and the Assembly in Brandenburg.[68] SO RUNS THE EPITAPH OF THE HOUSE OF BRANDENBURG!

Emperor Charles V was admired because he arranged his funeral while he was still alive.[69] But to carve a bad joke on your own gravestone! That is to go one better than Charles V, even including his Criminal Court Decrees.[70]

Brandenburg in the Assembly and the Assembly in Brandenburg!

Once upon a time a king of Prussia appeared in the Assembly. He was not the real Brandenburg. The Marquess of Brandenburg,[71] who appeared in the Assembly the day before yesterday, was the real king of Prussia.

The guard-room in the Assembly, the Assembly in the guard-room! That is to say: *Brandenburg in the Assembly, the Assembly in Brandenburg!*

Or will the *Assembly in Brandenburg* – as is well-known, Berlin lies in the province of Brandenburg – attain mastery over . . . the

---

67. The Pfuel ministry expressed a 'misunderstanding' between the Crown and the people about the significance and extent of the counter-revolution; the Brandenburg ministry cleared up this misunderstanding by expressing the true meaning of the counter-revolution.

Friedrich, Graf von Brandenburg was a Prussian general and the natural son of Frederick William II. He was a military man without previous political experience or ambitions. On 2 November 1848 the king appointed Brandenburg as Prime Minister and Baron Manteuffel as Minister of the Interior; on 9 November the Prussian National Assembly was prorogued and its place of meeting changed from Berlin to the small provincial town of Brandenburg.

68. A reference to Frederick William IV's phrase about the Brandenburg ministry: 'Either Brandenburg in the Chamber or the Chamber in Brandenburg.'

69. According to the legend, Emperor Charles V is said to have made the arrangements for his own funeral shortly before his death.

70. The Constitutio Criminalis Carolina, accepted in 1532 by the Diet of Regensburg. It was notorious for the exceptionally severe punishments it imposed.

71. Count (not Marquess) Brandenburg announced the move from Berlin to Brandenburg himself when he appeared in the Assembly on 9 November.

Brandenburg in the Assembly? Will Brandenburg seek protection in the Assembly just as Capet once did in another Assembly?[72]

BRANDENBURG IN THE ASSEMBLY AND THE ASSEMBLY IN BRANDENBURG is an ambiguous phrase, an equivocal phrase, heavy with destiny.

Clearly, the people find it infinitely easier to deal with *kings* than with *legislative assemblies*. History possesses a whole catalogue of vain popular uprisings against national assemblies. It offers only two great exceptions. The English people, in the person of Cromwell, dispersed the Long Parliament. The French people, in the person of Bonaparte, dispersed the Council of the Five Hundred. But the Long Parliament had already long been a *rump*, the Council of the Five Hundred had long been a *corpse*.

Have *kings* been more fortunate than peoples in *coups directed against legislative assemblies*?

Charles I, James II, Louis XVI and Charles X are not very promising predecessors.

But there are better precedents in Spain and Italy. And most recently in Vienna?

Nevertheless, it should not be forgotten that the parliament sitting in Vienna was a *congress of peoples*,[73] and that the *representatives of the Slav peoples*, with the exception of the Poles, joined the imperial camp with fifes playing and drums beating.

The war of the Vienna camarilla with the Reichstag was at the same time the war of the Slav Reichstag with the German Reichstag. In the Berlin Assembly, on the other hand, there is no Slav schism, only a *slave* schism, and slaves are not a party. They are at most the camp-followers of a party. The withdrawal of the Berlin Right[74] does not strengthen the enemy camp, it infects it rather with a fatal weakness – *treachery*.

In Austria, the Slav party *conquered alongside* the camarilla; it will now *fight against* the camarilla for the spoils of victory. If the Berlin camarilla wins, it will not have to share the victory with the Right and enforce it against the Right; it will give the Right a *tip* – and then *kick it out*.

72. Louis XVI ('Capet') took refuge from the wrath of the people of Paris in the French National Assembly on 10 August 1792.

73. The Austrian Reichstag of 1848 represented most of the Austrian nationalities, and could therefore be described in this way.

74. After the proclamation of 9 November 1848 on the prorogation and transfer of the Assembly, 96 deputies of the Right obediently left the building; the other 263 deputies voted to continue sitting in Berlin, and did so.

The Prussian Crown is *in the right* in so far as it opposes itself to the Assembly as an *absolute Crown*. But the Assembly is in the wrong because it does not oppose itself to the Crown as an *absolute Assembly*. It ought to have had the ministers arrested for *high treason*, as betrayers of the *sovereignty of the people*. It ought to have *outlawed and proscribed* every official who obeyed commands other than its own.

Yet it may well be that the *political* weakness displayed by the National Assembly in *Berlin* will turn into *civil* strength in the *provinces*.

The bourgeoisie would have liked to transform the *feudal kingdom* into a *bourgeois kingdom* in the *amicable* way. After it had torn away from the feudal party the coats-of-arms and titles which offended its bourgeois pride, as well as the revenues pertaining to feudal property and offensive to the bourgeois mode of appropriation, the bourgeoisie would only too willingly have joined the feudal party and enslaved the people in alliance with it. But the old bureaucracy refuses to sink to the level of servant of a bourgeoisie it previously ruled as a despotic schoolmaster. The feudal party refuses to make a bonfire of its honours and interests on the altar of the bourgeoisie. And, finally, the Crown sees its true, indigenous social foundation in the elements of the old feudal society, whose supreme outgrowth it is, whereas it considers the bourgeoisie to be an alien, artificial soil, in which it can only achieve a stunted growth.

The bourgeoisie would transform the intoxicating '*grace of God*' into a sobering *legal title*, the rule of blue blood into the rule of white paper, the royal sun into a bourgeois astral lamp.

The monarchy therefore refused to let the bourgeoisie mislead it. It replied to the bourgeois semi-revolution with a complete counter-revolution. It threw the bourgeoisie back into the *arms of the revolution, of the people*, by making the call: 'Brandenburg in the Assembly and the Assembly in Brandenburg.'

While admitting that we do not expect an appropriate answer to the situation from the bourgeoisie, we should on the other side not omit to remark that the Crown too, in its coup against the National Assembly, had recourse to hypocritical inconsistency, and hid behind apparent constitutionalism at the very moment when it was endeavouring to slough off this burdensome semblance of reality.

It is the German Central Authority which gave the order for

Brandenburg's coup d'état (on Brandenburg's instructions). *The Guards regiments entered Berlin at the command of the Central Authority*. The Berlin counter-revolution is taking place at the orders of the German Central Authority.[75] Brandenburg gave Frankfurt the order to give him this order. Frankfurt denies its own sovereignty in the act of asserting it. Bassermann naturally seized the opportunity of playing the servant as master.[76] But he has the satisfaction of seeing that the master, for his part, is playing the servant.

Whatever the immediate outcome of the struggle in Berlin, the *dilemma* is posed – *king* or *people* – and the people will win, with the slogan 'Brandenburg in the Assembly and the Assembly in Brandenburg'.

We may well yet have a rough schooling to go through, but this will be preparatory training for – THE REVOLUTION AS A WHOLE.

II *N.Rh.Z.*, 12 November 1848, *second edition*

Cologne, 11 November

The *European revolution* is describing a *circular course*. It began in Italy, it assumed a European character in Paris, Vienna felt the first impact of the February revolution, the Berlin revolution was in its turn influenced by the Vienna revolution. It was in Italy – in Naples – that the European counter-revolution struck its first blow, in Paris – the June days – that it assumed a European character, in Vienna that the first impact of the June counter-revolution was felt, and in Berlin that the counter-revolution was completed and compromised. *But it is from Paris that the crowing of the Gallic cock will once more awaken Europe.*[77]

In Berlin the counter-revolution has compromised itself. Everything compromises itself in Berlin, even the counter-revolution.

In Naples, the counter-revolution was the lumpenproletariat allied with the monarchy, against the bourgeoisie.

75. There is no evidence that the Central Authority in Frankfurt gave such an order. However the removal of the Prussian National Assembly was seen by some of Frederick William's advisers as the precondition for an alliance between the king and Frankfurt.

76. On 7 November Bassermann was sent to Berlin by the Reich ministry to mediate between the king and the Assembly.

77. Heine wrote of the French revolution of 1830: 'The Gallic cock has crowed a second time, and now it is daybreak even in Germany.' H. Heine, *Sämmtliche Werke*, vol. 14, Hamburg, 1867–8.

In Paris, it was the greatest historical battle which has ever taken place. The bourgeoisie, allied with the lumpenproletariat, against the working class.

In Vienna, it was a whole swarm of nationalities which imagined the counter-revolution would bring emancipation, as well as secret treachery by the bourgeoisie against the workers and the Academic Legion. In addition to this, conflict within the citizens' militia itself, and finally, the attack from the people which gave the Court an excuse for its own attack.

In Berlin, *nothing of the kind*. The bourgeoisie and the people on one side; the non-commissioned officers on the other.

Wrangel and Brandenburg, two men without heads, without hearts, without a political tendency, with nothing but the pure military moustache – that is the opposition to this querulous, indecisive, too-clever-by-half National Assembly.

The will! – whether it be the will of the donkey, the ox, or the military moustache – this is all that is needed to oppose the will-less grumblers of the March revolution. And the Prussian court, which has no more will than the National Assembly, seeks out the two most stupid men in the kingdom and says to these lions: *represent the will*. Even Pfuel had a few atoms of grey matter. But in face of *absolute stupidity*, the argumentative grumblers who are defending the achievements of March must shrink back.

'The Gods themselves fight in vain against stupidity',[78] exclaims the afflicted National Assembly.

And these Wrangels, these Brandenburgs, these blockheaded numbskulls, who are able to *will* because they lack a will of their own, because they will what they are *ordered* to will, who are too stupid to diverge from orders given to them with trembling voice and quivering lips, these people too are *compromising* themselves in so far as they omit to engage in *skull-bashing*, the sole activity these *bulldozers* are capable of.

Wrangel can do no more than confess that he knows of only one National Assembly, a National Assembly which obeys orders. Brandenburg takes lessons in parliamentary procedure, and after enraging the Chamber with his blunt and repulsive sergeant-major's language, allows 'the tyrant to be tyrannized by others' and obeys the order of the National Assembly, by most humbly *requesting* the right to speak, which he had only shortly before

78. Schiller, *The Maid of Orleans*, III, vi.

wanted to *take*. 'I had rather be a tick in a sheep, than such a valiant ignorance.'[79]

The calm attitude of Berlin *delights* us; in this way the ideals of the Prussian officer corps are being destroyed.

But what of the National Assembly? Why does it not issue an excommunication, why does it not declare Wrangel to be outside the law, why does no deputy step into the midst of Wrangel's bayonets, declare the illegality of the position, and harangue the soldiery?

The Berlin National Assembly should look through the *Moniteur*, the *Moniteur* of 1789 to 1795.[80]

And what shall *we* do on this occasion?

We shall refuse to pay taxes. A Wrangel, a Brandenburg comprehends – for these beings are learning Arabic from the Hyghlans[81] – that he wears a sword and receives a uniform and his pay. He does *not* understand, however, where sword, uniform and pay come from.

There is now only one way left to defeat the monarchy, at least until the epoch of the anti-June revolution in Paris, which will take place in December.[82]

The monarchy is defying the bourgeoisie as well as the people. Let us therefore defeat it in the bourgeois manner.

How does one defeat a monarchy in a bourgeois manner?

By starving it out.

And how does one starve it out?

By refusing to pay the taxes.

Keep this point well in mind! All the princes of Prussia, the Brandenburgs, the Wrangels, produce no *soldiers' rations*. You yourselves produce the rations.

79. Shakespeare, *Troilus and Cressida*, III, iii.

80. *Le Moniteur Universel*, a daily paper, first appeared in Paris in 1789 and published the proceedings and decrees of the revolutionary institutions. It later became, as from 1799, the official organ of the French government.

81. On 3 November the *Kölnische Zeitung* printed an account of an imaginary African tribe called the 'Hyghlans', which contained the words, 'Many of them are learning the Arabian language.'

82. A reference to the election of the French President, which was to take place on 10 December 1848.

III *N.Rh.Z.*, 14 November 1848

Cologne, 13 November

Just as the French National Assembly once found its official meeting-place locked, and had to continue its sittings in an indoor tennis court, so the Prussian National Assembly must meet in the Berlin shooting-gallery.[83]

The decision taken there, as our Berlin correspondent will report in this morning's special edition, is that *Brandenburg has committed high treason*. The *Kölnische Zeitung* has not reported this.

In the meantime we have just received a letter from a *member of the National Assembly*, containing these words:

The National Assembly has unanimously declared (with 242 members present) that Brandenburg has committed high treason by this measure (the dissolution of the militia), and anyone who cooperates actively or passively in the execution of this measure must be considered as a traitor.[84]

Dumont's credibility is well known.

Now that the National Assembly has declared Brandenburg to be a traitor, the **obligations to pay taxes automatically ceases.** *No taxes are owed to a government of traitors.* Tomorrow we shall explain to our readers in detail how *in England, the oldest constitutional country*, they deal with similar confrontations by using the weapon of tax-refusal.[85] In any case, the treacherous government has itself shown the people the right way by immediately refusing the National Assembly its attendance allowances, and thereby seeking to starve it out.

The above-mentioned deputy also informs us that **the militia will not surrender its weapons.**

The struggle therefore appears to be unavoidable, and it is **the duty of the Rhineland to hurry to the aid of the Berlin National Assembly with men and weapons.**

83. From 11 to 13 November 1848 the Prussian National Assembly met in a shooting-gallery, having been driven from their normal meeting-place on 10 November.

84. The resolution of 11 November, adopted at the ninety-eighth sitting of the National Assembly.

85. The explanation was given in the *Neue Rheinische Zeitung* of 15 November; see also pp. 261–3.

NO MORE TAXES!!!

N.Rh.Z., 17 November 1848 (*Extraordinary Supplement*)
                                            Cologne, 16 November

No newspapers from Berlin have come out, with the exception of the *Preussischer Staats-Zeitung*, the *Vossische Zeitung*[86] and the *Neue Preussische Zeitung*.[87]

The militia has been disarmed in the district where the state officials live, but not elsewhere. Their battalion is the one which massacred the engineering workers on 31 October.[88] Its disarming is thus in fact a victory for the people's cause.

The National Assembly was once again driven out of its meeting-place, in this case the city hall. It then assembled in the Mielenz Hotel and finally, with all its 226 votes, adopted the following resolution on tax-refusal:

> The Brandenburg ministry is not entitled to dispose of the state's money and to raise taxes as long as the National Assembly is unable freely to continue its sittings in Berlin. This resolution enters into force as from 17 November.
>
> *National Assembly of 15 November 1848.*

All taxes are therefore abolished as from today! The payment of taxes is high treason, the refusal to pay taxes is the first duty of the citizen!

THE FRANKFURT ASSEMBLY

N.Rh.Z., 23 November 1848

                                            Cologne, 22 November

The Frankfurt parliament has annulled the resolution of the Berlin Assembly on tax-refusal on the ground that it is illegal. In doing this it has declared for Brandenburg, for Wrangel, for all

86. A Berlin newspaper, which adopted a moderate liberal attitude in the 1840s.

87. An explicitly reactionary newspaper founded in Berlin in June 1848 by the camarilla and the junkers associated with it (including Bismarck). More commonly known as the *Kreuzzeitung*.

88. On 31 October 1848 a demonstration took place in Berlin, sparked off by the Assembly's rejection of the proposal that the Prussian government be asked to aid Vienna with money and soldiers. In its course the 8th battalion of the militia shot at an unarmed crowd of engineering workers.

that is Prussian. Frankfurt has moved to Berlin, Berlin has moved to Frankfurt. The German parliament is in Berlin, the Prussian parliament is in Frankfurt. The Prussian parliament has become a German parliament, the German parliament has become a Brandenburg-Prussian parliament. Prussia was supposed to merge into Germany,[89] and now the German parliament in Frankfurt wants Germany to merge into Prussia.

The German parliament! How could one speak of a German parliament after the terrible events in Berlin and Vienna? No one thought any longer of the life of the noble Gagern[90] after the death of Robert Blum.[91] No one thought any longer of a Schmerling[92] after the Brandenburg-Manteuffel ministry. The professorial gentlemen who 'made history' for their private satisfaction had to permit the bombardment of Vienna, the murder of Robert Blum, and the barbarisms of Windischgrätz. The gentlemen who were so concerned with the history of German civilization left the practical application of civilization to Jellačić and his Croats. Whilst the professors made the theory of history, history itself went on its own stormy way and worried very little about the history of the professors.

This resolution has destroyed the Frankfurt parliament. It has thrown it into the arms of the traitor Brandenburg. The Frankfurt parliament has made itself guilty of high treason, and it must be judged. When a whole people rises up, in order to protest against an act of royal despotism, when this protest takes the entirely legal form of a refusal to pay taxes, and an assembly of professors – without any authority – declares this refusal of taxes, this uprising of the whole people, to be illegal, then this assembly is outside all the laws, it is an assembly of traitors.

It is the duty of all those members of the Frankfurt Assembly

89. In the royal manifesto of 21 March 1848 Frederick William IV stated: 'Prussia is henceforth merged into Germany.'

90. Heinrich von Gagern was one of the leading figures of south German liberalism, in 1848 a Right-Centre deputy, President of the Frankfurt National Assembly, and from December 1848 to March 1849 President of the Reich ministry.

91. Robert Blum was a journalist from Leipzig and the leader of the Left in the Frankfurt Assembly. He took part in the Vienna revolution of October 1848 and was afterwards court-martialled and shot.

92. Anton, Ritter von Schmerling was an Austrian liberal, in 1848 a member of the Frankfurt Assembly (Right Centre), and Minister of the Interior from July to September 1848, President and Foreign Minister from September to December 1848, in the Reich ministry.

who voted against the resolution to withdraw from this 'deceased Federal Diet'. It is the duty of all democrats to elect these 'Prussians' who have resigned from Frankfurt as members of the German National Assembly in Berlin, as representatives of the departed 'Germans'. The National Assembly in Berlin is not a 'part': it is the whole, for it is capable of making decisions. The Brandenburgian Assembly in Frankfurt will however become a 'part'; for certainly the 150 members who will have to withdraw will be followed by others who have no wish to constitute a Frankfurt Federal Diet. The Frankfurt parliament! It fears a red republic and decrees a *red monarchy*! We do not want a *red* monarchy, we do not want the purple-coloured Crown of Austria to be placed over Prussia, and we therefore declare that the German parliament is guilty of high treason. Yet even this would be to rate it too highly, by ascribing to it a political importance it lost long ago. The severest judgement has already been passed on the Frankfurt Assembly: people have disregarded its resolutions and . . . forgotten it.

THE BOURGEOISIE AND THE COUNTER-REVOLUTION

I *N.Rh.Z.*, 10 December 1848

Cologne, 9 December

We have never concealed the fact that we stand on a *revolutionary*, not on a *legal foundation*. Now the government, for its part, has abandoned the hypocrisy of the legal foundation. It has placed itself on the revolutionary foundation, for the counter-revolutionary foundation is also revolutionary.

Paragraph 6 of the law of 6 April 1848[93] lays down:

It is the responsibility of the future representatives of the people in all cases to agree on the laws and on the budget, and to exercise the right to grant supply.

In paragraph 13 of the law of 8 April 1848[94] there is the following passage:

93. 'An Ordinance on Certain Foundations of the Future Prussian Constitution' issued by the Camphausen ministry on 6 April 1848.
94. 'The Electoral Law for the Assembly to be Called to Agree with the King on the Prussian State Constitution', was passed by the second United Diet on 8 April 1848.

The Assembly which meets together on the basis of the present law is authorized to *establish the future constitution of the state* by agreement with the Crown, and to exercise the existing powers of the estates, namely in relation to the grant of supply, for the duration of its session.

The government chases the *Vereinbarungsversammlung* out of existence, dictates a so-called constitution[95] to the country on its own authority, and itself grants the taxes denied to it by the representatives of the people.

The Prussian government has put a sensational end to the Camphausen saga, which was a kind of solemn right-wing saga of Job.[96] In revenge, the inventor of this epic tale, the great Camphausen, calmly continues to sit in Frankfurt as the envoy of that same Prussian government, and continues to intrigue with the Bassermanns in the service of that same Prussian government. This Camphausen, who invented the theory of *Vereinbarung* in order to rescue the legal foundation, i.e. in order to swindle the revolution of the honours owing to it, simultaneously invented the mines which would later explode the legal foundation and the theory of *Vereinbarung* as well.

This man gave us the *indirect* elections which produced an Assembly to which the government could thunder 'too late' at the moment of its momentary resistance. He brought back the prince of Prussia, the head of the counter-revolution, and sank so low as to transform the prince of Prussia's flight into an educational trip, by issuing an official lie.[97] He kept the old Prussian legislation on political crimes in force and the old courts in operation. Under Camphausen the old bureaucracy and the old army won a breathing-space in which to recover from their terror and completely reconstitute themselves. All the chief men of the *ancien régime* remained at their posts undisturbed. The camarilla waged war in Posen while Camphausen himself was waging war in Denmark. The purpose of the Danish war was to provide a diversion for the surplus patriotic energy of the youth of Germany, which was subjected to appropriate disciplinary measures

95. On 5 December 1848 the National Assembly was dissolved and a new constitution was issued setting up two legislative chambers and giving the king an absolute right of veto on all laws.

96. A reference to the satirical poem by Karl Arnold Kortum, *Die Jobsiade. Ein komisches Heldengedicht* (*The saga of Job. A comical heroic poem.*)

97. In Camphausen's speech of 6 June 1848 to the National Assembly Prince William of Prussia's flight to England in March was presented as an educational trip which had already been arranged before the revolution.

by the police after its return. The war was also supposed to provide General Wrangel and his celebrated Guards regiments with a certain popularity, and to rehabilitate the Prussian soldiery in general. As soon as this aim had been fulfilled, the pseudo-conflict had to be smothered at any cost. This was the reason for the shameful armistice which Camphausen himself brought the German National Assembly to accept.[98] The result of the Danish war was the appointment of the 'Supreme Commander of both Marks',[99] and the return to Berlin of the Guards regiments driven out in March.

And then there is the war which the Potsdam camarilla waged in Posen under Camphausen's auspices!

The war in Posen was more than a war against the Prussian revolution. It spelled the fall of Vienna, the fall of Italy, the defeat of the June heroes. It was the first decisive triumph gained over the European revolution by the Russian tsar. And all this occurred under the auspices of the great Camphausen, 'the thinking friend of history', the knight of the great debate, the hero of mediation.

The counter-revolution had thus taken control of all important positions under Camphausen's ministry and through his agency. It had prepared its army for battle, while the *Vereinbarungsversammlung* debated. Under Hansemann-Pinto,[1] the Minister of the Deed, the old police force was newly accoutred, and the bourgeoisie carried on a war against the people as bitter as it was petty. Under Brandenburg the conclusion was drawn from these premises. All that was needed now was – a military moustache and a sabre instead of a head.

When Camphausen resigned, we made this statement: 'He sowed reaction in the interests of the big bourgeoisie, but he will reap it in the interests of the aristocracy and absolutism.[2]

We do not doubt that his excellency the Prussian envoy Camp-

98. The Armistice of Malmö between Prussia and Denmark, concluded on 26 August, provided for the setting up of a mixed Prussian-Danish administrative commission in Schleswig-Holstein, and thus meant the abandonment of the German Provisional Government for the Duchies at Kiel. The Frankfurt Assembly ratified the decision on 16 September, thus reversing its own vote of 4 September.

99. See p. 161, n. 44.

1. An ironical allusion to the similarity between Hansemann's financial proposals and those of the eighteenth-century Dutch financier Pinto, who saw speculation on the stock-exchange as a means of speeding up the circulation of money.

2. See the article 'The Fall of the Camphausen Ministry', p. 129.

hausen counts himself at this moment as one of the feudal lords, and will have reconciled himself with his 'misunderstanding' in the most peaceful way.

However, no mistake should be made here: one should not ascribe any world-historical initiative to a Camphausen or a Hansemann; these are men of very subordinate importance. They were nothing but the instruments of a class. Their language and activities were merely the official echo of the class which had pushed them into the foreground. They were simply the big bourgeoisie – in the foreground.

It was the representatives of this class who formed the *liberal opposition* at the United Diet, that sweetly sleeping institution momentarily reawakened by Camphausen.

The gentlemen of this liberal opposition have been reproached with being untrue to their principles after the March revolution. This is an error.

The big landowners and capitalists, in other words the moneybags, who alone were represented in the United Diet, had grown in wealth and in general culture. The old divisions between the estates of the realm had lost their material foundation with the development of bourgeois society in Prussia, i.e. with the development of industry, trade and agriculture, and the nobility itself had become fundamentally bourgeoisified. Instead of dealing in devotion, love and piety, it now dealt above all in sugar beet, liquor and wool. Its chosen jousting-ground had become the wool market. Against these forces stood the absolutist state, whose old social foundation had been conjured away from beneath its feet by the course of historical development; it had become a fetter and a hindrance for the new bourgeois society, with its changed mode of production and its changed needs. The bourgeoisie had to lay claim to a share in political power, if only to assert its purely material interests. It alone was capable of bringing its commercial and industrial interests to bear through legislation. It had to take the administration of these its 'holiest interests' out of the hands of an outdated, ignorant and arrogant bureaucracy. It had to assert its control of the resources of the state, resources which it considered to be its own creation. It was also ambitious enough to wish to conquer a political position commensurate with its social position, once it had deprived the bureaucracy of the monopoly of so-called culture, and had become conscious of the extent of its superiority over the bureaucracy in real understanding of the requirements of bourgeois society. In order to attain its goal, it had to allow free discussion of its own interests and views, and of the actions of the government. It called this 'the right of freedom of the press'. It had to be able to *associate* freely. This was called 'the right of freedom of association'. *Religious freedom* and so on had equally to be demanded, as the necessary consequence of *free competition*. And before March 1848 the Prussian bourgeoisie was firmly set on the road to the realization of all its wishes.

The Prussian state was in a condition of financial need. Its credit had dried up. This was the secret of the convocation of the United Diet. It is true that the government struggled against its fate, and that the 'United' was unceremoniously dismissed. But the shortage of money and the absence of credit would infallibly have thrown the government ever further into the arms of the bourgeoisie. Like feudal barons, kings by the grace of God have exchanged their privileges for hard cash from time immemorial. The emancipation of the serfs was the first, the constitutional monarchy the second great act of this world-historical bargain in all the Christian-Germanic states. 'Money has no master', but masters cease to be masters once their money has run out.

The liberal opposition in the United Diet was therefore nothing other than the opposition of the bourgeoisie to a form of government which no longer corresponded to its interests and needs. In order to oppose the Court, they had to pay court to the people.

Perhaps they really imagined that their opposition was *on behalf of* the people.

They could at any rate only claim from the government the rights and freedoms they were striving to attain for themselves under the rubric of the *rights of the people* and the *freedom of the people*.

This opposition was well on the way to success, as we have said, when the *storm of February* burst forth.

II *N.Rh.Z.*, 15 December 1848

Cologne, 11 December

After the March deluge – a deluge in miniature – had subsided, it left behind no monsters on the surface of the Berlin earth, no revolutionary colossi, but rather creatures of the old style, thickset bourgeois shapes: the liberals of the United Diet, the representatives of the class-conscious Prussian bourgeoisie. The provinces which have the most developed bourgeoisie, the Rhineland and Silesia, provided the greater part of the new ministries. Behind them a whole train of Rhenish lawyers. In the same measure as the bourgeoisie was forced into the background by the feudal party, the Rhineland and Silesia made room in the ministries for the old Prussian provinces. The Brandenburg ministry only retains a connection with the Rhineland through a Tory from Elberfeld. Hansemann and von der Heydt![3] The whole difference between March and December 1848 is contained for the Prussian bourgeoisie in these two names.

The Prussian bourgeoisie was thrown to the highest position in the state, not as it would have liked, through a *peaceful transaction with the Crown*, but through a *revolution*. Against the Crown it had to represent not its own interests but the people's interests, i.e. it had to act against itself, for a *popular movement* had cleared the way for it. However, in the bourgeoisie's eyes the Crown was only the divine umbrella behind which its own profane interests were concealed. The inviolability of *its own* interests and the corresponding political forms had the following meaning when translated into constitutional language: the inviolability of the Crown. Hence the enthusiasm of the German and in particular the Prussian bourgeoisie for *constitutional monarchy*. If therefore the February revolution and its German after-effects were welcomed by the Prussian bourgeoisie because the direction of the state was thereby thrown into its hands, the revolution was also and just as much a disappointment, because it attached to bourgeois rule conditions the bourgeoisie was both unwilling and unable to fulfil.

The bourgeoisie had not moved a muscle. It had allowed the people to fight on its behalf. The power handed over to it was not therefore the power of a general who has defeated his opponents, but rather that of a committee of public safety to which the victorious people has entrusted the maintenance of its own interests.

Camphausen was always aware of the inconveniences involved in this position; the whole weakness of his ministry arose from this awareness and the circumstances which conditioned it. A kind of blush of shame therefore transfigured even the most shameless acts of Camphausen's government. Frank shamelessness and

3. August, Freiherr von der Heydt, a banker from Elberfeld in the Rhineland, was appointed Minister of Trade in the Brandenburg ministry (December 1848).

impertinence were the privilege of the Hansemann government. The tint of red constitutes the only difference between these two painters.

The Prussian March revolution must not be confused either with the English revolution of 1648 or with the French revolution of 1789.

In 1648 the bourgeoisie was in alliance with the modern nobility against the monarchy, the feudal nobility and the established church.

In 1789 the bourgeoisie was in alliance with the people against the monarchy, the nobility and the established church.

The revolution of 1789 was (at least in Europe) only prefigured by the revolution of 1648, which in turn was only prefigured by the rising of the Netherlands against Spain.[4] Both revolutions were approximately a century in advance of their predecessors, not only in time but also in content.

In both revolutions, the bourgeoisie was the class which was *genuinely* to be found at the head of the movement. The proletariat, and the other sections of the town population which did not form a part of the bourgeoisie, either had as yet no interests separate from those of the bourgeoisie, or they did not yet form independently developed classes or groups within classes. Therefore, where they stood in opposition to the bourgeoisie, as for example in 1793 and 1794 in France, they were in fact fighting for the implementation of the interests of the bourgeoisie, although not *in the manner* of the bourgeoisie. The *whole of the French terror* was nothing other than a *plebeian manner* of dealing with the *enemies of the bourgeoisie*, with absolutism, feudalism and parochialism.

The revolutions of 1648 and 1789 were not *English* and *French* revolutions; they were revolutions of a *European* pattern. They were not the victory of a *particular* class of society over the *old political order*; they were the *proclamation of the political order for the new European society*. In these revolutions the bourgeoisie gained the victory; but the *victory of the bourgeoisie* was at that time the *victory of a new social order*, the victory of bourgeois property over feudal property, of nationality over provincialism, of competition over the guild, of the partition of estates over primogeniture, of the owner's mastery of the land over the land's mastery of its owner, of enlightenment over superstition, of the family over the family name, of industry over heroic laziness, of

4. The Dutch war of liberation began in 1572.

civil law over privileges of medieval origin. The revolution of 1648 was the victory of the seventeenth century over the sixteenth century, the revolution of 1789 was the victory of the eighteenth century over the seventeenth century. Still more than expressing the needs of the parts of the world in which they took place, England and France, these revolutions expressed the needs of the whole world, as it existed then.

Nothing of this is to be found in the *Prussian March revolution*.

The February revolution had *done away with* the constitutional monarchy in reality and the rule of the bourgeoisie in the mind. The purpose of the Prussian March revolution was to *establish* the constitutional monarchy in the mind and the rule of the bourgeoisie in reality. Far from being a *European revolution* it was merely the stunted echo, in a backward country, of a European revolution. Instead of being in advance of its own age it was behind it by more than half a century. It was *secondary* from the very beginning, but, as is well known, secondary diseases are more difficult to cure, and at the same time, ravage the body more, than original ones. Here it was not a matter of setting up a new social order, but of the rebirth in Berlin of the society which had expired in Paris. The Prussian March revolution was not even *national* and *German*; it was from its inception *provincial* and *Prussian*. All kinds of provincial uprisings – e.g. those in Vienna, Kassel and Munich – swept along beside it and contested its position as the main German revolution.

Whereas 1648 and 1789 had the infinite self-confidence that springs from standing at the summit of creativity, it was Berlin's ambition in 1848 to form an anachronism. Its light was like the light of those stars which first reaches the earth when the bodies which radiated it have been extinct for a hundred thousand years. The Prussian March revolution was such a star for Europe – only on a small scale, just as it was everything on a small scale. Its light was light from the corpse of a society long since putrefied.

The German bourgeoisie had developed so sluggishly, so pusillanimously and so slowly, that it saw itself threateningly confronted by the proletariat, and all those sections of the urban population related to the proletariat in interests and ideas, at the very moment of its own threatening confrontation with feudalism and absolutism. And as well as having this class *behind* it, it saw *in front of* it the enmity of all Europe. The Prussian bourgeoisie was not, like the French bourgeoisie of 1789, the class which represented the *whole* of modern society in face of the representatives of the old society, the monarchy and the nobility. It had sunk to the level of a type of *estate*, as clearly marked off from the people as from the Crown, happy to oppose either, irresolute against each of its opponents, taken individually, because it always saw the other one in front of it or to the rear; inclined from the outset to treachery against the people and compromise with the crowned representative of the old society, because it itself already belonged to the old society; representing not the interests of a new society against an old but the renewal of its own interests within an obsolete society; at the steering-wheel of the revolution, not because the people stood behind it but because the people pushed it forward; at the head of the movement, not because it represented the initiative of a new social epoch, but only because it represented the malice of an old; a stratum of the old state which had not been able to break through to the earth's surface but had been thrown up by an earthquake; without faith in itself, without faith in the people, grumbling at those above, trembling before those below, egoistic in both directions and conscious of its egoism, revolutionary in relation to the conservatives and conservative in relation to the revolutionaries, mistrustful of its own slogans, which were phrases instead of ideas, intimidated by the storm of world revolution yet exploiting it; with no energy in any respect, plagiaristic in all respects; common because it lacked originality, original in its commonness; making a bargaining-counter of its own wishes, without initiative, without faith in itself, without faith in the people, without a world-historical function; an accursed old man, who found himself condemned to lead and mislead the first youthful impulses of a robust people in his own senile interests – sans teeth, sans eyes, sans taste, sans everything – this was the nature of the *Prussian bourgeoisie* which found itself at the helm of the Prussian state after the March revolution.

III *N.Rh.Z.*, 16 December 1848

Cologne, 15 December

The theory of *Vereinbarung*, which the bourgeoisie, having entered the government in the shape of the Camphausen ministry, immediately proclaimed as the 'broadest' basis of the Prussian *contrat social*, was by no means an empty theory; it had grown on the tree of 'golden' life.

The March revolution by no means subjected the sovereign by the grace of God to the sovereign people. It only compelled the Crown, the absolutist state, to come to terms with the bourgeoisie, to *make an agreement* [*sich vereinbaren*] with its old rival.

The Crown would sacrifice the nobility to the bourgeoisie, the bourgeoisie would sacrifice the people to the Crown. On this condition, the monarchy would become bourgeois and the bourgeoisie would become royal.

After March there existed only these two powers. They did each other mutual service as lightning conductors of the revolution. All this naturally happened on the '*broadest democratic basis*'.

That was the *secret of the theory of Vereinbarung*.

The dealers in oil and wool[5] who formed the first ministry after the March revolution fancied themselves in their role, which was to hide the compromised Crown beneath their plebeian wings. They revelled in the luxury of being presentable at Court, and, reluctantly and out of sheer generosity, they abandoned their raw Roman virtues – the Roman virtues of the United Diet – and bridged the chasm which threatened to swallow up the throne with the corpse of their former popularity. What airs Camphausen gave himself as the *midwife* of the constitutional throne! The good man was openly moved by himself, by his own magnanimity. The Crown and its party unwillingly tolerated this humiliating protectorate; it made the best of a bad job in the expectation of better days.

The half-dissolved army, the bureaucracy shaking for its positions and emoluments, the humiliated feudal estate, whose leader was on a trip abroad to study constitutions,[6] all these people easily deceived the '*bourgeois gentilhomme*' with a few polite words and courtesies.

The Prussian bourgeoisie was *nominally* in possession of power, and it did not doubt for a moment that the forces of the old state had placed themselves unreservedly at its disposal and become transformed into devoted servants of its own omnipotence.

Not just in the ministry, but over the whole extent of the kingdom, the bourgeoisie was intoxicated by this delusion. Did it not find willing and submissive accomplices in the army, the bureaucracy,

5. Camphausen dealt in oil and corn before attaining political prominence, Hansemann began as a wool-merchant.

6. See p. 181, n. 97.

and even among the feudal nobility, for its only post-March deeds of heroism, namely the often bloody provocations of the militia against the unarmed proletariat? The local representatives of the bourgeoisie, the *municipal councillors* – whose importunately servile baseness was later trampled on in an appropriate fashion by such people as Windischgrätz, Jellačić and Welden[7] – braced themselves for only one kind of endeavour, their patriarchally serious words of warning to the people. And were not these words of warning, the only heroic deeds of the municipal councillors after the March revolution, gazed at in admiration by the district presidents who had been struck dumb and the divisional generals who had withdrawn into themselves? Was there still any room for the Prussian bourgeoisie to doubt that the old resentment of the army, the bureaucracy and the feudal nobility had died away and been replaced by respectful devotion towards itself, the magnanimous victor, the bridle both of anarchy and of its own excessive claims?

The position was clear. The Prussian bourgeoisie had only one more task, that of making its power secure, removing troublesome anarchists, restoring 'law and order' and regaining the profits lost during the March storm. Now it could only be a question of restricting to a minimum the *costs of production* of its rule and of the March revolution which was the condition of that rule. In its struggle with feudal society and the Crown the Prussian bourgeoisie had been compelled to lay claim in the name of the people to a number of weapons, such as the right of association, freedom of the press, etc. Would these weapons not inevitably be destroyed, once they were in the hands of a deluded people which no longer needed to carry them *on behalf of* the bourgeoisie and was demonstrating a regrettable inclination to carry them *against* the bourgeoisie?

There was obviously only one more obstacle in the way of the *agreement* between the bourgeoisie and the Crown, the bargain between the bourgeoisie and the old state now resigned to its fate. The bourgeoisie was convinced of this. And that obstacle was the people, *puer robustus sed malitiosus*[8] as Hobbes put it. The *people*, and the *revolution*!

---

7. Franz, Freiherr von Welden was an Austrian general, governor of Vienna from November 1848 to April 1849, and supreme commander of the Austrian troops fighting against Hungary, April-June 1849.

8. 'A strong but malicious boy', from the preface to Hobbes's *De Cive*.

The *revolution* was the *legal title of the people*; the people based their vehement claims on the revolution. The revolution was the bill of exchange the people had drawn on the bourgeoisie. The bourgeoisie had come to power through the revolution. The bill of exchange fell due on the first day of bourgeois rule. The bourgeoisie had to dishonour it.

The meaning of the *revolution* in the popular mind was: you bourgeois are the *comité du salut public*, the committee of public safety in whose hands we have placed the power, not so that you may *reach a compromise with* the Crown in your own interests, but so that you may enforce our interests, the interests of the people, *against* the Crown.

The *revolution* was the people's protest against the bourgeoisie's compromise with the Crown. While it compromised with the Crown, therefore, the bourgeoisie *had to protest* against the *revolution*.

And this happened under the great Camphausen. The *March revolution was not recognized*. The representatives of the nation in Berlin constituted themselves as the *representatives of the Prussian bourgeoisie*, as the *Vereinbarungsversammlung*, by rejecting the motion for the recognition of the March revolution.

The Berlin Assembly turned what had happened into a non-event. It openly proclaimed to the Prussian people that it had not compromised with the bourgeoisie in order to make a revolution against the Crown, but that it had made a revolution so that the Crown might make an agreement with the bourgeoisie directed against itself! In this way, the *legal title* of the revolutionary people was annulled and the *legal foundation* of the conservative bourgeoisie was attained.

The *legal foundation*!

Brüggemann, and through him the *Kölnische Zeitung*, have prattled, yarned and whined so much about the 'legal foundation', so often lost and regained it, perforated it, patched it up, tossed it from Berlin to Frankfurt and then back to Berlin, contracted it, extended it, changed it from a simple foundation into an inlaid foundation, from an inlaid foundation into a false floor – the chief instrument of the stage magician – and from a false floor into a trap-door with no floor at all, with the result that our readers have rightly come to view the legal foundation as the foundation of the *Kölnische Zeitung*, they have come to confuse the shibboleth of the Prussian bourgeoisie with the private shibboleth of Joseph Dumont, a necessary idea of the world history of Prussia with an arbitrary hobby-horse of the *Kölnische Zeitung*, and to see in the legal foundation only the soil in which the *Kölnische Zeitung* grows.

The *legal foundation*, and, what is more, the *Prussian legal foundation*!

The *legal foundation*, upon which, *after* March, there danced the knight of the grand debate, Camphausen, the reawakened spectre of the United Diet, and the *Vereinbarungsversammlung*! Was this the Constitutional Law of 1815,[9] the Diet Law of 1820,[10] the Patent of 1847, or the law of 8 April 1848 for the election of an assembly to make an agreement with the king on a constitution?

It was none of these.

The 'legal foundation' meant simply that the revolution had not gained its foundation, and the old society had not lost its foundation, that the March revolution was merely an 'occurrence', which had given the 'impulse' to an 'agreement' between the throne and the bourgeoisie. This 'agreement' had long been under preparation within the old Prussian state, the Crown itself had already expressed the need for it in earlier royal decrees, although before March it had not considered the matter to be '*urgent*'. The 'legal foundation', to put it briefly, meant that the bourgeoisie wished to negotiate with the Crown on the same footing *after* March as *before* March, as if no revolution had taken place and the United Diet would have achieved its goal without the revolution. The 'legal foundation' meant that the legal title of the people, the *revolution*, did not exist in the social contract between the government and the bourgeoisie. *The bourgeoisie derived its claims from the old Prussian legislation, in order to prevent the people from deriving any claims from the new Prussian revolution*.

It is obvious that the *ideological half-wits* retained by the bourgeoisie, their newspapermen and the like, had to present this veneer of bourgeois interest as the actual interest of the bourgeoisie, and to persuade themselves and others of this. In the head of

9. The 'Ordinance Concerning the Creation of a Representation of the People' of 22 May 1815; a promise to call a general Prussian parliament which was not fulfilled.

10. The 'Ordinance Concerning the Future Organization of the State Debt', 17 January 1820. This promised that any future loans would require the consent of a Diet.

a Brüggemann, the phrase of the legal foundation became transformed into a real substance.

The Camphausen ministry had accomplished its task, a task of *mediation* and *transition*. That is to say, it formed the *mediating link* between the bourgeoisie which had been raised up on the shoulders of the people and the bourgeoisie which no longer needed the shoulders of the people; between the bourgeoisie which, in appearance, represented the people against the Crown, and the bourgeoisie which, in reality, represented the Crown against the people; between the bourgeoisie which had peeled itself off from the revolution and the bourgeoisie which, as the kernel of the revolution, had itself been peeled.

In accordance with its role, the Camphausen ministry limited itself with virginal modesty to *passive resistance* to the revolution.

Admittedly, it rejected it in theory. But in practice it only *fought* against its forms of appearance and merely *tolerated* the reconstitution of the old powers in the state.

In the meantime the bourgeoisie believed it had arrived at the point where *passive resistance* must go over to *active attack*. The Camphausen ministry resigned, not because it had committed this or that blunder, but for the simple reason that it was the *first* ministry after the March revolution, it was the ministry *of* the March revolution, and, true to its origins, still had to conceal its representation of the bourgeoisie beneath the dictatorship of the people. The equivocal origin and ambiguous character of the Camphausen ministry continued to impose on it certain proprieties, certain reservations and allowances towards the sovereign people, which the bourgeoisie began to find irksome. A second ministry, chosen directly from the Assembly, would no longer have to observe these proprieties.

Camphausen's resignation was therefore a puzzle for the coffee-house politicians. The Ministry of the Deed, the *Hansemann ministry*, followed after Camphausen because the bourgeoisie had decided to go over from the period of passive betrayal of the people to the Crown to the period of *active* subjection of the people to its own rule, as agreed on with the Crown. The Ministry of the Deed was the *second* ministry *after* the March revolution. That was its whole secret.

IV *N.Rh.Z.*, 31 December 1848

Cologne, 29 December

Gentlemen! In matters of money, there is no room for soft-heartedness! [11]

Hansemann summed up the whole of the liberalism of the United Diet in these few words. This man was the necessary head of the ministry which emerged from the *Vereinbarungsversammlung* itself, the ministry which was to change *passive resistance* against the people into an *active attack* on the people, the Ministry of the Deed.

In no Prussian ministry have there been so many *middle-class* names! Hansemann, Milde, Märker, Kühlwetter, [12] Gierke! Even the ministry's presentable master of ceremonies, von Auerswald, belonged to the liberal nobility, i.e. the Königsberg opposition, which had espoused the bourgeois cause. [13] Among this rabble, only Roth von Schreckenstein [14] represented the old, bureaucratized, Prussian feudal nobility. *Roth von Schreckenstein!* Surviving title of a lost historical novel by the late Hildebrandt! [15] But Roth von Schreckenstein was only the feudal mounting of the bourgeois jewel. Roth von Schreckenstein, placed in the middle of a bourgeois ministry, signified, in gigantic letters: the feudality, the army, the bureaucracy of Prussia follow the newly risen star of the Prussian bourgeoisie. These magnates have put themselves at its disposal, and it has planted them in front of its throne, just as bears were planted in front of monarchs on old heraldic emblems. Roth von Schreckenstein is only supposed to be the bear of the bourgeois ministry.

On 26 June the Hansemann ministry presented itself to the

11.   A phrase from Hansemann's speech of 8 June 1847 to the United Diet, in which he opposed the granting of a loan to the king to build the Berlin-Königsberg railway.

12.   Friedrich von Kühlwetter was Minister of the Interior in Prussia from June to September 1848.

13.   The Königsberg (now Kaliningrad) Provincial Diet had been an important centre of opposition in the 1840s, under the leadership of liberal members of the local nobility, such as Count Schwerin and the brothers Auerswald. The East Prussian representatives in the United Diet of 1847 cooperated with the Rhenish liberals in their opposition to the king's policy.

14.   Ludwig, Freiherr von Roth von Schreckenstein was a Prussian general, and Minister of War from June to September 1848.

15.   A reference to the historical novel *Kuno von Schreckenstein, oder die weissagende Traumgestalt* (*Kuno von Schreckenstein, or the Prophetic Vision*) by C. Hildebrandt, Quedlinburg, 1821.

National Assembly. Its serious existence first began in July. The *June revolution* was the background of the Ministry of the Deed, just as the *February revolution* was the background of the Ministry of Mediation.[16]

As the Prussian crown exploited the bloody victory of the Croats over the Viennese bourgeoisie, so the Prussian bourgeoisie, in its fight against the people, exploited the bloody victory of the Paris bourgeoisie over the Paris proletariat. The agony of the Prussian bourgeoisie after the Austrian November[17] is *retribution* for the agony of the Prussian people after the French June. The German philistines, in their short-sighted narrow-mindedness, confused themselves with the French bourgeoisie. They had overthrown neither the throne nor feudal society, much less removed its last remnants. They did not have to maintain a society they had created. In their inborn egoism and craftiness they believed after June (as after February, indeed, ever since the beginning of the sixteenth century) that they could draw three quarters of the profit from the labour of others. They did not realize that the Austrian November lay in wait behind the French June, and Prussian December behind the Austrian November. They did not realize that if in France the bourgeoisie, having smashed the throne, only saw one enemy before it, the proletariat, the situation was reversed in Prussia. There the bourgeoisie possessed only one ally in its struggle with the Crown – the people. Not that the bourgeoisie and the people had no interests which brought them into opposition as enemies. But one *identical* interest cemented them together against a third power which oppressed both of them simultaneously.

The Hansemann ministry saw itself as a *ministry of the June revolution*. And in every Prussian town the philistines changed into 'honest republicans' in face of the 'red brigands' – although they did not cease to be honest royalists, and occasionally over-looked that their 'reds' bore – the black and white cockade.[18]

In the speech from the throne on 26 June, Hansemann made

16. The Camphausen ministry.

17. I.e. the repressive measures taken by the Habsburg authorities against the population of Vienna after the defeat of the revolution on 31 October, and the definitive assumption of power by the counter-revolution, signalized by the formation of Prince Schwarzenberg's ministry of 21 November.

18. The meaning of this sentence is unclear. Black and white were the colours of the Prussian state flag, and Marx thus seems to be alluding to the limited, 'Prussian' character of the alleged revolutionaries of the time.

short work of Camphausen's mysterious and nebulous 'monarchy on the *broadest democratic basis*'.

'*Constitutional monarchy on the basis of the bicameral system* and the joint exercise of the legislative power by both Chambers and the Crown' – this is the dry formula to which he reduced the prophetic declaration of his enthusiastic predecessor. 'Alteration where necessary of a situation which cannot be brought into consonance with the new constitution of the state, liberation of property from the fetters which restrict its *advantageous utilization* in a large part of the kingdom, reorganization of the administration of justice, reform of tax laws, in particular *removal of tax exemptions* etc.', and above all 'the *strengthening of the state power*, which is necessary for the protection of the *freedom* gained' (by the bourgeoisie) 'against reaction' (exploitation of freedom in the interests of the feudal nobility) 'and anarchy' (exploitation of freedom in the interests of the people), 'and for the *restoration of the confidence which has been disturbed*.' This was the ministerial programme, this was the programme of the ministry of the Prussian bourgeoisie, whose classical representative is Hansemann.

In the United Diet, Hansemann was the bitterest and most cynical opponent of confidence, for '*there is no room for soft-heartedness in matters of money*'. In the ministry, Hansemann proclaimed that the '*restoration of the confidence which has been disturbed*' was the main necessity, for – and this time his remarks were directed to the *people*, not, as before, to the *throne* – '*there is no room for soft-heartedness in matters of money*'.

Then it was a question of the confidence which *gives* money, now it is a question of the confidence which *makes* money; there it was *feudal* confidence, loyal confidence in God, King, and Fatherland, here it is *bourgeois* confidence, confidence in trade and traffic, in the interest on capital, in the solvency of business associates, in short, commerical confidence; not faith, hope and charity, but *credit*.

'*Restoration of the confidence which has been disturbed*': Hansemann expressed with these words the *idée fixe* of the Prussian bourgeoisie.

Credit depends on the certainty that the exploitation of wage labour by capital, of the proletariat by the bourgeoisie, and of the small citizen by the great citizen, will continue in its customary manner. Consequently, every political stirring of the proletariat, whatever its nature, even if it has occurred directly at the behest of the bourgeoisie, disturbs confidence, i.e. credit. When Hansemann spoke of the 'restoration of the confidence which has been disturbed', his real meaning, therefore, was the *suppression of any political stirring by the proletariat* and those sections of society whose interests do not directly coincide with the interests of the class which considers itself to be at the helm of the state.

Hansemann therefore placed the '*strengthening of the state power*' close beside the 'restoration of the confidence which has been disturbed'. He was mistaken only in the nature of this 'state power'. He believed he was strengthening that state power which is worthy of credit, of bourgeois confidence, but he only strengthened the state power which simply insists on confidence, and, where necessary, obtains it with grape-shot because it possesses no credit. He wanted to be niggardly with the costs of production of bourgeois rule, and as a result he burdened the bourgeoisie with the exorbitant millions which were the cost of the restoration of feudal rule in Prussia.

With the workers Hansemann was very convincing. He had, he said, just the medicine for them in his pocket. But before he could take it out, it was above all necessary to restore 'confidence'. This could be done if the working class put a stop to its political agitation and intervention in the affairs of the state, and returned to its old habits. If it followed his advice, confidence would be restored, and the secret medicine would already be effective precisely because it was no longer necessary or applicable, for in this case the malady, i.e. the disturbance of bourgeois order, would have been removed. What need is there of a medicine where there is no illness? But if the people remained obstinate, he would '*strengthen* the state power', the police, the army, the courts, the bureaucracy, he would set his dogs at the people's throat, for 'confidence' has become a 'matter of money', and:

Gentlemen! In matters of money, there is no room for soft-heartedness!

However much Hansemann might smile about this now, his programme was in fact an *honourable*, a well-meant programme.

He wanted to strengthen the state power not only against anarchy, i.e. the people, but also against the reaction, i.e. against the Crown and the feudal interests, in so far as they might attempt to oppose the money-bags, and the 'most necessary', i.e. the most modest political pretensions of the bourgeoisie.

The Ministry of the Deed, in its very composition, was a protest against this 'reaction'.

It was distinguished from all earlier Prussian ministries by the fact that its real Prime Minister was the Minister of Finance. For centuries, the Prussian state had very carefully concealed the subordination of war, internal affairs, external affairs, church and school affairs, even the royal household, faith, hope and charity, to the profane matter of the *finances*. The Ministry of the Deed made this tiresome, bourgeois truth its motto, by placing at its head Hansemann, the man whose ministerial programme, like his opposition programme, could be summed up in the following words:

Gentlemen! In matters of money, there is no room for soft-heartedness!

The monarchy had become a 'matter of money' in Prussia.

Let us now go over from the programme of the Ministry of the Deed to its deeds.

A serious attempt was made to carry out the threat of 'strengthening the state power' against 'anarchy', i.e. against the working class and all those sections of the bourgeoisie which did not stick to Hansemann's programme. It can indeed be said that with the exception of the increase of the beet tax and the brandy tax, this *reaction* against so-called *anarchy*, i.e. against the revolutionary movement, was the sole serious deed of the Ministry of the Deed.

A mass of press trials on the basis of the Landrecht, or, in default of that, the Code Pénal, numerous arrests on the same 'adequate basis' (von Auerswald's formula), the introduction of a constabulary in Berlin [19] with a proportion of one constable to two houses, police attacks on the freedom of association, letting loose the militia on proletarians who became uppish, examples of a state of siege, all these brave deeds from the Olympian days of Hansemann are still fresh in our memory. There is no need to give details.

Kühlwetter summed up this side of the endeavours of the Ministry of the Deed in the following utterance: 'A state which wishes to be absolutely free must have an absolutely immense supply of policemen as its executive power,' and Hansemann

19. The Auerswald-Hansemann ministry introduced a detachment of armed special constables in addition to the ordinary police force.

himself murmured the gloss which became a fixed system under his ministry: 'This would make an important contribution to the *establishment of confidence*, and to the *resuscitation of the trading activities which are at present languishing*.'[20]

Under the Ministry of the Deed the old Prussian police, the state prosecutor's office, the bureaucracy in general and the army were all 'strengthened' because, in Hansemann's deluded view, since they were in the *pay* of the bourgeoisie, they were therefore at its *service*. The important thing is that they were 'strengthened'.

On the other side, the attitude of the proletariat and of the bourgeois democrats can be characterized by *one* event. Because some reactionaries had mishandled certain democrats in Charlottenburg, the people stormed the Prime Minister's residence in Berlin. The Ministry of the Deed had become as popular as that. The next day Hansemann proposed a law against riots and public assemblies.[21] This is the clever way in which he intrigued against the reaction.

The real, palpable, popular action of the Ministry of the Deed was therefore purely a *police* action. In the eyes of the proletariat and the *urban* democrats, the ministry and the *Vereinbarungsversammlung*, whose majority was represented in the ministry, as well as the Prussian bourgeoisie, whose majority in turn formed the majority in the *Vereinbarungsversammlung*, constituted nothing other than a part of the *old*, and now revived, *state of policemen and officials*. Their hostility to the bourgeoisie was increased by the fact that the bourgeoisie was in power and had formed itself into an integral part of the police by means of the citizen's militia.

In the people's eyes, this was the 'conquest of March': the liberal gentlemen of the bourgeoisie also took over the functions of the *police*. A double police force, in other words!

It emerges, not from the deeds of the ministry, but from its proposal for organic laws, that it '*strengthened*' the police, the ultimate expression of the old state, and urged it on to deeds of valour, exclusively in the interests of the bourgeoisie.

20. Extracts from speeches made on 7 August to the National Assembly by Kühlwetter and Hansemann.

21. Members of a democratic club were attacked in Charlottenburg on 20 August; the next day there were demonstrations in Berlin against the residence of the Minister of the Interior (Kühlwetter) and against Auerswald's residence. On 22 August Hansemann introduced his bill forbidding unauthorized public assemblies and gatherings, passed by a large majority on 24 August.

In the Hansemann ministry's proposals on local government, juries and the militia, it is *ownership* in one form or another which determines the section of the population that is brought within the constitution. Admittedly, the most servile concessions are made in all these proposals to the power of the king, for the bourgeois ministry believed that it possessed in the king an ally who was now harmless. However, in compensation for this, the rule of capital over labour emerges all the more mercilessly.

The militia law which the *Vereinbarungsversammlung* accepted has now been turned against the bourgeoisie and has provided the legal pretext for its disarmament. Of course the bourgeoisie imagined that the militia law would only become effective after the municipal regulations had been issued and the constitution had been promulgated, i.e. after its own rule had been consolidated. The experiences the Prussian bourgeoisie has undergone in connection with the militia law should contribute towards its enlightenment; it ought to learn from this that, for the present, when it thinks it is acting against the people, it is only acting against itself.

For the people, therefore, the Hansemann ministry was summed up *in practice* in old-fashioned Prussian police measures, and *in theory* in offensive distinctions of the Belgian type between bourgeois and non-bourgeois citizens.[22]

Let us now go over to the other part of the ministerial programme, to its support of *anarchy against the reaction*.

In this direction the ministry has more pious wishes to show for itself than deeds.

The division of the Crown domains and their sale to private owners, the opening up of banking to free competition, the transformation of the Seehandlung[23] into a private body, all these measures come into the category of pious *bourgeois* wishes.

The Ministry of the Deed suffered the misfortune that all its economic attacks on the feudal party took place under the aegis of

22. The Belgian constitution of 1831 made this distinction by establishing a high property qualification for electors, reduced but not abolished by the liberal ministry of Rogier in 1848.

23. The full title of this body was the Preussische Seehandlungsgesellschaft (Prussian Company for Maritime Affairs). It was founded in 1772 as a private credit company, and was made the Prussian state's own finance house in 1820, as a means of circumventing the Diet Law of that year by providing a secret source of loans.

the *forced loan*, and that its reforming measures in general therefore appeared to the people to be merely financial expedients to fill the coffers of the strengthened 'state power'. The result was that Hansemann reaped the hatred of one party without gaining the favour of the other. And it cannot be denied that he only risked a serious attack on feudal privileges where he was confronted with the problem which touched him most closely, the *money problem*, the *money problem as interpreted by the Ministry of Finance*. It was in this narrow sense that he called out to the feudal party:

> *Gentlemen! In matters of money, there is no room for soft-heartedness!*

His positive bourgeois endeavours to combat the feudal party thus bore the same colouring as his negative measures for the '*resuscitation of trading activities*' – they appeared to be police interventions. In political economy, *police* means *treasury*. The increases in the beet tax and the brandy tax, which Hansemann pushed through the National Assembly and raised to the level of laws, enraged the money-bags 'with God for King and Fatherland' [24] in Silesia, Brandenburg, Saxony, East and West Prussia, etc. However, while these measures brought down the wrath of the industrial landowners in the old Prussian provinces, they did not stir up any less dissatisfaction amongst the bourgeois brandy manufacturers of the Rhineland, who saw that they had been placed in still more unfavourable conditions for competing with the old Prussian provinces. And, filling the cup to overflowing, they embittered the workers of the old provinces, for whom they meant, and could mean, nothing other than *an increase in the price of an essential foodstuff*. The only positive result of these measures, then, was the replenishment of the coffers of the 'strengthened state power'. And this example is sufficient, for it is the only anti-feudal deed of the Ministry of the Deed, the only deed which was *genuinely* carried out, the only bill with this intention which actually became law.

Hansemann's 'proposals' for the abolition of *tax exemptions on landed property and on certain classes of people*, as also his projected income tax, called forth fits of rage among the landed enthusiasts for 'God, King and Fatherland'. They decried him as a

---

24. The words at the mast-head of every issue of the *Kreuzzeitung*.

communist and even now the Knight of the Prussian Cross crosses himself three times whenever he hears the name of Hansemann.[25] It sounds to him like Fra Diavolo.[26] The abolition of the land tax exemption, the only significant measure proposed by a Prussian minister during the magnificent reign of the *Vereinbarungsversammlung*, came to grief through the *principled obtuseness of the Left*, for which Hansemann himself had provided the justification. Should the Left open up new sources of financial assistance for the ministry of the 'strengthened state power' before the constitution had been constructed and sworn in?

The bourgeois ministry *par excellence* was unfortunate enough to see its most radical measures paralysed by the radical members of the *Vereinbarungsversammlung*. It was so petty that its whole crusade against feudalism culminated in a *tax increase* equally hateful to all classes, while its financial wizardry resulted in the abortion of the *forced loan*: two measures which in the end only provided *subsidies for the campaign of the counter-revolution against the bourgeoisie itself.* The *feudal party*, however, had become convinced of the 'malevolent' intentions of the *bourgeois* ministry. And so Hansemann's original slogan proved its accuracy in the financial struggle of the Prussian bourgeoisie against feudalism, since in its condition of powerless unpopularity it could only exact *money which would be used against it*!

The bourgeois ministry had succeeded in arousing the equally bitter enmity of the urban proletariat, the bourgeois democrats and the feudal party; then, with the eager support of the *Vereinbarungsversammlung*, it managed to alienate even the peasant class, subjected as that class was to the yoke of feudalism. It should by no means be forgotten that for half its life this Assembly saw the Hansemann ministry as a suitable representative and that the bourgeois martyrs of today are Hansemann's henchmen of yesterday.

The proposal for emancipation from feudal burdens, laid before the Assembly by Patow on 20 June, was criticized by us at the

25. Knight of the Prussian Cross: an allusion to the title of the *Kreuzzeitung* (literally: newspaper of the cross). In November 1848 it published a number of articles attacking Hansemann as a 'leader of the extreme Left', discussed in detail by Marx in the 17 November issue of the *Neue Rheinische Zeitung* (*MECW* 7, pp. 30–4).

26. The nickname of Michele Pezza, the leader of a south Italian robber band which fought against the occupying French forces from 1798 to 1806.

time.[27] It was a most miserable concoction, combining the power-less bourgeois desire to remove feudal privileges because they were 'incompatible with the new constitution of the state' with the bourgeois fear of laying one's hands in a revolutionary fashion on any kind of property. Lamentable, cowardly, narrow-minded egoism deluded the Prussian bourgeoisie to such an extent that it pushed aside its *necessary ally* – the *peasant class*.

On 3 June 1848 deputy Hanow[28] put the motion

that all negotiations in progress for the purpose of settling relations between landowners and peasants, and for the redemption of services, be stopped at once on the application of either party, until a new law can be issued on this matter, based on fair principles.

And only *at the end of September*, four months later, under the Pfuel ministry did the *Vereinbarungsversammlung* accept the bill for the cessation of pending negotiations between landowners and peas-ants, after it had rejected all liberal amendments and retained clauses for the 'reservation of provisional assessments of current services' and the 'recovery of disputed taxes and outstanding debts'.

In *August*, if we are not mistaken, the *Vereinbarungsversammlung* decided that Nenstiel's motion for 'the *immediate abolition of compulsory labour services*' was *not urgent*.[29] How then could the peasants regard it as an urgent matter to fight for that Assembly, when it had thrown them back behind the actual situation they themselves had conquered in March?

The French bourgeoisie began with the liberation of the peasants. With the peasants it conquered Europe. The Prussian bourgeoisie was so caught up in its own most immediate, *narrowest* interests that it forfeited even this ally and made it into an instrument in the hands of the feudal counter-revolution.

The *official* history of the dissolution of the bourgeois ministry is well known.

The 'state power' was so far 'strengthened' under its protec-tive wings, the energy of the people so far suppressed, that the

27. In a number of articles in the *Neue Rheinische Zeitung*, of which 'The Bill for the Abolition of Feudal Burdens' is printed above. For the others see *MECW* 7, pp. 117–18 and 327–32 (Engels).

28. Friedrich Hanow was the director of an orphanage in Brandenburg. In 1848 he sat with the Left Centre in the Prussian National Assembly.

29. Johann Nenstiel was a Silesian merchant, who sat with the Centre in the Prus-sian Assembly. It was on 1 September 1848, in fact, that the Assembly voted that Nen-stiel's motion was not urgent and could be added to the ordinary agenda of business.

Dioscuri,[30] Kühlwetter and Hansemann, had already on 15 July to issue a warning to all the provincial presidents of the kingdom about the reactionary machinations of the administration's officials, especially the district presidents. Later on, an 'Assembly of the Nobility and the Possessors of Large Estates for Protection' – i.e. of their privileges[31] – was able to sit in Berlin alongside the *Vereinbarungsversammlung*, and finally, on 4 September 1848, a 'Communal Diet for the Maintenance of the Threatened Property Rights of Landownership', clearly handed down from the Middle Ages, was able to assemble in Oberlausitz in opposition to the so-called Berlin National Assembly.

The energy displayed by the government and the so-called National Assembly against these ever more threatening symptoms of counter-revolution found its appropriate expression in paper admonitions. The Citizen Ministry[32] only had bayonets, bullets, prisons and bailiffs for the people, *'for the restoration of the confidence which has been disturbed and the resuscitation of trading activities'*.

The Schweidnitz affair, in which the soldiery directly massacred the bourgeoisie in the militia,[33] at last awakened the National Assembly from its apathy. On 9 August it braced itself for a deed of heroism, the Stein-Schultze army order, which used the tactfulness of the Prussian officer as the ultimate instrument of compulsion. What a coercive measure! Did not the honour of the royalist forbid the officers to consider the honour of the citizen?

On 7 September, a month after the *Vereinbarungsversammlung* had adopted the Stein-Schulze army order, it decided once again that its decision had been a genuine decision and must be implemented by the ministers. Hansemann refused, and on 11 September resigned, having previously had himself appointed as a bank director at an annual salary of 6000 thalers – for *there is no room for softheartedness in matters of money*.

Finally, on 25 September, the *Vereinbarungsversammlung* gratefully accepted a wholly watered-down formula of recognition from Pfuel. In the meantime, the Stein-Schultze army order had

30. Castor and Pollux, the twin sons of Leda in Greek myth.

31. A reference to the General-Versammlung zur Wahrung der materiellen Interessen aller Klassen des preussischen Volks, also called the Junkerparlament, a congress of big landowners which met in Berlin on 18 August 1848.

32. The Auerswald-Hansemann ministry.

33. On 31 July the troops of the garrison of Schweidnitz fired on the citizens' militia, killing fourteen people.

sunk to the level of a *bad joke* owing to the concentration of masses of troops around Berlin, and the fact that the Wrangel army order ran parallel to it.[34]

It is only necessary to skim over the dates given above and the history of the Stein-Schultze army order to be convinced that this order was not the *real* reason for Hansemann's resignation. Would Hansemann, who did not shrink from recognizing the revolution, have shrunk from that paper proclamation? Would Hansemann, who managed to recapture his ministerial portfolio every time it slipped from his hands, on this occasion have left it lying on the ministerial bench for all comers out of sheer honest irritation? No, our Hansemann is no dreamer! He was simply duped, just as he represented the duped bourgeoisie as a whole. He was led to believe that the Crown would not let him go in any circumstances. He was permitted to lose the last appearance of popularity, so that he could then be sacrificed to the rancour of the backwoods junkers, while the Crown freed itself from bourgeois tutelage. Moreover, the plan of campaign agreed on with Russia and Austria required a general of the camarilla, outside the *Vereinbarungsversammlung*, at the head of the cabinet. Under the Citizen Ministry the old 'state power' had been sufficiently 'strengthened' to be able to risk this coup.

Pfuel did not come up to expectations. The victory of the Croats in Vienna made even a Brandenburg a suitable instrument.

The *Vereinbarungsversammlung* was ignominiously dispersed, hoaxed, ridiculed, humiliated and persecuted under the Brandenburg ministry, and the *people* remained *indifferent* at the decisive moment. Its *defeat* was the *defeat of the Prussian bourgeoisie*, of the *constitutionalists*, and therefore a victory for the *democratic party*, however dearly the latter had to pay for this victory.

But what of the *octroi* of a constitution?[35]

It used to be said that a 'piece of paper' would never force itself between the king and *his* people.[36] Now it is said: *only a piece*

---

34. See p. 161, n. 44.

35. The term *octroi* was used widely in nineteenth-century Europe to refer to a solemn act done by a king out of the plenitude of his power, usually, as in this case, the grant of a constitution. The constitution in question is that issued by Frederick William IV on 5 December 1848.

36. In his speech at the opening of the first United Diet (11 April 1847), Frederick William IV said that he would never allow a piece of paper to be inserted between the Lord God in heaven and this land, as a second providence, so to speak.

of paper shall force itself between the king and *his* people. Prussia's *real* constitution is the *state of siege.* The dictated French constitution contained only one paragraph 14, providing for its abolition. [37] Every paragraph of the dictated Prussian constitution is a paragraph 14.

By this constitution, the Crown grants privileges – but only to itself.

It grants itself the freedom to dissolve the Chambers for an indefinite period. It grants the ministers the freedom to issue appropriate laws in the interval (even laws on property, etc.). It grants the deputies the freedom to impeach the ministers for this, at the risk of being declared 'internal enemies' in a state of siege. Finally, it grants itself the freedom to replace this dangling 'piece of paper', when the shares of counter-revolution are buoyant in the spring, with a Christian-Germanic Magna Carta *organically* emerging from the medieval differentiation of estates, or indeed to give up the constitutional game altogether. Even in the last instance, the conservative part of the bourgeoisie would fold its hands and pray: '*The Lord giveth, the Lord taketh away, blessed be the name of the Lord.*'

The history of the Prussian bourgeoisie demonstrates, as indeed does that of the whole German bourgeoisie from March to December, that a purely *bourgeois revolution*, along with the establishment of *bourgeois hegemony* in the form of a *constitutional monarchy*, is impossible in Germany. What *is* possible is either the feudal and absolutist counter-revolution or the *social-republican revolution.*

However, we have a guarantee that the more active part of the bourgeoisie will have to awaken again from its apathy, in the shape of the *monstrous bill* with which the counter-revolution will surprise the bourgeoisie in the spring. As our friend Hansemann so sensibly said:

Gentlemen! In matters of money, there is no room for soft-heartedness!

37. Paragraph 14 of the French constitutional charter of 1815 (another *octroi*) provided that the king could issue ordinances without the consent of parliament in case of necessity.

THE MAGYAR STRUGGLE[38]

N.Rh.Z., 13 January 1849   Frederick Engels
                                   Cologne, January 1849

Whereas in Italy the revolution's first rejoinder to the counter-revolution of last summer and autumn has already begun,[39] on the Hungarian plains the last fight to suppress the movement which proceeded directly out of the February revolution is coming to an end. The new Italian movement is the prelude of the movement of 1849, the war against the Magyars is the sequel of the movement of 1848. This sequel will probably stretch out into the new drama which is silently being prepared.

The sequel is heroic, as was the first rapid kaleidoscope of the tragedy of the 1848 revolution, or the fall of Paris and Vienna, comfortingly heroic indeed after the feeble and petty interlude between June and October. The last act of 1848 is joined to the first act of 1849 by means of *terrorism*.

For the first time in the revolutionary movement of 1848, for the first time since 1793, a nation encircled by a numerically superior counter-revolution has dared to oppose craven counter-revolutionary fury with revolutionary passion, to oppose white terror with red terror. For the first time for a long while we come upon a really revolutionary character, a man who has dared to pick up the gauntlet to fight a last-ditch struggle in the name of his people, a man who for his nation is Danton and Carnot rolled into one – Louis Kossuth.[40]

The odds are terrible. The whole of Austria, headed by sixteen million fanaticized Slavs, against four million Magyars.

The *levée en masse*, the national manufacture of weapons, the *assignats*, short shrift for anyone who obstructs the revolutionary movement, the revolution in permanence, in short all the chief characteristics of the glorious year 1793 are to be seen again in

38. The political and constitutional conflict between the Magyars and the Austrian government finally developed into open war in December 1848 with the advance of Windischgrätz's troops into Hungary.

39. The Italian revolution flared up again in November 1848, with the victory of the radical republicans in Rome and the flight of the Pope to Gaeta, and repeated disturbances in Florence directed against the Grand Duke.

40. Lajos Kossuth was a Magyar nationalist and revolutionary who dominated the Hungarian Diet in 1848, and led Magyar resistance against the Habsburgs. After the defeat of Hungary in 1849 he lived in exile.

Hungary as armed, organized and galvanized by Kossuth. Vienna lacked this revolutionary organization, which must be set up within twenty-four hours so to speak, on pain of destruction, otherwise Windischgrätz would never have entered the city. We shall see whether he can penetrate into Hungary in spite of this revolutionary organization.

Let us look more closely at the struggle and the parties engaged in it.

The Austrian monarchy emerged out of the attempt to unite Germany into a single kingdom in the way that the French kings up to Louis XI had accomplished this in France. The attempt came to grief on the wretched locally oriented narrow-mindedness of both Germans and Austrians, and the correspondingly petti-fogging spirit of the House of Habsburg. Instead of the whole of Germany, the Habsburgs obtained only those south German districts which were in direct conflict with isolated Slav tribes or in which a German feudal nobility and German burghers [41] jointly ruled over subjugated Slav tribes. In both cases the Germans of each province needed support from outside. They obtained this support by associating against the Slavs, and this association was in fact the result of the unification of the provinces in question under the Habsburg sceptre.

This was the origin of German Austria. One only needs to look up in the nearest available textbook how the Austrian monarchy came into existence, how it split up and then again united, and all this in the course of the struggle against the Slavs, in order to see the correct-ness of this account.

Hungary is attached to German Austria. The Magyars waged the same struggle in Hungary as the Germans in German Austria. The Archduchy of Austria and Styria, a German wedge thrust forward between Slav barbarians, held out its hand across the Leitha [42] to the Magyar wedge, similarly thrust forward between Slav barbarians. Just as the German nobility dominated and germanized the Slav tribes to the south and north, in Bohemia, Moravia, Carinthia and Carniola, and thereby drew them into the movement of Europe as a whole, so also did the Magyar

41. 'Burghers' is a rendering of '*Bürgerschaft*' (strictly 'burgherdom'), Engels's term for the urban proprietors of pre-capitalist times.

42. A tributary of the Danube, which formed the historic boundary between the hereditary lands of the Austrian emperor (Cisleithania) and the lands of the Crown of St Stephen (Transleithania, or Hungary).

nobility dominate the Slav tribes of Croatia, Slavonia and the Carpathian lands. Their interests were the same, and their enemies were natural allies. The alliance of the Magyars and the Austrian Germans was a necessity. All that was lacking was one great event, a fierce attack on both of them, in order to make this alliance indissoluble. This development occurred with the conquest of the Byzantine empire by the Turks. The Turks threatened Hungary and in the second instance Vienna, and for centuries Hungary was riveted indissolubly to the House of Habsburg.

But the common enemies of both gradually lost their strength. The Turkish empire declined into impotence, and the Slavs lost the power to make insurrections against the Magyars and the Germans. Indeed, in the Slav lands a section of the ruling German and Magyar nobility assumed a Slav nationality, and with this the Slav nations themselves gained an interest in the preservation of a monarchy which had increasingly to protect the nobility against the developing German and Magyar bourgeoisie. The national antagonisms vanished and the House of Habsburg adopted a different policy. The same House of Habsburg that had swung itself into the throne of the German empire on the shoulders of the German burghers became, more emphatically than any other dynasty, the representative of the feudal nobility against the burghers.

It was in accordance with this policy that Austria took part in the partition of Poland. The grand Galician *starosts* and *voivods*, [43] the Potockis, Lubomirskis and Czartoryskis, betrayed Poland to Austria and became the most loyal supporters of the House of Habsburg, which, in return, guaranteed their possessions against the attacks of the lesser nobility and the burghers.

But the burghers of the towns gained more and more wealth and influence, and agriculture, as it progressed alongside industry, put the peasants in a different position in relation to the owners of the land. The movement of these bourgeois and their peasant allies against the nobility became ever more threatening. And since the movement of the peasants, who are always the bearers of national and local narrow-mindedness, is necessarily a local and national movement, the old national conflicts re-emerged at the same time.

This was the state of affairs when Metternich played his master stroke. He deprived the nobility, with the exception of the most

43. *Starost, voivod*: administrative divisions of the old kingdom of Poland and, by extension, the great nobles in charge of them.

powerful feudal barons, of all influence on the direction of state policy. He deprived the bourgeoisie of its power, while winning over the most powerful financial barons – the state of the finances compelled him to do this. In this way, resting on high feudality and high finance, as also on the bureaucracy and the army, he attained the ideal of absolute monarchy more completely than all his rivals. The bourgeoisie and peasants of each nation were restrained by the nobility of that nation and the peasants of every other nation, whilst the nobility of each nation was restrained by their fear of the bourgeoisie and peasants of their own nation. The different class interests, limited national attitudes and local prejudices, in all their complexity, held each group in a position of total reciprocal stalemate, and allowed that old rogue Metternich complete freedom of movement. The Galician massacres [44] show how far he had succeeded in inflaming the peoples against each other. In that instance, Metternich suppressed the democratic Polish movement, which had been begun in the interests of the peasants, by using the religious [45] and national fanaticism of the Ruthenian peasants themselves.

At first the year 1848 brought the most frightful confusion to Austria, by momentarily freeing all these different peoples who had hitherto been in thrall to each other through Metternich's agency. Germans, Magyars, Czechs, Poles, Moravians, [46] Slovaks, Croats, Ruthenes, Romanians, Illyrians [47] and Serbs all came into conflict, whilst the individual classes within each of these nations also fought each other. But order soon came into this confusion. The disputants divided into two huge armed camps: on one side, the side of revolution, were the Germans, Poles and Magyars; on the other side, the side of counter-revolution, were the others, i.e.

44. In February 1846 a Polish nationalist rising broke out in Galicia and Cracow. At the same time the Ruthenian peasants rose against the Polish nationalist nobles, with the encouragement and aid of the Austrian authorities, and massacred large numbers of them.

45. The Ruthenes mostly adhered to the Uniate Church, which had Orthodox rites although it recognized the supermacy of the Pope; this made for conflict with the Roman Catholic Poles.

46. There was no separate Moravian nationality in the nineteenth century; the word 'Moravian' refers here to the Czech inhabitants of Moravia.

47. There has never been an Illyrian nationality; Illyria was the area on the east coast of the Adriatic inhabited in the nineteenth century by Slovenes, Croats and Serbs. The poet Ljudevit Gaj invented the 'Illyrian nationality' in the 1830s in order to give the south Slavs a sense of unity. In view of later developments, 'Yugoslav' would be a reasonable but anachronistic translation.

all the Slavs with the exception of the Poles, plus the Romanians and the Saxons of Transylvania.

What is the origin of this line of separation according to nationality? On what facts is it based?

It corresponds to the whole previous history of the peoples in question. It is the beginning of the decision on whether all these great and small nations will live or die.

The whole previous history of Austria up to the present day is a demonstration of this, and the year 1848 has confirmed it. Amongst all the nations and nationalities of Austria there are only three bearers of progress, which have actively intervened in history and are still capable of independent life: Germans, Poles and Magyars. They are therefore revolutionary now.

The chief mission of all the other great and small nationalities and peoples is to perish in the universal revolutionary storm. They are therefore now counter-revolutionary.

As far as the Poles are concerned, we refer the reader to our articles on the Frankfurt debate on Poland.[48] In order to tame their revolutionary spirit Metternich had already appealed to the Ruthenes, a nationality distinguished from the Poles by a somewhat different dialect and in particular by the Greek religion, who had belonged to Poland from time immemorial and first learned by the agency of Metternich that the Poles were their oppressors. As if the Poles themselves had not been oppressed just as much as the Ruthenes in the old Poland, and as if Metternich were not their common oppressor under Austrian rule!

This is enough on the subject of the Poles and Ruthenes, who are in any case so clearly divided from Austria proper by history and by geographical position that we had to deal with them first of all before we could settle accounts with the rest of the jumble of peoples.

However, let us point out that the Poles are displaying great political insight and a truly revolutionary attitude in fighting, as they do now, in alliance with their old enemies the Germans and Magyars, against the pan-Slav counter-revolution. A Slav people to which freedom is dearer than Slavdom has demonstrated its viability by that very decision, and has in this way already made certain of its future.

And now we come to Austria proper.

48. *MECW* 7, pp. 337–81. The third article, which is particularly relevant in this context, is printed above.

In the early Middle Ages, Austria south of the Sudeten and Carpathian Mountains, i.e. the regions of the upper Elbe valley and the middle Danube, was a land inhabited exclusively by Slavs. These Slavs belonged in language and customs to the same stock as the Slavs of Turkey, the Serbs, Bosnians, Bulgars, Thracian and Macedonian Slavs – that of the South Slavs, so called to distinguish them from the Poles and the Russians. Apart from these related Slav tribes, the immense area which stretches from the Black Sea to the Bohemian Forest and the Tyrolese Alps was inhabited only by a few Greeks (in the south of the Balkan peninsula) and scattered Wallachians speaking a Romance language (in the lower Danube region).

From the west, the Germans thrust themselves like a wedge between this compact Slavic mass; the Magyars did the same from the east. The German element conquered the western part of Bohemia and penetrated on both sides of the Danube beyond the Leitha. The Archduchy of Austria, part of Moravia and most of Styria were all germanized, and the Czechs and Moravians were thus separated from the Carinthians and Carniolans. In the same way the Magyars entirely cleared out the Slavs from Transylvania and central Hungary as far as the German border and occupied the area, thus separating the Slovaks and some Ruthenian districts (in the north) from the Serbs, Croats and Slavonians, and subjecting all these peoples to themselves. Finally the Turks, following in the footsteps of the Byzantines, subjugated the Slavs living south of the Danube and the Save. The historical role of the South Slavs had thus come to an end for all time.

The last attempt of the South Slavs to intervene independently in history was the Hussite War, a Czech nationalist peasant war fought under a religious flag against the German nobility and German imperial suzerainty. The attempt failed and since then the Czechs have remained continuously in tow to the German Reich.

The victorious Germans and Magyars then took over the historical initiative in the Danube region. The South Slavs would have become Turkish without the Germans and, in particular, without the Magyars; a part of them actually did become Turkish, indeed Mohammedan, as the Slav Bosnians still are today. And that is a service for which the Austrian South Slavs have not paid too dearly even by exchanging their nationality for that of the Germans or Magyars.

The Turkish invasion of the fifteenth and sixteenth centuries was the second edition of the Arabian invasion of the eighth century. The victory of Charles Martel was repeated again and again under the walls of Vienna and on the Hungarian plains. The whole development of Europe was threatened again at Wahlstatt [49] by the Mongolian invasion, just as it had been at Poitiers. [50] And where it was a matter of saving this development, could the decision indeed have depended on a few long-decayed and impotent nationalities, such as the Austrian Slavs, which received their own salvation into the bargain?

As in external affairs, so too internally. The class which provided the driving force, the bearer of further development, the burgher class, was everywhere German or Magyar. The Slavs experienced difficulties in producing a national class of burghers. The South Slavs could only manage this occasionally. And with the burghers, industrial power, capital, was in German or Magyar hands, German culture advanced, and the Slavs came under German domination intellectually as well, right down as far as Croatia. The same thing happened, only later and therefore to a lesser degree, in Hungary, where the Magyars took over intellectual and commercial leadership together with the Germans. The Hungarian Germans, however, have become true Magyars in sentiment, character and customs, despite their retention of the German language. The only exceptions are the newly introduced peasant colonists, [51] the Jews, and the Saxons of Transylvania, who persist in retaining an absurd nationality in the middle of a foreign country.

And if the Magyars remained somewhat behind the German Austrians in civilization, they have made up for this brilliantly by their political activity of more recent times. From 1830 to 1848 there existed in Hungary alone more political life than in the whole of Germany, the feudal forms of the old Hungarian constitution were better exploited in the interests of democracy than the modern forms of the south German constitutions. And who stood

49. At the battle of Wahlstatt (Silesia) in 1241 the Mongols were defeated by German and Slav armies, and their westward penetration was halted.

50. The victory of Charles Martel over the Arabs took place in 732 at Poitiers.

51. German peasant colonists were introduced into Hungary in the late eighteenth century.

at the head of this movement? The Magyars. Who supported the Austrian reaction? The Croats and Slavonians.[52]

The Austrian Slavs founded a separatist movement in opposition to this Magyar movement as well as to the reawakening political movement in Germany: *pan-Slavism*.

Pan-Slavism arose in Prague and Zagreb, not in Russia or Poland. Pan-Slavism is an alliance of all the small Slav nations and nationalities of Austria and secondarily of Turkey, for the purpose of fighting against the Austrian Germans, the Magyars and ultimately the Turks. The Turks are only involved in this accidentally and can remain entirely outside our discussion, being a similarly decayed nation. Pan-Slavism is fundamentally directed against the revolutionary elements in Austria and is therefore reactionary from the outset.

Pan-Slavism immediately demonstrated this reactionary tendency with a double betrayal: it sacrificed the sole Slav nation to have played a revolutionary role so far, the Poles, to its petty nationalist narrow-mindedness, and it *sold* itself and Poland *to the Russian tsar*.

Pan-Slavism leads directly to the establishment of a Slav empire under Russian domination, from the Erzgebirge and the Carpathians to the Black, Aegean and Adriatic Seas, an empire which would include about a dozen Slav languages and chief dialects, in addition to German, Italian, Magyar, Wallachian, Turkish, Greek and Albanian. The whole thing would be held together not by the elements which have so far held together and developed Austria, but by the abstract characteristic of Slavdom and the so-called Slav language, which is of course supposed to be common to the majority of the inhabitants. But where does this Slavdom exist except in the heads of a few ideologists, where does the 'Slav language' exist except in the imagination of Herr Palacký,[53] Herr Gaj and their confederates, and, roughly speaking, in the Old Slav litany of the Russian church, which no Slav understands any more? In reality all these peoples have the most varied levels of civilization, from Bohemia's modern industry and culture, which has been developed (by Germans) to a relatively high degree,

52. Inhabitants of Slavonia, a province attached to the kingdom of Croatia. They were largely Croat in nationality.

53. František Palacký was a Czech historian and liberal politician, the proponent of 'Austro-Slavism' and the leader of the Czech national movement in the mid nineteenth century.

down to the well-nigh nomadic barbarism of the Croats and the Bulgars; these nations therefore really have the most opposed interests. In reality, the Slav language of these ten or twelve nations is composed of so many dialects, for the most part mutually incomprehensible; although these can be reduced to a number of main branches (Czech, Illyrian, Serbian and Bulgarian), they have turned into mere patois owing to the complete neglect of all literature and the crudeness of most of the peoples, who, with few exceptions, have always used a *foreign* non-Slavic language as their written language. The unity of pan-Slavism is therefore either a mere fantasy or . . . *the Russian knout*.

And which nations are supposed to head this great Slav empire? Precisely those which have been scattered and split up for a thousand years, for which elements capable of life and development had *forcibly* to be imported by other, non-Slavic peoples, and which were saved from succumbing to Turkish barbarism by the victorious arms of non-Slavic peoples. Small, powerless nationalities ranging in number from a few thousands to not quite two millions, everywhere separated from each other and robbed of their national strength! So weak have they become that, for example, the people which were most powerful and most terrifying in the Middle Ages, the Bulgars, now have a reputation in Turkey for their meekness and faint-heartedness and regard it as an honour to be called *dobre chrisztian*, good Christian! Does a single one of these peoples, Czechs and Serbs not excepted, possess a national historical tradition which lives in the minds of the people and transcends the pettiest local conflicts?

The time for pan-Slavism was the eighth and ninth centuries, when the South Slavs still controlled the whole of Hungary and Austria and threatened Byzantium. If they could not resist the German and Magyar invasion then, if they could not win their independence and form a stable empire at a time when their two enemies, the Magyars and the Germans, were tearing each other to pieces, how will they do this now, after a thousand years of subjection and de-nationalization?

There is no country in Europe that does not possess, in some remote corner, at least one remnant-people, left over from an earlier population, forced back and subjugated by the nation which later became the repository of historical development. These remnants of a nation, mercilessly crushed, as Hegel said, by the course of history, this *national refuse*, is always the fanatical representative of the counter-revolution and remains so until it is completely exterminated or de-nationalized, as its whole existence is in itself a protest against a great historical revolution.

In Scotland, for example, the Gaels, supporters of the Stuarts from 1640 to 1745.

In France the Bretons, supporters of the Bourbons from 1792 to 1800.

In Spain the Basques, supporters of Don Carlos.

In Austria the pan-Slav South Slavs, who are nothing more than the *national refuse* of a thousand years of immensely confused development. It is the most natural thing in the world that this national refuse, itself as entangled as the development which brought it into existence, sees its salvation solely in a reversal of the entire development of Europe, which according to it must proceed not from west to east but from east to west, and that its weapon of liberation, its unifying bond, is the *Russian knout*.

The South Slavs had already shown their reactionary character before 1848. The year of revolution itself exposed this quite openly.

Who made the Austrian revolution when the February storm broke loose? Vienna or Prague? Budapest or Zagreb? The Germans and Magyars or the Slavs?

It is true that a small democratic party existed among the more educated South Slavs, who, while not wishing to give up their nationality, nevertheless wished to place it at the disposal of freedom. Owing to this illusion, the movement succeeded in awakening the sympathies of the democrats of western Europe as well, sympathies which were entirely justified as long as the Slav democrats fought together with them against the common foe; but the illusion was destroyed by the bombardment of Prague. From this event onwards, all the South Slav peoples placed themselves at the disposal of the Austrian reaction, following the precedent set by the Croats. Those leaders of the South Slav movement who are still spinning yarns about national equality and a democratic Austria are either blockheaded dreamers, as for example many of the journalists, or scoundrels like Jellačić. Their democratic assurances mean no more than the democratic assurances of the official Austrian counter-revolution. Suffice it to say that in practice the re-establishment of South Slav nationality begins with the most furious brutality against the Austrian and Magyar revolutions, with the first of many great services to be performed for the Russian tsar.

Apart from the high nobility, the bureaucracy and the soldiery, the Austrian camarilla only found support among the Slavs. The Slavs caused the fall of Italy, the Slavs stormed Vienna, and it is the Slavs who are now falling upon the Magyars from all sides. They are led by two peoples: the Czechs, under Palacký, wielding the pen; and the Croats, under Jellačić, wielding the sword.

This is the thanks for the general sympathy displayed by the German democratic press in June for the Czech democrats when they were shot down with grape-shot by the same man, Windischgrätz, who is now their hero.

To sum up: in Austria, leaving aside the Poles and the Italians, the Germans and the Magyars have assumed the historical initiative, in the year 1848 as in the previous thousand years. They represent the *revolution*.

The South Slavs, who have trailed behind the Germans and Magyars for a thousand years, only rose up to establish their national independence in 1848 in order to suppress the German-Magyar revolution at the same time. They represent the *counter-revolution*. Two similarly decayed nations, entirely lacking in active historical forces, have attached themselves to the South Slavs: the Saxons and Romanians of Transylvania.

The House of Habsburg, which founded its strength on the union of Germans and Magyars in the fight against the South Slavs, is now eking out the last moments of its existence by uniting the South Slavs in the fight against the Germans and Magyars.

That is the political side of the question. Now for the military side.

The area exclusively inhabited by Magyars does not even comprise a third of Hungary and Transylvania taken together. From Bratislava onwards, to the north of the Danube and the Tisza, up to the crest of the Carpathians, there live several million Slovaks and a number of Ruthenes. In the south, between the Save, the Danube and the Drave, there live Croats and Slavonians; further east, along the Danube, there is a Serbian colony of over half a million. These two Slav belts are joined together by the Wallachians and Saxons of Transylvania.

The Magyars are therefore surrounded on three sides by natural enemies. The Slovaks who hold the mountain passes would be dangerous opponents, in view of the terrain, which is perfect for partisan warfare, if they were less lethargic in character.

In the north, then, the Magyars have merely to fend off the attacks of armies which have broken through from Galicia and Moravia. However, in the east the Romanians and Saxons rose up *en masse* and joined the local Austrian army corps. Their position is excellent, partly owing to the mountainous nature of the country, partly because they control most of the towns and fortresses.

Finally, in the south, the Serbs of the Banat, supported by German colonists, Wallachians and, like the Romanians, by an Austrian army corps, are covered by the immense morass of Alibunar and are almost unassailable.

The Croats are covered by the Drave and the Danube, and as they have at their disposal a strong Austrian army with all its resources, they had already pushed forward onto Magyar territory before October [54] and they are now holding their line of defence on the lower Drave with ease.

From the fourth side, from Austria, Windischgrätz and Jellačić are advancing in close columns. The Magyars are surrounded on all sides, surrounded by an enemy with an enormous numerical superiority.

The struggle is reminiscent of the struggle against France in the year 1793. There is only the difference that the thinly populated and only semi-civilized land of the Magyars has far fewer resources than the French republic had in those days.

Weapons and munitions manufactured in Hungary must necessarily be of very bad quality; in particular it is impossible to manufacture artillery quickly. The country is much smaller than France, and every inch of land lost is a correspondingly greater blow. The Magyars have nothing left but their revolutionary enthusiasm, their courage, and the energetic, fast moving organization Kossuth was able to give them.

Nevertheless, Austria has not yet won.

If we do not beat the emperor's troops on the Leitha, we shall beat them on the Répce; if not on the Répce, we shall beat them at Pest; if not at Pest, we shall beat them on the Tisza – but, at all events, we shall beat them. [55]

54. Jellačić invaded Hungary on 11 September 1848, acting on his own initiative, although the Habsburg court did not disavow him. Croat forces were advancing on Budapest in October when they were recalled to take part in the siege of Vienna.

55. Quoted from Kossuth's speech on 9 November 1848 to the Hungarian parliament.

So said Kossuth, and he is doing his best to keep his word. Even with the fall of Budapest[56] the Magyars still have the huge heath of lower Hungary, an area made, as it were, for partisan warfare on horseback, which offers numerous almost impregnable positions between the swamps where the Magyars can establish themselves. And, since they almost all have mounts, they possess all the qualifications for waging such a war. If the imperial army ventures into this desolate district, it will have to import all its provisions from Galicia or Austria, because it will find nothing there, absolutely nothing, and it cannot be foreseen how it will maintain itself. It will accomplish nothing in close formation, and if it is divided up into flying squads it will be lost. Its unwieldiness would irretrievably deliver it into the hands of the fast-moving bands of Magyar horsemen, and even in case of victory there would be no possibility of pursuit; while each imperial straggler would meet with the deathly enmity of every peasant and every shepherd. The war in these steppes would be similar to the Algerian war,[57] and the ungainly Austrian army would need years to bring it to an end. And the Magyars will be saved if they only hold out for a couple of months.

The Magyar cause therefore stands far better than the paid enthusiasts for black and yellow[58] would have us believe. They have not yet been defeated. However, if they do fall, they fall with honour as the last heroes of the 1848 revolution, and only for a short time. Then the Slav counter-revolution, with all its barbarism, will momentarily overwhelm the Austrian monarchy and the camarilla will see what kind of ally it has. But at the first victorious uprising of the French proletariat, which Louis Napoleon is doing his best to conjure up, the Austrian Germans and the Magyars will gain their freedom and take a bloody revenge on the Slav barbarians. The general war which will then break out will scatter this Slav Sonderbund,[59] and annihilate all these small pigheaded nations even to their very names.

The next world war will not only cause reactionary classes and

56. On 5 January 1849.

57. The French conquest of Algeria occupied in all a period of seventeen years, from the first expedition in 1830 to the final surrender in 1847.

58. The Austrian imperial colours.

59. Literally, 'separate league', from the alliance formed by the seven Catholic cantons of Switzerland in defence of the Jesuits and clerical privilege against the centralizing, democratic and anti-clerical tendencies of the majority. It was defeated in the Sonderbund War of November 1847.

dynasties to disappear from the face of the earth, but also entire reactionary peoples. And that too is an advance.

DEMOCRATIC PAN-SLAVISM

I *N.Rh.Z.*, 15 February 1849   Frederick Engels
                                                                 Cologne, 14 February

We have pointed out often enough that the sweet dreams which came to the surface after the February and March revolutions, the fantasies of universal brotherhood between peoples, of a European federal republic and of everlasting world peace, were fundamentally nothing more than a cover for the helplessness and the inactivity of the spokesmen of that time. They did not see, or did not want to see, what had to be done to make the revolution secure; they could not implement, or did not want to implement any really revolutionary measures. The narrowness of one side, the counter-revolutionary intrigues of the other side, produced a tacit agreement that the people should merely be given sentimental phrases instead of revolutionary deeds. The magniloquent scoundrel Lamartine was the classic *hero* of this epoch of betrayal of the people concealed beneath the flowers of poetry and the frippery of rhetoric.

The peoples which have passed through the revolution know how dearly they have had to pay for the fact that at that time, in their generosity, they believed the fine words and the haughty assurances of their spokesmen. Instead of the securing of the revolution, they were everywhere given the undermining of the revolution by reactionary parliaments; instead of the implementation of the promises given on the barricades, they were given the counter-revolutions of Naples, Paris, Vienna and Berlin, the fall of Milan and the war against Hungary; instead of the brotherhood of peoples, they were given the renewal of the Holy Alliance on the broadest basis under the patronage of England and Russia. And the same men who were in April and May still applauding the bombastic phrases of the epoch, now only redden when they think of how they let themselves be cheated by idiots and scoundrels.

We have learnt through painful experience that the 'European brotherhood of peoples' will come to pass not through mere phrases and pious wishes but only as a result of thorough revolutions and bloody struggles; that it is not a matter of fraternization between all European peoples underneath a republican flag, but of the alliance of revolutionary peoples against counter-revolutionary peoples, an alliance which does not happen on *paper* but on the *field of battle*.

All over western Europe these bitter but necessary experiences have robbed Lamartine's phrases of all credit. In the east however there still exist parties, supposedly democratic, revolutionary parties, which never weary of echoing these phrases and sentimentalities and preaching the gospel of the European brotherhood of peoples.

These parties (leaving out of consideration certain ignorant German enthusiasts such as Herr A. Ruge, etc.) are the *democratic pan-Slavists* of the various Slav peoples.

The programme of democratic pan-Slavism lies before us in a pamphlet entitled: '*Proclamation to the Slavs*. By a Russian patriot, Michael Bakunin, Member of the Slav Congress in Prague' (Köthen, 1848).

Bakunin is our friend. That will not prevent us from subjecting his pamphlet to criticism.

Listen how, right at the beginning of his proclamation, Bakunin harks back to the illusions of March and April last:

> The revolution's very first sign of life was a cry of hatred against the old oppression, a cry of sympathy and love for all oppressed nationalities. The peoples . . . finally felt the shame with which the old diplomacy had laden mankind, and recognized that the welfare of nations will never be secure as long as a single people in Europe lives under oppression . . . Away with the oppressors, was the cry which resounded as from a single mouth. Hail to the oppressed, the Poles, the Italians and all! No more wars of conquest, but just the one last war, fought out to the end, the good fight of the revolution for the final liberation of all peoples! Down with the artificial barriers which have been forcibly erected by congresses of despots in accordance with so-called historical, geographical, commercial and strategic necessities! Let there be no other boundaries but those which correspond to nature, boundaries drawn justly and in a democratic sense, boundaries which the sovereign will of the peoples itself prescribes on the basis of its national qualities. This is the call which issues forth from all peoples (pp. 6–7).

Already in this passage we meet again all the visionary enthusiasm of the first months after the revolution. There is no mention here of the obstacles which are really in the way of such a general liberation, of the utterly different levels of civilization of the

individual peoples and the equally different political needs conditioned by those levels. The word 'freedom' replaces all of this. Of
reality itself there is either no discussion at all, or, in so far as it
does come into consideration, it is portrayed as something absolutely
abominable, the arbitrary creation of 'congresses of despots' and
'diplomats'. The supposed will of the people confronts this bad reality with its categorical imperative, with its absolute demand for plain
and simple 'freedom'.

We have seen who was the stronger. The supposed will of the
people was duped so outrageously precisely because it accepted such
an imaginary abstraction from the relations which actually existed at
the time.

Out of the plenitude of its own power, the revolution proclaimed the
dissolution of the despotic states, the dissolution of the Prussian kingdom . . . Austria . . . the Turkish empire . . . finally the dissolution of
the last consolation of the despots, the Russian empire . . . and as the
ultimate aim of all this – the general federation of European republics
(p. 8).

In actual fact it must appear peculiar to us here in the west that
all these fine plans, after the failure of the *first* attempt to carry them
out, can still be counted as something of great merit. That was indeed
precisely the worst feature of the revolution, that it 'proclaimed
the dissolution of the despotic states out of the plenitude of its own
power', but at the same time did not move a muscle 'out of the plenitude of its own power' to execute its decree.

The Slav Congress was called at that time. It completely adopted
the standpoint of these illusions. Listen to this:

Keenly feeling the common bond of history (?) and blood, we swear never
to let our destinies be separated again. Execrating politics, of which we have
so long been the victims, *we ourselves stood up* for our right to complete
independence and *made the vow* that this would henceforth be *common to all
Slav peoples*. We recognized the independence of Bohemia and Moravia . . .
we held out our fraternal hand to the German people, to democratic Germany.
In the name of those of us who lived in Hungary, we offered a fraternal
alliance . . . to the Magyars, the furious foes of our race. In our alliance of
liberation we also did not forget those of our brothers who sigh beneath the
Turkish yoke. We solemnly condemned that criminal policy which thrice tore
Poland apart . . . All this we said, and we demanded with all the democrats of
all peoples (?): liberty, equality and the fraternity of all nations (p. 10).

Democratic pan-Slavism is still making these demands today:

Then we felt certain of our cause ... *justice* and *humanity* were entirely on our side, and on the side of our foes was nothing but illegality and barbarism. These were *no empty dreams* which we devoted ourselves to, but rather the ideas of the *only true and necessary policy*, the policy of *revolution*.

'Justice', 'humanity', 'liberty', 'equality', 'fraternity', 'independence' – so far we have found nothing more in the pan-Slav manifesto than these more or less moral categories, which admittedly sound very fine, but *prove absolutely nothing* in historical and political matters. 'Justice', 'humanity', 'liberty', etc., may demand this or that a thousand times over; but if the cause is an impossible one, nothing will happen and it will remain, despite everything, 'an empty dream'. The pan-Slavists could have learned something about their illusions from the role the mass of the Slavs has played since the Prague Congress, they could have realized that there is nothing to be achieved against iron reality with all the pious wishes and beautiful dreams in the world, and that their policy was as little a 'policy of revolution' as that of the French Second Republic. And yet they come to us now, in January 1849, with the same old phrases about whose content western Europe was disillusioned by a most bloody counter-revolution!

Just one word about 'the universal brotherhood of peoples' and the drawing of 'boundaries, which the sovereign will of the peoples itself prescribes on the basis of its national qualities'. The United States and Mexico are two republics; the people are sovereign in both of them.

How did it happen that a war broke out over Texas [60] between these two republics, which are supposed to be 'united' and 'federated' according to the *moral theory*, how did it happen that the 'sovereign will' of the American people, supported by the courage of the American volunteers, moved the naturally drawn boundaries some hundreds of miles further south for reasons of 'geographical, commercial and strategic necessity'? And will Bakunin reproach the Americans with this 'war of conquest', which admittedly gives a hard knock to his theory based on

60. The war of 1845–7 between Mexico and the United States, after which large areas of Mexico were ceded to the U.S. (February 1848).

'justice and humanity', but which was waged simply and solely in the interests of civilization? Or is it perhaps a misfortune that magnificent California was snatched from the lazy Mexicans, who did not know what to do with it? Or that the energetic Yankees are increasing the means of circulation by the rapid exploitation of the Californian gold mines, have concentrated a thick population and extensive commerce on the most suitable stretch of the Pacific coast within a few years, are building big cities, opening steamship communications, laying a railway from New York to San Francisco, opening the Pacific for the first time to actual civilization, and are about to give world trade a new direction for the third time in history? The 'independence' of a few Spanish Californians and Texans may suffer by this, 'justice' and other moral principles may be infringed here and there; but what does that matter against such world-historical events?

Let us remark in passing that the editors of the *Neue Rheinische Zeitung* were fighting long before the revolution against this theory of the universal brotherhood of peoples, which is aimed at nothing but a random fraternization without regard for the historical position or the social level of development of the individual peoples, and that we had indeed to fight against our best friends, the English and French democrats. The proofs of this are contained in the English, French and Belgian democratic newspapers of that time. [61]

As far as pan-Slavism specifically is concerned, we have developed the point in Number 194 of, the *Neue Rheinische Zeitung* [62] that, leaving aside the well meant self-deceptions of the democratic pan-Slavists, it has in reality no other aim than to give a point of support to the fragmented Austrian Slavs, who are at present dependent on the Germans and the Magyars for their history, literature, politics, commerce and industry. On one side this was to be provided by Russia, on the other side by the Austrian monarchy, dominated by its Slav majority and dependent on Russia. We have explained how such small nations, dragged along for centuries by history against their will, must necessarily be counter-revolutionary, and how their whole position in the 1848 revolution was in truth counter-revolutionary. In dealing with this manifesto of democratic pan-Slavism, which

61. See for example Marx and Engels's 'Speeches on Poland', above, also *MECW* 6, pp. 3–14 and 409–11 (by Engels), and 450–65.
62. See 'The Magyar Struggle', above.

demands independence for all Slavs without differentiation, we must return to this point.

By the way, one must admit that the political romanticism and sentimentality of the democrats at the Slav Congress was highly excusable. With the exception of the Poles – and the Poles are not pan-Slavists, for obvious reasons – they all belong to nationalities which are either, as in the case of the South Slavs, necessarily counter-revolutionary owing to their whole historical position, or, as in the case of the Russians, still far removed from a revolution and therefore at least at present still counter-revolutionary. These parties, having become democratic through receiving an education abroad, endeavoured to harmonize their democratic convictions with their feeling of nationalism, which is very pronounced among the Slavs, as is well known; and since the positive world, the real situation of their country, offered no points of contact for this reconciliation, or only simulated ones, there was nothing left to them but the other-worldly 'kingdom of the dream',[63] the realm of pious wishes, the politics of delirium. How wonderful it would be, if Croats, Pandours[64] and Cossacks formed the vanguard of European democracy, if the ambassador of the Siberian republic could present his credentials in Paris! A pleasant prospect indeed; but the most enthusiastic pan-Slavist will not demand that European democracy should await its realization – and at present it is precisely the nations whose particular independence is demanded by the manifesto that are the particular enemies of democracy.

We repeat: apart from the Poles, the Russians, and at most the Slavs of Turkey, no Slav people has a future, for the simple reason that all the other Slavs lack the primary historical, geographical, political and industrial conditions for a viable independence.

Peoples which have never had a history of their own, which come under foreign domination the moment they have achieved the first, crudest level of civilization, or are *forced onto* the first level of civilization by the yoke of the foreigner, have no capacity for survival and will never be able to attain any kind of independence.

And that has been the fate of the Austrian Slavs. The Czechs,

63. H. Heine, 'Germany: A Winter's Tale,' *The Poetry and Prose of Heinrich Heine*, ed. F. Ewen, ch. 7.

64. A force of brutal soldiery of South Slav origin, raised and enrolled under the Habsburg banner in the mid eighteenth century.

amongst whom we ourselves should like to count the Moravians and the Slovaks, although they are linguistically and historically distinct, never had a history. Since Charlemagne Bohemia has been bound to Germany. The Czech nation emancipated itself for one moment and formed the Great Moravian Empire, but was immediately subjugated again and tossed back and forth like a football for five hundred years between Germany, Hungary and Poland. Then Bohemia and Moravia became definitively attached to Germany, and the Slovak areas remained with Hungary. Is this 'nation', with absolutely no historical existence, actually making a claim for independence?

It is the same with the so-called South Slavs proper. Where is the history of the Illyrian Slovenes, the Dalmatians,[65] the Croats and the Schokazen?[66] They lost the last trace of political independence after the eleventh century, and since then have been partly under German, partly under Venetian and partly under Magyar rule. Is it really intended to botch together a powerful, independent and viable nation out of these tattered rags?

But there is worse to come. If the Austrian Slavs formed a compact mass like the Poles, Magyars or Italians, if they were in a position to gather from twelve to twenty million people in a state, their claims would have a serious character despite everything. But the actual situation is the precise opposite of this. The Germans and the Magyars have inserted themselves between the Slavs like a broad wedge up to the outermost ends of the Carpathians, and separated the Czechs, Moravians and Slovaks from the South Slavs by a zone some sixty to eighty miles wide. Five and a half million Slavs live to the north of this zone; five and a half million Slavs live to the south of it. They are divided by a compact mass of ten to eleven million Germans and Magyars, who are allies by history and by necessity.

But why shouldn't the five and a half million Czechs, Moravians and Slovaks be able to form a state? And the five and a half million South Slavs, together with the Turkish Slavs?

Inspect the distribution of the Czechs and their linguistically related neighbours on the first linguistic map you find. They are inserted into Germany like a wedge, but they are gnawed at and

65. Inhabitants of the Austrian crownland of Dalmatia, of mainly Croat nationality, with some Serbs in the south.

66. A small South Slav national group which in the seventeenth century fled from the advance of the Turks into Bosnia to settle in southern Hungary.

forced back on both sides by the German element. A third of Bohemia speaks German; there are seventeen Germans to every twenty-four Czechs in Bohemia. And it is precisely the Czechs who are to form the nucleus of the intended Slav state; for the Moravians are just as heavily mixed with Germans, the Slovaks with Germans and Magyars, and moreover they are entirely demoralized as far as nationality is concerned. What a Slav state, which would be ultimately *dominated by the German bourgeoisie of the towns*!

The same is true of the South Slavs. The Slovenes and Croats cut off Germany and Hungary from the Adriatic; and Germany and Hungary *cannot* allow themselves to be cut off from the Adriatic, owing to 'geographical and commercial necessities' which are admittedly no obstacle for Bakunin's imagination, but which exist all the same and are just as much matters of life and death for Germany and Hungary as the Baltic coast from Danzig to Riga is for Poland. And where the existence of great nations and the free development of their resources is at stake, nothing will be decided by such sentimental factors as deference to a few dispersed Germans or Slavs. Not to mention the fact that these South Slavs are similarly mixed up with German, Magyar and Italian elements, that here too the projected South Slav state breaks up into disconnected fragments with the first glance at the language map, and that, at best, the whole state would be delivered into the hands of the Italian bourgeoisie of Trieste, Fiume and Zara, and the German bourgeoisie of Agram, Laibach, Karlstadt, Semlin, Pancsova and Weisskirchen.

But couldn't the Austrian South Slavs link up with the Serbs, Bosniaks,[67] Morlaks[68] and Bulgars? Certainly, if, apart from the difficulties already mentioned, the age-old hatred of the people of the Austrian borderlands for the Turkish Slavs beyond the Save and the Unna did not exist; but these people have related to each other for centuries as rogues and bandits, and, despite all their racial affinities, their mutual hatred is infinitely greater than that between Slavs and Magyars.

In actuality the Germans and Magyars would be in an *extremely* pleasant situation if the Austrian Slavs were put in possession of their so-called 'rights'. An independent Bohemian-Moravian

---

67. The Mohammedan inhabitants of Bosnia, usually Serb in nationality.

68. A national group descended from the old romanized population of Illyria, Serb in language, and living in north Dalmatia and south Istria.

state wedged in between Silesia and Austria, Austria and Styria cut off by the 'South Slav republic' from the Adriatic and the Mediterranean, their natural trade outlets, eastern Germany torn to pieces like a loaf gnawed by rats! And all this would be out of gratitude for the pains the Germans have taken to civilize the obstinate Czechs and Slovenes, and to introduce amongst them trade, industry, a tolerable agriculture and education!

But it is precisely this yoke forced upon the Slavs under the pretext of civilization which constitutes one of the greatest crimes committed by the Germans, as also by the Magyars! Listen to this:

> You were right to boil with anger, and right to pant for revenge against that *execrable German policy*, which was directed at nothing other than your ruin, which *has enslaved you for centuries* (p. 5) ... The Magyars, the *furious enemies* of our race, who, though they numbered hardly four millions, had the presumption to impose their yoke on eight million Slavs (p. 9) ...
>
> What the Magyars have done against our Slav brothers, what crimes they have committed against our nationality, how they have trampled our language and our independence underfoot, all this I know (p.30).

What then are the immense and terrible crimes of the Germans and the Magyars against the Slav nation? We are not referring here to the partition of Poland, which does not belong in this context, but to the 'centuries of injustice' that are supposed to have been perpetrated against the Slavs.

In the north the Germans have conquered back from the Slavs the region between the Elbe and the Warta, which was previously German and later became Slav; this conquest was conditioned by the 'geographical and strategic necessities' which emerged from the division of the Carolingian empire. These Slav districts have been completely germanized; the thing is done and cannot be redressed, even if the pan-Slavists were to rediscover the lost languages of the Sorbs, Wends and Obotrians [69] and impose them on the people of Leipzig, Berlin and Stettin. Up to now it has not been denied that this conquest was in the interests of civilization.

In the south the Germans found that the Slav peoples had

69. Three West Slav peoples, which settled between the Elbe and the Oder after the fifth century, and were later forcibly germanized, with the partial exception of the Sorbs of Lausitz, who still survive in eastern Germany as a distinct national group.

already been scattered. The non-Slav Avars [70] had taken care of this when they occupied the region later seized by the Magyars. The Germans made these Slavs their tributaries and waged a number of wars against them. They also fought against the Avars and the Magyars, and deprived them of the whole country between the Ems and the Leitha. Whereas here they germanized forcibly, the germanization of the Slav lands proceeded on a much more peaceful footing, through migration and the influence of the more developed nation on the undeveloped nation. German industry, German trade, German education automatically brought the German language into the country. As far as 'oppression' is concerned, the Slavs were no more oppressed by the Germans than the mass of the Germans themselves were.

If we look at Hungary, we find that there are many Germans there too, yet the Magyars have never had cause to complain of an 'execrable German policy', even though there were 'hardly four million' of them. And if the 'eight million Slavs' had to allow the four million Magyars to impose their yoke on them for *eight centuries*, this alone is sufficient proof that the few Magyars had more vitality and energy than the many Slavs.

But of course the greatest 'crime' of the Germans and the Magyars was that they prevented these twelve million Slavs from becoming Turkish! What would have happened to these small and fragmented nationalities, which have played such a wretched role in history, if the Magyars and Germans had not held them together and led them against the armies of Mohammed and Suleiman, if their so-called 'oppressors' had not fought the decisive battles in defence of these weak semi-nations? Does not the fate of the 'twelve million Slavs, Wallachians and Greeks' who have been 'trodden underfoot by seven hundred thousand Ottomans' (p. 8) right up to the present day speak loudly enough?

And finally was it not a 'crime', was it not an 'execrable policy' that, at the time when great monarchies were a 'historical necessity' throughout Europe, the Germans and the Magyars united all these small, crippled, powerless nationalities into a great empire and enabled them to take part in an historical development which would have been entirely foreign to them had they been left to themselves? Naturally, that kind of thing cannot be

70. A Tartar people which settled in the Balkans from the sixth to the ninth century. They were finally defeated by Germans, Slavs, Turks and Magyars, and disappeared from the historical record.

accomplished without forcibly crushing the occasional sensitive specimen of national plant life. But nothing is accomplished in history without force and pitiless ruthlessness, and what indeed would have happened to history if Alexander, Caesar and Napoleon had had the same quality of compassion now appealed to by pan-Slavism on behalf of its decayed clients! And are the Persians, the Celts and the Germanic Christians [71] not worth the Czechs, the Oguliner [72] and the Sereschaner. [73]

Now, however, as a result of the immense progress in industry, trade and communications, political centralization has become a far more urgent need than it was in the fifteenth and sixteenth centuries. Anything which has yet to be centralized is being centralized now. And *now* the pan-Slavists come to us and demand that we should let these half-germanized Slavs 'go free', that we should abolish a centralization which is forced on these Slavs by all their material interests!

It appears, in short, that these 'crimes' of the Germans and the Magyars against the Slavs in question are some of the best and most commendable of the deeds we and the Magyar people can pride ourselves on in the course of our history.

By the way, we should add that the Magyars have been too forbearing and too weak towards the arrogant Croats, especially since the revolution. It is notorious that Kossuth conceded everything possible to them, except that their deputies might speak Croat at the Diet. And this forbearance towards a naturally counter-revolutionary nation is the only thing the Magyars can be reproached with.

II *N.Rh.Z.*, 16 February 1849   Frederick Engels
                                                     Cologne, 15 February

We finished yesterday by showing that the Austrian Slavs have never had a history of their own, that they are dependent on the

---

71. *Christliche Germanen*, a simultaneous reference to the defeat of Prussian resistance by Napoleon in the 1800s, and the insistence of the romantic reaction, and Frederick William IV in particular, on the 'Christian' and 'Germanic' character of Prussia.

72. Oguliner: the members of a detachment of infantry on the military border of Croatia, created in 1746, and stationed at Ogulin.

73. Sereschaner: the members of a special cavalry detachment attached to Austrian border regiments from 1700 onwards for purposes of reconnaissance and minor skirmishes with the Turks.

Germans and Magyars for their history, literature, politics, commerce and industry, that they are already partially germanized, magyarized or italianized, that if they set up independent states those states will be ruled not by them but by the German and Italian bourgeoisie of their towns, and finally, that neither Hungary nor Germany can tolerate the forcible detachment and independent establishment of such small and unviable intermediate states.

However, all that would not in itself be decisive. If the Slavs had begun a *new revolutionary history* at any time within the period of their oppression, they would have proved their capacity for independent existence by that very act. The revolution would have had an interest in their liberation from that moment onwards, and the particular interest of the Germans and Magyars would vanish in face of the greater interest of the European revolution.

But that did not happen at any time. The Slavs – let us recall again that we exclude the Poles from all this – were always precisely the *chief tools of the counter-revolutionaries*. Being oppressed at home, they were the *oppressors of all revolutionary nations* abroad, as far as the influence of the Slavs extended.

Let no one reply to this that we are acting in the interest of German nationalist prejudices. There are proofs available in German, French, Belgian and English newspapers that it was precisely the editors of the *Neue Rheinische Zeitung* who were attacking all German nationalist stupidity in the most decisive fashion long *before* the revolution.[74] Admittedly they did not, like some other people, scold the Germans in a wildly exaggerated way and on the basis of mere hearsay; instead of this they mercilessly laid bare, with historical proofs, the shabby role Germany has played in history thanks to its nobility and its burghers, and, of course, to its stunted industrial development; they have always recognized the justified position of the great historical nations of the west, of the English and the French, in contrast to the backward Germans. But precisely on account of that, we must be permitted not to share the enthusiastic illusions of the Slavs and to judge other peoples just as strictly as we have judged our own nation.

It has always been said that the Germans were the shock troops of despotism throughout Europe. We are far from denying the

74. See 'Speeches on Poland', above; also *MECW* 6, pp. 15–33, 235–73, 540–4 and 553–5 (all by Engels).

shameful role of the Germans in the shameful wars against the French revolution from 1792 to 1815, in the oppression of Italy since 1815 and of Poland since 1772; but who stood behind the Germans, who used them as their mercenaries or their vanguard? England and Russia. Indeed, the Russians have boasted up to the present day that they decided the overthrow of Napoleon with their innumerable armies, and this of course is largely correct. One thing at least is certain, and that is that three quarters of the armies which by their numerical superiority forced Napoleon back from the Oder to Paris were composed of Slavs, either Russian or Austrian.

And what about the oppression of the Italians and Poles by the Germans? A wholly Slav and a half Slav power rivalled each other in partitioning Poland; the armies which overwhelmed Kościuszko [75] contained a majority of *Slavs*; the armies of Diebitsch and Pask-ievitch [76] were exclusively *Slav* armies. In Italy, the *tedeschi* [77] have for long years borne alone the disgrace of counting as oppressors; but, once again, what was the composition of the armies which could best be used for the suppression of the Italian revolutions and whose brutalities could be laid at the door of the Germans? They were composed of Slavs. Go to Italy and ask who suppressed the revolution in Milan. They will no longer say '*i tedeschi*' – since the *tedeschi* made a revolution in Vienna they are not hated any more – but rather '*i croati*'. That is how the Italians now sum up the whole Austrian army, i.e. everything for which they have the deepest hatred: *i croati*.

And yet these accusations would be irrelevant and unjustified if the Slavs had taken a serious part anywhere in the movement of 1848, if they had hastened to enter the ranks of the revolutionary peoples. One single courageous attempt at a democratic revolu-tion, even if it is stifled, will expunge whole centuries of infamy and cowardice from the memory of other peoples and will instantly rehabilitate a nation, however deeply it may have been despised. The Germans discovered that last year. But while the French, the

75. Tadeusz Kośçiuszko was a Polish general and patriot who took part in the war of 1791–2 and led the insurrection of 1794.

76. Count Hans Diebitsch and Ivan Fedorovich Paskievitch were both Russian field-marshals. Diebitsch commanded the war against the Poles in 1831, and on his death was replaced by Paskievitch, who served as viceroy of Poland from 1832 to 1856. In 1849 Paskievitch commanded the Russian troops against Hungary.

77. Germans.

Germans, the Italians, the Poles and the Magyars were raising the banner of revolution, the Slavs fell in as *one* man under the banner of *counter-revolution*. In the van the South Slavs, who had already defended their own particular counter-revolutionary wishes against the Magyars for many years; then the Czechs; and behind them, armed for battle and ready to appear on the field at the decisive moment . . . the Russians.

It is known that in Italy the Magyar hussars went over in great numbers to the Italians, just as in Hungary whole Italian battalions placed themselves at the disposal of the Magyar revolutionary government and are still fighting under the Magyar flag; it is known that in Vienna the German regiments sided with the people, and were absolutely unreliable even in Galicia; it is known that Austrian and non-Austrian Poles fought in their masses in Italy, in Vienna and in Hungary against the Austrian armies, and are still fighting in the Carpathians; but has anyone ever heard of Czech or South Slav troops rebelling against the black and yellow flag?

On the contrary, so far we know only that an Austria shaken to its very foundation was kept in being and momentarily secured by the enthusiasm of the Slavs for black and yellow; that it was precisely the Croats, Slovenes, Dalmatians, Czechs, Moravians and Ruthenes who provided such men as Windischgrätz and Jellačić with their contingents for the suppression of the revolution in Vienna, Cracow, Lvov and Hungary, and, as we have now learnt from Bakunin, that the Slav Congress in Prague was not dispersed by Germans but by Galician, Czech and Slovak Slavs and '*nothing but Slavs*' (p. 33).

The revolution of 1848 compelled all the European peoples to declare for it or against it. In one month all the peoples which were ripe for revolution had made their revolution, all the unripe peoples had formed an alliance against the revolution. At that time, it was necessary to disentangle eastern Europe's confused ravel of peoples. Everything depended on which nation seized the revolutionary initiative, which nation developed the greatest revolutionary energy and thereby secured its future. The Slavs remained dumb, the Germans and the Magyars, true to their previous historical position, placed themselves in the forefront. And in this way the Slavs were thrown completely into the arms of the counter-revolution.

But the Slav Congress at Prague?

We repeat: the so-called democrats among the Austrian Slavs are either rogues or visionaries, and the visionaries, who can find no basis in their own people for these ideas introduced from abroad, have been continuously led around by the nose by the rogues. At the Prague Slav Congress the visionaries had the upper hand. As soon as their fantasies appeared to threaten the *aristocratic* pan-Slavists, Count Thun,[78] Palacký and their associates, they betrayed the visionaries to Windischgrätz and the black and yellow counter-revolution. Is there not a bitter, striking irony in the fact that this congress of enthusiasts, defended by the enthusiastic youth of Prague, was dispersed by soldiers of their own nation, that the visionary Slav Congress was so to speak confronted with a military Slav Congress! The Austrian army, the conqueror of Prague, Vienna, Lvov, Cracow, Milan and Budapest: that is the real, the active Slav Congress!

The unprincipled and unclear nature of the fantasies of the Slav Congress is shown by its fruits. The bombardment of a town like Prague would have filled any other nation with an inextinguishable hatred of the oppressors. What did the Czechs do? They kissed the rod which had chastised them till the blood came, they enthusiastically took the oath to the flag beneath which their brothers had been massacred and their women violated. The battle in the streets of Prague was the turning point for the Austrian democratic pan-Slavists. In return for the promise of their miserable 'national autonomy' they betrayed democracy and revolution to the Austrian monarchy, to 'the centre', 'the systematic realization of despotism in the heart of Europe', as Bakunin himself says on p. 29. And one day we shall take a bloody revenge on the Slavs for this cowardly and base betrayal of the revolution.

It has finally become clear to these traitors that, despite their treason, they have been taken in by the counter-revolution, that there is no intention of creating either a 'Slav Austria' or a 'federal state on the basis of national equality', least of all of setting up democratic institutions for the Austrian Slavs. Jellačić, who is no greater scoundrel than most of the democratic Austrian Slavs, bitterly regrets having been exploited; and Stratimiro-

---

78. Leo, Graf von Thun was a member of that section of the high Bohemian nobility which was allied with the Czech nationalists (later described as the 'feudals'). In 1848 he was Governor of Bohemia, from 1849 to 1860 he was Minister of Religious Affairs.

vić [79] has openly rebelled against Austria in order to avoid being exploited any further. Once more the Slovanská Lípa unions [80] are everywhere coming up against the government and daily undergoing painful experiences which show them the trap they allowed themselves to be enticed into. But now it is too late; in their own homeland they are powerless against the Austrian soldiery they themselves reorganized, they are rebuffed by the Germans and Magyars they betrayed, they are rebuffed by revolutionary Europe, and they will have to endure the same military despotism they helped to impose on the Viennese and the Magyars. 'Be submissive to the emperor, so that the imperial troops don't treat you as if you were rebellious Magyars.' With these words Patriarch Rajačić [81] showed what they must expect now.

How differently the Poles have behaved! Oppressed, enslaved, bled dry for eighty years, they have always placed themselves on the side of the revolution, they have declared that the independence of Poland is inseparable from the revolutionizing of Poland. The Poles have joined in the fight in Paris, Vienna, Berlin, Italy and Hungary, in all the revolutions and revolutionary wars, without worrying whether they were fighting against Germans, Slavs, Magyars, or even against Poles. The Poles are the only Slav nation which is free from all tendencies towards pan-Slavism. But they have very good reasons for this: they have mainly been subjugated by *their own* so-called *Slav brothers*, and among the Poles hatred for the Russians precedes hatred for the Germans, quite justifiably. For this reason, then, because the liberation of Poland is inseparable from the revolution, because Pole and revolutionary have become identical words, the Poles can be as certain of the sympathy of the whole of Europe and the restoration

79. Džordže Stratimirović was an Austrian general of Serbian extraction. In 1848 he led the Serbian national movement and was president of the Provisional Government of the Voivodina (May–August 1848). He was then made supreme commander of all Serbian troops in the Voivodina, and took part in the campaign against Hungary.

80. 'Slav Linden': Czech nationalist society, founded in April 1848, with branches all over Bohemia. The Prague centre was in the hands of moderate liberals, who went over to the reaction after June 1848, but the provincial unions were often led by radical nationalists, who continued to agitate against the Austrian government up to the middle of 1849.

81. Josif Rajačić was appointed Patriarch of the Austrian Serbs in 1848. He strongly upheld Habsburg authority and fiercely opposed the Hungarian revolution. In 1849 he was appointed Regent of the Voivodina.

of their nationality as the Czechs, the Croats and the Russians can be certain of the hatred of the whole of Europe and the bloodiest revolutionary war of the whole West against them.

The Austrian pan-Slavists ought to realize that all their wishes are fulfilled, in so far as they can be fulfilled at all, in the restoration of the 'united Austrian monarchy' [82] under Russian protection. If Austria collapses, they have in store for them the revolutionary terrorism of the Germans and the Magyars, but not, as they imagine, the liberation of all the nations enslaved under the Austrian sceptre. They are therefore bound to want Austria to remain united, indeed, to want Galicia to remain part of Austria so that the Slavs may retain their majority in the state. In this respect the interests of pan-Slavism are *directly opposed* to the restoration of Poland; for a Poland without Galicia, a Poland which does not stretch from the Baltic to the Carpathians, is no Poland. It follows however that a 'Slav Austria' will similarly remain a mere dream; for without the supremacy of the Germans and the Magyars, without the two centres of Vienna and Budapest, Austria falls to pieces again, as proved by its whole history up to the last few months. The realization of pan-Slavism would therefore have to be limited to a Russian protectorate over Austria. The openly reactionary pan-Slavists were therefore quite right to cling to the maintenance of the whole monarchy; it was the only way to save anything. The so-called democratic pan-Slavists were in a difficult dilemma: either abandonment of the revolution and at least partial salvation of their nationality by the Austrian monarchy, or abandonment of their nationality and salvation of the revolution by the collapse of that monarchy. At that time the fate of revolution in eastern Europe depended on the attitude of the Czechs and the South Slavs; we shall not forget that at the decisive moment they betrayed the revolution to St Petersburg and Olmütz for the sake of their petty nationalist aspirations.

What would be said if the democratic party in Germany placed at the head of their programme the demand for the return of Alsace, Lorraine, and also Belgium, which belongs in every respect to France, on the pretext that the majority of the population there is Germanic? How ridiculous the German democrats would make themselves if they wanted to set up a pan-German

82. Engels made an ironical use here of the official Austrian expression for the monarchy as a whole (*österreichische Gesamtmonarchie*), including both the hereditary Austrian lands and the kingdom of Hungary.

alliance of Germans, Danes, Swedes, Englishmen and Dutchmen, for the 'liberation' of all German-speaking lands! Luckily German democracy has advanced beyond these fantasies. The German students of 1817 and 1830 nursed similar reactionary fantasies and are now evaluated throughout Germany according to their deserts. The German revolution first came into existence, the German nation first began to be something, when people had entirely freed themselves from these futilities.

But pan-Slavism is just as childish and reactionary as pan-Germanism. If one re-reads the history of the pan-Slav movement in Prague last spring, one has the feeling of being carried back thirty years: tricolour ribbons, Old Frankish costume, Old Slav masses, a complete restoration of the era and the customs of the primeval forest, the Svornost – a complete copy of the Burschenschaft [83] the Slav Congress – a new edition of the Wartburg Festival, [84] the same phrases, the same wild enthusiasm, the same lamentations afterwards: 'We a stately edifice had built,' [85] etc. Anyone who wants to see this famous song translated into Slav prose should read Bakunin's pamphlet.

Just as, in the long run, there emerged from the German Burschenschaften the most emphatically counter-revolutionary attitude, the most furious hatred of the French and the most narrow-minded nationalism, just as they later all became traitors to the cause for which they had pretended to enthuse, precisely in the same way, only more quickly, because the year 1848 was a year of revolution, did the democratic appearance of the democratic pan-Slavists dissolve into fanatical hatred of the Germans and Magyars, indirect opposition to the restoration of Poland (Lubomirsky), [86] and direct attachment to the counter-revolution.

And if a few upright Slav democrats now called on the Austrian

83. Svornost: Czech nationalist student organization, set up in Bohemia in March 1848. Burschenschaften: German student organizations, set up in the 1810s, which agitated for German unification.

84. The Wartburg Festival was a celebration of the three-hundredth anniversary of the Reformation, held on 18 October 1817, at which the students demonstrated against Metternich and in favour of German unification.

85. *Wir hatten gebauet ein staatliches Haus*; the title of a song by August Daniel Binzer mourning the dissolution of the Jena Burschenschaft in 1819.

86. Jerzy, Prince Lubomirsky was a reactionary and pan-Slavist Polish magnate who took part in the Slav Congress and later in 1848 sat in the Austrian Reichstag.

Slavs to join the revolution, to look on the Austrian monarchy as their main enemy, and indeed to side with the Magyars in the interests of the revolution, this reminds one of the hen which runs around at the edge of the pond in despair over the young ducks it has itself incubated, which now suddenly escape into an environment utterly foreign to it, where it cannot follow them.

Let us in any case have no illusions about this. With all pan-Slavists, nationality, i.e. imaginary, general Slav nationality, *comes before the revolution*. The pan-Slavists want to join the revolution on condition that they are permitted to constitute all Slavs without exception, and without regard for the most vital necessities, into independent Slav states. We Germans would have gone far in March if we had wanted to lay down the same absurd conditions! However, the revolution does not allow conditions to be dictated to it. Either one is a revolutionary and accepts the consequences of the revolution, whatever they may be, or one is thrown into the arms of the counter-revolution and is one morning to be found arm in arm with Nicholas and Windischgrätz, perhaps entirely unknowingly and unwillingly.

The Magyars and ourselves should guarantee the Austrian Slavs their independence – this is what Bakunin demands, and people of the calibre of a Ruge are actually capable of making him such promises in secret. They are demanding of us and the other revolutionary nations of Europe that we should guarantee an existence without let or hindrance to the centres of counter-revolution situated close by our door, a right freely to conspire and bear arms against the revolution; that we should constitute a counter-revolutionary Czech state right in the heart of Germany, that we should break the power of the German, Polish and Magyar revolutions by thrusting between them Russian advance posts on the Elbe, in the Carpathians and on the Danube!

We would not even think of it. We reply to the sentimental phrases about brotherhood which are offered to us here in the name of the most counter-revolutionary nations in Europe that hatred of the Russians was, and still is, the *first revolutionary passion* of the Germans; that since the revolution a hatred of the Czechs and the Croats has been added to this, and that, in common with the Poles and the Magyars, we can only secure the revolution against these Slav peoples by the most decisive acts of terrorism. We now know where the enemies of the revolution are concentrated: in Russia and in the Slav lands of Austria; and no phrases, no references to an indefinite democratic future of these lands will prevent us from treating our enemies as enemies.

And if Bakunin finally proclaims the following:

Truly, the Slav must not *lose* anything, he must *gain*! Truly, he must live! And we *shall* live. *As long as the smallest part* of our rights is contested, as long as *a single member is divided off from our general body or kept torn away* from it, just so long will we fight *to the utmost*, an implacable, life-and-death struggle, until finally Slavdom is great and free and stands in the world independently –

if revolutionary pan-Slavism means this passage seriously, and leaves the revolution entirely out of the picture where it is a question of the imaginary Slav nationality, then we too know what we have to do.

Then we shall fight 'an implacable life-and-death struggle' with Slavdom, which has betrayed the revolution; a war of annihilation and ruthless terrorism, not in the interests of Germany but in the interests of the revolution!

THE TRIAL OF THE RHINELAND DISTRICT COMMITTEE OF DEMOCRATS. SPEECH BY KARL MARX IN HIS OWN DEFENCE[87]

N.Rh.Z., 25 February 1849

Gentlemen of the jury!

If the action now in progress had been brought *before* 5 December, I should have understood the charge made by the public prosecutor. Now, *after* 5 December, I do not understand how the public prosecutor still dares to call on laws which the Crown itself has trodden underfoot.

On what has the ministry based its criticism of the National Assembly, of the decision to refuse to pay taxes? On the laws of 6 April and 8 April 1848. And what did the government do on 5 December 1848, when it unilaterally promulgated a constitution and imposed a new electoral law on the country? It thereby tore up the laws of 6 April and 8 April. These laws no longer exist for

87. The trial of the Rhineland District Committee of Democrats took place on 8 February 1849. Marx, Karl Schapper, and the lawyer Karl Schneider II were accused in connection with the Proclamation of 18 November 1848, signed by the three men, calling on citizens to forcibly resist attempts to collect taxes (printed in *MECW* 8, p. 24). They were all acquitted by the jury.

the supporters of the government. Should they continue to exist for its opponents? On 5 December, the government put itself on a *revolutionary* footing, namely the footing of *counter-revolution*. In this situation there are only accomplices and revolutionaries. The government itself changed the mass of citizens into rebels, in so far as they based themselves on existing laws and defended those laws against the government's breach of them. *Before* 5 December it was possible to disagree about the meaning of the National Assembly's transfer to Brandenburg, its dissolution, and the state of siege in Berlin. *After* 5 December it became an authentic fact that these measures formed the introduction to the counter-revolution, that any modes of action were permissible against a party which itself no longer recognized the conditions under which it *was* the government, and therefore could no longer be recognized by the country as the government. Gentlemen! The Crown could at least have saved the appearance of legality; it has disdained even to do this. It could have dispersed the National Assembly and then had its ministry appear before the country and say: 'We have ventured on a coup d'état. The situation forced us to do this. Formally speaking, we have disregarded the law, but there are moments of crisis when the very existence of the state is at risk. There is only *one* inviolable law on such occasions, the law of the state's own preservation. When we dissolved the Assembly, no constitution existed. Therefore, we could not have broken the constitution. However, two organic laws do exist, those of 6 April and 8 April 1848. In point of fact only *a single* organic law exists, the *electoral law*. We invite the country to participate in new elections in accordance with *this* law. We, the *responsible ministry*, will appear before the Assembly which emerges from these elections. We expect this Assembly to recognize the coup d'état as a *deed of deliverance* necessitated by the circumstances. It will give its retrospective sanction to the coup. It will say that we have infringed against a legal formula in order to save the fatherland. Let the Assembly decide our fate!'

If the ministry had acted in this way, it could have brought us before its tribunal with some *apparent* justification. The Crown would have saved the appearance of legality. It was not able to do this, nor did it *wish* to.

In the eyes of the Crown, the March revolution was a brute fact. One brute fact can only be extirpated by another. In annulling the new elections due to be held on the basis of the law of April 1848, the ministry *denied* its *responsibility*, *annulled the very court it was responsible to*. In this way it transformed the National Assembly's appeal to the people from the outset into mere appearance, fiction, an imposture. In inventing a Chamber resting on a property qualification as an integral part of the legislative assembly, the ministry tore up the organic laws, abandoned the legal foundation, falsified the elections and denied the people any possibility of judging the Crown's 'deed of deliverance'.

It follows, gentlemen, that one fact cannot be denied, and no later historian will deny it: the Crown has made a revolution, it has thrown the existing legal situation overboard, and it cannot appeal to the laws it has so shamefully invalidated. After the successful conclusion of a revolution, one can hang one's opponents but not condemn them. One can clear them out of the way as defeated foes, but not judge them as criminals. After a successful revolution or counter-revolution one cannot apply the laws one had invalidated against the *defenders* of those same laws. This is a cowardly semblance of legality, which you, gentlemen of the jury, will not sanction by your final judgement.

I have told you, gentlemen, that the government has falsified the judgement of the people on the Crown's 'deed of deliverance'. Nevertheless, the people have already decided *against* the Crown and *for* the National Assembly. The elections to the Second Chamber are the only legally valid elections, because they alone took place on the basis of the law of 8 April 1848. And almost all the tax-refusers have been re-elected to the Second Chamber, many of them two or three times over. The deputy for Cologne, Schneider II,[88] is in fact one of the accused in this trial. The question of the right of the National Assembly to resolve to refuse to pay taxes has therefore already been confirmed in practice by the people.

Leaving aside this supreme judgement, you will all concede, gentlemen, that you are not confronted here with a crime in the ordinary sense, that there is here absolutely no conflict with the laws, such as is relevant to this forum. In normal circumstances, the public power executes the existing laws; the criminal is he who breaks those laws or violently opposes the public power in its

88. Karl Schneider II was a Cologne lawyer and sat as a Radical-Democrat in the Prussian National Assembly. He was chairman of the Cologne Democratic Society, and a member of the Cologne Committee of Public Safety formed during the September crisis as the nucleus of a revolutionary government.

execution of those laws. In our case, one public power has broken the law, and the other public power, it is unimportant which one, has upheld it. A conflict between two state powers does not lie within the jurisdiction of either private law or criminal law. The question as to who is in the right, the Crown or the National Assembly, is a historical question. All the juries, all the courts of Prussia, cannot decide this question. There is only one power which can decide it: history. I do not understand, therefore, how we can be accused on the basis of the Code Pénal.

We are dealing here with a struggle between two powers, and only superior power can decide between two powers. This has been pointed out equally by the revolutionary and by the counter-revolutionary press, gentlemen. An organ of the government itself proclaimed the same fact shortly before the decisive phase of the struggle. The *Neue Preussische Zeitung*, the organ of the present ministry, saw this point very clearly. A few days before the crisis, it made approximately the following statement: this is no longer a matter of law, but of force, and we shall see whether the old kingdom by the grace of God still has the force. The *Neue Preussische Zeitung* grasped the situation correctly. Force versus force. A physical victory had to decide the issue. The counter-revolution has won, but this only concludes the first act of the drama. In England, the struggle lasted for more than twenty years. After repeated victories, Charles I finally mounted the scaffold. And what guarantee can there be, gentlemen, that the present ministry and the officials who have made themselves into its instruments will not be condemned as traitors by the present Chamber or by its successors?

Gentlemen! The public prosecutor has sought to base his accusation on the laws of 6 and 8 April. I was therefore compelled to demonstrate that those very laws speak against a conviction. But I shall not conceal the fact that I do not recognize these laws, and will never recognize them. They were never even valid for the deputies who emerged from the popular elections; still less could they prescribe a path for the March revolution to follow.

How did the laws of 6 April and 8 April arise? Through an agreement reached between the government and the United Diet. In this way they hoped to establish continuity with the old legal situation and suppress the revolution which had swept away this situation. Men like Camphausen, etc. considered it important to preserve the appearance of lawful progress. And how did they do this? By a series of obvious and inept contradictions. Let us dwell for a moment on the old legal position, gentlemen. Was not the very existence of Prime Minister Camphausen a breach of the law, since he was a *responsible minister*, a minister without a previous official career in the Prussian administration? Camphausen's position as a *responsible Prime Minister* was illegal. This *legally* non-existent official recalled the United Diet in order to have it pass laws it was not *legally* entitled to pass. And this self-condemning formalistic game was described as progress through the law, as the maintenance of the legal foundation!

But let us disregard the formal aspect, gentlemen. What was the United Diet? The representative of old, decayed social relations. The revolution had taken place in opposition to these relations. The representative of the defeated society was then presented with organic laws which were supposed to recognize, regulate and organize the revolution against that old society. What an absurd contradiction! The Diet had collapsed with the old monarchy.

Now, gentlemen, let us look squarely at the so-called *legal foundation*. I am all the more compelled to discuss this point because we are rightly considered to be the foes of the legal foundation, apart from the fact that the laws of 6 April and 8 April owe their existence merely to the formal recognition of the legal foundation.

First and foremost, the Diet represented big landed property. Big landed property was in reality the basis of the medieval, *feudal society*. In contrast to this, *our* society, *modern bourgeois society*, rests on industry and trade. Landed property itself has lost all the previous conditions of its existence, it has become dependent on trade and industry. Agriculture is consequently now carried on in an industrial fashion, and the old feudal lords have sunk to the position of manufacturers of cattle, wool, corn, sugar beet, schnapps and so on, in other words to people who engage in trade with the products of their industries, just like any other tradesman! However much they might hold fast to their old prejudices, they have in practice become members of the bourgeoisie, who produce as much as possible as cheaply as possible, who buy where they can get the best bargain and sell at the highest possible price. These gentlemen's mode of life, of production and of appropriation therefore gives the lie to their inherited and grandiloquent delusions. Landed property requires *medieval modes of production and commercial intercourse* to be the dominating element in society. The United Diet represented this medieval mode of production and intercourse, which had long ceased to exist, and whose representatives in equal measure held onto their old privileges and joined in the enjoyment and exploitation of the advantages of the new society. The new bourgeois society, which rests on entirely different foundations and on a changed mode of production, had to seize political power for itself; it had to snatch this power from the hands of those who represented the interests of the foundering society, and whose political power, in its entire organization, had proceeded from entirely different material relations of society. *Hence the revolution.* The revolution was directed against the *absolute monarchy*, the highest political expression of the old society. But it was directed just as much against the *representation of the estates*, a social order long since destroyed by modern industry, or, at the most, existing in the form of a few pretentious remnants daily further outstripped by bourgeois society and driven into the background in a state of dissolution. Why then was the view taken that the new society which asserted its rights in the revolution should allow the United Diet, the representative of the old society, to dictate laws to it?

In order to maintain the *legal foundation*, it is alleged. But what do you understand by the maintenance of the legal foundation, gentlemen? The maintenance of laws which belong to a bygone social epoch, which were made by the representatives of extinct or declining social interests, and which therefore also convert interests contradictory to the general need into laws. However, society does not depend on the law. That is a legal fiction. The law depends rather on society, it must be the expression of society's communal interests and needs, arising from the existing material mode of production, and not the arbitrary expression of the will of the single individual. I have here in my hands the Code Napoléon, but it is not the Code which created modern bourgeois society. Instead, it is bourgeois society, as it originated in the eighteenth century and underwent further development in the nineteenth century, which finds its merely legal expression in the Code. As soon as the Code ceases to correspond to social relations, it is no more than a bundle of paper. Social relations cannot make old laws the foundation of the new development of society; nor could these old laws have created the old social circumstances.

These laws emerged from these old circumstances, and they

must perish with them. They must necessarily alter in line with changes in the condition of life. The defence of old laws against the new needs and claims of social development is fundamentally nothing but a hypocritical defence of outdated particular interests against the contemporary interest of the whole. This *attempt to maintain the legal foundation* involves treating particular interests as *dominant* when they are in fact *no longer dominant*; it involves the imposition on a society of laws which are themselves condemned by that society's conditions of life, its mode of appropriation, its trade and its material production; it involves the prolongation of the activities of legislators who only serve particular interests; it involves the misuse of the state power in order to forcibly subordinate the interests of the majority to the interests of the minority. At every moment, therefore, this attempt comes into conflict with existing needs, hinders trade and industry, and sets the stage for *social crises* which come to a head in *political revolutions*.

This is the true meaning of this attachment to the legal foundation, of maintenance of the legal foundation. And this phrase 'the legal foundation', involving either conscious deception or unconscious self-deception, was used to support the recall of the United Diet, and the fabrication by it of organic laws for the National Assembly made necessary by the revolution and created by it. And these laws are supposed to provide the guidelines for the National Assembly!

The National Assembly represented modern bourgeois society as opposed to the feudal society represented in the United Diet. It was elected by the people in order independently to establish a constitution which would correspond to the conditions of life which had come into conflict with the previous political organization and the previous laws. It was therefore sovereign from the outset, a constituent assembly. If it nevertheless condescended to adopt the standpoint of compromise and negotiation, this was a purely formal act of politeness towards the Crown, a mere ceremony. It is not necessary here for me to examine the question whether the Assembly had the right to act on behalf of the people in becoming the *Vereinbarungsversammlung*. In the judgement of the Assembly, a conflict with the Crown could be avoided with the good will of both parties.

This much however is certain: the laws of 6 and 8 April, negotiated with the United Diet, were formally invalid. Materially, they were only significant in so far as they expressed and laid down the conditions under which the National Assembly could be a real expression of popular sovereignty. The 'United Diet legislation' was only a form of words which spared the Crown the humiliation of proclaiming: *I have been defeated*.

N.Rh.Z., 27 February 1849

Gentlemen of the jury,

I shall now proceed to the closer elucidation of the prosecution's case.

The public prosecutor said:

> The Crown has alienated a part of the power which lay entirely in its hands. Even in private life, an act of renunciation does not go beyond the clear words in which the renunciation is made. But the law of 8 April 1848 does not concede to the National Assembly the right to refuse to pay taxes, nor does it fix on Berlin as the National Assembly's necessary place of residence.

Gentlemen! The power in the hands of the Crown had been *smashed to pieces*; it surrendered power to save what fragments it could. You will recall, gentlemen, how shortly after his accession to the throne, the king gave a formal pledge in Königsberg and Berlin that he would concede a constitution. You will recall how the king swore high and low, in 1847, at the opening of the United Diet, that he would permit no piece of paper to come between him and *his* people. After March 1848, the king himself, through the medium of the constitution he promulgated, proclaimed that he was a *constitutional* king. He inserted this abstract piece of foreign frippery, this piece of paper, between his people and himself. Will the public prosecutor dare to assert that the king voluntarily contradicted his solemn promises in such a striking way, that he voluntarily rendered himself guilty before all Europe of the intolerable inconsistency of consenting to negotiate with the Assembly or to issue a constitution? The king made the concessions *enforced* on him by the revolution. No more, no less!

The prosecution's vulgar comparison unfortunately proves nothing. Of course, if I renounce something, I renounce nothing more than I renounce *expressly*. If I present you with a gift, it would be sheer impudence if you endeavoured to extract further favours on the basis of my deed of gift. But after March it was the people who gave, the Crown which received the gift. It is obviously true that the gift must be interpreted in the sense given it by the giver and not the receiver, by the people and not by the Crown.

The Crown's absolute power had been broken. The people had won the victory. The two sides concluded an armistice, and the people were deceived. The public prosecutor has himself taken pains to demonstrate thoroughly to you, gentlemen, that the people were deceived. In order to contest the National Assembly's right to refuse to pay taxes, the public prosecutor pointed out in detailed fashion that if something of the kind was contained in the law of 6 April, it is no longer to be found in the law of 8 April. The intervening period was therefore used for the purpose of removing from the representatives of the people the rights conceded to them two days before. Could the public prosecutor possibly have compromised the Crown's *reputation for honesty* more strikingly? Could there be any more irrefutable proof that the intention was to *deceive* the people?

The public prosecutor continued: 'The right to *transfer* and *prorogue* the National Assembly emanates from the executive power, and is recognized in all constitutional countries.'

As far as the *executive power's* right to *transfer* the legislative chambers is concerned, I would invite the public prosecutor to indicate a single law or example in favour of this assertion. In England, for example, the king had an old-established historical right to call Parliament together wherever he pleased. There is no law which lays down that London is the English Parliament's place of meeting. You know, gentlemen, that in general in England the main political freedoms are sanctioned by common law, not by written law. An example is the freedom of the press. But if an English ministry had the idea of transferring Parliament from London to Windsor or Richmond . . . it is sufficient merely to formulate this for its impossibility to be recognized.

In constitutional countries the Crown has of course the right to *prorogue* parliament. However, do not forget that on the other side all constitutions specify the *length of time* during which parliament may be prorogued and the point at which they must be recalled. No constitution exists in Prussia, this is yet to be established; there is no legal time-limit for the recall of a prorogued parliament, but for that reason there is also no royal right of prorogation. Otherwise the Crown could have prorogued the Chambers for ten days, or for ten years, or for ever. Wherein lay the guarantee that the Chambers would ever be called, or, once called, remain in session? The continued existence of the Chambers side by side with the Crown was left to the Crown's own discretion. The legislative power, if indeed one is entitled to speak here of a legislative power, had become a fiction.

Gentlemen! Here, on the basis of a single example, you can see the result of the attempt to compare the conflict between the Prussian crown and the Prussian National Assembly with the situation in constitutional countries. It leads to the *defence of monarchical absolutism*. On the one hand the public prosecutor vindicates the Crown's rights as the rights of a constitutional executive; but on the other hand there exists no law, no custom, no organic institution, to impose on the Crown the limitations proper to a constitutional executive. This is the demand put to the people's representatives: that they should play the role of a *constitutional* parliament *vis-à-vis* an *absolute* monarch!

Does it still need to be shown that the case we are dealing with is not one of an executive and a legislature confronting one another, and that the doctrine of the constitutional separation of powers cannot be applied to the Prussian National Assembly and the Prussian crown? Disregard the revolution, stick merely to the official *theory of Vereinbarung*. Even according to this theory, two sovereign powers confronted each other. One of these powers had to destroy the other, there is no doubt about that. Two sovereign powers cannot function simultaneously, side by side, *in one state*. This would be a self-contradiction, like squaring the circle. Material force had to decide between the two sovereignties. But we ourselves are not required to investigate here the possibility or the impossibility of *Vereinbarung*. Enough of that! Two powers enter into relations in order to conclude a treaty. Camphausen himself implied there was a possibility that the treaty would not come into existence. Speaking from the ministerial bench itself to the *Vereinbarungsversammlung*, he indicated the imminent danger to the country if the compromise did not materialize. The danger lay in the original relationship between the compromising National Assembly and the Crown, and now, after the event, the intention is to make the National Assembly responsible for this danger, by denying this original relationship and presenting the Assembly as a *constitutional body*. To solve the difficulty by passing straight over it!

I believe I have proved to you, gentlemen, that the Crown had neither the right to transfer the Assembly nor the right to prorogue it.

But the public prosecutor did not confine himself to investigating the *legality* of the Crown's transfer of the National Assembly; he endeavoured to demonstrate the *expediency* of this action. 'Would it not have been expedient', he said, 'if the National Assembly had obeyed the Crown and moved to Brandenburg?' The public prosecutor bases this expediency on the situation of the Chamber itself. It was not free in Berlin, etc.

Was not the Crown's intention in making this transfer as clear as day? Has it not stripped all the reasons given officially for the transfer of their apparent justification? It was not a matter of freedom of deliberation, but of the choice between sending the Assembly home and arbitrarily issuing a new constitution, and creating a sham representation by choosing docile deputies. When a quorum of deputies unexpectedly turned up in Brandenburg, hypocrisy was abandoned and the dissolution of the National Assembly was proclaimed.

It is clear in any case that the Crown did not have the right to declare the National Assembly free or unfree. No one but the Assembly itself could decide whether it enjoyed or did not enjoy the freedom necessary for its deliberations. There was nothing more convenient for the Crown than to be able to declare the National Assembly unfree and not accountable for its actions whenever it took a decision obnoxious to the Crown, and then to place it under an interdict.

The public prosecutor has also spoken of the government's duty to protect the dignity of the National Assembly against the terrorism of the Berlin population.

This argument sounds like a satire on the government itself. I do not wish to speak of its behaviour towards individual persons: these persons were after all the elected representatives of the people. The government sought to humiliate them in every way. It persecuted them in the most infamous manner, and set on foot a kind of ferocious hunt against them. Let us leave aside personalities, and ask how it preserved the dignity of the National Assembly in its *work*. Its archives – the documents of the committees, the royal embassies, the legislative proposals, the preliminary drafts – have been abandoned to the solidery, who have turned them into pipe-lighters, heated stoves with them, and trodden them underfoot.

Even the forms of judicial process were not observed; the archives were simply seized without any inventory being taken.

The plan was to destroy this work which had cost the people so much, in order to be able to slander the National Assembly more effectively, and to remove from view those plans for reform which were hateful to the government and the aristocrats. After all this, is it not well-nigh ridiculous to assert that the government transferred the National Assembly from Berlin to Brandenburg out of tender care for its dignity?

I come now to the public prosecutor's arguments on the question of the *formal validity* of the resolution against the payment of taxes.

This resolution could only have attained formal validity, says the prosecution, if the Assembly had obtained for it the *sanction of the Crown*.

But, gentlemen, the Crown confronted the Assembly in the person of the Brandenburg ministry, not in its own person. This then is the nonsensical act the public prosecutor demands of the Assembly: it should have reached an agreement with the Brandenburg ministry to proclaim it guilty of treason and to refuse to grant it any taxes! What does this suggestion mean other than that the National Assembly should have decided on unconditional submission to every demand made by the Brandenburg ministry?

The resolution against the payment of taxes was formally invalid for another reason, says the public prosecutor, for a bill can only become law on the *second reading*.

On the one hand the government ignored the *essential* forms it was bound to observe towards the National Assembly; on the other hand it expects the National Assembly to observe the most inessential *formalities*. Nothing could be simpler! A proposal objectionable to the Crown passes its first reading; the second reading is prevented by the use of armed force. The law is and remains invalid because it lacks a second reading. The public prosecutor has overlooked the exceptional situation which prevailed when the representatives of the people passed that resolution, while threatened by bayonets in their place of meeting. The government has committed outrage after outrage. It has recklessly broken very important laws, including the Habeas Corpus Act [89]

89. On 28 August 1848 the Berlin Assembly passed a form of Habeas Corpus Act, entitled 'A Law for the Protection of Personal Freedom'.

and the law on the militia.[90] It has arbitrarily introduced an unrestricted military despotism, in the form of the state of siege. The people's representatives have been chased from pillar to post. And while *all the laws* are shamelessly broken, they demand that a mere *rule of procedure* should be observed to the letter.

I do not know, gentlemen, whether it is a case of intentional falsification (far be it from me to suppose the public prosecutor would do this) or merely ignorance, when he says that 'the National Assembly never wanted any compromise, it never sought any compromise'.

If the people have any reproach to make of the Berlin National Assembly, it is precisely its lust for compromise. If the members of the Assembly themselves have any regrets, these are regrets over its mania for compromise. It was the mania for compromise which gradually alienated the people, which led to the loss of all its positions of strength, and which finally exposed it to the attacks of the Crown without the defence of a nation behind it. When it wanted at last to assert its will, it stood there isolated and powerless, precisely because it failed to have a will and to assert it at the proper time. It first announced its mania for compromise when it denied the revolution and sanctioned the theory of *Vereinbarung*, when it degraded itself from a revolutionary National Assembly to an ambiguous association of compromisers. It carried its weakness for compromise to an extreme when it accepted von Pfuel's apparent recognition of Stein's army order at its face value. The announcement of this army order had by then become a farce, as it could only be seen as the comic echo of Wrangel's army order. And yet instead of ignoring it, the Assembly eagerly grabbed hold of the Pfuel ministry's toned-down version, which reduced the original to complete meaninglessness. In order to avoid any serious conflict with the Crown it accepted the shadow of a demonstration against the old, reactionary army as a real demonstration. It affected to consider something which was no longer even an apparent solution to the conflict as the real solution. So little desirous of struggle, so much inclined towards compromise, was this Assembly, though presented by the public prosecutor as quarrelsome and mischievous.

Should I point out yet another symptom of the Chamber's

90. On 13 October 1848 the Assembly passed the 'Law on the Creation of a Citizens' Militia'. The militia was dissolved on 11 November after Wrangel's troops entered Berlin.

conciliatory character? Cast your minds back, gentlemen, to the agreement reached by the National Assembly with Pfuel over the law for the cessation of redemption negotiations. If the Assembly was unable to crush the enemy represented by the army, it was of vital importance to win over the friend represented by the peasantry. But the Assembly renounced this friendship. It was more concerned to avoid a conflict with the Crown, to avoid a conflict under all circumstances, to compromise. It considered it to be more important to compromise than to act in the interests of its own self-preservation. And now they reproach this Assembly with not wanting any compromise, with not trying to achieve one!

Even when the conflict had broken out, the Assembly still sought a compromise. Gentlemen, you know the pamphlet produced by Unruh,[91] a man of the Centre. You will have learned from it how many attempts were made to avoid a break, how deputations were sent to the Crown and not allowed an audience, how individual deputies tried to prevail upon ministers who thrust them aside with aristocratic pride, how concessions were made and laughed to scorn. The Assembly wanted to make peace at a time when the only suitable thing was to prepare for war. And the public prosecutor accuses this Assembly of not having wanted a compromise, of not having tried to achieve one!

The Berlin National Assembly clearly abandoned itself to a gigantic illusion, it showed its failure to understand its own position and its own conditions of existence, when it held an amicable understanding, a compromise with the Crown to be possible, and endeavoured to put this into effect, both *before* and *during* the conflict.

The Crown did not want a compromise. It could not. Let us make no mistake, gentlemen of the jury, about the nature of the struggle which erupted in March and was later waged between the National Assembly and the Crown. Here it was not a matter of an ordinary conflict between a ministry and a parliamentary opposition, a conflict between people who were ministers and people who wanted to become ministers, a battle between two political parties in a legislative chamber. Members of the National

91. Hans von Unruh, *Skizzen aus Preussens neuester Geschichte* (*Sketches from Prussia's Most Recent History*), Madgeburg, 1849. Unruh was a Prussian engineer and moderate liberal politician. In 1848 he led the Left Centre in the Prussian Assembly, from October 1848 he was its chairman. In 1849 he was elected to the Second Chamber.

Assembly, belonging either to the minority or the majority, may well have imagined this to be so. It is the real historical position of the National Assembly, as it emerged from the European revolution and from the March revolution conditioned by the latter, which is the sole decisive factor, and not the opinion of the *Vereinbarungsversammlung*. This was not a case of a political conflict between two parties standing on the ground of *one* society, it was a *conflict between two societies*, a *social* conflict which had taken on a political form, *it was the struggle of modern bourgeois society with the old feudal-bureaucratic society*, the struggle between the society of *free competition* and the society of *guild organization*, between the society of industry and the society of landownership, between the society of knowledge and the society of belief. The Crown by the grace of God, the paternalistic bureaucracy, the independent army, all these institutions formed the appropriate *political* expression of the old society. The appropriate *social* foundation of this old political power was formed by the privileged landowning nobility with its peasants in a state of serfdom or semi-serfdom, small-scale industry organized in a patriarchal or corporate fashion, the mutually exclusive estates, the brutal contrast between town and country, and above all the domination of the country over the town. The old political power – composed of the Crown by the grace of God, the paternalistic bureaucracy, the independent army – saw its actual material foundation vanish from beneath its feet as soon as attacks were made on the privileged estates of the nobility, on the nobility itself, on the domination of country over town, on the subjection of the country people, and on the legislation which corresponded to all these conditions of life, such as the municipal regulations, the criminal law, etc.; in short, on the foundations of the old society.

It was the National Assembly which committed these criminal attacks. And the old society saw that political power had been snatched from its hands when the Crown, the bureaucracy and the army lost their feudal privileges. The National Assembly wanted to abolish these privileges. No wonder, then, that the army, the bureaucracy, and the nobility jointly pressed the Crown to make a coup d'état. No wonder that the Crown, knowing the intimate connection between its own interests and those of the old feudal-bureaucratic society, allowed itself to succumb to this pressure. The Crown was precisely the representative of the feudal and aristocratic society; the National Assembly was the representative of modern bourgeois society. It was a condition of existence for the latter that it should demote the bureaucracy and the army from the position of masters of trade and industry to that of their instruments, that it should *make* them into mere organs of bourgeois commerce. It cannot allow agriculture to be restricted by feudal privileges, or industry by bureaucratic tutelage. This would contradict its fundamental principle of free competition. It cannot allow external trade relations to be regulated by considerations of international dynastic politics instead of by the interests of national production. It must subordinate the organization of finance to the needs of production, whereas the old state had to subordinate production to the needs of the Crown by the grace of God, in particular the need to patch up the royal ramparts, the social supports of the Crown. Just as modern industry is in fact a leveller, so must modern society tear down all legal and political barriers between town and country. In modern society there still exist *classes*, but not *estates*. Its development consists in the struggle between these classes, but the classes are united against the estates and their monarchy by the grace of God.

The monarchy by the grace of God, the highest political expression, the highest political representative of the old feudal-bureaucratic society, can therefore make no *genuine* concessions to modern bourgeois society. Its drive for self-preservation, and the society which stands behind it and on which it rests, will force it again and again to take back the concessions which have been made, to reassert its feudal character, to risk a counter-revolution. After a revolution, counter-revolution is the Crown's constantly self-renewing condition of existence.

On the other side, modern society cannot rest until it has destroyed and removed the official state power inherited from past ages, with which the old society still violently maintains itself. The hegemony of the Crown by the grace of God is precisely the hegemony of the obsolete social elements.

There can therefore be no peace between these two societies. Their material interests and needs require a life-and-death struggle in which one society must win, the other go under. That is the only possible relationship between them. It follows that there can be no peace between the Crown and the popular assembly, the highest political representatives of these two societies. The National Assembly had the choice of either giving way to the old society or stepping forth as an independent power in relation to the Crown.

Gentlemen! The public prosecutor has described the *refusal to pay taxes* as an action 'which shatters the innermost *citadels of society*'. It has nothing to do with the citadels of society.

Why do taxes play such an important part in the history of constitutionalism, gentlemen? This can be explained very simply. Just as the serfs purchased their privileges from the feudal barons with hard cash, so did whole peoples purchase their privileges from the feudal kings. The kings needed money for their wars with foreign nations and also, in particular, for their struggles with the feudal lords. The more trade and industry developed, the more money they required. To the same degree, however, the third estate, the burghers, grew and developed, and came to possess more and more financial resources. The third estate then bought progressively increasing liberties from the kings by means of taxes. In order to make sure of these liberties it reserved for itself the right to renew the grants of money at specific intervals – known as the right to grant and to refuse supply. In English history, in particular, this process can be traced in all its details.

In medieval society, then, taxes were the only bond between the emergent bourgeois society and the ruling feudal state. They formed the bond through which the feudal state was compelled to make concessions to the development of bourgeois society, and to adapt itself to the latter's requirements. In modern state the right to grant and refuse supply has changed into a form of surveillance exercised by bourgeois society over that committee to administer its general interests which is the government.

You will therefore find that a *partial refusal to pay taxes* is an integral part of any constitutional mechanism. This kind of tax-refusal occurs as often as the *budget* is thrown out. The current budget is only granted for a definite period of time; moreover, parliament must be recalled after only a very short interval has elapsed from its prorogation. It is therefore impossible for the Crown to make itself independent. By the rejection of a budget supply is definitively *refused*, unless the new parliament brings the ministry a majority, or the Crown appoints a new ministry in line with the wishes of the new parliament. The rejection of the budget is therefore a *refusal to pay taxes which takes a parliamentary form*. In the present conflict this form was not applicable, because the constitution did not yet exist and was still to be created.

But a refusal to pay taxes such as we have in the present case, which not only rejects the new budget but also forbids the payment of the current taxes, is by no means unheard of. This was a very frequent occurrence in the Middle Ages. Even the old German Diet and the old feudal Estates of Brandenburg made decisions to refuse to pay taxes. And there is no lack of examples in modern constitutional countries. In 1832 in England the refusal to pay taxes led to the fall of the Wellington cabinet.[92] And bear in mind, gentlemen, that it was not the English Parliament which decided on a refusal to pay taxes, it was the people who proclaimed this and accomplished it on their own authority. And England is the historic land of constitutionalism.

The English revolution, which brought Charles I to the scaffold, began with a refusal of supply. The North American revolution, which ended with the Declaration of Independence from England, began with a refusal of supply. In Prussia, too, the refusal to pay taxes may be the harbinger of very terrible things. However, it was not John Hampden who brought Charles I to the scaffold but rather Charles I's own obstinacy, his dependence on the feudal estate, his arrogance in wishing to put down with violence the imperative demands of the newly emerging society. The refusal of supply is only a symptom of the conflict between Crown and people, only a proof that the conflict between the government and the people has reached a high and threatening level. It does not itself produce this conflict and this dissension, but only expresses the existence of such a situation. In the worst case, there follows the fall of the existing government, of the given form of the state. This does not touch the innermost citadels of society. Indeed, in the present case, the refusal to pay taxes was society's act of self-defence against a government which threatened its innermost citadels.

Finally, the public prosecutor accuses us of having gone further than the National Assembly itself, in the incriminating appeal: 'In the first place, the National Assembly did not publish its resolution.' Do I seriously have to reply to this, gentlemen, that the resolution to refuse to pay taxes was not even published in the statute-book?

92. The Grey Cabinet resigned in 1832 after the king's refusal to create enough peers to carry through the Reform Bill; for a few days Wellington attempted to form a cabinet, but the threat of a tax-strike (put into effect in some places) was sufficient to compel the return of Grey and the passing of the Reform Bill.

Moreover, it is said, the National Assembly did not call for violence, did not place itself on a revolutionary footing, as we did, but rather wanted to remain on legal ground.

Previously, the public prosecutor had presented the National Assembly as illegal. Now he presented it as legal. In each case the aim was to present us as criminals. If the collection of taxes is declared to be illegal, must I not violently resist the violent accomplishment of this illegality? Even from this point of view, we should be justified in driving out force with force. Anyway, it is absolutely true that the National Assembly wished to remain on purely legal ground, on the ground of passive resistance. There were two courses open to it: the revolutionary course – which it did not adopt, as the gentlemen did not want to risk their necks – and the course of refusing to pay taxes, which remained at the level of passive resistance. It chose the latter course. But in order to carry out this decision the people had to place themselves on revolutionary ground. The attitude of the National Assembly was by no means authoritative for the people. The National Assembly has no rights for itself, it only has the rights handed over by the people for it to maintain. If it fails to execute its mandate, it is extinguished. The people themselves then enter the stage in their own right, and act out of the plenitude of their power. If for example a National Assembly sold itself to a treasonable government, the people would have to drive away both the government and the National Assembly. If the Crown makes a counter-revolution, the people have the right to reply with a revolution. They do not need the permission of any National Assembly. But in fact the Prussian National Assembly has itself stated that the Prussian government attempted a treasonable and criminal act.

I shall briefly sum up, gentlemen of the jury. The public prosecutor cannot apply the laws of 6 and 8 April 1848 against us, after the Crown itself has torn them up. These laws are not decisive in any case, since they were arbitrarily concocted by the United Diet. The National Assembly's resolution against the payment of taxes was formally and materially valid. In our Proclamation we went further than the National Assembly. This was our right and our duty.

Finally, I repeat that only the first act of the drama has come to an end. The struggle between two societies, medieval and bourgeois, will be fought anew in political forms. The same conflicts will return as soon as the Assembly meets again. The organ of the ministry, the *Neue Preussische Zeitung*, has already prophesied this: the same people have been re-elected, it will be necessary to drive away the Assembly a second time.

However, whatever new course the new National Assembly may adopt, the necessary result can be nothing other than this: *complete victory for the counter-revolution* or a *new and victorious revolution*. The victory of the revolution will perhaps first become possible only after the completion of the counter-revolution.

TO THE WORKERS OF COLOGNE

N.Rh.Z., 19 May 1849 [93]

At this final moment we warn you against attempting any putsch in Cologne. Owing to Cologne's military situation you would be hopelessly defeated. You have seen in Elberfeld how the bourgeoisie sends the workers into the firing-line and afterwards betrays them in the basest manner. [94] A state of siege in Cologne would demoralize the whole Rhine province, and a state of siege would be the necessary consequence of any uprising from your side at this time. The Prussians will despair at your calm attitude.

The editors of the *Neue Rheinische Zeitung* give you their parting thanks for the concern you have shown for them. Their last word, always and everywhere, will be: *the emancipation of the working class*.

The Editorial Board of the Neue Rheinische Zeitung

93. This final issue of the *Neue Rheinische Zeitung* was printed in red.

94. There was a rising of workers and petty bourgeois at Elberfeld against the dissolution of the Second Chamber, which had been elected under the constitution of 5 December 1848, but passed a vote of no confidence in the Brandenburg ministry. The rising lasted from 9 to 14 May 1849, and ended with the heroes' welcome given to the invading Prussian troops by the respectable bourgeois of the town.

Reviews from the *Neue Rheinische Zeitung Revue*[1]

REVIEW: JANUARY–FEBRUARY 1850

Karl Marx and Frederick Engels

'*A tout seigneur, tout honneur.*'[2] Let us begin with Prussia.

The king of Prussia is doing his best to provoke a crisis out of the present period of lukewarm agreements and unsatisfactory compromises. He grants a constitution, then after a little unpleasantness[3] he creates two Chambers which revise this constitution. To ensure that the constitution is acceptable to the Crown, whatever the cost, the Chambers erase every article to which the king might in any way take exception; now, they believe, he will immediately take an oath to this constitution. But on the contrary: in order to give the Chamber proof of his 'royal zeal', Frederick William issues a proclamation in which he makes new suggestions to improve the constitution, the acceptance of which would rob this document of the last semblance of even the least, so-called constitutional, bourgeois guarantees. The king hopes the Chambers will reject these suggestions. Far from it. Though the Chambers may have been mistaken in the Crown, they have now taken care that the Crown will not be mistaken in them. They have accepted everything, but everything: an Upper Chamber, an emergency

---

1. These three reviews, for January–February, March–April and May–October 1850, first appeared in the *Neue Rheinische Zeitung. Politisch-Ökonomische Revue*, which Marx and Engels edited from London and which was published in Hamburg and New York, in issues 2 (February), 4 (April) and 5–6 (May–October) respectively, the latter double number being the final issue of the *Revue*. They are translated here from the texts printed in *MEW* 7.

2. To every lord the honour he is due.

3. The elections of January 1849 to the Second Chamber, held on the basis of universal suffrage, resulted in a victory for the liberal opposition. Frederick William IV therefore dissolved the Second Chamber in April 1849 and ordered new elections on the basis of the electoral law of 30 May 1849, which laid down a high property qualification as well as unequal representation for different social groups. In this way he secured a Second Chamber consisting largely of big landowners and high state officials, which was prepared to do his will.

court, a veteran reserve and entailed estates[4] – merely so as not to be sent home, merely in order to force the king into finally taking a 'solemn and holy' oath. This is the way the Prussian constitutional bourgeoisie revenges itself.

It will be difficult for the king to invent a humiliation that these Chambers would find too severe. In the end he will feel obliged to declare that 'the more sacred he holds the vow which he is to swear, the more sensible does his soul become of the duties with which God has entrusted him in the interests of the beloved Fatherland',[5] and the less his 'royal zeal' will allow him to swear an oath to a constitution which offers him everything, but his country nothing.

What the gentlemen of the late lamented United Diet, now reunited in the Chambers, are so afraid of, is being driven back to their old position before 18 March;[6] this would mean that the revolution still lay before them, and this time their rewards would be few. Furthermore, in 1847 they were able to refuse the loan supposedly intended for the Eastern Railway,[7] whereas in 1849 they actually voted the government the loan in question first, and made representations afterwards for the theoretical right to grant money.

Meanwhile, outside the Chambers, the bourgeoisie sitting on the juries is taking pleasure in aquitting those accused of political crimes, thereby demonstrating its opposition to the government. In these trials the government is regularly compromising itself, but so are the representatives of democracy – the accused and those in the public gallery. We call to mind the trial of Waldeck, the 'unfailing constitutionalist', the trial in Trier,[8] etc.

---

4. The constitution as finally accepted by the Chambers and issued by Frederick William on 31 January 1850 retained the following elements of the old pre-revolutionary system: the Upper Chamber, the right to set up emergency courts for high treason trials, the universal obligation to do military service (*Landsturm*), and the entailed and inalienable estates (*Fideikommiss*).

5. Words from Frederick William's message of 7 January 1850 to the Chambers.

6. 18 March 1848: the outbreak of the revolution in Berlin.

7. The loan for the Ostbahn from Berlin to Königsberg (now Kaliningrad) was rejected by the United Diet on 9 June 1847 on the ground that the king had 'totally ignored the rights of the Diet'.

8. Benedict Waldeck was a Left deputy in the Prussian National Assembly, and later in the Second Chamber. He was tried in Berlin in December 1849 for his political activity, but, instead of firmly defending his views, he insisted on his loyalty to the Prussian crown. Karl Grün, the former 'true socialist', behaved similarly at his trial in Trier.

In reply to the question of old Ernst Moritz Arndt,[9] 'Where is the German's fatherland?', Frederick William IV replied: 'Erfurt.'[10] It was not so difficult to parody the *Iliad* in the *Batrachomyomachia*, but no one up till now ever ventured to conceive of a parody of this parody. The Erfurt plan, however, manages to travesty even the *Batrachomyomachia* of the Paulskirche.[11] It is of course completely immaterial whether this incredible assembly convenes in Erfurt or whether the Orthodox tsar forbids it, just as immaterial as the protest against its competency which Herr Vogt will doubtless agree to issue with Herr Venedey.[12] The whole scheme is only of interest to those profound politicians for whom the 'great German' versus 'little German' question[13] was a source of material for their leading articles as productive as it was indispensable, and to the Prussian bourgeoisie, who live in the blissful belief that the king of Prussia, having rejected everything in Berlin,[14] will grant everything in Erfurt.

If the Frankfurt 'National Assembly' will be more or less accurately reflected in Erfurt, the old Federal Diet is reborn in the 'Interim'[15] and reduced to its simplest expression in the

9. In the struggle against Napoleon, nationalist German intellectuals such as Arndt had looked to Prussia as 'the German's fatherland' and to Frederick William III as the national saviour.

10. The Erfurt 'parliament' of March to April 1850 consisted of a number of representatives of the Right in the Frankfurt National Assembly (dissolved the previous year) who supported the Prussian plan to create a 'little German' federal state headed by Prussia, from which Austria would be excluded. Frederick William IV was compelled to abandon this plan almost immediately by joint Russian-Austrian pressure.

11. The *Batrachomyomachia* (Battle of Frogs and Mice), by an unknown author, was a parody of Homer's *Iliad*. The Paulskirche was the meeting-place of the Frankfurt Assembly of 1848–9.

12. Karl Vogt was a natural scientist and a Radical-Democrat deputy in the Frankfurt National Assembly. In 1849 he emigrated to Switzerland and became a professor in Geneva.

13. The problem of whether to exclude Austria from Germany (thus forming a 'little Germany' or *Kleindeutschland*, or to include Austria in part or as a whole, thus forming a 'great Germany' or *Grossdeutschland*, considerably exercised the Frankfurt Assembly in 1849, after it seemed certain to the majority that Germany could only be unified by agreement with either Prussia or Austria.

14. On 3 April 1849 Frederick William IV refused the crown of Germany offered to him by a deputation from Frankfurt.

15. The treaty of 30 September 1849 between Prussia and Austria which provisionally settled the administration of the affairs of Germany, on the basis of the 'maintenance of the German Confederation'.

form of an Austro-Prussian Federal Commission. The 'Interim' has already intervened in Wurtemberg and will soon intervene in Mecklenburg and Schleswig-Holstein.[16]

While Prussia has long been barely scraping its budget together out of issues of paper money, surreptitious loans from the 'Seehandlung'[17] banking house and the remains of the exchequer, and has only now been forced to resort to loans, Austria is in the full flower of national bankruptcy. A deficit of 155 million Austrian florins in the first nine months of the year 1849, which must have risen to 210 or 220 million by the end of December; the complete ruin of government credit at home and abroad following the spectacularly abortive attempt to raise a new loan; the total exhaustion of domestic financial resources – conventional taxes, fire insurance premiums, issues of paper money; the necessity of imposing, on a land already sucked dry, new taxes born of desperation, which will probably never be paid – these are the main characteristics of Austria's financial debility. At the same time the Austrian body politic is decaying more and more rapidly. The government's attempts to resist this process by frantic centralization are in vain; the decomposition has already reached the body politic's outer extremities. Austria is becoming intolerable in the eyes of the most barbarian of its peoples, the mainstays of old Austria – the South Slavs in Dalmatia, Croatia and Banat – intolerable even for the 'loyal' border people.[18] Only an act of desperation still holds out a slight chance of salvation: a foreign war. This foreign war, towards which Austria is being irresistibly propelled, cannot but bring about its rapid and complete disintegration.

Nor has Russia been wealthy enough to pay for its glory, which, moreover, it has had to finance with ready money. Despite the much vaunted gold mines in the Urals and Altai, despite the inexhaustible treasures in the vaults of Petropavlovsk, despite the purchase of government bonds in London and Paris – allegedly motivated by a sheer surplus of money – the Orthodox tsar finds himself obliged to withdraw 5 million silver roubles, under all sorts of false pretexts, from the cash reserves deposited in Petro-

16. See the Review of May–October 1850, below, p. 306.

17. See p. 200, n. 23.

18. 'Border people' (*Grenzer*): the inhabitants of the historic military border districts of Austria, who did military service on the border in return for the right to farm the land.

pavlovsk, in order to cover the paper issue, and he is obliged to have his government bonds sold on the Paris Bourse. Not only this, he also finds it necessary to approach the unbelieving City of London for an advance of 30 million silver roubles.

As a result of the movements of 1848 and 1849 Russia has become so deeply entangled in European politics that it must now urgently execute its old plans with regard to Turkey and Constantinople, 'the key to its house',[19] if they are not to become impracticable for ever. The progress of the counter-revolution, the strength of the revolutionary party in western Europe, which is increasing daily, the internal situation in Russia and the unfavourable state of its finances – all this is forcing it to act rapidly. We recently witnessed the diplomatic prelude to this new and heroic oriental drama.[20] In a few months we shall see the drama itself.

The war against Turkey will necessarily be a European war. This is all the better for Holy Russia, which thereby gains an opportunity of setting a firm foot in Germany, of completing the counter-revolution with the utmost vigour, of helping the Prussians to capture Neuchâtel,[21] and finally, of marching on the centre of the revolution, Paris.

In such a European war England cannot remain neutral. It must take sides against Russia and, for Russia, England is the most dangerous adversary of all. Even if the continental armies must inevitably suffer from overextension as they penetrate further into Russia, and even if they must come to a virtual standstill after crossing the eastern borders of the old Poland – with the risk of the punishment of 1812 being repeated – England nevertheless has the means of striking Russia where it is most vulnerable. Apart

19. Alexander I's description of Constantinople, in a conversation with the French Ambassador Caulaincourt in 1808.

20. In August 1849 the Russian and Austrian governments jointly demanded from the Turkish government the extradition of Hungarians and Poles who had fled to Turkey after the defeat of Hungary.

21. Neuchâtel (Neuenburg), the town and canton of northern Switzerland, was the object of especial Prussian hatred, first because it had thrown off the sovereignty of the king of Prussia and made itself independent in 1848, second because it was the refuge of the revolutionary democrats of south-west Germany after the defeat of the campaign of May and June 1849 in defence of the constitution of the German Reich. In September 1849 the Prince of Prussia told a French agent that the further presence of these elements in Switzerland was intolerable, but that it would take too many troops to recapture Neuchâtel.

from the fact that it can force the Swedes to reconquer Finland, St Petersburg and Odessa have no protection against its fleet. The Russian fleet, as is well known, is the worst in the world, and Kronstadt and Schlüsselberg are just as vulnerable as Saint Jean d'Acre[22] and San Juan de Ulua.[23] But without St Petersburg and Odessa Russia is a giant with severed hands. Furthermore, it cannot do without England even for six months, either for the sale of its raw materials or for the purchase of industrial goods; this became evident even at the time of Napoleon's continental blockade, and is even more the case today. Severance from the English market would drive Russia into the most violent convulsions within a few months. England, on the other hand, can not only do without the Russian market for some time, but can obtain all Russian raw materials from other markets. It is evident that the dreaded might of Russia is by no means as dangerous as is thought. It must nevertheless assume a fearsome form for the German bourgeois, because he rightly suspects that the barbarian hordes from Russia will shortly flood into Germany and play there, as it were, a messianic role.

Switzerland is behaving towards the Holy Alliance in general as the Prussian Chambers behave towards their king in particular. But Switzerland has at least a scapegoat to fall back on, to whom it can pass on two or three times over the blows it receives from the Holy Alliance – a scapegoat, into the bargain, defenceless and at the mercy of its favour and disfavour – the German refugees. It is true that a section of the 'Radical' Swiss in Geneva, Vaud and Berne protested against the cowardly policy of the Federal Council – cowardly both towards the Holy Alliance and towards the refugees; equally true, however, was the Federal Council's assertion that its policy was 'that of the vast majority of the Swiss people'. Meanwhile, on the domestic front, the central government quietly continues to carry out minor bourgeois reforms: the centralization of the customs, coinage, posts, weights and measures – reforms which ensure the applause of the petty bourgeoisie. Of course it has not dared to implement the decision to suspend the

22. A fortress on the Syrian coast, which was taken by Egyptian troops in 1832, and retaken by the English, Austrian, and Turkish fleets jointly in 1840.
23. The fortress of Veracruz on the east coast of Mexico. It was the last fortress to remain in Spanish hands and was finally taken by the Mexicans in 1825.

military treaties[24] and the inhabitants of the founding cantons[25] are still going in droves to Como to sign up for the Neapolitan military service. But for all its humility and complaisance towards the Holy Alliance, Switzerland is threatened by a disastrous storm. In their initial over-confidence after the Sonderbund War,[26] and then completely after the February revolution, the Swiss, who are otherwise so timid, allowed themselves to be seduced into an act of imprudence. They dared something monstrous by wanting to be independent for once; they gave themselves a new constitution in place of that guaranteed by the great powers in 1814, and they recognized the independence of Neuchâtel in spite of the treaties. For this they will be chastised regardless of all their obeisances, favours and police services. And once it is involved in the European war Switzerland's is not the most pleasant of situations. It may have insulted the Holy Alliance; on the other hand, it has also betrayed the revolution.

The suppression of the revolution is being carried out most shamelessly and brutally in France, where the bourgeoisie is leading the forces of reaction in its own interests, and where the republican form of government is allowing these forces to develop with the greatest freedom and consistency. In the short space of a month the reimposition of the wine tax – which immediately and completely ruined half the rural population – was followed in rapid succession by d'Hautpoul's circular, which appoints the police to spy even on civil servants; the law on schoolteachers, which declares that all primary teachers are subject to arbitrary dismissal by the prefects; the education law, which places the schools in the hands of the priests; the transportation law, in which the bourgeoisie vents all its unexpiated desire for revenge upon the June insurgents and, for want of another executioner, delivers them up to the deadliest climate in the whole of Algeria. We shall not mention the innumerable deportations of even the most innocent foreigners, which have continued without a break since 13 June.[27]

24. These treaties (*Militärkapitulationen*) obliged the Swiss cantons to furnish mercenary troops for various foreign powers; article 11 of the Constitution of 1848 forbade the cantons to make such treaties.

25. The three cantons (*Urkantonen*) which founded the Swiss Confederation in the fourteenth century (Schwyz, Uri, and Unterwalden) and took the side of the Sonderbund in the war of 1847.

26. See p. 97, n. 3.

27. On the French events referred to here see 'The Class Struggles in France', below, pp. 369–476.

The object of this violent bourgeois reaction is, of course, the restoration of the monarchy. But a considerable obstacle is put in the way of a monarchist restoration by the different pretenders themselves and their parties inside the country. The Legitimists and Orleanists, the two strongest monarchist parties, more or less balance each other out. The third party, the Bonapartists, are by far the weakest. In spite of his seven million votes, Louis Napoleon does not even have a real party, but only a coterie. Always supported by the majority of the Chamber in the general exercise of reactionary rule, he finds himself deserted as soon as his own particular interests as a pretender come into view – deserted not just by the majority in the Chamber but even by his own ministers, who first leave him in the lurch and then force him to declare the next day in writing that – in spite of everything – they enjoy his confidence. Serious though the consequences of these disagreements may be, until now they have only been comic episodes, in which the President of the Republic always comes off the loser. Meanwhile, it can be taken for granted that each monarchist group is conspiring on its own account with the Holy Alliance. The National Assembly has the effrontery to threaten the people openly with the Russians, while there is already enough evidence to prove that Louis Napoleon is plotting with Tsar Nicholas.

To the same extent that the forces of reaction advance the strength of the revolutionary party naturally grows. Ruined by the fragmentation of landownership, by the tax burden and the narrow governmental character of most of the taxes, which are detrimental even from the point of view of the bourgeoisie; disappointed by the promises of Louis Napoleon and the reactionary deputies, the mass of the rural population has embraced the revolutionary party and professes a form of socialism, albeit still very crude and bourgeois. How strong the revolutionary mood is even in the Legitimist departments is demonstrated by the last election in the department of Gard, the centre of royalism and the 1815 'white terror', where a red deputy was elected. Under pressure from big capital, which in the world of commerce and politics has assumed the very same position it had under Louis Philippe, the petty bourgeoisie has followed the lead of the rural population. The situation has changed so radically that even the traitor Marrast and the journal of the *épiciers*,[28] *Le Siècle*, has had

28. Literally 'grocers', a derogatory term for the small shopkeepers. In 'The Class Struggles in France' Marx refers to *Le Siècle* as the 'literary

to come out in favour of the socialists. The position of the different classes towards each other – for which the opposition of the political parties is only another expression – is almost identical with that of 22 February 1848,[29] except that other issues are at stake: the workers have a deeper consciousness of their strength and the peasants, hitherto a politically moribund class, have been swept up into the movement and won over for the revolution.

It is for this reason that the ruling bourgeoisie must attempt to abolish universal suffrage as quickly as possible. In this necessity, on the other hand, lies the certainty of an imminent victory for the revolution, whatever the situation abroad.

The dramatic nature of the situation as a whole is revealed in the strange legislative proposal of deputy Pradié, who in some 200 clauses attempts to prevent coups d'état and revolutions by a decree of the National Assembly. The lack of trust with which high finance regards the apparent restoration of 'order' – here as well as in other capitals – can be seen in the fact that a few months ago the various branches of the House of Rothschild extended their partnership agreement for only *one year* – a period of unprecedented brevity in the annals of commerce.

While the Continent has been occupied for the last two years with revolution and counter-revolution, and the inevitable torrent of words which has accompanied these events, industrial England has been busy with quite another commodity: prosperity. Here, the commercial crisis which broke out *in due course*[30] in the autumn of 1845 was twice interrupted – at the beginning of 1846 by the free trade legislation,[31] and at the beginning of 1848 by the February revolution. Between these two events, a large proportion of the commodities which had been flooding markets abroad gradually found new market outlets, and the February revolution then removed the competition of continental industry in these markets, while English industry did not lose much more from the disruption of the continental market than it would have lost without the revolution from a continuation of the crisis. The

representative of the constitutional-monarchist petty bourgeoisie'; see below, p. 438.

29. The first day of the disturbances in Paris which led up to the February revolution. At this time the parties were all united on the objective of removing Guizot, though divided on further objectives.

30. In English in the original.

31. I.e. the repeal of the Corn Laws.

February revolution, by temporarily bringing continental industry almost to a standstill, helped the English to weather a crisis year quite tolerably; it contributed substantially to clearing accumulated stocks on the overseas markets and made a new industrial boom possible in the spring of 1849. This boom which, moreover, has extended to a large part of continental industry, has reached such a level in the last three months that the manufacturers claim that they have never known such good times – a claim which is always made on the eve of a crisis. The factories are overwhelmed with orders and are operating at an accelerated rate; they are resorting to every possible means to circumvent the Ten Hours Act and to increase working hours; scores of new factories are being built throughout the industrial districts, and old ones are being extended. Ready money is being loaded onto the market, idle capital is striving to take advantage of this period of general profit; the discount rate is giving rise to speculation and quick investments in manufacturing or in trade in raw materials; almost all articles are rising absolutely in price; all prices are rising relatively.

In short, England is enjoying the full bloom of 'prosperity'. The only question is how long this intoxication will last. Not very long, at any rate. Many of the larger markets – particularly the East Indies – are already almost saturated. Even now exports are being directed less to the really large markets than to the entrepots of world trade, from where goods can be directed to the more favourable markets. As a result of the colossal productive forces which English industry added in the years 1846, 1847 and particularly 1849 to those which already existed in the period 1843–45, and which it still continues to add to, the remaining markets, particularly in North and South America and Australia, will be likewise saturated; and with the first news of their saturation '*panic*' [32] will ensue in speculation and in production simultaneously – perhaps as early as the end of spring, at the latest in July or August. However, as this crisis will inevitably coincide with great clashes on the Continent, it will bear fruit of a very different type from all preceding crises. Whereas hitherto every crisis has been the signal for further progress, for new victories by the industrial bourgeoisie over the landowners and financial bourgeoisie, this crisis will mark the beginning of the modern

32. In English in the original.

English revolution, a revolution in which Cobden will assume the role of Necker.[33]

Now we come to America. The most important thing which has happened here, still more important than the February revolution, is the discovery of the California gold mines. Even now, after scarcely eighteen months, it can be predicted that this discovery will have much greater consequences than the discovery of America itself. For three hundred and thirty years all trade from Europe to the Pacific Ocean has been conducted with a touching, long-suffering patience around the Cape of Good Hope or Cape Horn. All proposals to cut through the Isthmus of Panama have come to grief because of the narrow-minded jealousy of the trading nations. The Californian gold mines were only discovered eighteen months ago and the Yankees have already set about building a railway, a great overland road and a canal from the Gulf of Mexico, steamships are already sailing regularly from New York to Chagres, from Panama to San Francisco, Pacific trade is already concentrating in Panama and the journey around Cape Horn has become obsolete. A coastline which stretches across thirty degrees of latitude, one of the most beautiful and fertile in the world and hitherto more or less unpopulated, is now being visibly transformed into a rich, civilized land thickly populated by men of all races, from the Yankee to the Chinese, from the Negro to the Indian and Malay, from the Creole and Mestizo to the European. Californian gold is pouring in torrents over America and the Asiatic coast of the Pacific and is drawing the reluctant barbarian peoples into world trade, into the civilized world. For the second time world trade has found a new direction. What Tyre, Carthage and Alexandria were in antiquity, Genoa and Venice in the Middle Ages, what London and Liverpool have been hitherto, the emporia of world trade – this is what New York, San Francisco, San Juan del Norte, Léon, Chagres and Panama will now become. The focal point of international traffic – in the Middle Ages, Italy; in modern times, England – is now the southern half of the North American peninsula: industry and

33. The financial reforms of the banker Jacques Necker in the 1780s were both a contributory factor to the outbreak of the first French revolution and an attempt to prevent it. Richard Cobden, along with John Bright, was the leader of the Anti-Corn-Law League of the 1840s, and the political leader of the industrial bourgeoisie generally. He subsequently became a Liberal minister. For Marx's views on English political development, see the Introduction to *Surveys from Exile*, pp. 352–8.

commerce in the Old World must make tremendous efforts if they are to avoid falling into the same state of decline as the industry and commerce of Italy since the sixteenth century, if England and France are not to become what Venice, Genoa and Holland are today. In a few years we shall have a regular steam-packet line from England to Chagres, from Chagres and San Francisco to Sydney, Canton and Singapore. Thanks to the Californian gold and the untiring energy of the Yankees both coastlines of the Pacific Ocean will be just as populated, just as open to trade, and just as industrialized as is the coast from Boston to New Orleans at present. Then the Pacific Ocean will perform the same role as the Atlantic does now and the Mediterranean did in antiquity and the Middle Ages – the great sea-route for international traffic – and the Atlantic Ocean will decline to a mere inland lake, such as the Mediterranean is today. The only chance for the civilized countries of Europe to avoid falling into the same industrial, commercial and political dependence which characterizes Italy, Spain and Portugal today, lies in a social revolution which, so long as there is still time, will transform the mode of production and exchange according to those requirements of production which arise from the modern productive forces; which will thus make possible the generation of new productive forces which will guarantee the superiority of European industry and so compensate for the disadvantages of Europe's geographical location.

In conclusion a characteristic curiosity from China, which the well-known German missionary, Gützlaff, has brought back with him. The slowly but steadily increasing over-population of the country has long made social conditions in China very oppressive for the great majority of the nation. When the English came they won for themselves the right to conduct free trade with five ports. Thousands of English and American ships sailed to China and within a short time the country was saturated with cheap products manufactured in Britain and America. Chinese industry based on handicraft succumbed to the competition of the machine. The unshakeable Middle Kingdom underwent a social crisis. Taxes could no longer be collected, the state came to the brink of bankruptcy, the population sank into poverty, erupted in rebellion, and scorned, mistreated and killed the emperor's mandarins and bonzes. The country is on the verge of ruin and is threatened by a mighty revolution. But even worse, among the rebellious plebs people appeared who pointed to the poverty of some and the wealth of others, who demanded and still demand a different distribution of property – indeed the total abolition of private property. When Herr Gützlaff came back among civilized people and Europeans after twenty years' absence, he heard talk of socialism and asked what it was. When he was told, he exclaimed in alarm: 'Am I nowhere to escape this ruinous doctrine? Precisely the same thing has been preached for some time in China by many people from the mob.'

Chinese socialism may, of course, bear the same relation to European socialism as Chinese to Hegelian philosophy. But it is still amusing to note that the oldest and most unshakeable empire on earth has, within eight years, been brought to the brink of a social revolution by the cotton bales of the English bourgeoisie; in any event, such a revolution cannot help but have the most important consequences for the civilized world. When our European reactionaries, in the course of their imminent flight through Asia, finally arrive at the Great Wall of China, at the gates which lead to the home of primal reaction and primal conservatism, who knows if they will not find written thereon the legend:

République chinoise
Liberté, Egalité, Fraternité

London, 31 January 1850

*

The wishes of the Prussian bourgeoisie have been fulfilled: the 'man of honour' has taken an oath to the constitution, on condition that it is 'made possible for him to rule with this constitution'.[34] And the bourgeois in the Chambers have already satisfied this desire completely in the few days which have passed since 6 February. Before 6 February they said: 'We must make concessions so that the constitution is ratified on oath; once the oath has been given we can proceed quite differently.' After 6 February they say: 'The king has sworn an oath to the constitution; we have all the guarantees possible; we can safely make concessions.' Eighteen millions have been approved for armaments, without debate, without opposition and almost unanimously for the

34. On 6 February 1850, Frederick William IV took the oath to the constitution of 31 January 1850, and the words quoted are from his speech on that occasion.

mobilization of 500,000 men against an enemy who is still unknown; the budget has been passed in four days, and all government bills pass through the Chambers in less than no time. It is clear that the German bourgeoisie, as always, lacks nothing in cowardice and in pretexts for cowardice.

These compliant Chambers have given the king of Prussia ample opportunity to recognize the advantages of the constitutional system over the absolutist system, not only for the subjects but also for the rulers. If we think back to the financial troubles of 1842–8, to the abortive attempts to borrow money through the Seehandlung and the Bank, to Rothschild's dismissive replies, to the loan refused by the United Diet, to the exhaustion of the exchequer and public funds, and if we compare all this with the financial surplus of 1850 – three budgets with a deficit of seventy millions covered by consent of the Chambers, the mass circulation of loan certificates and treasury bills, the safer financial footing provided for the state by the Bank of Prussia, as against the Seehandlung, and over and above all this, a reserve of thirty-four millions in approved loans – what a contrast!

According to statements made by the War Minister, the Prussian government regards as probable certain eventualities which might force it to mobilize its whole army in the interests of European 'peace and order'. Prussia has proclaimed its renewed membership of the Holy Alliance loudly and clearly enough with this declaration. It is also evident what enemy this new crusade is directed against. The centre of anarchy and revolution, the Gallic Babel is to be destroyed. Whether France is to be attacked directly or whether this attack is to be preceded by diversionary campaigns against Switzerland and Turkey, will depend entirely upon how the situation develops in Paris. At all events the Prussian government now has the means to increase its 180,000 soldiers to 500,000 within two months; 400,000 Russian troops have been marshalled in Poland, Volhynia and Bessarabia; Austria has at least 650,000 men at the ready. Merely in order to feed these colossal forces Russia and Austria must begin a war of invasion this year. And on the question of the initial direction to be taken by this invasion, a remarkable document has just reached the public.

In one of its latest issues the *Schweizerische Nationalzeitung* has published a memorandum attributed to the Austrian general Schönhals, which contains a complete plan to invade Switzerland. The principal elements of this plan are as follows:

Prussia concentrates around 60,000 men on the Main near the railways; an army corps from Hesse, Bavaria and Wurtemberg concentrates partly near Rottweil and Tuttling and partly near Kempten and Memmingen. Austria draws up 50,000 men in Vorarlberg and in the region of Innsbruck and forms a second corps in Italy between Sesto-Calende and Lecco. In the meantime, Switzerland is delayed by diplomatic negotiations. When the moment comes to attack, the Prussians speed by rail to Lörrach, and the smaller German contingents to Donaueschingen; the Austrians concentrate at Bregenz and Feldkirch, and position their Italian army at Como and Lecco. One brigade stops at Varese and threatens Bellinzona. The ambassadors hand over an ultimatum and depart. Operations begin: the main pretext for the invasion is to restore the federal constitution of 1814 and the freedom of the Sonderbund cantons. The attack itself takes place in a concentric formation against Lucerne. The Prussians advance via Basle towards the River Aar, the Austrians via St Gallen and Zurich towards the River Limmet. The former take up positions from Solothurn to Zurzach, the latter from Zurzach through Zurich as far as Uznach. At the same time a detachment of 15,000 Austrians advances via Chur to the Splügen Pass and combines with the Italian corps, whereupon both advance along the upper Rhine valley towards the St Gotthard Pass; here they join forces with the corps which has moved through Varese and Bellinzona and incite the founding cantons to rebellion. Meanwhile these cantons are cut off from the west of Switzerland by the advance of the main armies, which the smaller contingents make contact with via Schaffhausen, and by the capture of Lucerne; thus the sheep are separated from the goats. At the same time France, which is committed by the 'secret treaty of 30 January' to muster 60,000 men at Lyons and Colmar, occupies Geneva and the Jura under the same pretext which it used to occupy Rome. Thus Berne becomes untenable and the 'revolutionary' government is forced either to capitulate immediately or to starve with its troops in the Bernese Alps.

As can be seen, the project is not bad. It takes into account the lie of the land and proposes taking the flatter and more fertile north of Switzerland first and capturing the only tenable position in the north, that behind the rivers Aar and Limmet, with the combined main forces. It has the advantage of cutting off the Swiss army's main granary and of leaving it for the time being the most difficult mountain terrain. Thus the plan can be put into operation as early as the beginning of spring, and the earlier it is executed the more difficult is the position of the Swiss, who will be forced back into the mountains.

It is extremely difficult on the basis of internal evidence to determine whether the document was published against the will of its authors, or whether it was deliberately composed to find its way into the hands of a Swiss newspaper and be published. Should the latter be the case, its intention could only be to cause the Swiss to exhaust their finances by a rapid and large-scale mobilization of troops – thus producing greater Swiss compliance towards the Holy Alliance – and to confuse public opinion in general as to the intentions of the allies. This would be supported by the ostentatious sabre-rattling accompanying the mobilization of Russia and Prussia and the war plans against Switzerland, and, in addition, by a sentence in the memorandum itself, which recommends the greatest rapidity in the execution of all operations, so that as large an area as possible can be taken before the contingents have concentrated again and moved out. On the other hand there are just as many internal considerations which argue in favour of the memorandum's genuine character as a real proposal to invade Switzerland.

This much is certain: the Holy Alliance will march this year, whether first of all against Switzerland or Turkey, or directly against France; in both cases the Swiss Federal Council can pack its bags. Whether the Holy Alliance or the revolution reach Berne first, it has brought about its own ruin by its craven neutrality. The counter-revolution cannot be satisfied with the Federal Council's concessions, because its very origins are more or less revolutionary; the revolution cannot for one moment tolerate such a treacherous and cowardly government in the heart of Europe between the three nations most closely involved in the movement. The behaviour of the Swiss Federal Council offers the most blatant and, we hope, the last example of what the alleged 'independence' and 'autonomy' of small states between the modern great nations really means.

As far as recent events in France are concerned we refer the reader to the section of the article '1848–1849' contained in this number.[35] In the next number we shall publish a special

35. Chapter II of 'The Class Struggles in France' in *Surveys from Exile*.

article on the virtual abolition of the Ten Hours Act in England.[36]

REVIEW: MARCH–APRIL 1850

Karl Marx and Frederick Engels

(In our previous number the monthly review had to be omitted due to lack of space. We now publish from this review only the part which has reference to England.)

Shortly before the anniversary of the February revolution, when Carlier had the liberty trees cut down, *Punch* published a cartoon of a liberty tree which had bayonets for leaves and bombs for fruit; opposite the French liberty tree, bristling with bayonets, a song is printed in praise of the English liberty tree, which bears the only fruit of reliable quantity: pounds, shillings and pence. But this irritating attempt at wit pales beside the immoderate fits of rage in which *The Times* has been slandering the triumphs of 'anarchy' since 10 March. The reactionary party in England, as in all countries, feels the blow struck in Paris as if it had been actually dealt the blow itself.[37]

But at the moment the greatest threat to 'order' in England does not lie in the dangers emanating from Paris but is a direct consequence of this order itself, a fruit from the English liberty tree: a *commercial crisis*.

We already pointed out in our review for January that a crisis was approaching. It has been precipitated by several factors. Before the last crisis in 1845 surplus capital found an outlet in railway speculation. However, overproduction and excess speculation reached such a pitch that the railway market did not even recover during the prosperity of 1848–9, and even the shares of the most respectable firms in this sector of business are still quoted at extremely low prices. Nor did the low prices for corn and the harvest prospects for 1850 offer any opportunity for the investment of capital, and the various government bonds were subject to too extreme a risk to form the object of large-scale speculation. Thus the surplus capital of the period of prosperity found its usual outlets blocked. For the speculators there remained only the possibility

36. Engels's article 'The Ten Hours Bill' is translated in *MECW* 10, pp. 288–300.

37. See *The Class Struggles in France*, in *Surveys from Exile*, pp. 457–62.

of unloading all their capital either into industrial production, or into speculative ventures in colonial foodstuffs and the key industrial raw materials, cotton and wool. With the direct influx of such huge amounts of capital – normally employed in other ways – industrial production naturally grew with extraordinary speed, and as a result the markets became saturated. Thus the outbreak of the crisis was significantly accelerated. Even now the first symptoms of the crisis are becoming evident in the most important sections of industry and speculation. For four weeks the situation in the key industry, cotton, has been completely depressed and within this industry it is the main branches – in particular the spinning and weaving of coarse fabrics – which are suffering most. Cotton yarn and coarse calico have already fallen in price far more than raw cotton. Production is being cut back, and almost without exception the factories are working short time. A temporary revival of industrial activity is hoped for as a result of the spring orders from the Continent; but while the orders already placed for the domestic market, the East Indies, China and the Levant are largely being cancelled again, the continental orders, which always provided work for two months, are hardly coming in at all because of the unsettled political situation. In the woollen industry there are symptoms here and there which indicate that the still more or less 'healthy' state of this business is about to come to an end. Iron production is suffering likewise. Manufacturers think it inevitable that prices will soon fall and they are attempting to prevent too rapid a fall by means of mergers. So much for the state of industry. Let us now turn our attention to speculation. The prices of cotton are falling, partly as a result of new increases in supply, partly as a result of the slump in the industry itself. The same is true of colonial foodstuffs. Supplies are increasing, consumption on the home market is dropping. In the last two months twenty-five shiploads of tea alone have arrived in Liverpool. The consumption of colonial produce, which was held back even during the period of prosperity as a result of the distressed state in the agricultural districts, is all the more subject to the similar pressure which is now making itself felt in the industrial districts. One of the most important colonial traders in Liverpool has already succumbed to this adverse turn of events.

The results of the commercial crisis now impending will be more serious than ever before. It coincides with the agricultural crisis which began with the abolition of corn tariffs in England and has increased as a result of the recent good harvests. For the first time England is experiencing *at the same time* an *industrial* and an *agricultural* crisis. This dual crisis in England will be accelerated, widened in scope and made even more explosive by the convulsions which are now simultaneously imminent on the Continent; and the continental revolution will take on an unprecedentedly socialist character as a result of the repercussions of the English crisis on the world market. It is a known fact that no European country will be hit so directly, to such an extent and with such intensity as Germany. The reason is simple: Germany represents England's biggest continental market, and the main German exports, wool and grain, have by far their most important outlet in England. History is most happily summed up in this epigram addressed to the apostles of order: while inadequate consumption drives the working classes to revolt, overproduction drives the upper classes to bankruptcy.

The Whigs will naturally be the first victims of the crisis. As in the past, they will abandon the helm of state as soon as the threatening storm breaks. And this time they will say farewell for ever to the offices of Downing Street. A short-lived Tory ministry may follow them at first, but the ground will quake under their feet; all the parties of the opposition will unite against them, with the industrialists at their head. The Tories have no popular universal panacea for the crisis, such as the repeal of the Corn Laws. They will be forced at least to carry out a parliamentary reform. This means that they cannot avoid assuming power under conditions which will open the doors of Parliament to the proletariat, place its demands on the agenda of the House of Commons and pitch England into the European revolution.

*

We have little to add to these notes written one month ago on the subject of the impending commercial crisis. The temporary upward trend in business which regularly occurs in spring has finally appeared this year, too, but on a much smaller scale than usual. French industry has particularly profited from this, as it supplies excellent summer fabrics, but in Manchester, Glasgow and the West Riding increased orders have also been received. This temporary revival in industry, it must be remembered, occurs every year and will only delay the development of the crisis a little.

There has been a temporary upward trend in business in the East Indies. The more favourable market situation in England has allowed merchants to sell off their supplies below earlier prices and the situation on the Bombay market has eased a little as a result. These temporary and local improvements in trade are also typical of the episodic movements which occur from time to time, particularly at the beginning of every crisis, and which have only an insignificant effect on its general course.

News has just arrived from America describing the market situation there as completely depressed. America, however, is the most important market; the saturation of this market, the stagnation of business and the drop in prices there mark the actual beginning of the crisis, which will have direct, rapid and inevitable repercussions on England. We need only call to mind the crisis of 1837. Only one article continues to rise in value in America: U.S. Bonds, the only government bonds which offer a safe refuge for the capital of our European apostles of order.

After America's involvement in the downward movement caused by overproduction, we can expect the crisis to develop more rapidly than hitherto in the months to come. Political events on the Continent are likewise daily forcing matters to a head, and the coincidence of economic crisis and revolution, which has already been mentioned several times in this *Revue*, will become more and more inescapable. *Que les destins s'accomplissent!* [38]

London, 18 April 1850

REVIEW: MAY–OCTOBER 1850

Karl Marx and Frederick Engels

The political activity of the last six months has been essentially different from that which preceded it. The revolutionary party has everywhere been driven from the field, and the victors – the various fractions of the bourgeoisie in France, the various princes in Germany – are squabbling over the fruits of their victory. The quarrel is being conducted with a great deal of noise; and it might seem inevitable that there will be an open rupture, and that a decision can only be reached by force of arms. Yet the swords are doomed to remain in their sheaths, and the indeterminacy of

38. Let destiny take its course.

the situation will be repeatedly concealed behind peace treaties, while ever new preparations are made for a phoney war.

Let us first consider the basic *reality* underlying this superficial turbulence.

The years 1843–5 were years of industrial and commercial prosperity, a necessary sequel to the almost uninterrupted industrial depression of 1837–42. As is always the case, prosperity very rapidly encouraged speculation. Speculation regularly occurs in periods when overproduction is already in full swing. It provides overproduction with temporary market outlets, while for this very reason precipitating the outbreak of the crisis and increasing its force. The crisis itself first breaks out in the area of speculation; only later does it hit production. What appears to the superficial observer to be the cause of the crisis is not overproduction but excess speculation, but this is itself only a symptom of overproduction. The subsequent disruption of production does not appear as a consequence of its own previous exuberance but merely as a setback caused by the collapse of speculation. However, as we cannot at this moment give a complete history of the post-1845 crisis, we shall enumerate only the most significant of these *symptoms* of overproduction.

In the years of prosperity from 1843 to 1845, speculation was concentrated principally in railways, where it was based upon a real demand, in corn, as a result of the price rise of 1845 and the potato blight, in cotton, following the bad crop of 1846, and in the East Indian and Chinese trade, where it followed hard on the heels of the opening up of the Chinese market by England.

The extension of the English railway system had already begun in 1844 but did not get fully under way until 1845. In this year alone the number of bills presented for the formation of railway companies amounted to 1,035. In February 1846, even after countless of these projects had been abandoned, the money to be deposited with the government for the remainder still amounted to the enormous sum of £14 million and even in 1847 the total amount of the payments called up in England was over £42 million of which over £36 million was for English railways, and £5½ million for foreign ones. The heyday of this speculation was the summer and autumn of 1845. Stock prices rose continuously, and the speculators' profits soon sucked all social classes into the whirlpool. Dukes and earls competed with merchants and manufacturers for the lucrative honour of sitting on the boards of directors of the various companies; members of the House of Commons, the legal profession and the clergy were also represented in large numbers. Anyone who had saved a penny, anyone who had the least credit at his disposal, speculated in railway stocks. The number of railway journals rose from three to twenty. The large daily papers often each earned £14,000 per week from railway advertisements and prospectuses. Not enough engineers could be found, and they were paid enormous salaries. Printers, lithographers, bookbinders, paper-merchants and others, who were mobilized to produce prospectuses, plans, maps, etc; furnishing manufacturers who fitted out the mushrooming offices of the countless railway boards and provisional committees – all were paid splendid sums. On the basis of the actual extension of the English and continental railway system and the speculation which accompanied it, there gradually arose in this period a superstructure of fraud reminiscent of the time of Law and the South Sea Company.[39] Hundreds of companies were promoted without the least chance of success, companies whose promoters themselves never intended any real execution of the schemes, companies whose sole reason for existence was the directors' consumption of the funds deposited and the fraudulent profits obtained from the sale of stocks.

In October 1848 a reaction ensued, soon becoming a total panic. Even before February 1848, when deposits had to be paid to the government, the most unsound projects had gone bankrupt. In April 1846 the setback had already begun to affect the continental stock markets; in Paris, Hamburg, Frankfurt and Amsterdam there were compulsory sales at considerably reduced prices, which resulted in the bankruptcy of bankers and brokers. The railway crisis lasted into the autumn of 1848, prolonged by the successive bankruptcies of less unsound schemes as they were gradually affected by the general pressure and as demands for payment were made. This crisis was also aggravated by developments in other areas of speculation, and in commerce and industry; the prices of the older, better-established stocks were gradually forced down, until in October 1848 they reached their lowest level.

In August 1845 public attention first turned to the potato blight, which appeared not only in England and Ireland but also

39. John Law, the economist and financier, was one of the key figures associated with the 'South Sea Bubble' which burst in 1720.

on the Continent – the first symptom that the roots of existing society were rotten. At the same time reports were received which no longer left people in any doubt about the huge loss in the corn harvest that had already been expected. These two factors caused corn prices to rise considerably on all European markets. In Ireland total famine broke out, obliging the English government to give the province a loan of £8 million – exactly £1 for each Irishman. In France, where the calamity was increased by the floods, which caused about £4 million worth of damage, the crop failure was of the utmost gravity. It was no less so in Holland and Belgium. The crop failure of 1845 was followed by an even worse one in 1846, and the potato blight appeared again too, although this time it was not as widespread. Speculation in corn thus had a real basis; it flourished all the more since the rich harvests of 1842–4 had long held it back almost completely. From 1845 to 1847 more corn was imported than ever before. Corn prices rose continuously until spring 1847, when, because of the changing news from various countries about the coming harvest, and because of the measures taken by various governments (the opening of ports to the free import of corn, etc.), a period of fluctuation began. Finally in May 1847 prices reached their highest point. In this month the average price of a quarter of wheat in England rose as high as 102s. 6d. and on single days as high as 115s. and 124s. But considerably more favourable reports soon came in about the weather and the growing crops; prices fell, and in the middle of July the average price stood at only 74s. Unfavourable weather drove prices up again somewhat, until finally, in the middle of August, it was certain that the 1847 harvest would produce an above average yield. The fall in prices could now no longer be stopped; supplies to England increased beyond all expectation, and on 18 September the average price had fallen to 49s. 6d. In the course of sixteen weeks, therefore, the average price had varied by no less than 53s.

During this whole period, not only had the railway crisis continued but, on top of all this, the whole credit system collapsed at the very moment when the corn prices were at their highest, in April and May 1847, and the money market was completely ruined. The corn speculators nevertheless held out through the fall in prices until 2 August. On this day the Bank raised its lowest discount rate to 5 per cent and, for all bills of exchange over more than two months, to 6 per cent. Immediately a series of most spectacular bankruptcies ensued on the Corn Exchange, headed by that of Mr Robinson, Governor of the Bank of England. In London alone, eight great corn merchants went bankrupt, their total liabilities amounting to more than £1½ million. The provincial corn exchanges were totally paralysed; bankruptcies followed one after another at a similar rate, especially in Liverpool. Corresponding bankruptcies took place sooner or later on the Continent according to the distance from London. However, by 18 September, when the price of corn fell to its lowest point, the corn crisis can be regarded as being over in England.

We now come to the commercial crisis proper, the monetary crisis. In the first four months of 1847 the general state of trade and industry still seemed to be satisfactory, with the exception of iron production and the cotton industry. Iron production, given an enormous boost by the railway bubble of 1845, suffered proportionately as this outlet for the excess supply of iron contracted. The cotton industry, the main branch of industry for the East Indian and Chinese markets, had been overproducing for these markets as early as 1845, and very soon a relative recession began. The bad cotton crop of 1846, the rise in prices for both raw material and finished commodity, and the consequent reduction in consumption, all increased pressure on the industry. In the first few months of 1847 production was cut back considerably throughout Lancashire, and the cotton workers were hit by the crisis.

On 15 April 1847 the Bank of England raised its lowest discount rate for short-term bills to 5 per cent, and set a limit to the total amount of discountable bills irrespective of the character of the drawee houses. It also made a peremptory announcement to its customers that, contrary to previous practice, it would no longer renew advances made when these fell due, but would demand repayment. Two days later the publication of its weekly balance sheet showed that the reserves of the Banking Department had dropped to £2½ million. The Bank had therefore taken the above measures to stop the drain of gold from its vaults and to replenish its cash reserves.

The drain of gold and silver from the Bank had various causes. Rising consumption and the considerably higher prices of almost all articles required added means of circulation, particularly gold and silver for retail trade. Further, the continuous payment of instalments for railway construction, which in April alone amounted to £4,314,000, had led to a mass withdrawal of deposits from the Bank. That part of the money called up which was intended for foreign railways, flowed directly abroad. The considerable excess import of sugar, coffee and other colonial produce (consumption and prices having risen even more as a result of speculation), of cotton (following the speculative purchases made since it had become clear that the crop would be scarce), and, in particular, of corn (as a result of repeated harvest failures), had to be paid for mostly in ready cash or bullion, and in this way, too, a considerable amount of gold and silver flowed abroad. This drain of precious metals from England, it may be added, continued until the end of August, despite the Bank's measures mentioned above.

The Bank's decisions, and the news of the low level of its reserves, immediately produced pressure on the money market and a panic throughout English commerce matched in intensity only by that of 1845. In the last week of April and the first four days of May almost all credit transactions were paralysed. However no unusual bankruptcies occurred; trading houses kept their heads above water with enormous interest payments and by the forced sale of supplies, government stocks, etc. at ruinous prices. A whole series of well-established firms saved themselves in this way during the first act of the crisis only by paving the way for their subsequent collapse. But the fact that the first and most threatening danger had been overcome contributed to the raising of confidence; after 5 May pressure on the money market noticeably eased, and towards the end of May the alarm was more or less over.

A few months later, however, at the beginning of August, the bankruptcies mentioned above occurred in the corn trade. Lasting until September, they were hardly over when the general commercial crisis broke out with concentrated force, particularly in the East Indian, West Indian and Mauritian trade. The crisis broke simultaneously in London, Liverpool, Manchester and Glasgow. During September twenty concerns were ruined in London alone, their total liabilities amounting to between £9 and £10 million. 'There were uprootings of commercial dynasties in England not less striking than the fall of those political houses of which we have lately heard so much,' said Disraeli on 30 August 1848 in the House of Commons. The epidemic of bankruptcies in the East Indian trade raged incessantly until the end of the year and was resumed in the first months of 1848 when news arrived of the bankruptcy of the corresponding concerns in Calcutta, Bombay, Madras and Mauritius.

This series of bankruptcies, unprecedented in the history of commerce, was caused by general over-speculation and the resulting excess import of colonial produce. The prices of this produce, which had been kept at an artificially high level for a long time, dropped somewhat before the panic in April 1847, but were subject to a general and steep drop only *after* this panic, when the whole credit system collapsed and one house after the other was forced to sell on a mass scale. This fall was so considerable, particularly from June and July until November, that even the oldest and most reputable concerns were ruined.

The bankruptcies in September were still limited exclusively to *actual merchant houses*. On 1 October the Bank raised its lowest discount rate for short-term bills to 5½ per cent, and declared at the same time that it would henceforth make no more advances against government stocks of any kind. The *joint stock banks* and *private bankers* were now no longer able to withstand the pressure. The Royal Bank of Liverpool, the Liverpool Banking Company, the North and South Wales Bank, the Newcastle Union Joint Stock Bank and others were ruined, one after the other, within a few days. At the same time declarations of insolvency were issued by a large number of smaller private bankers throughout the English provinces.

A considerable number of stock-jobbers, stockbrokers, billbrokers, shipping agents, tea and cotton brokers, iron manufacturers and iron merchants, cotton and wool spinners, calico printers, etc. in Liverpool, Manchester, Oldham, Halifax, Glasgow and elsewhere went bankrupt following the general suspension of payments by the banks which characterized the month of October. According to Mr Tooke,[40] these bankruptcies were without precedent in the history of English commerce, both in their number and in the amount of capital involved, and the crisis far exceeded that of 1825. The crisis reached its peak between 22 and 25 October, when all commercial transactions had come to a standstill. A deputation from the City then brought about a suspension of the Bank Act of 1844, which had been the fruit of

40. Thomas Tooke, the economist, was the author of *A History of Prices* . . ., London, 1848, from which Marx made numerous extracts, and which he drew on extensively for this review.

the deceased Sir Robert Peel's sagacity. With this suspension, the division of the Bank of England into two completely independent departments with separate cash reserves instantly came to an end; another few days of the old arrangement and the Banking Department would have been forced into bankruptcy while £6 million in gold lay stored in the Issue Department.

As early as October the crisis caused the first setback on the Continent. Serious bankruptcies occurred simultaneously in Brussels, Hamburg, Bremen, Elberfeld, Genoa, Livorno, Courtrai, St Petersburg, Lisbon and Venice. While the crisis eased in England, it increased in intensity on the Continent, affecting places hitherto untouched. During the worst period, the exchange rate was favourable for England, and from November on England continuously attracted imports of gold and silver, not only from Russia and the Continent, but also from America. The immediate result was that as the money market eased in England, it tightened in the rest of the commercial world and the crisis grew. Thus the number of bankruptcies outside England rose in November; equally important bankruptcies now occurred in New York, Rotterdam, Amsterdam, Le Havre, Bayonne, Antwerp, Mons, Trieste, Madrid and Stockholm. In December the crisis broke in Marseilles and Algiers and took on a new severity in Germany.

We have now arrived at the point where the February revolution broke out in France. If one looks at the list of bankruptcies which Mr D. M. Evans appends to his *Commercial Crisis of 1847–48* (London, 1848), one finds that in England *not a single concern of any importance* was ruined as a result of this revolution. The only bankruptcies connected with it occured in stock-jobbing, as a result of the sudden devaluation of all government stocks on the Continent. There were, of course, similar stock-jobbing bankruptcies in Amsterdam, Hamburg, etc. English consols fell by 6 per cent, whereas they had fallen by 3 per cent after the July revolution. Thus, as far as stock-jobbers were concerned, the February republic was only twice as dangerous as the July monarchy.

The panic which broke out in Paris after February, and swept across the whole Continent together with the revolution, was very similar in the course it took to the London panic of April 1847. Credit disappeared suddenly and business transactions came almost to a standstill; in Paris, Brussels and Amsterdam everyone hurried to the bank to change notes for gold. On the whole, however, very few bankruptcies ensued outside the field of stock-jobbing, and it cannot easily be proved that these few cases were necessarily the result of the February revolution. The suspensions of payment by the Paris brokers, most only temporary, were only partly connected with stock-jobbing; some were precautionary measures, by no means caused by insolvency, the rest were attributable to pure chicanery, aimed at making difficulties for the Provisional Government in order to force concessions from it. As far as the banking and commercial bankruptcies in other parts of the Continent were concerned it is impossible to determine to what extent they resulted from the duration and gradual spread of the commercial crisis, how far the situation at the time was used by already unsound firms to make a judicious exit, and how far they were really the result of losses caused by the panic atmosphere of the revolution. At any rate, it is certain that the commercial crisis contributed far more to the revolution of 1848 than the revolution to the commercial crisis. Between March and May England enjoyed direct advantages from the revolution, which supplied her with a great deal of continental capital. From this moment on the crisis can be regarded as over in England; there was an improvement in all branches of business and the new industrial cycle began with a decided movement towards prosperity. How little the continental revolution held back the industrial and commercial boom in England can be seen from the fact that the amount of cotton manufactured here rose from 475 million lb. in 1847 to 713 million lb. in 1848.

In England this renewed prosperity developed visibly during 1848, 1849 and 1850. For the eight months January–August, England's total exports amounted to £31,633,214 in 1848; £39,263,322 in 1849 and £43,851,568 in 1850. In addition to this considerable improvement, manifest in all branches of business with the exception of iron production, rich harvests were gathered everywhere during these three years. The average price of wheat in 1848–50 was 36s. per quarter in England, 32s. in France. This period of prosperity is characterized by the fact that three major outlets for speculation were blocked. Railway production had been reduced to the slow development of a normal branch of industry, corn offered no opportunities due to a series of good harvests, and, as a result of the revolution, government stocks had lost the reliable character without which large speculative transactions in securities are not possible. During every period of prosperity capital accumulates. On the one hand increased production generates new capital; on the other, capital which was available but idle during the crisis is released from its inactivity and unloaded onto the market. With the lack of speculative outlets this *additional* capital was forced during these years to flow into actual industry, thus increasing production even more rapidly. How apparent this is in England, without anyone being able to explain it, is demonstrated by this naive statement in the *Economist* of 19 October 1850:

It is remarked that the present prosperity differs from that of former periods within recollection, in all of which there was some baseless speculation exciting hopes that were destined not to be realized. At one time it was foreign mines, at another more railways than could be conveniently made in half a century. Even when such speculations were well founded, they contemplated a realization of income, from raising metals or creating new conveniences, at the end of a considerable period, and afforded no immediate reward. But at present our prosperity is founded on the production of things immediately useful, and that go into consumption nearly as fast as they are brought to market, returning to the producers a fair remuneration and stimulating more production.

Cotton manufacturing, the dominant branch of industry, provides the most striking proof of the extent to which industrial production has increased in 1848 and 1849. The United States cotton crop of 1849 produced a higher yield than in any previous year, amounting to 2¾ million bales, or about 1,200 million lb. The expansion of the cotton industry has kept pace with this increase in imports to such an extent that at the end of 1849 stocks were lower than ever before, even after the years of the crop failures. In 1849 over 775 million lb. of cotton were spun, as against 721 million lb. in 1845, the year of the greatest prosperity hitherto. The expansion of the cotton industry is further shown by the great rise in cotton prices (55 per cent) resulting from a relatively minor loss in the 1850 crop. At least the same progress can be seen in all other branches, such as the spinning and weaving of silk, shoddy and linen. Exports in these industries have risen so considerably, particularly in 1850, that they have produced a large increase in the total export figures for the first eight months of this year (£12 million above the corresponding figure for 1848, £4 million above that for 1849), even though in 1850 the export of cotton products has dropped noticeably as a result of the bad cotton crop. In spite of the considerable increase in wool prices, which seems to have been caused by speculation in 1849, but which has now levelled out, the woollen industry has expanded continuously, and new looms are continually being brought into operation. The export of linen textiles in 1844, the highest previously, amounted to 91 million yards, at a value of over £2,800,000, while in 1849 it reached 107 million yards at a value of over £3,000,000.

Another proof of the growth of English industry is the continuously rising consumption of basic colonial produce, particularly coffee, sugar and tea, at continuously rising prices – at least for the first two articles. This increase in consumption is a direct result of the expansion of industry, the more so, as the exceptional market situation created since 1845 by the extraordinary railway investments has long since been reduced to its normal scale, and as the low corn prices of the last few years have not allowed any increase in consumption in the agricultural areas.

In the last few months the broad expansion of the cotton industry has led to renewed attempts to saturate the East Indian and Chinese markets. But the quantity of old stocks still awaiting sale in these areas soon again obstructed these attempts. At the same time, in view of the rising consumption of raw materials and colonial produce, an attempt was made to speculate in these commodities, but a stop was very quickly put to this by the temporary increase in imports, and by the memory of the wounds sustained in 1847, which are still too fresh.

Industrial prosperity will be further increased by the recent opening up of the Dutch colonies, by the impending establishment of trading routes across the Pacific Ocean (to which we shall return) and by the great industrial exhibition of 1851. This exhibition was announced by the English bourgeoisie already in 1849, with the most impressive cold-bloodedness, at a time when the whole Continent was still dreaming of revolution. For this exhibition they have summoned all their vassals from France to China to a great examination, in which they are to demonstrate how they have been using their time; and even the omnipotent tsar of Russia feels obliged to order his subjects to appear in large numbers at this great examination. This great world congress of products and producers is quite different in its significance from the absolutist Congresses of

Bregenz and Warsaw,[41] which have caused our narrow-minded continental democrats so much sweat; different also from the European democratic congresses which the various provisional governments *in partibus infidelium*[42] repeatedly project for the salvation of the world. This exhibition is a striking proof of the concentrated power with which modern large-scale industry is everywhere demolishing national barriers and increasingly blurring local peculiarities of production, society and national character among all peoples. By putting on show the massed resources of modern industry in a small concentrated space, just at a time when modern bourgeois society is being undermined from all sides, it is also displaying materials which have been produced, and are still being produced day after day in these turbulent times, for the construction of a new society. With this exhibition, the bourgeoisie of the world has erected in the modern Rome its Pantheon, where, with self-satisfied pride, it exhibits the gods which it has made for itself. It thus gives a practical proof of the fact that the 'impotence and vexation of the citizen', which German ideologists preach about year in year out, is only these gentlemen's own impotent failure to understand the modern movement, and their own vexation at this impotence. The bourgeoisie is celebrating this, its greatest festival, at a moment when the collapse of its social order in all its splendour is imminent, a collapse which will demonstrate more forcefully than ever how the forces which it has created have outgrown its control. In a future exhibition the bourgeoisie will perhaps no longer figure as the owners of these productive forces but only as their ciceroni.

The loss of the cotton crop has been spreading general alarm among the bourgeoisie since the beginning of the year, just as the potato blight did in 1845 and 1846. This alarm has increased considerably since it became clear that the cotton crop of 1851,

41. The Bregenz meeting of 11–12 October 1850 between the rulers of Austria, Bavaria and Wurtemberg resulted in the signature of the treaty of 12 October by which the three states agreed to oppose Prussia's attempts to gain the headship of the German Confederation. At the Warsaw meeting of 28 October 1850 between Nicholas I, Francis Joseph and Count Brandenburg, the last-named, as Prussia's representative, was put under considerable pressure, and compelled to make concessions to Austria.

42. 'In the lands of the infidels': a favoured expression of Marx's, taken from the title of Catholic bishops appointed to non-Christian territories where they could not reside, and applied here to the impotent governments-in-exile formed after the defeat of the revolutions of 1848, generally by democratic refugees.

too, will not turn out to be much richer than that of 1850. The loss, which would have been insignificant in earlier periods, now represents a very serious threat to the present expansion of the cotton industry, and it has already impeded production considerably. The bourgeoisie, having scarcely recovered from the shattering discovery that one of the central pillars of its social order – the potato – was endangered, now sees the second pillar – cotton – threatened. If just a moderate loss in one year's cotton crop and the prospect of a second has been enough to excite serious alarm amidst the rejoicing over prosperity, a few consecutive years in which the cotton crop really does fail are bound to reduce the whole of civilized society to a temporary state of barbarism. The golden age and the iron age are long past; it was reserved for the nineteenth century, with its intelligence, world markets and colossal productive resources, to usher in the *cotton age*. At the same time, the English bourgeoisie has felt more forcefully than ever the power which the United States exercises over it, as a result of its hitherto unbroken monopoly of cotton production. It has immediately applied itself to the task of breaking this monopoly. Not only in the East Indies, but also in Natal, the northern region of Australia and all parts of the world where climate and conditions allow cotton to be grown, it is to be encouraged in every way. At the same time, that section of the English bourgeoisie kindly disposed towards the Negro has made the following discovery: 'That the prosperity of Manchester is dependent on the treatment of slaves in Texas, Alabama and Louisiana is as curious as it is alarming.' (*Economist*, 21 September 1850). That the decisive branch of English industry is based upon the existence of slavery in the southern states of the American union, that a Negro revolt in these areas could ruin the whole system of production as it exists today is, of course, an extremely depressing fact for the people who spent £20 million [43] a few years ago on Negro emancipation in their own colonies. However, this fact leads to the only realistic solution of the slave question, which has recently again been the cause of such long and violent debate in the American Congress. American cotton production is based on slavery. As soon as the industry reaches a point where it cannot tolerate the United States' cotton monopoly any longer, cotton

43. This was the sum of money voted by Parliament in 1833 to be paid to the plantation-owners in compensation for the abolition of slavery in the West Indies and other British colonies.

will be successfully mass-produced in other countries, and it is hardly possible to achieve this anywhere today except with *free workers*. But as soon as the free labour of other countries can deliver sufficient supplies of cotton to industry more cheaply than the slave labour of the United States, then American slavery will be broken together with the American cotton monopoly and the slaves will be emancipated, because they will have become useless as slaves. Wage labour will be abolished in Europe in just the same way, as soon as it becomes not only unnecessary for production, but in fact a hindrance to it.

If the new cycle of industrial development which began in 1848 takes the same course as that of 1843–7, the crisis will break out in 1852. As a symptom that the excess speculation which is caused by overproduction, and which precedes each crisis, will not be long in coming, we can quote the fact that the discount rate of the Bank of England has not risen above 3 per cent for two years. But when the Bank of England keeps its interest rates down in times of prosperity, the other money dealers have to reduce their rates even more, just as in times of crisis when the Bank raises the rate considerably, they have to raise their rates above the Bank's. The additional capital which, as we have seen above, is always unloaded onto the bond market in times of prosperity, is enough by itself to force down the interest rate, as a result of the laws of competition; but the interest rate is reduced to a much larger extent by the enormous expansion of credit produced by general prosperity, which lowers the demand for capital. In these periods a government is in a position to reduce the interest rate on its funded debts, and the landowner is able to renew his mortgage on more favourable terms. The capitalists with investments in loan capital thus see their income reduced by a third or more, at a time when the income of all other classes is rising. The longer this situation lasts, the more they will be under pressure to look for more profitable capital investments. Overproduction gives rise to numerous new projects, and the success of a few of them is sufficient to attract a whole mass of capital in the same direction, until gradually the bubble becomes general. But, as we have seen, speculation has at this point of time only two outlets: cotton growing and the new world market routes created by the development of California and Australia. It is evident that this time the scope for speculation will assume far greater dimensions than in any earlier period of prosperity.

Let us take a look at the situation in the English agricultural districts. The general pressure produced by the repeal of the Corn Laws and the simultaneous rich harvests has here become chronic, although it has been alleviated somewhat by the considerable increase in consumption caused by prosperity. In addition, with low corn prices the agricultural workers at least are in a relatively better position, although the improvement in England has been more limited than in other countries, where land parcelling is the rule. Under these circumstances the agitation of the Protectionists [44] for the reimposition of corn duties continues in the agricultural areas, although less shrilly and overtly than before. It is evident that this agitation will remain quite insignificant so long as the relatively tolerable position of the agricultural workers continues. But as soon as the crisis breaks, with repercussions in the farming areas, the agricultural depression on the land will provoke considerable unrest. The industrial and commercial crisis will then coincide with the agricultural crisis for the first time, and in all issues which give rise to conflict between town and country, manufacturers and landowners, the two parties will be supported by two great armies: the manufacturers by the mass of the industrial workers, and the landowners by the mass of the agricultural workers.

We now come to the United States of America. The crisis of 1836, which broke out there first and raged most violently, lasted almost without interruption until 1842 and led to a complete transformation of the American credit system. The commerce of the United States recovered on this more solid foundation, if at first very slowly, until from 1842 to 1845 prosperity significantly increased there, too. The rise in prices and the revolution in Europe only brought benefits for America. From 1845 to 1847 it profited from the enormous export of grain and from the 1846 rise in cotton prices. In 1849 it produced the largest cotton crop to date, and in 1850 it made about $20 million from the loss in the cotton crop, which coincided with the new boom in the European cotton industry. The revolutions of 1848 caused a large-scale flow of European capital to the United States, which arrived partly with the immigrants themselves and was partly attributable to European investments in American treasury bonds. This increase in

44. When the Tory party split in 1846 over the repeal of the Corn Laws, the majority group adopted the name 'Protectionist'.

demand for American bonds has forced up their price to such an extent that recently in New York speculators have been seizing on them quite feverishly. Thus, despite all assertions to the contrary in the reactionary bourgeois press, we still maintain that the only form of state to enjoy the confidence of our European capitalists is the *bourgeois republic*. There is only one expression of bourgeois confidence in any form of state; *its quotation on the stock exchange*.

However, the prosperity of the United States increased even more for other reasons. The populated area, the *home market* of the North American union, extended with surprising rapidity in two directions. The population increase, due both to reproduction within America and to the continuing increase in immigration, led to the settlement of whole states and territories. Wisconsin and Iowa were comparatively densely populated within a few years, and there was a significant increase in immigrants to all states in the upper Mississippi region. The exploitation of the mines on Lake Superior and the rising grain production in the whole area around the Great Lakes produced a new boom in commerce and shipping on this system of great inland waterways, which will expand further as a result of an act passed during the last session of Congress, by which trade with Canada and Nova Scotia has been greatly facilitated. While the north-western states have thus gained a new importance, Oregon has been colonized within a few years, Texas and New Mexico annexed and California conquered. The discovery of the Californian gold mines has set the cap on American prosperity. In the second number of this *Revue* – before any other European journal – we drew attention to the importance of this discovery and its necessary consequences for the whole of world trade.[45] This importance does not lie in the increased supply of gold from the newly discovered mines, although this increase in the means of exchange was bound to have consequences for commerce in general. It lies rather in the spur given to investment on the world market by the mineral wealth of California, in the activity into which the whole west coast of America and the eastern coast of Asia has been plunged, in the new market outlets created in California and in all the other countries affected by California. Even taken by itself the Californian market is very important; a year ago there were 100,000 people there; now there are at least 300,000 people, who are producing almost nothing but

45. 'Review: January–February 1850', above, pp. 269–70.

gold, and who are exchanging this gold for their basic living requirements from foreign markets. But the Californian market itself is unimportant compared to the continual expansion of all the markets on the Pacific coast, compared to the striking increase in trade with Chile and Peru, western Mexico and the Sandwich Islands, and compared to the traffic which has suddenly arisen between Asia, Australia and California. Because of California, completely new international routes have become necessary, routes which will inevitably soon surpass all others in importance. The main trading route to the Pacific Ocean – which has really only now been opened up, and which will become the most important ocean in the world – will, from now on, go across the Isthmus of Panama. The establishment of links across the Isthmus by highways, railways and canals is now the most urgent requirement of world trade and has already been tackled in places. The railway from Chagres to Panama is already being built. An American company is having the river basin of San Juan del Norte surveyed with a view to connecting the two oceans, first of all by an overland route and then by a canal. Other routes – across the Isthmus of Darien, the Atrato route in New Granada, across the Isthmus of Tehuantepec – are being discussed in English and American journals. The ignorance in the whole civilized world about the conditions of the terrain in Central America, which has now suddenly been exposed, makes it impossible to determine which route is the most advantageous for a great canal; according to the little information available, the Atrato route and the way across Panama seem to offer the best opportunities. The rapid expansion of the ocean steamer lines has become equally urgent, in order to connect up with the lines of communication across the Isthmus. Steamers are already sailing between Southampton and Chagres, New York and Chagres, Valparaiso, Lima, Panama, Acapulco and San Francisco; but these few lines, with their small number of steamers, are by no means adequate. The increase in steamer lines between Europe and Chagres becomes daily more urgent, and the growing traffic between Asia, Australia and America requires great new steamship lines from Panama and San Francisco to Canton, Singapore, Sydney, New Zealand and the most important station in the Pacific, the Sandwich Islands. Of all the areas in the Pacific Australia and New Zealand in particular have expanded most, as a result of both the rapid progress of colonization and the influence of California, and they do not want to be divided from the civilized world a moment longer by a four to six-month sea voyage. The total population of the Australian colonies (excluding New Zealand) rose from 170,676 in 1839 to 333,764 in 1848; that is, it increased in nine years by 95½ per cent. England itself cannot leave these colonies without steamship links; and the government is negotiating at this moment for a line connecting with the Indian overland post. Whether this line comes about or not, the sheer necessity of a steamship connection with America, and particularly California, where 3,500 people from Australia emigrated to last year, will itself produce a solution. It may be said that the world has only become round since the necessity has arisen for this global steam shipping.

This imminent expansion in steam shipping will be increased further by the opening up of the Dutch colonies already mentioned and by the increase in screw steamers, with which – as is becoming increasingly clear – emigrants can be transported more rapidly, relatively cheaper and more profitably than with sailing ships. Apart from the screw steamers which already sail from Glasgow and Liverpool to New York, new ones are to be employed on this line and a shipping line is to be established between Rotterdam and New York. How universal is the present tendency for capital to flow into oceanic steam shipping is proved by the continuous increase in the number of steamers competing between Liverpool and New York, the establishment of entirely new lines from England to the Cape and from New York to Le Havre, and a whole series of similar schemes which are being hawked around New York.

With the investment of capital in oceanic steam shipping and the building of canals across the American isthmus the ground has already been laid for excess speculation in this area. The centre of this speculation is necessarily New York, which receives the great mass of Californian gold. It has already taken control of the main trade with California and in general performs the same function for the whole of America as London does for Europe. New York is already the centre of all transatlantic steam shipping. All the Pacific steam ships belong to New York companies, and almost all new projects in this branch of industry start in New York. Speculation in foreign steamship lines has already begun in these, and the Nicaragua Company, which was launched in New York, similarly represents the beginning of speculation in the isthmus canals. Over-speculation will soon develop, and even though English capital is flowing *en masse* into all such undertakings, even though the London Stock Exchange will be inundated with all sorts of similar schemes, New York will still remain the centre of the whole bubble, this time as in 1836, and will be the first to experience its collapse. Innumerable schemes will be ruined, but as with the English railway system in 1845, at least the *outline* of a universal shipping system will this time emerge from this over-speculation. No matter how many companies go bankrupt, the steamships – which are doubling the Atlantic traffic, opening up the Pacific, connecting up Australia, New Zealand, Singapore and China with America and are reducing the journey around the world to four months – the steamships will remain.

The prosperity in England and America soon made itself felt on the European continent. As early as summer 1849 the factories in Germany, particularly in the Rhine province, were quite busy again, and since the end of 1849 there has been a general recovery of business. This renewed prosperity, which our German bourgeois naively attribute to the restoration of stability and order, is based in reality only upon the renewed prosperity in England and upon the increased demand for industrial products on the American and tropical markets. In 1850 industry and trade have recovered even further. Just as in England, there has been a temporary surplus of capital and an extraordinary easing of the money market, and the reports of the Frankfurt and Leipzig autumn fairs have reportedly been extremely satisfactory for the bourgeoisie taking part. The troubles in Schleswig-Holstein and Electoral Hesse,[46] the quarrels within the Prussian Union and the threatening notes exchanged between Austria and Prussia have

46. The first war in Schleswig-Holstein had closed with the armistice of Malmö (August 1848); but war broke out again in April 1849, and lasted until July. Prussia finally concluded a peace treaty with Denmark on 2 July 1850 by which all Prussian troops were to be withdrawn from the duchies; the local army of Schleswig-Holstein endeavoured to resist the Danish army, but was defeated at the Battle of Idstedt (5 July 1850). In Electoral Hesse a conflict broke out in September 1850 between the Elector and his parliament; the Elector appealed for help not to Prussia but to Austria and the Federal Diet. Since Hesse was a member of the Erfurt Union, Frederick William replied by occupying Kassel; this was the reason for the threatening exchange of notes between September and November 1850. However the whole affair ended with Prussia's complete submission to the Austrians, the so-called humiliation of Olmütz (29 November 1850). See also below, pp. 304–308.)

not been able to hold back the development of all these symptoms of prosperity for a moment, as even the *Economist* noted, with mocking cockney smugness . . .[47]

We now turn to the political events of the last six months.

In England periods of economic prosperity are always periods of political prosperity for Whiggery – aptly embodied in the person of the smallest man in the kingdom, Lord John Russell.[48] The ministry brings before Parliament little petti-fogging reforms which it knows will fail to pass the House of Lords, or which it itself withdraws at the end of the session under the pretext of lack of time. The lack of time is always induced by the previous excess of boredom and empty talk, which the Speaker only brings to an end as late as possible, with the remark that there is no question before the House. At such times the struggle between Free Traders[49] and Protection-ists degenerates into pure humbug. The majority of the Free Traders are too preoccupied with the material exploitation of free trade to have the time or inclination to fight further for its logical political extensions; faced with the boom in urban industry, the Protectionists resort to burlesque jeremiads and threats. The parties continue the struggle merely for propriety's sake, in order not to forget each other's existence. Before the last session the industrial bourgeoisie created a huge fuss about financial reform; in Parliament itself they confined themselves to theoretical expostulations. Before the session, Mr Cobden repeated his declaration of war on the tsar on the occasion of the Russian loan, and he almost ran short of sarcasm, so much

47. The passage omitted here forms the opening five paragraphs of Chapter IV of 'The Class Struggles in France', below, pp. 462–5. In this passage Marx brings his economic analysis to the extremely impor-tant conclusion, 'While this general prosperity lasts, enabling the productive forces of bourgeois society to develop to the full extent possible within the bourgeois system, there can be no question of a real revolution. Such a revolution is only possi-ble at a time when *two factors* come into *conflict*: the *modern productive forces* and the *bourgeois forms of production* . . . *A new revolution is only possible as a result of a new crisis; but it will come, just as surely as the crisis itself.'*

48. Lord John Russell was the leader of the Whig party, and Prime Minister in 1846–52 and 1865–6. For Marx's opinion of him, see *MECW* 14, pp. 371–93.

49. The free trade majority in the House of Commons was composed of Whigs and Peelites as well as the relatively small party led by Cobden that Marx described as 'Free Traders, *par excellence*' (*Surveys from Exile*, pp. 590, 596–8).

did he heap upon the great pauper of St Petersburg. Six months later he was reduced to taking part in the scandalous Peace Congress farce,[50] whose only outcome was that an Ojibway Indian handed a pipe of peace to Herr Jaup[51] – to the great horror of Herr Haynau[52] on the platform – and that the Yankee temperance swindler, Elihu Burrit,[53] went to Schleswig-Holstein and Copenhagen in order to assure the governments concerned of his good intentions. As if the whole Schleswig-Holstein war could ever take a serious turn so long as Herr von Gagern takes part in it and Herr Venedey does not![54]

The great political issue of the past session was actually the *Greek debate*.[55] All the forces of absolutist reaction on the Continent had formed a coalition with the English Tories to overthrow Palmerston.[56] Louis Napoleon had even recalled the French ambassador from London, as much to flatter Tsar Nicholas as French national pride. The whole French National Assembly fanatically applauded this bold break with the traditional English alliance. The affair gave Mr Palmerston the opportunity to present himself in the Commons as the *champion*[57] of civil liberty throughout Europe; he received a majority of forty-six votes, and the result of the coalition, which was as impotent as it was silly, was the non-renewal of the Aliens Bill.[58]

50. In August 1850 an international congress of pacifists met in Frankfurt-am-Main. It was attended by prominent free-traders, philanthropists, and Quakers.

51. Heinrich Jaup was the liberal Prime Minister of Hesse-Darmstadt from 1848 to 1850, and presided over the Frankfurt peace congress.

52. Julius Jakob, Freiherr von Haynau was the Austrian field-marshal notorious for his cruel reprisals against the Hungarians after their defeat in 1849.

53. Elihu Burrit was an American bourgeois philanthropist and pacifist, who organized the Frankfurt peace congress and numerous others.

54. Marx is presumably making a dig here at Venedey's inflated idea of his own importance.

55. The debates of June 1850 on Greece are known in English history as the Don Pacifico debates, since the affair stemmed from Palmerston's handling of Don Pacifico's claim for compensation from the Greek government for damage done to his house by an anti-semitic Greek mob.

56. Viscount Palmerston was at this time Foreign Secretary, and later became Prime Minister (1855–65).

57. In English in the original.

58. The Aliens Bill, first carried in 1793 and sporadically renewed, had empowered the government to expel foreign nationals at its discretion. During the latter half of the nineteenth century the British government did not enjoy this power.

If in his demonstration over Greece and his speeches in Parliament Palmerston confronted European reactionaries as a bourgeois liberal, the English people used the presence of Herr Haynau in London to give a striking demonstration of *its* foreign policy.[59]

While Austria's military representative was chased through the streets of London by the people, Prussia, in the person of its diplomatic representative, suffered a misfortune equally appropriate to its position. It will be recalled how the most ridiculous figure in England, the garrulous man of letters Lord Brougham, ejected the man of letters Bunsen from the gallery of the House of Lords on account of his tactless and offensive behaviour[60] – to the general accompaniment of laughter from all the ladies present. Herr Bunsen, in the spirit of the great power which he represents, calmly put up with this humiliation. He will simply not leave the country, whatever happens to him. He is tied to England by all his private interests; he will continue to exploit his diplomatic post in order to speculate in English religion, to find a place for his sons in the Church of England and for his daughters on one of the social rungs of the English gentry.

The death of Sir Robert Peel has contributed considerably to the accelerated disintegration of the old parties. The party which had formed his main support since 1845, the so-called Peelites, has subsequently disintegrated.[61] Since his death Peel himself has been apotheosized in the most exaggerated fashion by almost all parties as England's greatest statesman. One thing at least distinguished him from the European 'statesmen' – he was no mere careerist. Beyond this, the statesmanship of this son of the bourgeoisie who rose to be leader of the aristocracy consisted in the view that there is today only one real aristocracy: the bourgeoisie. In the light of this belief he continually used his leadership of the landed aristocracy to wring concessions from it for the bourgeoisie. This became evident in the question of Catholic emancipation and the reform of the police, by means of which he increased the bourgeoisie's political power; in the Bank Acts of

59. Haynau visited London in September 1850, and was recognized by some draymen, who attacked him.

60. Henry, Lord Brougham was a former Whig Lord Chancellor; Christian von Bunsen was the Prussian ambassador in London; the exact circumstances of the incident alluded to here are not clear.

61. Sir Robert Peel, leader of the liberal wing of the Tory party, and Prime Minister in 1834–5 and 1841–6, split his party by repealing the Corn Laws in 1846 with Whig and Free Trade support.

1818 and 1844, which strengthened the financial aristocracy; in
the tariff reform of 1842 and the free trade legislation of 1846,
with which the aristocracy was nothing short of sacrificed to the
industrial bourgeoisie. The second supporting pillar of the aristocracy, the 'Iron Duke', the hero of Waterloo,[62] stood faithfully
beside the cotton knight Peel, a disappointed Don Quixote. Since
1845 Peel had been treated as a traitor by the Tory party. His
power over the House of Commons was based upon the extraordinary *plausibility of his eloquence*. If one reads his most
famous speeches, one finds that they consist of a massive accumulation of common-places, skilfully interspersed with a large
amount of statistical data. Almost all the towns in England want
to erect a monument to the man who repealed the Corn Laws. A
Chartist journal has remarked, referring to the police trained by
Peel in 1829: 'What do we want with these monuments to Peel?
Every police officer in England and Ireland is a living monument
to Peel.'[63]

The most recent event to cause a controversy in England is the
elevation of Mr Wiseman to the position of Cardinal Archbishop of
Westminster and the Pope's division of England into thirteen Catholic dioceses.[64] This step taken by the Vicar of Christ, which has been
a great surprise for the Church of England, proves once again the
illusions to which European reactionaries are subject; as if, after the
victories which they have recently won in the service of the bourgeoisie, the restoration of the whole feudal, absolutist order, with all
its religious trappings, must now automatically follow. In England
Catholicism has its few supporters in the two extremes of society, the
aristocracy and the lumpenproletariat. The lumpenproletariat, the mob,
which is either Irish or of Irish ancestry, is Catholic by descent. The
aristocracy conducted its fashionable flirtation with Puseyism until
conversion to Catholicism finally began to become the fashion.[65] At a
time when the English aristocracy was being forced in the course of its
struggle with the advancing bourgeoisie to flaunt ever more brazenly

62. The Duke of Wellington became a Tory politician, and was Prime Minister in
1828–30.

63. From the article entitled 'The Peel Monument', in the Chartist *Red Republican*,
17 August 1850.

64. On 29 September 1850 the Pope re-established the Roman Catholic hierarchy
in England, setting up an archbishopric and twelve bishoprics.

65. After E. B. Pusey; the Oxford movement as it is now known. J. H. Newman,
the original leader of this Anglo-Catholic movement, was converted to Rome in
1845.

the religious ideologues of the aristocracy, the orthodox theologians of the High Church were also being forced in their struggle with the theologians of the bourgeois dissenters to recognize more and more the logical consequences of their semi-Catholic dogma and ritual. Indeed the conversion of individual reactionary Anglicans to the original Church, with its monopoly on grace, inevitably also increased in frequency. These insignificant phenomena produced in the minds of the English Catholic clergy the most sanguine hopes for the imminent conversion of all England. The new papal bull, which once again treated England as a Roman province, and which was intended to give a new impetus to this trend towards conversion, is now producing the opposite effect. The Puseyites, suddenly confronted with the serious consequences of their medieval dabbling, are recoiling in horror, and the Puseyite Bishop of London has lost no time in issuing a declaration in which he recants all his errors and declares a war to the death on the Pope. The whole comedy is of interest to the bourgeoisie only in so far as it presents them with an opportunity for new attacks on the High Church and its universities. The commission which is to report on the state of the universities will give rise to furious debates in the next session. The mass of the people is naturally not interested, and is neither for nor against Cardinal Wiseman. With the present dearth of news the papers are presented with welcome material for long articles and vehement diatribes against Pius IX. *The Times* even demands that the government should incite an insurrection in the Papal States and unleash Mazzini and the Italian refugees against the Pope to punish his interference. The *Globe*, Palmerston's press organ, drew an extremely witty parallel between the papal bull and Mazzini's latest manifesto.[66] The Pope, it says, claims spiritual supremacy over England and names bishops *in partibus infidelium*.[67] Here in London an Italian government sits *in partibus infidelium*, headed by the anti-pope, Mr Mazzini. The supremacy which Mr Mazzini does not only claim but actually exercises in the Papal States is at the moment equally of a purely spiritual nature. Like the papal bulls, Mazzini's manifestos are also purely religious in content. They preach a religion, they make an appeal to faith,

66. Guiseppe Mazzini was the ideological leader of the Italian national movement. In 1849 he led the Provisional Government of the Roman republic, and subsequently lived in exile in England.

67. In the lands of the infidels; see p. 289, n. 42.

they bear the motto: *Dio ed il popolo*, God and the people. We wonder whether there is any difference between the claims made by each, other than that – in contrast to the Pope – Mr Mazzini at least represents the religion of the majority of the people to whom he speaks – for there is scarcely any religion in Italy any longer except that of *Dio ed il popolo*. Moreover, Mazzini has used this opportunity to go a step further. In London, together with the other members of the Italian National Committee he has floated a loan of 10 million francs – approved by the Roman Constituent Assembly[68] – in the form of shares of 100 francs each and, what is more, for the sole purpose of buying weapons and war materials. It cannot be denied that this loan has more chance of succeeding than the abortive voluntary loan of the Austrian government in Lombardy.[69]

England recently delivered Rome and Austria a really serious blow by its trade agreement with Piedmont-Sardinia. This treaty destroys the Austrian scheme for an Italian customs union and secures a considerable area of operation for English trade and the policies of the English bourgeoisie in northern Italy.

The existing organization of the Chartist party is also disintegrating. Those petty bourgeois who are still in the party, allied with the labour aristocracy, form a purely democratic tendency, whose programme is limited to the People's Charter and a few other petty-bourgeois reforms.[70] The mass of the workers living in really proletarian conditions belong to the revolutionary Chartist tendency. At the head of the first group is Feargus O'Connor; at the head of the second, Julian Harney and Ernest Jones. Old O'Connor, an Irish squire and supposedly a descendant of the old kings of Munster, is, in spite of his ancestry and his political standpoint, a genuine representative of Old England. He is essentially conservative, and feels a highly determined hatred not only for industrial progress but also for the revolution. His

68. The Roman Constituent Assembly was elected in January 1849; after the fall of the Roman republic in July 1849 many of its deputies went into exile in England, and it was there that it granted the loan referred to.

69. The Austrian government of Lombardy and Venetia asked for a 'voluntary loan' in the spring of 1850, which turned into a forced loan when it became clear that the inhabitants were unwilling to subscribe to it.

70. The six points of the People's Charter were manhood suffrage, the ballot, equal electoral districts, payment of MPs, abolition of property qualifications, and annual parliaments. Cf. 'The Chartists', *Surveys from Exile*, p. 598.

ideals are patriarchal and petty-bourgeois through and through. He unites in his person an inexhaustible number of contradictions, which find their fulfilment and harmony in a certain blunt *common sense*,[71] and which enable him year in year out to write his interminable weekly letters in the *Northern Star*, each successive letter always in open conflict with the previous one. For this very reason O'Connor claims to be the most consistent man in Great Britain and to have prophesied everything that has happened during the last twenty years. His shoulders, his roaring voice, his great pugilistic skill, with which he is said to have defended Nottingham Market against 20,000 people – all this is an essential part of the representative of Old England. It is clear that a man like O'Connor is bound to be a great obstacle in a revolutionary movement; but such people serve a useful purpose, in that the many old, ingrained prejudices which they embody and propagate disappear with them – with the result that the movement, once it has rid itself of these people, can free itself from these prejudices once and for all. O'Connor will come to grief in the movement; but for that reason he will possess an even stronger claim to the title of 'a martyr in a good cause', like Lamartine and Marrast.

The main point of conflict between the two Chartist tendencies is the land question. O'Connor and his followers want to use the Charter to settle part of the working-class on smallholdings, and eventually to make smallholding property universal in England. It is well known how he failed in his attempt to establish smallholding property on a small scale through a joint-stock company. The tendency of every bourgeois revolution to destroy large-scale landed property might make this division into small-holdings appear to the English workers for a while as something very revolutionary, although it is regularly accompanied by the unfailing tendency of small property to become concentrated and to meet with economic ruin in the face of large-scale agriculture. The revolutionary Chartist tendency opposes this demand for division of the land with a demand for the confiscation of all landed property. The land is not to be distributed but to remain national property.

Despite this split and the emergence of more extreme demands, the Chartists, remembering the circumstances under which the Corn Laws were repealed, still suspect that in the next crisis they will once again have to form an alliance with the industrial bourgeoisie, the

---

71. In English in the original.

Financial Reformers,[72] and that they will have to help them defeat their enemies, forcing concessions from them in return. This will certainly be the position of the Chartists in the next crisis. The actual revolutionary movement in England can only begin when the Charter has been won, just as the June battle in France was possible only when the republic had been won . . .[73]

In Germany the political events of the last six months are epitomized in the spectacle of Prussia duping the liberals and Austria duping Prussia.

In 1849 Prussia's hegemony in Germany seemed to be the issue, in 1850 the division of power between Austria and Prussia. In 1851 all that is still in question is the form in which Prussia submits to Austria and returns as a repentant sinner to the bosom of the completely restored Federal Diet. The 'little Germany' which the king of Prussia hoped to obtain in compensation for his unfortunate imperial procession through Berlin on 21 March 1848[74] has transformed itself into 'little Prussia'. Prussia has had to bear every humiliation patiently, and has disappeared from the ranks of the great powers. The perfidious narrowness of its policies has again reduced even the modest dream of the Union[75] to nothing. It falsely ascribed to the Union a liberal character and thus duped the wise men of the Gotha party[76] with constitutional phantas-

72. I.e. the National Association for Parliamentary and Financial Reform, founded in 1849 by Cobden and Bright. This body campaigned on the basis of the so-called 'Little Charter' whose demands included household suffrage, triennial parliaments and the ballot.

73. The passage omitted here forms the bulk of Chapter IV of Engels's edition of 'The Class Struggles in France', in *Surveys from Exile*, from 'Let us now return to France' (p. 465) to the end.

74. See p. 119, n. 28.

75. The Union of Three Kings (i.e. of Prussia, Saxony, and Hanover) was the first fruit of Radowitz's policy of uniting Germany under Prussian headship on a federal basis (26 May 1849). During 1849 it extended rapidly to cover a total of twenty-eight states; however, in 1850 the larger states began to desert Prussia, leaving the smaller states in the Erfurt Union (April 1850), which received a constitution, but had in its turn to be dissolved under Austrian pressure (November 1850).

76. The Gotha party was founded in June 1849 by some prominent members of the monarchist Right in the Frankfurt National Assembly (such as Dahlmann, Bassermann, the brokers Gagern and Brüggemann), after Frederick William IV's refusal to accept the German crown from the Assembly. Its aim was the union of Germany without Austria under a Prussia transformed into a constitutional monarchy.

magoria which were never seriously meant; yet Prussia had become so bourgeois as a result of its whole industrial development, its permanent deficit and its national debt that, twist and turn as it might, it fell even more irredeemably a victim of constitutionalism. While the wise men of Gotha finally discovered how shamefully Prussia had dealt with their dignity and prudence, while even Gagern and Brüggeman finally turned their backs in noble outrage on a government which played such outrageous games with the freedom and unity of the fatherland, Prussia was having just as little joy in the chickens which it had gathered under its protective wings in the shape of the petty princes. Only in their moment of direst distress and defencelessness had they delivered themselves into the claws of the Prussian eagle – claws eager for annexation – and they had to pay dearly for the return of their subjects to their old obedience to the state as a result of Prussian intervention, threats and demonstrations. They had to pay with oppressive military treaties, expensive billeting and the prospect of being mediatized by the Union constitution. But Prussia itself had seen to it that they were to escape this new predicament. Prussia had restored the rule of the forces of reaction everywhere and the more these forces re-established themselves the more the petty princes deserted Prussia to throw themselves into the arms of Austria. Now that they could again rule as they had done before March, absolutist Austria was closer to them than a power whose ability to be absolutist was no greater than its desire to be liberal. Furthermore, Austrian policy did not lead to the mediatization of small states but, on the contrary, to their protection as integral components of the Federal Diet which was to be revived. Thus Prussia watched as Saxony, which a few months earlier had been saved by Prussian troops, deserted her, as did Hanover and Electoral Hesse. Now Baden has followed the rest despite its Prussian garrison. Prussia can see quite clearly from events in the two Hesses that its support of the reactionary forces in Mecklenburg, Hamburg and Dessau was not to its own but to Austria's advantage. Thus the unsuccessful German kaiser has come to realize that he is indeed living in an age of perfidy. But even though he must now stand by while 'his right arm, the Union', is taken from him, the fact is that this arm had already withered away some time before. Thus Austria has already brought the whole of southern Germany under its hegemony and even in north Germany the most important states oppose Prussia.

Austria had finally made such progress that, supported by Russia, it was able to oppose Prussia openly. It did this over two issues: Schleswig-Holstein and Electoral Hesse.

In Schleswig-Holstein 'Germany's sword'[77] has concluded a genuine Prussian separate peace[78] and delivered its allies up to the hands of the hostile superior force. England, Russia and France decided to put an end to the independence of the duchies and recorded this intention in a treaty which Austria also signed. Austria and the other governments, in accordance with the London Treaty, have argued in the restored Federal Diet for a Federal intervention in Holstein in favour of Denmark. Meanwhile Prussia has sought to continue its policy of procrastination by urging the parties to submit to a Federal court of arbitration, which is not yet defined nor in existence and which has been rejected by most of the major governments. It has achieved nothing with all its manoeuvring other than that the major powers have come to suspect it of revolutionary machinations and that it has received a series of threatening notes, which will soon mar its pleasure in an 'independent' foreign policy. The people of Schleswig-Holstein will soon have their father and sovereign restored to them. A people which allows itself to be governed by Herr Beseler and Herr Reventlow,[79] despite having the whole army on its side, shows that it still needs the Danish whip for its upbringing.

The movement in Electoral Hesse gives us an inimitable example of what an 'uprising' in a small German state can lead to. The virtuous bourgeois resistance to the double-dealer, Hassenpflug,[80] had produced everything that could be demanded of such a spectacle. The Chamber was unanimous, the country was unanimous, the civil servants and the army were on the side of the

---

77. A reference to Frederick William IV's speech of 3 April 1849 in reply to the German National Assembly's offer of the imperial Crown: 'If the Prussian shield and sword is needed against internal or external enemies, I shall not be found missing.'

78. The Prussians were famous for making this move both in the course of the eighteenth century and at the time of the Napoleonic Wars.

79. Wilhelm Beseler was the head of the provisional government of Schleswig-Holstein set up in Kiel in 1848, and a Right Centre deputy at Frankfurt; Graf Friedrich von Reventlow was a reactionary Prussian noble and a member of the provisional government of Schleswig-Holstein.

80. Hans Daniel Hassenpflug was a supporter of the despotic rule of the Elector of Hesse before and after 1848; he was Prime Minister of Electoral Hesse from 1850 to 1855.

citizens; all opposing forces had been removed, the demand 'Out with the prince' had been fulfilled spontaneously, the double-dealer Hassenpflug had disappeared with his whole ministry; everything was going smoothly, all parties kept strictly within the bounds of the law, all excesses were avoided and the opposition had achieved the finest victory in the annals without lifting a finger. And now that the bourgeoisie had all the power in their hands, now that their Committee of Estates met not the least resistance anywhere, now they were for the first time really needed. Now they saw that, instead of Electoral troops, foreign troops were standing at their borders, ready to march in to put an end to this splendid show of bourgeois power within twenty-four hours. Only now did the helplessness and disgrace begin. Whereas earlier the bourgeoisie had not been able to retreat, now they were not able to advance. The refusal to pay taxes in Electoral Hesse proves more strikingly than any earlier event how all clashes within small states end in pure farce. They only result in foreign intervention, and the conflict is brought to an end not only by the removal of the prince but also of the constitution. It proves how ludicrous all these momentous struggles are, in which the petty bourgeoisie of the petty states seeks with patriotic loyalty to save every little achievement left over from the March days from its inevitable destruction.

In Electoral Hesse, in a state of the Union which had to be torn away from the Prussian embrace, Austria was involved in a direct confrontation with its rival. It was Austria who more or less incited the Elector into his attack on the constitution and then placed him under the protection of the Federal Diet. In order to add weight to this protective relationship, to use the business in Electoral Hesse to break Prussian resistance to Austrian hegemony, and to coerce Prussia into rejoining the Federal Diet, Austrian and south German troops have now been marshalled in Franconia and Bohemia. Prussia is also mobilizing its forces. The newspapers are bursting with reports of marches and countermarches by the army corps. All this noise will lead to nothing, just like the quarrel between the French party of Order and Bonaparte. Neither the king of Prussia nor the emperor of Austria is his own master – only the Russian tsar is. At the tsar's command rebellious Prussia will finally give way without a drop of blood being spilt. The parties will meet peacefully seated in the Federal Diet, without any interruption in the petty jealousy which exists between them, in their conflict with their subjects, or in their vexation at Russian supremacy.

We now come to the abstract country, the European nation, the nation of the *exiles*. We shall not mention the individual groups of exiles, the Germans, French, Hungarians, etc; their *haute politique* is limited to pure *chronique scandaleuse*. But Europe and the people as a whole have recently been given a provisional government in the form of the European Central Committee,[81] consisting of Joseph Mazzini, Ledru-Rollin, Albert Darasz (the Pole)[82] and – Arnold Ruge, who modestly justifies his presence by writing 'member of the Frankfurt National Assembly' after his name. Although it is impossible to say which democratic council has called these four evangelists to office, their manifesto undeniably contains the creed of the broad mass of the exiles and summarizes in fitting form the intellectual achievements which this mass owes to the recent revolution.

The manifesto begins with a pompous enumeration of the strengths of democracy.

What does democracy lack for the achievement of its victory? ... Organization ... We have sects but no church, incomplete and contradictory philosophies but no religion, no collective belief which can assemble the believers under a single sign and harmonize their work ... The day on which we find ourselves all united, marching together under the eyes of the best among us ... will be the eve of the struggle. On this day we shall have counted our numbers, we shall know who we are, we shall be conscious of our power.

Why has the revolution not yet succeeded? Because the organization of revolutionary power has been weak. This is the first decree of the exiles' provisional government.

This state of affairs is to be remedied by the organization of an army of believers, and the founding of a religion.

But to achieve this two great obstacles must be surmounted, two great errors overcome: the exaggeration of the rights of individuality,

81. The Central Committee of European Democracy was set up in June 1850 in London on the initiative of Mazzini, but only lasted until March 1852 owing to ideological differences between its various members. Its manifesto, 'To the Peoples', was published in the Committee's journal, *Le Proscrit*, on 6 August 1850. The italics in Marx's quotations are his own.

82. Albert Darasz took part in the Polish rising of 1830, and after its defeat went into exile, becoming an important figure in a number of Polish exile nationalist organizations. Alexandre Ledru-Rollin had been editor of *La Reforme* (see p. 91, n. 31).

the narrow-minded exclusiveness of theory ... We must not say 'I': we must learn to say 'we' ... those who follow their individual suscepti-bilities refuse to make the small sacrifices demanded by organization and discipline and deny the total body of beliefs which they preach, as a result of the habits of the past ... Exclusiveness in theory is the negation of our basic dogma. He who says, 'I have discovered a political truth,' and who makes the acceptance of his system into a condition of acceptance into the fraternal association, disavows the people – the only progressive interpreter of the world law – merely in order to assert his own ego. He who maintains that he is able today to discover a defini-tive solution to the problems which activate the masses, by means of the isolated labour of his intellect, however powerful it may be, condemns himself to the error of incompleteness by abandoning one of the eternal sources of truth: the collective intuition of the people in action. The definitive solution is the secret of our victory ... For the most part our systems can be nothing but a dissection of corpses, a discovery of evil and an analysis of death, incapable of perceiving or comprehending life. Life is the people in movement, the instinct of the masses raised to an extraordinary power by common contact, by the prophetic feeling of great things to be achieved, by spontaneous, sudden, electric asso-ciation in the street. It is action, exciting to their highest pitch all the latent powers of hope, devotion, love and enthusiasm which are now dormant, revealing man in the unity of his nature, in the full vigour of his potency. The handshake of a worker at one of those historic moments which begin an epoch will teach us more about the organization of the future than can be taught today by the cold and heartless labour of reason or by knowledge of the illustrious dead of the last two millenia – of the old society.

So, in the end, all this highfalutin nonsense amounts to the highly vulgar and philistine view that the revolution failed because of the jealous ambition of the individual leaders, and because of the conflicting opinions of the various popular teachers.

The struggles of the different classes and fractions of classes with one another, which in their development through specific phases is precisely what constitutes the revolution, are, for our evangelists, only the unhappy consequence of divergent systems. However, the divergent systems are in reality the result of the existence of class struggles. It becomes clear even from this that the authors of the manifesto deny the existence of the class struggle. Under the pretext of fighting the doctrinaire they dispense with all specific realities of the situation, all specific partisan views. They forbid the individual classes to formulate their interests and demands in the face of other classes. They expect the classes to forget their conflicting interests and to reconcile themselves under the banner of something hollow and brazenly vague, which, in the guise of reconciling the interests of all parties, only conceals the domination by one party and its interests – the party of the bourgeoisie. After what these gentlemen must have experienced in France, Germany and Italy during the last two years it cannot even be said that the hypocrisy by means of which they wrap bourgeois interests in a Lamartinian rhetoric of brotherhood is unconscious. How much the gentlemen know about 'systems' is shown, moreover, by the fact that they imagine each of these systems to be merely a fragment of the wisdom compiled in the manifesto, and to be based solely on one of the rhetorical phrases assembled here: freedom, equality, etc. Their notions of social organization are highly striking: a riot in the street, a brawl, a shake of the hand, and that is that! For them the whole revolution consists merely in the overthrow of the existing governments; once this aim has been achieved, 'victory' will have been won. The movement, the development, the struggle then comes to an end, and under the aegis of the then ruling European Central Committee the golden age of the European Republic and the permanent rule of the night-cap can begin. Just as they hate development and struggle, these gentlemen hate thought, callous thought – as if any thinker, including Hegel and Ricardo, would ever have achieved that degree of callousness with which this mealy-mouthed swill is poured over the heads of the public. The people are not to worry about the morrow, they must empty their heads of ideas. When the great day of decision comes, they will be electrified by mere physical contact and the riddle of the future will be solved for the people by a miracle. This summons to empty-headedness is a direct attempt to swindle precisely those classes who are most oppressed. One member of the European Central Committee asks,

In saying this, do we mean that we are to march on without a banner; do we mean that we wish to inscribe a negation on our banner? Such a suspicion cannot be directed at us. As men of the people, who have been part of the struggle for many years, we do not for one moment consider leading them into an *empty future*.

On the contrary, to prove the *fullness* of their *future* these gentlemen present a record – worthy of Leporello[83] himself – of

83. In Mozart's opera *Don Juan*, the hero's servant and chronicler of his sexual achievements.

eternal truths and achievements from the whole course of history. This record is put forward as the common ground of 'democracy' in our day and age and is summed up in the following edifying paternoster:

We believe in the progressive development of human ability and strength towards the moral law which has been imposed upon us. We believe in association as the only means to achieve this end. We believe that the interpretation of this moral law and the law of progress can be entrusted to the charge of neither a caste nor an individual, but to the people, enlightened by national education, led by those from its midst whom virtue and the people's genius show to be the best. We believe in the sacredness of both individuality and society, which should never exclude nor conflict with each other, but should harmonize for the betterment of all by all. We believe in freedom, without which all human responsibility disappears; in equality, without which freedom is only an illusion; in brotherhood, without which freedom and equality would be means without an end; in association, without which brotherhood would be an unrealizable programme; in *family, community, state* and *fatherland* as equally progressive spheres which man must successively grow into, in the knowledge and application of freedom, equality, brotherhood and association. We believe in the sanctity of work and in *property* which arises from work as its symbol and fruit; we believe in the duty of society to provide the means for material work through credit and the means for mental work through education . . . to sum up, we believe in a social condition which has God and His law as its apex, and the people as its base . . .

So: progress – association – moral law – freedom – equality – brotherhood – association – family, community, state – sanctity of property – credit – education – God and the people – *Dio e popolo*. These phrases figure in all the manifestos of the 1848 revolutions, from the French to the Wallachian, and it is precisely for that reason that they figure here as the common basis of the new revolution. In none of these revolutions was the sanctity of property, here sanctified as the product of work, forgotten. Eighty years before their time Adam Smith knew much better than our revolutionary pioneers the precise extent to which bourgeois property is 'the fruit and symbol of work'. As for the socialist concession that society shall grant everyone the material means for work through credit, every manufacturer is accustomed to give his worker credit for as much material as he can process in a week. The credit system is as widely extended nowadays as is compatible with the inviolability of property, and credit itself is after all only a form of bourgeois property.

Summarized, this gospel teaches a social order in which God forms the apex and the people – or, as is said later, *humanity* – the base. That is, they believe in society as it exists, in which, as is well known, God is at the apex and the mob at the base. Although Mazzini's creed, God and the people, *Dio e popolo*, may have a meaning in Italy, where the Pope is equated with God and the princes with the people, it is a bit much to offer this plagiarism of Johannes Ronge,[84] the most insipid swill of the German pseudo-Enlightenment, as the key which will solve the riddle of the century. Furthermore, how easily the members of this school accustom themselves to the small sacrifices which organization and discipline demand, how willingly they give up the narrow exclusiveness of theory is demonstrated by our friend, Arnold Winkelried Ruge, who, to Leo's great joy, has this time been able to recognize the difference between divinity and humanity.[85]

The manifesto ends with the words:

What is needed is a constitution for European democracy, and the foundation of a people's budget or exchequer. What is needed is the organization of an army of initiators.

In order to be one of the first initiators of the people's budget Ruge has turned to '*de demokratische Jantjes van Amsterdam*'[86] – the democratic citizens of Amsterdam – to explain to them their special vocation and duty to provide money. Holland is in distress!

London, 1 November 1850

84. Johannes Ronge was a German priest, the founder of the 'German Catholic' movement of the 1840s, which was an attempt to purge the Roman Catholic church of superstition and bring it into harmony with the modern age.

85. A reference to Ruge's controversy with the reactionary clericalist historian Heinrich Leo at the end of the 1830s. Leo asserted in his pamphlet *Die Hegelingen* (Halle, 1838) that the Young Hegelians were atheists because they were unable to recognize the difference between divinity and humanity.

86. Jantjes: nickname for the Dutch.

Address of the Central Committee to the Communist League (March 1850)[1]

Karl Marx and Frederick Engels

THE CENTRAL COMMITTEE TO THE LEAGUE

Brothers,

In the two revolutionary years of 1848–9 the League proved itself in two ways. First, its members everywhere involved themselves energetically in the movement and stood in the front ranks of the only decisively revolutionary class, the proletariat, in the press, on the barricades and on the battlefields. The League further proved itself in that its understanding of the movement, as expressed in the circulars issued by the Congresses and the Central Committee of 1847[2] and in the *Manifesto of the Communist Party*, has been shown to be the only correct one, and the expectations expressed in these documents have been completely fulfilled. This understanding of the conditions of modern society, which was previously only propagated by the League in secret, is now on everyone's lips and is preached openly in the market place. At the same time, however, the formerly strong organization of the League has been considerably weakened. A large number of members who were directly involved in the movement thought that the time for secret societies was over and that public action alone was sufficient. The individual districts and communes[3]

1. This Address was printed in London and clandestinely distributed within the Communist League network in Germany, then published in the German press after its seizure consequent on the arrest of the Cologne Central Committee of the Communist League in April 1851. It is translated here from the version published by Engels as an appendix to the 1885 edition of Marx's book *The Cologne Communist Trial*, as printed in *MEW* 7.

2. Some of these documents are printed as appendices to *MECW* 6.

3. The basic group of the Communist League was the 'commune' (*Gemeinde*), consisting of between three and twenty members. A 'district' (*Kreis*) was formed by between two and ten communes falling within a specified geographical area, its committee (*Kreisbehörde*) being an aggregate of the elected commune committees. The Central Committee (*Zentralbehörde*) appointed certain districts as 'central districts' (*leitende Kreise*), their committees being

allowed their connections with the Central Committee to weaken and gradually become dormant. So, while the democratic party, the party of the petty bourgeoisie, has become more and more organized in Germany, the workers' party has lost its only firm foothold, remaining organized at best in individual localities for local purposes; within the general movement it has consequently come under the complete domination and leadership of the petty-bourgeois democrats. This situation cannot be allowed to continue; the independence of the workers must be restored. The Central Committee recognized this necessity and it therefore sent an emissary, Joseph Moll, to Germany in the winter of 1848–9 to reorganize the League. Moll's mission, however, failed to produce any lasting effect, partly because the German workers at that time had not had enough experience and partly because it was interrupted by the insurrection last May.[4] Moll himself took up arms, joined the Baden-Palatinate army and fell on 29 June in the battle of the River Murg. The League lost in him one of its oldest, most active and most reliable members, who had been involved in all the Congresses and Central Committees and had earlier conducted a series of missions with great success. Since the defeat of the German and French revolutionary parties in July 1849,[5] almost all the members of the Central Committee have reassembled in London: they have replenished their numbers with new revolutionary forces and set about reorganizing the League with renewed zeal.

This reorganization can only be achieved by an emissary, and the Central Committee considers it most important to dispatch the emissary at this very moment, when a new revolution is imminent, that is, when the workers' party must go into battle with the maximum degree of organization, unity and independence, so that it is not exploited and taken in tow by the bourgeoisie as in 1848.

We told you already in 1848, brothers, that the German liberal bourgeoisie would soon come to power and would immediately

---

charged with the common affairs of a group of districts. See 'Rules of the Communist League', *MECW* 6, pp. 585–8.

4. This refers to the Reich Constitution Campaign; see Introduction, pp. 47–8.

5. For the French side see 'The Class Struggles in France', *Surveys from Exile*, pp. 92–101.

turn its newly won power against the workers. You have seen how this forecast came true. It was indeed the bourgeoisie which took possession of the state authority in the wake of the March movement of 1848 and used this power to drive the workers, its allies in the struggle, back into their former oppressed position. Although the bourgeoisie could accomplish this only by entering into an alliance with the feudal party, which had been defeated in March, and eventually even had to surrender power once more to this feudal absolutist party, it has nevertheless secured favourable conditions for itself. In view of the government's[6] financial difficulties, these conditions would ensure that power would in the long run fall into its hands again and that all its interests would be secured, if it were possible for the revolutionary movement to assume from now on a so-called peaceful course of development. In order to guarantee its power the bourgeoisie would not even need to arouse hatred by taking violent measures against the people, as all of these violent measures have already been carried out by the feudal counter-revolution. But events will not take this peaceful course. On the contrary, the revolution which will accelerate the course of events is imminent, whether it is initiated by an independent rising of the French proletariat or by an invasion of the revolutionary Babel[7] by the Holy Alliance.

The treacherous role that the German liberal bourgeoisie played against the people in 1848 will be assumed in the coming revolution by the democratic petty bourgeoisie, which now occupies the same position in the opposition as the liberal bourgeoisie did before 1848. This democratic party, which is far more dangerous for the workers than were the liberals earlier, is composed of three elements: 1) The most progressive elements of the big bourgeoisie, who pursue the goal of the immediate and complete overthrow of feudalism and absolutism. This fraction is represented by the former Berlin *Vereinbarer*, the tax-resisters;[8] 2) The constitutional-democratic petty bourgeois, whose main aim during the previous movement was the formation of a more or less

6. Marx seems to be referring to the Prussian government, but the same reasoning would presumably apply to other German governments.

7. I.e. France.

8. The *Vereinbarer* were the members of the Prussian National Assembly, which Marx nicknamed the *Vereinbarungsversammlung* (assembly of agreement); see p. 118, n. 22. After the royal coup d'état of November 1848, the left wing of the prorogued Prussian Assembly called on citizens to refuse taxes. The tax-resisters were thus only a section of the *Vereinbarer*.

democratic federal state; this is what their representatives, the Left in the Frankfurt Assembly and later the Stuttgart parliament, worked for, as they themselves did in the Reich Constitution Campaign;[9] 3) The republican petty bourgeois, whose ideal is a German federal republic similar to that in Switzerland and who now call themselves 'red' and 'social-democratic' because they cherish the pious wish to abolish the pressure exerted by big capital on small capital, by the big bourgeoisie on the petty bourgeoisie. The representatives of this fraction were the members of the democratic congresses and committees, the leaders of the democratic associations and the editors of the democratic newspapers.

After their defeat all these fractions claim to be 'republicans' or 'reds', just as at the present time members of the republican petty bourgeoisie in France call themselves 'socialists'. Where, as in Wurtemberg, Bavaria, etc., they still find a chance to pursue their ends by constitutional means, they seize the opportunity to retain their old phrases and prove by their actions that they have not changed in the least. Furthermore, it goes without saying that the changed name of this party does not alter in the least its relationship to the workers but merely proves that it is now obliged to form a front against the bourgeoisie, which has united with absolutism, and to seek the support of the proletariat.

The petty-bourgeois democratic party in Germany is very powerful. It not only embraces the great majority of the urban middle class, the small industrial merchants and master craftsmen; it also includes among its followers the peasants and rural proletariat in so far as the latter has not yet found support among the independent proletariat of the towns.

The relationship of the revolutionary workers' party to the petty-bourgeois democrats is this: it cooperates with them against the party which they aim to overthrow; it opposes them wherever they wish to secure their own position.

The democratic petty bourgeois, far from wanting to transform the whole of society in the interests of the revolutionary proletarians, only aspire to a change in social conditions which will make the existing society as tolerable and comfortable for them-

9. In May 1849 the German National Assembly had to flee Frankfurt after inaugurating the Reich Constitution Campaign. On 6 June about one hundred members of its left wing reconvened in Stuttgart, but on 18 June they were finally dispersed by Prussian troops.

selves as possible. They therefore demand above all else a reduction in government spending through a restriction of the bureaucracy and the transference of the major tax burden onto the large landowners and bourgeoisie. They further demand the removal of the pressure exerted by big capital on small capital through the establishment of public credit institutions and the passing of laws against usury, whereby it would be possible for themselves and the peasants to receive advances on favourable terms from the state instead of from capitalists; also, the introduction of bourgeois property relationships on the land through the complete abolition of feudalism. In order to achieve all this they require a democratic form of government, either constitutional or republican, which would give them and their peasant allies the majority; they also require a democratic system of local government to give them direct control over municipal property and over a series of political offices at present in the hands of the bureaucrats.

The rule of capital and its rapid accumulation is to be further counteracted, partly by a curtailment of the right of inheritance, and partly by the transference of as much employment as possible to the state. As far as the workers are concerned one thing, above all, is definite: they are to remain wage labourers as before. However, the democratic petty bourgeois want better wages and security for the workers, and hope to achieve this by an extension of state employment and by welfare measures; in short, they hope to bribe the workers with a more or less disguised form of alms and to break their revolutionary strength by temporarily rendering their situation tolerable. The demands of petty-bourgeois democracy summarized here are not expressed by all sections of it at once, and in their totality they are the explicit goal of only a very few of its followers. The further particular individuals or fractions of the petty bourgeoisie advance, the more of these demands they will explicitly adopt, and the few who recognize their own programme in what has been mentioned above might well believe they have put forward the maximum that can be demanded from the revolution. But these demands can in no way satisfy the party of the proletariat. While the democratic petty bourgeois want to bring the revolution to an end as quickly as possible, achieving at most the aims already mentioned, it is our interest and our task to make the revolution permanent until all the more or less propertied classes have been driven from their ruling positions, until the proletariat has conquered state power and until the association of the proletarians has progressed sufficiently far – not only in one country but in all the leading countries of the world – that competition between the proletarians of these countries ceases and at least the decisive forces of production are concentrated in the hands of the workers. Our concern cannot simply be to modify private property, but to abolish it, not to hush up class antagonisms but to abolish classes, not to improve the existing society but to found a new one. There is no doubt that during the further course of the revolution in Germany, the petty-bourgeois democrats will for the moment acquire a predominant influence. The question is, therefore, what is to be the attitude of the proletariat, and in particular of the League towards them: 1) While present conditions continue, in which the petty-bourgeois democrats are also oppressed; 2) In the coming revolutionary struggle, which will put them in a dominant position; 3) After this struggle, during the period of petty-bourgeois predominance over the classes which have been overthrown and over the proletariat.

1. At the moment, while the democratic petty bourgeois are everywhere oppressed, they preach to the proletariat general unity and reconciliation; they extend the hand of friendship, and seek to found a great opposition party which will embrace all shades of democratic opinion; that is, they seek to ensnare the workers in a party organization in which general social-democratic phrases prevail, while their particular interests are kept hidden behind, and in which, for the sake of preserving the peace, the specific demands of the proletariat may not be presented. Such a unity would be to their advantage alone and to the complete disadvantage of the proletariat. The proletariat would lose all its hard-won independent position and be reduced once more to a mere appendage of official bourgeois democracy. This unity must therefore be resisted in the most decisive manner. Instead of lowering themselves to the level of an applauding chorus, the workers, and above all the League, must work for the creation of an independent organization of the workers' party, both secret and open, alongside the official democrats, and the League must aim to make every one of its communes a centre and nucleus of workers' associations in which the position and interests of the proletariat can be discussed free from bourgeois influence. How serious the bourgeois democrats are about an alliance in which the proletariat has equal power and equal rights is demonstrated

by the Breslau democrats, who are conducting a furious campaign in their organ, the *Neue Oder-Zeitung*,[10] against independently organized workers, whom they call 'socialists'. In the event of a struggle against a common enemy a special alliance is unnecessary. As soon as such an enemy has to be fought directly, the interests of both parties will coincide for the moment and an association of momentary expedience will arise spontaneously in the future, as it has in the past. It goes without saying that in the bloody conflicts to come, as in all others, it will be the workers, with their courage, resolution and self-sacrifice, who will be chiefly responsible for achieving victory. As in the past, so in the coming struggle also, the petty bourgeoisie, to a man, will hesitate as long as possible and remain fearful, irresolute and inactive; but when victory is certain it will claim it for itself and will call upon the workers to behave in an orderly fashion, to return to work and to prevent so-called excesses, and it will exclude the proletariat from the fruits of victory. It does not lie within the power of the workers to prevent the petty-bourgeois democrats from doing this; but it does lie within their power to make it as difficult as possible for the petty bourgeoisie to use its power against the armed proletariat, and to dictate such conditions to them that the rule of the bourgeois democrats, from the very first, will carry within it the seeds of its own destruction, and its subsequent displacement by the proletariat will be made considerably easier. Above all, during and immediately after the struggle the workers, as far as it is at all possible, must oppose bourgeois attempts at pacification and force the democrats to carry out their terroristic phrases. They must work to ensure that the immediate revolutionary excitement is not suddenly suppressed after the victory. On the contrary, it must be sustained as long as possible. Far from opposing so-called excesses – instances of popular vengeance against hated individuals or against public buildings with which hateful memories are associated – the workers' party must not only tolerate these actions but must even give them direction. During and after the struggle the workers must at every opportunity put forward their own demands against those of the bourgeois democrats. They must demand guarantees for the workers as soon as the democratic bourgeoisie sets about taking over the

10. Founded in 1849, the *Neue Oder-Zeitung* passed in the 1850s as the most radical newspaper published in Germany. Marx contributed to this paper in 1855, the last year of its existence, though basically for economic reasons.

government. They must achieve these guarantees by force if necessary, and generally make sure that the new rulers commit themselves to all possible concessions and promises – the surest means of compromising them. They must check in every way and as far as is possible the victory euphoria and enthusiasm for the new situation which follow every successful street battle, with a cool and cold-blooded analysis of the situation and with undisguised mistrust of the new government. Alongside the new official governments they must simultaneously establish their own revolutionary workers' governments, either in the form of local executive committees and councils or through workers' clubs or committees, so that the bourgeois-democratic governments not only immediately lose the support of the workers but find themselves from the very beginning supervised and threatened by authorities behind which stand the whole mass of the workers. In a word, from the very moment of victory the workers' suspicion must be directed no longer against the defeated reactionary party but against their former ally, against the party which intends to exploit the common victory for itself.

2. To be able forcefully and threateningly to oppose this party, whose betrayal of the workers will begin with the very first hour of victory, the workers must be armed and organized. The whole proletariat must be armed at once with muskets, rifles, cannon and ammunition, and the revival of the old-style citizens' militia,[11] directed against the workers, must be opposed. Where the formation of this militia cannot be prevented, the workers must try to organize themselves independently as a proletarian guard, with elected leaders and with their own elected general staff; they must try to place themselves not under the orders of the state authority but of the revolutionary local councils set up by the workers. Where the workers are employed by the state, they must arm and organize themselves into special corps with elected leaders, or as a part of the proletarian guard. Under no pretext should arms and ammunition be surrendered; any attempt to disarm the workers must be frustrated, by force if necessary. The destruction of the bourgeois democrats' influence over the workers, and the enforcement of conditions which will compromise the rule of bourgeois democracy, which is for the moment inevitable, and make it as difficult as possible – these are the main points which the

11. See p. 160, n. 36.

proletariat and therefore the League must keep in mind during and after the approaching uprising.

3. As soon as the new governments have established themselves, their struggle against the workers will begin. If the workers are to be able to forcibly oppose the democratic petty bourgeois it is essential above all for them to be independently organized and centralized in clubs. At the soonest possible moment after the overthrow of the present governments the Central Committee will come to Germany and will immediately convene a Congress, submitting to it the necessary proposals for the centralization of the workers' clubs under a directorate established at the movement's centre of operations. The speedy organization of at least provincial connections between the workers' clubs is one of the prime requirements for the strengthening and development of the workers' party; the immediate result of the overthrow of the existing governments will be the election of a national representative body. Here the proletariat must take care: 1) that by sharp practices local authorities and government commissioners do not, under any pretext whatsoever, exclude any section of workers; 2) that workers' candidates are nominated everywhere in opposition to bourgeois-democratic candidates. As far as possible they should be League members and their election should be pursued by all possible means. Even where there is no prospect of achieving their election the workers must put up their own candidates to preserve their independence, to gauge their own strength and to bring their revolutionary position and party standpoint to public attention. They must not be led astray by the empty phrases of the democrats, who will maintain that the workers' candidates will split the democratic party and offer the forces of reaction the chance of victory. All such talk means, in the final analysis, that the proletariat is to be swindled. The progress which the proletarian party will make by operating independently in this way is infinitely more important than the disadvantages resulting from the presence of a few reactionaries in the representative body. If the forces of democracy take decisive, terroristic action against the reaction from the very beginning, the reactionary influence in the election will already have been destroyed.

The first point over which the bourgeois democrats will come into conflict with the workers will be the abolition of feudalism; as in the first French revolution, the petty bourgeoisie will want to give the feudal lands to the peasants as free property; that is, they will try to perpetuate the existence of the rural proletariat, and to form a petty-bourgeois peasant class which will be subject to the same cycle of impoverishment and debt which still afflicts the French peasant. The workers must oppose this plan both in the interest of the rural proletariat and in their own interest. They must demand that the confiscated feudal property remain state property and be used for workers' colonies, cultivated collectively by the rural proletariat with all the advantages of large-scale farming and where the principle of common property will immediately achieve a sound basis in the midst of the shaky system of bourgeois property relations. Just as the democrats ally themselves with the peasants, the workers must ally themselves with the rural proletariat.

The democrats will either work directly towards a federated republic, or at least, if they cannot avoid the one and indivisible republic they will attempt to paralyse the central government by granting the municipalities[12] and provinces the greatest possible autonomy and independence. In opposition to this plan the workers must not only strive for the one and indivisible German republic, but also, within this republic, for the most decisive centralization of power in the hands of the state authority. They should not let themselves be led astray by empty democratic talk about the freedom of the municipalities, self-government, etc. In a country like Germany, where so many remnants of the Middle Ages are still to be abolished, where so much local and provincial obstinacy has to be broken down, it cannot under any circumstances be tolerated that each village, each town and each province may put new obstacles in the way of revolutionary activity, which can only be developed with full efficiency from a central point. A renewal of the present situation, in which the Germans have to wage a separate struggle in each town and province for the same degree of progress, can also not be tolerated. Least of all can a so-called free system of local government be allowed to perpetuate a form of property which is more backward than modern private property and which is everywhere and inevitably being transformed into private property; namely communal property, with its consequent disputes between poor and rich communities. Nor can this so-called free system of local government be allowed to

---

12. The German *Gemeinde* (literally commune or community) here refers equally to an urban municipality or a rural district.

perpetuate, side by side with the state civil law, the existence of communal civil law with its sharp practices directed against the workers. As in France in 1793, it is the task of the genuinely revolutionary party in Germany to carry through the strictest centralization.[13]

We have seen how the next upsurge will bring the democrats to power and how they will be forced to propose more or less socialistic measures. It will be asked what measures the workers are to propose in reply. At the beginning, of course, the workers cannot propose any directly communist measures. But the following courses of action are possible:

1. They can force the democrats to make inroads into as many areas of the existing social order as possible, so as to disturb its regular functioning and so that the petty-bourgeois democrats compromise themselves; furthermore, the workers can force the concentration of as many productive forces as possible – means of transport, factories, railways, etc. – in the hands of the state.

2. They must drive the proposals of the democrats to their logical extreme (the democrats will in any case act in a reform-ist and not a revolutionary manner) and transform these proposals into direct attacks on private property. If, for instance, the petty bourgeoisie propose the purchase of the railways and factories, the workers must demand that these railways and factories simply be confiscated by the state without compensation as the property

13. It must be noted today that this passage is based on a misunderstanding. At that time, thanks to Bonapartist and liberal falsifiers of history, it was considered an established fact that the centralized administrative machine in France was in-troduced by the Great Revolution and was used, particularly by the Convention, as an independent and decisive weapon with which to defeat the royalist and fed-eralist forces of reaction as well as the enemy abroad. However, it is now known that during the entire revolution, up to 18 Brumaire, the whole administration of the departments, districts and municipalities consisted of authorities elected by the local population, and that the authorities acted with complete freedom within the limits of the general state legislation. This provincial and local self-government, resembling the American, indeed became the strongest instrument of the revolu-tion, so much so that immediately after the coup d'état of 18 Brumaire Napoleon hurried to replace it by the prefectural rule which still exists and which was thus, from its very beginning, simply a tool of reaction. But just as local and provincial self-government does not necessarily contradict political and national centraliza-tion, no more is it bound up with that narrow cantonal or municipal selfishness which we encounter in such a repugnant form in Switzerland and which all south German federal republicans wanted to make the rule in Germany in 1849. [Note by Engels to the 1885 edition.]

of reactionaries. If the democrats propose a proportional tax, then the workers must demand a progressive tax; if the democrats themselves propose a moderate progressive tax, then the workers must insist on a tax whose rates rise so steeply that big capital is ruined by it; if the democrats demand the regulation of the state debt, then the workers must demand national bankruptcy. The demands of the workers will thus have to be adjusted according to the measures and concessions of the democrats.

Although the German workers cannot come to power and achieve the realization of their class interests without passing through a protracted revolutionary development, this time they can at least be certain that the first act of the approaching revolutionary drama will coincide with the direct victory of their own class in France and will thereby be accelerated.

But they themselves must contribute most to their final victory, by informing themselves of their own class interests, by taking up their independent political position as soon as possible, by not allowing themselves to be misled by the hypocritical phrases of the democratic petty bourgeoisie into doubting for one minute the necessity of an independently organized party of the proletariat. Their battle-cry must be: The Permanent Revolution.

London, March 1850

Address of the Central Committee to the Communist League (June 1850)[1]

Karl Marx and Frederick Engels

THE CENTRAL COMMITTEE TO THE LEAGUE

Brothers,

In our last circular, delivered to you by the League's emissary,[2] we discussed the position of the workers' party and, in particular, of the League, both at the present moment and in the event of revolution.

The main purpose of this letter is to present a report on the state of the League.

For a while, following the defeats sustained by the revolutionary party last summer, the League's organization almost completely disintegrated. The most active League members involved in the various movements were dispersed, contacts were broken off and addresses could no longer be used; because of this and because of the danger of letters being opened, correspondence became temporarily impossible. The Central Committee was thus condemned to complete inactivity until around the end of last year.

As the immediate after-effects of our defeats gradually passed, it became clear that the revolutionary party needed a strong secret organization throughout Germany. The need for this organization, which led the Central Committee to decide to send an emissary to Germany and Switzerland, also led to an attempt to establish a new secret association in Switzerland, and to an attempt by the Cologne commune to organize the League in Germany itself.

Around the beginning of the year several more or less well-known refugees from the various movements formed an organization[3] in Switzerland which intended to overthrow the governments

---

1. The June Address was first published in the same circumstances as the March Address, and is translated from the same source.

2. This refers to the March Address. The emissary was Heinrich Bauer.

3. The organization in question was known as Revolutionary Centralization. Former League members in it included Karl d'Ester.

at the right moment and to keep men at the ready to take over the leadership of the movement and even the government itself. This association did not possess any particular party character; the motley elements which it comprised made this impossible. The members consisted of people from all groups within the movement, from resolute Communists and even former League members to the most faint-hearted petty-bourgeois democrats and former members of the Palatinate government.[4]

In the eyes of the Baden-Palatinate careerists and lesser ambitious figures who were so numerous in Switzerland at this time, this association presented an ideal opportunity for them to advance themselves.

The instructions which this association sent to its agents – and which the Central Committee has in its possession – give just as little cause for confidence. The lack of a definite party standpoint and the attempt to bring all available opposition elements together in a sham association is only badly disguised by a mass of detailed questions concerning the industrial, agricultural, political and military situations in each locality. Numerically, too, the association was extremely weak; according to the complete list of members which we possess, the whole society in Switzerland consisted, at the height of its strength, of barely thirty members. It is significant that workers are hardly represented at all among the membership. From its very beginning, it was an army of officers and N.C.O.'s without any soldiers. Its members include A. Fries and Greiner from the Palatinate, Körner from Elberfeld, Sigel, etc.[5]

They sent two agents to Germany. The first agent, Bruhn,[6] a member of the League, managed by false pretences to persuade certain League members and communes to join the new association for the time being, as they believed it to be the resurrected League. While reporting on the League to the Swiss Central Commitee in Zurich, he simultaneously sent us reports on the Swiss association. He cannot have been content with his role as an

4. I.e. the provisional revolutionary government of the Palatinate formed during the Reich Constitution Campaign of May–July 1849.

5. A. Fries and Theodor Greiner had been members of the Palatinate provisional revolutionary government; Hermann Körner had organized the Elberfeld insurrection of May 1849 (see p. 258, n. 94); Franz Sigel had been commander-in-chief of the Baden revolutionary army.

6. Karl von Bruhn, a journalist, had participated in the 1848 revolution, and was to edit in the 1860s the Lassallean paper *Nordstern*.

informer, for while he was still corresponding with us, he wrote outright slanders to the people in Frankfurt, who had been won over to the Swiss association, and he ordered them not to enter into any contacts whatsoever with London. For this he was immediately expelled from the League. Matters in Frankfurt were settled by an emissary from the League. It may be added that Bruhn's activities on behalf of the Swiss Central Committee remained fruitless. The second agent, the student Schurz[7] from Bonn, achieved nothing because, as he wrote to Zurich, he found that all the people of any use were already in the hands of the League. He then suddenly left Germany and is now hanging around Brussels and Paris, where he is being watched by the League. The Central Committee does not see this new association as a danger, particularly as a completely reliable member of the League[8] is on its committee, with instructions to observe and report on the actions and plans of these people, in so far as they operate against the League. Furthermore, we have sent an emissary[9] to Switzerland in order to recruit the people who will be of value to the League, with the help of the aforementioned League member, and in order to organize the League in Switzerland in general. This information is based on fully authentic documents.

Another attempt of a similar nature had already been made earlier by Struve, Sigel and others, at the time that they joined forces in Geneva. These people had no compunction about claiming quite flatly that the association they were attempting to found was the League, nor about using the names of League members for precisely this end. Of course, they deceived nobody with this lie. Their attempt was so fruitless in every respect that the few members of this abortive association who stayed in Switzerland eventually had to join the organization previously mentioned. But the more impotent this coterie became, the more it showed off with pretentious titles like the 'Central Committee of European Democracy'[10] etc. Struve, together with a few other

7. Karl Schurz had fought in the Baden-Palatinate insurrection; he emigrated to the U.S.A. in 1852, and later became a diplomat, senator, and Secretary of the Interior.

8. Wilhelm Wolff.

9. Ernst Dronke, a collaborator of Marx and Engels on the *Neue Rheinische Zeitung*.

10. Marx and Engels discussed the 'Central Committee of European Democracy' in their Review of May–October 1850, above, pp. 308–12.

disappointed great men, has continued these attempts here in London.[11] Manifestos and appeals to join the 'Central Bureau of German Refugees' and the 'Central Committee of European Democracy' have been sent to all parts of Germany, but this time, too, without the least success.

The contacts which this coterie claims to have made with French and other non-German revolutionaries do not exist. Their whole activity is limited to a few petty intrigues among the German refugees here in London, which do not affect the League directly and which are harmless and easy to keep under surveillance. All these attempts have either the same purpose as the League, namely the revolutionary organization of the workers' party, in which case they are undermining the centralization and strength of the party by fragmenting it and are therefore of a decidedly harmful, separatist character, or else they can only serve to misuse the workers' party for purposes which are foreign or straightforwardly hostile to it. Under certain circumstances the workers' party can profitably use other parties and groups for its own purposes, but it must not subordinate itself to any other party. Those people who were in government during the last movement,[12] and used their position only to betray the movement and to crush the workers' party where it tried to operate independently, must be kept at a distance at all costs.

The following is a report on the state of the League:

i. Belgium

The League's organization among the Belgian workers, as it existed in 1846 and 1847,[13] has naturally come to an end, since the leading members were arrested in 1848 and condemned to death, having their sentences commuted to life imprisonment with hard labour. In general, the League in Belgium has lost strength since

11. Gustav Struve, a member of the Baden revolutionary committee of May 1849, was later one of the leaders of the German democratic emigration in London. He founded the 'Central Bureau of All-German Refugees' in conjunction with other petty-bourgeois democrats, including Marx's one-time collaborator Arnold Ruge, in opposition to Marx and Engels's 'Social-Democratic Refugee Committee'.

12. I.e. the Reich Constitution Campaign.

13. The Belgian organization of the League had been set up by Marx himself during his Belgian exile (see Introduction, p. 28).

the February revolution and since most of the members of the German Workers Association were driven out of Brussels. The police measures which have been introduced have prevented its reorganization. Nevertheless one commune in Brussels has carried on throughout; it is still in existence today and is functioning to the best of its ability.

ii. Germany

In this circular the Central Committee intended to submit a special report on the state of the League in Germany. However, this report can not be made at the present time, as the Prussian police are even now investigating an extensive network of contacts in the revolutionary party. This circular, which will reach Germany safely but which, of course, may here and there fall into the hands of the police while being distributed within Germany, must therefore be written so that its contents do not provide them with weapons which could be used against the League. The Central Committee will therefore confine itself, for the time being, to the following remarks:

In Germany the League has its main centres in Cologne, Frankfurt am Main, Hanau, Mainz, Wiesbaden, Hamburg, Schwerin, Berlin, Breslau, Liegnitz, Glogau, Leipzig, Nuremberg, Munich, Bamberg, Würzburg, Stuttgart and Baden.

The following towns have been chosen as central districts: Hamburg for Schleswig-Holstein; Schwerin for Mecklenburg; Breslau for Silesia; Leipzig for Saxony and Berlin; Nuremberg for Bavaria, Cologne for the Rhineland and Westphalia.

The communes in Göttingen, Stuttgart and Brussels will remain in direct contact with the Central Committee for the time being, until they have succeeded in widening their influence to the extent necessary to form new central districts.

A decision will not be made on the position of the League in Baden until the report has been received from the emissary sent there and to Switzerland.

Wherever peasant and agricultural workers' associations exist, as in Schleswig-Holstein and Mecklenburg, members of the League have succeeded in exercising a direct influence upon them and, in some cases, in gaining complete control. For the most part, the workers and agricultural workers' associations in Saxony, Franconia, Hesse and Nassau are also under the leadership of the

League. The most influential members of the Workers Brotherhood [14] also belong to the League. The Central Committee wishes to point out to all communes and League members that it is of the utmost importance to win influence in the workers' sports, peasants' and agricultural workers' associations, etc. everywhere. It requests the central districts and the communes corresponding directly with the Central Committee to give a special report in their subsequent letters on what has been achieved in this connection.

The emissary to Germany, who has received a vote of commendation from the Central Committee for his activities, has everywhere recruited only the most reliable people into the League and left the expansion of the League to their greater local knowledge. It will depend upon the local situation whether convinced revolutionaries can be enlisted. Where this is not possible a second class of League members must be created for those people who are reliable and make useful revolutionaries but who do not yet understand the full communist implications of the present movement. This second class, to whom the association must be represented as a merely local or regional affair, must remain under the continuous leadership of actual League members and committees. With the help of these further contacts the League's influence on the peasants' and sports associations in particular can be very firmly organized. Detailed arrangements are left to the central districts; the Central Committee hopes to receive their reports on these matters, too, as soon as possible.

One commune has proposed to the Central Committee that a Congress of the League be convened, indeed in Germany itself. The communes and districts will certainly appreciate that under the present circumstances even regional congresses of the central districts are not everywhere advisable, and that a general Congress of the League at this moment is a sheer impossibility. However, the Central Committee will convene a Congress of the Communist League in a suitable place just as soon as circumstances allow. Prussian Rhineland and Westphalia recently received a visit from

14. The Workers Brotherhood was founded by the Communist League member Stephan Born in Berlin in September 1848. It was composed primarily of handicraft workers and tended to follow an economist line rather than the revolutionary line of Marx and the *Neue Rheinische Zeitung* (see Introduction, p. 40). It survived the defeat of the revolution, and maintained a semi-clandestine organization for some years after its banning in 1851.

an emissary of the Cologne central district. The report on the result of this trip has not yet reached Cologne. We request all central districts to send similar emissaries round their regions and to report on their success as soon as possible. Finally we should like to report that in Schleswig-Holstein contacts have been established with the army: we are still awaiting the more detailed report on the influence which the League can hope to gain here.

iii. Switzerland

The report of the emissary is still being awaited. It will therefore not be possible to provide more exact information until the next circular.

iv. France

Contacts with the German workers in Besançon and other places in the Jura will be re-established from Switzerland. In Paris Ewerbeck,[15] the League member who has been up till now at the head of the commune there, has announced his resignation from the League, as he considers his literary activities to be more important. Contact has therefore been interrupted for the present and must be resumed with particular caution, as the Parisians have enlisted a large number of people who are absolutely unfitted for the League and who were formerly even directly opposed to it.

v. England

The London district is the strongest in the whole League. It has earned particular credit by covering single-handedly the League's expenses for several years – in particular those for the journeys of the League's emissaries. It has been strengthened recently by the recruitment of new elements and it continues to lead the German Workers Educational Association[16] here, as well as the more resolute section of the German refugees in England.

15. August Ewerbeck was a doctor of medicine, and a leading member of the League of the Just in Paris before its transformation into the Communist League.
16. See p. 20, n. 35.

The Central Committee is in touch with the decisively revolutionary parties of the French, English and Hungarians by way of members
delegated for this purpose.

Of all the parties involved in the French revolution it is in particular the genuine proletarian party headed by Blanqui which has
joined us. The delegates of the Blanquist secret society are in regular and official contact with the delegates of the League, to whom
they have entrusted important preparatory work for the next French
revolution.[17]

The leaders of the revolutionary wing of the Chartists are also in
regular and close contact with the delegates of the Central Committee.
Their journals are being made available to us.[18] The break between
this revolutionary, independent workers' party and the faction headed
by O'Connor,[19] which tends more towards a policy of reconciliation,
has been considerably accelerated by the delegates of the League.

The Central Committee is similarly in contact with the most
progressive section of the Hungarian refugees. This party is important because it includes many excellent military experts, who would
be at the League's disposal in the event of revolution.

The Central Committee requests the central districts to distribute
this letter among their members as soon as possible and to submit
their own reports soon. It urges all League members to the most
intense activity, especially now that the situation has become so
critical that it cannot be long before another revolution breaks out.

17. See p. 51.
18. Ibid. This refers in particular to Harney's *Red Republican*, in which the first
English translation of the Communist Manifesto was published in November 1850.
19. Feargus O'Connor was the founder and editor of the *Northern Star*, the most
influential Chartist newspaper, to which Engels had contributed before 1848. Marx
and Engels discussed the different Chartist tendencies in their Review of May–
October 1850, above, pp. 302–304.

Minutes of the Central Committee Meeting of 15 September 1850[1]

Meeting of the Central Committee held on 15 September 1850
Present: Marx, Engels, Schramm, Pfänder, Bauer, Eccarius, Schapper, Willich, Lehmann
Apologies from Fränkel.[2]

The minutes of the previous meeting were not at hand, because this was an extraordinary meeting. They were therefore not read out.

MARX: It was not possible to hold the Friday meeting because of a clash with the meeting of the Association's committee.[3] The meeting has to take place today because Willich called a district assembly, the legality of which I won't go into here. I want to present the following motion, which divides into three articles:

1. As soon as this meeting is concluded, the seat of the Central Committee shall be transferred from London to Cologne and its powers handed over to the district committee there. This decision

1. This document was first published in the *International Review of Social History*, vol. I, part 2. Amsterdam, 1956, and is translated here from the text of that journal.
2. Konrad Schramm was a journalist and the publisher of the *Neue Rheinische Zeitung Revue*; Karl Pfänder was a miniature painter, a member of the old League of the Just and later a member of the General Council of the First International; Johann Georg Eccarius was a tailor, also a member of the old League and a future member of the General Council of the International; Albert Lehmann was a worker, formerly a leading member of the League of the Just, and Fränkel was also a worker. When the Communist League split, Schramm, Pfänder and Eccarius took the side of Marx and Engels, Lehmann, Fränkel and Willich that of Schapper; Bauer joined neither side, and emigrated to Australia soon after. Though a majority in the Central Committee, Marx's group were a minority in the London district of the League, also in the German Workers Educational Association and the Social-Democratic Refugee Committee, both of which they left consequent on the split.
3. I.e. the committee of the German Workers Educational Association.

shall be transmitted to members of the League in Paris, Belgium and Switzerland. The new Central Committee shall itself be responsible for transmitting the decision within Germany.

Reason: I was opposed to Schapper's proposal for an all-German district committee in Cologne, because it would destroy the unity of the central authority. Our motion makes this unnecessary. There are a number of further reasons. The minority of the Central Committee is in open rebellion against the majority. This was manifested both in the vote of censure at the last meeting and in the general assembly now called by the district, as well as in the Association and among the refugees.[4] It is therefore impossible to keep the Central Committee here. The unity of the Central Committee can no longer be preserved: it would have to split and two leagues would be set up. Since the interest of the party[5] must take precedence, however, I suggest this as a way out.

2. The existing statutes of the League shall be repealed. The new Central Committee shall be assigned the task of drawing up new statutes.

Reason: The statutes adopted at the 1847 Congress were altered by the London Central Committee. The political situation has now changed once more. The last London statutes watered down the articles which dealt with matters of principle. Both sets of statutes are in use in one place or another; in some places neither is used, or people have taken it upon themselves to produce their own, i.e., there is total anarchy in the League. Furthermore, the more recent statutes have been made public and are thus of no further use. The essence of my motion is therefore that genuine statutes should replace this situation in which there are really none.[6]

3. In London, two districts shall be set up, which are to have absolutely no relations with one another. The only link between them shall be that they both belong to the League and correspond with the same Central Committee.

4. Presumably a reference to the Social-Democratic Refugee Committee.

5. I.e. the workers movement, see p. 22 n. 43.

6. The original statutes of the Communist League are those printed in *MECW* 6, pp. 585–8. The statement of principles contained in the first paragraph is quoted in the Introduction to this volume, above, p. 22. The 'watering down' was done by the new London Central Committee formed in autumn 1848, after Marx had dissolved the Cologne Central Committee in May. These new statutes were published consequent on their seizure by the Prussian police in March 1849.

Reason: It is precisely for the unity of the League that two districts must be set up here. Besides personal antagonisms, differences of principle have come to light, even within the Association. During our last debate in particular,[7] on the question of 'The position of the German proletariat in the next revolution', views were expressed by members of the minority of the Central Committee which directly contradict our second-to-last circular[8] and even the Manifesto. A national German approach has replaced the universal conception of the Manifesto, flattering the national sentiments of German artisans. The *will*, rather than the actual conditions, was stressed as the chief factor in the revolution. We tell the workers: If you want to change conditions and make yourselves capable of government, you will have to undergo fifteen, twenty or fifty years of civil war. Now they are told: We must come to power immediately or we might as well go to sleep. The word 'proletariat' has been reduced to a mere phrase, like the word 'people' was by the democrats. To make this phrase a reality one would have to declare the entire petty bourgeoisie to be proletarians, i.e. *de facto* represent the petty bourgeoisie and not the proletariat. In place of actual revolutionary development one would have to adopt the revolutionary phrase. This debate has finally exposed the differences of principle which underlie the personal animosities, and the time has come for intervention. It is these very differences which the two groups have taken as their slogans, and various League members have described the defenders of the Manifesto as reactionaries. An attempt has been made to make them unpopular through this, but this doesn't bother them at all, since they are not after popularity. In this situation the majority would have the right to dissolve the London district and expel the members of the minority for contradicting the principles of the League. I do not propose this course, because it would lead to fruitless quarrelling and because by conviction these people are communists, even though the views they have expressed are anti-communist and could at most be called social-democratic. It will be seen, however, that to stay together would be a pure waste of time. Schapper has often spoken of separation, well, I am taking separation seriously. I believe I have found a way for us to separate without destroying the party.

I want to state that, as far as I am concerned, I have no wish for

7. There seems to be no record of this debate.
8. The March Address.

more than a dozen people to be in our district, as few as possible, and I gladly leave the whole troop to the minority. If you accept this suggestion, we shall clearly be unable to remain in the same Association: I and the majority will resign from the Great Windmill Street Association. Finally, it is not a question of hostile relations between the two groups; on the contrary, we want to abolish the tension by abolishing all relations whatsoever. We shall still be together in the League and in the party, but we shall not maintain relations which can only be injurious.

SCHAPPER: Just as the proletariat cut itself off from the Montagne and the press in France, so here the people who speak for the party on matters of principle are cutting themselves off from those who organize within the proletariat. I am in favour of moving the Central Committee, and also of altering the statutes. I also believe that the new revolution will bring forth people who themselves will lead it, and do so better than all the people who had a name in 1848. As far as splits on questions of principle are concerned, it was Eccarius who proposed the question which provoked this debate. I expressed the view which is being challenged here because I have always had strong feelings on the matter. It boils down to whether we do the beheading at the outset or whether we are ourselves beheaded. The workers will have their turn in France, and thereby *we* will in Germany. If that was not the case I would certainly give the whole thing up and then I could have a different material position. If our turn comes, we can take the measures necessary to secure the power of the proletariat. I am a fanatical supporter of this view. No doubt I shall be sent to the guillotine in the next revolution but I shall return to Germany. If you want to set up two districts, well and good. The League will cease to exist and then we shall meet again in Germany and perhaps be able to come together again there. Marx is a personal friend of mine, but if you want separation, well and good. We'll go alone and you'll go alone. But then two leagues ought to be set up – one for those whose influence derives from their pens and the other for those who work in other ways. I don't hold with the view that the bourgeoisie will come to power in Germany, and I am a fanatical enthusiast in this respect. If I wasn't, I wouldn't give an iota for the whole business. But if we have two districts here in London, two associations, two refugee committees, then we might as well have two leagues and complete separation.

MARX: Schapper has misunderstood my motion. As soon as the motion is accepted we will separate, the two districts will separate, and the people involved will have no further connection with each other. They will be in the same League, however, and under the same Central Committee. You will even retain the great mass of the League membership. As far as personal sacrifices are concerned, I have made as many as anyone else, but they have been for the class and not for individual people. As for enthusiasm, there is not much enthusiasm involved in belonging to a party which you believe will become the government. I have always resisted the momentary opinion of the proletariat. We are devoted to a party which would do best not to assume power just now. The proletariat, if it should come to power, would not be able to implement proletarian measures immediately, but would have to introduce petty-bourgeois ones. Our party can only become the government when conditions allow *its* views to be put into practice. Louis Blanc provides the best example of what happens when power is assumed prematurely.[9] Moreover, in France the proletarians will not come to power alone, but with the peasants and the petty bourgeoisie, and it is the latter's measures that they will have to implement, not their own. The Paris Commune[10] is proof that it is not necessary to be part of the government in order to get something done. Anyway, why don't some of the other members of the minority say what they think, especially Citizen Willich, since at the time they all unanimously approved the circular. We *cannot* and do not want to split the League; we merely want to divide the London district into two separate districts.

ECCARIUS: I proposed the question, and intended to bring the matter up for discussion anyway. As far as Schapper's view is concerned, I have elaborated in the Association why I regard it as illusory and why I do not believe that our party will come to power immediately in the next revolution. Our party will be more important in the clubs than in the government.

9. Marx is referring to Blanc's membership of the Provisional Government set up in France after the February revolution, and the false position Blanc put himself in as a representative of the Paris working class in a bourgeois government; see 'The Class Struggles in France', in *Surveys from Exile*, pp. 378, 387–8.

10. Not, of course, the Commune of 1871, but the Commune (i.e. municipal council) of Paris which played a major role during the first French revolution.

Citizen Lehmann left without a word, as did Citizen Willich.

Article 1 accepted by all. Schapper abstained.
Article 2 accepted by all. Schapper the same.
Article 3 similarly accepted. Schapper the same.

SCHAPPER [*expressing his protest against us all*]: We are now completely separated. I have my acquaintances and friends in Cologne, who will follow me rather than you.
MARX: We have concluded the matter in accordance with the statutes, and the decisions of the Central Committee are valid.

After the minutes had been read Marx and Schapper stated that neither had written to Cologne on the subject.

Schapper was asked if he had any objections to the minutes. He said he had none, since he regarded all objections as superfluous.

Eccarius proposed that the minutes be signed by everyone. Schapper said he would not sign.

These proceedings took place in London, 15 September 1850. Read out, approved and signed.

K. MARX, *Chairman of the Central Committee*
F. ENGELS, *Secretary*
HENRY BAUER
C. SCHRAMM
J. G. ECCARIUS
C. PFÄNDER

Volume II
Surveys from Exile

Introduction to Volume II

The Triumph of Reaction

In August 1850 Marx recognized that the revolutionary period of 1848 was at an end. A new revolutionary outbreak was not possible until the next cyclical trade crisis, and if Marx still believed that revolution would surely follow in the wake of this crisis, he no longer believed that a proletarian revolution could succeed in Germany until modern industry had developed more substantially. The development of the revolution, which had earlier seemed a matter of a few years, had now to be counted in decades.[1]

If the 1850s and early 1860s found Marx essentially a spectator of the political scene, this was by force of circumstance, not his own choice. After the split in the Communist League in September 1850, Marx continued to work at rebuilding the League as the nucleus of a proletarian party in Germany and at propagating the ideas of scientific communism on an international scale. But as the reaction consolidated itself throughout Europe, he found himself fighting a losing battle. The Central Committee of the Communist League, which was moved to Cologne following the split, was arrested en bloc in May 1851, and the League's German organization completely destroyed. Marx still attempted to hold together the London district, now once again the League's centre. However, the atmosphere of exile, always demoralizing, was doubly so for the German Communist refugees now that they were cut off from their comrades in Germany. Their community was riven by petty suspicion and intrigue, and many of the best Communists left to start a new life in North America. Marx and Engels themselves suffered the effects of exile. They collaborated with a Hungarian, Bangya, in producing a text attacking their political rivals among the German exiles,[2] and had a nasty shock

1. See the Introduction to *The Revolutions of 1848*, above, pp. 51–54.
2. 'The Great Men of the Exile', in *MECW* 11, pp. 227–326.

when this Bangya turned out to be himself an agent of the Prussian police.

A great deal of Marx's energy was devoted to the defence campaign for the Cologne Communist prisoners, who were only brought to trial in October 1852. After the trial, at which seven of the eleven accused were sentenced to between three and six years' imprisonment for 'attempted high treason', Marx wrote an exposé of the case and of the Prussian political police in general.[3] But the Cologne convictions sealed the fate of the Communist League, and on 17 November the League was formally dissolved, on Marx's proposal.

The dissolution of the Communist League and the virtual disappearance of the German workers' movement for a whole decade indicates the immense gap between the programme Marx and Engels laid down in the *Manifesto of the Communist Party* and the real development of the proletariat at that time. With the collapse of the League Marx was plunged into twelve years of almost complete political isolation. Exiled in London, he had next to no contact with events in Germany, while the greater part of the German Communist workers in London had followed Schapper and Willich.[4] Marx and Engels could have counted scarcely a dozen allies in the 1850s, and only one or two non-Germans. Yet Marx's confidence in the future that his theory predicted for the workers' movement never abated, and in their most extreme isolation he and Engels continued to regard themselves as the true representatives of the workers' party.

His political isolation in the 1850s was compounded by much personal suffering. The first decade of exile was an extremely hard time for Marx and his family. They experienced grinding poverty and had frequently to resort to the pawnshop for loans. Marx was already troubled with the liver disease that was to plague him for the rest of his life, and several of the children that his wife bore died in infancy. In November 1850 Engels moved to Manchester, where he was to work for his family's cotton business for the next twenty years. He was thus able to prevent the Marx household from starving, and consistently sent financial help until Marx's circumstances improved. While Marx and Engels were geographically separated they exchanged letters regularly, sometimes daily. By far the greater

3. 'Revelations Concerning The Communist Trial in Cologne,' in *MECW* 11, pp. 395–456.

4. On Schapper and Willich, see above, pp. 52–3, 333–9.

part of the Marx-Engels correspondence dates from the 1850s and 1860s, and it provides a valuable supplement to their other writings, on both general theoretical and political questions.

Classes and the State

Marx and Engels began to analyse the experience of the 1848 revolution in the *Neue Rheinische Zeitung Revue*, five issues of which were produced during 1850. Besides the Reviews of international economic and political developments that they wrote for the *Revue*,[5] this journal also contained Marx's articles later known as *The Class Struggles in France* and Engels's on the Reich Constitution Campaign. After the demise of the *Revue*, Engels wrote the series of articles *Revolution and Counter-Revolution in Germany*[6] and Marx *The Eighteenth Brumaire of Louis Bonaparte*.

Engels called *The Class Struggles in France*, 'Marx's first attempt to explain a section of contemporary history by means of his materialist conception.'[7] Here Marx began, for the first time, to develop a systematic set of concepts for coming to grips with the phenomena of a politics which is certainly that of class struggle – the struggle of groups whose existence and interests are defined by the relations of production – but which is nevertheless politics, practised in the field of ideology and coercion that gives it its specific character. Marx continued his analysis of French developments in *The Eighteenth Brumaire of Louis Bonaparte*. In this work, dealing with the coup d'état of December 1851, he confronts the paradox of a state power that appears not to express the rule of a social class at all, but to dominate civil society completely and to arbitrate class struggles from above.

In the Communist Manifesto, Marx had described the executive of the modern state as simply 'a committee for managing the common affairs of the whole bourgeoisie'.[8] In the rather rarefied presentation of the Manifesto the development of industrial

5. These Reviews are translated in *The Revolutions of 1848*, with the exception of the excerpts that comprise Chapter IV of Engels's 1895 edition of *The Class Struggles in France*, which is followed here. The original *Neue Rheinische Zeitung* was the daily newspaper edited by Marx in Cologne during the German revolution of 1848.

6. These were originally published under Marx's name in the *New York Daily Tribune*; *MECW* 11, pp. 3–96.

7. Introduction to the 1895 edition of *The Class Struggles in France*, in *MECW* 27, p. 506.

8. Above, p. 63.

344   *Introduction to Volume II*

capitalism is seen as having simplified class distinctions, to the point that a numerically small bourgeoisie and an 'immense majority' of proletarians confront one another, with intermediate classes rapidly disappearing. Furthermore, the rapid social changes of bourgeois society have swept away all 'ancient and venerable prejudices and opinions',[9] so that the class struggle can be fought out in explicit and demystified terms. The proletariat can unashamedly avow its class interest, and the ideologies that attempt to present the particular interest of the ruling class as the general interest increasingly fail to deceive the masses. To turn from the Manifesto to *The Class Struggles in France* and the *Eighteenth Brumaire* is to turn from a theory that is abstract, although valid at its own level, to a concrete analysis that is correspondingly complex. In the space of less than four years France experienced a whole series of political transformations. The actors that appeared on the political stage were by no means readily identifiable as representatives of social interests, but included such heteroclite and esoteric entities as the Legitimist and Orleanist monarchists, the Montagne and the party of Order, the 'pure' republicans, the Society of 10 December, and the almost comic figure of Louis Napoleon himself. Marx's project in these essays is essentially to decode these and other political forces, to explain why the different classes in French society represented themselves in this way in the political arena, and why their struggles were fought out as struggles between different forms of state.[10]

The starting-point of Marx's explanation is the relatively undeveloped character of French capitalism. 'The struggle against capital in its highly developed modern form – at its crucial point, the struggle of the industrial wage-labourer against the industrial bourgeois – is in France a partial phenomenon.'[11] Industrial capitalism, in other words, was only one of the modes of production found concurrently in France, and the great majority of the French population were still involved either in peasant or petty-bourgeois (i.e., artisan) production. The lower strata of the middle class had not yet sunk into the proletariat, and in place of the industrial bourgeoisie and proletariat, which the Manifesto presents as the only two classes characteristic of developed

9. Ibid., p. 70.
10. The rest of this section draws heavily on Nicos Poulantzas, *Political Power and Social Classes*, London, 1975.
11. *The Class Struggles in France*, below, p. 380.

industrial capitalism, Marx distinguished a much richer variety of classes and fractions of classes, of which *great landowners*, *financial bourgeoisie*, *industrial bourgeoisie*, *petty bourgeoisie* (of various gradations), *industrial proletariat*, *lumpenproletariat* and *small peasant proprietors* are only the most prominent. (The German '*Fraktion*' has the primary meaning of a parliamentary party, but Marx also uses it for sections of a class that are the basis of different political parties. In order to preserve Marx's concept, we have used the English 'fraction' even in some contexts where it is not in general usage, as indeed Marx himself did when he wrote in English [see below, p. 593].)

Given this plurality of classes, it is not surprising that Marx had to qualify the simple model of *one* ruling class presented in the Manifesto. Marx's analyses of France imply rather the existence, on the one hand, of a *ruling bloc* composed of a plurality of classes or fractions of classes; on the other hand, within this ruling bloc, of a single dominant class or fraction. The Orleanist monarchy of 1830–48 was the rule of the 'financial aristocracy' (i.e., financial bourgeoisie) and the big industrial bourgeoisie, while the Restoration monarchy of 1815–30 had been the rule of the large landowners. In the bourgeois republic of 1848–51 these two wings of the bourgeoisie, still organized under their monarchist banners, 'had found the form of state in which they could rule jointly'.[12] However, within this ruling bloc Marx identifies the financial bourgeoisie as the dominant fraction, under both the Orleanist monarchy and the 1848 republic. 'Our whole account has shown how the republic, from the first day of its existence, did not overthrow the financial aristocracy, but consolidated it.'[13] Although the economic interests of the industrial bourgeoisie were opposed to those of the 'financial aristocracy', and they had even supported the February revolution, they were forced, when the revolution brought with it the threat of the proletariat, to rally round the class that had recently been their adversary.

Since every propertied minority must rely on the exploited masses to fight its battles for it, it can only exert political power by presenting its own particular interest as the interest of society in general. It is thus always necessary for the propertied classes to appear on the political stage in ideological disguise. If 'the

12. *The Eighteenth Brumaire of Louis Bonaparte*, below, p. 499.
13. *The Class Struggles in France*, p. 443.

legitimate monarchy was simply the political expression of the immemorial domination of the lords of the soil' and 'the July monarchy was only the political expression of the usurped rule of the bourgeois parvenus',[14] Marx goes on to stress that this ideological disguise also imprisons those who wear it. Although the 'superstructure of different and specifically formed feelings, illusions, modes of thought and views of life' is created by a class 'out of its material foundations and the corresponding social relations', yet 'the single individual, who derives these feelings, etc., through tradition and upbringing, may well imagine that they form the real determinants and the starting-point of his activity'. The disguise, therefore, has its specific effects on the political struggle. Although as the party of Order, the coalesced bourgeoisie 'ruled over the other classes of society more harshly and with less restriction than ever they could under the Restoration or the July monarchy', at the same time the republic undermined the 'social foundation' of this political rule, since the two fractions of the bourgeoisie 'had now to confront the subjugated classes and contend with them without mediation, without being concealed by the Crown, without the possibility of diverting the national attention by their secondary conflicts among themselves and with the monarchy'.[15]

Moreover, the ideological representation of class interests defines a distinct stratum of ideologists attached to each class. Writing about the Montagne, Marx stresses that what made the democratic ideologists representatives of the petty bourgeoisie was not that they were themselves shopkeepers, but that:

Their minds are restricted by the same barriers which the petty bourgeoisie fails to overcome in real life, and ... they are therefore driven in theory to the same problems and solutions to which material interest and social situation drive the latter in practice. This is the general relationship between the *political and literary representatives* of a class and the class which they represent.[16]

In certain circumstances the ideological forms in which the class struggle is necessarily fought out can place a party in power that does not represent a well-defined class or fraction at all. After the

14. *The Eighteenth Brumaire of Louis Bonaparte*, p. 507.
15. Ibid., pp. 508–9.
16. Ibid., pp. 510–11.

defeat of the June insurgents, political power was temporarily held by the 'republican fraction of the bourgeoisie', which Marx explicitly notes 'was not a fraction of the bourgeoisie bound together by great common interests and demarcated from the rest by conditions of production peculiar to it', but rather a coterie of 'writers, lawyers, officers and officials'.[17]

What enabled these 'pure republicans' to hold power was the fact that the class bloc that was overthrown by the February revolution had ruled through the political form of the monarchy. The ideologists who stood for republicanism as such, and who did so for specific reasons of French history, thus found themselves in a privileged position in the new order, but, resting on no firm class base, their reign was soon brought to an end with the developing class struggle.

This brings us to the key question of representative democracy. How in Marx's theory can a minoritarian propertied class stably exercise political power through a democratic constitution?

The first point to note is that Marx consistently refuses to idealize the forms of political democracy, to see this particular form of state as privileged in the expression it gives to the forces of civil society. It is not and cannot be in the parliamentary arena that class struggles are resolved. Marx repeats in his more substantial autopsies of the French 1848 revolution what he had stressed as a practical imperative in the *Neue Rheinische Zeitung*: political democracy is brought into being by the struggle of classes and is overthrown by the same struggle. Any illusion to the contrary is *parliamentary cretinism* – 'that peculiar epidemic which has prevailed over the whole continent of Europe since 1848 ... which holds its victims spellbound in an imaginary world and robs them of all sense, all memory, and all understanding of the rough external world'.[18]

Marx by no means dismisses the value of parliamentary democracy for the exploited classes, and indeed he refers to it as 'political emancipation'.[19] He insists only that the social antagonisms that survive political emancipation cannot be resolved by pure reason or the vote of representatives within this particular emancipated sphere.

Rather than defending the results of universal suffrage, Marx directly attacks the 'magical power' which 'republicans of the old

17. Ibid., p. 491.
18. Ibid., pp. 544–5.
19. *The Class Struggles in France*, p. 405.

school' had attributed to it,[20] and brings his bitter irony to bear against the attempt to set abstract standards of justice against the outcome of the class struggle. When the Provisional Government disputed 'the right of the barricade fighters to declare a republic' on the grounds that 'only a majority of the French people had that authority', Marx commented that 'the bourgeoisie allows the proletariat only one form of usurpation – that of fighting'.[21] The possible contradiction between universal suffrage and the class interests of the proletariat was highlighted by the events of May and June 1848. When the Constituent Assembly elected in April proved to have a large reactionary majority, the Paris proletariat attempted to overthrow the Assembly, unleashing against it the desperate insurrection of the June days. Far from condemning the Paris proletariat for attempting to force its will on French society, Marx extolled its 'bold, revolutionary battle-cry . . . *Overthrow of the bourgeoisie! Dictatorship of the working class!*'[22]

That said, Marx does not present in these texts an explanation of how capitalist class rule can be stably maintained through a representative state with universal suffrage. Indeed he was not to be confronted with such a phenomenon until late in his life, precisely because universal suffrage was not conceded in any country (as opposed to being won briefly in periods of revolution) until and unless the threat of working-class revolution had been allayed. In 1850, therefore, universal suffrage appears in Marx's theory of the state as an internally contradictory phenomenon. 'It gives political power to the classes whose social slavery it is intended to perpetuate: proletariat, peasants and petty bourgeoisie. And it deprives the bourgeoisie, the class whose old social power it sanctions, of the political guarantees of this power.'[23] Marx does not just imply that universal suffrage has to be set aside eventually 'by revolution or by reaction',[24] but that it produces of itself an untenable situation, and in fact he goes as far as to assert:

In the older civilized countries, with their highly developed class formation, modern conditions of production, and an intellectual consciousness in which

20. Ibid., p. 56.
21. Ibid., p. 42.
22. Ibid., p. 61.
23. Ibid., p. 71.
24. Ibid., p. 134.

all traditional ideas have been dissolved through the work of centuries, the republic is generally only the political form for the revolutionizing of bourgeois society, and not its conservative form of existence.[25]

In the case of the Second Republic, universal suffrage certainly was an unstable form, even if Marx's generalization from this was to be proved wrong. The disaffection of the proletariat, peasantry and petty bourgeoisie led the bourgeoisie to trust in monarchy as against parliamentary democracy, and the only monarchy that could find a viable popular base was that of Bonaparte.

Bonapartism, at first sight, seems to upset Marx's theory of the state as the organized rule of a class, or even a class bloc. Marx himself wrote, 'France therefore seems to have escaped the despotism of a class only to fall back beneath the despotism of an individual, and indeed beneath the authority of an individual without authority. The struggle seems to have reached the compromise that all classes fall on their knees, equally mute and impotent, before the rifle butt.'[26] However, Marx goes on to resolve this paradox by analysing the Bonapartist regime, if not as the organized rule of a class bloc, nevertheless as the determined product of the class struggle.

There are three basic elements to Marx's analysis of Bonapartism: the opposition *state/society*, the bourgeoisie and the peasantry. Marx's formulations as to the relations between these elements are often rather clumsy, as his concepts are being painfully born out of the analysis of contemporary political phenomena, but the basic relationships are clear enough. Firstly, Marx stresses the continuity of the French state apparatus from its perfection by the first Napoleon through to the 1848 republic. This executive power had been gradually strengthened by the struggle against revolution, until it became a 'frightful parasitic body, which surrounds the body of French society like a caul and stops up all its pores',[27] and indeed strives for power of its own. Under Louis Bonaparte the executive power appeared to have cut quite adrift from any class base, but Marx defines its relationship to two distinct social classes.

On the one hand, Marx introduces the peasantry as the passive class base of Bonapartism: 'Bonaparte represents a class, indeed he represents the most numerous class of French society, the small

25. *The Eighteenth Brumaire*, p. 489.
26. Ibid., p. 570.
27. Ibid., p. 571.

peasant proprietors.'[28] This representation, however, despite the term used, is of a quite distinctive kind. If the peasantry were a necessary precondition of Bonaparte's rule, Marx assuredly does not see the Bonapartist regime as a 'dictatorship of the peasantry' in the way that he speaks of the 'dictatorship of the bourgeoisie' and 'dictatorship of the working class'. In fact, due to their isolation in the productive process, and France's poor means of communication, the peasants were 'incapable of asserting their class interest in their own name', so that 'their representative must appear simultaneously as their master, as an authority over them, an unrestricted governmental power that protects them from the other classes and sends them rain and sunshine from above'. Indeed, Marx goes so far as to say, 'The political influence of the small peasant proprietors is therefore ultimately expressed in the executive subordinating society to itself.'[29]

But this being so, Bonaparte's 'representation' of the peasants complements without the least contradiction his representation, in a quite different sense, of the bourgeoisie itself. Marx not only sees the bourgeois parliamentarians as having paved the way for Bonaparte by their attack on universal suffrage, but more crucially presents the 'extra-parliamentary mass of the bourgeoisie' as having 'invited Bonaparte to suppress and annihilate its speaking and writing part, its politicians and intellectuals . . . [in order] to pursue its private affairs with full confidence under the protection of a strong and unrestricted government'.[30]

How is it that the bourgeoisie can entrust political rule to a power other than itself? How can it be sure that Bonaparte will protect its interests so well, especially given that, once the state machine dominates civil society, depriving all – including the bourgeoisie – of political rights, the class that has voluntarily abandoned political power cannot similarly win it back? Marx does not explicitly answer this question, but the answer in fact lies in the nature of the capitalist mode of production itself. As Marx was to explain in *Capital*, political violence is not continuously needed to extract surplus-value and ensure the expanded reproduction of capitalist relations, which in this respect differ fundamentally from the feudal or slave modes of production. All that is needed is the basic juridical framework that protects the free exchange of commodities, labour-power being

28. Ibid., p. 477.
29. Ibid., p. 478.
30. Ibid., p. 558.

itself an exchangeable commodity. Once pre-capitalist obstacles to capitalist development have been cleared away, the bourgeoisie does not have to direct the state itself, as long as the state power is one that will maintain this juridical framework and repress any revolutionary challenge to it.

In these circumstances, however, the executive power for its part is just as dependent on the capitalist mode of production, for as a 'parasitic body' it itself lives off the surplus-value produced by the workers and is as threatened as the bourgeoisie by proletarian revolution. Bonapartist state and French bourgeoisie thus shared a fundamental unity of interest; while there was certainly room for conflict between them, this could only be secondary in relation to their common antagonism to the proletariat. The peasantry, on the other hand, were only an instrument for Bonaparte's ambition. Unable to organize themselves independently, they needed only the few token gestures in their direction required to avert spontaneous revolt. It is thus not surprising that the Bonapartist regime, besides maintaining the basic functions of the capitalist state, took active measures to further the development of French capitalism, measures probably more far-reaching than a bourgeois-democratic regime would have been able to carry out.

If Marx's mature theory adequately explains the symbiotic relationship between bourgeoisie and Bonapartist state, he was still unwilling, in 1852, to accept this as a viable situation. The early formulations of historical materialism, *The German Ideology* and the Manifesto in particular, assume an identity between what Marx was later to distinguish as the (economically) 'ruling class' and the (politically) 'governing caste'.[31] Only with the further development during the 1850s of Marx's theory of modes of production did economy and polity emerge as fully distinct levels of the social formation.

Marx accordingly underestimated the tenacity of Louis Bonaparte's regime. He optimistically predicted that a rapidly intensifying crisis would arise from the allegedly contradictory demands placed on Bonaparte by his need to appear as the the 'patriarchal benefactor of all classes'[32] – surely a normal functional requisite for any government. Marx's hope that Bonaparte would 'bring the whole bourgeois economy into confusion'[33] was not to be fulfilled, and

31. 'Parties and Cliques', below, p. 613.
32. *The Eighteenth Brumaire*, p. 581.
33. Ibid., p. 582.

indeed Marx offers no satisfactory reason why this should have happened.

Finally, it is clear from Marx's analysis of the French executive that he saw the state as something more than just the instrument of ruling-class power. For Marx, the very existence of a state apparatus separate from civil society – which the bourgeoisie needs in order to maintain its supremacy – involves a specific oppression of civil society by the state, over and above the exploitation of the proletariat by capital which it perpetuates. The task of the proletarian revolution is not merely the abolition of capitalist exploitation, but also the liberation of civil society from domination by its state apparatus. In this context Marx introduces for the first time the concept of the revolution destroying the state apparatus, although still only in an oblique way, and as a task implicitly peculiar to France.[34] Only in 1871 was Marx to spell out, with reference to the Paris Commune, what precisely was involved in 'smashing' the state machine, and what form of organization the proletariat had to put in its place.

England

After completing his book on the Cologne Communist Trial, in December 1852, Marx returned to his economic studies, at least in so far as the needs of earning a living allowed him to do. The results of Marx's theoretical work were slow to appear, and during the 1850s he published only the first two chapters of what was later to be *Capital*.[35] However, in the journalistic work that he undertook, particularly for the *New York Daily Tribune*, Marx was of necessity prolific, and the articles that he and Engels wrote for this paper between 1852 and 1862 fill several volumes of their collected works. Needless to say, there is much in these pieces, which range over a great part of the contemporary economic and political scene, that is not of lasting value, and there are even many issues on which Marx's judgement turned out to be mistaken. Equally, however, there is much in Marx's journalistic work that is of durable importance, and this work is important is a whole, as a moment of Marx's political practice.

When Marx settled permanently in London, in 1849, he was

34. Ibid., p. 571.
35. *A Contribution to the Critique of Political Economy*, in *MECW* 29.

thirty-one years old, and it was in England that he was to spend three-quarters of his adult life. In the 1850s this fact was of course not yet apparent, and Marx's connections with the English working-class movement were not to blossom until the next decade, with the foundation of the International Working Men's Association. Marx's only real comrade in the English workers' movement in the 1850s was Ernest Jones.[36] Marx passed on to Jones's *People's Paper* many of his *Tribune* articles and discussed his political work with him regularly until the Chartist movement finally collapsed in 1858.

It was unfortunate for the development of Marx's politics that he found himself exiled in a country that was, in the third quarter of the nineteenth century, the most stable and crisis-free in the bourgeois world. English Chartism had been mortally wounded in 1848, and it was to be four decades before the period of mid-Victorian prosperity came to an end and a new socialist workers' movement developed. The sluggish English environment undoubtedly acted as a brake on the development of Marx's politics. While the worst years of reaction saw the steady maturation of Marx's general theory and his critique of bourgeois economics, his political theory made little progress compared with the heady developments of the 1848 period. Revolutionary political theory can only develop in response to the new problems and tasks raised by mass struggle, and this was completely lacking in Marx's England.

In England, the relationship between political power and civil society was quite different from that which Marx had studied in France and Germany. In Marx's native land civil society was to a notorious extent dominated by the state, and Marx had attacked Hegel's defence of the state bureaucracy as early as 1843.[37] In his writings on France, also, Marx had isolated the bureaucratic-military apparatus as the key bastion of the rule of capital. The British state of the mid-Victorian period did not possess the immense standing army and bureaucracy of its Continental neighbours, a fact which Marx was to interpret as facilitating the proletarian revolution. Yet the political rule of capital was none the less firmly established in Britain, though the forms it took were subtler and less conspicuous. In the absence of the stormy class struggles that had unveiled to him

36. On Ernest Jones, see the Introduction to *The Revolutions of 1848*, p. 16.

37. In his 'Critique of Hegel's Doctrine of the State'; Karl Marx, *Early Writings*, Harmondsworth, 1975, pp. 57–198.

the nature of bourgeois rule in France, Marx was never able to get to the root of the peculiarities of the British state.

The starting point of Marx's writings on Britain was a review of Guizot's pamphlet on the English revolution of the seventeenth century, which Marx saw as an attempt by Guizot to explain why bourgeois society in England had developed in the form of constitutional monarchy longer than in France. The stable political structure introduced by the English revolution of 1688, which Guizot could only ascribe to the superior intelligence of the English bourgeoisie, Marx attributed to the existence in England of a class of large landowners which had arisen under Henry VIII (from the confiscation and sale of church lands), whose estates were not feudal but bourgeois property, and who could therefore enter into a 'lasting alliance' with the developing commercial and financial bourgeoisie.[38]

In 1852, in his first series of articles for the *New York Daily Tribune*, Marx turned his attention to the two-party system that had dominated British politics since the 1688 revolution. The Tory party was the class party of the large landed proprietors, 'distinguished from the other bourgeois in the same way as rent of land is distinguished from commercial and industrial profit. Rent of land is conservative, profit is progressive.' 'The Tories recruit their army from the farmers ... [and] are followed and supported by the Colonial Interest, the Shipping Interest, the State Church party,' in fact all the sections of the ruling class opposed to the dominance of industrial capital. The Whig party, 'a species which, like all those of the amphibious class, exists very easily, but is difficult to describe', consisted in fact of 'the oldest, richest, and most arrogant portion of English landed property', but were defined politically by serving as 'the *aristocratic representatives* ... of the industrial and commercial middle class'. 'Under the condition that the bourgeoisie should abandon to them, to an oligarchy of aristocratic families, the monopoly of government and the exclusive possession of office, they make to the middle class, and assist it in conquering, all those concessions which in the course of social and political development have shown themselves to have become *unavoidable* and *undelayable*.'[39] Thus a symbiotic relationship is defined between the 'economically ruling class' and

38. 'Review of Guizot's Book on the English Revolution', below, p. 588.
39. 'Tories and Whigs', below, pp. 591–3.

the 'politically governing caste' which in some ways parallels that between Bonaparte and the French bourgeoisie.

Thus far, Marx's analysis is indisputable. The problems begin when he comes on to deal with the perspectives for future development. Marx held that constitutional monarchy was not the final political form of bourgeois society in England. Before the English propertied classes were mortally threatened by the proletariat, Marx believed that the industrial bourgeoisie would itself be forced to overthrow the traditional structures of the constitution, because its own 'new requirements' clashed with the interests of the landed proprietors and the old commercial and financial bourgeoisie.

For Marx, the highly mediated political expression of the power of capital provided by the Whig party was an anachronism which corresponded to a more backward state of capitalist development. Marx believed that as industrial capital grew to increasing pre-eminence over other forms of bourgeois property, the industrial bourgeoisie would push aside the old structures of the constitution that represented so many *'faux frais'* (overhead costs) of production – the monarchy, Lords, colonies, standing army and Established Church – and take power directly into its own hands in the form of a democratic republic. The Free Traders were therefore 'the party of the self-conscious bourgeoisie' (in this sense, industrial bourgeoisie), which would necessarily strive 'to make available its social power as a political power as well, and to eradicate the last arrogant remnants of feudal society'.[40] The economic strength of the Tories had been broken by the repeal of the Corn Laws in 1846, but Marx held that the Tories still attempted 'to maintain a political power, the social foundation of which has ceased to exist' by means of 'a *counter-revolution*, that is to say, by a reaction of the state against society', an attempt which Marx believed 'must bring on a crisis'.[41]

Even though the manufacturers, faced as they were with the working class as their own 'arising enemy', might 'strive to avoid every forcible collision with the aristocracy', yet 'historical necessity and the Tories press them onwards. They cannot avoid fulfilling their mission, battering to pieces Old England.' 'When they will have conquered exclusive political dominion ... the struggle against

40. 'The Chartists', below, p. 596.
41. 'Tories and Whigs', p. 592.

356 Introduction to Volume II

capital will no longer be distinct from the struggle against the existing government.'[42]

As for the English working class, Marx believed that the Chartist programme of universal suffrage was the direct road to its supremacy. Universal suffrage was 'the equivalent for political power for the working class of England, where the proletariat forms the large majority of the population, where, in a long, though underground civil war, it has gained a clear consciousness of its position as a class'.[43] Marx was of course wrong in his predictions. The industrial bourgeoisie managed to integrate itself politically and culturally into the old ruling bloc, and the aristocratic 'mask'[44] was to remain for at least a further half-century to camouflage and mystify the rule of capital. The Chartists' six points were one by one conceded by the ruling classes, but they did not lead, as Marx had hoped, to working-class political power.

The root of Marx's error was his application to England of a political model worked out on the basis of Continental experience.[45] On the Continent, particularly in France, which Marx saw as the paradigm of bourgeois political development, the industrial bourgeoisie had joined more than once in revolution against the old ruling classes, and the Communist Manifesto indeed presents the 'battering to pieces' of the old regime by the industrial bourgeoisie as part of a historically necessary process. Marx had already had to recognize, with respect to Germany, that the general schema of the Manifesto could be distorted by relative backwardness;[46] he did not yet understand that it could be equally distorted, in a different direction, by England's relative precocity.

The constitutional settlement of 1688 had a firmer basis than Marx ascribed to it. As the first capitalist nation, England acquired in the eighteenth century the unrivalled mastery of the world market that stimulated the industrial revolution. Under the constitutional monarchy, and with its market secured by the sea power already developed by the commercial bourgeoisie, the industrial capitalist class that began to form in the late eighteenth

42. 'The Chartists', p. 598.

43. Ibid.

44. 'The British Constitution', below, p. 588.

45. The critique of Marx's analysis of English politics presented here is indebted to arguments developed by Tom Nairn, particularly in 'The Fateful Meridian', *New Left Review* I/60.

46. See the Introduction to *The Revolutions of 1848*, above, pp. 29, 40.

century had no fundamental quarrel with the traditional ruling classes. Significantly, it remained untouched by the rationalist ideology of the Enlightenment, which logically 'should' have expressed its interests, as, despite the *'faux frais'* represented by the trappings of state, it did not face the obstacle to its development represented by the absolutist state that its counterparts on the Continent had to overcome. The industrialists rallied behind their elders and betters in the Napoleonic wars, which, for the English ruling classes, were less motivated by counter-revolutionary zeal than a continuation of the trade wars against the French monarchy. Jacobinism did evoke a certain response among the English artisans and petty bourgeoisie, but it was crushed by a united front of all the exploiting classes. The contradiction between the industrialists and the old ruling classes was already a secondary one, and the campaigns over the Reform Bill and the Corn Laws in no way ruptured the underlying alliance. Indeed, the repeal of the Corn Laws weakened the landlords' economic strength only marginally (grain prices were only to fall substantially with the opening-up of the American prairies in the 1870s) and was a price that the Tories were prepared to pay. Further, the absence of a bureaucratic-military state apparatus in England made Marx's expectations of a Tory counter-revolution, a 'reaction of the state against society', rather far-fetched. In April 1848, after all, the government could only resist the threat of Chartist insurrection by enrolling the bourgeois citizens of London en masse as a special constabulary.

The English working class were held in check by mechanisms just as effective as the Continental forces of repression. The industrial workers of the nineteenth century had no revolutionary tradition within historic memory to draw on, and the half-hearted reluctance of the Chartists to employ 'physical force' witnesses to the hold that the ideology of the 'British Constitution', Anglo-Saxon liberty and the rule of law had for them. Furthermore, the Chartist party consistently represented the 'aristocracy of labour', the 10–15 per cent of skilled craftsmen who, in the heyday of English capitalism's world monopoly, enjoyed a highly privileged position over the unorganized mass of the working class. After the moral defeat of 1848 most former Chartists turned their energies away from politics and into building the 'new model unions' whose very existence depended on this division among the working class and ultimately on British imperialism. Two decades later, when it became clear to the ruling class that working-class suffrage was not a threat but that the great majority of workers would vote for the ruling-class parties, the Second Reform Bill enfranchised the bulk of the male working class. The Chartist demands, revolutionary had they been won by force, proved recuperative when they were given by grace of the ruling classes who allowed the workers into the hallowed pale of the British Constitution.

India, China and Imperialism

In his articles on India and China, written between 1853 and 1858, Marx confronted for the first time the relationship between the capitalist metropolises and their colonies and satellites. In the Manifesto, Marx and Engels had portrayed bourgeois society as spreading homogeneously out from its original base and held that national differences were being abolished as the bourgeoisie of the most advanced nations forced other nations 'to become bourgeois themselves'.[47] This analysis had obvious implications for the proletarian movement. If the lands that European capitalism drew into its world market were destined to run through the same development as the capitalist heartlands, then the proletariat could only wish to speed the process of colonization, as a necessary condition for the transition to communism on a world scale. It was on these grounds that Engels could write in 1848, for example: 'The conquest of Algeria is an important and fortunate fact for the progress of civilization.'[48]

In the early 1850s, Marx and Engels had still not freed themselves from the Eurocentric view of human development that imperialism itself had engendered. It was not that they had any illusions about the bourgeoisie's 'civilizing' mission. When Marx first turned his attention to India, he wrote, 'The profound hypocrisy and inherent barbarism of bourgeois civilization lies unveiled before our eyes, turning from its home, where it assumes respectable forms, to the colonies, where it goes naked.'[49] But quite ignorant of Asian social history, Marx could describe Hindu society as 'undignified, stagnatory and vegetative', as a 'passive sort of existence'[50] that

47. Above, p. 65.
48. 'Extraordinary Revelations.–Abd-El-Kader.–Guizot's Foreign Policy', *Northern Star*, 22 January 1848; *MECW* 6, p. 471.
49. 'The Future Results of the British Rule in India', below, p. 658.
50. 'The British Rule in India', below, p. 640.

had 'no history at all' and was 'the predestined prey of conquest'.[51] It was only European capitalism, he believed, that had drawn Asia into world history. Marx did not realize that capitalist exploitation in India was not simply more barbaric than its domestic form, but essentially different in nature. Thus, analysing the benefits that Britain derived from the Indian empire, Marx distinguished between the interests of the traditional ruling class – the 'moneyocracy' and 'oligarchy' that had 'directly exploited' India – and the interest of the industrial bourgeoisie. He argued that although it was the cheap cotton textiles of Lancashire that had been responsible for the ruin of native Indian industry, the British industrial bourgeoisie had itself eventually lost by this, and stood to gain by the creation of 'fresh productive powers'[52] in India as the basis of extended trade. Although capitalism, in its most vicious form, was imposed on colonized territories such as India from without, Marx still predicted for these countries the same historical trajectory as that of the capitalist metropolises themselves; the only possible course of development for backward Asia was to follow in the wake of the advanced Europe that exploited it. Industrialization within capitalist relations was the precondition for Indian liberation, and Marx believed that the British were laying the basis for all-round industrialization with the building of railways.[53] British capital, which by its initial impact had ruined India, would in the long run rebuild the Indian economy, as part of the global 'material basis of the new world' that it was the bourgeoisie's historical mission to create. The social revolution that was to 'master the results of the bourgeois epoch' for human needs was still in the hands of the 'most advanced peoples' of western Europe.[54]

On this premise, Marx could only see in the revolt that broke out in 1857 a blind reaction to the misery inflicted by the British. Although he denounced the oppression that had provoked the uprising, and the atrocities that accompanied its suppression, Marx did not acclaim the 'Indian mutiny' as a revolutionary struggle, as he did not accept that an independent India could have a viable path of national development ahead of it.[55]

An exchange of letters between Marx and Engels in October

51. 'The Future Results of the British Rule in India', pp. 653–4.
52. 'The East India Company – Its History and Results', below, p. 649.
53. 'The Future Results of the British Rule in India', pp. 655–7.
54. Ibid., p. 659.
55. Marx's articles on the Indian revolt are printed in *MECW* 15.

1858 shows their momentary awareness that international capitalist relations posed a problem for their theory of the proletarian revolution which they had not yet solved. Writing to Marx on 7 October, Engels explained Ernest Jones's concessions to the bourgeois Reform movement in the following terms:

It seems to me that Jones's new move, taken in conjunction with the former more or less successful attempts at such an alliance, is really bound up with the fact that the English proletariat is actually becoming more and more bourgeois, so that this most bourgeois of all nations is apparently aiming ultimately at the possession of a bourgeois aristocracy and a bourgeois proletariat alongside the bourgeoisie. For a nation that exploits the whole world this is of course to a certain extent justifiable.[56]

The next day Marx wrote to Engels: 'The difficult question for us is this: on the Continent the revolution is imminent and will immediately assume a socialist character. Is it not bound to be crushed in this little corner, considering that in a far greater territory the movement of bourgeois society is still in the ascendant?'[57] The problem that Marx posed here and the implications of Engels's remarks on the 'bourgeoisification' of the English proletariat are both momentous for the theory of scientific communism. Indeed, Engels's thesis runs quite counter to the Communist Manifesto. It is very strange, then, that neither Marx nor Engels seriously attempted to solve this complex of problems. This gap in their theory was later to have dire consequences for the Marxist movement, as the European workers' parties came to value their imperialist privilege so highly that they blindly followed their respective ruling classes into inter-imperialist war.

In his later years Marx was to revise considerably his views on the stagnant character of Indian society, and also to deny that the west European path of historical development was a necessary model for all societies.[58] But if in this respect he overcame his

56. *MECW* 40, p. 343.
57. Ibid., p. 346.
58. On the latter point see Marx's letter to the editorial board of *Otechestvenniye Zapiski*, November 1877; *MECW* 24, pp. 196–201. Although Marx did not deal explicitly with India in his later writings, Kovalevsky's theory of the rural commune, which Marx accepted, showed Indian society in a quite different perspective. For an account of the development of Marx and Engels's theories of Asiatic and pre-class societies, see Maurice Godelier's Preface to *Sur les sociétés pré-capitalistes*, Éditions sociales, Paris, 1970.

initial Eurocentrism, Marx still did not develop a theory of the way in which metropolis and colony are linked by capitalism in a relationship which substantially modifies the course of development of both.

From today's vantage point, and with the development of the Marxist theory of imperialism from Lenin onwards, we can see the answer to Marx's 'difficult question'. The specific exploitation of what are now the 'third world' countries by the imperialist metropolises is not necessarily dependent on direct political occupation, but is effected quite adequately through market relationships and the movements of trade and capital. Capitalist relations of production force the underdeveloped countries into a vicious specialization in primary products, often turning over entire countries to a single crop. Industrial development in these countries is generally impossible without a strong protectionist policy, even a state monopoly of foreign trade, and comprehensive economic planning. The local bourgeoisie, however, typically remains weak and tied to imperialism, and is unable to overcome the imperialist division of labour. At the same time imperialism fosters in the metropolis a working-class interest in colonial exploitation, whether part of the proceeds is passed to a privileged 'labour aristocracy', as Lenin held, or whether, as seems more probable today, it enables the metropolitan working class as a whole to enjoy a more tolerable standard of living. On top of this economic base an ideology is built up that ties the working class disastrously to its own exploiters. Imperialism determines the historical trajectories of both metropolis and colony, in opposed directions. Those countries oppressed by imperialism cannot simply share in the 'ascendant movement of bourgeois society', but can only develop by throwing off imperialist domination. After the socialist revolution in Russia it became possible for countries that made anti-imperialist revolutions to escape from the tyranny of the world market and industrialize within socialist relations of production. There is thus no problem of the proletarian revolution in the capitalist metropolises being 'crushed in this little corner'. The problem is rather that as long as these countries dominate a great part of the world, the overthrow of capitalism in its heartlands is much more difficult, and indeed has nowhere yet taken place.[59] While Marx equated

59. Czechoslovakia and the German Democratic Republic, where socialist trans-

'civilization' with Europe and expected the socialist revolution to spread across the world in the same direction as capitalism, the course of the revolution has been the exact opposite: not from West to East, but from East to West.

Marx paid less attention to China than to India, partly no doubt because of its less direct relationship with Britain. His articles on China deal mainly with the immediate political events of the Taiping rebellion and the Second Opium War of 1856–8, and their repercussions in the British political arena. Occasionally, however, there are some comments that are of general interest for Marx's politics. In the Review from the *Neue Rheinische Zeitung Revue* for January–February 1850 Marx noted the reported existence of a 'Chinese socialism', which he maintained 'may bear the same relation to European socialism as Chinese to Hegelian philosophy'.[60] It was 'the cotton bales of the English bourgeoisie' that had brought 'the oldest and most unshakeable empire on earth ... to the brink of a social revolution', and 'such a revolution cannot help but have the most important consequences for the civilized world'. Despite the 'socialist' ideology, Marx seems to ascribe to the impending Chinese revolution a bourgeois character of the classical European kind, imagining written on the Great Wall of China 'the legend: *République chinoise; Liberté, Égalité, Fraternité*'. In 'Revolution in China and in Europe', written in 1853, Marx again posits a dialectical relationship between Chinese and European developments.[61] Yet while at an abstract level he makes great play with this theme, the only concrete mediation that he cites is that the loss of the Chinese market through political chaos would precipitate the next trade crisis in Europe. China did indeed turn out to have a distinctive socialist revolution, though its ultimate impact on Europe is still uncertain.

Russia, Europe and America

Between 1853 and 1856, Marx and Engels's contributions to the *New York Daily Tribune* were dominated by the 'Eastern question' – the conflict between Russia and Turkey, and the ensuing Crimean War. They insisted that the defeat of Turkey by Russia would lead to a

formation was conducted in the 1940s under the protection of the Soviet defence 'umbrella', are exceptions that prove the rule.

60. Above, p. 271.
61. Below, pp. 659–67.

great expansion of Russian power in Europe, and would therefore be 'an unspeakable calamity for the revolutionary cause'. 'In this instance the interests of the revolutionary democracy and of England go hand in hand.'[62]

Marx and Engels undoubtedly made a great error of judgement here. If Russia was the main enemy of the revolution in Europe, it was not the only one, and its ability to intervene in Europe was not unlimited. There is at least a trace of paranoia in Marx and Engels's vigorous support for the anti-Russian alliance of three other empires – Britain, France and Turkey. Marx systematically condemned the British government for failing to prosecute the Crimean War with sufficient vigour, and attempted to show that Palmerston, Foreign Minister and later Prime Minister, was in fact in the pay of the Russian cabinet. Marx's diatribes against Palmerston, quite inadequately founded, were eagerly seized upon by the demagogic anti-Russian faction of the Tory party and reprinted as fly-posters in large editions. Marx also wrote for the *Free Press*, a paper belonging to the prominent Tory Turkophile David Urquhart, a series of articles titled 'Revelations of the Diplomatic History of the Eighteenth Century', in which he sought to demonstrate the peculiarly and permanently expansionist character of tsarist foreign policy and the continuous connivance of the English governing caste with it.[63]

It is particularly sad that Marx's contributions to Ernest Jones's *People's Paper*, the one revolutionary organ of the British working class in this period, should have consisted to a large extent of articles encouraging British workers to support the victory of their government in what was essentially an inter-imperialist war.

Throughout Europe the 1850s were a period of reaction, though also one of rapid economic development. All through this decade the workers' and democratic movements were almost completely silenced by the counter-revolution. But the tasks that the defeated bourgeois revolutions had failed to carry out were not simply ignored. They were instead carried out by a 'revolution from above', to the extent essential for capitalist development, but in a distorted and anti-popular way. Under the shock of 1848, and in

62. 'The Real Issue in Turkey', in *MECW* 12, pp. 13–17.
63. Marx's 'The Story of the Life of Lord Palmerston' is printed in *MECW* 12, and 'Revelations of the Diplomatic History of the Eighteenth Century' in *MECW* 15.

response to the pressure of the bourgeoisie, the forces of reaction undertook extensive modernization in the 1850s. The Prussian state actively promoted industrial development through its direction of the banking system; the Austrian empire destroyed remaining local privileges and built up a highly efficient bureaucracy; Bonaparte used his 'unrestricted government' to foster the development of commerce and industry.

The economic crisis that broke out in 1857 did not have the revolutionary results Marx anticipated. Instead of detonating popular uprising throughout Europe, it led, in the first instance, to international war, when Louis Bonaparte sought to allay the threat of popular discontent by attacking Austria in the name of Italian unification. After the defeat of the 1848 revolutionary movement in Italy the kingdom of Piedmont-Sardinia, comparatively advanced economically, set out to unify Italy under its hegemony, with Cavour setting the model that Bismarck was to follow in Germany a decade later. Under the guise of the 'principle of nationalities' Bonaparte allied with Cavour to drive Austria out of Venice and Lombardy, for which France was rewarded with two Piedmontese provinces with a mixed Franco-Italian population: Savoy and Nice. After the Austrian defeat, Bonaparte, under pressure from the other powers, reneged on his bargain with Cavour and agreed to leave Venice in Austrian possession. A popular movement now broke out in central and southern Italy, inspired by Garibaldi's landing in Sicily, which brought the whole country except Venice and Rome into the new kingdom of Italy.

The international political crisis of 1859 led Marx and Engels to intervene with a pamphlet, written by Engels and published anonymously in Germany,[64] which betrays some basic misconceptions about the nature of European politics in this transitional period. In his pamphlet Engels countered the specious argument of the pro-Austrian 'great Germans' that, for military reasons, Germany must be defended on the Po. But although he declared that a united Germany would not need an inch of Italian soil for its defence, he accepted the Habsburg argument that Bonaparte aimed to annex the left bank of the Rhine and that Germany (which at this moment meant Austria) should not concede its positions in Italy while the Bonapartist threat still obtained. Engels not only made German national unification

64. 'Po and Rhine', in *MECW* 16, pp. 211–54.

the only touchstone of the international conflict; he grossly overestimated France's military potential as against Austria and Prussia, and exaggerated the counter-revolutionary character of the Bonapartist regime. He also failed to understand the importance of the Italian Risorgimento. Besides accomplishing the important result of Italian unity, this had, in fact, a far more popular character than did the German unification movement of the 1860s.

Although Marx recognized that 'the reaction carries out the programme of the revolution',[65] he and Engels did not appreciate the extent to which the revolutionary programme of 1848 had been overtaken by history. Their judgement on the crisis of 1859 would no doubt have been different had they seen that the revolutionary-democratic road to national unity in Germany had been closed, instead of expecting a rebirth of the movement of 1848. Distanced from events in Germany, they failed to realize how far the national movement of the bourgeoisie had been co-opted by the Prussian state. But elsewhere, as in Italy, where there were still weak absolutist regimes which did not enjoy bourgeois support, a revolutionary-democratic nationalism of the 1848 type was still possible. Although Marx and Engels had little chance of influencing events in Italy at this period, it would surely have been more consistent of them to have supported Mazzini and Garibaldi, despite their limitations and the bombastic rhetoric that Marx justifiably detested.[66]

Marx's last journalistic articles, written mainly for the Viennese *Die Presse*, cover the civil war in the United States. Marx's position on the American Civil War is notable for his unconditional support of the Northern side. Marx saw the war as 'nothing less than a struggle between two social systems: the system of slavery and the system of free labour. The struggle has broken out because the two systems can no longer peacefully co-exist on the North American continent. It can only be ended by the victory of the one system or the other.'[67]

---

65. '"Erfurtery" in the Year 1859', in *MECW* 16, pp. 404–6.

66. Ferdinand Lassalle, who was soon to found the German social-democratic movement and was at this time in frequent correspondence with Marx, had a more realistic judgement of the state of affairs in Germany and refused to support Austria in any way in its defence of German territory and power. (See the Introduction to Volume III, below, pp. 704–706.)

67. 'The Civil War in the United States', below, p. 685.

Marx's analysis of the conflict, as far as it goes, is accurate, and his support for the North basically justified from the standpoint of the working class. Nevertheless, matters were not as simple as Marx portrayed them. From today's perspective it is impossible to ignore both the popular character of the resistance of the Southern smallholders and the imperialist dimension of the war aims of the North, of which the devastation and exploitation of the Southern territories were an inevitable by-product. Further, Marx was highly susceptible to Lincoln's demagogy, and even though Lincoln was only forced by the logic of the war to proclaim the abolition of slavery, Marx referred to him as a 'single-minded son of the working class'.[68]

Marx's enthusiasm for Lincoln and the Northern cause was excessive, and rested on an inadequate understanding of the nature of the American social formation and the federal state. It is easy to see how in the 1860s Marx could enthusiastically compare the achieved bourgeois democracy of the USA with the bureaucratic states of Continental Europe and even aristocratic England. In the circumstances where the English ruling classes were firmly united in support of the Southern slave-owners and it was necessary to struggle to win the English workers away from ruling-class ideology, it is understandable that Marx bent the stick a little too far in the opposite direction. But the populist rhetoric of American capitalism veiled a reality which was predatory and imperialist even in the 1860s, and the war against the South was undoubtedly part of its imperial expansion.

During the 1850s and early 1860s Marx was faced with several political phenomena of a new kind, and extended his horizon from a European to a global one. Yet he made several errors of judgement. He did not understand the peculiarities of the British social and political system. He did not understand the general character of European development after the defeat of the 1848 revolution. He exaggerated the negative role of tsarist Russia and the positive role of federal America. Most seriously, he did not develop a theory of imperialism.

By contrast to the brilliance of Marx's analyses of the class struggles in France, his other surveys from exile provide us with some particular important insights, but no major development

68. 'Address of the International Working Men's Association to Abraham Lincoln, President of the United States', in *MECW* 20, pp. 19–21.

of political theory. In the last instance, the relative weakness of Marx's political writings from 1852 to 1863 must be ascribed to his isolation from political activity, itself due to the absence of open class struggle. With the resurgence of the workers' movement in the 1860s and 1870s, Marx's political theory was also to advance to new ground.

If it had not been for his need to earn a living by journalistic work, Marx would in fact have written very little on politics during this decade, as he concentrated his creative energies in a different direction: the development of his theory of historical materialism and of his critique of bourgeois economics. The *Grundrisse* was written in 1857–8, *A Contribution to the Critique of Political Economy* published in 1859, and in 1861 Marx began work on *Capital* itself. These are his real achievements during the years of reaction.

The Italian Risorgimento, which meant so little to Marx, in fact marked the beginning of the revival of the democratic and workers' movements. This was given a strong stimulus by the Polish insurrection of 1863, which evoked a long-unprecedented gesture from Marx in the form of a 'Proclamation' which he drew up on behalf of the German Workers Educational Association.[69] In 1864, the new tide was to bring Marx back into organized political activity. Marx's exile was to be ended, not by his return to Germany, but by the foundation, in England itself, of a new centre of the proletarian movement: the International Working Men's Association.

*

All texts written by Marx in German have been newly translated for this volume. Historical annotation for *The Class Struggles in France* and *The Eighteenth Brumaire of Louis Bonaparte* was provided by Ben Fowkes.

DAVID FERNBACH
1973 AND 2010

---

69. Marx's position on the Polish question is discussed in the Introductions to *The Revolutions of 1848* (pp. 43–6) and *The First International and After* (pp. 747–50). On the German Workers Educational Association, see below, p. 688, n. 1.

The Class Struggles in France: 1848–50[1]

With the exception of only a few chapters, every important section in the annals of the revolution from 1848 to 1849 carries the heading: *Defeat of the Revolution!*

What was overcome in these defeats was not the revolution. It was the pre-revolutionary, traditional appendages, the products of social relationships which had not yet developed to the point of sharp class antagonisms – persons, illusions, ideas and projects from which the revolutionary party was not free before the February revolution, from which it could be freed not by the *February victory*, but only by a series of *defeats*.

In a word: revolutionary progress cleared a path for itself not by its immediate, tragi-comic achievements, but, on the contrary, by creating a powerful and united counter-revolution; only in combat with this opponent did the insurrectionary party mature into a real party of revolution.

To demonstrate this is the task of the following pages.

I. THE DEFEAT OF JUNE 1848

From February to June 1848

After the July revolution,[2] as the liberal banker Laffitte[3] was

---

1. The first three chapters of *The Class Struggles in France* were originally published in numbers 1, 2 and 3 of the *Neue Rheinische Zeitung. Politisch-ökonomische Revue*, Hamburg, 1850. The fourth chapter consists of two excerpts from the 'Review: May–October 1850' in the final double number 5/6 of the *Revue*, added by Engels when *The Class Struggles in France* was first published as a separate pamphlet in 1895 (see p. 462). *The Class Struggles in France* is translated here from the text of the 1895 pamphlet, as printed in *MEW* 7.

2. The revolution of July 1830 overthrew the legitimate Bourbon monarchy restored in 1815 and replaced it with the constitutional Orleanist or July monarchy, with Louis Philippe as its king (1830–48).

3. Jacques Laffitte became Louis Philippe's first Prime Minister (August 1830–March 1831).

escorting his *compère*,[4] the Duke of Orleans,[5] in triumph to the Hôtel de Ville,[6] he dropped the remark: 'From now on the bankers will rule.' Laffitte had betrayed the secret of the revolution.

Under Louis Philippe it was not the French bourgeoisie as a whole which ruled but only one fraction of it – bankers, stock-market barons, railway barons, owners of coal and iron mines and forests, a section of landed proprietors who had joined their ranks – the so-called *financial aristocracy*. It sat on the throne, it dictated laws in parliament and made official appointments from the ministries to the tobacco bureaux.

The actual *industrial bourgeoisie* formed part of the official opposition; that is, it was represented in parliament only as a minority. Its opposition became increasingly determined as the autocracy of the financial aristocracy became more absolute and as the latter grew more secure in its domination of the working class after the revolts of 1832, 1834 and 1839 had been choked in blood.[7] Grandin,[8] the factory-owner from Rouen, the fanatical mouthpiece of bourgeois reaction both in the Constituent and Legislative National Assemblies, was Guizot's[9] sharpest opponent in the Chamber of Deputies. In the last days of Louis Philippe Léon Faucher,[10] later known for his impotent efforts to make a name for himself as the Guizot of the French counter-revolution, conducted a journalistic campaign in the name of industry against the speculators and their train-bearer, the government.

4. Accomplice.
5. Louis Philippe's previous title.
6. The town hall of Paris.
7. The Paris rising of June 1832 was an attempted republican insurrection by the secret societies; the Lyons workers' rising of April 1834 was led by the Société des Droits de l'Homme (Society of the Rights of Man), a republican secret society, but supported by the workers' mutual aid associations; the Paris rising of May 1839 was an attempted revolutionary putsch led by Blanqui and Barbès, and animated by re-pub-lican and semi-socialist ideas (such as the introduction of a system of progressive taxation and a declaration of state bankruptcy).
8. Victor Grandin was a leading member of the 'dynastic', i.e., loyal, opposition under Louis Philippe.
9. François Guizot was an historian, and *de facto* Prime Minister from 1840 to 1848.
10. Léon Faucher, a journalist and economist, was originally an Orleanist, but later went over to Bonaparte. He was a member of both the Constituent and Le-gis-lative National Assemblies, and Minister of the Interior from December 1848 to May 1849.

Bastiat[11] agitated in the name of Bordeaux and the whole of wine-producing France against the ruling system.

The *petty bourgeoisie* in all its social gradations, just like the *peasant class*, was completely excluded from political power. Finally, in the official opposition, or completely outside the *pays légal*,[12] were the *ideological* representatives and spokesmen of the classes mentioned, their scholars, lawyers, doctors, etc., in a word, their so-called *authorities*.

As a result of its financial difficulties the July monarchy was from the very beginning dependent upon the big bourgeoisie,[13] and this dependence became the inexhaustible source of increasing financial difficulties. It was impossible to subordinate the state administration to the interests of national production without balancing the budget, without balancing state expenditure and state revenue. And how was it to establish this balance without damaging interests which were, every one of them, pillars of the ruling system, and without organizing the redistribution of taxes, which meant shifting a considerable part of the tax burden on to the shoulders of the big bourgeoisie?

The indebtedness of the state was, on the contrary, in the *direct interest* of that fraction of the bourgeoisie which ruled and legislated in parliament. The *state deficit* was, in fact, the actual object of its speculation and its main source of enrichment. At the end of each year a new deficit. After four or five years a new loan. And every new loan gave the financial aristocracy a fresh opportunity to swindle the state, which was artificially kept hovering on the brink of bankruptcy and was forced to do business with the bankers on the most unfavourable terms. Every new loan provided yet another opportunity to plunder that section of the public which invested its money in government securities by means of manoeuvres on the Bourse, into the secrets of which the government and the parliamentary majority were initiated. In general, the uncertain position of government bonds and the bankers' possession of state secrets put them and their associates in parliament and on the throne in a position to create sudden,

11. Frédéric Bastiat was a leading *laissez-faire* economist, active in the free-trade agitation of the late 1840s.

12. Literally 'legal country', i.e., the political nation, those who enjoyed the right to vote under the narrow franchise of the Restoration and the July monarchy.

13. I.e., the financial bourgeoisie or 'financial aristocracy'.

unusual fluctuations in the price of government securities, which invariably resulted in the ruin of a mass of smaller capitalists and in the fabulously speedy enrichment of the big gamblers. The fact that the state deficit served the direct interests of the ruling fraction of the bourgeoisie explains why the *extraordinary* state expenditure in the last years of Louis Philippe's reign was more than double the extra-ordinary state expenditure under Napoleon, indeed almost reaching the annual sum of 400 million francs, while France's total average exports rarely reached 750 million francs. The enormous sums of money which thus flowed through the hands of the state gave rise, moreover, to crooked delivery contracts, bribery, embezzlement and roguery of all kinds. The wholesale swindling of the state through loans was repeated on a retail basis in public works. The relationship between parliament and government was reproduced in the relation-ship between individual administrative departments and individual entrepreneurs.

In the same way that it exploited government spending in general and government loans in particular, the ruling class exploited the *construction of railways*. Parliament heaped the main burdens on the state and secured the golden fruit for the speculating financial aris-tocracy. We recall the scandals in the Chamber of Deputies when by chance it came to light that all members of the majority, includ-ing a number of ministers, were stockholders in the same railway projects which, as legislators, they subsequently had carried out at state expense.

On the other hand, the smallest financial reforms came to grief as a result of the bankers' influence. Thus, for instance, Rothschild[14] protested, over the question of *postal reform*, whether the state was to be allowed to reduce the sources of revenue with which to pay interest on its ever-increasing debt.

The July monarchy was nothing more than a joint-stock company for the exploitation of France's national wealth, whose dividends were divided among ministers, parliament, 240,000 voters and their adherents. Louis Philippe was the director of this company – a Robert Macaire[15] of the throne. Commerce, industry, agriculture, shipping – the interests of the industrial

14. James, baron de Rothschild, head of the Paris banking house, possessed great political influence under the July monarchy.

15. Robert Macaire was the character created by the contemporary actor Frédérick Lemaître as a satire on the clever swindlers who flourished in this epoch.

I. The Defeat of June 1848

bourgeoisie were inevitably in permanent peril and at a permanent disadvantage under this system. Cheap government, *gouvernement à bon marché*, is what it had written on its banner in the July days.

While the financial aristocracy made the laws, controlled the state administration, exercised authority in all public institutions, and controlled public opinion by actual events and through the press, the same prostitution, the same blatant swindling, the same mania for self-enrichment – not from production but by sleight-of-hand with other people's wealth – was to be found in all spheres of society, from the Court to the Café Borgne.[16] The same unbridled assertion of unhealthy and vicious appetites broke forth, appetites which were in permanent conflict with the bourgeois law itself, and which were to be found particularly in the upper reaches of society, appetites in which the wealth created by financial gambles seeks its natural fulfilment, in which pleasure becomes *crapuleux*,[17] in which money, filth and blood commingle. In the way it acquires wealth and enjoys it the financial aristocracy is nothing but the *lumpenproletariat reborn at the pinnacle of bourgeois society*.

And the non-ruling fractions of the French bourgeoisie cried, 'Corruption!' The people cried, '*À bas les grands voleurs! À bas les assassins!*'[18] when in 1847, on the most honoured stages of French society, the same scenes were publicly enacted which regularly lead the lumpenproletariat into brothels, workhouses, lunatic asylums, before the courts, into the dungeons and onto the scaffold.[19] The industrial bourgeoisie saw its interests endangered, the petty bourgeoisie was incensed, the popular imagination was outraged, Paris was inundated with pamphlets – *La dynastie Rothschild, Les juifs – rois de l'époque*, etc. – in which the rule of the financial aristocracy was denounced and castigated with varying degrees of wit.

Rien pour la gloire! Glory doesn't bring any profit. *La paix partout et toujours!*[20]

War lowers the prices of the 3 and 4 per cent bonds! This is what

16. This term was applied in Paris to disreputable bars and cafés.
17. Debauched.
18. 'Down with the great thieves! Down with the murderers!'
19. A number of high-level scandals occurred in France in 1847, including the suicide of the duc de Choiseul-Praslin, and the condemnation of Teste, former Minister of Public Works, for embezzlement.
20. 'Peace everywhere and always.'

the France of the stock-exchange sharks had inscribed on its banner. Its foreign policy thus dissolved in a series of insults to French national pride, and this national pride responded all the more vigorously as the rape of Poland ended with the annexation of Cracow by Austria and as Guizot became actively involved in the Swiss Sonderbund war on the side of the Holy Alliance. The victory of the Swiss liberals in this sham war strengthened the self-respect of the bourgeois opposition in France; the bloody revolt of the people in Palermo affected the paralysed mass of the people like an electric shock and reawakened their great revolutionary memories and passions.[21]

The outbreak of general discontent was finally accelerated and brought to the pitch of revolt by two economic events of world importance.

The *potato blight* and the *crop failures* of 1845 and 1846 aggravated the general ferment among the people. In France, as on the rest of the Continent, the rising prices of 1848 provoked bloody conflicts. While the people struggled for basic necessities, the financial aristocracy indulged in shameless orgies. In Buzançais starving rebels were executed,[22] in Paris surfeited *escrocs*[23] were snatched out of the hands of the courts by the royal family!

The second great economic event to accelerate the outbreak of the revolution was a *general commercial and industrial crisis* in England. Heralded as early as autumn 1845 by the wholesale ruin of speculators in railway shares, delayed during 1846 by a series of circumstantial factors such as the imminent abolition of the corn duties, this crisis finally broke out in autumn 1847 with the bankruptcies of the great London wholesale grocers. They were rapidly followed by the insolvencies of the land banks and the closure of factories in the English industrial districts. The after-effects of this crisis on the Continent were not yet at an end when the February revolution broke out.

21. Annexation of Cracow by Austria in agreement with Russia and Prussia on 11 November 1846; Swiss Sonderbund [separatist] war from 4 to 28 November 1847; rising in Palermo on 12 January 1848; at the end of January, a nine-day bombardment of the town by the Neapolitan regime. [*Note by Engels to the 1895 edition.*]

22. In January 1847, at Buzançais in central France, the starving local inhabitants attacked a consignment of corn supplies. This resulted in a battle with the troops, for which in March 1847 a number of rioters were condemned to death, and others to forced labour.

23. Swindlers.

The devastation of commerce and industry resulting from the economic epidemic made the rule of the financial aristocracy even more intolerable. Throughout France the bourgeois opposition campaigned for *electoral reform* with a series of banquets, aiming to win a parliamentary majority and overthrow the ministry of the Bourse. In Paris the industrial crisis had the particular effect of forcing a huge number of manufacturers and wholesale merchants, who could not conduct business with foreign markets under the existing circumstances, onto the domestic market. They set up large establishments, whose competition ruined masses of *épiciers* and *boutiquiers*.[24] Hence the innumerable bankruptcies among this section of the Paris bourgeoisie; hence their revolutionary behaviour in February. It is well known how Guizot and the Chambers replied to the proposed reforms with an unmistakable challenge, how Louis Philippe decided too late to form a government under Barrot,[25] how it came to hand-to-hand fighting between the people and the army, how the army was disarmed by the passive behaviour of the National Guard,[26] and how the July monarchy was forced to make way for a provisional government.

In its composition the Provisional Government which arose from the February barricades inevitably reflected the different parties who shared the victory. It could be nothing other than a *compromise between the various classes* who together overthrew the July monarchy, but whose interests were mutually hostile. In its *great majority* it consisted of representatives of the bourgeoisie: the republican petty bourgeoisie was represented by Ledru-Rollin and Flocon,[27] the republican bourgeoisie by the people

24. Grocers and small shopkeepers.

25. Odilon Barrot led the 'dynastic' opposition under the July monarchy, and was Prime Minister from December 1848 to October 1849.

26. The National Guard had existed since 1789, with some interruptions. As reorganized by Louis Philippe in 1831 it was limited to property-owning citizens. In 1848, however, it abandoned the July monarchy and joined the republican forces. It was democratized in February 1848 by the admission of all (male) citizens between the ages of 20 and 60.

27. Alexandre Ledru-Rollin was the editor of the newspaper *La Réforme* and the leader of the radical-democratic party. In 1848 he was Minister of the Interior in the Provisional Government, a member of the Executive Commission and a deputy in the Constituent Assembly. After 13 June 1849 he went into exile in England. Ferdinand Flocon was a journalist and politician, associated with the *Réforme*.

from the *National*,[28] the dynastic opposition by Crémieux, Dupont de l'Eure,[29] etc. The working class had only two representatives, Louis Blanc and Albert.[30] Finally, Lamartine's[31] presence in the Provisional Government did not really represent any actual interests, any particular class; he represented the February revolution itself, the common uprising with its illusions, its poetry, its imaginary content, and its phrases. But this spokesman of the February revolution also belonged to the *bourgeoisie* – both in his social position and in his views.

If Paris, as a result of political centralization, rules France, in moments of revolutionary upheaval the workers rule Paris. The Provisional Government's first act was to attempt to free itself from this overpowering influence by sending out an appeal from drunken Paris to sober France. Lamartine disputed the right of the barricade fighters to declare a republic: only a majority of the French people had that authority; their vote must be awaited, the Paris proletariat must not tarnish its victory by an attempt at usurpation. The bourgeoisie allows the proletariat only *one* form of usurpation – that of fighting.

At midday on 25 February the republic had still not been declared; however, the ministries had already been divided up among the bourgeois elements of the Provisional Government and among the generals, bankers and lawyers of the *National*. But this time the workers were determined not to tolerate any trickery like that of July 1830.[32] They were ready to take up the

28. See p. 397.

29. Adolphe Crémieux was a liberal lawyer who had gained a reputation in the 1840s for defending republicans; he was Minister of Justice from February to May 1848, and a member of both Assemblies from 1848 to 1851. Jacques Dupont de l'Eure, a veteran of the 1789 and 1830 revolutions, was the head of the Provisional Government.

30. Louis Blanc pioneered modern 'democratic socialism' with his scheme for self-governing 'National Workshops' set up by government action, which were gradually to supersede the capitalist economy. In August 1848 he went into exile in England. Albert was the pseudonym of Alexandre Martin, a metal worker and a member of republican secret societies under the July monarchy.

31. Alphonse de Lamartine, the poet and author of a history of the Girondins (1847), was a moderate republican with radical leanings. He was made Foreign Minister in the Provisional Government of February 1848 and appointed in May to the National Assembly's Executive Commission.

32. In July 1830 the Paris workers were the main force in the revolution that overthrew the Bourbon dynasty, but their aspirations for a republic were thwarted by the big bourgeoisie.

struggle again and to gain a republic by force of arms. Raspail[33] went to the Hôtel de Ville with this message. In the name of the Paris proletariat he *ordered* the Provisional Government to declare the republic; if this order from the people was not carried out within two hours he would return at the head of 200,000 men. The corpses of the fallen were scarcely cold, the barricades had not been cleared away, the workers had not been disarmed, and the only force with which they could be met was the National Guard. Under these circumstances the Provisional Government's reservations, arising from diplomatic considerations and its legal scruples, disappeared. The time limit of two hours had not passed and on all the walls of Paris the gigantic, historic words shone forth:

République française! Liberté, Égalité, Fraternité!

With the proclamation of the republic based on universal suffrage even the memory of the limited aims and motives which had driven the bourgeoisie into the February revolution was forgotten. Not just a few fractions of the bourgeoisie but all classes of French society were suddenly propelled into the arena of political power; they were forced to quit the boxes, the pit, the gallery and to act for themselves on the revolutionary stage! The illusion of an arbitrary state power confronting bourgeois society had disappeared with the constitutional monarchy, as had the whole series of subordinate struggles provoked by this illusory power!

By dictating the republic to the Provisional Government, and through the Provisional Government to the whole of France, the proletariat immediately came into the foreground as an independent party; but at the same time it challenged the whole of bourgeois France to enter the lists against it. What it conquered was the ground on which to struggle for its revolutionary emancipation, by no means this emancipation itself.

The first task of the February republic was rather to *complete the rule of the bourgeoisie*, by allowing *all the property-owning classes* to enter the political arena along with the financial aristocracy. The majority of the great landowners, the Legiti-

---

33. François-Vincent Raspail was a natural scientist and a democratic journalist with Blanquist leanings; he took part in both 1830 and 1848. He was elected a member of the Constituent Assembly in 1848, and in 1849 condemned to five years' imprisonment for his role in the June days of 1848 – a sentence later commuted to exile.

mists, were freed from the political impotence to which they had been condemned by the July monarchy. The *Gazette de France*[34] had not campaigned with the opposition papers in vain; neither had La Rochejacquelein[35] sided in vain with the revolution during the 24 February sitting of the Chamber of Deputies. As a result of universal suffrage the nominal property-owners, the peasants, who form the vast majority of the French people, had been made arbiters of the fate of France. The February republic finally allowed the unadulterated power of the bourgeoisie to emerge by knocking aside the crown behind which capital had concealed itself.

Just as the workers, in the July days, had fought for and won the *bourgeois monarchy*, so in the February days they fought for and won the *bourgeois republic*. Just as the July monarchy was forced to proclaim itself a *monarchy surrounded by republican institutions*, so the February republic was forced to proclaim itself a *republic surrounded by social institutions*. The proletariat *forced* this concession to be made, too.

Marche, a worker, dictated the decree in which the newly formed Provisional Government pledged itself to guarantee the workers a livelihood by means of labour, to provide all citizens with employment, etc. A few days later, when it had forgotten its promises and seemed to have lost sight of the proletariat, a mass of 20,000 workers marched on the Hôtel de Ville, with the demand, '*Organize labour! Let us form our own Ministry of Labour!*' Reluctantly, and after long debate, the Provisional Government appointed a permanent special commission charged with *finding* means of improving the situation of the working classes! This commission was composed of delegates from the Paris trade corporations and was presided over by Louis Blanc and Albert. The Luxembourg Palace was assigned to it as a meeting place. In this way the representatives of the working class were banished from the seat of the Provisional Government, the bourgeois part of which retained the real government power and the administrative reins exclusively in its own hands. *Alongside* the Ministries of Finance, Trade and Public Works, alongside the Bank and the Bourse a *socialist synagogue* arose, whose high priests, Louis Blanc and Albert, had the task of discovering the promised land,

34. The press organ of the Legitimist (i.e., pro-Bourbon) party.
35. Henri, marquis de La Rochejacquelein was a Legitimist politician, a member of both Assemblies and later a Senator under Napoleon III.

proclaiming the new gospel and giving work to the Paris proletariat. Unlike any profane state power they had no budget or executive power at their disposal. They were supposed to dash the supporting pillars of bourgeois society to the ground by running their heads against them. While those in the Luxembourg sought the philosophers' stone, in the Hôtel de Ville they minted the coinage for circulation.

And yet it was impossible for the claims of the Paris proletariat – so far as they went beyond the bourgeois republic – to assume any form other than the nebulous one provided by the Luxembourg.

The workers had carried out the February revolution together with the bourgeoisie, and they tried to secure their interests *alongside* the bourgeoisie, just as in the Provisional Government itself they had installed a worker alongside the bourgeois majority. *Organize labour!* But the bourgeois form of organized labour is wage labour. Without it there would be no capital, no bourgeoisie, no bourgeois society. The workers' *own Ministry of Labour*! But the Ministries of Finance, Trade, Public Works – are these not the *bourgeois* ministries of labour? *Alongside* them a *proletarian* Ministry of Labour was bound to be a ministry of impotence, a ministry of pious wishes, a Luxembourg Commission. Just as the workers believed that they could emancipate themselves alongside the bourgeoisie, so they believed that they could accomplish a proletarian revolution within the national walls of France alongside the remaining bourgeois nations. But French relations of production are determined by France's foreign trade, by its position on the world market and by the laws of this market; how was France to break these laws without a European revolutionary war, which would have repercussions on the despot of the world market, England?

As soon as it has risen up, a class in which the revolutionary interests of society are concentrated finds the substance and material of its revolutionary activity in its own immediate situation: enemies to be struck down; measures to be taken, dictated by the needs of the struggle – the consequences of its own actions drive it on. It does not conduct theoretical investigations into its task. The French working class was not in a position to do this; it was still incapable of carrying out its own revolution.

In general, the development of the industrial proletariat is conditioned by the development of the industrial bourgeoisie.

Only under the rule of the bourgeoisie does it begin to exist on a broad national basis, which elevates its revolution to a national one; only under the rule of the bourgeoisie does it create the modern means of production, which also become the means of its revolutionary liberation. It is only the rule of the bourgeoisie which serves to tear up the material roots of feudal society and level the ground, thus creating the only possible conditions for a proletarian revolution. French industry is more highly developed and the French bourgeoisie more revolutionary than that of the rest of the Continent. But was not the February revolution aimed directly against the financial aristocracy? This fact proves that the industrial bourgeoisie did not rule France. The industrial bourgeoisie can only rule when modern industry adapts all property relations to suit its own requirements, and industry can only achieve this power when it has conquered the world market, for national boundaries do not suffice for its development. By and large, however, French industry is only able to retain its control even of the domestic market by a more or less modified system of protective duties. Thus, although in Paris the French proletariat possesses enough real power and influence at the moment of revolution to spur it to efforts beyond its means, in the rest of France it is crowded together in separate and dispersed industrial centres, and is almost submerged by the predominance of peasant farmers and petty bourgeois. The struggle against capital in its highly developed modern form – at its crucial point, the struggle of the industrial wage-labourer against the industrial bourgeois – is in France a partial phenomenon, which, after the days of February, was not able to provide the national substance of a revolution. All the less so, as the struggle against secondary forms of capitalist exploitation – the struggle of the peasant against usury and mortgages, of the petty bourgeois against the wholesale merchant, banker and manufacturer, in a word, against bankruptcy – was still hidden in the general uprising against the financial aristocracy. Nothing is more easily explained, then, than the fact that the Paris proletariat attempted to secure its interests *alongside* those of the bourgeoisie, instead of asserting them as the revolutionary interests of society itself, and that it lowered the *red* flag before the tricolour. The French workers could not move a step forward, nor cause the slightest disruption in the bourgeois order, until the course of the revolution had aroused the mass of the nation, the peasants and the petty bourgeoisie, located between the proletariat and the bourgeoisie, against this order, against the rule of capital, and until it had forced them to join forces with their protagonists, the proletarians. The workers were only able to gain this victory at the price of the terrible defeat of June.

It remains to the credit of the Luxembourg Commission, this creation of the Paris workers, that it disclosed the secret of the revolution of the nineteenth century from a European platform: *the emancipation of the proletariat.* The *Moniteur*[36] could not help blushing when it had officially to propagate the 'wild ravings' which hitherto had lain buried in the apocryphal writings of the socialists and had only reached the ears of the bourgeoisie from time to time as remote legends, half-terrifying, half-ludicrous. Europe started up in surprise from its bourgeois doze. Thus, in the ideas of the proletarians, who confused the financial aristocracy with the bourgeoisie in general, in the imagination of republican worthies, who even denied the existence of classes or who at most admitted them to be the result of the constitutional monarchy, in the hypocritical phrases of those bourgeois fractions which had been excluded from power up to now, the *rule of the bourgeoisie* was abolished with the establishment of the republic. At that time all the royalists turned into republicans and all the millionaires of Paris turned into workers. The phrase which corresponded to this imaginary abolition of class relations was *fraternité*, general fraternization and brotherhood. This pleasant abstraction from class antagonisms, this sentimental reconciliation of contradictory class interests, this fantastic transcendence of the class struggle, this *fraternité* was the actual slogan of the February revolution. The classes had been divided by a mere *misunderstanding*, and Lamartine christened the Provisional Government of 24 February '*un gouvernement qui suspend* ce malentendu terrible qui existe entre les différentes classes'.[37] The Paris proletariat revelled in this magnanimous intoxication of brotherhood.

Having been forced to proclaim the republic, the Provisional Government, for its part, did everything to make it acceptable to

36. *Le Moniteur universel,* the official newspaper of successive French regimes from 1799 to 1869.

37. 'A government which removes *this terrible misunderstanding which exists between the different classes*'; speech in the Chamber of Deputies, 24 February 1848.

the bourgeoisie and to the provinces. The bloody terror of the first French republic was disavowed with the abolition of the death penalty for political crimes; the press was opened to all opinions; the army, the courts and administration remained, with few exceptions, in the hands of the old dignitaries; none of the great culprits of the July monarchy was called to account. The bourgeois republicans of the *National* enjoyed themselves exchanging monarchist names and customs for those of the First Republic. As far as they were concerned the republic was only a new evening dress for the old bourgeois society. The young republic sought its chief virtue not in frightening others but rather in constantly taking fright itself, and in disarming resistance and ensuring its further existence by its own soft compliance and lack of resistance. It was loudly announced to the privileged classes at home and the despotic powers abroad that the republic was of a peaceable nature. Its motto was: Live and let live. In addition, shortly after the February revolution the Germans, Poles, Austrians, Hungarians, Italians – all peoples revolted in a manner corresponding to their own situations. Russia and England – the former intimidated, the latter itself agitated – were unprepared. The republic, therefore, was not confronted by a *national* enemy. Consequently there were no great foreign complications to kindle energy, to accelerate the revolutionary process, to drive forward or throw overboard the Provisional Government.

The Paris proletariat, which saw in the republic its own creation, naturally acclaimed every act of the Provisional Government, making it easier for the latter to establish itself in bourgeois society. It willingly allowed itself to be used by Caussidière[38] for police services, to protect property in Paris, just as it allowed Louis Blanc to arbitrate in wage disputes between workers and masters. It was a *point d'honneur* to keep the bourgeois honour of the republic unsullied in the eyes of Europe.

The republic encountered no resistance either at home or abroad. As a result it was disarmed. Its task was no longer to transform the world by revolution but only to adapt itself to the conditions of bourgeois society. The fanaticism with which the

38. Marc Caussidière, a socialist-inclined revolutionary democrat who had taken part in conspiratorial activity under the July monarchy, was appointed Prefect of Police in Paris by the Provisional Government, and also elected to the Constituent National Assembly. After the defeat of the June insurrection he emigrated to England.

Provisional Government undertook this task is testified to most eloquently of all by its *financial measures*.

Both *public credit* and *private credit* were, of course, shaken. *Public credit* is based on the confidence that the state will allow itself to be exploited by the financial sharks. But the old state had disappeared and the revolution was primarily directed against the financial aristocracy. The vibrations from the last European commercial crisis had not yet died away. Bankruptcy still followed on bankruptcy.

Private credit was therefore paralysed, circulation restricted, production at a standstill before the February revolution broke out. The revolutionary crisis intensified the commercial crisis. And if private credit is based on the confidence that bourgeois production – the full range of relations of production – and bourgeois order are inviolable and will remain unviolated, what sort of effect must a revolution have which calls into question the basis of bourgeois production, the economic slavery of the proletariat, and which sets up in opposition to the Bourse the sphinx of the Luxembourg Commission? The revolt of the proletariat is the abolition of bourgeois credit, for it signifies the abolition of bourgeois production and its social order. Public and private credit are the thermometers by which the intensity of a revolution can be measured. *They fall, the more the passion and potency of the revolution rises*.

The Provisional Government wanted to strip the republic of its anti-bourgeois appearance. It had to attempt, therefore, to peg the *exchange value* of this new form of state and its *quotation* on the Bourse. Private credit inevitably rose together with the daily quotation of the republic on the Bourse.

In order to remove even the *suspicion* that it would not or could not honour the obligations accepted by the monarchy, in order to encourage confidence in the bourgeois morality and solvency of the republic, the Provisional Government resorted to a form of boasting as undignified as it was childish. It paid out the interest on the 5, 4½ and 4 per cent bonds *before* the legal date of payment. The bourgeois aplomb and self-confidence of the capitalists suddenly awoke when they saw the anxious haste with which the Provisional Government sought to buy their confidence.

The financial embarrassment of the Provisional Government was, of course, not diminished by a theatrical stroke which robbed it of its stocks of ready cash. The financial predicament could no longer be concealed and the *petty bourgeoisie, domestic servants* and *workers* had to pay for the pleasant surprise which had been prepared for the state creditors.

It was declared that amounts exceeding one hundred francs could no longer be drawn on savings bank books. The sums of money deposited in the savings banks were confiscated and transformed by decree into an irredeemable national debt. In this way the *petty bourgeois*, who was already hard pressed, was embittered against the republic. As he received state debt certificates in place of his savings bank books he was forced to go to the Bourse to sell them, and thus to deliver himself up to the hands of the financial sharks against whom he had conducted the February revolution.

The financial aristocracy, which ruled under the July monarchy, had its high church in the Bank. Just as the Bourse controls state credit, the Bank controls commercial credit.

As it was directly threatened by the February revolution, not merely in its rule but in its very existence, the Bank tried from the outset to discredit the republic by fostering a general lack of credit. It suddenly terminated the credit of bankers, manufacturers and merchants. As this manoeuvre did not immediately provoke a counter-revolution it inevitably reacted on the Bank itself. The capitalists withdrew the money which they had deposited in the vaults of the Bank. The holders of banknotes rushed to its counter in order to change them for gold and silver.

The Provisional Government could have legally forced the Bank into bankruptcy without violently interfering in its dealings; it only needed to remain passive and to leave the Bank to its fate. The *bankruptcy of the Bank* would have been the deluge which in a trice would have swept from the soil of France the financial aristocracy, the mightiest and most dangerous enemy of the republic, the golden pedestal of the July monarchy. And once the Bank was bankrupt the bourgeoisie itself would have been forced to regard it as a last desperate chance of salvation if the government had formed a national bank and had placed national credit under the supervision of the nation.

But, on the contrary, the Provisional Government established a *compulsory rate* for the Bank's notes. It did more; it transformed all provincial banks into branches of the Banque de France and allowed it to cast its net over the whole of France. Later it pledged the *state forests* to the Bank as a guarantee for a loan which it contracted from it. Thus, the February revolution directly consolidated and extended the bankocracy which it was supposed to overthrow.

Meanwhile the Provisional Government was writhing under the incubus of a growing deficit. It begged in vain for patriotic sacrifices. Only the workers threw it alms. A new heroic step had to be taken: the imposition of a *new tax*. But who was to be taxed? The stock-exchange sharks, the Bank kings, the state creditors, the *rentiers*, the industrialists? That was not the way for the republic to curry favour with the bourgeoisie. It would have meant on the one hand endangering state and commercial credit, on the other hand, trying to purchase them with such great sacrifices and humiliations. But somebody had to cough up. Who was sacrificed to bourgeois credit? *Jacques le bonhomme*, the *peasant*.

The Provisional Government imposed a surcharge of 45 centimes in the franc on the four direct taxes. The government press tried to make the Paris proletariat believe that the new tax would primarily hit the big landed proprietors, the recipients of the milliard francs compensation paid by fiat of the Restoration.[39] But in reality it hit the *peasant class* above all, that is, the great majority of the French people. *It was they who had to pay the costs of the February revolution*, and among them the counter-revolution found its main material. The 45-centimes tax was a question of life and death for the French peasant; he made it a question of life and death for the republic. For the French peasant the republic represented, from this moment on, the 45-centimes tax, and in the Paris proletariat he saw the wastrel who was making himself comfortable at *his* expense.

While the revolution of 1789 began by relieving the peasant of his feudal burdens, the revolution of 1848 introduced itself to the rural population by levying a new tax, in order not to endanger capital and in order to keep the machinery of state running.

There was only *one* way for the Provisional Government to remove all these difficulties and force the state to change course – *declaring state bankruptcy*. The reader will remember how in the National Assembly Ledru-Rollin subsequently told of the virtuous indignation with which he had rejected this presumptuous

39. In 1825 the Restoration regime decreed this sum in compensation to the aristocratic landowners whose property had been confiscated during the first French revolution.

suggestion from the stock-exchange shark Fould,[40] the present French Minister of Finance. Fould had handed him the apple from the tree of knowledge.

The Provisional Government had succumbed to the old bourgeois society by honouring the bills which it had drawn on the state. It had become the harassed debtor of this bourgeois society instead of facing it as a threatening creditor, who had to collect the revolutionary debts of many years' standing. It had to strengthen the shaky structure of bourgeois relationships, in order to fulfil obligations which need only be fulfilled in the context of these relationships. Credit became a condition of its existence, and the concessions and promises made to the proletariat became just so many *fetters* which it *had to* break free of. The emancipation of the workers – even as a *phrase* – became intolerably dangerous for the republic, for it represented a permanent protest against the restoration of credit, which is based on the untroubled and unqualified acceptance of the existing economic class relationships. It was necessary, therefore, *to have done with the workers*.

The February revolution had thrown the army out of Paris. The National Guard, that is, the bourgeoisie in its various social gradations, was the only power. However, alone it did not feel itself a match for the proletariat. Moreover, gradually and piecemeal it was obliged to open its ranks and allow armed proletarians to join, albeit after the fiercest resistance and after creating a hundred different obstacles. Consequently there remained only one way out: *to set one section of the proletariat against the other*.

For this purpose the Provisional Government formed twenty-four battalions of Mobile Guards, each composed of a thousand young men between fifteen and twenty. For the most part they belonged to the lumpenproletariat, which, in all towns, forms a mass quite distinct from the industrial proletariat. It is a recruiting ground for thieves and criminals of all sorts, living off the garbage of society, people without a definite trace, vagabonds, *gens sans feu et sans aveu*,[41] varying according to the cultural level of their particular nation, never able to repudiate their *lazzaroni* character; during their youthful years – the age at which the Provisional Government recruited them – they are thoroughly tractable,

40. Achille Fould was a banker and Orleanist politician who switched his allegiance to Bonaparte in 1849. He sat in the Constitutional Assembly, and was Minister of Finance 1849–60 and 1861–7.

41. People without hearth or home.

capable of the greatest acts of heroism and the most exalted self-sacrifice as well as the lowest forms of banditry and the foulest corruption. The Provisional Government paid them 1 franc 50 centimes a day; that is, it bought them. It gave them their own uniform, thereby distinguishing them outwardly from the blouses of the workers. In part it assigned officers from the standing army to lead them and in part they themselves elected young sons of the bourgeoisie, who entranced them with rodomontades about dying for the fatherland and devotion to the republic.

Thus the Paris proletariat was confronted by an army of 24,000 youthful, strong, foolhardy men, drawn from its own midst. The workers *cheered* the Mobile Guard as it marched through Paris! They recognized in it their protagonists on the barricades. They regarded it as the *proletarian* guard in contrast to the bourgeois National Guard. Their error was pardonable.

Besides the Mobile Guard the government decided to rally around itself an army of industrial workers. Minister Marie[42] enrolled hundreds of thousands of workers thrown on the streets by the crisis and the revolution into so-called National Workshops. Hidden behind this grandiose name was nothing other than the use of workers for tedious, monotonous, unproductive *earthworks* for a daily wage of 23 sous. *English workhouses in the open* – this is all these National Workshops were. In them the Provisional Government thought it had formed *a second proletarian army against the workers*. However, the bourgeoisie was mistaken in the National Workshops, just as the workers were mistaken in the Mobile Guard. It had created an *army for mutiny*.

But *one* object was achieved.

National Workshops was also the term used for the people's workshops which Louis Blanc preached about in the Luxembourg Palace. By virtue of their common designation the Marie workshops, which were planned in direct *opposition* to the Luxembourg proposals, presented the occasion for a plot of errors worthy of a Spanish servants' comedy.[43] The Provisional Government itself

42. Alexandre Marie de Saint-Georges, a lawyer and bourgeois republican politician, was Minister of Public Works in the Provisional Government of 1848, Chairman of the Constituent National Assembly, and Minister of Justice in Cavaignac's govern-ment (October–December 1848).

43. In the seventeenth-century comedies of Lope de Vega and Calderón, a humor-ous effect was often obtained by masters' masquerading as their servants and *vice versa*.

surreptitiously spread the rumour that these National Workshops were the invention of Louis Blanc, and this seemed all the more plausible as Louis Blanc, the prophet of national workshops, was a member of the Provisional Government. And in the half-naïve, half-deliberate confusion of the Paris bourgeoisie, in the artificially moulded public opinion of France and Europe, these *workhouses*[44] were seen as the first realization of socialism, which was pilloried together with the National Workshops.

It was not in what they were but in their name that the National Workshops embodied the protest of the proletariat against bourgeois industry, bourgeois credit and the bourgeois republic. As a result the whole hatred of the bourgeoisie descended upon them. In the National Workshops it had also found the target against which it could direct its attack as soon as it had gathered its strength sufficiently to break openly with the February illusions. All dissatisfaction, all resentment on the part of the *petty bourgeois* was also directed against these National Workshops, which became the common target. With veritable fury they reckoned up the money which the proletarian idlers were consuming while their own situation was becoming more intolerable day by day. 'A state income for sham work – so that's socialism!' they grumbled to themselves. They sought the reason for their predicament in the National Workshops, the declamations of the Luxembourg Commission, the processions of workers marching through Paris. And nobody was more fanatical about the alleged machinations of the communists than the petty bourgeois, who tottered helplessly on the brink of bankruptcy.

Thus, in the approaching fray between bourgeoisie and proletariat all the advantages, all decisive positions, all the middle strata of society were in the hands of the bourgeoisie, at the same time as the waves of the February revolution broke high over the whole Continent and every postal delivery brought a fresh report of revolution, now from Italy, now from Germany, now from the remotest south-east of Europe, and sustained the general intoxication of the people by delivering continual testimony of a victory which it had already forfeited.

17 March and *16 April* saw the first skirmishes in the great class struggle which the bourgeois republic hid beneath its wing.

17 March revealed the ambiguous situation of the proletariat, which prevented it from taking any decisive action. Its demonstra-

44. In English in the original.

tion was originally intended to drive the Provisional Government back onto a revolutionary course, if possible, to bring about the exclusion of its bourgeois members and to force the postponement of the election dates for the National Assembly and the general staff of the National Guard.[45] But on 16 March the bourgeoisie represented in the National Guard organized a hostile demonstration directed against the Provisional Government. Shouting '*À bas Ledru-Rollin!*' it forced its way to the Hôtel de Ville. And on 17 March the people were forced to shout, 'Long live Ledru-Rollin! Long live the Provisional Government!' They were forced to take sides with the bourgeois republic, which seemed to be in danger, *against* the bourgeoisie. The people strengthened the position of the Provisional Government instead of seizing control of it. 17 March fizzled out in a melodramatic scene, and although the Paris proletariat once again displayed its giant body on this day, the bourgeoisie both inside and outside the Provincial Government was all the more determined to break it.

16 April was a *misunderstanding* engineered by the Provisional Government with the help of the bourgeoisie. The workers had gathered in large numbers on the Champ de Mars and in the Hippodrome in order to prepare for the elections for the general staff of the National Guard. Suddenly the rumour spread from one end of Paris to the other, with lightning speed, that the workers had armed themselves and gathered on the Champ de Mars, led by Louis Blanc, Blanqui,[46] Cabet[47] and Raspail, with the intention of marching from there to the Hôtel de Ville to overthrow the Provisional Government and to proclaim a communist government. The general alarm was sounded – later Ledru-Rollin, Marrast[48] and Lamartine all fought for the honour of having taken this initiative – and within one hour 100,000 men

45. This demonstration was organized by Blanqui and his party, who hoped to delay the elections, due on 9 April and 18 April respectively, until they had won over a greater section of the plebeian classes.

46. Auguste Blanqui was the outstanding French workers' leader of the nineteenth century, but still believed that the overthrow of the bourgeois state could be accomplished by conspiratorial means. See the Introduction to *The Revolutions of 1848*, pp. 18–9.

47. Étienne Cabet was the author of the communist utopia *Voyage en Icarie*.

48. Armand Marrast, a journalist and bourgeois republican, was editor-in-chief of *Le National* (see below, p. 397). After the February revolution he became a member of the Provisional Government and Mayor of Paris, and later chairman of the Constituent National Assembly.

were under arms, the Hôtel de Ville was occupied at all points by the National Guard, the cry, 'Down with the Communists! Down with Louis Blanc, Blanqui, Raspail, Cabet!' thundered through Paris and innumerable deputations paid homage to the Provisional Government, all of them ready to save the fatherland and society. When the workers finally appeared in front of the Hôtel de Ville to hand the Provisional Government a patriotic collection, taken at the Champ de Mars, they learnt to their amazement that bourgeois Paris had defeated their shadow in a carefully conducted mock battle. The terrible attempt of 16 April furnished the pretext *for the recall of the army to Paris* – the actual purpose of this clumsily arranged farce – and for reactionary federalist demonstrations in the provinces.

The National Assembly, elected by *direct, universal suffrage*, was convened on 4 May. Universal suffrage did not possess the magical power attributed to it by republicans of the old school. They saw throughout France, at least among the majority of Frenchmen, *citoyens* with the same interests, views, etc. This was their *cult of the people*. Instead of their *imaginary* people the electors revealed the *real* people, that is, the representatives of the different classes which comprised the people. We have seen why the peasants and petty bourgeois had to vote under the leadership of bourgeois spoiling for a fight and big landowners thirsty for restoration. But although universal suffrage was not the miracle-working magic wand which the republican worthies had assumed, it possessed the incomparably greater merit of unleashing the class struggle, of allowing the various middle strata of bourgeois society to get over their illusions and disappointments, of propelling all fractions of the exploiting class at one go to the heights of state power and thus tearing off their deceitful masks, while the monarchy, with its electoral system based on property qualifications, only allowed particular fractions of the bourgeoisie to compromise themselves, while it kept the others concealed backstage and adorned them with the halo of a common opposition.

In the Constituent National Assembly which met on 4 May the *bourgeois republicans*, the republicans of the *National*, had the upper hand. Even Legitimists and Orleanists at first only dared show themselves under the mask of bourgeois republicanism. The battle against the proletariat could only be joined in the name of the republic.

The republic dates from 4 May, not from 25 February – that is, the republic recognized by the French people; this is not the republic which the Paris proletariat thrust upon the Provisional Government, not the republic with social institutions, not the vision which hovered before the fighters on the barricades. The republic proclaimed by the National Assembly, the only legitimate republic, is not a revolutionary weapon against the bourgeois order but rather its political reconstitution, the political reconsolidation of bourgeois society – in a word, *the bourgeois republic*. This assertion rang out from the rostrum of the National Assembly and was re-echoed in the whole republican and anti-republican bourgeois press.

As we have seen, the February republic was in reality – and could be nothing else but – a *bourgeois* republic, but the Provisional Government was forced by direct pressure of the proletariat to proclaim it a *republic with social institutions*. The Paris proletariat was still incapable, except in its *imagination*, in its *fantasy*, of moving beyond the bourgeois republic; when it came to action it invariably acted in the service of the republic. The promises made to the proletariat came to represent an intolerable danger for the new republic, and the Provisional Government's entire existence took the form of a struggle against the demands of the proletariat.

In the National Assembly all France sat in judgement upon the Paris proletariat. The Assembly immediately broke with the social illusions of the February revolution; without beating about the bush it proclaimed the *bourgeois republic*, nothing but the bourgeois republic. It immediately excluded Louis Blanc and Albert, the representatives of the proletariat, from the Executive Commission which it appointed; it rejected the suggestion of a special Ministry of Labour; it received with stormy acclamation the statement by Minister Trélat:[49] 'It is now merely a question of *re-establishing labour on its old basis*.'

But all this was not enough. The February republic had been fought for and won by the workers with the passive assistance of the bourgeoisie. The proletarians rightly regarded themselves as the victors of February, and they made the arrogant claims of victors. They had to be defeated on the streets, they had to be shown that they would be defeated as soon as they fought not

49. Ulysse Trélat, a doctor and bourgeois republican, was deputy chairman of the Constituent National Assembly in 1848 and Minister of Public Works from May to June.

with but *against* the bourgeoisie. Just as the February republic with its socialist concessions had needed a battle conducted by the proletariat united with the bourgeoisie against the monarchy, a second battle was necessary in order to sever the republic from these socialist concessions, to assert the official dominance of the *bourgeois republic*. The bourgeoisie had to reject the demands of the proletariat arms in hand. The real birthplace of the bourgeois republic was not the *February victory* but the *June defeat*.

The proletariat accelerated the decision when it forced its way into the National Assembly on 15 May, seeking in vain to recapture its revolutionary influence, and only succeeded in handing over its energetic leaders to the jailors of the bourgeoisie.[50] *Il faut en finir!* This situation must end! With this cry the National Assembly gave vent to its determination to force the proletariat to the decisive battle. The Executive Commission issued a series of provocative decrees, such as the prohibition of public meetings, etc. From the rostrum of the Constituent National Assembly the workers were directly provoked, insulted and derided. But, as we have seen, the National Workshops represented the actual point of attack. Imperiously, the Constituent National Assembly brought them to the attention of the Executive Commission, which was only waiting to hear its own plan announced as the decree of the National Assembly.

The Executive Commission began by making entry into the National Workshops more difficult, by replacing the day wage by piece-work, by banishing workers not born in Paris to the Sologne, ostensibly for the construction of earthworks. These earthworks were only a rhetorical formula with which to disguise their expulsion, as the workers announced to their comrades when they returned, disillusioned. Finally, on 21 June a decree appeared in the *Moniteur* which ordered the forcible expulsion of all unmarried workers from the National Workshops, or their enrolment in the army.

The workers were left with no choice; they had either to starve or to strike out. They answered on 22 June with the gigantic insurrection, in which the first great battle was fought between the two great classes which divide modern society. It was a fight for

50. On 15 May Blanqui and the proletarian party led a mass assault on the newly elected National Assembly, aiming to overthrow it and set up a new Provisional Government. After the assault was repulsed by the National Guard, Blanqui, Barbès, Albert and Raspail were all arrested.

the preservation or destruction of the *bourgeois* order. The veil which shrouded the republic was torn asunder.

It is well known how the workers, with unheard-of bravery and ingenuity, without leaders, without a common plan, without supplies, and for the most part lacking weapons, held in check the army, the Mobile Guard, the Paris National Guard and the National Guard which streamed in from the provinces, for five days. It is well known how the bourgeoisie sought compensation for the mortal terror it had suffered in outrageous brutality, massacring over 3,000 prisoners.

The official representatives of French democracy were so immersed in republican ideology that the meaning of the June battle only began to dawn on them after a few weeks. It was as though they were stupefied by the powder and smoke in which their fantastic republic dissolved.

The immediate impression which the news of the June defeat made on us, the reader will allow us to describe in the words of the *Neue Rheinische Zeitung*.[51]

The last official remnant of the February revolution, the Executive Commission,[52] has melted away like an apparition before the seriousness of events. Lamartine's fireworks[53] have turned into Cavaignac's[54] incendiary rockets. '*Fraternité*', the brotherhood of opposing classes, one of which exploits the other, this '*fraternité*' was proclaimed in February and written in capital letters on the brow of Paris, on every prison and every barracks. But its true, genuine, prosaic expression is *civil war* in its most terrible form, the war between labour and capital. This fraternity flamed up in front of all the windows of Paris on the evening of 25 June. The Paris of the bourgeoisie was illuminated, while the Paris of the proletariat burned, bled and moaned in its death agony.

Fraternity lasted only as long as there was a fraternity of interests between bourgeoisie and proletariat. Pedants of the old revolutionary traditions of 1793; constructors of socialist systems, who went begging to the bourgeoisie on behalf of the people, and who were allowed to

51. The following passage is quoted from 'The June Revolution', above, pp. 124–5. It was first published in the *Neue Rheinische Zeitung* of 29 June 1848.

52. The Executive Commission set up by the Constituent Assembly replaced the Provisional Government on 10 May 1848 and lasted until 24 June.

53. An allusion to Lamartine's fiery declarations to the European governments.

54. Louis-Eugène Cavaignac, a general and moderate republican, was made Min-i-ster of War in May 1848, and in June was given dictatorial powers to suppress the Paris insurrection.

preach long sermons and to compromise themselves as long as the proletarian lion had to be lulled to sleep[55]; republicans, who wanted to keep the whole of the old bourgeois order, but remove the crowned head; supporters of the dynastic opposition, upon whom chance had foisted the fall of a dynasty instead of a change of ministers; Legitimists, who wanted not to cast aside the livery but to change its cut: all these were the allies with whom the people made its February. . . .

The February revolution was the *beautiful* revolution, the revolution of universal sympathy, because the conflicts which erupted in the revolution against the monarchy slumbered harmoniously side by side, as yet *undeveloped*, because the social struggle which formed its background had only assumed an airy existence – it existed only as a phrase, only in words. The June revolution is the *ugly* revolution, the repulsive revolution, because realities have taken the place of words, because the republic has uncovered the head of the monster itself by striking aside the protective, concealing crown.

Order! was Guizot's battle-cry. *Order!* screamed Sébastiani,[56] Guizot's follower, when Warsaw became Russian. *Order!* screamed Cavaignac, the brutal echo of the French National Assembly and the republican bourgeoisie. *Order!* thundered his grapeshot, as it lacerated the body of the proletariat.

None of the innumerable revolutions of the French bourgeoisie since 1789 was an attack on *order*; for they perpetuated class rule, the slavery of the workers, *bourgeois* order, no matter how frequent the changes in the political form of this rule and this slavery. June has violated this order. Woe unto June!

'Woe unto June!' the echo resounds from Europe.

The Paris proletariat was *forced* into the June insurrection by the bourgeoisie. This in itself sealed its fate. It was neither impelled by its immediate, avowed needs to fight for the overthrow of the bourgeoisie by force, nor was it equal to this task. It had to be officially informed by the *Moniteur* that the time was past when the republic found itself obliged to show deference to its illusions; only its defeat convinced it of the truth that the smallest improvement in its position remains a *utopia* within the bourgeois republic, a utopia which becomes a crime as soon as it aspires to become

55. See *Manifesto of the Communist Party*, section III, 3; in Volume I, above, pp. 88–1.

56. Horace, comte Sébastiani, was the French Minister of Foreign Affairs from 1830 to 1832. In 1831 he refused to protest against the tsar's suppression of the Polish revolution and called for a return by both parties to the treaty settlement of 1815. By this the greater part of Poland formed part of the Russian empire, with the tsar as its king.

reality. In place of demands which were exuberant in form but petty and even bourgeois in content, which it had hoped to wring from the February republic, the bold, revolutionary battle-cry appeared: *Overthrow of the bourgeoisie! Dictatorship of the working class!*

By making its burial place the birthplace of the *bourgeois republic*, the proletariat forced this republic to appear in its pure form, as the state whose avowed purpose it is to perpetuate the rule of capital and the slavery of labour. Permanently aware of its scarred, irreconcilable and invincible enemy – invincible because its existence is a precondition of its own life – bourgeois rule, freed from all fetters, was inevitably transformed, all at once, into bourgeois terrorism. Now that the proletariat was temporarily removed from the stage and the dictatorship of the bourgeoisie officially recognized, the middle strata of bourgeois society, the petty bourgeoisie and the peasant class, were obliged to ally themselves with the proletariat, as their own situation became more intolerable and their antagonism to the bourgeoisie sharper. As they had earlier sought the cause of their misfortune in the rise of the working class, they were now compelled to find it in its defeat.

If the June insurrection increased the self-confidence of the bourgeoisie all over the Continent and led it into an open alliance with the feudal monarchy against the people, who was the first victim of this alliance? The continental bourgeoisie itself. The June defeat prevented it from consolidating its rule and from bringing the people, half-satisfied, half-discontented, to a standstill at the lowest stage of the bourgeois revolution.

The June defeat finally betrayed to the despotic powers of Europe the secret that France must, at all costs, maintain peace abroad in order to be able to conduct civil war at home. Thus the peoples who had begun their struggle for national independence were abandoned to the superior power of Russia, Austria and Prussia, but at the same time the fate of these national revolutions was made subject to the fate of the proletarian revolution and they were robbed of their apparent autonomy, their independence of the great social upheaval. The Hungarian, the Pole, the Italian shall not be free as long as the worker remains a slave!

Finally, with the victories of the Holy Alliance, Europe has assumed a form in which any new proletarian uprising in France will immediately coincide with a *world war*. The new French revolution will be forced to leave its natural soil immediately and to *conquer the European* terrain, on which alone the social revolution of the nineteenth century can be carried out.

It is only as a result of the June defeat, therefore, that all the conditions have been created under which France can seize the *initiative* of the European revolution. Only since it has been dipped in the blood of the *June insurgents* has the tricolour become the flag of the European revolution – *the red flag*!

And we cry, *The revolution is dead! – Long live the revolution!*

II. 13 JUNE 1849

From June 1848 to 13 June 1849

25 February 1848 had brought France the *republic*; 25 June thrust *revolution* upon her. And whereas before February revolution had meant *the overthrow of the form of government*, after June it meant *the overthrow of bourgeois society*.

The June struggle had been led by the *republican* fraction of the bourgeoisie; as a result of its victory political power inevitably fell into its hands. The state of siege laid Paris at its feet, gagged and unable to resist; a moral state of siege prevailed in the provinces, which were ruled by the threatening, brutal arrogance of the victorious bourgeoisie and the unbounded property fanaticism of the peasants. There was no danger, therefore, from *below*!

Together with the revolutionary power of the workers the political influence of the *democratic republicans* was also broken – the republicans, that is, in the sense of the *petty bourgeoisie*, which was represented in the Executive Committee by Ledru-Rollin, in the Constituent National Assembly by the party of the Montagne[57] and in the press by the *Réforme*. On 16 April they had conspired together with the bourgeois republicans against the proletariat; in the June days they had jointly waged war against it. As a result, they themselves demolished the very basis on which their party existed as a power, for the petty bourgeoisie can only maintain a revolutionary attitude towards the bourgeoisie as long as the proletariat stands behind it. They were dismissed. The sham alliance which the bourgeois republicans had reluctantly and perfidiously made with them during the period of the Provisional

57. The radical-democratic party in the Second Republic (1848–51) was known as the Montagne (Mountain), after the name given to the Jacobin party in the First Republic.

Government and the Executive Commission was openly broken. Scorned and rejected as allies, they were reduced to the level of satellites to the men of the tricolour, from whom they could wring no concessions but whose rule they had to support whenever this rule, and with it the republic, seemed to be threatened by the anti-republican fractions of the bourgeoisie. Lastly, these fractions, the Orleanists and the Legitimists, were from the outset in the minority in the Constituent National Assembly. Before the June days they themselves only dared react beneath the mask of bourgeois republicanism; the June victory led the whole of bourgeois France for the moment to hail its saviour in the person of Cavaignac, and when, shortly after the June days, the anti-republican party re-established its independence, the military dictatorship and the state of siege in Paris only allowed it to stretch out its feelers very timidly and cautiously.

Since 1830 the *bourgeois republican* fraction, its writers, its spokesmen, its authorities, its men of ambition, its deputies, generals, bankers and lawyers, had gathered around a Paris journal, *Le National*. It had its subsidiary newspapers in the provinces. The coterie around the *National* represented the *dynasty of the tricolour republic*. It immediately took possession of all state dignities, the ministries, the prefecture of police, the post office directorship, the positions of prefect, the senior officers' posts now vacant in the army. At the head of the executive power stood its general, Cavaignac; its editor-in-chief, Marrast, became the permanent chairman of the Constituent National Assembly. As master of ceremonies he also did the honours of the worthy republic in his salons.

Even revolutionary French writers, awed, as it were, by the republican tradition, have reinforced the erroneous belief that in the Constituent National Assembly the royalists held sway. On the contrary, after the June days the Constituent Assembly remained the *exclusive representative of bourgeois republicanism*, and this aspect was all the more accentuated as the influence of the tricolour republicans outside the Assembly collapsed. In so far as it was a question of maintaining the *form* of the bourgeois republic the Assembly had the votes of the democratic republicans at its disposal; in so far as it was a question of maintaining the *substance*, then not even its manner of speech distinguished it any longer from the royalist fractions of the bourgeoisie, for it is precisely the interests of the bourgeoisie, the material conditions of its class rule and class exploitation, which form the substance of the bourgeois republic.

It was not royalism, therefore, but bourgeois republicanism which found expression in the life and activities of this Constituent Assembly, which, in the end, did not die and was not killed off, but simply decayed.

Throughout the duration of its rule, as long as it occupied the centre of the stage with its grand state drama, an uninterrupted sacrificial ceremony was being performed in the background – the June insurgents who had been taken prisoner were continually being sentenced by court martial or deported without trial. The Constituent National Assembly had the tact to admit that in the case of the June insurgents it was not trying criminals but crushing enemies.

The first act of the Constituent National Assembly was the appointment of a commission of inquiry into the events of June and 15 May and into the part played by the socialist and democratic party leaders during these days. The inquiry was aimed directly at Louis Blanc, Ledru-Rollin and Caussidière. The bourgeois republicans were burning with impatience to get rid of these rivals. They could not have entrusted the execution of their vengeance to any more suitable individual than M. Odilon Barrot, the former leader of the dynastic opposition, the embodiment of liberalism, the *nullité grave*,[58] the thorough nonentity, who had not only to revenge a dynasty but also to settle with the revolution for thwarting his period of office as premier. This was a sure guarantee of the inexorability of his vengeance. This same Barrot, then, was appointed chairman of the commission of inquiry and he instituted regular legal proceedings against the February revolution, which may be summarized as follows: 17 March, *demonstration*, 16 April, *conspiracy*, 15 May, *attempt*, 23 June, *civil war*! Why did he not extend his learned judicial investigations as far back as 24 February? The *Journal des Débats* answered that 24 February was the *founding of Rome*.[59] The origin of states becomes lost in a myth which must be believed and not discussed. Louis Blanc and Caussidière were handed over to the courts. The National Assembly completed the task of purging itself which it had begun on 15 May.

58. Pompous nobody.
59. A reference to the leader of 28 August; the *Journal des Débats* was the leading Orleanist paper.

The Provisional Government's plan of taxing capital by means of a mortgage tax – taken up again by Goudchaux[60] – was rejected by the Constituent Assembly; the law limiting the working day to ten hours was repealed; imprisonment for debt was reintroduced; the large majority of the French population, which can neither read nor write, was excluded from jury service. Why not from the franchise also? The deposit of caution money by journals was reintroduced; restrictions were imposed on the right of association.

But in their haste to provide the old bourgeois order with its old guarantees, and to erase every trace left behind by the revolutionary tide, the bourgeois republicans encountered a resistance which provided an unexpected threat.

No one had fought with more fanaticism in the June days for the salvation of property and the restoration of credit than the Parisian petty bourgeoisie – café and restaurant proprietors, *marchands de vins*, small traders, shopkeepers, craftsmen, etc. The shopkeeper had gathered his strength and had marched on the barricade in order to restore the flow of business from the street into the shop. But behind the barricade stood the customers and the debtors; in front of it the creditors. And when the barricades had been pulled down, the workers crushed, and the shop-keepers rushed back to their shops, drunk with victory, they found their entrances barricaded by one of the saviours of property, an official agent from the powers of credit, who handed them threatening notices: Overdue promissory notes! Overdue rents! Overdue bonds! Indeed, time had also run out for both shop and shopkeeper!

Salvation of property! But the houses in which they lived were not their property; the shops which they kept were not their property; the goods in which they dealt were not their property. Neither their business, nor the plate from which they ate, nor the bed in which they slept belonged to them any longer. They were the ones from whom *this property had to be saved* – in the interests of the house-owner who had let the house, the banker who had discounted the promissory notes, the capitalist who had advanced the cash, the manufacturer who had entrusted the goods to these shopkeepers for sale, the wholesale dealer who had sold the raw materials to the craftsmen on credit. *Restoration of credit!* But,

---

60. Michel Goudchaux, a banker and bourgeois republican, had been Minister of Finance in the Provisional Government.

having gathered its strength, credit proved to be a vigorous and jealous god, driving the insolvent debtor out of his four walls with wife and child, handing his supposed property over to capital and throwing the man himself into the debtors' prison, which had once more cast its threatening shadow over the corpses of the June insurgents.

The petty bourgeoisie realized with horror that by crushing the workers they had delivered themselves unresisting into the hands of their creditors. Since February their creeping bankruptcy, which they had apparently ignored, had become chronic, and after June it was declared openly.

Their *nominal property* had been left unchallenged as long as it had been a question of driving them to the battlefield *in the name of property*. Now that the great issue with the proletariat had been settled, the small business with the shopkeepers could be settled in turn. In Paris the mass of paper in default amounted to over 21 million francs, in the provinces to over 11 million. The proprietors of more than 7,000 Paris firms had not paid their rent since February.

While the National Assembly had set up an inquiry into the *political guilt*, which went back as far as the end of February, the petty bourgeoisie, for its part, now demanded an inquiry into the *civil debts* up to 24 February. They assembled *en masse* in the vestibule of the Bourse, and for every merchant who could prove that his insolvency was due solely to the commercial stagnation caused by the revolution and that his business had been on a sound footing on 24 February, they demanded with threats an extension of the period of payment by decree of the commercial court and an order compelling creditors to liquidate their claims in return for a moderate percentage payment. This question was debated as a legislative proposal in the National Assembly in the form of the *'concordats à l'amiable'*. The Assembly vacillated; then it suddenly learnt that at that moment at the Porte St Denis thousands of wives and children of the June insurgents had prepared a petition requesting an amnesty.

In the presence of the resurrected spectre of June the petty bourgeoisie trembled; the National Assembly recovered its implacable spirit. The main points of the *concordats à l'amiable*, the 'amicable agreements' between creditor and debtor, were rejected.

Thus, long after the democratic representatives of the petty bourgeoisie had been repulsed by the republican representatives of the bourgeoisie in the National Assembly, the actual economic significance of this parliamentary split became manifest in the sacrifice of the petty-bourgeois debtors to the bourgeois creditors. A large section of the petty bourgeoisie was completely ruined, and the rest were only allowed to continue their business on conditions which made them the absolute serfs of capital. On 22 August 1848 the National Assembly rejected the *concordats à l'amiable*; on 19 September 1848, in the middle of a state of siege, the prince, Louis Bonaparte,[61] and the prisoner of Vincennes, the communist Raspail, were elected representatives of Paris. But the bourgeoisie elected the usurious money-changer and Orleanist Fould. So from all sides at once there came an open declaration of war against the Constituent National Assembly, against bourgeois republicanism, against Cavaignac.

There is no need to elaborate on how the mass bankruptcy of the Paris petty bourgeoisie had inevitable repercussions far beyond those immediately hit, nor on how bourgeois commerce was inevitably shaken once again, while the state deficit was swollen further by the costs of the June insurrection, nor on how government revenues constantly declined as a result of the interruption in production, restricted consumption and decreasing imports. Cavaignac and the National Assembly could not resort to any other measure than a new loan, which forced them even further under the yoke of the financial aristocracy.

While the petty bourgeoisie reaped bankruptcy and liquidation by court order as the fruit of the June victory, Cavaignac's janissaries, the Mobile Guard, found their reward in the soft arms of the courtesans and, as 'the youthful saviours of society', they received homage of all kinds in the salons of Marrast, the *gentilhomme*[62] of the tricolour, who simultaneously played Amphitryon[63] and the troubadour of the worthy republic. The preferential social treatment and disproportionately higher pay given to the Mobile Guard embittered the *army* while, at the same time, all the national illusions disappeared with which bourgeois republicanism – by way of its paper, the *National* – had been able

61. Louis Bonaparte, nephew of the emperor Napoleon, was elected President of France in December 1848 for a four-year term; on 2 December 1851 he overthrew the republican constitution and ruled as emperor until 1870 under the title Napoleon III.

62. Knight.

63. Lavish host, after the son of Alkaios, king of Tyre, in the Greek legend.

to win the allegiance of a part of the army and the peasant class under Louis Philippe. The role of mediation which Cavaignac and the National Assembly played in *northern Italy* in order, together with England, to betray it to Austria – this one day of rule destroyed eighteen years of opposition for the *National*. No government was less national than that of the *National* and none was more dependent upon England, while under Louis Philippe it had lived according to a daily paraphrase of Cato's dictum: '*Delenda est Carthago*';[64] none was more servile towards the Holy Alliance, while from a Guizot it had demanded the tearing-up of the Treaty of Vienna.[65] An irony of history made Bastide, the former foreign affairs editor of the *National*, French Minister of Foreign Affairs, so that he could refute his articles, one by one, with each of his dispatches.

For a moment both the army and the peasant class had believed that with military dictatorship, foreign war and '*gloire*' were now the order of the day in France. But Cavaignac did not represent the dictatorship of the sabre over the bourgeoisie but the dictatorship of the bourgeoisie by the sabre, and they now required the soldier only as gendarme. Beneath the stern features of his anti-republican resignation Cavaignac concealed insipid submissiveness to the humiliating conditions of his bourgeois office. *L'argent n'a pas de maître!* Money has no master! He idealized this old election slogan of the *tiers-état*,[66] as did the Constituent Assembly in general, by translating it into political language: The bourgeoisie has no king; the true form of bourgeois rule is the republic.

And the development of this *form*, the preparation of a republican *constitution*, was the 'great organic task' of the Constituent National Assembly. The re-christening of the Christian calendar as a republican one, or of St Bartholomew as St Robespierre, no more changed wind and weather than this constitution changed, or was intended to change, bourgeois society. Where it went beyond a *change of costume*, it documented the *existing* facts. Thus it solemnly registered as fact the existence of the republic, the existence of universal suffrage, the existence of a

64. Carthage must be destroyed.

65. The Treaty of Vienna of June 1815, together with the Treaties of Paris (May 1814 and November 1815), confined France to its frontiers of 1790 and erected safeguards against French expansionism.

66. Third estate.

single sovereign National Assembly in place of two constitutionally limited Chambers. It registered and regulated the fact of Cavaignac's dictatorship by replacing the stationary, irresponsible, hereditary monarchy with an ambulatory, responsible, elective monarchy, with a quadrennial presidency. To the same degree, therefore, it elevated to the status of a constitutional law the extraordinary power which the National Assembly had providently invested in its chairman in the interests of its own safety after the terror of 15 May and 25 June. The rest of the Constitution was a work of terminology. The royalist labels were torn off the machinery of the old monarchy and republican labels were stuck on. Marrast, the former editor-in-chief of the *National*, now editor-in-chief of the Constitution, acquitted himself of this academic task not without talent.

The Constituent Assembly resembled that Chilean official who wanted to regulate property relations on the land more exactly by means of a cadastral survey at the very moment when subterranean rumblings had already heralded the volcanic eruption which was to rend asunder the ground beneath his very feet. While in theory it measured out the forms which gave republican expression to bourgeois rule, in reality it only retained its power by the suspension of all formulas, by force *sans phrase*,[67] by the *state of siege*. Two days before it began its work on the Constitution it proclaimed a prolongation of the state of siege. Earlier constitutions had been made and accepted as soon as the process of social upheaval had come to rest, as soon as the newly formed class relationships had become established, and at the same time as the warring fractions of the ruling class had resorted to a compromise which allowed them to continue the struggle among themselves and at the same time to exclude the exhausted masses from the struggle. This Constitution, on the other hand, did not sanction any social revolution; it sanctioned the momentary victory of the old society over the revolution.

In the first draft of the Constitution, composed before the June days, the *droit au travail*, the right to work, was contained as a preliminary, clumsy formula, summarizing the revolutionary claims of the proletariat. It was changed into the *droit à l'assistance*, the right to public assistance. And which modern state does not feed its paupers in one form or another? The right to work is, in the bourgeois sense, nonsense, a wretched, pious wish. But behind

67. Pure and simple.

the right to work stands power over capital, behind power over capital the appropriation of the means of production, their subjection to the associated working class, that is, the abolition of wage labour, capital and their mutual relationship. Behind the 'right to work' was the June insurrection. The Constituent Assembly, which placed the revolutionary proletariat *hors la loi*, outside the law, in reality, had to exclude its formula from the Constitution, the law of laws, as a matter of principle; it had to pronounce its anathema upon the 'right to work'. But it did not stop here. As Plato banished the poets from his republic, from its republic it banished for all time *progressive taxation*. And progressive taxation is not only a bourgeois measure, which can be applied on a large or small scale within the existing relations of production, it was the only means of tying the middle strata of bourgeois society to the 'respectable' republic, the only means of reducing the national debt and of holding the anti-republican majority of the bourgeoisie in check.

On the question of the *concordats à l'amiable* the tricolour republicans had indeed sacrificed the petty bourgeoisie to the big bourgeoisie. They raised this deed to the level of a principle with the legal prohibition of progressive taxation. They put bourgeois reform on a par with proletarian revolution. But which class, then, remained as the mainstay of their republic? The big bourgeoisie. And the mass of this class was anti-republican. While it exploited the republicans of the *National* with a view to consolidating the old economic order, it intended, on the other hand, to exploit the re-established social relations in order to restore the corresponding political forms. At the beginning of October Cavaignac already felt obliged to make Dufaure and Vivien,[68] former ministers under Louis Philippe, ministers of the republic, no matter how much the brainless puritans of his own party grumbled and raged.

While the tricolour Constitution rejected any compromise with the petty bourgeoisie and was unable to win the allegiance of any new social group to the new form of government, it hurried, on

68. Jules-Armand Dufaure, a lawyer and originally an Orleanist politician, sat in both Assemblies as a republican and was Minister of the Interior in Cavaignac's government (October–December 1848), and again under Louis Bonaparte's presidency (June–October 1849). Alexandre Vivien, also a lawyer and originally an Orleanist politician, became Minister of Public Works in Cavaignac's government.

the other hand, to restore to its traditional inviolability a body which represented the grimmest and most fanatical defender of the old state. It elevated the *irremovability of judges*, which had been called into question by the Provisional Government, to a constitutional law. Having removed *one* king, scores of kings arose again in the shape of irremovable inquisitors of legality.

The French press has dealt with the contradictions of Monsieur Marrast's Constitution from many points of view; for example, the coexistence of two sovereign powers, the National Assembly and the President, and so on.

But the most comprehensive contradiction in the Constitution consists in the fact that it gives political power to the classes whose social slavery it is intended to perpetuate: proletariat, peasants and petty bourgeoisie. And it deprives the bourgeoisie, the class whose old social power it sanctions, of the political guarantees of this power. It imposes on the political rule of the bourgeoisie democratic conditions which constantly help its enemies towards victory and endanger the very basis of bourgeois society. It demands from the one that it should not proceed from political emancipation to social emancipation and from the other that it should not regress from social restoration to political restoration.

The bourgeois republicans were bothered little by these contradictions. The less *indispensable* they became – and they were only indispensable as the protagonists of the old society against the revolutionary proletariat – the more they sank, a few weeks after their victory, from the position of a *party* to that of a *coterie*. And they treated the Constitution as a huge *intrigue*. What was to be constituted in it was above all the rule of the coterie. The President was to be a protracted Cavaignac and the Legislative Assembly a protracted Constituent Assembly. They hoped to be able to reduce the political power of the masses to a sham power and to manipulate the sham power sufficiently themselves to confront the majority of the bourgeoisie with the permanent dilemma of the June days: *the rule of the* National *or the rule of anarchy*.

Work on the Constitution began on 4 September and was finished on 23 October. On 2 September the Constituent Assembly had resolved not to dissolve itself until the organic laws which supplemented the Constitution had been enacted. None the less, it now decided to bring its very own creation, the President, to life as early as 10 December, long before the course of its own activity

had come to a close. So confident was it of hailing in the constitutional *homunculus* the son of his mother. As a precaution the
provision was made that should none of the candidates receive
two million votes, the election would pass from the nation to the
Constituent Assembly.

These precautions were in vain! The first day on which the
Constitution came into force was the last day of the Constituent
Assembly's rule. Its death sentence lay in the depths of the ballot
box. It sought the 'son of his mother' and found the 'nephew
of his uncle'. Saul Cavaignac slew one million votes but David
Napoleon slew six million. Saul Cavaignac was beaten six times
over.

10 December 1848 was the day of the *peasant insurrection*. The
symbol that expressed their entry into the revolutionary movement, clumsy but cunning, rascally but naïve, oafish but sublime, a
calculated superstition, a pathetic burlesque, an inspired but stupid
anachronism, a momentous, historic piece of buffoonery, an unde-
cipherable hieroglyph for the understanding of the civilized – this
symbol bore unmistakably the physiognomy of the class which
represents barbarism within civilization. The republic had announced
itself to the peasants with the *tax collector*; they announced themselves to the republic with the *emperor*. Napoleon was the only man
who had exhaustively represented the interests and the imagination
of the peasant class, newly created in 1789. By inscribing his name
on the frontispiece of the republic this class declared war abroad
and the enforcement of its class interests at home. For the peasants
Napoleon was not a person but a programme. They marched on the
polling stations with banners flying, drums beating and trumpets
sounding, shouting, '*Plus d'impôts, à bas les riches, à bas la république, vive l'empereur.*' No more taxes, down with the rich, down
with the republic, long live the emperor! Behind the emperor lurked
the peasant war. The republic which they voted down was the *republic of the rich*.

10 December was the coup d'état of the peasants, who overthrew
the existing government. And from this day forth, having taken a
government from France and given her a new one, their eyes were
immediately fixed on Paris. Having once been the active heroes of
the revolutionary drama they could no longer be thrust back into the
inactive, acquiescent role of the chorus.

The other classes contributed to the completion of the peasants' electoral victory. For the *proletariat* the election of Napoleon meant the removal of Cavaignac from office, the overthrow of the Constituent Assembly, the dismissal of bourgeois republicanism, the annulment of the June victory. For the *petty bourgeoisie* Napoleon represented the rule of the debtor over the creditor. For the majority of the *big bourgeoisie* Napoleon's election represented an open breach with the party which it had temporarily had to make use of against the revolution but which became intolerable to it as soon as this class tried to consolidate the temporary situation as the constitutional position. Napoleon in place of Cavaignac represented for them the monarchy in place of the republic, the beginning of the royalist restoration, a tentative hint given to Orleans, the Bourbon *fleur-de-lis* concealed beneath the Bonapartist violets. Finally, the *army*, in voting for Napoleon, voted against the Mobile Guard, against the idyll of peace and in favour of war.

Thus it happened, as the *Neue Rheinische Zeitung* put it,[69] that the simplest man in France acquired a significance of the most multifarious kind. Precisely because he was nothing he was able to signify everything, except what he in fact was. Meanwhile, no matter how different the meaning of the name Napoleon on the lips of the various classes, each of them used it to write on its ballot paper: Down with the party of the *National*, down with Cavaignac, down with the Constituent Assembly, down with the bourgeois republic. Minister Dufaure declared publicly in the Constituent Assembly that 10 December was a second 24 February.

The petty bourgeoisie and proletariat had voted *en bloc for* Napoleon in order to vote *against* Cavaignac and, by combining their votes, to rob the Constituent Assembly of the final decision. The most progressive sections of each class, however, put forward their own candidates. Napoleon was the *common name* for all the parties in coalition against the bourgeois republic; Ledru-Rollin and Raspail were the *proper names*, the former of the democratic petty bourgeoisie, the latter of the revolutionary proletariat. The votes for Raspail – as the proletarians and their socialist spokesmen declared aloud – were intended as a mere demonstration: each vote a protest against the presidency as such, that is, against the Constitution itself, each vote a vote against

69. Marx is referring to an article by Ferdinand Wolff in the *Neue Rheinische Zeitung* of 21 December 1848.

Ledru-Rollin, the first act by which the proletariat declared itself to be an independent political party distinct from the democratic party. This party, however – the democratic petty bourgeoisie and its parliamentary representative, the Montagne – treated the candidature of Ledru-Rollin with the seriousness which it habitually uses to solemnly dupe itself. This, it may be added, was its last attempt to set itself up against the proletariat as an independent party. The democratic petty bourgeoisie and its Montagne, as well as the republican bourgeois party, were beaten on 10 December.

Besides a Montagne France now possessed a Napoleon, a proof that both were only the lifeless caricatures of the great realities whose name they bore. Louis Napoleon, with the emperor's hat and the eagle, parodied the old Napoleon no more wretchedly than the Montagne, with its phrases borrowed from 1793 and its demagogic poses, parodied the old Montagne. The traditional superstitious belief in 1793 was thus shed with the traditional belief in Napoleon. The revolution could only come into its own when it had won its *own, original* name, and it could only do this when the modern revolutionary class, the industrial proletariat, came to the fore as a dominant force. It may be said that 10 December took the Montagne by surprise and sowed confusion in its mind precisely because on this day the classical analogy with the old revolution was interrupted, with a laugh, by a derisive peasant joke.

On 20 December Cavaignac laid down his office and the Constituent Assembly proclaimed Louis Napoleon President of the Republic. On 19 December, the last day of its exclusive rule, it rejected a proposal of amnesty for the June insurgents. Would not the revocation of the decree of 27 June, by which it had condemned 15,000 insurgents to deportation, having dispensed with legal sentences, mean the revocation of the June battle itself?

Odilon Barrot, Louis Philippe's last Prime Minister, became Louis Napoleon's first Prime Minister. Just as Louis Napoleon did not date his rule from 10 December, but from a decree of the Senate of 1804, he found a Prime Minister who did not date his ministry from 20 December but from a royal decree of 24 February. Like a legitimate heir of Louis Philippe, Louis Napoleon smoothed over the change of regime by retaining the old ministry, which, moreover, had not had time to wear itself out because it had not had time to embark on life.

The leaders of the royalist fractions of the bourgeoisie advised him to make this choice. The head of the old dynastic opposition, which had unconsciously been the stepping-stone to the republicans of the *National*, was even more suited to function fully consciously as the stepping-stone from the bourgeois republic to the monarchy.

Odilon Barrot led the only old opposition party which had not exhausted its strength in the unceasing but fruitless struggle for ministerial portfolios. In rapid succession the revolution propelled all the old opposition parties to the heights of state power so that they were obliged to deny and repudiate their old phrases not only in what they did but even in what they said, and so that finally, united in a repulsive conglomeration, they might be hurled by the people into the carrion-pit of history. And no apostasy was spared this Barrot, this embodiment of bourgeois liberalism, who for eighteen years had concealed the base hollowness of his mind beneath a studied solemnity of bearing.[70] When, at certain moments, the all too striking contrast between the thistles of the present and the laurels of the past startled even Barrot himself, a glance in the mirror restored his ministerial composure and his human self-admiration. What he saw reflected in the mirror was Guizot, whom he had always envied, who had always been his master, Guizot himself, but Guizot with the Olympian brow of Odilon. What he overlooked were the Midas' ears.

The Barrot of 24 February first became manifest in the Barrot of 20 December. Barrot, the Orleanist and Voltairean, was joined by the Legitimist and Jesuit Falloux – as Minister of Education.

A few days later the Ministry of the Interior was given to Léon Faucher, the Malthusian. Law, religion and political economy! The Barrot ministry contained all this and in addition a combination of Legitimists and Orleanists. Only the Bonapartist was missing. Bonaparte still concealed his desire to play Napoleon, for Soulouque did not yet play Toussaint-Louverture.[71]

The party of the *National* was immediately ejected from all the high posts in which it had made itself at home. The posts of Prefect

---

70. Marx is here paraphrasing a passage from Lawrence Sterne's novel *Tristram Shandy*, chapter 11.

71. Toussaint-Louverture led the black revolution in Haiti that secured independence from Spanish and English colonialism. Faustin Soulouque, President of the Haitian republic, foreshadowed Louis Bonaparte by proclaiming himself emperor on 26 August 1849, while distinguished only for his ignorance, cruelty and vanity.

of Police, Post Office Director, Public Prosecutor, Mayor of Paris, were all occupied by the old creatures of the monarchy. Changarnier,[72] the Legitimist, was given the joint supreme command of the National Guard of the department of Seine, the Mobile Guard and the regular troops of the First Army Division;[73] Bugeaud,[74] the Orleanist, was appointed commander-in-chief of the Army of the Alps. This change of officials continued without interruption under Barrot's government. The first action of his ministry was the restoration of the old royalist administration. In a trice the official scene changed – scenery, costumes, language, actors, supernumeraries, extras, prompters, the position of the parties, the dramatic motifs, the nature of the conflict, the total situation. Only the antediluvian Constituent Assembly still occupied its old position. But, from the moment the Assembly had installed Bonaparte, Bonaparte Barrot and Barrot Changarnier, France emerged from the period of republican constitution and entered the period of the constituted republic. And what was the point of a Constituent Assembly in a constituted republic? Once the earth had been created there remained nothing else for its Creator but to flee to heaven. The Constituent Assembly was determined not to follow His example; the Assembly was the last refuge of the bourgeois republican party. All control over the executive had been wrested from it, but did it not still possess constituent omnipotence? Its first thought was at all costs to secure the position of sovereignty which it occupied, and starting from here to reconquer the ground which it had lost. If the Barrot ministry could be displaced by a ministry of the *National*, the royal personnel would have to vacate the administrative palaces forthwith and the tricolour personnel would move in again in triumph. The Assembly decided on the overthrow of the ministry, and the ministry offered it an opportunity for attack which could not have been more suitable had the Constituent Assembly invented it itself.

It will be remembered what Louis Bonaparte signified for the peasants: no more taxes! He sat in the President's chair for six days and on the seventh, 27 December, he proposed to his ministry the *retention of the salt tax*, abolished by decree of the Provisional

72. Nicolas Changarnier, a general and a deputy in both Assemblies, was rewarded with this post for his part in the suppression of the June insurrection.

73. The First Army Division comprised the Paris garrison.

74. Thomas Bugeaud de la Piconerrie was a marshal of France and a deputy to the Legislative National Assembly.

Government. The salt tax shares with the wine tax the privilege of being the scapegoat of the old French financial system, particularly in the eyes of the rural population. The Barrot ministry could not have put into the mouth of the man chosen by the peasants a more biting epigram dedicated to his electors than the words: *Restoration of the salt tax!* With the salt tax Bonaparte lost his revolutionary salt – the Napoleon of the peasant insurrection dissolved like an apparition, and nothing remained but the great unknown of royalist, bourgeois intrigues. And it was not unintentional that the Barrot ministry made this act of tactlessly rough disillusionment the first administrative act of the President.

The Constituent Assembly, for its part, eagerly seized the double opportunity of overthrowing the ministry and setting itself up as the representative of the peasants' interests in opposition to the man elected by the peasantry. It rejected the proposal of the Minister of Finance, reduced the salt tax to a third of its earlier amount, thus increasing a national deficit of 560 million francs by 60 million francs, and after this *vote of no confidence* calmly awaited the resignation of the ministry. So little did it understand the new world around it and its own changed position. Behind the ministry stood the President and behind the President stood six million voters, each of whom had cast in the ballot box a vote of no confidence in the Constituent Assembly. The Constituent Assembly gave the nation its vote of no confidence back. What a ridiculous exchange! It forgot that its votes were no longer legal tender. The rejection of the salt tax only brought to maturity the decision of Bonaparte and his ministry '*to have done*' with the Constituent Assembly. The long duel now began which occupied the entire latter half of the Constituent Assembly's existence. 29 January, 21 March, 8 May are the *journées*, the great days of this crisis, each day a forerunner of 13 June.

The French, Louis Blanc for example, have seen in 29 January the day on which a constitutional contradiction emerged, the contradiction between a sovereign, indissoluble National Assembly created by universal suffrage, and a President who according to the letter of the Constitution was answerable to the Assembly, but who was in reality not only likewise sanctioned by universal suffrage – unifying in his person, furthermore, all those votes which were divided and split up a hundredfold among the individual members of the National Assembly – but who was also in full possession of the whole executive power over which the National Assembly hovered as a mere moral power. This interpretation of 29 January confuses the language of the struggle on the platform, in the press and in the clubs, with its real content. The confrontation between Louis Bonaparte and the Constituent National Assembly was not a confrontation between one one-sided constitutional power and another, it was not a confrontation between the executive and the legislature. It was a confrontation between the constituted bourgeois republic itself and the instruments of its constitution, the ambitions, intrigues and ideological demands of the revolutionary fraction of the bourgeoisie, which had founded it and now discovered to its amazement that its constituted republic looked like a restored monarchy. This revolutionary fraction of the bourgeoisie now found that it wanted to hold on by force to the constituent period with its conditions and illusions, its language and its personalities, and to prevent the mature bourgeois republic from assuming its complete and natural form. Just as the Constituent National Assembly was represented by Cavaignac who after his fall had rejoined its ranks, so Bonaparte represented the Legislative National Assembly, which had not yet parted company with him; that is, the National Assembly of the constituted bourgeois republic.

The significance of Bonaparte's election could only become clear when, in the repeat performance represented by the elections to the new National Assembly, the multifarious meanings of his name were substituted for the one word Bonaparte. The mandate of the old Assembly was annulled as a result of 10 December. Thus on 29 January it was not the President and the National Assembly of the *same* republic which faced each other; it was the National Assembly of the nascent republic and the President of the fully fledged republic: two powers which embodied two completely different periods in the life process of the republic. There was, on the one hand, the small republican fraction of the bourgeoisie which alone could proclaim the republic, wrest it from the revolutionary proletariat by street fighting and a reign of terror, and could draft in the Constitution its ideal fundamental features; and there was, on the other, the whole royalist mass of the bourgeoisie, which alone could rule in this constituted bourgeois republic, strip the Constitution of its ideological trimmings and bring about by its legislation and administration the indispensable conditions for the subjugation of the proletariat.

The storm which broke on 29 January had been gathering throughout the month. With its vote of no confidence the Constituent Assembly wanted to force the Barrot ministry to resign. The Barrot ministry, on the other hand, proposed to the Constituent Assembly that it pass a definitive vote of no confidence in itself, that it decide on suicide and decree its *own dissolution*. At the behest of the ministry Rateau,[75] one of the most obscure deputies, laid this motion before the Assembly on 6 January – before the same Constituent Assembly which had already resolved in August not to dissolve itself until it had issued a whole series of organic laws which would supplement the Constitution. The government supporter Fould declared outright before the Assembly that its dissolution was necessary *'to restore the stability of credit'*. And did it not impair the stability of credit by prolonging provisional rule and by calling Barrot – and with him Bonaparte and the constituted republic – into question? The Olympian Barrot became a raging Roland[76] at the prospect of having the premiership, which he had finally laid his hands on, torn from his grasp after enjoying the office for scarcely two weeks, the office which the republicans had already robbed him of for a decennium – that is, for ten months. Before this wretched Assembly he out-tyrannized the tyrant. The mildest of his words were: 'No future is possible with it.' It did indeed now only represent the past. 'It is incapable', he added ironically, 'of providing the republic with the institutions necessary for its consolidation.' Indeed, its categorical opposition to the proletariat was accompanied by a breakdown in its bourgeois energy, and in its opposition to the royalists its republican exuberance revived anew. Thus, it was doubly incapable of consolidating the bourgeois republic, which it no longer comprehended, with the necessary institutions.

Together with Rateau's proposal the ministry organized a *storm of petitions* throughout the country and daily, from all corners of France, bundles of *billets-doux* landed on the doorstep of the Constituent Assembly, more or less categorically requesting it to *dissolve* itself and make its will. The Assembly, for its part, organized counter-petitions, in which the petitioners requested its continuing existence. The electoral struggle between Bonaparte

75. Jean-Pierre Rateau was a lawyer and a deputy in both the Constituent and Legislative Assemblies. He was a Bonapartist.

76. After Charlemagne's nephew, famed for his audacious exploits.

and Cavaignac was renewed as a struggle of petitions for and against the dissolution of the National Assembly. The petitions were to be belated commentaries on 10 December. This agitation continued throughout January.

In its conflict with the President the Constituent Assembly could not refer back to the general election as its origin, for appeal was made to universal suffrage. It could not base itself on any regularly constituted power as it was a question of a struggle against legal power. It was not in a position to overthrow the ministry by a vote of no confidence, as it had attempted on 6 and 26 January, as the ministry did not ask for its confidence. Only *one* possibility was left to it, that of *insurrection*. The armed forces of insurrection were *the republican part of the National Guard*, the Mobile Guard and the centres of the revolutionary proletariat, the *clubs*. In December the Mobile Guard, heroes from the days of June, formed the organized armed forces of the republican bourgeois fraction, just as before June the National Workshops had formed the organized armed forces of the revolutionary proletariat. Just as the Executive Commission of the Constituent Assembly directed its brutal attack against the National Workshops when it felt compelled to put an end to the intolerable demands of the proletariat, so Bonaparte's ministry directed its attack against the Mobile Guard when it felt obliged to put an end to the intolerable demands of the republican bourgeois fraction. It ordered the *disbandment of the Mobile Guard*. One half was dismissed and thrown onto the streets; the other half was organized on monarchist instead of democratic lines, and its pay was reduced to the usual pay of the regular troops. The Mobile Guard found itself in the same situation as the June insurgents, and every day the press printed *public confessions*, in which it acknowledged its blame for June and implored the proletariat for forgiveness.

And the *clubs*? The moment the Constituent Assembly had called the President into question in the person of Barrot, and hence the constituted bourgeois republic and the bourgeois republic in general, all the constituent elements of the February republic ranged themselves around it – all the parties which wanted the overthrow of the existing republic and a process of violent retrogression in order to transform it into the republic of their class interests and principles. What had been done was undone; the crystallizations of the revolutionary period became fluid again;

II. 13 June 1849

the republic over which they were fighting was once more the undefined republic of the February days: and each party reserved for
itself the right to provide the definition. For a moment the parties
took up their old positions of February. The tricolour republicans
of the *National* leant once more on the democratic republicans of
the *Réforme* and pushed them as their protagonist into the forefront
of the parliamentary struggle. The democratic republicans leant
again on the socialist republicans – they announced their reconciliation and unity in a public manifesto on 27 January – and prepared
the background for insurrection in the clubs. The ministerial press
rightly treated the tricolour republicans of the *National* as the resurrected insurgents of June. In order to secure their position at the
head of the bourgeois republic they called the bourgeois republic
itself into question. On 26 January Minister Faucher proposed a
law on the right of association; the first paragraph ran: '*Clubs are
prohibited*.' He proposed that this bill be discussed immediately as
a matter of urgency. The Constituent Assembly rejected the motion
of urgency and on 27 January it put forward a resolution with 230
signatures proposing that the ministry be impeached for violating
the Constitution. *Impeachment* of the ministry at a moment when
such an act tactlessly exposed the impotence of the judge, namely
the majority in the Chamber, or served as an impotent protest by the
accuser against this majority itself – this was the great revolutionary trump card which the latter-day Montagne played from now on
whenever the crisis reached a peak. Poor Montagne, crushed by the
weight of its own name!

On 15 May Blanqui, Barbès, Raspail, etc., had tried to break up
the Constituent Assembly by forcing their way into the chamber
at the head of the Paris proletariat. Barrot intended to inflict a
moral 15 May on the Assembly with his plan to dictate its self-
dissolution and to close its meeting place. This same Assembly
had appointed Barrot to conduct an inquiry against the accused of
May, and now, at the moment that he confronted it like a royalist
Blanqui, as it sought allies against him in the clubs, among the
revolutionary proletariat and in Blanqui's party, at this moment
the implacable Barrot tormented it with the proposal to withdraw
the May prisoners from the jurisdiction of the Court of Assizes
and to transfer them to the High Court, the *haute cour* devised by
the party of the *National*. It was remarkable how his panic over
a ministerial portfolio could produce from the head of a Barrot

pearls worthy of a Beaumarchais! After long vacillation the National Assembly accepted his proposal. In its treatment of the May assailants it reverted to its normal character.

While the Constituent Assembly was forced into *insurrection* against the President and the ministers, President and ministers were forced into a coup against the Constituent Assembly, for they possessed no legal means of dissolving it. But the Constituent Assembly was the mother of the Constitution and the Constitution was the mother of the President. With a coup d'état the President would tear up the Constitution and invalidate his republican claim. He would then be forced to produce his imperial claim; but the imperial claim would call forth the Orleanist claim, and both paled before the claim of the Legitimists. The fall of the legal republic could only result in the rise of its extreme antipode, the Legitimist monarchy, at a moment when the Orleanists were still nothing more than the defeated party of February and Bonaparte the victor of 10 December, when both could only oppose the republican usurpation with their own equally usurped monarchist claims. The Legitimists were aware of the advantage of the hour; they conspired openly. In General Changarnier they hoped to find their General Monk.[77] The approach of the *white monarchy* was proclaimed as openly in their clubs as was that of the *red republic* in the proletarian clubs.

The ministry would have rid itself of all problems by means of a happily suppressed uprising. 'Legality is the death of us,' cried Odilon Barrot. An uprising would have allowed it to dissolve the Constituent Assembly under the pretext of the *salut public*[78] and to violate the Constitution itself in the interests of the Constitution. Odilon Barrot's brutal behaviour in the National Assembly, the motion to dissolve the clubs, the unceremonious removal of fifty tricolour prefects and their replacement by royalists, the disbandment of the Mobile Guard, the maltreatment of its leaders by Changarnier, the reinstatement of Professor Lerminier,[79] who had been intolerable even under Guizot, the toleration of Legitimist boasting – each of these was a provocation for an uprising. But the uprising did not take place. It awaited its

77. The English general who in 1660 used the troops under his command to secure the restoration of the Stuarts.

78. Public safety.

79. Jean Lerminier was an ultra-reactionary jurist who had resigned from the Collège de France in 1839 after protests from his students.

signal from the Constituent Assembly and not from the ministry.

Finally came 29 January, the day on which the motion of Mathieu de la Drôme,[80] proposing the categorical rejection of Rateau's motion, was to be put to the vote. Legitimists, Orleanists, Bonapartists, Mobile Guard, Montagne, clubs, all conspired on this day, each as much against its supposed ally as against its supposed enemy. Bonaparte, mounted on horseback, reviewed a section of the troops on the Place de la Concorde; Changarnier play-acted with a display of strategic manoeuvres; the Constituent Assembly found its building occupied by the military. This Assembly, the focal point of all conflicting hopes, fears, expectations, ferments, tensions, conspiracies, this lion-hearted Assembly did not hesitate for a moment when it came nearer than ever before to the *Weltgeist*.[81] It resembled the warrior who not only feared to use his own weapons, but also felt obliged to keep his opponent's intact. Scorning death it signed its own death warrant and rejected the categorical rejection of Rateau's motion. Even though itself in a state of siege, it imposed limits on a constituent activity whose necessary context had been the state of siege in Paris. It revenged itself in a worthy manner the next day by conducting an inquiry into the fright which the ministry had given it on 29 January. The Montagne demonstrated its lack of revolutionary energy and political intelligence by allowing itself to be used by the party of the *National* as the crier in this great comedy of intrigue. The party of the *National* had made its last attempt to maintain in the constituted republic the monopoly rule which it has possessed in the formative stage of the bourgeois republic. It had failed.

Whereas in the January crisis the existence of the Constitutional Assembly was at stake, in the crisis of 21 March the existence of the Constitution was at stake; in January it was a matter of the *National* party's personnel, in March it was a matter of its ideals. It goes without saying that the honourable republicans surrendered the noble sentiments of their ideology more cheaply than the worldly pleasures of governmental power.

On 21 March Faucher's bill against the right of association – *the suppression of the clubs* – was on the agenda of the National

80. Philippe Mathieu de la Drôme was a Montagne deputy in both Assemblies.

81. In Hegel's philosophy of history, the transpersonal force of historical reason.

Assembly. Article 8 of the Constitution guarantees all Frenchmen the right of association. This prohibition of the clubs, therefore, represented an unequivocal violation of the Constitution, and the Constituent Assembly itself was to canonize the profanation of its saints. But the clubs were the meeting points, the conspiratorial haunts of the revolutionary proletariat. The National Assembly itself had forbidden the union of the workers against the bourgeoisie. And what were these clubs other than a union of the whole working class against the whole bourgeois class – the formation of a workers' state against the bourgeois state? Were they not, every one of them, constituent assemblies of the proletariat and hard-hitting army divisions for revolt? What the Constitution had to constitute above all, was the rule of the bourgeoisie. Therefore the constitutional right of association could clearly refer only to those associations which were compatible with the rule of the bourgeoisie, that is, with bourgeois order. If, for the sake of theoretical propriety, the Constitution was expressed in general terms, were not the government and the National Assembly there to interpret and apply it in the specific case? And if in the primeval epoch of the republic the clubs were in fact prohibited by the state of siege, had they not, in an ordered, constituted republic, to be prohibited by law? The tricolour republicans had nothing with which to counter this prosaic interpretation of the Constitution except its own high-flown phrases. A section of them, Pagnerre, Duclerc,[82] etc., voted for the ministry and thus presented it with a majority. The other section, with the archangel Cavaignac and church father Marrast at their head, withdrew to a special room once the article prohibiting the clubs had been passed – and there they 'took counsel'. The National Assembly was paralysed; it no longer had a quorum. At the right moment Mr Crémieux reminded those gathered in the room that the way out led directly on to the street and that it was no longer February 1848 but March 1849. Suddenly enlightened, the party of the *National* returned to the chamber followed by the Montagne, who had been duped again. Constantly tormented by revolutionary desires, the Montagne no less constantly grasped at constitutional possibilities and still felt more at home behind the bourgeois republicans

82. Laurent Pagnerre, a publisher and bourgeois republican politician, was General Secretary of the Provisional Government in 1848. Charles Duclerc, a lawyer and former Orleanist politician who turned republican in 1848, was Minister of the Interior in Cavaignac's government.

than in front of the revolutionary proletariat. Thus the comedy was played out. And the Constituent Assembly itself had decreed that violation of the letter of the Constitution was the only appropriate way to realize its spirit.

Only one point remained to be settled: the relationship of the constituted republic to the European revolution – its *foreign policy*. On 8 May 1849 there was an unusually excited mood in the Constituent Assembly, whose term of life was due to come to an end in a few days. The attack by the French army on Rome, its repulse by the Romans, its political infamy and military disgrace, the assassination of the Roman republic by the French republic, the first Italian campaign of the second Bonaparte[83] was on the agenda once again. The Montagne had once more played its trump card; Ledru-Rollin had laid on the President's desk the inevitable bill of impeachment against the ministry, and this time against Bonaparte, too, for violation of the Constitution.

The motive of 8 May was repeated later as the motive of 13 June. Let us discuss the military expedition to Rome.

In the middle of November 1848 Cavaignac had dispatched a battle-fleet to Civitavecchia to protect the Pope, to take him on board and transport him to France. The Pope was to consecrate the worthy republic and to secure Cavaignac's election as President. With the Pope Cavaignac wanted to hook the priests, with the priests the peasants and with the peasants the presidency. Although it was in the first instance election propaganda, Cavaignac's expedition was also a protest and a threat issued against the Roman revolution. It contained in embryo the intervention of France on the side of the Pope.

This intervention, in company with Austria and Naples, on behalf of the Pope and against the Roman republic, was resolved upon in the first meeting of Bonaparte's ministerial council on 23 December. Falloux in the ministry meant the Pope in Rome – and in the Rome of the Pope. Bonaparte no longer needed the Pope to become the peasants' President, but he needed the conservation of the Pope in order to conserve the President's peasants. Their gullibility had made him President. With the loss of their faith they would lose their gullibility and with the loss of the Pope they would lose their faith. And the coalition of Orleanists and

83. An ironic allusion to Napoleon Bonaparte's first Italian campaign of 1796, in which the people of northern Italy welcomed him as their liberator from the Austrian yoke.

Legitimists who ruled in Bonaparte's name! Before the king was restored the power had to be restored which consecrates kings. Apart from their royalism, without the old Rome under his secular rule there would be no Pope; without the Pope there would be no Catholicism; without Catholicism there would be no French religion; and without religion what would become of traditional French society? The mortgage which the peasant has on heavenly possessions guarantees the mortgage which the bourgeois has on the peasant's possessions. The Roman revolution, therefore, was an attack on property and bourgeois order as dreadful as the June revolution. The re-establishment of bourgeois rule in France required the restoration of papal rule in Rome. Lastly, a blow struck against the Roman revolutionaries was a blow struck against the allies of the French revolutionaries; the alliance of the counter-revolutionary classes in the constituted French republic was inevitably continued in the alliance of the French republic with the Holy Alliance, with Naples and Austria. The decision of the ministerial council of 23 December was no secret to the Constituent Assembly. On 8 January Ledru-Rollin had already interpellated the ministry on the matter; the ministry had issued a denial and the National Assembly had proceeded with the agenda. Did it trust the ministry's word? We know that it spent the whole of January passing votes of no confidence in the government. But if it was part of the ministry's role to lie it was part of the National Assembly's role to feign belief in these lies and thereby to save the republican *dehors*.[84]

In the meantime Piedmont had been beaten, Charles Albert had abdicated, and the Austrian army was knocking at the gates of France.[85] Ledru-Rollin interpellated vehemently. The ministry proved that it had only continued Cavaignac's policy in northern Italy, just as Cavaignac had only continued the policy of the Provisional Government, that is, of Ledru-Rollin. This time it actually reaped a vote of confidence from the National Assembly and it was authorized to occupy temporarily a convenient point in northern Italy in order to give support to the peaceful negotiations with Austria over the integrity of Sardinian territory[86] and

84. Appearances.
85. By the end of August 1848 the Austrian army under Radetsky had defeated Charles Albert at Custozza and retaken Milan and all Lombardy.
86. I.e., the territory of the Sardinian monarchy, which, besides the island of Sardinia, comprised Piedmont, Savoy and Nice.

the Roman question. As is well known, the fate of Italy is decided on the battlefields of northern Italy. Thus either Rome would fall with Piedmont and Lombardy, or France would have to declare war on Austria and thus on the European counter-revolution. Did the National Assembly suddenly take the Barrot ministry for the old Committee of Public Safety, or itself for the Convention?[87] Why, then, the military occupation of a point in northern Italy? The expedition against Rome was concealed beneath this transparent veil.

On 14 April a force of 14,000 men under Oudinot sailed for Civitavecchia. On 16 April the National Assembly voted the ministry a credit of 1,200,000 francs in order to maintain a fleet of intervention in the Mediterranean for three months. It thus gave the ministry all the means it needed to intervene against Rome while pretending to allow it to intervene against Austria. It did not see what the ministry was doing; it only heard what it said. Such faith as this was not to be found in Israel; the Constituent Assembly was in the position of not daring to know what the constituted republic had to do.

Finally, on 8 May, the last scene in the comedy was played. The Constituent Assembly requested the ministry to take rapid measures to direct the Italian expedition back to the goal which had been planned for it. That same evening Bonaparte inserted a letter in the *Moniteur* in which he paid the highest tribute to Oudinot. On 11 May the National Assembly rejected the bill of impeachment against Bonaparte and his ministry. As for the Montagne, which, instead of rending this tissue of deceit, took the parliamentary comedy tragically in order to take part itself in the role of Fouquier-Tinville,[88] did it not reveal its natural petty-bourgeois calf's hide beneath the borrowed lion's skin of the Convention?

The latter half of the life of the Constituent Assembly can be resumed as follows: on 29 January it conceded that the royalist fractions of the bourgeoisie were the natural leaders of the republic which it had constituted; on 21 March that the violation of the Constitution was in fact its implementation; and on 11 May that the bombastically announced passive alliance of the French republic with the struggling peoples signified its active alliance with the European counter-revolution.

87. I.e., of 1792–4.
88. Antoine Fouquier-Tinville was the Public Prosecutor at the revolutionary tribunal under the rule of the Convention.

This wretched Assembly quit the stage after giving itself the satisfaction – two days before the anniversary of its establishment on 4 May – of rejecting the motion of amnesty for the June insurgents. With its power destroyed, mortally hated by the people, rejected, abused, contemptuously cast aside by the bourgeoisie whose tool it was, forced in the second half of its life to disavow the first half, robbed of its republican illusions, without any great achievements to its credit in the past, without hope in the future, its living body dying bit by bit, it was able to galvanize its own corpse back into life only by continually recalling and reliving the victory of June. Like a vampire living off the blood of the June insurgents it was only able to retain its self-confidence by constantly and repeatedly damning those who had already been damned!

It bequeathed a state deficit, increased by the costs of the June insurrection, by the loss of the salt tax, by compensation paid out to the plantation owners for the abolition of Negro slavery, by the costs of the Rome expedition, by the loss of the wine tax, which it repealed at its last gasp like a malicious old man who takes pleasure in burdening his laughing heir with a compromising debt of honour.

At the beginning of March the election campaign had begun for the Legislative National Assembly. Two main groups confronted each other: the *party of Order* and the *democratic socialist* or *Red party*. Between the two stood the *Friends of the Constitution*, the name under which the tricolour republicans of the *National* tried to present a party. The *party of Order* was formed immediately following the days of June; only after 10 December had allowed it to get rid of the *National* coterie, the bourgeois republicans, was the secret of its existence revealed: the *coalition of the Orleanists* and *Legitimists* in *one party*. The bourgeois class was divided into two great fractions which had alternately maintained a monopoly of power – *big landed property* under the *Restoration*, the *financial aristocracy* and the *industrial bourgeoisie* under the *July monarchy*. Bourbon was the royal name for the dominance of the interests of one fraction; Orleans was the royal name for the dominance of the interests of the other. The *nameless realm of the republic* was the only form of rule under which both fractions were able to maintain their common class interest with equal power and without giving up their mutual rivalry. Since the bourgeois republic could be nothing other than the perfected and most purely developed rule of the whole bourgeois class, could it be anything else but the rule of the Orleanists supplemented by the Legitimists, the rule of the Legitimists supplemented by the Orleanists, the *synthesis of the Restoration and the July monarchy*? The bourgeois republicans of the *National* did not represent any large economically based fraction of their class. As opposed to the two bourgeois fractions, which only understood their *particular* rule, their only significance and historical claim lay in having asserted, under the monarchy, the *general* rule of the bourgeois class, in having asserted the *nameless realm of the republic*, which they idealized and embellished with antique arabesques but in which they hailed above all the rule of their coterie. Although the party of the *National* could hardly believe its own eyes when it caught sight of the royalist coalition at the head of the republic which it had founded, the royalists deceived themselves no less as far as their joint rule was concerned. They did not realize that although each of their fractions, taken in isolation, was royalist, the product of their chemical fusion was inevitably *republican*, that the white and the blue monarchies could not help but neutralize each other in the tricolour republic. Although their opposition to the revolutionary proletariat and to the intermediate classes, which increasingly grouped themselves around the proletarian centre, forced them to summon their united strength and to conserve this strength in its organized form, each fraction of the party of Order had to oppose the restorationist and usurpatory desires of the other by asserting their joint rule – the *republican form* of bourgeois rule. Thus, we find the royalists initially believing in an imminent restoration, later conserving the republican form, while foaming with rage and uttering deadly invective against it, and finally confessing that they can only tolerate each other in the republic and postponing the restoration indefinitely. Their enjoyment of united rule itself strengthened the two fractions and made each of them even more unable and unwilling to subordinate itself to the other, unable and unwilling, that is, to restore the monarchy.

In its election programme the party of Order proclaimed outright the rule of the bourgeois class, the preservation, that is, of the vital conditions of its rule: *property, family, religion, order!* It naturally represented its class rule and the conditions of this class rule as the rule of civilization, as providing the necessary conditions for material production and for the social relationships which result from material production. The party of Order had enormous financial resources at its disposal; it had organized branches throughout France; it had all the ideologists of the old society in its pay; it had the influence of the existing government power at its disposal; it possessed an army of unpaid vassals in the mass of the petty bourgeoisie and peasants, who, still separated from the revolutionary movement, found in the high dignitaries of property the natural representatives of their petty property and their petty prejudices. Represented throughout the country by innumerable petty monarchs, the party of Order could punish the rejection of its candidates as insurrection and could dismiss rebellious workers, recalcitrant farm labourers, servants, clerks, railway officials, registrars and all the functionaries who are its social subordinates. Finally, here and there, it was able to maintain the myth that the republican Constituent Assembly had prevented the Bonaparte of 10 December from revealing his miraculous powers.

We have not considered the Bonapartists in connection with the party of Order. They were not a serious fraction of the bourgeois class but a collection of old, superstitious invalids and young, incredulous adventurers. The party of Order was victorious at the elections, and it sent a great majority into the Legislative Assembly.

Faced with the coalition of the counter-revolutionary bourgeoisie those sections of the petty bourgeoisie and peasantry which were already revolutionized naturally had to ally themselves with the high dignitaries of the revolutionary interests, the revolutionary proletariat. We have seen how the democratic spokesmen of the petty bourgeoisie in parliament, the Montagne, were driven, as a result of parliamentary defeats, to join the socialist spokesmen of the proletariat and how the petty bourgeoisie itself outside parliament was driven, as a result of the brutal assertion of bourgeois interests and by bankruptcy, to join the proletariat proper. On 27 January the Montagne and the socialists had celebrated their reconciliation; they repeated their act of union in the great February banquet of 1849. The socialist and the democratic parties, the party of the workers and the party of the petty bourgeoisie, united to form the *social-democratic party* – the *Red* party.

Although the French republic had been paralysed for a moment by the agony that followed the June days, since the raising of the state of siege on 19 October it had experienced an uninterrupted series of feverish excitements. First the struggle for the presidency; then the struggle between the President and the Constituent Assembly; the struggle over the clubs; the trial in Bourges,[89] which – by comparison with the petty figures of the President, the royalist coalition, the worthy republicans, the democratic Montagne and the socialist doctrinaires of the proletariat – made the real proletarian revolutionaries look like primordial monsters such as only a deluge could leave behind on the surface of society, or such as could only precede a social deluge; the election campaign; the execution of Bréa's murderers;[90] the continual prosecution of the press; the violent state interference with the banquets carried out by the police; the insolent royalist provocations; the exhibition of the portraits of Louis Blanc and Caussidière on the pillory; the uninterrupted struggle between the constituted republic and the Constituent Assembly, which continually brought the revolution back to where it had started, made the victors into vanquished, the vanquished into victors, and in a trice reversed the position of the parties and classes, their political disagreements and alliances; the rapid course of the European counter-revolution; the glorious Hungarian struggle; the armed uprisings in Germany; the Rome expedition; the ignominious defeat of the French army before Rome[91] – in this vortex of events, in this torment of historical unrest, in this dramatic ebb and flow of revolutionary passions, hopes and disappointments, the different classes in French society had to count the epochs of their development in weeks as they had previously counted them in half-centuries. A considerable section of the peasantry and the provinces had been revolutionized. They had become disappointed in Napoleon, and they were offered by the Red party the substance in place of the name, and in place of illusory freedom from taxation the repayment of the milliard

89. The High Court at Bourges sat from 7 March to 3 April to try the leaders of the 15 May attempt. Blanqui was condemned to ten years' imprisonment, Barbès and Albert to deportation for life, and others to long terms of imprisonment.

90. General Jean-Baptiste Bréa was killed while commanding a unit against the June insurgents; two men were convicted of his murder.

91. The Hungarian revolution was defeated in summer 1849 by Russian intervention; the German Reich Constitution Campaign was in May and June; and it was May 1849 when Oudinot first advanced on Rome, was soundly beaten by Garibaldi and retreated to Civitavecchia.

francs paid to the Legitimists, the settlement of mortgages and the abolition of usury.

The army itself was infected with revolutionary fever. In supporting Bonaparte it had voted for victory and he gave it defeat. In him it had voted for the Little Corporal[92] who concealed the great revolutionary commander, and he gave it back the great generals behind whom the pipe-clay corporal takes refuge. There was no doubt that the Red party, the democratic coalition, would inevitably celebrate, if not victory, at least great triumphs, that Paris, the army and a large part of the provinces were bound to vote for it. Ledru-Rollin, the leader of the Montagne, was elected in five departments; no leader of the party of Order, and no candidate of the actual proletarian party, achieved such a victory. This election reveals to us the secret of the democratic socialist party. On the one hand, the Montagne, the parliamentary protagonist of the democratic petty bourgeoisie, was forced to unite with the socialist doctrinaires of the proletariat. (The proletariat, forced by the terrible material defeat of June to recover its strength in intellectual victories and, as yet unable to seize the revolutionary dictatorship, had to embrace the doctrinaires of proletarian emancipation, the socialist sectarians.)[93] On the other hand, the revolutionary peasants, the army and the provinces ranged themselves behind the Montagne. Thus, the Montagne became lord and master in the revolutionary camp, and by coming to an understanding with the socialists it set aside all differences within the revolutionary party. In the latter half of the Constituent Assembly's existence it represented the republican pathos of this body and made people forget its sins in the Provisional Government, the Executive Commission and the June days. Just as the party of the *National*, true to its half-and-half nature, had allowed itself to be oppressed by the royalist ministry, the party of the Mountain, which had been pushed aside during the period of the *National* party's omnipotence, rose up and made its strength felt as the parliamentary representative of the revolution. In fact, the party of the *National* had nothing to oppose the royalist fractions with,

92. This was the pet name given to Napoleon I by his army.
93. By 'socialist sectarians' Marx refers to the Fourierists and Proudhonists who preached abstention from political struggle and sought to emancipate the proletariat by various utopian remedies; see the Introduction to *The Revolutions of 1848*, above, pp. 16–19, and section III of the Communist Manifesto, ibid., pp. 81–91.

except ambitious personalities and idealistic humbug. The party of the Mountain, on the other hand, represented a mass hovering between the bourgeoisie and the proletariat, whose material interests demanded democratic institutions. By comparison with the Cavaignacs and the Marrasts, therefore, Ledru-Rollin and the Montagne took up a position more truly within the revolutionary movement; from a consciousness of this momentous situation they drew all the greater courage, the more the expression of revolutionary energy was limited to parliamentary attacks, the tabling of bills of impeachment, threats, the raising of voices, thundering speeches and extremes which never went beyond phrases. The peasants were more or less in the same position as the petty bourgeoisie; they had more or less the same demands to make. All the middle strata of society, so far as they were driven to join the revolutionary movement, were bound to find their hero in Ledru-Rollin. Ledru-Rollin was the leading personage of the democratic petty bourgeoisie. To oppose the party of Order the half-conservative, half-revolutionary, and wholly utopian reformers of this social order had first to be pushed to the fore.

The party of the *National*, the 'Friends of the Constitution *quand même*',[94] the *républicains purs et simples*, were completely beaten in the elections. A tiny minority from this party was elected to the legislature; their most notorious leaders disappeared from the stage, even Marrast, editor-in-chief and Orpheus of the worthy republic.

On 28 May the Legislative Assembly gathered; 11 June brought a repetition of the collision of 8 May; in the name of the Montagne Ledru-Rollin tabled a bill of impeachment against the President and the ministry for violation of the Constitution, for the bombardment of Rome. On 12 June the Legislative Assembly rejected the bill of impeachment, just as the Constituent Assembly had rejected it on 11 May, but this time the proletariat drove the Montagne onto the streets, not, however, for a street battle but for a street procession. It should suffice to say that the Montagne was at the head of this movement to know that the movement was defeated and that June 1849 was a caricature, as ludicrous as it was contemptible, of June 1848. The great retreat of 13 June was eclipsed only by the even greater battle report of Changarnier, the great man improvised by the party of Order. Every social

94. Regardless.

epoch needs its great men, and if it does not find them it invents them, as Helvétius said.

On 20 December only one half of the constituted republic was in existence, the President; on 28 May it was completed by the other half, the Legislative Assembly. In June 1848 the constituent bourgeois republic had engraved its name in the birth register of history by an unspeakable battle against the proletariat; in June 1849 the constituted bourgeois republic had done the same by an ineffable comedy with the petty bourgeoisie. June 1849 was the Nemesis of June 1848. In June 1849 it was not the workers who were defeated; it was the petty bourgeois who stood between them and the revolution who were felled. June 1849 was not a bloody tragedy between wage labour and capital, but a lamentable prison-filling drama acted out between debtor and creditor. The party of Order had won; it was all-powerful. It now had to show what it was.

III. THE CONSEQUENCES OF 13 JUNE 1849

From 13 June 1849 to 10 March 1850

On 20 December [1848] the Janus head of the *constitutional republic* had shown only *one* face: the executive face with the indistinct, shallow features of Louis Bonaparte. On 28 May 1849 it showed its second face: the *legislative* face, pitted with scars left behind from the orgies of the Restoration and the July monarchy. With the Legislative National Assembly the phenomenon of the *constitutional republic* was completed, the republican form of government, that is, in which the rule of the bourgeois class is constituted – in other words, the joint rule of the two great royalist fractions which form the French bourgeoisie, the coalition of the Legitimists and the Orleanists, the *party of Order*. At the same time as the French republic thus became the property of the royalist coalition, the European coalition of counter-revolutionary forces embarked on a general crusade against the last sanctuaries of the March revolutions. Russia invaded Hungary; Prussia marched against the army upholding the Reich constitution, and Oudinot bombarded Rome. The European crisis was obviously approaching a decisive turning point; the eyes of all Europe were directed at Paris, and the eyes of Paris at the Legislative Assembly.

On 11 June Ledru-Rollin mounted the rostrum. He did not

make a speech; he formulated a requisitory against the ministers, naked, unadorned, factual, concentrated, forceful.

The attack on Rome is an attack on the Constitution; the attack on the Roman republic is an attack on the French republic. Paragraph V[95] of the Constitution reads, 'The French Republic will never employ its armed forces against the freedom of any people whatsoever' – and the President is using the French army against the freedom of Rome. Paragraph 54 of the Constitution forbids the executive to declare any war whatsoever without the consent of the National Assembly. The resolution of the Constituent Assembly of 8 May expressly orders the ministers to redirect the Roman expedition to its original purpose with all speed; it forbids them, therefore, no less expressly to wage war against Rome – and Oudinot is bombarding Rome. Ledru-Rollin thus called the Constitution itself as a witness for the prosecution against Bonaparte and his ministers. As the tribune of the Constitution he hurled a threat in the direction of the royalist majority of the National Assembly: 'The republicans will ensure that respect is paid to the Constitution – by every means possible, even by force of arms!' '*By force of arms!*' the Montagne re-echoed a hundred times over. The majority answered with a frightful tumult; the chairman of the National Assembly called Ledru-Rollin to order; Ledru-Rollin repeated his challenging declaration, and finally he laid on the chairman's desk a motion proposing the impeachment of Bonaparte and his ministers. By 361 votes to 203 the National Assembly resolved to move on from the bombardment of Rome to the regular agenda.

Did Ledru-Rollin believe he could defeat the National Assembly with the Constitution and the President with the National Assembly?

The Constitution, it is true, forbade any attack on the freedom of foreign peoples, but according to the ministry what the French army was attacking in Rome was not 'freedom' but the 'despotism of anarchy'. Despite all its experiences in the Constituent Assembly had the Montagne still not understood that the interpretation of the Constitution did not belong to those who had made it but only to those who had accepted it? That its wording was bound to be interpreted in accordance with its viable sense, and that the bourgeois sense was the only viable one? That Bonaparte and the royalist majority in the National Assembly were the authentic

95. The paragraphs of the French Constitution with roman numerals are from the introductory section.

interpreters of the Constitution, just as the priest is the authentic interpreter of the Bible and the judge the authentic interpreter of the law? Was the National Assembly, which had been given life by the general election, to feel bound by the testamentary provision of the dead Constituent Assembly, whose vital will had been broken by the likes of Odilon Barrot? By appealing to the resolution passed by the Constituent Assembly on 8 May, had Ledru-Rollin forgotten that on 11 May the same Constituent Assembly had rejected his first motion proposing the impeachment of Bonaparte and his ministers; that it had acquitted them; that it had thus sanctioned the attack on Rome as 'constitutional'; that he was only lodging an appeal against a judgement which had already been delivered; and that, lastly, he was appealing from the republican Constituent Assembly to the royalist Legislative Assembly? The Constitution itself calls insurrection to its assistance in a special paragraph, in which it summons every citizen to protect it. Ledru-Rollin based his position on this paragraph. But, at the same time, are the public powers not organized to protect the Constitution and is not the Constitution only violated the moment one of the public constitutional powers rebels against the others? And the President of the republic, the ministers of the republic, the National Assembly of the republic were all in the most harmonious agreement.

What the Montagne attempted on 11 June was '*an insurrection within the limits of pure reason*', that is, a purely *parliamentary insurrection*. The majority of the Assembly, intimidated by the prospect of an armed uprising by the popular masses, was supposed to destroy its own power and the significance of its own election in the persons of Bonaparte and his ministers. Had the Constituent Assembly not made a similar attempt to annul the election of Bonaparte by insisting so obstinately on the dismissal of the Barrot-Falloux ministry?

There was no lack of models from the time of the Convention for parliamentary insurrections which had suddenly and radically transformed the relation of majority and minority – and was the new Montagne to fail where the old Montagne had succeeded? – nor did the present circumstances seem unfavourable for such an undertaking. Popular unrest in Paris had reached an alarming pitch; the army did not seem favourably disposed towards the government, judging by its vote at the elections; the legislative majority itself was still too young to have consolidated its position, and, in addition, it consisted of old gentlemen. If the Montagne succeeded in bringing about a parliamentary insurrection, the helm of state would immediately fall into its hands. The democratic petty bourgeoisie, for its part, wished, as always, for nothing more fervently than to see the battle fought out above its head, in the clouds, between the departed spirits of parliament. Finally, both the democratic petty bourgeoisie and its representatives, the Montagne, would, by means of a parliamentary insurrection, fulfil their great ambition, that of breaking the power of the bourgeoisie without unleashing the proletariat or letting it appear other than in a reduced perspective; the proletariat would have been used without becoming dangerous.

After the vote of the National Assembly on 11 June a meeting took place between several members of the Montagne and delegates from the secret workers' societies. The latter urged that an attack be made that very evening. The Montagne decisively rejected this plan. On no account did it want to let the leadership slip out of its grasp; it suspected its allies as much as it suspected its opponents, and rightly so. The memory of June 1848 surged through the ranks of the Paris proletariat more vigorously than ever. Nevertheless, it was chained to the alliance with the Montagne. The latter represented the greater part of the departments; it exaggerated its influence in the army; it had the democratic section of the National Guard at its disposal; it had the moral strength of the shopkeepers behind it. To begin the insurrection at this moment against the will of the Montagne would have meant for the proletariat – decimated, moreover, by cholera and driven out of Paris in considerable numbers by unemployment – a useless repetition of the June days of 1848, without the situation which had forced that desperate struggle. The proletarian delegates did the only rational thing. They committed the Montagne to *compromise* itself, that is, to overstep the limits of the parliamentary struggle should its bill of impeachment be rejected. Throughout 13 June the proletariat maintained the same sceptically watchful position and waited for a serious, irrevocable clash between the democratic National Guard and the army in order to rush into the battle and to propel the revolution forward beyond the petty-bourgeois aim set for it. The proletarian commune which was to take its place beside the official government in the event of victory was already formed. The Paris workers had learnt their lesson in the bloody school of June 1848.

On 12 June Minister Lacrosse[96] himself proposed to the Legislative Assembly that they proceed at once to the discussion of the bill of impeachment. During the night the government had made every provision for defensive and offensive measures; the majority of the National Assembly was resolved to drive the rebellious minority out onto the street; the minority itself could no longer retreat; the die was cast. The bill of impeachment was rejected by 377 votes to eight. The Montagne, which had abstained, rushed furiously into the propaganda halls of 'peaceful democracy', into the newspaper offices of the *Démocratie pacifique*.[97]

This withdrawal from the parliament building robbed it of its strength, just as withdrawal from Earth robbed Antaeus, her giant son, of his strength. Though they were Samsons in the precincts of the Legislative Assembly, in the precincts of 'peaceful democracy' they were only Philistines. A long, noisy, aimless debate developed. The Montagne was determined to compel the observance of the Constitution by any means possible, '*except by force of arms*'. It was supported in this decision by a manifesto and by a deputation of the 'Friends of the Constitution', which was the name assumed by the wreckage left over from the coterie of the *National*, the bourgeois republican party. While six of its remaining parliamentary representatives had voted *against* and the others all *for* the rejection of the bill of impeachment, while Cavaignac placed his sabre at the disposal of the party of Order, the larger extra-parliamentary section of the coterie greedily seized the opportunity to emerge from its position as a political pariah and to push its way into the ranks of the democratic party. Did they not appear as the natural shield-bearers of this party, which concealed itself behind their shield, behind their *principle*, behind the *Constitution*?

The 'Mountain' laboured till daybreak. It gave birth to a '*Proclamation to the people*', which on the morning of 13 June occupied a more or less shamefaced place in two socialist journals.[98] It declared that the President, the ministers and the majority of

96. Bertrand, baron de Lacrosse, an Orleanist and later a Bonapartist, was Minister of Public Works in 1848–9 and 1851, and deputy chairman of the Constituent and Legislative National Assemblies.

97. *La Démocratie pacifique* was a Fourierist daily paper edited by Considérant. At a meeting in its offices, the Montagne deputies rejected armed struggle and decided to confine themselves to peaceful demonstration.

98. Marx is alluding to the poem (quoted by Athenaeus in the *Deipnosophistai*) in which a mountain gives birth to a mouse.

the Legislative Assembly were 'outside the Constitution' (*hors la constitution*) and summoned the National Guard, the army and finally the people to 'rise up'. '*Long live the Constitution!*' was the slogan which it issued, a slogan which meant nothing other than '*Down with the revolution!*'

In response to the Montagne's proclamation the petty bourgeoisie held a so-called *peaceful demonstration* on 13 June; that is, a street procession moved along from the Château d'Eau through the boulevards, 30,000 strong, mostly members of the National Guard, unarmed, interspersed with members of the secret workers' sections, shouting '*Long live the Constitution!*', a slogan which was uttered mechanically, ice-cold, and with a bad conscience by the demonstrators themselves, and which, instead of swelling up like thunder, was ironically tossed back by the echo of the people who milled about on the pavements. Deep-chested notes were missing from the many-voiced chorus. And as the procession turned by the meeting place of the 'Friends of the Constitution' and a hired herald of the Constitution appeared on the roof of the building violently cleaving the air with his *claqueur* hat, letting the slogan '*Long live the Constitution!*' fall like hail from his monstrous lungs onto the heads of the pilgrims, even they seemed to be overcome by the comedy of the situation. It is well known how, when the procession arrived at the corner of the rue de la Paix, it was met in the boulevards in a thoroughly unparliamentary manner by the dragoons and chasseurs of Changarnier, how, in an instant, it scattered in all directions, casting over its shoulder the occasional cry 'to arms' so that the parliamentary call to arms of 11 June might be fulfilled.

The majority of the Montagne, assembled in the rue du Hasard, scattered as the violent dispersion of the peaceful procession, the vague rumours of the murder of unarmed citizens on the boulevards, and the growing tumult on the streets seemed to herald the approach of an uprising. Ledru-Rollin, at the head of a small band of deputies, saved the honour of the Montagne. Under the protection of the Paris artillery, which had assembled in the Palais National, they betook themselves to the Conservatoire des Arts et Métiers[99] where the 5th and 6th legions of the National Guard were due to arrive. But the Montagnards waited for the 5th and 6th legions in vain. These cautious National Guards left

99. Museum of Arts and Trades.

their representatives in the lurch; the Paris artillery itself prevented the people from erecting barricades; chaotic disorder made any decision impossible, and the regular troops advanced with fixed bayonets. Some of the representatives were taken prisoner; others escaped. Thus ended 13 June.

If 23 June 1848 was the insurrection of the revolutionary proletariat, 13 June 1849 was the insurrection of the democratic petty bourgeoisie, each of these two insurrections the *classical* and *pure* expression of the class which had carried it out.

Only in Lyons did it come to an obstinate, bloody conflict. Here, where the industrial bourgeoisie and the industrial proletariat confront each other directly, where the workers' movement, unlike that in Paris, is not incorporated in, and determined by, the general movement, 13 June, in its repercussions, lost its original character. Wherever else it struck in the provinces it did not ignite – *a cold flash of lightning*.

13 June closes the first *period in the life of the constitutional republic*, which had begun its normal existence with the meeting of the Legislative Assembly on 28 May 1849. The whole course of this prologue was filled by the noisy struggle between bourgeoisie and petty bourgeoisie, as the latter resisted in vain the consolidation of the bourgeois republic, for which it had itself continuously conspired in the Provisional Government and the Executive Commission, for which it had fought desperately against the proletariat during the June days. 13 June broke its resistance and made the *legislative dictatorship* of the united royalists a *fait accompli*. From this moment on the National Assembly was only *the party of Order's Committee of Public Safety*.

Paris had put the President, the ministers and the majority of the National Assembly in a '*state of impeachment*'; they put Paris in a '*state of siege*'. The Montagne had declared the majority of the Legislative Assembly '*outside the Constitution*'; for violating the Constitution the majority handed the Montagne over to the High Court[1] and proscribed everything that still possessed any vitality. It was decimated to a rump without head or heart. The minority had gone so far as to attempt a *parliamentary insurrection*; the majority elevated its *parliamentary despotism* to a law. It

1. In a decree of 10 August 1849 the National Assembly decided to bring 'the accomplices and abettors of the conspiracy and attempt of 13 June' to the High Court.

decreed new *standing orders*, which abolished the freedom of the rostrum and empowered the chairman of the National Assembly to punish representatives who violated these standing orders with censorship, fines, confiscation of salaries, temporary expulsion or prison. Over the rump of the Montagne was hung the rod in place of the sword. The rest of the Montagne deputies owed it to their honour to quit the Assembly *en masse*. Such an act would have hastened the dissolution of the party of Order. It was bound to disintegrate into its original component parts the moment not even the semblance of an opposition existed to hold these together any longer.

At the same time as they lost their *parliamentary* power the democratic petty bourgeois were robbed of their *armed* power by the dissolution of the Paris Artillery and of the 8th, 9th and 12th legions of the National Guard. On the other hand, encouraging tribute was paid from the rostrum of the National Assembly to the legion of high finance, which, on 13 June, had raided the printing houses of Boulé and Roux, had smashed the presses, laid waste to the offices of the republican journals, and arbitrarily arrested editors, compositors, printers, forwarding clerks and errand boys. The disbandment of sections of the National Guard suspected of republicanism was repeated throughout the length and breadth of France.

A new *press law*, a new *law of association*, a new *law on the state of siege*, the Paris prisons overcrowded, political refugees driven out,[2] all journals which went beyond the limits of the *National* suspended, Lyons and the five surrounding departments delivered up to the brutal chicanery of military despotism, the ubiquitous courts, the often purged army of civil servants purged once again – these were the inevitable, the constantly recurring *commonplaces* of the victorious forces of reaction; they are only worth mentioning after the massacre and deportations of June, because this time they were directed not only against Paris but also against the departments, not only against the proletariat but, above all, against the middle classes.

The repressive laws, which left the declaration of a state of siege to the discretion of the government, which gagged the press more firmly and abolished the right of association, absorbed all

2. Marx had arrived in Paris on 3 June 1849 as a political refugee from Germany. On 19 July he was ordered to leave Paris, and after obtaining a stay of execution, he left Paris on 24 August for London.

the legislative activity of the National Assembly throughout June, July and August.

However, this period is characterized by the exploitation of victory, not *in fact* but *in principle*; not by resolutions passed by the National Assembly, but by the motivation of these resolutions; not by the matter itself, but by the phrase; not by the phrase, but by the accent and gesture which give life to the phrase. The ruthless and unashamed expression of *royalist sentiments*, the contemptuously superior insults aimed at the republic, the coquettishly frivolous divulging of restorationist aims, in a word, the boastful violation of *republican propriety* give this period its particular tone and colour. '*Long live the Constitution!*' was the battle-cry of the *vanquished* of 13 June. The *victors*, therefore, were absolved from the hypocrisy of constitutional, that is, republican, talk. The counter-revolution subjugated Hungary, Italy and Germany, and they believed that the restoration was already before the gates of France. Among the masters of ceremonies in the party of Order a veritable competition developed to document their royalism in the *Moniteur* and to confess, repent and ask the forgiveness of God and man for any liberal sins they might by chance have committed under the monarchy. No day went by without the February revolution being declared a public calamity from the rostrum of the National Assembly, without some Legitimist provincial squire solemnly maintaining that he had never recognized the republic, without one of the craven deserters of and traitors to the July monarchy relating the belated acts of heroism which he would have performed but for the philanthropy of Louis Philippe or for other misunderstandings. What was to be admired in the days of February was not the magnanimity of the victorious people but the self-sacrifice and moderation of the royalists, which had allowed the people to achieve their victory. One representative proposed donating part of the relief money intended for those wounded in February to the Municipal Guard,[3] which was alone in having earned the gratitude of the fatherland at that time. Another wanted a decree for the erection of an equestrian statue

3. Under the July monarchy the Municipal Guard put down a number of insurrections with ferocity, and was particularly hated by the people in February 1848. The Provisional Government at first intended to dissolve it, but a para-military force of this nature soon turned out to be necessary to suppress opposition from the left. It was therefore kept in being, from May 1848 under the name of Republican Guard.

of the Duke of Orleans in the Place du Carrousel. Thiers[4] called the Constitution a dirty piece of paper. One after the other they appeared at the rostrum: Orleanists who repented their conspiracy against the legitimate monarchy; Legitimists who accused themselves of having hastened the overthrow of monarchy in general by opposing the illegitimate monarchy; Thiers, who regretted having intrigued against Molé;[5] Molé, who regretted having intrigued against Guizot; Barrot, who regretted having intrigued against all three. The slogan, 'Long live the social-democratic republic!' was declared unconstitutional; the slogan, 'Long live the republic!' was prosecuted as social-democratic. On the anniversary of the Battle of Waterloo a representative declared, 'I fear the invasion of the Prussians less than the entry of revolutionary refugees into France.' To the complaints about the terrorism organized in Lyons and the neighbouring departments, Baraguey-d'Hilliers[6] answered, 'I prefer the white terror to the red terror.' (*J'aime mieux la terreur blanche que la terreur rouge*.) And the Assembly applauded wildly every time an epigram directed against the republic, against the revolution, against the Constitution, in favour of the monarchy, in favour of the Holy Alliance, fell from the lips of their speakers. Every slightest infringement of republican formalities, for example, that of addressing the representatives as '*citoyens*', aroused the enthusiasm of the knights of Order.

The Paris by-elections of 8 July, held under the influence of the state of siege and the abstention of a large section of the proletariat from the ballot box, the taking of Rome by the French army, the entry into Rome of the red eminences, with the inquisition and monkish terrorism in their train;[7] all these added new victories to the victory of June and heightened the intoxication of the party of Order.

Finally, in the middle of August, half with the intention of attending the Departmental Councils which had just assembled, half because of exhaustion from the orgy of tendentiousness,

4. Louis-Adolphe Thiers was an historian and politician. Twice Prime Minister under Louis Philippe, he was a leading Orleanist under the Second Republic and, after supervising the suppression of the Paris Commune of 1871, became the first President of the Third Republic (1871–3).

5. Louis, comte Molé was an Orleanist politician, Prime Minister from 1836 to 1839, and a deputy in both Assemblies.

6. Achille, comte Baraguey-d'Hilliers was a Bonapartist general, and a deputy in both Assemblies. In 1851 he commanded the Paris garrison.

7. This refers to the commission of three cardinals who entered Rome with the French army to restore the reactionary papal regime.

which had lasted for many months, the royalists decreed a two-month prorogation of the National Assembly. With transparent irony they left behind a Commission of twenty-five representatives,[8] the cream of the Legitimists and Orleanists, a Molé and a Changarnier, to represent the National Assembly and to serve as *guardians of the republic*. The irony was more profound than they suspected. Condemned by history to help in the overthrow of the monarchy which they loved, they were destined by history to conserve the republic which they hated.

The prorogation of the Legislative Assembly *closes the second period in the life of the constitutional republic, the period in which it sowed its royalist wild oats*.

The state of siege in Paris had been raised again, the press had resumed its activities once more. During the suspension of the social-democratic press, during the period of repressive legislation and royalist blustering, *Le Siècle*, the old literary representative of the *constitutional-monarchist petty bourgeoisie, became republicanized*; *La Presse*, the old literary advocate of the *bourgeois reformers, became democratized*; *Le National*, the old classical organ of the *bourgeois republicans*, became socialized.

The *secret societies* grew in extent and intensity the more the *public clubs* became impossible. Each of the workers' *industrial cooperatives*, tolerated as purely commercial societies, although economically of no significance, became politically a means of cementing the proletariat. 13 June had chopped off the official heads of the various semi-revolutionary parties; the masses that remained found their own head. The knights of Order had intimidated the country with prophesies of the terror of the red republic; the base excesses, the hyperborean barbarity of the victorious counter-revolution in Hungary, in Baden[9] and in Rome washed the '*red republic*' white. The discontented intermediate classes of French society began to prefer the promises of the 'red republic' with its problematic terrors to the terrors of the red monarchy with its actual hopelessness. No socialist spread more propaganda in France than Haynau.[10] *À chaque capacité selon ses œuvres*.[11]

8. The Standing Commission of the Assembly was provided for in the Constitution, to safeguard the latter during the Assembly's recess.

9. Baden was the chief stronghold of the German Reich Constitution Campaign.

10. Julius Jakob, Freiherr von Haynau was an Austrian field-marshal notorious for his cruel reprisals against the Hungarian nationalists in 1849.

11. To each according to his works.

Meanwhile Louis Napoleon exploited the National Assembly's recess to make princely tours in the provinces; the most hot-blooded Legitimists made pilgrimages to the descendant of St Louis[12] at Ems, and the mass of the party of Order's deputies intrigued in the Departmental Councils, which had just met. It was a matter of making them put forward what the majority of the National Assembly did not yet dare, a *motion of urgency for the immediate revision of the Constitution*. According to itself, the Constitution could not be revised until 1852, and then only by a National Assembly summoned for this specific purpose. But if the majority of the Departmental Councils expressed themselves in favour of revision, would the National Assembly not have to sacrifice the virginity of the Constitution to the voice of France? The National Assembly entertained the same hopes with regard to the provincial assemblies as the nuns in Voltaire's *La Henriade* with regard to the pandours. But the Potiphars of the National Assembly, with a few exceptions, found they were dealing with just so many provincial Josephs. The vast majority did not want to understand the importunate insinuation. The revision of the Constitution was thwarted by the very instruments with which it was to have been called into existence, by the votes of the Departmental Councils. The voice of France, namely the voice of bourgeois France, had spoken, and it had spoken against revision.

At the beginning of October the Legislative National Assembly assembled again – *tantum mutatus ab illo*.[13] Its physiognomy was completely changed. The unexpected rejection of revision by the Departmental Councils had placed it back within the limits of the Constitution and had indicated the limits of its term of life. The Orleanists had become suspicious as a result of the pilgrimages of the Legitimists to Ems; the Legitimists had become mistrustful as a result of the negotiations of the Orleanists with London;[14] the journals of both fractions had fanned the flames and weighed the rival claims of their pretenders. Orleanists and Legitimists grumbled in unison at the machinations of the Bonapartists, which became evident on the princely tours, in the more or less transparent emancipatory endeavours of the President, in the

12. This was Henri-Charles d'Artois, comte de Chambord, grandson of Charles X and pretender to the French throne under the title of Henri V. He lived at Ems near Wiesbaden.

13. How great a change since then.

14. The deposed Louis Philippe lived at Claremont near London.

presumptuous language of the Bonapartist newspapers; Louis Bonaparte grumbled at a National Assembly which found only the Legitimist and Orleanist conspiracies legitimate, and at a ministry which permanently betrayed him to this National Assembly. Finally, the ministry itself was split on the Rome policy and the *income tax*, which had been proposed by Minister Passy[15] and decried as socialist by the conservatives.

One of the first bills that the Barrot ministry presented to the re-assembled Legislative Assembly was a credit demand of 300,000 francs for a widow's pension for the Duchess of Orleans.[16] The National Assembly approved it and added to the French nation's list of debts a sum of 7 million francs. While Louis Philippe thus continued successfully to play the role of the *pauvre honteux*, the shamefaced beggar, the ministry neither dared move a salary increase for Bonaparte nor did the Assembly seem inclined to give it. And Louis Bonaparte, as ever, vacillated before the dilemma: *aut Caesar aut Clichy!*[17]

The second credit demand made by the ministry, for nine million francs to cover *the costs of the Rome expedition*, increased the tension between Bonaparte on the one hand and the ministers and the National Assembly on the other. Louis Bonaparte had inserted in the *Moniteur* a letter to his military aide, Edgar Ney, in which he tied the papal government to constitutional guarantees. The Pope, for his part, had issued an address, *motu proprio*,[18] in which he rejected any limits on his restored rule. Bonaparte's letter, a deliberate indiscretion, lifted the veil of his cabinet in order to reveal himself to the glances of the gallery as a benevolent genius, misunderstood and fettered in his own house. He flirted, not for the first time, with the 'furtively beating wings of a free soul'.[19] Thiers, the commission's *rapporteur*, completely ignored Bonaparte's beating wings and contented himself with translating

15. Hippolyte Passy, an economist and Orleanist politician, was Minister of Fin-ance from 1849 to 1850.

16. Helène, duchesse d'Orléans was the widow of Ferdinand, Louis Philippe's eldest son.

17. Either Caesar or Clichy. Clichy was the Paris debtors' prison during the mid-ni-neteenth century.

18. 'Of his own accord', the general name for a papal message sent without the collaboration of the cardinals and generally dealing with internal administrative arrangements of the papal state. This particular *motu proprio* was published on 12 September 1849.

19. A phrase from Georg Herwegh's poem 'From the Mountain'.

the papal allocution into French. It was not the ministry but Victor Hugo[20] who tried to save the President with an agenda in which the National Assembly was to express its agreement with Napoleon's letter.

Allons donc! Allons donc![21] With this disrespectful, flippant interjection the majority buried Hugo's motion. The President's policy? The President's letter? The President himself? *Allons donc! Allons donc!* Who the devil takes Monsieur Bonaparte *au sérieux*? Do you believe, Monsieur Victor Hugo, that we believe that you believe in the President? *Allons donc! Allons donc!*

The breach between Bonaparte and the National Assembly was finally accelerated by the discussion on the *recall of the Orleans and Bourbons*. In default of the ministry the President's cousin, the son of the ex-king of Westphalia,[22] had proposed this motion, which had no other function than that of reducing the Legitimist and Orleanist pretenders to the same level as, or even a *lower* one than, the Bonapartist pretender, who at least was already at the pinnacle of state power.

Napoleon Bonaparte was disrespectful enough to make the *recall of the banished royal families* and the *amnesty for the June insurgents* parts of one and the same motion. The indignation of the majority forced him immediately to apologize for this sacriligious juxtaposition of the holy and the impious, the royal races and the proletarian brood, the fixed stars of society and its swamp lights, and to assign to each of these its proper rank. The majority energetically rejected the recall of the royal family, and Berryer,[23] the Demosthenes of the Legitimists, left no doubt as to the significance of their vote. The public degradation of the pretenders, that is what they intend! They want to rob them of their halo, of the last trace of majesty which is left to them, the *majesty of exile*! What, declared Berryer, would the people think of the pretender who, forgetting his illustrious origins, came here to live as a simple private citizen! Louis Bonaparte could not be told more clearly that his presence in France did not mean that he had won, that while the royalist coalition needed him here in France on the President's chair as a *neutral man*, the serious pretenders to the

20. Victor Hugo, the novelist, was a deputy in both Assemblies. He originally supported the party of Order, but broke with it over the Rome expedition.
21. Come off it!
22. Jérôme Bonaparte was a deputy in both Assemblies.
23. Pierre-Antoine Berryer was a lawyer and a deputy in both Assemblies.

throne had to remain withdrawn from profane sight by the mists of exile.

On 1 November Louis Bonaparte answered the Legislative Assembly with a message which announced, in rather blunt terms, the dismissal of Barrot's ministry and the formation of a new one. The Barrot-Falloux ministry was the ministry of the royalist coalition: the Hautpoul[24] ministry was Bonaparte's own ministry, the organ of the President in his confrontation with the Legislative Assembly, the *ministry of clerks*.

Bonaparte was no longer merely the *neutral man* of 10 December 1848. His possession of executive power had caused a number of interests to group around him; the struggle against 'anarchy' forced the party of Order itself to increase his influence, and even if he was *no longer* popular, the party of Order was *unpopular*. Could he not hope to force the Orleanists and the Legitimists, as a result of their rivalry and the necessity of some sort of monarchist restoration, to a recognition of the *neutral pretender*?

The third period in the life of the constitutional republic dates from 1 November 1849 and ends with 10 March 1850. It did not only see the beginning of the regular play of constitutional institutions so admired by Guizot – the squabble between executive and legislature. In the face of the restorationist desires of the united Orleanists and Legitimists it saw Bonaparte defend his actual power: the republic. In the face of Bonaparte's restorationist desires the fractions of the party of Order defended their joint power: the republic. The Orleanists confronted the Legitimists, and the Legitimists the Orleanists, as the representatives of the status quo: the republic. All these fractions of the party of Order, each of which had its own king and restoration *in petto*, in turn enforced the joint rule of the bourgeoisie in opposition to the usurpatory and mutinous desires of the rival pretenders: they enforced that form of society in which particular claims of the various parties were held in check and neutralized – *the republic*.

The royalists made of *the monarchy* what Kant makes of the republic – the only rational form of state: a postulate of practical reason, which can never be realized but whose achievement must always be the goal striven for and adhered to in one's beliefs.

24. Alphonse, marquis d'Hautpoul was a Legitimist general, later a Bonapartist. He sat in the Legislative National Assembly and was Minister of War from 1849 to 1850.

Thus, the constitutional republic, which had been produced by the bourgeois republicans as a hollow ideological formula, became in the hands of the royalist coalition a form filled with substance and life. And Thiers spoke truer than he knew when he said, 'We, the royalists, are the true pillars of the constitutional republic.'

The overthrow of the coalition ministry and the appearance of the ministry of the clerks have a second significance. Its Minister of Finance was Fould. Fould's appointment to the Ministry of Finance represented the official surrender of French national wealth to the Bourse, the administration of public property by the Bourse and in the interests of the Bourse. With Fould's appointment the financial aristocracy announced its own restoration in the *Moniteur*. This restoration necessarily supplemented the other restorations, each forming a link in the chain of the constitutional republic.

Louis Philippe had never dared make a real *loup-cervier* (stock-exchange shark) Minister of Finance. Since his monarchy was the ideal name that covered the rule of the big bourgeoisie, the privileged interests had to bear ideologically disinterested names in his ministries. But the bourgeois republic, on all fronts, pushed into the foreground what the different monarchies, the Legitimist no less than the Orleanist, had kept concealed in the background. It brought back to earth what they had transferred to the heavens. It replaced the names of the saints with the bourgeois proper names of the dominant class interests.

Our whole account has shown how the republic, from the first day of its existence, did not overthrow the financial aristocracy but consolidated it. The concessions which were made to it were a fate passively submitted to rather than actively striven for. With Fould, however, governmental initiative fell back into the hands of the financial aristocracy.

It might be asked how the bourgeois coalition was able to bear and tolerate the rule of finance, which under Louis Philippe had been based on the exclusion or subordination of the other fractions of the bourgeoisie.

The answer is simple.

First of all, the financial aristocracy itself forms a decisive and substantial part of the royalist coalition, whose common governmental power is called a republic. Are not the spokesmen and authoritative figures of the Orleanists the old allies and accom-

plices of the financial aristocracy? Does it not itself represent the
golden phalanx of Orleanism? As far as the Legitimists are concerned,
even at the time of Louis Philippe they had taken a practical part in all
the speculative orgies on the Bourse, in mines and in railways. The
combination of large landed property and high finance is in general a
normal fact, as evidenced by England, and even Austria.

In a country such as France, where the volume of national
production is disproportionately smaller than the size of the
national debt, where government bonds form the most important
object of speculation and the Bourse forms the chief market for
the investment of capital which is intended to be turned to account
unproductively, in such a country a countless mass of people from
all bourgeois or semi-bourgeois classes inevitably have an interest
in the national debt, stock-market gambles and finance. Do not all
these subaltern interested parties find their natural supporters and
commanders in the fraction which represents these interests on the
broadest basis?

How does public property come to fall into the hands of high
finance? Due to the growing indebtedness of the state. And what
causes the indebtedness of the state? The constant excess of its
expenditure compared with its revenue, a disproportion which is both
the cause and the effect of the system of state loans.

One way for the state to free itself from this indebtedness would
be to curb its expenditure, that is, simplify and reduce the size of the
government organism, govern as little as possible, employ as small a
personnel as possible and have as few dealings with bourgeois society as possible. This course was impossible for the party of Order,
whose means of repression, official interference in the name of the
state and omnipresence through the organs of state, were bound to
increase the more the rule of its class and its conditions of life were
threatened from an increasing number of quarters. The *gendarmerie* cannot be reduced in size while attacks on persons and property
increase.

Alternatively, the state would have to try to avoid debt and
produce an immediate but temporary balance in the budget by placing *extraordinary taxes* on the shoulders of the richest classes. But
was the party of Order to sacrifice its own wealth on the altar of the
fatherland in order to withdraw the national wealth from exploitation
by the Bourse? *Pas si bête!*[25]

25. It is not so stupid.

Thus, without a total revolution in the French state there can be no revolution in the French state budget. This state budget inevitably led to state indebtedness and this inevitably led to the dominance of the trade in state securities, the rule of the state creditors, bankers, money-dealers and sharks of the Bourse. Only one fraction of the party of Order directly participated in the overthrow of the financial aristocracy – the *manufacturers*. We are not speaking of the medium-sized or smaller people engaged in industry, but rather the rulers of the manufacturing interests, who had formed the broad basis of the dynastic opposition under Louis Philippe. Their interests indubitably lie in a reduction of production costs, hence a reduction of taxation, which is a factor in production costs, hence a reduction of the state debt, the interest on which increases taxation, and hence in the overthrow of the financial aristocracy.

In England – and the largest French manufacturers are petty bourgeois compared with their English rivals – we really find the manufacturers, a Cobden, a Bright,[26] at the head of the crusade against the Bank and the stock-exchange aristocracy. Why not in France? In England industry predominates; in France, agriculture. In England industry requires *free trade*; in France, protective tariffs, a national monopoly alongside the other monopolies. French industry does not dominate French production; French industrialists, therefore, do not dominate the French bourgeoisie. In order to assert their interest against the other fractions of the bourgeoisie they cannot, as can the English, take the lead in a movement and at the same time pursue their own class interests to the extreme; they must follow in the train of the revolution and serve interests which are opposed to the overall interests of their class. In February they had misunderstood their position; February sharpened their wits. And who is more directly threatened by the workers than the employer, the industrial capitalist? In France, therefore, the manufacturer inevitably became the most fanatical member of the party of Order. What is the reduction of his *profit* by finance *compared with the abolition of profit by the proletariat*?

In France the petty bourgeois does what the industrial bourgeois would normally have to do; the worker does what would normally be the task of the petty bourgeois. Who then does the task of the worker? Nobody. It is not accomplished in France; it is only

26. Richard Cobden and John Bright were the leaders of the English 'Free Trade' party (see 'The Chartists', below, pp. 596–7).

proclaimed. And it will not be accomplished within any national walls. The class war within French society will be transformed into a world war in which nation confronts nation. The worker's task will begin to be accomplished only when the world war carries the proletariat to the fore in the nation that dominates the world market, i.e., England. The revolution which here finds not its end but its organizational beginning is no short-winded revolution. The present generation is like the Jews, whom Moses led through the wilderness. They not only have a new world to conquer; they must perish in order to make room for the men who are equal to a new world.

Let us return to Fould.

On 14 November Fould came to the rostrum of the National Assembly and explained his financial system: an apology for the old system of taxation! Retention of the wine tax! Withdrawal of Passy's income tax!

Passy, too, was no revolutionary; he was an old minister of Louis Philippe's. He was a puritan of the Dufaure school and one of the most intimate confidants of Teste, the scapegoat of the July monarchy.[27] Passy, too, had praised the old system of taxation and had recommended the retention of the wine tax; but he had also torn aside the veil from the state deficit. He declared a new tax, the income tax, to be necessary if state bankruptcy was to be avoided. Fould, who had recommended state bankruptcy to Ledru-Rollin, recommended to the Legislative Assembly a state deficit. He promised economies, the nature of which was later revealed as, for example, reducing expenditure by 60 million francs and increasing the floating debt by 200 million francs – conjuring tricks in the arrangement of figures, in the drawing up of accounts, which all finally added up to new loans.

Alongside the other jealous fractions of the bourgeoisie, the financial aristocracy under Fould did not behave in such a shamelessly corrupt manner as under Louis Philippe. But the system remained the same, with a steady increase in debts and the dis-

27. On 8 July 1847, before the Chamber of Peers in Paris, began the trial of Parmentier and General Cubières, charged with bribing civil servants with a view to obtaining a concession for a salt works, and of the then Minister of Public Works, Teste, for accepting such financial bribes. During the trial Teste attempted to commit suicide. All were sentenced to pay heavy fines and Teste, in addition, to three years imprisonment. [*Note by Engels to the 1895 edition.*]

guising of the deficit. And gradually the old Bourse swindling emerged more and more into the open, as evidenced by the law on the Avignon railway, by the mysterious fluctuations in government securities, for a moment the talk of all Paris, finally by Fould's and Bonaparte's abortive speculations on the elections of 10 March.

With the official restoration of the financial aristocracy the French people soon had to face a 24 February once again.

In an attack of misanthropy directed against its heir the Constituent Assembly had abolished the wine tax for the year of our Lord 1850. With the abolition of old taxes, new debts could not be paid. Creton,[28] a cretin of the party of Order, had already moved the retention of the wine tax before the prorogation of the Legislative Assembly. Fould took up this motion in the name of the Bonapartist ministry, and on 20 December 1849, on the anniversary of Bonaparte's proclamation as President, the National Assembly decreed the *restoration of the wine tax.*

The proposer of this resolution was not a financier but the Jesuit leader Montalembert.[29] His deduction was strikingly simple: taxes are the maternal breast at which the government is suckled. The government is represented by the instruments of repression, the organs of authority, the army, the police, the officials, the judges, the ministers, the *priests*. The attack on taxation is an attack by the anarchists on the sentinels of order, who protect the material and spiritual production of bourgeois society from the incursions of the proletarian vandals. Taxation is the fifth god beside property, family, order and religion. And the wine tax is indisputably a tax – furthermore, no ordinary one, but a traditional, a respectable tax, a tax with monarchist loyalties. *Vive l'impôt des boissons![30] Three cheers and one cheer more![31]*

When the French farmer talks of the devil, he pictures him in the guise of a tax collector. From the moment that Montalembert deified taxes the peasant became godless, an atheist, and threw himself into the arms of the devil, *socialism*. The religion of order had forfeited the allegiance of the peasant; the Jesuits had forfeited it; Bonaparte had forfeited it. 20 December 1849 had irrevocably

28. Nicolas Creton was a lawyer and Orleanist, and a deputy in both Assemblies.

29. Charles, comte de Montalembert was a member of both Assemblies and the leader of the clerical party. Originally an Orleanist, he went over to Bonaparte in 1861.

30. Long live the tax on drinks!

31. In English in the original.

compromised 20 December 1848. The 'nephew of his uncle' was not the first in his family to be defeated by this wine tax, which, in Montalembert's expression, smelt the revolutionary storm in the air. The true Napoleon, Napoleon the great, had declared on St Helena that the reintroduction of the wine tax had contributed more to his overthrow than anything else, as it had alienated the peasants of southern France from him. Already the favourite object of popular hatred under Louis XIV (see the writings of Boisguillebert and Vauban),[32] it had been abolished by the first revolution; Napoleon had reintroduced it in 1808 in a modified form. When the Restoration entered France it was not only the cossacks that trotted before it but also promises of the abolition of the wine tax. The *gentilhommerie* naturally did not need to keep its word to the *gent taillable à merci et miséricorde*.[33]

1830 had promised the abolition of the wine tax. It was not its nature to do what it said or to say what it would do. 1848 promised the abolition of the wine tax just as it promised everything. Finally, the Constituent Assembly, which promised nothing, made, as already mentioned, a testamentary provision according to which the wine tax was to disappear on 1 January 1850, and just ten days before 1 January 1850 the Legislative Assembly reintroduced it. The French people were thus in its perpetual pursuit. When they had thrown it out of the door, they saw it come in again through the window.

The popular hatred of the wine tax can be explained by the fact that it unites all that is odious about the French taxation system. The way it is levied is odious; the way it is distributed is aristocratic, for the rates of taxation remain the same for the most common and for the most expensive wines. It increases in geometric progression as the consumer's wealth decreases, an inverted progressive tax, and so directly provokes the poisoning of the working class as a premium on adulterated and imitation wines. It reduces consumption by establishing customs offices at the gates of all towns over 4,000 inhabitants and by transforming every town into a foreign country with protective tariffs against French wine. The great wine merchants, but even more so the small ones, the *marchands de vins*, the small wine-shop keepers

32. Pierre le Pesant, sieur de Boisguillebert, was the founder of classical political economy in France; Sebastien le Prêtre, marquis de Vauban, was a marshal, military engineer and economist.

33. People taxable at their pleasure and at their mercy.

whose livelihood is directly dependent upon the consumption of
wine are, every one of them, avowed enemies of the wine tax. And
lastly, by reducing consumption, the wine tax reduces the producers' market. While it prevents the workers in the towns from
paying for the wine, it prevents the wine growers from selling it.
And France numbers a wine-growing population of about twelve
million. The hatred of the people in general for the wine tax, and
the particular fanaticism of the peasants, is then understandable.
And, furthermore, they saw in its restoration not a particular or
more or less chance event. The peasants have a kind of historical
tradition, which is handed down from father to son, and in this
tradition the saying goes that whenever it wants to deceive the
peasants every government promises the abolition of the wine tax,
and that as soon as it had deceived the peasants it retains or reim-
poses the wine tax. On the question of the wine tax the peasants
test the bouquet, the inclination, of the government. The restoration of the wine tax on 20 December meant: *Louis Bonaparte is
like the others*. However, he was not like the others, he was an
invention of the peasants, and by petitioning in millions against the
wine tax they took back the votes which, a year before, they had
given to the 'nephew of his uncle'.

The rural population of France – over two thirds of the total –
consists for the most part of so-called free *landowners*. The first
generation, which was freed gratuitously from feudal burdens by
the revolution of 1789, did not have to pay for the soil. But the
following generations paid, in the form of the *price of the land*,
what their forefathers, as semi-serfs, had paid in the form of rent,
tithes, socage, etc. The more the population grew, the more the
land was partitioned. The plots of land became dearer, for the
smaller they became the more the demand for them increased. But
as the price which the peasant paid for the land rose, whether he
bought it directly or had it accounted as capital by his coparceners,
so in the same measure the *indebtedness of the peasant*, that is,
his *mortgage*, inevitably grew also. The debt claim with which
land is encumbered is called the *mortgage*, a pawn-ticket for
the land. Just as *privileges* accumulated on medieval estates,
so *mortgages* accumulate on modern plots of land. On the other
hand, under the parcelling system the land is purely an *instrument of production* for its owners. Now, the more the land is
divided, the more its fertility diminishes. The use of machinery on
the land, division of labour, and great soil enrichment measures

such as the digging of canals for drainage and irrigation and the like, become more and more impossible, while the *overhead costs* of cultivation grow proportionally, the more the instrument of production is itself divided up. All this happens regardless of whether the owner of the land possesses capital or not. But the more the land is partitioned, the more the plot of land with its utterly miserable inventory forms the total capital of the peasant farmer, the more capital investment in the land is reduced and the more the cottager lacks the land, money and education necessary to apply the advances in agronomy, so much the more the cultivation of the land retrogresses. Finally, the *net profit* decreases in the same proportion as the *gross consumption* increases, as the whole family of the peasant is held back by its holding from pursuing other occupations and yet is not placed in a position to live by it.

To the same degree, therefore, that the population, and with it the partitioning of the land, increases, the *instrument of production*, the soil, *becomes more expensive*, its *fertility* decreases, *agriculture declines and the peasant falls into debt*. What was an effect becomes in turn a cause. Each generation leaves the next even more indebted; each new generation begins under more unfavourable and more burdensome conditions; mortgages beget mortgages, and if it becomes impossible for the peasant to offer his smallholding as a security for *new debts*, that is, to encumber it with new mortgages, he falls a direct victim to *usury* and the *usurious interest rates* become all the more exorbitant.

And thus it has come about that the peasant cedes to the capitalist – in the form of *interest* on *mortgages* encumbering the soil, in the form of interest on *non-mortgaged usurious advances* – not only a ground rent, not only the industrial profit, in a word, not only the *whole net profit*, but even *a part of his wages*, so that he has sunk to the level of an *Irish tenant farmer* – and all under the pretext of being a *private proprietor*.

This process was accelerated in France by the ever-increasing *tax burden* and by *legal costs*, partly caused by the formalities with which French legislation surrounds landed property, partly by the innumerable conflicts between the smallholdings, which bound and cross each other on all sides, partly by the litigiousness of the peasants, whose enjoyment of property is limited to the fanatical defence of their imaginary property, their *property rights*.

According to a statistical tabulation for 1840, French agricultural production amounted to a gross value of 5,237,178,000 francs. Of this, 3,552,000,000 francs went on the costs of cultivation, including consumption by the labour force. There remains a net product of 1,685,178,000 francs, of which 550 million must be deducted for interest on mortgages, 100 million for legal officials, 350 million for taxes and 107 million for registration money, stamp duty, mortgage fees, etc. One third of the net product remains, 598 million francs;[34] when spread over the population this is not even 25 francs *per capita* net product. These calculations naturally include neither usury outside the field of mortgage nor the costs of lawyers, etc.

The position of the French peasants, after the republic had added new burdens to their old ones, is understandable. It is evident that their exploitation differs only in *form* from that of the industrial proletariat. The exploiter is the same: *capital*. The individual capitalists exploit the individual peasants by means of *mortgage* and *usury*; the capitalist class exploits the peasant class by means of *state taxes*. The peasant's claim to property is the talisman with which capital has hitherto held him under its spell, the pretext on which it set him against the industrial proletariat. Only the fall of capital can raise the peasant, only an anticapitalist, proletarian government can break his economic poverty and his social degradation. The *constitutional republic* is the dictatorship of his united exploiters; the *social-democratic* or *red* republic is the dictatorship of his allies. And the scales rise or fall according to the votes which the peasant casts into the ballot box. He himself has to decide his fate. This is the way the socialists spoke in pamphlets, almanacs, calendars and leaflets of all kinds. This language became more comprehensible to the peasant as a result of the counter-publications of the party of Order, which also addressed him and, striking the true peasant tone with their crude exaggeration and brutal interpretation and representation of the intentions and ideas of the socialists, over-stimulated his lust for forbidden fruit. But most comprehensible of all was the language of the actual experience which the peasant had gained from the use of the franchise and the disappointments which had overwhelmed him, blow upon blow, with revolutionary speed. *Revolutions are the locomotives of history.*

34. Either Marx or his source for these figures has made a mistake; the exact figure here would be 578,178,000. However, the *per capita* net product would then be even less.

There were various symptoms of the gradual revolutionizing of the peasants. It was already evident in the elections to the Legislative Assembly; it was evident in the state of siege in the five departments bordering Lyons; it was evident several months after 13 June in the election of a Montagnard in place of the former chairman of the Chambre introuvable[35] in the department of Gironde. It was evident on 20 December 1849 in the election of a red deputy in place of a deceased Legitimist deputy in the department of Gard,[36] the promised land of the Legitimists, scene of the most terrible atrocities against republicans in 1794 and 1795, and centre of the *terreur blanche* of 1815, when liberals and Protestants were murdered in public. This revolutionizing of the most stationary class has become most obvious since the reintroduction of the wine tax. The government measures and laws of January and February 1850 were directed almost exclusively against the departments and the *peasants*. This is the most striking proof of their progress.

Hautpoul's circular, in which the gendarme was appointed inquisitor of the prefect, of the sub-prefect and, above all, of the mayor, in which espionage was organized even into the hiding places of the remotest village community; *the law against school-teachers*, in which the authorities, the spokesmen, the educators and the interpreters of the peasant class were subjected to the arbitrary power of the prefect and were hounded like beasts, these proletarians of the educated class, from one community to another; *the bill against the mayors*, in which the Damocles sword of dismissal hung over their heads and they, the presidents of the peasant communities, were permanently confronted by the President of the republic and the party of Order; the *ordinance* which transformed the seventeen military divisions of France into four pashalics[37] and imposed the barracks and the bivouac of the French as their national salon; the *education law*, whereby the party of Order proclaimed the unconsciousness and forcible

35. This is the name given by history to the fanatically ultra-royalist, reactionary Chamber of Deputies elected immediately after the second overthrow of Napoleon in 1815. [*Note by Engels to the 1895 edition.*]

36. Favaune, the Montagne's candidate, was elected deputy for Beaune with an absolute majority.

37. By a decree of 10 March 1850 the government redivided France into five large military divisions, putting the most reactionary generals at the head of the Paris region. The republican press nicknamed these divisions pashalics, after the despotic power of the Turkish pasha.

stupefaction of France as conditions vital for its own existence under the rule of universal suffrage – what were all these laws and measures? Desperate attempts to reconquer the departments and their peasantry for the party of Order.

Regarded as *repression*, they were wretched measures which wrung the neck of their own intentions. The major measures, such as the retention of the wine tax, the 45-centime tax, the disdainful rejection of the peasants' petitions for the repayment of the thousand million francs,[38] etc., all these legislative thunderbolts struck the peasant class only once, wholesale, from the centre of government; the laws and measures quoted here made the attack and resistance *general*, the talking-point in every cottage; they inoculated every village with the revolution; *they made the revolution a local matter and a matter for the peasants*.

On the other hand, did these proposals of Bonaparte's and their acceptance by the National Assembly not demonstrate that the two powers of the constitutional republic were united as long as the problem was of repressing 'anarchy' – all classes, that is, that rose up against the bourgeois dictatorship? Had not Soulouque, directly after his harsh message, assured the Legislative Assembly of his *dévouements*[39] to order in the announcement which followed immediately from Carlier, a dirty, mean caricature of Fouché, like Bonaparte's shallow caricature of Napoleon?[40]

The *education law* shows us the alliance of the young Catholics and old Voltaireans. Could the rule of the united bourgeoisie be anything else but the despotic coalition of the pro-Jesuit Restoration and the July monarchy with its free-thinking pretensions? Had not the weapons which the one bourgeois fraction had distributed among the people for use against the other in their struggle for supremacy to be torn from the people again now that it confronted their united dictatorship? Nothing outraged the

38. See above, p. 385.
39. Devotion.
40. Bonaparte's message to the Legislative Assembly of 31 October 1849 announced the dismissal of the Barrot ministry and the formation of a new one. Pierre Carlier, the Bonapartist Prefect of Police in Paris, called on 10 November for the formation of a 'social league against socialism', in order to support 'religion, work, family, property and fidelity to the government'; this was to take living form as the Society of 10 December (see below, pp. 531–2). Joseph Fouché, a former Jacobin who ended up working for Louis XVIII, had been Police Minister under Napoleon and was distinguished by his lack of principles.

Paris shopkeepers more than the coquettish display of Jesuitism, not even the rejection of the *concordats à l'aimable*.

Meanwhile, the clashes between the various fractions of the party of Order, and between the National Assembly and Bonaparte, continued. The National Assembly was far from pleased when Bonaparte, immediately after his coup d'état, after securing his own, Bonapartist, ministry, summoned before him the invalids of the monarchy who had been newly appointed prefects and made their unconstitutional agitation for his re-election as President a condition of their office. It was far from pleased when Carlier celebrated his inauguration by banning a Legitimist club; when Bonaparte founded his own journal, *Le Napoléon*, which betrayed the secret desires of the President to the public, while his ministers had to deny them from the rostrum of the Legislative Assembly. It was far from pleased by the defiant retention of the ministry despite the various votes of no confidence; by the attempt to win the goodwill of NCOs by a daily increment of four sous, and the goodwill of the proletariat by a plagiarism of Eugène Sue's *Mystères*,[41] an honour loan bank. It was far from pleased, finally, by the effrontery with which the ministers were made to propose the deportation of the remaining June insurgents to Algiers in order to heap the unpopularity *en gros*[42] on the Legislative Assembly, while the President reserved popularity for himself *en détail*[43] by individual acts of clemency. Thiers dropped threatening references to 'coups d'état' and '*coups de tête*',[44] and the Legislative Assembly revenged itself on Bonaparte by rejecting every legislative proposal which he put forward on his own behalf, by investigating with a noisy display of mistrust every proposal he made in the public interest in order to see whether he was not aspiring to increase Bonaparte's personal power by increasing the executive power. In a word, it *revenged itself by a conspiracy of contempt*.

For its part, the Legitimist party was vexed to see the more talented Orleanists take control of almost all posts and to see *centralization* grow while it sought its salvation in the principle of *decentralization*. And this was what was happening. The counter-

41. The sentimental social-reformist novelist Eugène Sue, and his book *The Mysteries of Paris*, had been criticized by Marx in *The Holy Family*.

42. Wholesale.

43. Retail.

44. Rash acts.

revolution *centralized by force*; that is, it prepared the mechanism of revolution. It even *centralized* the gold and silver of France in the Paris Bank through the compulsory quotation of banknotes, and so created the *ready war chest* of the revolution.

Lastly, the Orleanists were vexed to see the principle of legitimacy emerge in opposition to their own bastard principle and to find themselves permanently snubbed and maltreated as the bourgeois *mésalliance* of a noble spouse.

Gradually we have seen peasants, petty bourgeois, the middle classes in general siding with the proletariat, driven into open conflict with the official republic and treated by it as antagonists. *Resistance to bourgeois dictatorship, need for a change in society, retention of democratic republican institutions as the means to this end, regrouping around the proletariat as the decisive revolutionary force* – these are the common characteristics of the *so-called party of social democracy, the party of the red republic*. This party of Anarchy, as its opponents christened it, is no less a coalition of various interests than the party of Order. From the smallest reform of the old social disorder to the overthrow of the old social order, from bourgeois liberalism to revolutionary terrorism – this is the distance between the extremes which form the starting point and the finishing point of the 'party of Anarchy'.

Abolition of the protective tariffs – socialism! For it strikes at the monopoly of the *industrial* fraction of the party of Order. Regulation of the state budget – socialism! For it strikes at the monopoly of the *financial* fraction of the party of Order. Free admission for foreign meat and corn – socialism! For it strikes at the monopoly of the third fraction of the party of Order, *large landed property*. In France the demands of the free-trade party, that is, of the most advanced English bourgeois party, appear as so many socialist demands. Voltaireanism – socialism! For it strikes at a fourth fraction of the party of Order – the Catholic fraction. Freedom of the press, freedom of association, universal public education – socialism, socialism! They strike at the general monopoly of the party of Order.

So rapidly had the course of the revolution ripened conditions that reformists of all shades, even the most moderate claimants of the middle classes, were forced to group themselves around the banner of the most extreme party of revolution, around the *red flag*.

Yet however manifold the *socialism* of the various major

sections of the party of Anarchy, according to the economic conditions and the consequent overall revolutionary demands of their class or class fraction, in *one* point it is in harmony: in proclaiming itself the *means of emancipating the proletariat*, and proclaiming the emancipation of the latter as its *aim*. Deliberate deception by some, self-deception by others, who give out the world transformed in accordance with their own needs as the best world for all, as the realization of all revolutionary claims and the removal of all revolutionary conflicts.

And concealed beneath the *general* socialist phrases of the 'party of Anarchy', all more or less identical, there is the socialism of the *National*, of the *Presse* and of the *Siècle*, which is more or less consistent in its desire to overthrow the rule of the financial aristocracy and to liberate industry and commerce from the forces which have fettered them hitherto. This is the socialism of industry, trade and agriculture, whose rulers in the party of Order deny these interests in so far as they no longer accord with their private monopolies. There is a distinction between this *bourgeois socialism*, to which, as to every variety of socialism, a section of the workers and the petty bourgeoisie rallies, and socialism proper, *petty-bourgeois socialism*, socialism *par excellence*. Capital hounds the members of this class mainly as a creditor, so they demand *credit institutions*; it crushes them by *competition*, so they demand *producers' cooperatives* supported by the state; it overwhelms them by *concentration*, so they demand *progressive taxation*, limitations on inheritance, the taking over of large construction projects by the state, and other measures that will *forcibly check the growth of capital*. Since they dream of the peaceful implementation of their socialism – allowing possibly for a second, brief February revolution – the coming historical process appears to them as an *application* of systems, which the thinkers of society, either in company with others, or as single inventors, devise or have devised. In this way they become the eclectics or adepts of existing socialist *systems*, of *doctrinaire socialism*, which was the theoretical expression of the proletariat only as long as it had not yet developed further and become a free, autonomous, historical movement.[45]

The *utopia*, *doctrinaire socialism*, subordinates the total movement to one of its elements, substitutes for common social pro-

45. See the Introduction to *The Revolutions of 1848*, above, pp. 16–19, and section III of the *Manifesto of the Communist Party*, above, pp. 87–91.

duction the brainwork of individual pedants and, above all, in its fantasy dispenses with the revolutionary struggle of classes and its requirements by means of small conjuring tricks or great sentimentalities; fundamentally it only idealizes the existing society, takes a picture of it free of shadows and aspires to assert its ideal picture against the reality of this society. While this socialism is thus left by the proletariat to the petty bourgeoisie, while the struggle of the various socialist leaders among themselves holds up each of the so-called systems in contrast to the others as a solemn adherence to one of the intermediate points along the path of social revolution – the proletariat rallies ever more around *revolutionary socialism*, around *communism*, for which the bourgeoisie itself has invented the name of Blanqui. This socialism is the *declaration of the permanence of the revolution*, the *class dictatorship* of the proletariat as a necessary intermediate point on the path towards the *abolition of class differences in general*, the abolition of all relations of production on which they are based, the abolition of all social relations which correspond to these relations of production, and the revolutionizing of all ideas which stem from these social relations.

The scope of this account does not allow further discussion of this subject.

We have seen: just as in the party of Order the *financial aristocracy* inevitably took the lead, so, too, in the 'party of Anarchy' did the *proletariat*. While the various classes which united in a revolutionary league rallied around the proletariat, while the departments became more and more unsafe and the Legislative Assembly itself became even more sullen towards the pretensions of the French Soulouque, the long-deferred and delayed by-elections approached which were to replace the Montagnards proscribed after 13 June.

The government, despised by its enemies, abused and humiliated daily by its supposed friends, saw only *one* means of escaping from the repugnant and untenable situation – a *revolt*. A revolt in Paris would have permitted it to proclaim a state of siege in Paris and the departments and thus to control the elections. On the other hand, the friends of order were obliged to make concessions to a government which had achieved a victory over anarchy, if they did not want to appear as anarchists themselves.

The government set to work. At the beginning of February 1850, provocation of the people by chopping down the liberty trees.[46] In vain. If the liberty trees lost their place the government itself lost its head and recoiled, frightened by its own provocation. The National Assembly, however, received this clumsy attempt at emancipation by Bonaparte with ice-cold mistrust. The removal of the wreaths of immortelles from the July Column[47] was no more successful. It gave a part of the army the opportunity for revolutionary demonstrations and the National Assembly cause for a more or less veiled vote of no confidence in the ministry. The government press threatened in vain the abolition of universal suffrage and the invasion of the cossacks. Hautpoul's direct challenge to the Left, issued in the middle of the Legislative Assembly, to betake itself onto the streets, and his declaration that the government was ready to receive it, was also in vain. Hautpoul received only a call to order from the chairman, and the party of Order, with silent, malicious pleasure, allowed a deputy of the Left to mock Bonaparte's usurpatory desires.[48] Finally, the prophesy of a revolution on 24 February was also in vain. The result of the government's prophesy was that the people ignored 24 February.

The proletariat did not allow itself to be provoked into a *revolt*, because it was about to carry out a *revolution*.

Unhindered by the provocations of the government, which only increased the general irritation at the existing situation, the election committee, completely under the influence of the workers, nominated three candidates for Paris: de Flotte, Vidal and Carnot. De Flotte was a June deportee, who had been amnestied as a result of one of Bonaparte's popularity-seeking schemes; he was a friend of Blanqui's and had taken part in the attempt of 15 May. Vidal, known as a communist writer by his book *On the Distribution of Wealth*, was a former secretary to Louis Blanc in the Luxembourg Commission. Carnot, the son of the Convention's organizer of victory, was the least compromised member of the *National* party, Minister of Education in the Provisional Government and the Executive Commission, with his democratic public

46. The tradition of planting liberty trees, generally oaks or poplars, dated back to the revolution of 1789; the trees in question here had been planted after February 1848.

47. The July Column, erected to celebrate the 1830 revolution, had been decked with immortelles after the February revolution.

48. When deputy Pascal Duprat stated on 16 February that Louis Bonaparte would have to choose between the role of his uncle or that of Washington, a Left deputy interrupted, 'Or Soulouque.'

education bill a living protest against the education law of the Jesuits. The three candidates represented the three allied classes. At the head, the June insurgent, the representative of the revolutionary proletariat; next to him, the doctrinaire socialist, the representative of the socialist petty bourgeoisie; finally, the third, the representative of the republican bourgeois party, whose democratic formulas had gained a socialist significance in the struggle with the party of Order and had long since lost their own significance. It was a *general coalition against the bourgeoisie and the government, as in February*. But this time the *proletariat was the head of the revolutionary league*.

In spite of all endeavours the socialist candidates won. The army itself voted for the June insurgent against its own War Minister, La Hitte.[49] The party of Order was thunderstruck. The departmental elections brought them no solace; they produced a majority for the Montagnards.

The election of 10 March 1850 was the revocation of June 1848! The butchers and deporters of the June insurgents returned to the National Assembly, but bowed down, in the wake of the deportees, with their principles on their lips. *It was the revocation of 13 June 1849*: the Montagne, proscribed by the National Assembly, returned to the National Assembly, but as the advanced trumpeters of the revolution, no longer as its commander. *It was the revocation of 10 December*: Napoleon had failed with his minister, La Hitte. There is only one analogy in the parliamentary history of France: the rejection of d'Haussez, a minister of Charles X, in 1830. Finally, the election of 10 March 1850 was the annulment of the election of 13 May [1849], which had given the party of Order a majority. The election of 10 March was a protest against the majority of 13 May. 10 March was a revolution. Behind the ballot slips lay the paving stones.

'The vote of 10 March means war,' cried Ségur d'Aguesseau,[50] one of the most advanced members of the party of Order.

With 10 March 1850 the constitutional republic entered a new phase, *the phase of its dissolution*. The different fractions of the majority are again at one with each other and with Bonaparte; they are again the saviours of order; he is again their *neutral man*.

49. Jean-Ernest Ducos, vicomte de La Hitte was a general and Bonapartist, Foreign Minister and Minister of War, 1849–51.

50. Raymond, comte de Ségur d'Aguesseau was a lawyer and an opportunist politician.

If they remember that they are royalists this only happens out of despair at the possibility of the bourgeois republic; if he remembers that he is a pretender, this only happens because he despairs of remaining President.

At the command of the party of Order Bonaparte answers the election of de Flotte, the June insurgent, with the appointment of Baroche[51] as Minister of the Interior – Baroche, the prosecutor of Blanqui and Barbès, Ledru-Rollin and Guinard.[52] The Legislative Assembly answers the election of Carnot with the adoption of the education law and the election of Vidal with the suppression of the socialist press. The party of Order seeks to dispel its own fear with trumpet blasts from its press. 'The sword is holy,' cries one of its organs. 'The defenders of order must take the offensive against the Red party,' declares another. 'Between socialism and society there is a duel to the death, an unceasing, relentless war; in this duel of desperation one or the other must perish; if society does not destroy socialism, socialism will destroy society,' crows another cock of order. Erect the barricades of order, the barricades of religion, the barricades of the family. An end must be made of the 127,000 voters of Paris![53] A Bartholomew's night for the socialists! And for a moment the party of Order believes its own confidence in its victory.

Their organs hold forth most fanatically against the '*shopkeepers of Paris*'. The June insurgent elected as a representative by the shopkeepers of Paris! This means a second June 1848 is impossible; it means a second 13 June [1849] is impossible; it means the moral influence of capital is broken; it means that the bourgeois Assembly now represents only the bourgeoisie, that big property is lost because its vassal, small property, seeks its salvation in the camp of the propertyless.

The party of Order, of course, returns to its inevitable *commonplace*: *More repression!* it calls, *Tenfold repression!* But its powers of repression have been reduced tenfold while resistance has increased a hundredfold. Must not the main instrument of repression itself, the army, be repressed? And the party of Order

51. Pierre-Jules Baroche, a lawyer and a deputy in both Assemblies, was originally an Orleanist, but had become a Bonapartist by 1850.

52. Auguste-Joseph Guinard was a Montagne deputy in the Constituent National Assembly, condemned to exile for life for his part in the demonstration of 13 June 1849.

53. De Flotte had gained 126,643 votes in the election of 15 March.

speaks its last word: 'The iron ring of stifling legality must be broken. The *constitutional republic is impossible*. We must fight with our true weapons; since February 1848 we have fought the revolution with *its* weapons on *its* terrain; we have accepted *its* institutions; the Constitution is a fortress which only protects the besiegers and not the besieged! By smuggling ourselves into holy Ilion in the belly of the Trojan horse we have, unlike our fore-fathers, the *Grecs*,[54] not conquered the hostile city but made prisoners of ourselves.'

However, the basis of the Constitution is *universal suffrage. The destruction of universal suffrage* – this is the last word of the party of Order, of the bourgeois dictatorship.

On 4 May 1848, 20 December 1848, 13 May 1849 and 8 July 1849, universal suffrage declared them right. On 10 March 1850 universal suffrage declared that it had itself been wrong. Bourgeois rule as the product and result of universal suffrage, as the express act of sovereign will of the people – this is what the bourgeois Constitution means.

But does the Constitution still have any meaning the moment that the content of this suffrage, this sovereign will, is no longer bourgeois rule? Is it not the duty of the bourgeoisie to regulate the franchise so that it demands what is reasonable, *its* rule? By repeatedly terminating the existing state power and by creating it anew from itself does not universal suffrage destroy all stability; does it not perpetually call all existing powers into question; does it not destroy authority; does it not threaten to elevate anarchy itself to the level of authority? Who could still doubt this after 10 March 1850?

By repudiating universal suffrage, with which it had draped itself hitherto and from which it drew its omnipotence, the bourgeoisie openly confesses: *Our dictatorship has existed hitherto by the will of the people; it must now be consolidated against the will of the people*. And, with all consistency, it no longer seeks its supports in France, but outside, abroad, in *invasion*.

With the invasion, like a second Coblenz,[55] with its seat established in France itself, it arouses all the national passions against itself. With this attack on universal suffrage it gives the new

54. Grecs – A play on words: Greeks, but also professional cheats. [*Note by Engels to the 1895 edition.*]

55. Coblenz had been the centre of the counter-revolutionary emigration during the first French revolution.

revolution a *general pretext*, and the revolution needs such a pretext. Every *particular* pretext would divide the fractions of the revolutionary league and expose their differences. The *general* pretext dulls the perceptions of the half-revolutionary classes; it enables them to deceive themselves as to the *specific character* of the coming revolution, as to the consequences of its own deeds. Every revolution needs a banquet question. Universal suffrage is the banquet question of the new revolution.

The bourgeois fractions in their coalition are already condemned, in so far as they take flight from the only possible form of their *joint* power, from the mightiest and most complete form of their *class rule*, the *constitutional republic*, by returning to the subordinate, incomplete, weaker form of the *monarchy*. They resemble that old man who, in order to regain his youthful strength, fetched out his boyhood clothes and tormented his withered limbs by trying to get them on. Their republic had only *one* merit; *it was the forcing house of the revolution*.

10 March 1850 bears the inscription: *Après moi le déluge!* After me the deluge!

IV. THE ABOLITION OF UNIVERSAL SUFFRAGE IN 1850

(The continuation of the three preceding chapters is to be found in the 'Review' in the double number 5/6 of the *Neue Rheinische Zeitung* [*Revue*], which was the last to appear. After a description of the great commercial crisis which broke out in England in 1847 and an explanation of how political complications came to a head in the revolutions of February and March 1848 as a result of its repercussions on the European continent, it is then shown how the commercial and industrial prosperity which set in again in the course of 1848 and increased still further in 1849 paralysed the revolutionary upsurge and made possible the simultaneous victories of the forces of reaction. Then, with particular reference to France, it is said:)[56]

The same symptoms have been evident in France since 1850. Parisian industry is working at full capacity, and even the cotton factories of Rouen and Mulhouse are in quite a good state, although here, as in England, high prices have had a dampening

56. Foreword written by Engels for the 1895 edition. This chapter is composed of two separate excerpts from the 'Review: May–October 1850', as indicated here by the asterisk on p. 131. The remainder of this 'Review' is printed in *The Revolutions of 1848*.

effect. The development of prosperity in France has been further encouraged, in particular, by comprehensive tariff reform in Spain and by reduction of duties on various luxury goods in Mexico. Exports of French goods to both markets have increased significantly. The accumulation of capital in France has led to a series of speculative ventures conducted on the pretext of the large-scale exploitation of the Californian gold-mines. A large number of companies have emerged whose low stock prices and prospectuses with socialist overtones have made a direct appeal to the purses of the petty bourgeoisie and workers, but which jointly and severally add up to that pure form of fraud which is peculiar to the French and Chinese. One of these companies is even under the patronage of the government. The French import duties brought in some 63 million francs in the first nine months of 1848, 95 million in the corresponding period of 1849 and 93 million in 1850. Moreover, in September 1850 this revenue rose again by more than a million francs over the same month in 1849. Exports have also risen in 1849 and even more so in 1850.

The most striking proof of the restored prosperity is the reintroduction of cash payments by the Bank following the law of 6 August 1850. On 15 March 1848 the Bank had been empowered to suspend its cash payments. At that time its notes in circulation, together with those of the provincial banks, amounted to 373 million francs (£14,920,000). On 2 November 1849 the circulation stood at 482 million francs, or £19,280,000, an increase of £4,360,000, and on 2 September 1850, 496 million francs, or £19,840,000, an increase of about £5 million. During this time no depreciation of the notes occurred; on the contrary, the increased note circulation was accompanied by a constant accumulation of gold and silver in the Bank's vaults, so that in summer 1850 its cash reserves ran to about £14 million, an incredible amount for France. The fact that the Bank was thereby in a position to increase its note issue, and thus its active capital, by 123 million francs, or £5 million, proves conclusively how correct was our assertion in an earlier number that the financial aristocracy was not only not overthrown by the February revolution but in fact actually strengthened by it.[57] This becomes even more evident from a survey of French bank legislation of the last few years. On 10 June 1847 the Bank was empowered to issue 200-franc notes; the lowest note until then had been 500 francs. A decree of 15

57. Above, p. 443.

March 1848 declared the notes of the Bank of France to be legal tender and relieved the Bank of the obligation to exchange them for cash. Its note issue was limited to 350 million francs, and it was now empowered to issue 100-franc notes. A decree of 27 April ordered the merger of the departmental banks with the Bank of France; another decree of 2 May 1848 raised the total note issue to 452 million francs, and a decree of 22 December 1849 further raised the maximum issue to 525 million francs. Finally the law of 6 August 1850 reintroduced the convertibility of notes into coin. These facts, the continuous increase in circulation and the concentration of all French gold and silver in the Bank vaults, led Monsieur Proudhon to the conclusion that the Bank would have to cast off its old skin and metamorphose itself into a Proudhon-type people's bank.[58] He did not even need to know the history of the English Bank restrictions of 1797–1819,[59] he needed only direct his attention across the Channel to see that this situation, unknown to him in the history of bourgeois society, was no more than an eminently normal bourgeois event, which was only now taking place in France for the first time. It is clear that the supposedly revolutionary theoreticians who talked so big, in the manner of the Provisional Government in Paris, were just as ignorant of the nature and outcome of the measures which had been taken as were the gentlemen of the Provisional Government themselves.

In spite of the industrial and commercial prosperity which France is enjoying at the moment, the mass of the population, the 25 million peasants, are in the throes of a great depression. The good harvests of the past few years have forced down corn prices in France even lower than in England, and the position of the debt-ridden peasants, sucked dry by usury and burdened by taxes, is by no means splendid! But the history of the last three years has sufficiently proved that this class is absolutely incapable of any revolutionary initiative.

Just as the period of crisis occurred later on the Continent than in England, so did the period of prosperity. The original process always takes place in England; it is the demiurge of the bourgeois cosmos. The different phases of the cyclical motion of bourgeois

58. Proudhon had currently put forward this position in a pamphlet directed against the bourgeois economist Frédéric Bastiat, entitled *Gratuité de crédit*. Marx had criticized Proudhon's doctrines in *The Poverty of Philosophy*.

59. Between 1797 and 1821, under the Bank Restriction Act of 1797, the British banks were absolved from the requirement of exchanging notes for specie.

society occur on the Continent in a secondary and tertiary form. On the one hand, the Continent exports far more to England than to any other country, and these exports depend on conditions in England, particularly with regard to the overseas market. England exports far more to countries overseas than does the whole Continent, so that the quantity of continental exports to these countries always depends on England's exports at the time. So, although the crises produce revolution on the Continent first, they nevertheless have their roots in England. These violent convulsions must necessarily occur at the extremities of the bourgeois organism rather than at its heart, where the possibility of restoring the balance is greater. On the other hand, the degree to which the continental revolutions have repercussions on England is also the thermometer by which one can measure how far they really challenge bourgeois conditions of life, rather than affecting only its political formations.

While this general prosperity lasts, enabling the productive forces of bourgeois society to develop to the full extent possible within the bourgeois system, there can be no question of a real revolution. Such a revolution is only possible at a time when *two factors* come into *conflict*: the *modern productive forces* and the *bourgeois forms of production*. Far from giving rise to new revolutions, the various squabbles in which the individual fractions of the continental party of Order now indulge and compromise themselves are, on the contrary, only possible because the basic situation at the moment is so secure and – what the forces of reaction do not know – so *bourgeois*. All reactionary attempts to hold up bourgeois development will rebound in the face of this basic situation, as will all the moral outrage and enthusiastic proclamations of the democrats. *A new revolution is only possible as a result of a new crisis; but it will come, just as surely as the crisis itself.*

*

Let us now return to France.

The victory which the people had won in alliance with the petty bourgeoisie in the election of 10 March was annulled by the people themselves when they provoked the new election of 28 April. Vidal was elected in the department of Bas-Rhin as well as in Paris.[60] The Paris committee, on which the Montagne and the

---

60. Bas-Rhin was one of the departments of Alsace, with Strasbourg as its capital.

petty bourgeoisie were strongly represented, induced him to accept for Bas-Rhin. The victory of 10 March ceased to be decisive. The date for a decision was postponed yet again, the people's resilient mood weakened, and they became used to legal triumphs instead of revolutionary ones. The revolutionary significance of 10 March, the rehabilitation of the June insurrection, was finally completely destroyed by the candidature of Eugène Sue, the sentimental petty-bourgeois social dreamer, whom the proletariat could at best accept as a joke, as a favour to the *grisettes*.[61] To oppose this well-intentioned candidature, the party of Order, which had become bolder as a result of its opponents' vacillating policy, put forward a candidate who was to represent their June *victory*. This strange candidate was the Spartan *paterfamilias* Leclerc,[62] whose heroic armour, however, was stripped from his body piece by piece by the press, and who was spectacularly defeated in the election. The new electoral victory of 28 April made the Montagne and the petty bourgeoisie over-confident. They were already rejoicing at the thought of being able to achieve their aims by purely legal means, without pushing the proletariat into the foreground again with a new revolution. They fully counted on bringing Monsieur Ledru-Rollin into the presidential chair and a majority of Montagnards into the Assembly by means of universal suffrage in the new elections of 1852. The party of Order, completely reassured by the forthcoming election, by Sue's candidature and by the mood of the Montagne and petty bourgeoisie that the latter were determined to remain peaceful whatever happened, answered both election victories with an *electoral law* which abolished universal suffrage.

The government took great care not to take responsibility for the presentation of this bill. It made an apparent concession to the majority by delegating the preparation of the bill to the high dignitaries of this majority, the seventeen burgraves.[63] Thus the

61. Working girls.

62. Alexandre Leclerc was a Paris merchant.

63. The Commission of Seventeen was set up by the Minister of the Interior on 1 May 1850 to draft a new electoral law. 'Burgraves' was the nickname given to the committee of the leading Orleanist and Legitimist parliamentarians which formulated the policy of the party of Order in the National Assembly. In fact the Commission of Seventeen included not only the five most important burgraves, Molé, Berryer, de Broglie, Montalembert and Thiers, but also a number of people chosen by the government from outside the Assembly.

abolition of universal suffrage was not proposed to the Assembly by the government; the majority of the Assembly itself made the proposal.

On 8 May the project was brought before the Chamber. The whole social-democratic press rose to a man to preach to the people dignified behaviour, *calme majestueux*, passivity, and trust in its elected representatives. Every article in these papers was an admission that a revolution would inevitably lead to the destruction of, above all, the so-called revolutionary press and that it was therefore now a question of self-preservation. The supposedly revolutionary press betrayed its whole secret. It signed its own death warrant.

On 21 May the Montagne opened the debate by moving the rejection of the entire proposal on the grounds that it violated the Constitution. The party of Order answered that the Constitution would be infringed if necessary, but that this was not necessary because the Constitution was capable of any interpretation and the majority alone had the authority to decide on the correct interpretation. The Montagne countered the uncontrolled and wild attacks of Thiers and Montalembert with a decent and educated humanism. They presented arguments based upon a legal foundation; the party of Order referred them to the foundations upon which the law stands – bourgeois property. The Montagne whimpered: *Did they really want to do their best to bring about a revolution?* The party of Order replied that they would wait and see.

On 22 May the preliminary question was settled by a vote of 462 to 227. The same men who had demonstrated so solemnly and thoroughly that the National Assembly and every single deputy would be abandoning their responsibility if they abandoned the people, their mandator, remained in their seats and sought to make the country act in their stead with petitions. They still remained seated and unmoved when the law was passed in spectacular fashion on 31 May. They tried to revenge themselves with a protest, in which they put on record their innocence of this gross violation of the Constitution, a protest which they did not even submit openly but smuggled into the chairman's pocket behind his back.

An army of 150,000 men in Paris, the long postponement of the decision, the calls for restraint from the press, the pusillanimity of the Montagne and the newly elected representatives, the majestic calm of the petty bourgeoisie and, above all, the commercial and industrial prosperity: all these prevented any attempt at revolution on the part of the proletariat.

Universal suffrage had fulfilled its mission, the only function which it can have in a revolutionary period. The majority of the people had passed through the school of development it provided. It had to be abolished – by revolution or by reaction.

On a subsequent occasion the Montagne soon expended even more energy. From the rostrum, War Minister Hautpoul had called the February revolution a dire catastrophe. The spokesmen of the Montagne, who distinguished themselves, as usual, by their noisy moral indignation, were prevented from speaking by the chairman, Dupin.[64] Girardin[65] proposed to the Montagne that they immediately leave *en masse*. Result: the Montagne remained seated, but Girardin was cast out from their midst as unworthy.

The electoral law required its completion by a new press law. This was not long in coming. A bill proposed by the government, considerably sharpened by the amendments of the party of Order, raised caution money, imposed an extra stamp duty on novels in magazine form (in answer to the election of Eugène Sue), taxed all publications up to a certain number of pages appearing in weekly or monthly editions and, in conclusion, decreed that every article in a journal had to bear the signature of its author. The regulations concerning caution money killed the so-called revolutionary press; the people regarded its demise as retribution for the abolition of universal suffrage. However, neither the purpose nor the effect of the new law was limited to this section of the press. So long as the press was anonymous it appeared as the organ of a public opinion without number or name; it was the third power in the state. With the signature of each article a newspaper became merely a collection of journalistic contributions by more or less well-known individuals. Every article sank to the level of an advertisement. Hitherto the newspapers had circulated as the paper money of public opinion; now they were reduced to more or less worthless promissory notes, whose value

64. André-Marie Dupin was a lawyer and an Orleanist politician, chairman of the Chamber of Deputies from 1832 to 1839 and of the Legislative Assembly from 1849 to 1851; subsequently a Bonapartist.

65. Émile de Girardin was a journalist and politician of varying political views. Before 1848 he opposed Guizot, during the revolution he was a 'pure republican', and later he became a Bonapartist. He sat in the Legislative Assembly from 1850 to 1851.

and circulation depended on the credit, not only of the issuer, but also of the endorser. The press of the party of Order, which had provoked the abolition of universal suffrage, had also urged the most extreme measures against the bad press. However, the good press itself, in its sinister anonymity, had become uncomfortable for the party of Order and even more so for its individual provincial representatives. The party of Order demanded to be confronted only by paid writers, with names, addresses and further personal particulars. The good press bewailed in vain the ingratitude with which their services were rewarded. The law was passed; the regulation concerning the inclusion of names hit them most of all. The names of the Republican daily columnists were fairly well known, but the respectable firms of the *Journal des Débats*, the *Assemblée nationale*, the *Constitutionnel*,[66] etc., with their loftily proclaimed political wisdom, cut wretched figures when the mysterious company suddenly turned out to be corrupt *penny-a-liners*[67] of long practice who defended all possible causes for ready cash, like Granier de Cassagnac, or spineless old scribblers who call themselves statesmen, like Capefigue, or coquettish fops, like Monsieur Lemoinne[68] of the *Débats*.

In the debate on the press law the Montagne had already sunk to such a level of moral degradation that it was obliged to limit itself to applauding the splendid tirades of an old notable from the days of Louis Philippe, Monsieur Victor Hugo.

With the election law and the press law the revolutionary and democratic party quits the official stage. Before its departure home, shortly after the end of the session, both fractions of the Montagne – the social democrats and the democratic socialists – issued manifestos, two declarations of incompetence, in which they proved that although force and success had never been on their side, they had nevertheless always been on the side of eternal justice and all the other eternal truths.

Let us now examine the party of Order. As the *Neue Rheinische Zeitung* said in its last issue:[69]

66. These were all daily papers which supported the party of Order.

67. English in the original.

68. Bernard-Adolphe Granier de Cassagnac was an Orleanist before the 1848 revolution, later a Bonapartist and a member of the Legislative Body under the Second Empire. Jean-Baptiste Capefigue was a novelist and historian, and an ultra-royalist. John-Emile Lemoinne was the English correspondent of the *Journal des Débats*.

69. See above, pp. 442–3.

In the face of the restorationist desires of the united Orleanists and Legitimists ... Bonaparte defend[ed] his actual power: the republic. In the face of Bonaparte's restorationist desires the fractions of the party of Order defended their joint power: the republic. The Orleanists confronted the Legitimists, and the Legitimists the Orleanists, as the representatives of the status quo: the republic. All these fractions of the party of Order, each of which had its own king and restoration *in petto*, in turn enforced the joint rule of the bourgeoisie in opposition to the usurpatory and mutinous desires of the rival pretenders: they enforced that form of society in which particular claim of the various parties were held in check and neutralized – the republic ... And Thiers spoke truer than he knew, when he said, 'We the royalists, are the true pillars of the constitutional republic.'

This comedy of these *republicains malgré eux* – the aversion to the status quo and the constant attempts to consolidate it; the incessant conflicts between Bonaparte and the National Assembly; the ever-renewed threat that the party of Order would split up into its component parts, and the ever repeated reunification of its fractions; the attempt made by each fraction to transform every victory against the common enemy into a defeat for its temporary allies; the petty jealousy on both sides, the vindictiveness, the harassment, the tireless drawing of swords, which always ends with the farcical *baiser Lamourette*[70] – this unedifying comedy of errors has never developed in a more classical fashion than in the last six months.

The party of Order also regards the electoral law as a victory against Bonaparte. Had the government not abdicated power by leaving the formulation and responsibility for its own proposal to the Commission of Seventeen? And was not Bonaparte's main strength against the Assembly based on the fact that he was the choice of six million voters? Bonaparte, for his part, treated the electoral law as a concession to the Assembly, with which he claimed to have bought harmony between the legislative and executive powers. By way of payment the base adventurer demanded an increase in his civil list of three million francs. Could the National Assembly enter into a conflict with the executive at a moment when it had divested the great majority of the French people of its rights? It rose up in anger, and it seemed prepared to

70. 'Lamourette's kiss': on 7 July 1792 Lamourette, a deputy, prevailed on his warring colleagues in the Constitutional Assembly to forget their differences and embrace one another; needless to say, this reconciliation was specious and transient.

bring matters to a head. Its Commission rejected the motion and the Bonapartist press issued warnings and pointed to the disinherited, disenfranchised people. After a large number of noisy transactions the Assembly finally gave way on the particular issue, but at the same time it gained its revenge on the question of principle. Instead of granting him the annual increase in the civil list of three million francs demanded on principle, it made him an accommodation of 2,160,000 francs. Not satisfied with this, it made this concession only after it had been supported by Changarnier, the general of the party of Order and the protector with whom they had saddled Bonaparte. So it actually approved the two million francs not for Bonaparte but for Changarnier.

This gift, flung at his feet *de mauvaise grâce*,[71] was picked up by Bonaparte in quite the same spirit as it was given. Again the Bonapartist press raged against the National Assembly. When the amendment on journalists' signatures – which was particularly aimed at the less important papers which represented Bonaparte's private interests – was first introduced during the debate on the press law, the main Bonapartist paper, *Le Pouvoir*, published an open and virulent attack on the National Assembly. The ministers had to disassociate themselves from the paper before the Assembly; the publisher of the *Pouvoir* was summoned before the bar of the Assembly and the highest possible fine, 5,000 francs, was imposed upon him. The next day the *Pouvoir* published an even more insolent article against the Assembly, and by way of governmental revenge the Public Prosecutor brought actions against several Legitimist papers for violating the Constitution.

Finally the question arose of the prorogation of parliament. Bonaparte wanted this in order to be able to operate unhindered by the Assembly. The party of Order wanted it, partly in order to complete its fractional intrigues and partly so that the individual deputies could pursue their private interests. Both needed it in order to consolidate and increase the victories of the forces of reaction in the provinces. The Assembly thus adjourned from 11 August until 11 November. However, as Bonaparte made absolutely no secret of the fact that his sole concern was to rid himself of the burdensome supervision of the National Assembly, it added to the vote of confidence a stamp of no confidence in the President. All Bonapartists were excluded from the Standing

71. In a bad spirit.

Commission of twenty-eight members who stayed on during the recess to act as the moral guardians of the republic. In place of the Bonapartists even a few republicans from the *Siècle* and the *National* were voted in, in order to demonstrate to the President the allegiance of the majority to the constitutional republic.

Shortly before and especially shortly after the parliamentary adjournment the two great fractions of the party of Order, Orleanists and Legitimists, showed signs of wanting reconciliation through an alliance of the two royal houses under whose banner they fought. The papers were full of suggestions for such a reconciliation, which had supposedly been discussed at Louis Philippe's sick bed at St Leonards, when Louis Philippe's death suddenly simplified the situation. Louis Philippe was the usurper, Henri V the usurped; the comte de Paris,[72] on the other hand, was the rightful heir to Henri V's throne, as the latter had no children. Now every pretext for opposition to the fusion of the dynastic interests was removed. But at precisely this moment the two fractions of the bourgeoisie discovered that it was not devotion to a particular royal house which divided them, but that it was rather their separate class interests which divided the two dynasties. The Legitimists, who had undertaken the pilgrimage to Henri V's royal camp at Wiesbaden, just as their rivals had gone to St Leonards, received the news there of Louis Philippe's death.[73] They immediately formed a ministry *in partibus infidelium*,[74] which consisted mostly of members of the commission of moral guardians of the republic and which, on the occasion of a domestic squabble in the bosom of the party, stepped forward with the most unequivocal proclamation of divine right.[75] The Orleanists rejoiced over the compromising scandal which this manifesto provoked in the press and did not disguise for one second their open enmity towards the Legitimists.

During the adjournment of the National Assembly the Departmental Councils met. The majority of them declared in favour of a revision of the Constitution hedged to a greater or lesser degree

72. Louis-Philippe-Albert, grandson of Louis Philippe.

73. On 26 August 1850.

74. 'In the lands of the infidels': a favoured expression of Marx's, taken from the title of Catholic bishops appointed to non-Christian territories where they could not reside.

75. Marx refers to the Wiesbaden manifesto of August 1850, in which the comte de Chambord rejected the idea of an appeal to the people as the basis of monarchist restoration.

by clauses and safeguards; that is, they declared themselves in favour of a 'solution' in the form of a monarchist restoration, which was not more closely defined. At the same time they admitted that they were not authorized and, in fact, too cowardly to find such a solution. The Bonapartist fraction immediately interpreted this wish for revision as meaning an extension of Bonaparte's presidency.

The constitutional solution – Bonaparte's retirement in May 1852, the simultaneous election of a new President by the whole electorate, the revision of the Constitution by a revisionary chamber in the first four months of the new presidency – is completely intolerable for the ruling class. The day of the new presidential election would be the day of decision for all the opposing parties: Legitimists, Orleanists, bourgeois republicans and revolutionaries. A decision between the different parties would have to be reached by force. If the party of Order succeeded in joining forces through the candidature of a neutral man outside the dynastic families, he would still be faced with Bonaparte. In its struggle with the people the party of Order is continually obliged to increase the power of the executive. Every increase in the power of the executive office increases the power of its bearer, Bonaparte. To the same degree, therefore, that the fractions of the party of Order strengthen their joint power, they increase the strength behind Bonaparte's dynastic pretensions and increase his chances of frustrating the constitutional solution by force on the day of decision. Despite the party of Order he will no more bother about the one supporting pillar of the Constitution than they – despite the people – bothered about the other supporting pillar on the question of the electoral law. Bonaparte would apparently appeal to universal suffrage against the National Assembly. In a word, the constitutional solution puts the whole status quo in question, and behind this danger to the status quo the bourgeois sees chaos, anarchy and civil war. He sees his purchases, his sales, his bills, his marriage, his notarial contracts and agreements, his mortgages, his ground rents, his house rents, his profits and all his sources of income endangered in May 1852, and he cannot expose himself to this risk. Behind the threat to the political status quo there lies the hidden danger that the whole of bourgeois society will collapse. The only possible solution for the bourgeoisie is the postponement of a solution. It can only save the constitutional republic by a violation of the Constitution, by a prolongation of the powers of the President. This is also the last word of the press of the party of Order after the long-drawn-out and profound debates about 'solutions' which they involved themselves in after the session of the Departmental Councils. Thus to its shame the mighty party of Order finds itself obliged to take seriously the ludicrous, vulgar and hated person of the pseudo-Bonaparte.

This sordid figure has also deceived himself as to why he has increasingly assumed the character of the man of destiny. While his party had enough insight to ascribe his growing importance to circumstances, he believed it to be due solely to the magic power of his name and his unceasing caricature of Napoleon. He became more enterprising day by day. He countered the pilgrimages to St Leonards and Wiesbaden with his tours of France. The Bonapartists had so little trust in the magic effect of his personality that everywhere they sent along crowds of people from the Society of 10 December[76] – that organization of the Paris lumpenproletariat – packed into railway trains and post-chaises, to function as hired applauders. They fed this marionette with speeches which, according to the reception in the various towns, proclaimed republican resignation or unflagging resilience as the electoral slogan of presidential policy. In spite of all these manoeuvres these journeys were anything but triumphal processions.

Believing he had inspired the people with enthusiasm, Bonaparte set about winning the army. He had great reviews held on the plain of Satory near Versailles, in which he sought to buy the soldiers with garlic sausage, champagne and cigars. If the genuine Napoleon was able to raise the spirits of his soldiers, flagging from the hardships of his conquering campaigns, by the occasional show of patriarchal familiarity, the pseudo-Napoleon thought that the grateful troops would shout: '*Vive Napoleon, vive le saucisson!*' that is, hurrah for the sausage [*Wurst*], hurrah for the clown [*Hanswurst*]!

These reviews brought to a head the long-restrained conflict between Bonaparte and his War Minister, Hautpoul, on the one hand, and Changarnier on the other. In Changarnier the party of Order had found its really neutral man, of whom there could be no question of his having his own dynastic claims. They had chosen him as Napoleon's successor. Furthermore, with his conduct on 29 January and 13 June 1849 Changarnier had become the party of Order's great general – a modern Alexander,

76. See *The Eighteenth Brumaire*, below, p. 531.

whose brutal intervention had in the eyes of the timid bourgeoisie severed the Gordian knot of the revolution. Basically just as ludicrous as Bonaparte, he had thus come to power in the cheapest possible way, and he was used by the National Assembly to supervise the President. He himself made a great show of the patronage which he gave Napoleon, for example in the matter of the civil list, and he behaved in an ever more domineering fashion towards the President and his ministers. When, during the discussion of the electoral law, an insurrection was expected, he forbade his officers to take any orders at all from the War Minister or from the President. The press also helped to magnify the figure of Changarnier. In view of its complete lack of great personalities the party of Order naturally felt urged to ascribe all the strength which its class lacked to one single individual and to build him up to a monstrous size. Thus the myth of Changarnier '*the bulwark of society*' was created. The presumptuous charlatanry and the mystique of self-importance with which Changarnier condescended to bear the world on his shoulders form a laughable contrast to the events during and after the review at Satory, which irrefutably proved that it required only a stroke of the pen from the infinitely small person of Bonaparte to reduce the colossus Changarnier, this fantastic offspring of bourgeois fear, to the dimensions of mediocrity and to transform him from the heroic saviour of society into a pensioned general.

Bonaparte had already been revenging himself on Changarnier for some time by provoking the War Minister to a disciplinary quarrel with the troublesome protector. The last review at Satory finally caused the old animosity to erupt. Changarnier's constitutional indignation knew no bounds when he saw the cavalry regiments ride past with the unconstitutional cry: '*Vive l'empereur!*' To forestall any unpleasant debates about this in the coming session of the Chamber Bonaparte dismissed the War Minister, Hautpoul, by appointing him Governor of Algiers. In his place he put a reliable old general from the days of the Empire – Changarnier's complete equal in brutality. However, in order that Hautpoul's dismissal might not appear to be a concession to Changarnier, he transferred General Neumayer[77] – the great saviour of society's right hand – from Paris to Nantes. It had been Neumayer who, at the last review, had caused the whole infantry to march past

77. Maximilian-George Neumayer was a general and a supporter of the party of Order. He commanded the troops in Paris from 1848 to 1850.

Napoleon's successor in icy silence. Changarnier, feeling himself abused in the person of Neumayer, protested and threatened, but in vain. After negotiations lasting two days Neumayer's transfer orders appeared in the *Moniteur* and the hero of social order was left with the choice of either submitting to discipline or resigning.

Bonaparte's struggle with Changarnier is the continuation of his struggle with the party of Order. The re-opening of the National Assembly on 11 November is therefore overshadowed by dark omens. But it will be a storm in a teacup. Essentially, the old game cannot help but continue. In spite of the cries from the sticklers for principle in its various fractions the majority of the party of Order will be forced to prolong the power of the President. Similarly, despite all temporary protestations, Bonaparte will be obliged to accept this extension of power simply as a delegation from the National Assembly (if only for lack of money). Thus the solution will be postponed, the status quo preserved, one fraction of the party of Order compromised, weakened and rendered unacceptable to the other; the repression against the common enemy, the people, will be extended and exhausted, until the economic situation has again reached the point where a new explosion blows all these squabbling parties with their constitutional republic sky-high.

To reassure the bourgeoisie, it must be said that the scandal between Napoleon and the party of Order is resulting in many small capitalists being ruined on the Bourse and their wealth finding its way into the pockets of the big sharks there.

The Eighteenth Brumaire of Louis Bonaparte[1]

PREFACE TO THE SECOND EDITION (1869)

My friend Joseph Weydemeyer,[2] who died before his time, once had the intention of publishing a political weekly in New York, as from 1 January 1852. He invited me to provide a history of the coup d'état for this paper. Until the middle of February I therefore wrote him weekly articles under the title 'The Eighteenth Brumaire of Louis Bonaparte'. In the meantime Weydemeyer's original plan had fallen through. Instead he started a monthly, *Die Revolution*, in the spring of 1852, and its first number consists of my 'Eighteenth Brumaire'. A few hundred copies of this found their way into Germany at that time, without, however, entering the actual book trade. A German bookseller, who affected extremely radical airs, replied to my offer of the book with a truly virtuous horror at a 'presumption' so 'contrary to the times'.

It will be seen from these facts that the present work arose under the immediate pressure of events, and that its historical material does not extend beyond the month of February (1852). It is now republished, partly because of the demand of the book trade, and partly because my friends in Germany have urgently requested it.

Of the writings dealing with the same subject at about the *same time* as mine, only two are worthy of notice: Victor Hugo's *Napoléon le petit*[3] and Proudhon's *Coup d'état*.[4]

---

1. The circumstances in which the *Eighteenth Brumaire* was written and published are explained by Marx himself in the 'Preface' below. It is translated here from the text printed in *MEW* 8.
2. Joseph Weydemeyer was a member of the Communist League, a participant in the 1848 revolution, and the editor of the Frankfurt *Neue Deutsche Zeitung* from 1849 to 1850. In 1851 he emigrated to America. Marx's own footnote here reads, 'Military commander of the St Louis district during the American Civil War'.
3. London, 1852.
4. *La Révolution sociale demontrée par le coup d'état du 2 décembre*, Brussels, 1852. Pierre-Joseph Proudhon was a petty-bourgeois socialist whom Marx had criticized in *The Poverty of Philosophy* (1847).

Victor Hugo confines himself to bitter and witty invective against the responsible author of the coup d'état. With him the event itself appears like a bolt from the blue. He sees in it only a single individual's act of violence. He does not notice that he makes this individual great instead of little by ascribing to him a personal power of initiative which would be without precedent in world history. Proudhon, for his part, seeks to portray the coup as the result of the preceding historical development. But his historical construction of the coup imperceptibly turns into a historical apology for its hero. Thus he falls into the error of our so-called *objective* historians. I show how, on the contrary, the *class struggle* in France created circumstances and conditions which allowed a mediocre and grotesque individual to play the hero's role.

To revise the present work would be to rob it of its particular coloration. I have therefore merely corrected printer's errors and struck out allusions which are now no longer intelligible.

The closing sentence of my work: 'But when the emperor's mantle finally falls on the shoulders of Louis Bonaparte, the bronze statue of Napoleon will come crashing down from the top of the Vendôme Column', has already been fulfilled.[5]

Colonel Charras opened the attack on the cult of Napoleon in his work on the campaign of 1815.[6] Since then, and particularly in the last few years, French literature has knocked the Napoleonic legend on the head with the weapons of historical research, criticism, satire and wit. This violent rupture with traditional popular belief, this immense intellectual revolution, has been little noticed and less understood outside France.

Finally, I hope that my work will contribute towards eliminating the current German scholastic phrase which refers to a so-called *Caesarism*. This superficial historical analogy ignores the main point, namely that the ancient Roman class struggle was only fought out within a privileged minority, between the free rich and

5. This is meant in the metaphorical sense of the general attack on the Napoleon cult in the 1860s. In fact, the statue of Napoleon I came down two years later, in 1871, when the Paris Commune ordered its removal as a 'monument to barbarism and a symbol of brute force'.

6. *Histoire de la campagne de 1815, Waterloo*, Brussels, n.d. Jean-Baptiste Charras was a soldier and a moderate bourgeois republican. He took part in the suppression of the June insurrection and was a deputy in both Assemblies of the Second Republic. After attempting to resist Bonaparte's coup d'état, he was exiled from France.

the free poor, while the great productive mass of the population, the slaves, formed a purely passive pedestal for the combatants. People forget Sismondi's significant expression: the Roman proletariat lived at the expense of society, while modern society lives at the expense of the proletariat. The material and economic conditions of the ancient and the modern class struggles are so utterly distinct from each other that their political products also can have no more in common with each other than the Archbishop of Canterbury has with the High Priest Samuel.

London, 23 June 1869   KARL MARX

I

Hegel remarks somewhere that all the great events and characters of world history occur, so to speak, twice.[7] He forgot to add: the first time as tragedy, the second as farce. Caussidière in place of Danton, Louis Blanc in place of Robespierre, the Montagne of 1848–51 in place of the Montagne of 1793–5, the Nephew in place of the Uncle.[8] And we can perceive the same caricature in the circumstances surrounding the second edition of the eighteenth Brumaire![9]

Men make their own history, but not of their own free will; not under circumstances they themselves have chosen but under the given and inherited circumstances with which they are directly confronted. The tradition of the dead generations weighs like a nightmare on the minds of the living. And, just when they appear to be engaged in the revolutionary transformation of themselves and their material surroundings, in the creation of something which does not yet exist, precisely in such epochs of revolutionary crisis they timidly conjure up the spirits of the past to help them; they borrow their names, slogans and costumes so as to stage the new world-historical scene in this venerable disguise and borrowed language. Luther put on the mask of the apostle Paul; the Revolu-

7. It is doubtful whether Hegel ever wrote these words. This theme, which Marx elaborates on in the ensuing paragraphs, is an expansion of a number of hints thrown out by Engels in his letter to Marx of 3 December 1851. See *MECW 38*, p. 505: 'It really seems as if old Hegel in his grave were acting as World Spirit and directing history, ordaining most conscientiously that it should all be unrolled twice over, once as a great tragedy and once as a wretched farce.'

8. Louis Bonaparte was the nephew of Napoleon I.

9. Napoleon I's coup d'état against the Directory took place on 9 November 1799, i.e., on 18 Brumaire of the year VIII by the revolutionary calendar. Marx therefore described Louis Bonaparte's coup of 2 December 1851 as the second edition of the eighteenth Brumaire.

tion of 1789–1814 draped itself alternately as the Roman republic and the Roman empire; and the revolution of 1848 knew no better than to parody at some points 1789 and at others the revolutionary traditions of 1793–5. In the same way, the beginner who has learnt a new language always retranslates it into his mother tongue: he can only be said to have appropriated the spirit of the new language and to be able to express himself in it freely when he can manipulate it without reference to the old, and when he forgets his original language while using the new one.

If we reflect on this process of world-historical necromancy, we see at once a salient distinction. Camille Desmoulins, Danton, Robespierre, Saint-Just and Napoleon, the heroes of the old French Revolution, as well as its parties and masses, accomplished the task of their epoch, which was the emancipation and establishment of modern *bourgeois* society, in Roman costume and with Roman slogans. The first revolutionaries smashed the feudal basis to pieces and struck off the feudal heads which had grown on it. Then came Napoleon. Within France he created the conditions which first made possible the development of free competition, the exploitation of the land by small peasant property, and the application of the unleashed productive power of the nation's industries. Beyond the borders of France he swept away feudal institutions so far as this was necessary for the provision on the European continent of an appropriate modern environment for the bourgeois society in France. Once the new social formation had been established, the antediluvian colossi disappeared along with the resurrected imitations of Rome – imitations of Brutus, Gracchus, Publicola, the tribunes, the senators, and Caesar himself. Bourgeois society in its sober reality had created its true interpreters and spokesmen in such people as Say,[10] Cousin,[11] Royer-Collard,[12] Benjamin Constant[13] and Guizot. The real leaders of the bourgeois army

10. Jean-Baptiste Say was a French economist who popularized the doctrines of Adam Smith in the early nineteenth century.

11. Victor Cousin was a French philosopher, appointed Minister of Education in Thiers's short-lived cabinet of 1840. He endeavoured to combine the ideas of Descartes, Hume and Kant into a system he himself described as 'eclecticism'.

12. Pierre-Paul Royer-Collard was a political theorist and politician under the Restoration and the July monarchy. He supported constitutional monarchy as, quite explicitly, the organ of bourgeois rule.

13. Benjamin Constant was a liberal writer and politician, a leading figure in the opposition of the 1820s to the rule of Charles X and the ultras.

sat behind office desks while the fathead Louis XVIII served as the bourgeoisie's political head. Bourgeois society was no longer aware that the ghosts of Rome had watched over its cradle, since it was wholly absorbed in the production of wealth and the peaceful struggle of economic competition. But unheroic as bourgeois society is, it still required heroism, self-sacrifice, terror, civil war, and battles in which whole nations were engaged, to bring it into the world. And its gladiators found in the stern classical traditions of the Roman republic the ideals, art forms and self-deceptions they needed in order to hide from themselves the limited bourgeois content of their struggles and to maintain their enthusiasm at the high level appropriate to great historical tragedy. A century earlier, in the same way but at a different stage of development, Cromwell and the English people had borrowed for their bourgeois revolution the language, passions and illusions of the Old Testament. When the actual goal had been reached, when the bourgeois transformation of English society had been accomplished, Locke drove out Habakkuk.

In these revolutions, then, the resurrection of the dead served to exalt the new struggles, rather than to parody the old, to exaggerate the given task in the imagination, rather than to flee from solving it in reality, and to recover the spirit of the revolution, rather than to set its ghost walking again.

For it was only the ghost of the old revolution which walked in the years from 1848 to 1851, from Marrast, the *républicain en gants jaunes*[14] who disguised himself as old Bailly,[15] right down to the adventurer who is now hiding his commonplace and repulsive countenance beneath the iron death-mask of Napoleon.

An entire people thought it had provided itself with a more powerful motive force by means of a revolution; instead, it suddenly found itself plunged back into an already dead epoch. It was impossible to mistake this relapse into the past, for the old dates arose again, along with the old chronology, the old names, the old edicts, long abandoned to the erudition of the antiquaries, and the old minions of the law, apparently long decayed. The nation might well appear to itself to be in the same situation as that mad Englishman in Bedlam, who thought he was living in the time of the pharaohs. He moaned every day about the hard work he had to

14. Yellow-gloved republican.

15. Jean-Sylvain Bailly was a leader of the liberal and constitutionalist bourgeoisie in the first French revolution; guillotined in 1793.

perform as a gold-digger in the Ethiopian mines, immured in his subterranean prison, by the exiguous light of a lamp fixed on his own head. The overseer of the slaves stood behind him with a long whip, and at the exits was a motley assembly of barbarian mercenaries, who had no common language and therefore understood neither the forced labourers in the mines nor each other. 'And I, a freeborn Briton,' sighed the mad Englishman, 'must bear all this to make gold for the old pharaohs.' 'To pay the debts of the Bonaparte family,' sighed the French nation. As long as he was in his right mind, the Englishman could not free himself of the obsession of making gold. As long as the French were engaged in revolution, they could not free themselves of the memory of Napoleon. The election of 10 December 1848[16] proved this. They yearned to return from the dangers of revolution to the fleshpots of Egypt, and 2 December 1851 was the answer. They have not merely acquired a caricature of the old Napoleon, they have the old Napoleon himself, in the caricature form he had to take in the middle of the nineteenth century.

The social revolution of the nineteenth century can only create its poetry from the future, not from the past. It cannot begin its own work until it has sloughed off all its superstitious regard for the past. Earlier revolutions have needed world-historical reminiscences to deaden their awareness of their own content. In order to arrive at its own content the revolution of the nineteenth century must let the dead bury their dead. Previously the phrase transcended the content; here the content transcends the phrase.

The February revolution was a surprise attack; it took the old society *unawares*. The people proclaimed this unexpected *coup de main*[17] to be an historic deed, the opening of a new epoch. On 2 December the February revolution was conjured away by the sleight of hand of a cardsharper. It is no longer the monarchy that appears to have been overthrown but the liberal concessions extracted from it by a century of struggle. Instead of *society* conquering a new content for itself, it only seems that the *state* has returned to its most ancient form, the unashamedly simple rule of the military sabre and the clerical cowl. The answer to the coup *de main* of February 1848 was the *coup de tête*[18] of December

16. On 10 December 1848 Louis Bonaparte was elected President of the French Republic by a large majority.

17. Surprise attack.

18. Impulsive act.

1851. Easy come, easy go! However, the intervening period has not gone unused. Between 1848 and 1851 French society, using an abbreviated because revolutionary method, caught up on the studies and experiences which would in the normal or, so to speak, textbook course of development have had to precede the February revolution if it were to do more than merely shatter the surface. Society now appears to have fallen back behind its starting-point; but in reality it must first create the revolutionary starting-point, i.e., the situation, relations and conditions necessary for the modern revolution to become serious.

Bourgeois revolutions, such as those of the eighteenth century, storm quickly from success to success. They outdo each other in dramatic effects; men and things seem set in sparkling diamonds, and each day's spirit is ecstatic. But they are short-lived; they soon reach their apogee, and society has to undergo a long period of regret until it has learnt to assimilate soberly the achievements of its period of storm and stress. Proletarian revolutions, however, such as those of the nineteenth century, constantly engage in self-criticism, and in repeated interruptions of their own course. They return to what has apparently already been accomplished in order to begin the task again; with merciless thoroughness they mock the inadequate, weak and wretched aspects of their first attempts; they seem to throw their opponent to the ground only to see him draw new strength from the earth and rise again before them, more colossal than ever; they shrink back again and again before the indeterminate immensity of their own goals, until the situation is created in which any retreat is impossible, and the conditions themselves cry out:

Hic Rhodus, hic salta! Here is the rose, dance here![19]

In any case, every observer of any competence must have suspected, even without having followed the course of French development step by step, that the revolution was about to meet with an unheard-of humiliation. It was enough to hear the self-satisfied yelps of victory with which the gentlemen of the democratic party congratulated one another on the anticipated happy

---

19. The Latin phrase comes from one of Aesop's fables. It is the reply made to a boaster who claimed he had once made an immense leap in Rhodes: 'Rhodes is here. Leap here and now.' But the German phrase, '*Hier ist die Rose, hier tanze!*' ('here is the rose, dance here'), is Hegel's variant, in the Preface to the *Philosophy of Right*. The Greek '*Rhodos*' can mean both Rhodes and rose.

consequences of the second Sunday in May 1852.[20] In their minds the second Sunday in May 1852 had become an obsession, a dogma, like the day of Christ's Second Coming and the beginning of the millennium in the minds of the Chiliasts. As always, weakness had found its salvation in a belief in miracles. The democrats thought the enemy had been overcome when they had conjured him away in imagination, and lost all understanding of the present in their inactive glorification of the anticipated future, and of the deeds they had up their sleeves but did not yet wish to display publicly. Those heroes who seek to disprove their well-established incapability by presenting each other with their sympathy and gathering together in a crowd had tied up their bundles and grabbed their laurel wreaths as advance payment. They were just then engaged in discounting on the exchange market the republics of a purely titular character for which they had already quietly, modestly and providently organized the governing personnel. The second of December struck them like lightning from a clear sky, and the people who in periods of despondency willingly let their inner fears be drowned by those who could shout the loudest will now perhaps have convinced themselves that the time has gone by when the cackle of geese could save the Capitol.

The Constitution, the National Assembly, the dynastic parties,[21] the blue and the red republicans, the heroes of Africa,[22] the thunder from the platform, the sheet lightning of the daily press, all the other publications, the political names and intellectual reputations, the civil law and the penal code, *liberté, égalité, fraternité* and the second Sunday in May – all have vanished like a series of optical illusions before the spell of a man whom even his enemies do not claim to be a magician. Universal suffrage seems to have survived for a further moment[23] so as to sign its testament with its own hand before the eyes of the whole world,

20. On the second Sunday in May 1852 the presidential term was to end and new elections were to be held, according to the Constitution of 4 November 1848.

21. A common name for the Legitimists (supporters of a Bourbon restoration) and Orleanists (supporters of an Orleans restoration).

22. The republican generals, Cavaignac, Lamoricière and Bedeau, who had commanded in the colonial wars in Algeria in the 1830s and 1840s.

23. The plebiscite of 20 December 1851, which sanctioned the coup d'état of 2 December by 7,500,000 votes to 650,000, according to the official figures, was held on a basis of universal (male) suffrage.

and to declare in the name of the people themselves: *All that exists deserves to perish.*[24]

It is not sufficient to say, as the French do, that their nation was taken by surprise. A nation and a woman are not forgiven for the unguarded hour in which the first available adventurer is able to violate them. Expressions of that kind do not solve the problem; they merely give it a different formulation. It remains to be explained how a nation of thirty-six millions could be taken by surprise by three swindlers[25] and delivered without resistance into captivity.

Let us recapitulate in their general features the phases the French revolution passed through from 24 February 1848 to December 1851.

Three main periods are unmistakable: *the February period*; *the period of the constitution of the republic* or *of the Constituent National Assembly*, from 4 May 1848 to 28 May 1849; and *the period of the constitutional republic* or *of the Legislative National Assembly*, from 28 May 1849 to 2 December 1851.

The *first period*, from the fall of Louis Philippe on 24 February 1848 to the meeting of the Constituent Assembly on 4 May, the *February period* proper, can be described as the *prologue* to the revolution. Its character was officially expressed by the declaration of its own improvised government that it was merely *provisional*, and, like the government, everything that was suggested, attempted or enunciated in this period proclaimed itself to be merely *provisional*. Nobody and nothing took the risk of claiming the right to exist and take real action. The dynastic opposition, the republican bourgeoisie, the democratic and republican petty bourgeoisie, and the social-democratic working class, i.e., all the elements that had prepared or determined the revolution, provisionally found their place in the February government.

It could not have been otherwise. The original aim of the February days was electoral reform, to widen the circle of the politically privileged within the possessing class itself and to overthrow the exclusive domination of the aristocracy of finance. However, when it came to the actual conflict, when the people mounted the barricades, the National Guard maintained a passive attitude, the army offered no serious resistance, and the monarchy

24. A saying of Mephistopheles in the first part of Goethe's *Faust*.

25. The three swindlers were no doubt Bonaparte, his half-brother Morny, and Eugène Rouher, Minister of Justice from 1849 to 1852.

ran away, the republic appeared to be a matter of course. But every party interpreted it in its own way. The proletariat had secured the republic arms in hand and now imprinted it with its own hallmark, proclaiming it to be a *social republic*. In this way the general content of the modern revolution was indicated, but this content stood in the strangest contradiction with everything which could immediately and directly be put into practice in the given circumstances and conditions, with the material available and the level of education attained by the mass of the people. On the other hand, the claims of all the other elements which had contributed to the February revolution were recognized in that they secured the lion's share of the posts in the new government. In no period, therefore, do we find a more variegated mixture of elements, more high-flown phrases, yet more actual uncertainty and awkwardness; more enthusiastic striving for innovation, yet a more fundamental retention of the old routine; a greater appearance of harmony throughout the whole society, yet a more profound alienation between its constituent parts. While the Paris proletariat was still basking in the prospect of the wide perspectives which had opened before it and indulging in earnest discussions on social problems, the old powers of society regrouped themselves, assembled, reflected on the situation, and found unexpected support from the mass of the nation, the peasants and the petty bourgeoisie, who all rushed onto the political stage once the barriers of the July monarchy had collapsed.

The *second period*, from 4 May 1848 to the end of May 1849, was the period of the *constitution* or *foundation* of the *bourgeois republic*. Immediately after the February days, the dynastic opposition had been taken unawares by the republicans, and the republicans by the socialists. But France too had been taken unawares by Paris. The National Assembly which met on 4 May 1848 had emerged from elections held throughout the nation; it therefore represented the nation. It was a living protest against the pretensions of the February days and an attempt to reduce the results of the revolution to the standards of the bourgeoisie. In vain did the Paris proletariat (which had grasped the nature of this National Assembly straightaway) endeavour on 15 May, a few days after the Assembly had met, to deny its existence by force, to dissolve it, to tear apart the organic and threatening form taken on by the nation's counteracting spirit and to scatter its individual constituents to the winds.[26] As is well known, 15 May had no other result than to remove Blanqui and his comrades, i.e., the real leaders of the proletarian party, from the public stage for the entire duration of the cycle with which we are dealing.

The *bourgeois monarchy* of Louis Philippe could only be followed by a *bourgeois republic*. In other words, if a limited section of the bourgeoisie previously ruled in the name of the king, the whole of the bourgeoisie would now rule in the name of the people. The demands of the Paris proletariat are examples of utopian humbug, which must be finished with. The Paris proletariat replied to this declaration by the Constituent National Assembly with the *June insurrection*, the most colossal event in the history of European civil wars. The bourgeois republic was victorious. It had on its side the financial aristocracy, the industrial bourgeoisie, the middle class, the petty bourgeoisie, the army, the Mobile Guard (i.e., the organized lumpenproletariat), the intellectual celebrities, the priests and the rural population. On the side of the Paris proletariat stood no one but itself. Over 3,000 insurgents were butchered after the victory, and a further 15,000 were transported without having been convicted. With this defeat the proletariat passed into the *background* of the revolutionary stage. Whenever the movement appeared to be making a fresh start the proletariat tried to push forward again, but it displayed less and less strength and achieved ever fewer results. As soon as one of the higher social strata got into a revolutionary ferment, the proletariat would enter into alliance with it and so share all the defeats successively suffered by the different parties. But the wider the area of society that these additional blows affected, the weaker they became. One by one the proletariat's more important leaders in the Assembly and in the press fell victim to the courts, and ever more dubious figures stepped forward to lead it. In part it threw itself into *doctrinaire experiments, exchange banks and workers' associations,*[27] *i.e., into a movement which renounces the hope of overturning the old world by using the huge combination of means provided by the latter, and seeks rather to achieve its salvation in a private manner, behind the back of society, within its own limited conditions of existence; such a movement necessarily fails.* It seems

26. See p. 392.

27. Exchange banks based on 'labour money' were the Proudhonist panacea. The workers' associations referred to here were early craft unions, lacking broad revolutionary perspectives.

that until *all the classes* that the proletariat fought against in June themselves lie prostrate beside it, it will be unable either to recover its own revolutionary greatness or to win new energy from the alliances into which it has recently entered. But at least it was defeated with the honours attaching to a great world-historical struggle; not just France, but the whole of Europe trembled in face of the June earthquake, whereas the later defeats of the higher social classes were bought so cheaply that the victorious party had to exaggerate them impudently to make them pass for events at all, and were the more shameful the greater the distance between the defeated party and that of the proletariat.

The defeat of the June insurgents certainly prepared and flattened the ground on which the bourgeois republic could be founded and erected, but at the same time it showed that there are other issues at stake in Europe besides that of 'republic or monarchy'. It revealed that the bourgeois republic signified here only the unrestricted despotism of one class over other classes. It proved that in the older civilized countries, with their highly developed class formation, modern conditions of production, and their intellectual consciousness in which all traditional ideas have been dissolved through the work of centuries, *the republic is generally only the political form for the revolutionizing of bourgeois society*, and not its *conservative form of existence*, as for example in the United States of America. There, although classes already exist, they have not yet become fixed, but rather continually alter and mutually exchange their component parts; the modern means of production make up for the relative scarcity of heads and hands instead of coinciding with a stagnant surplus population; finally, the feverish and youthful movement of a material production which has to appropriate a new world has left neither time nor opportunity for the abolition of the old spiritual world.

During the June days all other classes and parties joined together to form the *party of Order*, in opposition to the proletarian class, the *party of Anarchy*, of socialism and communism. They 'saved' society from 'the enemies of society'. They handed out the catchphrases of the old society – 'property, family, religion, order' – among their soldiers as passwords, and proclaimed to the counter-revolutionary crusading army: 'In this sign shalt thou conquer.'[28] From this moment onwards, as soon as one of the

28. Christian legend has it that a cross appeared to the Emperor Constantine before the battle fought in 312 against Maxentius, bearing these words.

numerous parties which had assembled under this sign against the June insurgents sought to defend its own class interest on the revolutionary battlefield, it succumbed in face of the cry of 'property, family, religion, order'. Society was saved as often as the circle of its rulers contracted, as often as a more exclusive interest was upheld as against the wider interest. Every demand for the simplest bourgeois financial reform, every demand of the most ordinary liberalism, the most formal republicanism, or the most commonplace democracy, was simultaneously punished as an 'attack on society' and denounced as 'socialism'. And, finally, the high priests of the cult of 'religion and order' are themselves kicked off their Delphic stools, hauled from their beds at the dead of night, put in prison vans, and thrown into jail or sent into exile. Their temple is levelled to the ground, their mouths are sealed, their pens smashed, and their law torn to pieces in the name of religion, property, family and order. Bourgeois fanatics for order are shot down on their balconies by drunken bands of troops, their sacred domesticity is profaned, their houses are bombarded for the fun of it, all in the name of property, the family, religion and order. Last of all, the dregs of bourgeois society form themselves into the *holy phalanx of order*, and the hero Crapulinski[29] moves into the Tuileries as the 'saviour of society'.

II

Let us pick up the threads of this historical process once again.

After the June days, the history of the *Constituent National Assembly* was the *history of the domination and the dissolution of the republican fraction of the bourgeoisie*, that fraction which goes under the various names of tricolour republicans, pure republicans, political republicans, formal republicans, etc.

Under the bourgeois monarchy of Louis Philippe, this fraction had formed the *official* republican *opposition* and was therefore a recognized component of the contemporary political world. It had its representatives in parliament and a considerable field of influence in the press. Its Paris organ, *Le National*, was considered

29. 'Crapulinski' comes from the French word '*crapule*' (scoundrel) and was used by Heine as the name of the spendthrift Polish nobleman in his poem 'Two Knights'.

to be just as respectable in its own way as the *Journal des Débats*.[30] Its position under the constitutional monarchy was in accordance with its character. This was not a fraction of the bourgeoisie bound together by great common interests and demarcated from the rest by conditions of production peculiar to it; it was a coterie of republican-minded members of the bourgeoisie, writers, lawyers, officers and officials. Its influence rested on the personal antipathies of the country towards Louis Philippe, on memories of the old republic, on the republican faith of a number of enthusiasts, and, above all, on *French nationalism*, for it constantly kept alive hatred of the Vienna treaties[31] and the alliance with England. This concealed imperialism[32] accounted for a large part of the support the *National* possessed under Louis Philippe, but later, under the republic, it was to confront it as a deadly rival in the person of Louis Bonaparte. Like the rest of the bourgeois opposition, it fought the financial aristocracy. Polemics against the budget, which in France coincided exactly with the struggle against the financial aristocracy, provided popularity too cheaply and material for puritanical *leading articles*[33] too plentifully for the opposition not to exploit the issue. The industrial bourgeoisie was grateful to it for its slavish defence of the French system of protective tariffs, although it took up this defence more on nationalist than on economic grounds. The bourgeoisie as a whole was grateful for its venomous denunciations of communism and socialism. Apart from this, the party of the *National* was *purely republican*, i.e., it demanded a republican instead of a monarchical form of bourgeois rule, and it demanded above all the lion's share of this rule. It was absolutely unclear about the conditions of this transformation. What was as clear as day, and publicly declared at the reform banquets held in the last days of Louis Philippe, was that the official opposition was unpopular with the petty-bourgeois democrats and, more so, with the revolutionary proletariat. The oppositional pure republicans were already on the point of making

30. The leading Orleanist paper, which had a semi-official character under the July monarchy.

31. See above, p. 402, n. 65.

32. Marx uses the term 'imperialism' not in its present-day sense, but to refer to the form of French nationalism which looked back to the exploits of Napoleon I, i.e., to the First Empire, and expressed itself in support for Louis Bonaparte in the 1850s. Where the words 'imperialism' and 'imperialist' appear in this translation, they are used in this sense.

33. In English in the original.

do initially with a regency of the Duchess of Orleans[34] when the February revolution broke out and assigned their best-known representatives a place in the Provisional Government; in this they showed themselves to be typical of all pure republicans. They naturally possessed in advance the confidence of the bourgeoisie and the majority of the Constituent National Assembly. The *socialist* elements of the Provisional Government were straightaway excluded from the Executive Commission which the National Assembly formed when it met, and the party of the *National* made use of the outbreak of the June insurrection to dismiss the Executive Commission as well and thereby to free itself of its closest rivals, the *petty-bourgeois* or *democratic republicans* (Ledru-Rollin, etc.). Cavaignac, the general of the bourgeois republican party, who had commanded the June battle, replaced the Executive Commission with a kind of dictatorial authority. The former editor-in-chief of the *National*, Marrast, became the permanent chairman of the Constituent National Assembly, and the ministries, as well as all the other important posts, fell to the pure republicans.

The republican fraction of the bourgeoisie, which had long seen itself as the legitimate heir to the July monarchy, thus found its dearest expectations exceeded. But it had achieved power through the grape-shot which suppressed a rising of the proletariat against capital; not through a liberal revolt of the bourgeoisie against the throne. What it had imagined would be the *most revolutionary* event turned out to be in reality the *most counter-revolutionary*. The fruit fell into its lap from the tree of knowledge, not the tree of life.

The exclusive *rule of the bourgeois republicans* only lasted from 24 June to 10 December 1848. Its results can be summarized as the *drafting of a republican constitution* and the *state of siege in Paris*.

Fundamentally, the new Constitution was merely a republicanized version of the constitutional Charter of 1830.[35] The narrow electoral qualification of the July monarchy, which excluded even a large section of the bourgeoisie from political rule, was incom-

34. On the morning of 24 February 1848 Louis Philippe abdicated in favour of his young grandson, the comte de Paris. The child's mother, the duchesse d'Orléans, was to be regent for the time being.
35. The Charter of 1830 was the basic constitutional law of the July monarchy. It proclaimed the sovereignty of the people but retained the monarchy as well as the limited franchise of the previous regime, merely increasing the number eligible to vote to approximately two hundred thousand.

patible with the existence of the bourgeois republic. The February revolution had immediately proclaimed direct universal suffrage in place of the property qualification. The bourgeois republicans could not treat this event as not having happened. They had to content themselves with the addition of an ordinance limiting the electorate to those people who had resided for six months in the relevant constituency. The old organization of the administration, the municipalities, courts, the army, etc., continued to exist intact, or, where the Constitution did make a change, this change concerned the table of contents, not the content; the name, not the thing.

The inevitable general staff of the liberties of 1848, personal freedom, freedom of the press, speech, association, assembly, education, religion, etc., received a constitutional uniform which made it impossible to establish any cases where they might have been infringed. Each of these liberties is proclaimed to be the *unconditional* right of the French citizen, but there is always the marginal note that it is unlimited only in so far as it is not restricted by the *'equal rights of others* and the *public safety'*, or by 'laws' which are supposed to mediate precisely this harmony of the individual liberties with each other and with the public safety. For example: 'Citizens have the right to form associations, to assemble peaceably and without weapons, to petition, and to express their opinions through the press or in any other manner. *The enjoyment of these rights has no other restriction than the equal rights of others and the public safety'* (Chapter II of the French Constitution, paragraph 8). Or: 'Education is free. Freedom of education shall be *enjoyed* under the conditions fixed by law and the supreme control of the state' (paragraph 9). Or: 'The domicile of every citizen is inviolable *except* in the forms laid down by law' (paragraph 3). And so on. The Constitution therefore constantly refers to future *organic* laws which are to implement the above glosses and regulate the enjoyment of these unrestricted liberties in such a way that they do not come up against each other or against the public safety. These organic laws were later brought into existence by the friends of order, and all liberties were regulated so as to make sure that the bourgeoisie was not hindered in its enjoyment of them by the equal rights of the other classes. Where the Constitution entirely forbade these liberties to the 'others' or allowed them to be enjoyed under conditions which were simply traps set by the police, this always happened solely

in the interests of 'public safety', i.e., the safety of the bourgeoisie as laid down by the Constitution. In the period which followed,
both sides had therefore a perfect right to appeal to the Constitution:
the friends of order, who did away with all those liberties, and the
democrats, who demanded their retention. For each paragraph of the
Constitution contains its own antithesis, its own upper and lower
house, namely, freedom in the general phrase, abolition of freedom
in the marginal note. In this way, as long as the *name* of freedom
was respected and only its actual implementation was prevented
(in a legal way, it goes without saying), its constitutional existence
remained intact and untouched however fatal the blows dealt to it in
its actual physical existence.

This Constitution, so cleverly made inviolable, could nevertheless, like Achilles, be wounded at one point. Not in the heel, but
in the head, or rather the two heads at its top – the Legislative
Assembly on the one hand and the President on the other. If one
skims through the Constitution, one finds that the only paragraphs
which are absolute, positive, consistent, and incapable of distortion, are those which determine the relation between the President
and the Legislative Assembly. For here the bourgeois republicans
were concerned to secure their own position. Paragraphs 45 to 70
of the Constitution are drawn up in such a way that the National
Assembly can remove the President constitutionally, whereas the
President can only remove the National Assembly unconstitutionally, by sweeping away the Constitution itself. Here, therefore,
the Constitution provokes its own forcible destruction. Not
only does it sanctify the separation of powers, like the Charter
of 1830; it extends this into an intolerable contradiction. The
game of constitutional powers, as Guizot described the parliamentary squabble between the legislature and the executive, is
continually played for the maximum possible stake in the 1848
Constitution. On one side are the seven hundred and fifty representatives of the people, who are elected by universal suffrage
and are re-eligible; they form an uncontrollable, indissoluble,
indivisible National Assembly, an all-powerful legislature which
decides in the last instance on war, peace and commercial treaties, alone possesses the right of amnesty, and unceasingly holds
the front of the stage owing to its permanent character. On the
other side is the President, with all the attributes of royal power,
with the authority to appoint and dismiss his ministers independently of the National Assembly, with all the instruments of

executive power in his hands, and finally with the right of appointment to every post, which means in France the right to decide on the livelihood of at least a million and a half people, for this is the number who depend on the five hundred thousand officials and officers of every rank. He has the whole of the armed forces behind him. He has the privilege of pardoning individual criminals, suspending members of the National Guard, and, with the agreement of the Council of State,[36] dismissing the departmental, cantonal and municipal councils elected by the citizens themselves. The right to initiate and negotiate all treaties with foreign countries is reserved to him. While the Assembly constantly performs on the public stage and is exposed to the daylight of public criticism, the President lives a secluded life in the Elysian Fields,[37] though admittedly he has before his eyes and in his heart paragraph 45 of the Constitution, which daily calls out to him: '*Frère, il faut mourir.*'[38] Your power will cease on the second Sunday of the beautiful month of May in the fourth year after your election! Then your glory is at an end! The play will not be performed twice, and if you have debts make sure in good time that you pay them off with the 600,000 francs the Constitution has granted you, unless you prefer to move to Clichy[39] on the second Monday of the beautiful month of May!

Thus, if the Constitution assigns the real power to the President, it endeavours to secure moral power for the National Assembly. Leaving aside the fact that it is impossible to create moral authority by legislative fiat, the Constitution also provides for its own abolition by having the President elected by the direct suffrage of all Frenchmen. Whereas in the case of the National Assembly the votes of France are divided among its seven hundred and fifty members, they are here, on the contrary, concentrated on *one* individual. While each individual deputy represents only this or that party, this or that town, this or that bridgehead, or merely the necessity of electing some appropriate member of the seven

36. The Council of State was originally set up by Napoleon I, as a body of experts – administrative, scientific, diplomatic and military – to plan legislation. It has since found a place in most French regimes, being particularly important under the Second Empire and the Fifth Republic.

37. The President's palace is the Elysée, adjacent to the Avenue des Champs Elysées. The original Elysian Fields are the abode of the blessed after death in Greek mythology.

38. Brother, you must die.

39. Clichy was the Paris debtors' prison during the mid-nineteenth century.

hundred and fifty, in which case neither the issue nor the man is closely inspected, *he*, the President, is the elect of the nation, and the act of electing him is the great trump which the sovereign people plays once every four years. The elected National Assembly stands in a metaphysical relation to the nation, but the elected President stands in a personal relation to it. No doubt the National Assembly manifests in its individual deputies the multifarious aspects of the national spirit, but the President is its very incarnation. Unlike the Assembly, he possesses a kind of divine right; he is there by the grace of the people.

Thetis, the sea goddess, prophesied to Achilles that he would die in the bloom of youth. The Constitution, which, like Achilles, had its weak point, had also, like Achilles, a foreboding that it would have to go early to its death. The constitution-making pure republicans needed only to direct their gaze from the heavenly clouds of their ideal republic to the profane world in order to see how the insolence of the royalists, the Bonapartists, the democrats and the communists, as well as their own discredit, grew daily in the same measure that their great legislative artefact neared completion. They did not need Thetis to emerge from the sea and inform them of this secret. They endeavoured to cheat fate with constitutional cunning by inserting paragraph 111, according to which any motion for the *revision of the Constitution* had to be carried in three successive debates, with an interval of a whole month between each, by at least three quarters of the votes cast, and with no less than 500 members of the National Assembly voting. This was merely an impotent attempt to prolong their exercise of power as a parliamentary minority, which they prophetically saw their own future to be. Even at this time, when they had at their disposal a parliamentary majority and all the resources of governmental authority, power was daily slipping further from their feeble grasp.

Finally, in a melodramatic paragraph, the Constitution entrusts itself 'to the vigilance and the patriotism of the whole French people as well as every individual Frenchman', after it had previously, in a different paragraph, entrusted the 'vigilant' and 'patriotic' Frenchman to the tender and painstakingly penal care of the '*haute cour*', the special High Court invented for that very purpose.

This, then, was the Constitution of 1848, overthrown on 2 December 1851 not by a head, but by coming into contact with a mere hat; this hat was of course of the three-cornered Napoleonic variety.

Inside the Assembly the bourgeois republicans were engaged in discussing, voting and adding refinements to the Constitution; outside the Assembly Cavaignac was maintaining Paris in a *state of siege*. The state of siege in Paris was the midwife of the Constituent Assembly in its labour of creating the republic. If the Constitution was later put out of existence by bayonets, it should not be forgotten that it had to be protected in its mother's womb by bayonets, bayonets turned against the people, and brought into the world by them. The forefathers of the 'respectable republicans' had sent their symbol, the tricolour, on a grand tour round Europe. The republicans of 1848 in their turn made an invention which found its way unaided over the whole Continent, but returned to France with ever renewed love, so that by now it has obtained citizenship in half her departments – the *state of siege*. An excellent invention which has found periodic application in every successive crisis in the course of the French revolution. The barracks and the bivouac were thus periodically deposited on the head of French society in order to compress its brain and keep it quiet; the sabre and the musket were periodically made to judge and administer, to guard and to censor, to play the part of policeman and night-watchman; the military moustache and the service uniform were periodically trumpeted forth as the highest wisdom and the spiritual guide of society. Was it not inevitable that barracks and bivouac, sabre and musket, moustache and uniform, would finally hit on the idea of saving society once and for all by proclaiming the supremacy of their own regime and thus entirely freeing civil society from the trouble of ruling itself? They had the more reason to hit on this idea in that they could then expect a better cash payment in return for their elevated services, while the merely periodic states of siege and temporary rescues of society at the behest of this or that fraction of the bourgeoisie produced little solid payment apart from one or two dead and wounded and a few friendly bourgeois grimaces. Was the military not bound to finally play at state of siege in its own interests and for its own interests, and at the same time lay siege to the bourgeois purse? It should not be forgotten, by the way, that Colonel Bernard, the man who presided over the military commission which under Cavaignac deported 15,000 insurgents without trial, is at this moment again at the head of the military commissions active in Paris.

Although, with the state of siege in Paris, the respectable pure republicans founded the nursery in which the praetorian guards[40] of 2 December 1851 were to grow up, they nevertheless deserve our praise for one thing: instead of over-doing nationalist sentiment as they had done under Louis Philippe, now that they had control of the nation's armed forces they crawled before the foreigner, and instead of liberating Italy, they allowed the Austrians and Neapolitans to reconquer it.[41] The election of Louis Bonaparte as President on 10 December 1848 put an end to the dictatorship of Cavaignac and the Constituent Assembly.

It is stated in paragraph 44 of the Constitution that 'the President of the French Republic must never have lost his status as a French citizen'. The first President of the French Republic, L. N. Bonaparte, had, in addition to losing his status as a French citizen, been an English special constable, and he had even been naturalized in Switzerland.[42]

I have dealt elsewhere[43] with the significance of the election of 10 December, and I shall not return to the issue here. Suffice it to say that it was a *reaction of the peasants*, who had had to pay the costs of the February revolution, against the other classes of the nation, a *reaction of the country against the town*. It found great favour with the army, for which the republicans of the *National* had provided no glory and no extra pay, with the big bourgeoisie, who saw Bonaparte as a bridge to the monarchy, and with the proletarians and petty bourgeois, who hailed him as a scourge for Cavaignac. I shall find an opportunity later on to examine more closely the relation of the peasants to the French revolution.

The period from 20 December 1848[44] to the dissolution of the

40. A reference to the Society of 10 December (see below, p. 531). The original praetorian guards were attached to the person of the Roman emperors.

41. The Austrian victory of Custozza (25 July) was followed by the armistice of Vigevano (9 August) between Austria and Piedmont. On 25 August Cavaignac publicly rejected any idea of intervening against Austria, offering instead French mediation. The Neapolitan army reconquered half of Sicily in September 1848, but was compelled to conclude an armistice before the conquest was complete, as a result of joint Anglo-French pressure.

42. In 1832 Louis Bonaparte had adopted Swiss citizenship, and in 1848 he joined the special constabulary organized to defend London against the Chartists.

43. See above, p. 406–10.

44. On 20 December 1848 Cavaignac laid down his office, Louis Bonaparte was proclaimed President, and his first cabinet, under Odilon Barrot, was sworn in.

Constituent Assembly in May 1849 comprises the history of the fall of the bourgeois republicans. After they had founded a republic for the bourgeoisie, driven the revolutionary proletariat from the field, and temporarily reduced the democratic petty bourgeoisie to silence, they were themselves pushed aside by the mass of the bourgeoisie, which quite rightly confiscated the republic as being *its property*. This bourgeois mass was however *royalist*. One section of it, the great landowners, had ruled during the Restoration and was therefore Legitimist. The other, the aristocracy of finance and the big industrialists, had ruled under the July monarchy and was therefore Orleanist. The high dignitaries of the army, the university, the church, the bar, the academy and the press, were to be found on both sides, though in varying proportions. Here in the bourgeois republic, which bore neither the name 'Bourbon' nor the name 'Orleans', but the name 'Capital', they had found the form of state in which they could rule *jointly*. They had already been brought together into the 'party of Order' by the June insurrection. The first requirement now was the removal of the clique of bourgeois republicans who still occupied the seats in the National Assembly. These pure republicans had brutally misused physical force against the people; they were now just as cowardly, faint-hearted, spiritless, and incapable of resistance in their retreat as they had previously been brutal, when it was necessary to assert their republicanism and their legislative rights against the executive power and the royalists. I need not relate here the shameful history of their collapse. They did not go under; they faded away. Their history has been played out once and for all. In the following period they figured, whether inside or outside the Assembly, merely as memories, although these memories appeared to take on new life as soon as the mere name of Republic was at issue once more, and whenever the revolutionary conflict threatened to sink down to the lowest level. It might be pointed out in passing that the journal which gave this party its name, the *National*, was converted to socialism in the succeeding period.

Before we finish with this period we must cast a glance back at the two powers, one of which destroyed the other on 2 December 1851, although from 20 December 1848 to the exit of the Constituent Assembly they had lived in a conjugal relationship. We mean Louis Bonaparte, on the one hand, and the party of the royalist coalition, the party of Order, the party of the big bourgeoisie, on the other. At the beginning of his term of office Bonaparte immediately formed a ministry of the party of Order, placing at its head Odilon Barrot, the old leader – mark this well – of the most liberal fraction of the parliamentary bourgeoisie. Barrot had at last hunted down the ministerial position whose spectre had haunted him since 1830, and what is more, the premiership of that ministry; not, however, as he had imagined under Louis Philippe, as the most advanced leader of the parliamentary opposition, but with the task of killing off a parliament in alliance with all his arch-enemies, the Jesuits and Legitimists. He had finally brought his bride home, but only after she had become a prostitute. Bonaparte seemed to have completely effaced himself. The party of Order acted for him.

The Council of Ministers decided at its very first meeting on the expedition to Rome, agreeing that it should take place behind the back of the National Assembly. The means for the expedition were to be obtained from the Assembly on false pretences. It thus began with a fraud perpetrated on the National Assembly and a secret conspiracy with the absolutist powers abroad against the revolutionary Roman republic. In the same way and with the same manoeuvres Bonaparte was to prepare his coup of 2 December against the royalist Legislative Assembly and its constitutional republic. It should not be forgotten that the same party which formed Bonaparte's ministry on 20 December 1848 formed the majority of the Legislative Assembly on 2 December 1851.

The Constituent Assembly had decided in August that it would only dissolve when it had worked out and promulgated a whole series of organic laws which were to supplement the Constitution. The party of Order had the deputy Rateau propose on 6 January 1849 that the Assembly should forget the organic laws and instead resolve on its *own dissolution*. Odilon Barrot's ministry and all the royalist deputies bullied the National Assembly with the argument that its dissolution was necessary for the restoration of credit, for the consolidation of order, for the cessation of the indefinite provisional situation, for the establishment of a definitive state of affairs; that it hindered the new government's productivity and sought to prolong its existence out of mere spite; and that the country was tired of it. Bonaparte took note of all this invective against the legislative power, learnt it by heart, and on 2 December 1851 demonstrated to the parliamentary royalists that he had learnt his lessons well. He repeated their own catchwords against them.

The Barrot ministry and the party of Order went further. They were behind the *petitions to the National Assembly* which arrived from all over France, politely requesting the Assembly to disappear. Thus against the National Assembly, the constitutionally organized expression of the people, they led into the attack the unorganized masses. They taught Bonaparte to appeal from parliamentary assemblies to the people. Finally, on 29 January 1849, there came the day on which the Constituent Assembly was supposed to decide on its own dissolution. The Assembly found its meeting-place under military occupation; Changarnier, the party of Order's general who held the supreme command of both the National Guard and the troops of the line, held a big military review in Paris, as if in expectation of a battle, and the royalist coalition threatened the Constituent Assembly that force would be used if it was unwilling to submit. It was willing, but only obtained the very short extension of life it bargained for. What was 29 January if not the coup d'état of 2 December 1851, only carried out by the royalists in alliance with Bonaparte against the republican National Assembly? These gentlemen did not notice, or did not want to notice, that Bonaparte made use of 29 January 1849 by having a section of the troops march past him in front of the Tuileries, and eagerly seized on this first public display of the power of the military against the power of parliament to intimate that he would act the part of Caligula.[45] Of course, the royalists saw only their Changarnier.

One important factor which led the party of Order forcibly to cut short the Constituent Assembly's life was the question of the *organic* laws supplementing the Constitution, such as the laws on education, on religious worship, etc. It was of vital importance to the royalist coalition that it should make these laws itself and not allow them to be made by the now mistrustful republicans. Among these organic laws there was also a law on the responsibility of the President of the republic. In 1851, indeed, the Legislative Assembly was engaged in drafting a law of that kind when Bonaparte forestalled this coup with the coup of 2 December. What would the royalist coalition not have given in its parliamentary winter campaign of 1851 to find the law on responsibility ready

45. The Roman emperor Caligula (37–41) declared himself a god and established a regime of complete absolutism. He relied on the support of the military, and in particular on the praetorian guard.

and waiting, no matter that it had been drafted by a suspicious and malevolent republican Assembly?

After 29 January 1849, when the Constituent Assembly destroyed its own last weapon,[46] the Barrot ministry and the friends of order hounded it to death, did everything possible to humiliate it, and, making use of its weakness and self-despair, wrung from it laws which cost it its last remnant of public esteem. Bonaparte, occupied with his Napoleonic obsession, was impertinent enough to exploit this degradation of the power of parliament in public. When, on 8 May 1849, the National Assembly censured the ministry for Oudinot's occupation of Civitavecchia and gave orders for the Roman expedition to be brought back to its alleged purpose,[47] Bonaparte published a letter to Oudinot in the *Moniteur* the same evening, in which he congratulated him on his heroic deeds, and already acted the part of the magnanimous protector of the army against the pen-pushing parliamentarians. The royalists smiled at this. They simply considered Napoleon their dupe. Finally, when Marrast, the chairman of the Constituent Assembly, momentarily thought its safety was in danger and, basing himself on the Constitution, requisitioned a colonel with his regiment, the colonel refused the request with a reference to discipline, and referred Marrast to Changarnier, who scornfully turned him away with the remark that he did not like *bayonets which thought*. In November 1851, when the royalist coalition wanted to start the decisive struggle with Bonaparte, they tried to push through the principle of the direct requisition of troops by the chairman of the National Assembly, with their notorious Quaestors Bill.[48] One of their generals, Le Flô,[49] had signed the bill. Changarnier voted for it, and Thiers paid homage to the prudent wisdom of the former Constituent Assembly, but all to no purpose. The War Minister,

46. On 29 January 1849 the Constituent Assembly rejected a motion from Mathieu de la Drôme calling for the unconditional rejection of Rateau's motion of 6 January that the Assembly decree its own dissolution.

47. See above, pp. 419–21.

48. The name given, by analogy with the old Roman office, to the National Assembly's commissioners for finance and security. The quaestors Le Flô, Baze and Panat moved that the Assembly be given the exclusive right to command the troops. This motion was rejected on 17 November 1851 owing to the refusal of the Montagne to vote for it.

49. Adolphe Le Flô was a general and a diplomat. During the Second Republic he supported the party of Order.

Saint-Arnaud,[50] replied as Changarnier had replied to Marrast – and the Montagne applauded!

Thus when the party of Order did not yet control the National Assembly, when it was still only the ministry, it had itself stigmatized the parliamentary regime. And now it makes an outcry because 2 December 1851 has banished the parliamentary regime from France!

We wish it a pleasant journey.

III

The Legislative National Assembly met on 28 May 1849. It was dispersed on 2 December 1851. The period between these dates covers the life-span of the *constitutional* or *parliamentary republic*.

In the first French revolution the rule of the Constitutionalists was followed by the rule of the Girondins, and the rule of the Girondins by the rule of the Jacobins. Each of these parties leant on the more progressive party. As soon as it had brought the revolution to the point where it was unable to follow it any further, let alone advance ahead of it, it was pushed aside by the bolder ally standing behind it and sent to the guillotine. In this way the revolution moved in an ascending path.

In the revolution of 1848 this relationship was reversed. The proletarian party appeared as the appendage of petty-bourgeois democracy. It was betrayed and abandoned by the latter on 16 April,[51] on 15 May, and in the June days. The democratic party, for its part, leant on the shoulders of the bourgeois-republican party. As soon as the bourgeois republicans thought they had found their feet, they shook off this burdensome comrade and relied in turn on the shoulders of the party of Order. The party of Order hunched its shoulders, allowed the bourgeois republicans to tumble off, and threw itself onto the shoulders of the armed forces. It believed it was still sitting on those shoulders when it noticed one fine morning that they had changed into bayonets. Every party kicked out behind at the party pressing it forward

50. Armand de Saint-Arnaud was a Bonapartist general and an organizer of the coup d'état of 2 December. He was Minister of War from 1851 to 1854.

51. On 16 April 1848 a large body of workers was prevented by the National Guard from marching to the Hôtel de Ville to present a patriotic collection owing to the Provisional Government's fear that the demonstration might turn into a Blanquist coup directed against it.

and leant on the party in front, which was pressing backward. No wonder each party lost its balance in this ridiculous posture, and collapsed in the midst of curious capers, after having made the inevitable grimaces. In this way the revolution moved in a descending path. Before the last February barricade had been cleared away and the first revolutionary authority constituted, the parties found themselves enmeshed in this retrogressive process.

The period we have now to deal with contains the most variegated mixture of crying contradictions: constitutionalists who openly conspire against the Constitution; revolutionaries who are by their own admission constitutionalists; a National Assembly which aspires to supreme power but throughout remains parliamentary; a Montagne which finds its vocation in patience and parries its present defeats by prophesying future victories; royalists who are *patres conscripti*[52] of the republic and are compelled by the situation to keep the mutually hostile royal houses they support abroad and the republic they hate in France; an executive which draws strength from its very weakness and respectability from the contempt it inspires; a republic with imperialist trappings, which is nothing but the combined infamy of two monarchies, the Restoration and the July monarchy; alliances whose first condition is separation, and struggles whose first law is their indecisiveness; wild and empty agitation in the name of tranquillity, the most solemn preaching of tranquillity in the name of revolution; passions without truth, truths without passion; heroes without deeds of heroism, history without events; a course of development apparently only driven forward by the calendar, and made wearisome by the constant repetition of the same tensions and relaxations; antagonisms which seem periodically to press forward to a climax, but become deadened and fall away without having attained their resolution; exertions pretentiously put on show and bourgeois terror at the danger that the world may end, and at the same time the pettiest intrigues and courtly comedies played by the world's saviours, who in their *laissez-aller* are more reminiscent of the era of the Fronde[53] than of the Day of Judgement; the official collective genius of France brought to ruin by

52. The ancient Roman term for senators.
53. The movement of opposition on the part of the French nobility to the absolut-ism of the French monarchy, in the years 1648–53. The Fronde became a byword for aristocratic frivolity.

the cunning stupidity of a single individual; the collective will of the nation seeking its appropriate expression through the superannuated enemies of the interests of the masses, whenever it spoke through universal suffrage, until finally it found expression in the self-will of a freebooter. If any section of history has been painted grey on grey, it is this. Men and events appear as Schlemihls in reverse,[54] as shadows which have become detached from their bodies. The revolution paralyses its own representatives and endows only its opponents with passion and forcefulness. The 'red spectre' is continually conjured up and exorcized by the counter-revolutionaries; when it finally appears it is not with the Phrygian cap[55] of anarchy on its head, but in the uniform of order, in *red breeches*.

As we have seen, the ministry which Bonaparte installed on 20 December 1848, the day of his ascension into the Elysian Fields, was a ministry of the party of Order, of the Legitimist and Orleanist coalition. The Barrot-Falloux ministry outlasted the republican Constituent Assembly, whose life it had more or less violently curtailed, and was still at the helm when the Legislative Assembly met. Changarnier, the general of the royalist alliance, continued to combine in his own person the general command of the First Army Division and of the Paris National Guard. Finally, the general elections had secured for the party of Order the vast majority of the seats in the National Assembly. Here the former deputies and peers of Louis Philippe's reign met with a holy host of Legitimists, for whom many of the nation's voting cards had become transformed into cards of admission to the political stage. The Bonapartist deputies were too thin on the ground to be able to form an independent parliamentary party. They appeared only as the *mauvaise queue*[56] of the party of Order. Thus the party of Order was in possession of the power of government, of the army, and of the legislative body, in short, of all the power of the state. It had been morally strengthened by the general elections, which made it appear that it ruled by the will of the people, and also by the simultaneous victory of the counter-revolution all over the continent of Europe.

54. After the hero of *Peter Schlemihl*, by Adalbert von Chamisso. Schlemihl sold his shadow for a magic purse.

55. The conical peaked cap worn by the Jacobins; frequently used in the nineteenth century as a symbol of liberty.

56. Dubious hangers-on.

Never did a party open its campaign with greater resources or under more favourable auspices.

The shipwrecked *pure republicans* found that in the Legislative National Assembly they had shrunk to a clique of approximately fifty men, headed by the African generals Cavaignac, Lamoricière and Bedeau.[57] However, the main opposition party was formed by the Montagne. This was what the *social-democratic* party had baptized itself for parliamentary purposes. It had at its disposal more than 200 of the 750 votes in the National Assembly and was therefore at least as powerful as any one of the fractions of the party of Order taken in isolation. The fact that it was in a minority as against the royalist coalition as a whole seemed to be outweighed by special circumstances. It was not just that the elections in the departments showed that it had won considerable support among the rural population. It counted in its ranks almost all the deputies from Paris; the army had sworn its faith in democracy by electing three non-commissioned officers, and Ledru-Rollin, the leader of the Montagne, had, unlike any of the party of Order's deputies, been elected to parliament by five different departments. Thus on 28 May 1849 the Montagne seemed to possess all the requirements for success, in view of the inevitability of clashes between the rival royalists, and between Bonaparte and the party of Order in general. A fortnight later it had lost everything, including its honour.

Before we follow the parliamentary history any further, some remarks are necessary in order to avoid certain common delusions about the overall character of the epoch which lies before us. If we look at this in the fashion of the democrats, the issue during the period of the Legislative National Assembly was the same issue as in the period of the Constituent Assembly: a simple struggle between republicans and royalists. However, the democrats sum up the whole course of development itself in *one* slogan: '*reaction*' – a night in which all cats are grey and which allows them to reel off their useless platitudes. And of course an initial inspection reveals the party of Order to be a conglomeration of different royalist fractions, which not only intrigue against each other to

57. See above, p. 485. Christophe Juchault de Lamoricière was a deputy in both Assemblies, and War Minister in Cavaignac's government (June–December 1848). Marie-Adolphe Bedeau was vice-chairman of both Assemblies. Both generals actively participated in the suppression of the June insurrection.

raise their own pretender to the throne and exclude the pretender of the opposing fraction, but also unite together in a common hatred of the 'republic' and in common attacks on it. The Montagne for its part appears as the representative of the 'republic' in opposition to this royalist conspiracy. The party of Order appears to be constantly engaged in a 'reaction' directed, neither more nor less than in Prussia, against the press, the right of association, and similar things, and which is accomplished, as in Prussia, by means of the brutal police interventions of the bureaucracy, the *gendarmerie* and the courts. The Montagne for its part is just as continually engaged in fighting off these attacks and in this way defending the 'eternal rights of man', more or less in the same way as every so-called people's party has done for a century and a half. But this superficial appearance veils the *class struggle* and the peculiar physiognomy of this period, and it vanishes on a closer examination of the situation and the parties.

As we have said, Legitimists and Orleanists formed the two great fractions of the party of Order. Was it nothing but the *fleur-de-lis* and the tricolour, the House of Bourbon and the House of Orleans, the different shades of royalism, which held the fractions fast to their pretenders and apart from each other? Was it their royalist creed at all? Under the Bourbons, *big landed property* had ruled, with its priests and lackeys; under the July monarchy, it had been high finance, large-scale industry, large-scale trade, i.e., *capital*, with its retinue of advocates, professors and fine speech-makers. The legitimate monarchy was simply the political expression of the immemorial domination of the lords of the soil, just as the July monarchy was only the political expression of the usurped rule of the bourgeois parvenus. It was therefore not so-called principles which kept these fractions divided, but rather their material conditions of existence, two distinct sorts of property; it was the old opposition between town and country, the old rivalry between capital and landed property. Who would deny that at the same time old memories, personal enmities, fears and hopes, prejudices and illusions, sympathies and antipathies, convictions, articles of faith and principles bound them to one or the other royal house? A whole superstructure of different and specifically formed feelings, illusions, modes of thought and views of life arises on the basis of the different forms of property, of the social conditions of existence. The whole class creates and forms these out of its material foundations and the corresponding social relations.

The single individual, who derives these feelings, etc., through tradition and upbringing, may well imagine that they form the real determinants and the starting-point of his activity. The Orleanist and Legitimist fractions each tried to make out to their opponents and themselves that they were divided by their adherence to the two royal houses; facts later proved that it was rather the division between their interests which forbade the unification of the royal houses. A distinction is made in private life between what a man thinks and says of himself and what he really is and does. In historical struggles one must make a still sharper distinction between the phrases and fantasies of the parties and their real organization and real interests, between their conception of themselves and what they really are. Orleanists and Legitimists found themselves side by side in the republic, making equal claims. Each side wanted to secure the *restoration* of its *own* royal house against the other; this had no other meaning than that each of the *two great interests* into which the bourgeoisie is divided – landed property and capital – was endeavouring to restore its own supremacy and the subordination of the other interest. We refer to the two interests of the bourgeoisie because big landed property in fact has been completely bourgeoisified by the development of modern society, despite its feudal coquetry and racial pride. The Tories in England long imagined they were enthusiastic about the monarchy, the church, and the beauties of the old English constitution, until the day of danger wrung from them the confession that they were only enthusiastic about *ground rent*.[58]

The members of the royalist coalition intrigued against each other outside parliament: in the press, at Ems, and at Claremont.[59] Behind the scenes they dressed up again in their old Orleanist and Legitimist liveries and went back to their old tournaments. But on the public stage, in their grand national performances as a great parliamentary party, they put off their respective royal houses with mere bows and adjourned the restoration of the monarchy to an indefinite point in the future. They did their real business as

58. This is a reference to the effect of the abolition of the Corn Laws in 1846 on the Tory party: the party's name was changed to that of Protectionist, and for some years it campaigned on the single issue of the restoration of the Corn Laws, with a view to keeping ground rents at the highest possible level. (See 'Tories and Whigs', p. 591.)

59. Ems, near Wiesbaden, was the residence of the comte de Chambord (Henri V), the Legitimist claimant; Claremont, near London, was the residence of Louis Philippe.

the *party of Order*, i.e., under a *social* and not a *political* title, as representatives of the bourgeois world order, not as knights of errant princesses, as the bourgeois class against other classes, not as royalists against republicans. And as the party of Order they ruled over the other classes of society more harshly and with less restriction than ever they could under the Restoration or the July monarchy. This was only possible given the governmental form of the parliamentary republic, for the two great subdivisions of the French bourgeoisie could only unite under this form, thus placing on the agenda the rule of their class instead of the regime of a privileged fraction of it. If, nevertheless, as the party of Order, they also insulted the republic and expressed their abhorrence of it, this did not happen merely as a result of royalist memories. They realized instinctively that although the republic made their political rule complete it simultaneously undermined its social foundation, since they had now to confront the subjugated classes and contend with them without mediation, without being concealed by the Crown, without the possibility of diverting the national attention by their secondary conflicts amongst themselves and with the monarchy. It was a feeling of weakness which caused them to recoil when faced with the pure conditions of their own class rule and to yearn for the return of the previous forms of this rule, which were less complete, less developed and, precisely for that reason, less dangerous. But whenever the royalists in coalition came into conflict with the pretender who confronted them, with Bonaparte, whenever they thought the executive power was endangering their parliamentary omnipotence, whenever, in other words, they had to produce the political title-deeds of their domination, they came forward as *republicans*, not *royalists*, from the Orleanist Thiers, who warned the National Assembly that the republic divided them least, to the Legitimist Berryer, who, on 2 December 1851, swathed in the tricoloured sash, harangued the people assembled in front of the town hall of the tenth *arrondissement* as a tribune speaking in the name of the republic.[60] Admittedly a mocking echo called back to him: *Henri V! Henri V!*[61]

The petty bourgeoisie and the workers had formed their own coalition, the so-called *social-democratic* party, in opposition to the coalition of the bourgeoisie. The petty bourgeoisie saw that they had done badly out of the June days. Their material interests were in danger, and the counter-revolution called into question

60. See p. 567.   61. See p. 439, n. 12.

the democratic guarantees which were supposed to secure the assertion of those interests. They therefore drew closer to the workers. Their parliamentary representatives, on the other hand, the Montagne, had improved their position. After being pushed aside during the dictatorship of the bourgeois republicans, they had reconquered their lost popularity in the latter half of the session of the Constituent Assembly by their struggle with Bonaparte and the royalist ministers. They had concluded an alliance with the socialist leaders, celebrated in February 1849 with banquets of reconciliation. A joint programme was drafted, joint election committees were set up, and joint candidates put forward. The social demands of the proletariat lost their revolutionary point and gained a democratic twist, while the democratic claims of the petty bourgeoisie were stripped of their purely political form and had their socialist point emphasized. In this way arose *social-democracy*. Apart from some working-class extras, and a few members of the socialist sects, the new Montagne, the result of this combination, contained the same elements as the old Montagne, but more of them. However, it had changed along with the class it represented in the course of historical development. The peculiar character of social-democracy can be summed up in the following way: democratic republican institutions are demanded as a means of softening the antagonism between the two extremes of capital and wage labour and transforming it into harmony, not of superseding both of them. However varied the measures proposed for achieving this goal, however much it may be edged with more or less revolutionary conceptions, its content remains the same. This content is the reformation of society by democratic means, but a reformation within the boundaries set by the petty bourgeoisie. Only one must not take the narrow view that the petty bourgeoisie explicitly sets out to assert its egoistic class interests. It rather believes that the *particular* conditions of its liberation are the only *general* conditions within which modern society can be saved and the class struggle avoided. Nor indeed must one imagine that the democratic representatives are all *shopkeepers*[62] or their enthusiastic supporters. They may well be poles apart from them in their education and their individual situation. What makes them representatives of the petty bourgeoisie is the fact that their minds are restricted by the same barriers which the petty bourgeoisie fails to overcome in real life, and that

62. In English in the original.

they are therefore driven in theory to the same problems and solutions to which material interest and social situation drive the latter in practice. This is the general relationship between the *political and literary representatives* of a class and the class which they represent.

After the analysis we have given, it should be self-evident that the ultimate goal of the Montagne in its fight with the party of Order on behalf of the republic and the so-called rights of man was neither of these things; just as little as an army which resists those who want to deprive it of its weapons has joined battle in order to remain in possession of those weapons.

The party of Order provoked the Montagne as soon as the National Assembly met. The bourgeoisie now felt it necessary to settle accounts with the democratic petty bourgeoisie, just as, a year earlier, it had realized the necessity of dealing with the revolutionary proletariat. Only this time the situation of the opponent was different. The strength of the proletarian party lay in the streets; the strength of the petty-bourgeois party lay in the National Assembly. The petty bourgeoisie had, therefore, to be enticed out of the National Assembly and into the streets, so that they would themselves destroy their parliamentary power before there was time or opportunity to consolidate it. The Montagne rushed into the trap at a full gallop.

The bombardment of Rome by French troops[63] was the bait thrown to it. This violated paragraph V of the Constitution, which forbade the French republic to employ its armed forces against the liberties of another people. On top of this, paragraph 54 forbade the executive to declare war without the agreement of the National Assembly, and the Constituent Assembly had expressed its disapproval of the Roman expedition by the resolution of 8 May 1849. On these grounds, therefore, Ledru-Rollin introduced a bill of impeachment against Bonaparte and his ministers on 11 June 1849. Infuriated by the wasp-stings of Thiers, he allowed himself to be carried away to the point of threatening to defend the Constitution by all means, even with weapons. The Montagne rose to a man and repeated this call to arms. On 12 June the National Assembly rejected the bill of impeachment and the Montagne left the Assembly. The events of 13 June are well known: the proclamation of one section of the Montagne by which Bona-

---

63. The seige of Rome began on 3 June 1849. It mainly consisted of a bombardment of the city, which lasted throughout the month (see pp. 419–21).

parte and his ministers were declared to be 'outside the Constitution'; the street procession of the democratic National Guards, who, being unarmed, dispersed when they came up against Changarnier's troops, and so on. Some of the Montagne fled abroad, others were handed over to the High Court at Bourges, and a parliamentary regulation subjected the rest of them to the schoolmasterly supervision of the chairman of the National Assembly.[64] Paris was again placed in a state of siege and the democratic part of its National Guard was dissolved. In this way the influence of the Montagne in parliament was broken together with the power of the petty bourgeoisie in Paris.

Lyons, where 13 June had given the signal for a bloody workers' uprising, was similarly proclaimed in a state of siege, together with the five surrounding departments, and this situation has lasted up to the present time.

The bulk of the Montagne had left its vanguard in the lurch by refusing to sign its proclamation. The press had deserted, only two newspapers having dared to publish it. The individual petty bourgeois betrayed their representatives, for the National Guards either stayed away or, where they appeared, hindered the building of barricades. The petty bourgeois had in turn been deceived by their representatives, in that their alleged allies from the ranks of the army were nowhere to be seen. Finally, instead of gaining increased strength from the proletariat, the democratic party had infected it with its own weakness; as is usual with the exploits of the democrats, the leaders had the satisfaction of being able to charge their 'people' with desertion, and the people had the satisfaction of being able to charge its leaders with fraud.

Seldom had an action been announced more noisily than the impending campaign of the Montagne; seldom had an event been trumpeted with greater certainty or longer in advance than the inevitable victory of democracy. The democrats certainly believe in the trumpets whose blasts made the walls of Jericho collapse. Whenever they are confronted with the ramparts of despotism, they endeavour to imitate that miracle. If the Montagne wanted a parliamentary victory, it ought not to have given the call to arms. If it gave the call to arms in parliament, it ought not to have

64. A new order of business was adopted by the National Assembly under the impact of the events of 13 June. It gave the chairman of the Assembly the right to exclude deputies for infringing due parliamentary forms and provided for the loss of half a deputy's salary if he was censured three times in a month.

behaved in a parliamentary fashion in the streets. If the peaceful demonstration was meant seriously, it was foolish not to foresee that it would be received in a warlike manner. If a real struggle was intended, it was very odd to lay down the weapons with which it would have to be fought. But the revolutionary threats of the petty bourgeoisie and their democratic representatives are merely attempts to intimidate the opponent. And when they have run into a blind alley, when they have compromised themselves sufficiently to be compelled to carry out their threats, they do this in an ambiguous way, avoiding the means to the end like the plague and clutching at excuses for their failure. The blaring overture which announced the struggle dies away into a subdued grumbling as soon as it is due to begin, the actors cease to take themselves *au sérieux*, and the action totally collapses like a balloon pricked by a needle.

No party exaggerates the means at its disposal more than the democratic party; no party deludes itself more frivolously about the situation. Since part of the army had voted for it, the Montagne was now convinced that the army would revolt in its favour. And on what occasion was this supposed to happen? On an occasion which had no other meaning, from the troops' point of view, than that the revolutionaries had taken the side of Roman soldiers against French soldiers. On the other hand, the memory of June 1848 was still too fresh for the proletariat to feel anything but a deep aversion towards the National Guard, or for the leaders of the secret societies[65] to feel anything but complete mistrust for the democratic leaders. Important common interests had to be at stake to offset these differences, and the violation of an abstract paragraph of the Constitution did not provide a common interest of this kind. Did the democrats themselves not insist that the Constitution had been repeatedly violated? Had the most popular newspapers not branded it as a counter-revolutionary concoction? But because the democrat represents the petty bourgeoisie, a *transitional class* in which the interests of two classes meet and become blurred, he imagines he is elevated above class antagonisms generally. The democrats admit that they are confronted with a privi-

65. The organizations that Marx is referring to here are not, strictly speaking, the revolutionary secret societies that existed before the February revolution, but rather their open descendants, the 'Republican clubs' that were set up by revolutionary militants such as Blanqui, Barbès, etc., after February 1848.

leged class, but assert that they, along with all the rest of the nation, form the *people*. What they represent is the *right of the people*; what interests them is the *interest of the people*. Therefore, when a struggle approaches, they do not need to examine the interests and positions of the various classes. They do not need to weigh up the means at their disposal too critically. They have only to give the signal for the people, with all its inexhaustible resources, to fall upon the oppressors. If in the sequel their interests turn out to be uninteresting and their power turns out to be impotence, either this is the fault of dangerous sophists, who split the *indivisible people* into different hostile camps, or the army was too brutalized and deluded to understand that the pure goals of democracy were best for it too, or a mistake in one detail of implementation has wrecked the whole plan, or indeed an unforeseen accident has frustrated the game this time. In each case the democrat emerges as spotless from the most shameful defeat as he was innocent when he went into it, fresh in his conviction that he must inevitably be victorious, taking the view that conditions must ripen to meet his requirements, rather than that he and his party must abandon their old standpoint.

Consequently, we must not imagine that the Montagne felt particularly miserable, although it was decimated, broken and humiliated by the new parliamentary regulations. If 13 June had removed its leaders, it had nevertheless made room for men of an inferior stamp, who were flattered by this new position. If their powerlessness in parliament could no longer be doubted, they were now justified in confining their activities to outbursts of moral indignation and blustering declamation. The party of Order pretended to see all the horrors of anarchy embodied in them, as the last official representatives of the revolution; they could therefore be all the more insipid and modest in reality. Thus, they consoled each other for 13 June along the following lines: But if they dare to attack universal suffrage, then we shall show them what kind of people we are! *Nous verrons!*

As far as those members of the Montagne who fled abroad are concerned, it is sufficient here to point out that because Ledru-Rollin had succeeded, in barely two weeks, in irretrievably ruining the powerful party he headed, he now considered it his mission to form a French government *in partibus*.[66] As the level of the revolution sank and the official celebrities of official France be-

66. See p. 472, n. 74.

came more dwarf-like, Ledru-Rollin's figure in the distance, removed from the scene of action, seemed to increase in magnitude; he was able to figure as the republican pretender for 1852, periodically issuing circulars to the Wallachians and other peoples in which he threatened to take action, along with his confederates, against the continental despots. Was Proudhon completely wrong to exclaim to these gentlemen: '*Vous n'êtes que des blagueurs*'?[67]

The party of Order had broken the Montagne on 13 June; it had also succeeded in *subordinating the Constitution to the majority decision of the National Assembly*. That was its interpretation of the republic: the rule of the bourgeoisie in parliamentary forms, without the restrictions characteristic of a monarchy, such as the executive veto or the possibility of dissolving parliament. This was the *parliamentary republic*, as Thiers put it. But when, on 13 June, the bourgeoisie had secured its own supremacy within the parliament building, had it not also afflicted parliament itself with an incurable weakness *vis-à-vis* the executive and the people by expelling its most popular part? By surrendering numerous deputies on the demand of the courts, and without making a great deal of fuss, it abolished its own parliamentary immunity. The humiliating procedural rules to which it subjected the Montagne exalted the status of the President of the republic in the same measure as it degraded the individual deputies. By stigmatizing an insurrection for the protection of constitutional provisions as an anarchistic attempt to overthrow society, it forbade any appeal to the weapon of insurrection on its own part if ever the executive power should behave unconstitutionally towards it. And the irony of history would have it that Oudinot, the general who bombarded Rome on Bonaparte's instructions and so provided the immediate occasion for the constitutionalist revolt of 13 June, was the man vainly and imploringly offered to the people by the party of Order on 2 December 1851 as the general to defend the Constitution against Bonaparte. Another hero of 13 June was Vieyra,[68] who reaped a harvest of congratulations from the tribune of the National Assembly for the brutalities he had committed in the offices of democratic newspapers at the head of a band of National Guards belonging to high financial circles. This same Vieyra was a party

67. 'You are nothing but humbugs,' a phrase from an article of 20 July 1850; P.-J. Proudhon, *Correspondence*, vol. 14, p. 297.

68. Vieyra, a French colonel, was in 1851 the Chief of Staff of the National Guard and a Bonapartist. He took part in the coup d'état of 2 December.

to Bonaparte's conspiracy and played a very important part in depriving the National Assembly of any protection by the National Guard in the hour of its final agony.

13 June had yet another meaning. The Montagne had wanted to force the impeachment of Bonaparte. Its defeat was thus a direct victory for him, a personal triumph over his democratic enemies. The party of Order had won that victory; Bonaparte had only to cash in on it, and he did. On 14 June a proclamation could be read on the walls of Paris in which the President, reluctantly and almost against his will, compelled, as it were, by the sheer force of events, emerged from his cloistered seclusion as the incarnation of misunderstood virtue, and complained of the slanders of his opponents. While appearing to identify his person with the cause of order, he in fact identified the cause of order with his person. In addition to this, Bonaparte had himself taken the initiative in the matter of the expedition against Rome, whereas the National Assembly had only retrospectively approved it. After reinstalling the High Priest Samuel in the Vatican, he could hope to enter the Tuileries as King David.[69] He had won over the priests.

As we have seen, the revolt of 13 June was limited to a peaceful street procession. There were therefore no military laurels to be won against it. Despite this, the party of Order was able to transform a bloodless battle into a second Austerlitz[70] in this period so poor in heroes and events. On public platforms and in the press the army was praised as the force of order against the anarchic impotence of the popular masses, and Changarnier was praised as the 'bulwark of society'; in the end he believed in this mystification himself. Secretly, however, the corps that seemed doubtful were transferred from Paris, the regiments which had voted for democratic candidates at the elections were banished from France to Algeria, restless elements among the troops were assigned to penal detachments, and finally the press was systematically isolated from the barracks and the barracks from civil society.

We have now arrived at the decisive turning point in the history of the French National Guard. In 1830 its attitude had decided the fate of the Restoration. Under Louis Philippe every rebellion in which the National Guard stood on the side of the troops was a

69. Louis Bonaparte, it was rumoured, hoped to receive the French crown from the hands of Pius IX after he had restored the Pope's temporal power.

70. The first Austerlitz was the battle of that name in 1805, at which Napoleon I defeated the allied Russian and Austrian armies.

failure. In the February days of 1848, when the National Guard behaved passively towards the insurrection and ambiguously towards Louis Philippe, he admitted defeat, and indeed he was defeated. In this way the conviction became rooted that the revolution could not win *without* the National Guard, and that the army could not win *against* it. This was the army's superstitious belief in civilian omnipotence. The June days of 1848, when the whole National Guard put down the insurrection alongside the troops of the line, had strengthened this belief. After Bonaparte took office the importance of the National Guard was to some extent reduced by the unification of its command with that of the First Army Division in the person of Changarnier, in defiance of the Constitution.

Command of the National Guard thus appeared as an attribute of the military commander-in-chief, and the National Guard appeared as no more than an addition to the troops of the line. Its power was finally broken on 13 June. Not simply because of its partial dissolution, which was later to be repeated all over France, leaving only fragments behind. The demonstration of 13 June had been above all a demonstration by the democratic wing of the National Guard. To be sure, they had not confronted the army with their weapons, but only with their uniforms; however, the talisman lay precisely in the uniform. Once the army reached the conviction that it was a woollen rag like any other uniform, the charm lost its power. In the June days the bourgeoisie and petty bourgeoisie, as the National Guard, were united with the army against the proletariat; on 13 June 1849 the bourgeoisie let the army disperse the petty-bourgeois sections of the National Guard; on 2 December 1851 the bourgeois National Guard itself vanished, and Bonaparte merely bore witness to this fact when he subsequently signed the decree dissolving it. Thus the bourgeoisie smashed its own last weapon against the army. However, it was compelled to do so from the moment when the petty bourgeoisie ceased to stand behind it as its vassal, and instead stood before it as a rebel, just as, in general, it had to destroy all its instruments of defence against absolutism with its own hand as soon as it had itself become absolute.

In the meantime the party of Order celebrated the reconquest of a power only apparently lost in 1848, and recovered in 1849 free from its previous restrictions. It celebrated with invective against the republic and the Constitution, execration of all revolutions, whether present, past or future, including that made by its own leaders, and legislation muzzling the press, destroying the right of association, and establishing the state of siege as an organic institution. Then, after appointing a Standing Commission to sit in its absence, the National Assembly adjourned from the middle of August to the middle of October. During this recess the Legitimists intrigued with Ems, the Orleanists with Claremont, Bonaparte went on princely tours of the country, and the Departmental Councils discussed the possibility of revising the Constitution. These incidents regularly recurred every time the National Assembly went into recess, but I shall only discuss them where they became real events. Let us merely point out here that the National Assembly acted imprudently in disappearing from the stage for considerable intervals, leaving only *one* figure in sight at the head of the republic, even though it was the pitiful figure of Louis Bonaparte, at a time when the party of Order, to the scandal of the public, was splitting up into its royalist components and pursuing mutually contradictory desires for a restoration. As soon as the confusing din of the Assembly fell silent during these recesses, and its body merged into that of the nation, it became obvious that only *one thing* was needed to complete the true form of this republic: the *former's* recess must be made permanent, and the *latter's* motto, *liberté, égalité, fraternité*, must be replaced with the unambiguous words *infantry, cavalry, artillery!*

IV

The National Assembly resumed its sittings in the middle of October 1849. On 1 November[71] Bonaparte surprised it with a message announcing the dismissal of the Barrot-Falloux ministry and the formation of a new one. Lackeys have never been sacked with less ceremony than Bonaparte used with his ministers. For the time being Barrot and company received the kicks that were intended for the National Assembly.

As we have seen, the Barrot ministry had been made up of Legitimists and Orleanists; it was a ministry of the party of Order. Bonaparte had needed such a ministry so as to dissolve the republican Constituent Assembly, carry out the expedition against Rome, and break the democratic party. He had seemed to efface

71. The date of the dismissal of the Barrot-Falloux ministry and the formation of the Hautpoul ministry was in fact 31 October.

himself behind this ministry, resigning the power of government into the hands of the party of Order and assuming the modest character mask worn by responsible newspaper editors in the time of Louis Philippe, the mask of the *straw man*.[72] Now he threw away the mask, for it was no longer a light veil behind which he could hide his features, but an iron mask which prevented him from displaying any features of his own. He had appointed the Barrot ministry so as to disperse the republican National Assembly in the name of the party of Order; he dismissed it so as to declare his own name to be independent of the party of Order's National Assembly.

There was no shortage of plausible pretexts for this dismissal. The Barrot ministry even neglected to observe the proprieties which would have let the President of the republic appear as a power alongside the National Assembly. During the National Assembly's recess Bonaparte published a letter to Edgar Ney[73] in which he seemed to object to the illiberal attitude of the Pope; in the same way he had opposed the Constituent Assembly by publishing a letter commending Oudinot for the attack on the Roman republic. Now, when the National Assembly voted the budget for the Roman expedition, Victor Hugo brought this letter up for discussion, for supposedly liberal reasons. The party of Order drowned the idea that Bonaparte's notions might have any political weight with cries of scornful disbelief. None of the ministers took up the gauntlet on his behalf. On another occasion Barrot let fall from the platform, with his usual hollow pathos, words of indignation about the 'abominable machinations' which were going on, according to him, in the immediate entourage of the President. On top of this the ministry rejected any proposal for an increase in the presidential civil list, whilst it obtained a widow's pension for the Duchess of Orleans from the National Assembly. And the imperial pretender in Bonaparte was so intimately mingled with the adventurer who has fallen on bad times that his one great idea, that it was his destiny to restore the empire, was always supplemented by the other, that it was the mission of the French people to pay his debts.

72. The severe press law of September 1835 laid down that the responsible editor of a newspaper had personally to sign each issue. Since many of the real editors of republican journals were in prison, 'straw men' (*hommes de paille*) had to be employed, men who lent their names to the paper while in practice having nothing to do with it.

73. General Edgar Ney was Louis Bonaparte's military aide.

The Barrot-Falloux ministry was the first and last *parliamentary ministry* called to life by Bonaparte. Its dismissal therefore marked a decisive turning point. With it the party of Order lost the lever of executive power, an indispensable position for the maintenance of the parliamentary regime, and it never re-conquered it. In France the executive has at its disposal an army of more than half a million individual officials, and it therefore constantly maintains an immense mass of interests and livelihoods in a state of the most unconditional dependence; the state enmeshes, controls, regulates, supervises and regiments civil society from the most all-embracing expressions of its life down to its most insignificant motions, from its most general modes of existence down to the private life of individuals. This parasitic body acquires, through the most extraordinary centralization, an omnipresence, an omniscience, an elasticity and an accelerated rapidity of movement which find their only appropriate complement in the real social body's helpless irresolution and its lack of a consistent formation. One realizes immediately that in such a country the National Assembly lost all real influence when it lost control of the ministerial portfolios, because it failed at the same time to simplify the state administration, reduce the army of officials as much as possible, and finally let civil society and public opinion create their own organs independent of the power of the government. But the *material interest* of the French bourgeoisie is most intimately imbricated precisely with the maintenance of that extensive and highly ramified state machine. It is that machine which provides its surplus population with jobs, and makes up through state salaries for what it cannot pocket in the form of profits, interest, rents and fees. Its *political interest* equally compelled it daily to increase the repression, and therefore to increase the resources and the personnel of the state power; it had simultaneously to wage an incessant war against public opinion and mistrustfully mutilate and cripple society's independent organs of movement where it did not succeed in entirely amputating them. The French bourgeoisie was thus compelled by its class position both to liquidate the conditions of existence of all parliamentary power, including its own, and to make its opponent, the executive, irresistible.

The new ministry was known as the Hautpoul ministry. It was not that General Hautpoul had received the rank of Prime Minister. Bonaparte had abolished this dignitary when he removed

Barrot, for the existence of a Prime Minister condemned the President of the republic to the legal nullity of a constitutional monarch, though in this case a monarch with neither throne nor crown, neither sceptre nor sword, neither irresponsibility nor the indefeasible possession of the highest state dignity – worst of all, without a civil list. The Hautpoul ministry contained only one man with a parliamentary reputation, the moneylender Fould, one of the most notorious members of the clique of high financiers. The Ministry of Finance was allotted to him. Look up the quotations of the Paris Bourse, and you will find that from 1 November 1849 onwards, French government securities rose and fell with the rise and fall of the Bonapartist stocks. Bonaparte had found his ally in the Bourse; at the same time he gained control of the police through the appointment of Carlier as Prefect of Police in Paris.

The consequences of this change of ministries could only emerge in the further course of development. Bonaparte seemed to have first taken a step forwards only to be driven all the more conspicuously backwards. His blunt message was followed by the most servile declaration of allegiance to the National Assembly. Whenever his ministers dared to make the timid attempt to introduce his personal fads as proposals for legislation, it was apparent that they were being compelled by their position to unwillingly fulfil peculiar commissions which they were convinced in advance would be unsuccessful. His own ministers disavowed him from the platform of the National Assembly whenever he blurted out his intentions behind their backs, playing with his 'Napoleonic ideas'.[74] His desire to usurp power only seemed to be expressed aloud so that the malicious laughter of his opponents might never fall silent. He behaved like the misunderstood genius proclaimed by all the world to be a simpleton. He never enjoyed the hatred of all classes to a greater degree than in this period. The rule of the bourgeoisie was never more unconditional, and it never wore the insignia of domination more ostentatiously.

I do not need to write the history of the bourgeoisie's legislative activity here: it can be summed up for this period in two laws, the one restoring the *wine tax*[75] and the other abolishing unbelief:

74. Louis Bonaparte expressed his theory of government in a book entitled *Des idées napoléoniennes*, published in Paris in 1839.

75. The Constituent Assembly had resolved to abolish the wine tax as from 1 January 1850, but on 20 December 1849 the Legislative Assembly reintroduced the tax. On the political significance of this decision, see *The Class Struggles in France*, above, pp. 447–49.

the *education law*.[76] If wine-drinking was made harder for the French, they were endowed all the more richly with the water of true life. With the law on the wine tax the bourgeoisie declared the inviolability of the old and hated French tax system, but they endeavoured by means of the education law to ensure the continuance of the old state of mind which allowed the masses to tolerate it. It is astounding to see the Orleanists, liberal members of the bourgeoisie, old apostles of Voltaireanism and eclecticism in philosophy, entrusting the control of the French mind to their hereditary enemies, the Jesuits. However, although Orleanists and Legitimists might be deeply divided as regards the pretenders to the throne, they understood that they now needed to unite the repressive instruments of two epochs in order to secure their joint domination, supplementing and strengthening the means of subjugation characteristic of the July monarchy with those of the Restoration.

The peasants had been disappointed in all their hopes; they were oppressed more than ever, on the one hand, by the low level of grain prices, on the other hand, by the growing burden of taxes and mortgage debts, and they started to stir in the departments. The government replied by starting a campaign against school-masters, who were made subject to the priests, a campaign against mayors, who were made subject to the prefects, and a system of informers, to which everyone was subject. In Paris and the big towns the reaction itself bears the features of its epoch, and challenges more than it strikes down. In the countryside it becomes dull, common, petty, fatiguing and plodding; it becomes, in one word, a *gendarme*. It is understandable how three years of rule by the *gendarme*, consecrated by the rule of the priests, were bound to demoralize the immature peasant masses.

Whatever quantity of passion and declamation the party of Order employed against the minority from the tribune of the National Assembly, its actual speech remained as monosyllabic as that of the Christian, with his 'yea, yea, nay, nay'. The party of Order was as monosyllabic in parliament as in the press, and as boring as a riddle whose solution is known in advance. One slogan constantly recurred, one theme always stayed the same, one

76. The education law (*loi Falloux*), which was adopted on 15 March 1850, placed all state schools under the joint supervision of the clergy and the mayors, as well as making numerous other provisions designed to strengthen clerical influence in the educational system.

verdict was always ready, whether it was a question of the right of petition, the tax on wine, the freedom of the press, trade, the clubs, or the charter of a municipality, the protection of personal freedom or the regulation of the state budget: the invariable word '*socialism*'. Even bourgeois liberalism was declared *socialist*, as well as bourgeois enlightenment and bourgeois financial reform. It was socialist to build a railway where a canal already existed, and it was socialist to defend oneself with a stick when attacked with a rapier.

This was not merely a figure of speech, a fashion or a piece of party tactics. The bourgeoisie correctly saw that all the weapons it had forged against feudalism were turning their points against the bourgeoisie itself, that all the means of education it had produced were rebelling against its own civilization, and that all the gods it had created had abandoned it. It understood that all the so-called bourgeois liberties and organs of progress were attacking and threatening its *class rule* both at the social foundation and the political summit, and had therefore become '*socialist*'. It rightly discerned the secret of socialism in this threat and this attack.

The bourgeoisie judges the meaning and tendency of socialism more correctly than so-called socialism itself can; this is why the latter cannot understand the bourgeoisie's obdurate resistance to it, whether it snivels sentimentally about the sufferings of mankind, prophesies the millennium and universal brotherly love in the Christian manner, drivels about the mind, education and freedom in the humanistic style, or, finally, in doctrinaire fashion, cooks up a system for the reconciliation and welfare of all classes.[77] However, what the bourgeoisie did not grasp was the logical conclusion that its *own parliamentary regime*, its *political rule* in general, must now succumb to the general verdict of condemnation for being *socialist*. As long as the rule of the bourgeois class was not completely organized and had not attained its pure political expression, the antagonism of the other classes could not emerge in its pure form, and, when it did emerge, it could not take the dangerous turn which transforms every struggle against the

77. In the 1848 period the term 'socialism' generally referred to the various middle-class schools of social reform, while 'communism' referred to the revolutionary working-class movement. See *Manifesto of the Communist Party*, section III, in *The Revolutions of 1848*, above, pp. 81–91; Engels's preface to the English edition, above, pp. 58–9; and *The Class Struggles in France*, above, p. 456.

state power into a struggle against capital. If it saw 'tranquillity' endangered by every sign of life in society, how could it want to retain a *regime of unrest*, its own *parliamentary regime*, at the head of society? A regime which lives in struggle and by struggle, as one of its orators expressed it. If the parliamentary regime lives by discussion, how can it forbid discussion? In it all interests and social institutions are transformed into general ideas, and debated in that form. How can any interest or institution then assert itself to be above thought, and impose itself as an article of faith? The struggle of the parliamentary orators calls forth the struggle of the scribblers of the press; the parliamentary debating club is necessarily supplemented by debating clubs in the salons and alehouses; the deputies, by constantly appealing to the opinion of the people, give the people the right to express their real opinion in petitions. The parliamentary regime leaves everything to the decision of majorities; why then should the great majority outside parliament not want to make the decisions? When you play the fiddle at the summit of the state, what else is there to expect than that those down below should dance?

Thus, by now branding as 'socialist' what it had previously celebrated as 'liberal', the bourgeoisie confesses that its own interest requires its deliverance from the peril of its own self-government; that to establish peace and quiet in the country its bourgeois parliament must first of all be laid to rest; that its political power must be broken in order to preserve its social power intact; that the individual bourgeois can only continue to exploit the other classes and remain in undisturbed enjoyment of property, family, religion and order on condition that his class is condemned to political insignificance along with the other classes; and that in order to save its purse the crown must be struck off its head and the sword which is to protect it must be hung over it like the sword of Damocles.

The National Assembly proved to be so unproductive in the area of the general interests of the bourgeoisie that its proceedings on the Paris–Avignon railway, for example, which began in the winter of 1850, were still not ready to be concluded on 2 December 1851. Wherever it was not engaged in measures of repression or reaction, the Assembly was cursed with incurable barrenness.

While his ministry partly seized the initiative in proposing laws in the spirit of the party of Order, and partly even outdid its severity in implementing and administering them, Bonaparte also sought to win popularity in another direction, to demonstrate his opposition to the National Assembly and hint at a secret reserve which was only temporarily prevented by the situation from making its hidden treasures available to the French people, by making childishly absurd proposals, such as the proposal to decree a pay increase of four sous a day for non-commissioned officers, or the proposal to establish a bank which would loan money to workers on the security of their honour. Money as a gift and money on tick, these were the perspectives with which he hoped to entice the masses. The financial science of the lumpenproletariat, of both the genteel and the common variety, is restricted to gifts and loans. These were the only springs Bonaparte knew how to set in motion. Never has a pretender speculated in a more vulgar fashion on the gullibility of the masses.

The National Assembly repeatedly became enraged at these unmistakable attempts to gain popularity at its expense, and at the growing danger that this adventurer, whipped on by his debts and not held back by an established reputation, would risk a desperate stroke. The discord between the party of Order and the President had assumed a threatening character when an unexpected occurrence threw him back, repentant, into its arms. We are referring to the *by-elections of 10 March 1850*. These elections took place in order to fill the seats made vacant after 13 June either by imprisonment or exile. The only candidates elected in Paris were social-democrats. Indeed, most of the Parisian votes went to de Flotte, one of the insurgents of June 1848. In this way the petty bourgeoisie of Paris, in alliance with the proletariat, had its revenge for the defeat of 13 June 1849. It seemed to have disappeared from the battlefield at the moment of danger only in order to return at more favourable opportunity with fighting forces of a more mass character and a bolder battle-cry. There was one circumstance that appeared to heighten the danger of this electoral victory: the army voted in Paris for the June insurgent and against La Hitte, one of Bonaparte's ministers, and in the departments largely for the Montagnards, who maintained their numerical preponderance over their opponents here as well, though not so decisively as in Paris.

Bonaparte suddenly saw himself confronted once again with the revolution. As on 29 January and 13 June 1849, so also on 10 March 1850 he disappeared behind the party of Order. He bowed to it submissively, he humbly begged its pardon, he offered to appoint any ministry whatsoever at the command of the parliamentary majority, he even implored the Orleanist and Legitimist party leaders such as Thiers, Berryer, de Broglie[78] and Molé, in short the so-called burgraves,[79] to seize the helm of state themselves. This moment was irretrievable, but the party of Order did not know how to make use of it. Instead of boldly taking possession of the power offered, it did not even force Bonaparte to reinstate the ministry dismissed on 1 November. It contented itself with humiliating him with its forgiveness and attaching M. Baroche to the Hautpoul ministry. This Baroche had twice put on a rabid performance as public prosecutor before the High Court at Bourges, once against the revolutionaries of 15 May [1848], the other time against the democrats of 13 June [1849], each time because of an attack on the National Assembly's position. Yet none of Bonaparte's ministers later contributed more greatly to the degradation of the National Assembly, and after 2 December we rediscover him as the duly installed and highly paid vice-chairman of the Senate. He had spat in the soup of the revolutionaries so that Bonaparte might eat it up.

The social-democratic party, for its part, seemed to be simply straining after pretexts to put its own victory in question again and take the sting out of it. Vidal, one of the newly elected representatives for Paris, had been elected simultaneously in Strasbourg. He was persuaded to decline the Paris mandate and accept that of Strasbourg. And so, instead of giving its electoral victory a definitive character and thereby compelling the party of Order immediately to contest it in parliament, instead of driving its opponent into a conflict at a moment of enthusiasm among the people and favour among the army, the democratic party bored Paris during the months of March and April with renewed electoral agitation, allowed the excited passions of the people to be worn out in this repetition of the provisional voting game, allowed the energy of the revolution to be satiated with constitutional successes and wasted on petty intrigues, empty declamations and sham movements, allowed the bourgeoisie to rally and make its preparations, and finally allowed the subsequent election of April to weaken the significance of the March elections by making

78. Achille, duc de Broglie was an Orleanist politician, Prime Minister from 1835 to 1836, and a deputy in the Legislative Assembly from 1849 to 1851.

79. See p. 466, n. 63.

a sentimental commentary on them in the form of the election of Eugène Sue. To put it succinctly, the democratic party made an April fool of 10 March.

The parliamentary majority knew its opponent's weaknesses. Bonaparte had left it to direct the attack and take responsibility for it, and its seventeen burgraves worked out a new electoral law to be proposed by M. Faucher, who had begged for the honour of being entrusted with it. On 8 May he introduced the law, which abolished universal suffrage, imposed a three-year residence requirement for the electors, and made proof of residence dependent in the case of workers on a certificate from their employers.

The democrats had stormed and raged in a revolutionary fashion during the constitutional electoral contest; but now, when it was necessary to demonstrate the seriousness of that electoral victory arms in hand, they preached in a constitutional fashion, in favour of order, majestic calm (*calme majestueux*) and lawful behaviour, i.e., blind subjection to the will of the counter-revolution which had imposed itself as law. During the debate the Montagne shamed the party of Order by upholding the dispassionate attitude of the philistine who sticks to the legal basis as against the revolutionary passion of the upholders of order, and struck them down with the frightful reproach that their acts were revolutionary. Even the newly elected deputies took care to show by their respectable and discreet behaviour how wrong it was to decry them as anarchists and interpret their election as a victory for revolution. The new electoral law went through on 31 May. The Montagne was content to smuggle a protest into the chairman's pocket. The electoral law was followed by a new press law, which completely got rid of the revolutionary newspapers.[80] They had deserved their fate. The *National* and the *Presse*, both bourgeois organs, were left behind after this deluge as the most extreme outposts of the revolution.

We have seen how the democratic leaders had done everything to embroil the people of Paris in a sham fight throughout March and April, and how they did all they could to hold them back from a real struggle after 8 May. In addition to this, we should not forget that 1850 was a year of the most splendid industrial and commercial prosperity, and the Paris proletariat was therefore

80. The press law of 16 July 1850 increased the amount of caution money required for any newspaper to 24,000 francs and imposed a stamp duty on all periodicals of less than ten sheets.

fully employed. But it was excluded from any share in political power by the electoral law of 31 May 1850. This barred the proletariat from the very arena of the struggle. It threw the workers back into the position they had occupied before the February revolution: they were again outcasts. By allowing themselves to be led by the democrats in face of such an event, by their ability to forget their revolutionary class interest in a situation which was momentarily comfortable, they renounced the honour of being a conquering power, gave themselves up to their fate, and proved that the defeat of June 1848 had rendered them incapable of fighting for years; they proved that, for the time being, the historical process would again have to go forward *over* their heads. As for the petty-bourgeois democrats, who on 13 June had exclaimed, 'But if they touch universal suffrage, then we'll show them,' they now consoled themselves with the assertion that the counterrevolutionary blow they had been struck was not a blow and that the law of 31 May was not a law. On the second Sunday of May 1852, they said, every Frenchman would appear at the polling station with a voting card in one hand and a sword in the other. They thought this prophecy was sufficient. Lastly, the army was punished by its superiors for the elections of March and April 1850, just as it had been punished for the elections of 29 May 1849. This time, however, it said to itself emphatically, 'The revolution will not swindle us a third time.'

The law of 31 May 1850 was the bourgeoisie's coup d'état. All its previous victories over the revolution had only a provisional character. They were put in question as soon as the existing National Assembly withdrew from the stage. They depended on the chance result of a new general election, and the history of elections since 1848 proved irrefutably that the moral domination of the bourgeoisie over the masses declined in direct proportion to the development of its physical domination. On 10 March universal suffrage declared directly against the rule of the bourgeoisie, and the bourgeoisie replied by outlawing it. The law of 31 May was therefore a necessity of the class struggle. Moreover, the Constitution required a minimum of two million votes to make the election of a President of the republic valid. If none of the presidential candidates received this minimum, the National Assembly was to choose the President from among the three candidates who received the most votes. At the time when the Constituent Assembly made this law, ten million electors were registered on the voting lists. In the Constituent Assembly's sense, then, a fifth of the voting strength was sufficient to make the election of the President valid. The law of 31 May struck at least three million electors from the voting lists, reducing the number of people entitled to vote to seven million, but it nevertheless retained the legal minimum of two million for the election of the President. It therefore raised the legal minimum from a fifth to nearly a third of the possible votes, i.e., it did everything to smuggle the election of the President out of the hands of the people and into the hands of the National Assembly. Thus the party of Order seemed to have made its rule doubly secure by the electoral law of 31 May; it placed both the election of the National Assembly and the election of the President of the republic in the hands of the stationary part of society.

v

The struggle between the National Assembly and Bonaparte broke out again immediately after the revolutionary crisis had been weathered and universal suffrage abolished.

The Constitution had fixed Bonaparte's salary at 600,000 francs. Hardly six months after his installation he had succeeded in doubling this sum of money. For Odilon Barrot had extracted from the Constituent Assembly an annual supplement of 600,000 francs for so-called official expenses. After 13 June 1849 Bonaparte had had similar requests aired, but this time Barrot did not give them a hearing. Now, after 31 May 1850, he immediately made use of the favourable moment and made his ministers propose a civil list of three million in the National Assembly. In the course of a long and adventurous life of vagabondage he had developed very sensitive feelers for sensing the weak moments when he might extort money from the bourgeoisie. He practised real *chantage*.[81] The National Assembly had violated popular sovereignty with his aid and his connivance; he threatened to denounce its crime to the tribunal of the people if it did not open its purse and buy his silence with three million a year. It had robbed three million Frenchmen of their franchise; he demanded a franc in circulation for every Frenchman withdrawn from circulation, precisely three million francs. Six million had voted for him; he demanded compensation for the votes of which he had been retrospectively

81. Blackmail.

cheated. The Commission of the National Assembly sent this importunate person away; the Bonapartist press began to make threats.
Could the National Assembly break with the President of the republic at a time when it had broken fundamentally with the mass of the
nation? Admittedly, it rejected the annual civil list, but it granted an
allowance, which was intended to be unique, of 2,160,000 francs. It
thus made itself guilty of the double weakness of granting the money
and simultaneously showing, by its annoyance, its unwillingness to
grant it. Later on we shall see what Bonaparte needed the money for.

After this tiresome sequel to the abolition of universal suffrage,
in which Bonaparte exchanged his humble bearing during the crisis
of March and April for an impertinent provocation of the usurping
parliament, the National Assembly adjourned for three months, from
11 August to 11 November. It left behind it a Standing Commission
of twenty-eight members, which contained no Bonapartists at all but
did include some moderate republicans. The Standing Commission
of 1849 had only included gentlemen of order and Bonapartists.
But at that time the party of Order had declared itself in permanent
session against the revolution. This time the parliamentary republic
declared itself in permanent session against the President. After the
law of 31 May the President was the only rival still confronting the
party of Order.

The National Assembly met again in November 1850. It now
seemed that in place of the previous petty skirmishes a great and
ruthless struggle with the President, a life-and-death struggle between
the two powers, had become inevitable.

During the parliamentary recess of 1850, just as in 1849, the
party of Order had split up into its separate fractions, each busy
with its own restorationist intrigues; these had now been reinforced by the death of Louis Philippe.[82] Henri V, the king of the
Legitimists, had even appointed a formal ministry which resided in
Paris, and which included members of the Standing Commission.
Bonaparte was therefore justified for his part in making circular tours through the French departments, canvassing votes for
himself and blurting out his own restorationist plans, sometimes
publicly and sometimes in secret, according to the mood of the
town he happened to be favouring with his presence. On these
expeditions, which the grand official *Moniteur* and the small
private *Moniteurs* belonging to Bonaparte naturally had to cele-

82. On 26 August 1850.

brate as triumphs, he was constantly accompanied by affiliates of the Society of 10 December.[83] This society dated from 1849. Under the pretext of founding a charitable organization, the Paris lumpen-proletariat had been organized into secret sections, each section led by Bonapartist agents and the whole headed by a Bonapartist general. Alongside decayed roués of doubtful origin and uncertain means of subsistence, alongside ruined and adventurous scions of the bourgeoisie, there were vagabonds, discharged soldiers, discharged criminals, escaped galley slaves, swindlers, confidence tricksters, *lazzaroni*, pickpockets, sleight-of-hand experts, gamblers, *maquereaux*,[84] brothel-keepers, porters, pen-pushers, organ-grinders, rag-and-bone merchants, knife-grinders, tinkers and beggars: in short, the whole indeterminate fragmented mass, tossed backwards and forwards, which the French call *la bohème*; with these elements, so akin to himself, Bonaparte formed the backbone of the Society of 10 December. This was a 'charitable organization' in that all its members, like Bonaparte, felt the need to provide themselves with charity at the expense of the nation's workers. This Bonaparte, who has set himself up as the *head of the lumpenproletariat*, who can only in that class find a mass reflection of the interests he himself pursues, who perceives in the scum, the leavings, the refuse of all classes the only class which can provide him with an unconditional basis, this is the real Bonaparte, the Bonaparte *sans phrase*.[85] An old, cunning roué, he conceives the historical life of nations and their state proceedings as comedy in the most vulgar sense, as a masquerade in which the grand costumes, words and postures merely serve as a cover for the most petty trickery. On his expedition to Strasbourg a trained Swiss vulture represented the Napoleonic eagle. For his landing in Boulogne he put some London flunkeys into French uniforms to represent the army.[86] In his Society of 10 December he assembled ten thousand rogues, who were supposed to represent the people in the way that Snug the joiner represented the lion.[87] At a time when the bourgeoisie

83. Founded by Carlier, the Paris Prefect of Police, and headed by Louis Bona-parte's friend, General Piat.

84. Pimps.

85. Unextenuated.

86. In October 1836 Louis Bonaparte attempted to seize the town of Strasbourg and was expelled from France; in August 1840 he landed at Boulogne and tried to start a Bonapartist mutiny in the Boulogne garrison.

87. In *A Midsummer Night's Dream*.

itself was playing the most complete comedy, but in the most serious manner in the world, without infringing any of the pedantic requirements of French dramatic etiquette, and was itself half duped and half convinced of the serious character of its own state proceedings, the adventurer had to win, because he treated the comedy simply as a comedy. Only now that he has removed his solemn opponent, now that he himself takes his imperial role seriously and imagines that the Napoleonic mask represents the real Napoleon, does he become the victim of his own conception of the world, the serious clown who no longer sees world history as a comedy but his comedy as world history. What the National Workshops[88] were for the socialist workers, what the Mobile Guard was for the bourgeois republicans, the Society of 10 December was for Bonaparte: the characteristic fighting force of his party. On his journeys detachments of the Society had to pack the trains and improvise a public for him, had to stage public enthusiasm, scream the words *vive l'empereur*, insult and beat up republicans, all with the protection of the police, of course. When he returned to Paris they had to form the advance guard and forestall or disperse counter-demonstrations. The Society of 10 December belonged to him, it was *his* work, his very own idea. Whatever else he laid hold of was put into his hands by the force of circumstances, whatever else he did either circumstances did for him or he copied from the deeds of others; but he himself became an original author when he combined official turns of phrase about order, religion, family and property, spoken publicly before the citizens, with the secret society of the Schufterles and the Spiegelbergs,[89] the society of disorder, prostitution and theft, behind him. The history of the Society of 10 December is his own history.

Now it happened by way of exception that some deputies belonging to the party of Order got in the way of the Decembrists' sticks. There was worse to come. Police Commissioner Yon, who was assigned to the National Assembly with the job of looking after its security, informed the Standing Commission, acting on the deposition of a certain Allais, that a section of the Decembrists had resolved to assassinate General Changarnier and the Chairman of the National Assembly, Dupin, and had already

88. See pp. 384–8.
89. Two characters from Schiller's drama *The Robbers*, who were portrayed as complete rogues, lacking all moral principles.

chosen the individuals who were to accomplish this. One can well understand how terrified Monsieur Dupin was. A parliamentary investigation into the Society of 10 December, i.e., the profanation of the secret world of Bonapartism, seemed unavoidable. Just before the National Assembly met Bonaparte prudently dissolved his society, only on paper of course, for even at the end of 1851 Police Prefect Carlier sent him an exhaustive memorandum in which he vainly endeavoured to persuade him to break up the Decembrists in actual fact.

The Society of 10 December was to remain Bonaparte's private army until he succeeded in turning the public army into a Society of 10 December. He made the first attempt at this shortly after the adjournment of the National Assembly, and indeed with the money he had just extracted from it. As a fatalist he believed that there are certain higher powers which man, and the soldier in particular, cannot withstand. Among these powers he counted above all cigars and champagne, cold poultry and garlic sausage. He therefore began by entertaining officers and NCOs in the Elysée apartments with cigars and champagne, cold poultry and garlic sausage. On 3 October he repeated this manoeuvre with the mass of the troops at a review held at St Maur, and on 10 October, on a still larger scale, at a review held at Satory. The uncle recalled the campaigns of Alexander in Asia, the nephew recalled the conquests of Bacchus in the same land. Alexander was of course a demigod; but Bacchus was a god, in fact he was the god of the Society of 10 December.

After the review of 3 October the Standing Commission summoned the War Minister, Hautpoul, to appear before it. He promised that these acts of indiscipline would not recur. We know how on 10 October Bonaparte kept Hautpoul's word. Changarnier had been in command at both reviews, as commander-in-chief of the Paris army. He was simultaneously a member of the Standing Commission and the head of the National Guard, the 'saviour' of 29 January and 13 June, the 'bulwark of society', the party of Order's presidential candidate, and the anticipated Monk[90] of two monarchies. So far he had never recognized that he was subordinate to the Minister of War; he had always openly scoffed at the republican Constitution and clothed Bonaparte with an

90. Changarnier had been expected both by the Legitimists and the Orleanists to invite their king back to the throne, as General Monk had invited Charles II in 1660.

ambiguously lordly protection. Now he was eager to uphold discipline against the Minister of War and the Constitution against Bonaparte. Whereas a section of the cavalry raised the cry '*Vive Napoléon! Vivent les saucissons!*'[91] on 10 October, Changarnier arranged that the infantry at least, which was marching past under the command of his friend Neumayer, should observe an icy silence. As a punishment, and at Bonaparte's instigation, the Minister of War relieved General Neumayer of his post in Paris, on the pretext of installing him as commanding general of the Fourteenth and Fifteenth Army Divisions. Neumayer rejected this exchange of commands and had therefore simply to take his leave.

Changarnier for his part published an order of the day on 2 November in which he forbade the troops to shout political slogans or engage in demonstrations of any kind while bearing arms. The Elysée newspapers attacked Changarnier; the newspapers of the party of Order attacked Bonaparte; the Standing Commission held repeated secret sessions and it was repeatedly proposed that a state of emergency be declared; the army seemed to be divided into two antagonistic camps with two antagonistic general staffs, one in the Elysée, Bonaparte's residence, the other in the Tuileries, Changarnier's residence. Only the meeting of the National Assembly seemed necessary and the signal for battle would resound. The French public judged this friction between Bonaparte and Changarnier like the English journalist who characterized it in the following words:

The political housemaids of France are sweeping away the glowing lava of the revolution with old brooms and squabbling while they work.

Meanwhile Bonaparte quickly removed his Minister of War, dispatching him precipitately to Algeria, and appointing General Schramm[92] in his place. On 12 November he sent the National Assembly a message of American elaborateness, overloaded with details, reeking of order, anxious for conciliation, resigned to the Constitution, dealing with every possible question except the *questions brûlantes*[93] of the hour. As if in passing, he let fall the remark that, according to the express provisions of the Constitu-

91. Long live Napoleon! Long live the sausages!
92. Jean-Paul Schramm was a Bonapartist general, and Minister of War from October 1850 to 1851.
93. Burning questions.

tion, the President alone had the army at his disposal. The message closed with this solemn declaration:

Above all else France demands tranquillity ... I alone am bound by my oath, and I shall keep within the narrow limits the Constitution has drawn for me. ... As far as I am concerned, I am elected by the people and owe my power to them alone, and I shall always submit to their lawfully expressed will. Should you resolve at this session on a revision of the Constitution, a Constituent Assembly will regulate the position of the executive power. If not, then the nation will solemnly proclaim its decision in 1852. But whatever the solutions of the future may be, let us come to an understanding, so that passion, surprise, or violence will never decide the destiny of a great nation ... My attention is claimed not by the question of who is to rule France in 1852 but by the question of how to employ the time at my disposal so that the intervening period may pass by without agitation or disturbance. I have opened my heart to you with sincerity; you will answer my frankness with your trust, my good endeavours with your cooperation, and God will do the rest.

The respectable, hypocritically moderate, virtuously commonplace language of the bourgeoisie revealed its deepest level of meaning when used by the autocrat of the Society of 10 December, the picnic hero of St Maur and Satory.

The burgraves of the party of Order were not for a moment deluded about the kind of confidence this outpouring deserved. They had long been cynical about oaths; they could count veterans and virtuosos of political perjury in their midst, and they had not failed to overhear the passage about the army. They noticed with indignation that in its long-winded enumeration of the latest laws the message had passed over the most important law, the electoral law, with an affected silence and, moreover, that the election of the President in 1852 was left to the hands of the people, provided there was no revision of the Constitution in the meantime. The electoral law was the party of Order's ball and chain, which prevented it from walking and, *a fortiori*, from storming forward! Moreover, with the official dissolution of the Society of 10 December and the dismissal of War Minister Hautpoul, Bonaparte had sacrificed the scapegoats with his own hand on the altar of the country. He had taken the sting out of the expected conflict. Finally, the party of Order itself anxiously sought to avoid, mitigate or conceal any decisive conflict with the executive. It allowed its rival to win the fruits of its victories over the revolution, out of its own fear of losing them. 'Above all else, France demands tranquillity': the party of Order had proclaimed this to the revolution ever since February, and now Bonaparte's message proclaimed it to the party of Order. 'Above all else, France demands tranquillity': Bonaparte committed acts which aimed at usurpation, but the party of Order upset the 'tranquillity' if it raised the alarm about these acts and interpreted them in hypochondriac fashion. The sausages of Satory were as quiet as mice if no one referred to them. 'Above all else, France demands tranquillity.' Bonaparte thus demanded to be left alone to do as he liked, and the parliamentary party was paralysed by a double fear – by the fear of conjuring up new revolutionary disorders, and by the fear of appearing in the eyes of the bourgeoisie, in the eyes of its own class, as itself the instigator of unrest. Since France demanded tranquillity above all else, the party of Order did not dare to answer 'war' after Bonaparte had spoken in his message of 'peace'. The public, which had looked forward to seeing great scenes of scandal at the opening of the National Assembly, was disappointed in its hopes. The opposition deputies, who demanded that the minutes of the Standing Commission's discussions on the October events be laid on the table, were outvoted by the majority. On principle, all debates that could cause excitement were avoided. The activities of the National Assembly during November and December 1850 were without interest.

At last, towards the end of December, guerrilla warfare began over some particular parliamentary prerogatives. The movement could only get bogged down in such petty quarrels over the prerogatives of the two powers because the bourgeoisie had done away with the class struggle for the time being by abolishing universal suffrage.

A verdict of debt had been obtained against a deputy, Mauguin.[94] The Minister of Justice, Rouher,[95] replied to an inquiry from the president of the court that a warrant for the debtor's arrest should be made out without further formalities. Mauguin was therefore thrown into the debtors' prison. The National Assembly was furious when it learnt of this outrage. It not only ordered Mauguin's immediate release, but also had

94. François Mauguin was a lawyer and a deputy in both Assemblies.

95. Eugène Rouher was a Bonapartist deputy in both Assemblies, intermittently Minister of Justice between 1849 and 1852, and later a leading official of the Second Empire.

him forcibly brought back from Clichy the same evening by its *greffier*.[96] But in order to show its faith in the sacredness of private property, and with the *arrière pensée* of providing an asylum for troublesome Montagnards in case of need, it declared that deputies could be imprisoned for debt with the prior consent of the National Assembly. It forgot to decree that the President could also be locked up for debts incurred. It destroyed the last appearance of immunity surrounding its own members.

It will be recalled that Police Commissioner Yon, acting on the deposition of a certain Allais, had denounced a section of the Decembrists for planning the murder of Dupin and Changarnier. In relation to this, the quaestors proposed at the Assembly's very first sitting that it should form its own parliamentary police force, paid out of its private budget and completely independent of the Prefect of Police. The Minister of the Interior, Baroche, protested against this encroachment on his province. At this point a wretched compromise was concluded, by which the Assembly's police commissioner was to be paid out of its private budget and appointed and dismissed by its quaestors, but only after previous agreement with the Ministry of the Interior. Meanwhile the government had taken criminal proceedings against Allais, and here it was easy to present his deposition as an invention, and to put Dupin, Changarnier, Yon and the whole National Assembly in a ridiculous light through the speeches of the public prosecutor. On 29 December Baroche wrote a letter to Dupin demanding Yon's dismissal. The bureau of the National Assembly decided to retain Yon in his position, but the Assembly itself, alarmed by its own violence in the Mauguin affair and accustomed to receiving two blows in return for every one it ventured to strike at the executive power, failed to sanction this decision. As a reward for his professional zeal Yon was dismissed, and the Assembly robbed itself of a parliamentary prerogative indispensable against a man who, rather than deciding by night and striking by day, decides by day and strikes by night.[97]

We have already seen how during the months of November and December the National Assembly circumvented or suppressed any struggle with the executive over important and striking issues. We now see it forced to take up the struggle over the pettiest

96. The clerk to the Assembly, a fairly lowly position. In fact, however, it was Jean-Didier Baze, a quaestor, who was sent to fetch Mauguin.

97. Bonaparte's coup d'état took place on the night of 1–2 December 1851.

questions. In the Mauguin affair it confirmed in principle the liability of deputies to imprisonment for debt, but it reserved the right to have it applied only to deputies it disliked, and wrangled over this infamous privilege with the Minister of Justice. Instead of utilizing the alleged murder plot to start an investigation into the Society of 10 December and utterly discredit Bonaparte before France and Europe by revealing his true character as the head of the Paris lumpenproletariat, it let the conflict sink down to a level at which the only point at issue between itself and the Minister of Interior was the question of competence to appoint and dismiss a police commissioner. So, throughout the whole of this period we see the party of Order compelled by its ambiguous position to dissipate and fragment its struggle with the executive into petty conflicts of competence, chicaneries, legalistic hair-splitting and demarcation disputes, and to make the most preposterous formal questions about the content of its activity. It did not dare take up the conflict at a moment when it would have had a principled significance, when the executive had really compromised itself and the cause of the National Assembly would have been the cause of the nation, because by doing that it would have given the nation its marching orders, and a nation on the move was what it feared most of all. It accordingly rejected the motions put forward by the Montagne on such occasions, and proceeded to the order of the day. Having thus escaped the broader dimensions of the issue, the executive calmly awaited the time when it could take up the disputed question again in connection with some petty and insignificant issue, one of merely local parliamentary interest as it were. Then the pent-up rage of the party of Order could break out, they could tear down the stage curtains, they could denounce the President, they could declare the republic in danger, but then too their passion would appear absurd and the occasion of the struggle a hypocritical pretext, not worth fighting for. The parliamentary storm became a storm in a teacup, the fight became an intrigue, the confrontation became a scandal. The revolutionary classes gloated with malicious joy over the humiliation of the National Assembly, for they were as enthusiastically in favour of its parliamentary prerogatives as the Assembly was in favour of public liberties; the bourgeoisie outside parliament did not understand how the bourgeoisie inside parliament could waste its time on such petty squabbles and compromise public tranquillity over such pitiful rivalries with the President. The bourgeoisie was confused by a strategy which made peace at the moment when all the world expected battles, and launched an attack at the moment when all the world thought peace had been made.

On 20 December Pascal Duprat[98] questioned the Minister of the Interior about the Gold Bars lottery. This lottery was a 'daughter of Elysium'. Bonaparte had brought it into the world with the aid of his faithful followers, and Police Prefect Carlier had placed it under his official protection, although in France the law forbids all lotteries with the exception of raffles for charitable purposes. Seven million lottery tickets were to be sold at one franc each. The profits were supposedly earmarked for the transportation of Parisian vagabonds to California. In part, this was an attempt to supplant the Paris proletariat's dreams of socialism with dreams of gold, the doctrinaire right to work with the seductive prospect of the big win. The Paris workers naturally did not recognize the inconspicuous francs enticed out of their own pockets when they saw the glitter of the Californian gold bars. However, the main object was a straightforward swindle. The vagabonds who wanted to open the gold mines of California without bothering to leave Paris were Bonaparte himself and his debt-ridden knights of the round table. The three million francs granted by the National Assembly had been squandered in riotous living; the coffers had to be refilled in one way or another. In vain had Bonaparte opened a national subscription for the building of so-called *cités ouvrières*,[99] with himself figuring at the top of the list for a substantial sum. The hard-hearted members of the bourgeoisie suspiciously awaited the payment of his share in hard cash, and as this was naturally not forthcoming, the speculation in socialist castles in the air fell flat on the ground. The gold bars were a better draw. It was not enough for Bonaparte and his confederates to pocket part of the surplus of seven millions over the value of the bars to be given out as prizes; they manufactured false lottery tickets; they issued ten, fifteen, even twenty tickets with the same number. This was a financial operation in the spirit of the Society of 10 December! Here the National Assembly was confronted not with the nominal President of the republic but with the flesh and blood Bonaparte. It could catch him red-handed, transgressing not the Constitution but the Code Pénal. If it proceeded with the

98. Pascal Duprat was a republican journalist and politician, and a deputy in both Assemblies.

99. Workers' settlements.

day's agenda, ignoring Duprat's question, this did not just happen because Girardin's motion that the Assembly should declare itself '*satisfait*' reminded the party of Order of its own systematic corruption. The bourgeois, and above all the bourgeois puffed up into a statesman, supplements his practical vulgarity with theoretical extravagance. As a statesman, he becomes a higher being, like the state power which confronts him, and a higher being can only be fought in a higher, consecrated fashion.

Precisely because Bonaparte was a bohemian, a princely lumpenproletarian, he had the advantage over the bourgeois scoundrels that he could wage the struggle in vulgar fashion. He now saw that the moment had come, after the Assembly had led him with its own hand over the treacherous ground of the military banquets, the reviews, the Society of 10 December and the Code Pénal, to go over from the apparent defensive to the real offensive. He was hardly embarrassed by the minor defeats sustained in the meantime by the Ministers of Justice, War, the Navy and Finance, through which the National Assembly displayed its irritation and dissatisfaction. Not only did he prevent the ministers from resigning and thus recognizing the subjection of the executive to parliament; he was now able to finish off what he had begun during the National Assembly's recess: the severance of the military power from parliament, the *dismissal of Changarnier*.

An Elysée newspaper published an order of the day, allegedly directed to the First Army Division during the month of May, and therefore proceeding from Changarnier, in which officers were recommended to give no quarter to traitors in their own ranks in case of an insurrection, to shoot them immediately and to refuse troops to the National Assembly if it should requisition them. The cabinet was questioned about this order of the day on 3 January 1851. It demanded first three months, then a week, and finally only twenty-four hours for the consideration and examination of the matter. The Assembly insisted on an immediate explanation. Changarnier got up and declared that this order of the day had never existed. He added that he would always hasten to comply with any summons the Assembly made and that it could count on him in case of a conflict. It received his declaration with a huge ovation and passed a vote of confidence in him. By placing itself under the private protection of a general, the Assembly abdicated: it decreed its own powerlessness and the army's omnipotence. But the general was deceiving himself when he put at the Assembly's disposal against Bonaparte a power he only held in fief from that same Bonaparte, when he himself expected protection from this parliament which needed him to protect it. However, Changarnier believed in the mysterious power which the bourgeoisie had vested in him on 29 January 1849. He held himself to be the third power, existing alongside the two other powers in the state. He shared the fate of the other heroes, or rather saints, of that epoch, whose greatness consisted precisely in the high opinion of them which was spread abroad by their party in its own interests, and who collapsed into ordinary mortals as soon as the situation required them to perform miracles. Scepticism is generally the deadly enemy of these presumed heroes and real saints. This is the reason for their dignified moral indignation at unenthusiastic wits and scoffers.

The same evening the ministers were ordered to go to the Elysée. Bonaparte insisted on Changarnier's dismissal, which five ministers refused to sign; the *Moniteur* announced that there was a ministerial crisis, and the press supporting the party of Order threatened to form a parliamentary army under the command of Changarnier. The party of Order had the constitutional authority to take this step. It only needed to appoint Changarnier as Chairman of the National Assembly and requisition any number of troops it pleased for its protection. It could do this all the more safely in that Changarnier was still in fact the head of the army and the Paris National Guard, and was only waiting for the opportunity to be requisitioned along with the army. The Bonapartist press did not as yet even dare to question the right of the National Assembly to requisition troops directly, in view of the likely lack of success, under the given circumstances, of legalistic discussions of this kind. It appears likely that the army would have obeyed the orders of the National Assembly, if one bears in mind that Bonaparte had to search the whole of Paris for eight days to find two generals – Baraguay d'Hilliers and Saint-Jean d'Angely[1] – who were ready to countersign Changarnier's dismissal. But it appears more than doubtful whether the party of Order would have found the necessary number of votes in its own ranks and in parliament, when one considers that eight days later 286 votes separated themselves from that party, and that the

1. Auguste, comte Regnault de Saint-Jean d'Angely was a Bonapartist general and a deputy in both Assemblies. He was made Minister of War in January 1851.

542   *The Eighteenth Brumaire of Louis Bonaparte*

Montagne rejected a proposal of this nature even in December 1851, at the final and decisive hour. Nevertheless, the burgraves might perhaps have succeeded in inspiring the mass of their party to a heroism consisting in feeling secure behind a forest of bayonets and accepting the services of an army which had deserted to their camp. Instead, these gentlemen proceeded to the Elysée on the evening of 6 January[2] to make Bonaparte forgo the sacking of Changarnier by using diplomatic phrases and objections. He who seeks to persuade someone acknowledges him as the master of the situation. Bonaparte was therefore reassured by this action, and on 12 January[3] he appointed a new ministry in which the leaders of the old ministry, Fould and Baroche, retained their seats. Saint-Jean d'Angely became Minister of War, the *Moniteur* published the decree dismissing Changarnier, and his command was divided between Baraguay d'Hilliers, who received the First Army Division, and Perrot,[4] who received the National Guard. The bulwark of society had been dismissed, and while this did not cause a great stir, it did cause the quotations on the Bourse to rise.

By rejecting the army which was placed at its disposal in the person of Changarnier, and so irrevocably delivering it into the hands of the President, the party of Order declared that the bourgeoisie had lost its vocation to rule. The parliamentary ministry had already ceased to exist. Since it had now lost its grip on the army and the National Guard, what instruments of power remained for it to maintain both the usurped power of the Assembly over the people and its constitutional power against the President? None. All it had left now was the appeal to principles without the support of force, principles it had always interpreted as general rules to be prescribed for others so as to improve one's own freedom of movement. With the dismissal of Changarnier and the devolution of military power into Bonaparte's hands we come to the end of the first section of the period we are considering, the period of the struggle between the party of Order and the executive. The war between the two powers was now openly declared and openly waged, but only after the party of Order had lost both weapons and soldiers. Without a ministry, without an army, without the people, without public opinion, no longer the repre-

2. The correct date is 8 January 1851.
3. The correct date is 10 January 1851.
4. Benjamin-Pierre Perrot was a general who took part in the suppression of the June insurrection.

sentative of the sovereign nation since its electoral law of 31 May, sans teeth, sans eyes, sans taste, sans everything, the National Assembly had gradually become transformed into an old French *parlement*,[5] which had to leave action to the government and make do with growling and remonstrating after the deed was done.

The party of Order received the new ministry with a storm of indignation. General Bedeau reminded the Assembly of the meekness of the Standing Commission during the recess and the excessive consideration for the President which had led it to give up the idea of publishing its proceedings. The Minister of the Interior himself now insisted on the publication of these minutes, which had of course become as dull as ditchwater, revealed no new facts, and made no impact whatsoever on a bored public. The National Assembly accepted Rémusat's[6] proposal to withdraw into its offices and appoint a 'Committee for Extraordinary Measures'. The dislocation of Parisian daily routine caused by the Assembly was the less effective in that trade was now prosperous, factories and workshops were fully employed, the price of corn was low, foodstuffs were available in abundance, and the saving banks received new deposits every day. The 'extraordinary measures' announced so noisily by the parliament fizzled out into a vote of no confidence against the ministers on 18 January, a vote in which General Changarnier was not even mentioned. The party of Order had been forced to word its resolution in this way in order to secure the republican vote, as the dismissal of Changarnier was the single one of all the ministry's measures that the republicans approved of, whereas the party of Order could not reproach the ministry with any of its other acts, since it had dictated them itself.

The no-confidence resolution of 18 January was passed by 415 votes to 286. In other words, it was carried only by a *coalition* between the staunch Legitimists and Orleanists, the pure republicans, and the Montagne. This demonstrated that in its conflicts with Bonaparte the party of Order had lost not only the ministry and the army, but also its independent parliamentary majority, that a detachment of representatives had deserted its camp out of

5. The regional assembly of magistrates in the France of the *ancien régime*. It registered the king's decrees and had the right to refuse registration if the decree went against the customs of the realm. In practice the king was able to override such a refusal, although this power was disputed by the parlements in the eighteenth century.

6. Charles, comte de Rémusat was a writer and an Orleanist politician, Minister of the Interior in 1840. He sat in both Assemblies.

fear of struggle, fanaticism for compromise, boredom, family regard for relatives holding state salaries, speculation on coming vacancies in ministerial positions (Odilon Barrot), and finally the simple egoism which always inclines the ordinary bourgeois citizen to sacrifice the general interest of his class to this or that private motive. From the beginning, the Bonapartist representatives had belonged to the party of Order only in its struggle against the revolution. The leader of the Catholic party, Montalembert, had already thrown his influence onto the scales on Bonaparte's side, since he despaired of the Assembly's prospects of survival. Finally, the parliamentary leaders, the Orleanist Thiers and the Legitimist Berryer, were compelled to proclaim openly that they were republicans, to admit that though their hearts were royalist their minds were republican, since the parliamentary republic was the only possible form for the rule of the bourgeoisie as a whole. They were thus forced, before the eyes of the bourgeois class itself, to brand the plans for restoration which they unwearyingly continued to pursue behind the Assembly's back as intrigues as dangerous as they were thoughtless.

The no-confidence resolution of 18 January struck at the ministers, not the President. But it was the President, not the ministers, who had dismissed Changarnier. Should the members of the party of Order impeach Bonaparte himself? What for? For his desire to carry out a restoration? This only supplemented their own. For conspiracy, in the matter of the military reviews and the Society of 10 December? They had buried these themes long ago beneath the normal order of business. For the dismissal of the hero of 29 January and 13 June 1849, the man who in May 1850 threatened to set fire to all four corners of Paris in case of an uprising? Their allies, the supporters of the Montagne and of Cavaignac, did not even allow them to set the fallen bulwark of society on his feet with an official declaration of sympathy. Indeed, they could not deny that the President had the constitutional authority to dismiss a general. They were only furious because he made an unparliamentary use of his constitutional right. But had they not repeatedly made an unconstitutional use of their parliamentary prerogative, in particular when they abolished universal suffrage? They were therefore thrown back onto manoeuvres which took place entirely within parliamentary bounds. This attitude was supported by that peculiar epidemic which has prevailed over the whole continent of Europe since 1848, *parliamentary cretinism*, which holds its victims spellbound in an imaginary world and robs them of all sense, all memory, and all understanding of the rough external world. It required this parliamentary cretinism to make the party of Order view its parliamentary victories as real victories and imagine it was touching the President when it struck at his ministers, for its members had themselves destroyed the whole basis of parliamentary power with their own hands, indeed had been forced to destroy it in their struggle with the other classes. They merely gave Bonaparte the opportunity of humiliating the National Assembly once again in the eyes of the nation. On 20 January the *Moniteur* announced that the resignation of the entire ministry had been accepted. On the pretext that no parliamentary party had a majority any longer, as demonstrated by the vote of 18 January, this fruit of a coalition between the Montagne and the royalists, and in expectation of the later formation of a new majority, Bonaparte appointed a so-called transitional ministry which contained not a single member of parliament and consisted exclusively of entirely unknown and insignificant individuals, a ministry of mere clerks and copyists. The party of Order could now wear itself out in playing games with these puppets; the executive no longer saw the point of being seriously represented in the National Assembly. The more his ministers were reduced to playing mere walk-on parts, the more obviously did Bonaparte concentrate the whole executive power in his own person and the more latitude did he have to exploit it for his own purposes.

The party of Order, in coalition with the Montagne, revenged itself by rejecting the presidential grant of 1,800,000 francs which the head of the Society of 10 December had forced his ministerial clerks to propose. This time the issue was decided by a majority of only 102 votes; another twenty-seven votes had therefore fallen away since 18 January. The dissolution of the party of Order was proceeding apace. At the same time, in order to make sure that there was not even a momentary mistake made about the meaning of its coalition with the Montagne, it disdained even to take into consideration a proposal signed by 189 members of the Montagne for a general amnesty of political offenders. It was sufficient for the Minister of the Interior, a certain Vaïsse,[7] to declare that the present tranquillity was only apparent, and that

7. Claude-Marius Vaïsse, a typical nonentity in Bonaparte's 'ministry of clerks'.

in secret a great agitation was going on, secret societies were being organized everywhere, the democratic papers were making arrangements to reappear, the reports from the departments sounded unfavourable, the exiles in Geneva were leading a conspiracy which was spreading via Lyons over the whole of southern France, that France stood on the edge of an industrial and commercial crisis, that the manufacturers of Roubaix had reduced the hours of work, that the prisoners of Belle Isle[8] were in revolt – even a mere Vaïsse could conjure up the red spectre and make the party of Order reject without discussion a proposal which would have won immense popularity for the National Assembly and thrown Bonaparte back into its arms. Instead of letting itself be intimidated by the executive's perspective of new disorders, it should rather have allowed the class struggle some latitude, so as to keep the executive dependent on itself. But it did not feel equal to the task of playing with fire.

The so-called transitional ministry continued to vegetate until the middle of April. Bonaparte wearied and teased the National Assembly with constantly renewed ministerial combinations. Sometimes he seemed to want to form a republican ministry with Lamartine and Billault,[9] at other times a parliamentary ministry with the inevitable Odilon Barrot, whose name is always there when a dupe is needed, at other times a Legitimist ministry with Vatimesnil[10] and Benoist d'Azy,[11] and at still other times an Orleanist ministry with Maleville.[12] While he maintained the tension between the different fractions of the party of Order in this way, and alarmed them all with the prospect of a republican ministry and the return of universal suffrage which would inevitably follow, he simultaneously created among the bourgeoisie as a whole the conviction that his honest endeavours to form a parliamentary ministry were being wrecked by the irreconcilability of the royalist

8. The revolutionaries arrested during the previous three years had been impris-o-ned on the island of Belle Isle, off the west coast of France.

9. August-Adolphe Billault was a lawyer and an Orleanist, who sat in both Assemblies and became a Bonapartist after the coup d'état. He was Minister of the Interior from 1854 to 1858.

10. Antoine Lefebvre de Vatimesnil was a Legitimist politician, Minister of Education under Charles X. He sat in the Legislative Assembly.

11. Denis, comte Benoist d'Azy was a financier and industrialist, and a Legitimist deputy and vice-chairman in the Legislative Assembly, 1849–51.

12. Léon de Maleville was an Orleanist deputy in both Assemblies, and Minister of the Interior in December 1848.

fractions. The bourgeoisie cried out all the more loudly for a 'strong government'. It found it all the more unforgivable to leave France 'without administration' in that a general commercial crisis now seemed to be setting in, winning recruits for socialism in the towns while the ruinously low price of corn did the same for the country-side. Trade became daily more stagnant, and the number of hands without work increased noticeably. In Paris at least 10,000 workers were without bread; in Rouen, Mulhouse, Lyons, Roubaix, Tourcoing, St Etienne, Elbeuf, etc., innumerable factories stood idle. Under these circumstances Bonaparte could take the risk, on 11 April, of restoring the ministry of 18 January, i.e., Messrs Rouher, Fould, Baroche, etc., reinforced by Monsieur Léon Faucher, whom the Constituent Assembly at the end of its life had unanimously (with the exception of five ministerial votes) branded with a vote of no confidence for the dissemination of false dispatches by telegraph.[13] In other words, the National Assembly had won a victory over the ministry of 18 January, and it had struggled with Bonaparte for three months, only for Fould and Baroche to admit the puritan Faucher as the third member of their ministerial alliance on 11 April.

In November 1849 Bonaparte had been satisfied with an *unparliamentary* ministry; in January 1851 he had been satisfied with an *extra-parliamentary* ministry; now, on 11 April 1851, he felt strong enough to form an *anti-parliamentary* ministry, which harmoniously combined within itself the votes of no confidence passed by both Assemblies, the Constituent and the Legislative, the Assembly of the republicans and the Assembly of the royalists. This graduated scale of ministries was the thermometer with which the Assembly could measure the decline in its own vital heat. This thermometer had fallen so low by the end of April that Persigny[14] could invite Changarnier in a personal interview to go over to the presidential camp. He assured him that Bonaparte regarded the influence of the National Assembly as completely annihilated and that a proclamation had already been prepared

13. On 11 May 1849 the Constituent Assembly rebuked Faucher for announcing in a dispatch that the deputies who had voted against the government were 'just waiting to mount the barricades and start the June business again'.

14. Jean Fialin, duc de Persigny was a Bonapartist and a deputy in the Legislative Assembly. He helped to organize the coup d'état of 2 December and was Minister of the Interior from 1852 to 1854 and again from 1860 to 1863.

for publication after the coup d'état, which was his constant aim but which had to be postponed again for accidental reasons. Changarnier informed the leaders of the party of Order of this obituary notice, but who believes that the bites of a bed-bug are fatal? And the Assembly, in its defeated, disintegrated and putrescent condition, could not bring itself to see in its duel with the grotesque head of the Society of 10 December anything other than a duel with a bed-bug. But Bonaparte answered the party of Order as Agesilaus answered King Agis: 'I seem an ant to you, but one day I shall be a lion.'[15]

VI

In its vain endeavours to maintain possession of the military and to reconquer supreme control of the executive, the party of Order was condemned to remain in coalition with the Montagne and the pure republicans. This proved incontrovertibly that it had lost its independent *parliamentary majority*. The mere power of the calendar, of the hour hand of the clock, gave the signal for its complete disintegration on 28 May. The last year of the National Assembly's life began on 28 May. It had now to decide whether the Constitution was to continue unchanged or be revised. But the revision of the Constitution did not just involve the question of bourgeois rule or petty-bourgeois democracy, democracy or proletarian 'anarchy', parliamentary republic or Bonaparte, it also posed the question of Orleans or Bourbon! Thus there fell into the Assembly's midst the apple of discord which would openly arouse the conflict of interests and split the party of Order into opposing fractions. The party of Order was a combination of heterogeneous social substances. The question of revision produced a level of political temperature at which the mixture decomposed into its original constituents.

The Bonapartists' interest in revision was simple. For them it was above all a question of the abolition of paragraph 45, which forbade Bonaparte's re-election, and the prolongation of his authority. The position of the republicans was just as simple. They were unconditionally opposed to any revision; they saw in revision a general conspiracy against the republic. As they disposed of

15. From Athenaeus' *Deipnosophistai*. In fact it was Tachos, king of Egypt, whom Agesilaus, king of Sparta, answered in that way, and he referred to a mouse rather than an ant.

more than a quarter of the votes in the National Assembly, and as, according to the Constitution, three quarters of the votes were required for a resolution in favour of revision to be legally valid and for the convocation of a special revising Assembly, they only needed to count their votes to be sure of victory. And they were sure of victory.

As against these clear positions, the party of Order found itself involved in inextricable contradictions. If it rejected revision, it endangered the status quo by leaving Bonaparte only one way out, the way of force, and by abandoning France at the moment of decision, the second Sunday of May 1852, to revolutionary anarchy, with a President who had lost his authority, a parliament which had long lacked authority, and a people which meant to reconquer its authority. It knew that to cast its vote for revision as the Constitution laid down was a waste of time, as it would be defeated, in accordance with the Constitution, by the veto of the republicans. If it unconstitutionally declared a simple majority vote to be binding, it could only hope to master the revolution by subordinating itself unconditionally to the domination of the executive. In that case, it would make Bonaparte the master of the Constitution, of its revision, and of the party of Order itself. A merely partial revision, prolonging the authority of the President, would pave the way to imperialist usurpation. A general revision, cutting short the existence of the republic, would inevitably bring the dynastic claims into conflict, for the conditions of a Bourbon and an Orleanist restoration were not just different, but mutually exclusive.

The *parliamentary republic* was more than the neutral territory where the two fractions of the French bourgeoisie, Legitimists and Orleanists, big landed property and industry, could live side by side with equal rights. It was the inescapable condition of their *joint* rule, the only form of state in which both the claims of these particular fractions and the claims of all other classes of society were subjected to the general interest of the bourgeois class. As royalists, they fell back into their old antagonism, into the struggle between landed property and money for supremacy, and their kings and dynasties formed the highest expression of this antagonism, its personification. Hence the opposition of the party of Order to the *recall of the Bourbons*.

Between 1849 and 1851 the Orleanist deputy Creton had periodically introduced a motion to rescind the decree exiling the royal families. The Assembly just as regularly offered the spectacle of an assembly of royalists obstinately barring the door through which their exiled kings could return home. Richard III had murdered Henry VI, remarking that he was too good for this world and belonged in heaven.[16] They, in turn, declared that France was too bad to have her kings back. They had become republicans under the compulsion of circumstances, and they repeatedly sanctioned the popular decision that banished their kings from France.

A revision of the Constitution – and the circumstances compelled them to consider this possibility – would put in question not only the republic but also the joint rule of the two bourgeois fractions, and the possibility of a monarchy recalled to life the rivalry of the interests it had preferentially represented by turns, and the struggle for the supremacy of one fraction over the other. The party of Order's diplomats thought they could settle the conflict by merging the two dynasties, by a so-called *fusion* of the royalist parties and their respective houses. The genuine fusion of the Restoration and July monarchies was the parliamentary republic, in which the Orleanist and the Legitimist colours were extinguished and the various species of bourgeois disappeared into the bourgeois as such, the bourgeois genus. But now the Orleanist was supposed to become a Legitimist and the Legitimist an Orleanist. Royalty, the personification of their antagonism, was now to embody their unity; the expression of their exclusive fractional interests was to become the expression of their common class interest; the monarchy was to accomplish what could only be, and had been, accomplished by the abolition of two monarchies, i.e., the republic. This was the philosophers' stone the doctors of the party of Order racked their brains to produce. As if the Legitimist monarchy could ever become the monarchy of the industrial bourgeoisie or the bourgeois monarchy could ever become the monarchy of the hereditary landed aristocracy! As if landed property and industry could fraternize beneath a *single* crown which could only be placed on a single head, the head of the elder brother or the younger! As if industry could make a compromise with landed property at all, as long as landed property did not decide to become industrial

16. Marx's reference here is to Shakespeare rather than historical fact. In *Henry VI*, V, vi Gloucester (later Richard III) kills Henry VI, and in *Richard III*, I, ii he justifies his action with the line that Henry 'was fitter for that place than Earth'.

itself! If Henri V were to die tomorrow, the comte de Paris[17] would not for that reason become the king of the Legitimists, unless he ceased to be the king of the Orleanists. However, the philosophers of fusion, who became more prominent as the question of revision came further into the foreground, who had created their own official daily organ in the shape of the *Assemblée nationale*,[18] and who are again at work even at this very moment (February 1852), explain the whole problem as a result of the antagonism and rivalry between the two dynasties. The attempts to reconcile the Orleans family with Henri V had begun with the death of Louis Philippe, but, like all the dynastic intrigues, they were games played only during the recesses of the National Assembly, in the intervals of the drama and behind the scenes, more a case of sentimental coquetry with old superstitions than seriously meant business. Now, however, these intrigues became important state proceedings, performed by the party of Order on the public stage, instead of in amateur theatricals, as hitherto. The couriers rushed from Paris to Venice,[19] from Venice to Claremont, from Claremont to Paris. The comte de Chambord issued a manifesto announcing not his, but the 'national' restoration, 'with the help of all members of his family'. The Orleanist Salvandy[20] threw himself at the feet of Henri V. The Legitimist leaders Berryer, Benoist d'Azy and Saint-Priest[21] travelled to Claremont in order to persuade the Orleans clique, but without success. Too late the fusionists realized that the interests of the two fractions of the bourgeoisie did not lose in exclusiveness or gain in flexibility when brought to their quintessential form of family interests, the interests of two royal houses. If Henri V were to recognize the comte de Paris as his successor – the only success fusion could achieve in the best circumstances – the House of Orleans would not win any claim not already secured by the childlessness of Henri V, but it would lose all the claims conquered by the July revolution. It would have abandoned its original claims, all the titles it had

17. Louis-Philippe-Albert, the grandson of Louis Philippe.
18. A newspaper of a Legitimist tendency, which appeared in Paris between 1848 and 1857.
19. The comte de Chambord, 'Henri V', lived in Venice in the 1850s.
20. Narcisse, comte de Salvandy was an Orleanist politician of the 1830s and 1840s, and Minister of Education from 1837 to 1839 and from 1845 to 1848.
21. Louis, vicomte de Saint-Priest was a general and a diplomat, and a deputy in the Legislative National Assembly.

wrung from the elder branch of the Bourbons in almost a hundred years of struggle, it would have exchanged its historical prerogative, the prerogative of the modern monarchy, for the prerogative of its lineage. Fusion was therefore nothing but a voluntary abdication by the House of Orleans, its resignation in face of legitimism, a repentant withdrawal from the Protestant state church back into the Catholic. Moreover, this withdrawal would not even bring it to the throne it had lost but to the steps of the throne, where it had been born. The old Orleanist ministers (Guizot, Duchâtel,[22] etc.), who also hastened to Claremont to put in their word for fusion, only represented the retrospective regret felt for the July revolution, the despair felt for the bourgeois monarchy and the monarchical character of the ordinary citizen, and the superstitious belief in legitimacy as the last charm against anarchy. They imagined they were mediators between Orleans and Bourbon; in fact they were merely Orleanists who had abandoned Orleans, and the prince de Joinville[23] received them as such. On the other hand, the lively and combative section of the Orleanists, Thiers, Baze,[24] etc., found it so much the easier to convince the family of Louis Philippe that if any direct restoration of the monarchy presupposed the fusion of the two dynasties, and if any such fusion presupposed the abdication of the House of Orleans, it corresponded entirely to the traditions of their predecessors to recognize the republic provisionally and to wait until events permitted the transformation of the President's chair into a throne. Rumours of Joinville's candidature were spread abroad, public curiosity was kept in suspense, and a few months later, in September, after the rejection of revision, his candidature was publicly proclaimed.

The attempt at a royalist fusion between Orleanists and Legitimists had thus not only failed; it had broken up their *parliamentary fusion*, their common republican form, and disintegrated the party of Order into its original constituents; but as the estrangement between Claremont and Venice grew, their attempted compromise collapsed, and agitation in favour of Joinville gained

22. Charles, comte Duchâtel had been Minister of Trade in 1834–6 and Minister of the Interior in 1839 and 1840–48.

23. François, duc d'Orléans, prince de Joinville was the son of Louis Philippe and the cousin of the Orleanist pretender.

24. Jean-Didier Baze was a lawyer and an Orleanist politician. He sat in both Assemblies.

ground, so the negotiations between Bonaparte's minister Faucher and the Legitimists became all the more eager and serious.

The dissolution of the party of Order did not stop short when its original elements had re-emerged. Each of the two great fractions itself underwent a new decomposition. It was as if all the old nuances which had previously fought and pressed against each other within each of the two circles, whether Legitimist or Orleanist, had become reactivated through contact with water, like dried infusoria, as if they had regained enough vital energy to form their own groups and indulge in their own independent antagonisms. The Legitimists dreamed they were back among the disputes between the Tuileries and the Pavillon Marsan,[25] between Villèle and Polignac,[26] while the Orleanists relived the golden epoch of the jousting matches between Guizot, Molé, de Broglie, Thiers and Odilon Barrot.[27]

The section of the party of Order which was eager for revision, but divided on the limits of this revision – a section composed of the two groups of Legitimists led respectively by Berryer and Falloux, and by La Rochejaquelein, together with the war-weary Orleanists such as Molé, Broglie, Montalembert and Odilon Barrot – agreed with the Bonapartist representatives on the following indefinite and broadly framed motion: 'The undersigned representatives move that the Constitution be revised, with the aim of restoring to the nation the full exercise of its sovereignty.'

However, at the same time they unanimously declared through their *rapporteur*, de Tocqueville,[28] that the National Assembly did not have the right to propose the *abolition of the republic*, for

25. The disputes of the period between 1815 and 1824 between Louis XVIII, who resided in the Tuileries, and the comte d'Artois, later Charles X, who resided at the Pavillon Marsan.

26. Jean-Baptiste, comte de Villèle, Prime Minister from 1822 to 1827, was regarded as representing the main body of the ultra-royalists, and Auguste, prince de Polignac, Prime Minister from 1829 to 1830, as representing the most reactionary and politically naïve faction of that party.

27. The 1830s were a period of confused faction-fighting, while the continuous presence of Guizot as Prime Minister from 1840 to 1848 later provid-ed the elements of a division between right and left, with Thiers and Barrot representing different currents of the Orleanist 'left' against the other politicians mentioned by Marx.

28. Alexis de Tocqueville was an historian and a constitutional monarchist politician, a supporter of the Orleanist 'third party' in the 1840s, Foreign Minister from June to October 1849, and a deputy in both Assemblies.

this right belonged exclusively to the Revising Chamber.[29] In any case, the Constitution could only be revised in a '*legal*' manner, only if the constitutionally prescribed three quarters of the votes cast were in favour of revision. On 19 July, after six days of stormy debate, the motion for revision failed to secure the necessary majority, as was only to be expected. 446 votes were cast in favour and 278 against. The rigid Orleanists such as Thiers, Changarnier, etc., voted with the republicans and the Montagne.

Thus a majority of the Assembly had proclaimed its opposition to the Constitution, but the Constitution itself opted in favour of the minority, and declared its decision to be binding. But had not the party of Order subordinated the Constitution to the parliamentary majority on 13 June 1849 and again on 31 May 1850? Did not its whole previous policy rest on the subordination of paragraphs of the Constitution to the decisions of a parliamentary majority? Had it not left the Old Testament-style faith in the letter of the law to the democrats, and punished them for that faith? At the present moment, however, the revision of the Constitution meant nothing but the continuation of the President's authority, just as the continued existence of the Constitution meant nothing but the deposition of the President. Bonaparte was therefore acting in accordance with the will of the Assembly when he tore up the Constitution, and he followed the spirit of the Constitution when he broke up the Assembly.

The Assembly had declared the Constitution to be 'beyond the province of a majority', and its own rule along with it; by its vote it had abolished the Constitution and prolonged the President's power, while declaring at the same time that it was impossible either for the former to die or for the latter to live as long as it, the Assembly, continued to exist. The feet of its intended gravediggers could be heard just outside the door. While it debated the question of revision, Bonaparte removed General Baraguay d'Hilliers, who had shown himself to be irresolute, from the command of the First Army Division. He appointed instead General Magnan,[30] the victor of Lyons and the hero of the December days, one of his

29. This would be a new Constituent Assembly, elected for the purpose of revising the 1848 Constitution.

30. Bernard-Pierre Magnan was a Bonapartist general, prominent in suppressing the Lyons risings of 1831 and 1849 and the Paris rising of June 1848. He sat in both Assemblies and helped to organize the coup d'état of 2 December.

creatures, who had already more or less compromised himself for him in the days of Louis Philippe in connection with the Boulogne expedition.

By its decision on revision, the party of Order proved that it could neither rule nor serve, neither live nor die, neither tolerate the republic nor overthrow it, neither uphold the Constitution nor throw it overboard, neither cooperate with the President nor break with him. From whom, then, did it expect the resolution of all these contradictions? The calendar, the course of events, was supposed to bring the solution. The party of Order no longer had the impertinence to claim that it controlled events, and it therefore challenged the events to assume control over it, for the events were the power to which it had surrendered one position after another in the struggle against the people, until it stood impotent before it. It now chose this critical moment to retire from the stage and adjourn for three months, from 10 August to 4 November. The result was that the head of the executive was able to draw up his plan of campaign without disturbance, to strengthen his means of attack, select his instruments of attack, and fortify his positions.

Not only was the parliamentary party of Order split into its two great fractions, and each of these fractions divided within itself, but the party of Order within the parliament had also fallen out with the party of Order *outside* parliament. The spokesmen and writers of the bourgeoisie, its platform and its press, to put it briefly the ideologists of the bourgeoisie, had become alienated from the bourgeoisie itself. Representatives and represented faced each other in mutual incomprehension.

The Legitimists in the provinces, with their limited horizons and unlimited enthusiasm, censured their parliamentary leaders, Berryer and Falloux, for deserting to the Bonapartist camp and abandoning Henri V. Their understanding restricted to the level of the *fleur-de-lis*, they believed in the fall of man but not in diplomacy.

The commercial bourgeoisie's break with its politicians was far more fateful and decisive. The bourgeoisie did not reproach its representatives, as the Legitimists had reproached theirs, with having abandoned principles, but rather with having clung to principles which had become useless.

I pointed out earlier that after Fould's entry into the ministry the section of the commercial bourgeoisie which had held the lion's share of power under Louis Philippe, the *financial aristocracy*, had become Bonapartist. Fould represented Bonaparte's interests in the Bourse and the Bourse's interests before Bonaparte. A quotation from the European organ of the financial aristocracy, the London *Economist*, portrays its position most strikingly. In the issue of 1 February 1851, its Paris correspondent had this to say:

Now we have it stated from numerous quarters that France wishes above all things for repose. The President declares it in his message to the Legislative Assembly; it is echoed from the tribune; it is asserted in the journals; it is announced from the pulpit; *it is demonstrated by the sensitiveness of the public funds at the least prospect of disturbance, and their firmness the instant it is made manifest that the executive is victorious.*

In the issue of 29 November 1851, the *Economist* declared in its own name: '*The President is the guardian of order, and is now recognized as such on every Stock Exchange of Europe.*'[31]

The financial aristocracy thus condemned the party of Order's parliamentary struggle against the executive as a *disturbance of order*, and celebrated every victory of the President over its own supposed representatives as a *victory of order*. By the 'financial aristocracy' must be understood not merely the big loan promoters and speculators in public funds, whose interests, it is immediately apparent, coincide with the interests of the state power. The whole of the modern money market, the whole of the banking business, is most intimately interwoven with public credit. A part of their business capital is necessarily put out at interest in short-term public funds. Their deposits, the capital put at their disposal by merchants and industrialists and distributed by them among the same people, flow in part from the dividends of holders of government bonds. If in every epoch the stability of the state power has constituted the most essential requirement for the entire money market and its high priests, why should this not be even truer today, when every deluge threatens to sweep away the old state debts along with the old states?

The *industrial bourgeoisie* shared this fanaticism for order, and was also angered by the bickering between the parliamentary party of Order and the executive power. After their vote on 18 January, in connection with the dismissal of Changarnier,

---

31. The italics in these quotations are Marx's own.

Thiers, Anglès, Sainte-Beuve,[32] etc., received public admonitions in which their coalition with the Montagne was particularly scourged as a betrayal of order – criticism received indeed precisely from the industrial districts. As we have seen, the ostentatious bantering and petty intrigues which marked the struggle of the party of Order with the President deserved no better reception than this. Equally, however, this bourgeois party, which demanded that its representatives should let military power slip from its own parliament to an adventurer and pretender without the slightest resistance, was not even worth the intrigues which were wasted in its interests. The struggle to maintain its *public* interests, its own *class interests*, its *political power*, only troubled and upset it, as it was a disturbance of private business.

With scarcely any exception, the bourgeois dignitaries of the chief departmental towns, the municipal authorities, the judges of the commercial courts, etc., received Bonaparte in the most servile manner wherever his tours carried him, even when, as in Dijon, he roundly attacked the National Assembly, and the party of Order in particular.

When trade was good, as it still was at the beginning of 1851, the commercial bourgeoisie raged against any parliamentary struggle, lest trade be put out of sorts. When trade was bad, as it was continuously from the end of February 1851, the commercial bourgeoisie accused the parliamentary struggles of being the cause of stagnation and screamed for them to fall silent so that the voice of trade could again be heard. The revision debates fell precisely in this bad period for trade. Since it was the existence or non-existence of the present form of the state which was at stake here, the bourgeoisie felt it had all the more justification for demanding that its representatives finish with this excruciating interregnum and yet simultaneously maintain the status quo. There was no contradiction here. The end of the interregnum was understood to mean precisely its continuation, the postponement to a remote future of the moment of decision. The status quo could only be maintained in two ways: by the prolongation of Bonaparte's authority or by his retirement in accordance with the Constitution and the election of Cavaignac. One section of the bourgeoisie desired the latter solution and could give its representatives no

32. François-Ernest Anglès was a landed proprietor, and a deputy in the Legislative National Assembly. Pierre-Henri Sainte-Beuve was a manufacturer and landed proprietor, and a deputy in both Assemblies.

better advice than to keep quiet and steer clear of the burning question. They took the view that if their representatives did not speak, Bonaparte would not act. They wanted a parliamentary ostrich which would hide its head in order to remain invisible. Another section of the bourgeoisie wanted to leave Bonaparte sitting in the presidential chair because he was already there, and thus keep everything in the same old rut. They were indignant that their parliament had not openly broken the Constitution and abdicated without further ado.

The General Councils of the departments, those provincial representative bodies of the big bourgeoisie, met during the recess of the National Assembly from 25 August onwards. They declared for revision almost unanimously, thus against the Assembly and for Bonaparte.

The bourgeoisie demonstrated its anger with its literary representatives, its own press, even more unambiguously than its break with its *parliamentary representatives*. Not only France but the whole of Europe was astonished by the sentences of ruinous fines and shameless terms of imprisonment inflicted, on verdicts brought in by bourgeois juries, for every attack by bourgeois journalists on Bonaparte's usurpationist desires, and for every attempt by the press to defend the political rights of the bourgeoisie against the executive power.

As I have shown, the *parliamentary party of Order* condemned itself to acquiescence by its clamour for tranquillity. It declared the political rule of the bourgeoisie to be incompatible with the bourgeoisie's own safety and existence by destroying with its own hands the whole basis of its own regime, the parliamentary regime, in the struggle against the other classes of society. Similarly, the *extra-parliamentary mass of the bourgeoisie* invited Bonaparte to suppress and annihilate its speaking and writing part, its politicians and intellectuals, its platform and its press, by its own servility towards the President, its vilification of parliament, and its brutal mistreatment of its own press. It hoped that it would then be able to pursue its private affairs with full confidence under the protection of a strong and unrestricted government. It declared unequivocally that it yearned to get rid of its own political rule so as to be free of the attendant troubles and dangers.

And this bourgeoisie, which had already rebelled against the purely parliamentary and literary struggle for the rule of its own class and betrayed the leaders of that struggle, now dares to indict the proletariat retrospectively for failing to rise in a bloody life-and-death struggle on its behalf! This bourgeoisie, which had at every moment sacrificed its general class interests, i.e., its political interests, to the narrowest and most sordid private interests, and expected its representatives to make a similar sacrifice, now bewails the fact that the proletariat has sacrificed the bourgeoisie's ideal political interests to its own material interests. It poses as a pure soul, misunderstood and deserted at the decisive hour by a proletariat led astray by socialists. And it finds a general echo in the bourgeois world. Here I am not speaking, of course, of obscure German politicians or riff-raff of similar opinions. I refer, for example, to the *Economist*, as already quoted, which declared as late as 29 November 1851, that is, four days before the coup d'état, that Bonaparte was the 'guardian of order' and Thiers and Berryer were 'anarchists', and which on 27 December, after Bonaparte had quietened down these anarchists, was already screaming of the betrayal committed by the 'masses of ignorant, untrained, and stupid *proletaires*' against 'the skill, knowledge, discipline, mental influence, intellectual resources and moral weight of the middle and upper ranks'. The stupid, ignorant and vulgar mass was nothing other than the bourgeoisie itself.

In the year 1851 France had admittedly undergone a kind of minor trade crisis. At the end of February it emerged that there was a decline in exports in comparison with 1850; in March trade suffered and factories closed down; in April the position of the industrial departments appeared to be as desperate as after the February days; in May business had still not revived; as late as 28 June the portfolio of the Bank of France showed by the immense growth of deposits and the similarly great decrease in advances on bills of exchange that production was at a standstill. It was not until the middle of October that a progressive improvement of business again set in. The French bourgeoisie attributed this stagnation in trade to purely political causes, to the struggle between the legislature and the executive, to the insecurity of a merely provisional form of state, to the terrifying prospect of the second Sunday in May 1852. I do not wish to deny that all these circumstances had a depressing effect on a number of branches of industry in Paris and the provinces. But in every case the impact of political conditions was only local and inconsiderable. Does this need any other proof than the fact that the improvement of trade occurred towards the middle of October, at the precise moment when the political situation grew worse, the political horizon darkened, and a thunderbolt from Elysium was expected at any time? Let it be said in passing that the French bourgeois, whose 'skill, knowledge, mental insight and intellectual resources' reach no further than the end of his nose, could have found the cause of his commercial misery right under his nose for the whole duration of the Great Exhibition in London. While factories were closed down in France, commercial bankruptcies broke out in England. The industrial panic reached a climax in France in April and May; the commercial panic reached a climax in England in April and May. The English woollen industry suffered alongside the French woollen industry; English silk manufacture suffered alongside French silk manufacture. The English cotton mills continued to operate, but without producing the same profits as in 1849 and 1850. The only difference was that the crisis in France was industrial, in England commercial; that in France the factories stood still, while in England they extended their operations, but under less favourable conditions than in the preceding years; that in France it was exports which received the fiercest blows, in England imports. The reason for both situations was obvious, although not to be found within the confines of the French political horizon. 1849 and 1850 were years of very great material prosperity, and of an overproduction which only made itself apparent in 1851. At the beginning of the year this trend was very much strengthened by the prospect of the Industrial Exhibition.[33] Special circumstances also made their contribution: the initial partial failure of the cotton crop in 1850 and 1851, followed by the certainty that there would be a bigger cotton crop than expected; the initial rise followed by the sudden fall, in other words, the fluctuations, in the price of cotton; the fact that the raw silk crop, in France at least, had turned out below the average yield; and finally the fact that woollen manufacture had expanded so much since 1848 that wool production could not keep up with it, so that the price of raw wool rose out of all proportion to the price of woollen manufactures. Here, then, in the raw material of three industries producing for the world market we already have three reasons for a stagnation in trade. Leaving aside these special circumstances, the apparent crisis of 1851 was simply the halt which overproduction and excessive speculation always have to come to in the course of the industrial cycle, before they collect together all their

33. The London 'Great Exhibition' of 1851.

reserves of strength in order to drive feverishly through the final phase of the cycle and return to their starting-point, the *general trade crisis*. During such interruptions in the course of trade commercial bankruptcies break out in England, while in France industry itself is reduced to immobility, partly because it is forced into retreat by the competition of the English in all markets, which becomes intolerable at precisely such moments, partly because, producing luxury goods, it is a preferential target of attack in every business stagnation. Thus, apart from the general crises, France undergoes her own national trade crises, which are nevertheless determined and conditioned far more by the general state of the world market than by French local influences. It will not be without interest to contrast the sober judgement of the English bourgeois with the prejudiced view of the French bourgeois. One of the biggest Liverpool trading firms wrote in its annual trading report for 1851:

Few years have more thoroughly belied the anticipations formed at their commencement than the one just closed; instead of the great prosperity which was almost unanimously looked for it has proved one of the most discouraging that has been seen for the last quarter of a century – this, of course, refers to the mercantile, not the manufacturing classes. And yet there certainly were grounds for anticipating the reverse at the beginning of the year – stocks of produce were moderate, money was abundant, and food was cheap, a plentiful harvest well secured, unbroken peace on the Continent, and no political or fiscal disturbances at home; indeed, the wings of commerce were never more unfettered . . . To what source, then, is this disastrous result to be attributed? We believe to *over-trading* both in imports and exports. Unless our merchants will put more stringent limits to their freedom of action, nothing but a triennial panic can keep us in check.[34]

Now imagine the French bourgeois, imagine how in the midst of this business his trade-crazy brain is tortured, whirled around and stunned by rumours of a coup d'état, by rumours that universal suffrage will be restored, by the struggle between parliament and the executive, by the Fronde-like war between Orleanists and Legitimists, by the communist conspiracies in southern France, by alleged *jacqueries* in the departments of Nièvre and Cher, by the publicity campaigns of the various presidential candidates, by the cheap and showy slogans of the newspapers, by the threats of the republicans to uphold the Constitution and universal suffrage

34. *Economist*, 10 January 1852.

by force of arms, by the preaching of the *émigré* heroes *in partibus*, who announced that the world would come to an end on the second Sunday in May 1852 – think of all this, and you will understand why the bourgeois, in this unspeakable, clamorous chaos of fusion, revision, prorogation, constitution, conspiration, coalition, emigration, usurpation and revolution, madly snorts at his parliamentary republic: *Rather an end with terror than a terror without end.*

Bonaparte understood this cry. His powers of comprehension had been sharpened by the growing vehemence of creditors who saw in every sunset a movement of the stars in protest against their terrestrial bills of exchange, since every sunset brought nearer settlement day, the second Sunday in May 1852. They had turned into veritable astrologers. The National Assembly had deprived Bonaparte of any hope of a constitutional prolongation of his authority; the candidature of the prince de Joinville did not permit any further hesitation.

If ever an event cast its shadow forward well in advance of its occurrence, it was Bonaparte's coup d'état. Scarcely a month after his election, on 29 January, he had already made a proposal to Changarnier to this effect. His own Prime Minister, Odilon Barrot, had secretly denounced the policy of coup d'état in the summer of 1849, and Thiers had denounced it openly in the winter of 1850. In May 1851 Persigny had tried once more to win Changarnier for the coup; the *Messager de l'Assemblée*[35] had published a report of this negotiation. During every parliamentary storm, the Bonapartist newspapers threatened a coup d'état, and the nearer the crisis approached, the louder their tone became. In the orgies at which Bonaparte celebrated every night in company with the men and women of the *swell mob*,[36] when the hour of midnight approached and rich libations had loosened tongues and heated imaginations, the coup d'état was fixed for the following morning. Swords were drawn, glasses clinked, deputies were thrown out of the window, and the imperial mantle fell on Bonaparte's shoulders, until the following morning once more exorcized the ghost, and an astounded Paris learnt of the danger it had once again escaped from vestals who lacked reserve and paladins who lacked discretion. During the months of September and October rumours of a coup came thick and fast.

35. A newspaper which appeared in Paris from February to December 1851.
36. In English in the original.

At the same time the shadow took on colour, like a variegated daguerreotype. If one looks up the European daily newspapers for the months of September and October one finds, word for word, suggestions like the following: 'Paris is full of rumours of a coup d'état. The capital is to be filled with troops during the night, and the next morning decrees will be issued dissolving the National Assembly, declaring the department of Seine in a state of siege, restoring universal suffrage and appealing to the people. Bonaparte is said to be looking for ministers who will execute these illegal decrees.' The news reports which brought this information always closed with the fateful word '*postponed*'. The coup d'état was always Bonaparte's obsession. It was with this idea in his mind that he had again set foot on French soil. He was possessed by it to such an extent that he repeatedly betrayed it and blurted it out. He was so weak that he gave it up just as often. The shadow of the coup had become so familiar to the Parisians as a spectre that they were unwilling to believe in it when it finally appeared as flesh and blood. It was therefore neither the discreet reticence of the head of the Society of 10 December nor the unexpected nature of the attack on the National Assembly which allowed the coup d'état to succeed. If it succeeded, it was as a necessary and inevitable result of the previous course of development, which occurred in spite of Bonaparte's indiscretion and with the Assembly's foreknowledge.

On 10 October Bonaparte announced to his ministers his decision to restore universal suffrage; on 16 October they resigned, and on 26 October Paris learnt of the formation of the Thorigny[37] ministry. At the same time Carlier was replaced by Maupas[38] as Prefect of Police, and the head of the First Army Division, Magnan, concentrated the most reliable regiments in the capital. On 4 November the National Assembly resumed its sittings. It could do no more than repeat the course it had gone through in a short, succinct summary, and prove that it was buried only after it had died.

The first outpost it had lost in the struggle with the executive was the ministry. It had solemnly to admit this loss by accepting at full value the Thorigny ministry, which was a ministry in

37. Pierre-François Thorigny was a lawyer and a Bonapartist, appointed Minister of the Interior in October 1851.

38. Charlemagne de Maupas was a lawyer and a Bonapartist, Paris Prefect of Police in 1851, one of the organizers of the coup d'état of 2 December, and later Minister of Police.

appearance only. The Standing Commission received Monsieur Giraud[39] with laughter when he presented himself in the name of the new ministers. Such a weak ministry for such strong measures as the restoration of universal suffrage! But that was precisely the intention, to accomplish nothing *in* the Assembly and to accomplish everything *against* the Assembly.

On the very first day of the new session, the National Assembly received Bonaparte's message demanding the restoration of universal suffrage and the abolition of the law of 31 May 1850. On the same day his ministers introduced a decree to this effect. The Assembly immediately rejected the ministers' motion of urgency, and on 13 November rejected the law itself by 355 votes to 348. Thus it tore up its mandate once more; it confirmed once again that it had transformed itself from the freely elected representation of the people into the usurping parliament of a class; and it acknowledged once again that the muscles which connected the parliamentary head with the body of the nation had been cut in two by the parliament itself.

While the executive appealed from the National Assembly to the people with its motion to restore universal suffrage, the legislature appealed from the people to the army by its Quaestors Bill. The aim of the Quaestors Bill was to establish its right to requisition troops directly and to set up a parliamentary armed force. But by appointing the army as arbitrator between itself and the people, between itself and Bonaparte, by recognizing the army as the decisive power in the state, the Assembly only confirmed the fact that it had long since abandoned any claim to rule over the army. By debating its right to requisition troops, instead of immediately requisitioning them, it revealed its doubts about its own power. By rejecting the Quaestors Bill it publicly admitted its powerlessness. The bill was defeated by 108 votes, and it was the Montagne which decided the issue. It found itself in the position of Buridan's ass, though in this case it had not to decide which was the more attractive of two bundles of hay but which was the harder of two showers of blows. On the one side there was the fear of Changarnier; on the other side there was the fear of Bonaparte. One must admit that the circumstances were not conducive to heroism.

39. Charles-Joseph Giraud was a lawyer who was made Minister of Education in the Thorigny cabinet.

On 18 November an amendment was moved to the law on municipal elections introduced by the party of Order, providing for a
reduction of the residence requirement for municipal electors from
three years to one year. The amendment was defeated by a single
vote, but it immediately became apparent that this single vote had
been a mistake. By splitting up into its hostile fractions, the party
of Order had long ago lost its independent parliamentary majority.
It now showed that there was no longer any parliamentary majority
at all. The National Assembly had become *incapable of transacting
business*. Its atomized constituents were no longer held together by
any cohesive force; it had used up its last supply of breath. It was
dead.

Finally, a few days before the catastrophe, the extra-parliamentary
mass of the bourgeoisie once more solemnly confirmed its breach
with the bourgeoisie in parliament. Thiers, as a parliamentary hero,
had received an exceptionally strong dose of the incurable sickness
of parliamentary cretinism. After the Assembly itself had died, he
devised a new parliamentary intrigue together with the Council of
State. This was a law of responsibility, which was supposed to confine
the President firmly within the limits of the Constitution. Bonaparte,
however, had other ideas. On 15 September, when he laid the foundation stone of the new market halls in Paris, he had, like a second
Masaniello,[40] enchanted the *dames des halles*, the fishwives – of
course, one fishwife outweighed seventeen burgraves in real power.
A little later, after the introduction of the Quaestors Bill, he roused
the enthusiasm of the lieutenants being entertained in the Elysée.
And now, on 25 November, he swept off their feet the members of
the industrial bourgeoisie who had assembled at the Circus to receive
from his hands prize medals for the London Industrial Exhibition. I
give here the significant section of his speech, in the version given by
the *Journal des Débats*:

With such unhoped-for successes, I am justified in saying once more
how great the French republic would be if it were permitted to pursue
its real interests and reform its institutions, instead of being constantly
disturbed by demagogues on one side and monarchical hallucinations
on the other. [*Loud, stormy and repeated applause from all parts of the
amphitheatre.*] The monarchical hallucinations hinder all progress and
all important branches of industry. In place of progress there is only

40. Masaniello was a Neapolitan fisherman, leader of a popular rising against Spanish rule in 1647.

struggle. One sees men who were previously the most zealous upholders of the royal authority and prerogative become partisans of a Convention merely in order to weaken the authority that has sprung from universal suffrage. [*Loud and repeated applause*.] We see men who have suffered most from the revolution, and have deplored it most, provoke a new one, and do this merely in order to fetter the will of the nation ... I promise you tranquillity for the future, *etc. etc.* [*Cries of bravo, stormy acclamations*.]

The industrial bourgeoisie thus applauded the coup d'état on 2 December, the destruction of the Assembly, the downfall of its own rule, and the dictatorship of Bonaparte, with servile cries of bravo. The thunder of applause on 25 November was answered by the thunder of cannon on 4 December, and it was on the house of Monsieur Sallandrouze,[41] who had clapped most, that they clapped most of the bombs.

When Cromwell dissolved the Long Parliament, he went alone into its midst, drew out his watch so that it should not exist a minute beyond the time limit he had set, and drove out the members of parliament individually with jovial and humorous invective. Napoleon, though smaller than his model, at least went to the Council of the Five Hundred on 18 Brumaire and read out its sentence of death, albeit in an uneasy voice. The second Bonaparte, who, by the way, found himself in possession of an executive power very different from that of Cromwell or Napoleon, sought his model not in the annals of world history but in the annals of the Society of 10 December, in the annals of the criminal courts. He robbed the Bank of France of twenty-five million francs; he bought General Magnan with a million and the soldiers with fifteen francs each and liquor; he held a meeting with his accomplices in secret, like a thief in the night; he had the houses of the most dangerous parliamentary leaders broken into and Cavaignac, Lamoricière, Le Flô, Changarnier, Charras, Thiers, Baze, etc., dragged from their beds; he had the main squares of Paris and the parliament buildings occupied by troops; and then, early in the morning, he had ostentatious placards put up on all the walls, proclaiming the dissolution of the National Assembly and the Council of State, the restoration of universal suffrage, and the imposition of a state of siege in the Seine depart-

---

41. Charles Sallandrouze de Lamornais was an industrialist, and a deputy in the Constituent Assembly; at first an Orleanist, he later supported the coup d'état.

ment. Shortly afterwards he also inserted a false document in the *Moniteur*, purporting to show that some influential parliamentary names had grouped themselves around him and formed a consultative commission.

The rump parliament, assembled in the *mairie* of the tenth arrondissement and composed mainly of Legitimists and Orleanists, voted the deposition of Bonaparte amid repeated cries of 'Long live the republic', vainly harangued the gaping crowds in front of the building, and was finally dragged away, escorted by a company of the African infantry, first to the d'Orsay barracks, and later, after being packed into prison vans, to the prisons of Mazas, Ham and Vincennes. Thus ended the party of Order, the Legislative Assembly, and the February revolution. Before we hurry on to our conclusion, let us give a short summary of the history of the February revolution:

1. *First period*. From 24 February to 4 May 1848. February period. Prologue. Universal brotherhood swindle.

2. *Second period*. Period of the establishment of the republic and of the Constituent National Assembly.

(a) 4 May to 25 June 1848. Struggle of all classes against the proletariat. Defeat of the proletariat in the June days.

(b) 25 June to 10 December 1848. Dictatorship of the pure bourgeois republicans. Drafting of the Constitution. Proclamation of a state of siege in Paris. The bourgeois dictatorship ended on 10 December by the election of Bonaparte as President.

(c) 20 December 1848 to 28 May 1849. Struggle of the Constituent Assembly with Bonaparte and with the party of Order in alliance with him. End of the Constituent Assembly. Fall of the republican bourgeoisie.

3. *Third period*. Period of the *constitutional republic* and the *Legislative National Assembly*.

(a) 28 May 1849 to 13 June 1849. Struggle of the petty bourgeoisie with the bourgeoisie and with Bonaparte. Defeat of petty-bourgeois democracy.

(b) 13 June 1849 to 31 May 1850. Parliamentary dictatorship of the party of Order. It completes its supremacy by abolishing universal suffrage but loses the parliamentary ministry.

(c) 31 May 1850 to 2 December 1851. Struggle between the parliamentary bourgeoisie and Bonaparte.

(i) 31 May 1850 to 12 January 1851. The Assembly loses the supreme command of the army.

(ii) 12 January 1851 to 11 April 1851. It fails in its attempts to regain the administrative power. The party of Order loses its independent parliamentary majority. Its coalition with the republicans and the Montagne.

(iii) 11 April to 9 October 1851. Attempts at revision, fusion and prorogation. The party of Order dissolves into its individual components. The breach between the bourgeois parliament and press and the mass of the bourgeoisie is consolidated.

(iv) 9 October to 2 December 1851. Open breach between the Assembly and the executive. The Assembly performs its dying act and succumbs, left in the lurch by its own class, by the army, and by all other classes. End of the parliamentary regime and of bourgeois rule. Victory of Bonaparte. The empire is restored as a parody.

VII

The *social republic* appeared on the threshold of the February revolution as a phrase, as a prophecy. In the June days of 1848 it was drowned in the blood of the Paris proletariat, but it haunted the succeeding acts of the drama like a ghost. The *democratic republic* also announced its appearance on the stage. On 13 June 1849 it fizzled out, together with its *petty-bourgeois* supporters, who took flight, but at the same time advertised themselves with redoubled boastfulness. The *parliamentary republic*, together with the bourgeoisie, took possession of the entire stage and enjoyed its existence to the full, but it was buried on 2 December 1851 while the coalition of royalists cried out in anguish: 'Long live the republic!'

The French bourgeoisie revolted at the prospect of the rule of the labouring proletariat; it has brought the lumpenproletariat into power, led by the head of the Society of 10 December. The bourgeoisie held France in breathless fear of the future terrors of red anarchy; Bonaparte discounted this future for it when, on 4 December, he had the refined bourgeois citizens of the Boulevard Montmartre and the Boulevard des Italiens shot down at their windows in alcoholic enthusiasm by the army of order. It deified the sword; it is ruled by the sword. It destroyed the revolutionary press; its own press has been destroyed. It placed popular meetings under police supervision; its salons are under the supervision of the police. It dissolved the democratic National Guard; its own National Guard has been dissolved. It imposed a state of siege; a state of siege has been imposed upon it. It replaced juries with military commissions; its juries have been replaced with military commissions. It subjected the education of the people to the priests; the priests have subjected it to their own education. It transported without trial; it is being transported without trial. It suppressed every stirring in society by means of the state power; every stirring in its society is crushed by means of the state power. It rebelled against its own politicians and intellectuals out of enthusiasm for its purse; its politicians and intellectuals have been swept away, but its purse is being plundered now that its mouth is gagged and its pen broken. The bourgeoisie indefatigably cried out to the revolution what Saint Arsenius cried out to the Christians: '*Fuge, tace, quiesce!*' 'Run away, keep quiet, and don't make a disturbance!'[42] Bonaparte cries to the bourgeoisie: '*Fuge, tace, quiesce!*' 'Run away, keep quiet, and don't make a disturbance!'

The French bourgeoisie long ago solved Napoleon's dilemma: '*Dans cinquante ans l'Europe sera républicaine ou cosaque.*'[43] Their solution was the 'Cossack republic'. That work of art, the bourgeois republic, has not been distorted into a monstrous shape by the black magic of a Circe. It has lost nothing but the appearance of respectability. The parliamentary republic contained present-day France in finished form. It only required a bayonet thrust for the abscess to burst and the monster to spring forth before our eyes.

Why did the Paris proletariat not rise in revolt after 2 December?

As yet, the overthrow of the bourgeoisie had only been decreed, the decree had not been carried out. Any serious proletarian rising would at once have revived the bourgeoisie, reconciled it with the army, and ensured a second June defeat for the workers.

On 4 December the proletariat was incited to fight by the bourgeois and the *épicier*.[44] On the evening of that day several legions of the National Guard promised to appear on the scene of battle armed and uniformed. For the bourgeois and the shop-

42. This was the advice given by Arsenius when he left Rome to become a hermit in the Egyptian desert in the early fifth century.
43. In fifty years Europe will be republican or Cossack.
44. Shopkeeper – a rather pejorative term.

keeper had found out that in one of the decrees of 2 December Bonaparte had abolished the secret ballot and advised them to record their 'yes' or their 'no' in the official registers after their names. Bonaparte was intimidated by the resistance of 4 December. During the night he had placards posted on all the street corners of Paris, announcing the restoration of the secret ballot. The bourgeois and the shopkeeper believed they had achieved their aim. It was the bourgeois and the shopkeeper who failed to appear next morning.

Bonaparte had robbed the Paris proletariat of its leaders, the barricade commanders, by a surprise attack during the night of 1–2 December. The proletariat was an army without officers, and it was in any case unwilling to fight under the banner of the Montagnards because of the memories of June 1848, June 1849, and May 1850. It left its vanguard, the secret societies, to save the insurrectional honour of Paris, which the bourgeoisie had so unresistingly abandoned to the soldiery, so that Bonaparte was later able to disarm the National Guard with the derisive justification that he was afraid its weapons would be misused against itself by the anarchists!

'*C'est le triomphe complet et définitif du socialisme.*'[45] This was Guizot's characterization of 2 December. But if the overthrow of the parliamentary republic contains within itself the germ of the triumph of the proletarian revolution, its first tangible result was *the victory of Bonaparte over the Assembly, of the executive over the legislature, of force without words over the force of words*. In the Assembly the nation raised its general will to the level of law, i.e., it made the law of the ruling class its general will. It then renounced all will of its own in face of the executive and subjected itself to the superior command of an alien will, to authority. The opposition between executive and legislature expresses the opposition between a nation's heteronomy and its autonomy. France therefore seems to have escaped the despotism of a class only to fall back beneath the despotism of an individual, and indeed beneath the authority of an individual without authority. The struggle seems to have reached the compromise that all classes fall on their knees, equally mute and equally impotent, before the rifle butt.

But the revolution is thorough. It is still on its journey through purgatory. It goes about its business methodically. By 2 December

45. It is the complete and final triumph of socialism.

1851 it had completed one half of its preparatory work; it is now completing the other half. First of all it perfected the parliamentary power, in order to be able to overthrow it. Now, having attained this, it is perfecting the *executive power*, reducing it to its purest expression, isolating it, and pitting itself against it as the sole object of attack, in order to concentrate all its forces of destruction against it. And when it has completed this, the second half of its preliminary work, Europe will leap from its seat and exultantly exclaim: 'Well worked, old mole!'[46]

The executive power possesses an immense bureaucratic and military organization, an ingenious and broadly based state machinery, and an army of half a million officials alongside the actual army, which numbers a further half million. This frightful parasitic body, which surrounds the body of French society like a caul and stops up all its pores, arose in the time of the absolute monarchy, with the decay of the feudal system, which it helped to accelerate. The seignorial privileges of the landowners and towns were transformed into attributes of the state power, the feudal dignitaries became paid officials, and the variegated medieval pattern of conflicting plenary authorities became the regulated plan of a state authority characterized by a centralization and division of labour reminiscent of a factory. The task of the first French revolution was to destroy all separate local, territorial, urban and provincial powers in order to create the civil unity of the nation. It had to carry further the centralization that the absolute monarchy had begun, but at the same time it had to develop the extent, the attributes and the number of underlings of the governmental power. Napoleon perfected this state machinery. The Legitimist and July monarchies only added a greater division of labour, which grew in proportion to the creation of new interest groups, and therefore new material for state administration, by the division of labour within bourgeois society. Every *common* interest was immediately detached from society, opposed to it as a higher, *general* interest, torn away from the self-activity of the individual members of society and made a subject for governmental activity, whether it was a bridge, a schoolhouse, the communal property of a village community, or the railways, the

46. Hamlet's actual words in *Hamlet* I, v, 162, are, 'Well said old mole, canst work i' th' ground so fast?' Marx's '*Brav gewühlt, alter Maulwurf*' is a condensation, with the twist that *wühlen*, besides meaning to work, grub, burrow, also means to agitate, stir up, foment discontent. See below, p. 634.

national wealth and the national university of France. Finally, the parliamentary republic was compelled in its struggle against the revolution to strengthen by means of repressive measures the resources and centralization of governmental power. All political upheavals perfected this machine instead of smashing it. The parties that strove in turn for mastery regarded possession of this immense state edifice as the main booty for the victor.

However, under the absolute monarchy, during the first French revolution, and under Napoleon, bureaucracy was only the means of preparing the class rule of the bourgeoisie. Under the Restoration, Louis Philippe, and the parliamentary republic, on the other hand, it was the instrument of the ruling class, however much it strove for power in its own right.

Only under the second Bonaparte does the state seem to have attained a completely autonomous position. The state machine has established itself so firmly *vis-à-vis* civil society that the only leader it needs is the head of the Society of 10 December, an adventurer who has rushed in from abroad and been chosen as leader by a drunken soldiery, which he originally bought with liquor and sausages, and to which he constantly has to throw more sausages. This explains the shamefaced despair, the feeling of terrible humiliation and degradation which weighs upon France's breast and makes her catch her breath. France feels dishonoured.

But the state power does not hover in mid-air. Bonaparte represents a class, indeed he represents the most numerous class of French society, the *small peasant proprietors*.

Just as the Bourbons were the dynasty of big landed property and the Orleans the dynasty of money, so the Bonapartes are the dynasty of the peasants, i.e., of the mass of the French people. The chosen hero of the peasantry is not the Bonaparte who submitted to the bourgeois parliament but the Bonaparte who dispersed it. For three years the towns succeeded in falsifying the meaning of the election of 10 December and swindling the peasants out of the restoration of the empire. The election of 10 December 1848 was completed only with the coup d'état of 2 December 1851.

The small peasant proprietors form an immense mass, the members of which live in the same situation but do not enter into manifold relationships with each other. Their mode of operation isolates them instead of bringing them into mutual intercourse. This isolation is strengthened by the wretched state of France's means of communication and by the poverty of the peasants.

Their place of operation, the smallholding, permits no division of labour in its cultivation, no application of science and therefore no diversity of development, variety of talent, or wealth of social relationships. Each individual peasant family is almost self-sufficient; it directly produces the greater part of its own consumption and therefore obtains its means of life more through exchange with nature than through intercourse with society. The smallholding, the peasant and the family; next door, another smallholding, another peasant and another family. A bunch of these makes up a village, and a bunch of villages makes up a department. Thus the great mass of the French nation is formed by the simple addition of isomorphous magnitudes, much as potatoes in a sack form a sack of potatoes. In so far as millions of families live under economic conditions of existence that separate their mode of life, their interests and their cultural formation from those of the other classes and bring them into conflict with those classes, they form a class. In so far as these small peasant proprietors are merely connected on a local basis, and the identity of their interests fails to produce a feeling of community, national links or a political organization, they do not form a class. They are therefore incapable of asserting their class interest in their own name, whether through a parliament or through a convention.[47] They cannot represent themselves; they must be represented. Their representative must appear simultaneously as their master, as an authority over them, an unrestricted governmental power that protects them from the other classes and sends them rain and sunshine from above. The political influence of the small peasant proprietors is therefore ultimately expressed in the executive subordinating society to itself.

Historical tradition produced the French peasants' belief that a miracle would occur, that a man called Napoleon would restore all their glory. And an individual turned up who pretended to be that man, because he bore the name of Napoleon, thanks to the stipulation of the Code Napoléon that '*la récherche de la paternité est interdite*'.[48] After twenty years of vagabondage and a series of grotesque adventures the prophecy was fulfilled and the man became Emperor of the French. The nephew's obsession was realized, because it coincided with the obsession of the most numerous class of the French people.

47. I.e., a revolutionary assembly like that of 1792–5.
48. Inquiry into paternity is forbidden.

But the objection will be made: What about the peasant risings in half of France, the army's murderous forays against them, and their imprisonment and transportation *en masse*?

Since Louis XIV, France has experienced no corresponding persecution of the peasants 'for demagogic practices'.

This point should be clearly understood: the Bonaparte dynasty represents the conservative, not the revolutionary peasant: the peasant who wants to consolidate the condition of his social existence, the smallholding, not the peasant who strikes out beyond it. It does not represent the country people who want to overthrow the old order by their own energies, in alliance with the towns, but the precise opposite, those who are gloomily enclosed within this old order and want to see themselves and their small-holdings saved and given preferential treatment by the ghost of the Empire. It represents the peasant's superstition, not his enlightenment; his prejudice, not his judgement; his past, not his future; his modern Vendée, not his modern Cevennes.[49]

Three years of hard rule by the parliamentary republic had freed some of the French peasants from the Napoleonic illusion and revolutionized them, if only superficially, but they were violently suppressed by the bourgeoisie whenever they started to move. Under the parliamentary republic the modern consciousness of the peasant fought with his traditional consciousness. The process moved forward in the form of an unceasing struggle between the schoolmasters and the priests. The bourgeoisie struck down the schoolmasters. For the first time the peasants endeavoured to take up an independent attitude in face of the government's activities. This was shown in the continual conflict between the mayors and the prefects. The bourgeoisie deposed the mayors. Finally, during the period of the parliamentary republic the peasants of various localities rose against their own offspring, the army. The bourgeoisie punished them with states of siege and military expeditions. And this same bourgeoisie is now exclaiming over the stupidity of the masses, the *vile multitude*[50] which allowed them to betray it to Bonaparte. The bourgeoisie itself violently strength-

49. Vendée, in Brittany, was the focus of royalist revolt during the first French revolution. Cevennes was the area of southern France in which the peasant rising of the years 1702–5 took place, the 'revolt of the Camisards'. It was a rising of Protestants for freedom of conscience, and also against feudal dues.

50. In English in the original.

ened the imperialist leanings of the peasant class and kept in being the conditions that form the breeding-ground of this peasant religion. The bourgeoisie is naturally bound to fear the stupidity of the masses as long as they remain conservative, and the discernment of the masses as soon as they become revolutionary.

In the risings after the coup d'état a section of the French peasantry protested, arms in hand, against its own vote of 10 December 1848. The school these peasants had gone through since 1848 had sharpened their wits. But they had signed themselves away to the underworld of history, and history kept them to their word. Moreover, the majority was still so prejudiced that the peasant population of precisely the reddest departments voted openly for Bonaparte. In its view the National Assembly had hindered his progress. He had now merely broken the fetters imposed by the towns on the will of the country. Here and there the peasants even entertained the grotesque idea that a convention could co-exist with Napoleon.

After the first revolution had transformed the peasants from a state of semi-serfdom into free landed proprietors, Napoleon confirmed and regulated the conditions under which they could exploit undisturbed the soil of France, which had now devolved on them for the first time, and satisfy their new-found passion for property. But the French peasant is now succumbing to his smallholding itself, to the division of the land, the form of property consolidated in France by Napoleon. It was the material conditions which made the feudal French peasant a small proprietor and Napoleon an emperor. Two generations have been sufficient to produce the inevitable consequence: a progressive deterioration of agriculture and a progressive increase in peasant indebtedness. The 'Napoleonic' form of property, which was the condition for the liberation and enrichment of the French rural population at the beginning of the nineteenth century, has developed in the course of that century into the legal foundation of their enslavement and their poverty. And precisely this law is the first of the 'Napoleonic ideas' which the second Bonaparte has to uphold. If he still shares with the peasants the illusion that the cause of their ruin is to be sought, not in the smallholding itself, but outside it, in the influence of secondary circumstances, his experiments will burst like soap bubbles at their first contact with the relations of production.

The economic development of the smallholding has profoundly

distorted the relation of the peasants to the other classes of society. Under Napoleon the fragmentation of landed property in the countryside supplemented free competition and the beginning of large industry in the towns. The peasant class was the ubiquitous protest against the landed aristocracy which had just been overthrown. The roots which the smallholding struck in French soil deprived feudalism of all nutriment. Its fences formed the bourgeoisie's system of natural fortifications against surprise attacks on the part of its old overlords. But in the course of the nineteenth century the urban usurer replaced the feudal lord; the mortgage on the land replaced its feudal obligations; bourgeois capital replaced aristocratic landed property. The peasant's smallholding is now only the pretext that allows the capitalist to draw profits, interest and rent from the soil, while leaving the tiller himself to work out how to extract the wage for his labour. The mortgage debt burdening the soil of France imposes on the French peasantry an interest payment equal to the annual interest on the entire British national debt. Owing to this enslavement by capital, inevitably brought about by its own development, small peasant property has transformed the mass of the French nation into troglodytes. Sixteen million peasants (including women and children) live in hovels, many of which have only one opening, others only two, and the rest, the most fortunate cases, only three. Windows are to a house what the five senses are to a head. The bourgeois order, which at the beginning of the century made the state do sentry duty over the newly arisen smallholding, and manured it with laurels, has become a vampire that sucks out its blood and brains and throws them into the alchemist's cauldron of capital. The Code Napoléon is now merely the lawbook for distraints on chattels, forced sales and compulsory auctions. To the four million (including children, etc.) officially admitted paupers, vagabonds, criminals and prostitutes in France must be added five million who totter on the precipice of non-existence and either wander around the countryside itself or, with their rags and their children, continually desert the country for the towns and the towns for the country. The interests of the peasants are therefore no longer consonant with the interests of the bourgeoisie, as they were under Napoleon, but in opposition to those interests, in opposition to capital. They therefore find their natural ally and leader in the *urban proletariat*, whose task is the overthrow of the bourgeois order. But the *strong and unrestricted government* – and this is the second '*Napoleonic idea*' which the second Napoleon has to implement – is required to defend this 'material' order by force. This '*ordre matériel*' also serves as the catchword in all Bonaparte's proclamations against the rebellious peasants.

Besides the mortgage which capital imposes on it, the small-holding is burdened by *taxation*. Taxation is the source of life for the bureaucracy, the army, the priests and the court; in short, it is the source of life for the whole executive apparatus. Strong government and heavy taxes are identical. By its very nature, small peasant property is suitable to serve as the foundation of an all-powerful and innumerable bureaucracy. It creates a uniform level of relationships and persons over the whole surface of the land. Hence it also allows a uniformity of intervention from a supreme centre into all points of this uniform mass. It annihilates the aristocratic intermediate levels between the mass of the people and the state power. On all sides, therefore, it calls forth the direct interference of this state power and the interposition of its organs without mediation. Finally, it produces an unemployed surplus population which can find room neither on the land nor in the towns, and which accordingly grasps at state office as providing a kind of respectable charity, thus provoking the creation of state posts. Napoleon repaid the forced taxes with interest by the new markets he opened with the bayonet, and by plundering the European continent. Previously these taxes were an incentive to peasant industry, but now they rob it of its last resources and put the finishing touch to the peasant's inability to resist pauperism. And an enormous bureaucracy, with gold braid and a fat belly, is the 'Napoleonic idea' which is most congenial of all to the second Bonaparte. It could not be otherwise, for he has been forced to create, alongside the real classes of society, an artificial caste for which the maintenance of his regime is a question of self-preservation. One of his first financial operations was therefore to raise officials' salaries to their old level and to create new sinecures.

Another 'Napoleonic idea' is the rule of the *priests* as an instrument of government. But if the newly arisen smallholding was naturally religious in its accord with society, its dependence on natural forces, and its subjection to the authority protecting it from on high, it is naturally irreligious when ruined by debts, at variance with society and authority, and driven beyond its own limitations. Heaven was a very nice addition to the narrow strip of land just obtained, especially as it produced the weather; it becomes an insult as soon as it is offered as a substitute for the small-holding. The priest then appears as merely the anointed bloodhound of the terrestrial police – another 'Napoleonic idea'. Next time the expedition against Rome will take place in France itself, but in a sense opposite to that of Monsieur Montalembert.[51]

Lastly, the culminating point of the 'Napoleonic idea' is the predominance of the *army*. The army was the small peasant proprietors' *point d'honneur*, the peasant himself transformed into a hero, defending his new possessions against external enemies, glorifying his recently won nationhood, and plundering and revolutionizing the world. The uniform was the peasant's national costume, the war was his poetry, the smallholding, extended and rounded off in imagination, was his fatherland, and patriotism was the ideal form of his sense of property. But the French peasant now has to defend his property, not against the Cossacks, but against the *huissier*[52] and the tax collector. The smallholding lies no longer in the so-called fatherland, but in the register of mortgages. The army itself is no longer the flower of peasant youth, but the dregs of the peasant lumpenproletariat. To a large extent it consists of *remplaçants*, substitutes, just as the second Bonaparte is himself only a substitute for Napoleon. It now performs its deeds of valour by driving and hunting the peasants like chamois or pheasants, in the course of *gendarme* duty, and if the internal contradictions of his system drive the head of the Society of 10 December to send his army over the French border, it will reap not laurels but a sound thrashing, after committing a few acts of brigandage.

All the 'Napoleonic ideas' are ideas of the undeveloped smallholding in its heyday. So much is evident. It is equally true that they are an absurdity for the smallholding that has outlived its day. They are only the hallucinations of its death agony, words made into phrases, spirits made into ghosts. But this parody of the empire was necessary to free the mass of the French nation from the burden of tradition and to bring out the antagonism between the state power and society in its pure form. With the progressive disintegration of small peasant property the state structure erected upon it begins to collapse. The political centraliza-

51. Montalembert was a leading supporter of the expedition to crush the Roman republic and restore the temporal power of the Pope (April–July 1849).
52. Bailiff.

tion that modern society requires can arise only on the debris of the military and bureaucratic government machinery originally forged in opposition to feudalism.[53]

The situation of the French peasantry reveals the solution to the riddle of the *general elections of 20 and 21 December*, which bore the second Bonaparte onto Mount Sinai, not to receive laws, but to make them.

Clearly, the bourgeoisie now had no other choice than to elect Bonaparte. When the puritans at the Council of Constance[54] complained of the dissolute lives of the Popes and moaned about the necessity of moral reform, Cardinal Pierre d'Ailly thundered at them: 'The Catholic Church can only be saved now by the Devil in person, and you ask for angels.' Similarly, after the coup d'état, the French bourgeoisie cried, 'Bourgeois society can only be saved now by the head of the Society of 10 December! Only theft can save property; perjury, religion; bastardy, the family; disorder, order!'

Bonaparte is the executive authority which has attained power in its own right, and as such he feels it to be his mission to safeguard 'bourgeois order'. But the strength of this bourgeois order lies in the middle class. He therefore sees himself as the representative of the middle class and he issues decrees in this sense. However, he is only where he is because he has broken the political power of this middle class, and breaks it again daily. He therefore sees himself as the opponent of the political and literary power of the middle class. But by protecting its material power he recreates its political power. The cause must accordingly be kept alive, but the effect must be done away with wherever it appears. However, this cannot occur without slight confusions of cause and effect, since both lose their distinguishing characteristics when they interact. New decrees are issued that obliterate the boundary between the

53. In the first edition this paragraph ended with the following lines, which Marx omitted from the 1869 edition: 'The destruction of the state machine will not endanger centralization. Bureaucracy is only the low and brutal form of a centralization still burdened with its opposite, feudalism. In despair and disappointment at the Napoleonic restoration, the French peasant will abandon his faith in his smallholding, the entire state edifice erected on the smallholding will fall to the ground, and *the proletarian revolution will obtain the chorus without which its solo will prove a requiem* in all peasant countries.'

54. A council of the Catholic Church, held between 1414 and 1418, at which the position of the Pope was restored after the disturbances of the previous century, and the doctrines of the reformers Wycliffe and Hus were declared heretical.

two. As against the bourgeoisie, Bonaparte sees himself simultaneously as the representative of the peasants and of the people in general, as the man who wants to make the lower classes happy within the framework of bourgeois society. New decrees are issued that swindle the 'true socialists'[55] out of their statecraft in advance. But, above all, Bonaparte sees himself as the head of the Society of 10 December, as the representative of the lumpenproletariat to which he himself, his entourage, his government and his army belong, and whose chief concern is to do well for himself and extract California lottery prizes from the treasury. And he confirms that he is the head of the Society of 10 December with decrees, without decrees and despite decrees.

The contradictory task facing the man explains the contradictions of his government, the confused and fumbling attempts to win and then to humiliate first one class and then another, the result being to array them all in uniform opposition to him. This practical uncertainty forms a highly comic contrast to the peremptory and categorical style of the government's decrees, a style faithfully copied from the uncle.

Industry and trade, i.e., the business affairs of the middle class, are to flourish under the strong government as in a hothouse. Hence the grant of innumerable railway concessions. But the Bonapartist lumpenproletariat is to enrich itself. Hence fraudulent manipulation of the Bourse with the railway concessions, by those already initiated. But no capital is forthcoming for the railways. Hence the Bank is obliged to make advances on the railway shares. But the Bank must simultaneously be exploited by Bonaparte, and therefore must be cajoled. Hence it is released from the obligation to publish its report every week. The government makes a leonine agreement[56] with the Bank. The people are to be given employment. Hence instructions are issued for public works. But the public works raise the tax burden on the people. Hence the taxes are reduced by attacking the *rentiers*, by conversion of the 5 per cent bonds to 4½ per cent. But the middle class must again receive a sop. Hence the wine tax is doubled for the people, who

55. A reference to the ideas of the German socialists of the 1840s, who preached a sentimental and humanistic variety of socialism, subjected to a devastating critique by Engels in the second part of *The German Ideology*. (See also *The Manifesto of the Communist Party*, section III in Volume I, above, pp. 84–7.)

56. An agreement from which one partner secures all the gains, the other partner suffers all the losses. From Aesop's fable of the lion.

buy it in small quantities, and halved for the middle class, who drink it in bulk. The existing workers' associations are dissolved, but miracles of association are promised for the future. The peasants are to be helped. Hence mortgage banks are set up to accelerate their indebtedness, on the one hand, and the concentration of capital, on the other. But these banks are to be used to make money out of the confiscated estates of the House of Orleans, and no capitalist wishes to accept this condition, which is not contained in the decree. Hence the mortgage bank remains a mere decree, etc., etc.

Bonaparte would like to appear as the patriarchal benefactor of all classes. But he cannot give to one class without taking from another. At the time of the Fronde, it was said of the duc de Guise that he was the most obliging man in France, because he had turned all his estates into obligations of his supporters towards himself. In the same way Bonaparte would like to be the most obliging man in France and turn all the property and labour of the country into a personal obligation towards himself. He would like to steal the whole of France in order to be able to give it back to France, or rather to be able to buy France again with French money, for as the head of the Society of 10 December he must buy what ought to belong to him. And all the institutions of the state, the Senate,[57] the Council of State, the Legislative Body,[58] the Legion of Honour, the military medals, the wash-houses, the public works, the railways, the general staff of the National Guard (without privates) and the confiscated estates of the House of Orleans – all these things become part of the Institute of Purchase. Every place in the army and the government apparatus becomes a means of purchase. But the most important aspect of this process of taking France in order to give France back is the percentage that finds its way into the pockets of the head and the members of the Society of 10 December during the transaction. The *bon mot* with which Countess L., the mistress of Monsieur de Morny,[59]

57. The Senate was the upper house set up by the constitution of 14 January 1852, with the task of protecting the constitution and the power to modify it if the President (as 'Napoleon III' still regarded himself) proposed this. Its members were appointed by the President.

58. The Legislative Body (Corps Législatif) of the Second Empire was elected by universal suffrage, but had very restricted power.

59. Charles, duc de Morny was the half-brother of Louis Bonaparte, a deputy in the Legislative National Assembly and one of the organizers of the coup of 2 December.

characterized the confiscation of the Orleans estates, '*C'est le premier vol*[60] *de l'aigle*,'[61] fits every flight of this *eagle*, which is more like a *raven*. Every day he and his adherents call out to each other like that Carthusian monk in Italy who said to the miser ostentatiously counting up the goods he could live on for years to come, '*Tu fai conto sopra i beni, bisogna prima far il conto sopra gli anni.*'[62] So as not to get the years wrong, they count in minutes. A gang of shady characters pushes its way forward to the court, into the ministries, to the chief positions in the administration and the army. Of even the best of them it must be said that no one knows where they come from. They are a noisy, disreputable, rapacious crowd of bohemians, crawling into gold-braided coats with the same grotesque dignity as the high dignitaries of Soulouque's empire.[63] One can gain a shrewd idea of this upper stratum of the Society of 10 December if one bears in mind that Véron-Crevel[64] preaches its morals and Granier de Cassagnac is its thinker. When Guizot utilized this Granier at the time of his ministry in an obscure provincial paper against the dynastic opposition, he used to boast of him with the phrase, '*C'est le roi des drôles*' – 'he is the king of buffoons.' It would be a mistake to call to mind the Regency[65] or Louis XV in connection with the court and the clan of Louis Bonaparte. For 'France has often experienced a government of mistresses, but never before a government of kept men.'[66]

Driven on by the contradictory demands of his situation, Bonaparte, like a conjuror, has to keep the eyes of the public fixed on himself, as Napoleon's substitute, by means of constant surprises, that is to say by performing a coup d'état in miniature every day. He thereby brings the whole bourgeois economy into confusion, violates everything that seemed inviolable to the revolution of 1848, makes some tolerant of revolution and others

60. *Vol* means flight and theft. [*Footnote by Marx.*]

61. It is the first flight of the eagle.

62. You are reckoning up your goods, but you should first reckon your years. [*Footnote by Marx.*]

63. See p. 409, n. 71.

64. In the character of Crevel in *Cousine Bette*, drawn after Dr Véron, the owner of *Le Constitutionnel*, Balzac portrayed the thoroughly dissolute Parisian philistine. [*Footnote by Marx.*]

65. The regency of Philippe of Orleans, during the minority of Louis XV (1715–23).

66. Madame Girardin's remark. [*Footnote by Marx.*]

desirous of revolution, creates anarchy itself in the name of order, and at the same time strips the halo from the state machine, profaning it and making it both disgusting and ridiculous. He repeats the cult of the Holy Tunic at Trier[67] in the form of the cult of the Napoleonic imperial mantle in Paris. But when the emperor's mantle finally falls on the shoulders of Louis Bonaparte, the bronze statue of Napoleon will come crashing down from the top of the Vendôme Column.

67. One of the sacred relics exhibited in Trier Cathedral in 1844 as part of the Catholic revival of the 1840s.

Articles on Britain

REVIEW OF GUIZOT'S BOOK ON THE
ENGLISH REVOLUTION[1]

It is the intention of Monsieur Guizot's pamphlet to demonstrate why Louis Philippe and the policies of Guizot should not really have been overthrown on 24 February 1848, and how the shameful character of the French is to blame for the fact that the July monarchy collapsed ignominiously after eighteen troubled years and did not achieve that durability which the English monarchy has enjoyed since 1688.

We can see from this pamphlet how even the most able figures of the *ancien régime*, even those whom in their way possess an unquestionable talent for history, have been so completely bewildered by the fateful events of February that they have lost all historical understanding, even of their own earlier actions. Instead of the February revolution bringing him to recognize the completely different historic conditions, the completely different situation of the social classes under the French monarchy of 1830 and the English monarchy of 1688, M. Guizot resolves the difference in a few moral phrases and asserts in conclusion that the policy overthrown on 24 February 'can overcome revolutions, just as it preserves states'.

Clearly formulated, the question which M. Guizot is trying to answer is this: Why has bourgeois society in England developed in the form of a constitutional monarchy longer than in France?

The following passage serves to characterize M. Guizot's familiarity with bourgeois development in England:

Under the reigns of George I and George II public attention turned elsewhere: foreign policy ceased to be its main consideration; domestic

1. François Guizot, *Pourquoi la révolution d'Angleterre a-t-elle réussi?* Paris, 1850. Marx wrote this review for the February 1850 issue of the *Neue Rheinische Zeitung Revue*, and it is translated here from the text printed in *MEW* 7.

administration, the maintenance of peace, financial, colonial, commercial questions, parliamentary development and parliamentary struggles became the main preoccupation of government and public (p. 168).

In the reign of William III M. Guizot finds only two factors worthy of mention: the maintenance of the balance of power between Parliament and the Crown, and the maintenance of the European balance of power in the struggle against Louis XIV. Suddenly, during the Hanoverian dynasty, 'public attention turned elsewhere'; we do not know how or why. It is evident here how M. Guizot transfers the most commonplace phrases from French parliamentary debate to English history and how, by doing so, he imagines that he has provided an explanation. In precisely the same way M. Guizot imagined, as a minister, that he could carry on his shoulders both the equilibrium between parliament and Crown and the European equilibrium, whereas in reality he did nothing except sell off the whole French state and the whole of French society, piece by piece, to the financial sharks of the Paris Bourse.

M. Guizot does not regard it as worth mentioning that the wars against Louis XIV were wars of competition, pure and simple, aimed at destroying French trade and French sea-power; that under William III the rule of the financial bourgeoisie was given its first legitimation with the establishment of the Bank of England and the introduction of the national debt;[2] and that the manufacturing bourgeoisie was given a new impetus by the consistent application of the protective tariff system. Only political phrases have any meaning for him. He does not even mention that under Queen Anne the ruling parties were able to preserve themselves and the constitutional monarchy only by force, by extending the life of Parliament to seven years, and thus almost destroying the influence of the people upon the government.[3]

Under the Hanoverian dynasty England had already developed to such an extent that it was able to conduct the war of competition against France in the modern fashion. England itself continued to fight France only in America and the East Indies, while contenting itself on the Continent with financing foreign princes like

2. The charter of the Bank of England, granted in 1694, was conditional on its providing loans to the government.
3. The Septennial Act was not in fact passed until May 1716, by which time George I had succeeded to the throne.

Frederick II in their wars against France. And because foreign wars thus assumed another form, M. Guizot says that 'foreign policy ceased to be the main consideration' and that its place was taken by 'the maintenance of peace'. The extent to which 'parliamentary development and parliamentary struggles became the main preoccupation of government and public' should be measured against the cases of bribery under Walpole's ministry,[4] which, it must be said, resemble to a 'T' the scandals which were the order of the day under M. Guizot.

M. Guizot ascribes the fact that the English revolution fared better than the French to two particular causes: the first is that the English revolution had a distinctly religious character and thus by no means broke with all the traditions of the past; the second is that from its inception it operated not as a destructive but as a conservative force, in that Parliament was defending old existing laws against the encroachments of the Crown.

As far as the first point is concerned, M. Guizot forgets that free thought, which causes his flesh to creep so badly in connection with the French revolution, was exported to France from England, no less. Locke had been its father, and in Shaftesbury and Bolingbroke it had already assumed that intellectually acute form which was later developed so brilliantly in France. We thus come to the strange conclusion that this same free thought which, according to M. Guizot, caused the French revolution to come to grief, was one of the most important products of the religious revolution in England.

As for the second point, M. Guizot completely forgets that the French revolution began just as conservatively, if not more so, than the English revolution. Absolutism, particularly as it finally manifested itself in France, was also an innovation there, and the *parlements* rose up against this innovation in defence of the old laws, the *us et coutumes*[5] of the old monarchy based on the estates. And whereas the first step taken by the French revolution was to revive the Estates General, which had lain dormant since Henri IV and Louis XIII, the English revolution does not reveal any evidence of the same classical conservatism.

According to M. Guizot, the main result of the English revolution was that it became impossible for the king to govern against the will of Parliament, in particular the House of Commons. The

4. Sir Robert Walpole was Whig Prime Minister from 1721 to 1742.
5. Practices and customs.

significance of the whole revolution, as he sees it, lies in the fact that initially both sides, Crown and Parliament, overstepped the limits of their power and went too far until, finally, under William III, they found the right balance and neutralized each other. M. Guizot finds it superfluous to mention that the subjection of the monarchy to Parliament amounts to its subjection to the rule of a class. He is therefore also absolved from having to investigate how this class finally acquired the necessary power to make the Crown its servant. In his account the whole struggle between Charles I and Parliament turned around purely political privileges. As to why Parliament and the class which it represents needed these privileges, we hear not a word. No more does M. Guizot speak of Charles I's direct interference in free competition, which made things increasingly impossible for English commerce and industry, or of Charles I's dependence upon Parliament, which resulted from his continual financial difficulties and which increased the more he tried to defy Parliament. Thus, for M. Guizot, the whole revolution is to be explained simply by the malevolence and religious fanaticism of individual troublemakers, who could not content themselves with moderate freedom. He is equally unable to enlighten us about the connection between the religious movement and the development of bourgeois society. The Commonwealth, of course, is likewise merely the work of a few ambitious, fanatical and malevolent individuals. That around the same time in Lisbon, Naples and Messina attempts were also made to establish republics,[6] and that, as in England, this was under the influence of the Dutch example, is a fact which goes without mention. Although M. Guizot never loses sight of the French revolution, he never once comes to the simple conclusion that everywhere the transition from an absolute to a constitutional monarchy only comes about after a violent struggle and by way of a form of republic, and that even then the old obsolete dynasty has to make way for a usurpatory collateral branch. Consequently, he is only able to produce the most trivial commonplaces about the overthrow of the English Restoration monarchy. He does not even mention the most immediate causes: the fear felt among the new great landowners created by the Reformation of the re-establishment of Catholicism, in which case they would, of course, have had to surrender all their stolen Church property, as a result

6. Republican uprisings against the Spanish monarchy took place in Lisbon in 1640, in Naples in 1647–8 and in Messina (Sicily) in 1674–6.

of which seven tenths of the total acreage of England would have changed owners; the fear of Catholicism felt by the commercial and industrial bourgeoisie, since it by no means suited their business interests; the nonchalance with which the Stuarts, to their own advantage and that of their court nobility, sold the whole of English industry and commerce to the government of France – the only country which at that time was endangering England with its competition, in many respects successfully. Consequently, as M. Guizot everywhere omits the most important factors, there is nothing left for him but to present a highly unsatisfactory and banal narration of the merely political events.

The great puzzle of the conservative character of the English revolution, which M. Guizot can solve only by attributing it to the superior intelligence of the English, is in fact explained by the lasting alliance of the bourgeoisie with the great landowners, an alliance which fundamentally distinguishes the English from the French revolution, the latter having destroyed large landed property by dividing it up into smallholdings. This class of large landowners allied with the bourgeoisie, which, it may be added, had already arisen under Henry VIII, was not, as were the French feudal landowners of 1789, in conflict with the vital interests of the bourgeoisie, but rather in complete harmony with them. Their estates were indeed not feudal but bourgeois property. On the one hand, they provided the industrial bourgeoisie with the population necessary to operate the manufacturing system, and, on the other hand, they were in a position to raise agricultural development to the level corresponding to that of industry and commerce. Hence their common interests with the bourgeoisie; hence their alliance.

As far as M. Guizot is concerned, English history comes to an end with the consolidation of the constitutional monarchy. Subsequent events are limited to a pleasant interchange between Whigs and Tories, on the lines of the great debate between M. Guizot and M. Thiers. In reality, however, the momentous development and transformation of bourgeois society in England only began with the consolidation of the constitutional monarchy. Where M. Guizot sees only a gentle tranquillity and an idyllic peace, in reality the most tremendous conflicts and far-reaching revolutions were taking place. At first, manufacturing expanded under the constitutional monarchy to an extent hitherto unknown, later making way for large-scale industry, the steam-engine and the gigantic factories. Whole classes disappeared from the population, new classes taking their place with a new basis of existence and new needs. A new bourgeoisie of colossal proportions arose; while the old bourgeoisie struggled with the French revolution, the new one conquered the world market. It became so omnipotent that, even before it gained direct political power as a result of the Reform Bill,[7] it forced its opponents to legislate in *its* interests and in accordance with *its* requirements. It captured direct representation in Parliament and used this to destroy the last remnants of real power left to the landed proprietors. Finally, at this moment, it is busy completely demolishing the beautiful edifice of the English constitution before which M. Guizot stands in admiration.

And while M. Guizot compliments the English on the failure of republicanism and socialism – those base, tumorous growths of French society – to shake the foundations of an infinitely beneficent monarchy, class conflicts in English society have reached a pitch unequalled in any other country: a bourgeoisie with unprecedented wealth and productive forces is confronted here by a proletariat which equally has no precedent in power and concentration. So the respectful tribute which M. Guizot pays to England really amounts to this: that under the protection of the constitutional monarchy elements of social revolution have developed which are far more radical and far greater in number than in all other countries of the world put together. Whenever the strands which make up the course of English history become intertwined in a conjunctural knot, which he cannot even give the appearance of severing with mere political phrases, M. Guizot takes refuge in religious phrases, in the armed intervention of God. Thus the spirit of God, for instance, moves over the army and prevents Cromwell from proclaiming himself king, etc., etc. Guizot seeks refuge from his conscience in God; he seeks refuge from a profane public in style.

Indeed, it is not merely that *les rois s'en vont*, but also that *les capacités de la bourgeoisie s'en vont*.[8]

7. Of 1831–2.
8. Not only do kings disappear, but so do the leading authorities of the bourgeoisie.

TORIES AND WHIGS[9]

London, 6 August 1852

The results of the general election for the British Parliament are now known. These results I shall analyse more fully in my next letter.[10]

What were the parties which during this electioneering agitation opposed or supported each other?

Tories, Whigs, Liberal Conservatives (Peelites), Free Traders, *par excellence* (the men of the Manchester School, Parliamentary and Financial Reformers),[11] and lastly, the Chartists.

Whigs, Free Traders and Peelites coalesced to oppose the Tories. It was between this coalition on one side, and the Tories on the other, that the real electoral battle was fought. Opposed to Whigs, Peelites, Free Traders and Tories, and thus opposed to entire official England, were the Chartists.

The political parties of Great Britain are sufficiently known in the United States. It will be sufficient to bring to mind, in a few strokes of the pen, the distinctive characteristics of each of them.

Up to 1846 the Tories passed as the guardians of the traditions of Old England. They were suspected of admiring in the British Constitution the eighth wonder of the world; to be *laudatores*

9. The following three articles were Marx's first authentic contributions to the *New York Daily Tribune*, although Engels's articles on 'Germany: Revolution and Counter-Revolution' had been appearing since October 1851 under Marx's name. As Marx had not yet mastered the English language sufficiently, he drafted these articles in German, and Engels translated them into English and sent them to New York. A small number of obvious mistranslations and grammatical mistakes have here been corrected. Within a few months, however, Marx was able to write fluently in English. This article appeared in the *New York Daily Tribune* of 21 August 1852.

10. Marx's article 'Result of the Elections' was published in the *New York Daily Tribune* of 11 September 1852.

11. The name 'Manchester School', which strictly speaking denoted the economists who ideologically represented the industrial bourgeoisie, was often used by extension for the Free Trade party of Liberals and Radicals. The significance of Marx's tag '*par excellence*' is that Whigs and Peelites also supported free trade and in particular the repeal of the Corn Laws, but without this being the guiding principle of their politics. The National Association for Parliamentary and Financial Reform was founded in 1849 by Cobden and Bright, and lasted until 1855. Its programme, the 'Little Charter', included household suffrage, triennial parliaments and the ballot. The Association was supported by the Free Traders, and also by the reformist wing of the Chartists.

temporis acti,[12] enthusiasts for the throne, the High Church, the privileges and liberties of the British subject. The fatal year, 1846, with its repeal of the Corn Laws, and the shout of distress which this repeal forced from the Tories, proved that they were enthusiasts for nothing but the rent of land, and at the same time disclosed the secret of their attachment to the political and religious institutions of Old England. These institutions are the very best institutions, with the help of which *large landed property* – the landed interest – has hitherto ruled England, and even now seeks to maintain its rule. The year 1846 brought to light in its nakedness the *substantial class interest* which forms the *real base* of the Tory party. The year 1846 tore down the traditionally venerable lion's hide, under which Tory class interest had hitherto hidden itself. The year 1846 transformed the Tories into *Protectionists*.[13] Tory was the sacred name, Protectionist is the profane one; Tory was the political battle-cry, Protectionist is the economical shout of distress; Tory seemed an idea, a principle, Protectionist is an interest. Protectionists of what? Of their own revenues, of the rent of their own land. Then the Tories, in the end, are bourgeois as much as the remainder, for where is the bourgeois who is not a protectionist of his own purse? They are distinguished from the other bourgeois in the same way as rent of land is distinguished from commercial and industrial profit. Rent of land is conservative, profit is progressive; rent of land is national, profit is cosmopolitical; rent of land believes in the State Church, profit is a dissenter by birth. The repeal of the Corn Laws in 1846 merely recognized an already accomplished fact, a change long since enacted in the elements of British civil society, viz., the subordination of the landed interest to the moneyed interest, of property to commerce, of agriculture to manufacturing industry, of the country to the city. Could this fact be doubted since the country population stands, in England, to the towns' population in the proportion of one to three? The substantial foundation of the power of the Tories was the rent of land. The rent of land is regulated by the price of food. The price of food, then, was artificially maintained at a high rate by the Corn Laws. The

12. Those who extol the past.

13. In 1846 Sir Robert Peel, the Tory Prime Minister, split his party by repealing the Corn Laws with Whig and Radical support. The majority fraction of the Tory party (anti-Peelite) campaigned in the 1852 election under the 'Protectionist' banner.

repeal of the Corn Laws brought down the price of food, which in its turn brought down the rent of land, and with sinking rent broke down the real strength upon which the political power of the Tories reposed.

What, then, are they trying to do now? To maintain a political power, the social foundation of which has ceased to exist. And how can this be attained? By nothing short of a *counter-revolution*, that is to say, by a reaction of the state against society. They strive to retain forcibly institutions and a political power which were condemned from the very moment at which the rural population found itself outnumbered three times by the population of the towns. And such an attempt must necessarily end with their destruction; it must accelerate and make more acute the social development of England; it must bring on a crisis.

The Tories recruit their army from the farmers, who have either not yet lost the habit of following their landlords as their natural superiors, or who are economically dependent upon them, or who do not yet see that the interest of the farmer and the interest of the landlord are no more identical than the respective interests of the borrower and of the usurer. They are followed and supported by the Colonial Interest, the Shipping Interest, the State Church party, in short, by all those elements which consider it necessary to safeguard their interests against the necessary results of modern manufacturing industry, and against the social revolution prepared by it.

Opposed to the Tories, as their hereditary enemies, stand the Whigs, a party with whom the American Whigs have nothing in common but the name.

The British Whig, in the natural history of politics, forms a species which, like all those of the amphibious class, exists very easily, but is difficult to describe. Shall we call them, with their opponents, Tories out of office or, as continental writers love it, take them for the representatives of certain *popular* principles? In the latter case we should get embarrassed in the same difficulty as the historian of the Whigs, Mr Cooke, who, with great naiveté, confesses in his *History of Parties*[14] that it is indeed a certain number of 'liberal, moral and enlightened principles' which constitutes the Whig party, but that it was greatly to be regretted that during the more than a century and a half that the Whigs have

14. G. W. Cooke, *The History of the Parties* (3 volumes), London, 1836–7.

existed, they have been, when in office, always prevented from carrying out these principles. So that in reality, according to the confession of their own historian, the Whigs represent something quite different from their professed 'liberal and enlightened principles'. Thus they are in the same position as the drunkard brought up before the Lord Mayor who declared that he represented the temperance principle but from some accident or other always got drunk on Sundays.

But never mind their principles; we can better make out what they are in historical fact; what they carry out, not what they once believed, and what they now want other people to believe with respect to their character.

The Whigs, as well as the Tories, form a fraction of the large landed proprietors of Great Britain. Nay, the oldest, richest and most arrogant portion of English landed property is the very nucleus of the Whig party.

What, then, distinguishes them from the Tories? The Whigs are the *aristocratic representatives* of the bourgeoisie, of the industrial and commercial middle class. Under the condition that the bourgeoisie should abandon to them, to an oligarchy of aristocratic families, the monopoly of government and the exclusive possession of office, they make to the middle class, and assist it in conquering, all those concessions which in the course of social and political development have shown themselves to have become *unavoidable* and *undelayable*. Neither more nor less. And as often as such an unavoidable measure has been passed, they declare loudly that herewith the end of historical progress has been obtained; that the whole social movement has carried its ultimate purpose, and then they 'cling to finality'.[15] They can support more easily than the Tories a decrease of their rental revenues, because they consider themselves as the heaven-born farmers of the revenues of the British Empire. They can renounce the monopoly of the Corn Laws, as long as they maintain the monopoly of government as their family property. Ever since the 'Glorious Revolution' of 1688 the Whigs, with short intervals caused principally by the first French revolution and the consequent reaction, have found themselves in the enjoyment of the public offices. Whoever recalls to his mind this period of English history will find

15. In 1837 Lord John Russell, the Whig leader, had characterized the Reform Bill of 1832 as the final point of constitutional reform. The Radicals thereupon nicknamed him 'Finality John'.

no other distinctive mark of Whigdom but the maintenance of their family oligarchy. The interests and principles which they represent besides, from time to time, do not belong to the Whigs; they are forced upon them by the development of the industrial and commercial class, the bourgeoisie. After 1688 we find them united with the Bankocracy, just then rising into importance, as we find them in 1846 united with the Millocracy. The Whigs as little carried the Reform Bill of 1831 as they carried the Free Trade Bill of 1846. Both reform movements, the political as well as the commercial, were movements of the bourgeoisie. As soon as either of these movements had ripened into irresistibility, as soon as, at the same time, it had become the safest means of turning the Tories out of office, the Whigs stepped forward, took up the direction of the government, and secured to themselves the governmental part of the victory. In 1831 they extended the political portion of reform as far as was necessary in order not to leave the middle class entirely dissatisfied; after 1846 they confined their free-trade measures so far as was necessary in order to save to the landed aristocracy the greatest possible amount of privileges. Each time they took the movement in hand in order to prevent its forward march, and to recover their own posts at the same time.

It is clear that from the moment when the landed aristocracy is no longer able to maintain its position as an independent power, to fight, as an independent party, for the government position, in short, that from the moment when the Tories are definitively overthrown, British history has no longer any room for the Whigs. The aristocracy once destroyed, what is the use of an aristocratic representation of the bourgeoisie against this aristocracy?

It is well known that in the Middle Ages the German emperors put the just then arising towns under imperial governors, '*advocati*', to protect these towns against the surrounding nobility. As soon as growing population and wealth gave them sufficient strength and independence to resist, and even to attack the nobility, the towns also drove out the noble governors, the *advocati*.

The Whigs have been these *advocati* of the British middle class, and their governmental monopoly must break down as soon as the landed monopoly of the Tories is broken down. In the same measures as the middle class has developed its independent strength, they have shrunk down from a party to a coterie.

It is evident what a distastefully heterogeneous mixture the character of the British Whigs must turn out to be: feudalists, who are at the same time Malthusians, money-mongers with feudal prejudices, aristocrats without point of honour, bourgeois without industrial activity, finality-men with progressive phrases, progressists with fanatical conservatism, traffickers in homeopathical fractions of reforms, fosterers of family-nepotism, grand masters of corruption, hypocrites of religion, Tartuffes of politics. The mass of the English people have a sound aesthetical common sense. They have an instinctive hatred against everything motley and ambiguous, against bats and Russellites. And then, with the Tories, the mass of the English people, the urban and rural proletariat, has in common the hatred against the 'money-monger'. With the bourgeoisie it has in common the hatred against aristocrats. In the Whigs it hates the one and the other, aristocrats and bourgeois, the landlord who oppresses, and the money lord who exploits it. In the Whig it hates the oligarchy which has ruled over England for more than a century, and by which the people is excluded from the direction of its own affairs.

The Peelites (Liberal Conservatives) are no party; they are merely the souvenir of a partyman, of the late Sir Robert Peel. But Englishmen are too prosaical for a souvenir to form, with them, the foundation for anything but elegies. And now that the people have erected brass and marble monuments to the late Sir Robert Peel in all parts of the country, they believe they are able so much the more to do without those perambulant Peel monuments, the Grahams, the Gladstones, the Cardwells, etc.[16] The so-called Peelites are nothing but this staff of bureaucrats which Robert Peel had schooled for himself. And because they form a pretty complete staff, they forget for a moment that there is no army behind them. The Peelites, then, are old supporters of Sir Robert Peel, who have not yet come to a conclusion as to what party to attach themselves to. It is evident that a similar scruple is not a sufficient means for them to constitute an independent power.

Remain the Free Traders and the Chartists, the brief delineation of whose character will form the subject of my next.

16. William Gladstone, the future Liberal Prime Minister, had been President of the Board of Trade in Peel's second ministry of 1841–6. Edward Cardwell and Sir James Graham, who had been respectively Secretary to the Treasury and Home Secretary, were also to hold ministerial office as Liberals.

THE CHARTISTS[17]

London, 10 August 1852

While the Tories, the Whigs, the Peelites – in fact, all the parties we have hitherto commented upon – belong more or less to the past, the Free Traders (the men of the Manchester School, the Parliamentary and Financial Reformers) are the *official representatives of modern English society*, the representatives of that England which rules the market of the world. They represent the party of the self-conscious bourgeoisie, of industrial capital striving to make available its social power as a political power as well, and to eradicate the last arrogant remnants of feudal society. This party is led on by the most active and most energetic portion of the English bourgeoisie – the *manufacturers*. What they demand is the complete and undisguised ascendancy of the bourgeoisie, the open, official subjection of society at large to the laws of modern, bourgeois production, and to the rule of those men who are the directors of that production. By free trade they mean the unfettered movement of capital; freed from all political, national and religious shackles. The soil is to be a marketable commodity, and the exploitation of the soil is to be carried on according to the common commercial laws. There are to be manufacturers of food as well as manufacturers of twist and cottons, but no longer any lords of the land. There are, in short, not to be tolerated any political or social restrictions, regulations or monopolies, unless they proceed from 'the eternal laws of political economy', that is, from the conditions under which capital produces and distributes. The struggle of this party against the old English institutions, products of a superannuated, an evanescent stage of social development, is resumed in the watchword: *Produce as cheap as you can, and do away with all the* faux frais *of production* (with all superfluous, unnecessary expenses in production). And this watch-word is addressed not only to the private individual, but to the *nation at large* principally.

Royalty, with its 'barbarous splendors', its court, its civil list and its flunkeys – what else does it belong to but to the *faux frais* of production? The nation can produce and exchange without royalty; away with the crown. The sinecures of the nobility, the House of Lords? *Faux frais* of production. The large standing army? *Faux frais* of production. The colonies? *Faux frais* of

17. Published in the *New York Daily Tribune* of 25 August 1852.

production. The State Church, with its riches, the spoils of plunder or of mendicity? *Faux frais* of production. Let parsons compete freely with each other, and everyone pay them according to his own wants. The whole circumstantial routine of English law, with its Court of Chancery? *Faux frais* of production. National wars? *Faux frais* of production. England can exploit foreign nations more cheaply while at peace with them.

You see, to these champions of the British bourgeoisie, to the men of the Manchester School, every institution of Old England appears in the light of a piece of machinery as costly as it is useless, and which fulfils no other purpose but to prevent the nation from producing the greatest possible quantity at the least possible expense, and to exchange its products in freedom. Necessarily, their last word is the bourgeois republic, in which free competition rules supreme in all spheres of life; in which there remains altogether that *minimum* only of government which is indispensable for the administration, internally and externally, of the common class interest and business of the bourgeoisie; and where this minimum of government is as soberly, as economically organized as possible. Such a party, in other countries, would be called *democratic*. But it is necessarily revolutionary, and the complete annihilation of Old England as an aristocratic country is the end which it follows up with more or less consciousness. Its nearest object, however, is the attainment of a parliamentary reform which should transfer to its hands the legislative power necessary for such a revolution.

But the British bourgeois are not excitable Frenchmen. When they intend to carry a parliamentary reform they will not make a February revolution. On the contrary. Having obtained, in 1846, a grand victory over the landed aristocracy by the repeal of the Corn Laws, they were satisfied with following up the material advantages of this victory, while they neglected to draw the necessary political and economic conclusions from it, and thus enabled the Whigs to reinstate themselves into their hereditary monopoly of government. During all the time from 1846 to 1852, they exposed themselves to ridicule by their battle-cry: Broad principles and practical (read *small*) measures. And why all this? Because in every violent movement they are obliged to appeal to the *working class*. And if the aristocracy is their vanishing opponent, the working class is their arising enemy. They prefer to compromise with the vanishing opponent rather than to strengthen the arising enemy, to whom the future belongs, by concessions of a more than apparent importance. Therefore, they strive to avoid every forcible collision with the aristocracy; but historical necessity and the Tories press them onwards. They cannot avoid fulfilling their mission, battering to pieces Old England, the England of the past; and the very moment when they will have conquered exclusive political dominion, when political dominion and economic supremacy will be united in the same hands, when, therefore, the struggle against capital will no longer be distinct from the struggle against the existing government – from that very moment will date the *social revolution of England*.

We now come to the Chartists, the politically active portion of the British *working class*. The six points of the Charter which they contend for contain nothing but the demand of universal suffrage, and of the conditions without which universal suffrage would be illusory for the working class, such as the ballot, payment of members, annual general elections. But universal suffrage is the equivalent for political power for the working class of England, where the proletariat forms the large majority of the population, where, in a long, though underground, civil war, it has gained a clear consciousness of its position as a class, and where even the rural districts know no longer any peasants, but only landlords, industrial capitalists (farmers) and hired labourers. The carrying of universal suffrage in England would, therefore, be a far more socialistic measure than anything which has been honoured with that name on the Continent.

Its inevitable result, here, is *the political supremacy of the working class*.

I shall report, on another occasion, on the revival and the reorganization of the Chartist party. For the present I have only to treat of the recent election.

To be a voter for the British Parliament, a man must occupy, in the boroughs, a house rated at £10 for the poor rate, and, in the counties, he must be a freeholder to the annual amount of 40 shillings, or a leaseholder to the amount of £50. From this statement alone it follows that the Chartists could take, officially, but little part in the electoral battle just concluded. In order to explain the actual part they took in it, I must recall to mind a peculiarity of the British electoral system:

Nomination day and declaration day! Show of hands and poll!

When the candidates have made their appearance on the day of election, and have publicly harangued the people, they are elected, in the first instance, by the show of hands, and every hand has the right to be raised, the hand of the non-elector as well as that of the elector. For whomsoever the majority of the hands are raised, that person is declared, by the returning officer, to be (provisionally) elected by show of hands. But now the medal shows its reverse. The election by show of hands was a mere ceremony, an act of formal politeness towards the 'sovereign people', and the politeness ceases as soon as privilege is menaced. For if the show of hands does not return the candidates of the privileged electors, these candidates demand a poll; only the privileged electors can take part in the poll, and whosoever has there the majority of votes is declared duly elected. The first election, by show of hands, is a show satisfaction allowed, for a moment, to public opinion, in order to convince it, the next moment, the more strikingly of its impotency.

It might appear that this election by show of hands, this danger-ous formality, had been invented in order to ridicule universal suffrage, and to enjoy some little aristocratic fun at the expense of the 'rabble' (expression of Major Beresford, Secretary at War). But this would be a delusion, and the old usage, common originally to all Teutonic nations, could drag itself traditionally down to the nineteenth century, because it gave to the British class-parliament, cheaply and without danger, an appearance of popularity. The ruling classes drew from this usage the satisfaction that the mass of the people took part, with more or less passion, in their sectional interests as its national interests. And it was only since the bour-geoisie took an independent station at the side of the two official parties, the Whigs and Tories, that the working masses stood up on the nomination days in their own name. But in no former year the contrast of show of hands and poll, of nomination day and declara-tion day, has been so serious, so well defined by opposed principles, so threatening, so general, upon the whole surface of the country, as in this last election of 1852.

And what a contrast! It was sufficient to be named by show of hands in order to be beaten at the poll. It was sufficient to have had the majority at a poll, in order to be saluted by the people with rotten apples and brickbats. The duly elected members of Parliament, before all [else], had a great deal to do in order to keep their own parliamentary bodily selves in safety. On one side the majority of the people, on the other the twelfth part of the whole population, and the fifth part of the sum total of the male adult inhabitants of the country. On one side enthusiasm, on the other bribery. On one side parties disowning their own distinctive signs, liberals pleading the conservatism, conservatives proclaiming the liberalism of their views; on the other, the people, proclaiming their presence and pleading their own cause. On one side a worn-out engine which, turning incessantly in its vicious circle, is never able to move a single step forward, and the impotent process of friction by which all the official parties gradually grind each other into dust; on the other, the advancing mass of the nation, threatening to blow up the vicious circle and to destroy the official engine.

I shall not follow up, over all the surface of the country, this contrast between nomination and poll, between the threatening electoral demonstration of the working class and the timid electioneering manoeuvres of the ruling classes. I take one borough from the mass, where the contrast is concentrated in a focus: the Halifax election. Here the opposing candidates were: [Henry] Edwards (Tory); Sir Charles Wood (late Whig Chancellor of the Exchequer, brother-in-law to Earl Grey); Frank Crossley (Manchester man); and finally Ernest Jones, the most talented, consistent and energetic representative of Chartism. Halifax being a manufacturing town, the Tory had little chance. The Manchester man, Crossley, was leagued with the Whigs. The serious struggle, then, lay only between Wood and Jones, between the Whig and the Chartist.[18]

Sir Charles Wood made a speech of about half an hour, perfectly inaudible at the commencement and during its latter half for the disapprobation of the immense multitude. His speech, as reported by the reporter, who sat close to him, was merely a recapitulation of the free-trade measures passed, an attack on Lord Derby's government,[19] and a laudation of '*the unexampled prosperity of the country and the people!*' ('Hear, hear.') He did not propound one single new measure of reform; and but faintly, in very few words, hinted at Lord John Russell's bill for the franchise.[20]

I give a more extensive abstract of E. Jones's speech, as you will

18. The following passages are quoted from the *People's Paper*, 14 July 1852.

19. Edward Stanley, Earl of Derby, was the leader of the Tory party from 1846 until his death in 1869, and Prime Minister in 1852, 1858–9 and 1866–8.

20. In February 1852 Russell announced a bill for further electoral reform, but he never introduced it.

not find it in any of the great London ruling-class papers.

Ernest Jones, who was received with immense enthusiasm, then spoke as follows:

'Electors and non-electors, you have met upon a great and solemn festival. Today the constitution recognizes universal suffrage in theory, that it may perhaps deny it in practice on the morrow [. . .] Today the representatives of two systems stand before you, and you have to decide beneath which you shall be ruled for seven years. Seven years – a little life! [. . .] I summon you to pause upon the threshold of those seven years: today they shall pass slowly and calmly in review before you: today decide, you 20,000 men!, that perhaps five hundred may undo your will tomorrow.' ('Hear, hear.') 'I say the representatives of two systems stand before you. Whig, Tory, and money-monger are on my left, it is true, but they are all as one. The money-monger says, buy cheap and sell dear. The Tory says, buy dear, sell dearer. Both are the same for labour. But the former system is in the ascendant, and pauperism rankles at its root. That system is based on foreign competition. Now I assert that under the buy-cheap-and-sell-dear principle, brought to bear on foreign competition, the ruin of the working and small trading classes must go on. Why? Labour is the creator of all wealth. A man must work before a grain is grown, or a yard is woven. But there is no self-employment for the working man in this country. Labour is a hired commodity – labour is a thing in the market that is bought and sold; consequently, as labour creates all wealth, labour is the first thing bought – "Buy cheap! Buy cheap!" Labour is bought in the cheapest market. But now comes the next: "Sell dear! Sell dear!" Sell what? *Labour's produce.* To whom? To the foreigner – aye! and to *the labourer himself* – for labour, not being self-employed, the labourer is *not* the partaker of the first fruits of his toil. "Buy cheap, sell dear." How do you like it? "Buy cheap, sell dear." Buy the working man's labour cheaply, and sell back to that very working man the produce of his own labour dear! The principle of inherent loss is in the bargain. The employer buys the labour cheap – he sells, and on the sale he must make a profit; he sells to the working man himself – and thus every bargain between employer and employed is a deliberate cheat on the part of the employer. Thus labour has to sink through eternal loss, that capital may rise through lasting fraud. But the system stops not here. *This is brought to bear on foreign competition – which means, we must ruin the trade of other countries, as we have ruined the labour of our own.*[21] How does it work? The high-taxed country has to undersell the low-taxed. Competition abroad is constantly increasing – consequently cheapness must increase constantly also. Therefore, wages in England must keep constantly falling. And how do they effect the fall? By *surplus labour*. How do they obtain the surplus labour? By monopoly of the land, which drives more hands than are wanted into the factory. By monopoly of machinery, which drives those hands into the street – by woman labour which drives the man from the shuttle – by child labour, which drives the woman from the loom. Then planting their foot upon that living base of surplus, they press its aching heart beneath their heel, and cry "Starvation! Who'll work? A half loaf is better than no bread at all" – and the writhing mass grasps greedily at their terms.' (Loud cries of 'Hear, hear.') 'Such is the system for the working man. But electors! How does it operate on you? How does it affect home trade, the shopkeeper, poor rate and taxation? For every increase of competition abroad, there must be an increase of cheapness at home. Every increase of cheapness in labour is based on increase of labour surplus – and this surplus is obtained by an increase of machinery. I repeat, how does this operate on you? The Manchester Liberal on my left establishes a new patent, and throws three hundred men as a surplus in the streets. Shopkeepers! Three hundred customers less. Ratepayers! Three hundred paupers more.' (Loud cheers.) 'But mark me! The evil stops not there. These three hundred men operate first to bring down the wages of those who remain at work in their own trade. The employer says, "Now I reduce your wages." The men demur. Then he adds: "Do you see those three hundred men who have *just* walked out – you *may change places if you like*, they're sighing to come in on any terms, for they're starving." The men feel it, and are crushed. Ah! You Manchester Liberal! Pharisee of politics! those men are listening – have I got you now? But the evil stops not yet. Those men, driven from their own trade, seek employment in others, when they swell the surplus, and bring wages down. The low-paid trades of today were the high-paid once – the high paid of today will be the low paid soon. Thus the purchasing power of the working classes is diminished every day, and with it dies home trade. Mark it, shopkeepers! Your customers grow poorer, and your profits less,

21. Marx's italics.

while your paupers grow more numerous and your poor rates and your taxes rise. Your receipts are smaller, your expenditure is more large. You get less and pay more. How do you like the system? On you the rich manufacturer and landlord throw the weight of poor rate and taxation. Men of the middle class! You are the tax-paying machine of the rich. They create the poverty that creates their riches, and they make you pay for the poverty they have created. The landlord escapes it by privilege, the manufacturer by repaying himself out of the wages of his men, and that reacts on you. How do you like the system? Well, that is the system upheld by the gentlemen on my left. What then do I propose? I have shown the wrong. That is something. But I do more; I stand here to show the right, and prove it so.' (Loud cheers.)

Ernest Jones then went on to expose his own views on political and economic reform, and continued as follows:

'Electors and non-electors, I have now brought before you some of the social and political measures, the immediate adoption of which I advocate now, as I did in 1847. But, because I tried to extend *your* liberties, *mine* were curtailed.' ('Hear, hear.') 'Because I tried to rear the temple of freedom for you all, I was thrown into the cell of a felon's jail;[22] and there, on my left, sits one of my chief jailers.' (Loud and continued groans, directed towards the left.) 'Because I tried to give voice to truth, I was condemned to silence. For two years and one week he cast me into a prison in solitary confinement on the silent system, without pen, ink or paper, but oakum picking as a substitute. [. . .] Ah!' (turning to Sir Charles Wood) 'it was your turn for two years and one week; it is mine this day. I summon the angel of retribution from the heart of every Englishman here present.' (An immense burst of applause.) 'Hark! you feel the fanning of his wings in the breath of this vast multitude!' (Renewed cheering, long continued.) [. . .] 'You may say this is not a public question. But it is!' ('Hear, hear.') 'It is a public question, for the man who cannot feel for the wife of the prisoner will not feel for the wife of the working man. He who will not feel for the children of the captive will not feel for the children of the labour-slave.' ('Hear, hear,' and cheers.) 'His past life proves it, his promise of today does not contradict it.

22. Ernest Jones and other leaders of the revolutionary wing of the Chartist party were imprisoned in 1850; two of Jones's comrades died of the mistreatment they received.

Who voted for Irish coercion,[23] the gagging bill,[24] and tampering with the Irish press? The Whig! There he sits! Turn him out! Who voted fifteen times against Hume's motion for the franchise; Locke King's on the counties; Ewart's for short Parliaments; and Berkeley's for the ballot?[25] The Whig, there he sits; turn him out! Who voted against the release of Frost, Williams and Jones?[26] The Whig, there he sits; turn him out! Who voted against inquiry into colonial abuses and in favour of Ward and Torrington, the tyrants of Ionia and Ceylon?[27] The Whig, there he sits; turn him out! Who voted against reducing the Duke of Cambridge's salary of £12,000,[28] against all reductions in the army and navy, against the repeal of the window-tax, and forty-eight times against every other reduction of taxation, his own salary included? The Whig, there he sits; turn him out! Who voted against a repeal of the paper duty, the advertisement duty, and the taxes on knowledge? The Whig, there he sits; turn him out! Who voted for the batches of new bishops, vicar rate, the Maynooth grant,[29] against its reduction, and against absolving dissenters from paying Church rates? The Whig, there he sits; turn him out! Who voted against all inquiry into the adulteration of food? The Whig, there he sits; turn him out! Who voted against lowering the duty on sugar, and repealing the tax on malt? The Whig, there he sits; turn him out! Who voted against shortening the nightwork of bakers, against inquiry into the condition of framework knitters, against medical inspectors of workhouses, against preventing little children from working before six in the morning, against parish relief for preg-

23. This refers to the act of April 1833 which gave the Lord Governor of Ireland arbitrary powers of repression.

24. The 'gagging bill' was the popular name for Castlereagh's 'six acts' passed in winter 1819, which among other repressive measures banned public meetings and imposed a heavy tax on newspapers.

25. These bills were all introduced as part of the campaign for the Parliamentary and Financial Reformers' 'Little Charter'.

26. John Frost and Zephaniah Williams were Chartist militants transported to Australia for life for their part in the Welsh miners' revolt of 1839.

27. Henry George Ward and George Byng, Viscount Torrington, were both Whig politicians, respectively Lord High Commissioner of the Ionian Islands (1849–55) and Governor of Ceylon (1847–50).

28. The Duke of Cambridge was Queen Victoria's cousin, a general, and Commander-in-Chief of the British army from 1856 to 1895.

29. This was a government grant to an Irish Catholic college, part of the British government's attempt to win the Irish clergy away from the national movement.

nant women of the poor, and against the Ten Hours Bill?[30] The Whig, there he sits; turn him out! Turn him out, in the name of humanity and of God! Men of Halifax! Men of England! The two systems are before you. Now judge and choose!' (It is impossible to describe the enthusiasm kindled by this speech, and especially at the close; the voice of the vast multitude, held in breathless suspense during each paragraph, came at each pause like the thunder of a returning wave, in execration of the representative of Whiggery and class rule. Altogether, it was a scene that will long be unforgotten in Halifax. On the show of hands being taken, very few, and those chiefly of the hired or intimidated, were held up for Sir C. Wood; [. . .] but almost every one present raised both hands for Ernest Jones, amidst cheering and enthusiasm it would be impossible to describe.)

The Mayor declared Mr Ernest Jones and Mr Henry Edwards to be elected by show of hands. Sir C. Wood and Mr Crossley then demanded a poll.

What Jones had predicted took place; he was nominated by 20,000 votes, but the Whig Sir Charles Wood and the Manchester man Crossley were elected by 500 votes.

CORRUPTION AT ELECTIONS[31]

London, 20 August 1852

Just before the late House of Commons separated, it resolved to heap up as many difficulties as possible for its successors in their way to Parliament. It voted a Draconian law against bribery, corruption, intimidation, and electioneering sharp practices in general.

A long list of questions is drawn up, which, by this enactment, may be put to petitioners of sitting members, the most searching and stringent that can be conceived. They may be required on oath to state who were their agents, and what communications they held with them. They may be asked and compelled to state, not only what they know, but what they 'believe, conjecture, and

30. The Ten Hours Bill, passed in 1847, set a statutory limit on the working day of women and young people under eighteen, and thereby indirectly affected the working hours of many adult male workers as well. See Engels's article 'The Ten Hours Bill' in *MECW* 10, pp. 288–300.

31. From the *New York Daily Tribune*, 4 September 1852.

suspect,' as to money expended either by themselves or anyone else acting – authorized or not authorized – on their behalf. In a word, no member can go through the strange ordeal without risk of perjury, if he have the slightest idea that it is possible or likely that anyone has been led to overstep on his behalf the limits of the law.

Now, even supposing this law to take it for granted that the new legislators will use the same liberty as the clergy, who only believe *some* of the Thirty-Nine Articles, yet contrive to sign them *all*, yet there remain, nevertheless, clauses sufficient to make the new Parliament the most virginal assembly that ever made speeches and passed laws for the three kingdoms. And in juxtaposition with the general election immediately following, this law secures to the Tories the glory that under their administration the greatest purity of election has been theoretically proclaimed, and the greatest amount of electoral corruption has been practically carried out.

A fresh election is proceeded with, and here a scene of *bribery, corruption, violence, drunkenness and murder* ensues, *unparalleled* since the times when old Tory monopoly reigned supreme before. We actually hear of soldiers with loaded guns, and bayonets fixed, taking liberal electors by force, dragging them under the landlords' eyes to vote against their own consciences, and those soldiers shooting with deliberate aim, the people who dared to sympathize with the captive electors, and committing wholesale murder on the unresisting [. . .] people! [Allusion to the event at Six Mile Bridge, Limerick, County Clare.] It may be said: That was in Ireland! Aye! and in England they have employed their police to break the stalls of those opposed to them; they have sent their organized gangs of midnight ruffians prowling through the streets to intercept and intimidate the Liberal electors; they have opened the cesspools of drunkenness; they have showered the gold of corruption, as at Derby, and in almost every contested place they have exercised systematic intimidation.

Thus far Ernest Jones's *People's Paper*.[32] Now, after this Chartist weekly paper, hear the weekly paper of the opposite party, the most sober, the most rational, the most moderate organ of the industrial bourgeoisie, the London *Economist*:[33]

We believe we may affirm, at this general election, there has been more *truckling*, more *corruption*, more *intimidation*, more *fanaticism* and more *debauchery*[34] than on any previous occasion. It is reported

32. 14 August 1852.   33. 7 August 1852.   34. Marx's italics.

that bribery has been more extensively resorted to at this election than for many previous years . . . Of the amount of intimidation and undue influence of every sort which has been practised at the late election, it is probably impossible to form an exaggerated estimate . . . And when we sum up all these things – the brutal drunkenness, the low intrigues, the wholesale corruption, the barbarous intimidation, the integrity of candidates warped and stained, the honest electors who are ruined, the feeble ones who are suborned and dishonoured; the lies, the stratagems, the slanders which stalk abroad in the daylight, naked and not ashamed; the desecration of holy words; the soiling of noble names – we stand aghast at the holocaust of victims – of destroyed bodies and lost souls – on whose funeral pile a new Parliament is reared.

The means of corruption and intimidation were the usual ones: direct government influence. Thus on an electioneering agent at Derby, arrested in the flagrant act of bribing, a letter was found from Major Beresford, the Secretary at War, wherein that same Beresford opens a credit upon a commercial firm for electioneering monies. The *Poole Herald* publishes a circular from Admiralty House to the half-pay officers, signed by the commander-in-chief of a naval station, requesting their votes for the ministerial candidates. Direct force of arms has also been employed, as at Cork, Belfast, Limerick (at which latter place eight persons were killed). Threats of ejection by landlords against their farmers, unless they voted with them. The land agents of Lord Derby herein gave the example to their colleagues. Threats of exclusive dealing against shopkeepers, of dismissal against workmen, intoxication, etc., etc. To these *profane* means of corruption *spiritual* ones were added by the Tories; the royal proclamation against Roman Catholic processions was issued in order to inflame bigotry and religious hatred; the No Popery cry was raised everywhere. One of the results of this proclamation were the Stockport riots.[35] The Irish priests, of course, retorted with similar weapons.

The election is hardly over, and already a single Queen's Counsel has received from twenty-five places instructions to invalidate the returns to Parliament on account of bribery and intimidation. Such petitions against elected members have been signed, and the expenses of the proceedings raised, at Derby, Cockermouth, Barnstaple, Harwich, Canterbury, Yarmouth, Wakefield, Boston, Huddersfield, Windsor and a great number of

35. On 29–30 June 1852, at Stockport, Cheshire, a Protestant mob conducted a terrorist attack on the local Irish population, with police connivance.

other places. Of eight to ten Derbyite members it is proved that, even under the most favourable circumstances, they will be rejected on petition.

The principal scenes of this bribery, corruption and intimidation were, of course, the agricultural counties and the peers' boroughs; for the conservation of the greatest possible number of the latter the Whigs had expended all their acumen in the Reform Bill of 1831. The constituencies of large towns and of densely populated manufacturing counties were, by their peculiar circumstances, very unfavourable ground for such manoeuvres.

Days of general election are in Britain traditionally the baccha-nalia of drunken debauchery, conventional stock-jobbing terms for the discounting of political consciences, the richest harvest times of the publicans. As an English paper says, 'These recurring saturnalia never fail to leave enduring traces of their pestilential presence.'[36] Quite naturally so. They are saturnalia in the ancient Roman sense of the word. The master then turned servant, the servant turned master. If the servant be master for one day, on that day brutality will reign supreme. The masters were the grand dignitaries of the ruling classes, or sections of classes, the servants formed the mass of these same classes, the privileged electors encircled by the mass of the non-electors, of those thousands that had no other calling than to be mere hangers-on, and whose support, vocal or manual, always appeared desirable, were it only on account of the theatrical effect.

If you follow up the history of British elections for a century past or longer, you are tempted to ask not why British Parliaments were so bad, but on the contrary, how they managed to be even as good as they were, and to represent as much as they did, though in a dim refraction, the actual movement of British society. Just as opponents of the representative system must feel surprised on finding that legislative bodies in which the abstract majority, the accident of the mere number, is decisive, yet decide and resolve according to the necessities of the situation – at least during the period of their full vitality. It will always be impossible, even by the utmost straining of logical deductions, to derive from the relations of mere numbers the necessity of a vote in accordance with the actual state of things; but from a given state of things the necessity of certain relations of numbers will always follow as of itself. The traditional bribery of British elections, what else was

36. *Economist*, 7 August 1852.

it but another form, as brutal as it was popular, in which the relative strength of the contending parties showed itself? Their respective means of influence and of dominion, which on other occasions they used in a *normal* way, were here enacted for a few days in an abnormal and more or less burlesque manner. But the premise remained, that the candidates of the rivalling parties represented the interests of the mass of the electors, and that the privileged electors again represented the interests of the nonvoting mass, or rather, that this voteless mass had, as yet, no specific interest of its own. The Delphic priestesses had to become intoxicated by vapours to enable them to find oracles; the British people must intoxicate itself with gin and porter to enable it to find its oracle-finders, the legislators. And where these oracle-finders were to be looked for, that was a matter of course.

This relative position of classes and parties underwent a radical change from the moment the industrial and commercial middle classes, the bourgeoisie, took up its stand as an official party at the side of the Whigs and Tories, and especially from the passing of the Reform Bill in 1831. These bourgeois were in no wise fond of costly electioneering manoeuvres, of *faux frais* of general elections. They considered it cheaper to compete with the landed aristocracy by general moral, than by personal pecuniary means. On the other hand they were conscious of representing a universally predominant interest of modern society. They were, therefore, in a position to demand that electors should be ruled by their common national interests, not by personal and local motives, and the more they recurred to this postulate, the more the latter species of electoral influence was, by the very composition of constituencies, centred in the landed aristocracy but withheld from the middle classes. Thus the bourgeoisie contended for the principle of moral elections and forced the enactment of laws in that sense, intended, each of them, as safeguards against the local influence of the landed aristocracy; and indeed, from 1831 down, bribery adopted a more civilized, more hidden form, and general elections went off in a more sober way than before. When at last the mass of the people ceased to be a mere chorus, taking a more or less impassioned part in the struggle of the official heroes, drawing lots among them, rioting, in bacchantic carouse, at the creation of parliamentary divinities, like the Cretan centaurs at the birth of Jupiter, and taking pay and treat for such participation in their glory – when the Chartists surrounded in threatening

masses the whole circle within which the official election struggle must come off, and watched with scrutinizing mistrust every
movement taking place within it – then an election like that
of 1852 could not but call for universal indignation, and elicit
even from the conservative *Times*, for the first time, some words
in favour of general suffrage, and make the whole mass of the
British proletariat shout as with one voice: The foes of Reform,
they have given Reformers the best arguments; such is an election
under the class system; such is a House of Commons with such a
system of election!

In order to comprehend the character of bribery, corruption and
intimidation, such as they have been practised in the late election,
it is necessary to call attention to a fact which operated in a parallel
direction.

If you refer to the general elections since 1831, you will find
that, in the same measure as the pressure of the voteless majority
of the country upon the privileged body of electors was increasing,
as the demand was heard louder, from the middle classes, for an
extension of the circle of constituencies, from the working class,
to extinguish every trace of a similar privileged circle – that in the
same measure the number of electors who actually voted grew less
and less, and the constituencies thus more and more contracted
themselves. Never was this fact more striking than in the late
election.

Let us take, for instance, London. In the City the constituency
numbers 26,728; only 10,000 voted. The Tower Hamlets number
23,534 registered electors; only 12,000 voted. In Finsbury, of 20,025
electors, not one half voted. In Liverpool, the scene of one of the
most animated contests, of 17,433 registered electors, only 13,000
came to the polls.

These examples will suffice. What do they prove? The apathy
of the privileged constituencies. And this apathy, what proves it?
That they have outlived themselves – that they have lost every
interest in their own political existence. This is in no wise apathy
against politics in general, but against a species of politics, the
result of which, for the most part, can only consist in helping the
Tories to oust the Whigs, or the Whigs to conquer the Tories. The
constituencies feel instinctively that the decision lies no longer
either with Parliament, or with the making of Parliament. Who
repealed the Corn Laws? Assuredly not the voters who had elected
a Protectionist Parliament, still less the Protectionist Parliament

itself, but only and exclusively the pressure from without. In this pressure from without, in other means of influencing Parliament than by voting, a great portion even of electors now believe. They consider the hitherto lawful mode of voting as an antiquated formality, but from the moment Parliament should make front against the pressure from without, and dictate laws to the nation in the sense of its narrow constituencies, they would join the general assault against the whole antiquated system of machinery.

The bribery and intimidation practised by the Tories were, then, merely violent experiments for bringing back to life dying electoral bodies which have become incapable of production, and which can no longer create decisive electoral results and really national Parliaments. And the result? The old Parliament was dissolved, because at the end of its career it had dissolved into sections which brought each other to a complete standstill. The new Parliament begins where the old one ended; it is paralytic from the hour of its birth.

LETTER TO THE LABOUR PARLIAMENT[37]

London, 9 March 1854

I regret deeply to be unable, for the moment at least, to leave London, and thus to be prevented from expressing verbally my feelings of pride and gratitude on receiving the invitation to sit as Honorary Delegate at the Labour Parliament. The mere assembling of such a Parliament marks a new epoch in the history of the world. The news of this great fact will arouse the hopes of the working classes throughout Europe and America.

Great Britain, of all other countries, has seen developed on the greatest scale the despotism of capital and the slavery of labour. In no other country have the intermediate stations between the millionaire commanding whole industrial armies and the wage slave living only from hand to mouth so gradually been swept away from the soil. There exist here no longer, as in continental countries, large classes of peasants and artisans almost equally

37. The Labour Parliament held in Manchester from 6 to 18 March 1854 was part of an unsuccessful attempt by the Chartist left wing to create a broad workers' organization out of the widespread strike movement of 1853–4. Marx was elected an honorary delegate, no doubt on Ernest Jones's proposal. His 'Letter' was read to the Labour Parliament on 10 March, and published in the *People's Paper* on 18 March 1854.

dependent on their own property and their own labour. A complete divorce of property from labour has been effected in Great Britain. In no other country, therefore, the war between the two classes that constitute modern society has assumed so colossal dimensions and features so distinct and palpable.

But it is precisely from these facts that the working classes of Great Britain, before all others, are competent and called for to act as leaders in the great movement that must finally result in the absolute emancipation of labour. Such they are from the conscious clearness of their position, the vast superiority of their numbers, the disastrous struggles of their past, and the moral strength of their present.

It is the working millions of Great Britain who first have laid down the real basis of a new society – modern industry, which transformed the destructive agencies of nature into the productive power of man. The English working classes, with invincible energies, by the sweat of their brows and brains, have called into life the material means of ennobling labour itself, and of multiplying its fruits to such a degree as to make general abundance possible.

By creating the inexhaustible productive powers of modern industry they have fulfilled the first condition of the emancipation of labour. They have now to realize its other condition. They have to free those wealth-producing powers from the infamous shackles of monopoly, and subject them to the joint control of the producers, who, till now, allowed the very products of their hands to turn against them and be transformed into as many instruments of their own subjugation.

The labouring classes have conquered nature; they have now to conquer man. To succeed in this attempt they do not want strength, but the organization of their common strength, organization of the labouring classes on a national scale – such, I suppose, is the great and glorious end aimed at by the Labour Parliament.

If the Labour Parliament proves true to the idea that called it into life, some future historian will have to record that there existed in the year 1854 two parliaments in England, a parliament at London, and a parliament at Manchester – a parliament of the rich, and a parliament of the poor – but that men sat only in the parliament of the men and not in the parliament of the masters.

Yours truly,

KARL MARX

PARTIES AND CLIQUES[38]

London, 5 February

The duration of the present government crisis[39] is more or less normal, as such crises in England have in the past lasted an average of nine to ten days. In his famous work *On Man and the Development of his Faculties*[40] [Adolphe] Quételet amazes the reader with the demonstration that the annual number of accidents, crimes, etc., in civilized countries can be determined in advance with almost mathematical accuracy. There is nothing amazing, however, about the normal duration of the English government crises typical of various periods of the nineteenth century; it is well known that a definite series of ministerial permutations must be attempted, a definite number of offices must be haggled over, and a definite number of intrigues must be allowed to cancel each other out. Only the character of the present political permutations is unusual, a character that is due to the dissolution of the old parties. It was, indeed, this very dissolution which made possible and inevitable the formation of the Coalition ministry which has now collapsed. The governing caste, which in England is by no means identical with the ruling class, will now be driven from one coalition to the next until it has given conclusive proof that it is no longer destined to govern. As is known, the Derbyites had declared their opposition to coalitions in highly solemn tones. Yet Lord Derby's first step, as soon as the Queen had charged him with the formation of a new Cabinet, was to try to form a coalition, not only with Palmerston (and Disraeli had explicitly declared during the Roebuck debate that the vote of censure which had been moved was no longer directed against the Duke of Newcastle[41] or Aberdeen but against Palmerston himself),

38. The following five articles were written by Marx in 1855 for the *Neue Oder-Zeitung*, a German newspaper with democratic leanings published in Breslau. They are translated here from the texts printed in *MEW* 11. 'Parties and Cliques' first appeared in the *Neue Oder-Zeitung* of 8 February 1855.

39. This government crisis followed the resignation of Lord Aberdeen's Coalition ministry (of Whigs and Peelites) on 29 January 1855. The Aberdeen ministry was defeated in the Commons over the 'Roebuck motion', which appointed a Select Committee to investigate the government departments responsible for the mismanagement of the British army in the Crimea.

40. English translation published in Edinburgh, 1842.

41. The Duke of Newcastle was Minister of War in the Aberdeen ministry.

but also with Gladstone and Sidney Herbert – that is, with the Peelites. The Tories pursued the Peelites with particular hatred as they saw in them the most immediately identifiable instruments of their party's dissolution. Russell was then charged with the formation of a Cabinet, and he attempted a coalition with the same Peelites whose presence in the old ministry had served as a pretext for his resignation and who had deserted him in a solemn parliamentary sitting. When Palmerston finally forms his ministry he will only produce a second, slightly altered version of the old Coalition ministry. The Whig Grey clan will perhaps replace the Whig Russell clan, and so on.

The old parliamentary parties with their monopoly on government exist now only in the form of coteries; but the same causes which have robbed these coteries of the power to form parties, to distinguish themselves from each other, also rob them of the power to unite. As a result, no period of English parliamentary history has demonstrated such a fragmentation into a mass of insignificant and fortuitous cliques as the period of the Coalition ministry. Only two of these cliques, the Derbyites and the Russellites, are numerically significant. Their followers include an extremely ramified group of powerful old families with a wide patronage. But it is precisely this numerical strength which constitutes the weakness of the Derbyites and Russellites. They are too small to form an independent parliamentary majority; yet they are too large and nourish too many careerists at their breasts to be able to purchase sufficient support from outside their ranks by bestowing important positions. The numerically weak cliques of Peelites, Greyites, Palmerstonians, etc., are therefore more suited to form coalition ministries. But the very thing that enables them to form ministries – the weakness of each of these cliques individually – makes their parliamentary majority a matter of chance, which can be broken any day, whether by an alliance of Derbyites and Russellites or by a combination of the Derbyites with the Manchester School.

The recent attempts to form ministries have been equally interesting from another point of view. In all these ministerial combinations members of the old Cabinet have been included, and the most important member of this Cabinet now heads the latest combination. Yet does not the passage of the Roebuck motion, which censured all the members of the old Coalition, imply that the vote of no confidence will be followed by a committee of inquiry, as Palmerston himself declared in his answer to Disraeli?

Are the accused to take over the helm of state again before the committee has been appointed, before the investigation has opened? But although Parliament has the power to bring down the ministry, the ministry has the power to *dissolve* Parliament. How the prospect of a dissolution must affect the present Parliament can be seen from the statement made on 1 March 1853 by Sir John Trollope, who observed that as many as fourteen Commons committees were already sitting to investigate the cases of corruption in the last parliamentary elections. If this continued, every Member of Parliament would be fully occupied with committees of inquiry. Indeed, the number of members accused was so overwhelming that the rest, whose election was not contested, would not suffice to pass judgement on them, or even to conduct an inquiry.

It would be a bitter blow if the seats so dearly bought were to be lost at the very beginning of the third parliamentary session – for patriotism's sake.

THE BRITISH CONSTITUTION[42]

London, 2 March

While the British Constitution has failed all along the line wherever the war has put it to the test, on the home front the Coalition ministry – the most constitutional in English history – has disintegrated. 40,000 British soldiers have died on the shores of the Black Sea, victims of the British Constitution! Officers, Command Headquarters, Commissariat, Medical Corps, Transport Corps, Admiralty, Horse Guards, Ordnance Department, the Army and Navy – all have collapsed. They have completely ruined their reputation in the eyes of the world; but all have the satisfaction of knowing that they were only doing their duty in the eyes of the British Constitution! *The Times* spoke truer than it knew when it declared that it was the British Constitution itself that was on trial. It has stood trial and has been found guilty.

But what is this British Constitution? Are its essential features to be found in the laws governing representation and the limitations imposed on the executive power? These characteristics distinguish it neither from the Constitution of the United States nor from the constitutions of the countless joint-stock companies in England which know 'their business'. The British Constitution

42. From the *Neue Oder-Zeitung*, 6 March 1855.

is, in fact, only an antiquated and obsolete compromise made between the bourgeoisie, which rules in actual practice, although *not officially*, in all the decisive spheres of bourgeois society, and the landed aristocracy, which forms the *official government*. After the 'Glorious Revolution' of 1688 only one section of the bourgeoisie, the *financial aristocracy*, was originally included in the compromise. The Reform Bill of 1831 opened the door to another group – the *millocracy*, as they are called in England: the high dignitaries of the *industrial* bourgeoisie. Legislative history since 1831 is the history of concessions made to the industrial bourgeoisie, from the Poor Law Amendment Act[43] to the repeal of the Corn Laws, and from the repeal of the Corn Laws to the Succession Duty on landed property.[44]

Although the bourgeoisie – itself only the highest social stratum of the middle classes – thus also gained general *political* recognition as the *ruling class*, this only happened on one condition; namely that the whole business of government in all its details – including even the executive branch of the legislature, that is, the actual making of laws in both Houses of Parliament – remained the guaranteed domain of the landed aristocracy. In 1830 the bourgeoisie preferred a renewal of the compromise with the landed aristocracy to a compromise with the mass of the English people. Now, subjected to certain principles laid down by the bourgeoisie, the aristocracy (which enjoys exclusive power in the Cabinet, in Parliament, in the Civil Service, in the Army and Navy, and which is thus one half, and comparatively the most important one, of the British nation) is being forced at this very moment to sign its own death warrant and to admit before the whole world that it is no longer destined to govern England. Observe the attempts being made to galvanize the corpses of the aristocracy into life! Ministry after ministry is formed, only to dissolve itself after governing for a few weeks. The crisis is permanent; the government only provisional. All political action has been suspended, and everyone admits that his only concern is to keep the political machine adequately oiled so that it does not come to a complete standstill. Not even the House of Commons recognizes itself in the ministries which are created in its own image.

43. The Poor Law Amendment Act of 1834 abolished outdoor relief and set up a standardized system of poor relief based on workhouses.
44. Succession Duty was introduced in 1853.

In this general state of helplessness there is not only a war to be waged but an enemy even more dangerous than Tsar Nicholas to be fought. This enemy is the *commercial* and *industrial* crisis, which since last September has been increasing in force and scope with every day that passes. Its iron hand has stopped the mouths of the superficial apostles of free trade who have been preaching for years that, since the repeal of the Corn Laws, saturated markets and social crises have been banished for ever into the shadowy realm of the past. The markets are saturated again, and no one is decrying the lack of caution which has prevented manufacturers from curbing production louder than the same economists who were lecturing us five months ago, with dogmatic infallibility, that it was impossible to produce too much.

The sickness appeared in a chronic form at the time of the Preston strike.[45] Shortly afterwards saturation of the American market brought the crisis to a head in the United States. Although saturated, India and China, just like California and Australia, continued to function as outlets for overproduction. As the English manufacturers could no longer sell their goods on the domestic markets without forcing down prices, they resorted to the danger-ous expedient of sending their products abroad on consignment, particularly to India, China, Australia and California. These evasive measures enabled trade to continue for a while with less disruption than if the goods had been dumped on the market all at once. But as soon as these goods arrived at their destination they immediately affected prices, and towards the end of September the effects were also felt here in England.

The crisis then moved from a chronic to an acute stage. The first firms to collapse were calico printers, among them old-established firms in and around Manchester. It was next the turn of the ship-owners, the Australian and Californian traders, then the Chinese and finally the Indian firms. Everyone was hit, and most suffered heavy losses; many firms have had to suspend busi-ness, and the danger is not over for any of them in this area of commerce. On the contrary, it continues to grow. Silk manu-

45. The strike of cotton spinners and weavers in Preston and the surrounding dis-tricts, which began in August 1853, was one of the largest strikes of the 1850s. The workers' basic demand was a wage rise of 10 per cent. The manufacturers responded with a lock-out, which lasted until February 1854. The Chartists played a prominent role in the strike, which was eventually broken by the arrest of its leaders in March 1854 and the importing of Irish strike-breakers.

facturers have been similarly hit; for the moment their industry has almost come to a standstill, and the districts where silk is manufactured are suffering terrible hardships. It is now the turn of the cotton spinners and manufacturers: some have already succumbed and a good many more will inevitably share their fate. We have already mentioned[46] that the fine-spun producers are still working short time and the manufacturers of coarse-spun will soon have to resort to the same measures. Even now some of them are only working for a few days per week. How long will they be able to last?

Another few months and the crisis in the manufacturing districts will reach the severity of 1842, if it does not exceed it. But as soon as its effects are generally felt among the working classes there will be a revival of the political movements which for six years have been more or less dormant among these classes and have only left behind the cadres for new agitation. The conflict between the industrial proletariat and the bourgeoisie will begin again at the same time as the conflict between bourgeoisie and aristocracy reaches its climax. The mask will then drop, which until now has hidden from the foreigner the real features of Great Britain's political physiognomy. However, only those who are unacquainted with this country's rich human and material resources will doubt that it will emerge victorious and rejuvenated from the impending great crisis.[47]

46. In an article in the *Neue Oder-Zeitung* of 20 February 1855; see *MEW* 11, pp. 66–8.

47. In a variant of this article published in the *New York Daily Tribune* on 24 March 1855, this paragraph is replaced by the following: 'A few months more and the crisis will be at a height which it has not reached in England since 1846, perhaps not since 1842. When its effects begin to be fully felt among the working classes, then will that political movement begin again, which has been dormant for six years. Then will the working men of England rise anew, menacing the middle classes at the very time that the middle classes are finally driving the aristocracy from power. Then will the mask be torn off which has hitherto hid the real political features of Great Britain. Then will the two real contending parties in that country stand face to face – the middle class and the working class, the bourgeoisie and the proletariat – and England will at last be compelled to share in the gen-e-ral social evolutions of European society. When England entered into the French alliance she finally abandoned that isolated character which her insular position had created for her, but which the commerce of the world, and the increasing facilities for intercourse, had long since undermined. Henceforth she can hardly help undergoing the great internal movements of the other European nations.' 'The Crisis in England', *MECW* 14, pp. 61–2.

THE CHARACTER OF THE WHIGS AND TORIES[48]

London, 14 May

The *anti-aristocratic* movement in England[49] can only have one *immediate* result: to bring the Tories, that is, the *specifically aristocratic party, to power*. If not, it is bound, first of all, to peter out in a few Whig platitudes, a few administrative sham reforms not worth mentioning. Layard's[50] announcement of his resolutions on the 'State of the Nation' and the reception given to this announcement in the House of Commons led to the holding of the City meetings. But hot on the heels of the City meetings came Ellenborough's motion in the House of Lords by means of which the Tories have taken control of the new Reform agitation and have transformed it into a ladder for their rise to government power. In his motion Layard himself has changed the words '*aristocratic influence*' to '*family influence*' – a concession to the Tories. Every movement outside the House assumes *within* the House the form of a squabble between the two fractions of the ruling class. In the hands of the Whigs the Anti-Corn-Law League became a means of overthrowing the Tories. In the hands of the Tories the Administrative Reform Association has become a means of overthrowing the Whigs.[51] It must not be forgotten that in this way both fractions in turn have sacrificed one basic element of the old regime after another, while, it may be added, the regime itself has been preserved. We have already expressed our view that only the Tories can be forced into making large concessions because only under them does the pressure from outside assume a threatening, and even a revolutionary, character. The Whigs represent the actual oligarchy in England, the rule of a few great families such as the Sutherlands, the Bedfords, the Carlisles, the

---

48. From the *Neue Oder-Zeitung*, 18 May 1855. This is the second part of a composite article originally entitled '*Morning Post* against Prussia; Character of the Whigs and Tories'.

49. This anti-aristocratic movement was the Association for Administrative Reform, founded in May 1855 by City business circles. It attempted to use the unrest due to the Crimean catastrophe, and the exposures of official incompetence by the Roebuck Committee, to promote the appointment of more representatives of the commercial and financial bourgeoisie to official positions.

50. Sir Austen Henry Layard, an archaeologist and the Radical MP, was a member of the Roebuck Committee investigating the conduct of the Crimean War.

51. The Whig government of Palmerston in fact survived until 1858.

Devonshires, etc.; the Tories represent the squireocracy, the Junker party, one might say, although broad lines of distinction must be drawn between the English squire and the north German Junker. The Tories, therefore, are the vehicles of all the Old English prejudices with regard to Church and state, patronage and anti-Catholicism. The Whigs, the oligarchs, are *enlightened* and have never hesitated to cast off prejudices which stand in the way of their hereditary tenure of state office. The Whigs have always prevented any movement within the middle classes by offering their friendship; the Tories have always driven the mass of the people into the arms of the middle classes with their friendship, having already placed the middle classes at the disposal of the Whigs. At this moment there is no longer any difference between Whigs and Tories except that the latter represent the plebs of the aristocracy, and the former its cream. The old aristocratic phrases are on the side of the aristocratic plebs; the liberal phrases on the side of the aristocratic upper crust. Indeed, since the decline of the old Tories (Lord Bolinbroke, etc.) the Tory party has always been ruled by parvenus, Pitt, Addington, Perceval, Canning, Peel and Disraeli. The *homines novi*[52] have always been found among the ranks of the Tories. When Lord Derby (himself a Whig turncoat) formed his ministry it contained besides him perhaps two other old names. All the rest were simple squires, apart from one man of letters. The Whigs, on the other hand, who have never hesitated for a second to change their coats and views with the times, who apparently can always rejuvenate and metamorphose themselves, have not needed any new people. They have been able to perpetuate the family names. If one reviews the whole of English history since the 'Glorious Revolution' of 1688, one finds that all the laws directed against the mass of the people have been initiated by the Whigs, from the Septennial Act to the most recent Poor Law and factory legislation. But Whig reaction has always been in harmony with the middle classes. Tory reaction has been directed even more against the middle classes than against the mass of the people. Hence the liberal reputation of the Whigs.

ON THE REFORM MOVEMENT[53]

London, 21 May

Today all the London newspapers have published an address from

---

52. New men.   53. From the *Neue Oder-Zeitung*, 24 May 1855.

the City Reformers, or rather from their executive committee, to the 'People of England'. The style of the document is dry, business-like and not quite as fulsome as the trade circulars which periodically appear from the same source offering to the world at large coffee, tea, sugar, spices and other tropical products wrapped up in tastefully arranged verbiage. The Association promises to produce material for a thorough physiological examination of the different government departments and to reveal all the mysteries of Downing Street and its heritage of wisdom. That is what it promises. What it demands in return is that, instead of sending candidates to Parliament who, as hitherto, have been imposed on them by aristocratic clubs, the English electorates should elect candidates of their own choosing, who recommend themselves solely by their merit. Thus the Association recognizes as normal those same privileged electorates which – with their corruption, their dependence upon a few clubs and their total lack of freedom – it admits to be the birthplace of the present House of Commons and therefore of the government. The members of the Association have no desire to abolish these exclusive electoral bodies nor even to widen them; they merely wish to exercise a moral influence on them. Why do they not have done with it and appeal to the conscience of the oligarchy instead of threatening to abolish its privileges? It must surely be an easier task to convert the heads of the oligarchy than its electoral bodies. Evidently the City Association would like to provoke an anti-aristocratic movement, but a movement *within* the bounds of *legality* (as Guizot put it), a movement within official England. And how does it intend to stir up the stagnant morass of the constituencies? How does it intend to bring about their emancipation from interests and practices which make them the vassals of a few select clubs and the supporting pillars of the governing oligarchy? By means of a physiology of Downing Street? Not quite; but nevertheless by means of *pressure from without*, mass meetings and the like. And how does the Association intend to mobilize the unofficial and unfranchised masses, in order to exert pressure on the privileged electoral circle? By inviting them to abandon the People's Charter (which basically contains nothing less than the demand for *universal suffrage* and the necessary conditions for its genuine realization in England); by inviting them to acknowledge the privileges of these electorates, which, as the City Reformers themselves admit, are in the process of decay. The City Association has before it the example of the Parliamentary and Financial Reformers. It knows that this movement, led by Hume, Bright, Cobden, Walmsley and Thompson, failed because it tried to replace the People's Charter by the so-called 'Little Charter', because it tried to make a compromise with the masses, because it tried to fob them off with mere concessions. Does the Association imagine that it can achieve *without* concessions what these men were not able to achieve *despite* concessions? Or does it conclude from the Anti-Corn-Law movement that it is possible to mobilize the English people for partial reforms? The object of that movement was very general, very popular, very palpable. The symbol of the Anti-Corn-Law League was, of course, a large and substantial loaf of bread, in contrast to the diminutive loaf of the Protectionists. The popular idiom naturally responded more readily to the idea of a loaf of bread – particularly in the famine year of 1845 – than it would to the notion of a 'physiology of Downing Street'. We need not remind our readers of a famous brochure, *The City; or, the Physiology of London Business*,[54] which demonstrated with the greatest accuracy that no matter how well the gentlemen of the City conduct their individual business, in the management of their *common* business, like all *insurance companies*, they follow more or less faithfully the official line laid down by Downing Street. Their management of the *railways*, with its blatant fraud, swindling and total neglect of safety precautions, is so notorious that more than once the question has been raised in and outside Parliament, and in the press, as to whether the railways should not be put under direct state control and taken out of the hands of the private capitalists! The physiology of Downing Street, therefore, will not 'do', as the English say. *'This will not do, sir!'*[55]

AGITATION AGAINST THE SUNDAY TRADING BILL[56]

London, 25 June

Obsolete social forces, nominally still in possession of all the attributes of power long after the basis of their existence has rotted away under their feet, continue to vegetate as their heirs begin to quarrel over their claims to the inheritance – even before

54. By D. M. Evans, London, 1845.   55. In English in the original.
56. From the *Neue Oder-Zeitung*, 28 June 1855.

the obituary notice has been printed and the testament unsealed; and it is an old maxim, borne out by history, that before their final death agony these social forces summon up their strength once more and move from the defensive to the offensive, issuing challenges instead of giving ground, and attempting to draw the most extreme conclusions from premises which have not only been called into question but have already been condemned. Such is the case today with the English oligarchy; and such is the case with its twin sister, the Church. There have been innumerable attempts at reorganization within the Established Church, both High and Low, and attempts to come to terms with the dissenters so that the profane masses can be confronted with a compact force. Measures of religious coercion have followed each other in rapid succession – in the House of Lords the pious Lord Ashley bewailed the fact that in England alone five million people had become estranged not only from the Church but from Christianity. The Established Church replies, '*Compelle intrare*'.[57] It leaves it to Lord Ashley and similar dissenting, sectarian and hysterical pietists to pull out of the fire the chestnuts which it intends to eat itself.

The Beer Bill, which closed all places of public amusement on Sundays except between 6 and 10 p.m., was the first example of religious coercion. It was smuggled through a sparsely attended House at the end of a sitting, after the pietists had bought the support of the larger London publicans by guaranteeing them the continuation of the licensing system – the continued monopoly of big capital. Then came the Sunday Trading Bill, which has now passed its third reading in the Commons and which has just been debated clause by clause by the Committee of the Whole House. In this new coercive measure, too, the interest of big capital has been heeded, as only small shopkeepers do business on Sundays and the big shops are quite willing to eliminate the Sunday competition of the small traders by parliamentary means. In both cases we find a conspiracy between the Church and the capitalist monopolies, and in both religious penal laws aimed at the lower classes to set at rest the conscience of the privileged classes. The aristocratic clubs were no more hit by the Beer Bill than the Sunday occupations of fashionable society are by the Sunday Trading Bill. The working class receives its wages late on Satur-

57. From the biblical phrase, 'Compel them to come in, that my house may be filled.'

days; Sunday trading, therefore, exists solely for them. They are the only section of the population forced to make their small purchases on Sundays, and the new bill is directed against them alone. In the eighteenth century the French aristocracy said, 'For us, Voltaire; for the people, mass and tithes.' In the nineteenth century the English aristocracy says, 'For us, pious phrases; for the people, Christian practice.' The classical saints of Christianity mortified their bodies to save the souls of the masses; the modern, educated saints mortify the *bodies of the masses* to save their own souls.

This alliance between a degenerate, dissipated and pleasure-seeking aristocracy and the Church – built on a foundation of filthy and calculated profiteering on the part of the beer magnates and monopolistic wholesalers – gave rise to a *mass demonstration* in Hyde Park yesterday, such as London has not seen since the death of George IV, the 'first gentleman of Europe'. We witnessed the event from beginning to end and believe we can state without exaggeration that *yesterday in Hyde Park the English revolution began*. The latest news from the Crimea acted as an important ferment in this *'unparliamentary'*, *'extra-parliamentary'* and *'anti-parliamentary'* demonstration.

The instigator of the Sunday Trading Bill, Lord Robert Grosvenor, had answered the objection that his bill was directed only against the poor and not against the rich classes by saying that the aristocracy was largely refraining from employing its servants and horses on Sundays. At the end of last week the following poster issued *by the Chartists* could be seen on all the walls in London announcing in large print:

New Sunday Bill prohibiting newspapers, shaving, smoking, eating and drinking and all other kinds of recreation and nourishment both corporal and spiritual, which the *poor people* still enjoy at the present time. *An open-air meeting* of artisans, workers and *'the lower orders'* generally of the capital will take place in Hyde Park on Sunday afternoon to see how religiously the aristocracy is observing the Sabbath and how anxious it is not to employ its servants and horses on that day, as Lord Robert Grosvenor said in his speech. The meeting is called for three o'clock on the right bank of the Serpentine, on the side towards Kensington Gardens. Come and bring your wives and children in order that they may profit by the example their 'betters' set them!

It should be realized that what Longchamps means to the Parisians, the road along the Serpentine means to English high society:

it is the place where in the afternoons, particularly on Sundays, they parade their magnificent carriages with all their trappings and exercise their horses followed by swarms of lackeys. It will be evident from the poster quoted above that the struggle against clericalism, like every serious struggle in England, is assuming the character of a *class struggle* waged by the poor against the rich, by the people against the aristocracy, by the 'lower orders' against their 'betters'.

At 3 o'clock about 50,000 people had gathered at the appointed spot on the right bank of the Serpentine in the huge meadows of Hyde Park. Gradually the numbers swelled to at least 200,000 as people came from the left bank too. Small knots of people could be seen being jostled from one spot to another. A large contingent of police was evidently attempting to deprive the organizers of the meeting of what Archimedes had demanded in order to move the earth: a fixed place to stand on. Finally, a large crowd made a firm stand and the Chartist [James] Bligh constituted himself chairman on a small rise in the middle of the crowd. No sooner had he begun his harangue than Police Inspector Banks at the head of forty truncheon-swinging constables explained to him that the Park was the private property of the Crown and that they were not allowed to hold a meeting in it. After some preliminary exchanges, in the course of which Bligh tried to demonstrate that the Park was public property and Banks replied he had strict orders to arrest him if he persisted in his intention, Bligh shouted amidst the tremendous roar of the masses around him: 'Her Majesty's police declare that Hyde Park is the private property of the Crown and that Her Majesty is not inclined to lend her land to the people for their meetings. So let us adjourn to Oxford Market.'

With the ironic cry of '*God save the Queen!*' the throng dispersed in the direction of Oxford Market. But meanwhile [James] Finlen, a member of the Chartist leadership, had rushed to a tree some distance away. A crowd followed him and surrounded him instantly in such a tight and compact circle that the police abandoned their attempts to force their way through to him. 'We are enslaved for six days a week', he said, 'and Parliament wants to rob us of our bit of freedom on the seventh. These oligarchs and capitalists and their allies, the sanctimonious clerics, want to do *penance* – not by mortifying themselves but by mortifying us – for the unconscionable murder committed against the sons of the people sacrificed in the Crimea.'

We left this group to approach another where a speaker, stretched out on the ground, was haranguing his audience from this horizontal position. Suddenly from all sides came the cry: 'Let's go to the road. Let's go to the carriages.' Meanwhile people had already begun heaping insults on the carriages and riders. The constables, who were steadily receiving reinforcements, drove the pedestrians back from the road. They thus helped to form a dense avenue of people on either side which extended for more than a quarter of an hour's walk from Aspley House, up Rotten Row, and along the Serpentine as far as Kensington Gardens. The public gathering consisted of about two thirds workers and one third members of the middle class, all with their wives and children. The reluctant actors – elegant gentlemen and ladies, 'commoners and lords' in high coaches-and-four with liveried servants in front and behind, elderly gentlemen alone on horseback, a little flushed from their port wine – this time did not pass by in review. They ran the gauntlet. A babel of jeering, taunting and discordant noises – in which no language is so rich as the English – soon closed in upon them from all sides. As the concert was improvised there was a lack of instrumental accompaniment. The chorus, therefore, had to make use of its own organs and to confine itself to vocal music. And what a diabolical concert it was: a cacophony of grunting, hissing, whistling, squawking, snarling, growling, croaking, yelling, groaning, rattling, shrieking, gnashing sounds. Music to drive a man out of his mind, music to move a stone. Added to this came outbursts of genuine Old English humour strangely mixed with boiling and long-constrained anger. 'Go to church!' was the only recognizable articulate sound. In a conciliatory fashion one lady stretched out an orthodoxly bound prayerbook from the coach. 'Give it to your horses to read!' the thunder of a thousand voices echoed back. When the horses shied, reared, bucked and bolted, endangering the lives of their elegant burdens, the mocking cries became louder, more menacing, more implacable. Noble lords and ladies, among them Lady Granville, wife of the President of the Privy Council, were forced to alight and make use of their feet. When elderly gentlemen rode by whose dress – in particular the broad-brimmed hat – envinced a special claim to purity of faith, all the sounds of fury were extinguished, as at a command – by inextinguishable laughter. One of these gentlemen lost his patience. Like Mephistopheles he made an indecent gesture: he stuck his tongue out at the enemy. 'He is a wordcatcher! a parliamentary man! He fights with his own weapons!' someone called out from one side of the road. 'He is a saint! he is psalm singing!' came the antistrophe from the other side. Meanwhile the metropolitan electric telegraph had announced to all police stations that a riot was imminent in Hyde Park and ordered the police to the theatre of war. So at short intervals one police detachment after another marched between the two rows of people from Aspley House to Kensington Garden, each being met with the popular ditty:

> Where are the geese?
> Ask the police!

This refers to a notorious theft of geese which a constable recently committed in Clerkenwell.

The spectacle lasted for three hours. Only English lungs are capable of such a feat. During the performance opinions such as 'This is only the beginning!' 'This is the first step!' 'We hate them!' etc., could be heard from various groups. While hatred could be read in the faces of the workers we have never seen such smug, self-satisfied smiles as those that covered the faces of the middle classes. Just before the end the demonstration increased in violence. Sticks were shaken at the carriages, and through the endless discordant din the cry could be heard: 'You rascals!' Zealous Chartist men and women battled their way through the crowds throughout these three hours, distributing leaflets which declared in large type:

Reorganization of Chartism! A big public meeting will take place next Tuesday, 26 June, in the Literary and Scientific Institute in Friar Street, Doctor's Commons, to elect delegates to a conference for the reorganization of Chartism in the capital. Admission free.

Today's London papers carry on average only a short account of the events in Hyde Park. There have been no leading articles yet with the exception of Lord Palmerston's *Morning Post*. This paper writes:

A scene, in the highest degree disgraceful and dangerous, was enacted yesterday in Hyde Park ... [an] outrage on law and decency ... It was distinctly illegal to interfere, by physical force, in the free action of the legislature ... We must have no repetition of violence on Sunday next, as has been threatened.

But at the same time it declares that the 'fanatical' Lord Grosvenor is solely 'responsible' for the trouble and that he has provoked the 'just indignation of the people'! As if Parliament has not given Lord Grosvenor's Bill its three readings! Has he perhaps also exerted pressure 'by physical force in the free action of the legislature'?

II[58]

London, 2 July

The demonstration against the Sunday Bill was repeated in Hyde Park yesterday on a larger scale, under a more ominous sign and with more serious consequences, as is witnessed by the sombre but agitated mood in London today.

The posters calling for the repetition of the meeting also contained an invitation to assemble on Sunday at 10 a.m. before the house of the pious Lord Grosvenor and to accompany him to church. The pious gentleman, however, had left London on Saturday in a private carriage – in order to travel incognito. That he is by nature destined to make martyrs of others rather than to be a martyr himself had been demonstrated by his circular in all the London newspapers, in which he on the one hand upheld his Bill and on the other took pains to show that it is without meaning, function or significance. On Sunday his house was occupied all day not by psalm singers but by constables, 200 in number. Such was the case, too, at the house of his brother, the Marquess of Westminster, a man famous for his wealth.

On Saturday the head of the London police, Sir Richard Mayne, had posters stuck on all the walls in London in which he '*prohibited*' not only a meeting in Hyde Park but also the gathering of any 'large numbers' and the manifestation of any signs of approval or disapproval. The result of these decrees was that as early as 3 o'clock – even according to the report of the *Police Gazette* – 150,000 people of *every* age and social position were milling about. Gradually the crowds swelled to gigantic proportions unbelievable even by London standards. Not only did London appear *en masse*; an avenue of spectators formed again on both sides of the road along the Serpentine; only this time the crowd was denser and deeper than last Sunday. High society, however, stayed away. Altogether perhaps twenty vehicles put in

58. From the *Neue Oder-Zeitung*, 5 July 1855.

an appearance, most of them gigs and phaetons, which drove by without hindrance. Their more stately and better upholstered brethren, who displayed larger paunches and more livery, were greeted with the old shouts and with the old babel of noise; and this time the sound waves made the air vibrate for at least a mile around. The police decrees were given a rebuttal by the mass gathering and by the chorus of noise from a thousand throats. High society had avoided the field of battle, and by its absence it had acknowledged the sovereignty of the *vox populi*.

It was 4 o'clock. The demonstration seemed to be fizzling out into a harmless Sunday outing for want of any combustible elements. But the police had other plans. Were they to withdraw to the accompaniment of general laughter, casting wistful parting glances at their own posters, which could be read in large print at the entrance to the park? Besides, their high dignitaries were present: Sir Richard Mayne and Superintendents Gibbs and Walker on horseback, Inspectors Banks, Darkin and Brennan on foot. 800 constables had been strategically deployed, for the most part hidden in buildings and concealed in ambush. Stronger detachments had been stationed in neighbouring districts as reinforcements. At a point of intersection where the road along the Serpentine crosses a path leading towards Kensington Gardens, the Ranger's Lodge, the Magazine and the premises of the Royal Humane Society had been transformed into improvised blockhouses manned by a strong police contingent; each building had been prepared to accommodate prisoners and wounded. Cabs stood at the ready at the police station in Vine Street, Piccadilly, waiting to drive to the scene of battle and to take away the defeated demonstrators under safe escort. In short, the police had drawn up a plan of campaign 'more vigorous', as *The Times* said, 'than any of which we have yet had notice in the Crimea'. The police needed bloody heads and arrests so as not to stumble straight from the sublime into the ridiculous. So, as soon as the avenue of spectators had cleared somewhat, and the masses had dispersed away from the road into different groups on the huge expanse of the park, their senior officers took up positions in the middle of the road, between the rows of people, and from their horses they issued pompous orders right and left, supposedly for the protection of the carriages and horsemen passing by. As there were no carriages or horsemen, however, and therefore nothing to protect, they began to pick out individuals from the crowd 'on false pretexts' and to have them arrested on the pretext that they were pickpockets. As these experiments increased in number and the pretext lost its credibility the crowds raised a general cry, and the contingents of police broke out from their hiding places. Drawing their truncheons from their pockets they beat heads bloody, tore people out of the crowd here and there – altogether there were 104 such arrests – and dragged them to the improvised blockhouses. The left side of the road is separated only by a narrow piece of ground from the Serpentine. By manoeuvring his gang of constables a police officer managed to drive the spectators close to the edge of the water, where he threatened them with a cold bath. In order to escape the police truncheons one man swam across the Serpentine to the other bank; a policeman gave chase in a boat, caught him and brought him back in triumph.

How the scene had changed since the previous Sunday! Instead of elegant coaches-and-four, dirty cabs, which drove back and forth between the police station at Vine Street and the improvised jails in Hyde Park. Instead of lackeys on the boxes of carriages, constables sitting next to drunken cab drivers. Inside the vehicles, instead of elegant gentlemen and ladies, prisoners with bloody heads, dishevelled hair, half undressed and with torn clothes, guarded by dubious conscripts from the Irish lumpenproletariat who had been pressed into the London police. Instead of the wafting of fans, a hail of truncheons. Last Sunday the ruling classes had shown their fashionable face; this time the face they displayed was that of the state. In the background – behind the affably grinning old gentlemen, the fashionable dandies, the elegantly infirm widows and the perfumed beauties in their cashmeres, ostrich feathers, and garlands of flowers and diamonds – stood the constable with his waterproof coat, greasy oilskin hat and truncheon – the reverse side of the coin. Last Sunday the ruling classes had confronted the masses as individuals. This time they assumed the form of state power, law and truncheon. This time resistance amounted to insurrection, and the Englishman must be subjected to long, slow provocation before he is moved to insurrection. Thus, the counter-demonstration was limited, on the whole, to hissing, grunting and whistling at the police vehicles, to isolated attempts to free the prisoners but, above all, to passive resistance, as the crowds phlegmatically stood their ground on the field of battle.

Soldiers – partly from the Guard, partly from the 66th Regiment – assumed a characteristic role in this spectacle. They had appeared in force. Twelve of them, some decorated with medals from the Crimea, stood among a group of men, women and children on whom the police truncheons were descending. An old man fell to the ground, struck by a blow. 'The London stiffstaffs' (a term of abuse for the police) 'are worse than the Russians at Inkerman,' called out one of the Crimean heroes. The police seized him. He was immediately freed to the accompaniment of shouts from the crowd: 'Three cheers for the army!' The police deemed it advisable to move off. Meanwhile, a number of Grenadiers had arrived; the soldiers fell into line and with the crowd milling about them shouting, 'Hurrah for the army, down with the police, down with the Sunday Bill,' they paraded up and down in the park. The police stood about irresolutely, when a sergeant of the Guard appeared and loudly called them to account for their brutality, calmed the soldiers and persuaded some of them to follow him to the barracks to avoid more serious collisions. But the majority of the soldiers remained behind, and from among the people they gave vent to their anger at the police in no uncertain terms. In England the opposition between the police and the army is an old one. The present moment, when the army is the 'pet child' of the masses, is certainly not likely to reduce this opposition.

An old man named Russell is said to have died today as a result of the wounds he suffered yesterday; half a dozen people are in St George's Hospital suffering from injuries. During the demonstration different attempts were again made to hold smaller meetings. In one of them, near the Albert Gate outside the section of the park originally occupied by the police, an anonymous speaker harangued his public something like this:

Men of Old England! Awake, rise up from your slumber or fall for ever; resist the government every Sunday! Observe the Sunday Bill as you have done today. Do not be afraid to demand those rights to which you are entitled. Cast off the fetters of oligarchical oppression and tyranny. If you do not, you will be hopelessly crushed. Is it not outrageous that the inhabitants of this great metropolis, the greatest in the civilized world, must surrender their freedom into the hands of a Lord Grosvenor or a man like Lord Ebrington! His Lordship feels obliged to drive us to Church and to make us religious by means of an act of Parliament. His attempts are in vain. Who are we, and who are they? Look at the war which is being fought. Is it not being waged at the expense and with the blood of the productive classes? And what about the unproductive classes? They have bungled it from start to finish.

Speaker and meeting were, of course, interrupted by the police.

In Greenwich, near the Observatory, Londoners also held a meeting of ten to fifteen thousand people, which was likewise broken up by the police.

Speech at the Anniversary of the *People's Paper*[1]

The so-called revolutions of 1848 were but poor incidents – small fractures and fissures in the dry crust of European society. However, they denounced the abyss. Beneath the apparently solid surface they betrayed oceans of liquid matter, only needing expansion to rend into fragments continents of hard rock. Noisily and confusedly they proclaimed the emancipation of the proletarian, i.e., the secret of the nineteenth century, and of the revolution of that century. That social revolution, it is true, was no novelty invented in 1848. Steam, electricity, and the self-acting mule were revolutionists of a rather more dangerous character than even citizens Barbès, Raspail and Blanqui. But, although the atmosphere in which we live weighs upon every one with a 20,000 lb. force, do you feel it? No more than European society before 1848 felt the revolutionary atmosphere enveloping and pressing it from all sides. There is one great fact, characteristic of this our nineteenth century, a fact which no party dares deny. On the one hand, there have started into life industrial and scientific forces which no epoch of former human history had ever suspected. On the other hand, there exist symptoms of decay, far surpassing the horrors recorded of the latter times of the Roman empire. In our days everything seems pregnant with its contrary. Machinery, gifted with the wonderful power of shortening and fructifying human labour, we behold starving and overworking it. The newfangled sources of wealth, by some strange weird spell, are turned into sources of want. The victories of art seem bought by the loss of character. At the same pace that mankind masters nature, man seems to become enslaved to other men or to his own infamy. Even the pure light of science seems unable to shine but on the

1. Marx delivered this speech at a dinner commemorating the fourth anniversary of Ernest Jones's *People's Paper*, in London on 14 April 1856. It was published in the *People's Paper* on 19 April 1856.

dark background of ignorance. All our invention and progress seem to result in endowing material forces with intellectual life, and in stultifying human life into a material force. This antagonism between modern industry and science on the one hand, modern misery and dissolution on the other hand; this antagonism between the productive powers and the social relations of our epoch is a fact, palpable, overwhelming, and not to be controverted. Some parties may wail over it; others may wish to get rid of modern arts, in order to get rid of modern conflicts. Or they may imagine that so signal a progress in industry wants to be completed by as signal a regress in politics. On our part, we do not mistake the shape of the shrewd spirit that continues to mark all these contradictions. We know that to work well the new-fangled forces of society, they only want to be mastered by new-fangled men – and such are the working men. They are as much the invention of modern time as machinery itself. In the signs that bewilder the middle class, the aristocracy and the poor prophets of regression, we do recognize our brave friend, Robin Good-fellow, the old mole that can work in the earth so fast, that worthy pioneer – the Revolution.[2] The English working men are the first-born sons of modern industry. They will then, certainly, not be the last in aiding the social revolution produced by that industry, a revolution which means the emancipation of their own class all over the world, which is as universal as capital-rule and wages-slavery. I know the heroic struggles the English working class have gone through since the middle of the last century – struggles [no] less glorious because they are shrouded in obscurity, and burked by the middle-class historian. To revenge the misdeeds of the ruling class, there existed in the Middle Ages, in Germany, a secret tribunal called the 'Vehmgericht'. If a red cross was seen marked on a house, people knew that its owner was doomed by the 'Vehm'. All the houses of Europe are now marked with the mysterious red cross. History is the judge – its executioner, the proletarian.

2. Robin Goodfellow is a character of English folklore, used by Shakespeare in *A Midsummer Night's Dream*. On the 'old mole', see above, p. 571, n. 46.

Articles on India and China

THE BRITISH RULE IN INDIA[1]

London, 10 June 1853

Hindustan is an Italy of Asiatic dimensions, the Himalayas for the Alps, the Plains of Bengal for the Plains of Lombardy, the Deccan for the Apennines, and the Isle of Ceylon for the Island of Sicily. The same rich variety in the products of the soil, and the same dismemberment in the political configuration. Just as Italy has, from time to time, been compressed by the conqueror's sword into different national masses, so do we find Hindustan, when not under the pressure of the Mohammedan, or the Mogul, or the Briton, dissolved into as many independent and conflicting states as it numbered towns, or even villages. Yet, in a social point of view, Hindustan is not the Italy, but the Ireland of the East. And this strange combination of Italy and Ireland, of a world of voluptuousness and a world of woes, is anticipated in the ancient traditions of the religion of Hindustan. That religion is at once a religion of sensualist exuberance and a religion of self-torturing asceticism; a religion of the Lingam and of the Juggernaut; the religion of the monk, and of the bayadere.

I share not the opinion of those who believe in a golden age of Hindustan, without recurring, however, like Sir Charles Wood,[2] for the confirmation of my view, to the authority of Khuli Khan.[3] But take, for example, the times of Aurungzeb;[4] or the epoch when the Mogul appeared in the north, and the Portuguese in the

1. For this article Marx made use of ideas expressed by Engels in his letter to Marx of 6 June 1853 (*MECW* 39, pp. 335–41). The article first appeared in the *New York Daily Tribune* of 25 June 1853.

2. Sir Charles Wood, later Lord Halifax, was President of the Board of Control, the British minister responsible for the supervision of the East India Company. Marx refers to a speech by Wood in the House of Commons on 3 June 1853.

3. Khuli Khan, also known as Nadir Shah, invaded India from Afghanistan in 1739 and dealt the Mogul empire its death blow.

4. Aurungzeb, the sixth Mogul emperor, reigned from 1658 to 1707.

south;[5] or the age of Mohammedan invasion, and of the heptarchy in southern India;[6] or, if you will, go still more back to antiquity, take the mythological chronology of the Brahmin himself, who places the commencement of Indian misery in an epoch even more remote than the Christian creation of the world.

There cannot, however, remain any doubt but that the misery inflicted by the British on Hindustan is of an essentially different and infinitely more intensive kind than all Hindustan had to suffer before. I do not allude to European despotism, planted upon Asiatic despotism, by the British East India Company, forming a more monstrous combination than any of the divine monsters startling us in the Temple of Salsette.[7] This is no distinctive feature of British colonial rule, but only an imitation of the Dutch, and so much so that in order to characterize the working of the British East India Company, it is sufficient to literally repeat what Sir Stamford Raffles, the *English* Governor of Java, said of the old Dutch East India Company.

The Dutch Company, actuated solely by the spirit of gain, and viewing their Javan subjects with less regard or consideration than a West India planter formerly viewed the gang upon his estate, because the latter had paid the purchase money of human property, which the other had not, employed all the pre-existing machinery of despotism to squeeze from the people their utmost mite of contribution, the last dregs of their labour, and thus aggravated the evils of a capricious and semi-barbarous government, by working it with all the practised ingenuity of politicians, and all the monopolizing selfishness of traders.[8]

All the civil wars, invasions, revolutions, conquests, famines, strangely complex, rapid and destructive as the successive action in Hindustan may appear, did not go deeper than its surface. England has broken down the entire framework of Indian society, without any symptoms of reconstitution yet appearing. This loss

5. This would be the early sixteenth century. The Portuguese annexed Goa in 1510. Babar, the founder of the Mogul empire, conquered the Punjab in 1525.

6. The Islamic conquest of India began with Mahmud's invasion of Lahore in 1001. This first wave of Islamic rule decomposed in the mid-fourteenth century. By 'heptarchy' Marx refers to the fragmentation that preceded the Islamic conquest. The original heptarchy was England of the sixth to eighth century, divided into seven kingdoms.

7. The Isle of Salsette, north of Bombay, is celebrated for its 109 cave temples.

8. T. S. Raffles, *The History of Java*, London, 1871, vol. 1, p. 168.

of his old world, with no gain of a new one, imparts a particular kind of melancholy to the present misery of the Hindu, and separates Hindustan, ruled by Britain, from all its ancient traditions, and from the whole of its past history.

There have been in Asia, generally, from immemorial times, but three departments of government: that of finance, or the plunder of the interior; that of war, or the plunder of the exterior; and, finally, the department of public works. Climate and territorial conditions, especially the vast tracts of desert, extending from the Sahara, through Arabia, Persia, India and Tartary, to the most elevated Asiatic highlands, constituted artificial irrigation by canals and waterworks the basis of Oriental agriculture. As in Egypt and India, inundations are used for fertilizing the soil of Mesopotamia, Persia, etc.; advantage is taken of a high level for feeding irrigative canals. This prime necessity of an economical and common use of water, which in the Occident drove private enterprise to voluntary association, as in Flanders and Italy, necessitated in the Orient, where civilization was too low and the territorial extent too vast to call into life voluntary association, the interference of the centralizing power of government. Hence an economical function devolved upon all Asiatic governments, the function of providing public works. This artificial fertilization of the soil, dependent on a central government, and immediately decaying with the neglect of irrigation and drainage, explains the otherwise strange fact that we now find whole territories barren and desert that were once brilliantly cultivated, as Palmyra, Petra, the ruins in Yemen, and large provinces of Egypt, Persia and Hindustan; it also explains how a single war of devastation has been able to depopulate a country for centuries, and to strip it of all its civilization.

Now, the British in East India accepted from their predecessors the departments of finance and of war, but they have neglected entirely that of public works. Hence the deterioration of an agriculture which is not capable of being conducted on the British principle of free competition, of *laissez-faire* and *laissez-aller*. But in Asiatic empires we are quite accustomed to see agriculture deteriorating under one government and reviving again under some other government. There the harvests correspond to good or bad governments, as they change in Europe with good or bad seasons. Thus the oppression and neglect of agriculture, bad as it is, could not be looked upon as the final blow dealt to Indian society by the

British intruder, had it not been attended by a circumstance of quite different importance, a novelty in the annals of the whole Asiatic world. However changing the political aspect of India's past must appear, its social condition has remained unaltered since its remotest antiquity, until the first decennium of the nineteenth century. The hand-loom and the spinning-wheel, producing their regular myriads of spinners and weavers, were the pivots of the structure of that society. From immemorial times Europe received the admirable textures of Indian labour, sending in return for them her precious metals, and furnishing thereby his material to the goldsmith, that indispensable member of Indian society, whose love of finery is so great that even the lowest class, those who go about nearly naked, have commonly a pair of golden earrings and a gold ornament of some kind hung round their necks. Rings on the fingers and toes have also been common. Women as well as children frequently wore massive bracelets and anklets of gold or silver, and statuettes of divinities in gold and silver were met with in the households. It was the British intruder who broke up the Indian hand-loom and destroyed the spinning-wheel. England began with driving the Indian cottons from the European market; it then introduced twist into Hindustan and in the end inundated the very mother country of cotton with cottons. From 1818 to 1836 the export of twist from Great Britain to India rose in the proportion of 1 to 5,200. In 1824 the export of British muslins to India hardly amounted to 1,000,000 yards, while in 1837 it surpassed 64,000,000 yards. But at the same time the population of Dacca decreased from 150,000 inhabitants to 20,000. This decline of Indian towns celebrated for their fabrics was by no means the worst consequence. British steam and science uprooted, over the whole surface of Hindustan, the union between agriculture and manufacturing industry.

These two circumstances – the Hindu, on the one hand, leaving, like all Oriental peoples, to the central government the care of the great public works, the prime condition of his agriculture and commerce, dispersed, on the other hand, over the surface of the country, and agglomerated in small centres by the domestic union of agricultural and manufacturing pursuits – these two circumstances had brought about, since the remotest times, a social system of particular features – the so-called *village system*, which gave to each of these small unions their independent organization and distinct life. The peculiar character of this system may be judged from the following description, contained in an old official report of the British House of Commons on Indian affairs:[9]

A village, geographically considered, is a tract of country comprising some hundred or thousand acres of arable and waste lands; politically viewed it resembles a corporation or township. Its proper establishment of officers and servants consists of the following descriptions: the *potail*, or head inhabitant, who has generally the superintendence of the affairs of the village, settles the disputes of the inhabitants, attends to the police, and performs the duty of collecting the revenue within his village, a duty which his personal influence and minute acquaintance with the situation and concerns of the people render him the best qualified for this charge. The *kurnum* keeps the accounts of cultivation, and registers everything connected with it. The *tallier* and the *totie*, the duty of the former of which consists in gaining information of crimes and offences, and in escorting and protecting persons travelling from one village to another; the province of the latter appearing to be more immediately confined to the village, consisting, among other duties, in guarding the crops and assisting in measuring them. The *boundaryman*, who preserves the limits of the village, or gives evidence respecting them in cases of dispute. The superintendent of tanks and watercourses distributes the water for the purposes of agriculture. The Brahmin, who performs the village worship. The schoolmaster, who is seen teaching the children in a village to read and write in the sand. The calendar-Brahmin, or astrologer, etc. These officers and servants generally constitute the establishment of a village; but in some parts of the country it is of less extent; some of the duties and functions above described being united in the same person; in others it exceeds the above-named number of individuals. Under this simple form of municipal government, the inhabitants of the country have lived from time immemorial. The boundaries of the villages have been but seldom altered; and though the villages themselves have been sometimes injured, and even desolated by war, famine or disease, the same name, the same limits, the same interests, and even the same families, have continued for ages. The inhabitants gave themselves no trouble about the breaking up and divisions of kingdoms; while the village remains entire, they care not to what power it is transferred, or to what sovereign it devolves; its internal economy remains unchanged. The *potail* is still the head inhabitant, and still acts as the petty judge or magistrate, and collector or rentor of the village.

These small stereotype forms of social organism have been to the greater part dissolved, and are disappearing, not so much

9. Marx quotes this report of 1812 from G. Campbell, *Modern India: A Sketch of the System of Civil Government*, London, 1852, pp. 84–5.

through the brutal interference of the British tax-gatherer and the British soldier, as to the working of English steam and English free trade. Those family-communities were based on domestic industry, in that peculiar combination of hand-weaving, hand-spinning and hand-tilling agriculture which gave them self-supporting power. English interference having placed the spinner in Lancashire and the weaver in Bengal, or sweeping away both Hindu spinner and weaver, dissolved these small semi-barbarian, semi-civilized communities by blowing up their economical basis, and thus produced the greatest and, to speak the truth, the only *social* revolution ever heard of in Asia.

Now, sickening as it must be to human feeling to witness those myriads of industrious patriarchal and inoffensive social organizations disorganized and dissolved into their units, thrown into a sea of woes, and their individual members losing at the same time their ancient form of civilization and their hereditary means of subsistence, we must not forget that these idyllic village communities, inoffensive though they may appear, had always been the solid foundation of Oriental despotism, that they restrained the human mind within the smallest possible compass, making it the unresisting tool of superstition, enslaving it beneath traditional rules, depriving it of all grandeur and historical energies. We must not forget the barbarian egotism which, concentrating on some miserable patch of land, had quietly witnessed the ruin of empires, the perpetration of unspeakable cruelties, the massacre of the population of large towns, with no other consideration bestowed upon them than on natural events, itself the helpless prey of any aggressor who deigned to notice it at all. We must not forget that this undignified, stagnatory and vegetative life, that this passive sort of existence evoked on the other part, in contradistinction, wild, aimless, unbounded forces of destruction, and rendered murder itself a religious rite in Hindustan. We must not forget that these little communities were contaminated by distinctions of caste and by slavery, that they subjugated man to external circumstances instead of elevating man to be the sovereign of circumstances, that they transformed a self-developing social state into never-changing natural destiny, and thus brought about a brutalizing worship of nature, exhibiting its degradation in the fact that man, the sovereign of nature, fell down on his knees in adoration of Kanuman, the monkey, and Sabbala, the cow.

England, it is true, in causing a social revolution in Hindustan was actuated only by the vilest interests, and was stupid in her manner of enforcing them. But that is not the question. The question is, can mankind fulfil its destiny without a fundamental revolution in the social state of Asia? If not, whatever may have been the crimes of England she was the unconscious tool of history in bringing about that revolution.

Then, whatever bitterness the spectacle of the crumbling of an ancient world may have for our personal feelings, we have the right, in point of history, to exclaim with Goethe:

> *Sollte diese Qual uns quälen,*
> *Da sie unsre Lust vermehrt,*
> *Hat nicht Myriaden Seelen*
> *Timurs Herrschaft aufgezehrt?*[10]

THE EAST INDIA COMPANY – ITS HISTORY AND RESULTS[11]

London, 24 June 1853

The debate on Lord Stanley's motion to postpone legislation for India has been deferred until this evening.[12] For the first time since 1783 the Indian question has become a ministerial one in England.[13] Why is this?

The true commencement of the East India Company cannot be dated from a more remote epoch than the year 1702, when the different societies, claiming the monopoly of the East India trade, united together in one single company. Till then the very existence of the original East India Company was repeatedly endangered, once suspended for years under the protectorate of Cromwell, and once threatened with utter dissolution by parliamentary interference under the reign of William III. It was under the ascendancy of that Dutch prince when the Whigs became the farmers

10.   'Should this torture then torment us
            Since it brings us greater pleasure?
            Were not through the rule of Timur
            Souls devoured without measure?'
From Goethe's *Westöstlicher Diwan. An Suleika*.

11. From the *New York Daily Tribune*, 11 July 1853.

12. The motion proposed by Lord Stanley, a Tory, was designed to block the further progress of the Aberdeen Coalition's Government of India Bill, which with its minor reforms satisfied neither the Tories nor the Radicals.

13. In 1783 Fox had proposed the transfer of the East India Company's political powers to the Crown, and his government had been defeated on this issue.

of the revenues of the British Empire, when the Bank of England sprang into life, when the protective system was firmly established in England and the balance of power in Europe was definitively settled, that the existence of an East India Company was recognized by Parliament. That era of apparent liberty was in reality the era of monopolies not created by royal grants, as in the times of Elizabeth and Charles I, but authorized and nationalized by the sanction of Parliament. This epoch in the history of England bears, in fact, an extreme likeness to the epoch of Louis Philippe in France, the old landed aristocracy having been defeated, and the bourgeoisie not being able to take its place except under the banner of moneyocracy, or the *haute finance*. The East India Company excluded the common people from the commerce with India, at the same time that the House of Commons excluded them from parliamentary representation. In this, as well as in other instances, we find the first decisive victory of the bourgeoisie over the feudal aristocracy coinciding with the most pronounced reaction against the people, a phenomenon which has driven more than one popular writer, like Cobbett, to look for popular liberty rather in the past than in the future.

The union between the constitutional monarchy and the monopolizing moneyed interest, between the Company of East India and the 'Glorious Revolution' of 1688 was fostered by the same force by which the liberal interests and a liberal dynasty have at all times and in all countries met and combined, by the force of corruption, that first and last moving power of constitutional monarchy, the guardian angel of William III and the fatal demon of Louis Philippe. So early as 1693, it appeared from parliamentary inquiries that the annual expenditure of the East India Company, under the head of 'gifts' to men in power, which had rarely amounted to above £1,200 before the revolution, reached the sum of £90,000. The Duke of Leeds was impeached for a bribe of £5,000, and the virtuous king himself convicted of having received £10,000. Besides these direct briberies, rival companies were thrown out by tempting the government with loans of enormous sums at the lowest interest, and by buying off rival directors.

The power the East India Company had obtained by bribing the government, as did also the Bank of England, it was forced to maintain by bribing again, as did the Bank of England. At every epoch when its monopoly was expiring, it could only effect a renewal of its charter by offering fresh loans and by fresh presents made to the government.

The events of the Seven Years' War[14] transformed the East India Company from a commercial into a military and territorial power. It was then that the foundation was laid of the present British empire in the East. Then East India stock rose to £263, and dividends were then paid at the rate of 12½ per cent. But then there appeared a new enemy to the Company, no longer in the shape of rival societies, but in the shape of rival ministers and a rival people. It was alleged that the Company's territory had been conquered by the aid of British fleets and British armies, and that no British subjects could hold territorial sovereignties independent of the Crown. The ministers of the day and the people of the day claimed their share in the 'wonderful treasures' imagined to have been won by the last conquests. The Company only saved its existence by an agreement made in 1767 that it should annually pay £400,000 into the national exchequer.

But the East India Company, instead of fulfilling its agreement, got into financial difficulties and, instead of paying a tribute to the English people, appealed to Parliament for pecuniary aid. Serious alterations in the charter were the consequence of this step. The Company's affairs failing to improve, notwithstanding their new condition, and the English nation having simultaneously lost their colonies in North America, the necessity of elsewhere regaining some great colonial empire became more and more universally felt. The illustrious Fox thought the opportune moment had arrived, in 1783, for bringing forward his famous India Bill, which proposed to abolish the Courts of Directors and Proprietors, and to vest the whole Indian government in the hands of seven commissioners appointed by Parliament. By the personal influence of the imbecile king[15] over the House of Lords, the bill of Mr Fox was defeated, and made the instrument of breaking down the then Coalition government of Fox and Lord North, and of placing the famous Pitt at the head of the government. Pitt carried in 1784 a bill through both Houses, which directed the establishment of the Board of Control, consisting of six members of the Privy Council, who were 'to check, superintend

14. For England, the dominant theatre of the Seven Years' War (1756–63) was in the colonial territories. Among other English gains France was forced to abandon her conquests in India.
15. George III.

and control all acts, operations and concerns which in any wise related to the civil and military Government, or revenues of the territories and possessions of the East India Company'.

On this head, Mill, the historian, says:

> In passing that law two objects were pursued. To avoid the imputation of what was represented as the heinous object of Mr Fox's bill, it was necessary that the principal part of the power should *appear* to remain in the hand of the Directors. For ministerial advantage it was necessary that it should in *reality* be all taken away. Mr Pitt's bill professed to differ from that of his rival, chiefly in this very point, that while the one destroyed the power of the Directors, the other left it almost entire. Under the act of Mr Fox the powers of the ministers would have been avowedly held. Under the act of Mr Pitt, they were held in secret and by fraud. The bill of Fox transferred the power of the Company to Commissioners appointed by Parliament. The bill of Mr Pitt transferred it to Commissioners appointed by the King.[16]

The years of 1783 and 1784 were thus the first, and till now the only years, for the Indian question to become a ministerial one. The bill of Mr Pitt having been carried, the charter of the East India Company was renewed, and the Indian question set aside for twenty years. But in 1813 the Anti-Jacobin war, and in 1833 the newly introduced Reform Bill, superseded all other political questions.

This, then, is the first reason of the Indian question's having failed to become a great political question, since and before 1784; that before that time the East Indian Company had first to conquer existence and importance; that after that time the oligarchy absorbed all of its power which it could assume without incurring responsibility; and that afterwards the English people in general were at the very epochs of the renewal of the charter, in 1813 and in 1833, absorbed by other questions of overbearing interest.

We will now take a different view. The East India Company commenced by attempting merely to establish factories for their agents and places of deposit for their goods. In order to protect them they erected several forts. Although they had, even as early as 1689, conceived the establishment of a dominion in India, and of making territorial revenue one of their sources of emolument, yet, down to 1744, they had acquired but a few unimportant districts around Bombay, Madras and Calcutta. The war which

16. James Mill, *The History of the British India*, London, 1826, vol. IV, p. 488 & vol. V, pp. 68, 75, 150–51.

subsequently broke out in the Carnatic[17] had the effect of rendering them, after various struggles, virtual sovereigns of that part of India. Much more considerable results arose from the war in Bengal and the victories of Clive. These results were the real occupation of Bengal, Bihar and Orissa. At the end of the eighteenth century, and in the first years of the present one, there supervened the wars with Tippoo Sahib,[18] and in consequence of them a great advance of power and an immense extension of the subsidiary system.[19] In the second decennium of the nineteenth century the first convenient frontier, that of India within the desert, had at length been conquered. It was not till then that the British empire in the East reached those parts of Asia which had been, at all times, the seat of every great central power in India. But the most vulnerable points of the empire, from which it had been overrun as often as old conquerors were expelled by new ones, the barriers of the western frontier, were not in the hands of the British. During the period from 1838 to 1849, in the Sikh and Afghan wars, British rule subjected to definitive possession the ethnographical, political and military frontiers of the East Indian continent, by the compulsory annexation of the Punjab and of Scinde. These were possessions indispensable to repulse any invading force issuing from Central Asia, and indispensable against Russia advancing to the frontiers of Persia. During this last decennium there have been added to the British Indian territory 167,000 square miles, with a population of 8,572,630 souls. As to the interior, all the native states now became surrounded by British possessions, subjected to British *suzeraineté* under various forms, and cut off from the sea-coast, with the sole exception of Gujarat and Scinde. As to its exterior, India was now finished. It is only since 1849 that the one great Anglo-Indian empire has existed.

17. The war between England and France in India, which broke out in 1744 and ended in 1761 with the complete withdrawal of the French, was fought mainly in the Carnatic (the south-eastern coastal region).

18. Tippoo was the Sultan of Mysore. The defeat of Tippoo in 1799 and the Second Mahratta War of 1803 left Britain the paramount power in the Indian subcontinent.

19. The system of 'subsidiary treaties' developed by the British to secure their position in India involved the British government guaranteeing a native ruler protection against attack in return for a sum of money. The British would raise, train and command the necessary number of sepoys, and leave internal affairs in the ruler's hands. States that accepted these treaties were known as 'native states', by far the largest being Hyderabad.

Thus the British government has been fighting, under the Company's name, for two centuries, till at last the natural limits of India were reached. We understand now, why during all this time all parties in England have connived in silence, even those which had resolved to become the loudest with their hypocritical peace cant, after the *arrondissement*[20] of the one Indian empire should have been completed. Firstly, of course, they had to get it, in order to subject it afterwards to their sharp philanthropy. From this view we understand the altered position of the Indian question in the present year, 1853, compared with all former periods of charter renewal.

Again, let us take a different view. We shall still better understand the peculiar crisis in Indian legislation on reviewing the course of British commercial intercourse with India through its different phases.

At the commencement of the East India Company's operations, under the reign of Elizabeth, the Company was permitted, for the purpose of profitably carrying on its trade with India, to export an annual value of £30,000 in silver, gold and foreign coin. This was an infraction against all the prejudices of the age, and Thomas Mun was forced to lay down in *A Discourse of Trade, from England unto the East-Indies*,[21] the foundation of the 'mercantile system', admitting that the precious metals were the only real wealth a country could possess, but contending at the same time that their exportation might be safely allowed, provided the *balance of payments* was in favour of the exporting nation. In this sense, he contended that the commodities imported from East India were chiefly re-exported to other countries, from which a much greater quantity of bullion was obtained than had been required to pay for them in India. In the same spirit, Sir Josiah Child wrote *A Treatise Wherein Is Demonstrated I. That the East India Trade Is the Most National of all Foreign Trades*.[22] By and by the partisans of the East India Company grew more audacious, and it may be noticed as a curiosity, in this strange Indian history, that the Indian monopolists were the first preachers of free trade in England.

Parliamentary intervention, with regard to the East India Company, was again claimed, not by the commercial but by the

20. Rounding off.
21. London, 1621, published under the initials T.M.
22. London, 1681, published under the pseudonym Philopatros.

industrial class, at the latter end of the seventeenth century, and during the greater part of the eighteenth, when the importation of East Indian cotton and silk stuffs was declared to ruin the poor British manufacturers, an opinion put forward in John Pollexfen's *England and East-India Inconsistent in Their Manufactures*, London, 1697,[23] a title strangely verified a century and a half later, but in a very different sense. Parliament did then interfere. By the Act 11 and 12, William III, cap. 10, it was enacted that the wearing of wrought silks and of printed or dyed calicoes from India, Persia and China should be prohibited, and a penalty of £200 imposed on all persons having or selling the same. Similar laws were enacted under George I, II and III, in consequence of the repeated lamentations of the afterwards so 'enlightened' British manufacturers. And thus, during the greater part of the eighteenth century, Indian manufactures were generally imported into England in order to be sold on the Continent, and to remain excluded from the English market itself.

Besides this parliamentary interference with East India, solicited by the greedy home manufacturer, efforts were made at every epoch of the renewal of the charter, by the merchants of London, Liverpool and Bristol, to break down the commercial monopoly of the Company and to participate in that commerce, estimated to be a true mine of gold. In consequence of these efforts, a provision was made in the Act of 1773 prolonging the Company's charter till 1 March 1814, by which private British individuals were authorized to export from, and the Company's Indian servants permitted to import into, England almost all sorts of commodities. But this concession was surrounded with conditions annihilating its effects, in respect to the exports to British India by private merchants. In 1813 the Company was unable to further withstand the pressure of general commerce, and, except the monopoly of the Chinese trade, the trade to India was opened, under certain conditions, to private competition. At the renewal of the Charter in 1833, these last restrictions were at length superseded, the Company forbidden to carry on any trade at all – their commercial character destroyed, and their privilege of excluding British subjects from the Indian territories withdrawn.

Meanwhile the East Indian trade had undergone very serious

23. This book was published anonymously.

revolutions, altogether altering the position of the different class interests in England with regard to it. During the whole course of the eighteenth century the treasures transported from India to England were gained much less by comparatively insignificant commerce than by the direct exploitation of that country, and by the colossal fortunes there extorted and transmitted to England. After the opening of the trade in 1813 the commerce with India more than trebled in a very short time. But this was not all. The whole character of the trade was changed. Till 1813 India had been chiefly an exporting country, while it now became an import-ing one; and in such a quick progression that already in 1823 the rate of exchange, which had generally been 2s. 6d. per rupee, sunk down to 2s. per rupee. India, the great workshop of cotton manufacture for the world since immemorial times, became now inundated with English twists and cotton stuffs. After its own produce had been excluded from England, or only admitted on the most cruel terms, British manufactures were poured into it at a small and merely nominal duty, to the ruin of the native cotton fabrics once so celebrated. In 1780 the value of British produce and manufactures [exported to India] amounted only to £386,152, the bullion exported during the same year to £15,041, the total value of exports during 1780 being £12,648,616, so that the Indian trade amounted to only one thirty-second of the entire foreign trade. In 1850 the total exports to India from Great Britain and Ireland were £8,024,000, of which cotton goods alone amounted to £5,220,000, so that it reached more than one eighth of the whole export, and more than one quarter of the foreign cotton trade. But the cotton manufacture also employed now one eighth of the population of Britain, and contributed one twelfth of the whole national revenue. After each commercial crisis the East Indian trade grew of more paramount importance for the British cotton manufacturers, and the East Indian continent became actually their best market. At the same rate at which the cotton manufactures became of vital interest for the whole social frame of Great Britain, East India became of vital interest for the British cotton manufacture.

Till then the interests of the moneyocracy which had converted India into its landed estates, of the oligarchy who had conquered it by their armies, and of the millocracy who had inundated it with their fabrics, had gone hand in hand. But the more the industrial interest became dependent on the Indian market, the more it felt the necessity of creating fresh productive powers in India, after having ruined her native industry. You cannot continue to inundate a country with your manufactures, unless you enable it to give you some produce in return. The industrial interest found that their trade declined instead of increasing. For the four years ending with 1846, the imports to India from Great Britain were to the amount of 261 million rupees, for the four years ending 1850 they were only 253 millions, while the exports for the former period [were] 274 million rupees, and for the latter period, 254 millions. They found out that the power of consuming their goods was contracted in India to the lowest possible point, that the consumption of their manufactures by the British West Indies was of the value of about 14s. per head of the population per annum, by Chile of 9s. 3d., by Brazil of 6s. 5d., by Cuba of 6s. 2d., by Peru of 5s. 7d., by Central America of 10d., while it amounted in India only to about 9d. Then came the short cotton crop in the United States, which caused them a loss of £11,000,000 in 1850, and they were exasperated at depending on America, instead of deriving a sufficiency of raw cotton from the East Indies. Besides, they found that in all attempts to apply capital to India they met with impediments and chicanery on the part of the Indian authorities. Thus India became the battlefield in the contest of the industrial interest on the one side, and of the money-ocracy and oligarchy on the other. The manufacturers, conscious of their ascendancy in England, ask now for the annihilation of these antagonistic powers in India, for the destruction of the whole ancient fabric of Indian government, and for the final eclipse of the East India Company.

And now to the fourth and last point of view, from which the Indian question must be judged. Since 1784 Indian finances have got more and more deeply into difficulty. There exists now a national debt of £50 million, a continual decrease in the resources of the revenue, and a corresponding increase in the expenditure, dubiously balanced by the gambling income of the opium tax, now threatened with extinction by the Chinese beginning themselves to cultivate the poppy, and aggravated by the expenses to be anticipated from the senseless Burmese war.[24]

'As the case stands,' says Mr Dickinson, 'as it would ruin

24. As Marx wrote this, a new Burmese war was anticipated as a result of the Burmese refusal to recognize the British annexation of Pegu in the Second Burmese War (1852). In the event, peace with Burma was signed before Marx's article was published.

England to lose her Empire in India, it is stretching our own finances with ruin, to be obliged to keep it.'[25]

I have shown thus, how the Indian question has become for the first time since 1783 an English question and a ministerial question.

INDIAN AFFAIRS[26]

London, 19 July 1853

The progress of the India Bill through the committee has little interest. It is significant that all amendments are thrown out now by the Coalition[27] coalescing with the Tories against their own allies of the Manchester School.

The actual state of India may be illustrated by a few facts. The home establishment absorbs 3 per cent of the net revenue, and the annual interest for home debt and dividends 14 per cent – together 17 per cent. If we deduct these annual remittances from India to England, the *military charges* amount to about two thirds of the whole expenditure available for India, or to 66 per cent, while the charges for *public works* do not amount to more than 2¾ per cent of the general revenue, or for Bengal 1 per cent, Agra 7¾, Punjab ⅛, Madras ½, and Bombay 1 per cent of their respective revenues. These figures are the official ones of the Company itself.

On the other hand nearly three fifths of the whole net revenue is derived from the *land*, about one seventh from *opium*, and upwards of one ninth from *salt*. These resources together yield 85 per cent of the whole receipts.

As to minor items of expenditure and charges, it may suffice to state that the *moturpha* revenue maintained in the Presidency of Madras and levied on shops, looms, sheep, cattle, sundry professions, etc., yields somewhat about £50,000 while the yearly dinners of the East India House cost about the same sum.

The great bulk of the revenue is derived from the land. As the various kinds of Indian land tenure have recently been described

25. John Dickinson, *The Government of India under a Bureaucracy*, London and Manchester, 1853, p. 50. Dickinson was a founder of the radical Indian Reform Association.

26. This is the final part of a composite article originally entitled 'The War Questions – Doings of Parliament – India'. From the *New York Daily Tribune*, 5 August 1853.

27. The same Coalition ministry referred to above, p. 613.

in so many places, and in popular style, too, I propose to limit my observations on the subject to a few general remarks on the *zemindari* and *ryotwari* systems.

The zemindari and the ryotwari were both of them agrarian revolutions, effected by British ukases, and opposed to each other: the one aristocratic, the other democratic; the one a caricature of English landlordism, the other of French peasant proprietorship; but pernicious, both combining the most contradictory character – both made not for the people who cultivate the soil, nor for the holder who owns it, but for the government that taxes it.

By the zemindari system, the people of the Presidency of Bengal were depossessed at once of their hereditary claims to the soil, in favour of the native tax-gatherers called *zemindars*. By the ryotwari system introduced into the Presidencies of Madras and Bombay, the native nobility, with their territorial claims, *merassis*, *jagirs*, etc., were reduced with the common people to the holding of minute fields, cultivated by themselves, in favour of the Collector[28] of the East India Company. But a curious sort of English landlord was the zemindar, receiving only one tenth of the rent, while he had to make over nine tenths of it to the government. A curious sort of French peasant was the *ryot*, without any permanent title in the soil, and with the taxation changing every year in proportion to his harvest. The original class of zemindars, notwithstanding their unmitigated and uncontrolled rapacity against the dispossessed mass of the ex-hereditary landholders, soon melted away under the pressure of the Company, in order to be replaced by mercantile speculators who now hold all the land of Bengal, with exception of the estates returned under the direct management of the government. These speculators have introduced a variety of the zemindari tenure called *patni*. Not content to be placed with regard to the British Government in the situation of middlemen, they have created in their turn a class of 'hereditary' middlemen called *patnidars*, who created again their subpatnidars, etc., so that a perfect scale of hierarchy of middlemen has sprung up, which presses with its entire weight on the unfortunate cultivator. As to the ryots in Madras and Bombay, the system soon degenerated into one of forced cultivation, and the land lost all its value.

28. A Collector was an official of the East India Company who combined the functions of tax collector, governor and judge.

'The land', says Mr Campbell, 'would be sold for balances by the Collector, as in Bengal, but generally is not, for a very good reason, viz.: that nobody will buy it.'[29]

Thus, in Bengal, we have a combination of English landlordism, of the Irish middleman system, of the Austrian system, transforming the landlord into the tax-gatherer, and of the Asiatic system, making the state the real landlord. In Madras and Bombay we have a French peasant proprietor who is at the same time a serf and a *métayer* of the state. The drawbacks of all these various systems accumulate upon him without his enjoying any of their redeeming features. The ryot is subject, like the French peasant, to the extortion of the private usurer; but he has no hereditary, no permanent title in his land, like the French peasant. Like the serf he is forced to cultivation, but he is not secured against want like the serf. Like the *métayer* he has to divide his produce with the state, but the state is not obliged, with regard to him, to advance the funds and the stock, as it is obliged to do with regard to the *métayer*. In Bengal, as in Madras and Bombay, under the zemindari as under the ryotwari, the ryots – and they form eleven twelfths of the whole Indian population – have been wretchedly pauperized; and if they are, morally speaking, not sunk as low as the Irish cottiers, they owe it to their climate, the men of the south being possessed of less wants, and of more imagination, than the men of the north.

Conjointly with the land tax we have to consider the salt tax. Notoriously, the Company retains the monopoly of that article which they sell at three times its mercantile value – and this in a country where it is furnished by the sea, by the lakes, by the mountains and the earth itself. The practical working of this monopoly was described by the Earl of Albemarle in the following words[30]: 'A great proportion of the salt for inland consumption throughout the country is purchased from the Company by large wholesale merchants at less than 4 rupees per *maund*;[31] these mix a fixed proportion of sand, chiefly got a few miles to the south-west of Dacca, and send the mixture to a second, or counting the government as the first, to a third monopolist at about 5 or 6 rupees. This dealer adds more earth or ashes, and thus passing

29. G. Campbell, *Modern India: A Sketch of the System of Civil Government*.

30. In a speech in the House of Lords on 18 July 1853.

31. An Indian dry measure of approximately twenty-six pounds.

through more hands, from the large towns to villages, the price is still raised from 8 to 10 rupees and the proportion of adulteration from 25 to 40 per cent. It appears then that the people pay from £21 17s. 2d. to £27 6s. 2d. for their salt, or in other words, from thirty to thirty-six times as much as the wealthy people of Great Britain.'

As an instance of English bourgeois morals, I may allege that Mr Campbell defends the opium monopoly because it prevents the Chinese from consuming too much of the drug, and that he defends the brandy monopoly (licences for spirit-selling in India) because it has wonderfully increased the consumption of brandy in India.

The zemindar tenure, the ryotwar and the salt tax, combined with the Indian climate, were the hotbeds of the cholera – India's ravages upon the Western world – a striking and severe example of the solidarity of human woes and wrongs.

THE FUTURE RESULTS OF THE BRITISH RULE IN INDIA[32]

London, 22 July 1853

I propose in this letter to conclude my observations on India. How came it that English supremacy was established in India? The paramount power of the Great Mogul was broken by the Mogul viceroys. The power of the viceroys was broken by the Mahrattas.[33] The power of the Mahrattas was broken by the Afghans, and while all were struggling against all, the Briton rushed in and was enabled to subdue them all. A country not only divided between Mohammedan and Hindu, but between tribe and tribe, between caste and caste; a society whose framework was based on a sort of equilibrium, resulting from a general repulsion and constitutional exclusiveness between all its members. Such a country and such a society, were they not the predestined prey of conquest? If we knew nothing of the past history of Hindustan, would there not be the one great incontestable fact, that even at

32. From the *New York Daily Tribune*, 8 August 1853.

33. The Mahrattas were a people from the north-western Deccan, who rose up against Mogul rule in the mid-seventeenth century and formed the Mahratta Confederacy. The Mahrattas' power was broken by the Afghan invasion of 1761 under Ahmad Khan, which also broke up the Mogul empire and created the conditions for British supremacy over the whole of India established after the Anglo-Mahratta war of 1803–5.

this moment India is held in English thraldom by an Indian army maintained at the cost of India? India, then, could not escape the fate of being conquered, and the whole of her past history, if it be anything, is the history of the successive conquests she has undergone. Indian society has no history at all, at least no known history. What we call its history is but the history of the successive intruders who founded their empires on the passive basis of that unresisting and unchanging society. The question, therefore, is not whether the English had a right to conquer India, but whether we are to prefer India conquered by the Turk, by the Persian, by the Russian, to India conquered by the Briton.

England has to fulfil a double mission in India: one destructive, the other regenerating – the annihilation of old Asiatic society, and the laying of the material foundations of Western society in Asia.

Arabs, Turks, Tartans, Moguls, who had successively overrun India, soon became *Hinduized*, the barbarian conquerors being, by an eternal law of history, conquered themselves by the superior civilization of their subjects. The British were the first conquerors superior and therefore inaccessible to Hindu civilization. They destroyed it by breaking up the native communities, by uprooting the native industry, and by levelling all that was great and elevated in the native society. The historic pages of their rule in India report hardly anything beyond that destruction. The work of regeneration hardly transpires through a heap of ruins. Nevertheless, it has begun.

The political unity of India, more consolidated and extending further than it ever did under the Great Moguls, was the first condition of its regeneration. That unity, imposed by the British sword, will now be strengthened and perpetuated by the electric telegraph. The native army, organized and trained by the British drill-sergeant, was the *sine qua non* of Indian self-emancipation, and of India ceasing to be the prey of the first foreign intruder. The free press, introduced for the first time into Asiatic society, and managed principally by the common offspring of Hindus and Europeans, is a new and powerful agent of reconstruction. The zemindari and ryotwari themselves, abominable as they are, involve two distinct forms of private property in land – the great desideratum of Asiatic society. From the Indian natives, reluctantly and sparingly educated at Calcutta under English superintendence, a fresh class is springing up, endowed with the requirements for government and imbued with European science. Steam has brought India into regular and rapid communication with Europe, has connected its chief ports with those of the whole south-eastern ocean, and has revindicated it from the isolated position which was the prime law of its stagnation. The day is not far distant when, by a combination of railways and steam vessels, the distance between England and India, measured by time, will be shortened to eight days, and when that once fabulous country will thus be actually annexed to the Western world.

The ruling classes of Great Britain have had, till now, but an accidental, transitory and exceptional interest in the progress of India. The aristocracy wanted to conquer it, the moneyocracy to plunder it, and the millocracy to undersell it. But now the tables are turned. The millocracy have discovered that the transformation of India into a reproductive country has become of vital importance to them, and that, to that end, it is necessary, above all, to gift her with means of irrigation and of internal communication. They intend now drawing a net of railways over India. And they will do it. The results must be inappreciable.

It is notorious that the productive powers of India are paralysed by the utter want of means for conveying and exchanging its various produce. Nowhere more than in India do we meet with social destitution in the midst of natural plenty, for want of the means of exchange. It was proved before a Committee of the British House of Commons, which sat in 1848, that 'when grain was selling from 6s. to 8s. a quarter at Khandesh, it was sold at 64s. to 70s. at Poona, where the people were dying in the streets of famine, without the possibility of gaining supplies from Khandesh, because the clay roads were impracticable'.

The introduction of railways may be easily made to subserve agricultural purposes by the formation of tanks, where ground is required for embankment, and by the conveyance of water along the different lines. Thus irrigation, the *sine qua non* of farming in the East, might be greatly extended, and the frequently recurring local famines, arising from the want of water, would be averted. The general importance of railways, viewed under this head, must become evident when we remember that irrigated lands, even in the districts near Ghauts, pay three times as much in taxes, afford ten or twelve times as much employment, and yield twelve or fifteen times as much profit, as the same area without irrigation.

Railways will afford the means of diminishing the amount and the cost of the military establishments. Col. Warren, Town Major of the Fort St William, stated before a Select Committee of the House of Commons: 'The practicability of receiving intelligence from distant parts of the country in as many hours as at present it requires days and even weeks, and of sending instructions with troops and stores, in the more brief period, are considerations which cannot be too highly estimated. Troops could be kept at more distant and healthier stations than at present, and much loss of life from sickness would by this means be spared. Stores could not to the same extent be required at the various depots, and the loss by decay, and the destruction incidental to the climate, would also be avoided. The number of troops might be diminished in direct proportion to their effectiveness.'

We know that the municipal organization and the economical basis of the village communities have been broken up, but their worst feature, the dissolution of society into stereotype and disconnected atoms, has survived their vitality. The village isolation produced the absence of roads in India, and the absence of roads perpetuated the village isolation. On this plan a community existed with a given scale of low conveniences, almost without intercourse with other villages, without the desires and efforts indispensable to social advance. The British having broken up this self-sufficient *inertia* of the villages, railways will provide the new want of communication and intercourse. Besides, 'one of the effects of the railway system will be to bring into every village affected by it such knowledge of the contrivances and appliances of other countries, and such means of obtaining them, as will first put the hereditary and stipendiary village artisanship of India to full proof of its capabilities, and then supply its defects.' (Chapman, *The Cotton and Commerce of India*.)[34]

I know that the English millocracy intend to endow India with railways with the exclusive view of extracting at diminished expenses the cotton and other raw materials for their manufacturers. But when you have once introduced machinery into the locomotion of a country which possesses iron and coals, you are unable to withhold it from its fabrication. You cannot maintain a net of railways over an immense country without introducing all those industrial processes necessary to meet the immediate and

34. John Chapman, *The Cotton and Commerce of India* ..., London, 1851.

current want of railway locomotion, and out of which there must grow the application of machinery to those branches of industry not immediately connected with railways. The railway system will therefore become, in India, truly the forerunner of modern industry. This is the more certain as the Hindus are allowed by British authorities themselves to possess particular aptitude for accommodating themselves to entirely new labour, and acquiring the requisite knowledge of machinery. Ample proof of this fact is afforded by the capacities and expertness of the native engineers in the Calcutta mint, where they have been for years employed in working the steam machinery, by the natives attached to the several steam-engines in the Hurdwar coal districts, and by other instances. Mr Campbell himself, greatly influenced as he is by the prejudices of the East India Company, is obliged to avow 'that the great mass of the Indian people possesses a great *industrial energy*, is well fitted to accumulate capital, and remarkable for a mathematical clearness of head and talent for figures and exact sciences'. 'Their intellects', he says, 'are excellent.'[35]

Modern industry, resulting from the railway system, will dissolve the hereditary divisions of labour, upon which rest the Indian castes, those decisive impediments to Indian progress and Indian power.

All the English bourgeoisie may be forced to do will neither emancipate nor materially mend the social condition of the mass of the people, depending not only on the development of the productive powers, but on their appropriation by the people. But what they will not fail to do is to lay down the material premises for both. Has the bourgeoisie ever done more? Has it ever effected a progress without dragging individuals and peoples through blood and dirt, through misery and degradation?

The Indians will not reap the fruits of the new elements of society scattered among them by the British bourgeoisie till in Great Britain itself the now ruling classes shall have been supplanted by the industrial proletariat, or till the Hindus themselves shall have grown strong enough to throw off the English yoke altogether. At all events, we may safely expect to see, at a more or less remote period, the regeneration of that great and interesting country, whose gentle natives are, to use the expression of Prince Saltykov, even in the most inferior classes, '*plus fins et plus*

35. George Campbell, *Modern India: A Sketch of the System of Civil Government*, London, 1852, pp. 59–60.

adroits que les Italiens',[36] whose submission even is counterbalanced by a certain calm nobility, who, notwithstanding their natural languor, have astonished the British officers by their bravery, whose country has been the source of our languages, our religions, and who represent the type of the ancient German in the Jat and the type of the ancient Greek in the Brahmin.

I cannot part with the subject of India without some concluding remarks.

The profound hypocrisy and inherent barbarism of bourgeois civilization lies unveiled before our eyes, turning from its home, where it assumes respectable forms, to the colonies, where it goes naked. They are the defenders of property, but did any revolutionary party ever originate agrarian revolutions like those in Bengal, in Madras, and in Bombay? Did they not, in India, to borrow an expression of that great robber, Lord Clive himself, resort to atrocious extortion, when simple corruption could not keep pace with their rapacity? While they prated in Europe about the inviolable sanctity of the national debt, did they not confiscate in India the dividends of the rajahs, who had invested their private savings in the Company's own funds? While they combated the French revolution under the pretext of defending 'our holy religion', did they not forbid, at the same time, Christianity to be propagated in India, and did they not, in order to make money out of the pilgrims streaming to the temples of Orissa and Bengal, take up the trade in the murder and prostitution perpetrated in the temple of Juggernaut? These are the men of 'Property, Order, Family and Religion'.

The devastating effects of English industry, when contemplated with regard to India, a country as vast as Europe and containing 150 millions of acres, are palpable and confounding. But we must not forget that they are only the organic results of the whole system of production as it is now constituted. That production rests on the supreme rule of capital. The centralization of capital is essential to the existence of capital as an independent power. The destructive influence of that centralization upon the markets of the world does but reveal, in the most gigantic dimensions, the inherent organic laws of political economy now at work in every civilized town. The bourgeois period of history has to create the material basis of the new world – on the one hand the universal

36. 'More subtle and adroit than the Italians.' Marx is quoting from A. D. Saltykov, *Lettres sur l'Inde*, Paris, 1848, p. 61.

intercourse founded upon the mutual dependency of mankind, and the means of that intercourse; on the other hand the development of the productive powers of man and the transformation of material production into a scientific domination of natural agencies. Bourgeois industry and commerce create these material conditions of a new world in the same way as geological revolutions have created the surface of the earth. When a great social revolution shall have mastered the results of the bourgeois epoch, the market of the world and the modern powers of production, and subjected them to the common control of the most advanced peoples, then only will human progress cease to resemble that hideous pagan idol, who would not drink the nectar but from the skulls of the slain.

REVOLUTION IN CHINA AND IN EUROPE[37]

A most profound yet fantastic speculator on the principles which govern the movements of humanity[38] was wont to extol as one of the ruling secrets of nature what he called the law of the contact of extremes. The homely proverb that 'extremes meet' was, in his view, a grand and potent truth in every sphere of life; an axiom with which the philosopher could as little dispense as the astronomer with the laws of Kepler or the great discovery of Newton.

Whether the 'contact of extremes' be such a universal principle or not, a striking illustration of it may be seen in the effect the Chinese revolution[39] seems likely to exercise upon the civilized world. It may seem a very strange and a very paradoxical assertion that the next uprising of the people of Europe, and their next movement for republican freedom and economy of government, may depend more probably on what is now passing in the Celestial

37. This article was written by Marx on 20 May 1853, and printed in the *New York Daily Tribune* as an unsigned leader on 14 June 1853.

38. Hegel.

39. Marx is referring here to the Taiping Heavenly Kingdom, a broadly based peasant revolt against the Manchu dynasty which broke out in Kwangsi province in 1851 and spread to include the central provinces of China and the lower and middle Yangtse region. The Taiping rebellion abolished the Manchu system of taxation, land tenure and political control, and also attacked, in the name of religion, the Buddhist monasteries which were a base of Manchu power. In the conditions of mid-nineteenth-century China a new feudal ruling class rapidly formed within the Taiping movement which was ready to compromise with the Manchus, and, thus weakened, the Heavenly Kingdom was finally defeated by English, American and French intervention in 1864.

Empire, the very opposite of Europe, than on any other political cause that now exists – more even than on the menaces of Russia and the consequent likelihood of a general European war. But yet it is no paradox, as all may understand by attentively considering the circumstances of the case.

Whatever be the social causes, and whatever religious, dynastic or national shape they may assume, that have brought about the chronic rebellions subsisting in China for about ten years past, and now gathered together in one formidable revolution, the occasion of this outbreak has unquestionably been afforded by the English cannon forcing upon China that soporific drug called opium.[40] Before the British arms the authority of the Manchu dynasty fell to pieces; the superstitious faith in the eternity of the Celestial Empire broke down; the barbarous and hermetic isolation from the civilized world was infringed; and an opening was made for that intercourse which has since proceeded so rapidly under the golden attractions of California and Australia. At the same time the silver coin of the Empire, its lifeblood, began to be drained away to the British East Indies.

Up to 1830, the balance of trade being continually in favour of the Chinese, there existed an uninterrupted importation of silver from India, Britain and the United States into China. Since 1833, and especially since 1840, the export of silver from China to India has become almost exhausting for the Celestial Empire. Hence the strong decrees of the emperor against the opium trade, responded to by still stronger resistance to his measures. Besides this immediate economical consequence, the bribery connected with opium smuggling has entirely demoralized the Chinese state officers in the southern provinces. Just as the emperor was wont to be considered the father of all China, so his officers were looked upon as sustaining the paternal relation to their respective districts. But this patriarchal authority, the only moral link embracing the vast machinery of the state, has gradually been corroded by the corruption of those officers, who have made great gains by conniving at opium smuggling. This has occurred principally in the

40. The first Opium War was precipitated by the Chinese government's burning shipments of opium in Canton harbour in 1839. Three years later, Britain forced on China the treaty of Nanking (August 1842), which opened five major ports to British trade, ceded Britain Hongkong island in perpetuity, exacted from China a war indemnity, and was supplemented the following year by an agreement granting Westerners the right of extra-territoriality.

same southern provinces where the rebellion commenced. It is almost needless to observe that, in the same measure in which opium has obtained the sovereignty over the Chinese, the emperor and his staff of pedantic mandarins have become dispossessed of their own sovereignty. It would seem as though history had first to make this whole people drunk before it could rouse them out of their hereditary stupidity.

Though scarcely existing in former times, the import of English cottons, and to a small extent of English woollens, has rapidly risen since 1833, the epoch when the monopoly of trade with China was transferred from the East India Company to private commerce, and on a much greater scale since 1840, the epoch when other nations, and especially our own,[41] also obtained a share in the Chinese trade. This introduction of foreign manufactures has had a similar effect on the native industry to that which it formerly had on Asia Minor, Persia and India. In China the spinners and weavers have suffered greatly under this foreign competition, and the community has become unsettled in proportion.

The tribute to be paid to England after the unfortunate war of 1840, the great unproductive consumption of opium, the drain of the precious metals by this trade, the destructive influence of foreign competition on native manufactures, the demoralized condition of the public administration, produced two things: the old taxation became more burdensome and harassing, and new taxation was added to the old. Thus in a decree of the emperor, dated Peking, 5 January 1853, we find orders given to the viceroys and governors of the southern provinces of Wuchang and Hanyang[42] to remit and defer the payment of taxes and especially not in any case to exact more than the regular amount; for otherwise, says the decree, 'how will the poor people be able to bear it?' 'And thus, perhaps,' continues the emperor, 'will my people, in a period of general hardship and distress, be exempted from the evils of being pursued and worried by the tax-gatherer.'

Such language as this, and such concessions, we remember to have heard from Austria, the China of Germany, in 1848.

41. I.e., the United States. This is presumably an interpolation by the *Tribune* editor. Marx frequently had occasion to complain of editorial distortion of his contributions, especially when, as with the present piece, they were used as leading articles.

42. Wuchang and Hanyang are in fact cities in Hupei province.

All these dissolving agencies, acting together on the finances, the morals, the industry and political structure of China, received their full development under the English cannon in 1840, which broke down the authority of the emperor and forced the Celestial Empire into contact with the terrestrial world. Complete isolation was the prime condition of the preservation of old China. That isolation having come to a violent end by the medium of England, dissolution must follow as surely as that of any mummy carefully preserved in a hermetically sealed coffin whenever it is brought into contact with the open air. Now, England having brought about the revolution of China, the question is how that revolution will in time react on England, and through England on Europe. This question is not difficult of solution.

The attention of our readers has often been called to the unparalleled growth of British manufactures since 1850. Amid the most surprising prosperity, it has not been difficult to point out the clear symptoms of an approaching industrial crisis. Notwithstanding California and Australia,[43] notwithstanding the immense and unprecedented emigration, there must ever, without any particular accident, in due time arrive a moment when the extension of the markets is unable to keep pace with the extension of British manufactures, and this disproportion must bring about a new crisis with the same certainty as it has done in the past. But if one of the great markets suddenly becomes contracted, the arrival of the crisis is necessarily accelerated thereby. Now, the Chinese rebellion must, for the time being, have precisely this effect upon England. The necessity for opening new markets, or for extending the old ones, was one of the principal causes of the reduction of the British tea duties, as, with an increased importation of tea, an increased exportation of manufactures to China was expected to take place. Now, the value of the annual exports from the United Kingdom to China amounted, before the repeal in 1833 of the trading monopoly possessed by the East India Company, to only £600,000; in 1836 it reached the sum of £1,326,388; in 1845 it had risen to £2,394,827; in 1852 it amounted to about £3,000,000. The quantity of tea imported from China did not exceed, in 1793, 16,167,331 lb.; but in 1845 it amounted to 50,714,657 lb.; in 1846 to 57,584,561 lb.; it is now above 60,000,000 lb.

The tea crop of the last season will not prove short, as shown

43. I.e., the gold discoveries of 1848 and 1851 respectively.

already by the export lists from Shanghai, of 2,000,000 lb. above the preceding year. This excess is to be accounted for by two circumstances. On one hand, the state of the market at the close of 1851 was much depressed, and the large surplus stock left has been thrown into the export of 1852. On the other hand, the recent accounts of the altered British legislation with regard to imports of tea reaching China have brought forward all the available teas to a ready market, at greatly enhanced prices. But with respect to the coming crop the case stands very differently. This is shown by the following extracts from the correspondence of a large tea firm in London:

In Shanghai the terror is extreme. Gold has advanced upward of 25 per cent, *being eagerly sought for hoarding*; silver has so far disappeared that *none could be obtained* to pay the China dues on the British vessels requiring port clearance; and in consequence of which Mr Alcock[44] has consented to become responsible to the Chinese authorities for the payment of these dues, on receipt of East India Company's bills, or other approved securities. *The scarcity of the precious metals* is one of the most unfavourable features, when viewed in reference to the immediate future of commerce, as this abstraction occurs precisely at that period when their use is most needed, to enable the tea and silk buyers to go into the interior and effect their purchases, for which a *large portion of bullion is paid in advance, to enable the producers to carry on their operations* ... At this period of the year it is usual to begin making arrangements for the new teas, whereas at present nothing is talked of but the means of protecting person and property, all transactions being at a stand ... If the means are not applied to secure the leaves in April and May, the early crop, which includes all the finer descriptions, both of black and green teas, will be as much lost as unreaped wheat at Christmas.[45]

Now the means for securing the tea leaves will certainly not be given by the English, American or French squadrons stationed in the Chinese seas, but these may easily, by their interference, produce such complications as to cut off all transactions between the tea-producing interior and the tea-exporting sea ports. Thus, for the present crop, a rise in the prices must be expected – speculation has already commenced in London – and for the crop to come a large deficit is as good as certain. Nor is this all. The Chinese, ready though they may be, as are all people in

44. Sir Rutherford Alcock was the British consul at Peking.

45. This is quoted from a circular of Moffat & Co., published in the *Economist*, 21 May 1853. The italics are Marx's.

periods of revolutionary convulsion, to sell off to the foreigner all the bulky commodities they have on hand, will, as the Orientals are used to do in the apprehension of great changes, set to hoarding, not taking much in return for their tea and silk except hard money. England has accordingly to expect a rise in the price of one of her chief articles of consumption, a drain of bullion, and a great contraction of an important market for her cotton and woollen goods. Even the *Economist*, that optimist conjuror of all things menacing the tranquil minds of the mercantile community, is compelled to use language like this: 'We must not flatter ourselves with finding as extensive a market for our exports to China as hitherto ... It is more probable that our export trade to China should suffer, and that there should be a diminished demand for the produce of Manchester and Glasgow.'[46]

It must not be forgotten that the rise in the price of so indispensable an article as tea, and the contraction of so important a market as China, will coincide with a deficient harvest in western Europe and, therefore, with rising prices of meat, corn, and all other agricultural produce. Hence contracted markets for manufactures, because every rise in the prices of the first necessaries of life is counterbalanced, at home and abroad, by a corresponding reduction in the demand for manufactures. From every part of Great Britain complaints have been received on the backward state of most of the crops. The *Economist* says on this subject:

In the South of England not only will there be left much land unsown, until too late for a crop of any sort, but much of the sown land will prove to be foul, or otherwise in a bad state for corn-growing. On the wet or poor soils destined for wheat, signs that mischief is going on are apparent. The time for planting mangel-wurzel may now be said to have passed away, and very little has been planted, while the time for preparing land for the turnip is rapidly going by, without any adequate preparation for this important crop having been accomplished ... Oat-sowing has been much interfered with by the snow and rain. Few oats were sown early, and late sown oats seldom produce a large crop ... In many districts losses among the breeding flocks have been considerable.[47]

The price of other farm-produce than corn is from 20 to 30, and even 50 per cent higher than last year. On the Continent, corn has risen comparatively more than in England. Rye has risen in

46. 21 May 1853.   47. 14 May 1853.

Belgium and Holland full 100 per cent. Wheat and other grains are following suit.

Under these circumstances, as the greater part of the regular commercial circle has already been run through by British trade, it may safely be augured that the Chinese revolution will throw the spark into the overloaded mine of the present industrial system and cause the explosion of the long-prepared general crisis, which, spreading abroad, will be closely followed by political revolutions on the Continent. It would be a curious spectacle, that of China sending disorder into the Western world while the Western powers, by English, French and American war-steamers, are conveying 'order' to Shanghai, Nanking, and the mouths of the Great Canal. Do these order-mongering powers, which would attempt to support the wavering Manchu dynasty, forget that the hatred against foreigners and their exclusion from the Empire, once the mere result of China's geographical and ethnographical situation, have become a political system only since the conquest of the country by the race of the Manchu Tartars?[48] There can be no doubt that the turbulent dissensions among the European nations who, at the latter end of the seventeenth century, rivalled each other in the trade with China, lent a mighty aid to the exclusive policy adopted by the Manchus. But more than this was done by the fear of the new dynasty, lest the foreigners might favour the discontent existing among a large proportion of the Chinese during the first half century or thereabouts of their subjection to the Tartars. From these considerations, foreigners were then prohibited from all communication with the Chinese except through Canton, a town at a great distance from Peking and the tea districts, and their commerce restricted to intercourse with the Hong[49] merchants, licensed by the government expressly for the foreign trade, in order to keep the rest of its subjects from all connection with the odious strangers. In any case an interference on the part of the Western governments at this time can only serve to render the revolution more violent and protract the stagnation of trade.

48. The Manchu dynasty was established in 1644, by which time the Manchus had conquered the greater part of the country.

49. Ko Hong was a Canton merchants' guild, responsible to the Chinese government for import and export control, and therefore for the attempts to curb the opium trade. By the Nanking treaty the Chinese government undertook to dissolve the Hong.

At the same time it is to be observed with regard to India that the British government of that country depends for full one seventh of its revenue on the sale of opium to the Chinese, while a considerable proportion of the Indian demand for British manufactures depends on the production of that opium in India. The Chinese, it is true, are no more likely to renounce the use of opium than are the Germans to forswear tobacco. But as the new emperor is understood to be favourable to the culture of the poppy and the preparation of opium in China itself, it is evident that a death-blow is very likely to be struck at once at the business of opium-raising in India, the Indian revenue, and the commercial resources of Hindustan. Though this blow would not immediately be felt by the interests concerned, it would operate effectually in due time, and would come in to intensify and prolong the universal financial crisis whose horoscope we have cast above.

Since the commencement of the eighteenth century there has been no serious revolution in Europe which had not been preceded by a commercial and financial crisis. This applies no less to the revolution of 1789 than to that of 1848. It is true, not only that we every day behold more threatening symptoms of conflict between the ruling powers and their subjects, between the state and society, between the various classes; but also the conflict of the existing powers among each other gradually reaching that height where the sword must be drawn, and the *ultima ratio* of princes be recurred to. In the European capitals, every day brings dispatches big with universal war, vanishing under the dispatches of the following day, bearing the assurance of peace for a week or so. We may be sure, nevertheless, that to whatever height the conflict between the European powers may rise, however threatening the aspect of the diplomatic horizon may appear, whatever movements may be attempted by some enthusiastic fraction in this or that country, the rage of princes and the fury of the people are alike enervated by the breath of prosperity. Neither wars nor revolutions are likely to pull Europe by the ears, unless in consequence of a general commercial and industrial crisis, the signal of which has, as usual, to be given by England, the representative of European industry in the market of the world.

It is unnecessary to dwell on the political consequences such a crisis must produce in these times, with the unprecedented extension of factories in England, with the utter dissolution of her official parties, with the whole state machinery of France transformed into one immense swindling and stock-jobbing concern, with Austria on the eve of bankruptcy, with wrongs everywhere accumulated to be revenged by the people, with the conflicting interests of the reactionary powers themselves, and with the Russian dream of conquest once more revealed to the world.

Articles on the North American Civil War[1]

THE NORTH AMERICAN CIVIL WAR

London, 20 October 1861

For months now the leading London papers, both weekly and daily, have been repeating the same litany on the American Civil War. While they insult the free states of the North, they anxiously defend themselves against the suspicion of sympathizing with the slave states of the South. In fact, they continually write two articles: one in which they attack the North, another in which they excuse their attacks on the North. *Qui s'excuse, s'accuse*.[2]

Their extenuating arguments are basically as follow. The war between North and South is a tariff war. Furthermore, the war is not being fought over any issue of principle; it is not concerned with the question of slavery but in fact centres on the North's lust for sovereignty. In the final analysis, even if justice is on the side of the North, does it not remain a futile endeavour to subjugate eight million Anglo-Saxons by force! Would not a separation from the South release the North from all connection with Negro slavery and assure to it, with its 20 million inhabitants and its vast territory, a higher level of development up to now scarcely dreamt of? Should the North not then welcome secession as a happy event, instead of wanting to crush it by means of a bloody and futile civil war?

Let us examine point by point the case made out by the English press.

The war between North and South – so runs the first excuse – is merely a tariff war, a war between a protectionist system and a

1. The following two articles began a series of thirty-seven that Marx and Engels wrote on events in North America for the liberal Vienna paper *Die Presse*. They are translated here from the texts printed in *MEW* 15. This article appeared in the paper's edition of 25 October 1861.

2. He who excuses himself, accuses himself.

free-trade system; and England, of course, is on the side of free trade. Is the slave-owner to enjoy the fruits of slave labour to the full, or is he to be cheated of part of these fruits by the Northern protectionists? This is the question at issue in the war. It was reserved for *The Times* to make this brilliant discovery; the *Economist*, *Examiner*, *Saturday Review* and the like have elaborated on the same theme. It is characteristic that this discovery was made, not in Charleston, but in London. In America everyone knew, of course, that between 1846 and 1861 a system of free trade prevailed and that Representative Morrill only carried his protectionist tariff through Congress after the rebellion had already broken out. Secession did not take place, therefore, because Congress had passed the Morrill tariff; at most, the Morrill tariff was passed by Congress because secession had taken place. To be sure, when South Carolina had its first attack of secessionism in 1832 the protectionist tariff of 1828 served as a pretext; but that a pretext is all it was is shown by a statement made by General Jackson. This time, however, the old pretext has in fact not been repeated. In the secession Congress at Montgomery[3] every mention of the tariff question was avoided because in Louisiana, one of the most influential Southern states, the cultivation of sugar is based entirely on protection.

But, the London press pleads further, the war in the United States is nothing but a war aimed at preserving the Union by force. The Yankees cannot make up their minds to strike off fifteen stars from their banner.[4] They want to cut a colossal figure on the world stage. Indeed, it would be quite a different matter if the war were being fought in order to abolish slavery. But the slavery question, as the *Saturday Review*, among others, categorically declares, has absolutely nothing to do with this war.

It must be remembered above all that the war was started not by the North but by the South. The North is on the defensive. For months it had quietly stood by and watched while the secessionists took possession of forts, arsenals, shipyards, customs houses, pay offices, ships and stores of arms belonging to the Union, insulted its flag, and took Northern troops prisoner. The

3. The Congress of Montgomery founded, on 4 February 1861, the Confederate States of America, with eleven member states, under the presidency of Jefferson Davis.

4. This total includes the contested border states which the South also claimed.

secessionists finally decided to force the Union government out of its passive stance by means of a blatant act of war; *for no other reason than this* they proceeded to bombard Fort Sumter near Charleston. On 11 April [1861] their General Beauregard had learnt in a meeting with Major Anderson, the commander of Fort Sumter, that the fort only had rations for three more days and that it would therefore have to be surrendered peacefully after this period. In order to forestall this peaceful surrender the secessionists opened the bombardment early the next morning (12 April), bringing about the fall of the place after a few hours. Hardly had this news been telegraphed to Montgomery, the seat of the secession Congress, when War Minister Walker declared publicly in the name of the new Confederacy: 'No man can say where *the war opened today* will end.' At the same time he prophesied that before the first of May the flag of the Southern Confederacy would wave from the dome of the old Capitol in Washington and within a short time perhaps also from the Faneuil Hall in Boston. Only then did Lincoln issue the proclamation summoning 75,000 men to protect the Union. The bombardment of Fort Sumter cut off the only possible constitutional way out: the summoning of a general convention of the American people, as Lincoln had proposed in his inaugural address. As it was, Lincoln was left with the choice of fleeing from Washington, evacuating Maryland and Delaware, surrendering Kentucky, Missouri and Virginia, or of answering war with war.

The question as to the principle underlying the American Civil War is answered by the battle slogan with which the South broke the peace. [Alexander H.] Stephens, the Vice-President of the Southern Confederacy, declared in the secession Congress that what fundamentally distinguished the constitution recently hatched in Montgomery from that of Washington and Jefferson was that slavery was now recognized for the first time as an institution good in itself and as the foundation of the whole political edifice, whereas the revolutionary fathers, men encumbered by the prejudices of the eighteenth century, had treated slavery as an evil imported from England and to be eradicated in the course of time. Another Southern matador, Mr Spratt, declared, 'For us it is a question of the foundation of a great slave republic.' Thus if the North drew its sword only in defence of the Union, had not the South already declared that the continuance of slavery was no longer compatible with the continuance of the Union?

Just as the bombardment of Fort Sumter gave the signal for the opening of the war, the electoral victory of the Northern Republican party, Lincoln's election to the presidency, had given the signal for secession. Lincoln was elected on 6 November 1860. On 8 November the message was telegraphed from South Carolina, 'Secession is regarded here as an accomplished fact'; on 10 November the Georgia legislature occupied itself with plans for secession, and on 13 November a special sitting of the Mississippi legislature was called to consider secession. But Lincoln's election was itself only the result of a split in the Democratic camp. During the election campaign the Northern Democrats concentrated their votes on Douglas, the Southern Democrats on [John C.] Breckinridge; the Republican party owed its victory to this split in the Democratic vote. How, on the one hand, did the Republican party achieve this dominant position in the North; how, on the other hand, did this division arise *within* the Democratic party, whose members, North and South, had operated in conjunction for more than half a century?

Buchanan's presidency[5] saw the control which the South had gradually usurped over the Union as a result of its alliance with the Northern Democrats, reach its peak. The last Continental Congress of 1787 and the first constitutional Congress of 1789–90 had legally excluded slavery from all territories of the republic north-west of Ohio. (Territories are the colonies lying within the United States which have not yet achieved the population level laid down in the Constitution for the formation of autonomous states.) The so-called Missouri Compromise (1820), as a result of which Missouri entered the ranks of the United States as a slave-owning state, excluded slavery from all other territories north of 36° 30′ latitude and west of the Missouri. As a result of this compromise the area of slavery was extended by several degrees of longitude while, on the other hand, quite definite geographical limits seemed to be placed on its future propagation. This geographical barrier was in turn torn down by the so-called Kansas-Nebraska Bill, whose author, Stephen A. Douglas, was at the time leader of the Northern Democrats. This bill, which passed both Houses of Congress, repealed the Missouri Compromise, placed slavery and freedom on an equal footing, enjoined the Union government to treat both with indifference, and left it to the

5. James Buchanan was U.S. President from 1857 to 1861.

sovereign people to decide whether slavery was to be introduced in a territory or not. Thus, for the first time in the history of the United States, every geographical and legal barrier in the way of an extension of slavery in the territories was removed. Under this new legislation the hitherto free territory of New Mexico, an area five times greater than New York state, was transformed into a slave territory, and the area of slavery was extended from the Mexican republic to latitude 38° north. In 1859 New Mexico was given a legal slave code which vies in barbarity with the statute-books of Texas and Alabama. However, as the 1860 census shows, New Mexico does not yet have fifty slaves in a population of about 100,000. The South therefore only had to send over the border a few adventurers with some slaves and, with the help of the central government in Washington, get its officials and contractors to drum up a sham representative body in New Mexico, in order to impose slavery and the rule of the slave-holders on the territory.

However, this convenient method proved inapplicable in the other territories. The South, therefore, went one step further and appealed from Congress to the Supreme Court of the United States. This Supreme Court, which numbers nine judges, five of whom are Southerners, had long been the most amenable instrument of the slave-holders. In 1857, in the notorious Dred Scott case, it decided that every American citizen had the right to take with him into any territory any property recognized by the Constitution. The Constitution recognizes slaves as property and commits the Union government to the protection of this property. Consequently, on the basis of the Constitution, slaves could be forced by their owners to work in the territories and thus every individual slave-holder was entitled to introduce slavery into territories hitherto free against the will of the majority of the settlers. The territorial legislatures were denied the right to exclude slavery, and Congress and the Union government were charged with the duty of protecting the pioneers of the slave system.

While the Missouri Compromise of 1820 had extended the geographical boundaries of slavery in the territories, and while the Kansas-Nebraska Bill of 1854 had eliminated all geographical boundaries and replaced them by a political barrier – the will of the majority of the settlers – the Supreme Court's decision of 1857 tore down even this political barrier and transformed all territories of the republic, present and future, from nurseries of free states into nurseries of slavery.

At the same time, under Buchanan's administration, the more severe law of 1850 on the extradition of fugitive slaves was ruthlessly carried out in the Northern states. It seemed to be the constitutional calling of the North to play slave-catcher for the Southern slave-holders. On the other hand, in order to hinder as far as possible the colonization of the territories by free settlers, the slave-holders' party frustrated all so-called free-soil measures, that is, measures intended to guarantee the settlers a fixed amount of uncultivated public land free of charge.

As in domestic policy, so also in the foreign policy of the United States the interests of the slave-holders served as the guiding star. Buchanan had in fact purchased the presidential office by issuing the Ostend Manifesto,[6] in which the acquisition of Cuba, whether by payment or by force of arms, is proclaimed as the great political task of the nation. Under his administration northern Mexico had already been divided up among American land speculators, who were impatiently awaiting the signal to fall upon Chihuahua, Coahuila and Sonora. The incessant piratical filibusters against the Central American states were no less carried out under the direction of the White House in Washington.[7] Closely connected with this foreign policy, which was manifestly aimed at conquering new territory for the expansion of slavery and the rule of the slave-holders, was the *resumption of the slave trade*, secretly supported by the Union government. Stephen A. Douglas himself declared in the American Senate on 20 August 1859 that during the previous year more Negroes had been requisitioned from Africa than ever before in any single year, even at the time when the slave trade was still legal. The number of slaves imported in the last year amounted to fifteen thousand.

Armed propaganda abroad on behalf of slavery was the avowed aim of national policy; the Union had in fact become the slave of the 300,000 slave-holders who rule the South. This state of affairs had been brought about by a series of compromises which the South owed to its alliance with the Northern Democrats. All the periodic attempts made since 1817 to resist the ever-increasing

6. The Ostend Manifesto was issued in 1854 by the United States ambassadors to Spain, France and England (the latter being Buchanan); it contained an offer to purchase Cuba from Spain and threatened to seize it by force if Spain refused.

7. Nicaragua was the particular object of these expeditions.

encroachments of the slave-holders had come to grief against this alliance. Finally there came a turning point.

Hardly had the Kansas-Nebraska Bill been passed, erasing the geographical boundary of slavery and making its introduction into new territories subject to the will of the majority of the settlers, when armed emissaries of the slave-holders, border rabble from Missouri and Arkansas, fell upon Kansas, a bowie-knife in one hand and a revolver in the other, and with the most atrocious barbarity tried to drive out its settlers from the territory which they had colonized. As these raids were supported by the central government in Washington, a tremendous reaction ensued. In the whole of the North, but particularly in the North-west, a relief organization was formed to provide support for Kansas in the shape of men, weapons and money. Out of this relief organization grew the Republican party, which thus has its origins in the struggle for Kansas. After the failure of the attempts to transform Kansas into a slave territory by force of arms the South tried to achieve the same result by way of political intrigue. Buchanan's administration, in particular, did its utmost to manoeuvre Kansas into the ranks of the United States as a slave state by the imposition of a slave constitution. Hence a new struggle took place this time conducted for the most part in the Washington Congress. Even Stephen A. Douglas, leader of the Northern Democrats, now (1857–8) entered the lists, against the administration and against his Southern allies, because the imposition of a slave constitution would contradict the principle of settlers' sovereignty passed in the Nebraska Bill of 1854. Douglas, Senator for Illinois, a north-western state, would naturally have forfeited all his influence if he had wanted to concede to the South the right to steal by force of arms or acts of Congress the territories colonized by the North. Thus while the struggle for Kansas gave birth to the Republican party, it simultaneously gave rise to the first split within the Democratic party itself.

The Republican party issued its first programme for the presidential election of 1856. Although its candidate, John Frémont, did not win, the huge number of votes cast for him demonstrated the rapid growth of the party, particularly in the North-west. In their second national convention for the presidential election (17 May 1860), the Republicans repeated their programme of 1856, enriched by only a few additional points. Its main contents were that not a foot of new territory would be conceded to slavery, and that the filibustering policy abroad must cease; the resumption of the slave trade was condemned, and lastly, free-soil laws would be enacted in order to further free colonization.

The point of decisive importance in this programme was that slavery was not to be conceded another foot of new ground; rather it was to remain confined once and for all within the limits of the states where it already legally existed. Slavery was thus to be interned for good. However, permanent territorial expansion and the continual extension of slavery beyond its old borders is a law of existence for the slave states of the Union.

The cultivation of the Southern export crops, i.e., cotton, tobacco, sugar, etc., by slaves is only profitable so long as it is conducted on a mass scale by large gangs of slaves and in wide areas of naturally fertile soil requiring only simple labour. Intensive cultivation, which depends less on the fertility of the soil and more on capital investment and on intelligent and energetic labour, runs contrary to the nature of slavery. Hence the rapid transformation of states such as Maryland and Virginia, which in earlier times employed slavery in the production of export commodities, into states which raise slaves in order to export them to states lying further south. Even in South Carolina, where slaves form four sevenths of the population, the cultivation of cotton has remained almost stationary for years due to the exhaustion of the soil. Indeed, South Carolina has become partly transformed into a slave-raising state by pressure of circumstances in so far as it already sells slaves to the states of the deep South and South-west to a value of four million dollars annually. As soon as this point is reached the acquisition of new territory becomes necessary, so that one section of the slave-holders can introduce slave labour into new fertile estates and thus create a new market for slave-raising and the sale of slaves by the section it has left behind. There is not the least doubt, for example, that without the acquisition of Louisiana, Missouri and Arkansas by the United States, slavery would long ago have disappeared in Virginia and Maryland. In the secession Congress at Montgomery one of the Southern spokesmen, Senator Toombs, strikingly formulated the economic law that necessitates the constant expansion of the slave territory. 'In fifteen years more,' he said, 'without a great increase in slave territory, either the slaves must be permitted to flee from the whites, or the whites must flee from the slaves.'

As is well known, individual states are represented in the

Congressional House of Representatives according to the size of their respective populations. Since the population of the free states is growing incomparably more quickly than that of the slave states, the number of Northern representatives has inevitably overtaken the number of Southerners. The actual seat of Southern political power, therefore, is being transferred more and more to the American Senate, where every state, whether its population is great or small, is represented by two senators. In order to assert its influence in the Senate and, through the Senate, its hegemony over the United States, the South thus needed a continual formation of new slave states. But this could only be brought about by conquering foreign countries, as in the case of Texas, or by transforming the United States territories first into slave territories, later into slave states, as in the case of Missouri, Arkansas, etc. John Calhoun, whom the slave-holders admire as their statesman *par excellence*, declared in the Senate as early as 19 February 1847 that only the Senate offered the South the means of restoring a balance of power between South and North, that the extension of the slave territory was necessary to restore this balance and that therefore the attempts of the South to create new slave states by force were justified.

When it comes down to it the number of actual slave-holders in the South of the Union is not more than 300,000; an exclusive oligarchy confronted by the many million so-called 'poor whites', whose number has constantly grown as a result of the concentration of landed property, and whose situation can only be compared with that of the Roman plebeians in the direst period of Rome's decline. Only with the acquisition of new territories, the prospect of such acquisition, and filibustering expeditions, is it possible to harmonize the interests of these 'poor whites' successfully with those of the slave-holders, to channel their restless thirst for action in a harmless direction and to tempt them with the prospect of becoming slave-holders themselves one day.

As a result of economic laws, then, to confine slavery to the limits of its old terrain would inevitably have led to its gradual extinction; politically it would have destroyed the hegemony exercised by the slave states by way of the Senate; and finally it would have exposed the slave-holding oligarchy to ominous dangers within their own states from the 'poor whites'. With the principle that every further extension of slave territories was to be prohibited by law the Republicans therefore mounted a radical attack on the rule of the slave-holders. Consequently, the Republican election victory could not help but lead to open struggle between North and South. However, as has already been mentioned, this election victory was itself conditioned by the split in the Democratic camp.

The Kansas struggle had already provoked a split between the slave party and its Democratic allies in the North. The same quarrel now broke out again in a more general form with the presidential election of 1860. The Northern Democrats, with Douglas as their candidate, made the introduction of slavery into the territories dependent upon the will of the majority of settlers. The slave-holders' party, with Breckinridge as its candidate, asserted that the Constitution of the United States, as the Supreme Court had also declared, made legal provision for slavery; slavery was in actual fact already legal in all territories and did not require special naturalization. Thus, while the Republicans prohibited any growth of slave territories, the Southern party laid claim to all territories as legally warranted domains. What they had tried, for instance, with Kansas – imposing slavery on a territory against the will of the settlers themselves, by way of the central government – they now held up as a law for all Union territories. Such a concession lay beyond the power of the Democratic leaders and would only have caused their army to desert to the Republican camp. On the other hand Douglas's 'settlers' sovereignty' could not satisfy the slave-holders' party. What the slave-holders wanted to achieve had to be brought about in the next four years under the new President; it could only be brought about by means of the central government and could not be delayed any longer. It did not escape the slave-holders' notice that a new power had arisen, the North-west, whose population, which had almost doubled between 1850 and 1860, was already more or less equal to the white population of the slave states – a power which neither by tradition, temperament nor way of life was inclined to let itself be dragged from compromise to compromise in the fashion of the old Northern states. The Union was only of value for the South in so far as it let it use federal power as a means of implementing its slave policy. If it did not, it was better to break now than to watch the development of the Republican party and the rapid growth of the North-west for another four years, and to begin the struggle under less favourable conditions. The slave-holders' party, therefore, now staked its all!

When the Northern Democrats refused to play the role of the Southern 'poor whites' any longer, the South brought about Lincoln's victory by splitting the votes and used this victory as an excuse for drawing the sword.

As is clear, the whole movement was and is based on the *slave question*. Not in the sense of whether the slaves within the existing slave states should be directly emancipated or not, but whether the twenty million free Americans of the North should subordinate themselves any longer to an oligarchy of 300,000 slave-holders; whether the vast territories of the Republic should become the nurseries of free states or of slavery; finally whether the foreign policy of the Union should take the armed propaganda of slavery as its device throughout Mexico, Central and South America.

In a foreign article we shall examine the assertion of the London press that the North should sanction secession as the most favourable and only possible solution of the conflict.

THE CIVIL WAR IN THE UNITED STATES[8]

'Let him go, he is not worth thine ire!'[9] This advice from Leporello to Don Juan's deserted love is now the repeated call of English statesmanship to the North of the United States – recently voiced anew by Lord John Russell. If the North lets the South go, it will free itself from any complicity in slavery – its historical original sin – and it will create the basis for a new and higher stage of development.

Indeed, if North and South formed two autonomous countries like England and Hanover, for instance, their separation would be no more difficult than was the separation of England and Hanover. 'The South', however, is neither geographically clearly separate from the North nor is it a moral entity. It is not a country at all, but a battle-cry.

The advice of an amicable separation presupposes that the Southern Confederacy, although it took the offensive in the Civil War, is at least conducting it for defensive purposes. It presupposes that the slave-holders' party is concerned only to unite the areas it has controlled up till now into an autonomous group of states, and to release them from the domination of the Union. Nothing could be more wrong. '*The South needs its entire territory*. It will

8. From *Die Presse* of 7 November 1861.
9. From Byron's *Don Juan*. Leporello's advice was mischievous in its intent.

and must have it.' This was the battle-cry with which the secessionists fell upon Kentucky. By their 'entire territory' they understand primarily all the so-called *border states*: Delaware, Maryland, Virginia, North Carolina, Kentucky, Tennessee, Missouri and Arkansas. Moreover, they claim the whole territory south of the line which runs from the north-west corner of Missouri to the Pacific Ocean. Thus what the slave-holders call 'the South' covers more than three quarters of the present area of the Union. A large part of the territory which they claim is still in the possession of the Union and would first have to be conquered from it. But none of the so-called border states, including those in Confederate possession, was ever *an actual slave state*. The border states form, rather, that area of the United States where the system of slavery and the system of free labour exist side by side and struggle for mastery: the actual battle-ground between South and North, between slavery and freedom. The war waged by the Southern Confederacy is, therefore, not a war of defence but a war of conquest, aimed at extending and perpetuating slavery.

The chain of mountains which begins in Alabama and stretches North to the Hudson River – in a manner of speaking the spinal column of the United States – cuts the so-called South into three parts. The mountainous country formed by the Allegheny Mountains with their two parallel ranges, the Cumberland Range to the west and the Blue Ridge Mountains to the east, forms a wedgelike division between the lowlands along the western coast of the Atlantic Ocean and the lowlands of the southern valleys of the Mississippi. The two lowland regions separated by this mountain country form, with their vast rice swamps and wide expanses of cotton-plantations, the actual area of slavery. The long wedge of mountain country which penetrates into the heart of slavery, with its correspondingly freer atmosphere, invigorating climate and soil rich in coal, salt, limestone, iron ore and gold – in short, every raw material necessary for diversified industrial development – is for the most part already a free country. As a result of its physical composition the soil here can only be successfully cultivated by free small farmers. The slave system vegetates here only as a sporadic growth and has never struck roots. In the largest part of the so-called border states it is the inhabitants of these highland regions who comprise the core of the free population, which out of self-interest, if nothing else, has sided with the Northern party.

Let us consider the contested area in detail.

Delaware, the north-easternmost of the border states, belongs to the Union both morally and in actual fact. Since the beginning of the war all attempts on the part of the secessionists to form even a faction favourable to them have come to grief against the unanimity of the population. The slave element in this state has long been dying out. Between 1850 and 1860 alone the number of slaves declined by a half, so that Delaware now has only 1,798 slaves out of a total population of 112,218. Nevertheless, the Southern Confederacy lays claim to Delaware, and it would in fact be militarily untenable as soon as the South took control of Maryland.

Maryland exhibits the above-mentioned conflict between highlands and lowlands. Out of a total population of 687,034 there are in Maryland 87,188 slaves. The recent general elections to the Washington Congress have again forcefully proved that the overwhelming majority of the people sides with the Union. The army of 30,000 Union troops at present occupying Maryland is not only to serve as a reserve for the army on the Potomac, but also to hold the rebellious slave-holders in the interior of the state in check. Here a phenomenon can be seen similar to those in other border states, i.e., that the great mass of the people sides with the North and a numerically insignificant slave-holders' party sides with the South. What the slave-holders' party lacks in numbers it makes up for in the instruments of power, secured by many years' possession of all state offices, an hereditary preoccupation with political intrigue, and the concentration of great wealth in a few hands.

Virginia at present forms the great cantonment where the main secessionist army and the main Unionist army confront each other. In the north-west highlands of Virginia the slaves number 15,000, while the free majority, which is twenty times as large, consists for the most part of independent farmers. The eastern lowlands of Virginia, on the other hand, have almost half a million slaves. The raising and selling of Negroes represents its main source of income. As soon as the lowland ringleaders had carried through the secession ordinance in the state legislature at Richmond, by means of intrigue, and had in all haste thrown open the gates of Virginia to the Southern army, north-western Virginia seceded from the secession and formed a new state; it took up arms under the banner of the Union and is now defending its territory against the Southern invaders.

Tennessee, with 1,109,847 inhabitants, of whom 275,784 are slaves, is in the hands of the Southern Confederacy, which has placed the whole state under martial law and imposed a system of proscription which recalls the days of the Roman triumvirate. In the winter of 1860–61, when the slave-holders suggested a general people's convention to vote on the question of secession, the majority of the people turned down a convention in order to forestall any pretext for the secessionist movement. Later, when Tennessee had been militarily overrun by the Southern Confederacy and had been subjected to a system of terror, a third of the voters in the elections still declared themselves in favour of the Union. As in most of the border states, the actual centre of resistance to the slave-holders' party here is to be found in the mountainous country, in east Tennessee. On 17 June 1861 a general convention of the people of east Tennessee assembled in Greenville, declared itself for the Union, delegated the former Governor of the state, Andrew Johnson, one of the most ardent Unionists, to the Senate in Washington and published a 'declaration of grievances', which exposes all the deception, intrigue and terror used to 'vote out' Tennessee from the Union. Since then the secessionists have held east Tennessee in check by force of arms.

Similar situations to those in West Virginia and east Tennessee are to be found in the north of Alabama, north-west Georgia and the north of North Carolina.

Farther west in the border state of Missouri, whose population of 1,173,317 includes 114,965 slaves – the latter mostly concentrated in the north-western area of the state – the people's convention of August 1861 decided in favour of the Union. Jackson, the Governor of the state and tool of the slave-holders' party, rebelled against the Missouri legislature and was outlawed; he then put himself at the head of the armed hordes which fell upon Missouri from Texas, Arkansas and Tennessee in order to bring it to its knees before the Confederacy and to sever its bond with the Union by the sword. Next to Virginia, Missouri represents the main theatre of the civil war at the moment.

New Mexico – not a state, but merely a territory, whose twenty-five slaves were imported under Buchanan's presidency so that a slave constitution could be sent after them from Washington – has felt no enthusiasm for the South, as even the South concedes. But the South's enthusiasm for New Mexico caused it to spew a band of armed adventurers over the border from Texas. New

Mexico has entreated the Union government for protection against these liberators.

As will have been noticed, we lay particular stress on the numerical proportion of slaves to free citizens in the individual border states. This proportion is in fact of decisive importance. It is the thermometer with which the vitality of the slave system must be measured. The very soul of the whole secessionist movement is to be found in South Carolina. It has 402,541 slaves to 301,127 free men. Second comes Mississippi, which gave the Southern Confederacy its dictator, Jefferson Davis. It has 436,696 slaves to 354,699 free men. Third comes Alabama, with 435,132 slaves to 529,164 free men.

The last of the contested border states which we still have to mention is Kentucky. Its recent history is particularly characteristic of the policy of the Southern Confederacy. Kentucky, with 1,135,713 inhabitants, has 225,490 slaves. In three successive general elections (in winter 1860–61, when delegates were elected for a congress of the border states; June 1861, when the elections for the Washington Congress were held; and finally in August 1861 in the elections for the Kentucky state legislature) an increasing majority decided in favour of the Union. On the other hand, Magoffin, the Governor of Kentucky, and all the state dignitaries are fanatical supporters of the slave-holders' party, as is Breckinridge, Kentucky's representative in the Senate at Washington, Vice-President of the United States under Buchanan and presidential candidate of the slave-holders' party in 1860. Although the influence of the slave-holders' party was too weak to win Kentucky for secession, it was powerful enough to tempt it into a declaration of neutrality at the outbreak of war. The Confederacy recognized its neutrality as long as it suited its purpose, as long as it was busy crushing the resistance in east Tennessee. No sooner had this been achieved when it hammered on the gates of Kentucky with the butt-end of a gun: '*The South needs its entire territory*. It will and must have it!'

At the same time a corps of Confederate freebooters invaded the 'neutral' state from the south-west and south-east. Kentucky awoke from its dream of neutrality; its legislature openly sided with the Union, surrounded the treacherous Governor with a committee of public safety, called the people to arms, outlawed Breckinridge and ordered the secessionists to withdraw immediately from the area which they had invaded. This was the signal for war. A Confederate army is moving in on Louisville while volunteers stream in from Illinois, Indiana and Ohio to save Kentucky from the armed missionaries of slavery.

The attempts made by the Confederacy to annex Missouri and Kentucky, for example, expose the hollowness of the pretext that it is fighting for the rights of the individual states against the encroachment of the Union. To be sure, it acknowledges the rights of the individual states which it counts as belonging to the 'South' to break away from the Union, but by no means their right to remain in the Union.

No matter how much slavery, the war without and military dictatorship within give the actual slave states a temporary semblance of harmony, even they are not without dissident elements. Texas, with 180,388 slaves out of 601,039 inhabitants is a striking example. The law of 1845, by virtue of which Texas entered the ranks of the United States as a slave state, entitled it to form not just one but five states out of its territory. As a result the South would have won ten instead of two new votes in the American Senate; and an increase in the number of its votes in the Senate was a major political objective at that time. From 1845 to 1860, however, the slave-holders found it impracticable to split up Texas – where the German population plays a great part[10] – into even two states without giving the party of free labour the upper hand over the party of slavery. This is the best proof of how strong the opposition to the slave-holders' oligarchy is in Texas itself.

Georgia is the biggest and most populous of the slave states. With a total of 1,057,327 inhabitants it has 462,230 slaves; that is, nearly half the population. Nevertheless, the slave-holders' party has not yet succeeded in having the constitution which it imposed on the South at Montgomery sanctioned in Georgia by a general vote of the people.

In the Louisiana state convention, which met on 21 March 1861 at New Orleans, Roselius, the state's political veteran, declared: 'The Montgomery constitution is not a constitution, but a conspiracy. It does not inaugurate a government by the people, but *a detestable and unrestricted oligarchy*. The people were not permitted to play any part in this matter. The Convention of

10. The German Texans, who formed in the 1850s about one fifth of the state's white population, included a large proportion of refugees from the 1848 revolution.

Montgomery has dug the grave of political liberty and now we are summoned to attend its funeral.'

The oligarchy of 300,000 slave-holders used the Montgomery Congress not only to proclaim the separation of the South from the North; it also exploited the Congress to overturn the internal system of government of the slave states, to completely subjugate that part of the white population which had still maintained some degree of independence under the protection of the democratic Constitution of the Union. Even between 1856 and 1860 the political spokesmen, lawyers, moralists and theologians of the slave-holders' party had tried to prove not so much that Negro slavery is justified but rather that colour is immaterial and that slavery is the lot of the working class everywhere.

It can be seen, then, that the war of the Southern Confederacy is, in the truest sense of the word, a war of conquest for the extension and perpetuation of slavery. The larger part of the border states and territories are still in the possession of the Union, whose side they have taken first by way of the ballot-box and then with arms. But for the Confederacy they count as 'the South', and it is trying to conquer them from the Union. In the border states which the Confederacy has for the time being occupied it holds the relatively free highland areas in check by means of martial law. Within the actual slave states themselves it is supplanting the democracy which existed hitherto by the unbridled oligarchy of 300,000 slave-holders.

By abandoning its plans for conquest the Southern Confederacy would abandon its own economic viability and the very purpose of secession. Indeed, secession only took place because it no longer seemed possible to bring about the transformation of the border states and territories within the Union. On the other hand, with a peaceful surrender of the contested area to the Southern Confederacy the North would relinquish more than three quarters of the entire territory of the United States to the slave republic. The North would lose the Gulf of Mexico completely, the Atlantic Ocean with the exception of the narrow stretch from the Penobscot estuary to Delaware Bay, and would even cut itself off from the Pacific Ocean. Missouri, Kansas, New Mexico, Arkansas and Texas would be followed by California. Unable to wrest the mouth of the Mississippi from the hands of the strong, hostile slave republic in the South, the great agricultural states in the basin between the Rocky Mountains and the Alleghenies, in the valleys of the Mississippi, Missouri and Ohio, would be forced by economic interests to secede from the North and to join the Southern Confederacy. These North-western states would in turn draw the other Northern states lying further east after them – with the possible exception of New England – into the same vortex of secession.

The Union would thus not in fact be dissolved, but rather *reorganized*, a *reorganization on the basis of slavery*, under the acknowledged control of the slave-holding oligarchy. The plan for such a reorganization was openly proclaimed by the leading Southern spokesmen at the Montgomery Congress and accounts for the article of the new constitution which leaves open the possibility of each state of the old Union joining the new Confederacy. The slave system would thus infect the whole Union. In the Northern states, where Negro slavery is, in practice, inoperable, the whole working class would be gradually reduced to the level of helotry. This would be in full accord with the loudly proclaimed principle that only certain races are capable of freedom, and as in the South actual labour is the lot of the Negroes, so in the North it is the lot of the Germans and Irish or their direct descendants.

The present struggle between South and North is thus nothing less than a struggle between two social systems: the system of slavery and the system of free labour. The struggle has broken out because the two systems can no longer peacefully co-exist on the North American continent. It can only be ended by the victory of one system or the other.

While the border states, the contested areas in which the two systems have so far fought for control, are a thorn in the flesh of the South, it cannot, on the other hand, be overlooked that they have formed the North's main weak point in the course of the war. Some of the slave-holders in these districts feigned loyalty to the North at the bidding of the Southern conspirators; others indeed found that it accorded with their real interests and traditional outlook to side with the Union. Both groups have equally crippled the North. Anxiety to keep the 'loyal' slave-holders of the border states in good humour and fear of driving them into the arms of the secession, in a word, a tender regard for the interests, prejudices and sensibilities of these ambiguous allies, have afflicted the Union government with incurable paralysis since the beginning of the war, driven it to take half-measures, forced it to hypocritically disavow the principle at issue in the war and to spare the enemy's most vulnerable spot – the root of the evil – *slavery itself*.

When Lincoln recently was faint-hearted enough to revoke Frémont's Missouri proclamation emancipating Negroes belonging to the rebels,[11] this was only in deference to the loud protest of the 'loyal' slave-holders of Kentucky. However, a turning point has already been reached. With Kentucky the last border state has been pressed into the series of battlefields between South and North. With the real war for the border states being conducted in the border states themselves, the question of winning or losing them has been withdrawn from the sphere of diplomatic and parliamentary negotiations. One section of the slave-holders will cast off its loyalist mask; the other will content itself with the prospect of compensation, such as Great Britain gave the West Indian planters.[12] Events themselves demand that the decisive pronouncement be made: *the emancipation of the slaves*.

Several recent declarations demonstrate that even the most obdurate Northern Democrats and diplomats feel themselves drawn to this point. In an open letter General Cass, War Minister under Buchanan and hitherto one of the South's most ardent allies, declares the emancipation of the slaves to be the *sine qua non* for the salvation of the Union. Dr Brownson, the spokesman of the Northern Catholic party, and according to his own admission the most energetic opponent of the emancipation movement between 1836 and 1860, published in his last *Review* for October an article *in favour of* abolition. Among other things he says, 'If we have opposed Abolition heretofore because we would preserve the Union, we must *a fortiori* now oppose slavery whenever, in our judgement, its continuance becomes incompatible with the maintenance of the Union, or of the nation as a free republican state.'[13]

Finally, the *World*, a New York organ of the Washington

---

11. General Frémont, the first Republican candidate for the presidency in 1856, issued this proclamation in August 1861 and began granting freedom to slaves on his military authority. Lincoln soon ordered Frémont to stop these measures.

12. In 1833 the British government paid West Indian planters £2 for every slave set free.

13. *Brownson's Quarterly Review*, 3rd New York Series, New York, 1861, vol. II, pp. 510–46.

Cabinet's diplomats, closes one of its latest tirades against the abolitionists with these words: 'On the day when it shall be decided that either slavery or the Union must go down, on that day sentence of death is passed on slavery. If the North cannot triumph *without* emancipation, it will triumph *with* emancipation.'

Proclamation on Poland by the German Workers Educational Association in London[1]

October 1863

In agreement with an agent of the Polish National Government,[2] the German Workers Educational Association in London has authorized the undersigned committee to organize a collection for Poland among the German workers in England, Germany, Switzerland and the United States. Even though the material support given to the Poles in this way will be but little, the moral support provided by the collection will be great.

The Polish question and the German question are identical. Without an independent Poland there can be no independent and united Germany, nor can Germany be emancipated from Russian domination, which began with the first partition of Poland.[3] The German aristocracy have long regarded the tsar as the secret master of their nation. Mute, inactive and indifferent, the German bourgeoisie stands by and watches the butchery of the heroic nation which alone continues to protect Germany from the Muscovite deluge. Another section of the bourgeoisie realizes the danger but

1. This proclamation was written by Marx at the request of the German Workers Educational Association and distributed as a leaflet among the German workers in England and elsewhere. It is translated here from the text reproduced in *MEW* 15. The German Workers Educational Association had been a front organization for the secret Communist League, but survived the latter's dissolution in 1852. When the League split in 1850, Marx and his followers withdrew from the Association, but in the late 1850s there was a rapprochement. Marx's position on the Polish question is discussed in the Introductions to Volumes II and III.

2. The Polish National Committee, which directed the insurrection of January 1863, transformed itself in May into the Polish National Government. The insurrection had by this time been to all intents crushed by Prussian and Russian forces, although sporadic resistance continued until the end of 1864.

3. In 1772 Poland was first partitioned between Russia, Austria and Prussia. The third and final partition, which completely abolished Poland as an independent state, was in 1795.

readily sacrifices German interests to the interests of the particular
German states, whose survival is conditional upon the fragmentation of Germany and the maintenance of Russian hegemony. Another
section of the bourgeoisie regards the autocracy in the east in the
same light as the rule of the coup d'état in the west[4] – a necessary
buttress of *Order*. Finally, a third section is so utterly and completely
subservient to the important business of making money that it has
completely forfeited its ability to understand and recognize situations of great historical importance. With its noisy demonstrations
on behalf of Poland the German citizens of 1831 and 1832 at least
forced the Federal Diet to take forceful measures.[5] Today Poland
finds its most zealous opponents and Russia its most useful tools
among the liberal celebrities of the so-called National Association.[6]
Each can decide for himself how far this liberal pro-Russian sentiment is connected with the *Prussian élite*.

In this fateful hour the German working class owes it to the
Polish people, to countries abroad and to its own honour, to utter
the loudest possible protest against the German betrayal of Poland,
which is also a betrayal of Germany and Europe. It must inscribe
the *reunification of Poland* in flaming letters upon its banner now
that bourgeois liberalism has erased this glorious device from its
own. The English working class has reaped everlasting historic
honour by its enthusiastic mass meetings held to crush the repeated
attempts of the ruling classes to intervene on the side of the
American slave-holders, although the continuation of the American
Civil War has inflicted the most terrible suffering and privation on
a million English workers.[7]

Even though the activities of the police prevent the working
class in Germany from holding such large demonstrations for

4. I.e., the French Second Empire.

5. The national and democratic agitation of 1830–33 in Germany was sparked off
by the French revolution of July 1830, and solidarity with the Polish insurrection of
1831–2 was only one aspect of it. The 'forcible measures' referred to were the 'Six
Acts' which the German Federal Diet passed in 1832 under Prussian and Austrian
pressure, and which re-established repressive measures throughout the German
Confederation.

6. The National Association was formed by the pro-Prussian wing of the German
liberal bourgeoisie in September 1850 to campaign for a 'little Germany' under
Prussian hegemony.

7. This suffering was caused by the Northern blockade of Southern ports preventing the export of cotton. See Marx's article 'A London Workers' Meeting', *MECW*
19, pp. 153–6.

Poland, this by no means forces them to remain mutely inactive, to be branded in the eyes of the world as accessories to treason.

The undersigned committee requests contributions of money to be sent to Herr Bolleter, the owner of the Association Tavern, 2, Nassau Street, Soho, London. The money will be used under the supervision of the [German Workers Educational] Association, and as soon as the purpose for which this collection is intended allows, public account will be rendered.

BOLLETER	BERGER
ECCARIUS	KRÜGER
LINDEN	MATZRATH
TATSCHKY	TOUPS
WOLFF	

Volume III
The First International and After

Introduction to Volume III

The International Working Men's Association

After an interval of twelve years, Marx returned to organized politics when the International Working Men's Association was founded in 1864. The setting for this second major phase of his political work had changed considerably since the days of 1848, and Marx had to face new problems of political theory and tactics. The Communist Manifesto, in which Marx had formulated the principles of scientific communism, had been far in advance of the actual development of the proletarian movement at the time, and this disparity led to problems which were discussed in the Introduction to *The Revolutions of 1848*. In this period Marx had had to deal first and foremost with the tactics that the proletariat should pursue during a bourgeois revolution, when the industrial working class was a small fraction of the population on the European continent, and only a tiny minority of advanced workers were conscious of the historical tasks that faced them.

By the 1860s, however, modern industry had begun to make substantial headway throughout western Europe. The industrial workers were increasing rapidly in numbers, and had in many parts overshadowed the ranks of pre-industrial artisans and journeymen. Whereas in the 1840s English Chartism was the only mass movement specifically characteristic of the modern proletariat, during the 1860s such movements began to develop in several countries of western and central Europe, as well as in the United States. The theory of scientific communism could now find for the first time a substantial material base. But while the Communist League of the 1840s could easily be very principled in its practice, as a small theoretical vanguard with little effect on the historical process, the broad workers' movements that developed in the 1860s had slowly to undergo the difficult development of theoretical consciousness, each starting from ideologies that reflected their different national experience of economic and political struggle. Working with such movements, Marx found himself called on to apply the tactic he had laid down in the Manifesto: to point out from within the developing proletarian movement its own international and long-term interests, attempting to educate it step by step to the positions of scientific communism.

The organizational initiative that founded the International was taken jointly by representatives of the English and French working classes. On the English side the protagonists were the trade-union leaders involved in the London Trades Council formed in 1860. These trade-unionists were by no means revolutionary or even socialist, and they represented not the broad mass of the English working class but the skilled and relatively privileged 'labour aristocracy' that comprised around ten to fifteen per cent of the English workers. Their chief political aim was to win the suffrage, and on most questions they tended to follow the lead of the bourgeois Radicals. But as workers they had their own specific interests that extended into the international arena, in particular preventing the import of foreign workers to break strikes, which was a quite common practice in the mid nineteenth century. And when a series of strikes in the building trades over the demand for a nine-hour day signalled an upsurge of working-class militancy, the London Trades Council felt its strength and began to extend its activity into political agitation, filling the vacuum in working-class politics left by the demise of Chartism in 1858.

Three events in the international arena helped focus the political consciousness of the English workers in the early 1860s and prepared the way for the formation of the First International. If the Italian Risorgimento aroused the sympathy of the Radical lower-middle class in England, it was followed yet more keenly by the politicized workers. When the exiled Garibaldi arrived in England in 1864 he was fêted by the London Working Men's Garibaldi Committee, and when the British government forced him to leave the country after a short stay, a workers' demonstration in London led to clashes with the police. More crucial was the political question raised by the American civil war, which impinged directly on a large section of the English working class through the cotton famine. At first both major working-class newspapers, *Reynolds'* and the *Beehive*, followed the bourgeois parties in support for the South, but after much controversy Lincoln's abolition of slavery in January 1863 finally swung working-class opinion to override immediate economic considerations, and a campaign of pro-Northern mass meetings helped deter the British government from intervening on the Southern side. Finally, the Polish insurrection of 1863 once more brought into prominence this old touchstone of democratic allegiance, and here again the increasingly confident skilled workers organized their own rallies in support of Poland, and a trade-union deputation called on Palmerston to press for British intervention against Russia.[1]

The actions over Italy, America and Poland were all led by the London Trades Council, in particular by Odger, Cremer and Howell, who were to play important roles in the International.[2] At the same time the suffrage movement gathered steam with the formation of the Trade Union Manhood Suffrage Association in November 1862, and a campaign of mass meetings during 1863. Even though this agitation lacked the revolutionary overtones of Chartism and was carried out in conjunction with the bourgeois Radicals, it marked a definite political renascence.

The campaign of solidarity with Poland was instrumental in forging the link between English and French workers that led to the founding of the International. Under the repression of the Bonapartist regime, the French workers' movement was slow to recover from its defeats of 1848. Blanqui[3] had been released from prison in 1859, but soon went into exile in Belgium; although he left some small groups of followers, they were perforce deep underground and had very little foothold in the growing industrial working class. But although there was at this time no right of

1. For Marx's views on these international developments, see the Introduction to Volume II, above, pp. 363–7.

2. George Odger was a shoemaker, one of the founders of the London Trades Council and its secretary from 1862 to 1872. He was a member of the International's General Council from its foundation until 1871, and its president until 1867, when the office was abolished. William Cremer, a carpenter, was a member of the International's General Council and its general secretary from 1864 to 1866. He later became a Liberal MP. George Howell, a mason, was secretary of the London Trades Council from 1861 to 1862, and a member of the International's General Council from 1864 to 1869.

3. Auguste Blanqui was the outstanding French workers' leader of the nineteenth century, but still believed that the overthrow of the bourgeois state could be accomplished simply by conspiratorial means (see the Introduction to *The Revolutions of 1848*, above, p. 18). Blanqui's Société des Saisons organized the uprising of May 1839, and he and his followers played an important role in the revolutions of 1848 and 1870–1. In all, Blanqui spent thirty-six years of his life in prison.

association or assembly, and no freedom of the press, Louis Napoleon tolerated cooperatives and mutual benefit societies as a safety valve for working-class discontent, and in these conditions Proudhon's ideas of social transformation through 'mutualism' took firm root.[4] In 1862 the emperor subsidized the visit of an elected delegation of Parisian workers to the London International Exhibition, and despite the rather compromising circumstances the Proudhonist leaders Tolain and Fribourg[5] made contact for the first time with the English workers' movement. By the following year Bonaparte had inaugurated the 'liberal empire' policy, attempting to stave off the danger of revolution by tolerating a constitutional opposition. In the new political climate the first workers' candidates stood for election to the legislature, and in February 1864, when strikes were legalized, the Proudhonists issued the 'Manifesto of Sixty', which spoke of the conflict between labour and capital. In July 1863 Tolain and four other delegates again travelled to London, this time to speak at a meeting in support of Poland organized by the London Trades Council. At this meeting Odger took the opportunity to raise the question of the import of lower-paid workers into England from the Continent to break strikes, and proposed 'regular and systematic communication between the industrious classes of all countries' as the solution to this problem.[6] From now on this communication was established at least between English and French workers, and on 28 September 1864 a further Anglo-French public meeting was held at St Martin's Hall, where it was agreed to form an international association.

The foundation of the International caught Marx at a transitional stage in his life. In 1862, thanks to a legacy, he became able for the first time since his arrival in England to support his family at a tolerable standard of comfort, and no longer had to undertake journalistic work. Marx had spent the greater part of the years

4. On Pierre-Joseph-Proudhon and his ideas, see the Introduction to *The Revolutions of 1848*, above, p. 17, and below, pp. 700–703 and 1014–16.

5. Henri Tolain, an engraver, became the leading figure of the International's Paris Federation. During the Paris Commune, however, he sat in the Versailles National Assembly and was expelled from the International. E. Fribourg, also an engraver, was his close collaborator.

6. H. J. Collins and C. Abramsky, *Karl Marx and the British Labour Movement*, London, 1965, p. 24.

1861–3 writing the immense manuscript of one and a half million words out of which the great bulk of all four volumes of *Capital* (i.e. including *Theories of Surplus-Value*) was constructed. During this period Marx was frequently ill, and withdrew into almost complete isolation. From the beginning of 1863 to the foundation of the International he published nothing, and only nine letters of his have been found other than those to his family and Engels. When the International was founded in September 1864, Marx's health was still poor, but his economic circumstances and the progress of his theoretical work permitted him to engage once more in organizational activity, and the circumstances in which the International was founded encouraged him to do so. Marx realized that the long night of reaction was now over and that a new upsurge of working-class struggle had finally begun. After the founding meeting he wrote to Engels that he had departed from his usual custom and involved himself in the new organization as 'I knew on this occasion "people who really count" were appearing, both from London and Paris'.[7]

The International was founded without Marx, but it would not have held together had it not been for the leadership he provided. Not only were the European workers' movements at very different stages of ideological development, but the General Council in London, consisting of English trade-unionists on the one hand and Continental émigrés on the other, needed Marx's unifying perspective in order to speak for the international proletariat. For instance, the French representatives elected at the St Martin's Hall meeting were republican democrats, and the Italians were followers of Mazzini; both groups actively opposed an independent workers' movement. Marx was able by skilful manoeuvring to force the resignation of these explicitly non-working-class tendencies, but he realized that to build a united international organization, and to maintain his own position, he would have to tread extremely carefully. The English trade-unionists, though politicized, were indifferent to socialism and hostile to revolution, and the French Proudhonists, who professed a form of socialism, were hostile not only to revolution but to all forms of politics. The Proudhonists also, in their reaction against the rhetorical revolutionism of the republican democrats, were hostile to the presence of intellectuals in a workers' organization. As Marx wrote to Engels, 'It will take time before the revival of the movement

7. Marx to Engels, 4 November 1864; *MECW* 42, p. 16.

allows the old boldness of language to be used. We must be *fortiter
in re, suaviter in modo*.'[8]

In line with this tactic, Marx drew up for the General Council
the Inaugural Address and Provisional Rules. These were
particularly designed to present at least a part of the ideas of
scientific communism in a form acceptable to the pragmatic
English trade-unionists, from which base Marx hoped to win
over the Proudhonists of the French-speaking countries and the
German Lassalleans.[9] The Address was privately described by
Marx as 'a sort of review of the adventures of the Working Classes
since 1845',[10] and he took as his starting-point the uncontentious
thesis of the ever widening gap between the wealth produced by
modern industry and the poverty of the working class that had
characterized the previous two decades, and the 'solidarity of
defeat' that united the English and Continental working classes
after the failures of 1848.

The programmatic formulations of the Inaugural Address read
rather tamely beside the declamatory language of the Manifesto,
and although the essential thesis of Marxian communism is hinted
at in the Address, it is couched in veiled and cautious terms.
Thus after referring to the Ten Hours Act passed in 1846 as 'the
victory of a principle . . . the first time that in broad daylight the
political economy of the middle class succumbed to the political
economy of the working class', and to the producers' cooperative
movement as 'a still greater victory',[11] Marx goes on to argue
that capitalism cannot be transformed by purely economic means.
'National means' are necessary to develop cooperative labour
to national dimensions, 'yet the lords of land and the lords of
capital will always use their political privileges for the defence
and perpetuation of their economical monopolies . . . To conquer
political power has therefore become the great duty of the working
classes.'[12] Marx's insistence on conquering political power may
seem decisive in our hindsight, but in the context of the Address
it was ambiguous enough, and the majority of the International's
English supporters undoubtedly interpreted it simply as winning

8. 'Strong in deed, gentle in style'; ibid., p. 17.
9. On Ferdinand Lassalle and the movement he founded, see below, pp. 704–7.
10. Marx to Engels, 4 November 1864; *MECW* 42, p. 18.
11. 'Inaugural Address of the International Working Men's Association', below,
p. 763.
12. Ibid., p. 764.

the suffrage. Although Marx had once written, in the days of the Chartist movement, that 'universal suffrage is the equivalent for political power for the working class in England',[13] he certainly did not see the Second Reform Bill of 1867, which satisfied present trade-union aspirations, as 'equivalent for political power', especially in the circumstances in which it was carried. However, Marx was convinced that the commitment of the working class to political activity would necessarily lead it onto the road of communist revolution, and he was certainly correct in counting it a significant advance to bring the working classes of Europe together into a common political organization. Marx ended the Address by stressing the importance of the 'heroic resistance' of the English working class to the government's aspirations for war with the Northern states of America, and asserted that the indifference with which the upper classes of Europe had allowed the assassination of the Polish insurrection had 'taught the working classes the duty to master themselves the mysteries of international politics'.[14]

As Marx had anticipated, the Address struck a particularly favourable chord in the ranks of the English trade-unionists. They were proud of the internationalist record they had built up over the past few years, they were once more engaged in struggle for the suffrage, and they expected the International they had set up to provide the material benefits of international cooperation. With the Address Marx proved himself a friend of the English workers, and this alliance provided the political centre of the International up to the split of 1871–2.

Following the General Council's acceptance of the Address and the Provisional Rules, Marx set to work to build up the International's organization. He was able to use the General Council's power of cooption to bring on some former members of the Communist League and other exiles more or less under his influence, and a particularly valuable role was played in the International's early years by Eccarius,[15] a German exile and former League member who had integrated himself into the English trade-union movement.

13. 'The Chartists', above, p. 632.

14. 'Inaugural Address . . .', below, p. 765.

15. Johann Georg Eccarius, a tailor and writer, was at the time one of Marx's closest followers, but in the later 1860s fell into the reformism of his English colleagues.

Two more of Marx's supporters, Jung and Dupont,[16] became the corresponding secretaries for Switzerland and France, while Marx himself acted as corresponding secretary for Germany. As one of his first initiatives on the General Council, Marx drew up an 'Address to President Lincoln',[17] congratulating Lincoln on his re-election, which gave the International its first burst of publicity when a cordial reply sent via the US legation was published in *The Times*. Marx intervened consistently to stress the importance of solidarity with Poland, and began to conduct some basic educational work among the General Council members, notably producing in spring 1865 his paper *Value, Price and Profit*,[18] in which he presented for the first time his theory of surplus-value.

The main ideological struggle during the first four years of the International's life was between the ideas of Marx and those of Proudhon. Proudhon's characteristic doctrine of mutualism envisaged the transformation of capitalism by means of producer cooperatives financed by a 'people's bank'. The Proudhonists rejected strikes as a 'forcible' interference into economic relations, and they rejected *a fortiori* all political struggle. Despite the working-class social base of Proudhonism, Marx had already characterized it in 1847 as a petty-bourgeois ideological tendency,[19] and in the 1860s it continued to express the outlook of a proletariat that still had a strong artisanal consciousness, not least in its insistence on relegating women to their 'proper' place in the home.[20]

16. Hermann Jung was a Swiss watchmaker, Eugène Dupont a French musical instrument maker; both were political exiles.

17. In *MECW* 20, pp. 19–21. For Marx's attitude to Lincoln, see also the Introduction to Volume II, above, p. 366.

18. In *MECW* 20, pp. 101–48.

19. In *The Poverty of Philosophy*. After Proudhon's death, Marx wrote a shorter critique of his ideas in a letter to Schweitzer of 24 January 1865; *MECW* 20, pp. 26–33.

20. The International, based as it was on an alliance between the exclusively male 'labour aristocracy' in England and the militantly anti-feminist Proudhonists of the French-speaking countries, was essentially male in its outlook, as its very name implies. But this was not unchallenged. A women's section of the International was founded in Paris in April 1871, during the Commune, and in August 1871 Victoria Woodhull and Tennessee Claflin founded a section of the International in New York on an explicitly feminist programme. Marx responded to the French development by moving a resolution at the London Conference of 1871 recommending the formation of working women's branches, which was not to 'interfere with the existence or formation of branches composed of both sexes' (*IWMA* IV, p. 442). However, he would have no truck with the American feminists, noting Victoria Woodhull as a 'banker's

The first round in this battle was prepared at the London Conference of the International in September 1865, and fought out at its first Congress, held in Geneva a year later. For the Geneva Congress Marx drafted a set of instructions for the delegates of the General Council, on the basis of a series of preliminary discussions. This document amounts to a concrete programme of action for the International. It emphasizes the importance of the struggle to win reforms from the existing bourgeois state, with particular regard to labour legislation (the eight-hour day, etc.), and the role of the trade unions in this struggle. Marx argued against the Proudhonists that the working class could win valuable reforms before it could bring about socialism, and that there was no other method at present of achieving these than through '*general laws*, enforced by the power of the state'. He stressed that 'in enforcing such laws, the working class do not fortify governmental power. On the contrary, they transform that power, now used against them, into their own agency.'[21] However, although Marx was to be historically vindicated in his insistence that the working class could win concessions from the capitalist state, these formulations, if taken in isolation, lay themselves open to a reformist interpretation. Marx did not make clear here to what extent the workers could transform the existing governmental power into their own agency, and what the limits of this transformation were. The revisionist Social-Democrats were later to use texts such as these to justify their claim that the working class could gradually take over the existing state and wield it to its own purposes. As we shall see, Marx rejected this possibility in the two most important political texts of this later period, *The Civil War in France* and the 'Critique of the Gotha Programme'. In the International's early years, however, Marx was forced to operate '*suaviter in modo*', and this fact must be taken into account in interpreting the documents he wrote for the International.

In the 'Instructions for Delegates' Marx went on to argue that trade unions were legitimate and necessary, while simultaneously insisting with an eye to his English audience that the present trade unions had

woman, free-lover, and general humbug' (*MECW* 23, p. 636). Marx's general attitude towards the nineteenth-century women's movement is difficult to discover, as it emerges only in asides such as this; Victoria Woodhull's section did undoubtedly have a definite middle-class character.

21. 'Instructions for Delegates to the Geneva Conference', below, p. 779.

'not yet fully understood their power of acting against the system of wage slavery itself', and 'must now learn to act deliberately as organizing centres of the working class in the broad interest of its *complete emancipation*. They must aid every social and political movement tending in that direction.'[22] Marx certainly had no illusion that the English trade-unionists of this time represented more than a minority of relatively privileged skilled workers, and he specifically stressed that they had to learn to 'consider themselves and act as the champions and representatives of the whole working class', to 'enlist the non-society men in their ranks' and 'convince the world at large that their efforts, far from being narrow and selfish, aim at the emancipation of the downtrodden millions'.[23] However, Marx was to be deceived in the expectations he held out for the English 'new model unions'. At this time these were the only working-class organizations in England, and therefore the only working-class representatives with whom Marx could make contact, but the stake that the labour aristocracy's privilege gave it in bourgeois society was to lead the trade unions into firm alliance with the Liberal party once the 1867 Reform Bill had been won.

Marx's struggle against Proudhonism carried over from the Geneva Congress of 1866 to the Congresses of Lausanne in 1867 and Brussels in 1868. At Geneva Marx's alliance of English trade-unionists, German Social-Democrats and his personal supporters among the London exiles carried through most of his resolutions, with certain minor concessions to the Proudhonists; but at Lausanne, where only a few English delegates attended, the Proudhonists were in a majority and easily dominated the Congress. However, the Brussels Congress of 1868, the largest and most representative of the International's Congresses to date, marked Marx's decisive victory. Although lip-service was still paid to 'mutual credit', the capitalist tendencies of existing cooperative experiments were denounced, and for the first time the Congress went on record in favour of the public ownership of land, including mines, railways, forests, canals, roads and telegraphs. This resolution was passed by a considerable majority, though in view of its importance, the subject was tabled for further discussion the following year. The International had thus developed a long way from its original conception as simply a workers' defence society.

22. Ibid., pp. 91–2.
23. Ibid., p. 92.

During the late 1860s the International gradually extended its organization. The structure it adopted was one of branches that corresponded with the General Council in London either directly, or via a national federal council. The General Council itself filled the function of a federal council for England. Besides individual membership, trade unions and other workers' societies that endorsed the aims of the International could affiliate. Even at its peak, the individual membership of the International does not seem to have run into more than a few thousands, although affiliated membership in England, where this was most important, reached over 50,000. However, the International steadily acquired influence and support well beyond the limits of its formal adherents. It did this in large measure through the support it was able to provide for strikes in different countries, both financially and, more important, by preventing the import of foreign blacklegs and by mobilizing international solidarity. In 1866 the Sheffield Conference of trade unions, forerunner of the TUC, called on its member societies to support the International, and the General Council steadily gained affiliations. It is noteworthy, however, that the English affiliations to the International came almost entirely from the craft unions in small-scale traditional industries and the building trades, and scarcely at all from unions engaged in mining, engineering and heavy industry, where the threat of foreign competition was at this time minimal.

On the Continent the International was at first slower to gain ground, but began to make rapid headway from 1867 onwards, when an upsurge of strike activity across most of western Europe followed in the wake of economic recession. In France, Switzerland and Belgium, successful intervention by the International in local strikes led to the building of strong sections, and these strikes also dealt a severe blow to Proudhonist ideology, as became visible at the Brussels Congress. In turn, the French Internationalists' involvement in successful strikes brought down on them severe repression from the Bonapartist regime, and the Paris Federation was crippled by three trials and the imprisonment of most of its leaders. This led to a section of left-wing Proudhonists taking a further step towards understanding the need for political action, and this group, led by Varlin,[24] was to play an important role in the Paris Commune of 1871.

24. Eugène Varlin, a bookbinder and the leader of the left-wing Proudhonists, played a prominent role in the organization of the Commune's defence, and was captured and shot by the Versailles forces.

German Social-Democracy

A major weakness of the International was the relative indifference it met with in Germany. Although the 1860s saw the development in Germany of a political workers' movement stronger in numbers and possibly more advanced in its ideology than elsewhere in Europe, Marx's influence on German Social-Democracy remained minimal, although this movement was later to present itself as the paradigm of a Marxist workers' party. German Social-Democracy arose in a political conjuncture dominated by the struggle between Prussia and Austria for German hegemony, and was at first strongly marked by its Prussian origins. After the defeat of the 1848 revolution, heavy political reaction had reigned in Prussia until 1859, when the regency of Prince William (later William I) inaugurated the 'New Era'. Opposition activity was once more tolerated, and in 1861 the liberal bourgeoisie formed the Progressive party, which demanded parliamentary government, though not universal suffrage. The German working class was slow to develop any political consciousness after the period of reaction, and the first workers' organizations were only a tail of the liberal bourgeoisie. However, German politics were polarized in October 1862, when the Prussian Diet refused Bismarck, the newly appointed Chancellor, the army credits he requested. Bismarck then announced his intention to unify Germany by 'blood and iron', and proceeded for the next four years to levy taxation unconstitutionally.

It was against this background that Ferdinand Lassalle conducted his agitation. Lassalle had taken part in the 1848 revolution, but, less compromised than most, he remained in Germany during the 1850s and was Marx and Engels's most regular correspondent there. Although he claimed to accept the Communist Manifesto, Lassalle was personally ambitious and lapsed into opportunism, seeing himself in the role of heroic saviour of the working class. However, Lassalle had already shown, in the international crisis of 1859, that he understood earlier than Marx and Engels the changed balance of forces within Germany.[25] Realizing that a renewed attempt at a democratic revolution of the 1848 type was no longer possible, he premised his campaign on the acceptance of German unification from

25. See the Introduction to Volume II, above, pp. 364–5.

above by Prussian arms. In May 1863 Lassalle founded the General Association of German Workers (ADAV) and conducted a series of mass meetings calling for universal suffrage and state-financed 'cooperative factories'. Lassalle's historic merit, as Marx recognized, was to have reawakened the German working class and formed the first socialist workers' party,[26] but in the circumstances of the time and under Lassalle's leadership this took a highly distorted form. Lassalle was even in secret correspondence with Bismarck, and hoped to secure working-class support for Bismarck's annexationist plans in return for universal suffrage and state-supported cooperatives – a deal that Bismarck rejected, realizing that Lassalle could not deliver the goods. Soon after, in August 1864, Lassalle was killed in a duel.

As far as perspectives for German development were concerned, Marx was most probably mistaken in holding that the liberal bourgeoisie could not be dismissed as a revolutionary force, and that the working class could successfully spur it onwards in the constitutional struggle against Bismarck. However, Marx was unquestionably right in insisting that the workers' party should attack as its main enemy the feudal and absolutist state, and not hedge this fundamental issue as Lassalle did by concentrating simply on the workers' exploitation by capital. Marx saw Lassalle's failure to demand the repeal of the anti-combination laws as particularly pernicious, since this did not just follow from Lassalle's mistaken theory of the 'iron law of wages', but expressed his refusal to accept and encourage the direct expression of working-class self-activity. The right of combination was 'a means of breaking the rule of the police and bureaucracy, and of smashing the "*Gesindeordnung*" and the rule of the aristocracy on the land'.[27]

Marx did not attack Lassalle publicly during his agitation, which took place while he had completely withdrawn from political activity. But the International brought Marx back into political life only one month after Lassalle's death. The ADAV was thrown into crisis by the loss of its charismatic leader, and Marx took the opportunity to attempt to counteract the pernicious legacy of the 'workers' dictator'.[28] As a first step, Marx allowed himself to be

26. Marx to Schweitzer, 13 October 1868; below, p. 838.

27. Marx to Schweitzer, 13 February 1865; below, p. 831. The *Gesindeordnung* (farm servants' code) was the semi-feudal legal code in force in east-Elbian Prussia.

28. Marx to Kugelmann, 23 February 1865; below, p. 832.

nominated for the ADAV presidency in December 1864, though only for propaganda purposes, as he had no intention of returning to Prussia. However this move failed, and only signalled the fact that Marx was virtually unknown to the new generation of German working-class militants. Secondly, Marx attempted to obtain ADAV affiliation to the International, but this also drew a blank, as the party would not risk contravening the law that prohibited such international affiliation. Marx's final attempt to influence the ADAV was to accept an offer that he and Engels should collaborate with the Lassallean newspaper *Social-Demokrat*, making the one condition that the paper should follow an uncompromising line towards the Prussian government, and attack the feudal-absolutist regime at least as strongly as it attacked the bourgeoisie. However it was not long before J. B. von Schweitzer, who now led the Lassallean party, openly expressed ADAV support for Bismarck's national policy in the columns of the paper, whereupon Marx and Engels publicly broke off all relations with the Lassallean organization.[29]

In February 1865, therefore, Marx had to abandon for the time being his hopes of winning the ADAV for the International, and for the next three years he had only a minimal entry into the German workers' movement, through the work of Wilhelm Liebknecht and Johann Philipp Becker. Liebknecht, later the leader of the German Social-Democratic Party, had been a protégé of Marx in London during the 1850s. Back in Germany in the 1860s, he worked with the Union of German Workers' Societies, although this was composed primarily of artisans rather than industrial workers, had been formed as a loose federation on a specifically non-socialist programme, and was allied to the petty-bourgeois People's Party of south Germany. Marx corresponded regularly with Liebknecht, and attempted to guide his work. It cannot be denied that Liebknecht and his comrade August Bebel[30] did valuable work in drawing sections of the working class outside of Prussia towards the International, and in 1868 their Union adopted the preamble to the International's

29. See Marx and Engels's letter 'To the Editor of the *Social-Demokrat*', 23 February 1865; *MECW* 20, p. 80.
30. August Bebel, a manual worker by origin, first proved himself as a workers' leader in this period. He later became both the leading tactician of the German Social-Democratic Party and a socialist theorist, publishing in particular *Woman and Socialism* (1883).

Rules[31] as its own statement of principles. However, in the face of the unresolved problem of German unification, Liebknecht acted as a 'great German' and anti-Prussian first, and a workers' leader second. Marx had frequent occasion to criticize him for his uncritical attitude towards the south German petty bourgeoisie, and his inability to attack simultaneously both the pro-Prussian and pro-Austrian bourgeois fractions. Throughout this period the International could not exist as a public organization in Germany, and J. P. Becker coordinated the German-speaking sections from Geneva, where he published *Die Vorbote* [*The Herald*]. It was largely Becker's work that prepared the Union of German Workers' Societies to adopt the International's programme, and his influence was also felt within the ADAV. However, Becker, despite the advice he received from Marx, was considerably more confused ideologically than Liebknecht – in 1868 he temporarily switched his allegiance to Bakunin – and could not hope to provide an effective leadership from outside Germany.

During the critical years of German unification, Marx thus had no real influence on the growing German workers' movement. However, after Prussian hegemony became a *fait accompli* with the defeat of Austria in 1866, the ADAV was no longer imprisoned by its position on the national question and began to function far more independently. When Liebknecht, along with his petty-bourgeois friends in the People's Party, refused to recognize the irreversible character of the Prussian victory, Marx established friendly relations with Schweitzer, advising him in particular on the formation of trade unions.[32] In 1869 the ADAV split (Schweitzer remaining with the dogmatic Lassalleans), and the ADAV opposition joined forces with Liebknecht and Bebel's Union to form the Social-Democratic Workers' Party (SDAP) on a programme that rather confusedly amalgamated Marxist, Lassallean and democratic ideas. However, the SDAP, although it now affiliated formally to the International, maintained what Engels called a 'purely platonic relationship'[33] to it. It thus showed itself, even before the Franco-Prussian war of 1870, to be the new strictly national type of workers' party that was to characterize the period between the Franco-Prussian war and the First World War.

31. I.e. the first six paragraphs of the Rules; below, p. 766.
32. Marx to Schweitzer, 13 October 1868; below, pp. 840–1.
33. Engels to Cuno, 7–8 May 1872; *MECW* 44, p. 371.

England and Ireland

After Marx's failure to influence the German workers' movement, he turned his attention primarily to England. On the General Council Marx had the ear of a considerable section of influential English trade-unionists, and over the years he led them through a series of discussions which included the theory of surplus-value, the role of trade unions, the Polish question, suffrage reform, land nationalization, cooperatives, etc. However, despite his initial optimism, Marx failed to make any real progress in winning the English workers' leaders towards the ideas of scientific communism. His first setback with the English was the course taken by the Reform League. This organization was formed in spring 1865 by the same trade-unionists who were involved in the International, and based itself on the principle of manhood suffrage as opposed to the Radical platform of household suffrage. Marx was highly enthusiastic, and wrote to Engels on 1 May 1865, 'The great success of the International Association is this: the Reform League is our work . . . We have baffled all attempts of the middle class to mislead the working class.'[34]

In the summer of 1866 the Reform League led militant demonstrations in Trafalgar Square and Hyde Park, and on 6 May 1867 a Reform League meeting in Hyde Park, which with 150,000 participants was the most massive workers' demonstration in Britain since 1848, ended in a riot. Certainly in the 1860s the English workers had not entirely lost the revolutionary potential they had shown in the 1840s. However, the Reform League was never the independent working-class organization that Marx at first believed. It was financed by the same sources as the middle-class Reform Union (i.e. far-sighted industrial capitalists) and it qualified its demand for manhood suffrage with the phrase 'registered and residential', thus deliberately excluding the large 'dangerous class' of casual workers and unemployed. By May 1867 the Reform League leaders had already accepted household suffrage as a compromise for the time being, and worked in conjunction with Walpole, the Home Secretary, to contain the 6 May demonstration. The Hyde Park riot led nevertheless to Walpole's resignation and forced Disraeli to insert the 'lodger clause' in his Reform Bill as a

34. *MECW* 42, p. 150.

concession, and the Reform League now counted its members in six figures. But Howell, Cremer and Applegarth[35] had quite literally 'sold out' to the bourgeoisie,[36] and after the passage of the 1867 Reform Act they worked secretly and successfully – in exchange for Home Office bribes – to mobilize the working class behind the Liberal party in the 1868 general election. During this period Applegarth, for example, was still actively involved in the General Council, and Marx saw him as a promising workers' leader. This contradiction illustrates the fact that the English trade-unionists basically used the International as a surrogate international department of the newly formed TUC. They were already well set on a reformist course, and thus were *a priori* unsusceptible to Marx's ideological influence.

From the time of the 'Fenian outrages'[37] in 1867 Marx and Engels took an increased interest in the Irish question, which was acquiring an ever greater importance in English politics. The General Council of the International discussed Ireland on several occasions in the late 1860s, and the evolution of Marx's position is of particular interest here. In November 1867, when Marx first introduced a discussion on Ireland at a meeting of the General Council, he explained his position to Engels in the following terms: the repeal of the Corn Laws (1846) marked the beginning of a new phase of English rule, characterized by Ireland's transition from a privileged position as England's corn supplier to the production of wool and meat. The 'sole significance of English rule' in Ireland was now 'Clearing of the Estate of Ireland', and it was because of this that Fenianism was 'characterized by a socialistic tendency' and 'a lower orders movement'. What the Irish needed, therefore, was self-government, an agrarian revolution, and protective tariffs against England, and Marx would advise the English workers to 'make the *repeal of the Union* ... an article of their *pronunziamento*',[38] for English landlordism was the common

35. Robert Applegarth, a cabinet-maker, was a member of the London Trades Council and of the General Council of the International (1865, then 1868–72).

36. Marx created a stir by denouncing the reformist trade-union leaders in these terms at the Hague Congress of 1872. (See H. Gerth, ed., *The First International*, Madison, 1958, p. 186.) The truth of this allegation is conclusively proved by Rodney Harrison in *Before the Socialists*, London, 1965, Chapter IV.

37. The Fenians, or Irish Republican Brotherhood, were a conspiratorial organization with little explicit ideology, but reflecting the agrarian and national aspirations of the Irish peasantry. They attempted an armed uprising against the British in February –March 1867.

38. Marx to Engels, 30 November 1867; below, pp. 844–5.

enemy of both English workers and Irish peasants. However, by 1869 Marx gave the Irish struggle a far more fundamental place in the English revolution, a change no doubt related to the political experience of the intervening years – in particular the unwillingness of most English trade-unionists to solidarize with the Irish Fenian movement, and the defection of the Reform League leaders to the Liberal party.

Now disaffected with his former allies in the English trade unions, Marx was led to attribute partial responsibility for their betrayals to the national antagonism between England and Ireland. Thus on 29 November 1869, while he was mobilizing the General Council of the International in support of the Irish amnesty movement (to free a group of Fenians condemned for terrorist activities), Marx wrote to his German correspondent Kugelmann that, without dissolution of the Union,

the English people will be kept in tether by the ruling classes, because they will have to establish a common front with them against Ireland. Every one of its movements in England itself remains paralysed by the quarrel with the Irish, who form a very considerable section of the working class in England itself.[39]

This had a striking strategic implication, which Marx spelled out in a letter to Engels a few days later:

I long believed it was possible to overthrow the Irish regime by way of English working-class ascendancy . . . A deeper study has now convinced me of the opposite. The English working class will never achieve anything before it has got rid of Ireland. The lever must be applied in Ireland. This is why the Irish question is so important for the social movement in general.[40]

Marx elaborated this new position in the General Council's letter to the Federal Council of French Switzerland of January 1870, and in a letter to the German-Americans Meyer and Vogt some three months later. His argument in these texts falls into two parts. Firstly, Marx presents Ireland as the weak link of the English ruling classes. 'Ireland is the bulwark of the *English landed aristocracy*', and

39. Below, p. 849.
40. Marx to Engels, 10 December 1869; below, pp. 850–1.

the overthrow of the English aristocracy in Ireland involves and would necessarily be followed by its overthrow in England. Thus one prerequisite for the proletarian revolution in England would be fulfilled . . . the destruction of the English landed aristocracy in Ireland is an infinitely easier operation than in England itself, because in Ireland the *land question* has up till now been the *exclusive form* which the social question has taken, because it is a question of existence, a *question of life and death* for the majority of the Irish people, because at the same time it is inseparable from the *national* question.[41]

On top of this:

Ireland is the only excuse the English government has for keeping up a large regular army which can, as we have seen, in case of need attack the English workers after having done its basic training in Ireland.[42]

But the English ruling classes were not merely more vulnerable in Ireland. Most important of all, according to Marx, was the privileged position that the national oppression of Ireland gave the English workers vis-à-vis their Irish brothers. This was why 'the English working class will never achieve anything before it has got rid of Ireland'. In England, the English and the Irish workers formed 'two *hostile* camps'. This division had an economic basis, as 'the ordinary English worker hates the Irish worker because he sees in him a competitor who lowers his standard of life,' but Marx also laid particular stress on ideological factors:

Compared with the Irish worker [the English worker] feels himself a member of the *ruling nation*, and for this very reason he makes himself into a tool of the aristocrats and capitalists *against Ireland* and thus strengthens their domination *over himself*.

The English worker also 'cherishes religious, social and national prejudices against the Irish worker', which are 'artificially sustained and intensified by the press, the pulpit, the comic papers, in short, by all the means at the disposal of the ruling classes'.

The antagonism between English and Irish workers, Marx claimed, was '*the secret of the impotence of the English working class*, despite

41. Marx to Meyer and Vogt, 9 April 1870; below, p. 852.
42. 'The General Council to the Federal Council of French Switzerland', below, p. 802.

its organization. It is the secret which enables the capitalist class to maintain its power, as this class is perfectly aware.' In this situation, and given the special importance of England as the 'metropolis of capital', the International had 'to bring the conflict between England and Ireland into the foreground, and everywhere to side openly with Ireland.'[43]

Marx's writings on the relationship between England and Ireland mark a significant new departure for his political theory. Marx and Engels had previously seen the exploitation of the colonies as invariably a secondary feature of capitalism's international dimension. Capitalism, despite its barbarous side-effects, was the only means of bringing the more backward countries into 'civilization', and so colonization was in the last instance progressive. When Engels first put forward a position on the Irish question, in 1848, he presented Irish liberation as a by-product of the English revolution. The future of the Irish people lay in their alliance with the English Chartists, whose victory would transform the association between England and Ireland from an exploitative to an egalitarian one.[44] But twenty years later, Marx came to ascribe to the Irish national struggle a determining role in the English revolution. The 'lever' had to be applied in Ireland, and the English workers would be tied to the leading-strings of their own ruling class until Irish national liberation was achieved.

This seems to presage the theory of imperialism founded by Lenin half a century later. However, there is a crucial difference. Lenin's innovation was to argue from a general economic relationship between metropolises and colonies to general political effects, including the corruption of a section of the metropolitan working class that benefited from colonial exploitation. Even though Marx's assertion that national liberation in Ireland had actually to precede proletarian revolution in England appears to go further than Lenin, Marx presented this relation between metropolis and colony as a particular case, the product of specific local circumstances. Marx certainly never held that the 'lever' of the revolution had as a general rule to be applied in the colonies. On the contrary, he was never to revise his initial assumption that the non-European colonies would have to follow the historical trajectory of the exploiting nations.[45]

43. Marx to Meyer and Vogt, 9 April 1870; below, pp. 853–54.

44. See Engels's articles of January 1848, 'The Coercion Bill for Ireland and the Chartists' and 'Feargus O'Connor and the Irish People', in *MECW* 6, pp. 445–9.

45. See the Introduction to Volume II, above, pp. 358–62, and below, p. 752.

Lacking an adequate theory of capitalism's international dimension, Marx did not satisfactorily account for the failure of the English working class to fulfil the expectations he had entertained in the mid 1860s. The role Marx attributed to Ireland in 1869–70 was almost certainly too great, and after 1870 he never again adduced this as an explanation of English reformism. Indeed, even in 1870 Marx would seem not to have ruled out altogether the beginnings, at least, of a revolutionary workers' movement in England before Irish emancipation was achieved. Furthermore, in the section of the letter to the Federal Council of French Switzerland that discusses perspectives for the English working class, Marx's argument is vitiated by a highly untypical voluntarism. Marx claimed here, 'The English have all that is needed *materially* for social revolution', and lacked only '*the sense of generalization and revolutionary passion*'.[46] Marx saw this spiritual lack as remediable by the efforts of the General Council of the International, ascribing to it powers far beyond any feasible attainment. The General Council could take initiatives, such as the foundation of the Land and Labour League,[47] 'which as they develop further appear to the public to be spontaneous movements of the English working class',[48] and by this sleight of hand the English workers would allegedly be imbued with the revolutionary passion in which they were deficient. Marx's resort to such an implausible explanation is clearly a sign of uncertainty, and signals the fact that he had not developed – and indeed was never to develop – a satisfactory theory of imperialism and working-class reformism.

46. Below, p. 800.

47. The Land and Labour League was formed in November 1869 by the more left-wing English members of the General Council. It based itself on the demand for land nationalization which had recently been ratified by the Basle Congress, and on republicanism, and campaigned in solidarity with the Irish movement and on issues such as unemployment. Its significance was that it did reach down to organize sections of the working class outside the labour aristocracy, particularly in east London, where several branches of the International were also formed in 1870–1. However, the League was split by the Paris Commune, and subsequently went into decline, with its left wing falling for the sectarian panacea of currency reform. Its experience suggests that the conditions for a new independent political movement of the English proletariat, which was to come into existence in the 1890s with the formation of the independent Labour Party, were not yet present at this stage.

48. Below, p. 800.

The Paris Commune

On 19 July 1870 Louis Napoleon declared war on the North German Confederation, set up under Prussian hegemony after the defeat of Austria in 1966. It is now known that Bismarck lured Bonaparte into war with the Ems telegram. At the time, however, Marx, in common with democratic and socialist opinion generally, saw Bonaparte as the aggressor, and justified the Prussian campaign in its first stage as a war of defence.[49] However, Marx certainly did not succumb to German chauvinism, and in the 'First Address of the General Council on the Franco-Prussian War', written only four days after the war was declared, he specifically put the onus on the German working class to prevent the war from losing its initial defensive character and degenerating into a war against the French people. Marx equally insisted that the German workers must counter the annexation of Alsace and Lorraine, as soon as such a plan became evident.[50]

On 1 September the French army capitulated at Sedan and Louis Napoleon was himself taken prisoner. Three days later the republic was proclaimed in Paris, and a Government of National Defence set up. On 9 September Marx wrote for the General Council a Second Address, which called on the workers of Europe and North America to agitate for the recognition of the French republic, and exposed Prussian annexationist plans. The SDAP, which had been temporarily split by the war, now rallied to the anti-annexationist position taken by Liebknecht and Bebel in the Reichstag, and conducted a campaign which brought down on it severe repression.

The Paris Commune of spring 1871 was the product of a patriotic movement of the workers and petty bourgeoisie against the ruling classes' capitulation to the Prussians. It took its title from the elected municipal council of Paris first established in 1792, whose revolutionary and patriotic role was of crucial importance in the first French revolution. With the fall of the Second Empire, the

49. Engels, in his manuscript 'The Role of Force in History', written in 1887–8, accepted that Louis Napoleon had attempted to avert the war, but had 'walked into a trap'; *MECW* 26, p. 487.

50. See Marx's letter to the Brunswick Committee of the SDAP, c. 1 September 1870; below, pp. 861–3. In this letter Marx forecast, with striking clarity, that the German annexationist policy of 1870 would necessarily lead to a war of France and Russia against Germany.

question of a revolutionary working-class initiative was inevitably raised. In Lyon, Bakunin and Cluseret[51] seized the town hall and proclaimed the 'abolition of the state'. They were soon rebuffed, though insurrectionary attempts also took place in Marseilles and Toulouse. At first the Government of National Defence succeeded in organizing new armies from its base in Tours, but the balance of forces soon shifted decisively in the Prussians' favour. From the end of September the Prussian army occupied all France north and east of Orleans, and laid siege to Paris. Two attempts were made in Paris during the siege to set up a revolutionary government, the first on 31 October, and the second on 22 January, both after unsuccessful attempts to break the siege. The initiative in both these attempts, as in the successful revolution of 18 March, was taken by the Blanquists, in alliance with the petty-bourgeois democrats or 'Jacobins'.

By the end of January the Government of National Defence recognized defeat, and on 8 February elections were held to a National Assembly, entrusted with making peace with the Prussians. The siege of Paris was now lifted, but the Assembly preferred to sit under Prussian protection in Versailles. The remaining obstacle in the way of a peace treaty was the disarmament of Paris, and Thiers's[52] attempt to effect this led to the seizure of power by the Central Committee of the National Guard,[53] the evacuation of all government bodies from Paris, and the election of the Commune. The second siege of Paris now began, and on 21 May the Versailles forces, strengthened by prisoners of war released for the purpose by the Prussians, began their invasion, defeating the last resistance after eight days of bitter fighting. The massacre of prisoners perpetrated by the Thiers government followed in the tradition of June 1848, but on a larger scale. Altogether, several tens of thousands of victims were killed, wounded or deported.

From September 1870 to the fall of the Commune eight months later, Marx's activity was oriented to events in France. After Sedan Marx roused the General Council to campaign for recognition of

51. Gustave Cluseret, a French officer influenced by Bakunin, was later chief of staff of the Paris Conmunard forces. On Bakunin see below, pp. 727–37.

52. Adolphe Thiers, a historian and Orleanist politician, and twice Prime Minister under Louis Philippe, headed the Government of National Defence, supervised the bloody repression of the Commune, and was President of the French Republic from 1871 to 1873.

53. The citizens' militia, formed in Paris on a district basis.

the French republic, and in this he worked closely with the English Positivists (intellectual followers of Comte). Up to the Communard revolution of March 1871, Marx had to steer a difficult course on the General Council against Odger, who identified recognition of the French republic with support for the government of Thiers and Favre, and against the Land and Labour League, who called for British intervention against Germany. Marx's attitude towards the demand for a Commune government, raised by the Blanquists immediately after Sedan, was quite unambiguous. He realized that the Paris workers did not have the strength to defeat the combined forces of the bourgeoisie and the Prussians, and bent himself to forestalling a revolutionary attempt. The General Council's Second Address specifically stated, 'Any attempt at upsetting the new government in the present crisis, when the enemy is almost knocking at the doors of Paris, would be a desperate folly,' and called on the French workers to 'calmly and resolutely improve the opportunities of republican liberty, for the work of their own class organization.'[54]

Contrary to the legend later propagated by the French government, the Communard revolution was not the work of the International. The fall of the Second Empire found the International's Paris Federation severely weakened after three successive prosecutions; it was now also divided by the issues raised by the war. The right-wing Proudhonists supported the republic, and their leader Tolain was to sit in the Versailles Assembly right through the rise and fall of the Commune. The left-wing Proudhonists still opposed revolutionary action in principle, although under Varlin's leadership they served on the Commune when this was set up, and fought valiantly in its defence. From September through to May, the revolutionary initiative remained in the hands of the Blanquists and their middle-class allies, and in the last stage of the Commune these two parties were to take political power into their own hands with a Committee of Public Safety. Blanquists and Jacobins formed a substantial majority on the elected Commune, with fifty-seven members against the Proudhonist minority of twenty-two, seventeen of whom were members of the International.[55]

The Paris Commune roused considerable support from the

54. Below, p. 869.
55. Only one member of the Commune was in any sense a Marxist, the Hungarian Leo Frankel, a protégé of Marx's in London, who served as the Commune's Minister of Labour, and later founded the Hungarian Social-Democratic party.

European working classes, and meetings and demonstrations of solidarity were held across the Continent and in England. Yet the General Council of the International, while participating in solidarity actions, issued no statement on the Commune during its two-month life. This fact is probably attributable to Marx's realization that the heroic attempt of the Communards to 'storm heaven'[56] was doomed in advance to failure. Marx wrote *The Civil War in France* while the Commune was fighting its losing battle against the Versailles army. It was approved by the Council on 30 May, two days after the Commune's defeat, and immediately printed.

The Civil War in France is the most crucial political text of Marx's later years, and contains his most substantial addition to the theory of the proletarian revolution worked out more than two decades previously. Like Marx's earlier writings, *The Class Struggles in France* and *The Eighteenth Brumaire of Louis Bonaparte*,[57] *The Civil War in France* presents an analysis of contemporary history. In this text, however, Marx's theoretical conclusions are less deeply embedded in the historical analysis. In the third section, Marx explains quite straightforwardly why the Commune was such an important revolutionary model, and what its essential features were. A valuable supplement to the published text of *The Civil War in France* is provided by two manuscript drafts[58] in which Marx elaborated at greater length some of the key theoretical questions raised by the Commune.

The starting point of Marx's analysis of the Commune is where *The Eighteenth Brumaire* left off – with the executive power and its 'immense bureaucratic and military organization'.[59] Now, more clearly than in 1852, Marx explained that the subjugation of bourgeois society by its own executive power was the inevitable result of the development of capitalism and the ever increasing threat presented by the working class. The thesis that the Empire was 'the only form of government possible at a time when the bourgeoisie had already lost, and the working class had not yet acquired, the faculty of ruling the nation',[60] does not imply that it was in any

56. Marx to Kugelmann, 12 April 1871; *MECW* 44, p. 132.

57. Both of these are printed in Volume II, above.

58. An extract from the first of these drafts is printed below, pp. 920–52. For the complete texts, see *MECW* 22, pp. 435–551.

59. Above, p. 571.

60. *The Civil War in France*: 'Address of the General Council', below, p. 892.

way neutral between bourgeoisie and proletariat. Although Marx presented the Bonapartist state as endowed with a certain measure of autonomy, he insisted more clearly than he had in *The Eighteenth Brumaire* that Bonapartism was a variety of the bourgeois state, defined by its function in maintaining the exploitation of labour by capital:

At the same pace at which the progress of modern industry developed, widened, intensified the class antagonism between capital and labour, the state power assumed more and more the character of the national power of capital over labour, of a public force organized for social enslavement, of an engine of class despotism.[61]

Imperialism is, at the same time, the most prostitute and the ultimate form of the state power ... which full-grown bourgeois society had finally transformed into a means for the enslavement of labour by capital.[62]

In *The Eighteenth Brumaire* Marx had predicted that the next act of the French revolution would be 'to concentrate all its forces of destruction' against the executive power, and to smash the bureaucratic and military apparatus.[63] What is new in 1871 is Marx's theoretical development, on the basis of the experience of the Commune, of the 'governmental machinery' with which the proletariat must replace the bourgeois state in order to carry out its own aims, i.e. the expropriation of the capitalist class.[64]

Marx introduces his analysis of the Commune with a quotation from the National Guard Central Committee's Manifesto of 18 March, that 'the proletarians of Paris' were herewith 'seizing upon the governmental power'.[65] In his first draft of *The Civil War in France*, Marx elaborated on this signal fact, implicitly seeing the Commune as embodying the tactical recommendations he had laid down in the March Address of 1850, i.e. that the workers, after the overthrow of the existing governments, must not lay down their arms:[66]

61. Ibid., p. 891.

62. Ibid., p. 892. Here, and in general, Marx uses the term 'Imperialist' not in its later sense, but as an adjective for the Bonapartist Empire.

63. Above, p. 571.

64. Below, p. 945.

65. Below, p. 890.

66. Above, p. 319.

That the workmen of Paris have taken the initiative of the present revolution and in heroic self-sacrifice bear the brunt of this battle, is nothing new . . . That the revolution is made in *the name of* and confessedly *for* the popular masses, that is the producing masses, is a feature this revolution has in common with all its predecessors. The new feature is that the people, after the first rise, have not disarmed themselves and surrendered their power into the hands of the republican mountebanks of the ruling classes, that, by the constitution of the *Commune*, they have taken the actual management of their revolution into their own hands and found at the same time, in the case of success, the means to hold it in the hands of the people itself, displacing the state machinery, the governmental machinery of the ruling classes by a governmental machinery of their own.[67]

According to Marx, the 'true secret' of the Commune was:

It was essentially a working-class government, the produce of the struggle of the producing against the appropriating class, the political form at last discovered under which to work out the economical emancipation of labour.[68]

Marx's presentation of the basic structural features of the Commune can be summarized as follows:

1. The abolition of an armed force separate from and hence opposed to the people. 'The first decree of the Commune, therefore, was the suppression of the standing army, and the substitution for it of the armed people.'[69]

2. The vesting of all political functions not in representatives but in recallable delegates. 'The Commune was formed of the municipal councillors, chosen by universal suffrage in the various wards of the town, responsible and revocable at short terms.' 'The police was at once stripped of its political attributes, and turned into the responsible and at all times revocable agent of the Commune. So were the officials of all other branches of the administration.' 'Instead of deciding once in three or six years which member of the ruling class was to misrepresent the people in parliament, universal suffrage was to serve the people, constituted in communes, as individual

67. 'First Draft of *The Civil War in France*', below, p. 945.
68. *The Civil War* . . . : 'Address', below, p. 896.
69. Ibid., p. 893. All the quotations under these five headings are from pp. 893–5 below.

suffrage serves every other employer in the search for the workmen and managers in his business.'

3. The absence of all material privileges for the delegated officials. 'From the members of the Commune downwards, the public service had to be done at *workmen's wages*. The vested interests and the representation allowances of the high dignitaries of state disappeared along with the high dignitaries themselves.'

4. The union of executive, legislative and judicial power in the same organs. 'The Commune was to be a working, not a parliamentary body, executive and legislative at the same time.' 'The judicial functionaries were to be divested of that sham independence which had but served to mask their abject subserviency to all succeeding governments ... Like the rest of public servants, magistrates and judges were to be elective, responsible and revocable.'

5. The organization of national unity from the base upwards. 'The commune was to be the political form of even the smallest country hamlet ... The rural communes of every district were to administer their common affairs by an assembly of delegates in the central town, and these district assemblies were again to send deputies to the national delegation in Paris ... The few but important functions which still would remain for a central government were not to be suppressed ... but were to be organized by Communal, and therefore strictly responsible agents.' 'While the merely repressive organs of the old governmental power were to be amputated, its legitimate functions were to be wrested from an authority usurping pre-eminence over society itself, and restored to the responsible agents of society.'

It is important to note that these structural features of the Commune do not explicitly demarcate a privileged position for the industrial working class, any more than the corresponding features of the bourgeois state, in either its parliamentary, Bonapartist or fascist variants, do for the bourgeoisie. But just as the maintenance of the power of capital over labour requires a state machinery which is divorced from the mass of the people and uncontrollable by them, so the working class, in order to expropriate the bourgeoisie and set up a communist order, requires a form of government through which the political power of the mass of the people can be directly expressed. And this is what all the institutions of the Commune were designed to do, backed in the last instance by the armed people themselves. Marx makes this distinction between ruling class and form of state in the following terms:

As the state machinery and parliamentarism are not the real life of the ruling classes, but only the organized general organs of their dominion, the political guarantees and forms and expressions of the old order of things, so the Commune is not the social movement of the working class and therefore of a general regeneration of mankind, but the organized means of action.[70]

The distinction is an important one, as throughout his life Marx always held that a new class, including the working class, could only come to power and transform society to its design if it represented, not merely its own particular interest, but a universal interest of historical development, so that only those with a vested interest in the old order would stand in its way. The Commune was thus 'a thoroughly expansive political form, while all previous forms of government had been emphatically repressive',[71] although by this Marx does not mean that the Commune government did not need to repress the minority who resisted the progress it represented. Indeed, Marx specifically states:

The Communal organization once firmly established on a national scale, the catastrophes it might still have to undergo would be sporadic slaveholders' insurrections, which, while for a moment interrupting the work of peaceful progress, would only accelerate the movement, by putting the sword into the hand of the social revolution.[72]

In the 'political form' of the Commune, Marx found the historical experience necessary to develop and concretize his theory of proletarian political power. The theory of scientific communism, as formulated in the Communist Manifesto, presents the proletarian revolution as passing through a sequence of stages: seizure of political power, expropriation of the bourgeoisie, disappearance of the political state. In the 1848 period, for lack of a concrete model of proletarian political power, Marx left it unclear what relation there is between the dictatorship of the proletariat and the disappearance of the state. In 1871, however, using the model of the Commune, Marx developed more clearly

70. 'First Draft . . .', below, pp. 936–7.
71. *The Civil War* . . . : 'Address', below, p. 896.
72. 'First Draft . . .', below, p. 937. 'Slaveholders' insurrection' refers to the recent North American Civil War. (See the Introduction to Volume II, above, pp. 365–6.)

the concept of the transient nature of the proletarian dictatorship. The substantive change in his position is that he no longer presented the inauguration of the proletarian dictatorship and the 'withering away' of the state as two discrete and unrelated stages. Throughout his writing on the Commune, Marx stresses that the political power which the proletariat puts in place of the smashed bourgeois state machine is a power of a fundamentally different kind to that of the bourgeois state. The Commune form of government, which mediates the class rule of the proletariat, is already no longer a state in the former sense of the term, because it is no longer separate from and antagonistic to civil society. This is why Marx deliberately refrains from calling the Commune a state, and precisely uses the terms 'Commune' and 'state' as opposites, e.g. 'this new Commune, which breaks the modern state power'.[73] While the Second Empire represented for Marx the highest level of absorption of civil functions by the state, the Commune, as its 'direct antithesis', 'would have restored to the social body all the forces hitherto absorbed by the state parasite feeding upon, and clogging the free movement of, society'.[74]

In his manuscript draft, Marx is even more explicit on the opposition between Commune and state. Here he describes the Commune as 'a revolution against the *state* itself, this supernaturalist abortion of society, a resumption by the people for the people of its own social life'.[75] It is this attribute of the Commune, its restoration to civil society of the social functions usurped by the state, and its delegation of political functions, including the 'few but important functions which would still remain for a central government' to 'strictly responsible agents', that differentiates it from the bourgeois state machine with its drive to dominate and control civil society, a drive that Marx had explained as the product of the class struggle. The working class still needs political power to overcome the bourgeoisie's resistance to its expropriation, but the repressive role of this power gradually disappears of itself with the cessation of the bourgeoisie's resistance, as it is not entrusted to a power separate from and uncontrolled by the mass of the people. Thus Marx saw the dictatorship of the proletariat as, right from the start, a political form that tends to wither away of itself, and the Paris Commune

73. *The Civil War* . . . : 'Address', below, p. 895.
74. Ibid., pp. 892 and 895.
75. 'First Draft of . . .', below, p. 933.

which first institutionalized this political form was henceforth to serve Marx and Engels, and the Marxist movement after them, as a basic reference point.

If the Commune was 'essentially a working-class government', and provided a general model for the proletarian dictatorship, Marx also recognized that, in a country in which the industrial working class was still a minority of the population, the Commune depended for its survival on the workers maintaining alliances with other classes – particularly a section of the middle class, and the peasantry. Part of the middle class in fact spontaneously rallied to the side of the proletariat, and Marx presents this as a sign of the Commune's strength and the workers' historical mission. The peasantry was never more than a potential ally, although Marx believed that the Commune would have won over the peasants if it had been given time. In his manuscript draft, Marx elaborated in greater detail the character of these alliances, actual and hypothetical, bringing the same kind of analysis to bear on the proletarian revolution itself, in terms of a ruling class bloc and a dominant class or class fraction within it, as he had employed in *The Class Struggles in France* to analyse the state of the exploiting classes.[76]

Marx summarizes this analysis under a very significant heading, 'The Communal Revolution as the Representative of all Classes of Society not Living on Foreign Labour'.[77] This category clearly includes the great majority of the peasantry, and divides the middle class between its 'true vital elements'[78] who played a necessary role in production, and the 'wealthy capitalists'[79] who had fled to Versailles. Working class, peasantry and petty bourgeoisie thus formed the ruling class bloc that would have come into existence if the Commune revolution had been able to survive and spread across France as a whole. Towards the peasantry, the Commune's relationship was in the circumstances a completely hypothetical one. The Commune had no chance to develop any real relationship with the peasants, although Marx believed that it could soon have won them over on the basis of its ability to stave off a war indemnity, abolish conscription, provide cheap government and local self-government. Marx was in fact too optimistic in holding that 'being immediately benefited by

76. See the Introduction to Volume II, above, pp. 344–8.
77. 'First Draft . . .', below, p. 942.
78. Ibid., p. 941.
79. *The Civil War* . . . : 'Address', below, p. 898.

the Communal republic, [the peasant] would soon confide in it',[80] and that three months of rule by the Versailles government would provoke a peasant rebellion. In the event, it was the peasantry that defeated the Commune, passively, since this greater part of the French nation did not mobilize in its defence, and actively, as soldiers in the army that overran Paris at the end of May. However, Marx's theoretical model of a worker-peasant alliance remains an important one, and was later to be developed and put into practice by Lenin.[81]

In contrast to the projected alliance with the peasantry, the Commune did establish a working alliance between working class and petty bourgeoisie, partly on the basis of patriotism, but above all on the question of the war indemnity of five billion francs demanded by the Prussians, which the Commune insisted should be paid primarily by the upper classes responsible for the war.[82] This gave the petty bourgeoisie a direct material incentive for 'rallying round the working class'.[83] It is clear from Marx's drafts that he saw this alliance as an intimate one. The workers did not just pacify the lower middle class with economic concessions, but actually gave them a share in the Communal government proportional to their numbers:

For the first time in history the petty and middling middle class has openly rallied round the workmen's revolution, and proclaimed it as the only means of their own salvation and that of France! It forms with them the bulk of the National Guard, it sits with them in the Commune, it mediates for them in the Union Républicaine![84]

80. 'First Draft of. . .', below, p. 941.

81. Although Marx certainly maintained that the communist revolution could only be led by the proletariat, he was far from ruling out the possibility of pro-letarian revolutions in countries where the majority of the population were still peasants – as was evidently the case in the France of 1871 – and consistently stressed that the success of such revolutions depended on peasant participation. Besides Marx's formulations on the peasant problem in *The Civil War in France* and particularly in the first draft, see also *The Eighteenth Brumaire*, above, p. 579, n. 53, and 'Conspectus of Bakunin's *Statism and Anarchy*', below, pp. 1017–19. Regarding Russia, Marx even maintained in his last years that the peasantry could in certain special circumstances be the main force of a communist revolution; see below, p. 751.

82. 'First Draft . . .', below, p. 938.

83. *The Civil War* . . . : 'Address', below, p. 898.

84. 'First Draft . . .', below, p. 942. On the 'Union Républicaine', see below, p. 898, n. 63.

But within the ruling bloc of workers and lower middle class, with potential space for the peasants, Marx leaves no doubt that the dominant class, that which determines the character of the ruling bloc as a whole, is the industrial proletariat. It is the 'workmen's revolution' that the middle class rallies around, and, as Marx writes in *The Civil War in France* itself, 'The working class was openly acknowledged as the only class capable of social initiative, even by the great bulk of the Paris middle class – shopkeepers, tradesmen, merchants – the wealthy capitalists alone excepted.'[85]

Had the Commune survived, i.e. had it been able to win peasant support, Marx believed that the working class could have gone on to build socialism in France.[86] Naturally this would eventually have broken its alliance with the urban and rural petty bourgeoisie, and Marx refers to this obliquely when he writes, 'The Commune does not do away with the class struggles, through which the working classes strive to the abolition of all classes . . . It could start violent reactions and as violent revolutions.' Yet Marx held that the Commune 'affords the rational medium in which that class struggle can run through its different phases in the most rational and humane way'.[87] Class struggle of this kind arose in a highly acute form in Russia after a proletarian revolution had been made in alliance with the peasantry, but where, despite Marx's warning that the proletariat 'must not hit the peasant over the head',[88] the working class did not manage to ease the peasants' transition to socialism by economic incentives, but forcibly appropriated the peasants' surplus in order to obtain the funds for industrial development. In these circumstances, the ensuing class struggle was far from conducted in 'the most rational and humane way' that Marx had hoped for.

In the conditions prevailing in spring 1871, the Commune had little time to carry out measures of a socialist character. Marx himself noted that 'the principal measures taken by the Commune

85. Below, p. 898.

86. In conformity with modem usage, 'socialism' is used here for the 'lower stage of communism', i.e. the collectivized economy constructed by the expropriation of the capitalist class, but still dominated by material scarcity. See 'Critique of the Gotha Programme', below, pp. 1030–1.

87. 'First Draft . . .', below, p. 937.

88. 'Conspectus of Bakunin's *Statism and Anarchy*', below, pp. 1018.

are taken for the salvation of the middle class'.[89] The measures that the Commune took in the particular interest of the working class were limited to such things as the prohibition on employers levying fines and the abolition of night work for bakers. Workshops and factories closed by renegade employers were indeed handed over to workers' self-management, but as a temporary measure and with the proviso of compensation. The Commune's two working-class parties, Blanquists and Proudhonists, were both highly confused in their economic theories, and would no doubt have made many errors in the course of building socialism. But for Marx, the fundamental premise of this development had already been achieved in the Commune. 'The great social measure of the Commune was its own working existence.'[90] If it had been able to develop, Marx held that the Commune government would necessarily tend towards communism, as

The political rule of the producer cannot coexist with the perpetuation of his social slavery. The Commune was therefore to serve as a lever for uprooting the economical foundations upon which rests the existence of classes, and therefore of class rule.[91]

In the style of much of *The Civil War in France*, Marx's phrase here – 'was therefore to serve' – does not simply refer to the subjective intent of the Communards, but to the objective tendency within the Communal form of government, which the working class, having political power in its hands, could not avoid furthering. Throughout this text and the preliminary drafts for it, Marx constantly moves from present actuality to theoretical conclusions. As in his earlier works on France, analysis of contemporary history was always for Marx the raw material of theoretical development.

In Lenin's influential commentary on Marx's writings on the state, he stressed that Marx in no sense 'made up or invented a "new" society', but that

he studied the birth of the new society out of the old, and the forms of transition from the latter to the former, as a natural-historical process. He examined the actual experience of a mass proletarian movement and tried to draw practical lessons from it. He 'learned' from the Commune, just as all

89. 'First Draft . . .', below, p. 942.
90. *The Civil War* . . . : 'Address', below, p. 901.
91. Ibid., p. 896.

the great revolutionary thinkers learned unhesitatingly from the experience of great movements of the oppressed classes.[92]

In the Manifesto Marx and Engels had not been able to see what formal political transformation would be needed in order for the proletariat to constitute itself as the ruling class. When the Manifesto was reprinted in 1872, Marx and Engels added a Preface in which they found it necessary to make only one significant qualification: 'One thing especially was proved by the Commune, viz. that "the working class cannot simply lay hold of the ready-made state machinery, and wield it for its own purposes"', and they refer to the section of *The Civil War in France* from which this quote is taken.[93]

If Marx had warned the Paris workers before the revolution of 18 March that any attempt to seize power in one isolated city was doomed to defeat, the Commune government of Blanquists, Proudhonists and Jacobins certainly made many mistakes that worsened its position. It failed to take the offensive against Versailles when this was still possible, and even to seize the Bank of France, which Marx believed would have put it in a position where it could have forced a compromise settlement on the Versaillais.[94] By the end of May 1871 the Paris Commune, 'glorious harbinger of a new society',[95] had been ruthlessly crushed, with the massacre of some 14,000 workers and the imprisonment or deportation of more than 10,000 others.

Marx and Bakunin

The vicious reaction triumphant in France found an echo in the persecution of the Commune's supporters in almost all Continental countries. Marx's brilliant vindication of the Commune led to the International being identified as its instigator, and its strength was ludicrously inflated by the hysterical propagandists of reaction. Martial law was declared throughout France, and in March 1872 Thiers passed through the French Assembly a special bill that made membership in the International a crime punishable

92. *The State and Revolution*, in Lenin, *Selected Works*; online at www.marxists.org/archive/lenin/works/sw/index.htm
93. Above, p. 60.
94. See Marx's letter to Ferdinand Domela-Nieuwenhuis, 22 February 1881; *MECW* 46, p. 65.
95. *The Civil War in France*, below, p. 917.

by imprisonment. In June 1872 Jules Favre, the French foreign minister, circularized the European governments calling for joint action to stamp out the International, and Bismarck proposed a European alliance against the International a month later. The following year not only the chancellors of Austria and Germany, but the two emperors themselves, discussed the threat of the International at two conferences, and the same theme was taken up by the Pope. In the prevailing conditions of repression, the International had to forgo holding its annual Congress for the second year running, but the General Council called instead, as in 1865, a Conference in London with the explicit aim of consolidating the International's organization in this difficult period. The London Conference marks the beginning of the International's internal crisis, and this cannot be discussed without returning to the period before the Franco-Prussian war and the entry of Michael Bakunin into the ranks of the International.

Bakunin's political career had been interwoven with that of Marx from the days of the Young Hegelian movement in the 1840s. He had been a member of the *Deutsche-Französische Jahrbücher* circle in 1844,[96] and had taken an active part in the German revolution of 1848. Despite Bakunin's differences with Marx and Engels over the Slav question, they disputed with him in 1849 as a friend, and respected the revolutionary militancy which led him to sacrifice himself in the Dresden insurrection during the Reich Constitution Campaign.[97] From 1849 to 1863 Bakunin was imprisoned, passing from Prussia through Austria to Russia, and spending years in solitary confinement in the Schüsselberg fortress before being exiled to Siberia. In 1863 Bakunin made a dramatic escape, and soon after arrived in London. At first he worked with Alexander Herzen, the then leader of the Russian emigration, whom Marx detested as a liberal with an ambiguous attitude towards tsarism, but in 1865 Bakunin broke with Herzen and left for Italy. Before leaving London he re-established friendly relations with Marx, and agreed to work in Italy for the International.

Once installed in Italy, however, Bakunin did not devote himself to the workers' movement, which was in its earliest stage of development there, and about which Bakunin still understood very

96. See the Introduction to *The Revolutions of 1848*, above, pp. 7–8.
97. Ibid., pp. 48–9, and 'Democratic Pan-Slavism', ibid., p. 227.

little. Instead, he bent his efforts to conspiratorial organization among the young Italian intelligentsia who had rallied to the cause of the Risorgimento and been subsequently disaffected by its anti-democratic outcome. The aims of Bakunin's secret International Brotherhood were vague, but it worked publicly not within the workers' International, but within the bourgeois-democratic organization known as the League of Peace and Freedom. At the League's Congress in September 1868, however, when its anti-working-class nature became evident, Bakunin organized some of the more left-wing elements of the League into the Alliance of Socialist Democracy, and as such wrote to the General Council applying for affiliation.

The starting-point of Bakunin's political practice was not commitment to the proletariat in its struggle against capital, but opposition to the state as such. Bakunin only rallied to the proletarian movement when he realized that the single class with an interest in the overthrow of the modern bourgeois state was the industrial working class. This realization coincided with the first stirrings of an independent workers' movement in Italy, and Bakunin went on to establish the doctrine of anarcho-communism which he is historically remembered as a tendency within the workers' movement, and attempted to dominate the International from his Italian base.

Bakunin's essential thesis was that the proletariat, while it must overthrow the existing state apparatus in order to liberate itself, must not set up in its place its own political power, as by doing so it necessarily substitutes a new authoritarian apparatus which will perpetuate its oppression. The workers' movement must therefore refrain from organizing as a political party, and from activity that involves it in working through the existing political state (e.g. the struggle for reforms, participation in parliament). The only permissible relationship to the state is the revolution that overthrows all political authority once and for all. Instead of the proletariat becoming the ruling class (which for Bakunin was almost a contradiction in terms), and using its political power to transform society, it must build the organization of the new society within the old in the form of the International. This must therefore be based on the principle of complete local autonomy, and Bakunin launched his attack on Marx over the question of the International's organization, thereby managing to unite behind his banner of 'anti-authoritarianism' all those elements, including English trade-unionists, who for their own reasons resented the 'authoritarian' interference of the General Council into their affairs.

Despite Bakunin's attack on the General Council's 'authoritarianism', he recognized as clearly as did Marx the need for revolutionary leadership. The inevitable counterpart of Bakunin's insistence that the working class organize not an 'authoritarian' party but an embryonic new society was his construction of a hidden leadership, immune to democratic control, to carry out the insurrectionary overthrow of the state. Bakunin's network of secret societies, the greater part of which existed only in his scheming brain, is legendary. When Bakunin first attempted to take over the International, he formed the Alliance as a public front, arrogating to it 'the special mission of studying political and philosophical questions on the basis of the great principle of equality'.[98] However, when the General Council refused affiliation to the Alliance on the grounds that an 'International within the International' was not permissible, Bakunin was quite happy to abandon this paper organization, reducing the Alliance to a 'central section' in Geneva, as his real concern was to organize his supporters into secret societies, and infiltrate the International in this way.

Bakunin and Marx first came into conflict at the time of the Basle Congress, over the 'abolition of the right of inheritance', the means proposed by Bakunin to transform capitalism into socialism. This was opposed by Marx, firstly because it was bound to antagonize the peasantry, and secondly because it reflected Bakunin's mistaken notion that the state, and not the economy, was the fundamental social structure and the basis of proletarian oppression. Bakunin carried the day at Basle, although this was in itself a relatively minor defeat for the Marxists. But shortly after the Basle Congress, Bakunin launched a general offensive against the General Council on several points, and it is these attacks, made in the Swiss papers *Égalité* and *Progrès* which he controlled, that Marx replied to in January 1870 with a 'Circular' to the Federal Council of French Switzerland. In the following months Bakunin succeeded in winning over a section of the Federal Council of French Switzerland, which then split. The overthrow of Louis Bonaparte provided Bakunin's followers with the

98. *Programme and Rules of the International Alliance of Socialist Democracy*, printed in *IWMA* III, pp. 273–8, together with Marx's marginal comments. See also 'The Alleged Splits in the International', below, pp. 956–998.

opportunity to work in the southern part of France, and in the wake of the Commune the Bakuninists' revolutionary militancy attracted the growing numbers of workers that joined the International's sections in Spain and Italy.

The internal crisis of the International, leading up to the Hague Congress and the subsequent split, is one of the most important periods of Marx's political activity, and, as Engels later wrote, 'the least amenable to accurate portrayal from printed sources'.[99] Marx was not merely fighting a defensive struggle against Bakunin's attempt to take over the International. It is evident that he had his own plans for its further development, and although these are not explicitly formulated in any written document, it seems that Marx hoped to transform the International's organizations in the various countries into political parties centred on London. Already in 1867, when the International first began to develop into a significant force on the Continent, Marx had written to Engels, 'And when the next revolution comes, and that will perhaps be sooner than might appear, we (i.e. you and I) will have this mighty Engine *at our disposal*',[1] and in the Circular of January 1870 Marx again emphasized, indeed overemphasized,[2] the role that the General Council could play. Meanwhile, as Marx wrote in the General Council's 'Report to the Brussels Congress':

The year 1867–8 will mark an epoch in the history of the Association. After a period of peaceable development it has assumed dimensions powerful enough to provoke the bitter denunciations of the ruling classes and the hostile demonstrations of governments. It has entered upon the phases of strife.[3]

Marx thus probably intended the International to become, in the event of revolution, a tactical weapon, and by 1868 he already saw a new revolutionary crisis on the horizon. The remaining condition for transforming the International into a more centralized and disciplined

99. Engels to Kautsky, 25 March 1895; *MECW* 50, p. 481. In September 1870 Engels sold his share in his family's business and moved from Manchester to London, where he became an active member of the General Council. During the critical period of 1870–72, Marx and Engels were thus able to work directly together for the first time since 1850.
   1. Marx to Engels, 11 September 1867; *MECW* 42, pp. 423–4.
   2. See above, p. 713.
   3. Below, p. 778.

body was a certain degree of ideological homogeneity, and the Brussels Congress marked a great victory for Marx in this regard, in that he succeeded in winning over a section of the Proudhonists to his own positions and defeating the Proudhonist diehards. The stage was now set for Marx's organizational plans: at the Basle Congress of 1869, held before Bakunin's operations became evident, Marx obtained passage of a resolution that considerably increased the powers of the General Council, in particular giving it the right to suspend, pending the decision of the Congress, branches of the International that contravened its principles and decisions. Marx did not in fact make use of this power vis-à-vis the Bakuninists, although the General Council did use it against the London French branch of the International, which was in Blanquist hands, and compromised the International by calling for terrorist actions such as the assassination of Bonaparte.

After the Basle Congress, the Bakuninist campaign against the General Council got under way, and by the time the London Conference met in September 1871 Marx responded by obtaining a further increase in the powers of the Council, giving it the right to appoint delegates to attend any branch or committee of the International, prohibiting groups of the International to call themselves by other than geographical titles, or to 'pretend to accomplish special missions within the International', and specifically excluding secret societies.[4] Marx thus hoped to block both the secret and the public activity of Bakunin's Alliance. However, the battle between Bakunin and Marx was no mere personal struggle for power, but a struggle of principles. The key issue at stake was that of working-class political action, and on this vital question Bakunin was diametrically opposed to the direction in which Marx was attempting to move the International. The most important result of the London Conference was therefore the passage of Marx's resolution on 'Working-Class Political Action'. This resolution reminded the International of the preamble to its own Rules which Marx had drafted in 1864 and which had spoken of the need to conquer political power, and went on to define this in more concrete terms. It argued from the 'presence of an unbridled reaction which ... pretends to maintain by brute force the distinction of classes and the political domination of the propertied classes resulting from it',

---

4. The Resolutions of the London Conference are printed in *IWMA* IV, pp. 440–50.

853.

that 'the working class cannot act, as a class, except by constituting itself into a political party, distinct from, and opposed to, all old parties formed by the propertied classes,' and that 'this constitution of the working class into a political party is indispensable in order to ensure the triumph of the social revolution and its ultimate end – the abolition of classes'.[5]

From the London Conference resolutions Marx evidently hoped to go forward to defeat Bakunin both organizationally and ideologically. But the growth of the International in southern Europe, and the accumulated minor grievances of other sections against the General Council, made it possible for Bakunin to rally a considerable force behind his 'anti-authoritarian' banner. At the Hague Congress in September 1872, which both sides prepared for by rather dubious means, and the greater part of which was spent in challenging credentials, Marx won a paper victory, but also a Pyrrhic one. The Hague Congress ratified the decisions of the London Conference and expelled Bakunin and Guillaume[6] from the International on the grounds that they had attempted to organize a secret society within it. Bakunin's expulsion is unlikely to have been passed had not Marx and Engels presented circumstantial evidence that appeared to implicate Bakunin in the 'Nechayev affair'; they were certainly not above using foul means when political necessity demanded.[7]

By the time the Hague Congress met, however, it was already obvious to Marx that, despite formal majorities, he had failed to win sufficient support to make his envisaged transformation of the International possible, or even to guarantee that Bakunin would

5. Below, p. 954.

6. James Guillaume, a Swiss schoolteacher, was the organizer of Bakunin's faction within the International.

7. Sergei Nechayev, a leading figure in the St Petersburg student movement of 1868–9, travelled to Switzerland in 1869 and established contact with Bakunin. In Nechayev Bakunin found a fellow-conspirator in whose mind fantasy and reality merged even more intimately than in his own. On the basis of the secret societies that he concocted with Bakunin, on returning to Russia Nechayev claimed to represent the International while he made himself notorious for his unscrupulous manipulation of revolutionary comrades, a practice he justified in his *Catechism of the Revolutionist*. Nechayev's arrest in 1871, and the exposure of his activities, threatened to discredit the International, and the London Conference therefore declared, 'Netschajeff has never been a member or an agent of the International Working Men's Association' (*IWMA* IV, p. 434). At the Hague Congress, Marx and Engels successfully used against Bakunin his connections with Nechayev, although they knew that Bakunin was guilty of nothing worse than crass misjudgement and gullibility. See p. 966 below, n. 34.

not take over the International at a future date. As Marx wrote to Kugelmann, the Hague Congress was 'a matter of life and death for the International; and before I retire I want at least to protect it from disintegrating elements'.[8] For this reason, Marx travelled in person to The Hague, his only attendance at one of the International's Congresses. Marx's majority at The Hague was composed chiefly of Germans, the exiled French Blanquists and a part of the English delegates, as well as his personal supporters on the General Council. Against Marx were ranged forces that counted for at least as much in real terms: the Spanish, the Belgians, the French-Swiss, and some of the English. The Italians, although Bakunin's most loyal disciples, refused to attend the Hague Congress in the same company as the 'authoritarians'. In order to prevent the General Council from falling into Bakuninist hands, Marx played his master-stroke: Engels proposed its removal to New York, which was carried by a narrow majority against both Bakuninist and Blanquist opposition. In New York the General Council was in the safe hands of Marx's German-American followers, until it died a natural death. The 'anti-authoritarians' called their own conference a week later, but they set up no executive body and, although their International nominally survived until 1881, it never developed a coherent unity. The Marxist International was finally wound up at the Philadelphia Congress of 1876.

Marx held an extremely poor opinion of Bakunin as a theorist, which was abundantly justified by Bakunin's muddled ideas. Thus in the programme of the Alliance of Socialist Democracy Bakunin demanded the 'social and economic equality of classes',[9] a nonsensical phrase which Marx made great play with. He also declared the Alliance atheist, which Marx saw as archaic and ridiculous posturing, as he had held ever since the 1840s that religion could only disappear when society was transformed. In one crucial respect, however, Marx underrated Bakunin, classing his theory together with Proudhonism as a variety of 'political indifferentism'. It is true that Bakunin inherited from Proudhon his view of political authority as an unmitigated evil; Marx saw this as an ideological position that reflected the recent artisanal background of the Latin working classes. However, Marx failed to make the significant

8. Marx to Kugelmann, 29 July 1872; *MECW* 44, p. 413.
9. *IWMA* III, p. 273.

distinction that while Proudhon's abstentionism was a purely passive one, Bakunin, for all his errors, was a socialist revolutionary who aimed, like Marx (and like Blanqui whom Marx always respected), at the overthrow of the bourgeois state and the abolition of private property. Bakunin's abstentionism, however mistaken, reflected his almost instinctive fear of reformist diversion from the revolutionary goal, and of bureaucratic authority in the post-revolutionary society.

In their articles 'Political Indifferentism' and 'On Authority', Marx and Engels made short work of Bakunin's politics. Marx wrote ironically that

if the workers replace the dictatorship of the bourgeois class with their own revolutionary dictatorship, then they are guilty of the terrible crime of *lèse-principe*; for, in order to satisfy their miserable profane daily needs and to crush the resistance of the bourgeois class, they, instead of laying down their arms and abolishing the state, give to the state a revolutionary and transitory form.[10]

And Engels asked the anarchists:

Have these gentlemen ever seen a revolution? A revolution is certainly the most authoritarian thing there is; it is the act whereby one part of the population imposes its will on the other part by means of rifles, bayonets and cannons . . . [and] it must maintain this rule by means of the terror which its arms inspire in the reactionaries.[11]

The mistake of the anti-authoritarians was that they 'demand that the authoritarian political state be abolished at one stroke even before the social conditions that gave birth to it have been destroyed'.[12] But however correct Marx was to insist that the working class can only expropriate the bourgeoisie and establish socialism by itself becoming the ruling class, and that political authority can only disappear consequent on the abolition of classes, Bakunin's rejection of working-class participation in the bourgeois political system, and his warning of the dangers involved in the proletarian seizure of political power, raise questions that Marx did not solve altogether satisfactorily. The former leads on to the question of reformism, which is the subject of the next section of this Introduction. As

10. 'Political Indifferentism', below, p. 1012.
11. 'On Authority', in *MECW* 23, p. 425.
12. Ibid.

for Bakunin's criticisms of his alleged 'state communism', Marx
countered this charge in his 'Conspectus of Bakunin's *Statism and
Anarchy*', with a series of comments interspersed between excerpts
of Bakunin's book that he copied out.

Bakunin's key attack on Marx is a classic anarchist formulation:

> The election of people's representatives and rulers of the state . . . [is] a lie,
> behind which is concealed the despotism of the *governing minority*, and only
> the more dangerously in so far as it appears as expression of the so-called
> people's will.

No matter that the workers may elect representatives from their
own number, Bakunin claims that such representatives, once
elected, '*cease to be workers* . . . and look down on the whole
common workers' world from the height of the state . . . Anyone
who can doubt this knows nothing of the nature of men.'[13] On the
contrary, Marx claims that the relation between electors and elected
depends on the 'economic foundation, the economic situation of
the voters'. In communist society, Marx holds, 'the distribution
of the general functions has become a business matter, that gives
no one domination', and 'election has nothing of its present
political character'.[14] Marx gives the examples of a trade-union
executive committee, the manager of a cooperative factory, and the
Russian village commune and *artel* to show how in the absence
of antagonistic interests there is no domination involved in the
election of representatives, which is always necessary in order to
carry out the 'general functions'.

Marx was certainly not oblivious of the dangers of political
bureaucracy. In the context of the International he had attacked
the dictatorial leadership of Lassalle and Schweitzer, and stressed
the importance of trade unions as a school for proletarian self-
government. He saw the form of direct democracy adopted by
the Paris Commune, with its revocability of representatives,
the absence of material privileges and the unity of executive
and legislative powers, as important precisely because it made
possible political control by the direct producers. Bakunin
was certainly misguided in seeing a workers' government as
necessarily leading to the formation of a new governing caste, and

13. Below, pp. 1020–1.
14. Ibid., p. 1020.

in founding the equation of political coercion and governing caste in 'human nature'. Indeed, from Bakunin's standpoint, a classless society would never be possible at all; at least Bakunin gives no adequate answer as to how the revolutionary proletariat is to overcome the resistance of the old ruling classes without using political coercion. But Bakunin, for all his errors, was conscious in advance of the revolution, albeit in a defective way, that there is a real problem of bureaucracy in the post-revolutionary period, a problem which the Marxist movement was only to begin seriously to deal with in Lenin's last writings on the bureaucratic deformations of the Soviet Russian state. Although the problems that the Russian revolution later posed could not have been solved in advance, it remains true that only through the solution of these problems can the withering away of the state that Marxism looks forward to become a reality.[15]

The Problem of Reformism

The defeat of the Second Empire marked the transition between two eras of working-class history. Up to 1870 European politics in general, and the workers' movement in particular, had been dominated by the Bonapartist regime in France and the unresolved problem of national unification in Germany and Italy. The French defeat consolidated the system of national states, and Marx realized even before Sedan that, '*This war has shifted the centre of gravity of the Continental workers' movement from France to Germany.*'[16] Despite the defeat of the Commune, the European proletariat of the 1870s found new opportunities open to it, and even in France the workers' movement recovered within a decade from this terrible blow. With the rapid growth of industry, it was no longer possible for the ruling classes of more advanced countries to contain the workers' movement by simple repression. Manhood suffrage had been granted in Bismarck's North German Confederation of 1867,

15. In this 'Conspectus', Marx accepted Bakunin's attribution to him of the concept of a 'workers' state, if he wants to call it that' (p. 1021). As Marx implies, it is not the word used that is important, but the concept it denotes. It is clear from this context, as also in the 'Critique of the Gotha Programme' (below, p. 1039), that where Marx does sometimes use the term 'state' to refer to the political form of workers' power, this represents no departure from his position in *The Civil War in France*, except at the level of terminology.

16. Marx to the Brunswick Committee of the SDAP, c. 1 September 1870; below, pp. 862–3.

and was extended to the German Reich established in 1871. The French Third Republic could also not avoid giving the working class freedom to organize politically within the legal framework of the bourgeois-democratic state. In those countries where democratic reforms were slower in coming, their attainment, proved possible by the German and French examples, provided the immediate goal of the socialist workers.

The tactics that Marx laid down for the workers' movement in the 1870s, and which Engels maintained until his death in 1895, were to provide the mass parties of the Second International (founded 1889) with their guiding principles. These parties, however, subordinated these tactical positions to an essentially reformist strategy, and failed completely to come to grips with the new problems and tasks that arose after Marx and Engels were dead, in the era of monopoly capitalism and modern imperialism. As Marx's dicta on the use of parliament, the peaceful road to socialism, and the proletarian party have been interpreted in a reformist as well as a revolutionary sense, it is necessary to examine his precise formulations and the contexts in which they arose, in order to judge the disputes over the Marxist legacy that have been fought now for over a century.

For Marx, the use that the working class could make of the suffrage and parliament, and the question of the peaceful road to socialism, were distinct and separate issues. Marx held that the working class should always make use of the representative institutions of bourgeois democracy, which, as a majority of the population, it could turn against the bourgeoisie itself. The franchise was to be 'transformed from the instrument of fraud that it has been up till now into an instrument of emancipation'.[17] The resolution of the London Conference on working-class political action referred to precisely this. Marx's insistence there, so infuriating to the anarchists, that the working class had to constitute itself 'into a political party, distinct from, and opposed to, all old parties formed by the propertied classes . . . in order to ensure the triumph of the social revolution',[18] implied that although the aims of the working class lay beyond the bourgeois state (as Marx had explained only a few months earlier in *The Civil War in France*), the way for the advanced workers to build up their strength and rally to them their class as a whole was through the

17. 'Introduction to the Programme of the French Workers' Party', below, p. 1061.
18. Below, p. 954.

electoral arena. The prototype of such a party was the German SDAP, which had been formed two years before the London Conference, and which served Marx as a living example. After the defeat of the Commune, the SDAP decisively emerged as the 'centre of gravity' of the European workers' movement. It had successfully used the parliamentary tribune as a forum for agitation, built up a disciplined mass membership, and survived undamaged the imprisonment of its leaders, Liebknecht and Bebel, for their campaign against the annexation of Alsace and Lorraine. The socialist workers' parties that grew up in almost every European country in the 1880s formed themselves more or less on the German example. Marx, and Engels after him, were to give every encouragement to the formation of these parties, and saw in them the organizational form through which to prepare the socialist revolution.

The theme of the 'peaceful road to socialism', on the other hand, emerges in Marx's work only in a strictly limited context. There were specific countries where Marx believed that the proletarian revolution could be carried out by peaceful means, but he presented these as exceptional cases. The key formulation of this 'peaceful road' position is in the speech Marx gave at a public meeting in Amsterdam after the Hague Congress, where he said:

We know that heed must be paid to the institutions, customs and traditions of the various countries, and we do not deny that there are countries, such as America and England, and if I was familiar with its institutions I might include Holland, where the workers may attain their goal by peaceful means.[19]

Marx also expressed this position, in rather stronger form, in a letter to his English friend and would-be disciple Henry Mayers Hyndman,[20] in 1880, claiming that, 'If the unavoidable evolution [i.e. to socialism in England] turn into a revolution, it would not only be the fault of the ruling classes, but also of the working class.'[21] However, Marx

19. 'Speech on the Hague Congress', below, p. 1008.

20. Shortly after Marx's death, Hyndman founded the first British Marxist organization, the Social Democratic Federation. However Hyndman led this group onto a highly sectarian course, and the SDF was repudiated by Engels. Hyndman himself, a former Tory, never relinquished either his high bourgeois lifestyle or his jingoism.

21. Marx to Hyndman, 8 December 1880; *MECW* 46, p. 49. Cf. however 'The Curtain Raised', below, p. 1084, for an example of Marx's thesis that, even if the working class in countries like England should take the parliamentary road to socialism, it would still be faced with a 'slave-owners' war'.

740 Introduction to Volume III

consistently contrasted these exceptional cases with the general rule. In this Amsterdam speech he stressed, 'We must recognize that in most continental countries the lever of the revolution will have to be force; a resort to force will be necessary one day in order to set up the rule of labour,'[22] and in the letter to Hyndman quoted above Marx contrasted the position in England with that of Germany, where 'military despotism' made a 'revolution' necessary. There are even occasional formulations of Marx's to the effect that 'the working classes would have to conquer the right to emancipate themselves on the battlefield',[23] unqualified by these exceptions; and there are no general statements whatever affirming the normal possibility of a 'peaceful road'.

Marx's basic determinant of the ability of the working class to make a non-violent revolution seems to be the absence of a bureaucratic-military state apparatus of the kind he had analysed for the French case in *The Eighteenth Brumaire*. Thus Marx wrote to Kugelmann in 1871, 'No longer, as before, to transfer the bureaucratic-military machine from one hand to another, but to *smash* it ... is essential for every real people's revolution on the Continent.'[24] In the 1870s England and the USA evidently appeared to Marx as the two major countries where there was no bureaucratic-military machine to enforce the power of capital over labour, and thus where the transformation from capitalism to communism could be achieved without having violently to smash the army and civil bureaucracy. Marx's position regarding England and America was therefore far from an ahistorical absolute. And as Lenin pointed out in *The State and Revolution*, the development of monopoly capitalism 'has clearly shown an extraordinary strengthening of the "state machine" and an unprecedented growth in its bureaucratic and military apparatus.'[25]

22. Below, p. 1008.
23. 'Speech on the Seventh Anniversary of the International', below, p. 956.
24. Marx to Kugelmann 12 April 1871; *MECW* 44, p. 131.
25. Lenin, *The State and Revolution*, loc. cit. Lenin's conclusion from this, which would most likely have been Marx's also, rings particularly true today for the USA, now that Britain has long since sunk to a minor power: 'Both Britain and America, the biggest and the last representatives – in the whole world – of Anglo-Saxon "liberty", in the sense that they had no militarist cliques and bureaucracy, have completely sunk into the all-European filthy, bloody morass of bureaucratic–military institutions which subordinate everything to themselves, and suppress everything. Today, in Britain and America too, the "precondition for every real people's revolution" is the smashing, the destruction of the "ready-made state machinery".'

The question that Marx never did deal with, however, and which became vitally important as international capitalism moved towards a cataclysmic crisis with the First World War, is how, in those countries which combine a bureaucratic-military machine with institutions of universal suffrage and parliamentary government, the working class is to make the transition from electoral politics to insurrection. In Marx's lifetime, to be sure, the workers' parties, even in Germany, were far from being immediately faced with this problem. In his letter to Hyndman of 1880, he typically combines an assertion of the eventual need for violent revolution in Germany with a vindication of the German party's present adherence to electoral politics as the means to build up its strength. The classic Marxist formulation on the transition from electoral politics to insurrection is in Engels's 1895 Introduction to *The Class Struggles in France*, where he argues the position (as Marx himself seems to have done) that the working class should wait for the ruling classes to break the rules of representative democracy and not take the initiative in a test of strength.[26] The reasons behind Engels's argument are evident: the working class will then enjoy the benefits of moral superiority, and it will be easier for it to win over sections of the intermediate classes and subvert the armed forces. However, this tactic has the drawback that it deprives the workers of the offensive, a vital advantage in insurrection. This question invariably presents a dilemma to revolutionary Marxists in bourgeois-democratic countries. But whatever choice is made, one essential precondition, if insurrection will or even may be necessary, is that the workers' party should carry out work well in advance to prepare for this contingency. Lenin therefore made the combination of legal and illegal work a condition for all parties wishing to join the Third International. The parties of the Second International, on the other hand, and the German Social-Democrats in particular, managed to combine a verbal orthodoxy that held to the letter of Marx's doctrines with a practical reformism quite alien to their spirit. (The classic representative of this tendency was the German Social-Democratic theorist Karl Kautsky, the 'pope of Marxism' after Engels's death.) It was possible, in other words, for these parties to claim, and even to believe, that they were moving to supersede capitalism and the bourgeois state, while the real direction of

26. *MECW* 27, pp. 506–24.

their practice led towards taking government office within it. Not one of the parties of the Second International that operated in a parliamentary democracy was to escape this degeneration.

With historical hindsight, we can see the failure of the Second International as already prepared by the circumstances in which the First International split. The International Working Men's Association did not split between revolutionaries and reformists, but between proponents of working-class political action and 'political indifferentists', as Marx referred to them. In the former camp, as also in the latter, there was a definite space for reformism, as revolutionary Marxists and 'political' reformists were united by agreement on the immediate tactical priority – the need to build up the workers' movement in the electoral arena. The label of 'Social-Democracy' thus concealed from the start the crucial question that divided revolutionaries from reformists, and neither Marx nor Engels ever fully realized the nature of the parties to which they gave their blessing.

Despite Marx's steadfast attack on all visible reformist manifestations, he seriously underestimated the strength of reformism and its underlying roots. In the Communist Manifesto Marx had presented the development of the proletarian movement as a two-stage process. In the first stage the proletariat develops from an unorganized mass, through local struggle against its immediate capitalist antagonists and the formation of 'combinations', into a constituted class subject; in the second stage it struggles as a class to overthrow capital on a national scale. Historical experience has certainly borne out the first part of Marx's model. In all countries where capitalist production has developed, the industrial proletariat has formed class organizations to defend its interests against capital: trade-union federations and political parties. But in by no means all cases has the whole organized working class struggled politically to overthrow capital. In general, a greater or smaller part of the working class, depending on specific conditions, has taken a revolutionary anti-capitalist path, while another part has struggled only for reforms within the capitalist system.

Marx's basic attitude towards working-class reformism is summed up in his aphorism 'The working class is revolutionary or it is nothing'.[27] What Marx meant by this emerges clearly from a letter he wrote in 1871 to his German-American follower Bolte,

27. Marx to Schweitzer, 13 February 1865; below, p. 832.

which provides an interesting gloss on the Communist Manifesto
from more than two decades later. It is surprising how firmly
Marx maintains in this letter the position on the development of
the proletarian movement put forward in the Manifesto, despite the
experience of the intervening years. On the one hand, 'the political
movement of the working class has as its ultimate object, of course,
the conquest of political power for this class', but in his definition,
'every movement in which the working class comes out as a *class*
against the ruling classes and tries to coerce them by pressure from
without is a political movement.'[28] No more than in the Manifesto
does Marx leave a theoretical space for the possibility of a workers'
movement that is organized politically as a class and yet struggles
solely for reforms within capitalism. Marx's sureness that the
political movement that 'has as its ultimate object, of course, the
conquest of political power', and the political movement that is
'every movement in which the working class comes out as a *class*
against the ruling classes', are one and the same may well be
true in the long run. Marx believed on the basis of his analysis of
capitalism that the imprisonment of the ever expanding productive
forces within the straitjacket of capitalist relations was bound to
become more and more intolerable to all but a small minority of
big capitalists. Yet while outlying portions of the capitalist world
have broken free, capitalism's imperialist trajectory has delayed
the second, revolutionary stage of the proletarian movement in the
heartlands for a whole historical epoch. In this era of imperialism,
it has been possible for vast numbers of workers in the advanced
capitalist countries to follow a reformist course continuously
reinforced by the material gains it has brought – the losses, from
world war to ecological crisis, being not self-evidently attributable
to capitalist relations of production.

The Gotha Programme on which Marx wrote his critical marginal
notes was drawn up in 1875 as the basis of the unification of the
SDAP with the Lassallean ADAV.[29] Marx, and the SDAP leaders
themselves, only countenanced this merger because the ADAV
had succeeded in throwing off the worst features of Lassalleanism.
After the settlement of the German national question, the ADAV

28. Marx to Bolte, 23 November 1871; *MECW* 44, p. 258.
29. The new party's name was for a while the German Socialist Workers' Party
(SAPD), later changed to the German Social-Democratic Party (SPD) by which it is
generally known.

proved its independence from Bismarckian manipulation by its anti-annexationist position in the Franco-Prussian war and its support for the Paris Commune, by its purchase on the everyday struggles of the German working class and its consequent quantitative growth. However, Marx was far from satisfied with the unity programme prepared for the Gotha Congress, which he considered 'thoroughly reprehensible and demoralizing for the party'.[30]

Of the Gotha Programme's Lassallean formulations, Marx singles out for his most bitter criticism the diagnosis 'in relation to [the working class,] all other classes are a *single reactionary mass*,' and the thesis 'the working class must initially work for its emancipation within the framework of the present-day national state'. The first of these only served, according to Marx, 'to extenuate [Lassalle's] alliance with the absolutist and feudal opponents of the bourgeoisie'. The Manifesto had never claimed that all other classes were 'a single reactionary mass', but only that 'of all the classes that stand face to face with the bourgeoisie today, the proletariat alone is a *really revolutionary class*', since 'the other classes decay and finally disappear in the face of modern industry; the proletariat is its special and essential product.' Marx reminds his German comrades that the 'Manifesto adds . . . that the lower middle class is becoming revolutionary "in view of (its) impending transfer into the proletariat"'. Conscious as always of the need to make alliances appropriate to each stage of the proletarian movement, Marx asks, 'At the last elections, did we proclaim to the artisans, small manufacturers, etc. and *peasants*: In relation to us you, together with the bourgeoisie and the feudal lords, form a single reactionary mass?'[31] As for the formulation that 'the working class must initially work for its emancipation *within the framework of the present-day national state*', Marx pointed out that the 'present-day national state' was in fact the German Reich. Even though the Gotha Programme proclaimed that 'the result of their efforts "will be *the international brotherhood of peoples*"', its damning omission was that there was 'not a word . . . of the *international role* of the German working class', i.e. how it was 'to challenge . . . Herr Bismarck's international policy of conspiracy'. Running through the whole of Marx's Critique is the suspicion that the Gotha Programme tends, not to revolution, but to reformist

30. Marx to Bracke, 5 May 1875; below, p. 1024.
31. Below, pp. 1032–3.

accommodation with the German Empire, 'a state which is no more than a military despotism and a police state, bureaucratically carpentered, embellished with parliamentary forms and disguised by an admixture of feudalism although already under the influence of the bourgeoisie'.[32]

However, the 'Critique of the Gotha Programme' is not simply directed against the Lassallean elements of German Social-Democratic ideology, but equally against the 'vulgar democratic' tendencies that the new party inherited from the SDAP. Perhaps the most crucial of all Marx's critical remarks, therefore, are that 'there is nothing in its political demands beyond the old and generally familiar democratic litany: universal suffrage, direct legislation, popular justice, a people's army, etc.'; and that it does not ask what transformation the state will undergo in the transition period between capitalist and communist society, when 'the state can only take the form of a *revolutionary dictatorship of the proletariat*'.[33]

This is the best known instance of Marx's use of the phrase 'dictatorship of the proletariat', but this key concept, which has always marked the division between revolutionaries and reformists,[34] recurs at several places in Marx's political writings. In *The Class Struggles in France*, written in 1850, Marx had lauded the Blanquists of 1848 for raising the slogan *'Dictatorship of the working class!'*[35] In his letter to Weydemeyer of 5 March 1852, Marx claimed as one of his chief discoveries that 'the class struggle necessarily leads to the dictatorship of the proletariat'.[36] Referring to the Paris Commune in his speech on the seventh anniversary of the International, Marx spoke of the need for a 'proletarian dictature'[37] (in the original English), and in his article on 'Political Indifferentism' of 1873 he referred again to the workers' 'revolutionary dictatorship'.[38] What is important, as always, is not the words used but the concept involved. For Marx, the proletarian dictatorship means simply the unrestrained political power of the working class, expressed through whatever political

32. Ibid., pp. 1033–4 and 1040.
33. Ibid., p. 1039.
34. See Lenin's 'The Proletarian Revolution and the Renegade Kautsky', in *Selected Works*; online at www.marxists.org/archive/lenin/works/sw/index.htm
35. Above, p. 395.
36. *MECW* 39, pp. 62–3.
37. Below, p. 956.
38. Below, p. 1012.

forms it may need to suppress the opposition of the former ruling classes and to expropriate the owners of capital. Marx himself saw the Commune as the prototype of this political form, although the Commune model may not be applicable in all cases. It was to insist that, in general, the working class must replace the bourgeois state by its own form of political power, that Marx used the term 'dictatorship of the proletariat'.

Marx and Engels came near to breaking with their German comrades over the Gotha Programme, but held back from this ultimate step. When their threat to 'publish a short statement dissociating ourselves from the said programme of principles and stating that we have had nothing to do with it'[39] was ignored, they backed down and collaborated after all with the new party. However, in 1879 they had further occasion to return to the attack, as the reformist tendency of the Gotha Programme invaded the Social-Democratic Party's practice when Bismarck introduced the Anti-Socialist Law. This move to repress the party was induced by its growing strength and electoral support (it had polled almost half a million votes in the 1878 elections), and Bismarck found a pretext in two attempts by anarchists on the life of the emperor. The crisis highlighted the predominant reformist orientation of the party. When a 'minor state of siege' was declared in Berlin, as a preliminary to the deportation from the capital of dozens of Socialist leaders, Liebknecht declared in the Reichstag that the SAPD was a party of reform, was opposed to 'revolution-mongering', and would obey the Anti-Socialist Law. The SAPD parliamentary group began to follow a policy of conciliation, even giving opportunist support to Bismarck's protectionist tariff policy, and Marx declared, 'They are already so far affected by parliamentary idiotism that they think they are *above criticism*.'[40]

When the party leadership grudgingly accepted the need for a party organ to be published abroad and smuggled into Germany, the three comrades it appointed to produce this in Switzerland, who included Bernstein,[41] came out instead with a 'Yearbook for Social

39. Marx to Bracke, 5 May 1875; below, p. 1023.

40. Marx to Sorge, 19 September 1879; *MECW* 45, pp. 410–14.

41. Eduard Bernstein, later the grand doyen of revisionism, was already at this time a prominent figure in the SAPD. In the 1880s he became a close friend of Engels, who appointed him his literary executor. From 1881 until 1890, when the Anti-Socialist Law was repealed, Bernstein edited from exile the *Social-Demokrat*, the clandestinely distributed SAPD organ.

Science and Social Policy' which commenced with a criticism of the party's record from a bourgeois-democratic position, attacking it not, as Marx had done, for its reformism, but for its '*one-sided*' class character.[42]

In their 'Circular Letter' to the SAPD leadership written in response to this, Marx and Engels reiterated their basic theses on the class struggle as laid down in the Manifesto thirty years earlier. They stressed more clearly, however, in the light of the experience of the German party, the danger of the workers' party becoming contaminated by bourgeois ideology. Marx accepts, as always, that 'people from the hitherto ruling class [will] join the struggling proletariat and supply it with educative elements', but he insists that 'when such people from other classes join the proletarian party the first requirement is that they do not bring any remnants of bourgeois, petty-bourgeois etc. prejudices with them, but that they adopt the proletarian outlook without prevarication.'[43] Marx ascribes the party's errors to the presence in its ranks of bourgeois ideologists, and implies that alien elements may have to be purged from the party in order to keep it to its revolutionary course. In a letter written some two years earlier he had also made it clear that it is not merely from those of bourgeois social origin that this danger comes: 'The workers themselves, when ... they give up work and become *professional literary men*, always breed "theoretical" mischief and are always ready to join muddleheads from the allegedly "learned" caste.'[44]

However, lacking a structural explanation of working-class reformism, Marx and Engels continued to see this simply as the product of external bourgeois influence, and to believe that these false ideas could be rectified by ideological struggle within a united party, at most by excluding a few bourgeois intellectuals. In the last analysis, they did not believe that reformism could take serious and systematic root in the working class.

Poland and Russia

A constant element in Marx and Engels's politics, from 1846 through to the 1880s, was support for Polish national liberation. This was neither a merely sentimental solidarity nor an absolute general principle, but held an important place in their conception of the

42. 'Circular Letter to Bebel, Liebknecht, Bracke, et al.', below, p. 1052.
43. Ibid., pp. 1057–8.
44. Marx to Sorge, 19 October 1877; *MECW* 45, p. 282.

proletarian revolution, as this developed in the context of specific relations of international politics. As these relations changed, and Marx and Engels had to recommend new tactics to the proletarian movement, the significance they gave the Polish struggle shifted, but its overall importance remained.

As discussed in the Introduction to *The Revolutions of 1848*, the cardinal plank of Marx and Engels's foreign policy in 1848 was 'war with Russia, including the restoration of Poland'.[45] In the 1870s and after, however, the unification of Germany and the development of capitalism in eastern Europe substantially altered the terms of the Polish question.

In the mid 1860s, Marx and Engels still held to their line of 1848. In 1863 Marx argued that 'without an independent Poland there can be no independent and united Germany',[46] but this thesis was soon to be disproved in practice. Engels's articles of 1866 recapitulate those of 1849, including the differentiation between the 'great historic nations' and the minor nationalities, only directed against the Proudhonists instead of against Bakunin. However, there is already the hint of change to come, when Engels refers to the contingency that 'the working classes of Russia . . . form a political programme'.[47] Previously Marx and Engels had seen Russia purely as a monolithic barbarian presence in Europe. But after the emancipation of the serfs in 1861, the beginnings of capitalism and the development of the radical-democratic opposition represented at this time above all by Chernyshevsky,[48] whom Marx greatly admired, they took an ever greater interest in Russian developments. Both learned the Russian language, and Marx spent a great part of his energies in the last decade of his life on Russian studies. In the 1870s the tsarist regime, as reactionary as ever at home, could no longer arbitrate central European affairs as it had done in the past. Above all, it was the establishment of the German Reich that had changed things, but also of increasing importance was the intensification of contradictions within Russia.

45. Engels, 'Marx and the *Neue Rheinische Zeitung*', *MECW* 26, p. 124. See the Introduction to *The Revolutions of 1848*, above, pp. 43–46.

46. 'Proclamation on Poland', above, p. 354.

47. 'What Have the Working Class to Do with Poland?', below, p. 1065.

48. In the Afterword to the second German edition of *Capital* (1873), Marx pays an unparalleled tribute to Chernyshevsky for his critical *Outline of Political Economy according to Mill*; this, more than anything, indicates Marx's awareness of the rapid development of revolutionary socialist ideas in Russia.

As early as 1875 Engels could write, if too optimistically, 'Russia undoubtedly is on the eve of a revolution',[49] in which he saw the main force in overthrowing feudalism and absolutism as the peasantry. In 1882, a year after the assassination of Alexander II, Marx and Engels explicitly contrasted the contemporary state of affairs with that of 1848:

During the revolution of 1848–9 ... the tsar was proclaimed the chief of European reaction. Today he is a prisoner of war of the revolution, in Gatchina, and Russia forms the vanguard of revolutionary action in Europe.[50]

By the 1870s, then, the Polish struggle was no longer necessarily linked with the German revolution, as it had been in the past. Marx and Engels, as representatives of the international workers' party, continued to support the Poles, but the reasons that they adduced for this support gradually changed. In this period of transition, three out of four points that appear in Marx's and Engels's speeches of 1875 are of dubious validity.

Marx now presents, as 'the main reason for the sympathy felt by the working class for Poland', the participation of Poles in an essentially individual way as '*cosmopolitan soldier[s] of the revolution*'. Whatever the sympathy this evokes, it is highly uncharacteristic of Marx to argue a case like this, in no way based on an objective assessment of the Polish struggle. Seemingly more substantial is the argument that 'as long as the independent life of a nation is suppressed by a foreign conqueror it inevitably directs all its strength, all its efforts and all its energy against the external enemy',[51] and that therefore the social revolution in Poland can only proceed when the national question has been settled. But however correct the principle behind this, the assumption is still made, as in 1848, that unlike the other oppressed nationalities of eastern Europe, Poland belonged to a privileged category of 'great historic nations', an assumption which history has proved false. Indeed, Polish nationalism was sufficiently weak among the industrial proletariat that developed in the cities of Russian Poland towards the end of the century that the workers' party founded by

49. 'Social Relations in Russia', *MECW* 24, p. 50.
50. 'Preface to the Second Russian Edition of the Communist Manifesto', *MECW* 24, p. 426.
51. 'For Poland', below, p. 1075.

Rosa Luxemburg could reject the national question entirely and challenge the nationalism it considered petty-bourgeois by styling itself the Social-Democratic Party of the Kingdom of Poland and Lithuania – the official title of Russian Poland.

The 'particular geographic, military, and historical position' of Poland, so important in the 1848 period and after, is now relegated to merely 'another reason'. But even the weight that Marx gives this, as 'the cement which holds together the three great military despots: Russia, Prussia and Austria', is less than convincing. The previous significance given to the partition of Poland was precisely its role in keeping Germany weak and divided, with a restored Poland being needed as a bastion between Germany and Russia.[52] But after the foundation of the German Reich, there was no essential reason why the partition of Poland necessarily held the three partitioners together. Indeed, Marx had already predicted in 1870 that the very circumstances in which the Reich was founded were 'pregnant with a *war between Germany and Russia*'.[53]

But besides these less cogent justifications of their support for Poland, which should perhaps be seen as residues from a previous position, the genuine new objective significance of the Polish struggle in the 1870s and after is also present. Just as Polish liberation in 1848 was a vital interest of the German revolution, so in this later period it was a vital interest, for very different reasons, of the Russian revolution. Engels noted in his 1875 speech that, in 1863, 'Russian chauvinism . . . poured over Poland once the preservation of Russian rule in Poland was at stake'.[54] Polish liberation would therefore now more than anything weaken the tsarist empire. It was for this reason that Lenin was to take issue with Rosa Luxemburg on the national question, and uphold the right of self-determination for all national groups, a position that acquired a greater significance in the era of twentieth-century imperialism. The Bolshevik national policy towards Poland and other nationalities oppressed by tsarism contributed in no small way to the victory of the socialist revolution of 1917.[55]

When Marx and Engels recognized in 1882 that 'Russia forms

52. See Engels's 'Speech on Poland', above, pp. 99–102.
53. See 'Letter to the Brunswick Committee of the SDAP', below, p. 862.
54. 'For Poland', below, p. 1074.
55. See Lenin's article 'The Right of Nations to Self-Determination', in *Selected Works*, loc. cit.

the vanguard of revolutionary action in Europe', the form of the Russian revolution was already a point of debate among Russian revolutionaries, as it was to be for a long time ahead. In 1874 Engels took issue with the petty-bourgeois writer Tkachov, who derived his views on Russian exceptionalism from Bakunin, and believed that Russia could step over capitalism and build a socialist society on the basis of the peasant commune – the *obshchina*. Engels stressed that capitalist development was well under way in Russia and was already undermining this collective form of property. It was to be the position of the Russian Marxists, in particular of Plekhanov's Emancipation of Labour group founded in 1881, that Russia would have to go through a similar process of capitalist development as had western Europe, before it could make the transition to socialism. They were to be proved at least partly right; but in Marx's last years, neither he nor Engels saw this question as already closed. Engels wrote in 1875:

The possibility undeniably exists of raising this form of society [Russian communal ownership] to a higher one, if [among other factors] . . . before the complete break-up of communal ownership, a proletarian revolution is successfully carried out in western Europe, creating for the Russian peasant . . . the material conditions which he needs, if only to carry through the revolution necessarily connected therewith of his whole agricultural system.[56]

In a manuscript of 1881,[57] Marx investigated this possibility in great detail, and finally he and Engels set down their view in the Preface to the 1882 Russian edition of the Communist Manifesto:

If the Russian Revolution becomes the signal for a proletarian revolution in the West, so that the two complement each other, the present Russian common ownership of land may serve as the starting-point for communist development.[58]

The elaboration of his position towards Russia was to be the final milestone in Marx's political development. The last decade of his life had been one of incessant illness, and on 14 March 1883 Marx died at his home in Hampstead.

56. 'Social Relations in Russia', op. cit.
57. 'Drafts of the letter to Vera Zasulich', *MECW* 24, pp. 346–69.
58. *MECW* 24, pp. 425–6.

Conclusion

In his speech at Marx's funeral, Engels said that Marx was 'before all else a revolutionist'.[59] Marx's political work, backed up by his critique of bourgeois economics, was devoted to the liberation of the proletariat – the working class of capitalist society.

The great service that Marx had performed was rapidly demonstrated after his death, as mass working-class parties arose across the capitalist world, following Marx in their aim to take over the state and transform the economic system in a socialist direction. But their fatal weakness was shown in 1914, when the parties of the Second International, with very few exceptions, reneged on their commitment to proletarian internationalism and followed their respective governments into the First World War.

If this can be traced to a flaw in Marx's own thinking, it would be his inadequate appreciation of capitalism's international dimension. Marx was certainly aware that capitalism, from its very origins, involved the exploitation of some countries by others, and he described in *Capital* the role of colonialism in 'primitive accumulation'.[60] Where Marx was wrong was in holding that despite this exploitation, and even through it, metropolitan capitalism would develop the productive forces of the colonies and satellites essentially as it had done in the west European heartlands; and that socialism would have to spread from metropolis to colony in the wake of capitalism.[61] In fact, capitalist imperialism radically differentiated the historical trajectories of metropolis and colony, keeping the lands of the 'third world' as underdeveloped suppliers of raw materials and cheap labour from which the whole population of the advanced countries could benefit, including their working classes. In this context, the first successful proletarian revolution took place in Russia, on the fringe of European capitalism, and the direction of the process this set in motion was eastward to Asia rather than back to the heartlands of the west.

Marx believed that a mass workers' party would necessarily become increasingly conscious of its long-term interest and follow a revolutionary course. In the context of the advanced capitalist

59. 'Karl Marx's Funeral', in *MECW* 24, p. 467.

60. See in particular *Capital* Volume 1, chapter XXXI, and Volume 3, chapter XX.

61. See the Introduction to Volume II, above, pp. 358–62.

countries, however, this meant greatly underestimating a reformism fuelled by the privileges derived from imperialism. On this basis, the ruling classes in Europe and North America were able to concede demands for universal suffrage and a welfare state, and steadily integrate the working class into a consumer society. Remaining references in these parties' programmes to Marx or even socialism were eventually dropped altogether.

If Marx's ideas seemed for many decades to have triumphed in Russia and China, this was due to the distinctive development of Marx's politics that Lenin had undertaken in the Russian context. Lenin held that the proletarian party should be a much more unified and disciplined body, confined to those prepared to work both legally and illegally along an agreed tactical line. This was certainly the precondition for the success of the Bolshevik revolution in 1917, which opened a new phase of 'Marxism-Leninism'. Yet in the harsh conditions of civil war and foreign intervention, the proclaimed 'dictatorship of the proletariat' fell too easily into the dictatorship of a party, of its leadership, and even of an individual. Despite raising Russia to an industrial power with high standards of health and education, and despite the immense achievement of defeating European fascism, the Soviet Union degenerated into an unwieldy bureaucracy running an inefficient economy. And while China sought to escape this dynamic with the Cultural Revolution of the 1960s, after Mao's death the Communist leaders opted for a capitalist road of development as their preferred form of modernization.

When this edition of Marx's Political Writings was first published in the 1970s, it was tempting to succumb to surface appearance. For all their failings, governments from Prague to Hanoi still claimed to be Marxist, as did the mass workers' parties of France and Italy, revolutionary movements across Latin America, and a number of newly independent African states. Twenty years later, this illusion had been fatally punctured, with the collapse of the Soviet Union, the wave of neoliberal globalization, and the brutal reassertion of United States hegemony.

Re-issuing these volumes in 2010, however, the resurgent interest in Marxism is readily understandable. The world economy is experiencing a crisis unprecedented since the 1930s, making a mockery of the claim that capitalism can provide a decent life for all. Still more seriously, capitalist patterns of production threaten a planetary disaster triggered by global warming. Though working-class politics has still to recover from the setbacks of the late twentieth century, the transformation required to set the world on a sustainable course is increasingly urgent. For all the progress of the last hundred years, the situation today has similarities to the alternative that Rosa Luxemburg posed in the First World War – between socialism and barbarism. It is all too clear that the ecological crisis cannot be solved from the side of capital; only a movement from the side of labour can undertake the changes needed. If the first shoots of this movement are visible here and there, its precise form is still impossible to foresee, and will no doubt vary from one region of the world to another. But the reformist path of social-democracy seems inadequate to the task in hand, and the Leninist path too narrowly based. We rather need what Marx in the Communist Manifesto called a 'self-conscious, independent movement of the immense majority, in the interest of the immense majority',[62] today as an imperative of human survival. And however unprecedented the task we confront, Marx's Political Writings will remain a lasting point of reference.

*

Besides certain texts that Marx and Engels co-authored, a few articles written by Engels alone have been included in this volume where these are necessary to the understanding of Marx's own politics. Although Engels's positions sometimes diverged slightly from Marx's, the two did operate a very close division of labour from 1846 through to Marx's death, in which Marx generally left Engels the fields of international politics and military affairs. Not only did Marx and Engels invariably consult together before publishing any significant political statement, but Engels often wrote pieces at Marx's express request. Although Engels's individual work, these are nevertheless an essential dimension of Marx and Engels's joint political practice.

62. The Communist Manifesto, above, p. 72.

In the Introduction and Notes to this volume 'Marx' is sometimes used for 'Marx and Engels' in this sense, and when Marx alone is involved and it is necessary to avoid ambiguity, this is made explicit.

All texts written by Marx and Engels in German and French have been newly translated for this edition.

DAVID FERNBACH

1973 AND 2010

Documents of the First International: 1864–70

INAUGURAL ADDRESS OF THE INTERNATIONAL
WORKING MEN'S ASSOCIATION[1]

Fellow working men,

It is a great fact that the misery of the working masses has not diminished from 1848 to 1864, and yet this period is unrivalled for the development of its industry and the growth of its commerce. In 1850, a moderate organ of the British middle class, of more than average information, predicted that if the exports and imports of England were to rise fifty per cent, English pauperism would sink to zero. Alas! On 7 April 1864[2] the Chancellor of the Exchequer delighted his parliamentary audience by the statement that the total import and export trade of England had grown in 1863 'to £443,955,000, that astonishing sum about three times the trade of the comparatively recent epoch of 1843'. With all that, he was eloquent upon 'poverty'. 'Think,' he exclaimed, 'of those who are on the border of that region,' upon 'wages . . . not increased'; upon 'human life . . . in nine cases out of ten but a struggle of existence'. He did not speak of the people of Ireland, gradually replaced by machinery in the north, and by sheep-walks in the south, though even the sheep in that unhappy country are decreasing, it is true, not at so rapid a rate as the men. He did not repeat what then had been just betrayed by the highest representatives of the upper ten thousand in a sudden fit of terror. When the garotte[3] panic had reached a certain height, the House of Lords

1. Marx drafted the Inaugural Address and the Provisional Rules of the International during the last week of October 1864. They were adopted by the General Council on 1 November, and published as a pamphlet: *Address and Provisional Rules of the Working Men's International Association*, London, 1864. In this and other texts originally published in English, printers' errors and archaic orthography have been corrected where necessary.

2. The day of Gladstone's budget speech for 1864.

3. The garotte panic was over a series of violent street robberies, some involving murder, which led to a parliamentary inquiry. The resulting blue book was the *Report of the Commissioners . . . relating to Transportation and Penal Servitude*, vol. 1, London, 1863.

caused an inquiry to be made into, and a report to be published upon, transportation and penal servitude. Out came the murder in the bulky blue book of 1863, and proved it was, by official facts and figures, that the worst of the convicted criminals, the penal serfs of England and Scotland, toiled much less and fared far better than the agricultural labourers of England and Scotland. But this was not all. When, consequent upon the civil war in America, the operatives of Lancashire and Cheshire were thrown upon the streets, the same House of Lords sent to the manufacturing districts a physician commissioned to investigate into the smallest possible amount of carbon and nitrogen, to be administered in the cheapest and plain-est form, which on an average might just suffice to 'avert starvation diseases'. Dr Smith, the medical deputy, ascertained that 28,000 grains of carbon and 1,330 grains of nitrogen were the weekly allowance that would keep an average adult just over the level of starvation diseases, and he found furthermore that quantity pretty nearly to agree with the scanty nourishment to which the pressure of extreme distress had actually reduced the cotton operatives.[4] But now mark! The same learned doctor was later on again deputed by the Medical Officer of the Privy Council to inquire into the nourish-ment of the poorer labouring classes. The results of his researches are embodied in the *Sixth Report on Public Health*, published by order of Parliament in the course of the present year. What did the doctor discover? That the silk weavers, the needle women, the kid glovers, the stocking weavers, and so forth, received, on an average, not even the distress pittance of the cotton operatives, not even the amount of carbon and nitrogen 'just sufficient to avert starvation diseases'. 'Moreover,' we quote from the report,

as regards the examined families of the agricultural population, it appeared that more than a fifth were with less than the estimated sufficiency of carbonaceous food, that more than one-third were with less than the estimated sufficiency of nitrogenous food, and that in three counties (Berkshire, Oxfordshire, and Somersetshire) insufficiency of nitrogenous food was the average local diet.

4. We need hardly remind the reader that, apart from the elements of water and certain inorganic substances, carbon and nitrogen form the raw materials of human food. However, to nourish the human system, those simple chemical constituen-ts must be supplied in the form of vegetable or animal substances. Potatoes, for instance, contain mainly carbon, while wheaten bread contains carbonaceous and nitrogenous substances in a due proportion [Marx].

'It must be remembered,' adds the official report,

that privation of food is very reluctantly borne, and that, as a rule, great poorness of diet will only come when other privations have preceded it . . . Even cleanliness will have been found costly or difficult, and if there still be self-respectful endeavours to maintain it, every such endeavour will represent additional pangs of hunger . . . These are painful reflections, especially when it is remembered that the poverty to which they advert is not the deserved poverty of idleness; in all cases it is the poverty of working populations. Indeed, the work which obtains the scanty pittance of food is for the most part excessively prolonged.

The report brings out the strange, and rather unexpected fact, 'that of the divisions of the United Kingdom', England, Wales, Scotland, and Ireland, 'the agricultural population of England', the richest division, 'is considerably the worst fed'; but that even the agricultural labourers of Berkshire, Oxfordshire, and Somersetshire, fare better than great numbers of skilled indoor operatives of the east of London.

Such are the official statements published by order of Parliament in 1864, during the millennium of free trade, at a time when the Chancellor of the Exchequer[5] told the House of Commons that: 'The average condition of the British labourer has improved in a degree we know to be extraordinary and unexampled in the history of any country or any age.'

Upon these official congratulations jars the dry remark of the official *Public Health Report*: 'The public health of a country means the health of its masses, and the masses will scarcely be healthy unless, to their very base, they be at least moderately prosperous.'

Dazzled by the 'Progress of the Nation' statistics dancing before his eyes, the Chancellor of the Exchequer exclaims in wild ecstasy: 'From 1842 to 1852 the taxable income of the country increased by 6 per cent; in the eight years from 1853 to 1861, it has increased from the basis taken in 1853 20 per cent. The fact is so astonishing to be almost incredible . . . This intoxicating augmentation of wealth and power,' adds Mr Gladstone, 'is entirely confined to classes of property'.[6]

5. Gladstone, in his 1864 budget speech.
6. This quotation is from Gladstone's budget speech of 16 April 1863. Marx was at one time accused of having invented the last sentence of this quotation, which he also cites in *Capital*. But although the sentence in question is not to be found in *Hansard*, whether by accident, or, as Marx believed,

If you want to know under what conditions of broken health, tainted morals, and mental ruin, that 'intoxicating augmentation of wealth and power entirely confined to classes of property' was, and is being, produced by the classes of labour, look to the picture hung up in the last *Public Health Report* of the workshops of tailors, printers, and dressmakers! Compare the *Report of the Children's Employment Commission* of 1863, where it is stated, for instance, that:

> The potters as a class, both men and women, represent a much degenerated population, both physically and mentally ... The unhealthy child is an unhealthy parent in his turn ... A progressive deterioration of the race must go on ... The degenerescence of the population of Staffordshire would be even greater were it not for the constant recruiting from the adjacent country, and the intermarriages with more healthy races.

Glance at Mr Tremenheere's blue book on *The Grievances complained of by the Journeymen Bakers!*[7] And who has not shuddered at the paradoxical statement made by the inspectors of factories, and illustrated by the Registrar General, that the Lancashire operatives, while put upon the distress pittance of food, were actually improving in health because of their temporary exclusion by the cotton famine from the cotton factory, and that the mortality of the children was decreasing, because their mothers were now at last allowed to give them, instead of Godfrey's cordial, their own breasts.[8]

Again reverse the medal! The Income and Property Tax Returns laid before the House of Commons on 20 July 1864 teach us that the persons with yearly incomes valued by the tax-gatherer at £50,000 and upwards, had, from 5 April 1862 to 5 April 1863, been joined by a dozen and one, their number having increased in that single year from 67 to 80. The same returns disclose the fact that about 3,000 persons divide amongst themselves a yearly income of about £25,000,000 sterling, rather more than the total revenue doled out annually to the whole mass of the agricultural labourers of England and Wales. Open the Census of 1861, and

---

by Gladstone's censorship, it appears in the parliamentary reports of both *The Times* and the *Morning Star*, and Marx was thus able to vindicate himself. See Engels's Preface to the fourth German edition of *Capital*, Volume 1, Harmondsworth 1976, pp. 115–20.

7. London, 1862.

8. *Report of the Inspectors of Factories ... for the half-year ending 31 October 1863*, London, 1864.

you will find that the number of the male landed proprietors of England and Wales had decreased from 16,934 in 1851, to 15,066 in 1861, so that the concentration of land had grown in 10 years 11 per cent. If the concentration of the soil of the country in a few hands proceeds at the same rate, the land question will become singularly simplified, as it had become in the Roman empire, when Nero grinned at the discovery that half the province of Africa was owned by six gentlemen.

We have dwelt so long upon these 'facts so astonishing to be almost incredible', because England heads the Europe of commerce and industry.[9] It will be remembered that some months ago one of the refugee sons of Louis Philippe publicly congratulated the English agricultural labourer on the superiority of his lot over that of his less florid comrade on the other side of the Channel. Indeed, with local colours changed, and on a scale somewhat contracted, the English facts reproduce themselves in all the industrious and progressive countries of the Continent. In all of them there has taken place, since 1848, an unheard-of development of industry, and an undreamed-of expansion of imports and exports. In all of them 'the augmentation of wealth and power entirely confined to classes of property' was truly 'intoxicating'. In all of them, as in England, a minority of the working classes got their real wages somewhat advanced; while in most cases the monetary rise of wages denoted no more a real access of comforts than the inmate of the metropolitan poor-house or orphan asylum, for instance, was in the least benefited by his first necessaries costing £9 15s. 8d. in 1861 against £7 7s. 4d. in 1852. Everywhere the great mass of the working classes were sinking down to a lower depth, at the same rate, at least, that those above them were rising in the social scale. In all countries of Europe it has now become a truth demonstrable to every unprejudiced mind, and only denied by those whose interest it is to hedge other people in a fool's paradise, that no improvement of machinery, no appliance of science to production, no contrivances of communication, no new colonies, no emigration, no opening of markets, no free trade, nor all these things put together, will do away with the miseries of the industrious masses; but that, on the present false base, every fresh development of the productive powers of labour must tend to deepen social contrasts and point

9. Marx's own German translation adds here: '. . . and in fact represents it on the world market'.

social antagonisms. Death of starvation rose almost to the rank of an institution, during this intoxicating epoch of economical progress, in the metropolis of the British empire. That epoch is marked in the annals of the world by the quickened return, the widening compass, and the deadlier effects of the social pest called a commercial and industrial crisis.

After the failure of the revolutions of 1848, all party organizations and party journals of the working classes were, on the Continent, crushed by the iron hand of force, the most advanced sons of labour fled in despair to the transatlantic republic, and the short-lived dreams of emancipation vanished before an epoch of industrial fever, moral marasmus, and political reaction. The defeat of the continental working classes, partly owed to the diplomacy of the English government, acting then as now in fraternal solidarity with the cabinet of St Petersburg, soon spread its contagious effects on this side of the Channel. While the rout of their continental brethren unmanned the English working classes, and broke their faith in their own cause, it restored to the landlord and the money-lord their somewhat shaken confidence. They insolently withdrew concessions already advertised. The discoveries of new goldlands led to an immense exodus, leaving an irreparable void in the ranks of the British proletariat. Others of its formerly active members were caught by the temporary bribe of greater work and wages, and turned into 'political blacks'. All the efforts made at keeping up, or remodelling, the Chartist movement, failed signally; the press organs of the working class died one by one of the apathy of the masses, and, in point of fact, never before seemed the English working class so thoroughly reconciled to a state of political nullity. If, then, there had been no solidarity of action between the British and the continental working classes, there was, at all events, a solidarity of defeat.

And yet the period passed since the revolutions of 1848 has not been without its compensating features. We shall here only point to two great facts.

After a thirty years' struggle, fought with most admirable perseverance, the English working classes, improving a momentaneous split between the landlords and money-lords, succeeded in carrying the Ten Hours Bill.[10] The immense physical, moral, and intellectual benefits hence accruing to the factory operatives,

10. Lord Shaftesbury's Act instituting the ten-hours limitation for women and children in textile factories was passed in June 1847.

half-yearly chronicled in the reports of the inspectors of factories, are now acknowledged on all sides. Most of the continental
governments had to accept the English Factory Act in more or
less modified forms, and the English Parliament itself is every
year compelled to enlarge its sphere of action. But besides its
practical import, there was something else to exalt the marvel-
lous success of this working men's measure. Through their most
notorious organs of science, such as Dr Ure, Professor Senior,[11]
and other sages of that stamp, the middle class had predicted, and
to their heart's content proved, that any legal restriction of the
hours of labour must sound the death knell of British industry,
which vampire-like, could but live by sucking blood, and children's blood, too. In olden times, child murder was a mysterious
rite of the religion of Moloch, but it was practised on some very
solemn occasions only, once a year perhaps, and then Moloch had
no exclusive bias for the children of the poor. This struggle about
the legal restriction of the hours of labour raged the more fiercely
since, apart from frightened avarice, it told indeed upon the great
contest between the blind rule of the supply and demand laws
which form the political economy of the middle class, and social
production controlled by social foresight, which forms the political economy of the working class. Hence the Ten Hours Bill was
not only a great practical success; it was the victory of a principle;
it was the first time that in broad daylight the political economy
of the middle class succumbed to the political economy of the
working class.

But there was in store a still greater victory of the political
economy of labour over the political economy of property. We
speak of the cooperative movement, especially the cooperative
factories raised by the unassisted efforts of a few bold 'hands'.
The value of these great social experiments cannot be overrated.
By deed, instead of by argument, they have shown that production
on a large scale, and in accord with the behests of modern science,
may be carried on without the existence of a class of masters
employing a class of hands; that to bear fruit, the means of labour
need not be monopolized as a means of dominion over, and of

11. Dr Andrew Ure and Professor Nassau Senior were characteristic representatives of what Marx termed 'vulgar economy', the degenerate form of bourgeois political
economy that, after 1830, abandoned the attempt of scientific explanation for mere
apologetics, as a result of the development of the class struggle between capital and
labour. See *Capital*, Volume 1, pp. 96–7.

extortion against, the labouring man himself; and that, like slave labour, like serf labour, hired labour is but a transitory and inferior form, destined to disappear before associated labour plying its toil with a willing hand, a ready mind, and a joyous heart. In England, the seeds of the cooperative system were sown by Robert Owen; the working men's experiments, tried on the Continent, were, in fact, the practical upshot of the theories, not invented, but loudly proclaimed, in 1848.

At the same time, the experience of the period from 1848 to 1864 has proved beyond doubt[12] that, however excellent in principle, and however useful in practice, cooperative labour, if kept within the narrow circle of the casual efforts of private workmen, will never be able to arrest the growth in geometrical progression of monopoly, to free the masses, nor even to perceptibly lighten the burden of their miseries. It is perhaps for this very reason that plausible noblemen, philanthropic middle-class spouters, and even keen political economists, have all at once turned nauseously complimentary to the very cooperative labour system they had vainly tried to nip in the bud by deriding it as the utopia of the dreamer, or stigmatizing it as the sacrilege of the socialist. To save the industrious masses, cooperative labour ought to be developed to national dimensions, and, consequently, to be fostered by national means. Yet the lords of land and the lords of capital will always use their political privileges for the defence and perpetuation of their economical monopolies. So far from promoting, they will continue to lay every possible impediment in the way of the emancipation of labour. Remember the sneer with which, last session, Lord Palmerston put down the advocates of the Irish Tenants' Right Bill. The House of Commons, cried he, is a house of landed proprietors.[13]

To conquer political power has therefore become the great duty of the working classes. They seem to have comprehended this, for in England, Germany, Italy and France there have taken place simultaneous revivals, and simultaneous efforts are being made at the political reorganization of the working men's party.

12. Marx's German translation adds: '– what the most intelligent leaders of the English working class already maintained in 1851–2, regarding the cooperative movement –'.

13. This refers to Palmerston's speech of 23 June 1863, in which he described the moderate reforms in the land tenure system proposed by Maguire and the Irish MPs, designed to guarantee an outgoing tenant compensation for the value of improvements made, as 'communist doctrines'.

One element of success they possess – numbers; but numbers weigh only in the balance, if united by combination and led by knowledge. Past experience has shown how disregard of that bond of brotherhood which ought to exist between the workmen of different countries, and incite them to stand firmly by each other in all their struggles for emancipation, will be chastised by the common discomfiture of their incoherent efforts. This thought prompted the working men of different countries assembled on 28 September 1864, in public meeting at St Martin's Hall, to found the International Association.

Another conviction swayed that meeting.

If the emancipation of the working classes requires their fraternal concurrence, how are they to fulfil that great mission with a foreign policy in pursuit of criminal designs, playing upon national prejudices, and squandering in piratical wars the people's blood and treasure? It was not the wisdom of the ruling classes, but the heroic resistance to their criminal folly by the working classes of England, that saved the west of Europe from plunging headlong into an infamous crusade for the perpetuation and propagation of slavery on the other side of the Atlantic. The shameless approval, mock sympathy, or idiotic indifference, with which the upper classes of Europe have witnessed the mountain fortress of the Caucasus falling a prey to, and heroic Poland being assassinated by, Russia;[14] the immense and unresisted encroachments of that barbarous power, whose head is at St Petersburg, and whose hands are in every cabinet of Europe, have taught the working classes the duty to master themselves the mysteries of international politics; to watch the diplomatic acts of their respective governments; to counteract them, if necessary, by all means in their power; when unable to prevent, to combine in simultaneous denunciations, and to vindicate the simple laws of morals and justice, which ought to govern the relations of private individuals, as the rules paramount of the intercourse of nations.

The fight for such a foreign policy forms part of the general struggle for the emancipation of the working classes.

Proletarians of all countries, unite!

14. In January 1863 a new national uprising broke out in Poland. It was crushed within two months by Russian forces, in alliance with Prussia. See 'Proclamation of Poland', above, pp. 688–90.

PROVISIONAL RULES[15]

Considering,

That the emancipation of the working classes must be conquered by the working classes themselves; that the struggle for the emancipation of the working classes means not a struggle for class privileges and monopolies, but for equal rights and duties, and the abolition of all class rule;

That the economical subjection of the man of labour to the monopolizer of the means of labour, that is, the sources of life, lies at the bottom of servitude in all its forms, of all social misery, mental degradation, and political dependence;

That the economical emancipation of the working classes is therefore the great end to which every political movement ought to be subordinate as a means;

That all efforts aiming at that great end have hitherto failed from the want of solidarity between the manifold divisions of labour in each country, and from the absence of a fraternal bond of union between the working classes of different countries;

That the emancipation of labour is neither a local nor a national, but a social problem, embracing all countries in which modern society exists, and depending for its solution on the concurrence, practical and theoretical, of the most advanced countries;

That the present revival of the working classes in the most industrious countries of Europe, while it raises a new hope, gives solemn warning against a relapse into the old errors and calls for the immediate combination of the still disconnected movements;

For these reasons –

The undersigned members of the committee, holding its powers by resolution of the public meeting held on 28 September 1864, at St Martin's Hall, London, have taken the steps necessary for founding the Working Men's International Association;

They declare that this International Association and all societies and individuals adhering to it, will acknowledge truth, justice,

15. The Provisional Rules of the International were ratified by the Geneva Congress of September 1866, and were later supplemented by the resolutions of the successive Congresses. The most significant amendment in the final General Rules published in November 1871 was the insertion of a paragraph 7a, which paraphrased Resolution IX of the London Conference of September 1871 (see below, pp. 953–4).

and morality, as the basis of their conduct towards each other, and towards all men, without regard to colour, creed, or nationality;

They hold it the duty of a man to claim the rights of a man and a citizen, not only for himself, but for every man who does his duty. No rights without duties, no duties without rights;

And in this spirit they have drawn up the following provisional rules of the International Association:

1. This association is established to afford a central medium of communication and cooperation between working men's societies existing in different countries, and aiming at the same end, viz., the protection, advancement, and complete emancipation of the working classes.

2. The name of the society shall be: 'The Working Men's International Association'.

3. In 1865 there shall meet in Belgium a general working men's Congress,[16] consisting of representatives of such working men's societies as may have joined the International Association. The Congress will have to proclaim before Europe the common aspirations of the working classes, decide on the definitive rules of the International Association, consider the means required for its successful working, and appoint the Central Council[17] of the Association. The General Congress is to meet once a year.

4. The Central Council shall sit in London, and consist of working men belonging to the different countries represented in the International Association. It shall from its own members elect the officers necessary for the transaction of business, such as a president, a treasurer, a general secretary, corresponding secretaries for the different countries, etc.

5. On its annual meetings, the General Congress shall receive a public account of the annual transactions of the Central Council. The Central Council, yearly appointed by the Congress, shall have power to add to the number of its members. In cases of urgency, it may convoke the General Congress before the regular yearly term.

6. The Central Council shall form an international agency be-

16. The first Congress of the International did not in fact meet until September 1866, in Geneva. In 1865 the General Council, on Marx's advice, judged it premature to hold a Congress, and called instead a private conference in London.

17. As from the Geneva Congress, the 'Central Council' was officially referred to as the General Council, the designation by which it is now more commonly known.

tween the different cooperating associations, so that the working men in one country be constantly informed of the movements of their class in every other country; that an inquiry into the social state of the different countries of Europe be made simultaneously, and under a common direction; that the questions of general interest mooted in one society be ventilated by all; and that when immediate practical steps should be needed, as, for instance, in case of international quarrels, the action of the associated societies be simultaneous and uniform. Whenever it seems opportune, the Central Council shall take the initiative of proposals to be laid before the different national or local societies.

7. Since the success of the working men's movement in each country cannot be secured but by the power of union and combination, while, on the other hand, the usefulness of the International Central Council must greatly depend on the circumstance whether it has to deal with a few national centres of working men's associations, or with a great number of small and disconnected local societies, the members of the International Association shall use their utmost efforts to combine the disconnected working men's societies of their respective countries into national bodies, represented by central national organs. It is self-understood, however, that the appliance of this rule will depend upon the peculiar laws of each country, and that, apart from legal obstacles, no independent local society shall be precluded from directly corresponding with the London Central Council.

8. Until the meeting of the first Congress, the committee chosen on 28 September 1864 will act as a Provisional Central Council, try to connect the different national working men's associations, enlist members in the United Kingdom, take the steps preparatory to the convocation of the General Congress, and discuss with the national and local societies the main questions to be laid before that Congress.

9. Each member of the International Association, on removing his domicile from one country to another, will receive the fraternal support of the associated working men.

10. While united in a perpetual bond of fraternal cooperation, the working men's societies, joining the International Association, will preserve their existent organizations intact.

INSTRUCTIONS FOR DELEGATES TO THE
GENEVA CONGRESS[18]

1. Organization of the International Association

Upon the whole, the Provisional Central Council recommend the *plan of organization* as traced in the Provisional Statutes.[19] Its soundness and facilities of adaptation to different countries without prejudice to unity of action have been proved by two years' experience. For the next year we recommend London as the seat of the Central Council, the continental situation looking unfavourable for change.

The members of the Central Council will of course be elected by Congress (5 of the Provisional Statutes) with power to add to their number.

The *General Secretary* to be chosen by Congress for one year and to be the only paid officer of the Association. We propose £2 for his weekly salary.

The *uniform annual contribution of each individual member of the Association* to be *one half penny* (perhaps one penny). The cost price of cards of membership (*carnets*) to be charged extra.

While calling upon the members of the Association to form benefit societies and connect them by an international link, we leave the initiation of this question (*établissement des sociétés de secours mutuels. Appui moral et matériel accordé aux orphelins de l'association*)[20] to the Swiss who originally proposed it at the conference of September last.[21]

18. Marx wrote these Instructions for the General Council's own delegates to the Geneva Congress of September 1866, following from discussion at the Council's meetings on the different questions. The 'Instructions' were read out at the Congress as the General Council's report, and published in the *International Courier*, the General Council's official organ, on 20 February and 13 March 1867. The full title given in the newspaper text is: 'Instructions for the Delegates of the Provisional General Council. The Different Questions'.

19. I.e. the Provisional Rules.

20. Setting up of benefit societies. Moral and material support for orphans of the association.

21. The London Conference of the International, September 1865.

2. International Combination of Efforts, by the Agency of the Association, in the Struggle between Labour and Capital

(*a*) From a general point of view, this question embraces the whole activity of the International Association which aims at combining and generalizing the till now disconnected efforts for emancipation by the working classes in different countries.

(*b*) To counteract the intrigues of capitalists always ready, in cases of strikes and lock-outs, to misuse the foreign workman as a tool against the native workman, is one of the particular functions which our society has hitherto performed with success. It is one of the great purposes of the Association to make the workmen of different countries not only *feel* but *act* as brethren and comrades in the army of emancipation.

(*c*) One great 'international combination of efforts' which we suggest is a *statistical inquiry into the situation of the working classes of all countries to be instituted by the working classes themselves*. To act with any success, the materials to be acted upon must be known. By initiating so great a work, the workmen will prove their ability to take their own fate into their own hands. We propose therefore:

That in each locality, where branches of our Association exist, the work be immediately commenced, and evidence collected on the different points specified in the subjoined scheme of inquiry.

That the Congress invite all workmen of Europe and the United States of America to collaborate in gathering the elements of the statistics of the working class; that reports and evidence be forwarded to the Central Council. That the Central Council elaborate them into a general report, adding the evidence as an appendix.

That this report together with its appendix be laid before the next annual Congress, and after having received its sanction, be printed at the expense of the Association.

General Scheme of Inquiry, which may of course be modified by each locality:

1. Industry, name of.
2. Age and sex of the employed.
3. Number of the employed.
4. Salaries and wages: (*a*) apprentices; (*b*) wages by the day or piece work; scale paid by middlemen. Weekly, yearly average.

5. (*a*) Hours of work in factories. (*b*) The hours of work with small employers and in homework, if the business be carried on in those different modes. (*c*) Nightwork and daywork.

6. Mealtimes and treatment.

7. Sort of workshop and work: overcrowding, defective ventilation, want of sunlight, use of gaslight. Cleanliness, etc.

8. Nature of occupation.

9. Effect of employment upon the physical condition.

10. Moral condition. Education.

11. State of trade: whether season trade, or more or less uniformly distributed over year, whether greatly fluctuating, whether exposed to foreign competition, whether destined principally for home or foreign competition, etc.

3. Limitation of the Working Day

A preliminary condition, without which all further attempts at improvement and emancipation must prove abortive, is the *limitation of the working day*.

It is needed to restore the health and physical energies of the working class, that is, the great body of every nation, as well as to secure them the possibility of intellectual development, sociable intercourse, social and political action.

We propose *eight hours' work* as the *legal limit* of the working day. This limitation being generally claimed by the workmen of the United States of America,[22] the vote of the Congress will raise it to the common platform of the working classes all over the world.

For the information of continental members, whose experience of factory law is comparatively short-dated, we add that all legal restrictions will fail and be broken through by capital if the *period of the day* during which the eight working hours must be taken, be not fixed. The length of that period ought to be determined by the eight working hours and the additional pauses for meals. For instance, if the different interruptions for meals amount to *one hour*, the legal period of the day ought to embrace nine hours, say from 7 a.m. to 4 p.m., or from 8 a.m. to 5 p.m., etc. Nightwork to be but exceptionally permitted, in trades or branches of trades specified by law. The tendency must be to suppress all nightwork.

22. The demand for the eight-hour day was first put forward by the National Labour Union at its Baltimore convention in August 1866.

This paragraph refers only to adult persons, male or female, the latter, however, to be rigorously excluded from all *nightwork whatever*, and all sort of work hurtful to the delicacy of the sex, or exposing their bodies to poisonous and otherwise deleterious agencies. By adult persons we understand all persons having reached or passed the age of eighteen years.

4. Juvenile and Children's Labour (Both Sexes)

We consider the tendency of modern industry to make children and juvenile persons of both sexes cooperate in the great work of social production, as a progressive, sound and legitimate tendency, although under capital it was distorted into an abomination. In a rational state of society *every child whatever*, from the age of nine years, ought to become a productive labourer in the same way that no able-bodied adult person ought to be exempted from the general law of nature, viz.: to work in order to be able to eat, and work not only with the brain but with the hands too.

However, for the present, we have only to deal with the children and young persons of both sexes [belonging to the working people. They ought to be divided][23] into three *classes*, to be treated differently; the first class to range from nine to twelve; the second, from thirteen to fifteen years; and the third, to comprise the ages of sixteen and seventeen years. We propose that the employment of the first class in any workshop or housework be legally restricted to *two*; that of the second, to *four*; and that of the third, to *six* hours. For the third class, there must be a break of at least one hour for meals or relaxation.

It may be desirable to begin elementary school instruction before the age of nine years; but we deal here only with the most indispensable antidotes against the tendencies of a social system which degrades the working man into a mere instrument for the accumulation of capital, and transforms parents by their necessities into slaveholders, sellers of their own children. The *right* of children and juvenile persons must be vindicated. They are unable to act for themselves. It is, therefore, the duty of society to act on their behalf.

23. The words in brackets were omitted in the original version of this text, apparently by printer's error. They are reinstated here after the pamphlet *The International Working Men's Association. Resolutions of the Congress of Geneva, 1866, and the Congress of Brussels, 1868*, London [1869].

If the middle and higher classes neglect their duties toward their offspring, it is their own fault. Sharing the privileges of these classes, the child is condemned to suffer from their prejudices.

The case of the working class stands quite different. The working man is no free agent. In too many cases, he is even too ignorant to understand the true interest of his child, or the normal conditions of human development. However, the more enlightened part of the working class fully understands that the future of its class, and, therefore, of mankind, altogether depends upon the formation of the rising working generation. They know that, before everything else, the children and juvenile workers must be saved from the crushing effects of the present system. This can only be effected by converting *social reason* into *social force*, and, under given circumstances, there exists no other method of doing so, than through *general laws*, enforced by the power of the state. In enforcing such laws, the working class do not fortify governmental power. On the contrary, they transform that power, now used against them, into their own agency. They effect by a general act what they would vainly attempt by a multitude of isolated individual efforts.

Proceeding from this standpoint, we say that no parent and no employer ought to be allowed to use juvenile labour, except when combined with education.

By education we understand three things.

Firstly: *Mental education*.

Secondly: *Bodily education*, such as is given in schools of gymnastics, and by military exercise.

Thirdly: *Technological training*, which imparts the general principles of all processes of production, and simultaneously initiates the child and young person in the practical use and handling of the elementary instruments of all trades.

A gradual and progressive course of mental, gymnastic, and technological training ought to correspond to the classification of the juvenile labourers. The costs of the technological schools ought to be partly met by the sale of their products.

The combination of paid productive labour, mental education, bodily exercise and polytechnic training, will raise the working class far above the level of the higher and middle classes.

It is self-understood that the employment of all persons from [nine] and to seventeen years (inclusively) in nightwork and all health-injuring trades must be strictly prohibited by law.

5. Cooperative Labour

It is the business of the International Working Men's Association to combine and generalize the *spontaneous movements* of the working classes, but not to dictate or impose any doctrinary system whatever. The Congress should, therefore, proclaim no *special system* of cooperation, but limit itself to the enunciation of a few general principles.

(*a*) We acknowledge the cooperative movement as one of the transforming forces of the present society based upon class antagonism. Its great merit is to practically show, that the present pauperizing and despotic system of the *subordination of labour* to capital can be superseded by the republican and beneficent system of *the association of free and equal producers*.

(*b*) Restricted, however, to the dwarfish forms into which individual wage slaves can elaborate it by their private efforts, the cooperative system will never transform capitalistic society. To convert social production into one large and harmonious system of free and cooperative labour, *general social changes* are wanted, *changes of the general conditions of society*, never to be realized save by the transfer of the organized forces of society, viz., the state power, from capitalists and landlords to the producers themselves.

(*c*) We recommend to the working men to embark in *cooperative production* rather than in *cooperative stores*. The latter touch but the surface of the present economical system, the former attacks its groundwork.

(*d*) We recommend to all cooperative societies to convert one part of their joint income into a fund for propagating their principles by example as well as by precept, in other words, by promoting the establishment of new cooperative fabrics, as well as by teaching and preaching.

(*e*) In order to prevent cooperative societies from degenerating into ordinary middle-class joint-stock companies (*sociétés par actions*), all workmen employed, whether shareholders or not, ought to share alike. As a mere temporary expedient, we are willing to allow shareholders a low rate of interest.

6. Trade Unions. Their Past, Present and Future

(A) Their Past

Capital is concentrated social force, while the workman has only to dispose of his working force. The *contract* between capital and labour can therefore never be struck on equitable terms, equitable even in the sense of a society which places the ownership of the material means of life and labour on one side and the vital productive energies on the opposite side. The only social power of the workmen is their number. The force of numbers, however, is broken by disunion. The disunion of the workmen is created and perpetuated by their *unavoidable competition amongst themselves*.

Trade unions originally sprang up from the *spontaneous* attempts of workmen at removing or at least checking that competition, in order to conquer such terms of contract as might raise them at least above the condition of mere slaves. The immediate object of trade unions was therefore confined to everyday necessities, to expediencies for the obstruction of the incessant encroachments of capital, in one word, to questions of wages and time of labour. This activity of the trade unions is not only legitimate, it is necessary. It cannot be dispensed with so long as the present system of production lasts. On the contrary, it must be generalized by the formation and the combination of trade unions throughout all countries. On the other hand, unconsciously to themselves, the trade unions were forming *centres of organization* of the working class, as the medieval municipalities and communes did for the middle class. If the trade unions are required for the guerrilla fights between capital and labour, they are still more important as *organized agencies for superseding the very system of wage labour and capital rule*.

(B) Their Present

Too exclusively bent upon the local and immediate struggles with capital, the trade unions have not yet fully understood their power of acting against the system of wage slavery itself. They therefore kept too much aloof from general social and political movements. Of late, however, they seem to awaken to some sense of their great historical mission, as appears, for instance, from their participation, in England, in the recent political movement, from the enlarged views taken of their function in the United States, and from the following resolution passed at the recent great conference of trade-union delegates at Sheffield:[24]

That this conference, fully appreciating the efforts made by the International Association to unite in one common bond of brotherhood the working men of all countries, most earnestly recommend to the various societies here represented, the advisability of becoming affiliated to that body, believing that it is essential to the progress and prosperity of the entire working community.

(c) Their Future

Apart from their original purposes, they must now learn to act deliberately as organizing centres of the working class in the broad interest of its *complete emancipation*. They must aid every social and political movement tending in that direction. Considering themselves and acting as the champions and representatives of the whole working class, they cannot fail to enlist the non-society men into their ranks. They must look carefully after the interests of the worst paid trades, such as the agricultural labourers, rendered powerless by exceptional circumstances. They must convince the world at large that their efforts, far from being narrow and selfish, aim at the emancipation of the downtrodden millions.

7. *Direct and Indirect Taxation*

(*a*) No modification of the form of taxation can produce any important change in the relations of labour and capital.

(*b*) Nevertheless, having to choose between two systems of taxation, we recommend the *total abolition of indirect taxes*, and the *general substitution of direct taxes*.

Because indirect taxes enhance the prices of commodities, the tradesmen adding to those prices not only the amount of the indirect taxes, but the interest and profit upon the capital advanced in their payment;

Because indirect taxes conceal from an individual what he is paying to the state, whereas a direct tax is undisguised, unsophisticated, and not to be misunderstood by the meanest capacity. Direct taxation prompts therefore every individual to

24. This conference was the forerunner of the TUC, which first met in 1869.

control the governing powers while indirect taxation destroys all tendency to self-government.

8. *International Credit*

Initiative to be left to the French.[25]

9. *Polish Question*[26]

(*a*) Why do the workmen of Europe take up this question? In the first instance, because the middle-class writers and agitators conspire to suppress it, although they patronize all sorts of nationalities on the Continent, [and] even Ireland. Whence this reticence? Because both, aristocrats and bourgeois, look upon the dark Asiatic power in the background as a last resource against the advancing tide of working-class ascendancy. That power can only be effectually put down by the restoration of Poland upon a democratic basis.

(*b*) In the present changed state of central Europe, and especially Germany, it is more than ever necessary to have a democratic Poland. Without it, Germany will become the outwork of the Holy Alliance, with it, the cooperator with republican France.[27] The working-class movement will continuously be interrupted, checked, and retarded, until this great European question be set at rest.

(*c*) It is especially the duty of the German working class to take

25. It was the French Proudhonists who had proposed this subject for discussion.

26. In the French translation of this text, made by Paul Lafargue (who later married Marx's daughter Laura) on Marx's authorization, and published in *Le Courrier International* of 16 March 1867, this section is headed, 'On the Need to Destroy Russian Influence in Europe in order to Apply the Right of Peoples to Self-Determination and to Reconstruct Poland on a Democratic and Social Basis.' This is taken from a resolution drafted by Marx and passed by the 1865 London Conference; see *IWMA* I, pp. 246–7.

27. Central Europe had recently been changed by the defeat of Austria in the Austro-Prussian war of June–July 1866, and the formation of the North German Confederation under Prussian hegemony. The Holy Alliance existed at this period only in a figurative sense; Marx's point is that Prussia/Germany was still tied to Austria and Russia by the partition of Poland. (See Engels's article, 'What Have the Working Classes to Do with Poland?', below, pp. 1064–5.)

the initiative in this matter, because Germany is one of the partitioners of Poland.

10. Armies[28]

(*a*) The deleterious influence of large standing armies upon *production* has been sufficiently exposed at middle-class congresses of all denominations, at peace congresses, economical congresses, statistical congresses, philanthropical congresses, sociological congresses. We think it, therefore, quite superfluous to expatiate upon this point.

(*b*) We propose the general armament of the people and their general instruction in the use of arms.

(*c*) We accept as a transitory necessity small standing armies to form schools for the officers of the militia; every male citizen to serve for a very limited time in those armies.

11. Religious Question[29]

To be left to the initiative of the French.

REPORT TO THE BRUSSELS CONGRESS[30]

The year 1867–8 will mark an epoch in the history of the Association. After a period of peaceable development it has assumed dimensions powerful enough to provoke the bitter denunciations of the ruling classes and the hostile demonstrations of governments. It has entered upon the phases of strife.

The French government took, of course, the lead in the reactionary proceedings against the working classes. Already last year we had to signalize some of its underhand manoeuvres. It meddled with our correspondence, seized our Statutes [Rules] and the Congress documents. After many fruitless steps to get them

28. In the French translation, this section is headed, 'Standing Armies: Their Relationship to Production.'

29. In the French translation, this section is headed, 'Religious Ideas: Their Influence on the Social, Political and Intellectual Movement.' This also had been proposed for discussion by the anti-clerical Proudhonists.

30. The General Council's report to the September 1868 Brussels Congress was drafted by Marx in English and approved by the General Council on 1 September 1868. It was published in *The Times*, 9 September 1868.

back, they were at last given up only under the official pressure of
Lord Stanley, the English Minister of Foreign Affairs.[31]

But the Empire has this year thrown off the mask and tried to
directly annihilate the International Association by *coups de police*
and judiciary prosecution. Begot by the struggle of classes, of
which the days of June 1848 are the grandest expression, it could
not but assume alternately the attitudes of the official saviour of
the bourgeoisie and of the paternal protector of the proletariat.
The growing power of the International having manifested itself
in the strikes of Roubaix, Amiens, Paris, Geneva, etc., reduced our
would-be patron to the necessity of turning our society to his own
account or of destroying it. In the beginning he was ready enough
to strike a bargain on very moderate terms. The manifesto of the
Parisians read at the Congress of Geneva[32] having been seized at
the French frontier, our Paris executive demanded of the Minister of
the Interior the reasons of this seizure. M. Rouher then invited one
of the members of the Committee to an interview, in the course of
which he declared himself ready to authorize the entry of the manifesto on the condition of some modifications being inserted. On the
refusal of the delegate of the Paris executive, he added, 'Still, if you
would introduce some words of gratitude to the emperor, who has
done so much for the working classes, one might see what could
be done.'

M. Rouher's, the sub-emperor's, insinuation was met by a blank
rebuff. From that moment the Imperial government looked out
for a pretext to suppress the Association. Its anger was heightened by the anti-chauvinist agitation on the part of our French
members after the German war.[33] Soon after, when the Fenian
panic had reached its climax, the General Council addressed to
the English government a petition demanding the commutation
of the sentence on the three victims of Manchester, and

31. The case referred to here involved the interception by French government
agents, in September 1866, of printed matter and correspondence being carried by a
Swiss, Jules Gottraux, from Geneva to London following the Geneva Congress. See
'The French Government and the International Association of Working Men', *IWMA*
II, pp. 271–6.

32. This document, which set out the views of the French Proudhonists
on the issues discussed at the Geneva Congress, was published in Brussels in
1866 under the title *Congrès de Genève, Mémoire des délégués français*. (It is
printed in J. Freymond (ed.), *La Première Internationale*, vol. I, Droz, Geneva,
1962.)

33. The Austro-Prussian war of 1866.

qualifying their hanging as an act of political revenge.[34] At the same time it held public meetings in London for the defence of the rights of Ireland. The Empire, always anxious to deserve the good graces of the British government, thought the moment propitious for laying hands upon the International. It caused nocturnal perquisitions to be made, eagerly rummaged the private correspondence, and announced with much noise that it had discovered the centre of the Fenian conspiracy, of which the International was denounced as one of the principal organs. All its laborious researches, however, ended in nothing. The public prosecutor himself threw down his brief in disgust. The attempt at converting the International Association into a secret society of conspirators having miserably broken down, the next best thing was to prosecute our Paris branch as a non-authorized society of more than twenty members. The French judges, trained by the Imperialist[35] discipline, hastened, of course, to order the dissolution of the Association and the imprisonment of its Paris executive. The tribunal had the *naïveté* to declare in the preamble of its judgement that the existence of the French Empire was incompatible with a working men's association that dared to proclaim truth, justice, and morality as its leading principles.[36] The consequences of these prosecutions made themselves felt in the departments, where paltry vexations on the part of the prefects succeeded to the condemnations of Paris. This governmental chicanery, however, so far from annihilating the Association, has given it a fresh impulse by forcing the Empire to drop its patronizing airs to the working classes.

In Belgium the International Association has made immense strides. The coal lords of the basin of Charleroi, having driven their miners to riots by incessant exactions, let loose upon those unarmed men the armed force which massacred many of them.[37] It was in the midst of the panic thus created that our Belgian branch took up the cause of the miners, disclosed their miserable economical condition, rushed to the rescue of the families of the

34. See below, pp. 842–3.

35. See p. 718, n. 62.

36. The first trial of the Paris Committee of the International took place in March 1868. Its fifteen members were fined, and the Paris sections declared dissolved. Meanwhile, a new Committee was elected, whose nine members were tried in May, and sentenced to three months' imprisonment and a fine.

37. In March 1868.

dead and wounded, and procured legal counsel for the prisoners, who were finally all of them acquitted by the jury. After the affair of Charleroi the success of the International in Belgium was assured. The Belgian Minister of Justice, Jules Bara, denounced the International Association in the Chamber of Deputies and made of its existence the principal pretext for the renewal of the law against foreigners. He even dared to threaten he should prevent the Brussels Congress from being held. The Belgium government ought at last to understand that petty states have no longer any *raison d'être* in Europe except they be the asylums of liberty.

In Italy, the progress of the Association has been impeded by the reaction following close upon the ambuscade of Mentana;[38] one of the first consequences was the restriction put upon the right of association and public meeting. But the numerous letters which have come to our hands fully prove that the Italian working class is more and more asserting its individuality quite independently of the old parties.

In Prussia, the International cannot exist legally, on account of a law which forbids all relations with foreign societies. Moreover, in regard to the General Union of the German Working Men,[39] the Prussian government has imitated Bonapartism on a shabby scale. Always ready to fall foul of each other, the military governments are cheek by jowl when entering upon a crusade against their common enemy, the working classes. In spite, however, of all these petty tribulations, small groups spread over the whole surface of Germany have long since rallied round our Geneva centre.[40] The General Union of the German Working Men, whose branches are mostly confined to northern Germany, have in their recent Congress held at Hamburg[41] decided to act in concert with the International Working Men's Association, although debarred from joining it officially. In the programme of the Nuremberg Congress, representing upwards of 100 working men's societies, which mostly belong to middle and southern Germany, the direct adhesion to the International has been put on the order

38. Garibaldi's expedition to secure Rome and the Papal State for the Kingdom of Italy was defeated at Mentana on 3 November 1867 by Papal guards backed by French forces.

39. I.e. the General Association of German Workers (ADAV); see the Introduction to this volume, pp. 21–3.

40. See the Introduction to this volume, p. 23.

41. The Hamburg Congress of the ADAV was held in August 1868.

of the day. At the request of their leading committee we have sent a delegate to Nuremberg.[42]

In Austria the working-class movement assumes a more and more revolutionary aspect. In the beginning of September a congress was to meet at Vienna, aiming at the fraternization of the working men of the different races of the empire. They had also sent an address to the English and French working men, in which they declared for the principles of the International. Your General Council had already appointed a delegate to Vienna[43] when the liberal government of Austria, on the very point of succumbing to the blows of the feudal reaction, had the shrewdness to stir the anger of the working men by prohibiting their congress.

In the struggle maintained by the building trades of Geneva the very existence of the International in Switzerland was put on its trial. The employers made it a preliminary condition of coming to any terms with their workmen that the latter should forsake the International. The working men indignantly refused to comply with this dictate. Thanks to the aid received from France, England, Germany, etc., through the medium of the International, they have finally obtained a diminution of one hour of labour and ten per cent increase of wages. Already deeply rooted in Switzerland, the International has witnessed since that event a rapid increase in the number of its members. In the month of August last the German working men residing in Switzerland (about fifty societies) passed at their Congress in Neuenburg [Neuchâtel] a unanimous vote of adhesion to the International.

In England the unsettled state of politics, the dissolution of the old parties, and the preparations for the coming electoral campaign have absorbed many of our most active members, and, to some degree, retarded our propaganda. Nevertheless, we have entered into correspondence with numerous provincial trade unions, many of which have sent in their adhesion. Among the more recent London affiliations those of the Curriers' Society and the City Men's Shoemakers are the most considerable as regards numbers.

Your General Council is in constant communication with the National Labour Union of the United States. On its last Congress

42. The Nuremberg Congress of the Union of German Workers' Societies was held in September 1868; see the Introduction to this volume, pp. 22–3. The General Council's delegate was J. G. Eccarius.

43. Peter Fox.

of August 1867, the American Union had resolved to send a delegate to the Brussels Congress, but, pressed for time, was unable to take the special measures necessary for carrying out the vote.

The latent power of the working classes of the United States has recently manifested itself in the legal establishment of a working day of eight hours in all the workshops of the federal government, and in the passing of laws to the same effect by many state legislatures. However, at this very moment the working men of New York, for example, are engaged in a fierce struggle for enforcing the eight hours' law, against the resistance of rebellious capital. This fact proves that even under the most favourable political conditions all serious success of the proletariat depends upon an organization that unites and concentrates its forces; and even its national organization is still exposed to split on the disorganization of the working classes in other countries, which one and all compete in the market of the world, acting and reacting the one upon the other. Nothing but an international bond of the working classes can ever ensure their definitive triumph. This want has given birth to the International Working Men's Association. That Association has not been hatched by a sect or a theory. It is the spontaneous growth of the proletarian movement, which itself is the offspring of the natural and irrepressible tendencies of modern society. Profoundly convinced of the greatness of its mission, the International Working Men's Association will allow itself neither to be intimidated nor misled. Its destiny, henceforward, coalesces with the historical progress of the class that bear in their hands the regeneration of mankind.

REPORT TO THE BASLE CONGRESS[44]

Citizens,

The delegates of the different sections will give you detailed reports on the progress of our Association in their respective countries. The report of your General Council will mainly relate to the guerrilla fights between capital and labour – we mean the strikes which during the last year have perturbed the continent of

44. The General Council's report to the September 1869 Basle Congress was drafted by Marx on the mandate of the General Council meeting of 31 August. It was published in the pamphlet *Report of the Fourth Annual Congress of the International Working Men's Association*, London, 1869.

Europe, and were said to have sprung neither from the misery of the labourer nor from the despotism of the capitalist, but from the secret intrigues of our Association.

A few weeks after the meeting of our last Congress, a memorable strike on the part of the ribbon-weavers and silk-dyers occurred in Basle, a place which to our days has conserved much of the features of a medieval town with its local traditions, its narrow prejudices, its purse-proud patricians, and its patriarchal rule of the employer over the employed. Still, a few years ago, a Basle manufacturer boasted to an English secretary of embassy, that 'the position of the master and the man was on a better footing here than in England', that 'in Switzerland the operative who leaves a good master for better wages would be *despised* by his own *fellow-workmen*', and that 'our advantage lies principally in the length of the working time and the moderation of the wages'. You see, *patriarchalism*, as modified by modern influences, comes to this – that the master is good, and that his wages are bad, that the labourer feels like a medieval vassal, and is exploited like a modern wage slave.

That patriarchalism may further be appreciated from an official Swiss inquiry into the factory employment of children and the state of the primary public schools. It was ascertained that 'the Basle school atmosphere is the worst in the world, that while in the free air carbonic acid forms only 4 parts of 10,000, and in closed rooms should not exceed 10 parts, it rose in Basle common schools to 20–81 parts in the forenoon, and to 53–94 in the afternoon'. Thereupon a member of the Basle Great Council, Mr Thurneysen, coolly replied, 'Don't allow yourselves to be frightened. The parents have passed through schoolrooms as bad as the present ones, and yet they have escaped with their skins safe.'

It will now be understood that an economical revolt on the part of the Basle workmen could not but mark an epoch in the social history of Switzerland. Nothing more characteristic than the starting-point of the movement. There existed an old custom for the ribbon-weavers to have a few hours' holiday on Michaelmas. The weavers claiming this small privilege at the usual time in the factory of Messrs Dubary & Sons, one of the masters declared, in a harsh voice and with imperious gesticulation, 'Whoever leaves the factory will be dismissed at once and for ever.' Finding their protestations in vain, 104 out of 172 weavers left the workshop without, however, believing in their definite dismissal, since master and men were bound by written contract to give a fourteen days' notice to quit. On their return the next morning they found the factory surrounded by gendarmes, keeping off the yesterday's rebels, with whom all their comrades now made common cause. Being thus suddenly thrown out of work, the weavers with their families were simultaneously ejected from the cottages they rented from their employers, who, into the bargain, sent circular letters round to the shopkeepers to debar the houseless ones from all credit for victuals. The struggle thus begun lasted from 9 November 1868 to the spring of 1869. The limits of our report do not allow us to enter upon its details. It suffices to state that it originated in a capricious and spiteful act of capitalist despotism, in a cruel lock-out, which led to strikes, from time to time interrupted by compromises, again and again broken on the part of the masters, and that it culminated in the vain attempt of the Basle 'High and Honourable State Council' to intimidate the working people by military measures and a quasi state of siege.

During their sedition the workmen were supported by the International Working Men's Association. But that was not all. That society, the masters said, had first smuggled the modern spirit of rebellion into the good old town of Basle. To again expel that mischievous intruder from Basle became, therefore, their great preoccupation. Hard they tried, though in vain, to enforce the withdrawal from it, as a condition of peace, upon their subjects. Getting generally worsted in their war with the International they vented their spleen in strange pranks. Owning some industrial branch establishments at Lörrach, in Baden, these republicans induced the grand-ducal official to suppress the International section at that place, a measure which, however, was soon after rescinded by the Baden government. The Augsburg *Allgemeine Zeitung*, a paper of world-wide circulation, presuming to report on the Basle events in an impartial spirit, the angry worthies threatened it in foolish letters with the withdrawal of their subscriptions. To London they expressly sent a messenger on the fantastic errand of ascertaining the dimensions of the International general 'treasury-box'. Orthodox Christians as they are, if they had lived at the time of nascent Christianity, they would, above all things, have spied into St Paul's banking accounts at Rome.

Their clumsily savage proceedings brought down upon them some ironical lessons of worldly wisdom on the part of the Geneva capitalist organs. Yet, a few months later, the uncouth

786 *Documents of the First International: 1864–70*

Basle vestrymen might have returned the compliment with usurious interest to the Geneva men of the world.

In the month of March there broke out in Geneva a building trades strike, and a compositors' strike, both bodies being affiliated to the International. The builders' strike was provoked by the masters setting aside a convention solemnly entered upon with their workmen a year ago. The compositors' strike was but the winding-up of a ten year quarrel which the men had during all that time in vain tried to settle by five consecutive commissions. As in Basle, the masters transformed at once their private feuds with their men into a state crusade against the International Working Men's Association.

The Geneva State Council dispatched policemen to receive at the railway stations, and sequestrate from all contact with the strikers, such foreign workmen as the masters might contrive to inveigle from abroad. It allowed the *'jeunesse dorée'*, the hopeful loafers of *'la jeune Suisse'*, armed with revolvers, to assault, in the streets and places of public resort, workmen and workwomen. It launched its own police ruffians on the working people on different occasions, and signally on 24 May, when it enacted at Geneva, on a small scale, the Paris scenes which Raspail has branded as *'les orgies infernales des casse-têtes'*.[45] When the Geneva workmen passed in public meeting an address to the State Council, calling upon it to inquire into these infernal police orgies, the State Council replied by a sneering rebuke. It evidently wanted, at the behest of its capitalist superiors, to madden the Geneva people into an *émeute*, to stamp that *émeute* out by the armed force, to sweep the International from the Swiss soil, and to subject the workmen to a Decembrist regime.[46] This scheme was baffled by the energetic action and moderating influence of our Geneva Federal Committee. The masters had at last to give way.

And now listen to some of the invectives of the Geneva capitalists and their press-gang against the International. In public meeting they passed an address to the State Council, where the following phrase occurs: 'The International Committee at Geneva ruins the Canton of Geneva *by decrees sent from London*

45. 'Hellish orgies with truncheons.' Thus François Raspail, a former associate of Blanqui, and at this time a republican deputy, referred to Bonapartist police violence in the elections of May–June 1869.

46. I.e. Bonapartist; Louis Napoleon's coup d'état was on 2 December 1851.

and Paris; it wants here to suppress all industry and all labour.'

One of their journals stated, 'The leaders of the International were secret agents of the emperor, who, at the opportune moment, were very likely to turn out public accusers against this little Switzerland of ours.'

And this on the part of the men who had just shown themselves so eager to transplant at a moment's notice the Decembrist regime to the Swiss soil, on the part of financial magnates, the real rulers of Geneva and other Swiss towns, whom all Europe knows to have long since been converted from citizens of the Swiss republic into mere feudatories of the French Crédit Mobilier[47] and other international swindling associations.

The massacres by which the Belgian government did answer in April last to the strikes of the puddlers at Seraing and the coal-miners of Borinage, have been fully exposed in the address of the General Council to the workmen of Europe and the United States.[48] We considered this address the more urgent since, with that constitutional model government, such working men's massacres are not an accident, but an institution. The horrid military drama was succeeded by a judicial farce. In the proceedings against our Belgian General Committee at Brussels, whose domiciles were brutally broken into by the police, and many of whose members were placed under secret arrest, the judge of instruction finds the letter of a workman, asking for 500 *'Internationales'*, and he at once jumps to the conclusion that 500 fighting-men were to be dispatched to the scene of action. The 500 *'Internationales'* were 500 copies of the *Internationale*, the weekly organ of our Brussels Committee.

A telegram to Paris by a member of the International, ordering a certain quantity of powder, is raked up. After a prolonged research, the dangerous substance is really laid hand on at Brussels. It is powder for killing vermin. Last, not least, the Belgian police flattered itself, in one of its domiciliary visits, to have got at that phantom treasure which haunts the great mind of the continental capitalist, viz.: the International treasure, the main stock of which is safely hoarded at London, but whose offsets travel con-

47. A government-sponsored bank set up in 1852, exposed by Marx in several articles in the *New York Daily Tribune* (e.g. 21 June, 24 June and 11 July 1856; 30 May and 1 June 1857).

48. 'The Belgian Massacres. To the Workmen of Europe and the United States', written by Marx; *IWMA* III, pp. 312–18.

tinually to all the continental seats of the Association. The Belgian official inquirer thought it buried in a certain strong box, hidden in a dark place. He gets at it, opens it forcibly, and there was found – some pieces of coal. Perhaps, if touched by the hand of the police, the pure International gold turns at once into coal.

Of the strikes that, in December 1868, infested several French cotton districts, the most important was that at Sotteville-lès-Rouen. The manufacturers of the department of the Somme had not long ago met at Amiens, in order to consult how they might undersell the English manufacturers in the English market itself. Having made sure that, besides protective duties, the comparative lowness of French wages had till now mainly enabled them to defend France from English cottons, they naturally inferred that a still further lowering of French wages would allow them to invade England with French cottons. The French cotton-workers, they did not doubt, would feel proud at the idea of defraying the expenses of a war of conquest which their masters had so patriotically resolved to wage on the other side of the Channel. Soon after it was bruited about that the cotton manufacturers of Rouen and its environs had, in secret conclave, agreed upon the same line of policy. Then an important reduction of wages was suddenly proclaimed at Sotteville-lès-Rouen, and then for the first time the Norman weavers rose against the encroachments of capital. They acted under the stir of the moment. Neither had they before formed a trade union nor provided for any means of resistance. In their distress they appealed to the International committee at Rouen, which found for them some immediate aid from the workmen of Rouen, the neighbouring districts, and Paris. Towards the end of December 1868, the General Council was applied to by the Rouen committee, at a moment of utmost distress throughout the English cotton districts, of unparalleled misery in London, and a general depression in all branches of British industry. This state of things has continued in England to this moment. Despite such highly unfavourable circumstances, the General Council thought that the peculiar character of the Rouen conflict would stir the English workmen to action. This was a great opportunity to show the capitalists that their international industrial warfare, carried on by screwing wages down now in this country, now in that, would be checked at last by the international union of the working classes. To our appeal the English workmen replied at once by a first contribution to Rouen, and the London Trades Council resolved to summon, in unison with the General Council, a metropolitan monster meeting on behalf of their Norman brethren. These proceedings were stopped by the news of the sudden cessation of the Sotteville strike. The miscarriage of that economical revolt was largely compensated for by its moral results. It enlisted the Norman cotton-workers into the revolutionary army of labour, it gave rise to the birth of trade unions at Rouen, Elboeuf, Darnétal, and the environs; and it sealed anew the bond of fraternity between the English and French working classes.

During the winter and spring of 1869 the propaganda of our Association in France was paralysed, consequent upon the violent dissolution of our Paris section in 1868,[49] the police chicaneries in the departments, and the absorbing interest of the French general elections.

The elections once over, numerous strikes exploded in the Loire mining districts, at Lyons, and many other places. The economical facts revealed during these struggles between masters and men struck the public eye like so many dissolving views of the high-coloured fancy pictures of working-class prosperity under the auspices of the Second Empire. The claims of redress on the part of the workmen were of so moderate a character and so urgent a nature that, after some show of angry resistance, they had to be conceded, one and all. The only strange feature about those strikes was their sudden explosion after a seeming lull, and the rapid succession in which they followed each other. Still, the reason of all this was simple and palpable. Having, during the elections, successfully tried their hands against their public despot, the workmen were naturally led to try them after the elections against their private despots. In one word, the elections had stirred their animal spirits. The governmental press, of course, paid as it is to misstate and misinterpret unpleasant facts, traced these events to a secret *mot d'ordre* from the London General Council, which, they said, sent their emissaries, from place to place, to teach the otherwise highly satisfied French workmen that it was a bad thing to be overworked, underpaid, and brutally treated. A French police organ, published at London, the *'International'* – (see its number of 3 August) – has condescended to reveal to the world the secret motives of our deleterious activity.

49. See above, p. 780.

The strangest feature is that the strikes were ordered to break out in such countries where misery is far from making itself felt. These unexpected explosions, occurring so opportunely for certain neighbours of ours, who had first had to apprehend war, make many people ask themselves whether these strikes took place on the request of some foreign Machiavelli, who had known how to win the good graces of this all-powerful Association.

At the very moment when this French police print impeached us of embarrassing the French government by strikes at home, in order to disembarrass Count Bismarck from war abroad, a Prussian paper accused us of embarrassing the North German Confederation with strikes, in order to crush German industry for the benefit of foreign manufactures.

The relations of the International to the French strikes we shall illustrate by two cases of a typical character. In the one case, the strike of Saint-Étienne and the following massacre at Ricamarie, the French government itself will no longer dare to pretend that the International had anything whatever to do with it. In the Lyons case, it was not the International that threw the workmen into strikes, but, on the contrary, it was the strikes that threw the workmen into the International.

The miners of Saint-Étienne, Rive-de-Giers, and Firminy had calmly, but firmly, requested the managers of the mining companies to reduce the working day, numbering twelve hours' hard underground labour, and revise the wages tariff. Failing in their attempt at a conciliatory settlement, they struck on 11 June. For them it was of course a vital question to secure the cooperation of the miners that had not yet turned out to combine with them. To prevent this, the managers of the mining companies requested and got from the prefect of the Loire a forest of bayonets. On 12 June, the strikers found the coal pits under strong military guard. To make sure of the zeal of the soldiers thus lent to them by the government, the mining companies paid each soldier a franc daily. The soldiers paid the companies back by catching, on 16 June, about sixty miners eager to get at a conversation with their brethren in the coal pits. These prisoners were in the afternoon of the same day escorted to Saint-Étienne by a detachment (150 men) of the fourth regiment of the line. Before these stout warriors set out, an engineer of the Dorian mines distributed them sixty bottles of brandy, telling them at the same time, they ought to have a sharp eye on their gang of prisoners, these miners being savages, barbarians, ticket-of-leave men. What with the brandy, and what with the sermon, a bloody collision was thus prepared for. Followed on their march by a crowd of miners, with their wives and children, surrounded by them on a narrow defile on the heights of the Moncel, Quartier Ricamarie, requested to surrender the prisoners, and, on their refusal, attacked by a volley of stones, the soldiers, without any preliminary warning, fired with their *chassepots* pell-mell into the crowd, killing fifteen persons, amongst whom were two women and an infant, and dangerously wounding a considerable number. The tortures of the wounded were horrible. One of the sufferers was a poor girl of twelve years, Jenny Petit, whose name will live immortal in the annals of the working-class martyrology. Struck by two balls from behind, one of which lodged in her leg, while the other passed through her back, broke her arm, and escaped through her right shoulder. '*Les chassepots avaient encore fait merveille*.'[50]

This time, however, the government was not long in finding out that it had committed not only a crime, but a blunder. It was not hailed as the saviour of society by the middle class. The whole municipal council of Saint-Étienne tendered its resignation in a document denouncing the scoundrelism of the troops and insisting upon their removal from the town. The French press rang with cries of horror! Even such conservative prints as the *Moniteur universel*[51] opened subscriptions for the victims. The government *had* to remove the odious regiment from Saint-Étienne.

Under such difficult circumstances, it was a luminous idea to sacrifice on the altar of public indignation a scapegoat always at hand, the International Working Men's Association. At the judicial trial of the so-called rioters, the act of accusation divided them into ten categories, very ingeniously shading their respective darkness of guilt. The first class, the most deeply tinged, consisted of workmen more particularly suspected to have obeyed some secret *mot d'ordre* from abroad, given out by the International. The evidence was, of course, overwhelming, as the following short extract from a French paper will show:

The interrogatory of the witnesses did not allow '*neatly*' to establish

50. '*Chassepots* [the French military rifle] had again worked wonders.'
51. The *Moniteur* had recently ceased to be the official organ of the French government.

the participation of the International Association. The witnesses affirm *only* the presence, at the head of the bands, of some *unknown* people, wearing white frocks and caps. *None of the unknown ones have been arrested, or appear in the dock.* To the question: do you *believe* in the intervention of the International Association? a witness replies: I *believe* it, but *without any proofs whatever*!

Shortly after the Ricamarie massacres, the dance of economical revolts was opened at Lyons by the silk-winders, most of them females. In their distress they appealed to the International, which, mainly by its members in France and Switzerland, helped them to carry the day. Despite all attempts at police intimidation, they publicly proclaimed their adhesion to our society, and entered it formally by paying the statutory contributions to the General Council. At Lyons, as before at Rouen, the female workers played a noble and prominent part in the movement. Other Lyons trades have since followed in the track of the silk-winders. Some 10,000 new members were thus gained for us in a few weeks amongst that heroic population which more than thirty years ago inscribed upon its banner the watchword of the modern proletariat: *'Vivre en travaillant ou mourir en combattant!'*[52]

Meanwhile the French government continues its petty tribulations against the International. At Marseilles our members were forbidden meeting for the election of a delegate to Basle. The same paltry trick was played in other towns. But the workmen on the Continent, as elsewhere, begin at last to understand that the surest way to get one's natural rights is to exercise them at one's personal risk.

The Austrian workmen, and especially those of Vienna, although entering their class movement only after the events of 1866,[53] have at once occupied a vantage-ground. They marched at once under the banners of socialism and the International, which, by their delegates at the recent Eisenach Congress,[54] they have now joined *en masse*.

If anywhere, the liberal middle class has exhibited in Austria its selfish instincts, its mental inferiority, and its petty spite

52. 'Live working or die fighting!' This slogan was raised by the Lyons silk workers in their revolt of 1831.

53. The Austro-Prussian war.

54. At the Eisenach Congress of August 1869 the dissident Lassalleans joined with Liebknecht and Bebel's group to form the Social-Democratic Workers's Party (SDAP); see the Introduction to this volume, pp. 23–4.

against the working class. Their ministry, seeing the empire distracted and threatened by an internecine struggle of races and nationalities, pounces upon the workmen who alone proclaim the fraternity of all races and nationalities. The middle class itself, which has won its new position not by any heroism of its own, but only by the signal disaster of the Austrian army, hardly able as it is, and knows itself to be, to defend its new conquests from the attacks of the dynasty, the aristocracy, and the clerical party, nevertheless wastes its best energies in the mean attempt to debar the working class from the rights of combination, public meeting, free press and free thought. In Austria, as in all other states of continental Europe, the International has supplanted the *ci-devant spectre rouge*.[55] When, on 13 July, a workmen's massacre on a small scale was enacted at Brünn [Brno], the cottonopolis of Moravia, the event was traced to the secret instigations of the International, whose agents, however, were unfortunately invested with the rare gift of rendering themselves invisible. When some leaders of the Vienna work-people figured before the judicial bench, the public accuser stigmatized them as tools of the foreigner. Only, to show how conscientiously he had studied the matter, he committed the little error of confounding the middle-class League of Peace and Freedom with the working man's International Association.

If the workmen's movement was thus harassed in Cis-Leithanian Austria, it has been recklessly prosecuted in Hungary. On this point the most reliable reports from Pest [Budapest] and Pressburg [Bratislava] have reached the General Council. One example of the treatment of the Hungarian workmen by the public authorities may suffice. Herr von Wenckheim, the Hungarian Home Minister, was just staying at Vienna on public business. Having for months been interdicted from public meetings and even from entertainments destined for the collection of the funds of a sick club, the Bratislava workmen sent at last delegates to Vienna, then and there to lay their grievances before the illustrious Herr von Wenckheim. Puffing and blowing his cigar, the illustrious one received them with the bullying apostrophe, 'Are you workmen? Do you work hard? For nothing else you have to care. You do not want public clubs; and if you dabble in politics, we shall know what measures to take against you. I shall do nothing for you. Let the workmen grumble to their hearts' content!' To the question of the workmen,

55. The former red spectre.

whether the good pleasure of the police was still to rule uppermost, the liberal minister replied: 'Yes, under my responsibility.' After a somewhat prolonged but useless explanation the workmen left the minister, telling him, 'Since state matters influence the workmen's condition, the workmen must occupy themselves with politics, and they will certainly do so.'

In Prussia and the rest of Germany, the past year was distinguished by the formation of trade unions all over the country. At the recent Eisenach Congress the delegates of 150,000 German workmen, from Germany proper, Austria and Switzerland, have organized a new democratic social party, with a programme literally embodying the leading principles of our Statutes. Debarred by law from forming sections of our Association, they have, nevertheless, formally entered it by resolving to take individual cards of membership from the General Council. At its congress at Barmen, the General Association of German Workers has also reaffirmed its adhesion to the principles of our Association, but simultaneously declared the Prussian law forbade them joining us.

New branches of our Association have sprung up at Naples, in Spain, and in Holland.

At Barcelona a Spanish, and at Amsterdam a Dutch organ of our Association is now being issued.[56]

The laurels plucked by the Belgian government on the glorious battlefields of Seraing and Frameries seem really to have roused the angry jealousy of the great powers. No wonder, then, that England also had this year to boast a workmen's massacre of its own. The Welsh coal-miners, at Leeswood Great Pit, near Mold, in Denbighshire, had received sudden notice of a reduction of wages by the manager of those works, whom, long since, they had reason to consider a most incorrigible petty oppressor. Consequently, they collected aid from the neighbouring collieries, and, besides assaulting him, attacked his house, and carried all his furniture to the railway station, these wretched men fancying in their childish ignorance thus to get rid of him for good and all. Proceedings were of course taken against the rioters; but one of them was rescued by a mob of 1,000 men, and conveyed out of the town. On 28 May, two of the ringleaders were to be taken before the magistrates of Mold by policemen under the escort of a detachment of the 4th Regiment of the line, 'The King's Own'.

56. *La Federación* and *De Werkman*.

A crowd of miners, trying to rescue the prisoners, and, on the resistance of the police and the soldiers, showering stones at them, the soldiers – without any previous warning – returned the shower of stones by a shower of bullets from their breachloaders (Snider fusils). Five persons, two of them females, were killed, and a great many wounded. So far there is much analogy between the Mold and the Ricamarie massacres, but here it ceases. In France, the soldiers were only responsible to their commander. In England, they had to pass through a coroner's jury inquest; but this coroner was a deaf and daft old fool, who had to receive the witnesses' evidence through an ear trumpet, and the Welsh jury, who backed him, were a narrowly prejudiced class jury. They declared the massacre 'justifiable homicide'.

In France, the rioters were sentenced to from three to eighteen months' imprisonment, and soon after, amnestied. In England, they were condemned to ten years' penal servitude! In France, the whole press resounded with cries of indignation against the troops. In England, the press was all smiles for the soldiers, and all frowns for their victims! Still, the English workmen have gained much by losing a great and dangerous illusion. Till now they fancied to have their lives protected by the formality of the Riot Act, and the subordination of the military to the civil authorities. They know now, from the official declaration of Mr Bruce, the Liberal Home Secretary, in the House of Commons – firstly, that without going through the premonitory process of reading the Riot Act, any country magistrate, some fox-hunter or parson, has the right to order the troops to fire on what he may please to consider a riotous mob; and, secondly, that the soldier may give fire on his own book, on the plea of self-defence. The Liberal minister forgot to add that, under these circumstances, every man ought to be armed, at public expense, with a breachloader, in self-defence against the soldier.

The following resolution was passed at the recent General Congress of the English trade unions at Birmingham:[57]

That as local organizations of labour have almost disappeared before organizations of a national character, so we believe the extension of the principle of free trade, which induces between nations such a competition that the interest of the workman is liable to be lost sight of and sacrificed in the fierce international race between capitalists, demands that such organizations should be still further extended and made inter-

57. The first TUC Congress.

national. And as the International Working Men's Association endeavours to consolidate and extend the interests of the toiling masses, which are everywhere identical, this Congress heartily recommends that Association to the support of the working men of the United Kingdom, especially of all organized bodies, and strongly urges them to become affiliated to that body, believing that the realization of its principles would also conclude to lasting peace between the nations of the earth.

During last May, a war between the United States and England seemed imminent. Your General Council, therefore, sent an address to Mr Sylvis, the President of the American National Labour Union, calling on the United States' working class to command peace where their would-be masters shouted war.[58]

The sudden death of Mr Sylvis, that valiant champion of our cause, will justify us in concluding this report, as an homage to his memory, by his reply to our letter:

Your favour of the 12th instant, with address enclosed, reached me yesterday. I am very happy to receive such kindly words from our fellow working men across the water: our cause is a common one. It is war between poverty and wealth: labour occupies the same low condition, and capital is the same tyrant in all parts of the world. Therefore I say our cause is a common one. I, in behalf of the working people of the United States, extend to you, and through you to those you represent, and to all the downtrodden and oppressed sons and daughters of toil in Europe, the right hand of fellowship. Go ahead in the good work you have undertaken, until the most glorious success crowns your efforts. That is our determination. Our late war resulted in the building up of the most infamous monied aristocracy on the face of the earth. This monied power is fast eating up the substance of the people. We have made war upon it, and we mean to win. If we can, we will win through the ballot-box; if not, then we will resort to sterner means. A little blood-letting is sometimes necessary in desperate cases.

58. This crisis followed the speech of the Republican Congressional leader Charles Summer on 13 April 1869, claiming 2 billion dollars compensation for the damage to US interests caused by English privateers during the civil war. In 1872 the dispute between England and the US was settled by an international tribunal, with England agreeing to pay 15½ million dollars. The General Council's 'Address to the National Labor Union of the United States', written by Marx, is printed in *IWMA* III, pp. 319–21.

THE GENERAL COUNCIL TO THE FEDERAL COUNCIL OF
FRENCH SWITZERLAND[59]

At its extraordinary meeting of 1 January 1870 the General Council
resolved:

1. We read in *Égalité*,[60] 11 December 1869:

> It is *certain* that the General Council is neglecting matters of great
> importance. We would remind it of its obligations under Regulation II/2:[61]
> 'The General Council is *bound* to execute the Congress resolutions, etc. . . .'
> We could ask the General Council enough questions for its answers to make
> a somewhat lengthy document. These will come later . . . Meanwhile, etc.
> etc. . . .

The General Council knows of no article, either in the Rules or
in the Regulations, which would oblige it to enter into correspondence or debate with *Égalité*, or provide any 'answers to
questions' from newspapers. Only the Federal Committee in
Geneva represents the branches of French Switzerland to the
General Council. Whenever the Federal Committee addresses
requests or objections to us by the one and only legitimate
channel, i.e. through its secretary, the General Council will
always be ready to reply. But the Federal Committee has no
right either to hand over its functions to the editors of *Égalité*
and *Progrès*,[62] or to permit those journals to usurp its functions.

59. This circular, sometimes known as the 'Confidential Communication', was written by Marx in French after the General Council's meeting of 1
January 1870, and distributed privately in hand-written copies. Marx's original text is not extant, and it is translated here from a manuscript copy made
by Marx's wife and corrected by Marx himself, as reproduced in *IWMA* III,
pp. 354–63.

60. *L'Égalité* was the official organ of the French-Swiss (*Romand*) Federal Council or Committee of the International, which was taken over by Bakunin's faction in
autumn 1869. Marx replies to the allegations in question point by point in the present
circular.

61. The Administrative Regulations of the International, adopted by the Geneva
Congress of 1866 as a supplement to the Rules, and modified by subsequent Congress decisions. This reference is to the 1871 English edition, printed in *IWMA* IV,
pp. 451–69.

62. *Le Progrès* was a Bakuninist paper, edited by James Guillaume in Le Locle,
Switzerland.

Generally speaking, administrative correspondence between the General Council and the national and local committees cannot be made public without doing considerable damage to the general interests of the Association. Therefore, if other organs of the International were to imitate *Progrès* and *Égalité*, the General Council would be forced either to remain silent and thus earn the discredit of the public, or to violate its obligations by making a public reply. *Égalité* has combined with *Progrès* in urging *Le Travail*[63] (a Paris newspaper) also to attack the General Council. This is virtually a *ligue du bien public*.[64]

2. Accepting that the questions posed by *Égalité* originate from the French-Swiss Federal Council, we shall reply to them, on condition that in future such questions do not reach us by the same route.

3. Question of the Bulletin

According to the resolutions of the Geneva Congress, inserted into the Administrative Regulations, the national committees are supposed to send the General Council *documents* relating to the proletarian movement, and '*as often as its means permit*, the General Council shall publish a report, etc.'[65] in the various languages.

The General Council's obligation is thus dependent on *conditions* which have never been fulfilled; even the statistical inquiry, provided for in the Rules, decided on by successive General Congresses, annually requested by the General Council, has never been carried out. No document has been sent to the General Council. As for *means*, the General Council would have long since ceased to exist without the English 'regional' contributions and the personal sacrifice of its own members.

Thus the regulation in question adopted at the Geneva Congress has remained a dead letter.

The Brussels Congress, for its part, never discussed the *execution* of this regulation; it discussed the possibility of a bulletin in due

63. *Le Travail* was the newspaper of the Paris sections of the International.

64. The original Ligue du Bien Public (League of Public Welfare) was an association of French barons founded in 1464 to resist Louis XI's centralizing policy.

65. *IWMA* II, p. 269.

time but *it adopted no resolution*. (See the *German report* printed at Basle under the eyes of the Congress.)[66]

For the rest, the General Council believes that the original aim of the bulletin is at the moment perfectly well served by the different organs of the International published in the various languages and mutually exchanged. It would be absurd to produce costly bulletins to do what is already done without expense. On the other hand, a bulletin which published things which are not said in the International's organs would only serve to admit our enemies behind the scenes.

4. *Question of the Separation of the General Council and the Regional Council for England*[67]

Long before the founding of *Égalité* this proposal arose from time to time in the General Council itself, put forward by one or two of its English members. It was always rejected almost unanimously.

Although the revolutionary *initiative* will probably start from France, only England can act as a *lever* in any seriously *economic* revolution. It is the only country where there are no longer any peasants, and where land ownership is concentrated in very few hands. It is the only country where almost all production has been taken over by the *capitalist form*, in other words with work combined on a vast scale under capitalist bosses. It is the only country *where the large majority of the population consists of wage-labourers*. It is the only country where the class struggle and the organization of the working class into *trade unions* have actually reached a considerable degree of maturity and universality. Because of its domination of the world market, it is the only country where any revolution in the economic system will have immediate repercussions on the rest of the world. Though landlordism and capitalism are most traditionally established in this country, on the other hand the *material conditions* for *getting rid of them* are also most ripe here. Given that the General Council is now in the happy position of *having its hand directly*

66. The corresponding English account is *Report of the Fourth Annual Congress of the International Working Men's Association*, London [1869].

67. From the foundation of the International the General Council also fulfilled the role of the leading body for Britain, until an English Federal Council was set up by decision of the London Conference of 1871.

upon this tremendous lever for proletarian revolution, what lunacy, we would almost say what a crime, to let it fall into purely English hands!

The English have all that is needed *materially* for social revolution. What they lack is *the sense of generalization and revolutionary passion*. These are things that only the General Council can supply, and it can thus speed up the genuinely revolutionary movement in this country, and consequently *everywhere else*. The tremendous results we have already achieved in this direction are attested to by the most intelligent and authoritative newspapers of the ruling class – as for instance the *Pall Mall Gazette*, the *Saturday Review*, the *Spectator* and the *Fortnightly Review* – to say nothing of the so-called Radical members of both Houses of Parliament who, not long ago, still exercised enormous influence over the English workers' leaders. They are publicly accusing us of having poisoned and almost extinguished the *English spirit* of the working class, and having thrust the workers into revolutionary socialism.

The only way we could have produced this change was to act as the General Council of the International Association. As the General Council we can initiate moves (such as the foundation of the Land and Labour League)[68] which as they develop further appear to the public to be spontaneous movements of the English working class.

If a Regional Council were to be formed as distinct from the General Council, what would be the immediate effects?

Caught between the General Council and the TUC, the Regional Council would lack authority. On the other hand, the General Council of the International would lose its present control of the great lever I have described. If we wanted to replace our important underground activity with the publicity of the theatre, then we would perhaps have made the mistake of publicly answering the question put in *Égalité* as to why the General Council submits to fulfilling such an inconvenient plurality of functions!

England can not be considered simply as one country among many others. It must be treated as the metropolis of capital.

68. See p. 713, n. 47.

5. Question of the General Council's Resolutions on the Irish Amnesty

If England is the bulwark of European landlordism and capitalism, the only point at which one can strike a major blow against official England is *Ireland*.

In the first place, Ireland is the bulwark of English landlordism. If it collapsed in Ireland, it would collapse in England. The whole operation is a hundred times easier in Ireland, because there the economic struggle is concentrated exclusively on landed property, because that struggle is at the same time a national one, and because the people have reached a more revolutionary and exasperated pitch there than in England. Landlordism in Ireland is kept in being solely by the *English army*. If the enforced union between the two countries were to cease, a social revolution would immediately break out in Ireland – even if of a somewhat backward kind. English landlordism would lose not only a major source of its wealth, but also its greatest moral force – the fact of *representing England's domination over Ireland*. On the other hand, by preserving the power of its landlords in Ireland, the English proletariat makes them invulnerable in England itself.

In the second place, in dragging down the working class in England still further by the forced immigration of poor Irish people, the English bourgeoisie has not merely exploited Irish poverty. It has also divided the proletariat into two hostile camps. The fiery rebelliousness of the Celtic worker does not mingle well with the steady slow nature of the Anglo-Saxon; in fact in all *the major industrial centres of England* there is a profound antagonism between the Irish and the English proletarians. The ordinary English worker hates the Irish worker as a competitor who brings down his wages and standard of living. He also feels national and religious antipathies for him; it is rather the same attitude that the poor whites of the Southern states of North America had for the Negro slaves. This antagonism between the two groups of proletarians within England itself is artificially kept in being and fostered by the bourgeoisie, who know well that this split is the real secret of preserving their own power.

This antagonism is reproduced once again on the other side of the Atlantic. The Irish, driven from their native soil by cattle and sheep, have landed in North America where they form a considerable, and increasing, proportion of the population. Their sole thought, their sole passion, is their hatred for England. The English and American governments (in other words, the classes they represent) nourish that passion so as to keep permanently alive the underground struggle between the United States and England; in that way they can prevent the sincere and worthwhile alliance between the working classes on the two sides of the Atlantic which would lead to their emancipation.

Furthermore, Ireland is the only excuse the English government has for keeping up a large regular army which can, as we have seen, in case of need attack the English workers after having done its basic training in Ireland.

Finally, what ancient Rome demonstrated on a gigantic scale can be seen in the England of today. A people which subjugates another people forges its own chains.

Therefore the International Association's attitude to the Irish question is absolutely clear. Its first need is to press on with the social revolution in England, and to that end, the major blow must be struck in Ireland.

The General Council's resolutions on the Irish Amnesty[69] are designed simply to lead into other resolutions which will declare that, quite apart from the demands of international justice, it is an essential precondition for the emancipation of the English working class to transform the present enforced union (in other words, the enslavement of Ireland) into a free and equal confederation, if possible, and into a total separation, if necessary.

In any case, the hyper-naive pronouncements of *Égalité* and *Progrès* as to the connection, or rather lack of connection, between the social movement and the political movement have never, as far as we know, been approved by any of our International Congresses. They are in fact contrary to our Rules, which state: 'The *economical emancipation* of the working classes is therefore the great end to which every *political movement ought* to be subordinate *as a means*'.[70]

The phrase 'as a means' was left out in the French translation made by the Paris Committee in 1864.[71] When taxed with this

69. These resolutions, adopted by the General Council on 16 November 1869, are reproduced by Marx in his letter to Engels of 18 November; below, p. 847.

70. Above, p. 766.

71. *Congrès Ouvrier. Association Internationale des Travailleurs. Règlement Provisoire* [Paris, 1864] (printed in Freymond, op. cit., vol. I).

by the General Council, the Paris Committee gave as its excuse the wretchedness of its political situation.

There are other distortions of the text. The first consideration of the Rules is framed thus: 'The struggle for the emancipation of the working classes means . . . a struggle . . . for equal rights and duties, and *the abolition of all class rule*.'

The Paris translation mentions the 'equal rights and duties', in other words, the general phrase which exists in nearly all the democratic manifestoes of the past hundred years, and which means something quite different to different classes; but it leaves out the concrete phrase, 'the abolition of all class rule'.

Again, in the second consideration of the Rules we read: '. . . the economical subjection of the *man of labour* to the *monopolizer of the means of labour*, that is, the *sources of life*, etc.'

The Paris translation has 'capital' instead of 'the means of labour, that is, the sources of life', an expression which includes the land as well as the other means of labour.

However, the original and authentic text has been restored in the French translation published in Brussels by *La Rive gauche* (in 1866), and printed in pamphlet form.[72]

6. *The Liebknecht–Schweitzer Problem*

Égalité says: 'These two groups belong to the International.'

That is not true. The Eisenach group[73] (which *Progrès* and *Égalité* are trying to turn into 'citizen Liebknecht's group') belongs to the International. *Schweitzer's group*[74] *does not belong to it*.

Schweitzer has even explained at length in his newspaper (*Social-Demokrat*) why the Lassallean organization could not be united with the International without destroying itself;[75] un-

72. This translation (*Manifeste de l'Association Internationale des Travailleurs suivi du Règlement Provisoire*) was made by Charles Longuet, who later married Marx's daughter Jenny.

73. The Social-Democratic Workers' Party (SDAP); see p. 707.

74. The General Association of German Workers (ADAV), founded by Lassalle; see pp. 705–7.

75. On 16 July 1869. After nominally moving closer to the International in 1868, Schweitzer swung the ADAV onto an ultra-sectarian course in June 1869, effecting a reconciliation with Countess Hatzfeld's splinter group (see below, p. 832, n. 29). This led to a large section of the ADAV breaking away, and uniting with Liebknecht and Bebel's group in September 1869 to form the Social-Democratic Workers' Party.

knowingly, he was speaking the truth. His artificial and sectarian organization is wholly opposed to the historic and spontaneous organization of the working class.

Progrès and *Égalité* have demanded that the General Council give a public statement of 'opinion' as to the personal differences between Liebknecht and Schweitzer. Since citizen Johann Philipp Becker (who is slandered along with Liebknecht in Schweitzer's paper) is one of the editorial committee of *Égalité*, it seems curious that its editors are not better informed as to the facts. They should know that Liebknecht, in the *Demokratisches Wochenblatt*,[76] publicly invited Schweitzer to accept the General Council as arbiter of their differences, and that Schweitzer equally publicly rejected the General Council's authority.[77]

On its side, the General Council has done everything in its power to bring this scandal to an end. It asked its secretary for Germany[78] to correspond with Schweitzer, which he did for two years, but all the Council's attempts have failed, thanks to Schweitzer's firm resolution to preserve at all costs his autocratic power over his own sectarian organization. It is for the General Council to decide at what moment its public intervention in the dispute will be of more value than harm.

7. Since *Égalité*'s accusations have been public, and might be thought to come from the Geneva (French-Swiss) Committee, the General Council will communicate this reply to all the committees with which it is in correspondence.

BY ORDER OF THE GENERAL COUNCIL

76. On 20 February 1869. The *Demokratisches Wochenblatt* had been the organ of Liebknecht's Union of German Workers' Societies. Marx erroneously referred here to the *Volksstaat*, the organ of the SDAP, which Liebknecht edited at the time of Marx's writing.

77. *Social-Demokrat*, 24 February 1869.

78. I.e. Marx.

On Germany

THE PRUSSIAN MILITARY QUESTION AND
THE GERMAN WORKERS' PARTY[1] [*Extract*]

Frederick Engels

II

The political existence of the Prussian bourgeoisie – the most advanced section and, as such, the representative of the whole German bourgeoisie – is characterized by a lack of courage which is unparalleled even in the history of this, not exactly bold, class and which can only be partially excused by what has been happening abroad. In March and April 1848 it was master of the situa-

1. Engels wrote this pamphlet at Marx's request early in February 1865, and it was published in Hamburg at the end of the month. It is translated here from the text printed in *MEW* 16. The first section of Engels's pamphlet, omitted here, is chiefly technical in character, and presents the details of the army reorganization along with a military critique of the measures involved. The aim of the army reorganization was to expand Prussian military strength as required by the Prussian regime's aspirations to German hegemony. It involved a large increase in the officer corps, the expansion of the peacetime army to a strength of 200,000, and the transformation of the Landwehr (territorial army) into an army reserve or a second field army.

Universal military service had been introduced in Prussia in 1814, although it was by no means consistently applied. Although the Prussian government presented the army reorganization as a more consistent application of universal military service, its real tendency was towards the French and Austrian system of a large regular army based on selective long-term military service. Engels held that the Prussian government could be forced, by dint of its own requirements, to make concessions to the bourgeois opposition that would give the reorganized army a more democratic character: the thorough application of the principle of universal military service, with a duration of two years in the colours followed by a period in the reserve and Landwehr duty, and the institution of non-professional Landwehr officers.

The proposed army reorganization marked the start of the constitutional conflict between the Prussian government and the liberal bourgeois majority in the Lower House of the Prussian Assembly. When the 'New Era' government had refused to make significant concessions to the bourgeoisie, the Progressive party deputies refused to vote for the military budget, in March

tion; but with the first independent stirrings on the part of the working class it immediately took fright and fled back to the protection of the very bureaucracy and feudal aristocracy which, with the help of the workers, it had just defeated. The Manteuffel period[2] was the inevitable consequence. At length the 'New Era'[3] began – without any assistance from the bourgeois opposition. This unhoped-for piece of luck turned the heads of the bourgeoisie. It completely forgot the position into which it had got itself as a result of its continual withdrawal from one position back to the next, its repeated revisions of the constitution and its surrender to the bureaucracy and feudalism – in which it even went so far as to accept the reinstitution of the feudal provincial and district diets. It believed itself once again master of the situation; it completely forgot that it had itself reinstated all the forces hostile to it, which, having gathered their strength, now controlled the real power in the state just as they had before 1848. The reorganization of the army thus hit the bourgeoisie as if a bomb had been tossed into its midst.

There are only two ways for the bourgeoisie to obtain political power. Since it is an army of officers, and can only recruit its troops from among the workers, it must either ensure the support of the workers or it must buy political power piecemeal from those forces confronting it from above, in particular, from the monarchy. The history of the English and French bourgeoisies shows that there is no other way.

1862. After new elections failed to break the deadlock, Bismarck was appointed chancellor, in October 1862, and proceeded with the military reform, levying taxation in defiance of the constitution. This situation still obtained when Engels wrote his pamphlet, but the conflict was resolved in August 1866, when, following the Prussian defeat of Austria and the formation of the North German Confederation, the Progressive party split, and the majority converted themselves into National Liberals and capitulated to Bismarck.

2. Otto, Freiherr von Manteuffel, was Prime Minister and Foreign Minister from 1850 to 1858. The Manteuffel period was a dictatorship of the junkers and the court camarilla, and even the reactionary 1850 constitution was repeatedly 'revised' from above.

3. In October 1858 Prince William became the prince regent, and succeeded to the throne when mad Frederick William IV died in 1861. His first act was to dismiss Manteuffel and appoint a moderate liberal government, which the bourgeois press optimistically saw as inaugurating a 'New Era'. However, William's aim was solely to contain bourgeois demands, and the 'New Era' brought no real reforms. It came to an end with the appointment of Bismarck in October 1862.

The Prussian bourgeoisie – for no reason at all – had lost all desire to enter into an honest alliance with the workers. In 1848 the German workers' party, at that time still at the beginning of its development and organization, was ready to do the bourgeoisie's work on very cheap terms; the bourgeoisie, however, feared the least independent activity on the part of the proletariat more than it feared the feudal lords and the bureaucracy.[4] Peace bought at the price of servitude seemed to the bourgeoisie more desirable than freedom with even the mere *prospect* of a struggle. This holy fear of the workers subsequently became traditional among the bourgeoisie until Herr Schulze-Delitzsch began his 'savings-box' agitation.[5] This was designed to prove to the workers that they could know no greater happiness than to devote their lives and even those of their offspring to industrial exploitation by the bourgeoisie, indeed that they must themselves contribute to this exploitation by creating a subsidiary source of income from industrial cooperatives of all kinds, thus giving the capitalists an opportunity of lowering their wages. Now, although the industrial bourgeoisie, together with cavalry lieutenants, are without doubt the least educated class in the German nation, such agitation was from the very beginning without the least prospect of lasting success among so intellectually advanced a people as the Germans. The more intelligent members of the bourgeoisie could not help but realize that nothing would come of their plans, and their alliance with the workers collapsed again.

All that was left was to haggle with the government over political power, which had to be paid for in ready cash – from the people's pocket, of course. The only *real* power which the bourgeoisie had in the state consisted in the right to vote taxes, although even this right was hedged by a great many provisos. This, at any rate, was where the pressure had to be applied, and a class so skilled in haggling over prices was bound to be at an advantage in such matters.

But no. The Prussian bourgeois opposition – in complete contrast to the classical English bourgeoisie of the seventeenth and

4. See 'The Bourgeoisie and the Counter-Revolution', in Volume I, above, pp. 180–206.

5. Franz Hermann Schulze-Delitzsch was a petty-bourgeois economist and a leading figure in the Progressive party. At the turn of the sixties he attempted to take the newly awakening workers' movement in tow by propagating harmless schemes for 'credit associations'.

eighteenth centuries – thought that it could get power on the cheap, *without* paying money for it.

What then was the correct policy for the bourgeois opposition, seen from a purely bourgeois standpoint and taking full account of the conditions under which the reorganization of the army was proposed? If it had been at all capable of judging its own strength it could not have failed to realize that, as a class which had just been raised up from the degradation it had suffered under Manteuffel – and without the least assistance from itself – it certainly did not have the power to prevent the actual *implementation* of the plan; this, indeed, was put into operation. It had to realize that the actual existence of the new institution was becoming increasingly difficult to reject with every fruitless session which passed; that is, it became more obvious from year to year that the government would offer less and less in order to gain the consent of the Chamber. It had also to realize that it was still far from having the power to appoint and dismiss ministers and that therefore the longer the conflict lasted the fewer ministers there would be who would be ready to compromise. Lastly it had to realize that it lay in its own interests not to bring matters to a head, for in view of the stage of development of the German working class, a serious conflict between the bourgeois opposition and the government was bound to give rise to an independent workers' movement. If the worst came to the worst, such a conflict would present the bourgeoisie with the old dilemma: either an alliance with the workers, but this time under much less favourable conditions than in 1848, or down on its knees before the government with a *pater, peccavi*![6]

Accordingly, the bourgeois liberals and Progressives[7] ought to have subjected the reorganization of the army, together with the inevitable rise in its peacetime size, to an unbiased and objective examination, in which it would probably have reached conclusions much the same as ours. It was important not to forget that the changes already made could not be prevented and that in view of the many correct and valuable elements contained in the plan its final implementation could at best be delayed. Above all, the

6. 'Father, I have sinned', the opening words of a Catholic prayer.
7. The Progressive party in Prussia stood for German unity under Prussian hegemony, an all-German parliament, to which the ministry should be responsible, and liberal economic reforms. It did not demand universal suffrage, or the unrestricted freedom of association, assembly and the press.

bourgeoisie should have been on its guard against taking up, right from the start, a position opposed to the reorganization; on the contrary, it should have made use of this reorganization and the money to be voted for it in order to purchase from the 'New Era' as many equivalent concessions as possible and to convert the nine or ten million thalers of new taxation into as much political power for itself as possible.

And there was no shortage of things still to be done! There was all the legislation passed under Manteuffel restricting the press and the freedom of association; the whole power structure of the police and bureaucracy, which had been taken over unchanged from the absolute monarchy; the ineffectiveness of the courts due to jurisdictional conflicts; the provincial and district diets; there was, above all, the interpretation of the constitution which had prevailed under Manteuffel and which now had to be challenged by a new constitutional practice; there was the atrophy of municipal self-government caused by the bureaucracy and a hundred other things, which any other bourgeoisie under similar circumstances would have willingly paid for with a tax increase of a half thaler *per capita* and all of which were within reach if the business were conducted with any degree of skill. But the bourgeois opposition did not think this way. As far as freedom of the press, association and assembly were concerned, Manteuffel's laws had given them just enough to make them feel comfortable. They were allowed moderate demonstrations against the government without hindrance; any increase in freedom would have brought less advantage to them than to the workers, and before the bourgeoisie would give the workers freedom to form an independent movement they preferred to put up with more pressure from the government. It was the same story with the restrictions imposed by the power of the police and bureaucracy. The bourgeoisie believed that, thanks to the government of the 'New Era', the bureaucracy had been subdued; but it was glad to see that this bureaucracy was still allowed to have a free hand against the workers. It completely forgot that the bureaucracy was much stronger and more vigorous than a government which happened to be well-disposed towards the bourgeoisie. It also imagined that with Manteuffel's fall the bourgeois millennium had begun and that it was now only a question of reaping the rich harvest of bourgeois hegemony without paying a penny in return.

But all the money which had to be voted, after the few years since 1848 had already cost so much, after the national debt had increased to such a size and taxes had risen so steeply! Gentlemen, you are the deputies of the most recent constitutional state in the world and you do not know that constitutionalism is the world's costliest form of government? It is almost costlier than Bonapartism, which, in the spirit of *après moi le déluge*[8] tries repeatedly to meet old debts with new ones and thus in the course of ten years consumes the financial resources of a century. The golden age of an absolutism kept within bounds, which you are still dreaming of, will never return.

But what about the constitutional provisos covering the continued raising of taxes already approved? Everyone knows how bashful the 'New Era' was in its demands for money. Little would have been lost by including the supplies for the army reorganization in the official budget in return for guaranteed concessions. It was a question of voting new taxes to cover this expenditure. It was possible for the bourgeoisie to be tight-fisted on fiscal matters; and, anyway, a better government than that of the 'New Era' could not have been wished for. The bourgeoisie was surely as much master of the situation as it had ever been, and it had won new power in other areas.

But could it then strengthen the forces of reaction by doubling the size of their main instrument of power, the army? This is an area in which the bourgeois Progressive party has become caught in an irresolvable contradiction. It demanded that Prussia play the part of a German Piedmont,[9] and to do this Prussia needs a powerful and well-organized army. It had the 'New Era' government, which secretly cherished the same hopes – the best government which, under the circumstances, it could have – but it *refuses* this government a stronger army. Day in day out, from morning till night the bourgeoisie talks of Prussia's glory, Prussia's greatness and the development of Prussian power; but it *refuses* to grant Prussia an increase in the size of its army which would even be comparable with that introduced by the other great powers since 1814. What is the reason for all this? The reason is that the bourgeois opposition fears that such an increase would only be to the advantage of the forces of reaction, that it would revitalize the

8. 'After me the deluge', a motto attributed to Louis XV.

9. Cavour, as Prime Minister of Piedmont/Sardinia, had successfully pioneered in Italy the tactic of national unification from above that was Bismarck's model in Germany.

decrepit aristocratic officers' corps and give the feudal and bureau-cratic–absolutist party in general the power to bury constitutionalism in its entirety by means of a coup d'état.

Admittedly, the bourgeois Progressives were right not to strengthen the reaction and they were correct in regarding the army as the securest stronghold from which this party could launch a coup. But was there ever a better opportunity of bringing the army under parliamentary control than that presented by this reorganization, proposed, as it had been, by the most pro-bourgeois government which Prussia had ever experienced in peacetime? As soon as the bourgeoisie declared its readiness to approve the expansion of the army on certain conditions, was that not just the time to settle the problem of the military academies, the preference given to the aristocracy in the officers' corps and all the other grievances; was that not the time to obtain guarantees which would give the officers' corps a more bourgeois character? The 'New Era' was sure of only one thing: that the army had to be strengthened. The devious ways it took to smuggle through the reorganization demonstrated most clearly its guilty conscience and its fear of the deputies. The bourgeoisie should have seized the opportunity with both hands, for such a chance could not be expected again in a hundred years. Detailed concessions could have been wrung from this government if the Progressives had approached the matter, not in a niggardly spirit, but as great speculators!

And now the practical consequences resulting from the reorganization of the officers' corps itself! Officers had to be found for twice the number of battalions. The military academies were then nowhere near adequate. Recruitment policy was liberal as never before in peacetime; lieutenancies were offered almost as awards to students, young lawyers and all young people with an education. Anyone who saw the Prussian army after its reorganization could not have recognized the officers' corps anymore. Our remarks are based not on hearsay but on our own observations. The characteristic lieutenants' jargon was submerged and the younger officers spoke their natural mother tongue; they did not in the least belong to an exclusive caste but represented to a greater extent than ever since 1815 all educated classes and all provinces of the state. This position had been won as a result of the necessity imposed by events themselves; it was only a question of holding it and making use of it. Instead the whole thing was ignored and dismissed by the bourgeois Progressives, as if all these officers were aristocratic cadets. And yet since 1815 there had never been so many bourgeois officers in Prussia as just at this time.

We must mention incidentally that we attribute the efficient conduct of the Prussian officers in the face of the enemy in the Schleswig-Holstein war[10] largely to this infusion of new blood. By themselves, the old class of subalterns would never have dared to act so often on their own initiative. In this respect the government is right in attributing to the military reorganization a considerable influence on the 'elegance' of the military successes; we are not in a position to judge whether the reorganization contributed in any other way to the defeat of the Danes.

Finally, the main point: could a coup d'état be more easily carried out if the peacetime army were strengthened? It is perfectly true that armies are the instruments with which coups are executed and that therefore every increase in the strength of an army also increases the practicability of a coup. But for a major country the military strength required by a great state depends not on the prospects – large or small – of a coup, but on the size of the armies of the other major states. In for a penny, in for a pound. If a Prussian deputy accepts his mandate, and takes Prussian greatness and Prussian power in Europe as his motto, then he must agree to make the means available without which there can be no talk of Prussian greatness and Prussian power. If the means cannot be provided without facilitating a coup, all the worse for the gentlemen of the Progressive party. If they had not conducted themselves in such a ludicrously craven and clumsy fashion in 1848, the period of coups d'état would probably be long past by now. Under the present circumstances nothing remains for them but to acknowledge the reorganization of the army in one form or another and to keep their reservations about coups to themselves.

However, there is another side to the matter. Firstly, it would have been more advisable to negotiate the approval of this instrument for a potential coup with a government of the 'New Era' than with a government under Bismarck. Secondly, it goes without saying that every further step towards a real implementation of universal military service makes the Prussian army less suitable as a tool for a coup d'état. Since the masses took up the demand

10. In spring 1864 Bismarck, in a short-lived alliance with Austria, went to war with Denmark and secured for Germany the duchies of Schleswig and Holstein.

for self-government and recognized the need for a struggle against all elements opposing this demand, the twenty- and twenty-one-year-olds have become part of the movement and, even under feudal and absolutist officers, it must have become increasingly difficult to use them to execute a coup. The further political education progresses in Prussia, the more recalcitrant will the mood of the recruits become. Even the present struggle between the government and the bourgeoisie must have demonstrated this.

Thirdly, the two-year period of military service is an adequate counterweight to the expansion of the army. The strengthening of the army increases the material capability of the government to carry out coups but, in the same degree, the two-year conscription period decreases its moral capability. In the third year of military service the incessant drumming of absolutist doctrines and habits of obedience into the soldiers' heads may bear fruit temporarily, as long as their military service lasts. In this third year, during which, militarily, the individual soldier has almost nothing more to learn, our conscript approaches, to a certain extent, the character of the soldier in the French and Austrian systems, who is trained for long years of service. He acquires something of the character of the professional soldier and, as such, he can be more easily used than the younger soldier. From the point of view of a military coup the distance of soldiers from civilian life in their third year of service would certainly more than balance out the recruitment of an additional 60,000 to 80,000 men over a period of two years.

But now we come to another point, the most decisive of all. It cannot be denied – we know our bourgeoisie too well – that a situation could arise in which, even without mobilization, even with an army at its peacetime level, a coup would be possible. However, it would still not be probable. In order to carry out a full-scale military coup an army mobilization would almost always be necessary. But when this happens a great change takes place. In peacetime the Prussian army may under certain circumstances become a mere tool which the government can use internally, but this can never happen in time of war! Anyone who has ever had an opportunity of seeing a battalion first in peacetime and then under war conditions knows the tremendous difference in the attitude of the military, in the character of the rank and file. People who joined the army as half-grown lads return to it as men;

they bring with them a store of self-respect, self-confidence, resolve and character, which benefits the whole battalion. The relationship of the ranks to the officers and of the officers to the ranks is transformed immediately. Militarily the battalion profits considerably; but politically it becomes – for absolutist purposes – completely unreliable. This was evident even during the invasion of Schleswig-Holstein, when, to the great surprise of the English newspaper correspondents, the Prussian soldiers openly took part in political demonstrations and expressed their by no means orthodox views without fear. And we owe the political corruption of the mobilized army, that is, its unreliability as an instrument of absolutist plans, mainly to the Manteuffel period and to the latest 'new' era. In 1848 things were quite different.

One of the best aspects of the Prussian military system both before and since the reorganization has been the fact that with *this* military system Prussia can neither conduct an unpopular war, nor can it carry out a coup d'état with any prospect of permanence. For, even if the peacetime army lent itself to a little coup, the first mobilization and the first threat of war would suffice to endanger all that had been 'achieved'. Without the ratification of the wartime army the heroic deeds of a peacetime army – a Battle of Düppel,[11] as it were, on the home front – would only be of passing significance; and the longer this ratification is needed the more difficult it will be to obtain. Some reactionary newspapers have declared the 'army' rather than the Chambers to be the true representative of the people. By this they meant, of course, only the officers. Should it happen one day that the gentlemen of the *Kreuz-Zeitung*[12] carry out a coup, and require for this a *mobilized* army, these representatives of the people will give them the shock of their lives, they can depend on it.

In the last instance, however, this is not the main guarantee against a coup. The main guarantee lies in that firstly, no government can assemble, by means of a coup, a Chamber of Deputies which will vote it new taxes and loans; secondly, even if it managed to produce such a compliant Chamber, no banker in Europe would grant it credit on the strength of that Chamber's resolutions. It would be a different case in most other European states. But

11. The battle of Düppel in April 1864 was the decisive defeat of Denmark in the Schleswig-Holstein war.
12. A nickname for the *Neue Preussische Zeitung*, the semi-official organ of the Prussian government, after the Prussian cross it used as its emblem.

since the promises of 1815 and all the vain manoeuvrings to obtain money up until 1848 Prussia happens to have a reputation such that no one would lend it a penny without a legally binding and unimpeachable resolution from the Chambers. Even Herr Raphael von Erlanger, who lent money to the American Confederates, would hardly entrust a Prussian government with ready cash if it had come to power by means of a coup. Prussia owes this state of affairs quite simply to the stupidity of absolutism.

The strength of the bourgeoisie lies in the fact that when the government gets into financial difficulties – as it must, sooner or later – it will be obliged to *turn to the bourgeoisie for money* and this time not to the political representatives of the bourgeoisie, who, in the last analysis, are quite aware that they are there to pay, but to the bourgeoisie of high finance, which is interested in doing good business with the government. The financial bourgeoisie measures the creditworthiness of a government by the same standards which it uses to measure the creditworthiness of a private individual and it is completely indifferent as to whether the Prussian state needs many soldiers or only a few. These gentlemen only grant credit against three signatures. If only the Upper Chamber has signed next to the government, and not the Chamber of Deputies, or if they only have the signature of a Chamber of Deputies full of government puppets, then they will regard the matter as kite-flying and decline with thanks.

At this point the military question becomes a constitutional question. It is immaterial which mistakes and complications have forced the bourgeois opposition into its present position; it must fight out the military question to the end or else it will lose what political power it still possesses. The government has already called its whole power of budgetary appropriation into question. But if the government will be *forced*, sooner or later, to make its peace with the Chamber, is it not the best policy simply to hold out until this moment arrives?

Since the conflict has gone so far, the answer must be an unqualified 'Yes'. It is more than doubtful whether an acceptable basis can be found for an agreement with this government. By overestimating its own strength the bourgeoisie has put itself in the position of having to discover by means of this military question whether it is the decisive power in the state or no power at all. If it wins the struggle, it will also win the power to appoint and dismiss ministers that the English House of Commons has. If it loses the struggle, it will no longer be able to achieve any position of importance by constitutional means.

But anyone who expects such powers of endurance does not know our bourgeoisie. In political matters the courage of the bourgeoisie is always in direct proportion to its importance in society. In Germany the social power of the bourgeoisie is far less than in England or even France; it has neither allied itself with the old aristocracy, as in England, nor has it destroyed the aristocracy with the help of the peasants and the workers, as in France. In Germany the feudal aristocracy is still hostile to the bourgeoisie, as well as being allied with the government. For all the enormous progress which it has made since 1848, industry, the basis of all the social power of the modern bourgeoisie, is still not as highly developed in Germany as in France and England. The colossal accumulation of capital in particular social strata, which can frequently be found in England and even in France, is much rarer in Germany. Hence the petty-bourgeois character of our whole bourgeoisie. The spheres of its activity and the mental horizons within which it operates are of a petty nature: it is no wonder that its whole mentality is equally petty! Where is it to find the courage to fight an issue out to the bitter end? The Prussian bourgeoisie knows only too well how dependent its industrial activity is upon the government. Industrial concessions[13] and administrative supervision weigh on it like a mountain. The government can put obstacles in the way of every new business project, and this is now true in the political sphere as well. During the conflict over the military question the bourgeois Chamber can only adopt a negative position; it is obliged to stay on the defensive. Meanwhile, the government assumes the offensive, interprets the Constitution in its own fashion, disciplines liberal officials, declares the liberal municipal elections null and void, employs all the machinery of bureaucratic power to make the bourgeoisie fully conscious of their position as Prussian subjects, in fact, captures one vantage point after another and thus occupies a position such as Manteuffel himself did not have. In the meantime expenditure and taxation continue their steady course without a budget and the army reorganization is consolidated with every year that passes. In short, while the government's victories in matters of detail accumulate daily in all fronts and assume the form of accomplished

13. At this time, bureaucratic regulation of industry in Prussia still required prospective entrepreneurs to obtain state concessions.

facts, the prospect of the final victory of the bourgeoisie assumes from year to year an increasingly revolutionary character. In addition, there is a workers' movement which is completely independent of both bourgeoisie and government and which forces the bourgeoisie either to make very awkward concessions to the workers or to be prepared to act without the workers at the decisive moment. Will the Prussian bourgeoisie have the courage to hold out until the bitter end under these circumstances? To do so it will have to have changed miraculously since 1848. The longing for a compromise daily audible in the sighs of the Progressive party since the beginning of this session is hardly evidence of such a change. We fear that this time, too, the bourgeoisie will not hesitate to betray itself.

III

'What is the proper attitude of the workers' party to this army reorganization and to the resulting conflict between the government and the bourgeois opposition?'

To develop their political activity fully the working class needs a much wider arena than that provided by the individual states of Germany in its present fragmented form. The multiplicity of states may be an obstacle to the proletarian movement, but it will never be regarded as justified and it will never be the object of serious concern. The German proletariat will never concern itself with Reich Constitutions, 'Prussian leadership', *Trias*[14] and such things, except when the time comes to make a clean sweep; it is completely indifferent as to how many soldiers the Prussian state needs in order to continue to survive as a great power. Whether the reorganization increases the military burden or not will not make much difference to the working class *as a class*. On the other hand, it is by no means indifferent as to whether universal military service is fully introduced. The more workers who are trained in the use of weapons, the better. Universal conscription is the necessary and natural extension of universal suffrage; it enables the electorate to carry out its resolutions arms in hand against any coup that might be attempted.

14. These references are to the Reich Constitution drawn up by the Frankfurt Assembly of 1848–9 (see the Introduction to *The Revolutions of 1848*, above, p. 18), the Prussian scheme for German hegemony first formulated by Frederick William IV on 20 March 1848, and the plan to reorganize the German Confederation into Austria, Prussia and a league of small and middle states, particularly canvassed by Bavaria and Saxony in the 1850s and 1860s.

The ever more complete introduction of military service is the only aspect of the Prussian army reorganization which interests the German working class.

But more important is the question of the position the workers' party should take with regard to the conflict between government and Chamber which this reorganization has produced.

The modern worker, the proletarian, is a product of the great industrial revolution, which, particularly during the last hundred years, has totally transformed all modes of production in all civilized countries, first in industry and afterwards in agriculture too, and as a result of which only two classes remain involved in production: the capitalists, who own means of production, raw materials and provisions, and the workers, who own neither means of production, nor raw materials nor provisions, but first have to buy their provisions from the capitalists with their labour. The modern proletarian, then, is only directly faced with *one* hostile and exploiting social class: the capitalist class, the bourgeoisie. In countries where this industrial revolution has been completely carried out, such as in England, *all* workers are faced only with capitalists, because on the land, too, the large tenant farmer is nothing but a capitalist; the aristocrat, who only consumes the ground rent from his properties, has absolutely no point of social contact with the worker.

It is a different matter in countries like Germany where the industrial revolution is still taking place. Here many elements have been left over from earlier feudal and post-feudal conditions, which, so to speak, cloud the social medium and rob the social situation of that simple, clear and classical character which typifies England's present stage of development. We find in Germany, in an atmosphere growing daily more modern and amidst highly modern capitalists and workers, the most amazing antediluvian fossils still alive and roaming society: feudal lords, patrimonial courts of justice, country squires, flogging, aristocratic government officials, district magistrates, jurisdictional disputes, executive power to issue punishment, and so on. We find that in the struggle for political power all these living fossils band together against the bourgeoisie; the latter, which, as a result of its property, is the most powerful class in the new epoch, demands, in the name of the new epoch, that they hand over political power.

Apart from the bourgeoisie and the proletariat modern large-scale industry produces a kind of intermediate class between the two others: the petty bourgeoisie. This class consists partly of the remnants of the earlier semi-medieval citizenry (*Pfahlbürgertum*), and partly of workers who to a certain extent have come up in the world. Its role is less in production than in the distribution of goods; its main line of business is the retail trade. While the old citizenry was the most stable social class, the modern petty bourgeoisie is the most unstable; among this class bankruptcy has become an institution. With its small capital it shares in the life of the bourgeoisie; with the insecurity of its existence it shares that of the proletariat. Its political position is as contradictory as its social existence; in general, however, its most adequate political expression is the demand for 'pure democracy'. Its political mission is to spur the bourgeoisie on in its struggle against the remnants of the old society and, in particular, against its own weaknesses and cowardice, as well as to help win those liberties – freedom of the press, association and assembly, universal suffrage, local self-government – without which, despite their bourgeois character, a timid bourgeoisie can probably manage, but without which the workers can never achieve emancipation.

At some time or another during the course of the struggle between the remnants of the old, antediluvian society and the bourgeoisie there always comes a point at which both combatants turn to the proletariat and seek its support. This moment usually coincides with the first stirrings of the working class itself. The feudal and bureaucratic representatives of the doomed society call upon the workers to join with them in attacking the capitalist parasites, the only enemies of the worker; the bourgeoisie points out to the workers that, both together, they represent the new social epoch and that therefore they at least share the same interests in their opposition to the *old* moribund form of society. At this point the working class gradually becomes conscious of the fact that it is a class in its own right, with its own interests and its own independent future. Hence the question arises which has been asked successively in England, France and Germany: what should be the attitude of the workers' party towards the combatants?

This will depend, above all, upon the particular aims which the workers' party, i.e. that section of the working class which has become conscious of the common class interest, strives for in the interest of its class.

As far as is known,[15] the most advanced workers in Germany demand the emancipation of the workers from the capitalists by the transfer of state capital to workers' associations, so that production can be carried on, without capitalists, on common account; and as a means of achieving this aim they seek to conquer political power by way of universal and direct suffrage.

This much is now clear: neither the feudal–bureaucratic party, generally simply referred to as the '*reaction*', nor the liberal–radical bourgeois party will be inclined to concede these demands voluntarily. But the proletariat will become a political force the moment an autonomous workers' party is formed and becomes a power to be reckoned with. The two hostile parties are aware of this and at the right moment, therefore, they will be disposed to make apparent or actual concessions to the workers. From which side can the workers exact the greatest concessions?

The existence of both bourgeoisie and proletariat is already a thorn in the flesh of the reactionary party. Its power depends on its ability to stop, or at least slow down modern social development. Otherwise all the property-owning classes will gradually become capitalists and all the oppressed classes proletarians and thus the reactionary party will disappear automatically. If it is consistent, the party of reaction certainly wants to do away with the proletariat, however not by moving forward to workers' associations but by transforming the modern proletariat back into journeymen and by reducing them partially or completely to the status of peasant bondsmen. Would such a transformation be in the interests of our proletarians? Do they wish themselves back under the patriarchal discipline of the guild master and the 'noble lord', even if such a thing were possible? Definitely not! It is precisely the release of the working class from the whole false system of property and all illusory privileges of earlier times, and the development of the naked conflict between capital and labour, which have made possible the existence of a single huge working class with common interests, the existence of a workers' movement and a workers' party. Such a reversal of history is, moreover, simply impossible. The steam engines, the mechanical spinning frames and weaving looms, the steam ploughs and threshing machines, the railways, the electric telegraph and the steam

15. This circumlocution follows Marx's advice to Engels in a letter of 11 February 1865 (*MECW* 42, p. 86–8), and was designed to avoid committing Engels to accepting the Lassallean demands.

presses of the present day totally exclude the possibility of such an absurd retrogression; indeed these developments are gradually but implacably destroying all residues left over from a feudal, guild-ridden society; they are dissolving all the petty social conflicts handed down from an earlier age into the one historic antagonism between capital and labour.

The bourgeoisie, on the other hand, has no historical function in modern society other than to increase on all fronts the gigantic forces of production and means of transport mentioned above and to put them to their fullest possible use; to lay its hands too – by way of its credit associations – on the means of production passed on from earlier times, in particular, on landed property; to introduce modern means of production into all branches of industry; to destroy all remnants of feudal production and feudal society and hence to reduce the whole of society to the simple opposition between a class of capitalists and a class of propertyless workers. This simplification of class antagonisms is accompanied to the same degree by a growth in the strength of the bourgeoisie, but to an even greater degree by the growth in the strength, class consciousness and potential for victory of the working class. Only as a result of this increase in the strength of the bourgeoisie will the proletariat gradually succeed in becoming the majority, the overwhelming majority in the state. This is already the case in England, but by no means so in Germany where, on the land, peasants of all kinds, and, in the towns, small craftsmen and shopkeepers etc. exist side by side with the proletariat.

Thus every victory gained by the forces of reaction obstructs social development and inevitably delays the day on which the workers will win the struggle. Every victory gained by the bourgeoisie over the reaction, however, is in one respect also a victory for the workers; it contributes to the final overthrow of capitalist rule and brings nearer the day when the workers will defeat the bourgeoisie.

Let us compare the present position of the German workers' party with that of 1848. There are still plenty of veterans in Germany who worked for the foundation of an embryonic German workers' party before 1848 and who helped to extend it after the revolution as long as conditions allowed. You all know what an effort it cost, even in those turbulent days, to create a workers' movement, to keep it going and to free it from reactionary guild elements, and how the whole movement became dormant again after a few years. If a workers' movement has now come into being, as it were, of its own accord, what is the reason for this? The reason is that since 1848 large-scale bourgeois industry in Germany has made tremendous progress, that it has destroyed a mass of small craftsmen and other people located between the worker and the capitalist, and that it has driven a mass of workers into direct opposition to the capitalist; in short, it has created a significant proletariat where no proletariat, or only one of limited size, existed. As a result of this industrial development a workers' party and a workers' movement has become a necessity.

This is not to say that there may not be moments when the forces of reaction find it advisable to make concessions to the workers. These concessions, however, are always of a specific kind. They are never political concessions. The forces of feudal–bureaucratic reaction will neither extend the suffrage nor tolerate the freedom of the press, association and assembly, nor will they curb the power of the bureaucracy. The concessions which they make are always directed against the bourgeoisie, but under no circumstances in such a way that they increase the political power of the workers. Thus, for instance, in England, the Ten Hours Act was passed for the factory workers against the will of the manufacturers.[16] The workers, therefore, could demand and possibly obtain from the Prussian government the strict observance of the regulations covering working hours in the factories – which, at present, only exist on paper – together with the right for workers to form combinations, etc. But in the event of the forces of reaction granting these concessions, their acceptance must not lead to any reciprocal concessions on the part of the workers. This must be made clear, and rightly so, for by making life uncomfortable for the bourgeoisie the party of reaction will have achieved its aim. The workers are not obliged to thank them, as indeed they never do.

There is another sort of reaction, which has met with great success in recent times and which has become very fashionable among certain people: the brand of reaction known as Bonapartism. Bonapartism is the necessary form of government in a country where the working class – highly developed in the towns but outnumbered by the small peasants on the land – has been defeated in a great revolutionary struggle by the capitalist class,

16. See Engels's article 'The Ten Hours Bill', *MECW* 10, pp. 288–301.

the petty bourgeoisie and the army. When the Parisian workers were defeated in the tremendous struggle of June 1848 the bourgeoisie, too, completely exhausted itself in achieving its victory. It was aware that it could not survive a second such victory. It ruled only in name; it was too weak to rule in reality. Leadership was assumed by the army, the actual victor in the struggle; it was supported by the class from which it chiefly recruited its strength, the small farmers, who wanted peace and protection from the town rowdies. It goes without saying that the form which this rule took was military despotism; its natural head was the ancestral heir of military despotism, Louis Bonaparte.

The characteristic role of Bonapartism *vis-à-vis* workers and capitalists is to prevent these two classes from engaging in open struggle. It protects the bourgeoisie from violent attack by the workers while encouraging minor skirmishes of a peaceful nature between them, and it robs both of all trace of political power. It does not tolerate free association, free assembly or a free press; it allows universal suffrage, but under such bureaucratic pressures that it is almost impossible to vote for an opposition candidate; it rules by means of a police system which is hitherto unprecedented even in police-ridden France. Moreover, a part of the bourgeoisie and a part of the workers are nothing short of *bought*; the former by colossal credit frauds, in which the money of small capitalists is lured into the pockets of large capitalists; the latter by colossal public works which lead to the creation of an artificial, Imperialist[17] proletariat, which is dependent upon the state and which exists side by side with the natural, independent proletariat in the large towns. Lastly, national pride is flattered by apparently heroic wars, which however are always sanctioned by higher European authority; they are waged against the general scapegoat of the day and only under conditions which guarantee victory from the outset.

The only advantage of such a government for the workers and the bourgeoisie is that they can rest from the struggle and that industry can develop vigorously under favourable conditions. The result is that the elements of a new and more violent struggle are now accumulating, a struggle which will break out as soon as there is no further need for this period of recovery. It would be the very height of folly to expect any more for the workers from

17. See p. 718, n. 62.

a government which exists merely to hold in check their struggle against the bourgeoisie.

Let us return now to the particular case which we are examining. What do the reactionary forces in Prussia have to offer the workers' party?

Can the reaction offer the working class a real share in political power? Not the slightest! Firstly, neither in the recent history of England nor France has a reactionary government ever done such a thing. Secondly, in the present struggle in Prussia the problem is precisely whether the government should concentrate all real power in its own hands or whether it should share it with parliament. One thing is certain: the government will never summon up all its strength and seize power from the bourgeoisie merely to hand over this power to the proletariat!

The feudal aristocracy and the bureaucracy can keep their real power in Prussia even without parliamentary representation. Their traditional position at court, in the army and in the civil service guarantees it to them. Indeed they would not wish for any particular form of representation because the Peers' and Civil Servants' Chambers such as Manteuffel had are absolutely impossible in Prussia in the long run. Thus, they want to be rid of the whole representative system.

On the other hand, both the bourgeoisie and the workers can only function as a really organized political force through parliamentary representation; and this parliamentary representation is only of value if they can have their say and make decisions, in other words, if they can 'keep the purse strings tight'. But this is precisely what Bismarck wants to prevent, as he himself admits. The question must arise whether it lies in the workers' interests for this parliament to be robbed of all political power, this parliament which they themselves hope to enter by gaining universal and direct suffrage and in which they hope to form a majority one day. Is it in their interests to set all the machinery of agitation in motion in order to elect their representatives to an assembly which, in the final analysis, has no say in matters anyway? Hardly.

But what if the government upset the existing electoral law and imposed by *octroi*[18] a system based on universal and direct suffrage? Yes, *if*! If the government played such a Bonapartist

18. A French term, denoting an act performed by the monarch out of the plenitude of his own power, and therefore reversible at will.

trick and the workers fell for it, they would acknowledge from the very outset the government's right to repeal universal and direct suffrage by a new *octroi* as soon as it suited its purpose. What would the fullest universal and direct suffrage be worth then?

If the government imposed a system based on universal and direct suffrage it would, from the very outset, so hedge it with clauses and provisos that it would no longer be universal and direct suffrage.

And even with regard to universal and direct suffrage, one need only go to France to be convinced of the harmless elections it is possible to hold on this basis in a country with a large and stupid rural population, a well organized bureaucracy and a tightly controlled press, in a country where there are absolutely no political meetings and where associations are satisfactorily suppressed by the police. How many workers' representatives have been elected into the French parliament despite the existence of universal and direct suffrage? And yet compared with Germany the French proletariat is a much more concentrated class and has a longer experience of struggle and organization.

This brings us to another point. In Germany the rural population is twice as large as the urban; that is, two thirds of the people live from farming and one third from industry. And as the large estate is the rule in Germany and the smallholding peasant the exception, this means, in other words, that a third of the workers are controlled by the capitalists, while two thirds are *controlled by the feudal lords*. Let those who continuously attack the capitalists but utter not the least angry word against feudalism take this to heart. The feudalists exploit twice as many workers in Germany as does the bourgeoisie; they are no less the direct enemy of the workers than are the capitalists. But that is by no means the whole story. Patriarchal rule on the old feudal estates has made the landless day-labourer hereditarily dependent upon his 'noble lord', and this makes it exceedingly difficult for the agricultural proletarian to join the movement of the urban workers. The priests, the systematic stupefaction of the countryside, bad schooling and isolation from the outside world do the rest. The agricultural proletariat is that section of the working class which is the last to become aware of its interests and social position and has the most difficulty in understanding them. In other words, it is that section of the working class which remains longest the unconscious tool of an exploiting and privileged class.

And which class is this? In Germany, not the bourgeoisie but the *feudal aristocracy*. Even in France, where, of course, almost only free peasant proprietors exist on the land, and where the feudal aristocracy has long since been robbed of all political power, universal suffrage has not brought the workers into parliament, but has almost totally excluded them. What would be the result of universal suffrage in Germany, where the feudal aristocracy still has real social and political power and where there are two landless agricultural labourers for every one industrial worker? The struggle against feudal and bureaucratic reaction – the two are inseparable in Germany – is synonymous with the struggle for the mental and political emancipation of the rural proletariat. For as long as the rural proletariat is not carried along in the movement, the urban proletariat in Germany will not achieve anything; universal and direct suffrage will not be a weapon for the proletariat but a *trap*.

Perhaps this very candid but necessary explanation will encourage the feudalists to support universal and direct suffrage. So much the better.

Or is the government only curtailing the bourgeois opposition press, its freedom of association and assembly (as though there were much left to curtail) in order to make the workers a gift of these basic rights? Indeed, is the workers' movement not being allowed to develop peacefully and without hindrance?

But there's the rub! The government *knows* and the bourgeoisie knows too that at the present the whole German workers' movement is only *tolerated* and will only survive as long as the government *wishes*. The government will tolerate the movement as long as its existence suits it, as long as it is in its interests for the bourgeois opposition to be confronted by new and independent opponents. As soon as the workers develop through this movement into an independent power, as soon as this movement poses a danger for the government, the matter will come to an end immediately. The way in which the government put an end to the agitation of the Progressives in the press, to their associations and meetings, may serve as a warning to the workers. The same laws, decrees and measures which were applied there can be used at any time against the workers to deal a death-blow to their agitation; this will happen as soon as this agitation becomes dangerous. It is crucially important for the workers to be clear on this point and not to become victims of the same illusions as the bourgeoisie in the New Era, who were likewise merely *tolerated* although they thought themselves in complete control of the situation. And anyone who imagines that the present government will lift the present restrictions on the freedom of the press, association and assembly, places himself outside the arena of rational discussion. But without the freedom of the press, and the freedom of association and assembly, no workers' movement is possible.

The present Prussian government is not so stupid as to cut its own throat. Should it happen that the forces of reaction toss a few sham political concessions to the German proletariat as a bait – then, it is to be hoped, the German proletariat will answer with the proud words of the old *Hildebrandslied*:[19]

> *Mit gêrû scal man geba infâhân, ort widar orte.*
> Gifts shall be accepted with the spear, point against point.

As for the *social* concessions which the reaction might make to the workers – shorter working hours in the factories, a better implementation of the factory laws, the right to form combinations, etc. – the experience of all countries shows that the reactionaries introduce such legislative proposals without the workers having to offer the least in return. The reactionaries need the workers but the workers do not need them. Thus, as long as the workers insist on these points in their own agitation they can count on the moment coming when reactionary elements will present these same demands merely in order to annoy the bourgeoisie; and as a result the workers will achieve a victory over the bourgeoisie without owing the reactionaries any thanks.

But if the workers' party has nothing to expect from the reactionaries except minor concessions, which they would gain anyway, without having to go begging – what can it expect, then, from the bourgeois opposition?

We have seen that both the bourgeoisie and the proletariat are children of a new epoch; that in their social activity both aim at clearing away the outmoded trappings which have survived from an earlier age. They have, it is true, a very serious struggle to settle between themselves, but this struggle can only be fought out when they are left to face each other alone. Only by throwing the old lumber overboard will they be able to 'clear the decks for battle'. But this time the battle will not be conducted between

19. An eighth-century Old High German heroic saga.

two ships but on board one and the same ship – between officers and crew.

The bourgeoisie cannot gain political supremacy and express this in the form of a constitution and laws without, at the same time, arming the proletariat. On its banner it must inscribe human rights in place of the old system of social position based on birth, freedom to pursue trades and commerce in place of the guild system, freedom and self-government in place of bureaucratic authoritarianism. Therefore, for consistency's sake, it must demand universal and direct suffrage, freedom of the press, association and assembly, and the repeal of all emergency laws directed against particular social classes. But this is all that the proletariat need demand from the bourgeoisie. It can not expect the bourgeoisie to stop being the bourgeoisie, but it can demand that it apply its own principles consistently. The result will be that the proletariat will lay its hands on all the weapons which it needs for its final victory. With the help of the freedom of the press and the right of association and assembly it will win universal suffrage, and by way of universal and direct suffrage, together with the means of agitation mentioned above, it will achieve everything else.

It is in the interests of the workers, therefore, to support the bourgeoisie in its struggle against all reactionary elements, *on condition that it remain true to itself*. Every victory gained by the bourgeoisie over the forces of reaction will ultimately benefit the working class. The instinct of the German workers has been correct. In all the German states they have quite rightly voted for the most radical candidates who have had a prospect of winning.

But what if the bourgeoisie is untrue to itself and betrays its own class interests and the principles arising from these interests?

Then there are two courses of action left to the workers!

On the one hand the workers can push the bourgeoisie against its will and force it, as far as possible, to extend the suffrage, to fight for a free press, free association and assembly so as to create a space in which the proletariat can freely move and organize itself. The English workers have been doing this since the Reform Bill of 1832, as have the French workers since the July revolution of 1830; they have furthered their own development and organization by using and acting within this movement, whose most immediate aims were of a purely bourgeois character, rather than by any other means. This will always happen, because the bourgeoisie, with its lack of political courage, is in all countries untrue to itself at some time or another.

Alternatively the workers can withdraw completely from the bourgeois movement and leave the bourgeoisie to its fate. This is what happened in England, France and Germany after the failure of the European workers' movement of 1840 to 1850. This course of action is only possible following violent and temporarily fruitless efforts, after which the class needs peace and quiet. As long as the working class is in a healthy condition such a situation is impossible; it would amount to a complete political abdication, and in the long run a naturally courageous class, a class which has nothing to lose and everything to gain, is incapable of this.

Even at the worst, if the bourgeoisie creeps under the skirts of the reactionary party for fear of the workers, appealing to the enemy for protection, even then the workers' party will have no choice but to continue the agitation, betrayed by the bourgeoisie, for bourgeois freedom – freedom of the press, association and assembly – despite the bourgeoisie. Without these freedoms the workers' party cannot move freely; in this struggle it is fighting for its own vital element, for the air it needs to breathe.

It goes without saying that in all these situations the workers' party will not merely act as the tail of the bourgeoisie, but as a completely separate and independent party. At every opportunity it will remind the bourgeoisie that the class interests of the workers are directly opposed to those of the capitalists and that the workers are conscious of this fact. It will retain and develop its own organization quite separately from the party organization of the bourgeoisie, and will only treat with the latter as one force with another. In this way it will assure itself of a position which commands respect and it will educate the individual workers as to their class interests. With the outbreak of the next revolutionary storm – and these storms now recur as regularly as commercial crises and equinoctial gales – it will be ready for action.

The policy of the workers' party in the Prussian constitutional conflict follows automatically from what has been said:

The workers' party must above all remain organized, as far as present circumstances allow.

It must press the Progressive party to campaign for *real* progress, as far as that is possible; force it to radicalize its own programme and to stick to it; pitilessly chastise and ridicule all inconsistencies and weaknesses.

The workers' party should allow the actual military question to take its own course, remembering that one day it will conduct its own *German* 'military reorganization'.

But the hypocritical temptations of the forces of reaction must be answered thus:

> Gifts shall be accepted with the spear, point against point.

MARX TO SCHWEITZER[20]

London, 13 February 1865

... As our statement is partly out of date following what M. Hess has written in no. 21 (received today), we shall leave the matter at that.[21] However, our statement contained another point: praise for the anti-Bonapartist stand of the Paris proletariat and a call to the German workers to follow this example. This was more important for us than the attack on Hess. However, we shall elsewhere elaborate in detail our views on the relation of the workers to the Prussian government.[22]

In your letter of 4 February you say that I myself warned Liebknecht against kicking over the traces so as not to be hounded by the authorities. Quite right. But at the same time I wrote that it is possible to say *anything* if one finds the right form.[23] Even a form of anti-government polemic which is possible by Berlin standards is certainly quite a different matter from a flirtation

20. The letter actually sent to Johann von Schweitzer in Berlin has not survived, and the text published here is an excerpt of Marx's draft, as quoted by him in a letter to Engels of 18 February 1865.

21. This refers to Marx and Engels's 'Statement to the Editorial Board of *Social-Demokrat*' of 6 February 1865 (*MECW* 20, p. 36), complaining at the insinuations of Moses Hess, the Paris correspondent of the paper, that the French members of the General Council, and the International's members in Paris, contained Bonapartist agents.

22. Engels had just finished writing 'The Prussian Military Question', which was published a few weeks later.

23. During Marx and Engels's short-lived collaboration with the Lassallean *Social-Demokrat*, Wilhelm Liebknecht served as the paper's acting editor. As the *Social-Demokrat* was produced in Berlin, and Liebknecht was not a Prussian citizen, he faced the constant threat of deportation, and he was in fact banned from Berlin shortly after this time. Marx refers here to his letter to Liebknecht of 2 February 1865 (see *MECW* 42, p. 75), which seems not to have survived.

with the government, let alone an apparent compromise. I wrote to you myself that the *Social-Demokrat* must avoid creating such appearances.[24]

I see from your paper that the government is equivocating and procrastinating on the matter of the abolition of the combination laws. On the other hand a *Times* report indicates that government plans holding out the prospect of state patronage for cooperatives have been abandoned.[25] I would be not in the least surprised if *The Times* had reported correctly for once!

Combinations, together with trade unions, which develop out of these, are not only of the greatest importance for the working class as a means of organization in its struggle against the bourgeoisie, although this importance is demonstrated, among other things, by the fact that even the workers of the United States cannot do without them, despite the franchise and the republic. In Prussia and in Germany in general the right of combination is also a means of breaking the rule of the police and bureaucracy, and of smashing the *'Gesindeordnung'*[26] and the rule of the aristocracy on the land; in short, it is a measure which will release the 'subjects' from state tutelage. It is something which the Progressive party or any bourgeois opposition party in Prussia, unless it is mad, would be a hundred times more likely to allow than the Prussian government, let alone a government led by Bismarck! On the other hand, support from the Royal Prussian Government for the cooperatives – and anyone who knows the situation in Prussia knows in advance the dwarf-like proportions of these cooperatives – is worthless as an economic measure and serves, furthermore, to extend the system of state tutelage, to bribe a section of the working class and to emasculate the movement. In the same way that the bourgeois party in Prussia made a singular fool of itself and brought about its present predicament by believing that with the advent of the 'New Era', government power had fallen into their hands by the grace of the prince regent, the workers' party will make an even greater fool of itself if it imagines that the Bismarck era or any other era will cause golden apples to drop into its mouth by the

24. Here again Marx refers to a letter that has not survived.

25. Marx refers to a speech by Count Itzenplitz, the Prussian Minister of Commerce, of 11 February, reported in *The Times* on the 13th.

26. The Prussian feudal code which gave the aristocracy almost absolute power over farm servants (*Gesinde*) on their estates.

grace of the king. There is not the least doubt that disappointment will follow Lassalle's wretched illusions of a socialist intervention by a Prussian government. The logic of things will tell. But the *honour* of the workers' party demands the rejection of such illusions even before they are burst by experience and their emptiness proved. The working class is revolutionary or it is nothing . . .

MARX TO KUGELMANN[27]

London, 23 February 1865
1, Modena Villas, Maitland Park,
Haverstock Hill

Dear Kugelmann,

I received your very interesting letter yesterday and I shall now reply to the individual points you make.

First of all I shall briefly describe my attitude to Lassalle. During his agitation our relations were suspended, 1) because of his self-opinionated bragging, compounded with the most shameless plagiarism from my writings etc.; 2) because I *condemned* his *political* tactics; 3) because I had explained and 'proved' to him here in London even *before* he began his agitation that to hope for *socialist* measures from a 'Prussian *state*' was nonsense. In his letters to me (1848–63), as in our personal meetings, he had always declared himself a supporter of the party which I represent.[28] As soon as he had become convinced in London (at the end of 1862) that he could not play his games *with* me, he decided to set himself up as the 'workers' dictator' *against* me and the old party. In spite of everything I recognized his merit as an agitator, although towards the end of his short career I found that even his agitation appeared in an increasingly ambiguous light. His sudden death, old friendship, grief-stricken letters from Countess Hatzfeld,[29]

27. Ludwig Kugelmann, a doctor in Hanover, was a personal friend of Marx and a regular correspondent.
28. After the dissolution of the Communist League in 1852, Marx and Engels belonged to no formal political organization. They nevertheless considered themselves the true representatives of the workers' party. 'Party' (*Partei*) was a rather loose word in mid-nineteenth-century usage, both German and English.
29. Sophie, Countess Hatzfeld, was Lassalle's lover and disciple, and led an ultra-sectarian splinter group from the Lassallean party from 1867 to 1869.

indignation at the *craven impudence* shown by the bourgeois press towards one whom they had feared so greatly during his lifetime – all this induced me to publish a short statement attacking the wretched Blind, which, however, did not deal with the *content* of Lassalle's activities. (Hatzfeld sent the statement to the *Nordstern*.)[30] For the same reasons and in the hope of being able to remove elements which seem dangerous to me, Engels and I promised to contribute to the *Social-Demokrat* (they have published a translation of the 'Address'[31] and at their request I wrote an article on Proudhon when he died[32]) and after Schweitzer had sent us a *satisfactory editorial programme* we gave permission for our names to be made known as contributors. The fact that W. Liebknecht was an unofficial member of the editorial board served as a further guarantee for us. However, it soon became clear – the evidence came into our possession – that Lassalle had in fact *betrayed* the party. He had entered into a formal contract with Bismarck (naturally *without the least* guarantee in *his* hand). At the end of September 1864 he was to go to Hamburg, where (together with the crazy Schramm[33] and the Prussian police spy Marr[34]) he was to *'force'* Bismarck to annex Schleswig-Holstein; that is, he was to proclaim its annexation in the name of the 'workers', etc. In return Bismarck promised universal suffrage and a bit of socialist charlatanry. It is a pity that Lassalle was not able to play this farce through to the end! It would have condemned him and made him look ridiculous! It would have put a stop to all attempts of that sort once and for all!

Lassalle went astray because he was a *'Realpolitiker'* of the Miquel[35] type, but on a larger scale and with grander aims! (By the bye, I had long since sufficiently made up my mind about Miquel to be able to explain his actions by the fact that the

30. Karl Blind was a German democratic refugee in London, who attacked Las-sal-le after his death in a purely personalistic way. The *Nordstern* was a Lassallean paper published in Hamburg.

31. I.e. the Inaugural Address of the International.

32. *MECW* 20, pp. 26–33.

33. Rudolph Schramm, a democratic refugee in London after the 1848 revolution, returned to Germany after the 1861 amnesty and became a supporter of Bismarck.

34. Wilhelm Marr was a journalist from Hamburg and a supporter of the 'Young Germany' movement in the 1840s.

35. Johannes Miquel was a former member of the Communist League who went over to the bourgeoisie in the 1850s, became a banker and eventually German Minister of Finance.

National Association[36] provided a splendid opportunity for a petty lawyer from Hanover to gain an audience in Germany beyond his own four walls and to bring the enhanced authority of a *Realpolitiker* to bear back home in Hanover – playing the role of a 'Hanoverian' Mirabeau under *'Prussian'* protection.) Miquel and his present friends seized the opportunity presented by the 'New Era' inaugurated by the Prussian prince regent and together with the members of the National Association they attached themselves to 'Prussian leadership', cultivating their 'civic pride' under *Prussian protection*; in the same way Lassalle intended to play the Marquis Posa of the proletariat to the Philip II of the Uckermark,[37] with Bismarck acting as the pimp between him and the Prussian monarchy. Lassalle only imitated the gentlemen of the National Association. But while they invoked Prussian 'reaction' in the interests of the middle class, he shook hands with Bismarck in the interests of the proletariat. Those gentlemen were more justified than Lassalle, in so far as the bourgeois is accustomed to regard the interests lying immediately before his nose as 'reality' and as this class has in fact everywhere made compromises, even with feudalism, while the working class, in the very nature of things, must be honestly 'revolutionary'.

For the theatrically vain nature of a Lassalle (who, however, could not be bribed with such trifles as political office, a position as mayor, etc.) it was a very seductive thought: a direct act on behalf of the proletariat, carried out by Ferdinand Lassalle! In fact he was too ignorant of the actual economic conditions involved in such an act to be critically true to himself! On the other hand, as a result of the base *'practical politics'* which led the German bourgeoisie to tolerate the reaction of 1849–59 and to watch the stupefaction of the people, the German workers had become too *'dispirited'* not to hail such a quack saviour who promised to lead them to the promised land overnight!

Well, to pick up the thread broken above. Hardly had the *Social-Demokrat* been founded than it became evident that old

36. The National Association was formed by the pro-Prussian wing of the German liberal bourgeoisie in September 1859, to campaign for a 'little Germany' under Prussian hegemony.

37. A reference to Schiller's drama *Don Carlos*. The Philip II of the Uckermark was evidently William I of Prussia. The Uckermark was a quintessentially junker district in Brandenburg, the heartland of the Prussian monarchy.

Hatzfeld wanted to execute Lassalle's 'testament'.[38] She was in touch with Bismarck through Wagener (of the *Kreuz-Zeitung*).[39] She placed the General Association of German Workers, the *Social-Demokrat* etc. at his disposal. The annexation of Schleswig-Holstein was to be proclaimed in the *Social-Demokrat*, Bismarck was to be generally recognized as patron etc. The whole merry plan was *frustrated*, as we had Liebknecht in Berlin on the editorial board of the *Social-Demokrat*. Although Engels and I did not like the editorial policy of the paper, the lickspittle Lassalle cult, the occasional flirtation with Bismarck etc., it was naturally more important to remain identified with the paper in public in order to thwart the intrigues of old Hatzfeld and the total compromising of the workers' party. We therefore made *bonne mine à mauvais jeu*[40] although privately we were always writing to the *Social-Demokrat* that they should oppose Bismarck just as much as they opposed the Progressives. We even tolerated the intrigues conducted *against* the International Working Men's Association by that affected fop Bernhard Becker,[41] who takes quite seriously the importance conferred on him in Lassalle's testament.

Meanwhile, Herr Schweitzer's articles in the *Social-Demokrat* became more and more Bismarckian. I had written to him before saying that the Progressives could be *intimidated* on the 'combination question' but that *neither now nor at any time* would the '*Prussian government*' concede the complete abolition of the combination laws.[42] Such an abolition would lead to a breach in the bureaucratic apparatus, the release of the workers from state tutelage, the overthrow of the *Gesindeordnung*,[43] the abolition of the aristocracy's flogging of rural backsides etc.: it would be altogether incompatible with the *bureaucratic* Prussian state, and

38. Lassalle did leave a political testament, which among other things recommended the election of Bernhard Becker as president of the ADAV. But Marx seems to be referring here to Lassalle's 'testament' in the broader sense, i.e. his unfulfilled political aspirations.

39. Hermann Wagener was the founder and editor of the *Neue Preussische Zeitung*. See p. 814, n. 12.

40. The best of a bad job.

41. Bernhard Becker was elected president of the ADAV on Lassalle's testamentary recommendation, but was soon forced to resign on the grounds of incompetence. His place was taken in December 1864 by Johann von Schweitzer. In a letter to Schweitzer of 16 January 1865 Marx complained of an article by Becker attacking the International.

42. On 13 February 1865. See above, p. 831.

43. See p. 831, n. 26.

Bismarck would never allow it. I added that if the Chamber rejected the combination laws the government would take refuge in empty phrases (for example, to the effect that the social question demands 'more fundamental' measures etc.) in order to preserve them. All this indeed proved to be the case. And what did Herr von Schweitzer do? He wrote an article *in support of* Bismarck[44] and now saves up all his heroic courage for such *infiniments petits*[45] as Schulze, Faucher, etc.[46]

I believe Schweitzer, etc. to be *sincere*, but they are *'Realpolitiker'*. They want to accommodate themselves to the *existing* situation and not leave this privilege of *'Realpolitik'* to Herr Miquel and Co. alone. The latter seem to want to reserve for themselves the right of intermixture with the Prussian government. They know that the workers' newspapers and workers' movement only exist *par la grâce de la police*.[47] So they want to take circumstances as they are and not provoke the government etc., just like our *'republican' Realpolitiker* who are willing to settle for a Hohenzollern kaiser. But as I am not a *'Realpolitiker'* I have found it necessary, together with Engels, to announce my withdrawal from the *Social-Demokrat* in a public statement[48] (which you will probably soon see in one paper or another).

You will see, therefore, why I can do *nothing* in Prussia at this moment. The government has flatly rejected my renaturalization in Prussia.[49] I would only be allowed to conduct *agitation* there in a form amenable to Herr von Bismarck.

I prefer a hundred times over to agitate here through the International Association. The influence on the *English* proletariat is direct and of the greatest importance. We are creating a stir

44. The third part of Schweitzer's article 'The Bismarck Ministry' appeared in the *Social-Demokrat* on 17 February 1865. Here Schweitzer explicitly came out in support of Bismarck's policy of unifying Germany under Prussian hegemony by 'blood and iron'. This led to Liebknecht's immediate resignation from the editorship, and to Marx and Engels withdrawing their collaboration.

45. Infinitely small fry.

46. Julius Faucher, like Schulze-Delitzsch, was a leader of the Progressive party.

47. By the grace of the police.

48. *MECW* 20, p. 80.

49. After the amnesty granted by William I in January 1861, following his accession to the throne, Marx applied for renaturalization, but his request was refused (see *MECW* 19, p. 339ff).

here at the present moment on the general suffrage question,[50] which naturally has *quite another significance* in England than it has in Prussia.

On the whole the progress of this Association is *beyond all expectations* – here, in Paris, in Belgium, Switzerland and Italy. Only in Germany, of course, do Lassalle's successors oppose me, 1. because they have a stupid fear of losing their importance; 2. because they are aware of my avowed opposition to what the Germans call *Realpolitik*. (It is this sort of '*reality*' which places Germany so far behind all civilized countries.)

As anyone who pays a shilling for a card can become a member of the Association; as the French have chosen the form of individual membership (as have the Belgians) because the law forbids them to join us as an 'association'; as the situation in Germany is similar, I have decided to call upon my friends to form small societies, irrespective of the number of members in each place, in which every member buys an English card of membership. As the English society is *public* nothing stands in the way of this procedure in France. I would welcome it if you would also establish contact with London in this way in your immediate area.

Thank you for your prescription. Strangely enough, three days before it arrived the disgusting illness broke out again. So the prescription was very convenient.

In a few days I shall send you twenty-four more 'Addresses'. I have just been interrupted by a friend and as I would like to send off this letter I shall take up the other points in your letter next time.

Yours truly,

K.M.

MARX TO SCHWEITZER[51]

London, 13 October 1868

Dear Sir,

The fact that you have not received a reply to your letter of 15 September is due to a misunderstanding on my part. I understood from your letter that you intended to send me your 'drafts' to

50. The day that Marx wrote this letter the Reform League was founded in London, on the initiative of the International's General Council, to campaign for manhood suffrage.

51. The actual letter sent to Schweitzer has not survived, and the following text is Marx's original draft.

look at. I waited for them. Then came your Congress[52] and (being much overworked) I no longer regarded an answer as pressing. In my capacity as secretary of the International for Germany I had *repeatedly* urged the necessity for *peace* before your letter of 8 October arrived. I received the answer (together with quotations from the *Social-Demokrat*) that you yourself were provoking the *war*. I declared that my role must necessarily be limited to that of the umpire in the duel.

I think that I cannot better repay the great confidence in me which you have expressed in your letter than by informing you openly and unequivocally of my view of the situation. I do this in the confidence that your only concern, as mine, is the success of the movement.

I recognize without reservation the intelligence and energy of your activities in the workers' movement. I have disguised this view from none of my friends. Whenever I have to speak in public – in the General Council of the International Working Men's Association and the German Workers' Educational Association here – I have always treated you as a man of our party and have never uttered *the least word about points of disagreement*.

Nevertheless, such points of disagreement exist.

D'abord,[53] as far as the Lassallean Association is concerned, it was founded in a period of reaction. It is to Lassalle's eternal credit that he re-awakened the workers' movement in Germany after it had slumbered for fifteen years. But he committed great mistakes. He allowed himself to be governed too much by the immediate circumstances of the day. He transformed a minor starting-point – his opposition to a dwarf like Schulze-Delitzsch – into the central point of his agitation: state aid versus self-help. In doing so he only re-adopted the slogan which Buchez, the leader of Catholic socialism, had issued against the real workers' movement in France in 1843 and the following years. As he was much too intelligent to regard this slogan as anything but a transitory *pis aller*,[54] he could only justify it by its (supposed) immediate practicability. For this purpose he had to maintain that it could be brought about in the near future. Thus, *the* 'state'

52. This was the congress called by the ADAV to found a trade-union federation, and held at Hamburg in September 1868. Supporters of Liebknecht's Union of German Workers Societies were not allowed to take part. The 'drafts' referred to above are Schweitzer's draft rules for the trade-union federation – see below.

53. First of all.   54. Makeshift.

transformed itself into the Prussian state. As a result he was forced to make concessions to the Prussian monarchy, the forces of Prussian reaction (the feudal party) and even the clerical party. He combined the Chartist cry of universal suffrage with Buchez's state aid for workers' associations. He overlooked the fact that conditions in Germany and England are different. He overlooked what the *bas-empire*[55] had taught about universal suffrage. Furthermore, he gave his agitation from the very beginning the character of a religious sect, as does every man who claims to have in his pocket a panacea for the suffering masses. In fact, every sect is religious. Furthermore, precisely because he was a founder of a sect, he denied any natural connection with the earlier movement in Germany or abroad. He fell into the same error as Proudhon, of not seeking the real basis for his agitation in the actual elements of the class movement, but of trying to prescribe the course of the movement according to a certain doctrinaire recipe.

Most of what I am now saying after the event I already told Lassalle when he came to London in 1862 and invited me to place myself with him at the head of the new movement.

You yourself have had personal experience of the contradictions between a sectarian and a class movement. The sect seeks its *raison d'être* and point of honour not in what it has in common with the class movement but in the *particular shibboleth* which distinguishes it from the class movement. When, therefore, in Hamburg[56] you proposed the congress for the foundation of trade unions you were only able to defeat the sectarian opposition by threatening to resign from the office of president. You were furthermore forced to play a dual role, to declare that you were acting on the one hand as the head of the sect and on the other as the organ of the class movement.

The dissolution of the General Association of German Workers[57] gave you the opportunity to accomplish a great step forward and to declare, *s'il le fallait*,[58] that a new stage of development had

55. Marx's name for the French Second Empire; the original 'lower empire' was the Byzantine.

56. The Hamburg Congress of the ADAV was held in August 1868. Its resolutions marked a weakening of that organization's sectarianism, and a rapprochement with the International.

57. On 16 September 1868 the ADAV headquarters in Leipzig were closed by the Saxon police. Three weeks later, however, a new ADAV headquarters was opened in Berlin, with the implicit tolerance of the Prussian authorities.

58. If it was necessary.

been reached and that the sectarian movement was now ready to merge into the class movement and to completely abandon its separation. As far as its true aims were concerned, the sect, like all earlier working-class sects, would bring them as an enriching element into the general movement. Instead you have in fact demanded of the class movement that it subordinate itself to a particular sectarian movement. Those who are not your friends have concluded from this that you are trying under all circumstances to preserve your 'own workers' movement'.

As far as the Berlin Congress is concerned, there was first of all no urgency, as there has not yet been a vote on the combination law.[59] So you should have come to a mutual understanding with the leaders *outside* the Lassallean circle and drawn up the plan and convened the Congress together with them. Instead, you left them only the alternative of joining *you* openly or of *opposing* you. The Congress itself seemed only a repetition of the Hamburg Congress.

As for the draft of the rules, I regard it as fundamentally misguided and I think I have as much experience as any contemporary in the field of trade unions. Without going into details here I would only remark that the *centralist* organization, no matter how valuable it may be for secret societies and sectarian movements, contradicts the essence of trade unions. Even if it were possible – and I declare *toute bonnement*[60] that it it is not – it would not be necessary, least of all in Germany. There, where the worker is subject to bureaucratic discipline from his infancy and believes in officialdom and higher authority, it is above all a question of teaching him to *walk by himself*.

Your plan is impractical anyway. In the 'Association' you have three independent authorities of different origin: 1) The *Committee* elected by the *trades*; 2) the President (a completely superfluous figure in this context)[61] elected by *all members*; 3) the

59. The law granting the right to form trade unions and to strike was passed by the North German Reichstag on 29 May 1869.

60. Quite frankly.

61. In the rules of the International Working Men's Association a president also figures. But in reality he never had any function other than chairing the meeting of the General Council. At my suggestion the office, which I turned down in 1866, was abolished completely and replaced by a chairman, who is elected at each weekly meeting of the General Council. The *London Trades Council* likewise only has a chairman. The secretary is its only permanent official, because he performs a continuous function [Marx].

Congress elected by the *localities*. The result – conflicts everywhere. And is this supposed to promote 'rapid action'! Lassalle made a big blunder when he borrowed the *'président élu du suffrage universel'*[62] from the French Constitution of 1852. And now the same sort of thing in a trade-union movement! Such a movement is largely concerned with questions of money, and you will soon discover that in such a situation all dictatorship has to come to an end.

However, whatever the mistakes in the organization, they can perhaps be more or less removed if affairs are conducted rationally. I am ready, as secretary of the International,[63] to function as arbitrator between you and the Nuremberg majority,[64] which has joined the International directly – on a rational basis, needless to say. I have written the same thing to Leipzig. I recognize the difficulties of your position and do not forget that each of us is guided more by the requirements of the situation than by his own will.

I promise you under all circumstances the neutrality which I feel to be my duty. On the other hand I cannot promise that one day, as a *private writer* – as soon as I regard it as absolutely necessary in the interests of the workers' movement – I will not openly criticize the superstitious doctrines of Lassalle, as I have criticized those of Proudhon.

Assuring you of my best wishes,
Yours respectfully,
K.M.

62. President elected by universal suffrage.

63. I.e. as the General Council's corresponding secretary for Germany.

64. The Union of German Workers Societies' Nuremberg Congress was held in September 1868. The minority of liberal bourgeois representatives left the Union at this point, and a programme was adopted that brought the Union into line with the International. The headquarters of the Union was in Leipzig.

Letters on Ireland[1]

MARX TO ENGELS

London, 2 November 1867

Dear Fred,
... I used to regard Ireland's separation from England as impossible. I now think it inevitable, although *federation* may follow separation. The policy of the English is revealed in the *Agricultural Statistics*[2] for this year, published a few days ago. Also the form which eviction is taking. The Irish viceroy, Lord Abicorn[3] (the name is *something* like that) has 'cleared' his estate in the last few weeks by forcibly evicting thousands of people, among them well-to-do tenant farmers whose improvements and capital investments have in this way been confiscated! Foreign rule has not taken this direct form of expropriation of the natives in any other European country. The Russians confiscate merely for political reasons; in West Prussia the Prussians buy out the land.

MARX TO ENGELS

London, 30 November 1867

Dear Fred,
... If you have read the papers you will have seen that 1) the International Council sent the Memorial for the Fenians to

---

1. Marx's letters to Engels and other close friends, basically written in German, sometimes lapse into an idiosyncratic composite of German and English. The frequent English words and phrases in the original have not been marked. These letters are translated from the texts printed in *MEW* 31 & 32.
2. *Agricultural Statistics, Ireland*, Dublin, 1867.
3. The name was in fact James Hamilton, Duke of Abercorn.

Hardy,[4] 2) the debate on Fenianism (the Tuesday before last) was public and *The Times* reported it. Reporters from the Dublin *Irishman* and *Nation* were there too. I didn't arrive until very late (I have had fever for about two weeks and it only disappeared two days ago) and in fact didn't intend to speak, firstly because of my uncomfortable state of health and secondly because of the ugly situation. However, Weston,[5] the chairman, wanted to force me to speak, and so I moved the adjournment, as a result of which I was obliged to speak last Tuesday. In fact I did not have a speech prepared for Tuesday last, but only the points of a speech.[6] However, the Irish reporters did not come and we waited until nine o'clock although the public house only remained open until 10.30 p.m. At my suggestion Fox[7] (he had not put in an appearance for two weeks because of a quarrel in the Council and had furthermore submitted his resignation as a member of the Council, accompanied by crude attacks on Jung) had prepared a long speech. After the sitting opened I thus announced that because of the belated hour I would allow Fox to speak in my place. In fact – as a result of the execution which had taken place in Manchester in the meantime – our topic, 'Fenianism', had become charged with passion and heated feeling, which would have forced me (though not the abstract Fox) to deliver a thundering revolutionary tirade instead of the intended sober analysis of the situation and the movement. Thus, by staying away and causing the sitting to begin late, the Irish reporters did me a great service. I don't like being involved with people like Roberts, Stephens, etc.[8]

Fox's speech was good, firstly because it was given by *an Englishman*, secondly, in its treatment of the purely political and

4. This refers to the General Council's 'Memorial' (written by Marx) sent on 20 November 1867 to Gathorne-Hardy, the Home Secretary, petitioning for the commutation of the death sentences on the five Fenian prisoners condemned at Manchester for the murder of a policeman in the course of an attempt to rescue two Fenian leaders. In the event, Michael Larkin, William Allen and Michael O'Brien were executed on 23 November.

5. John Weston, an Owenist, was a founding member of the International and its General Council.

6. Marx's 'Notes for an undelivered speech on Ireland' are printed in *MECW* 21, pp. 189–93.

7. Peter Fox, a journalist and a follower of Comte, was active in the Reform League and a member of the General Council.

8. James Stephens, a Fenian leader, had in fact emigrated to the United States in 1866. William Roberts was a lawyer prominent in the Fenians' defence.

international aspects. But with these he only touched the surface. The resolution which he submitted was insipid and vacuous. I opposed it and had it referred back to the Standing Committee.[9]

What the English do not yet know is that since 1846 the economic content of English rule in Ireland, and therefore also its political aims, has entered a new phase, and it is for this very reason that Fenianism is characterized by a socialist tendency (in a negative sense: in being opposed to the appropriation of the soil and as a lower orders movement). What could be more ridiculous than to confuse the barbarities of Elizabeth or Cromwell, who wanted to supplant the Irish by English colonists (in the Roman sense), with the present system, which is trying to supplant the Irish with sheep, pigs and oxen! The system from 1801 to 1846[10] (evictions during the period were exceptional, occurring most often in Leinster, where the land is particularly suited to cattle-raising), with its rackrents and middlemen, collapsed in 1846. The repeal of the Corn Laws, partly the result of the Irish famine, at any rate accelerated by it, deprived Ireland of its *monopoly* on corn supplies to England during normal times. Wool and meat became the watchword: that is, the conversion of tillage into pasture. Hence, from then on, the systematic consolidation of farms. The Encumbered Estates Act,[11] which turned a mass of earlier, enriched middlemen into landlords, accelerated the process. Clearing of the Estate of Ireland is now the sole significance of English rule there. Of course, the *stupid* English government in London itself knows nothing of this immense change since 1846. But the Irish know. From *Meagher's Proclamation* (1848)[12] down to the *election address of Hennessy* (Tory and Urquhartite) (1866), the Irish have expressed their awareness of it in the clearest and most forcible manner.

9. For Fox's speech and resolution see *IWMA* II, p. 181. The Standing Committee was the executive committee of the General Council.

10. In 1782 the Dublin Parliament, which represented the Protestant land-owners and bourgeoisie, had achieved a measure of independence from English control, and went on to pass various protectionist measures. Following the United Irishmen's rebellion of 1798, the Act of Union, operative from 1 January 1801, abolished the Irish Parliament. From 1801 onwards there was free trade between England and Ireland.

11. This Act, passed in 1853, accelerated the consolidation of Irish agriculture into larger units by facilitating the forced sale of the land of indebted farmers.

12. Thomas Meagher, of the Young Ireland movement, called in 1848 for a national armed uprising.

The question now is what advice *we* should give the *English* workers? In my view they must make the *Repeal of the Union* (in short, the *arrangement of* 1783, but democratized and adapted to the times) an article of their *pronunziamento*. This is the only *legal* and hence the only possible form of Irish emancipation which can be included in the programme of an *English* party. Experience must show later whether a mere personal union between the two countries could continue. I am half inclined to believe this, if it happens in time.

What the Irish need are:

1.   Self-government and independence from England.
2.   Agrarian revolution. With the best will in the world the English cannot make this revolution for them, but they can give them the legal means of making it for themselves.
3.   *Protective tariffs against England.* Between 1783 and 1801 all branches of Irish industry prospered. With the overthrow of the protective tariffs which the Irish Parliament had established, the Union destroyed all industrial life in Ireland. The small linen industry is in no way a substitute. The Union of 1801 affected Irish industry in just the same way as the measures passed by the English Parliament under Anne and George II for the suppression of the Irish woollen industry, etc. Once the Irish got their independence, need would immediately force them to turn protectionist, just like Canada and Australia etc. Before I present my views in the General Council (next Tuesday, this time fortunately *without* the presence of reporters)[13] I should be glad if you would give me your opinion in a few lines.

Salut.
Regards,
K.M.

MARX TO KUGELMANN

London, 6 April 1868

Dear Kugelmann,

... The Irish question is the dominant issue here at present. Gladstone and Co. have, of course, exploited the problem only

---

13. In the event, Marx did not deliver his speech to the General Council as planned, but used his notes for a speech to the German Workers Educational Association on 16 December 1867 (*MECW* 21, pp. 194–206).

in order to have an electoral cry at the next elections, which will be based on household suffrage.[14] *For the moment* this turn of events is harmful for the workers' party, as the *intriguers* among the workers who want to get into the next Parliament, such as Odger, Potter, etc., now have a new *pretext* for joining the bourgeois Liberals.

However, this is only a punishment which England – and therefore the English working class as well – is suffering in payment for the great crime which it has committed against Ireland over many centuries. And in the long run the English working class will itself profit. For the English Established Church in Ireland – or what they used to call here the Irish Church – is the religious bulwark of English landlordism in Ireland and at the same time the outpost of the Established Church in England itself (I am speaking of the Established Church as a *landowner*). With its overthrow in Ireland the Established Church will collapse in England, and both will be followed by the collapse of landlordism, first in Ireland and then in England. But I have always been convinced from the very first that the social revolution can only *seriously* begin from the bottom up; that is, with landlordism.[15]

However, the whole business will have the very useful result that, once the Irish Church is dead, the Protestant Irish tenants in the province of Ulster will join forces with the Catholic tenants and their movement in the other three provinces of Ireland, whereas hitherto landlordism has been able to exploit this *religious* antagonism . . .

Regards,

K. MARX

14. Household suffrage was granted by the Second Reform Act of 1867. It still left all women and two thirds of all adult males unfranchised, and did not apply in Scotland or Ireland. Gladstone, who won the General Election of December 1868 as leader of the Liberal party, had compared the repressive regime in Ireland to that of William the Conqueror.

15. The German, '*von Grund aus*' (from the bottom up) and '*Grund-und-Boden-Eigentum*' (landlordism), contains a play on words based on the dual meaning of the word '*Grund*'.

MARX TO ENGELS

London, 18 November 1869

Dear Fred,

. . . Last Tuesday I opened the discussion about point no. 1, *the attitude of the British government to the Irish Amnesty question*.[16] Made a speech lasting about one and a quarter hours, much cheered, and then proposed the following resolution on point no. 1.

Resolved,

That in his reply to the Irish demands for the release of the imprisoned Irish patriots – a reply contained in his letter to Mr O'Shea etc. etc. – Mr Gladstone deliberately insults the Irish nation;

That he clogs political amnesty with conditions alike degrading to the victims of misgovernment and the people they belong to;

That having, in the teeth of his responsible position, publicly and enthusiastically cheered on the American slaveholders' rebellion,[17] he now steps in to preach to the Irish people the doctrine of passive obedience;

That his whole proceedings with reference to the Irish Amnesty question are the true and genuine offspring of that *'policy of conquest'*, by the fiery denunciation of which Mr Gladstone ousted his Tory rivals from office;

That the *General Council* of the *'International Working Men's Association'* express their admiration of the spirited, firm and high-souled manner in which the Irish people carry on their Amnesty movement;

That these resolutions be communicated to all branches of, and working men's bodies connected with the *International Working Men's Association* in Europe and America.

16. Marx is referring to the meeting of the General Council on 16 November; see *IWMA* III, pp. 178–94. The amnesty movement, to press the British government to release Fenian prisoners, saw a new upsurge of popular struggle in Ireland, and Marx, for reasons that he states in his letter to Kugelmann of 29 November (below, pp. 848–50), actively mobilized the General Council in support of the Irish amnesty. 'Point no. 2', which Marx had also proposed that the General Council should discuss, was 'the attitude of the English working class towards the Irish' (*IWMA* III, p. 177), but Marx refrained from introducing this question into the debate.

17. This refers to Gladstone's speech at Newcastle on 7 October 1862, in which he sent greetings to Jefferson Davis, the Confederate president.

Harris (an O'Brien man[18]) agreed to second. But the president (Lucraft) pointed to the clock (we can only stay until eleven o'clock); hence meeting adjourned until next Tuesday. However, Lucraft, Weston, Hales, etc.,[19] in fact the whole Council, provisionally declared their agreement in [an] informal way.

Another O'Brienite – Milner – declared the language of the resolution was too weak (i.e. not declamatory enough); furthermore, he demands that everything that I said by way of an explanation should be included in the resolution. (That's asking quite a lot!)

So, as the debate continues on Tuesday, now [is] the time for you to say or write to me what you perhaps want *changed* or *added* in the resolutions. If, for example, you want another clause added about the amnesties throughout Europe, e.g. Italy, formulate it straightaway as a resolution . . .

Regards,
K.M.

MARX TO KUGELMANN

London, 29 November 1869

Dear Kugelmann,

. . . You will probably have seen in the *Volksstaat* the resolutions which I proposed against Gladstone on the Irish Amnesty question.[20] I have now attacked Gladstone – and it caused quite a stir here – in just the same way I attacked Palmerston earlier.[21]

18. The O'Brienite organization to which George Harris and George Milner belonged was the National Reform League. A former Chartist, Bronterre O'Brien through his League kept up a semi-socialist propaganda centred on land reform throughout the barren years of the 1850s. The National Reform League affiliated to the International in 1867, and its members played an important role in founding the Land and Labour League (see p. 713, n. 47).

19. Benjamin Lucraft was a leader of the furniture-workers' union, and a founder member of the General Council. In June 1871 he resigned from the International following the publication of *The Civil War in France*. John Hales was a leader of the weavers' union, a member of the General Council and its secretary from 1871–2.

20. The *Volksstaat*, edited by Wilhelm Liebknecht, was the official paper of the SDAP (Eisenach party), founded in August 1869 (see pp. 707–8). The resolution against Gladstone is that reproduced by Marx in his letter to Engels of 18 November 1869 (above, p. 847).

21. Marx is referring to his articles on Palmerston published in the *People's Paper*, the *New York Daily Tribune* and as a pamphlet in 1853 (*MECW* 12, pp. 341–406).

The demagogic refugees here are very fond of assailing the continental despots from a safe distance. That sort of thing only attracts me if it is done *vultu instantis tyranni*.[22]

Nevertheless, both my activities on this Irish Amnesty question and my further suggestion in the General Council that we discuss the relation of the English working class to Ireland and pass resolutions on the problem have, of course, other aims beyond that of speaking out loudly and decisively on behalf of the oppressed Irish against their oppressors.

I have become more and more convinced – and it remains a matter of driving the point home to the English working class – that it can never do anything decisive here in England until it makes a decisive break with the ruling class in its policy on Ireland, until it not only makes common cause with the Irish but actually takes the initiative in dissolving the *Union* founded in 1801 and replacing it with a free federal relationship. And, indeed, this must be done not as a matter of sympathy with Ireland but as a demand based on the interests of the English proletariat. Otherwise the English people will be kept in tether by the ruling classes, because they will have to establish a common front with them against Ireland. Every one of its movements in England remains paralysed by the quarrel with the Irish, who form a very considerable section of the working class in England itself. The *first condition* for emancipation here – the overthrow of the English landed oligarchy – remains an impossibility, because its bastion here cannot be stormed as long as it holds its strongly entrenched outpost in Ireland. But once the Irish people takes matters into its own hands there, once it is made its own legislator and ruler, once it becomes autonomous, the overthrow of the landed aristocracy (for the most part *the same people* as the English landlords) will be infinitely easier than here, because in Ireland it is not only a simple economic question but at the same time a *national* question, because the landlords there are not, as in England, the traditional dignitaries and representatives of the nation but its mortally hated oppressors. And not only England's inner social development but also its foreign policy, particularly with regard to Russia and the United States, remain paralysed by its present relationship with Ireland.

But, as the English working class undeniably casts the decisive weight into the scales of social emancipation in general, the

22. To the tyrant's face.

important thing is to apply the lever here. In fact the English republic under Cromwell came to grief – in Ireland.[23] *Non bis in idem!*[24] The Irish have played a delightful trick on the English government by electing the 'convict felon' O'Donovan Rossa[25] to Parliament. The government papers are already threatening a renewed suspension of the Habeas Corpus Act and a renewed system of terror! The fact is that England has never ruled and *can* never rule Ireland any other way, as long as the present relationship lasts – than by the most atrocious reign of terror and the most damnable corruption . . .

Regards,

K. MARX

MARX TO ENGELS

London, 10 December 1869

Dear Fred,

. . . *Ad vocem: Irish question.* Although I had undertaken to open the debates, I didn't go to the Central Council last Tuesday. My 'family' didn't allow me to go in this *fog* and in my present state of health . . .

The way I shall present the matter next Tuesday[26] is this: I shall say that quite apart from all the 'international' and 'humane' phrases about justice-for-Ireland – which are taken for granted in the International Council – it is in *the direct and absolute interests of the English working class* to get rid of their present connection with Ireland. And this is my firm conviction, for reasons which, in part, I *cannot* tell the English workers themselves. I long believed it was possible to overthrow the Irish regime by way of

23. From 1649 to 1652 Cromwell was engaged in reconquering Ireland, the greater part of which had been liberated from English rule by the insurrection of October 1641. Cromwell expropriated Irish land and allotted it to officers and soldiers in his army, but the effect of this was to weaken the resistance to the restoration of the Stuart monarchy.

24. Let this not happen a second time.

25. Jeremiah O'Donovan Rossa was co-founder of the Fenian movement, and published the *Irish People* from 1863 to 1865. In 1865 he was condemned to life imprisonment, but amnestied in 1870.

26. In fact the General Council's discussion of the Irish question came to an end at this point. On 14 December the council did not discuss the Irish question, but postponed it until 4 January, and on that day Marx proposed the adjournment of the discussion (see *IWMA* III, p. 200).

English working-class ascendancy. This is the position I always represented in the *New York Tribune*.[27] A deeper study has now convinced me of the opposite. The English working class will never achieve anything before it has got rid of Ireland. The lever must be applied in Ireland. This is why the Irish question is so important for the social movement in general ...

Regards,
K. MÖHR[28]

MARX TO MEYER AND VOGT

London, 9 April 1870

Dear Meyer and dear Vogt,[29]

... Among what I have sent you you will also find some copies of the familiar resolutions passed by the General Council on 30 November on the *Irish Amnesty* question[30] which I drew up; also an Irish pamphlet on the treatment of the Fenian convicts.

I intended to introduce more resolutions on the necessary transformation of the present Union (which amounts to the enslavement of Ireland) in[to] a free and equal federation with Great Britain. The prosecution of this matter has been suspended for the time being, as far as public resolutions go, because of my enforced absence from the General Council. No other member of the Council knows enough about Irish affairs and possesses enough authority in the eyes of the *English* members of the General Council to be able to replace me in this matter.

Meanwhile time has not passed unused and I would ask you to pay particular attention to what follows.

After occupying myself with the Irish question for many years I have come to the conclusion that the decisive blow against the English ruling classes (and it will be decisive for the workers' movement all over the world) *cannot* be struck *in England*, but *only in Ireland*.

On 1 January 1870 the General Council issued a secret circular

27. See for example Marx's article of 1853 on 'Forced Emigration', *MECW* 11, pp. 528–34.

28. 'The Moor' was a nickname of Marx's.

29. Siegfried Meyer and August Vogt were German supporters of Marx who emigrated to the US in the late 1860s and were active in the International in New York.

30. The resolutions proposed by Marx on 16 November 1869 (above, p. 847).

which I had drawn up in French[31] – for a reaction in England only the French, not the German papers are important – on the relation of the Irish national struggle to the emancipation of the working class and hence on the attitude which the International Working Men's Association should adopt on the Irish question.

I shall give you only the main points here quite briefly. Ireland is the bulwark of the *English landed aristocracy*. The exploitation of this country is not only one of the main sources of their material wealth; it is their greatest *moral* strength. They represent in fact *England's dominion over Ireland*. Ireland is, therefore, the *grand moyen*[32] by which the English aristocracy maintains *its rule in England* itself.

On the other hand, if the English army and police withdrew tomorrow, you would have an agrarian revolution in Ireland immediately. But the overthrow of the English aristocracy in Ireland involves and would necessarily be followed by its overthrow in England. Thus one prerequisite for the proletarian revolution in England would be fulfilled. Quite apart from the more passionate and more revolutionary character of the Irish compared with the English, the destruction of the English landed aristocracy in Ireland is an infinitely easier operation than in England itself, because in Ireland the *land question* has up till now been the *exclusive form* which the social question has taken, because it is a question of existence, a *question of life and death* for the majority of the Irish people, because at the same time it is inseparable from the *national* question.

As far as the English *bourgeoisie* is concerned, it has *d'abord*[33] a common interest with the English aristocracy in transforming Ireland into mere pasture land, to supply the English market with meat and wool at the cheapest possible prices. It has the same interest in reducing the Irish population to such a small number, by eviction and forcible emigration, that *English capital* (invested in leasehold farmland) can operate in this country with 'security'. It has the same interest in clearing the estate of Ireland that it had in the clearing of the agricultural districts of England and Scotland. The £6,000–£10,000 absentee and other Irish revenues which at present flow annually to London must also be taken into account.

31. 'The General Council to the Federal Council of French Switzerland'; see above, pp. 801–2.

32. Great means.   33. First of all.

But the English bourgeoisie has other, much more important interests in the present structure of the Irish economy. As a result of the steadily increasing concentration of farms Ireland supplies the English labour market with its surplus [labour] and thus lowers the wages and the material and moral position of the English working class.

And most important of all! All English industrial and commercial centres now possess a working class *split* into two *hostile* camps: English proletarians and Irish proletarians. The ordinary English worker hates the Irish worker because he sees in him a competitor who lowers his standard of life. Compared with the Irish worker he feels himself a member of the *ruling nation* and for this very reason he makes himself into a tool of the aristocrats and capitalists *against Ireland* and thus strengthens their domination *over himself*. He cherishes religious, social and national prejudices against the Irish worker. His attitude is much the same as that of the 'poor whites' towards the 'niggers' in the former slave states of the American Union. The Irishman pays him back with interest in his own money. He sees in the English worker both the accomplice and the stupid tool of *English rule in Ireland*.

This antagonism is artificially sustained and intensified by the press, the pulpit, the comic papers, in short, by all the means at the disposal of the ruling classes. *This antagonism* is the *secret of the impotence of the English working class*, despite its organization. It is the secret which enables the capitalist class to maintain its power, as this class is perfectly aware.

The evil does not stop here. It continues on the other side of the ocean. The antagonism between the English and the Irish is the secret basis of the conflict between the United States and England. It makes any serious and honest cooperation between the working classes of the two countries impossible. It allows the governments of the two countries, whenever they think fit, to blunt the edge of the social conflict by their mutual bullying and in case of need by going to war with one another.

England, as the metropolis of capital, as the power which has up to now ruled the world market, is for the time being the most important country for the workers' revolution; moreover it is the *only* country where the material conditions for this revolution have developed to a certain degree of maturity. To accelerate the social revolution in England is therefore the most important object of the International Working Men's Association. The only means of accelerating it is to bring about the independence of Ireland. It is therefore the task of the 'International' to bring the conflict between England and Ireland into the foreground and everywhere to side openly with Ireland. It is the special task of the General Council in London to arouse the consciousness in the English working class that *for them* the *national emancipation of Ireland* is not a question of abstract justice or humanitarian sentiment but the first condition of their own social emancipation.

These are roughly the main points contained in the circular, which are thus also the *raison d'être* of the General Council's resolutions on the Irish Amnesty. Shortly afterwards I sent an anonymous, vehement article[34] about the English treatment of the Fenians etc., attacking Gladstone etc., to the *Internationale* (the organ of our Belgian Central Committee in Brussels). In the article I also accused the French republicans – (the *Marseillaise* had printed some nonsense on Ireland by the wretched Talandier)[35] – of being led by their national egoism to save all their *colères*[36] for the Empire.

The article had an effect. My daughter, Jenny, under the pseudonym J. Williams (she called herself Jenny Williams in a private letter to the editor), wrote a series of articles for the *Marseillaise* and published, among other things, the letter from O'Donovan Rossa. Hence immense noise. *As a result*, after many years of cynical refusal, *Gladstone* has been forced to agree to a *parliamentary inquiry* into the treatment of the Fenian prisoners. She is now regular correspondent on Irish affairs for the *Marseillaise*. (*This is, of course, a secret between us.*) The English government and press are furious that the Irish question is thus *ordre du jour*[37] and that these scoundrels are now being watched and exposed via Paris all over the Continent.

We have killed another bird with the same stone. We have forced the Irish leaders and press people in Dublin to make contact with us, which the *General Council* had failed to achieve hitherto.

You have great scope in America to work in the same way. *A*

34. 'The English Government and the Fenian Prisoners'; *MECW* 21, pp. 101–7.

35. Pierre Talandier was a former member of the General Council, later a Bakuninist. The *Marseillaise* was a left republican newspaper.

36. Anger.

37. On the agenda.

combination between the German and Irish workers (and, of course, also with those English and American workers who show an interest) is the most important task to embark on now, and it must be done in the name of the 'International'. The social significance of the Irish question must be made clear.

I shall soon send you a special letter on the situation among the English workers.

Salut et fraternité![38]

KARL MARX

38. Greetings and brotherhood.

The Franco-Prussian War

*To the Members of the International Working Men's Association
in Europe and the United States*

In the Inaugural Address of the International Working Men's
Association, of November 1864, we said: 'If the emancipation of
the working classes requires their fraternal concurrence, how are
they to fulfil that great mission with a foreign policy in pursuit of
criminal designs, playing upon national prejudices, and squandering in piratical wars the people's blood and treasure?' We defined
the foreign policy aimed at by the International in these words:
'Vindicate the simple laws of morals and justice, which ought to
govern the relations of private individuals, as the rules paramount
of the intercourse of nations.'[2]

No wonder that Louis Bonaparte, who usurped his power by
exploiting the war of classes in France, and perpetuated it by
periodical wars abroad, should from the first have treated the
International as a dangerous foe. On the eve of the plebiscite
he ordered a raid on the members of the administrative committees of the International Working Men's Association throughout
France, at Paris, Lyons, Rouen, Marseilles, Brest, etc., on the
pretext that the International was a secret society dabbling in a
complot for his assassination, a pretext soon after exposed in its

1. The Franco-Prussian war broke out on 19 July 1870. The same day, the
General Council commissioned Marx to draft this Address, which was adopted at
the following council meeting of 26 July. It was published in the *Pall Mall Gazette*
on 28 July 1870, and a few days later as a leaflet. It is reproduced here from the
pamphlet, *The General Council of the International Working Men's Association on
the War*, Truelove, September 1870.

2. See above, p. 765.

full absurdity by his own judges.[3] What was the real crime of the French branches of the International? They told the French people publicly and emphatically that voting the plebiscite was voting despotism at home and war abroad. It has been, in fact, their work that in all the great towns, in all the industrial centres of France, the working class rose like one man to reject the plebiscite. Unfortunately the balance was turned by the heavy ignorance of the rural districts. The stock exchanges, the cabinets, the ruling classes and the press of Europe celebrated the plebiscite as a signal victory of the French emperor over the French working class; and it was the signal for the assassination, not of an individual, but of nations.

The war plot of July 1870 is but an amended edition of the coup d'état of December 1851.[4] At first view the thing seemed so absurd that France would not believe in its real good earnest. It rather believed the deputy[5] denouncing the ministerial war talk as a mere stock-jobbing trick. When, on 15 July, war was at last officially announced to the Corps Législatif,[6] the whole opposition refused to vote the preliminary subsidies, even Thiers branded it as 'detestable'; all the independent journals of Paris condemned it, and, wonderful to relate, the provincial press joined in almost unanimously.

Meanwhile, the Paris members of the International had again set to work. In the *Réveil* of 12 July they published their manifesto 'To the workmen of all nations', from which we extract the following few passages:

Once more, on the pretext of the European equilibrium, of national honour, the peace of the world is menaced by political ambitions. French, German, Spanish workmen! Let our voices unite in one cry of reprobation against war! ... War for a question of preponderance of a dynasty can, in the eyes of workmen, be nothing but a criminal

---

3. In the plebiscite of 8 May 1870, the French people were asked to approve Louis Napoleon's liberal reforms. The Paris Federation of the International called on the workers to boycott the plebiscite, an action which provoked the government to initiate this frame-up. In July 1870 thirty-eight members of the Paris Federation were imprisoned simply for belonging to the International, but the charges of conspiracy could not be made to stick.

4. Louis Bonaparte, elected president of the French republic in 1848, overthrew the constitution by his coup of 2 December 1851, and established the Second Empire.

5. Jules Favre.

6. The French legislature under the Second Empire.

absurdity. In answer to the warlike proclamations of those who exempt themselves from the impost of blood, and find in public misfortunes a source of fresh speculations, we protest, we who want peace, labour and liberty! . . . Brothers of Germany! Our division would only result in the complete triumph of *despotism* on both sides of the Rhine . . . Workmen of all countries! Whatever may for the present become of our common efforts, we, the members of the International Working Men's Association, who know of no frontiers, we send you as a pledge of indissoluble solidarity the good wishes and the salutations of the workmen of France.

This manifesto of our Paris section was followed by numerous similar French addresses, of which we can here only quote the declaration of Neuilly-sur-Seine, published in the *Marseillaise* of 22 July:

The war, is it just? – No! The war, is it national? – No! It is merely dynastic. In the name of humanity, of democracy, and the true interests of France, we adhere completely and energetically to the protestation of the International against the war.

These protestations expressed the true sentiments of the French working people, as was soon shown by a curious incident. The Society of 10 December,[7] first organized under the presidency of Louis Bonaparte, having been masqueraded into *blouses* and let loose on the streets of Paris, there to perform the contortions of war fever, the real workmen of the *faubourgs* came forward with public peace demonstrations so overwhelming that Piétri, the Prefect of Police, thought it prudent to at once stop all further street politics, on the plea that the real Paris people had given sufficient vent to their pent-up patriotism and exuberant war enthusiasm.

Whatever may be the incidents of Louis Bonaparte's war with Prussia, the death knell of the Second Empire has already sounded at Paris. It will end as it began, by a parody. But let us not forget that it is the governments and the ruling classes of Europe who enabled Louis Bonaparte to play during eighteen years the ferocious farce of the *restored Empire*.

On the German side, the war is a war of defence, but who put Germany to the necessity of defending herself? Who enabled

7. See *The Eighteenth Brumaire of Louis Bonaparte*, above, pp. 531–2. The Society had in fact been dissolved as early as 1850, but the Bonapartist police continued to organize secret paramilitary forces, which Marx assimilates to the original Society of 10 December.

Louis Bonaparte to wage war upon her? *Prussia!* It was Bismarck who conspired with that very same Louis Bonaparte for the purpose of crushing popular opposition at home, and annexing Germany to the Hohenzollern dynasty. If the battle of Sadowa[8] had been lost instead of being won, French battalions would have overrun Germany as the allies of Prussia. After her victory did Prussia dream one moment of opposing a free Germany to an enslaved France? Just the contrary. While carefully preserving all the native beauties of her old system, she superadded all the tricks of the Second Empire, its real despotism and its mock democratism, its political shams and its financial jobs, its high-flown talk and its low legerdemains. The Bonapartist regime, which till then only flourished on one side of the Rhine, had now got its counterfeit on the other. From such a state of things, what else could result but *war?*

If the German working class allow the present war to lose its strictly defensive character and to degenerate into a war against the French people, victory or defeat will prove alike disastrous. All the miseries that befell Germany after her war of independence[9] will revive with accumulated intensity.

The principles of the International are, however, too widely spread and too firmly rooted amongst the German working class to apprehend such a sad consummation. The voices of the French workmen have re-echoed from Germany. A mass meeting of workmen, held at Brunswick on 16 July, expressed its full concurrence with the Paris manifesto, spurned the idea of national antagonism to France, and wound up its resolutions with these words:

We are enemies of all wars, but above all of dynastic wars ... With deep sorrow and grief we are forced to undergo a defensive war as an unavoidable evil; but we call, at the same time, upon the whole German working class to render the recurrence of such an immense social misfortune impossible by vindicating for the peoples themselves the power to decide on peace and war, and making them masters of their own destinies.

At Chemnitz, a meeting of delegates representing 50,000 Saxon workers adopted unanimously a resolution to this effect:

8. The battle of Sadowa or Königgrätz, 3 July 1866, was Prussia's decisive victory in the Austro-Prussian war.

9. I.e. the war against Napoleon of 1813–14, which fired hopes for democracy and unification, but led to the reimposition of the old regimes.

In the name of the German democracy and especially of the workmen forming the Social-Democratic Workers' Party, we declare the present war to be exclusively dynastic . . . We are happy to grasp the fraternal hand stretched out to us by the workmen of France . . . Mindful of the watchword of the International Working Men's Association: *Proletarians of all countries, unite*, we shall never forget that the workmen of *all* countries are our *friends* and the despots of *all* countries our *enemies*.

The Berlin branch of the International has also replied to the Paris manifesto:

We join with heart and hand your protestation . . . Solemnly we promise that neither the sound of the trumpet, nor the roar of the cannon, neither victory nor defeat shall divert us from our common work for the union of the children of toil of all countries.

Be it so!

In the background of this suicidal strife looms the dark figure of Russia. It is an ominous sign that the signal for the present war should have been given at the moment when the Muscovite government had just finished its strategical lines of railway and was already massing troops in the direction of the Pruth. Whatever sympathy the Germans may justly claim in a war of defence against Bonapartist aggression, they would forfeit at once by allowing the Prussian government to call for, or accept, the help of the Cossacks. Let them remember that, after their war of independence against the first Napoleon, Germany lay for generations prostrate at the feet of the tsar.

The English working class stretch the hand of fellowship to the French and German working people. They feel deeply convinced that whatever turn the impending horrid war may take, the alliance of the working classes of all countries will ultimately kill war. The very fact that while official France and Germany are rushing into a fratricidal feud, the workmen of France and Germany send each other messages of peace and goodwill, this great fact, unparalleled in the history of the past, opens the vista of a brighter future. It proves that in contrast to old society, with its economical miseries and its political delirium, a new society is springing up, whose international rule will be *Peace*, because its national ruler will be everywhere the same – *Labour!* The pioneer of that new society is the International Working Men's Association.

LETTER TO THE BRUNSWICK COMMITTEE
OF THE SOCIAL-DEMOCRATIC WORKERS' PARTY[10]

... The military camarilla, professoriat, bourgeoisie and saloonbar politicians present this[11] as the way for Germany to prevent war with France permanently. On the contrary, it is the most certain way to convert this war into a *European institution*. It is in fact the surest way to perpetuate military despotism in the rejuvenated Germany, as a necessity for maintaining a *western Poland*, Alsace and Lorraine. It is the unfailing way to convert the approaching peace into a mere ceasefire, until France is sufficiently recovered to demand the lost territory back. It is the most unfailing way to ruin Germany and France by reciprocal self-mutilation.

The rogues and fools who have discovered these guarantees of perpetual peace, should know from Prussian history, from the results of Napoleon's Tilsit peace,[12] how such forcible measures of pacification have on a lively people the opposite of the planned effect. And look at France, even after the loss of Alsace and Lorraine, compared with Prussia after the Tilsit peace.

If French chauvinism had a certain material justification even in the context of the old state system, in that since 1815 Paris, the capital, and therefore France in general, was defenceless after a few lost battles – what new nourishment will it not derive once the frontier lies along the Vosges to the east, and at Metz to the north?

Even the most fanatical Teuton would not venture to maintain that the people of Alsace and Lorraine desire the blessings of *German* government. It is the principle of pan-Germanism and 'secure' frontiers that is being proclaimed, and what fine results this would have for Germany and Europe if applied on the eastern side.

10. The following excerpt from Marx and Engels's letter, the only extant part, was reproduced in a leaflet published by the Social-Democratic Workers' Party (SDAP). It is translated here from the text of the leaflet, as printed in *MEW* 17. A few words replaced in the leaflet by ellipses have been restored after markings by Engels in a copy of the leaflet.

11. The planned annexation by Prussia of Alsace and eastern Lorraine.

12. The Treaty of Tilsit, signed between France, Prussia and Russia in July 1807, after the defeat of the fourth anti-French coalition, confined Prussia to its territories east of the Elbe and formed western Germany into a confederation subordinate to the French Empire. This oppressive regime prepared the ground for the German national liberation movement of 1813–14.

Whoever is not completely deafened by the clamour of the moment, or does not have an *interest* in deafening the German people, must realize that the war of 1870 is just as necessarily pregnant with a *war between Germany and Russia* as the war of 1866 was with the war of 1870.

I say *necessarily, unavoidably*, except in the unlikely event of a prior outbreak of *revolution in Russia*. If this unlikely event does not occur, then a war between Germany and Russia must already be considered a *fait accompli*.

It depends completely on the behaviour of the German victors whether the present war will be useful or damaging.

If Alsace and Lorraine are taken, then France will later make war on Germany in conjunction with Russia. It is unnecessary to go into the unholy consequences.

If an honourable peace is made with France, then the war will have emancipated Europe from the Muscovite dictatorship, made Prussia merge into Germany, and allowed the western Continent a peaceful development; finally, it will have helped the outbreak of the Russian social revolution, whose elements only need such a push from outside in order to develop; it would thus also benefit the Russian people.

But I fear that the rogues and fools will drive on with their mad game unhindered, unless the German working class raises its voices *en masse*.

The present war opens a new world-historical epoch, in so far as Germany has shown that, even with the exclusion of German Austria, it is prepared to go its own way *independent of foreign influence*. If it has at first found its *unity* in *Prussian barracks*, this is a punishment that it has richly deserved. But *one* result has even so been directly achieved. Petty trivialities such as the conflict between National Liberal north Germans and Peoples' Party south Germans will no longer stand in the way.[13] Conditions will develop on a larger scale, and will be more unified. If the German working class does not play the historic role that has fallen to it, that will be its own fault. *This war has shifted the centre*

13. 'National Liberal' was the new title adopted by the majority of the bour-geois Progressive party in autumn 1866, when, following the defeat of Austria and the formation of the North German Confederation, they made their peace with Bismarck. The German Peoples' Party, formed in 1865, expressed the opposition of the south German bourgeoisie and petty bourgeoisie to Prussian hegemony, and their aspiration for a 'great Germany', including German Austria, with a federal constitution.

of gravity of the continental workers' movement from France to Germany. This has pinned on the German working class a greater responsibility . . .

SECOND ADDRESS OF THE GENERAL COUNCIL
ON THE FRANCO-PRUSSIAN WAR[14]

To the Members of the International Working Men's Association in Europe and the United States

In our first Manifesto of 23 July we said:

> The death knell of the Second Empire has already sounded at Paris. It will end as it began, by a parody. But let us not forget that it is the governments and the ruling classes of Europe who enabled Louis Napoleon to play during eighteen years the ferocious farce of the *restored Empire*.[15]

Thus, even before war operations had actually set in, we treated the Bonapartist bubble as a thing of the past.

If we were not mistaken as to the vitality of the Second Empire, we were not wrong in our apprehension lest the German war should 'lose its strictly defensive character and degenerate into a war against the French people'.[16] The war of defence ended, in point of fact, with the surrender of Louis Bonaparte, the Sedan capitulation, and the proclamation of the republic at Paris.[17] But long before these events, the very moment that the utter rottenness of the Imperialist[18] arms became evident, the Prussian military camarilla had resolved upon conquest. There lay an ugly obstacle in their way – *King William's own proclamations at the commencement of the war*. In his speech from the throne to the North German Reichstag, he had solemnly declared to make war upon

14. The Second Empire collapsed on 4 September 1870, after the defeat of Sedan. Two days later the General Council commissioned Marx to draft this Address, which was adopted at a special meeting on 9 September. It was issued as a leaflet on 11 September, and is reproduced here from the pamphlet *The General Council of the International Working Men's Association on the War*, Truelove, September 1870.

15. Above, p. 858.

16. Above, p. 859.

17. On 2 September 1870, at Sedan, 80,000 French soldiers, led by Louis Napoleon himself, surrendered to the Prussian army. The republic was declared two days later, following a workers' rising in Paris.

18. See p. 718, n. 62.

the emperor of the French, and not upon the French people. On 11
August he had issued a manifesto to the French nation, where he
said:

The emperor Napoleon having made, by land and sea, an attack on the
German nation, which desired and still desires to live in peace with the
French people, I have assumed the command of the German armies *to repel
his aggression*, and I have been led by *military events to cross the frontiers
of France*.

Not content to assert the defensive character of the war by the statement that he only assumed the command of the German armies '*to
repel aggression*', he added that he was only 'led by military events'
to cross the frontiers of France. A defensive war does, of course, not
exclude offensive operations dictated by 'military events'.

Thus this pious king stood pledged before France and the world
to a strictly defensive war. How to release him from his solemn
pledge? The stage-managers had to exhibit him as giving, reluctantly, way to the irresistible behest of the German nation. They
at once gave the cue to the liberal German middle class, with its
professors, its capitalists, its aldermen, and its penmen. That middle
class which in its struggle for civil liberty had, from 1846 to 1870,
been exhibiting an unexampled spectacle of irresolution, incapacity, and cowardice, felt, of course, highly delighted to bestride the
European scene as the roaring lion of German patriotism. It revindicated its civic independence by affecting to force upon the Prussian
government the secret designs of that same government. It does
penance for its long-continued and almost religious faith in Louis
Bonaparte's infallibility, by shouting for the dismemberment of the
French republic. Let us for a moment listen to the special pleadings
of those stout-hearted patriots!

They dare not pretend that the people of Alsace and Lorraine
pant for the German embrace; quite the contrary. To punish
their French patriotism, Strasbourg, a town with an independent citadel commanding it, has for six days been wantonly and
fiendishly bombarded by 'German' explosive shells, setting it
on fire, and killing great numbers of its defenceless inhabitants!
Yet the soil of those provinces once upon a time belonged to the
whilom German Empire.[19] Hence, it seems, the soil and the human

19. I.e. the Holy Roman Empire of the German Nation. France moved into Alsace
in 1639, and occupied Lorraine in 1670.

beings grown on it must be confiscated as imprescriptible German property. If the map of Europe is to be remade in the anti-quary's vein, let us by no means forget that the Elector of Branden-burg, for his Prussian dominions, was the vassal of the Polish republic.[20]

The more knowing patriots, however, require Alsace and the German-speaking part of Lorraine as a 'material guarantee' against French aggression. As this contemptible plea has bewil-dered many weak-minded people, we are bound to enter more fully upon it.

There is no doubt that the general configuration of Alsace, as compared with the opposite bank of the Rhine, and the presence of a large fortified town like Strasbourg, about halfway between Basle and Germersheim, very much favour a French invasion of south Germany, while they offer peculiar difficulties to an inva-sion of France from south Germany. There is, further, no doubt that the addition of Alsace and German-speaking Lorraine would give south Germany a much stronger frontier, inasmuch as she would then be master of the crest of the Vosges mountains in its whole length, and of the fortresses which cover its northern passes. If Metz were annexed as well, France would certainly for the moment be deprived of her two principal bases of operation against Germany, but that would not prevent her from constructing a fresh one at Nancy or Verdun. While Germany owns Coblenz, Mainz, Germersheim, Rastatt, and Ulm, all bases of operation against France, and plentifully made use of in this war, with what show of fair play can she begrudge France Strasbourg and Metz, the only two fortresses of any importance she has on that side? Moreover, Strasbourg endangers south Germany only while south Germany is a separate power from north Germany. From 1792 to 1795 south Germany was never invaded from that direc-tion, because Prussia was a party to the war against the French Revolution; but as soon as Prussia made a peace of her own in 1795, and left the south to shift for itself, the invasions of south Germany, with Strasbourg for a base, began, and continued till 1809. The fact is, a *united* Germany can always render Strasbourg and any French army in Alsace innocuous by concentrating all her troops, as was done in the present war, between Saarlouis and

20. The Electorate of Brandenburg grew into the Kingdom of Prussia. From 1618 to 1657, when the Elector first acquired the Duchy of Prussia, he was in respect of his Prussian lands a vassal of Poland.

Landau, and advancing, or accepting battle, on the line of road between Mainz and Metz. While the mass of the German troops is stationed there, any French army advancing from Strasbourg into south Germany would be outflanked, and have its communications threatened. If the present campaign has proved anything, it is the facility of invading France from Germany.

But, in good faith, is it not altogether an absurdity and an anachronism to make military considerations the principle by which the boundaries of nations are to be fixed? If this rule were to prevail, Austria would still be entitled to Venetia and the line of the Mincio, and France to the line of the Rhine, in order to protect Paris, which lies certainly more open to an attack from the north-east than Berlin does from the south-west. If limits are to be fixed by military interests, there will be no end to claims, because every military line is necessarily faulty, and may be improved by annexing some more outlying territory; and, moreover, they can never be fixed finally and fairly, because they always must be imposed by the conqueror upon the conquered, and consequently carry within them the seed of fresh wars.

Such is the lesson of all history. Thus with nations as with individuals. To deprive them of the power of offence, you must deprive them of the means of defence. You must not only garrotte but murder. If ever conqueror took 'material guarantees' for breaking the sinews of a nation, the first Napoleon did so by the Tilsit treaty,[21] and the way he executed it against Prussia and the rest of Germany. Yet, a few years later, his gigantic power split like a rotten reed upon the German people. What are the 'material guarantees' Prussia, in her wildest dreams, can, or dare impose upon France, compared to the 'material guarantees' the first Napoleon had wrenched from herself? The result will not prove the less disastrous. History will measure its retribution, not by the extent of the square miles conquered from France, but by the intensity of the crime of reviving, in the second half of the nineteenth century, *the policy of conquest*!

But, say the mouthpieces of Teutonic patriotism, you must not confound Germans with Frenchmen. What *we* want is not glory, but safety. The Germans are an essentially peaceful people. In their sober guardianship, conquest itself changes from a condition of future war into a pledge of perpetual peace. Of course, it is not Germans that invaded France in 1792, for the sublime purpose of

21. See p. 861, n. 12.

bayoneting the revolution of the eighteenth century. It is not Germans that befouled their hands by the subjugation of Italy, the oppression of Hungary, and the dismemberment of Poland. Their present military system, which divides the whole adult male population into two parts – one standing army on service, and another standing army on furlough, both equally bound in passive obedience to rulers by divine right – such a military system is, of course, a 'material guarantee' for keeping the peace, and the ultimate goal of civilizing tendencies! In Germany, as everywhere else, the sycophants of the powers that be poison the popular mind by the incense of mendacious self-praise.

Indignant as they pretend to be at the sight of French fortresses in Metz and Strasbourg, those German patriots see no harm in the vast system of Muscovite fortifications at Warsaw, Modlin and Ivangorod. While gloating at the terrors of Imperialist invasion, they blink at the infamy of autocratic tutelage.

As in 1865 promises were exchanged between Louis Bonaparte and Bismarck, so in 1870 promises have been exchanged between Gorchakov and Bismarck.[22] As Louis Bonaparte flattered himself that the war of 1866, resulting in the common exhaustion of Austria and Prussia, would make him the supreme arbiter of Germany, so Alexander flattered himself that the war of 1870, resulting in the common exhaustion of Germany and France, would make him the supreme arbiter of the western Continent. As the Second Empire thought the North German Confederation incompatible with its existence, so autocratic Russia must think herself endangered by a German empire under Prussian leadership. Such is the law of the old political system. Within its pale the gain of one state is the loss of the other. The tsar's paramount influence over Europe roots in his traditional hold on Germany. At a moment when in Russia herself volcanic social agencies threaten to shake the very base of autocracy, could the tsar afford to bear with such a loss of foreign prestige? Already the Muscovite journals repeat the language of the Bonapartist journals after the war of 1866. Do the Teuton patriots really believe that liberty and peace will be guaranteed to Germany by forcing France into the arms of Russia? If the fortune of her arms, the arrogance of success, and dynastic intrigue lead Germany to a dismemberment of France, there will then only remain two courses open to her. She

---

22. Prince Gorchakov was the Russian foreign minister under Tsar Alexander II.

must at all risks become the *avowed* tool of Russian aggrandizement, or, after some short respite, make again ready for another 'defensive' war, not one of those new-fangled 'localized' wars, but a *war of races* – a war with the combined Slavonian and Roman races.

The German working class has resolutely supported the war, which it was not in their power to prevent, as a war for German independence and the liberation of France and Europe from that pestilential incubus, the Second Empire. It was the German workmen who, together with the rural labourers, furnished the sinews and muscles of heroic hosts, leaving behind their half-starved families. Decimated by the battles abroad, they will be once more decimated by misery at home. In their turn they are now coming forward to ask for 'guarantees' – guarantees that their immense sacrifices have not been bought in vain, that they have conquered liberty, that the victory over the Imperialist armies will not, as in 1815, be turned into the defeat of the German people – and, as the first of these guarantees, they claim an *honourable peace for France*, and the *recognition of the French republic*.

The Central Committee of the German Social-Democratic Workers' Party issued, on 5 September, a manifesto, energetically insisting upon these guarantees.

> We protest against the annexation of Alsace and Lorraine. And we are conscious of speaking in the name of the German working class. In the common interest of France and Germany, in the interest of peace and liberty, in the interest of western civilization against eastern barbarism, the German workmen will not patiently tolerate the annexation of Alsace and Lorraine . . . We shall faithfully stand by our fellow-workmen in all countries for the common international cause of the Proletariat!

Unfortunately, we cannot feel sanguine of their immediate success. If the French workmen amidst peace failed to stop the aggressor, are the German workmen more likely to stop the victor amidst the clangour of arms? The German workmen's manifesto demands the extradition of Louis Bonaparte as a common felon to the French republic. Their rulers are, on the contrary, already trying hard to restore him to the Tuileries as the best man to ruin France. However that may be, history will prove that the German working class are not made of the same malleable stuff as the German middle class. They will do their duty.

Like them, we hail the advent of the republic in France, but at the same time we labour under misgivings which we hope will prove groundless. That republic has not subverted the throne, but only taken its place become vacant. It has been proclaimed, not as a social conquest, but as a national measure of defence. It is in the hands of a Provisional Government composed partly of notorious Orleanists,[23] partly of middle-class republicans, upon some of whom the insurrection of June 1848[24] has left its indelible stigma. The division of labour amongst the members of that government looks awkward. The Orleanists have seized the strongholds of the army and the police, while to the professed republicans have fallen the talking departments. Some of their first acts go far to show that they have inherited from the Empire, not only ruins, but also its dread of the working class. If eventual impossibilities are in wild phraseology demanded from the republic, is it not with a view to prepare the cry for a 'possible' government? Is the republic, by some of its middle-class managers, not intended to serve as a mere stopgap and bridge over [to] an Orleanist restoration?

The French working class moves, therefore, under circumstances of extreme difficulty. Any attempt at upsetting the new government in the present crisis, when the enemy is almost knocking at the doors of Paris, would be a desperate folly. The French workmen must perform their duties as citizens; but, at the same time, they must not allow themselves to be deluded by the national souvenirs of 1792, as the French peasants allowed themselves to be deluded by the national souvenirs of the First Empire.[25] They have not to recapitulate the past, but to build up the future. Let them calmly and resolutely improve the opportunities of republican liberty, for the work of their own class organization. It will gift them with fresh Herculean powers for the regeneration of

23. Supporters of the cadet branch of the French royal family, which ruled from 1830 to 1848 in the person of Louis Philippe. The Orleanists represented the 'aristocracy of finance' and the big bourgeoisie. See 'The Class Struggles in France', above, pp. 422–3 and 507–8.

24. The workers' uprising against the Provisional Government of 1848, acclaimed by Marx as 'the first great battle . . . between the two great classes which divide modern society' . . . 'a fight for the preservation or destruction of the bourgeois order'. 'The Class Struggles in France', above, pp. 392–3.

25. In 1792 the plebeian classes of Paris were instrumental in overthrowing the constitutional monarchy and convening the more radical Convention. The French peasantry had made the mistake of attempting to relive the past by electing Louis Bonaparte President of the Republic in 1848 and supporting his coup d'état of December 1851.

France, and our common task – the emancipation of labour. Upon their energies and wisdom hinges the fate of the republic.

The English workmen have already taken measures to overcome, by a wholesome pressure from without, the reluctance of their government to recognize the French republic.[26] The present dilatoriness of the British government is probably intended to atone for the anti-Jacobin war and its former indecent haste in sanctioning the coup d'état. The English workmen call also upon their government to oppose by all its power the dismemberment of France, which part of the English press is so shameless enough to howl for. It is the same press that for twenty years deified Louis Bonaparte as the providence of Europe, that frantically cheered on the slaveholders' rebellion.[27] Now, as then, it drudges for the slaveholder.

Let the sections of the International Working Men's Association in every country stir the working classes to action. If they forsake their duty, if they remain passive, the present tremendous war will be but the harbinger of still deadlier international feuds, and lead in every nation to a renewed triumph over the workman by the lords of the sword, of the soil, and of capital.

Vive la république.

26. Demonstrations for the recognition of the French republic were held in London and other English cities as early as 5 September.
27. I.e. the Confederate side in the United States civil war.

The Civil War in France

THE CIVIL WAR IN FRANCE:
ADDRESS OF THE GENERAL COUNCIL[1]

To All the Members of the Association in Europe and the United States

I

On 4 September 1870, when the working men of Paris proclaimed the republic, which was almost instantaneously acclaimed throughout France, without a single voice of dissent, a cabal of place-hunting barristers, with Thiers for their statesman and Trochu[2] for their general, took hold of the Hôtel de Ville.[3] At that time they were imbued with so fanatical a faith in the mission of Paris to represent France in all epochs of historical crisis, that, to legitimate their usurped titles as governors of France, they thought it quite sufficient to produce their lapsed mandates as representatives of Paris. In our second Address on the late war, five days after the rise of these men, we told you who they were.[4] Yet, in the turmoil of surprise, with the real leaders of the working class still shut up in Bonapartist prisons and the Prussians already marching upon Paris, Paris bore with their assumption of power, on the express condition that it was to be wielded for the single purpose of national defence. Paris, however, was not to be defended without arming its working class, organizing them into

1. On 18 April 1871 the General Council commissioned Marx to draft an address on the Paris Commune. Marx read *The Civil War in France* to the General Council meeting of 30 May 1871, two days after the final defeat of the Commune; it was adopted unanimously and published as a pamphlet on 13 June 1871, running through three editions in a matter of weeks. It is reproduced here from the third edition.

2. Louis Trochu was a general and Orleanist politician, Chairman of the Government of National Defence (September 1870–January 1871) and commander-in-chief of the Paris armed forces during the siege of Paris by the Prussians.

3. The Paris town hall.   4. See above, p. 869.

an effective force, and training their ranks by the war itself. But Paris armed was the revolution armed. A victory of Paris over the Prussian aggressor would have been a victory of the French workman over the French capitalist and his state parasites. In this conflict between national duty and class interest, the Government of National Defence did not hesitate one moment to turn into a Government of National Defection.

The first step they took was to send Thiers on a roving tour to all the courts of Europe, there to beg mediation by offering the barter of the republic for a king. Four months after the commencement of the siege,[5] when they thought the opportune moment had come for breaking the first word of capitulation, Trochu, in the presence of Jules Favre[6] and others of his colleagues, addressed the assembled mayors of Paris in these terms:

The first question put to me by my colleagues on the very evening of 4 September was this: Paris, can it with any chance of success stand a siege by the Prussian army? I did not hesitate to answer in the negative. Some of my colleagues here present will warrant the truth of my words and the persistence of my opinion. I told them, in these very terms, that, under the existing state of things, the attempt of Paris to hold out a siege by the Prussian army would be a folly. Without doubt, I added, it would be an heroic folly; but that would be all ... The events (managed by himself) have not given the lie to my prevision.

This nice little speech of Trochu was afterwards published by M. Corbon, one of the mayors present.[7]

Thus, on the very evening of the proclamation of the republic, Trochu's 'plan' was known to his colleagues to be the capitulation of Paris. If national defence had been more than a pretext for the personal government of Thiers, Favre, and Co., the upstarts of 4 September would have abdicated on the 5th – would have initiated the Paris people into Trochu's 'plan', and called upon them to surrender at once, or to take their own fate into their own hands. Instead of this, the infamous impostors resolved upon

5. Paris was besieged by the Prussians from 19 September 1870 to 28 January 1871, when the Government of National Defence signed an armistice. This provided, among other things, for the occupation of Paris, the payment of a large war indemnity, and the immediate election of a National Assembly to make peace.

6. Jules Favre was a lawyer and republican politician, and Foreign Minister in the Government of National Defence.

7. In *Le Figaro*, 19 March 1871.

curing the heroic folly of Paris by a regimen of famine and broken heads, and to dupe her in the meanwhile by ranting manifestoes, holding forth that Trochu, 'the governor of Paris, will never capitulate', and Jules Favre, the Foreign Minister, will 'not cede an inch of our territory, nor a stone of our fortresses'. In a letter to Gambetta,[8] that very same Jules Favre avows that what they were 'defending' against were not the Prussian soldiers, but the working men of Paris. During the whole continuance of the siege the Bonapartist cut-throats, whom Trochu had wisely entrusted with the command of the Paris army, exchanged, in their intimate correspondence, ribald jokes at the well-understood mockery of defence. (See, for instance, the correspondence of Adolphe Simon Guiod, supreme commander of the artillery of the army of defence of Paris and Grand Cross of the Legion of Honour, to Susane, general of division of artillery, a correspondence published by the *Journal officiel* of the Commune.)[9] The mask of imposture was at last dropped on 28 January 1871. With the true heroism of utter self-debasement, the Government of National Defence, in their capitulation, came out as the government of France by Bismarck's prisoners – a part so base that Louis Bonaparte himself had, at Sedan, shrunk from accepting it. After the events of 18 March, on their wild flight to Versailles, the *capitulards* left in the hands of Paris the documentary evidence of their treason, to destroy which, as the Commune says in its manifesto to the provinces, 'those men would not recoil from battering Paris into a heap of ruins washed by a sea of blood'.

To be eagerly bent upon such a consummation, some of the leading members of the Government of Defence had, besides, most peculiar reasons of their own.

Shortly after the conclusion of the armistice, M. Millière,[10] one of the representatives of Paris to the National Assembly, now shot

8. Léon Gambetta was a republican politician, Minister of War and of the Interior in the Government of National Defence. See p. 878, n. 27.

9. The *Journal officiel de la République française* was first published in Paris on 5 September 1870, as the official organ of the newly founded Government of Defence. From 20 March 1871 the Paris edition of this paper became the organ of the Commune, while the Versailles government continued to publish its own *Journal officiel*. On 30 March the Commune's paper was retitled *Journal officiel de la Commune de Paris*, and appeared under that title until 24 May. The letter referred to here was published on 25 April.

10. Jean-Baptiste Millière was a journalist and a left-wing Proudhonist, who sat in the Versailles Assembly but defended the Paris Commune.

by express order of Jules Favre, published a series of authentic legal documents in proof that Jules Favre, living in concubinage with the wife of a drunkard resident at Algiers, had, by a most daring concoction of forgeries, spread over many years, contrived to grasp, in the name of the children of his adultery, a large succession, which made him a rich man, and that, in a lawsuit undertaken by the legitimate heirs, he only escaped exposure by the connivance of the Bonapartist tribunals. As these dry legal documents were not to be got rid of by any amount of rhetorical horse-power, Jules Favre, for the first time in his life, held his tongue, quietly awaiting the outbreak of the civil war, in order, then, frantically to denounce the people of Paris as a band of escaped convicts in utter revolt against family, religion, order and property. This same forger had hardly got into power, after 4 September, when he sympathetically let loose upon society Pic and Taillefer, convicted, even under the Empire, of forgery, in the scandalous affair of the *'Étendard'*.[11] One of these men, Taillefer, having dared to return to Paris under the Commune, was at once reinstated in prison; and then Jules Favre exclaimed, from the tribune of the National Assembly, that Paris was setting free all her jailbirds!

Ernest Picard, the Joe Miller[12] of the Government of National Defence, who appointed himself Finance Minister of the Republic after having in vain striven to become the Home Minister of the Empire, is the brother of one Arthur Picard, an individual expelled from the Paris Bourse as a blackleg (see report of the Prefecture of Police, dated 31 July 1867), and convicted, on his own confession, of a theft of 300,000 francs, while manager of one of the branches of the Société Générale,[13] Rue Palestro, no. 5. (See report of the Prefecture of Police, 11 December 1868.) This Arthur Picard was made by Ernest Picard the editor of his paper, *L'Électeur libre*. While the common run of stock-jobbers were led astray by the official lies of this Finance Office paper, Arthur was running backwards and forwards between the Finance Office and the Bourse, there to discount the disasters of the French army. The whole financial correspondence of that worthy pair of brothers fell into the hands of the Commune.

11. *L'Étendard* was a Bonapartist newspaper, forced to close in 1868 after the exposure of its involvement in financial frauds.

12. Joe Miller was an eighteenth-century English comic actor.

13. The Société Générale du Crédit Mobilier; see above, p. 787, n. 47.

Jules Ferry, a penniless barrister before 4 September, contrived, as mayor of Paris during the siege, to job a fortune out of famine. The day on which he would have to give an account of his maladministration would be the day of his conviction.

These men, then, could find, in the ruins of Paris only, their tickets-of-leave: they were the very men Bismarck wanted. With the help of some shuffling of cards, Thiers, hitherto the secret prompter of the government, now appeared at its head, with the ticket-of-leave men for his ministers.

Thiers, that monstrous gnome, has charmed the French bourgeoisie for almost half a century, because he is the most consummate intellectual expression of their own class-corruption. Before he became a statesman he had already proved his lying powers as a historian. The chronicle of his public life is the record of the misfortunes of France. Banded, before 1830, with the republicans, he slipped into office under Louis Philippe by betraying his protector Laffitte,[14] ingratiating himself with the king by exciting mob riots against the clergy, during which the church of Saint Germain l'Auxerrois and the Archbishop's palace were plundered, and by acting the minister-spy upon, and the jail-*accoucheur* of, the Duchess de Berry.[15] The massacre of the republicans in the rue Transnonain, and the subsequent infamous laws of September against the press and the right of association, were his work.[16] Reappearing as the chief of the Cabinet in March 1840, he astonished France with his plan of fortifying Paris. To the republicans, who denounced this plan as a sinister plot against the liberty of Paris, he replied from the tribune of the Chamber of Deputies:

What! To fancy that any works of fortification could ever endanger liberty! And first of all you calumniate any possible government in supposing that it could some day attempt to maintain itself by bom-

14. Jacques Laffitte was a big banker and Louis Philippe's first Prime Minister (1830–31).
15. The Duchess de Berry was the mother of the Legitimist pretender, the Count de Chambord. In 1831 she attempted to organize a Legitimist revolt, and after its failure went into hiding. She was captured later in the year, and Thiers, as Minister of the Interior, had her officially examined to establish the fact of her pregnancy (she had in fact secretly re-married a minor Italian count) and thus discredit her.
16. A republican rising in April 1834 was suppressed by Thiers to the accompaniment of various atrocities. The September laws were passed in 1835.

barding the capital . . . but that government would be a hundred times more impossible after its victory than before.

Indeed, no government would ever have dared to bombard Paris from the forts, but that government which had previously surrendered these forts to the Prussians.

When King Bomba[17] tried his hand at Palermo, in January 1848, Thiers, then long since out of office, again rose in the Chamber of Deputies:

You know, gentlemen, what is happening at Palermo. You, all of you, shake with horror (in the parliamentary sense) on hearing that during forty-eight hours a large town has been bombarded – by whom? Was it by a foreign enemy exercising the rights of war? No, gentlemen, it was by its own government. And why? Because that unfortunate town demanded its rights. Well, then, for the demand of its rights it has got forty-eight hours of bombardment . . . Allow me to appeal to the opinion of Europe. It is doing a service to mankind to arise, and to make reverberate, from what is perhaps the greatest tribune in Europe, some words (indeed words) of indignation against such acts . . . When the regent Espartero, who had rendered services to his country (which M. Thiers never did), intended bombarding Barcelona, in order to suppress its insurrection, there arose from all parts of the world a general outcry of indignation.[18]

Eighteen months afterwards, M. Thiers was amongst the fiercest defenders of the bombardment of Rome by a French army.[19] In fact, the fault of King Bomba seems to have consisted in this only, that he limited his bombardment to forty-eight hours.

A few days before the revolution of February, fretting at the long exile from place and pelf to which Guizot[20] had condemned him, and sniffing in the air the scent of an approaching popular commotion, Thiers, in that pseudo-heroic style which won him the nickname of *Mirabeau-mouche*,[21] declared to the Chamber of Deputies:

17. Ferdinand II of Naples acquired his nickname from his bombardments of Palermo in January 1848 and Messina in the autumn of the same year, to suppress the Italian national movement.

18. This is quoted from *Le Moniteur universel*, 1 February 1848.

19. This was in May 1849, to overthrow the Roman republic and restore the temporal power of the Pope. See 'The Class Struggles in France', *Survey from Exile*, p. 85.

20. François Guizot was a historian and Orleanist politician, and Louis Philippe's chief minister from 1840 to 1848.

21. 'The fly-weight Mirabeau', an allusion to the hero of the first French revolution.

I am of the party of revolution, not only in France, but in Europe. I wish the government of the revolution to remain in the hands of moderate men . . . but if that government should fall into the hands of ardent minds, even into those of radicals, I shall, for all that, not desert my cause. I shall always be of the party of the revolution.[22]

The revolution of February came. Instead of displacing the Guizot cabinet by the Thiers cabinet, as the little man had dreamt, it superseded Louis Philippe by the republic. On the first day of the popular victory he carefully hid himself, forgetting that the contempt of the working men screened him from their hatred. Still, with his legendary courage, he continued to shy the public stage, until the June massacres had cleared it for his sort of action. Then he became the leading mind of the 'party of Order'[23] and its parliamentary republic, that anonymous interregnum, in which all the rival factions of the ruling class conspired together to crush the people, and conspired against each other to restore each of them its own monarchy. Then, as now, Thiers denounced the republicans as the only obstacle to the consolidation of the republic; then, as now, he spoke to the republic as the hangman spoke to Don Carlos:[24] 'I shall assassinate thee, but for thy own good.' Now, as then, he will have to exclaim on the day after his victory: *'L'empire est fait'* – the empire is consummated. Despite his hypocritical homilies about necessary liberties and his personal grudge against Louis Bonaparte, who had made a dupe of him, and kicked out parliamentarism – and outside of its factitious atmosphere the little man is conscious of withering into nothingness – he had a hand in all the infamies of the Second Empire, from the occupation of Rome by French troops to the war with Prussia, which he incited by his fierce invective against German unity – not as a cloak of Prussian despotism, but as an encroachment upon the vested right of France in German disunion. Fond of brandishing, with his dwarfish arms, in the face of Europe the sword of the first Napoleon, whose historical shoe-black he had

22. *Le Moniteur universel*, 3 February 1848.

23. The coalition of Legitimist and Orleanist monarchists, which represented the big bourgeoisie as a whole and was the preponderant force in the short-lived Second Republic of 1848–51. See 'The Class Struggles in France', above, pp. 422–4.

24. The rebellious son of Philip II of Spain. From Schiller's drama *Don Carlos*.

become, his foreign policy always culminated in the utter humiliation of France, from the London Convention of 1840[25] to the Paris capitulation of 1871 and the present civil war, where he hounds on the prisoners of Sedan and Metz[26] against Paris by special permission of Bismarck. Despite his versatility of talent and swiftness of purpose, this man has his whole lifetime been wedded to the most fossil routine. It is self-evident that to him the deeper undercurrents of modern society remained forever hidden; but even the most palpable changes on its surface were abhorrent to a brain all the vitality of which had fled to the tongue. Thus he never tired of denouncing as a sacrilege any deviation from the old French protective system. When a minister of Louis Philippe, he railed at railways as a wild chimera; and when in opposition under Louis Bonaparte, he branded as a profanation every attempt to reform the rotten French army system. Never in his long political career has he been guilty of a single – even the smallest – measure of any practical use. Thiers was consistent only in his greed for wealth and his hatred of the men that produce it. Having entered his first ministry under Louis Philippe poor as Job, he left it a millionaire. His last ministry under the same king (of 1 March 1840) exposed him to public taunts of peculation in the Chamber of Deputies, to which he was content to reply by tears – a commodity he deals in as freely as Jules Favre, or any other crocodile. At Bordeaux[27] his first measure for saving France from impending financial ruin was to endow himself with three millions a year, the first and the last word of the 'economical republic', the vista of which he had opened to his Paris electors in 1869. One of his former colleagues of the Chamber of Deputies of 1830, himself a capitalist and, nevertheless, a devoted member of the Paris

25. The European great powers, with the exclusion of France, signed the London Convention of July 1840 in aid of the Turkish Sultan against the French-supported Egyptian ruler Mohammed Ali, who was resisting Turkish suzerainty. The French government was forced to abandon its support of Mohammed.

26. An entire French army had also surrendered to the Germans at Metz, in October 1870.

27. When the siege of Paris cut the capital off from the rest of France, the Government of National Defence sent Gambetta by balloon across the German lines to establish a governmental delegation at Tours. In January 1871, under pressure from the German advance, the Tours delegation withdrew to Bordeaux, and it was at Bordeaux that the hastily elected National Assembly met soon after the armistice, before moving to Versailles.

Commune, M. Beslay,[28] lately addressed Thiers thus in a public placard:

> The enslavement of labour by capital has always been the cornerstone of your policy, and from the very day you saw the Republic of Labour installed at the Hôtel de Ville, you have never ceased to cry out to France: 'These are criminals!'

A master in small-state roguery, a virtuoso in perjury and treason, a craftsman in all the petty strategems, cunning devices, and base perfidies of parliamentary party-warfare; never scrupling, when out of office, to fan a revolution, and to stifle it in blood when at the helm of the state; with class prejudices standing him in the place of ideas, and vanity in the place of a heart; his private life as infamous as his public life is odious – even now, when playing the part of a French Sulla,[29] he cannot help setting off the abomination of his deeds by the ridicule of his ostentation.

The capitulation of Paris, by surrendering to Prussia not only Paris, but all France, closed the long-continued intrigues of treason with the enemy, which the usurpers of 4 September had begun, as Trochu himself said, on that very same day. On the other hand, it initiated the civil war they were now to wage, with the assistance of Prussia, against the republic and Paris. The trap was laid in the very terms of the capitulation. At that time above one third of the territory was in the hands of the enemy, the capital was cut off from the provinces, all communications were disorganized. To elect under such circumstances a real representation of France was impossible, unless ample time were given for preparation. In view of this, the capitulation stipulated that a National Assembly must be elected within eight days; so that in many parts of France the news of the impending election arrived on its eve only. This assembly, moreover, was, by an express clause of the capitulation, to be elected for the sole purpose of deciding on peace or war, and, eventually, to conclude a treaty of peace. The population could not but feel that the terms of the armistice rendered the continuation of the war impossible, and that for

28. Charles Beslay was a Proudhonist, and a member of the Commune's finance committee. As delegate to the Bank of France, he was especially responsible for the Commune's failure to establish political control over the Bank's activities.

29. The Roman dictator in 82–79 BC, notorious for his brutality towards the people.

sanctioning the peace imposed by Bismarck, the worst men in France were the best. But not content with these precautions, Thiers, even before the secret of the armistice had been broached to Paris, set out for an electioneering tour through the provinces, there to galvanize back into life the Legitimist party,[30] which now, along with the Orleanists, had to take the place of the then impossible Bonapartists. He was not afraid of them. Impossible as a government of modern France, and, therefore, contemptible as rivals, what party were more eligible as tools of counter-revolution than the party whose action, in the words of Thiers himself (Chamber of Deputies, 5 January 1833), 'had always been confined to the three resources of foreign invasion, civil war, and anarchy'?

They verily believed in the advent of their long-expected retrospective millennium. There were the heels of foreign invasion trampling upon France; there was the downfall of an empire, and the captivity of a Bonaparte; and there they were themselves. The wheel of history had evidently rolled back to stop at the *Chambre introuvable* of 1816.[31] In the Assemblies of the Republic, 1848 to 1851, they had been represented by their educated and trained parliamentary champions; it was the rank-and-file of the party which now rushed in – all the Pourceaugnacs[32] of France.

As soon as this Assembly of 'Rurals' had met at Bordeaux, Thiers made it clear to them that the peace preliminaries must be assented to at once, without even the honours of a parliamentary debate, as the only condition on which Prussia would permit them to open the war against the republic and Paris, its stronghold. The counter-revolution had, in fact, no time to lose. The Second Empire had more than doubled the national debt, and plunged all the large towns into heavy municipal debts. The war had fearfully swelled the liabilities, and mercilessly ravaged the resources of the nation. To complete the ruin, the Prussian Shylock was there with his bond for the keep of half a million of his soldiers on French soil, his indemnity of five milliards, and interest at

30. The Legitimists were the supporters of the elder branch of the French royal family, driven from the throne for the second and last time in 1830 in the person of Charles X. They represented the large landed proprietors. On the Orleanists see above, p. 869, n. 23.

31. The 'matchless' Chamber of 1815–16 was matchless only in its rabid reaction.

32. After Molière's Monsieur de Pourceaugnac, the typical philistine landed proprietor.

five per cent on the unpaid instalments thereof.[33] Who was to pay the bill? It was only by the violent overthrow of the republic that the appropriators of wealth could hope to shift on the shoulders of its producers the cost of a war which they, the appropriators, had themselves originated. Thus, the immense ruin of France spurred on these patriotic representatives of land and capital, under the very eyes and patronage of the invader, to graft upon the foreign war a civil war – a slaveholders' rebellion.

There stood in the way of this conspiracy one great obstacle – Paris. To disarm Paris was the first condition of success. Paris was therefore summoned by Thiers to surrender its arms. Then Paris was exasperated by the frantic anti-republican demonstrations of the 'Rural' Assembly and by Thiers's own equivocations about the legal status of the republic; by the threat to decapitate and decapitalize Paris; the appointment of Orleanist ambassadors; Dufaure's laws on overdue commercial bills and house-rents,[34] inflicting ruin on the commerce and industry of Paris; Pouyer-Quertier's[35] tax of two centimes upon every copy of every imaginable publication; the sentences of death against Blanqui and Flourens;[36] the suppression of the republican journals; the transfer of the National Assembly to Versailles; the renewal of the state of siege declared by Palikao,[37] and expired on 4 September; the appointment of Vinoy,[38] the *Décembriseur*, as governor of Paris – of Valentin,[39] the Imperialist *gendarme*,

33. The preliminary peace treaty signed at Versailles on 26 February ceded to the new German Reich Alsace and eastern Lorraine, and provided that France was to pay a war indemnity of five milliard francs. The final peace treaty was signed at Frankfurt on 10 May.

34. Jules Dufaure was an advocate and Orleanist politician, and Minister of Justice in 1871. The *loi Dufaure* of 10 March 1871 failed to provide the moratorium needed for the majority of those indebted as a result of the war and the siege of Paris.

35. Augustin Pouyer-Quertier was a large manufacturer, and Minister of Finance in 1871.

36. Gustave Flourens was a follower of Blanqui and a martyr of the Commune. Blanqui, who was imprisoned after the attempted insurrection of 31 October 1870, and Flourens, who organized the further attempt of 22 January 1871, were sentenced to death for their part in these actions.

37. Charles Cousin-Montauban, Count de Palikao, was a Bonapartist general, Minister of War and head of government in August–September 1870.

38. Joseph Vinoy was a general who had helped to organize Louis Bonaparte's coup d'état of December 1851.

39. Louis Valentin was another Bonapartist general.

as its prefect of police – and of d'Aurelle de Paladines,[40] the Jesuit general, as the commander-in-chief of its National Guard.

And now we have to address a question to M. Thiers and the men of national defence, his under-strappers. It is known that, through the agency of M. Pouyer-Quertier, his finance minister, Thiers had contracted a loan of two milliards. Now, is it true, or not –

1. That the business was so managed that a consideration of several hundred millions was secured for the private benefit of Thiers, Jules Favre, Ernest Picard, Pouyer-Quertier, and Jules Simon?[41] and –

2. That no money was to be paid down until after the 'pacification' of Paris?[42]

At all events, there must have been something very pressing in the matter, for Thiers and Jules Favre, in the name of the majority of the Bordeaux Assembly, unblushingly solicited the immediate occupation of Paris by Prussian troops. Such, however, was not the game of Bismarck, as he sneeringly, and in public, told the admiring Frankfurt[43] philistines on his return to Germany.

II

Armed Paris was the only serious obstacle in the way of the counter-revolutionary conspiracy. Paris was, therefore, to be disarmed. On this point the Bordeaux Assembly was sincerity itself. If the roaring rant of its Rurals had not been audible enough, the surrender of Paris by Thiers to the tender mercies of the triumvirate of Vinoy the *Décembriseur*, Valentin the Bonapartist *gendarme*, and d'Aurelle de Paladines the Jesuit general, would have cut off even the last subterfuge of doubt. But while insultingly exhibiting the true purpose of the disarmament of Paris, the conspirators asked her to lay down her arms on a

40. Louis d'Aurelle de Paladines was a supporter of the clericalist Legitimist party.

41. Jules Simon was a Republican politician, and Minister of Public Instruction in the Government of National Defence and Thiers's government of 1871.

42. These accusations against Thiers and his friends were made in the Communard press; Thiers himself admitted later that the prospective financiers were pressing for the rapid suppression of the Commune. The loan bill was passed by the National Assembly on 20 June 1871.

43. A reference to the German Federal Diet at Frankfurt, transformed by the new constitution of the German Reich into the Federal Council.

pretext which was the most glaring, the most barefaced of lies. The artillery of the Paris National Guard, said Thiers, belonged to the state, and to the state it must be returned. The fact was this: From the very day of the capitulation, by which Bismarck's prisoners had signed the surrender of France, but reserved to themselves a numerous bodyguard for the express purpose of cowing Paris, Paris stood on the watch. The National Guard reorganized themselves and entrusted their supreme control to a Central Committee elected by their whole body, save some fragments of the old Bonapartist formations.[44] On the eve of the entrance of the Prussians into Paris, the Central Committee took measures for the removal to Montmartre, Belleville, and La Villette of the cannon and mitrailleuses treacherously abandoned by the *capitulards* in and about the very quarters the Prussians were to occupy. That artillery had been furnished by the subscriptions of the National Guard. As their private property, it was officially recognized in the capitulation of 28 January, and on that very title exempted from the general surrender, into the hands of the conqueror, of arms belonging to the government. And Thiers was so utterly destitute of even the flimsiest pretext for initiating the war against Paris, that he had to resort to the flagrant lie of the artillery of the National Guard being state property!

The seizure of her artillery was evidently but to serve as the preliminary to the general disarmament of Paris, and, therefore, of the revolution of 4 September. But that revolution had become the legal status of France. The republic, its work, was recognized by the conqueror in the terms of the capitulation. After the capitulation, it was acknowledged by all the foreign powers, and in its name the National Assembly had been summoned. The Paris working men's revolution of 4 September was the only legal title of the National Assembly seated at Bordeaux, and of its executive. Without it, the National Assembly would at once have to give way to the Corps Législatif, elected in 1869, by universal suffrage under French, not under Prussian, rule, and forcibly dispersed by the arm of the revolution. Thiers and his ticket-

44. The Central Committee of the National Guard was elected by 215 out of 270 battalions, almost entirely working class or petty-bourgeois in composition, which formed themselves on 3 March 1870 into the Republican Federation of the National Guard. The Commune's soldiers were hence known as *fédérés* (Federals).

884   *The Civil War in France*

of-leave men would have had to capitulate for safe conducts signed by Louis Bonaparte, to save them from a voyage to Cayenne.[45] The National Assembly, with its power of attorney to settle the terms of peace with Prussia, was but an incident of that revolution, the true embodiment of which was still armed Paris, which had initiated it, undergone for it a five months' siege, with its horrors of famine, and made her prolonged resistance, despite Trochu's plan, the basis of an obstinate war of defence in the provinces. And Paris was now either to lay down her arms at the insulting behest of the rebellious slaveholders of Bordeaux, and acknowledge that her revolution of 4 September meant nothing but a simple transfer of power from Louis Bonaparte to his royal rivals; or she had to stand forward as the self-sacrificing champion of France, whose salvation from ruin, and whose regeneration were impossible, without the revolutionary overthrow of the political and social conditions that had engendered the Second Empire, and, under its fostering care, matured into utter rottenness. Paris, emaciated by a five months' famine, did not hesitate one moment. She heroically resolved to run all the hazards of a resistance against the French conspirators, even with Prussian cannon frowning upon her from her own forts. Still, in its abhorrence of the civil war into which Paris was to be goaded, the Central Committee continued to persist in a merely defensive attitude, despite the provocations of the Assembly, the usurpations of the executive, and the menacing concentration of troops in and around Paris.

Thiers opened the civil war by sending Vinoy, at the head of a multitude of *sergents-de-ville*[46] and some regiments of the line, upon a nocturnal expedition against Montmartre, there to seize, by surprise, the artillery of the National Guard. It is well known how this attempt broke down before the resistance of the National Guard and the fraternization of the line with the people.[47] Aurelle de Paladines had printed beforehand his bulletin of victory, and Thiers held ready the placards announcing his measures of coup d'état. Now these had to be replaced by Thiers's appeals, imparting his magnanimous resolve to leave

45. The penal settlement in French Guiana.
46. Police constables.
47. The women of Montmartre prevailed on the rank-and-file soldiers not to fire on the people, and thus assured the bloodless victory of the revolution of 18 March.

the National Guard in the possession of their arms, with which, he said, he felt sure they would rally round the government against the rebels. Out of 300,000 National Guards only 300 responded to this summons to rally round little Thiers against themselves. The glorious working men's revolution of 18 March took undisputed sway of Paris. The Central Committee was its provisional government. Europe seemed, for a moment, to doubt whether its recent sensational performances of state and war had any reality in them, or whether they were the dreams of a long bygone past.

From 18 March to the entrance of the Versailles troops into Paris, the proletarian revolution remained so free from the acts of violence in which the revolutions, and still more the counter-revolutions, of the 'better classes' abound, that no facts were left to its opponents to cry out about but the execution of Generals Lecomte and Clément Thomas, and the affair of the Place Vendôme.

One of the Bonapartist officers engaged in the nocturnal attempt against Montmartre, General Lecomte, had four times ordered the 81st line regiment to fire at an unarmed gathering in the Place Pigalle, and on their refusal fiercely insulted them. Instead of shooting women and children, his own men shot him. The inveterate habits acquired by the soldiery under the training of the enemies of the working class are, of course, not likely to change the very moment these soldiers changed sides. The same men executed Clément Thomas.

'General' Clément Thomas, a malcontent ex-quartermaster-sergeant, had, in the latter times of Louis Philippe's reign, enlisted at the office of the republican newspaper *Le National*, there to serve in the double capacity of responsible man-of-straw (*gérant responsable*) and of duelling bully to that very combative journal. After the revolution of February, the men of *Le National* having got into power, they metamorphosed this old quartermaster-sergeant into a general on the eve of the butchery of June, of which he, like Jules Favre, was one of the sinister plotters, and became one of the most dastardly executioners. Then he and his generalship disappeared for a long time, to again rise to the surface on 1 November 1870. The day before, the Government of Defence, caught at the Hôtel de Ville, had solemnly pledged their parole to Blanqui, Flourens and other representatives of the working class, to abdicate their usurped power into the hands of a

Commune to be freely elected by Paris. Instead of keeping their word, they let loose on Paris the Bretons of Trochu, who now replaced the Corsicans of Bonaparte.[48] General Tamisier alone, refusing to sully his name by such a breach of faith, resigned the commandership-in-chief of the National Guard, and in his place Clément Thomas for once became again a general. During the whole of his tenure of command, he made war, not upon the Prussians, but upon the Paris National Guard. He prevented their general armament, pitted the bourgeois battalions against the working men's battalions, weeded out the officers hostile to Trochu's 'plan', and disbanded, under the stigma of cowardice, the very same proletarian battalions whose heroism has now astonished their most inveterate enemies. Clément Thomas felt quite proud of having reconquered his June pre-eminence as the personal enemy of the working class of Paris. Only a few days before 18 March, he laid before the War Minister, Le Flô, a plan of his own for 'finishing off *la fine fleur* (the cream) of the Paris *canaille*'. After Vinoy's rout, he must needs appear upon the scene of action in the quality of an amateur spy. The Central Committee and the Paris working men were as much responsible for the killing of Clément Thomas and Lecomte as the Princess of Wales was for the fate of the people crushed to death on the day of her entrance into London.

The massacre of unarmed citizens in the Place Vendôme is a myth which M. Thiers and the Rurals persistently ignored in the Assembly, entrusting its propagation exclusively to the servants' hall of European journalism. 'The men of order', the reactionists of Paris, trembled at the victory of 18 March. To them it was the signal of popular retribution at last arriving. The ghosts of the victims assassinated at their hands from the days of June 1848 down to 22 January 1871,[49] arose before their faces. Their panic was their only punishment. Even the *sergents-de-ville*, instead of being disarmed and locked up, as ought to have been done, had the gates of Paris flung wide open for their safe retreat to Versailles.

48. On 31 October 1870, after the defeat of the French army and the rumours of capitulationist plans, Blanqui and his followers attempted to force the resignation of the Government of National Defence. The attempt was defeated by the middle-class sections of the National Guard, and by the Breton Mobile Guard, whom Trochu used to police Paris. Louis Napoleon had relied on similarly backward Corsicans.

49. The second attempted insurrection by the Blanquists during the siege of Paris was the signal for the violent suppression of the popular movement.

The men of order were left not only unharmed, but allowed to rally and quietly to seize more than one stronghold in the very centre of Paris. This indulgence of the Central Committee – this magnanimity of the armed working men – so strangely at variance with the habits of the 'party of Order', the latter misinterpreted as mere symptoms of conscious weakness. Hence their silly plan to try, under the cloak of an unarmed demonstration, what Vinoy had failed to perform with his cannon and mitrailleuses. On 22 March a riotous mob of swells started from the quarters of luxury, all the *petits crevés*[50] in their ranks, and at their head the notorious familiars of the Empire – the Heeckeren, Coëtlogon, Henri de Pène, etc. Under the cowardly pretence of a pacific demonstration, this rabble, secretly armed with the weapons of the bravo, fell into marching order, ill-treated and disarmed the detached patrols and sentries of the National Guards they met with on their progress, and, on debouching from the rue de la Paix, with the cry of 'Down with the Central Committee! Down with the assassins! The National Assembly for ever!' attempted to break through the line drawn up there, and thus to carry by surprise the headquarters of the National Guard in the Place Vendôme. In reply to their pistol-shots, the regular *sommations* (the French equivalent of the English Riot Act) were made, and, proving ineffective, fire was commanded by the general of the National Guard.[51] One volley dispersed into wild flight the silly coxcombs, who expected that the mere exhibition of their 'respectability' would have the same effect upon the revolution of Paris as Joshua's trumpets upon the wall of Jericho. The runaways left behind them two National Guards killed, nine severely wounded (among them a member of the Central Committee[52]), and the whole scene of their exploit strewn with revolvers, daggers, and sword-canes, in evidence of the 'unarmed' character of their 'pacific' demonstration. When, on 13 June 1849, the National Guard made a really pacific demonstration in protest against the felonious assault of French troops upon Rome,[53] Changarnier, then general of the party of Order, was acclaimed by the National Assembly, and especially by M. Thiers, as the saviour of society, for having launched his

50. Fops.
51. Jules Bergeret, a member of the Paris Commune.
52. Maljournal, also a member of the International.
53. See 'The Class Struggles in France', above, pp. 428–34.

troops from all sides upon these unarmed men, to shoot and sabre them down, and to trample them under their horses' feet. Paris, then, was placed under a state of siege. Dufaure hurried through the Assembly new laws of repression. New arrests, new proscriptions – a new reign of terror set in. But the lower orders manage these things otherwise. The Central Committee of 1871 simply ignored the heroes of the 'pacific demonstration'; so much so that only two days later they were enabled to muster under Admiral Saisset for that *armed* demonstration, crowned by the famous stampede to Versailles. In their reluctance to continue the civil war opened by Thiers's burglarious attempt on Montmartre, the Central Committee made itself, this time, guilty of a decisive mistake in not at once marching upon Versailles, then completely helpless, and thus putting an end to the conspiracies of Thiers and his Rurals. Instead of this, the party of Order was again allowed to try its strength at the ballot box, on 26 March, the day of the election of the Commune. Then, in the *mairies* of Paris, they exchanged bland words of conciliation with their too generous conquerors, muttering in their hearts solemn vows to exterminate them in due time.

Now look at the reverse of the medal. Thiers opened his second campaign against Paris in the beginning of April. The first batch of Parisian prisoners brought into Versailles was subjected to revolting atrocities, while Ernest Picard, with his hands in his trouser pockets, strolled about jeering them, and while Mesdames Thiers and Favre, in the midst of their ladies of honour (?), applauded, from the balcony, the outrages of the Versailles mob. The captured soldiers of the line were massacred in cold blood; our brave friend General Duval,[54] the iron-founder, was shot without any form of trial. Galliffet, the kept man of his wife, so notorious for her shameless exhibitions at the orgies of the Second Empire, boasted in a proclamation of having commanded the murder of a small troop of National Guards, with their captain and lieutenant, surprised and disarmed by his Chasseurs. Vinoy, the runaway, was appointed by Thiers Grand Cross of the Legion of Honour, for his general order to shoot down every soldier of the line taken in the ranks of the Federals. Desmarest, the gendarme, was decorated for the treacherous butcher-like chopping in pieces of the high-souled and chivalrous Flourens,

---

54. Émile Duval, a general of the National Guard, was an iron-founder, a member of the International and of the Paris Commune.

who had saved the heads of the Government of Defence on 31 October 1870. 'The encouraging particulars' of his assassination were triumphantly expatiated upon by Thiers in the National Assembly. With the elated vanity of a parliamentary Tom Thumb, permitted to play the part of a Tamerlane, he denied the rebels against his littleness every right of civilized warfare, up to the right of neutrality for ambulances. Nothing more horrid than that monkey, allowed for a time to give full fling to his tigerish instincts, as foreseen by Voltaire.[55] (See note I [pp. 233–4].)

After the decree of the Commune of 7 April, ordering reprisals and declaring it to be its duty 'to protect Paris against the cannibal exploits of the Versailles banditti, and to demand an eye for an eye, a tooth for a tooth',[56] Thiers did not stop the barbarous treatment of prisoners, moreover insulting them in his bulletins as follows: 'Never have more degraded countenances of a degraded democracy met the afflicted gazes of honest men' – honest like Thiers himself and his ministerial ticket-of-leave men. Still the shooting of prisoners was suspended for a time. Hardly, however, had Thiers and his Decembrist generals become aware that the Communal decree of reprisals was but an empty threat, that even their gendarme spies caught in Paris under the disguise of National Guards, that even *sergents-de-ville*, taken with incendiary shells upon them, were spared – when the wholesale shooting of prisoners was resumed and carried on uninterruptedly to the end. Houses to which National Guards had fled were surrounded by gendarmes, inundated with petroleum (which here occurs for the first time in this war), and then set fire to, the charred corpses being afterwards brought out by the ambulance of the press at the Ternes. Four National Guards having surrendered to a troop of mounted Chasseurs at Belle Épine, on 25 April, were afterwards shot down, one after another, by the captain, a worthy man of Galliffet's. One of his four victims, left for dead, Scheffer, crawled back to the Parisian outposts, and deposed to this fact before a commission of the Commune. When Tolain interpellated the War Minister upon the report of this commission, the Rurals drowned his voice and forbade Le Flô to answer. It would be an insult to their 'glorious' army to speak of its deeds. The flippant

55. In *Candide*, ch. 22.
56. The decree of reprisals was in fact adopted on 5 April. It provided for the killing of selected hostages in return for Communards executed by the Versaillais.

tone in which Thiers's bulletins announced the bayoneting of the Federals surprised asleep at Moulin Saquet, and the wholesale fusillades at Clamart shocked the nerves even of the not over-sensitive London *Times*. But it would be ludicrous today to attempt recounting the merely preliminary atrocities committed by the bombarders of Paris and the fomenters of a slaveholders' rebellion protected by foreign invasion. Amidst all these horrors, Thiers, forgetful of his parliamentary laments on the terrible responsibility weighing down his dwarfish shoulders, boasts in his bulletins that *l'Assemblée siège paisiblement* (the Assembly continues meeting in peace), and proves by his constant carousals, now with Decembrist generals, now with German princes, that his digestion is not troubled in the least, not even by the ghosts of Lecomte and Clément Thomas.

III

On the dawn of 18 March, Paris arose to the thunderburst of *'Vive la Commune!'* What is the Commune, that sphinx so tantalizing to the bourgeois mind? 'The proletarians of Paris,' said the Central Committee in its manifesto of 18 March,

amidst the failures and treasons of the ruling classes, have understood that the hour has struck for them to save the situation by taking into their own hands the direction of public affairs ... They have understood that it is their imperious duty and their absolute right to render themselves masters of their own destinies, by seizing upon the governmental power.

But the working class cannot simply lay hold of the readymade state machinery, and wield it for its own purposes.

The centralized state power, with its ubiquitous organs of standing army, police, bureaucracy, clergy, and judicature – organs wrought after the plan of a systematic and hierarchic division of labour – originates from the days of absolute monarchy, serving nascent middle-lass society as a mighty weapon in its struggles against feudalism. Still, its development remained clogged by all manner of medieval rubbish, seignorial rights, local privileges, municipal and guild monopolies and provincial constitutions. The gigantic broom of the French revolution of the eighteenth century swept away all these relics of bygone times, thus clearing simultaneously the social soil of its last hindrances to the superstructure of the modern state edifice raised under the First Empire, itself the offspring of the coalition wars of old semi-feudal Europe against modern France. During the subsequent regimes the government, placed under parliamentary control – that is, under the direct control of the propertied classes – became not only a hotbed of huge national debts and crushing taxes; with its irresistible allurements of place, pelf, and patronage, it became not only the bone of contention between the rival factions and adventurers of the ruling classes; but its political character changed simultaneously with the economic changes of society. At the same pace at which the progress of modern industry developed, widened, intensified the class antagonism between capital and labour, the state power assumed more and more the character of the national power of capital over labour, of a public force organized for social enslavement, of an engine of class despotism. After every revolution marking a progressive phase in the class struggle, the purely repressive character of the state power stands out in bolder and bolder relief. The revolution of 1830, resulting in the transfer of government from the landlords to the capitalists, transferred it from the more remote to the more direct antagonists of the working men. The bourgeois republicans, who, in the name of the revolution of February [1848], took the state power, used it for the June massacres, in order to convince the working class that 'social' republic meant the republic ensuring their social subjection, and in order to convince the royalist bulk of the bourgeois and landlord class that they might safely leave the cares and emoluments of government to the bourgeois 'republicans'. However, after their one heroic exploit of June, the bourgeois republicans had, from the front, to fall back to the rear of the 'party of Order' – a combination formed by all the rival fractions and factions of the appropriating class in their now openly declared antagonism to the producing classes. The proper form of their joint-stock government was the *parliamentary republic*, with Louis Bonaparte for its President. Theirs was a regime of avowed class terrorism and deliberate insult toward the 'vile multitude'. If the parliamentary republic, as M. Thiers said, 'divided them' (the different fractions of the ruling class) 'least', it opened an abyss between that class and the whole body of society outside their spare ranks. The restraints by which their own divisions had under former regimes still checked the state power, were removed by their union; and in view of the threatening upheaval of the proletariat, they now used that state power mercilessly and ostentatiously as the national war-engine of capital against labour. In their uninterrupted crusade against the producing masses they were, however, bound not only to invest the executive with continually increased powers of repression, but at the same time to divest their own parliamentary stronghold – the National Assembly – one by one, of all its own means of defence against the executive. The executive, in the person of Louis Bonaparte, turned them out. The natural offspring of the 'party-of-Order' republic was the Second Empire.

The Empire, with the coup d'état for its certificate of birth, universal suffrage for its sanction, and the sword for its sceptre, professed to rest upon the peasantry, the large mass of producers not directly involved in the struggle of capital and labour. It professed to save the working class by breaking down parliamentarism, and, with it, the undisguised subserviency of government to the propertied classes. It professed to save the propertied classes by upholding their economic supremacy over the working class; and, finally, it professed to unite all classes by reviving for all the chimera of national glory. In reality, it was the only form of government possible at a time when the bourgeoisie had already lost, and the working class had not yet acquired, the faculty of ruling the nation. It was acclaimed throughout the world as the saviour of society. Under its sway, bourgeois society, freed from political cares, attained a development unexpected even by itself. Its industry and commerce expanded to colossal dimensions; financial swindling celebrated cosmopolitan orgies; the misery of the masses was set off by a shameless display of gorgeous, meretricious and debased luxury. The state power, apparently soaring high above society, was at the same time itself the greatest scandal of that society and the very hotbed of all its corruptions. Its own rottenness, and the rottenness of the society it had saved, were laid bare by the bayonet of Prussia, herself eagerly bent upon transferring the supreme seat of that regime from Paris to Berlin. Imperialism is, at the same time, the most prostitute and the ultimate form of the state power which nascent middle-class society had commenced to elaborate as a means of its own emancipation from feudalism, and which full-grown bourgeois society had finally transformed into a means for the enslavement of labour by capital.

The direct antithesis to the Empire was the Commune. The cry of 'social republic', with which the revolution of February was ushered in by the Paris proletariat, did but express a vague aspiration after a republic that was not only to supersede the monarchical form of class rule, but class rule itself. The Commune was the positive form of that republic.

Paris, the central seat of the old governmental power, and, at the same time, the social stronghold of the French working class, had risen in arms against the attempt of Thiers and the Rurals to restore and perpetuate that old governmental power bequeathed to them by the Empire. Paris could resist only because, in consequence of the siege, it had got rid of the army, and replaced it by a National Guard, the bulk of which consisted of working men. This fact was now to be transformed into an institution. The first decree of the Commune, therefore, was the suppression of the standing army, and the substitution for it of the armed people.

The Commune was formed of the municipal councillors, chosen by universal suffrage in the various wards of the town, responsible and revocable at short terms. The majority of its members were naturally working men, or acknowledged representatives of the working class. The Commune was to be a working, not a parliamentary body, executive and legislative at the same time. Instead of continuing to be the agent of the central government, the police was at once stripped of its political attributes, and turned into the responsible and at all times revocable agent of the Commune. So were the officials of all other branches of the administration. From the members of the Commune downwards, the public service had to be done at *workmen's wages*. The vested interests and the representation allowances of the high dignitaries of state disappeared along with the high dignitaries themselves. Public functions ceased to be the private property of the tools of the central government. Not only municipal administration, but the whole initiative hitherto exercised by the state was laid into the hands of the Commune.

Having once got rid of the standing army and the police, the physical force elements of the old government, the Commune was anxious to break the spiritual force of repression, the 'parson-power', by the disestablishment and disendowment of all churches as proprietary bodies. The priests were sent back to the recesses of private life, there to feed upon the alms of the faithful in imitation of their predecessors, the apostles. The whole of the educational institutions were opened to the people gratuitously, and at the same time cleared of all interference of church and state. Thus, not only was education made accessible to all, but science itself freed from the fetters which class prejudice and governmental force had imposed upon it.

The judicial functionaries were to be divested of that sham independence which had but served to mask their abject subserviency to all succeeding governments to which, in turn, they had taken, and broken, the oaths of allegiance. Like the rest of public servants, magistrates and judges were to be elective, responsible, and revocable.

The Paris Commune was, of course, to serve as a model to all the great industrial centres of France. The communal regime once established in Paris and the secondary centres, the old centralized government would in the provinces, too, have to give way to the self-government of the producers. In a rough sketch of national organization which the Commune had no time to develop, it states clearly that the commune was to be the political form of even the smallest country hamlet, and that in the rural districts the standing army was to be replaced by a national militia, with an extremely short term of service. The rural communes of every district were to administer their common affairs by an assembly of delegates in the central town, and these district assemblies were again to send deputies to the national delegation in Paris, each delegate to be at any time revocable and bound by the *mandat impératif* (formal instructions) of his constituents. The few but important functions which still would remain for a central government were not to be suppressed, as has been intentionally misstated, but were to be discharged by Communal, and therefore strictly responsible agents. The unity of the nation was not to be broken, but, on the contrary, to be organized by the Communal constitution and to become a reality by the destruction of the state power which claimed to be the embodiment of that unity independent of, and superior to, the nation itself, from which it was but a parasitic excrescence. While the merely repressive organs of the old governmental power were to be amputated, its legitimate functions were to be wrested from an authority usurping pre-eminence over society itself, and restored to the responsible agents of society. Instead of deciding once in three or six years which member of the ruling class was to misrepresent the people in parliament, universal suffrage was to serve the people, constituted in communes, as individual suffrage serves every other employer in the search for the workmen and managers in his business. And it is well known that companies, like individuals, in matters of real business generally know how to put the right man in the right place, and, if they for once make a mistake, to redress it promptly. On the other hand, nothing could be more foreign to the spirit of the Commune than to supersede universal suffrage by hierarchic investiture.

It is generally the fate of completely new historical creations to be mistaken for the counterpart of older and even defunct forms of social life, to which they may bear a certain likeness. Thus, this new Commune, which breaks the modern state power, has been mistaken for a reproduction of the medieval communes, which first preceded, and afterwards became the substratum of, that very state power. The Communal constitution has been mistaken for an attempt to break up into a federation of small states, as dreamt of by Montesquieu and the Girondins,[57] that unity of great nations which, if originally brought about by political force, has now become a powerful coefficient of social production. The antagonism of the Commune against the state power has been mistaken for an exaggerated form of the ancient struggle against over-centralization. Peculiar historical circumstances may have prevented the classical development, as in France, of the bourgeois form of government, and may have allowed, as in England, to complete the great central state organs by corrupt vestries, jobbing councillors, and ferocious poor-law guardians in the towns, and virtually hereditary magistrates in the counties. The Communal constitution would have restored to the social body all the forces hitherto absorbed by the state parasite feeding upon, and clogging the free movement of, society. By this one act it would have initiated the regeneration of France. The provincial French middle class saw in the Commune an attempt to restore the sway their order had held over the country under Louis Philippe, and which, under Louis Napoleon, was supplanted by the pretended rule of the country over the towns. In reality, the Communal constitution brought the rural producers under the intellectual lead of the central towns of their districts, and these secured to them, in the working men, the natural trustees of their interests. The very existence of the Commune involved, as a matter of course, local municipal liberty, but no longer as a check upon the, now superseded, state power. It could only enter into the head of a Bismarck, who, when not engaged on his intrigues of blood and iron, always likes to resume his old trade, so befitting his mental

57. The party of the big bourgeoisie during the first French revolution.

calibre, of contributor to *Kladderadatsch* (the Berlin *Punch*), it could only enter into such a head, to ascribe to the Paris Commune aspirations after that caricature of the old French municipal organization of 1791, the Prussian municipal constitution which degrades the town governments to mere secondary wheels in the police machinery of the Prussian state.

The Commune made that catchword of bourgeois revolutions, cheap government, a reality, by destroying the two greatest sources of expenditure – the standing army and state functionarism. Its very existence presupposed the non-existence of monarchy, which, in Europe at least, is the normal incumbrance and indispensable cloak of class rule. It supplied the republic with the basis of really democratic institutions. But neither cheap government nor the 'true republic' was its ultimate aim; they were its mere concomitants.

The multiplicity of interpretations to which the Commune has been subjected, and the multiplicity of interests which construed it in their favour, show that it was a thoroughly expansive political form, while all previous forms of government had been emphatically repressive. Its true secret was this. It was essentially a working-class government, the produce of the struggle of the producing against the appropriating class, the political form at last discovered under which to work out the economical emancipation of labour.

Except on this last condition, the Communal constitution would have been an impossibility and a delusion. The political rule of the producer cannot coexist with the perpetuation of his social slavery. The Commune was therefore to serve as a lever for uprooting the economical foundations upon which rests the existence of classes, and therefore of class rule. With labour emancipated, every man becomes a working man, and productive labour ceases to be a class attribute.

It is a strange fact. In spite of all the tall talk and all the immense literature, for the last sixty years, about emancipation of labour, no sooner do the working men anywhere take the subject into their own hands with a will, than up rises at once all the apologetic phraseology of the mouthpieces of present society with its two poles of capital and wage slavery (the landlord now is but the sleeping partner of the capitalist), as if capitalist society was still in its purest state of virgin innocence, with its antagonisms still undeveloped, with its delusions still unexploded, with its prostitute realities not yet laid bare. The Commune, they exclaim, intends to abolish property, the basis of all civilization! Yes, gentlemen, the Commune intended to abolish that class property which makes the labour of the many the wealth of the few. It aimed at the expropriation of the expropriators. It wanted to make individual property a truth by transforming the means of production, land and capital, now chiefly the means of enslaving and exploiting labour, into mere instruments of free and associated labour. But this is communism, 'impossible' communism! Why, those members of the ruling classes who are intelligent enough to perceive the impossibility of continuing the present system – and they are many – have become the obtrusive and full-mouthed apostles of cooperative production. If cooperative production is not to remain a sham and a snare; if it is to supersede the capitalist system; if united cooperative societies are to regulate national production upon a common plan, thus taking it under their own control, and putting an end to the constant anarchy and periodical convulsions which are the fatality of capitalist production – what else, gentlemen, would it be but communism, 'possible' communism?

The working class did not expect miracles from the Commune. They have no ready-made utopias to introduce *par décret du peuple*.[58] They know that in order to work out their own emancipation, and along with it that higher form to which present society is irresistibly tending by its own economical agencies, they will have to pass through long struggles, through a series of historic processes, transforming circumstances and men. They have no ideals to realize, but to set free the elements of the new society with which old collapsing bourgeois society itself is pregnant. In the full consciousness of their historic mission, and with the heroic resolve to act up to it, the working class can afford to smile at the coarse invective of the gentlemen's gentlemen with the pen and inkhorn, and at the didactic patronage of well-wishing bourgeois doctrinaires, pouring forth their ignorant platitudes and sectarian crotchets in the oracular tone of scientific infallibility.

When the Paris Commune took the management of the revolution in its own hands; when plain working men for the first time dared to infringe upon the governmental privilege of their 'natural superiors', and, under circumstances of unexampled difficulty, performed their work modestly, conscientiously, and efficiently –

58. By decree of the people.

performed it at salaries the highest of which barely amounted to one fifth of what, according to high scientific authority,[59] is the minimum required for a secretary to a certain metropolitan school board – the old world writhed in convulsions of rage at the sight of the red flag, the symbol of the republic of labour, floating over the Hôtel de Ville.

And yet, this was the first revolution in which the working class was openly acknowledged as the only class capable of social initiative, even by the great bulk of the Paris middle class – shop-keepers, tradesmen, merchants – the wealthy capitalists alone excepted. The Commune had saved them by a sagacious settlement of that ever-recurring cause of dispute among the middle classes themselves – the debtor and creditor accounts.[60] The same portion of the middle class, after they had assisted in putting down the working men's insurrection of June 1848, had been at once uncer-emoniously sacrificed to their creditors by the then Constituent Assembly.[61] But this was not their only motive for now rallying round the working class. They felt that there was but one alterna-tive – the Commune, or the Empire – under whatever name it might reappear. The Empire had ruined them economically by the havoc it made of public wealth, by the wholesale financial swindling it fostered, by the props it lent to the artificially accelerated centrali-zation of capital, and the concomitant expropriation of their own ranks. It had suppressed them politically, it had shocked them morally by its orgies, it had insulted their Voltaireanism by hand-ing over the education of their children to the *frères ignorantins*,[62] it had revolted their national feeling as Frenchmen by precipi-tating them headlong into a war which left only one equivalent for the ruins it made – the disappearance of the Empire. In fact, after the exodus from Paris of the high Bonapartist and capi-talist *bohème*, the true middle-class party of Order came out in the shape of the 'Union Républicaine',[63] enrolling themselves

59. Professor Huxley [note by Marx to the German edition of 1871].

60. On 16 April 1871 the Commune decreed a three-year moratorium on all debts incurred as a result of the war, and the cancellation of interest payments.

61. This refers to the rejection of the *concordats à l'amiable* on 22 August 1848; see 'The Class Struggles in France', above, pp. 400–1.

62. The Brothers Ignoramus were an actual Catholic religious order. Marx uses the term here, however, to allude more generally to the clerical and obscurantist character of education under the Second Empire.

63. This was in fact the Alliance Républicaine des Départements, a petty-bourgeois group of provincial representatives in Paris loyal to the Commune.

under the colours of the Commune and defending it against the wilful misconstruction of Thiers. Whether the gratitude of this great body of the middle class will stand the present severe trial, time must show.

The Commune was perfectly right in telling the peasants that 'its victory was their only hope'.[64] Of all the lies hatched at Versailles and re-echoed by the glorious European penny-a-liner, one of the most tremendous was that the Rurals represented the French peasantry. Think only of the love of the French peasant for the men to whom, after 1815, he had to pay the milliard of indemnity![65] In the eyes of the French peasant, the very existence of a great landed proprietor is in itself an encroachment on his conquests of 1789. The bourgeois, in 1848, had burdened his plot of land with the additional tax of forty-five cents in the franc;[66] but then he did so in the name of the revolution; while now he had fomented a civil war against the revolution, to shift on to the peasant's shoulders the chief load of the five milliards of indemnity to be paid to the Prussian. The Commune, on the other hand, in one of its first proclamations, declared that the true originators of the war would be made to pay its cost. The Commune would have delivered the peasant of the blood tax,[67] would have given him a cheap government, transformed his present blood-suckers, the notary, advocate, executor, and other judicial vampires, into salaried communal agents, elected by, and responsible to, himself. It would have freed him of the tyranny of the *garde champêtre*,[68] the gendarme, and the prefect; would have put enlightenment by the schoolmaster in the place of stultification by the priest. And the French peasant is, above all, a man of reckoning. He would find it extremely reasonable that the pay of the priest, instead of being extorted by the tax-gatherer, should only depend upon the spontaneous action of the parishioners' religious instincts. Such were the great immediate boons which the rule of the Commune – and that rule alone – held out to the French peasantry. It is, therefore, quite superfluous here to expatiate upon the more com-

64. An apparent reference to the Commune's appeal 'To the rural workers', issued at the end of April.

65. In 1825 Louis XVIII's government granted landowners who had been expropriated during the first French revolution compensation of the order of a thousand million francs.

66. See 'The Class Struggles in France', above, p. 385.

67. I.e. conscription.

68. Village policeman.

plicated but vital problems which the Commune alone was able, and at the same time compelled, to solve in favour of the peasant, viz., the hypothecary debt, lying like an incubus upon his parcel of soil, the *prolétariat foncier* (the rural proletariat), daily growing upon it, and his expropriation from it enforced, at a more and more rapid rate, by the very development of modern agriculture and the competition of capitalist farming.

The French peasant had elected Louis Bonaparte President of the Republic; but the party of Order created the Empire. What the French peasant really wants he commenced to show in 1849 and 1850, by opposing his *maire* to the government's prefect, his schoolmaster to the government's priest, and himself to the government's gendarme. All the laws made by the party of Order in January and February 1850[69] were avowed measures of repression against the peasant. The peasant was a Bonapartist, because the great Revolution, with all its benefits to him, was, in his eyes, personified in Napoleon. This delusion, rapidly breaking down under the Second Empire (and in its very nature hostile to the Rurals), this prejudice of the past, how could it have withstood the appeal of the Commune to the living interests and urgent wants of the peasantry?

The Rurals – this was, in fact, their chief apprehension – knew that three months' free communication of Communal Paris with the provinces would bring about a general rising of the peasants, and hence their anxiety to establish a police blockade around Paris, so as to stop the spread of the rinderpest.

If the Commune was thus the true representative of all the healthy elements of French society, and therefore the truly national government, it was, at the same time, as a working men's government, as the bold champion of the emancipation of labour, emphatically international. Within sight of the Prussian army, that had annexed to Germany two French provinces, the Commune annexed to France the working people all over the world.

The Second Empire had been the jubilee of cosmopolitan blackleg-ism, the rakes of all countries rushing in at its call for a share in its orgies and in the plunder of the French people. Even at this moment the right hand of Thiers is Ganesco, the foul Wallachian, and his left hand is Markovsky, the Russian spy. The

69. See 'The Class Struggles in France', above, pp. 452–3.

Commune admitted all foreigners to the honour of dying for an immortal cause. Between the foreign war lost by their treason, and the civil war fomented by their conspiracy with the foreign invader, the bourgeoisie had found the time to display their patriotism by organizing police-hunts upon the Germans in France. The Commune made a German working man[70] its Minister of Labour. Thiers, the bourgeoisie, the Second Empire, had continually deluded Poland by loud professions of sympathy, while in reality betraying her to, and doing the dirty work of, Russia. The Commune honoured the heroic sons of Poland[71] by placing them at the head of the defenders of Paris. And, to broadly mark the new era of history it was conscious of initiating, under the eyes of the conquering Prussians, on the one side, and of the Bonapartist army, led by Bonapartist generals, on the other, the Commune pulled down that colossal symbol of martial glory, the Vendôme column.[72]

The great social measure of the Commune was its own working existence. Its special measures could but betoken the tendency of a government of the people by the people. Such were the abolition of the nightwork of journeymen bakers; the prohibition, under penalty, of the employers' practice to reduce wages by levying upon their work-people fines under manifold pretexts – a process in which the employer combines in his own person the parts of legislator, judge, and executor, and filches the money to boot. Another measure of this class was the surrender to associations of workmen, under reserve of compensation, of all closed workshops and factories, no matter whether the respective capitalists had absconded or preferred to strike work.

The financial measures of the Commune, remarkable for their sagacity and moderation, could only be such as were compatible with the state of a besieged town. Considering the colossal robberies committed upon the city of Paris by the great financial com-

70. Leo Frankel, in fact a German-speaking Hungarian, was an active member of the International, and the only member of the Commune who was in any sense a Marxist.

71. These were Jaroslaw Dombrowski and Walery Wroblewski, both revolutionary democrats in exile after the Polish insurrection of 1863. Dombrowski was appointed commander-in-chief of the Commune's forces during its last days, and died in its defence.

72. The Vendôme column was erected in 1806–10, out of melted-down cannons, to commemorate Napoleon's victories of 1805. It was pulled down on 16 May 1871, but restored after the Versailles victory.

panies and contractors, under the protection of Haussmann,[73] the Commune would have had an incomparably better title to confiscate their property than Louis Napoleon had against the Orleans family. The Hohenzollern[74] and the English oligarchs, who both have derived a good deal of their estates from church plunder, were, of course, greatly shocked at the Commune clearing but 8,000 francs out of secularization.

While the Versailles government, as soon as it had recovered some spirit and strength, used the most violent means against the Commune; while it put down the free expression of opinion all over France, even to the forbidding of meetings of delegates from the large towns; while it subjected Versailles and the rest of France to an espionage far surpassing that of the Second Empire; while it burned by its gendarme inquisitors all papers printed at Paris, and sifted all correspondence from and to Paris; while in the National Assembly the most timid attempts to put in a word for Paris were howled down in a manner unknown even to the *Chambre introuvable* of 1816; with the savage warfare of Versailles outside, and its attempts at corruption and conspiracy inside Paris – would the Commune not have shamefully betrayed its trust by affecting to keep up all the decencies and appearances of liberalism as in a time of profound peace? Had the government of the Commune been akin to that of M. Thiers, there would have been no more occasion to suppress party-of-Order papers at Paris than there was to suppress Communal papers at Versailles.

It was irritating indeed to the Rurals that at the very same time they declared the return to the church to be the only means of salvation for France, the infidel Commune unearthed the peculiar mysteries of the Picpus nunnery, and of the Church of Saint Laurent.[75] It was a satire upon M. Thiers that, while he showered grand crosses upon the Bonapartist generals in acknowledgement of their mastery in losing battles, signing capitulations, and turning cigarettes at Wilhelmshöhe,[76] the Commune dismissed and

73. Georges Haussmann, a Bonapartist politician and prefect of the Seine department, supervised the extensive planned rebuilding of Paris that was carried out under the Second Empire, which, among other things, created straight broad avenues for artillery fire, as a precaution against popular insurrection.   74. The Prussian royal family.

75. The Commune discovered at these places evidence of torture, incarceration and murder committed within religious orders.

76. The castle where the captured French generals, and Louis Napoleon himself, were interned.

arrested its generals whenever they were suspected of neglecting their duties. The expulsion from, and arrest by, the Commune of one of its members[77] who had slipped in under a false name, and had undergone at Lyons six days' imprisonment for simple bankruptcy, was it not a deliberate insult hurled at the forger, Jules Favre, then still the Foreign Minister of France, still selling France to Bismarck, and still dictating his orders to that paragon government of Belgium? But indeed the Commune did not pretend to infallibility, the invariable attribute of all governments of the old stamp. It published its doings and sayings, it initiated the public into all its shortcomings.

In every revolution there intrude, at the side of its true agents, men of a different stamp; some of them survivors of and devotees to past revolutions, without insight into the present movement, but preserving popular influence by their known honesty and courage, or by the sheer force of tradition; others mere bawlers, who, by dint of repeating year after year the same set of stereotyped declamations against the government of the day, have sneaked into the reputation of revolutionists of the first water. After 18 March, some such men did also turn up, and in some cases contrived to play pre-eminent parts. As far as their power went, they hampered the real action of the working class, exactly as men of that sort have hampered the full development of every previous revolution. They are an unavoidable evil: with time they are shaken off; but time was not allowed to the Commune.

Wonderful, indeed, was the change the Commune had wrought in Paris! No longer any trace of the meretricious Paris of the Second Empire. No longer was Paris the rendezvous of British landlords, Irish absentees, American ex-slaveholders and shoddy men, Russian ex-serfowners, and Wallachian boyards. No more corpses at the morgue, no nocturnal burglaries, scarcely any robberies; in fact, for the first time since the days of February 1848 the streets of Paris were safe, and that without any police of any kind. 'We', said a member of the Commune, 'hear no longer of assassination, theft and personal assault; it seems indeed as if the police had dragged along with it to Versailles all its conservative friends.'

The *cocottes*[78] had refound the scent of their protectors – the absconding men of family, religion, and, above all, of property.

---

77. Stanislas Blanchet, in fact a police agent.
78. High-class prostitutes.

In their stead, the real women of Paris showed again at the surface – heroic, noble, and devoted, like the women of antiquity. Working, thinking, fighting, bleeding Paris – almost forgetful, in its incubation of a new society, of the cannibals at its gates – radiant in the enthusiasm of its historic initiative!

Opposed to this new world at Paris, behold the old world at Versailles – that assembly of the ghouls of all defunct regimes, Legitimists and Orleanists, eager to feed upon the carcass of the nation – with a tail of antediluvian republicans, sanctioning, by their presence in the Assembly, the slaveholders' rebellion, relying for the maintenance of their parliamentary republic upon the vanity of the senile mountebank at its head, and caricaturing 1789 by holding their ghastly meetings in the Jeu de Paume.[79] There it was, this Assembly, the representative of everything dead in France, propped up to the semblance of life by nothing but the swords of the generals of Louis Bonaparte. Paris all truth, Versailles all lie; and that lie vented through the mouth of Thiers.

Thiers tells a deputation of the mayors of the Seine-et-Oise, 'You may rely upon my word, which I have *never* broken!'

He tells the Assembly itself that it was 'the most freely elected and most liberal Assembly France ever possessed'; he tells his motley soldiery that it was 'the admiration of the world, and the finest army France ever possessed'; he tells the provinces that the bombardment of Paris by him was a myth: 'If some cannon-shots have been fired, it is not the deed of the army of Versailles, but of some insurgents trying to make believe that they are fighting, while they dare not show their faces.'

He again tells the provinces that 'the artillery of Versailles does not bombard Paris, but only cannonades it'.

He tells the Archbishop of Paris that the pretended executions and reprisals (!) attributed to the Versailles troops were all moonshine. He tells Paris that he was only anxious 'to free it from the hideous tyrants who oppress it', and that, in fact, the Paris of the Commune was 'but a handful of criminals'.

The Paris of M. Thiers was not the real Paris of the 'vile multitude', but a phantom Paris, the Paris of the *francs-fileurs*,[80] the Paris of the boulevards, male and female – the rich, the

79. The tennis court where the French Third Estate met on 20 June 1789 and vowed to exact a constitution.

80. A pun on '*franc-tireur*' (sniper or guerrilla soldier). Literally, those who 'freely filed off'.

capitalist, the gilded, the idle Paris, now thronging with its lackeys, its blacklegs, its literary *bohème* and its *cocottes* at Versailles, Saint-Denis, Rueil, and Saint-Germain; considering the civil war but an agreeable diversion, eyeing the battle going on through telescopes, counting the rounds of cannon, and swearing by their own honour, and that of their prostitutes, that the performance was far better got up than it used to be at the Porte Saint Martin. The men who fell were really dead; the cries of the wounded were cries in good earnest; and, besides, the whole thing was so intensely historical.

This is the Paris of M. Thiers, as the emigration of Coblenz was the France of M. de Calonne.[81]

IV

The first attempt of the slaveholders' conspiracy to put down Paris by getting the Prussians to occupy it, was frustrated by Bismarck's refusal. The second attempt, that of 18 March, ended in the rout of the army and the flight to Versailles of the government, which ordered the whole administration to break up and follow in its track. By the semblance of peace negotiations with Paris, Thiers found the time to prepare for war against it. But where to find an army? The remnants of the line regiments were weak in number and unsafe in character. His urgent appeal to the provinces to succour Versailles, by their National Guards and volunteers, met with a flat refusal. Brittany alone furnished a handful of Chouans[82] fighting under a white flag, every one of them wearing on his breast the heart of Jesus in white cloth, and shouting '*Vive le roi!*' (Long live the king!). Thiers was, therefore, compelled to collect, in hot haste, a motley crew, composed of sailors, marines, Pontifical Zouaves,[83] Valentin's gendarmes, and Piétri's *sergents-de-ville* and *mouchards*.[84] This army, however, would have been ridiculously ineffective without the instalments of Imperialist war-prisoners, which Bismarck granted in

81. Coblenz was the main centre of the monarchist emigration during the first French revolution. Charles de Calonne, a former minister of Louis XVI, headed a government in exile there.

82. The name of the Breton royalist insurgents during the first French revolution.

83. A regiment of the Papal guard formed from the French aristocracy; the Pontifical Zouaves were sent to France in 1870 to fight the Prussians.

84. Police informers.

numbers just sufficient to keep the civil war a-going, and keep the Versailles government in abject dependence on Prussia. During the war itself, the Versailles police had to look after the Versailles army, while the gendarmes had to drag it on by exposing themselves at all posts of danger. The forts which fell were not taken, but bought. The heroism of the Federals convinced Thiers that the resistance of Paris was not to be broken by his own strategic genius and the bayonets at his disposal.

Meanwhile, his relations with the provinces became more and more difficult. Not one single address of approval came in to gladden Thiers and his Rurals. Quite the contrary. Deputations and addresses demanding, in a tone anything but respectful, conciliation with Paris on the basis of the unequivocal recognition of the republic, the acknowledgement of communal liberties, and the dissolution of the National Assembly, whose mandate was extinct, poured in from all sides, and in such numbers that Dufaure, Thiers's Minister of Justice, in his circular of 23 April to the public prosecutors, commanded them to treat 'the cry of conciliation' as a crime! In regard, however, of the hopeless prospect held out by his campaign, Thiers resolved to shift his tactics by ordering, all over the country, municipal elections to take place on 30 April, on the basis of the new municipal law dictated by himself to the National Assembly. What with the intrigues of his prefects, what with police intimidation, he felt quite sanguine of imparting, by the verdict of the provinces, to the National Assembly that moral power it had never possessed, and of getting at last from the provinces the physical force required for the conquest of Paris.

His banditti-warfare against Paris, exalted in his own bulletins, and the attempts of his ministers at the establishment, throughout France, of a reign of terror, Thiers was from the beginning anxious to accompany with a little by-play of conciliation, which had to serve more than one purpose. It was to dupe the provinces, to inveigle the middle-class element in Paris, and, above all, to afford the professed republicans in the National Assembly the opportunity of hiding their treason against Paris behind their faith in Thiers. On 21 March, when still without an army, he had declared to the Assembly: 'Come what may, I will not send an army to Paris.'

On 27 March he rose again: 'I have found the republic an accomplished fact, and I am firmly resolved to maintain it.'

In reality, he put down the revolution at Lyons and Marseilles[85] in the name of the republic, while the roars of his Rurals drowned the very mention of its name at Versailles. After this exploit, he toned down the 'accomplished fact' into an hypothetical fact. The Orleans princes, whom he had cautiously warned off Bordeaux, were now, in flagrant breach of the law, permitted to intrigue at Dreux. The concessions held out by Thiers in his interminable interviews with the delegates from Paris and the provinces, although constantly varied in tone and colour, according to time and circumstances, did in fact never come to more than the prospective restriction of revenge to the 'handful of criminals implicated in the murder of Lecomte and Clément Thomas', on the well-understood premise that Paris and France were unreservedly to accept M. Thiers himself as the best of possible republics, as he, in 1830, had done with Louis Philippe. Even these concessions he not only took care to render doubtful by the official comments put upon them in the Assembly through his ministers. He had his Dufaure to act. Dufaure, this old Orleanist lawyer, had always been the justiciary of the state of siege, as now in 1871, under Thiers, so in 1839 under Louis Philippe, and in 1849 under Louis Bonaparte's presidency. While out of office he made a fortune by pleading for the Paris capitalists, and made political capital by pleading against the laws he had himself originated. He now hurried through the National Assembly not only a set of repressive laws which were, after the fall of Paris, to extirpate the last remnants of republican liberty in France;[86] he foreshadowed the fate of Paris by abridging the, for him, too slow procedure of courts-martial, and by a new-fangled, Draconic code of deportation. The revolution of 1848, abolishing the penalty of death for political crimes, had replaced it by deportation. Louis Bonaparte did not dare, at least not in theory, to re-establish the regime of the guillotine. The Rural Assembly, not yet bold enough even to hint that the Parisians were not rebels, but assassins, had therefore to confine its prospective vengeance against Paris to Dufaure's new code of deportation. Under all these circumstances Thiers himself could not have gone on with his comedy of conciliation, had it not, as he intended it to do, drawn forth shrieks of rage from the

85. At Lyons and Marseilles Communard risings took place in the wake of Paris, but were defeated after only a few days.

86. Particularly a law curbing the press.

Rurals, whose ruminating mind did neither understand the play, nor its necessities of hypocrisy, tergiversation, and procrastination.

In sight of the impending municipal elections of 30 April, Thiers enacted one of his great conciliation scenes on 27 April. Amidst a flood of sentimental rhetoric, he exclaimed from the tribune of the Assembly:

There exists no conspiracy against the republic but that of Paris, which compels us to shed French blood. I repeat it again and again. Let those impious arms fall from the hands which hold them, and chastisement will be arrested at once by an act of peace excluding only the small number of criminals.

To the violent interruption of the Rurals he replied:

Gentlemen, tell me, I implore you, am I wrong? Do you really regret that I could have stated the truth that the criminals are only a handful? Is it not fortunate in the midst of our misfortunes that those who have been capable to shed the blood of Clément Thomas and General Lecomte are but rare exceptions?

France, however, turned a deaf ear to what Thiers flattered himself to be a parliamentary siren's song. Out of 700,000 municipal councillors returned by the 35,000 communes still left to France, the united Legitimists, Orleanists and Bonapartists did not carry 8,000. The supplementary elections which followed were still more decidedly hostile. Thus, instead of getting from the provinces the badly needed physical force, the National Assembly lost even its last claim to moral force, that of being the expression of the universal suffrage of the country. To complete the discomfiture, the newly chosen municipal councils of all the cities of France openly threatened the usurping Assembly at Versailles with a counter assembly at Bordeaux.

Then the long-expected moment of decisive action had at last come for Bismarck. He peremptorily summoned Thiers to send to Frankfurt plenipotentiaries for the definitive settlement of peace. In humble obedience to the call of his master, Thiers hastened to dispatch his trusty Jules Favre, backed by Pouyer-Quertier. Pouyer-Quertier, an 'eminent' Rouen cotton-spinner, a fervent and even servile partisan of the Second Empire, had never found any fault with it save its commercial treaty with England,[87]

---

87. The 'Cobden treaty' of January 1860, which substantially reduced French protective tariffs on imported industrial goods.

prejudicial to his own shop-interest. Hardly installed at Bordeaux as Thiers's Minister of Finance, he denounced that 'unholy' treaty, hinted at its near abrogation, and had even the effrontery to try, although in vain (having counted without Bismarck), the immediate enforcement of the old protective duties against Alsace, where, he said, no previous international treaties stood in the way. This man, who considered counter-revolution as a means to put down wages at Rouen, and the surrender of French provinces as a means to bring up the price of his wares in France, was he not *the one* predestined to be picked out by Thiers as the helpmate of Jules Favre in his last and crowning treason?

On the arrival at Frankfurt of this exquisite pair of plenipotentiaries, bully Bismarck at once met them with the imperious alternative: Either the restoration of the Empire, or the unconditional acceptance of my own peace terms! These terms included a shortening of the intervals in which the war indemnity was to be paid and the continued occupation of the Paris forts by Prussian troops until Bismarck should feel satisfied with the state of things in France; Prussia thus being recognized as the supreme arbiter in internal French politics! In return for this he offered to let loose, for the extermination of Paris, the captive Bonapartist army, and to lend them the direct assistance of Emperor William's troops. He pledged his good faith by making payment of the first instalment of the indemnity dependent on the 'pacification' of Paris. Such a bait was, of course, eagerly swallowed by Thiers and his plenipotentiaries. They signed the treaty of peace on 10 May, and had it endorsed by the Versailles Assembly on the 18th.

In the interval between the conclusion of peace and the arrival of the Bonapartist prisoners, Thiers felt the more bound to resume his comedy of conciliation, as his republican tools stood in sore need of a pretext for blinking their eyes at the preparations for the carnage of Paris. As late as 8 May he replied to a deputation of middle-class conciliators: 'Whenever the insurgents will make up their minds for capitulation, the gates of Paris shall be flung wide open during a week for all except the murderers of Generals Clément Thomas and Lecomte.'

A few days afterwards, when violently interpellated on these promises by the Rurals, he refused to enter into any explanations; not, however, without giving them this significant hint:

I tell you there are impatient men amongst you, men who are in too great a hurry. They must have another eight days; at the end of these eight days there will be no more danger, and the task will be proportionate to their courage and to their capacities.

As soon as MacMahon[88] was able to assure him that he could shortly enter Paris, Thiers declared to the Assembly that he would enter Paris with the *laws* in his hands, and demand a full expiation from the wretches who had sacrificed the lives of soldiers and destroyed public monuments.

As the moment of decision drew near he said – to the Assembly, 'I shall be pitiless!' – to Paris, that it was doomed; and to his Bonapartist banditti, that they had state licence to wreak vengeance upon Paris to their hearts' content. At last, when treachery had opened the gates of Paris to General Douay, on 21 May, Thiers, on the 22nd, revealed to the Rurals the 'goal' of his conciliation comedy, which they had so obstinately persisted in not understanding. 'I told you a few days ago that we were approaching *our goal*; today I come to tell you *the goal* is reached. The victory of order, justice and civilization is at last won!'

So it was. The civilization and justice of bourgeois order comes out in its lurid light whenever the slaves and drudges of that order rise against their masters. Then this civilization and justice stand forth as undisguised savagery and lawless revenge. Each new crisis in the class struggle between the appropriator and the producer brings out this fact more glaringly. Even the atrocities of the bourgeois in June 1848 vanish before the ineffable infamy of 1871. The self-sacrificing heroism with which the population of Paris – men, women and children – fought for eight days after the entrance of the Versaillais, reflects as much the grandeur of their cause, as the infernal deeds of the soldiery reflect the innate spirit of that civilization of which they are the mercenary vindicators. A glorious civilization, indeed, the great problem of which is how to get rid of the heaps of corpses it made after the battle was over!

To find a parallel for the conduct of Thiers and his bloodhounds we must go back to the times of Sulla and the two trium-

---

88. Marie Édmé MacMahon was a Bonapartist marshal, and commander-in-chief of the Versailles army that put down the Commune. He was subsequently President of the Third Republic (1873–9).

virates of Rome.[89] The same wholesale slaughter in cold blood; the same disregard, in massacre, of age and sex; the same system of torturing prisoners; the same proscriptions, but this time of a whole class; the same savage hunt after concealed leaders, lest one might escape; the same denunciations of political and private enemies; the same indifference for the butchery of entire strangers to the feud. There is but this difference, that the Romans had no mitrailleuses for the despatch, in the lump, of the proscribed, and that they had not 'the law in their hands', nor on their lips the cry of 'civilization'.

And after those horrors, look upon the other, still more hideous, face of that bourgeois civilization as described by its own press! The Paris correspondent of a London Tory paper writes:

With stray shots still ringing in the distance, and untended wounded wretches dying amid the tombstones of Père Lachaise – with 6,000 terror-stricken insurgents wandering in an agony of despair in the labyrinth of the catacombs, and wretches hurried through the streets to be shot down in scores by the mitrailleuse – it is revolting to see the *cafés* filled with the votaries of absinthe, billiards, and dominoes; female profligacy perambulating the boulevards, and the sound of revelry disturbing the night from the *cabinets particuliers*[90] of fashionable restaurants.

M. Edouard Hervé writes in the *Journal de Paris*, a Versaillist journal suppressed by the Commune:

The way in which the population of Paris (!) manifested its satisfaction yesterday was rather more than frivolous, and we fear it will grow worse as time progresses. Paris has now a *fête* day appearance, which is sadly out of place; and, unless we are to be called the *Parisiens de la décadence*, this sort of thing must come to an end.

And then he quotes the passage from Tacitus:

Yet, on the morrow of that horrible struggle, even before it was completely over, Rome – degraded and corrupt – began once more to wallow in the voluptuous slough which was destroying its body and polluting its soul – *alibi proelia et vulnera, alibi balnea popinaeque* [here fights and wounds, there baths and restaurants].

M. Hervé only forgets to say that the 'population of Paris' he speaks of is but the population of the Paris of M. Thiers – the

---

89. The first (60–53 BC) and second (46–43 BC) triumvirates were, like Sulla's dictatorship, notorious for their brutality against the Roman population.

90. Private rooms.

francs-fileurs returning in throngs from Versailles, Saint-Denis, Rueil and Saint-Germain – *the* Paris of the 'Decline'.

In all its bloody triumphs over the self-sacrificing champions of a new and better society, that nefarious civilization, based upon the enslavement of labour, drowns the moans of its victims in a hue-and-cry of calumny, reverberated by a world-wide echo. The serene working men's Paris is suddenly changed into a pandemonium by the bloodhounds of 'order'. And what does this tremendous change prove to the bourgeois mind of all countries? Why, that the Commune has conspired against civilization! The Paris people die enthusiastically for the Commune in numbers unequalled in any battle known to history. What does that prove? Why, that the Commune was not the people's own government but the usurpation of a handful of criminals! The women of Paris joyfully give up their lives at the barricades and on the place of execution. What does this prove? Why, that the demon of the Commune has changed them into Megaeras and Hecates! The moderation of the Commune during two months of undisputed sway is equalled only by the heroism of its defence. What does that prove? Why, that for months the Commune carefully hid, under a mask of moderation and humanity, the bloodthirstiness of its fiendish instincts, to be let loose in the hour of its agony!

The working men's Paris, in the act of its heroic self-holocaust, involved in its flames buildings and monuments. While tearing to pieces the living body of the proletariat, its rulers must no longer expect to return triumphantly into the intact architecture of their abodes. The government of Versailles cries, 'Incendiarism!' and whispers this cue to all its agents, down to the remotest hamlet, to hunt up its enemies everywhere as suspect of professional incendiarism. The bourgeoisie of the whole world, which looks complacently upon the wholesale massacre after the battle, is convulsed by horror at the desecration of brick and mortar!

When governments give state licences to their navies to 'kill, *burn* and destroy', is that a licence for incendiarism? When the British troops wantonly set fire to the Capitol at Washington and to the summer palace of the Chinese emperor,[91] was that in-

91. British troops fired on the Capitol and the White House in August 1814, during the war of 1812–14. The Summer Palace outside Peking was burned down by English and French troops during the expedition of 1860 to force China to ratify the oppressive treaty of Tsientsin.

cendiarism? When the Prussians, not for military reasons, but out of the mere spite of revenge, burned down, by the help of petroleum, towns like Châteaudun and innumerable villages, was that incendiarism? When Thiers, during six weeks, bombarded Paris, under the pretext that he wanted to set fire to those houses only in which there were people, was that incendiarism? In war, fire is an arm as legitimate as any. Buildings held by the enemy are shelled to set them on fire. If their defenders have to retire, they themselves light the flames to prevent the attack from making use of the buildings. To be burnt down has always been the inevitable fate of all buildings situated in the front of battle of all the regular armies of the world. But in the war of the enslaved against their enslavers, the only justifiable war in history, this is by no means to hold good! The Commune used fire strictly as a means of defence. They used it to stop up to the Versailles troops those long, straight avenues which Haussmann had expressly opened to artillery-fire; they used it to cover their retreat, in the same way as the Versaillais, in their advance, used their shells which destroyed at least as many buildings as the fire of the Commune. It is a matter of dispute, even now, which buildings were set fire to by the defence, and which by the attack. And the defence resorted to fire only then, when the Versaillais troops had already commenced their wholesale murdering of prisoners. Besides, the Commune had, long before, given full public notice that, if driven to extremities, they would bury themselves under the ruins of Paris, and make Paris a second Moscow, as the Government of Defence, but only as a cloak for its treason, had promised to do. For this purpose Trochu had found them the petroleum. The Commune knew that its opponents cared nothing for the lives of the Paris people, but cared much for their own Paris buildings. And Thiers, on the other hand, had given them notice that he would be implacable in his vengeance. No sooner had he got his army ready on one side, and the Prussians shutting up the trap on the other, than he proclaimed: 'I shall be pitiless! The expiation will be complete, and justice will be stern!' If the acts of the Paris working men were vandalism, it was the vandalism of defence in despair, not the vandalism of triumph, like that which the Christians perpetrated upon the really priceless art treasures of heathen antiquity; and even that vandalism has been justified by the historian as an unavoidable and comparatively trifling concomitant to the titanic struggle between a new society arising and an old one breaking down. It was still less the vandalism of Haussmann, razing historic Paris to make place for the Paris of the sightseer!

But the execution by the Commune of the sixty-four hostages, with the Archbishop of Paris at their head! The bourgeoisie and its army, in June 1848, re-established a custom which had long disappeared from the practice of war – the shooting of their defenceless prisoners. This brutal custom has since been more or less strictly adhered to by the suppressors of all popular commotions in Europe and India; thus proving that it constitutes a real 'progress of civilization'! On the other hand, the Prussians, in France, had re-established the practice of taking hostages – innocent men, who, with their lives, were to answer to them for the acts of others. When Thiers, as we have seen, from the very beginning of the conflict, enforced the humane practice of shooting down the Communal prisoners, the Commune, to protect their lives, was obliged to resort to the Prussian practice of securing hostages. The lives of the hostages had been forfeited over and over again by the continued shooting of prisoners on the part of the Versaillais. How could they be spared any longer after the carnage with which MacMahon's praetorians celebrated their entrance into Paris? Was even the last check upon the unscrupulous ferocity of bourgeois governments – the taking of hostages – to be made a mere sham of? The real murderer of Archbishop Darboy is Thiers. The Commune again and again had offered to exchange the archbishop, and ever so many priests in the bargain, against the single Blanqui, then in the hands of Thiers. Thiers obstinately refused. He knew that with Blanqui he would give to the Commune a head; while the archbishop would serve his purpose best in the shape of a corpse. Thiers acted upon the precedent of Cavaignac. How, in June 1848, did not Cavaignac and his men of order raise shouts of horror by stigmatizing the insurgents as the assassins of Archbishop Affre! They knew perfectly well that the archbishop had been shot by the soldiers of order. M. Jacquemet, the archbishop's vicar-general, present on the spot, had immediately afterwards handed them in his evidence to that effect.

All this chorus of calumny, which the party of Order never fail, in their orgies of blood, to raise against their victims, only proves that the bourgeois of our days considers himself the legitimate successor to the baron of old, who thought every weapon in his own hand fair against the plebeian, while in the hands of the plebeian a weapon of any kind constituted in itself a crime.

The conspiracy of the ruling class to break down the revolution by a civil war carried on under the patronage of the foreign invader – a conspiracy which we have traced from the very 4th of September down to the entrance of MacMahon's praetorians through the gate of Saint-Cloud – culminated in the carnage of Paris. Bismarck gloats over the ruins of Paris, in which he saw perhaps the first instalment of that general destruction of great cities he had prayed for when still a simple Rural in the Prussian *chambre introuvable* of 1849.[92] He gloats over the cadavers of the Paris proletariat. For him this is not only the extermination of revolution, but the extinction of France, now decapitated in reality, and by the French government itself. With the shallowness characteristic of all successful statesmen, he sees but the surface of this tremendous historic event. Whenever before has history exhibited the spectacle of a conqueror crowning his victory by turning into, not only the gendarme, but the hired bravo of the conquered government? There existed no war between Prussia and the Commune of Paris. On the contrary, the Commune had accepted the peace preliminaries, and Prussia had announced her neutrality. Prussia was, therefore, no belligerent. She acted the part of a bravo, a cowardly bravo, because incurring no danger; a hired bravo, because stipulating beforehand the payment of her blood-money of 500 millions on the fall of Paris. And thus, at last, came out the true character of the war, ordained by Providence as a chastisement of godless and debauched France by pious and moral Germany! And this unparalleled breach of the law of nations, even as understood by the old-world lawyers, instead of arousing the 'civilized' governments of Europe to declare the felonious Prussian government, the mere tool of the St Petersburg cabinet, an outlaw amongst nations, only incites them to consider whether the few victims who escape the double cordon around Paris are not to be given up to the hangman at Versailles!

That after the most tremendous war of modern times, the conquering and the conquered hosts should fraternize for the common massacre of the proletariat – this unparalleled event does indicate, not, as Bismarck thinks, the final repression of a new society upheaving, but the crumbling into dust of bourgeois society. The highest heroic effort of which old society is still capable is

92. Like the original *Chambre introuvable* of 1815–16 (see p. 880, n. 31), the Prussian Chamber elected in January 1849 was also noted for its arch-reactionary character.

916 The Civil War in France

national war; and this is now proved to be a mere governmental humbug, intended to defer the struggle of classes, and to be thrown aside as soon as that class struggle bursts out into civil war. Class rule is no longer able to disguise itself in a national uniform; the national governments are *one* as against the proletariat!

After Whit Sunday 1871, there can be neither peace nor truce possible between the working men of France and the appropriators of their produce. The iron hand of a mercenary soldiery may keep for a time both classes tied down in common oppression. But the battle must break out again and again in ever-growing dimensions, and there can be no doubt as to who will be the victor in the end – the appropriating few, or the immense working majority. And the French working class is only the advanced guard of the modern proletariat.

While the European governments thus testify, before Paris, to the international character of class rule, they cry down the International Working Men's Association – the international counter-organization of labour against the cosmopolitan conspiracy of capital – as the head fountain of all these disasters. Thiers denounced it as the despot of labour, pretending to be its liberator. Picard ordered that all communications between the French Internationalists and those abroad should be cut off; Count Jaubert,[93] Thiers's mummified accomplice of 1835, declares it the great problem of all civilized governments to weed it out. The Rurals roar against it, and the whole European press joins the chorus. An honourable French writer,[94] completely foreign to our Association, speaks as follows:

> The members of the Central Committee of the National Guard, as well as the greater part of the members of the Commune, are the most active, intelligent, and energetic minds of the International Working Men's Association . . . men who are thoroughly honest, sincere, intelligent, devoted, pure, and fanatical in the *good* sense of the word.

The police-tinged bourgeois mind naturally figures to itself the International Working Men's Association as acting in the manner of a secret conspiracy, its central body ordering, from time to time, explosions in different countries. Our association is, in fact,

93. Hippolyte François, Count Jaubert, served in Thiers's cabinet of 1840 and was a deputy to the National Assembly of 1871.

94. Apparently Jean Robinet, a physician and historian, and a follower of Comte, who attempted to mediate between Versailles and the Commune.

nothing but the international bond between the most advanced working men in the various countries of the civilized world. Wherever, in whatever shape, and under whatever conditions the class struggle obtains any consistency, it is but natural that members of our association should stand in the foreground. The soil out of which it grows is modern society itself. It cannot be stamped out by any amount of carnage. To stamp it out, the governments would have to stamp out the despotism of capital over labour – the condition of their own parasitical existence.

Working men's Paris, with its Commune, will be for ever celebrated as the glorious harbinger of a new society. Its martyrs are enshrined in the great heart of the working class. Its exterminators history has already nailed to that eternal pillory from which all the prayers of their priests will not avail to redeem them.

Notes

I

The column of prisoners halted in the avenue Uhrich, and was drawn up, four or five deep, on the footway facing to the road. General Marquis de Galliffet and his staff dismounted and commenced an inspection from the left of the line. Walking down slowly and eyeing the ranks, the general stopped here and there, tapping a man on the shoulder or beckoning him out of the rear ranks. In most cases, without further parley, the individual thus selected was marched out into the centre of the road, where a small supplementary column was, thus, soon formed . . . It was evident that there was considerable room for error. A mounted officer pointed out to General Galliffet a man and woman for some particular offence. The woman, rushing out of the ranks, threw herself on her knees, and, with outstretched arms, protested her innocence in passionate terms. The general waited for a pause, and then with most impassible face and unmoved demeanour, said, 'Madame, I have visited every theatre in Paris, your acting will have no effect on me' ('*ce n'est pas la peine de jouer la comédie*') . . . It was not a good thing on that day to be noticeably taller, dirtier, cleaner, older, or uglier than one's neighbours. One individual in particular struck me as probably owing his speedy release from the ills of this world to his having a broken nose . . . Over a hundred being thus chosen, a firing party told off, and the column resumed its march, leaving them behind. A few minutes afterwards a dropping fire in our rear commenced, and continued for over a quarter of an hour. It was the execution of these summarily convicted wretches – Paris Correspondent, *Daily News*, 8 June.

This Galliffet, 'the kept man of his wife, so notorious for her shameless exhibitions at the orgies of the Second Empire', went, during the war, by the name of the French 'Ensign Pistol'.

The *Temps* which is a careful journal, and not given to sensation, tells a dreadful story of people imperfectly shot and buried before life was extinct. A great number were buried in the square round Saint Jacques-la-Bouchière; some of them very superficially. In the daytime the roar of the busy streets prevented any notice being taken; but in the stillness of the night the inhabitants of the houses in the neighbourhood were roused by distant moans, and in the morning a clenched hand was seen protruding through the soil. In consequence of this, exhumations were ordered to take place . . . That many wounded have been buried alive I have not the slightest doubt. One case I can vouch for. When Brunel was shot with his mistress on the 24th ult. in the courtyard of a house in the Place Vendôme, the bodies lay there until the afternoon of the 27th. When the burial party came to remove the corpses, they found the woman living still and took her to an ambulance. Though she had received four bullets she is now out of danger – Paris Correspondent, *Evening Standard*, 8 June.

II

The following letter appeared in *The Times* of 13 June:

To the Editor of *The Times*

Sir, On 6 June 1871, M. Jules Favre issued a circular to all the European powers, calling upon them to hunt down the International Working Men's Association. A few remarks will suffice to characterize that document.

In the very preamble of our Statutes it is stated that the International was founded '28 September 1864, at a public meeting held at St Martin's Hall, Long Acre, London'. For purposes of his own Jules Favre puts back the date of its origin behind 1862.

In order to explain our principles, he professes to quote 'their (the International's) sheet of 25 March 1869'. And then what does he quote? The sheet of a society which is not the International. This sort of manoeuvre he already recurred to when, still a comparatively young lawyer, he had to defend the *National* newspaper, prosecuted for libel by Cabet.[95] Then he pretended to read extracts from Cabet's pamphlets while reading interpolations of his own – a trick exposed while the court was sitting, and which, but for the indulgence of Cabet, would have

95. Étienne Cabet was a utopian communist and the author of *Voyage en Icarie* (1839).

been punished by Jules Favre's expulsion from the Paris bar. Of all the documents quoted by him as documents of the International, not one belongs to the International. He says, for instance, ' "The Alliance declares itself Atheist," says the General Council, constituted in London in July 1869'.

The General Council never issued such a document. On the contrary, it issued a document which quashed the original statutes of the 'Alliance' – L'Alliance de la Démocratie Socialiste at Geneva – quoted by Jules Favre.[96]

Throughout his circular, which pretends in part also to be directed against the Empire, Jules Favre repeats against the International but the police inventions of the public prosecutors of the Empire, which broke down miserably even before the law courts of that Empire.

It is known that in its two Addresses (of July and September last) on the late war,[97] the General Council of the International denounced the Prussian plans of conquest against France. Later on, Mr Reitlinger, Jules Favre's private secretary, applied, though of course in vain, to some members of the General Council for getting up by the Council a demonstration against Bismarck, in favour of the Government of National Defence; they were particularly requested not to mention the republic. The preparations for a demonstration with regard to the expected arrival of Jules Favre in London were made – certainly with the best of intentions – in spite of the General Council, which, in its address of 9 September, had distinctly forewarned the Paris workmen against Jules Favre and his colleagues.

What would Jules Favre say if, in its turn, the International were to send a circular on Jules Favre to all the cabinets of Europe, drawing their particular attention to the documents published at Paris by the late M. Millière?[98]

I am, Sir, your obedient servant,

JOHN HALES.[99]
Secretary to the General Council
of the International Working Men's Association

London, 12 June 1871

In an article on 'The International Society and its aims', that pious informer, the London *Spectator* (24 June), amongst other similar tricks, quotes, even more fully than Jules Favre has done, the above document of the 'Alliance' as the work of the Inter-

96. This document was 'The International Working Men's Association and the International Alliance of Socialist Democracy'; see below, pp. 962–4.

97. Above, pp. 856–60 and 863–70.

98. Above, pp. 873–4.

99. This letter was in fact drafted by Marx and Engels.

national, and that eleven days after the refutation had been published in *The Times*. We do not wonder at this. Frederick the Great used to say that of all Jesuits the worst are the Protestant ones.

FIRST DRAFT OF *THE CIVIL WAR IN FRANCE*[1]   [*Extract*]

The Commune

1. Measures for the Working Class

Nightwork of Journeymen Bakers Suppressed (*20 April*). *The private jurisdiction*, usurped by the seigneurs of mills, etc. (manufacturers) (employers, great and small) being at the same time judges, executors, gainers and parties in the disputes, that right of *a penal code of their own*, enabling them to rob the labourers' wages by fines and deductions as punishment etc., abolished in public and private workshops; penalties impended upon the employers in case they infringe upon this law; *fines and deductions* extorted since 18 March to be paid back to the workmen (*27 April*). Sale of pawned articles at pawnshops suspended (*29 March*).

A great lot of workshops and manufactories have been closed in Paris, their owners having run away. This is the old method of the industrial capitalists, who consider themselves entitled 'by the spontaneous action of the laws of political economy' not only to make a profit out of labour, as the condition of labour, but to stop it altogether and throw the workmen on the pavement – to produce an artificial crisis whenever a victorious revolution threatens the 'order' of their 'system'. The Commune, very wisely, has appointed a Communal commission which, in cooperation with delegates chosen by the different trades, will inquire into the ways of handing over the deserted workshops and manufactories to cooperative workmen's societies with some indemnity for the capitalist

1. This text is a section of Marx's original draft of *The Civil War in France*, roughly corresponding to section III of the published version. It is reproduced here from the *Archiv Marksa i Engelsa* edited by Adoratsky, vol. III (VIII), Moscow, 1934. Adoratsky's text sticks very close to Marx's manuscript, which is in extremely unpolished and often ungrammatical English, with a lot of French words interspersed, and the present version has been somewhat edited in the interest of greater clarity. See p. 717, n. 58.

deserters (*16 April*); (this commission has also to make statistics of the abandoned workshops).

The Commune has given order to the *mairies*[2] to make no distinction between the wives called illegitimate, the mothers and widows of National Guards, as to the indemnity of seventy-five centimes.[3]

The public prostitutes till now kept for the 'men of order' at Paris, but for their 'safety' kept in personal servitude under the arbitrary rule of the police – the Commune has liberated the prostitutes from this degrading slavery, but swept away the soil upon which, and the men by whom, prostitution flourishes. The higher prostitutes – the *cocottes* – were of course, under the rule of order, not the slaves, but the masters of the police and the governors.

There was, of course, no time to reorganize public instruction (education); but by removing the religious and clerical element from it, the Commune has taken the initiative in the mental emancipation of the people. It has appointed a commission for the organization of education (primary – elementary – and professional) (*28 April*). It has ordered that all tools of instruction, like books, maps, paper, etc. be given gratuitously by the schoolmasters who receive them in their turn from the respective *mairies* to which they belong. No schoolmaster is allowed on any pretext to ask payment from his pupils for these instruments of instruction (*28 April*).

Pawnshops. All pawn tickets issued by the Mont-de-Piété[4] prior to 25 April 1871, pledging articles of clothing, furniture, linen, books, bedding and instruments of labour valued at not more than 20 francs, may be redeemed free of charge as from 12 May (*7 May*).

2. Measures for the Working Class, but Mostly for the Middle Classes

House-Rent for the Last Three Quarters up to April Wholly

2. The town halls of the *arrondissements* into which Paris is divided.
3. The significance of 'seventy-five centimes' is unclear. This seems to be a reference to the Commune's decree of 10 April, which granted a pension of 600 francs p.a. to the widows of National Guards killed in defence of the Commune, whether they were married or not – a very important point among the nineteenth-century Parisian working class. Widows were also entitled to 365 francs p.a. for each child under eighteen.
4. The Mont-de-Piété was a municipal pawnshop with several branches.

Remitted. Whoever had paid any of these three quarters shall have right of setting that sum against future payments. The same law to prevail in the case of furnished apartments. No notice to quit coming from landlords to be valid for three months to come (*29 March*).

Échéances. Payment of bills of exchange due (*expiration of bills*): all prosecutions for bills of exchange fallen due suspended (*12 April*).

All commercial papers of that sort to be repaid in (repayments spread over) two years, to begin 15 July next, the debt being not chargeable with interest. The total amount of the sums due divided in eight *equal instalments payable quarterly* (first quarter to be dated from *15 July*). Only on these partial payments when fallen due judicial prosecutions permitted (*16 April*). The Dufaure laws[5] on leases and bills of exchange entailed the bankruptcy of the majority of the respectable shopkeepers of Paris.

The notaries, bailiffs, auctioneers, bum-bailiffs and other judicial officers making till now a fortune of their functions, transformed into agents of the Commune receiving from it fixed salaries like other workmen.

As the professors of the École de Médecine have run away, the Commune appointed a commission for the foundation of *free universities*, no longer state parasites; given to the students that had passed their examination, means to practise independent of doctoral titles (titles to be conferred by the faculty).

Since the judges of the *Civil Tribunal of the Seine*, like the other magistrates always ready to function under any class government, had run away, the Commune appointed an advocate to do the most urgent business until the reorganization of tribunals on the basis of general suffrage (*26 April*).

3. General Measures

Conscription Abolished. In the present war every able man (National Guard) must serve. This measure excellent to get rid of all traitors and cowards hiding in Paris (*29 March*).

Games of Hazard Suppressed (*2 April*). Church separated from state; the religious budget suppressed; all clerical estates declared

5. See p. 881, n. 34.

national properties (*3 April*). The Commune, having made inquiries consequent upon private information, found that besides the old guillotine the '*government of order*' had commanded the construction of a new guillotine (more expeditious and portable) and paid in advance. The Commune ordered both the old and the new guillotines to be burned publicly on 6 April. The Versailles journals, re-echoed by the press of order all over the world, narrated that the Paris people, as a demonstration against the bloodthirstiness of the Communards, had burnt these guillotines! (*6 April*). All political prisoners were set free at once after the revolution of 18 March. But the Commune knew that under the regime of L. Bonaparte and his worthy successor the Government of Defence, many people were simply incarcerated on no charge whatever as political suspects. Consequently it charged one of its members – Protot[6] – to make inquiries. By him 150 people were set free who, being arrested six months before, had not yet undergone any judicial examination; many of them, already arrested under Bonaparte, had been for a year in prison without any charge or judicial examination (*9 April*). This fact, so characteristic of the Government of Defence, enraged them. They asserted that the Commune had liberated all felons. But who liberated convicted felons? The forger Jules Favre. Hardly got into power, he hastened to liberate Pic and Taillefer, condemned for theft and forgery in the affaire of the *Étendard*.[7] One of these men, Taillefer, daring to return to Paris, has been reinstated in his convenient abode. But this is not all. The Versailles government has delivered, in the Maisons Centrales[8] all over France, convicted thieves on the condition of entering M. Thiers's army.

Decree on the Demolition of the Column of the Place Vendôme. As 'a monument of barbarism, symbol of brute force and false glory, an affirmation of militarism, a negation of international right' (*12 April*).[9]

Election of Frankel[10] (German member of the International) to the Commune declared valid: 'considering that the flag of the Commune is that of the Universal Republic and that foreigners

6. Eugène Protot was a lawyer, doctor and journalist, a right-wing Blanquist and a member of the justice commission of the Paris Commune.
7. See p. 874, n. 11.   8. Prisons.
9. See p. 901, n. 72.   10. See p. 901, n. 70.

can have a seat in it' (*4 April*); Frankel afterwards chosen a member of the executive of the Commune (*21 April*).

The *Journal officiel* has inaugurated the publicity of the sittings of the Commune (*15 April*).

Decree of Pascal Grousset[11] for the protection of foreigners against requisitions. Never a government in Paris so courteous to foreigners (*27 April*).

The Commune has abolished political and professional oaths (*27 April*).

Destruction of the monument known as 'Chapelle expiatoire de Louis XVI'[12], rue d'Anjoy St Thérèse (the work of the *Chambre introuvable* of 1816) (*7 May*).

4. Measures of Public Safety

Disarmament of the 'loyal' National Guards (*30 March*); Commune declares incompatibility between seats in its ranks and at Versailles (*29 March*).

Decree of Reprisals. Never executed.[13] Only the fellows arrested, *Archbishop of Paris and Curé of the Madeleine*; whole staff of the college of Jesuits; incumbents of all the principal churches; *part of these fellows arrested* as hostages, part as conspirators with Versailles, part because they tried to save church property from the clutches of the Commune (*6 April*). 'The monarchists wage war like savages; they shoot prisoners, they murder the wounded, they fire on ambulances, troops raise the butt-end of their rifles in the air and then fire traitorously' (*Proclamation of Commune*).

In regard to these decrees of reprisals to be remarked:
    In the first instance men of all layers of the Paris society – after the exodus of the capitalists, the idlers and the parasites – have interposed at Versailles to stop the civil war – *except the Paris*

11. Pascal Grousset, a Blanquist, was chairman of the Commune's foreign relations commission.
12. Chapel of atonement for Louis XVI (i.e. for his execution by the French revolutionary Convention).
13. After Marx wrote this draft, during the last days of the Commune's resistance, 64 hostages were executed by order of the Committee of Public Safety (see above, pp. 716 and 914).

clergy. The Archbishop and the Curé of the Madeleine have only written to Thiers because averse to '*the effusion of their own blood,*' in their quality as hostages.

Secondly: after the publication by the Commune of the decree of reprisal, the taking of hostages etc., the atrocious treatment of the Versailles prisoners by Piétri's lambs[14] and Valentin's gendarmes did not cease, but the assassination of the captive Paris soldiers and National Guard was stopped, to set in with renewed fury as soon as the Versailles government had convinced itself that the Commune was too humane to execute its decree of 6 April. Then the assassination set in again wholesale. The Commune did not execute one hostage, not one prisoner, not even some gendarme officers who under the disguise of National Guard had entered Paris as spies and were simply arrested.

Surprise of the Redoubt of Clamart (2 May). Railway station in the hands of the Parisians, massacre, bayonetting, the 22nd battalion of Chasseurs (*Galliffet?*) shoots line soldiers offhand without any formality (*2 May*). *Redoubt of Moulin Saquet,* situated between Fort Issy and Montrouge, surprised in the night by treachery on the part of the commandant *Gallien* who had sold the password to the *Versaillaise* troops. Federals surprised in their beds asleep, great part of them massacred (*4 May?*).

25 April. Four National Guards (this established by commissaries sent to Bicêtre where the only survivor of the four men, at Belle Epine, near Villejuif. His name *Scheffer*). These men being surrounded by horse Chasseurs, on their order, unable to resist, surrendered, disarmed, nothing done to them by the soldiers. But then arrives the captain of the Chasseurs, and shoots them down one after the other with his revolver. Left there on the soil. Scheffer, fearfully wounded, survived.

Thirteen soldiers of the line made prisoners at the railway station of Clamart were shot offhand, and all prisoners wearing the line uniforms who arrive in Versailles will be executed whenever doubts about their identity are cleared up. (*Liberté* at Versailles.) Alexander Dumas *fils,* now at Versailles, tells that a young man exercising the functions, if not bearing the title, of a general, was shot, by order of a Bonapartist general, after having [been]

14. An ironic reference to the *sergents de ville* trained by Piétri as prefect of police in Paris (1866–70).

marched in custody a few hundred yards along a road. Parisian troops and National Guards surrounded in houses by gendarmes, who inundate the house with petroleum and then fire it. Some cadavers of National Guards burnt to ashes have been transported by the ambulance of the press of the Ternes (*Mot d'ordre, 20 April*). 'They have no right to ambulances'.

Thiers. Blanqui. Archbishop. General Chanzy.[15] (Thiers said his Bonapartists should have liked to be shot.)

Visitation in Houses, etc. Casimir Bouis[16] named chairman of a commission of inquiry into the doings of the dictators of 4 September (*14 April*). Private houses invaded and papers seized, but no furniture has been carried away and sold by auction. (Papers of the fellows of 4 September, Thiers, etc. and Bonapartist policemen in the house of Lafont, inspector-general of prisons) (*11 April*). The houses (properties) of Thiers and Co. invaded as traitors, but *only the papers* confiscated.

Arrests among Themselves. This shocks the bourgeois who wants political idols and 'great men' immensely.

'It is *provoking* (*Daily News, 6 May.* Paris Correspondence), however, and *discouraging*, that whatever be the authority possessed by the Commune, it is continually changing hands, and we know not today with whom the power may rest tomorrow . . . In all these eternal changes one sees more than ever the want of a presiding hand. The Commune is a concourse of equivalent atoms, each one jealous of another and *none endowed with supreme control over the others*'.

Suppression of newspapers!

5. Financial Measures

See Daily News, 6 May.
Principal outlay for war!
    Only 8928 francs from seizures – all taken from ecclesiastics, etc.

Vengeur, 6 May.

15. Antoine Chanzy, a general and a deputy in the 1871 National Assembly, was taken hostage by the Commune, but released when the Versailles troops temporarily withdrew.
16. Casimir Bouis was a Blanquist member of the Commune.

The Commune: The Rise of the Commune and the Central Committee

The Commune had been proclaimed at Lyons, then Marseilles, Toulouse, etc., after Sedan. Gambetta tried his best to break it down.[17]

The different movements at Paris in the beginning of October aimed at the establishment of the Commune, as a measure of defence against the foreign invasion, as the realization of the rise of 4 September. Its establishment by the movement of 31 October[18] failed only because Blanqui, Flourens and the other then leaders of the movement believed in the men of their word who had given their word of honour to abdicate and make room for a Commune freely elected by all the *arrondissements* of Paris. It failed because they saved the lives of those men so eager for the assassination of their saviours. Having allowed Trochu and Ferry to escape, they were surprised by Trochu's Bretons. It ought to be remembered that on 31 October the self-imposed 'Government of Defence' existed only on sufferance. It had not yet gone even through the farce of a plebiscite.[19] Under the circumstances, there was of course nothing easier than to misrepresent the character of the movement, to decry it as a treasonable conspiracy with the Prussians, to improve [?] the dismissal of the only man amongst them who would not break his word,[20] to strengthen Trochu's Bretons who were for the Government of Defence what the Corsican bravos had been for L. Bonaparte by the appointment of Clément Thomas as commander-in-chief of the National Guard; there was nothing easier for these old panic-mongers [than] – appealing to the cowardly fears of the middle class [towards] working[-class] battalions who had taken the initiative, throwing distrust and dissension amongst the working[-class] battalions themselves, by an appeal to patriotism – to create one of those days of blind reaction and disastrous misunderstandings by which they have

17. The Communard risings of October–November 1870 in the south of France were crushed by the Government of Defence after a few days.

18. See pp. 885–6.

19. After the crisis of 31 October, the Government of Defence attempted to retrieve the initiative by holding a plebiscite on 3 November; it succeeded in gaining a majority by demagogy and police pressure.

20. General François Tamisier; see above, p. 886.

always contrived to maintain their usurped power. As they had slipped into power on 4 September by a surprise, they were now enabled to give it a mock sanction by a plebiscite of the true Bonapartist pattern during days of reactionary terror.

The victorious establishment in Paris of the Commune at the beginning of November 1870 (then already initiated in the great cities of the country and sure to be imitated all over France) would not only have taken the defence out of the hands of traitors, and imprinted its enthusiasm on it as the present heroic war of Paris shows, it would have altogether changed the character of the war. It would have become the war of republican France, hoisting the flag of the social revolution of the nineteenth century, against Prussia, the banner-bearer of conquest and counter-revolution. Instead of sending the hackneyed old intriguer[21] a-begging at all courts of Europe, it would have electrified the producing masses in the old and the new world. By juggling away the Commune on 31 October, Jules Favre and Co. secured the capitulation of France to Prussia and initiated the present civil war.

But this much is shown: the revolution of 4 September was not only the reinstalment of the republic, because the place of the usurper had become vacant by his capitulation at Sedan, it not only conquered that republic from the foreign invader by the prolonged resistance of Paris although fighting under the leadership of its enemies – that revolution was working its way into the heart of the working classes. The republic had ceased to be a name for a thing of the past. It was impregnated with a new world. Its real tendency, veiled from the eye of the world through the deceptions, the lies and the vulgarizing of a pack of intriguing lawyers and word fencers, came again and again to the surface in the spasmodic movements of the Paris working classes (and the south of France) whose watchword was always the same, the *Commune*!

The Commune – the positive form of the revolution against the Empire and the conditions of its existence – first essayed in the cities of southern France, again and again proclaimed in spasmodic movements during the siege of Paris and juggled away by the sleight of hand of the Government of Defence and the Bretons of Trochu, the 'plan of capitulation' hero – was at last victoriously installed on 26 March, but it had not suddenly sprung into life on that day. It was the unchangeable goal of the workmen's

21. Thiers; see above, p. 872.

revolution. The capitulation of Paris, the open conspiracy against the republic at Bordeaux, the coup d'état initiated by the nocturnal attack on Montmartre, rallied around it all the living elements of Paris, no longer allowing the Defence men to limit it to the insulated efforts of the most conscious and revolutionary portions of the Paris working class.

The Government of Defence was only undergone as a makeshift of the first surprise, a necessity of the war. The true answer of the Paris people to the Second Empire, the empire of lies – was the Commune.

Thus also the rising of all living Paris – with the exception of the pillars of Bonapartism and its official opposition, the great capitalists, the financial jobbers, the sharpers, the loungers, and the old state parasites – against the Government of Defence does not date from 18 March, although it conquered on that day its first victory against the conspiration, it dates from 31 January,[22] from the very day of the capitulation. The National Guard – that is all the armed manhood of Paris – organized itself and really ruled Paris from that day, independently of the usurpatory government of the *capitulards* installed by the grace of Bismarck. It refused to deliver its arms and artillery, which were its property, and only left them in the capitulation because of its property. It was not the magnanimity of Jules Favre that saved these arms from Bismarck, but the readiness of armed Paris to fight for its arms against Jules Favre and Bismarck. In view of the foreign invader and the peace negotiations, Paris would not complicate the situation. It was afraid of civil war. It observed a mere attitude of defence and content with the *de facto* self-rule of Paris. But it organized itself quietly and steadfastly for resistance. Even in the terms of the capitulation itself the *capitulards* had unmistakably shown their tendency to make the surrender to Prussia at the same time the means of their domination over Paris. The only concession by Prussia they insisted upon, a concession which Bismarck would have imposed upon them as a condition, if they had not begged it as a concession – was 40,000 soldiers for subduing Paris. In the face of its 300,000 National Guards – more than sufficient for securing Paris from an attempt by the foreign enemy, and for the defence of its internal order – the demand of these 40,000 men – a thing which was besides avowed – could have no other purpose.

22. The armistice was in fact signed on 28 January; see above, p. 872, n. 5.

On its existing military organization it grafted a political federation according to a very simple plan. It was the alliance of all the National Guard, put in connection the one with the other *by the delegates* of each company, appointing in their turn the delegates of the battalions, who in their turn appointed general delegates, generals of legions, who were to represent an *arrondissement* and to cooperate with the delegates of the nineteen other *arrondissements*. Those twenty delegates, chosen by the majority of the battalions of the National Guard, composed the Central Committee, which on 18 March initiated the greatest revolution of this century and still holds its post in the present glorious struggle of Paris. Never were elections more sifted, never delegates fuller representing the masses from which they had sprung. To the objection of the outsiders that they were unknown – in point of fact, that they only were known to the working classes, but no old stagers, no men illustrious by the infamies of their past, by their chase after pelf and place – they proudly answered, 'So were the twelve apostles', and they answered by their deeds.

The Character of the Commune

The centralized state machinery which, with its ubiquitous and complicated military, bureaucratic, clerical and judiciary organs, entoils (enmeshes) the living civil society like a boa constrictor, was first forged in the days of absolute monarchy as a weapon of nascent modern society in its struggle of emancipation from feudalism. The seignorial privileges of the medieval lords and cities and clergy were transformed into the attributes of a unitary state power, displacing the feudal dignitaries by salaried state functionaries, transferring the arms from medieval retainers of the landlords and the corporations of townish citizens to a standing army; substituting for the checkered (parti-coloured) anarchy of conflicting medieval powers the regulated plan of a state power, with a systematic and hierarchic division of labour. The first French revolution with its task to found national unity (to create a nation) had to break down all local, territorial, townish and provincial independence. It was, therefore, forced to develop what absolute monarchy had commenced, the centralization and organization of state power, and to expand the circumference and the attributes of the state power, the number of its tools, its independence, and its supernaturalist sway over real society which in fact took the place of the medieval supernaturalist heaven, with its saints. Every minor solitary interest engendered by the relations of social groups was separated from society itself, fixed and made independent of it and opposed to it in the form of state interest, administered by state priests with exactly determined hierarchical functions.

This parasitical [excrescence upon] civil society, pretending to be its ideal counterpart, grew to its full development under the sway of the first Bonaparte. The Restoration and the monarchy of July [1830] added nothing to it but a greater division of labour, growing at the same measure in which the division of labour within civil society created new groups of interests, and therefore new material for state action. In their struggle against the revolution of 1848, the parliamentary republic of France and the governments of all continental Europe were forced to strengthen, with their measures of repression against the popular movement, the means of action and the centralization of that governmental power. All revolutions thus only perfected the state machinery instead of throwing off this deadening incubus. The fractions and parties of the ruling classes which alternately struggled for supremacy, considered the occupancy (control) (seizure) and the direction of this immense machinery of government as the main booty of the victor. It centred in the creation of immense standing armies, a host of state vermin, and huge national debts. During the time of the absolute monarchy it was a means of the struggle of modern society against feudalism, crowned by the French revolution, and under the first Bonaparte it served not only to subjugate the revolution and annihilate all popular liberties, it was an instrument of the French revolution to strike abroad, to create for France on the Continent, instead of feudal monarchies, more or less states after the image of France. Under the Restoration and the monarchy of July it became not only a means of the forcible class domination of the middle class, and a means of adding to the direct economic exploitation a second exploitation of the people by assuring to their families all the rich places of the state household. During the time of the revolutionary struggle of 1848 at last it served as a means of annihilating that revolution and all aspirations at the emancipation of the popular masses. But the state parasite received only its last development during the Second Empire. The governmental power with its standing army, its all-directing bureaucracy, its stultifying clergy and its servile tribunal hierarchy had grown so independent of society itself that a grotesquely mediocre adventurer with a hungry band of desperadoes behind him sufficed to wield it. It did no longer want the pretext of an armed coalition of old Europe against the modern world founded by the revolution of 1789. It appeared no longer as a means of class domination, subordinate to its parliamentary ministry or legislature. Humbling under its sway even the interests of the ruling classes, whose parliamentary show work it supplanted by self-elected Corps Législatifs and self-paid Senates,[23] sanctioned in its absolute sway by universal suffrage, the acknowledged necessity for keeping up 'order', that is the rule of the landowner and the capitalist over the producer, cloaking under the tatters of a masquerade of the past, the orgies of the corruption of the present and the victory of the most parasite fraction, the financial swindler, the *debauchery* of all the reactionary influences of the past let loose – a pandemonium of infamies – the state power had received its last and supreme expression in the Second Empire. Apparently the final victory of this governmental power over society, it was in fact the orgy of all the corrupt elements of that society. To the eye of the uninitiated it appeared only as the victory of the executive over the legislative, of the final defeat of the form of class rule pretending to be the autocracy of society by its form pretending to be a superior power to society. But in fact it was only the last degraded and the only possible form of that class ruling, as humiliating to those classes themselves as to the working classes which they kept fettered by it.

4 September was only the revindication of the republic against the grotesque adventurer that had assassinated it. The true antithesis to the *Empire itself* – that is to the state power, the centralized executive, of which the Second Empire was only the exhausting formula – was *the Commune*. This state power forms in fact the creation of the middle class, first a means to break down feudal-

---

23. The legislature of the Second Empire comprised the Corps Législatif (Legislative Body) and the Senate. The Corps Législatif was elected by universal male suffrage, but besides the absence of freedom of the press, association and assembly, and frequent police terrorism against the opposition, the Bonapartist regime constantly manipulated the elections. The Senate was partly elected, and partly consisted of government functionaries sitting *ex officio*.

ism, then a means to crush the emancipatory aspirations of the producers, of the working class. All reactions and all revolutions had only served to transfer that organized power – that organized force of the slavery of labour – from one hand to the other, from one fraction of the ruling classes to the other. It had served the ruling classes as a means of subjugation and of pelf. It had sucked new forces from every new change. It had served as the instrument of breaking down every popular rise and served it to crush the working classes after they had fought and been ordered to secure its transfer from one part of its oppressors to the others. This was, therefore, a revolution not against this or that Legitimate, Constitutional, Republican or Imperialist form of state power. It was a revolution against the *state* itself, this supernaturalist abortion of society, a resumption by the people for the people of its own social life. It was not a revolution to transfer it from one fraction of the ruling classes to the other, but a revolution to break down this horrid machinery of class domination itself. It was not one of those dwarfish struggles between the executive and the parliamentary forms of class domination, but a revolt against both these forms, integrating each other, and of which the parliamentary form was only the deceitful by-work of the executive. The Second Empire was the final form of this state usurpation. The Commune was its definite negation, and, therefore, the initiation of the social revolution of the nineteenth century. Whatever therefore its fate at Paris, it will make its way round the world. It was at once acclaimed by the working class of Europe and the United States as the magic word of delivery. The glories and the antediluvian deeds of the Prussian conqueror seemed only hallucinations of a bygone past.

It was only the working class that could formulate by the word 'Commune' – and initiate by the fighting Commune of Paris – this new aspiration. Even the last expression of that state power in the Second Empire, although humbling for the pride of the ruling classes and casting to the winds their parliamentary pretensions of self-government, had been only the last possible form of their class rule. While politically dispossessing them, it was the orgy under which all the economic and social infamies of their regime got full sway. The middling bourgeoisie and the petty middle class were by their economical conditions of life excluded from initiating a new revolution and induced to follow in the track of the ruling classes or be the followers of the working class. The peasants were the passive economical basis of the Second Empire, of that last triumph of a *state* separate of and independent from society. Only the proletarians, fired by a new social task to accomplish by them for all society, to do away with all classes and class rule, were the men to break the instrument of that class rule – the state, the centralized and organized governmental power usurping to be the master instead of the servant of society. In the active struggle against them by the ruling classes, supported by the passive adherence of the peasantry, the Second Empire, the last crowning at the same time as the most signal prostitution of the state – which had taken the place of the medieval church – had been engendered. It had sprung into life against them. By them it was broken, not as a peculiar form of governmental (centralized) power, but as its most powerful, elaborated into seeming independence from society, expression, and, therefore, also its most prostitute reality, covered by infamy from top to bottom, having centred in absolute corruption at home and absolute powerlessness abroad.

But this one form of class rule had only broken down to make the executive, the governmental state machinery, the great and single object of attack to the revolution.

Parliamentarism in France had come to an end. Its last term and fullest sway was the parliamentary republic from May 1848 to the coup d'état. The Empire that killed it was its own creation. Under the Empire with its Corps Législatif and its Senate – in this form it has been reproduced in the military monarchies of Prussia and Austria – it had been a mere farce, a mere by-word for despotism in its crudest form. Parliamentarism then was dead in France, and the workmen's revolution certainly was not to awaken it from this death.

The *Commune* – the reabsorption of the state power by society as its own living forces instead of as forces controlling and subduing it, by the popular masses themselves, forming their own force instead of the organized force of their suppression – the political form of their social emancipation, instead of the artificial force (appropriated by their oppressors) (their own force opposed to and organized against them) of society wielded for their oppression by their enemies. The form was simple, like all great things. The reaction of former revolutions – the time wanted for all historical developments, and in the past always lost in all revolutions, in the very days of popular triumph, whenever it had rendered its victorious arms, to be turned against itself – first by displacing the army by the National Guard. 'For the first time since 4 September the republic is liberated from the *government of its enemies* . . . to the city a national militia that defends the citizens against the power (the government) *instead of a permanent army that defends the government* against the citizens'. (Proclamation of Central Committee of 22 March.) (The people had only to organize this militia on a national scale, to have done away with the standing armies; the first economical condition *sine qua non* for all social improvements, discarding at once this source of taxes and state debt, and this constant danger to government usurpation of class rule – of the regular class rule or an adventurer pretending to save all classes); at the same time the safest guarantee against foreign aggression and making in fact the costly military apparatus impossible in all other states; the emancipation of the peasant from the blood-tax and [from being] the most fertile source of all state taxation and state debts. Here already the point in which the Commune is a *luck for the peasant*, the first word of his emancipation. With the 'independent police' abolished, and its ruffians supplanted by servants of the Commune. The general suffrage, till now abused either for the parliamentary sanction of the Holy State Power, or a play in the hands of the ruling classes, only employed by the people to sanction (choose the instruments of) parliamentary class rule once in many years, adapted to its real purposes, to choose by the communes their own functionaries of administration and initiation. The delusion as if administration and political governing were mysteries, transcendent functions only to be trusted to the hands of a trained caste – state parasites, richly paid sycophants and sinecurists, in the higher posts, absorbing the intelligence of the masses and turning them against themselves in the lower places of the hierarchy. Doing away with the state hierarchy altogether and replacing the haughty masters of the people by always removable servants, a mock responsibility by a real responsibility, as they act continuously under public supervision. Paid like skilled workmen, £12 a month, the highest salary not exceeding £240 a year, a salary somewhat more than a fifth, according to a great scientific authority, Professor Huxley, [of that needed] to satisfy a clerk for the Metropolitan School Board. The whole sham of state mysteries and state pretensions was done away with by a Commune, mostly consisting of simple working men, organizing the defence of Paris, carrying war against the praetorians of Bonaparte, securing the supplies for that immense town, filling all the posts hitherto divided between government, police, and prefecture, doing their work publicly, simply, under the most difficult and complicated circumstances, and doing it, as Milton did his *Paradise Lost*, for a few pounds, acting in bright daylight, with no pretensions to infallibility, not hiding itself behind circumlocution offices, not ashamed to confess blunders by correcting them. Making in one order the public functions – military, administrative, political – *real workmen's functions*, instead of the hidden attributes of a trained caste; (keeping order in the turbulence of civil war and revolution) (initiating measures of general regeneration). Whatever the merits of the single measures of the Commune, its greatest measure was its own organization, extemporized with the foreign enemy at one door, and the class enemy at the other, proving by its life its vitality, confirming its thesis by its action. Its appearance was a victory over the victors of France. Captive Paris resumed by one bold spring the leadership of Europe, not depending on brute force, but by taking the lead of the social movement, by giving body to the aspirations of the working class of all countries.

With all the great towns organized into communes after the model of Paris, no government could have repressed the movement by the surprise of sudden reaction. Even by this preparatory step the time of incubation, the guarantee of the movement [would have been won]. All France organized into self-working and self-governing communes, the standing army replaced by the popular militias, the army of state parasites removed, the clerical hierarchy displaced by the schoolmaster, the state judges transformed into Communal organs, the suffrage for the national representation not a matter of sleight of hand for an all-powerful government but the deliberate expression of organized communes, the state functions reduced to a few functions for general national purposes.

   Such is the *Commune – the political form of the social emancipation*, of the liberation of labour from the usurpations (slave-holding) of the monopolists of the means of labour, created by the labourers themselves or forming the gift of nature. As the state machinery and parliamentarism are not the real life of the ruling classes, but only the organized general organs of their dominion, the political guarantees and forms and expressions of the old order of things, so the Commune is not the social movement of the working class and therefore of a general regeneration of mankind, but the organized means of action. The Commune does not do away with the class struggles, through which the working classes strive to the abolition of all classes and, therefore, of all [class rule] (because it does not represent a peculiar interest. It represents the liberation of 'labour', that is the fundamental and natural condition of individual and social life which only by usurpation, fraud, and artificial contrivances can be shifted from the few upon the many), but it affords the rational medium in which that class struggle can run through its different phases in the most rational and humane way. It could start violent reactions and as violent revolutions. It begins the *emancipation of labour* – its great goal – by doing away with the unproductive and mischievous work of the state parasites, by cutting away the springs which sacrifice an immense portion of the national produce to the feeding of the state monster on the one side, by doing, on the other, the real work of administration, local and national, for workingmen's wages. It begins therefore with an immense saving, with economical reform as well as political transformation.

The Communal organization once firmly established on a national scale, the catastrophes it might still have to undergo would be sporadic slaveholders' insurrections, which, while for a moment interrupting the work of peaceful progress, would only accelerate the movement, by putting the sword into the hand of the social revolution.

The working class know that they have to pass through different phases of class struggle. They know that the superseding of the economical conditions of the slavery of labour by the conditions of free and associated labour can only be the progressive work of time (that economical transformation), that they require not only a change of distribution, but a new organization of production, or rather the delivery (setting free) of the social forms of production in present organized labour (engendered by present industry), of the trammels of slavery, of their present class character, and their harmonious national and international coordination. They know that this work of regeneration will be again and again relented and impeded by the resistance of vested interests and class egotisms. They know that the present 'spontaneous action of the natural laws of capital and landed property' – can only be superseded by 'the spontaneous action of the laws of the social economy of free and associated labour' by a long process of development of new conditions, as was the 'spontaneous action of the economic laws of slavery' and the 'spontaneous action of the economic laws of serfdom'. But they know at the same time that great strides may be [made] at once through the Communal form of political organization and that the time has come to begin that movement for themselves and mankind.

Peasantry

(*War indemnity*.) Even before the instalment of the Commune, the Central Committee had declared through its *Journal officiel*: '*The greater part of the war indemnity should be paid by the authors of war*'. This is the great 'conspiracy against civilization' the men of order are most afraid of. This is the most practical question. With the Commune victorious, the authors of the war will have to pay its indemnity; with Versailles victorious, the producing masses who have already paid in blood, ruin, and contribution, will have again to pay, and the financial dignitaries will even contrive to make a profit out of the transaction. The liquidation of the war costs is to be decided by the civil war. The Commune represents on this vital point not only the interests of the working class, the petty middle class, in fact, all the middle class with the exception of the *bourgeoisie* (the wealthy capitalists) (the rich landowners, and their state parasites). It represents above all the interest of the *French peasantry*. On them the greater part of the war taxes will be shifted, if Thiers and his 'Rurals' are victorious. And people are silly enough to repeat the cry of the 'Rurals' that they – the great landed proprietors – 'represent the peasant', who is of course, in the naivety of his soul, exceedingly anxious to pay for these good 'landowners' the milliards of the war indemnity, who made him already pay the milliard of indemnity: the revolution indemnity.[24]

The same men deliberately compromised the republic of February [1848] by the additional 45 centimes tax on the peasant,[25] but this they did in the name of the revolution, in the name of the 'Provisional Government' created by it. It is now in their own

24. See p. 899, n. 65. On the 'Rurals' see above, pp. 879–80.
25. See 'The Class Struggles in France', above, p. 385.

name that they wage a civil war against the Communal republic to shift the war indemnity from their own shoulders upon those of the peasant! He will of course be delighted by it!

The Commune will abolish conscription, the party of Order will fasten this blood-tax on the peasant. The party of Order will fasten upon him the tax-collector for the payment of a parasitical and costly state machinery, the Commune will give him a cheap government. The party of Order will continue to grind him down by the townish usurer, the Commune will free him of the incubus of the mortgages resting upon his plot of land. The Commune will replace the parasitical judiciary body eating the heart of his income – the notary, the bailiff, etc. – by Communal agents doing their work at workmen's salaries, instead of enriching themselves out of the peasant's work. It will break down this whole judiciary cobweb which entangles the French peasant and gives abodes to the judiciary bench and mayors of the bourgeois spiders that suck its blood! The party of Order will keep him under the rule of the gendarme, the Commune will restore him to independent social and political life! The Commune will enlighten him by the rule of the schoolmaster, the party of Order force upon him the stultification by the rule of the priest! But the French peasant is above all a man of reckoning! He will find it exceedingly reasonable that the payment of the clergy will no longer be exacted from him by the tax-collector, but will be left to the 'spontaneous action' of his religious instinct!

The French peasant had elected Louis Bonaparte President of the Republic, but the party of Order (during the anonymous regime of the republic under the Constituent and the Legislative Assemblies) was the creator of the Empire! What the French peasant really wants, he commenced to show in 1849 and 1852 by opposing his mayor to the government's prefect, his schoolmaster to the government's parson, himself to the government's gendarme! The nucleus of the reactionary laws of the party of Order in 1849 – and peculiarly in January and February 1850 – were specifically directed against the French peasantry! If the French peasant had made Louis Bonaparte President of the Republic because in his tradition all the benefits he had derived from the first revolution were fantastically transferred on the first Napoleon, the armed risings of peasants in some departments of France and the gendarme hunting upon them after the coup d'état proved that that delusion was rapidly breaking down! The Empire was founded on the delusions artificially nourished into power and traditional prejudices, the Commune would be founded on his living interests and his real wants.

The hatred of the French peasant is centring on the 'Rurals', the men of the *châteaux*, the men of the milliard of indemnity, and the townish capitalists masqueraded into landed proprietors, whose encroachment upon him marched never more rapidly than under the Second Empire, partly fostered by artificial state means, partly naturally growing out of the very development of modern agriculture. The 'Rurals' know that three months' rule of the republican Commune in France would be the signal for the rising of the peasantry and the agricultural proletariat against them. Hence their ferocious hatred of the Commune! What they fear even more than the emancipation of the townish proletariat is the emancipation of the peasants. The peasants would soon acclaim the townish proletariat as their own leaders and seniors. There exists of course in France as in most continental countries a deep antagonism between the townish and rural producers, between the industrial proletariat and the peasantry. The aspirations of the proletariat, the material basis of its movement, is labour organized on a grand scale, although now despotically organized, and the means of production centralized, although now centralized in the hands of the monopolist, not only as a means of production, but as a means of the exploitation and enslavement of the producer. What the proletariat has to do is to transform the present capitalist character of that organized labour and those centralized means of labour, to transform them from the means of class rule and class exploitation into forms of free associated labour and social means of production. On the other hand, the labour of the peasant is insulated and the means of production are parcelled, dispersed. On these economical differences rests super-constructed a whole world of different social and political views. But this peasant proprietorship has long since outgrown its normal phase, that is the phase in which it was a reality, a mode of production and a form of property which responded to the economical wants of society and placed the rural producers themselves in normal conditions of life. It has entered its period of decay. On the one side a large *prolétariat foncier* (rural proletariat) has grown out of it whose interests are identical with those of the townish wage labourers. The mode of production itself has become super-annuated by the modern progress of agronomy. Lastly – the peasant proprietorship itself has become nominal, leaving to the peasant the delusion of proprietorship and expropriating him from the fruits of his own labour. The competition of the great farm producers, the blood-tax, the state tax, the usury of the townish mortgagee and the multitudinous pilfering of the judiciary system thrown around him, have degraded him to the position of a Hindu ryot,[26] while expropriation – even expropriation from his nominal proprietorship – and his degradation into a rural proletarian is an every day fact. What separates the peasant from the proletarian is, therefore, no longer his real interest, but his delusive prejudice. If the Commune, as we have shown, is the only power that can give him immediate great loans even in its present economical conditions, it is the only form of government that can secure to him the transformation of his present economical conditions, rescue him from expropriation by the landlord on the one hand, save him from grinding, drudging and misery on the pretext of proprietorship on the other, that can convert his nominal proprietorship of the land into real proprietorship of the fruits of his labour, that can combine for him the profits of modern agronomy, dictated by social wants and every day now encroaching upon him as a hostile agency, without annihilating his position as a really independent producer. Being immediately benefited by the Communal republic, he would soon confide in it.

Union (Ligue) Républicaine

The party of disorder, whose regime topped [?] under the corruption of the Second Empire, has left Paris (exodus from Paris), followed by its appurtenances, its retainers, its menials, its state parasites, its *mouchards*,[27] its '*cocottes*', and the whole band of low *bohème* (the common criminals) that form the complement of that *bohème of quality*. But the true vital elements of the middle classes, delivered by the workmen's revolution from their sham representatives, have for the first time in the history of French revolutions separated from them and come out in their true colours. This is the 'League of Republican Liberty'[28] acting the inter-

26. An impoverished Indian peasant proprietor under a land tenure system introduced by the British. See Marx's article 'Indian Affairs', above, pp. 650–3.

27. Police spies.   28. See above, p. 898.

mediary between Paris and the provinces, disavowing Versailles and marching under the banners of the Commune.

The Communal Revolution as the Representative of all Classes of Society not Living upon Foreign Labour

We have seen that the Paris proletarian fights for the French peasant, and Versailles fights against him; that the greatest anxiety of the 'Rurals' is that Paris be heard by the peasants and no longer separated from them through the blockade; that at the bottom of its war upon Paris is the attempt to keep the peasant as its bondman and treat him as before as its material '*taillable à merci et miséricorde*'.[29]

For the first time in history the petty and middling middle class has openly rallied round the workmen's revolution, and proclaimed it as the only means of their own salvation and that of France! It forms with them the bulk of the National Guard, it sits with them in the Commune, it mediates for them in the Union Républicaine!

The principal measures taken by the Commune are taken for the salvation of the middle class – the debtor class of Paris against the creditor class! That middle class had rallied in the June insurrection (1848) against the proletariat under the banners of the capitalist class, their generals and their state parasites. It was punished at once on 19 September 1848 by the rejection of the '*concordats à l'amiable*'.[30] The victory over the June insurrection showed itself at once also as the victory of the creditor, the wealthy capitalist over the debtor, the middle class. It insisted mercilessly on its pound of flesh. On 13 June 1849 the National Guard of that middle class was disarmed and sabred down by the army of the bourgeoisie![31] During the Empire, [as a result of] the dilapidation of the state resources upon which the wealthy capitalist fed, this middle class was delivered to the plunder of the stock-jobbers, the railway kings, the swindling associations of the Crédit Mobilier,[32] etc., and expropriated by capitalist association (joint-stock company). If lowered in its political position, attacked in its economical interests, it was morally revolted by the orgies of that

29. Taxable at its pleasure and at its mercy.
30. See 'The Class Struggles in France', above, pp. 400–1.
31. Ibid., pp. 781–4.   32. See p. 787, n. 47.

regime. The infamies of the war gave the last shock and roused its feelings as Frenchmen. The disasters bestowed upon France by that war, its crisis of national breakdown and its financial ruin, this middle class feels that not the corrupt class of the would-be slave-holders of France, but only the manly aspirations and the herculean power of the working class, can come to the rescue!

They feel that only the working class can emancipate them from priest rule, convert science from an instrument of class rule into a popular force, convert the men of science themselves from the panderers to class prejudice, place-hunting parasites, and allies of capital into free agents of thought! Science can only play its genuine part in the republic of labour.

Republic Only Possible as Avowedly Social Republic

This civil war has destroyed the last delusions about the 'republic', as the Empire the delusion of unorganized 'universal suffrage' in the hands of the state gendarme and the parson. All vital elements of France acknowledge that a republic is only possible in France and Europe as a 'social republic', that is a republic which disowns the capital and landowner class of the state machinery to supersede it by the Commune, that frankly avows 'social emancipation' as the great goal of the republic and guarantees thus that social transformation by the Communal organization. The other republic can be nothing but the *anonymous* terrorism of all monarchical fractions, of the combined Legitimists, Orleanists, and Bonapartists, to land in an empire of some kind as its final goal, the *anonymous* terror of class rule which, having done its dirty work, will always burst into an empire!

The professional republicans of the Rural Assembly are men who really believe, despite the experiments of 1848–51, despite the civil war against Paris – the *republican form* of class despotism a possible, lasting form, while the 'party of Order' demands it only as a form of conspiracy for fighting the republic and reintroducing its only adequate form, monarchy or rather Imperialism,[33] as the form of class despotism. In 1848 these voluntary dupes were

33. See p. 718, n. 62.

pushed in the foreground till, by the insurrection of June, they had paved the way for the *anonymous* rule of all fractions of the would-be slave-holders in France. In 1871, at Versailles, they are from the beginning pushed into the background, there to figure as the 'republican' decoration of Thiers's rule and sanction by their presence the war of the Bonapartist generals upon Paris! In unconscious self-irony these wretches hold their party meeting in the Salle de Paume (tennis court) to show how they have degenerated from their predecessors in 1789! By their Schölchers,[34] etc. they tried to coax Paris into tendering its arms to Thiers and to force it into disarmament by the National Guard of 'order' under Saisset! We do not speak of the so-called socialist Paris deputies like Louis Blanc.[35] They undergo meekly the insults of a Dufaure and the Rurals, dote upon Thiers's 'legal' rights, and whining in the presence of the banditti cover themselves with infamy!

Workmen and Comte

If the workmen have outgrown the time of socialist sectarianism, it ought not [to] be forgotten that they have never been in the leading strings of Comtism. This sect has never afforded the International but a *branch* of about half a dozen men, whose programme was rejected by the General Council.[36] Comte is known to the Parisian workmen as the prophet in politics of Imperialism (of personal *dictatorship*), of capitalist rule in political economy, of hierarchy in all spheres of human action, even in the sphere of science, and as the author of a new catechism with a new pope and new saints in place of the old ones.

If his followers in England play a more popular part than those in France it is not by preaching their sectarian doctrines, but by their personal valour, and by the acceptance by their sect of the

34. Victor Schölcher was a left-wing republican deputy to the National Assembly of 1871. As the commander of an artillery legion of the National Guard in Paris, he attempted, on 17 March, to bring about the capitulation of Paris to the Versailles government.

35. This veteran social reformist of the 1840s, prominent in the Provisional Government of 1848, was elected to the 1871 National Assembly, and sat in Versailles during the rise and fall of the Commune.

36. Early in 1870 the Comtist 'Society of Positivist Proletarians' was allowed to affiliate to the International, although the General Council criticized its programme. See below, p. 972.

forms of working men's class struggle created without them, as for instance the trade unions and strikes in England which, by the bye, are denounced as heresy by their Paris co-religionists.

The Commune (*Social Measures*)

That the workmen of Paris have taken the initiative of the present revolution and in heroic self-sacrifice bear the brunt of this battle, is nothing new. It is the striking fact of all French revolutions! It is only a repetition of the past! That the revolution is made in *the name of* and confessedly *for* the popular masses, that is the producing masses, is a feature this revolution has in common with all its predecessors. The new feature is that the people, after the first rise, have not disarmed themselves and surrendered their power into the hands of the republican mountebanks of the ruling classes, that, by the constitution of the *Commune*, they have taken the actual management of their revolution into their own hands and found at the same time, in the case of success, the means to hold it in the hands of the people itself, displacing the state machinery, the governmental machinery of the ruling classes by a governmental machinery of their own. This is their ineffable crime! Workmen infringing upon the governmental privilege of the upper 10,000 and proclaiming their will to break the economical basis of that class despotism which for its own sake wielded the organized state force of society! This it is that has thrown the respectable classes in Europe as in the United States into a paroxysm of convulsions and accounts for their shrieks of abomination (it is blasphemy), their fierce appeals to assassination of the people and the Billingsgate of abuse and calumny from their parliamentary tribunes and their journalistic servants' hall!

The greatest measure of the Commune is its own existence, working, acting under circumstances of unheard-of difficulty! The red flag, hoisted by the Paris Commune, crowns in reality only the government of workmen for Paris! They have clearly, consciously proclaimed the emancipation of labour, and the transformation of society, as their goal! But the actual 'social' character of their republic consists only in this, that workmen govern the Paris Commune! As to their measures, they must, by the nature of things, be principally confined to the military defence of Paris and its supply!

Some patronizing friends of the working class, while hardly dissembling their disgust even at the few measures they consider as 'socialist', although there is nothing socialist in them except their tendency – express their satisfaction and try to coax genteel sympathies for the Paris Commune by the great discovery that, after all, workmen are rational men and whenever in power always resolutely turn their back upon socialist enterprises! They do in fact neither try to establish in Paris a *phalanstère* nor an *Icarie*.[37] Wise men of their generation! These benevolent patronizers, profoundly ignorant of the real aspirations and the real movement of the working classes, forget one thing. All the socialist founders of sects belong to a period in which the working classes themselves were neither sufficiently trained and organized by the march of capitalist society itself to enter as historical agents upon the world's stage, nor were the material conditions of their emancipation sufficiently matured in the old world itself. Their misery existed, but the conditions of their own movement did not yet exist. The utopian founders of sects, while in their criticism of present society clearly describing the goal of the social movement, the supersession of the wages system with all its economical conditions of class rule, found neither in society itself the material conditions of its transformation, nor in the working class the organized power and the conscience of the movement. They tried to compensate for the historical conditions of the movement by fantastic pictures and plans of a new society in whose propaganda they saw the true means of salvation. From the moment the working men's class movement became real, the fantastic utopias evanesced, not because the working class had given up the end aimed at by these utopians, but because they had found the real means to realize them, and in their place came a real insight into the historic conditions of the movement and a more and more gathering force of the militant organization of the working class. But the last two ends of the movement proclaimed by the utopians are the last ends proclaimed by the Paris revolution and by the International. Only the means are different, and the real conditions of the movement are no longer clouded in utopian fables. These patronizing friends of the proletariat, in glossing over the loudly proclaimed socialist tendencies of this revolution, are therefore but the dupes of their own ignorance. It is not the fault of the Paris proletariat, if for them the utopian creations of the prophets

---

37. Utopian communities envisaged by Charles Fourier and Étienne Cabet respectively.

of the working men's movement are still the 'social revolution', that is to say, if the social revolution is for them still 'utopian'.

*

Journal officiel of the Central Committee, 20 March:
'The proletarians of the capital, amidst the failures and the treasons of the governing (ruling) classes, have understood that the hour has arrived for them *to save the situation by taking into their own hands the direction (management) of public affairs* (the state business)'. They denounce 'the political incapacity and the moral decrepitude of the bourgeoisie' as the source of 'the misfortunes of France'.

'The workmen, who produce everything and enjoy nothing, who suffer from misery in the midst of their accumulated products, the fruit of their work and their sweat . . . *shall they never be allowed to work for their emancipation*? . . . The proletariat, in face of the permanent menace against its rights, of the absolute negation of all its legitimate aspirations, of the ruin of the country and all its hopes, has understood that it was its imperious duty and its absolute right to take into its hands its own destinies and to assure their triumph in seizing the state power'.

It is here plainly stated that the government of the working class is, in the first instance, necessary to save France from the ruins and the corruption impended upon it by the ruling classes, that the dislodgement of these classes from power (of these classes who have lost the capacity of ruling France) is *a necessity of national safety*.

But it is no less clearly stated that the government by the working class can only save France and do the national business by working for its *own emancipation*, the conditions of that emancipation being at the same time the conditions of the regeneration of France.

It is proclaimed as a war of labour upon the monopolists of the means of labour, upon capital.

The *chauvinism* of the bourgeoisie is only a vanity, giving a national cloak to all their own pretensions. It is a means, by permanent armies, to perpetuate international struggles, to subjugate in each country the producers by pitching them against their brothers in each other country, a means to prevent the international cooperation of the working classes, the first condition of their emancipation. The true character of that chauvinism (long since become a mere phrase) has come out during the war of defence after Sedan, everywhere paralysed by the chauvinist bourgeoisie in the capitulation of France, in the civil war carried on under that high priest of chauvinism, Thiers, on Bismarck's sufferance! It came out in the petty police intrigue of the Anti-German League, in foreigner-hunting in Paris after the capitulation. It was hoped that the Paris people (and the French people) could be stultified into the passion of national hatred and by factitious outrages to the foreigner forget its real aspiration and its home betrayers!

How has this factitious movement disappeared (vanished) before the breath of revolutionary Paris! Loudly proclaiming its international tendencies – because the cause of the producer is everywhere the same and its enemy everywhere the same, whatever its nationality (in whatever national garb) – it proclaimed as a principle the admission of foreigners into the Commune, it even chose a foreign workman (a member of the International) onto its executive,[38] it decreed [the destruction of] the symbol of French chauvinism – the Vendôme column!

And while the bourgeois *chauvins* have dismembered France, and act under the dictatorship of the foreign invasion, the Paris workmen have beaten the foreign enemy by striking at their own class rulers, have abolished fractions, in conquering the post as the vanguard of the workmen of all nations!

The genuine patriotism of the bourgeoisie – so natural for the real proprietors of the different 'national' estates – has faded into a mere sham consequent upon the cosmopolitan character imprinted upon their financial, commercial, and industrial enterprise. Under similar circumstances it would explode in all countries as it did in France.

Decentralization by the Rurals and the Commune

It has been said that Paris, and with it the other French towns, were oppressed by the rule of the peasants, and that its present struggle is for its emancipation from the rule of the peasantry! Never was a more foolish lie uttered!

Paris, as the central seat and the stronghold of the centralized government machinery, subjected the peasantry to the rule of the

38. Leo Frankel.

gendarme, the tax-collector, the prefect, the priest, and the rural magnates, that is to the despotism of its enemies, and deprived it of all life (took the life out of it). It repressed all organs of independent life in the rural districts. On the other hand, the government, the rural magnate, the gendarme and the priest, into whose hands the whole influence of the provinces was thus thrown by the centralized state machinery centring at Paris, brought this influence to bear for the government and the classes whose government it was, not against the Paris of the government, the parasite, the capitalist, the idle, the cosmopolitan stew, but against the Paris of the workman and the thinker. In this way, by the government centralization with Paris as its base, the peasants were suppressed by the Paris of the government and the capitalist, and the Paris of the workmen was suppressed by the provincial power handed over into the hands of the enemies of the peasants.

The Versailles *Moniteur* (29 March) declares that 'Paris cannot be a *free city*, because it is *the capital*'. This is the true thing. Paris, the capital of the ruling classes and its government, cannot be a 'free city', and the provinces cannot be 'free', because such a Paris is the capital. The provinces can only be free with the Commune at Paris. The party of Order is still less infuriated against Paris because it has proclaimed its own emancipation from them and their government, than because, by doing so, it has sounded the alarm signal for the emancipation of the peasant and the provinces from their sway.

Journal officiel de la Commune, 1 April: 'The revolution of 18 March had not for its only object the securing to Paris of communal representation elected, but subject to the *despotic tutelage of a national power strongly centralized. It is to conquer and secure independence for all the communes* of France, and also of all superior groups, departments, and provinces, united amongst themselves for their common interest by a really national pact; it is to guarantee and perpetuate the republic . . . Paris has *renounced her apparent omnipotence* which is identical with her forfeiture, she has not renounced that moral power, that intellectual influence, which so often has made her victorious in France and Europe in her propaganda.'

'This time again Paris works and suffers for all France, of which it prepares by its combats and its sacrifices the intellectual, moral, administrative and economical regeneration, the glory and the prosperity' (*Programme*[39] *of the Commune de Paris sent out by balloon*).

Mr Thiers, in his tour through the provinces, managed the elections, and above all, his own manifold elections. But there was one difficulty. The Bonapartist provincials had for the moment become impossible. (Besides, he did not want them, nor did they want him.) Many of the Orleanist old stagers had merged into the Bonapartist lot. It was therefore necessary to appeal to the rusticated Legitimist landowners who had kept quite aloof from politics and were just the men to be duped. They have given its apparent character to the Versailles assembly, its character of the '*Chambre introuvable*' of Louis XVIII, its 'Rural' character. In their vanity they believed, of course, that their time had at last come with the downfall of the second Bonapartist empire and under the shelter of foreign invasion, as it had come in 1814 and 1815. Still they are mere dupes. So far as they act, they can only act as elements of the 'party of Order' and its 'anonymous' terrorism, as in 1848–51. Their own party effusions lend only the comical character to that association. They are, therefore, forced to suffer as President the jail-*accoucheur* of the Duchess de Berry and as their ministers the pseudo-republicans of the Government of Defence. They will be pushed aside as soon as they have done their service. But – a trick of history – by this curious combination of circumstances they are forced to attack Paris for revolting against the '*republique une et indivisible*'[40] (Louis Blanc expresses it so, Thiers calls it unity of France), while their very first exploit was to revolt against unity by declaring for the 'decapitation and decapitalization' of Paris, by wanting the Assembly to sit in a provincial town. What they really want is to go back to what preceded the centralized state machinery, become more to less independent of its prefects and its ministers, and put into its place the provincial and local domainal influence of the *châteaux*. They want a reactionary *decentralization* of France. What Paris wants is to supplant that centralization which has done its service against feudality, but has become the mere unity of an artificial body, resting on gendarmes, red and black armies, repressing the life of real society, resting as an incubus upon it, giving Paris an 'apparent omnipotence' by enclosing it and leaving the provinces outside – to supplant this unitarian France which

39. This is quoted from the manifesto 'To the French People'.
40. One and indivisible republic.

exists besides the French society – by the political union of French society itself through the Communal organization.

The true partisans of breaking up the unity of France are therefore the Rurals, opposed to the united state machinery so far as it interferes with their own local importance (seignorial rights), so far as it is the antagonist of feudalism.

What Paris wants is to break up that factitious unitarian system, so far as it is the antagonist of the real living union of France and a mere means of class rule.

Comtist View

Men completely ignorant of the existing economical system are of course still less able to comprehend the workmen's negation of that system. They can of course not comprehend that the social transformation the working class aim at is the necessary, historical, unavoidable birth of the present system itself. They talk in deprecatory tones of the threatened abolition of 'property', because in their eyes their present class form of property – a transitory historical form – *is* property itself, and the abolition of that form would therefore be the abolition of property. As they now defend the 'eternity' of capital rule and the wages system, if they had lived in feudal times or in times of slavery they would have defended the feudal system and the slave system, as founded on the nature of things, as a spontaneous outgrowth [?] springing from nature, fiercely declaimed against their 'abuses', but at the same time from the height of their ignorance answering to the prophecies of their abolition by the dogma of their eternity righted by 'moral checks' ('constraints').

They are as right in their appreciation of the aims of the Paris working classes, as is Mr Bismarck in declaring that what the Commune wants is the Prussian municipal order.

Poor men! They do not even know that every *social form* of property has 'morals' of its own, and that the form of social property which makes property the attribute of labour, far from creating individual 'moral constraints', will emancipate the 'morals' of the individual from its class constraints.

*

How the breath of the popular revolution has changed Paris! The revolution of February was called the revolution of moral contempt. It was proclaimed by the cries of the people, '*À bas les grands voleurs! À bas les assassins!*'[41] Such was the sentiment of the people. But as to the bourgeoisie, they wanted broader sway for corruption! They got it under Louis Bonaparte's (Napoleon the little) reign. Paris, the gigantic town, the town of historic initiative, was transformed in[to] the *maison dorée*[42] of all the idlers and swindlers of the world, into a cosmopolitan stew! After the exodus of the 'better class of people', the Paris of the working class reappeared, heroic, self-sacrificing, enthusiastic in the sentiment of its herculean task! No cadavers in the morgue, no insecurity of the streets. Paris was never more quiet within. Instead of the *cocottes*, the heroic women of Paris! Manly, stern, fighting, working, thinking Paris! Magnanimous Paris! In view of the cannibalism of their enemies, making their prisoners only dangerless! . . . What Paris will no longer stand is yet the existence of the *cocottes* and *cocodès*.[43] What it is resolved to drive away or transform is this useless, sceptical and egotistical race which has taken possession of the gigantic town, to use it as its own. No celebrity of the Empire shall have the right to say, 'Paris is very pleasant in the best quarters, but there are too many paupers in the others.' (*Vérité*, 23 April): 'Private crime wonderfully diminished at Paris. The absence of thieves and *cocottes*, of assassinations and street attacks: all the conservatives have fled to Versailles!' 'There has not been signalized one single nocturnal attack even in the most distant and less frequented quarters since the citizens do their police business themselves'.

41. Down with the big thieves! Down with the murderers!
42. Brothel.   43. Fops.

Documents of the First International: 1871–2

RESOLUTION OF THE LONDON CONFERENCE ON
WORKING-CLASS POLITICAL ACTION[1]

Karl Marx and Frederick Engels

Considering the following passage of the preamble to the Rules:
'The economical emancipation of the working classes is the great
end to which every political movement ought to be subordinate *as
a means*';[2]

That the Inaugural Address of the International Working Men's
Association (1864) states: 'The lords of land and the lords of capital
will always use their political privileges for the defence and perpetuation of their economical monopolies. So far from promoting, they
will continue to lay every possible impediment in the way of the
emancipation of labour . . . To conquer political power has therefore
become the great duty of the working classes';[3]

That the Congress of Lausanne (1867) has passed this resolution:
'The social emancipation of the workmen is inseparable from their
political emancipation';[4]

That the declaration of the General Council relative to the
pretended plot of the French Internationalists on the eve of the
plebiscite (1870) says: 'Certainly by the tenor of our Statutes,[5]

1. This text is Resolution IX adopted by the London Conference of the International in September 1871, headed 'Political Action of the Working Class'. A draft
resolution on this question, originally introduced by the Blanquist Edouard Vaillant
on behalf of Marx's bloc, was passed in principle, and the final drafting left to the
General Council, a job that was in fact performed by Marx and Engels. The finished
resolution was published in the pamphlet *Resolutions of the Conference of Delegates
of the International Working Men's Association*, London, 1871.

2. Above, p. 766. (Emphasis added by Marx in the present text.)

3. Above, p. 764.

4. '*Procès-verbaux du congrès de l'Association Internationale des Travailleurs
réuni à Lausanne du 2 au 8 septembre 1867*', printed in J. Freymond (ed.), *La
Première Internationale*, vol. I, Geneva, 1962, p. 121.

5. By 'Statutes' Marx refers to the Rules of the International.

all our branches in England, on the Continent, and in America have the special mission not only to serve as centres for the militant organization of the working class, but also to support, in their respective countries, every political movement tending towards the accomplishment of our ultimate end – the economical emancipation of the working class';[6]

That false translations of the original Statutes have given rise to various interpretations which were mischievous to the development and action of the International Working Men's Association;[7]

In presence of an unbridled reaction which violently crushes every effort at emancipation on the part of the working men, and pretends to maintain by brute force the distinction of classes and the political domination of the propertied classes resulting from it;

Considering, that against this collective power of the propertied classes the working class cannot act, as a class, except by constituting itself into a political party, distinct from, and opposed to, all old parties formed by the propertied classes;

That this constitution of the working class into a political party is indispensable in order to ensure the triumph of the social revolution and its ultimate end – the abolition of classes;

That the combination of forces which the working class has already effected by its economical struggles ought at the same time to serve as a lever for its struggles against the political power of landlords and capitalists –

The Conference recalls to the members of the *International*:

That in the militant state of the working class, its economical movement and its political action are indissolubly united.

SPEECH ON THE SEVENTH ANNIVERSARY OF THE
INTERNATIONAL[8]

Concerning the International, [Marx] said that the great success which had hitherto crowned its efforts was due to circumstances

6. *IWMA* III, pp. 231–2.
7. See 'The General Council to the Federal Council of French Switzerland', above, pp. 802–3.
8. This text is an excerpt from a report published in the New York *World* on 15 October 1871, headed 'The Reds in Session. Authentic Account of the Seventh Anniversary of the International in London'. The anniversary cele-

over which the members themselves had no control. The foundation of the International itself was the result of these circumstances, and by no means due to the efforts of the men engaged in it. It was not the work of any set of clever politicians; all the politicians in the world could not have created the situation and circumstances requisite for the success of the International. The International had not put forth any particular creed. Its task was to organize the forces of labour and link the various working men's movements and combine them. The circumstances which had given such a great development to the association were the conditions under which the work-people were more and more oppressed throughout the world, and this was the secret of success. The events of the last few weeks had unmistakably shown that the working class must fight for its emancipation. The persecutions of the governments against the International were like the persecutions of ancient Rome against the primitive Christians. They, too, had been few in numbers at first, but the patricians of Rome had instinctively felt that if the Christians succeeded the Roman empire would be lost. The persecutions of Rome had not saved the empire, and the persecutions of the present day against the International would not save the existing state of things.

What was new in the International was that it was established by the working men themselves and for themselves. Before the foundation of the International all the different organizations had been societies founded by some radicals among the ruling classes for the working classes, but the International was established by the working men for themselves. The Chartist movement in this country had been started with the consent and assistance of middle-class radicals, though if it had been successful it could only have been for the advantage of the working class. England was the only country where the working class was sufficiently developed and organized to turn universal suffrage to its proper account. He then alluded to the revolution of February as a movement that had been favoured by a portion of the bourgeoisie against the ruling party. The revolution of February had only given promises to the working classes and had replaced one set of men of the

---

bration took the form of a dinner on 26 September, which the *World*'s correspondent, probably R. Landor who interviewed Marx three months before (see below, p. 393), apparently attended. The dinner was held two days after the close of the London Conference of the International, and the participants included many of the Conference delegates.

ruling class by another. The insurrection of June had been a revolt against the whole ruling class, including the most radical portion. The working men who had lifted the new men into power in 1848 had instinctively felt that they had only exchanged one set of oppressors for another and that they were betrayed.

The last movement was the Commune, the greatest that had yet been made, and there could not be two opinions about it – the Commune was the conquest of the political power of the working classes. There was much misunderstanding about the Commune. The Commune could not found a new form of class government. In destroying the existing conditions of oppression by transferring all the means of labour to the productive labourer, and thereby compelling every able-bodied individual to work for a living, the only base for class rule and oppression would be removed. But before such a change could be effected a proletarian dictature would become necessary, and the first condition of that was a proletarian army. The working classes would have to conquer the right to emancipate themselves on the battlefield. The task of the International was to organize and combine the forces of labour for the coming struggle.

THE ALLEGED SPLITS IN THE INTERNATIONAL[9]

Private Circular from the General Council of the International Working Men's Association

Karl Marx and Frederick Engels

Up to now the General Council has maintained a total reserve over struggles within the International, and has never made any public answer to the public attacks made against it over the past two years by members of the Association.

And still, had it only been a question of a few trouble-makers persisting in purposely sowing confusion between the International and a society which has from the first been hostile to it, that

9. Marx and Engels wrote this text in French between January and March 1872, as part of their preparations for the Hague Congress of September 1872. It was adopted by the General Council on 5 March, printed in Geneva in May, and distributed privately to the International's federations and sections. It is translated here from the pamphlet, *Les Prétendues Scissions dans l'Internationale. Circulaire privée du Conseil Général de l'Association Internationale des Travailleurs*, Geneva, 1872.

silence might have been preserved. But in view of the support given to reactionary forces all over Europe by the scandals that society has provoked – just at a moment when the International is passing through the most serious crisis it has faced since it was founded – it becomes necessary for the General Council to give a full account of these intrigues.

I

After the fall of the Paris Commune, the first act of the General Council was to publish its Address on *The Civil War in France*, in which it expressed its solidarity with everything done by the Commune, at a point when the bourgeoisie, the press and every government in Europe were all pouring out a stream of calumnies upon the defeated Communards. There were even some among the working class who failed to recognize their own cause, and joined in the abuse. The Council received one proof of this, among others, when two of its members, citizens Odger and Lucraft, resigned to dissociate themselves from the Address.[10] But in general it may be said that the united attitude of the working class towards the events in Paris dates from its publication in all the countries of the civilized world.

Furthermore, the International discovered a most powerful means of propaganda in the bourgeois press, and above all the leading English papers, because they felt obliged to attack the Address and the replies of the General Council maintained a full-scale debate in being.[11]

The arrival of numbers of Communard refugees in London made it necessary for the General Council to form itself into a relief committee, a function quite outside its normal activities which it carried on for over eight months. It goes without saying that the defeated and exiled Communards had nothing to hope for from the bourgeoisie; as for the working class, their calls for help came at a difficult time. Switzerland and Belgium had already received

10. After the Second Reform Bill of 1867 Odger worked for labour parliamentary representation through the Liberal party, and under pressure from his middle-class political allies he resigned from the General Council in June 1871, after the publication of *The Civil War in France*. Benjamin Lucraft, leader of the furniture-makers' union, was, like Odger, a founding member of the International and the General Council.

11. A selection of Marx and Engels's letters on behalf of the General Council is published in *MECW* 22, p. 285ff.

their contingents of refugees, whom they had either to support, or help on their way to London, and money collected in Germany, Austria and Spain was sent to Switzerland. In England, the battle for the nine-hour working day – whose final decisive engagement took place in Newcastle[12] – had absorbed both the individual contributions of the workers, and the organized funds of the trade unions; the latter, in any case, could statutorily only be used in the industrial struggle as such. However, by dint of continuous activity and correspondence, the Council managed to collect enough in small sums to distribute a little money each week. American working people responded most generously to its appeal. But, as so often, how wonderful it would have been if the Council had had anything like the millions attributed to it by the terrified imagination of the bourgeoisie!

After May 1871, a certain number of Communard refugees were called upon to replace the French members whom the war had removed from the Council. Among those thus brought in were former members of the International, and a minority of well-known revolutionaries whose election represented our homage to the Paris Commune.[13]

In the midst of such preoccupations, the Council had also to do the preparatory work for the Conference of delegates it had just convened.

The violent measures taken against the International by the Bonapartist government[14] had made it impossible to hold a Congress in Paris, as determined by the Basle Congress. The General Council, in virtue of the right conferred upon it in article 4 of the Rules,[15] sent out a circular on 12 July 1870, to convene the Congress in Mainz.[16] At the same time, in letters addressed to the various federations, it proposed that the seat of the General Council be transferred from England to another country, and

12. This refers to the Newcastle builders and engineers' strike of May–October 1871, led by the *ad hoc* Nine Hours League.

13. These 'well-known revolutionaries' who had formerly been outside of the International were Blanquists, who after the Commune accepted the Marxist position of the need for a working-class political party, and worked with Marx against Bakunin's intrigues.

14. See p. 857, n. 3.

15. References to the General Rules and Administrative Regulations of the International are given here according to the 1871 English edition, printed in *IWMA* IV, pp. 451–69.

16. 'The Fifth Annual Congress of the IWMA', *IWMA* III, pp. 372–3.

asked that the delegates be given a mandate to do this.[17] However the federations were unanimous in asking that it remain in London. The outbreak of the Franco-Prussian war, a few days later, made it impossible to hold any Congress at all, and the federations consulted gave us the power to fix a date for the next Congress as circumstances should allow.

As soon as the political situation seemed to make it possible, the General Council summoned a private Conference; the precedents for our doing this were the 1865 Conference, and the private administrative sessions of each Congress. It was impossible to hold a public Congress, for that would merely have served to get the continental delegates denounced at the height of the positive orgy of reaction then taking place in Europe: with Jules Favre demanding the extradition of refugees as common-law criminals from all other governments, even the English,[18] with Dufaure proposing in the Rural Assembly a law banning the International[19] – later plagiarized by Malou[20] for use against the Belgians; with a refugee from the Commune being taken into preventive custody in Switzerland while the Federal government was making up its mind whether or not to grant extradition; with a combined operation against Internationalists forming the ostensible basis for an alliance between Beust and Bismarck,[21] and Victor Emmanuel hurrying to adopt the clause directed against the International;[22] with the Spanish government doing everything demanded by the executioners of Versailles and forcing the Madrid Federal Coun-

17. The General Council in fact proposed Brussels as its future seat (see *IWMA* III, pp. 266–70). Marx's probable reason for this proposal, which there was little chance of the federations supporting, was to forestall objections to the strengthening of the General Council's authority.

18. Jules Favre, the French foreign minister, circularized the European governments on 6 June 1871, calling on them to hunt down the International.

19. Jules Dufaure was Minister of Justice in Thiers's government. The *loi Dufaure*, passed on 14 March 1872, made membership of the International in France an offence punishable by imprisonment. On the 'Rural Assembly' see above, pp. 879–80.

20. Jules Malou was the Belgian Prime Minister.

21. Friedrich, Count Beust, was the Austro-Hungarian chancellor. In August and September 1871, after preparatory exchanges between Beust and Bismarck, emperors Francis Joseph of Austria and William I of Germany held two meetings, in Bad Gastein and in Salzburg, specifically to coordinate measures against the International.

22. The Italian government banned the Naples section of the International in August 1871.

cil to seek refuge in Portugal.[23] In short, it was a situation in which the International's first task was to get its own organization back into order, so as to take up the challenge of the various governments.

All sections in regular communication with the General Council were invited to the Conference in good time; but even though it was not a public Congress, it still had serious difficulties to contend with. Obviously France, in its present state, could not elect delegates. The only section then functioning in Italy was the one in Naples, and just as it was appointing its delegate, it was dissolved by the army. In Austria and Hungary, all the most active members were in prison.[24] In Germany, some of the best-known members were wanted for the crime of high treason, while others were in prison, and all the party's funds were needed for the support of their families.[25] The Americans, though they sent the Conference a detailed memorandum on the situation of the International in their country, spent the money that could have paid for sending a delegation on supporting refugees. Clearly, all the federations recognized the need for holding a private Conference rather than a public congress.

The Conference, having sat in London from 17 to 23 September 1871, entrusted the General Council with the task of publishing its resolutions, of codifying the Administrative Regulations and putting them out, together with the revised and corrected General Rules, in three languages, of putting into effect the resolution to substitute adhesive stamps for membership cards, of reorganizing the International in England, and lastly, of finding the money needed for all these objects.[26]

The moment the Conference's activities were made public, the reactionary press – from Paris to Moscow, from London to New

23. The Spanish government moved to the offensive against the International in spring and summer 1871.

24. The leaders of the Austrian Social-Democratic party were arrested in July 1870, after a wave of strikes, and charged with high treason.

25. The Brunswick committee of the German Social-Democratic Workers' Party (SDAP) was arrested in September 1870 and its members held for over a year in prison, while Bebel and Liebknecht were arrested in December 1870, charged with high treason, and sentenced in March 1872 to two years' imprisonment.

26. See 'Resolutions of the London Conference', *IWMA* IV, pp. 440–50. The English reorganization involved the formation of an English Federal Council separate from the General Council.

York – attacked the resolution on working-class political action;[27] it enshrined, they said, designs so dangerous ('coldly calculated audacity', accused *The Times*) that it was vital that the International be outlawed at once. On the other hand, the resolution unmasking the fraudulent sectarian section[27a] provided a pretext for the ever-watchful international police to make loud demands in favour of the freedom of their protégés, the workers, as against the appalling despotism of the General Council and the Conference. So 'heavily oppressed' did the workers feel, indeed, that the General Council received new members, and notifications that new branches had been formed, from Europe, America, Australia and even the East Indies!

II

The attacks of the bourgeois press and the laments of the international police even found a certain sympathetic echo within our Association. Plots, directed apparently against the General Council, but in reality against the Association itself, began taking shape, and at the bottom of them all there was inevitably to be found the International Alliance of Socialist Democracy, that brain-child of the Russian Michael Bakunin. On his return from Siberia he preached pan-Slavism and racial war in Herzen's *Kolokol*, as the fruit of his long experience. Later, during his time in Switzerland, he was appointed to the governing committee of the 'League of Peace and Freedom' founded in opposition to the International. Since the affairs of this bourgeois society went from bad to worse, its president, Mr G. Vogt, acting on Bakunin's advice, proposed an alliance when the International's Congress met in Brussels in September 1868. But the Congress unanimously declared that *either* the League was pursuing the same aim as the International, in which case there was no point in its existing, *or* its aim was different, in which case no merger was possible. At the League's own congress in Berne a few days later, Bakunin underwent a conversion. He put forward an outworn programme, whose scientific value can be judged from this one phrase: '*the economic and social equalization of classes*'. With only a tiny minority supporting him, he broke with the League and joined the International, bent on replacing the International's General Rules with his own makeshift programme, which the League had rejected, and the General Council with himself as a virtual

27. See above, pp. 953–4.   27a. See above, p. 732.

dictator. With this object, he formed a new instrument, the 'International Alliance of Socialist Democracy', intending it to become an International within the International.

Bakunin found the people he needed to establish that society from among the friendships he had formed during his stay in Italy, and in a group of Russian exiles who acted as his emissaries and 'recruiting officers' among members of the International in Switzerland, France and Spain. However it was only the repeated refusals of the Belgian and Paris Federal Councils to recognize his 'Alliance' that made him decide to present the rules of his new society to the General Council for approval, rules which were simply a reproduction of his 'unappreciated' Berne programme. The Council replied with the following circular, dated 22 December 1868:

The International Working Men's Association and the International Alliance of Socialist Democracy[28]

About a month ago, a number of citizens established themselves in Geneva as the 'Inaugural Central Committee' of a new International society, known as 'The International Alliance of Socialist Democracy', which took as its '*special mission* the study of political and philosophical questions actually on the basis of this great principle of *equality*, etc . . .'

The printed programme and rules of this inaugural committee were only communicated to the General Council of the International Working Men's Association on 15 December 1868. According to these documents, the aforesaid Alliance is 'wholly founded within the International' – though at the same time it is wholly founded outside this Association. Alongside the General Council of the International, elected by the successive Congresses of Geneva, Lausanne and Brussels, there would seem, to judge by these documents, to be another General Council in Geneva, appointed by itself. Alongside the local groups of the International, there would seem to be local groups of the 'Alliance' which, through their own national bureaux functioning quite apart from the national bureaux of the International, 'will ask the Central Bureau of the Alliance to admit them into the International' – in other words, the Central Committee of the '*Alliance*' is taking upon itself the right to admit people into the *International*. Finally, the General Congress of the International Working Men's Association also has its counterpart in the 'General Congress of the Alliance', for, as the rules of the inaugural committee tell us, at the annual working men's Congress, the delegation of the International Alliance of Socialist Demo-

---

28. This circular was written by Marx in French, on the mandate of the General Council, and distributed by private letter.

cracy, as a branch of the International Working Men's Association, 'will hold its public sessions in another place'.

Considering:

That the presence of a second international body functioning both inside and outside the International Working Men's Association would infallibly succeed in reducing it to chaos;

That any other group of individuals living anywhere would have a right to imitate the Geneva inaugural group, and under various pretexts, whether expressed or not, to graft other International Associations with their own special missions onto the International Working Men's Association;

That in this way the International Working Men's Association could easily become the plaything of intriguers from all countries and all parties;

That in any case the Rules of the International Working Men's Association only include in its framework local and national branches (see articles 1 and 7 of the Rules);

That no section of the International Working Men's Association is allowed to adopt rules and administrative regulations contrary to the General Rules and Administrative Regulations of the International Working Men's Association (see article V/1 of the Administrative Regulations);

That the Rules and Administrative Regulations of the International Working Men's Association can only be revised by a General Congress at which two thirds of the delegates present are in favour (see article 12 of the General Rules);

That the question has already been settled by the resolutions unanimously adopted at the Brussels General Congress against the League of Peace;[29]

That in those resolutions Congress declared that the League of Peace served no purpose, given that its recent declarations made it clear that its aims and principles were identical with those of the International Working Men's Association;

That several members of the inaugural group of the Alliance, as delegates to the Brussels Congress, themselves voted for those resolutions;

The General Council of the International Working Men's Association, at its meeting of 22 December 1868, has unanimously resolved:

1. All the articles of the rules of the International Alliance of Socialist Democracy concerning its relationship with the International Working Men's Association are declared null and void;

29. See 'Resolutions of the First and Third Congresses of the International Working Men's Association', *IWMA* III, pp. 297–8.

2. The International Alliance of Socialist Democracy is not admitted as a branch of the International Working Men's Association.

G. ODGER, Chairman of the meeting

R. SHAW, General Secretary

London, 22 December, 1868

A few months later, the Alliance once again approached the General Council, asking whether or not its *principles* were acceptable to it. If the answer were 'Yes', then the Alliance declared itself ready to dissolve itself into sections of the International. In reply to this, it received the following circular of 9 March 1869:

The General Council to the Central Committee of the International Alliance of Socialist Democracy[30]

According to article 1 of our Rules, the Association admits all working men's societies 'aiming at the same end, viz. *the protection, advancement and complete emancipation of the working class*'.

Since the sections of the working class in various countries have reached different stages of development, it follows that their theoretical opinions, which reflect the real movement, will be equally divergent.

However, the community of action established by the International Working Men's Association, the exchange of ideas fostered by the publicity provided by the organs of the various national sections, and finally the face-to-face discussions at the general Congresses, cannot fail gradually to give rise to a common theoretical programme.

Thus it is no part of the functions of the General Council to make a critical study of the Alliance's programme. It is not for us to analyse whether or not it is a genuine expression of the proletarian movement. All we need to know is that it contains nothing counter to the *general tendency* of our Association, in other words, the *complete emancipation of the working class*. There is one sentence in your programme which fails this test. We read in article 2: 'It [the Alliance] desires above all the political, economic and social equalization of classes.'

The *equalization of classes*, if taken literally, amounts to the *harmony between capital and labour*, which is precisely what bourgeois socialists so unfortunately preach.[31] It is not the *equalization* of classes, a logical impossibility and therefore incapable of achievement, but on the con-

---

30. This circular was written by Marx and distributed by private letter. Since there are minor differences between the English original printed in *IWMA* III, pp. 310–11, and the French version reproduced by Marx in *Les Prétendues Scissions . . .* , we have followed the French text as published in the *Scissions* (the only contemporary published variant) rather than the English manuscript.

31. For Marx's critique of 'bourgeois socialism', see the 'Manifesto of the Communist Party', section III/2, *R1848*, pp. 93–4.

trary the *abolition* of classes which is the true secret of the proletarian movement, and the prime object of the International Working Men's Association. However, in view of the context in which the phrase 'equalization of classes' stands, it may perhaps have resulted merely from a slip of the pen. The General Council has no doubt that you would be willing to remove from your programme a phrase which could give rise to such dangerous misunderstanding. Apart from cases in which our Association's general tendency is positively contradicted, it is part of our principles to leave each section free to formulate its own theoretical programme.

Thus there is no obstacle to *converting* the sections of the Alliance into sections of the International Working Men's Association.

If it is definitely decided to *dissolve* the Alliance, and have its sections individually join the International, then by our Regulations it would become necessary to inform the Council of each new section's location and numerical strength.

Meeting of the General Council, 9 March 1869

The Alliance, having accepted these conditions, was admitted into the International by the General Council, which, owing to some of the signatures to the Bakunin programme, erroneously presumed it to be recognized by the French-Swiss[32] Federal Committee in Geneva – whereas in fact the opposite was the case. It had now achieved its immediate object of being represented at the Basle Congress. Despite the dishonest means used by his supporters (the only time such means were ever used in a Congress of the International), Bakunin was disappointed in his attempt to get the Congress to transfer the seat of the General Council to Geneva, and sanction officially the old Saint-Simonian rubbish of the immediate abolition of the right of inheritance, which Bakunin considered the practical starting-point of socialism. This marked the opening of the open and unremitting war waged by the Alliance not just against the General Council, but also against all sections of the International which refused to adopt the programme of their sectarian coterie, and above all the doctrine of total abstention from political activity.

Before the Basle Congress, when Nechayev came to Geneva, Bakunin had made contact with him and founded a secret society among students in Russia. Always concealing his own identity under the name of various 'revolutionary committees', he assumed autocratic powers, and adopted all the trickeries and

32. 'French-Swiss' has been used to translate *'Romand'*, the French name for the French-speaking districts and people of Switzerland.

mystifications from the time of Cagliostro.[33] This society's major means of propaganda consisted in compromising innocent people with the Russian police by sending them communications from Geneva in yellow envelopes, marked on the outside, in Russian, with the stamp of the Secret Revolutionary Committee. Public reports of the Nechayev trial show what infamous things were done in the name of the International.[34]

During that time, the Alliance began a public polemic against the General Council, first in *Progrès* (Le Locle), then in *Égalité* (Geneva), the official newspaper of the French-Swiss Federation, into which some members of the Alliance had followed Bakunin. The General Council paid no heed to the attacks in *Progrès*, Bakunin's own personal paper, but it could not ignore those in *Égalité* since these gave the appearance of having the Federation's approval. So it published the circular of 1 January 1870,[35] in which it said:

We read in *Égalité*, 11 December 1869: 'It is *certain* that the General Council is neglecting matters of great ·importance. We would remind it of its obligations under Regulation II/2: "The General Council is *bound* to execute the Congress resolutions, etc . . ." We could ask the General Council enough questions for its answers to make a somewhat lengthy document. These will come later . . . Meanwhile, etc. etc . . .' The General Council knows of no article, either in the Rules or the Regulations, which would oblige it to enter into correspondence or debate with *Égalité*, or provide any 'answers to questions' from newspapers. Only the Federal Committee in Geneva represents the branches of French Switzerland to the General Council. Whenever the Federal Committee addresses requests or objections to us by the one and only legitimate channel, i.e. through its secretary, the General Council will always be ready to reply. But the Federal Committee has no right either to hand over its functions to the editors of *Égalité* and *Progrès*, or to

33. Guiseppe Balsano, known as Allessandro Cagliostro, was an eighteenth-century Italian adventurer.

34. An extract from the trial will soon be published. There the reader will find a sample of the kind of maxims – at once ridiculous and evil – which through Bakunin's friends have been attributed to the International [Marx].

Nechayev's activities included the extortion of money under threat of assassination from a publisher with whom Bakunin had contracted to translate Marx's *Capital* into Russian. Evidence of this particular incident tipped the scales in securing Bakunin's expulsion from the International at the Hague Congress [Ed.].

35. 'The General Council to the Federal Council of French Switzerland'. See above, p. 797ff.

permit those journals to usurp its functions. Generally speaking, administrative correspondence between the General Council and the national and local committees cannot be made public without doing considerable damage to the general interests of the Association. Therefore, if other organs of the International were to imitate *Progrès* and *Égalité*, the General Council would be forced either to remain silent and thus earn the discredit of the public, or to violate its obligations by making a public reply. *Égalité* has combined with *Progrès* in urging *Le Travail* (a Paris newspaper) also to attack the General Council. This is virtually a *ligue du bien public*.

However, even before it learnt of this circular, the French-Swiss Federal Committee had already removed all Alliance supporters from editorial positions on *Égalité*.

The circular of 1 January 1870, like those of 22 December 1868 and 9 March 1869, was approved by all sections of the International.

It goes without saying that none of the conditions agreed by the Alliance was ever fulfilled. Its so-called sections remained a mystery to the General Council. Bakunin tried to keep under his personal authority the scattered groups in Spain and Italy, and the Naples section which he had prised away from the International. In the other towns of Italy, he was in correspondence with small groups made up not of working men, but of lawyers, journalists and other bourgeois doctrinaires. In Barcelona his influence was kept alive by a few friends. In certain towns in the south of France, the Alliance tried to establish separatist sections under the leadership of Albert Richard and Gaspard Blanc of Lyons, of whom we shall have more to say later on. In brief, the International within the International continued to stir up trouble.

The Alliance's master stroke, its attempt to seize the leadership of French Switzerland, was to take place at the Congress of La Chaux-de-Fonds, which opened on 4 April 1870.

Though, according to their own estimates, the supporters of the Alliance amounted to no more than one fifth of the members of the Federation, they managed, thanks to a repetition of the manoeuvres which had been so successful at Basle, to win an apparent majority of one or two votes – a majority which, on the admission of their own organ (see *Solidarité* for 7 May 1870), represented no more than *fifteen* sections, though there were thirty in Geneva alone! With this vote, the Congress split into two parts, which continued their sessions separately. The supporters of the

Alliance, considering themselves the legal representatives of the whole Federation, transferred the seat of the Federal Committee to La Chaux-de-Fonds, and established their official organ, *Solidarité*, edited by citizen Guillaume, in Neuchâtel. The special job of this young writer was to abuse the 'factory workers' of Geneva as disgraceful 'bourgeois', to attack *Égalité*, the Federation's own paper, and to urge total abstention from all political activity. The most trenchant articles on this latter subject were written by Bastelica[36] in Marseilles, and by those two great pillars of the Alliance in Lyons, Albert Richard and Gaspard Blanc.

On their return, the Geneva delegates convoked their sections to a general assembly which, despite the opposition of Bakunin and his friends, gave its approval to what they had done at the Chaux-de-Fonds Congress. Shortly afterwards, Bakunin and his most active disciples were expelled from the original French-Swiss Federation.

Barely had the Congress closed when the new La Chaux-de-Fonds Committee appealed to the General Council to intervene, in a letter signed by F. Robert, secretary, and Henri Chevalley, president – who, two months later was denounced as a *thief* by the Committee's organ, *Solidarité*, on 7 July. Having closely studied the apologias of both parties, the General Council decided on 28 June 1870 to maintain the Geneva Federal Committee in its former functions, and ask the new Federal Committee of La Chaux-de-Fonds to adopt a local title. For this decision, which ran wholly counter to their wishes, the Chaux-de-Fonds Committee denounced the General Council's *authoritarianism* – quite forgetting that it was they who had asked it to intervene in the first place. The problems created in the Swiss Federation by their continuing to usurp the title of the French-Swiss Federal Committee forced the General Council to suspend all official relations with them.

Louis Bonaparte had just surrendered his army at Sedan. Protests arose from the International's supporters everywhere against the continuance of the war. The General Council in its Address of 9 September,[37] denouncing Prussia's plans for conquest, showed

36. André Bastelica was a printer and a follower of Bakunin. He was active in the Communard risings in Marseilles, October–November 1870, then in the Paris Commune.

37. 'The Second Address of the General Council on the Franco-Prussian War', above, pp. 863–70.

how damaging its victory would be to the proletarian cause, and warned the workers of Germany that they would be the first to suffer. Meetings were called in England to create a counter-weight to the pro-Prussian leanings of the court. In Germany Internationalist workers organized demonstrations demanding the recognition of the republic, and 'a peace that would be honourable to France . . .'

The ebullient and bellicose Guillaume (in Neuchâtel) had the brilliant idea of producing an *anonymous* manifesto, published as a supplement to the official paper *Solidarité*, demanding the formation of a Swiss free corps to go and fight the Prussians – though when it came to the point, his abstentionist convictions would presumably have prevented his actually doing this.

Then came the Lyons uprising. Bakunin hastened to the spot, and with the support of Albert Richard, Gaspard Blanc and Bastelica, he established himself on 28 September in the town hall – though he made no attempt to guard the building in any way, since that would have been a political act. He was ignomini-ously driven out by a few National Guards just as, after a painful labour, he had at last given birth to his decree on the '*Abolition of the state*'.

In October 1870, the General Council, in the absence of its French members, coopted as a member citizen Paul Robin, a refugee from Brest, one of the best-known of the Alliance's supporters, and also the author of the attacks published against the General Council in *Égalité* – whose correspondent from the Chaux-de-Fonds Committee he still remained. On 14 March 1871, he suggested that a private conference of the International be summoned to settle the Swiss dispute. The Council, realizing that major events would soon be taking place in Paris, refused outright. Robin returned several times to the question, and even suggested that the Council itself pronounce a final settlement of the dispute. On 25 July, the General Council decided that this matter must be one of the questions laid before the Conference due to be convened in September 1871.

On 10 August, the Alliance, far from anxious to have its doings looked into closely by any conference, declared itself dissolved as from the sixth of that month. But on 15 September it reap-peared, and asked to be admitted to the Council in the guise of the 'Atheist Socialist Section'. According to Administrative Regulation II/5, adopted by the Basle Congress, the Council could not admit it without prior consultation with the Geneva Federal Committee, now worn out after two years of struggle with the various sectarian sections. Besides, the Council had already informed the Young Men's Christian Association that the International could not recognize any theological sections.

On 6 August, the date of the Alliance's 'dissolution', the Federal Committee of La Chaux-de-Fonds, while renewing its request to enter into official relations with the Council, informed it that it would continue to ignore the resolution of 28 June and present itself as the French-Swiss Federal Committee, as against Geneva – on the grounds 'that it is for the General Congress to judge the matter'. On 4 September, that same Committee sent a protest against the competence of the Conference – though it had been the first to demand that it be convened. The Conference might well have asked in return what competence the Paris Federal Committee possessed for judging the Swiss dispute, as the Chaux-de-Fonds Committee had also asked it to do before the siege.[38] However, it merely confirmed the General Council's decision of 28 June 1870. (See *Égalité*, 21 October 1871.)

III

The presence in Switzerland of some of the outlawed French who had found refuge there brought a fresh spark of life to the Alliance.

The Geneva members of the International did everything in their power for these people. They provided them with help and agitated strongly to prevent the Swiss authorities from conceding their extradition, as demanded by the Versailles government. Several people ran serious risks by going to France to help refugees to reach the frontier. One can therefore imagine the surprise with which the workers of Geneva saw certain such ringleaders as B. Malon[39] at once getting into contact with members

38. The first siege of Paris lasted from October 1870 to January 1871.

39. One wonders whether the friends of Malon who, in a mimeographed announcement three months later, described him as the 'founder of the International', and his book as the 'only independent work on the Commune', knew of the attitude taken by the deputy from Les Batignolles on the eve of the February elections. At that time, Malon, who did not anticipate the Commune, and was planning only for the success of his own election to the Assembly, was conspiring to get himself put on the list of the four committees as a member of the International. With this in mind, he had the effrontery to deny the existence of the Paris Federal Council, and submitted to the com-

of the Alliance, and, with the aid of N. Zhukovsky,[40] the former secretary of the Alliance, trying to establish a new 'Socialist Revolutionary Propaganda and Action Section' in Geneva, quite outside the French-Swiss Federation. In the first article of its rules, this organization 'declares its adherence to the General Rules of the International Working Men's Association, *while reserving to itself all the freedom of action* and initiative allowed it as a logical consequence of the principle of autonomy and federation recognized by the Rules and Congresses of the Association'. In other words, it held itself entirely free to carry on the work of the Alliance.

In a letter from Malon, dated 20 October 1871, this new section asked the General Council for the third time to admit it into the International. In conformity with Regulation II/5, adopted by the Basle Congress, the Council consulted the Geneva Federal Committee, which protested in no uncertain terms against the Council's granting recognition to this fresh 'centre of intrigue and dissension'. And, in fact, the Council *was* 'authoritarian' enough to refuse to impose the wishes of Malon and Zhukovsky upon an entire federation.

Solidarité no longer existed, so the new members of the Alliance founded *La Révolution sociale* under the chief editorship of Madame André Léo, who had just stated to the Peace Congress at Lausanne that 'Raoul Rigault and Ferré were the two sinister figures in the Commune who did not cease to demand bloodshed, albeit in vain up to the execution of the hostages'.[41]

---

mittees the names of a section founded by himself in Les Batignolles as though it came from the entire Association. Later, on 19 March, he insulted in a public document the leaders of the great revolution carried out the day before. Today this unbounded anarchist is printing or allowing to be printed what he said to the four committees a year ago: *'L'Internationale c'est moi!'* [I am the International!] Malon has thus managed to parody both Louis XIV, and Perron the chocolate-maker – though even Perron never claimed that his was the *only* edible chocolate [Marx].

Benoît Malon was a dyer, a left-wing Proudhonist and a member of the Paris Commune [Ed.].

40. Nikolai Zhukovsky was a Russian *émigré* and a close collaborator of Bakunin.

41. Marx's source here is the pamphlet, *La Guerre sociale*, Neuchâtel 1871. André Léo was the pseudonym of Léodile Champseix, the wife of Benoît Malon, who played an active part in the Commune. Raoul Rigault and Théophile Ferré were Blanquists, and respectively procurator and deputy-procurator of the Paris Commune. Both were shot by the Versailles forces.

From its first issue, this paper tried to equal or even out-do *Figaro, Gaullois, Paris-Journal* and other abusive papers, whose slanders against the General Council it was happy to repeat. It seemed an opportune moment to kindle, even within the International, the fire of nationalist hatreds. According to it, the General Council was a German committee with a Bismarckian brain behind it.[42]

Having clearly established that certain members of the General Council could not claim to be 'Gauls first and foremost', *La Révolution sociale* could do no more than adopt the second slogan of the European police, and attack the Council's 'authoritarianism'.

What then was the evidence on which these puerile attacks rested? The General Council had let the Alliance die a natural death, and in consort with the Geneva Federal Committee, had prevented its resurrection. In addition, it had asked that the Chaux-de-Fonds Committee take a title which would enable it to live in peace with the great majority of Swiss Internationalists.

Apart from these 'authoritarian' acts, what other use had the General Council made, from October 1869 to October 1871, of the wide-ranging powers granted it by the Basle Congress?

1. On 8 February 1870, the 'Society of Positivist Proletarians' in Paris asked the General Council for admission. The Council replied that the positivist principles enshrined in those rules of the society that dealt with capital were in flagrant contradiction with the preamble to the General Rules; that they must therefore strike them out, and join the International not as 'positivists' but as 'proletarians', though they would still be perfectly free to reconcile their theories with the general principles of the Association. The section, recognizing the justice of this ruling, joined the International.

2. In Lyons, there had been a split between the 1865 section and a section of recent origin in which, in addition to perfectly honest workers, the Alliance was represented by Albert Richard and Gaspard Blanc. As so often happens in such cases, the judgement of an arbitration court set up in Switzerland was not recognized. On 15 February 1870, the recently formed section did not merely

42. In point of fact that national make-up of the Council is as follows: 20 English, 15 French, 7 German (5 of them founders of the International), 2 Swiss, 2 Hungarian, 1 Polish, 1 Belgian, 1 Irish, 1 Danish and 1 Italian [Marx].

demand that the General Council should pronounce on the dispute in virtue of Regulation II/7, but actually sent it a 'judgement' to give – expelling and slandering the members of the 1865 section – to be signed and sent back *by return of post*! The Council deplored such an unheard-of proceeding, and demanded that some justification be given. To that demand, the 1865 section replied that the evidence for charges against Albert Richard had been laid before the arbitration court, but Bakunin had taken possession of it, and refused to return it, thus making it impossible to send it to the General Council. The Council's decision in this matter, dated 8 March, aroused no objection from either side.

3. The French branch in London, having accepted members of a doubtful character (to say the least), had gradually developed into the fief of M. Félix Pyat. He used it to organize highly compromising demonstrations in favour of the assassination of Louis Bonaparte, etc., and, under cover of the International, to get his ridiculous manifestoes sent all over France. The General Council merely stated in the Association's organs that M. Pyat was no longer a member of the International, and that it therefore bore no responsibility for anything he might say or do.[43] The French branch then declared that it recognized neither the General Council nor the Congresses; it stuck notices up all over London stating that apart from itself, the rest of the International was an anti-revolutionary society. The arrest of the French members on the eve of the plebiscite, on grounds of conspiracy (in fact contrived by the police, but given a certain semblance of probability by Pyat's manifestoes), forced the General Council to publish in *Marseillaise* and *Réveil* its resolution of 10 May 1870,[44] declaring that the so-called French branch had not belonged to the International for over two years, and that its actions were actually the work of the police. The need for this step was proved by the declaration in those same newspapers by the Paris Federal Committee, and those of the Parisian Internationalists during their trial – both of which were based on the Council's resolution.[45] The French branch had disappeared when the war began, but like

43. Félix Pyat was a petty-bourgeois democrat and a member of the Paris Commune. For the General Council's statement, see *IWMA* II, p. 224.

44. See *IWMA* III, pp. 235–6.

45. The resolution alluded to here is that of 7 July 1868, repudiating the actions of Félix Pyat. See *IWMA* II, p. 224.

the Alliance in Switzerland, it was to reappear in London, with new allies and under other names.

In the final days of the Conference, some of the exiled Communards formed a 'French section of 1871', some thirty-five strong. The first 'authoritarian' act of the General Council was a public denunciation of the secretary of that section, Gustave Durand, as a French police spy. The evidence in our possession proves that the police intended to help Durand, first of all at the Conference, and later by getting him onto the General Council. The rules of the new section bound its members to 'accept no delegation to the General Council other than from their own section', so citizens Theisz[46] and Bastelica resigned from the Council.

On 17 October, the section delegated two of its members to the Council, with formal instructions, one of whom was none other than M. Chautard, a former member of the artillery committee,[47] whom the Council refused to accept after an examination of the rules of the 1871 section.[48] It will be sufficient here to recall the major points in the debate to which these rules gave rise. They refer to article 2:

'To be accepted as a member of the section, one must justify one's means of existence, present guarantees of morality, etc.' In its resolution of 17 October 1871, the Council proposed that the phrase 'justify one's means of existence' be struck out. 'In cases of doubt,' said the Council, 'a section can certainly investigate a man's means of existence as a "guarantee of morality"; but in other cases, as with refugees, workers on strike etc., the absence of means of existence may well in itself be a guarantee of morality. To demand that candidates justify their means of existence as a general condition for joining the International would be a bourgeois innovation, contrary to both the spirit and the letter of the General Rules'. The section replied that the General Rules made the sections responsible for the morality of their members, and consequently allowed their right to secure such guarantees *as they thought fit*. To this the General Council replied on 7 November:[49]

46. Albert Theisz was a metal-cutter, a Proudhonist and a member of the Paris Commune.

47. I.e. the artillery committee of the Paris National Guard.

48. Shortly afterwards, this man whom they had tried to force upon the General Council was expelled from his section as being an agent of the Thiers police. He was accused by the very people who had earlier thought him the best man to represent them on the Council [Marx].

49. See *IWMA* V, pp. 339–45.

According to this view, an International section founded by teetotallers could insert in its special rules some such article as: 'To be a member of the section, one must swear to abstain from all alcoholic drink.' In short, the most ridiculous and extraordinary conditions of admission into the International could be laid down by the sections in their special rules, especially if this is done on the pretext of securing the morality of their members . . .

The French section of 1871 have added that 'the means of existence' of strikers are to be found in 'the strike fund'. To this one must reply, first that there is often no such 'fund'.

Further, official English inquiries have proved that the majority of English working men . . . are obliged, whether by strikes or lack of work, by inadequate wages or unfair terms of payment or a number of other possible causes, to have constant recourse to pawn-shops and money-lenders, 'means of existence' of which one cannot demand justification without making quite unacceptable inquiries into the private lives of citizens.

Now there can be one of two possibilities: either the section does not inquire into 'means of existence' as 'guarantees of morality', in which case the General Council's proposition is quite apt . . . Or the section, in article 2 of its rules, has intentionally made the justification of one's 'means of existence' a condition for admission in addition to 'guarantees of morality' . . . in which case the Council declares that this is a bourgeois innovation contrary in letter and spirit to the General Rules.

Article 11 of the section's rules reads: 'One or several delegates shall be sent to the General Council.' The Council asked that this article be struck out, 'because the General Rules of the International do not allow any sections the right to send delegates to the General Council'. It added:

The General Rules only recognize two means of electing members to the General Council: either they are elected by the Congress, or they are coopted by the General Council . . . It is quite true that the various sections existing in London were invited to send delegates to the General Council, but in order not to infringe the General Rules, they always did it as follows: The General Council first determined the number of delegates to be sent by each section, reserving to itself the right to accept or reject them in accordance with the Council's estimate of each one's ability to fulfil the general functions demanded of him. These delegates became members of the General Council not in virtue of being delegated by their sections, but in virtue of the Council's statutory right to coopt new members. Having until the decision of the last Conference functioned both as General Council of the International Association and as the Central Council for England, the London Council considered it valuable, in addition to the members it adopted directly, to accept members first delegated by their respective sections. It would be oddly mistaken to compare the method by which the General Council is elected to that used for the Paris Federal Council, which was not even a national Council appointed by a national Congress (as, for instance, the Federal Councils of Brussels or Madrid). The Paris Federal Council was entirely made up of delegates from the Paris sections . . . The way the General Council is elected is determined by the General Rules . . . and its members can accept no overriding mandate other than that of the Rules and Administrative Regulations . . . If one reads it in the light of the preceding paragraph, article 11 can only mean a complete change in the make-up of the General Council whereby, contrary to article 5 of the General Rules, it would consist only of delegates from the London sections, with the influence of local groups replacing that of the entire International Working Men's Association.

In conclusion, the General Council, whose prime duty is to carry out the resolutions of the Congresses (see Administrative Regulation II/2, adopted by the Geneva Congress), said that it considered as quite irrelevant to the question . . . the ideas put forward by the French section of 1871 concerning radical changes to be made in the articles of the General Rules bearing on its constitution.[50]

The Council further declared that it would admit two delegates from the section on the same conditions as those it accepted from the other London sections.

The '1871 section', far from finding this response satisfactory, put out a 'Declaration' on 14 December, signed by all its members – including the new secretary who was shortly afterwards expelled by the refugee society for unbefitting conduct. According to that declaration, the General Council, by refusing to usurp the functions of a legislative body, was guilty 'of a completely naturalistic distortion of the social idea' [*sic*].

Here then are a few examples of the kind of good faith which characterizes the formulation of this document.

The London Conference had approved the conduct of the German workers during the war. Obviously that resolution, proposed by a Swiss delegate, seconded by a Belgian, and accepted unanimously, referred only to those German members of the International who were – or still are – in prison for their anti-

50. This paragraph appears to continue quoting from the General Council's resolutions of 7 November, but the passages in question do not appear in Marx's manuscript as printed in *IWMA* V.

chauvinist activities during the war. In order further to avoid any possibility of its being interpreted pejoratively, the General Council's secretary for France had made very clear the exact meaning of the resolution in a letter published in *Qui Vive!*, *La Constitution*, *Le Radical*, *L'Émancipation*, *L'Europe*, and elsewhere. A week later, however, on 20 November 1871, fifteen members of the '1871 French section' sent to *Qui Vive!* a 'protest' filled with attacks on the German workers, and denouncing the resolution of the Conference as irrefutable proof that the General Council was possessed by 'the pan-Germanic idea'. The whole of the feudalist, liberal and police-controlled press of Germany was not slow to seize upon this incident to show the German workers how vain were their dreams of international unity. Finally, the protest of 20 November was endorsed by the entire 1871 section in its Declaration of 14 December.

To indicate 'the general tendency to authoritarianism into which the General Council was slipping', it referred to 'the publication by that same General Council of an *official* edition of the General Rules *revised by itself*'. A glance at the new edition of the Rules is enough to establish that every paragraph has a reference in the appendix to the sources proving its authenticity! As for the phrase '*official* edition', the first Congress of the International had decided that the '*official* and *obligatory* text of the Rules and Regulations is to be published by the General Council'. (See *Congrès ouvrier de l'Association Internationale des Travailleurs, tenu à Genève du 3 au 8 septembre 1866*,[51] p. 27, note.)

Needless to say, the 1871 section was in continuous contact with the dissidents of Geneva and Neuchâtel. One of its members – Chalain – who had used far more energy in attacking the General Council than he had ever used in defending the Commune, was suddenly rehabilitated by Malon, who had shortly beforehand made highly serious accusations against him in a letter to a member of the Council. In any case, the '1871 French section' had barely put out its declaration when civil war broke out within its ranks. First Theisz, Avrial and Camélinat[52] resigned. It then went on to break up into several small groups, one of which was led by a certain gentleman, Pierre Vesinier, who had been expelled from

51. Printed in Freymond, op. cit., vol. I.

52. Augustin Avrial was a mechanic, a left-wing Proudhonist and a member of the Paris Commune. Zephyrin Camélinat was a bronze-worker, a Proudhonist and a member of the Paris Commune.

the General Council for his slanders against Varlin and others, and then expelled from the International by the Belgian Commission appointed by the Brussels Congress in 1868.[53] Another of these groups was founded by B. Landeck, who was freed from his 'scrupulously regarded' commitment 'to take no further part in *political affairs or the International in France*' by the unexpected absconding of Prefect of Police Piétri on 4 September! (See *Troisième procès de l'Association Internationale des Travailleurs de Paris*, 1870, p. 4.) On the other hand, the mass of French refugees in London established a section which was completely in harmony with the General Council.

IV

The partisans of the Alliance, in the guise of the Neuchâtel Federal Committee,[54] trying yet another attempt to break up the International, this time on a far larger scale, summoned a Congress of their sections to be held at Sonvillier on 12 November 1871. Back in July, two letters from Master Guillaume to his friend Robin[55] had threatened the General Council with a campaign of this kind if it persisted in refusing to recognize them as against 'the Geneva brigands'.

The Sonvillier Congress consisted of sixteen delegates, representing nine sections in all, among them the new 'Socialist Revolutionary Propaganda and Action Section' in Geneva.

The Sixteen began with an anarchist decree, declaring the French-Swiss Federation dissolved – to which the Federation responded by immediately expelling the Alliance supporters from all its sections, and letting them go off to enjoy their own 'autonomy'. Apart from that, the Council had to admit that they had one flash of good sense in deciding to accept the title of 'Jura Federation' which the London Conference had bestowed on them.

This Congress of Sixteen then proceeded to the 'reorganization' of the International, putting out against the Conference and the General Council a 'Circular to all Federations of the International Working Men's Association'.[56]

53. Vesinier had nevertheless been a member of the Commune.

54. I.e. the Chaux-de-Fonds Committee.

55. Paul Robin, like Guillaume, was a schoolteacher and a leading member of Bakunin's Alliance.

56. Printed in Freymond, op. cit., vol. II, pp. 261–5.

The authors of this circular began by accusing the General Council of having summoned a Conference in 1871 instead of a Congress. From the explanations given above, it is clear that such attacks in fact involved the whole International since it had, as a body, accepted the summoning of a Conference – at which, furthermore, the Alliance had had no objection to being represented by citizens Robin and Bastelica.

The General Council has had delegates at each Congress; at Basle, for instance, there were six. The Sixteen now claimed that 'the majority of the Conference was rigged in advance by the admission of six delegates from the General Council with the right to vote'. The fact was that, of the delegates sent to the Conference by the General Council, the French refugees were none other than the representatives of the Paris Commune, while its English and Swiss members could not normally take any part in the sessions, as is clear from the minutes to be submitted to the next Congress. One Council delegate had a mandate from a national federation. According to a letter sent to the Conference, the mandate of another one was withdrawn because his death had been announced in the newspapers. There remained only one other, with the result that the Belgians alone outnumbered the General Council by six to one.[57]

The international police, watching from the sidelines in the person of Gustave Durand, complained bitterly that the General Rules had been violated by holding a 'secret' Conference. They did not even know our Administrative Regulations well enough to know that the administrative sessions of the Congresses *have* to be held in private.

Their complaints none the less found a sympathetic echo among the Sonvillier Sixteen, who declared: 'And to crown everything, one decision of this Conference allows the General Council itself to fix the date and place for the next Congress, or the *Conference to be held in its stead*; thus we are threatened with the suppression of general Congresses, those great public sessions of the International.'

The Sixteen refused to recognize that this decision was merely a way of informing all governments that, whatever repressive

57. Marx's statistics here are rather tendentious. Although several General Council members did hold mandates from sections or federations, thirteen of the twenty-two delegates at the London Conference were in fact on the General Council.

measures they might take, the International was unshakeably resolved to continue its general meetings by hook or by crook.

At the general assembly of the Geneva sections on 2 December 1871, which gave citizens Malon and Lefrançais a bad reception,[58] the latter submitted a proposition that would help to confirm the decrees passed by the Sonvillier Sixteen, and reinforce their complaint against the General Council and their rejection of the legitimacy of the Conference. The Conference had decided that 'the resolutions not intended for publicity will be communicated to the *Federal Councils or Committees of the various countries* by the corresponding secretaries of the *General Council*.'[59] This resolution, in complete conformity with the General Rules and Regulations, was falsified by Malon and his friends as follows: '*A part* of the resolutions of the Conference *will only be* communicated *to the* Federal Councils *and* to the corresponding secretaries'. Once again they accused the General Council of having 'failed in the *principle of sincerity*' by refusing to make use of 'publicity' which would inform the police of the resolutions whose sole object was the reorganization of the International in those countries where it was banned by law.

Citizens Malon and Lefrançais further objected, 'The Conference has infringed on freedom of thought and expression . . . by giving the General Council the right to denounce and disavow any press organ of the sections and federations that discusses either the principles on which the Association is based, or the respective interests of sections and federations, or finally the general interests of the whole Association (see *Égalité*, 21 October).' What do we find in *Égalité*? A resolution in which the Conference 'gives a warning that henceforth the General Council will be bound to publicly denounce and disavow organs of the International which, following the precedents of *Progrès* and *Solidarité*, should discuss in their columns, before the middle-class public, questions exclusively reserved for the local or Federal Committees and the General Council, or for the private and administrative sittings of the Federal or General Congresses'.[60]

To get the full flavour of Malon's lament, one must remember that this resolution has put an end once and for all to the efforts

58. Gustave Lefrançais was a teacher, a left-wing Proudhonist and a member of the Paris Commune.

59. *IWMA* IV, p. 449.

60. Resolution XVII/2 of the London Conference, ibid.

of certain journalists whose aim is to replace the official committees of the International, and play the same part there as the journalistic bohemia plays in the bourgeois world. Following an attempt of that kind, the Geneva Federal Committee were faced with members of the Alliance editing the official journal of the French-Swiss Federation, *Égalité*, in a manner that was totally hostile to them.

In any case, the General Council hardly needed the London Conference in order to publicly denounce and disavow such journalistic malpractice, for the Basle Congress had declared: 'Wherever attacks against the International are published, the nearest branch or committee is held to send at once a copy of such publication to the General Council' (Administrative Regulation V/7). 'It is obvious,' said the French-Swiss Federal Committee in its statement of 20 December 1871 (see *Égalité*, 24 December),

that this article did not imply that the General Council should simply file in its archives the newspapers which attack the Association, but should reply, and if need be, undo the harmful effect of slanders and malicious attacks. It is equally obvious that this article relates to all newspapers in general, and that if we are not prepared to put up freely with attacks from the bourgeois papers, then *a fortiori* we must use the instrument of our central delegation, the General Council, to disavow papers whose attacks upon us are made in the name of our own Association.

We may note, incidentally, that *The Times*, that Leviathan of the capitalist press, the Lyons *Progrès*, a newspaper of the liberal bourgeoisie, and the *Journal de Genève*, an ultra-reactionary paper, made the same attacks on the Conference, indeed in almost the same words, as citizens Malon and Lefrançais.

Having attacked first the calling of the Conference, then its membership and so-called secret character, the circular from Sonvillier went on to attack the resolutions themselves.

Declaring, first, that the Basle Congress had abdicated its authority 'by giving the General Council the right to refuse, to admit, or to suspend sections of the International', it goes on to impute this crime to the Conference: 'This Conference has . . . taken resolutions . . . which are directed towards turning the International, a free federation of autonomous sections, into a hierarchical and authoritarian organization of disciplined sections, entirely under the control of a General Council which may

at its own whim refuse to admit them or suspend their activity!'
Returning later to the Basle Congress, it describes it as having 'dena-
tured the powers of the General Council'.

All the contradictions in the Sonvillier circular boil down to this:
The 1871 Conference is accountable for the voting at the Basle
Congress of 1869, and the General Council is guilty of having
obeyed the Regulations which require it to carry out Congress
resolutions.

In point of fact, the true motive for all these attacks on the
Conference is something far less obvious than might seem at first.
To start with, the Conference had, by its resolutions, totally undermined the intrigues by the Alliance group in Switzerland. Then, the
supporters of the Alliance, in Italy, in Spain, in part of Switzerland
and in Belgium, had established and maintained with incredible
persistence a calculated confusion between Bakunin's outworn
programme and the programme of the International Working Men's
Association.

The Conference brought into the open this intentional misunderstanding in its two resolutions on working-class political action and
on sections with sectarian interests. The first, giving its due to the
political abstention preached in Bakunin's programme, was wholly
justified by all that had gone before, and supported by the General
Rules, the resolution of the Lausanne Congress and other similar
precedents.[61]

Let us now consider the question of the sectarian sections:

The first phase in the struggle of the proletariat against the
bourgeoisie is marked by sectarianism. This is because the
proletariat has not yet reached the stage of being sufficiently
developed to act as a class. Individual thinkers provide a critique
of social antagonisms, and put forward fantastic solutions which
the mass of workers can only accept, pass on, and put into practice. By their very nature, the sects established by these initiators
are abstentionist, strangers to all genuine action, to politics, to
strikes, to coalitions, in brief, to any unified movement. The mass
of the proletariat always remains unmoved by, if not hostile to,
their propaganda. The workers of Paris and Lyons did not want
the Saint-Simonians, Fourierists or Icarians, any more than the
Chartists and trade-unionists of England wanted the Owenists.

61. A footnote at this point in the text quotes in full Resolution IX of the London
Conference, on the political action of the working class. This resolution is printed
above, pp. 953-4.

All these sects, though at first they provide an impetus to the movement, become an obstacle to it once it has moved further forward; they then become reactionary, as witness the sects in France and England, and more recently the Lassalleans in Germany who, having for years hampered the organization of the proletariat, have finally become nothing less than tools of the police. In fact, we have here the proletarian movement still in its infancy, comparable perhaps to the time when astrology and alchemy were the infancy of science. For the founding of the International to become a possibility, the proletariat had to develop further.[62]

In comparison with the fantastic and mutually antagonistic organizations of the sects, the International is the real and militant organization of the proletarian class in every country, linked together in common struggle against the capitalists, the landowners, and their class power organized by the state. Thus the Rules of the International only speak of *workers'* societies, all seeking the same object, and all accepting the same programme – a programme limited to outlining the major features of the proletarian movement, and leaving the details of theory to be worked out as inspired by the demands of the practical struggle, and as growing out of the exchange of ideas among the sections, with an equal hearing given to all socialist views in their journals and congresses.

Just as in any other new stage of history, the old errors come to the surface for a time, only to disappear soon again; so the International has seen sectarian sections arise within it, though never in any very marked form.

By considering the resurrection of the sects as a great advance, the Alliance has shown conclusively that its time is past. For, though it did at first represent certain elements of progress, the Alliance's programme, like a kind of 'Mahommed without the Koran', amounts to no more than a collection of dead ideas, wrapped up in high-sounding phrases whose only function could be to frighten the more foolish of the bourgeois, or provide ammunition against the Internationalists for Bonapartist or other prosecutors.[63]

62. cf. 'Manifesto of the Communist Party', section III/3, in Volume I, above, pp. 88–91.

63. Comments published recently by the police about the International, not excepting Jules Favre's circular to the European powers, nor deputy Sacaze's report on Dufaure's draft law, are stuffed with quotations from the pompous manifestoes of the Alliance. The phraseology they use, radical only in its verbiage, provides reactionaries with just what they are looking for [Marx].

The Conference, at which every shade of socialism was represented, unanimously acclaimed the resolution against sectarian sections; everyone was convinced that that resolution, by bringing the International back onto its own ground, marked a new phase in its forward movement. The supporters of the Alliance, realizing that this resolution was their death-blow, could only see it in terms of a victory of the General Council over the International whereby, as their circular put it, it managed to win sole recognition for the 'special programme' of some members, 'their personal doctrine', 'the orthodox doctrine', 'the official theory alone having any right to be heard in the Association'. However, this was not the fault of those few members, but the necessary result, 'the corrupting effect' of their belonging to the General Council, for 'it is absolutely impossible for any man who has power (!) over his peers to remain a moral man. The General Council has become a circle of intrigue.'

According to the opinion of the Sonvillier Sixteen, the General Rules committed a very serious error in allowing the General Council to coopt new members. With that power, they said, 'the Council could afterwards coopt a whole group of people who would totally alter the tendency of the majority'. It would seem that to them, the mere fact of belonging to the General Council is enough to destroy not only a man's morality, but even his common sense. How else can it be supposed that a majority would transform itself voluntarily into a minority by coopting new members?

However, the Sixteen themselves do not appear wholly convinced on this point; for later on they complain that the General Council has been 'made up of *the same men, continually re-elected*, for five years running' – yet they go on to say that 'most of them are not our regularly elected delegates, since they were not chosen by any Congress'.

The truth of the matter is that the membership of the General Council has kept changing, though certain of the founding members have remained, as in the Federal Councils of Belgium, Switzerland, etc.

The General Council has to fulfil three essential conditions in order to carry out its mandate. First, there must be a large enough membership to do the amount of work involved; second, it must be made up of 'working men from the different countries represented in the International Association';[64] and finally, the

64. 'General Rules', *IWMA* IV, p. 453.

working-class element must predominate. Since, for workers, the demands of their jobs mean that there is inevitably a continual change in the membership of the General Council, how could it fulfil these conditions without having the right to coopt new members? However, more precise definition of that right seems needed, and this was raised at the recent Conference.

The re-election of the General Council as it stood, by successive Congresses – at which England was barely represented – would seem to prove that it was doing its duty within the limits of its possibilities. The Sixteen, however, saw this only as a proof of 'the blind faith of the Congresses', a faith which at Basle was pushed 'to the point of a voluntary abdication of power in favour of the General Council'.

According to them, the 'normal role' of the Council should be 'simply that of an office for correspondence and statistics'. This definition was derived from an incorrect translation of the Rules.

Unlike the rules of any bourgeois society, the General Rules of the International barely touch on its administrative organization. They leave that to be worked out through experience and formulated by future Congresses. None the less, since it is only unity and common action, among the sections in the various countries that can confer a distinctively international character, the Rules are more concerned with the General Council than with any other element in the organization.

Rule 6 states: 'The General Council shall form an international agency between the different national and local groups,' and goes on to give examples of the way in which it is to act. Actually among those examples is the instruction that the Council should see that, 'when immediate practical steps should be needed – as, for instance in the case of international quarrels – the action of the associated societies be simultaneous and uniform'. This article continues: 'Whenever it seems opportune, the General Council shall take the initiative of proposals to be laid before the different national or local societies'.[65] Furthermore, the Rules define the part the Council is to play in summoning and preparing for Congresses, and give it certain specific work to be done and laid before them. The Rules see so little opposition between the spontaneous action of groups and the unified action of the Association that they state:

Since the success of the working men's movement in each country

65. Ibid.

cannot be secured but by the power of union and combination, while, on the other hand, the usefulness of the International General Council must greatly depend [on the circumstance whether it has to deal with a few national centres of working men's associations, or with a great number of small and disconnected local societies]; the members of the International Association shall use their utmost efforts to combine the disconnected working men's societies of their respective countries into national bodies, represented by central national organs.[66]

Administrative Regulation II/2, adopted by the Geneva Congress, states: 'The General Council is *bound to execute* the Congress resolutions.'[67] This regulation rendered official the position occupied by the General Council from the first of being the Association's *executive arm*. It would be difficult to carry out orders without moral 'authority' in the absence of any other 'freely given authority'. The Geneva Congress also at that time ordered the General Council to publish 'the official and obligatory text of the Rules'.[68]

The same Congress also resolved: 'Every branch is at liberty to make rules and bye-laws for its local administration, adapted to local circumstances and the laws of its country. But these rules and bye-laws must not contain anything contrary to the General Rules and Regulations.'[69]

We may note first of all that there is not the slightest allusion to special declarations of principle, nor to special missions to be undertaken by any group on its own initiative outside the common objective being pursued by all the groups in the International. It is simply a matter of each section's right to adapt the General Rules and Regulations 'to local circumstances and the laws of its country'.

In the second place, who is to pronounce on the conformity of such special rules with the General Rules? Obviously if there does not exist any 'authority' empowered to do so, then the resolution is null and void. Not merely could hostile and police sections be formed, but the Association might also be infiltrated by bourgeois philanthropists and sectarians who have abandoned their own class; these would not only alter the whole character of the Association, but if there were enough of them, they could outnumber the workers at Congresses.

66. Ibid., p. 454.   67. Ibid., p. 457, Marx's emphasis.
68. See p. 766, n. 15.
69. 'General Rules', *IWMA* IV, p. 460.

From the first, the national or local federations have assumed the right in their respective areas to admit or refuse admittance to new sections, depending on whether or not the rules of those sections were in conformity with the General Rules. That this same function should be carried out by the General Council is envisaged in article 7 of the General Rules, which allows *local independent societies*, i.e. societies established outside the federal network of their country, the right to form their own direct links with it. The Alliance did not deign to make use of that right, and did not therefore fulfil the conditions for sending delegates to the Basle Congress.

Article 7 of the Rules also considers the legal obstacles which stand in the way of the formation of national federations in some countries, where the General Council is therefore called on to act as a substitute for a federal council.

Since the fall of the Commune, such legal obstacles have become more numerous in a number of countries, and made the action of the General Council more necessary still if dubious elements are to be kept out of the Association. Thus, recently, committees in France have asked the General Council to intervene to rid them of police spies; while in another major country,[70] the Internationalists have asked it to refuse recognition to any section not founded through a direct mandate either from itself or from them. Their request was motivated by the need to get rid of the kind of *agents provocateurs* whose overwhelming zeal took the form of setting up, one after another, new sections of unparalleled radicalism. From a different direction, certain so-called anti-authoritarian sections had no hesitation in appealing to the Council the moment any internal dispute arose, even demanding that it do all in its power to discipline the opposing side – as happened during the dispute in Lyons. More recently, since the Conference, the Turin 'Workers' Federation' resolved to declare itself a section of the International. There was then a split, with the minority group becoming a 'Society for the Emancipation of the Proletariat'. It joined the International and its first act was to pass a resolution in favour of the Jura Federation. Its paper, *Il Proletario*, was full of angry comments on all forms of authoritarianism. On sending in the subscriptions from the society, its secretary informed the General Council that the older Federation would probably also be sending in subscriptions. He continued:

70. This refers to Austria.

'As you will have read in *Il Proletario*, the Society for the Emancipation of the Proletariat . . . has determined . . . to reject all solidarity with the bourgeoisie who make up the Workers' Federation and pretend to be workers', and he asks the General Council to 'communicate this resolution to all the sections, and to refuse their ten-centime subscriptions should they be sent in'.[71]

Like all the International's groups, the General Council has the duty of issuing propaganda. This it does in its manifestoes, and through its agents who have established the foundations of the International in North America, Germany, and a number of towns in France.

Another of the General Council's functions is to assist during strikes, providing help on behalf of the entire International. (See the reports of the General Council to the various Congresses.) The following instance, among others, indicates how valuable its action has been during strikes. The English Iron-Founders' Resistance Society is in itself an international trade union, with branches in other countries, particularly the United States. However, in a strike by the American foundrymen, the latter found it necessary to get the General Council to intervene to stop English foundrymen being imported to take their places.

The development of the International has forced the General Council, as also the various Federal Councils, into the role of arbitrator.

The Brussels Congress resolved: 'The Federal Councils or Committees shall transmit to the General Council every three months a report on the administration and financial state of their respective branches' (Administrative Regulation IV/3).

Finally, the Basle Congress, which aroused such blind rage among the Sixteen, did no more than formalize the administrative relationship which had grown up as the Association developed. If it did extend the powers of the General Council excessively, whose fault was it if not that of Bakunin, Schwitzguebel, Robert,[72]

71. Such were at that time the *apparent* views of the Society for the Emancipation of the Proletariat, represented by its corresponding secretary, a friend of Bakunin's. In fact, the tendencies of this branch were very different. The society, having expelled this representative for the double disloyalty of mis-appropriating funds and being on terms of close friendship with the chief of police in Turin, provided further explanations which dispelled all mis-understanding between it and the General Council [Marx].

72. Adhemar Schwitzguebel was a Swiss engraver; Fritz Robert, a Swiss teacher.

Guillaume, and the other Alliance delegates, who were loud in demanding that very thing? Would they by chance accuse themselves of 'blind faith' in the General Council in London?

Here are two of the Administrative Regulations adopted by the Basle Congress:

II/4: 'Every new branch or society intending to join the International is bound immediately to announce its adhesion to the General Council;' and II/5: 'The General Council has the right to admit or to refuse the affiliation of any new branch or group, subject to appeal to the next Congress.' As for local independent societies coming into existence outside the federal networks, these articles merely confirm the practice observed from the very beginning of the International – a practice whose continuation is really a matter of life and death for the Association. But it would be going too far to generalize the practice by applying it without distinction to any section or society in the process of formation. What these articles really give the General Council is the right to interfere in the internal affairs of the federations, but they have never in fact been applied by the General Council in that way. Indeed it defies the Sixteen to find a single instance of its having interfered in the affairs of new sections wishing to become affiliated to existing federations or groups.

The resolutions just quoted relate to sections in the process of formation; the following refer to sections already granted recognition:

II/6: 'The General Council has also the right of suspending till the meeting of the next Congress any branch of the International.

II/7: 'In case of conflict between the societies or branches of a national group, or between groups of different nationalities, the General Council shall have the right to decide the conflict, subject to appeal at the next Congress, which will decide definitively.'

These two articles are necessary for extreme situations, but up to now the General Council has never in fact made use of them. The account given above shows that it has not suspended a single section, and that in any matter of dispute, it has done no more than act as an arbitrator at the request of both parties.

We come finally to one function which the needs of the struggle oblige the General Council to assume. However it may distress the supporters of the Alliance, the General Council, simply because of the persistence of the attacks made against it by all the enemies of the proletarian movement, stands in the forefront of those who must defend the International Working Men's Association.

v

Having shown the International in its true colours, the Sixteen go on to tell us what it *should* be like.

First, the General Council should officially be no more than an office for correspondence and providing statistics. Its administrative functions being abandoned, its correspondence would obviously be reduced simply to reproducing information already published in the Association's various journals. The correspondence office would therefore barely exist. As for providing statistics, that is a job that cannot be done without a powerful organization, and even more, as expressly stated in the original Rules, without a common objective. Now since these things smack strongly of 'authoritarianism', while there should perhaps *be* an office, it should not be a statistical office. In brief, the General Council should go. The same logic would also disband Federal Councils, local committees and all other centres of 'authority'. All that would remain would be autonomous sections.

And what would then be the mission of those 'autonomous sections', freely federated, and joyfully unshackled by any authority, 'even authority chosen and constituted by workers'?

At this point, one had to fill in the gaps in the Circular from the report of the Jura Federal Committee submitted to the Congress of the Sixteen. 'To make the working class the true representative of the new interests of mankind', their organization must be 'guided by the *idea* to which all else is subordinate. To *formulate* that idea out of the needs of our age, and the inner tendencies of human beings through a prolonged study of the phenomena of social life, and then to *bring that idea home* to our working men's organizations, such must be our object . . . etc.' Finally, there must be established 'within our working population a truly revolutionary socialist *school*'.

So, all of a sudden, our autonomous working men's sections have become so many *schools*, with these gentlemen from the Alliance as their teachers. They *formulate the idea* through 'prolonged study'. They then 'bring it home to our working men's associations'. To them, the working class is so much raw material, a chaos which needs the breath of their Holy Spirit to give it form.

All of this is simply a paraphrase of the Alliance's own old programme,[73] opening with the words: 'The socialist minority in the League of Peace and Freedom having left that League' proposes to found 'a new Alliance of Socialist Democracy . . . taking as its *special mission* the study of political and philosophical questions . . .' That is where their 'idea' first came from! 'Such an undertaking . . . will give the sincere socialist democrats of Europe and America the *means* of communicating with one another, and strengthening *their ideas*.'[74]

Thus, by their own admission, the minority group within a bourgeois society only wormed their way into the International shortly before the Basle Congress in order to use it *as a means* of presenting themselves to the mass of workers as the hieratic practitioners of a secret science, a science summed up in four sentences, culminating in the 'economic and social equality of the classes'.

Apart from this theoretical 'mission', there was also a practical side to the new organization being proposed for the International. 'The society of the future', says the Circular of the Sixteen, 'must be nothing but the universalization of the organization adopted by the International. We must therefore hasten to make that organization as close as possible to our ideal.'

'How can a free and egalitarian society emerge from an authoritarian organization? It is impossible. The International, the embryo of the future human society, must begin now to be the faithful reflection of our principles of liberty and federation.'

In other words, just as the monasteries of the Middle Ages were a reflection of the life of heaven, so the International must be a reflection of the new Jerusalem, whose 'embryo' is borne within

---

73. The original programme of the Alliance, which dates from October 1868, is reproduced in the German version as an appendix to Marx and Engels's pamphlet *Ein Komplott gegen die Internationale Arbeiterassoziation, MEW* 18, pp. 467–8, and in the French version, with Marx's marginal comments in *IWMA* III, pp. 273–8.

74. The Alliance supporters, who never stop reproving the General Council for having convened a private Conference at a time when summoning a public Congress would have been the height either of treason or idiocy, these absolute partisans of being open and above board, have – in complete disregard of our Rules – organized a truly secret society actually within the International, directed against the International, and aimed at getting the sections unwittingly under the priestly control of Bakunin. The General Council intends to demand an inquiry at the next Congress into this secret organization and those running it in certain countries, Spain for instance [Marx].

the womb of the Alliance. Had the Communards realized that the Commune was 'the embryo of the future human society', they would have thrown away all discipline and all weapons – things which must disappear as soon as there are no more wars – and they would not have been defeated!

But to make it quite clear that, despite their 'prolonged study', the Sixteen were not hatching this charming plan for disorganizing and disarming the International at a time when it was fighting for its life, Bakunin has just published the original text in his memorandum on the organization of the International.[75] (See *Almanach du Peuple pour 1872*, Geneva.)

VI

Now read the report presented by the Jura Committee to the Congress of the Sixteen. 'To read this', says their official journal, *La Révolution sociale* (16 November), 'will give the *true measure* of what may be expected in the way of dedication and practical intelligence from the members of the Jura Federation'. It begins by attributing to 'those terrible events', the Franco-Prussian war and the civil war in France, 'a somewhat *demoralizing* influence . . . on the situation of sections of the International'.

Though in fact the Franco-Prussian war may have tended to *disorganize* the sections by taking away a large number of workers into both armies, it is equally true to say that the fall of the Empire and Bismarck's open declaration of a war of conquest, gave rise in Germany and England to an impassioned struggle between the bourgeoisie who sided with the Prussians, and the proletariat who affirmed their internationalism more strongly than ever. In this way the International was to gain ground in both countries. In America, its doing so created a split in the vast body of German proletarian immigrants; the internationalist group broke away completely from the chauvinist one.

From yet another point of view, the advent of the Commune in Paris gave an unprecedented impulse to the external development of the International, and to the vigorous support for its principles by the sections in every country – except however the Jura Federation, whose report continues thus: since 'the beginning of the battle of the giants . . . we have been forced to reflect . . . that

75. English excerpts in G. D. Maximoff (ed.), *The Political Philosophy of Bakunin*, Collier-Macmillan, 1964.

some people are merely concealing their weakness ... To many people this situation (in their ranks) is a sign of decrepitude', but, 'on the contrary, it is ... an ideal situation *for a total transformation* of the International' – according to their image. A closer look at this advantageous situation will make their modest wish clearer.

Leaving aside the Alliance, which had been dissolved and its place taken by the Malon section, the Committee had to report on the situation in twenty sections. Among them, seven repudiated it totally; here is what the report has to say:

> The cabinet-makers' section, and the engravers' and engine-turners' section of Bienne, have never replied to *any* of the communications we have sent them.
>
> The trades' sections of Neuchâtel, consisting of carpenters, cabinet-makers, engravers and engine-turners, have made *no* reply to the communications of the Federal Committee.
>
> We have not been able to hear *any* news from the Val-de-Ruz section.
>
> The Le Locle section of engravers and engine-turners have given *no* reply to the communications of the Federal Committee.

This is presumably what is meant by the *free* relationship between autonomous sections and their Federal Committee.

Another section, that of 'the engravers and engine-turners of the district of Courtelary, after three years of stubborn persistence ... are now ... forming a resistance society' *outside the International*, a fact which did not deter them from sending two delegates to represent them at the Congress of the Sixteen.

We then come to four sections that are well and truly dead:

> The central Bienne section has for the moment collapsed; one of its keenest members however wrote recently that all hope of seeing the International born again in Bienne was not lost.
>
> The Saint-Blaise section has fallen.
>
> The Catébat section, after a splendid career, was forced to yield in face of the intrigues of the lords (!) of the district to dissolve this *valiant* section.
>
> Finally, the Corgémont section too fell victim to intrigues by the bosses.

We then come to the central section of the Courtelary district which 'took the wise step of *suspending* activities' – though it still sent two delegates to the Congress of the Sixteen.

There are then four sections whose existence is doubtful to say the least.

The Grange section has been reduced to a tiny kernel of socialist workers . . . Their local action is hampered by their small numbers.

The central section of Neuchâtel has had a great deal to suffer from circumstances, and had it not been for the dedication and activity of certain of its members, it would certainly have collapsed.

The central section of Le Locle, having hung between life and death for several months, finally broke up. Quite recently it has been reconstituted . . .

– clearly for the one object of sending two delegates to the Congress of the Sixteen!

The socialist propaganda section of La Chaux-de-Fonds is in a critical situation . . . Its position, far from improving, is in fact tending to grow worse.

Two sections then follow, the study circles of Saint-Imier and Sonvillier, which are only mentioned by the way, with nothing said as to their condition.

There remains one model section which, judging from its being called the '*central* section' would seem to be no more than the remainder of all the sections that no longer exist.

'The central section of Moutier has certainly suffered least . . . Its committee has been in continuous contact with the Federal Committee . . . (although) *sections are not yet consolidated . . .*' The explanation for this is that 'the action of the Moutier section is especially facilitated by the *excellent attitude* of a working-class population . . . with plebeian ways of living; we should like to see the working class of this district become still more independent of political elements.'

It is quite clear that this report does 'give the *precise measure* of what can be expected from the dedication and *practical intelligence* of the members of the Jura Federation'. They might have completed it by adding that the workers of La Chaux-de-Fonds, the original seat of their committee, have always refused to have any dealing with them! In fact, quite recently, at the general assembly of 18 January 1872, they replied to the Circular of the Sixteen with a unanimous vote confirming the resolution of the London Conference as well as that of the French-Swiss Congress of May 1871: 'to exclude permanently from the International Bakunin, Guillaume and their disciples'.

Does there remain anything more to be said as to the value of this so-called Sonvillier Congress, which, by its own admission caused 'an outbreak of war – open war – within the International'?

Undoubtedly these people, whose influence is out of all proportion to their numbers, have had considerable success. All the liberal and police press has openly supported them; they were echoed in their personal attacks on the General Council and their generalized attacks on the International by self-styled reformers from many countries; in England, by bourgeois republicans, whose intrigues had been unmasked by the General Council; in Italy, by dogmatic free-thinkers who have just founded a 'Universal Society of Rationalists' under the banner of Stefanoni,[76] to have its statutory headquarters in Rome, an 'authoritarian' and 'hierarchical' organization with its atheist monks and nuns, with statutes allowing for a marble bust to be placed in its congress hall of any bourgeois prepared to donate ten thousand francs or more; and finally in Germany, by Bismarckian socialists who not only run a police-backed paper, *Neuer Social-Demokrat*, but also sport the white shirts of the Prusso-German empire.[77]

In a touching appeal, the Sonvillier conclave asks that all International sections stress the urgency of holding an immediate Congress in order, as citizens Malon and Lefrançais put it, 'to fight off the successive encroachments of the London Council'; though what they really mean is to replace the International with the Alliance. This appeal received so encouraging a response that they were immediately reduced to falsifying one of the votes of the last Belgian Congress. They say in their official organ (*La Révolution sociale*, 4 January 1872): 'Finally, more important still, the Belgian sections met in Congress in Brussels on 24 and 25 December, and unanimously voted a resolution identical to that voted by the Sonvillier Congress, on the urgency of summoning a General Congress.' It is worth noting that this Belgian Congress did nothing of the kind: it charged the Belgian Congress, which is not due to meet until June, to work out a set of projected new General Rules to submit to the *next Congress* of the International.

In accordance with the wish of the vast majority of the Inter-

---

76. Luigi Stefanoni was a bourgeois democrat who had taken part in Garibaldi's campaign.

77. The *Neuer Social-Demokrat* was the organ of Schweitzer's die-hard Lassallean faction after the ADAV split in 1869 and the section led by Bracke united with Liebknecht and Bebel's Union of German Workers' Societies to form the SDAP ('Eisenach party'). The *blouses blanches* (white shirts) were working-class *provocateurs* organized by the Bonapartist police under the Second Empire.

national, the General Council is only convening the annual Congress for September 1872.

VII

A few weeks after the Conference, Messrs Albert Richard and Gaspard Blanc, the most influential and enthusiastic members of the Alliance, arrived in London with the task of recruiting from among the French refugees auxiliaries prepared to work for the restoration of the Empire, which seemed to them the only way of getting rid of Thiers without being reduced to penury. The General Council issued warnings to all whose interests might be at stake, including the Brussels Federal Council, of their Bonapartist manoeuvres.

In January 1872, they abandoned all pretence, and published a pamphlet: *'The Empire and the new France. An appeal to the French conscience from the people and youth'*.[78]

With the usual modesty of Alliance charlatans, they are loud in their own praise:

We who formed the great army of the French proletariat ... we, the most influential leaders of the International in France[79] ... having had the good fortune to be spared death by shooting, we remain here to set up against ... ambitious parliamentarians, well-fed republicans, and self-styled democrats of every kind ... the flag under which we fight and, despite all slanders, threats and attacks, we cry from the depths of our

---

78. Albert Richard and Gaspard Blanc, *L'Empire et la France nouvelle*, Brussels, 1872.

79. Under the headline 'To the Pillory!', *Égalité* said on 15 February:

'The time has not yet come when the whole story of the Communal movement's defeat in the south of France can be told; but what we can say now, we who have for the most part been witness to the deplorable defeat of the Lyons rising of 30 April, is that this rising failed partly because of the cowardice, the treason and the dishonesty of G. Blanc, who infiltrated everything, carrying out the orders of A. Richard who remained in the background. By their well-planned manoeuvres, these wretched men succeeded in compromising a number of those who took part in the preliminary work of the insurrectionary committees. Furthermore, these traitors succeeded in discrediting the International in Lyons – so much so that when the revolution took place in Paris, the workers in Lyons regarded the International with the utmost mistrust. Hence the total lack of organization; hence, further, the defeat of the rising, a defeat which inevitably brought with it the fall of the Commune, thus left isolated and defenceless. It was only this bloody lesson that made it possible for us to win the workers of Lyons over and get them to rally to the flag of the International. Albert Richard was the spoilt child, the prophet indeed, of Bakunin and his friends' [Marx].

hearts to an astonished Europe the call soon to resound in the hearts of all Frenchmen: 'Long live the Emperor!'.

For Napoleon III, dishonoured and scorned, there must be a magnificent rehabilitation.

So Messrs Albert Richard and Gaspard Blanc, paid out of the secret funds of Invasion III,[80] are, it appears, specially entrusted with that rehabilitation.

Furthermore, they admit: 'We have become Imperialists through the normal progression of our ideas.' There is a confession to warm the hearts of their co-religionists in the Alliance. As in the good old days of *Solidarité*, Richard and Blanc retail their old tags about 'political abstentionism' which, as is clear from their 'normal progression', only becomes a reality where there is absolute despotism, for then the workers abstain from all political activity in the same way as the prisoner abstains from going for walks in the sun.

'The age of the revolutionaries,' they say, 'is over ... communism is limited to Germany and England, Germany especially. It is there, certainly, that it has been receiving serious formulation for a long time before gradually spreading through the whole of the International; and this disquieting progress of *German influence* in the Association has contributed more than a little to hampering its development, or rather, to giving it a new direction in the sections of central and southern France which have never yet taken their slogans from a German.'

One might almost be listening to the great hierophant himself,[81] attributing to himself, as a Russian, a special mission to represent the *Latin races*, dating back to the foundation of the Alliance; or 'the genuine missionaries' of *La Révolution sociale* (2 November 1871) denouncing 'the backward movement which German and Bismarckian thinkers are trying to impose on the International'.

How fortunate that the genuine tradition has not been lost, and that Messrs Richard and Blanc were not shot! So their special 'work' consists in 'giving a new direction' to the International in central and southern France, trying to found Bonapartist sections which would *ipso facto* be essentially 'autonomous'.

As for forming the proletariat into a political party, as recommended by the London Conference, '*After the restoration of the Empire*, we', i.e. Richard and Blanc, 'will soon have done, not just

80. A nickname for Napoleon III.
81. I.e. Bakunin.

with socialist theories, but with the beginnings of their realization as seen in the revolutionary organization of the masses'.

In short, by exploiting the great 'principle of the autonomy of each section' which 'constitutes the real strength of the International . . . especially in *Latin countries*' (*La Révolution sociale*, 4 January), these gentlemen are counting on creating anarchy in the International.

Anarchy – that is the great warhorse of their master, Bakunin, whose doctrines only use certain catch-phrases from socialist theory. To all socialists anarchy means this: the aim of the proletarian movement – that is to say the abolition of social classes – once achieved, the power of the state, which now serves only to keep the vast majority of producers under the yoke of a small minority of exploiters, will vanish, and the functions of government become purely administrative. But to the Alliance it means something different. It designates anarchy in the ranks of the proletariat as *the* infallible means of destroying the powerful concentration of social and political forces in the hands of the exploiters. It is therefore demanding that the International replace its organization with anarchy – just at a time when the old world is in any case trying to destroy it. The international police could ask no better means to prolong the Thiers republic forever, while covering it with the mantle of empire.[82]

REPORT TO THE HAGUE CONGRESS[83]

Citizens,

Since our last Congress at Basle, two great wars have changed the face of Europe: the Franco-German war and the civil war in

82. In his report on the Dufaure law, deputy Sacaze makes his prime object of attack the International's 'organization'. That organization is his *bête noire*. Having noted 'the tremendous advance of this alarming Association', he goes on: 'That Association rejects . . . the shady practices of the sects which came before it. Its organization takes place and undergoes changes in the public view. Thanks to the power of that organization . . . it has gradually extended its sphere of action and influence. It is breaking new ground everywhere.' He then gives a summary description of that organization, and concludes: 'Such, in its carefully planned unity . . . is the plan of this vast organization. Its strength lies in its very conception. It also lies in the mass of its followers, joined in simultaneous action, and ultimately in the unconquerable impulse urging them on' [Marx].

83. This report was adopted by the General Council at a meeting in August 1872 (the precise date is unclear). The Hague Congress of September 1872 was

France. Both of these wars were preceded, accompanied, and followed by a third war – the war against the International Working Men's Association.

The Paris members of the International had told the French people, publicly and emphatically, that voting the plebiscite[84] was voting despotism at home and war abroad. Under the pretext of having participated in a plot for the assassination of Louis Bonaparte, they were arrested on the eve of the plebiscite, 23 April 1870. Simultaneous arrests of Internationalists took place at Lyons, Rouen, Marseilles, Brest, and other towns. In its declaration of 3 May 1870, the General Council stated:[85]

This last plot will worthily range with its two predecessors of grotesque memory. The noisy and violent measures against our French sections are exclusively intended to serve one single purpose – the manipulation of the plebiscite.

In point of fact, after the downfall of the December empire its governmental successors published documentary evidence to the effect that this last plot had been fabricated by the Bonapartist police itself,[86] and that on the eve of the plebiscite, Ollivier,[87] in a private circular, directly told his subordinates, 'The leaders of the International must be arrested or else the voting of the plebiscite can not be satisfactorily proceeded with.'

The plebiscitary farce once over, the members of the Paris Federal Council were indeed condemned, on 8 July, by Louis Bonaparte's own judges, but for the simple crime of belonging to the International and not for any participation in the sham plot. Thus the Bonapartist government considered it necessary to initiate the most ruinous war that was ever brought down upon

---

the only one of the International's Congresses that Marx personally attended, and he read the report in German translation to the open session of the Congress on 5 September. It was published in the *International Herald*, 5, 12 and 19 October.

84. See p. 857, n. 3.

85. *IWMA* III, p. 232. The two predecessors were the trials of the Paris Federal Committee of March and May 1868; see 'Report to the Brussels Congress', above, p. 780.

86. Marx is referring to the *Papiers et correspondance de la famille impériale*, published by the Government of Defence in 1870.

87. Émile Ollivier was Louis Napoleon's Prime Minister from January to August 1870.

France, by a preliminary campaign against the French sections of the International Working Men's Association. Let us not forget that the working class in France rose like one man to reject the plebiscite. Let us no more forget that 'the stock exchanges, the cabinets, the ruling classes and the press of Europe celebrated the plebiscite as a signal victory of the French emperor over the French working class'.[88] (See First Address of the General Council on the Franco-Prussian War, 23 July 1870.)

A few weeks after the plebiscite, when the Imperialist press commenced to fan the war-like passions amongst the French people, the Paris Internationalists, nothing daunted by the government persecutions, issued their appeal of 12 July, 'To the workmen of all nations', denounced the intended war as a 'criminal absurdity', telling their 'brothers of Germany' that their 'division would only result in the complete triumph of despotism on both sides of the Rhine', and declaring, 'We, the members of the International Association, know of no frontiers'.[89] Their appeal met with an enthusiastic echo from Germany, so that the General Council was entitled to state:

The very fact that while official France and Germany are rushing into a fratricidal feud, the workmen of France and Germany send each other messages of peace and goodwill, this great fact, unparalleled in the history of the past, opens the vista of a brighter future. It proves that in contrast to old society, with its economical miseries and its political delirium, a new society is springing up, whose international rule will be *Peace*, because its national ruler will be everywhere the same – *Labour!* The pioneer of that new society is the International Working Men's Association. – Address of 23 July 1870. [90]

Up to the proclamation of the republic, the members of the Paris Federal Council remained in prison, while the other members of the Association were daily denounced to the mob as traitors acting in the pay of Prussia.

With the capitulation of Sedan, when the Second Empire ended as it began, by a parody, the Franco-German war entered upon its second phase. It became a war against the French people. After her repeated solemn declarations to take up arms for the sole purpose of repelling foreign aggression, Prussia now dropped the

88. Above, p. 857.

89. This appeal was published in *Le Réveil*, a left republican Paris newspaper, on 12 July 1870.

90. Above, p. 860.

mask and proclaimed a war of conquest. From that moment she found herself compelled not only to fight the republic in France, but simultaneously the International in Germany. We can here but hint at a few incidents of that conflict.

Immediately after the declaration of war, the greater part of the territory of the North German Confederation, Hanover, Oldenburg, Bremen, Hamburg, Brunswick, Schleswig-Holstein, Mecklenburg, Pomerania, and the province of Prussia, were placed in a state of siege, and handed over to the tender mercies of General Vogel von Falkenstein. This state of siege, proclaimed as a safeguard against the threatening foreign invasion, was at once turned into a state of war against the German Internationalists.

The day after the proclamation of the republic at Paris, the Brunswick Central Committee of the German Social-Democratic Workers' Party, which forms a section of the International within the limits imposed by the law of the country, issued a manifesto[91] (5 September) calling upon the working class to oppose by all means in their power the dismemberment of France, to claim a peace honourable for that country, and to agitate for the recognition of the French republic. The manifesto denounced the proposed annexation of Alsace and Lorraine as a crime tending to transform all Germany into a Prussian barracks, and to establish war as a permanent European institution. On 9 September, Vogel von Falkenstein had the members of the Brunswick Committee arrested and marched off in chains, a distance of 600 miles, to Lötzen, a Prussian fortress on the Russian frontier, where their ignominious treatment was to serve as a foil to the ostentatious feasting of the Imperial guest at Wilhelmshöhe.[92] As arrests, the hunting of workmen from one German state to another, suppression of proletarian papers, military brutality, and police-chicane in all forms, did not prevent the International vanguard of the German working class from acting up to the Brunswick manifesto, Vogel von Falkenstein, by an ukase of 21 September, interdicted all meetings of the Social-Democratic Workers' Party. That interdict was cancelled by another ukase of 5 October, wherein he naively commands the police spies

... to denounce to him personally all individuals who, by public

91. The manifesto referred to here was based on Marx and Engels's letter to the Brunswick Committee of the SDAP (above, pp. 861–3).

92. Louis Napoleon, captured at Sedan, was imprisoned at this castle near Kassel from 5 September 1870 to 19 March 1871.

demonstrations, shall encourage France in her resistance against the conditions of peace imposed by Germany, so as to enable him to render such individuals innocuous during the continuance of the war.

Leaving the cares of the war abroad to Moltke,[93] the king of Prussia contrived to give a new turn to the war at home. By his personal order of 17 October, Vogel von Falkenstein was to lend his Lötzen captives to the Brunswick district tribunal, which, on its part, was either to find grounds for their legal durance, or else return them to the safe keeping of the dread general.

Vogel von Falkenstein's proceedings were, of course, imitated throughout Germany, while Bismarck, in a diplomatic circular, mocked Europe by standing forth as the indignant champion of the right of free utterance of opinion, free press, and free meetings, on the part of the peace party in France. At the very same time that he demanded a freely elected National Assembly for France, in Germany he had Bebel and Liebknecht imprisoned for having, in opposition to him, represented the International in the German parliament, and in order to get them out of the way during the impending general elections.[94]

His master, William the Conqueror, supported him by a decree from Versailles prolonging the state of siege, that is to say, the suspension of all civil law, for the whole period of the elections. In fact, the king did not allow the state of siege to be raised in Germany until two months after the conclusion of peace with France. The stubbornness with which he was insisting upon the state of war at home, and his repeated personal meddling with his own German captives, prove the awe in which he, amidst the din of victorious arms and the frantic cheers of the whole middle class, held the rising party of the proletariat. It was the involuntary homage paid by physical force to moral power.

If the war against the International had been localized, first in France, from the days of the plebiscite to the downfall of the Empire, then in Germany, during the whole period of the resistance of the republic against Prussia, it became general since the rise, and after the fall, of the Paris Commune.

On 6 June 1871, Jules Favre issued his circular to the foreign powers demanding the extradition of the refugees of the Com-

---

93. Helmuth Moltke was the Prussian commander-in-chief.

94. These elections were for the first Reichstag of the new German Empire, formed by the establishment of Prussian hegemony over the south German states and the annexation of Alsace and Lorraine.

mune as common criminals, and a general crusade against the International as the enemy of family, religion, order, and property, so adequately represented in his own person. Austria and Hungary caught the cue at once. On 13 June, a raid was made on the reputed leaders of the Pest [Budapest] Working Men's Union, their papers were seized, their persons sequestered, and proceedings were instituted against them for high treason. Several delegates of the Vienna [section of the] International, happening to be on a visit to Pest, were carried off to Vienna, there to undergo a similar treatment. Beust asked and received from his parliament a supplementary vote of £30,000, 'on behalf of expenses for political information that had become more than ever indispensable through the dangerous spread of the International all over Europe'.

Since that time a true reign of terror against the working class has set in in Austria and Hungary. In its last agonies the Austrian government seems still anxiously to cling to its old privilege of playing the Don Quixote of European reaction.

A few weeks after Jules Favre's circular, Dufaure proposed to his Rurals a law which is now in force, and punishes as a crime the mere fact of belonging to the International Working Men's Association, or of sharing its principles.[95] As a witness before the Rural committee of inquiry on Dufaure's bill, Thiers boasted that it was the offspring of his own ingenious brains and that he had been the first to discover the infallible panacea of treating the Internationalists as the Spanish Inquisition had treated the heretics. But even on this point he can lay no claim to originality. Long before his appointment as saviour of society, the true law which the Internationalists deserve at the hands of the ruling classes had been laid down by the Vienna courts.

On 26 July 1870, the most prominent men of the Austrian proletarian party were found guilty of high treason, and sentenced to years of penal servitude, with one fast day in every month. The law laid down was this:

The prisoners, as they themselves confess, have accepted and acted according to the programme of the German Working Men's Congress of Eisenach (1869). This programme embodies the programme of the International. The International is established for the emancipation of the working class from the rule of the propertied class, and from political dependence. That emancipation is incompatible with the existing institu-

95. On the *loi Dufaure*, see p. 959, n. 19. On the 'Rural Assembly', see above, pp. 879–80.

tions of the Austrian state. Hence, whoever accepts and propagates the principles of the International programme, commits preparatory acts for the overthrow of the Austrian government, and is consequently guilty of high treason.

On 27 November 1871, judgement was passed upon the members of the Brunswick Committee. They were sentenced to various periods of imprisonment. The court expressly referred, as to a precedent, to the law laid down at Vienna.

At Pest, the prisoners belonging to the Working Men's Union, after having undergone for nearly a year a treatment as infamous as that inflicted upon the Fenians by the British government, were brought up for judgement on 22 April 1872. The public prosecutor, here also, called upon the court to apply to them the law laid down at Vienna. They were, however, acquitted.

At Leipzig, on 27 March 1872, Bebel and Liebknecht were sentenced to two years' imprisonment in a fortress for attempted high treason upon the strength of the law as laid down at Vienna. The only distinctive feature of this case is that the law laid down by a Vienna judge was sanctioned by a Saxon jury.

At Copenhagen, the three members of the [Danish] Central Committee of the International, Brix, Pio, and Geleff, were thrown into prison on 5 May [1872] because they had declared their firm resolve to hold an open-air meeting in the teeth of a police order forbidding it. Once in prison they were told that the accusation against them was extended, that the socialist ideas in themselves were incompatible with the existence of the Danish state, and that consequently the mere act of propagating them constituted a crime against the Danish constitution. Again the law as laid down in Vienna! The accused are still in prison awaiting their trial.

The Belgian government, distinguished by its sympathetic reply to Jules Favre's demand of extradition, made haste to propose, through Malou, a hypocritical counterfeit of Dufaure's law.

His Holiness Pope Pius IX gave vent to his feelings in an allocation to a deputation of Swiss Catholics.[96] 'Your government,' said he,

which is republican, thinks itself bound to make a heavy sacrifice for what is called liberty. It affords an asylum to a goodly number of individuals of the worst character. It tolerates that sect of the Inter-

96. The source of this report is unclear, and it may possibly be apocryphal.

national which desires to treat all Europe as it has treated Paris. These gentlemen of the International, who are no gentlemen, are to be feared because they work for the account of the everlasting enemy of God and mankind. What is to be gained by protecting them! One must pray for them.

Hang them first and pray for them afterwards!

Supported by Bismarck, Beust, and Stieber,[97] the Prussian spy-in-chief, the emperors of Austria and Germany met at Salzburg in the beginning of September 1871, for the ostensible purpose of founding a Holy Alliance against the International Working Men's Association. 'Such a European alliance,' declared the *North German Gazette*,[98] Bismarck's private *Moniteur*, 'is the only possible salvation of state, church, property, civilization, in one word, of everything that constitutes European states.'

Bismarck's real object, of course, was to prepare alliances for an impending war with Russia, and the International was held up to Austria as a piece of red cloth is held up to a bull.

Lanza suppressed the International in Italy by simple decree.[99] Sagasta declared it an outlaw in Spain,[1] probably with a view to curry favour with the English stock exchange. The Russian government which, since the emancipation of the serfs, has been driven to the dangerous expedient of making timid concessions to popular claims today, and withdrawing them tomorrow, found in the general hue and cry against the International a pretext for a recrudescence of reaction at home. Abroad, with the intention of prying into the secrets of our Association, it succeeded in inducing a Swiss judge to search, in presence of a Russian spy, the house of Utin,[2] a Russian Internationalist, and the editor of the Geneva *Égalité*, the organ of our French-Swiss Federation. The republican

97. Wilhelm Stieber, as director of the Prussian political police, was an old enemy of Marx, who had exposed his earlier machinations in his book on *The Cologne Communist Trial* (*MECW* 11).

98. *Norddeutsche Allgemeine Zeitung*, a semi-official paper. *Le Moniteur universel* had been the official organ of the Bonapartist regime in France.

99. Giovanni Lanza, the Italian Prime Minister, banned the International on 14 August 1871 and had the Naples section forcibly closed on 20 August.

1. After the harassment that led the Madrid Federal Committee of the International to take refuge in Portugal in summer 1871, Praxedes Sagasta, the Spanish Minister of the Interior, gave instructions for the dissolution of the International's Spanish sections in January 1872.

2. Nikolai Utin was a Russian exile and a supporter of Marx in the International.

government of Switzerland has only been prevented by the agitation of the Swiss Internationalists from handing up to Thiers refugees of the Commune.

Finally, the government of Mr Gladstone, unable to act in Great Britain, at least set forth its good intentions by the police terrorism exercised in Ireland against our sections then in course of formation,[3] and by ordering its representatives abroad to collect information with respect to the International Working Men's Association.

But all the measures of repression which the combined government intellect of Europe was capable of devising, vanish into nothing before the war of calumny undertaken by the lying power of the civilized world. Apocryphal histories and mysteries of the International, shameless forgeries of public documents and private letters, sensational telegrams, followed each other in rapid succession; all the sluices of slander at the disposal of the venal respectable press were opened at once to set free a deluge of infamy in which to drown the execrated foe. This war of calumny finds no parallel in history for the truly international area over which it has spread, and for the complete accord in which it has been carried on by all shades of ruling-class opinion. When the great conflagration took place at Chicago, the telegraph round the world announced it as the infernal deed of the International; and it is really wonderful that to its demoniacal agency has not been attributed the hurricane ravaging the West Indies.

In its former annual reports, the General Council used to give a review of the progress of the Association since the meeting of the preceding Congress. You will appreciate, citizens, the motives which induce us to abstain from that course upon this occasion. Moreover, the reports of the delegates from the various countries, who know best how far their discretion may extend, will in a measure make up for this deficiency. We confine ourselves to the statement that since the Congress at Basle, and chiefly since the London Conference of September 1871, the International has been extended to the Irish in England and to Ireland itself, to Holland, Denmark, and Portugal, that it has been firmly organized in the United States, and that it has established ramifications in Buenos Aires, Australia, and New Zealand.

3. The General Council exposed this in a declaration entitled 'Police Terrorism in Ireland' (9 April 1872); *IWMA* V, pp. 149–50.

The difference between a working class without an International, and a working class with an International, becomes most evident if we look back to the period of 1848. Years were required for the working class itself to recognize the insurrection of June 1848 as the work of its own vanguard. The Paris Commune was at once acclaimed by the universal proletariat.

You, the delegates of the working class, meet to strengthen the militant organization of a society aiming at the emancipation of labour and the extinction of national feuds. Almost at the same moment, there meet at Berlin the crowned dignitaries of the old world in order to forge new chains and to hatch new wars.[4]

Long life to the International Working Men's Association!

SPEECH ON THE HAGUE CONGRESS[5]

In the eighteenth century, it was the custom of kings and potentates to gather in The Hague to discuss the interests of their dynasties.

Despite attempts to arouse our anxieties, we were determined to hold our workers' assembly in this selfsame place. We wanted to appear in the midst of the most reactionary population in order to reinforce the existence and expansion of our great Association and to fortify its hope in the future.

When our decision became known, people talked of the emissaries we had sent out to prepare the ground. Yes, we do not deny that we have such emissaries everywhere; but they are for the most part unknown to us. Our emissaries in The Hague were those workers whose jobs are as hard as those of our emissaries

4. In September 1872 the emperors of Germany, Austria-Hungary and Russia met in Berlin with a view to re-establishing their traditional Holy Alliance. They specifically discussed common action against the revolutionary movement.

5. After the Hague Congress of the International (2–7 September 1872) Marx and many other delegates visited Amsterdam at the invitation of the local section of the International. On 8 September Marx delivered the following speech in German and French at a public meeting. The most accurate report of Marx's speech, in French in *La Liberté*, was inaccessible to us, and it is therefore translated here from the German text printed in *MEW* 18, pp. 159–61. This is itself a translation from the French, checked against the less accurate German report given in the *Volksstaat*; the latter was bowdlerized in the places indicated.

in Amsterdam, and the latter are also workers who do a sixteen-hour working day. It is these men who are our emissaries; there are no others; and in all the countries where we show our face we find them prepared to give us a whole-hearted reception, for they very soon realize that we are fighting to improve their lot.

The Congress in The Hague produced three important results:

It proclaimed the need for the working class to fight the old, crumbling society in the political as in the social sphere; and we congratulate ourselves on the fact that this resolution of the London Conference will henceforth be included in our Rules.[6]

A group had formed in our midst which commended the abstention of the workers from political activity.

We saw it as our duty to point out how dangerous and fateful such principles seemed for the task in hand.

The workers will have to seize political power one day in order to construct the new organization of labour; they will have to overthrow the old politics which bolster up the old institutions, unless they want to share the fate of the early Christians, who lost their chance of heaven on earth because they rejected and neglected such action.

We do not claim, however, that the road leading to this goal is the same everywhere.

We know that heed must be paid to the institutions, customs and traditions of the various countries, and we do not deny that there are countries, such as America and England, and if I was familiar with its institutions, I might include Holland, where the workers may attain their goal by peaceful means. That being the case, we must recognize that in most continental countries the lever of the revolution will have to be force; a resort to force will be necessary one day in order to set up the rule of labour.[7]

The Hague Congress conferred new and even more extensive powers on the General Council.[8] Indeed, at a time when kings are gathering in Berlin for a meeting at which the powerful representatives of feudalism and of the past will plan new and more

6. Marx refers to Resolution IX of the London Conference, directed against the Bakuninists. See above, pp. 953–4.

7. In the *Volksstaat*, this sentence was replaced by, 'But this is not the case in all countries.'

8. The Basle Congress of 1869 had given the General Council power to suspend sections of the International that contravened its Rules, subject to ratification by the next Congress. The Hague Congress extended this power to whole federations.

determined repressive measures against us, at the very moment when persecution is being organized, the Hague Congress saw the appropriateness and necessity of extending the powers of the General Council and centralizing all actions for the coming struggle, because these actions would be helpless in isolation. Furthermore, who need worry about the delegation of power to the General Council except our enemies? Does the General Council have a bureaucracy or an armed police force to compel obedience? Is its authority not purely of a moral nature, and does it not submit its decisions to the judgement of the federations, which are entrusted with their implementation? If kings were forced to uphold their power under such conditions, without an army, without police and without courts, having only moral influence and moral authority, then they would present only a frail obstacle to the forward march of the revolution.

Finally, the Hague Congress moved the seat of the General Council to New York. Many people, even friends, showed surprise at this decision. Have they forgotten, then, that America is becoming the workers' part of the world *par excellence*, that each year half a million people – workers – emigrate to this other continent, and that the International must strike powerful roots into this soil, where the workers are the dominant force? Moreover, the Congress decision empowers the General Council to coopt members whose cooperation it regards as necessary and useful for the good of the common cause. Let us trust to their good judgement and expect that they will succeed in selecting people who are up to the task and who will know how to hold up the banner of our Association with a firm hand in Europe.

Citizens, let us remember the basic principle of the International: solidarity. We will only be able to attain the goal we have set ourselves if this life-giving principle acquires a secure foundation among the workers of all countries. The revolution requires solidarity, as the great example of the Paris Commune teaches us, for this most powerful uprising of the Parisian proletariat failed[9] because no great revolutionary movements equal in stature arose in any of the other centres such as Berlin, Madrid, etc.

As far as I am concerned, I shall continue my work and strive constantly to establish this solidarity, which will bear such rich

9. In the *Volksstaat*, the remainder of this sentence was replaced by, 'only because solidarity on the part of the workers of other countries was lacking'.

fruit in the future, amongst the entire working class. No, I shall not be withdrawing from the International, and all the rest of my life, like my efforts in the past, will be dedicated to the triumph of the social ideas which will one day – rest assured of this! – bring about the rule of the proletariat over the entire world.

Political Indifferentism[1]

'The working class must not constitute itself a political party; it must not, under any pretext, engage in political action, for to combat the state is to recognize the state: and this is contrary to eternal principles. Workers must not go on strike; for to struggle to increase one's wages or to prevent their decrease is like recognizing *wages*: and this is contrary to the eternal principles of the emancipation of the working class!

'If in the political struggle against the bourgeois state the workers succeed only in extracting concessions, then they are guilty of compromise; and this is contrary to eternal principles. All peaceful movements, such as those in which English and American workers have the bad habit of engaging, are therefore to be despised. Workers must not struggle to establish a legal limit to the working day, because this is to compromise with the masters, who can then only exploit them for ten or twelve hours, instead of fourteen or sixteen. They must not even exert themselves in order legally to prohibit the employment in factories of children under the age of ten, because by such means they do not bring to an end the exploitation of children over ten: they thus commit a new compromise, which stains the purity of the eternal principles.

'Workers should even less desire that, as happens in the United States of America, the state whose budget is swollen by what is taken from the working class should be obliged to give primary education to the workers' children; for primary education is not complete education. It is better that working men and working women should not be able to read or write or do sums than that they should receive education from a teacher in a school run by

1. This article was written in January 1873, and published in the Lodi *Almanacco Repubblicano per l'anno 1874*. Its companion piece in the *Almanacco* was Engels's *On Authority* (see *MECW* 23, pp. 422–5).

the state. It is far better that ignorance and a working day of sixteen hours should debase the working classes than that eternal principles should be violated.

'If the political struggle of the working class assumes violent forms and if the workers replace the dictatorship of the bourgeois class with their own revolutionary dictatorship, then they are guilty of the terrible crime of *lèse-principe*; for, in order to satisfy their miserable profane daily needs and to crush the resistance of the bourgeois class, they, instead of laying down their arms and abolishing the state, give to the state a revolutionary and transitory form. Workers must not even form single unions for every trade, for by so doing they perpetuate the social division of labour as they find it in bourgeois society; this division, which fragments the working class, is the true basis of their present enslavement.

'In a word, the workers should cross their arms and stop wasting time in political and economic movements. These movements can never produce anything more than short-term results. As truly religious men they should scorn daily needs and cry out with voices full of faith: "May our class be crucified, may our race perish, but let the eternal principles remain immaculate!" As pious Christians they must believe the words of their pastor, despise the good things of this world and think only of going to Paradise. In place of Paradise read the *social liquidation* which is going to take place one day in some or other corner of the globe, no one knows how, or through whom, and the mystification is identical in all respects.

'In expectation, therefore, of this famous social liquidation, the working class must behave itself in a respectable manner, like a flock of well-fed sheep; it must leave the government in peace, fear the police, respect the law and offer itself up uncomplaining as cannon-fodder.

'In the practical life of every day, workers must be the most obedient servants of the state; but in their hearts they must protest energetically against its very existence, and give proof of their profound theoretical contempt for it by acquiring and reading literary treatises on its abolition; they must further scrupulously refrain from putting up any resistance to the capitalist regime apart from declamations on the society of the future, when this hated regime will have ceased to exist!'

It cannot be denied that if the apostles of political indifferentism were to express themselves with such clarity, the working class would make short shrift of them and would resent being insulted by these doctrinaire bourgeois and displaced gentlemen, who are so stupid or so naive as to attempt to deny to the working class any real means of struggle. For all arms with which to fight must be drawn from society as it is and the fatal conditions of this struggle have the misfortune of not being easily adapted to the idealistic fantasies which these doctors in *social science* have exalted as divinities, under the names of *Freedom, Autonomy, Anarchy*. However the working-class movement is today so powerful that these philanthropic sectarians dare not repeat for the economic struggle those *great truths* which they used incessantly to proclaim on the subject of the political struggle. They are simply too cowardly to apply them any longer to strikes, combinations, single-craft unions, laws on the labour of women and children, on the limitation of the working day etc., etc.

Now let us see whether they are still able to be brought back to the good old traditions, to modesty, good faith and eternal principles.

The first socialists (Fourier, Owen, Saint-Simon, etc.), since social conditions were not sufficiently developed to allow the working class to constitute itself as a militant class, were necessarily obliged to limit themselves to dreams about the *model society* of the future and were led thus to condemn all the attempts such as strikes, combinations or political movements set in train by the workers to improve their lot. But while we cannot repudiate these patriarchs of socialism, just as chemists cannot repudiate their forebears the alchemists, we must at least avoid falling back into their mistakes, which, if we were to commit them, would be inexcusable.

Later, however, in 1839, when the political and economic struggle of the working class in England had taken on a fairly marked character, Bray, one of Owen's disciples and one of the many who long before Proudhon hit upon the idea of *mutualism*, published a book entitled *Labour's Wrongs and Labour's Remedy*.

In his chapter on the inefficacy of *all the remedies aimed for by the present struggle*, he makes a savage critique of all the activities, political or economic, of the English working class, condemns the political movement, strikes, the limitation of the working day, the restriction of the work of women and children in factories, since all this – or so he claims – instead of taking us out of the present state of society, keeps us there and does nothing but render the antagonisms more intense.

This brings us to the oracle of these doctors of social science, M. Proudhon. While the master had the courage to declare himself energetically opposed to all economic activities (combinations, strikes, etc.) which contradicted his redemptive theories of *mutualism*, at the same time through his writings and personal participation, he encouraged the working-class movement, and his disciples do not dare to declare themselves openly against it. As early as 1847, when the master's great work, *The System of Economic Contradictions*, had just appeared, I refuted his sophisms against the working-class movement.[2] None the less in 1864, after the *loi Ollivier*, which granted the French workers, in a very restrictive fashion, a certain right of combination, Proudhon returned to the charge in a book, *The Political Capacities of the Working Classes*, published a few days after his death.

The master's strictures were so much to the taste of the bourgeoisie that *The Times*, on the occasion of the great tailors' strike in London in 1866, did Proudhon the honour of translating him and of condemning the strikers with the master's very words. Here are some selections.

The miners of Rive-de-Gier went on strike; the soldiers were called in to bring them back to reason. Proudhon cries, 'The authority which had the miners of Rive-de-Gier shot acted disgracefully. But it was acting like Brutus of old caught between his paternal love and his consular duty: it was necessary to sacrifice his sons to save the Republic. Brutus did not hesitate, and posterity dare not condemn him.'[3] In all the memory of the proletariat there is no record of a bourgeois who has hesitated to sacrifice his workers to save his interests. What Brutuses the bourgeois must then be!

'Well, no: there is no right of combination, just as there is no right to defraud or steal or to commit incest or adultery.'[4] There is however all too clearly a right to stupidity.

2. P. J. Proudhon, *Système des contradictions economiques, ou philosophie de la misère* (1846). This was the work that Marx replied to with his book *The Poverty of Philosophy* (1847).

3. *De la Capacité politique des class ouvrières*, Paris, 1865, p. 413. To give Proudhon his due, he was not so much justifying the actions of the French authorities as exposing the 'contradictions' he saw as an inevitable evil of the present social order.

4. Ibid., p. 421.

What then are the eternal principles, in whose name the master fulminates his mystic anathema?

First eternal principle: 'Wage rates determine the price of commodities.'

Even those who have no knowledge of political economy and who are unaware that the great bourgeois economist Ricardo in his *Principles of Political Economy*, published in 1817, has refuted this long-standing error once and for all, are however aware of the remarkable fact that British industry can sell its products at a price far lower than that of any other nation, although wages are relatively higher in England than in any other European country.

Second eternal principle: 'The law which authorizes combinations is highly anti-juridical, anti-economic and contrary to any society and order.'[5] In a word 'contrary to the economic *right* of free competition'.

If the master had been a little less chauvinistic, he might have asked himself how it happened that forty years ago a law, thus contrary to the *economic rights of free competition*, was promulgated in England; and that as industry develops, and alongside it *free competition*, this law – so contrary to *any society and order* – imposes itself as a necessity even to bourgeois states themselves. He might perhaps have discovered that this right (with capital R) exists only in the *Economic Manuals* written by the Brothers Ignoramus of bourgeois political economy, in which manuals are contained such pearls as this: 'Property is the fruit of labour' ('of the labour', they neglect to add, 'of others').

Third eternal principle: 'Therefore, under the pretext of raising the working class from its condition of so-called social inferiority, it will be necessary to start by denouncing a whole class of citizens, the class of bosses, entrepreneurs, masters and bourgeois; it will be necessary to rouse workers' democracy to despise and to hate these unworthy members of the middle class; it will be necessary to prefer mercantile and industrial war to legal repression, and class antagonism to the state police.'[6]

The master, in order to prevent the working class from escaping from its so-called *social inferiority*, condemns the combinations that constitute the working class as a class antagonistic to the respectable *category of masters, entrepreneurs and bourgeois*, who for their part certainly prefer, as does Proudhon, *the state police to class antagonism*. To avoid any offence to this respectable class,

5. Ibid., p. 424.   6. Ibid., p. 426.

the good M. Proudhon recommends to the workers (up to the coming of the *mutualist regime*, and despite its serious disadvantages) freedom or competition, our 'only guarantee'.[7]

The master preached indifference in matters of economics – *so as to protect bourgeois freedom or competition*, our only guarantee. His disciples preach indifference in matters of politics – so as to protect bourgeois freedom, their only guarantee. If the early Christians, who also preached political indifferentism, needed an emperor's arm to transform themselves from oppressed into oppressors, so the modern apostles of political indifferentism do not believe that their own eternal principles impose on them abstinence from worldly pleasures and the temporal privileges of bourgeois society. However we must recognize that they display a stoicism worthy of the early Christian martyrs in supporting those fourteen or sixteen working hours such as overburden the workers in the factories.

7. Ibid., p. 422.

Conspectus of Bakunin's *Statism and Anarchy*[1]
[Extract]

We have already stated our deep opposition to the theory of Lassalle and Marx, which recommends to the workers, if not as final ideal then at least as the next major aim – *the foundation of a people's state*, which, as they have expressed it, will be none other than the proletariat *organized as ruling class*. The question arises, if the proletariat becomes the ruling class, over whom will it rule? It means that there will still remain another proletariat, which will be subject to this new domination, this new state.

It means that so long as the other classes, especially the capitalist class, still exists, so long as the proletariat struggles with it (for when it attains government power its enemies and the old organization of society have not yet vanished), it must employ *forcible* means, hence governmental means. It is itself still a class and the economic conditions from which the class struggle and the existence of classes derive have still not disappeared and must forcibly be either removed out of the way or transformed, this transformation process being forcibly hastened.

E.g. the *krestyanskaya chern*, the common peasant folk, the peasant mob, which as is well known does not enjoy the goodwill of the Marxists, and which, being as it is at the lowest level of culture, will apparently be governed by the urban factory proletariat.

I.e. where the peasant exists in the mass as private proprietor, where he even forms a more or less considerable majority, as in all states of the west European continent, where he has not disappeared and been replaced by the agricultural wage-labourer, as

1. During the latter part of 1874 Marx copied into a notebook, in the Russian, extensive extracts from Bakunin's recent book *Statism and Anarchy*, interspersing them, in the section reproduced below, with his own comments. This extract of Marx's 'Conspectus' is translated from the German text printed in *MEW* 18, pp. 630–36. English extracts of Bakunin's book are printed in G. P. Maximoff (ed.), *The Political Philosophy of Bakunin*.

1018 *Conspectus of Bakunin's* Statism and Anarchy

in England, the following cases apply: either he hinders each workers' revolution, makes a wreck of it, as he has formerly done in France, or the proletariat (for the peasant proprietor does not belong to the proletariat, and even where his condition is proletarian, he believes himself not to) must as government take measures through which the peasant finds his condition immediately improved, so as to win him for the revolution; measures which will at least provide the possibility of easing the transition from private ownership of land to collective ownership, so that the peasant arrives at this of his own accord, from economic reasons. It must not hit the peasant over the head, as it would e.g. by proclaiming the abolition of the right of inheritance or the abolition of his property. The latter is only possible where the capitalist tenant farmer has forced out the peasants, and where the true cultivator is just as good a proletarian, a wage-labourer, as is the town worker, and so has *immediately*, not just indirectly, the very same interests as him. Still less should small-holding property be strengthened, by the enlargement of the peasant allotment simply through peasant annexation of the larger estates, as in Bakunin's revolutionary campaign.

Or, if one considers this question from the national angle, we would for the same reason assume that, as far as the Germans are concerned, the Slavs will stand in the same slavish dependence towards the victorious German proletariat as the latter does at present towards its own bourgeoisie.

Schoolboy stupidity! A radical social revolution depends on certain definite historical conditions of economic development as its precondition. It is also only possible where with capitalist production the industrial proletariat occupies at least an important position among the mass of the people. And if it is to have any chance of victory, it must be able to do immediately as much for the peasants as the French bourgeoisie, *mutatis mutandis*, did in its revolution for the French peasants of that time. A fine idea, that the rule of labour involves the subjugation of land labour! But here Mr Bakunin's innermost thoughts emerge. He understands absolutely nothing about the social revolution, only its political phrases. Its economic conditions do not exist for him. As all hitherto existing economic forms, developed or undeveloped, involve the enslavement of the worker (whether in the form of wage-labourer, peasant, etc.), he believes that a *radical revolution* is possible in all such forms alike. Still more! He wants the European social revolution, premised on the economic basis of capitalist production, to take place at the level of the Russian or Slavic agricultural and pastoral peoples, not to surpass this level [. . .] The *will*, and not the economic conditions, is the foundation of his social revolution.

If there is a state [*gosudarstvo*], then there is unavoidably domination [*gospodstvo*], and consequently slavery. Domination without slavery, open or veiled, is unthinkable – this is why we are enemies of the state.
What does it mean, the proletariat organized as ruling class?

It means that the proletariat, instead of struggling sectionally against the economically privileged class, has attained a sufficient strength and organization to employ general means of coercion in this struggle. It can however only use such economic means as abolish its own character as salariat,[2] hence as class. With its complete victory its own rule thus also ends, as its class character has disappeared.

Will the entire proletariat perhaps stand at the head of the government?

In a trade union,[3] for example, does the whole union form its executive committee? Will all division of labour in the factory, and the various functions that correspond to this, cease? And in Bakunin's constitution, will all 'from bottom to top' be 'at the top'? Then there will certainly be no one 'at the bottom'. Will all members of the commune simultaneously manage the interests of its territory? Then there will be no distinction between commune and territory.

The Germans number around forty million. Will for example all forty million be members of the government?

Certainly![4] Since the whole thing begins with the self-government of the commune.

The whole people will govern, and there will be no governed.

If a man rules himself, he does not do so on this principle, for he is after all himself and no other.

2. In English in the original.   3. In English in the original.
4. In English in the original.

Then there will be no government and no state, but if there is a state, there will be both governors and slaves.

I.e. only if class rule has disappeared, and there is no state in the present political sense.

This dilemma is simply solved in the Marxists' theory. By people's government they understand (i.e. Bakunin) the government of the people by means of a small number of leaders, chosen (elected) by the people.

Asine![5] This is democratic twaddle, political drivel. Election is a political form present in the smallest Russian commune and artel. The character of the election does not depend on this name, but on the economic foundation, the economic situation of the voters, and as soon as the functions have ceased to be political ones, there exists 1) no government function, 2) the distribution of the general functions has become a business matter, that gives no one domination, 3) election has nothing of its present political character.

The universal suffrage of the whole people . . .

Such a thing as the whole people in today's sense is a chimera –

. . . in the election of people's representatives and rulers of the state – that is the last word of the Marxists, as also of the democratic school – [is] a lie, behind which is concealed the despotism of the *governing minority*, and only the more dangerously in so far as it appears as expression of the so-called people's will.

With collective ownership the so-called people's will vanishes, to make way for the real will of the cooperative.

So the result is: guidance of the great majority of the people by a privileged minority. But this minority, say the Marxists . . .

Where?

. . . will consist of workers. Certainly, with your permission, of former workers, who however, as soon as they have become representatives or governors of the people, *cease to be workers* . . .

As little as a factory owner today ceases to be a capitalist if he becomes a municipal councillor . . .

and look down on the whole common workers' world from the height

5. Asinine.

of the state. They will no longer represent the people, but themselves and their pretensions to people's government. Anyone who can doubt this knows nothing of the nature of men.

If Mr Bakunin only knew something about the position of a manager in a workers' cooperative factory, all his dreams of domination would go to the devil. He should have asked himself what form the administrative function can take on the basis of this workers' state, if he wants to call it that.

But those elected will be fervently convinced and therefore educated socialists. The phrase '*educated socialism*' . . .

. . . never was used.

. . . '*scientific socialism*' . . .

. . . was only used in opposition to utopian socialism, which wants to attach the people to new delusions, instead of limiting its science to the knowledge of the social movement made by the people itself; see my text against Proudhon.

. . . which is unceasingly found in the works and speeches of the Lasalleans and Marxists, itself indicates that the so-called people's state will be nothing else than the very despotic guidance of the mass of the people by a new and numerically very small aristocracy of the genuine or supposedly educated. The people are not scientific, which means that they will be entirely freed from the cares of government, they will be entirely shut up in the stable of the governed. A fine liberation!

The Marxists sense this (!) contradiction and, knowing that the government of the educated (*quelle rêverie*)[6] will be the most oppressive, most detestable, most despised in the world, a real dictatorship despite all democratic forms, console themselves with the thought that this dictatorship will only be transitional and short.

Non, mon cher![7] – That the *class rule* of the workers over the strata of the old world whom they have been fighting can only exist as long as the economic basis of class existence is not destroyed.

They say that their only concern and aim is *to educate and uplift* the *people* (saloon-bar politicians!) both economically and politically, to such a level that all government will be quite useless and the state will lose all political character, i.e. character of domination, and will change by itself into a free organization of economic interests and

6. What a daydream.   7. No, my dear.

communes. An obvious contradiction. If their state will really be popular, why not destroy it, and if its destruction is necessary for the real liberation of the people, why do they venture to call it popular?

Aside from the harping of Liebknecht's *Volksstaat*,[8] which is nonsense, counter to the Communist Manifesto etc., it only means that, as the proletariat still acts, during the period of struggle for the overthrow of the old society, on the basis of that old society, and hence also still moves within political forms which more or less belong to it, it has not yet, during this period of struggle, attained its final constitution, and employs means for its liberation which after this liberation fall aside. Mr Bakunin concludes from this that it is better to do nothing at all . . . just wait for the *day of general liquidation* – the last judgement.

8. On the *Volksstaat*, see p. 848, n. 20. Marx and Engels privately criticized Liebknecht for his failure to break decisively with the petty-bourgeois democrats.

Critique of the Gotha Programme[1]

Marx to Bracke[2]

London, 5 May 1875

Dear Bracke,

Please be so kind as to give the following critical marginal notes on the unity programme[3] to Geib, Auer,[4] Bebel and Liebknecht for their perusal after you have read them yourself. I have too much on my plate and have already been forced to overshoot the work limit prescribed by my doctor. It was therefore not a 'pleasure' by any means to write this long screed. It was necessary, however, so that friends in the party, for whom it is meant, will not misunderstand the steps I shall later have to take.

Namely, after the unity congress Engels and I are going to publish a short statement dissociating ourselves from the said programme of principles and stating that we have had nothing to do with it.

This is essential, because people abroad hold the completely erroneous view – carefully nurtured by enemies of the party – that we are secretly steering the movement of the so-called Eisenach party from here. In a very recent Russian publication,[5]

1. Marx wrote his marginal notes on the draft of the Gotha programme at the beginning of May 1875. When the 'Critique of the Gotha Programme' was first published, in 1891, Engels omitted certain passages as a concession to the German Social-Democratic Party. The Critique is translated here from Marx's manuscript, as printed in *MEW* 19.

2. Wilhelm Bracke had led the faction of the Lassallean ADAV which broke away in 1869, and joined with Liebknecht's group to form the SDAP ('Eisenach party').

3. The draft unity programme for the Gotha Congress, at which the SDAP and the ADAV were united to form the German Social-Democratic Workers' Party (SAPD, later SPD), was written by Wilhelm Liebknecht for the SDAP and Wilhelm Hasselmann for the ADAV, and published in both groups' papers on 7 March 1875. The Gotha Congress was held in late May.

4. August Geib and Ignaz Auer were prominent SDAP figures.

5. Bakunin's book *Statism and Anarchy*; see Marx's 'Conspectus', above, pp. 333–8.

Bakunin still makes me responsible, for example, not only for all the programmes, etc. of that party, but even for every step that Liebknecht has taken since the first day of his cooperation with the People's Party.[6]

Apart from that, it is my duty not to approve, even by diplomatic silence, a programme which in my opinion is thoroughly reprehensible and demoralizing for the party.

Every step of a real movement is more important than a dozen programmes. If it was not possible, therefore, to go *further* than the Eisenach programme – and, in the present conditions, it is not – then they should simply have concluded an agreement for action against the common enemy. Drawing up a programme of principle, however (instead of postponing this until such time as it has been prepared for by a considerable period of common activity), means erecting a milestone for all the world to see, by which the progress of the party will be measured.

Conditions forced the Lassallean leaders to come. If they had been told from the start that no haggling over principles would be tolerated, then they would have *had to be* satisfied with a programme of action or with an organizational plan for common action. Instead, they are being allowed to appear wielding mandates, and these mandates are being recognized as binding. This constitutes a surrender to the favour or disfavour of the people who are themselves most in need of help. To crown the matter, they turn around and hold a congress *before* the *compromise congress*, while our own party holds its congress *post festum*. Obviously the idea was to make all criticism ineffective, and to prevent our party from having second thoughts. It is clear that the mere fact of unification will satisfy the workers, but it is a mistake to believe that this momentary success has not been bought dearly.

Furthermore, the programme is no good, even when one disregards the hallowing of Lassalle's articles of faith.

In the near future, I shall be sending you the final instalment of the French edition of *Capital*. The rest of the printing was held up for a long while by the French government's ban. It should all be settled by this week or the beginning of next. Did you get the earlier six instalments? Please also send me Bernhard Becker's address, for I have to send him the final instalment as well.

6. See above, p. 706.

The *Volksstaat* bookshop has its own peculiar manners. Up to this moment, for example, they have not sent me a single copy of their edition of the *Cologne Communist Trial*.

With best wishes,

Yours,

KARL MARX

Marginal Notes on the Programme of the German Workers' Party

I

1. Labour is the source of all wealth and culture, *and since* useful labour can only be performed in and through society, all members of society have an equal right to the undiminished proceeds of labour.

First part of the paragraph: 'Labour is the source of all wealth and culture'.

Labour is *not the source* of all wealth. Nature is just as much the source of use-values (and surely these are what make up material wealth!) as labour. Labour is itself only the manifestation of a force of nature, human labour power. This phrase can be found in any children's primer; it is correct in so far as it is *assumed* that labour is performed with the objects and instruments necessary to it. A socialist programme, however, cannot allow such bourgeois formulations to silence the *conditions* which give them the only meaning they possess. Man's labour only becomes a source of use-values, and hence also of wealth, if his relation to nature, the primary source of all instruments and objects of labour, is one of ownership from the start, and if he treats it as belonging to him. There is every good reason for the bourgeoisie to ascribe *supernatural creative power* to labour, for when a man has no property other than his labour power it is precisely labour's dependence on nature that forces him, in all social and cultural conditions, to be the slave of other men who have taken the objective conditions of labour into their own possession. He needs their permission to work, and hence their permission to live.

Let us now leave this sentence as it stands, or rather hobbles. What sort of conclusion would one have expected? Obviously the following: 'Since labour is the source of all wealth, it follows that no one in society can appropriate wealth except as the product of labour. Thus, if a person does not work himself, he must live off the labour of others, and his culture, too, must be acquired at the cost of other people's labour.'

Instead of this the words *'and since'* are used to tack on a second proposition so that a conclusion can be drawn from this one rather than the first.

Second part of the paragraph: 'Useful labour can only be performed in and through society'.

According to the first proposition, labour was the source of all wealth and culture, so that a society could not exist without labour. Now we are told the opposite: 'useful' labour cannot exist without society.

One could just as well have said that it is only in society that useless labour, or even labour harmful to the community, can become a line of business, and that only in society is it possible to live from idleness, etc., etc. – in short, one could have copied down the whole of Rousseau.

And what is 'useful' labour? Surely simply labour which brings the desired useful result. A savage – and man was a savage after he ceased to be an ape – who kills an animal with a stone, gathers fruit, etc., is performing 'useful' labour.

Thirdly: the conclusion: 'And since useful labour can only be performed in and through society, all members of society have an equal right to the undiminished proceeds of labour.'

A beautiful conclusion! If useful labour can only be performed in and through society then the proceeds of labour belong to society – even if the individual worker only receives as much of them as is not required for the maintenance of the 'condition' of labour, society.

In fact, this sentence is not new: it has been used in all periods by the *champions of the existing state of society*. First come the claims of the government and all that goes with it, since it is the social organ for the maintenance of social order; then come the claims of the various kinds of private property, since the various kinds of private property form the foundations of society, etc. Hollow phrases such as these can clearly be twisted and turned at will.

The first and second parts of the paragraph would have some intelligible connection only if worded as follows: 'Labour becomes the source of all wealth and culture only when it is social labour,' or, which comes to the same thing, only 'in and through society'.

This proposition is indisputably correct, for although isolated labour (given its material conditions) can also create use-values, it cannot create either wealth or culture.

But this other proposition is equally indisputable: 'The social development of labour, and thus its development as a source of wealth and culture, proceeds in equal proportion to the development of poverty and destitution among the workers and of wealth and culture among the non-workers.'

Up to the present day all history has been governed by this law. What was needed here, therefore, was not generalizations about 'labour' and 'society' but concrete proof that in present capitalist society the material etc. conditions have finally been created which enable and compel the worker to break this historical curse.

In fact, however, the sole purpose of this paragraph, a mess both in style and content, is to inscribe the Lassallean catchword of 'the undiminished proceeds of labour' as a slogan at the top of the party banner. I shall return to the 'proceeds of labour', 'equal right', etc. below, where the same things reappear in a somewhat different form.

2. In present society the capitalist class has a monopoly of the instruments of labour; the resultant dependence of the working class is the cause of misery and servitude in all its forms.

This sentence has been lifted from the Rules of the International but is incorrect in this 'improved' version.

In present society the instruments of labour are the monopoly of the landowners (the monopoly of landed property is even the basis of the monopoly of capital) *and* of the capitalists. Neither class of monopolists is mentioned by name in the relevant passage of the Rules of the International. This text speaks of the *'monopolizer of the means of labour, that is, the sources of life'*; the addition of the 'sources of life' is adequate indication that land and soil are included under the instruments of labour.

The amendment was made because Lassalle, for reasons now generally known, *only* attacked the capitalist class and not the landowners. In England, the capitalist generally does not even own the land and soil on which his factory stands.

3. For the emancipation of labour the instruments of labour must be elevated to the common property of society and the whole of labour must be regulated on a cooperative basis, with a just distribution of the proceeds of labour.

'The instruments of labour must be elevated to common property'! This is probably meant to mean 'converted into common property'. But this just incidentally.

What are the 'proceeds of labour'? Are they the product of labour or its value? And in the latter case, is it the total value of the product or only that part of its value which labour has created over and above the value of the means of production consumed?

'Proceeds of labour' is a loose notion, used by Lassalle in place of definite economic concepts.

What is 'just' distribution?

Does not the bourgeoisie claim that the present system of distribution is 'just'? And given the present mode of production is it not, in fact, the only 'just' system of distribution? Are economic relations regulated by legal concepts of right or is the opposite not the case, that legal relations spring from economic ones? Do not the socialist sectarians themselves have the most varied notions of 'just' distribution?

To discover what we are meant to understand by the phrase 'just distribution' as used here we must take the opening paragraph and this one together. The latter presupposes a society in which 'the instruments of labour are common property and the whole of labour is regulated on a cooperative basis' and from the opening paragraph we learn that 'all members of society have an equal right to the undiminished proceeds of labour'.

'All members of society'? Including people who do not work? Then what remains of the 'undiminished proceeds of labour'? Only the working members of society? Then what remains of the 'equal right' of all members of society?

'All members of society' and 'equal right', however, are obviously mere phrases. The heart of the matter is that in this communist society every worker is supposed to receive the 'undiminished' Lassallean 'proceeds of labour'.

If we start by taking 'proceeds of labour' to mean the product of labour, then the cooperative proceeds of labour are the *total social product*.

From this the following must now be deducted:

Firstly: cover to replace the means of production used up.

Secondly: an additional portion for the expansion of production.

Thirdly: a reserve or insurance fund in case of accidents, disruption caused by natural calamities, etc.

These deductions from the 'undiminished proceeds of labour' are an economic necessity and their magnitude will be determined by the means and forces available. They can partly be calculated by reference to probability, but on no account by reference to justice.

There remains the other part of the total product, designed to serve as means of consumption.

But before this is distributed to individuals the following further deductions must be made:

Firstly: the general costs of all administration not directly appertaining to production.

This part will, from the outset, be very significantly limited in comparison with the present society. It will diminish commensurately with the development of the new society.

Secondly: the amount set aside for needs communally satisfied, such as schools, health services, etc.

This part will, from the outset, be significantly greater than in the present society. It will grow commensurately with the development of the new society.

Thirdly: a fund for people unable to work, etc., in short, for what today comes under so-called official poor relief.

Only now do we come to that 'distribution' which, under the influence of the Lassalleans, is the only thing considered by this narrow-minded programme, namely that part of the means of consumption which is distributed among the individual producers within the cooperative.

The 'undiminished proceeds of labour' have meanwhile already been quietly 'diminished', although as a member of society the producer still receives, directly or indirectly, what is withheld from him as a private individual.

Just as the phrase 'undiminished proceeds of labour' has vanished, the phrase 'proceeds of labour' now disappears altogether.

Within the cooperative society based on common ownership of the means of production the producers do not exchange their products; similarly, the labour spent on the products no longer appears *as the value* of these products, possessed by them as a material characteristic, for now, in contrast to capitalist society, individual pieces of labour are no longer merely indirectly, but directly, a component part of the total labour. The phrase 'proceeds of labour', which even today is too ambiguous to be of any value, thus loses any meaning whatsoever.

We are dealing here with a communist society, not as it has *developed* on its own foundations, but on the contrary, just as it *emerges* from capitalist society. In every respect, economically, morally, intellectually, it is thus still stamped with the birth-marks of the old society from whose womb it has emerged. Accordingly, the individual producer gets back from society – after the deductions – exactly what he has given it. What he has given it is his individual quantum of labour. For instance, the social working day consists of the sum of the individual hours of work. The individual labour time of the individual producer thus constitutes his contribution to the social working day, his share of it. Society gives him a certificate stating that he has done such and such an amount of work (after the labour done for the communal fund has been deducted), and with this certificate he can withdraw from the social supply of means of consumption as much as costs an equivalent amount of labour. The same amount of labour he has given to society in one form, he receives back in another.

Clearly, the same principle is at work here as that which regulates the exchange of commodities as far as this is an exchange of equal values. Content and form have changed because under the new conditions no one can contribute anything except his labour and conversely nothing can pass into the ownership of individuals except individual means of consumption. The latter's distribution among individual producers, however, is governed by the same principle as the exchange of commodity equivalents: a given amount of labour in one form is exchanged for the same amount in another.

Hence *equal right* is here still – in principle – a *bourgeois right*, although principle and practice are no longer at loggerheads, while the exchange of equivalents in commodity exchange only exists *on the average* and not in the individual case.

In spite of such progress this *equal right* still constantly suffers a bourgeois limitation. The right of the producers is *proportional* to the labour they do; the equality consists in the fact that measurement is *by the same standard*, labour. One person, however, may be physically and intellectually superior to another and thus be able to do more labour in the same space of time or work for a longer period. To serve as a measure labour must therefore be determined by duration or intensity, otherwise it ceases to be a standard. This *equal* right is an unequal right for unequal labour. It does not acknowledge any class distinctions, because everyone is just a worker like everyone else, but it gives tacit recognition to a worker's individual endowment and hence productive capacity as natural privileges. *This right is thus in its content one of inequality, just like any other right.* A right can by its nature only consist in the application of an equal standard, but unequal individuals (and they would not be different individuals if they were not unequal) can only be measured by the same standard if they are looked at from the same aspect, if they are grasped from one *particular* side, e.g., if in the present case they are regarded *only as workers* and nothing else is seen in them, everything else is ignored. Further: one worker is married, another is not; one has more children than another, etc., etc. Thus, with the same work performance and hence the same share of the social consumption fund, one will in fact be receiving more than another, one will be richer than another, etc. If all these defects were to be avoided rights would have to be unequal rather than equal.

Such defects, however, are inevitable in the first phase of communist society, given the specific form in which it has emerged after prolonged birth-pangs from capitalist society. Right can never rise above the economic structure of a society and its contingent cultural development.

In a more advanced phase of communist society, when the enslaving subjugation of individuals to the division of labour, and thereby the antithesis between intellectual and physical labour, have disappeared; when labour is no longer just a means of keeping alive but has itself become a vital need; when the all-round development of individuals has also increased their productive powers and all the springs of cooperative wealth flow more abundantly – only then can society wholly cross the narrow horizon of bourgeois right and inscribe on its banner: From each according to his abilities, to each according to his needs!

If I have dealt at some length with the 'undiminished proceeds of labour' on the one hand, and 'equal right' and 'just distribution' on the other, it is in order to show the criminal nature of what is being attempted: on the one hand, our party is to be forced to re-accept as dogmas ideas which may have made some sense at a particular time but which are now only a load of obsolete verbal rubbish; on the other hand, the realistic outlook instilled in our party at the cost of immense effort, but now firmly rooted in it, is to be perverted by means of ideological, legal and other humbug so common among the democrats and the French socialists.

Quite apart from the points made so far, it was a mistake anyway to lay the main stress on so-called *distribution* and to make it into the central point.

The distribution of the means of consumption at any given time is merely a consequence of the distribution of the conditions of production themselves; the distribution of the latter, however, is a feature of the mode of production itself. The capitalist mode of production, for example, rests on the fact that the material conditions of production are in the hands of non-workers in the form of property in capital and land, while the masses are only in possession of their personal condition of production, labour power. If the elements of production are distributed in this way, the present distribution of the means of consumption follows automatically. If the material conditions of production were the cooperative property of the workers themselves a different distribution of the means of consumption from that of today would follow of its own accord. Vulgar socialists (and from them, in turn, a section of the democrats) have followed the bourgeois economists in their consideration and treatment of distribution as something independent of the mode of production and hence in the presentation of socialism as primarily revolving around the question of distribution. Why go back a step when the real state of affairs has been laid bare?

4. The emancipation of labour must be the work of the working class, in relation to which all other classes are *a single reactionary mass*.

The first strophe is an 'improved' version of the preamble to the Rules of the International. There it is said: 'The emancipation of the working classes must be conquered by the working classes themselves';[7] here, in contrast, 'the working class' has to emancipate – what? – labour. Understand who may.

In compensation, however, the antistrophe is a Lassallean quote of the purest ilk: 'in relation to which (the working class) all other classes are *a single reactionary mass*'.

In the Communist Manifesto it is said, 'Of all the classes that stand face to face with the bourgeoisie today, the proletariat alone is a *really revolutionary class*. The other classes decay and

7. Above, p. 766.

finally disappear in the face of modern industry; the proletariat is its special and essential product.'[8]

The bourgeoisie is here conceived of as a revolutionary class – as the bringer of large-scale industry – in relation to the feudal lords and the lower middle class, who want to retain all the social positions created by obsolete modes of production. These do not, therefore, form a single reactionary mass *together with the bourgeoisie*.

On the other hand the proletariat is revolutionary in relation to the bourgeoisie because it has itself sprung up on the ground of large-scale industry; it is struggling to divest production of its capitalist character, which the bourgeoisie seeks to perpetuate. The Manifesto adds, however, that the lower middle class is becoming revolutionary 'in view of (its) impending transfer into the proletariat'.

From this point of view, therefore, it is once again nonsense to say that in relation to the working class it 'forms a single reactionary mass', 'together with the bourgeoisie' and with the feudal lords to boot.

At the last elections, did we proclaim to the artisans, small manufacturers, etc. and *peasants*: In relation to us you, together with the bourgeoisie and the feudal lords, form a single reactionary mass?

Lassalle knew the Communist Manifesto by heart, just as his faithful followers know his own gospels. The reason for such gross falsification can thus only be that he wanted to extenuate his alliance with the absolutist and feudal opponents of the bourgeoisie.

In the above paragraph, moreover, this oracular utterance is dragged in by the scruff of its neck, without any connection to the bowdlerized quote from the Rules of the International. It is therefore simply an impertinence to include it here and one that will by no means displease Herr Bismarck – a cheap swipe typical of Berlin's would-be Marat.[9]

5. The working class must initially work for its emancipation *within the framework of the present-day national state*, conscious that the necessary result of its efforts, common to the workers of all civilized countries, will be the international brotherhood of peoples.

8. Above, p. 77. Marx's emphasis in the present text.

9. Presumably Wilhelm Hasselmann, editor of the Lassallean *Neuer Social-Demokrat*.

In contrast to the Communist Manifesto and all earlier forms of socialism, Lassalle approached the workers' movement from the narrowest national point of view. His approach is followed here – and this after the work of the International!

It is perfectly self-evident that in order to be at all capable of struggle the working class must organize itself *as a class* at home and that the domestic sphere must be the immediate arena for its struggle. To this extent its class struggle is national, not in content, but as the Communist Manifesto says, 'in form'. But the 'framework of the present-day national state', e.g., the German Reich, is itself in turn economically 'within the framework of the world market' and politically 'within the framework of the system of states'. Any businessman will tell you that German trade is at the same time foreign trade, and the greatness of Herr Bismarck lies exactly in the *international* orientation of his policy.

And to what is the internationalism of the German workers' party reduced? To the consciousness that the result of their efforts 'will be *the international brotherhood of peoples*' – a phrase borrowed from the bourgeois League of Peace and Freedom[10] and which is intended to pass as an equivalent for the international brotherhood of the working classes in the joint struggle against the ruling classes and their governments. Not a word, therefore, of the *international role* of the German working class! And this is how it is meant to challenge its own bourgeoisie, which is already fraternally linked with the bourgeoisie in all other countries, and Herr Bismarck's international policy of conspiracy!

In fact, the programme's commitment to internationalism is *infinitely smaller* even than that of the free trade party. The latter also claims that the result of its efforts will be the 'international brotherhood of peoples'. It is also *doing* something, however, to internationalize trade and is certainly not content with the mere consciousness that all peoples are carrying on trade at home.

The international activity of the working classes is not in any way dependent on the existence of the International Working Men's Association. This was only the first attempt to create a central organ for such activity; an attempt which will be of lasting success because of the impetus it gave but which could not be continued in its *initial historical form* following the fall of the Paris Commune.

Bismarck's *Norddeutsche* was perfectly right when it declared,

10. See above, pp. 728–9.

to the satisfaction of its master, that the German workers' party had renounced internationalism in its new programme.[11]

II

Starting from these basic principles, the German workers' party will strive, by all legal means, for a *free state and* a socialist society; the abolition of the wage system *together with* the *iron law of wages*, and of exploitation in every form; the removal of all social and political inequality.

I will come back to the 'free' state below.

So, in future, the German workers' party will have to believe in Lassalle's 'iron law of wages'! To prevent it from being lost, the programme goes through the nonsense of speaking of the 'abolition of the wage system' (which should read 'the system of wage labour') '*together with* the iron law of wages'. If I abolish wage labour I naturally abolish all its laws as well, whether they are made of iron or sponge. Lassalle's attack on wage labour, however, revolves almost exclusively around this so-called law. As proof, therefore, that the Lassallean sect has come out on top, the 'wage system' must be abolished '*together with* the iron law of wages', and never without it.

It is common knowledge that Lassalle contributed nothing to the 'iron law of wages' except the word 'iron', which he pilfered from Goethe's 'great, eternal, iron laws'. The word 'iron' is a label by which the true believers can recognize each other. But if I take the law with Lassalle's stamp on it and thus in the way he meant it, then I must also take it with his supporting arguments. And what do I get? As Lange showed only a short time after Lassalle's death, the Malthusian theory of population (preached by Lange himself).[12] But if this theory is right, then I *cannot* abolish the law, even by abolishing wage labour a hundred times over, for this law then governs not only the system of wage labour but *all* social systems. This, precisely, has been the basis of economists' proofs, for fifty years or more, that socialism cannot abolish poverty, which has its basis in nature, but can only

11. The *Norddeutsche Allgemeine Zeitung*, in its leader of 20 March.

12. F. A. Lange was a neo-Kantian philosopher. Marx refers to his book *The Workers Question in its Significance for Present and Future*, Duisburg, 1865. Engels criticized Lange's book in a letter to him of 29 March 1865; *MECW* 42, pp. 135–9.

generalize it, distributing it simultaneously over the whole surface of society.

But all that is beside the main point. *Quite apart* from the *false* Lassallean formulation of the law, the really outrageous step back consists in the following:

Since Lassalle's death the scientific insight has made headway in our party that wages are not what they *appear* to be, namely the value or price of labour, but only a disguised form of the *value or price of labour power*.[13] Thereby the whole of the former bourgeois conception of wages was thrown overboard once and for all, as well as all criticisms of it, and it became clear that the wage labourer is only allowed to work for his own livelihood, i.e., *to live*, if he works a certain amount of time without pay for the capitalist (and thus also for the latter's fellow consumers of surplus value); that the whole capitalist system of production turns on the prolongation of this free labour through the extension of the working day and through the development of productivity, the increasing intensification of labour power, etc.; and that the system of wage labour is consequently a system of slavery, increasing in severity commensurately with the development of the social productive forces of labour, irrespective of whether the worker is then better or worse paid. And now, after this insight has gained more and more ground in our party, there comes this return to the dogmas of Lassalle, even though people must be aware that Lassalle *knew nothing* of the true nature of wages and that he followed the bourgeois economists in mistaking the appearance of the matter for its essence.

It is as if, among slaves who have finally got behind the secret of slavery and broken out in rebellion, one slave, still the prisoner of obsolete ideas, were to write in the programme of the rebellion: Slavery must be abolished because the provisioning of slaves in the slave system cannot exceed a certain low maximum!

The mere fact that the representatives of our party were capable of making such a monstrous attack on an insight which has gained wide acceptance among the mass of the party is surely sufficient proof of the criminal levity and complete lack of conscience with which they set to work on the formulation of the compromise programme.

Instead of the unspecific closing phrase of the paragraph, 'the

13. Marx is referring to his own scientific results, as presented in Volume 1 of *Capital*, first published in 1867.

removal of all social and political inequality', it should have been said that with the abolition of class distinctions all forms of social and political inequality will disappear of their own accord.

III

The German workers' party, *in order to pave the way for the solution of the social questsion*, demands the creation of producers' cooperatives *with state aid under the democratic control of the working people*. These producers' cooperatives are *to be called into being* for industry and agriculture to such an extent *that the socialist organization of the whole of labour will arise out of them*.

After Lassalle's 'iron law of wages', the prophet's remedy! The way is 'paved' for it in a suitably dignified manner! The existing class struggle is discarded in favour of the hack phrase of a newspaper scribbler – '*the social question*', for the solution of which one 'paves the way'. Instead of being the result of the revolutionary process of social transformation in society, the 'socialist organization of the whole of labour' 'arises' from 'state aid' to producers' cooperatives which the *state*, not the workers, is to 'call into being'. The notion that state loans can be used for the construction of a new society as easily as they can for the construction of a new railway is worthy of Lassalle's imagination!

A last remnant of shame induces them to put 'state aid' – 'under the democratic control of the working people'.

Firstly, the 'working people' in Germany are mainly peasants, and not proletarians.

Secondly, 'democratic' translates as 'by the rule of the people'. But what does 'control by the rule of the people of the working people' mean? Particularly in the case of a working people which in presenting the state with demands such as these is expressing its full awareness of the fact that it neither rules nor is mature enough to rule!

It would be superfluous to begin to criticize here a recipe which Buchez concocted under Louis Philippe *in opposition* to the French socialists and which was accepted by the reactionary workers of the *Atelier*.[14] The most offensive fact is not that this wonder cure has been included in the programme but that there

14. *L'Atelier* was a monthly journal published in the 1840s, influenced by Buchez's Christian socialism; it was edited by workers' representatives elected every three months.

has been a general retreat from the standpoint of a class movement to that of a sectarian one.

The workers' desire to create the conditions for cooperative production on a social and, by beginning at home, at first on a national scale, means nothing beyond that they are working to revolutionize the present conditions of production; it has nothing in common with the creation of cooperative societies with state aid! As far as the present cooperative societies are concerned, they are *only* valuable if they are independent creations of the workers, and not the protégés either of governments or of the bourgeoisie.

IV

I come now to the democratic section.

A. *The free basis of the state.*

According to section II, the first thing that the German workers' party strives for is 'a free state'.

A free state – what does that mean?

It is by no means the goal of workers who have discarded the narrow mentality of humble subjects to make the state 'free'. In the German Reich the 'state' has almost as much 'freedom' as in Russia. Freedom consists in converting the state from an organ superimposed on society into one thoroughly subordinate to it; and even today state forms are more or less free depending on the degree to which they restrict the 'freedom of the state'.

The German workers' party – at least if it adopts this programme – thus shows that its socialist values do not even go skin-deep, for instead of treating existing society (and the same holds good for any future one) as the *basis* of the existing *state* (or future state in the case of future society), it treats the state as an independent entity with its own 'intellectual, ethical and liberal foundations'.

And what of the wild misuse made in the programme of the words 'present state' and 'present society', or the even more riotous misconception of the state to which it addresses its demands?

The 'present society' is capitalist society, which exists in all civilized countries, freed in varying degrees from the admixture of medievalism, modified in varying degrees by the particular historical development of each country, and developed to a varying degree. In contrast to this, the 'present state' changes with each country's border. It differs between the Prusso-German empire and Switzerland, between England and the United States. '*The* present state' is thus a fiction.

Nevertheless, the various states of the various civilized countries, despite their motley diversity of form, do have this in common: they all stand on the ground of modern bourgeois society although the degree of capitalist development varies. They thus also share certain essential characteristics. In this sense one can speak of 'present states' in contrast to the future when their present root, bourgeois society, will have died off.

The question then arises: What transformation will the state undergo in a communist society? In other words, what social functions will remain that are analogous to the present functions of the state? This question can only be answered scientifically and even a thousandfold combination of the word 'state' and the word 'people' will not bring us a flea-hop nearer the problem.

Between capitalist and communist society lies a period of revolutionary transformation from one to the other. There is a corresponding period of transition in the political sphere and in this period the state can only take the form of a *revolutionary dictatorship of the proletariat*.

The programme, however, does not deal either with this or with the future public affairs of communist society.

There is nothing in its political demands beyond the old and generally familiar democratic litany: universal suffrage, direct legislation, popular justice, a people's army, etc. They merely echo the bourgeois People's Party or the League of Peace and Freedom. All these demands, unless exaggerated into fantastic dreams, have already been *realized*. It is just that the state to which they belong does not lie within the borders of the German Reich but in Switzerland, the United States, etc. This kind of 'state of the future' is a '*present state*', although it exists outside the 'framework' of the German Empire.

One thing has been forgotten, however. The German workers' party expressly declares that it acts within the 'present national state'. This means their own state, the Prusso-German empire. (Most of its demands would be meaningless if this were not so, for one can only demand what one has not already got.) Under these circumstances the main point should not have been forgotten, which is that all these pretty little gewgaws depend on the recognition of the so-called sovereignty of the people and are hence only appropriate in a *democratic republic*.

Although they lack the courage – and wisely so, for the circumstances demand caution – to call for a democratic republic after the manner of the French workers' programmes under Louis Philippe and Louis Napoleon, it was wrong to resort to the subterfuge which is neither 'honest'[15] nor decent of making demands which are only feasible in a democratic republic, and to address these demands to a state which is no more than a military despotism and a police state, bureaucratically carpentered, embellished with parliamentary forms and disguised by an admixture of feudalism although already under the influence of the bourgeoisie, and then to assure this same state into the bargain that they imagine they can impose these demands on it 'by legal means'.

Even vulgar democrats, who see the millennium in the democratic republic and who have no inkling that it is precisely in this final state form of bourgeois society that the class struggle must be fought to a conclusion, even they tower mountains above this kind of democratism which keeps within the bounds of what is allowed by the police and disallowed by logic.

The fact that the 'state' here stands for the government machine or for the state in so far as it forms through the division of labour a special organism separate from society is shown by the following words: 'The German workers' party demands *as the economic basis of* the state: a single progressive income tax, etc.' Taxes provide the economic basis of the government machinery and of nothing else. In the state of the future, already existing in Switzerland, this demand has been pretty well realized. Income tax presupposes varied sources of income for varied social classes, and hence capitalist society. It is thus not surprising that the Liverpool Financial Reformers, a bourgeois group led by Gladstone's brother, are putting forward the same demands as this programme.

B. The German workers' party demands as the intellectual and ethical basis of the state:

1. Universal and *equal elementary education* by the state. Universal compulsory school attendance. Free tuition.

'Equal elementary education'? What are we meant to under-

15. 'Honest' was a nickname for the Eisenachers (SDAP).

stand by these words? Is it believed that in our present society (and this is all we have to deal with here) education can be *equal* for all classes? Or is it demanded that the upper classes ought also to be reduced to the modicum of education – the elementary school – which is all that is compatible with the economic conditions of both wage-labourers and peasants?

'Universal compulsory school attendance. Free tuition.' The first of these exists even in Germany, and the second, in the case of elementary schools, in Switzerland and the United States. If in some states of the latter higher institutions of learning are also 'free', this in fact only means that the upper classes can defray the costs of their education out of the general taxpayer's pocket. Incidentally, the same is true of the 'free administration of justice' demanded under A/5. Criminal justice can be had free anywhere; civil justice is almost exclusively concerned with property conflicts and is hence almost exclusively the concern of the propertied classes. Should their cases be paid for out of public funds?

The paragraph on schools at least ought to have demanded technical schools (theoretical and practical) in combination with elementary schooling.

The idea of *'elementary education by the state'* is completely objectionable. Specifying the means available to elementary schools, the qualification of teaching staff, the subjects to be taught, etc. by a general law, as is done in the United States, and having state inspectors to supervise the observance of these regulations, is something quite different from appointing the state as educator of the people! Rather, government and church should alike be excluded from all influence on the schools. Indeed, in the Prusso-German Empire of all places (and the lame excuse that one is speaking of a future state is no way out; we have already seen what that means), it is inversely the state that could do with a rude education by the people.

Despite its democratic clang, the whole programme is thoroughly infested with the Lassallean sect's servile belief in the state, or, what is no better, by a democratic faith in miracles, or rather, it is a compromise between these two sorts of faith in miracles, both equally far removed from socialism.

'Freedom of science', says one paragraph of the Prussian Constitution. Then why here?

'Freedom of conscience'! If one should want, in this era of the

Kulturkampf,[16] to remind the liberals of their old catchwords, then surely it should only have been done in this form: Everyone should be free to relieve himself religiously as well as physically without the police sticking their noses in. But at this point the workers' party ought to have expressed its awareness that bourgeois 'freedom of conscience' only means the toleration of every possible kind of *religious freedom of conscience*, while its own goal is rather the liberation of the conscience from all religious spookery. But it chooses not to go further than the 'bourgeois' level.

I have now come to the end, for the appendix which now follows is not a *characteristic* part of the programme. I can thus be very brief here.

2. Normal working day.

In no other country has a workers' party restricted itself to such a vague demand. The length of the working day considered normal in the given circumstances has always been specified.

3. The restriction of female labour and the prohibition of child labour.

The standardization of the working day must anyway result in the restriction of female labour as far as this refers to the length of the working day, breaks, etc. Otherwise, the reference can only be to the exclusion of women from branches of labour which are specifically unhealthy for the female body or morally objectionable to the female sex. If this is what was meant, it should have been stated.

'*Prohibition of child labour*'! It was absolutely essential to give an *age-limit* here.

The *general prohibition* of child labour is incompatible with the existence of large-scale industry. It is thus only an empty, pious wish.

Its implementation – if possible – would be a reactionary step. With strict regulation of working hours according to age and with other precautionary measures to protect the children, the early combination of productive labour with education is one of the most powerful means for the transformation of present society.

16. The 'cultural struggle' was Bismarck's drive in the 1870s against the Catholic church and the Catholic Centre party.

4. State supervision of industry in the factory, workshop and home.

In the case of the Prusso-German state there should certainly have been a demand that inspectors be removable only by a court of law; that every worker should be able to take inspectors to court for neglect of duty; and that inspectors should only be recruited from the medical profession.

5. Regulation of prison labour.

A petty demand in a general workers' programme. In any case, it ought to have been made clear that there was no wish to see prisoners handled like animals for fear of competition, and especially no intention to deprive them of their only means of improvement, productive labour. Surely at least this much could have been expected from socialists.

6. An effective liability law.

What is meant by an 'effective' liability law should have been stated.

It could be noted in passing that, in speaking of the normal working day, the section of the factory laws relating to health regulations, safety measures, etc. has been overlooked. The liability law would only come into operation when these regulations were infringed.

In short, this appendix, too, is distinguished by its slovenly editing. *Dixi et salvavi animam meam.*[17]

17. I have spoken and saved my soul.

Circular Letter to Bebel, Liebknecht, Bracke, et al.[1]

Karl Marx and Frederick Engels

17–18 September 1879

Dear Bebel,

There has been a delay in replying to your letter of 29 August due on the one hand to the extended absence of Marx and on the other to several incidents: firstly the arrival of Richter's *Jahrbuch*[2] and then the arrival of Hirsch[3] himself.

I must assume that Liebknecht has not shown you my last letter to him, although I expressly requested him to do so. Otherwise you would certainly not have presented the same reasons which Liebknecht put forward and which I have already *answered* in that letter.[4]

Let us now go through the individual points at issue here.

I. The Negotiations with Karl Hirsch.

Liebknecht inquires whether Hirsch wants to take over the editorship of the newly founded party organ in Zurich.[5] Hirsch requests information about the founding of the paper: what funds are available and who is supplying them – the first question, in order to find out whether the paper will not have to cease publication after a few months; the other, in order to make sure who has his

1. This letter to the leadership of the German Social-Democratic Workers' Party was drafted by Engels and sent out over both Marx's and Engels's signatures after they had jointly revised it. It is translated here from the text printed in *MEW* 19.

2. The *Jahrbuch für Sozialwissenschaft und Sozialpolitik* was published in Zurich by Karl Höchberg, a philanthropist and reformist member of the SAPD, under the pseudonym Dr Ludwig Richter.

3. Karl Hirsch was a Social-Democratic publicist.

4. This interchange of letters has apparently not survived.

5. This was *Der Sozial-Demokrat*, the central organ of the SAPD published in Zurich from September 1879, and distributed clandestinely in Germany until the Anti-Socialist Law was repealed in 1890.

hand on the purse-strings and thus who has final control over the position of the paper. Liebknecht's answer to Hirsch: 'Everything in order, further information from Zurich' (Liebknecht to Hirsch, 28 July) does not arrive. But a letter from Bernstein to Hirsch does arrive from Zurich (24 July); Bernstein informs him that '*we* have been charged with the production and *supervision*' of the paper. He says a discussion has taken place 'between Viereck[6] and *us*' in which it was found, 'that your position would be made somewhat difficult by the differences of opinion which you had, as a *"Laterne"*[7] man, with individual comrades; however, *I* consider these reservations of no great importance'.

About the founding of the paper, not a word.

Hirsch answers on 26 July by return of post inquiring as to the financial position of the paper. Which comrades have pledged themselves to cover the deficit? Up to what amount and for how long a period? – The question of the editor's salary is of absolutely no importance in this connection; Hirsch merely wishes to know whether 'funds have been secured to guarantee the existence of the paper for at least one year'.

Bernstein answers on 31 July: Any potential deficit will be covered by voluntary contributions, of which *some* (!) have already been subscribed. In response to Hirsch's comments on the direction he intends to give the paper (of which more below), disapproving comments and *directives* are forthcoming:

> The *supervisory commission* must insist on this all the more, as it is itself subject to supervision, that is, is responsible. On this point, therefore, you would have to come to an agreement with the supervisory commission.

An immediate reply, if possible by telegraph, is requested.

Thus, instead of any answer to his justified questions Hirsch receives news that he is to carry on his editorial work under a *supervisory* commission with its seat in Zurich, a commission whose views differ very considerably from his own and whose members are not even named to him!

Hirsch, quite justifiably outraged at this treatment, prefers to come to an arrangement with the Leipzig people. You must be familiar with his letter of 2 August to Liebknecht, as Hirsch

6. Ludwig Viereck was a leader of the right wing of the SAPD.

7. *Die Laterne* was an anti-opportunist Social-Democratic satirical weekly, published by Karl Hirsch in Brussels from December 1878 to June 1879.

expressly demanded that you and Viereck be informed. Hirsch is even willing to place himself under a Zurich supervisory commission provided it makes comments to the editor in writing and is responsible to the Leipzig control commission.

Meanwhile Liebknecht writes to Hirsch on 28 July:

> *Of course* the undertaking has financial backing, as the whole party + (including) Höchberg are behind it. But I am not bothering about the details.

The next letter contains nothing about the financial backing either; on the other hand it contains the assurance that the Zurich commission is not an editorial commission but is only entrusted with *administration* and financial matters. On 14 August Liebknecht writes the same to me and demands that we persuade Hirsch to accept. On 29 August you yourself are so little informed about the true state of affairs that you write to me:

> In the editorial work of the newspaper he (Höchberg) has no more say than *any other prominent party comrade*.

Finally Hirsch receives a letter from Viereck on 11 August, in which he admits that

> ... the three men resident in Zurich were to tackle the founding of the paper as an *editorial commission* and to select an editor with the endorsement of the three Leipzig people ... *as far as I remember* it was also declared in the resolutions which were issued that the (Zurich) founding committee mentioned in clause 2 was to assume *the political as well as* the financial responsibility to the party ... Now this state of affairs seems to me to indicate that ... without the participation of the three men resident in Zurich, who have been charged by the party with the founding of the paper, an acceptance of the editorship cannot be considered.

Here Hirsch now has *something* definite at last, if only the information about the editor's position with regard to the Zurich people. They are an *editorial* commission; they also carry the *political* responsibility; it is not possible to take over the editorship without their participation. In short, Hirsch is simply directed to come to an arrangement with three people in Zurich whose names he has still not been given.

But so that the confusion is complete, Liebknecht writes a postscript to Viereck's letter:

Singer[8] has just been here from Berlin and has *reported*: The supervisory commission in Zurich is *not*, as Viereck thinks, an *editorial* commission but essentially an administrative commission, which is financially answerable to the party, i.e. to us, for the paper; of course the members have the right and the duty to discuss editorial matters with you (a right and a duty which, by the way, *every* party comrade has); they are *not* empowered to place you under *committee supervision*.

The three Zurich people and a member of the Leipzig executive – the only one who was present at the negotiations – insist that Hirsch is to be placed under the official direction of the Zurich commission; a second Leipzig member flatly denies this. And Hirsch is supposed to make up his mind before the gentlemen have reached an agreement among themselves? It does not seem to have occurred to anyone that Hirsch was entitled to be informed of the resolutions which had been passed containing the conditions which he was expected to comply with, the less so as it did not even occur to the Leipzig people to inform *themselves* reliably about those resolutions. Otherwise, how was the contradiction mentioned above possible?

Although the Leipzig people cannot agree on the powers delegated to the Zurich commission, the Zurich people are in absolutely no doubt.

Schramm[9] to Hirsch, 14 August:

If at that time you had not written that in the same case [as that of Kayser[10]] you would proceed in a similar fashion again, and if you had not thus held out the prospect of writing in the same manner, we would not consider the matter worth mentioning. But in view of your statement, we must reserve the right to cast a deciding vote on the acceptance of articles in the new journal.

The letter to Bernstein in which Hirsch is supposed to have said this is dated 26 July, *long* after the conference in Zurich in which the powers of the three Zurich people had been fixed. But in Zurich they are already revelling so much in the feeling of bureaucratic omnipotence that in reply to this later letter from Hirsch they are already laying claim to the new power to *decide* on the

8. Paul Singer was a leading Social-Democrat.

9. Karl Schramm, an economist and reformist Social-Democrat, edited the *Jahrbuch*.

10. Max Kayser was a right-wing Social-Democrat and Reichstag deputy; for his 'case' see below, pp. 1049–51.

acceptance of articles. The editorial commission has already become a commission of *censorship*.

Not until Höchberg came to Paris did Hirsch learn from him the *names* of the members of the two commissions.

What were the reasons that the negotiations with Hirsch came to nothing?

1. The obstinate refusal not only of the Leipzigers but also of the Zurichers to give him any substantive information about the financial basis and thus about the possibility of keeping the paper alive, if only for a year. He only learned of the amount subscribed from me here (after your communication to me). Thus it was scarcely possible to draw any other conclusion from the earlier information (the party + Höchberg) than that the paper either is already predominantly financed by Höchberg or will soon be completely dependent upon his contributions. And this latter possibility is even now still far from excluded. The sum of – if I read it correctly – 800 marks is *exactly* the same (£40 sterling) which the *Freiheit*[11] association here lost in the first *half-year*.

2. The repeated assurance by Liebknecht, which has since been proved to be totally inaccurate, that the Zurich people were not to exercise official supervision over the editor and the resultant comedy of errors.

3. Finally, the certainty that the Zurich commission was not only to supervise but actually to censor the editor and that all that fell to Hirsch was the role of a figurehead.

We can only agree with his decision thereupon to refuse. The Leipzig executive, as we have heard from Höchberg, has been augmented by two members who do not live in Leipzig and therefore it can only intervene when the three Leipzig members are in agreement. As a result, the real centre of gravity is transferred completely to Zurich; and Hirsch would not have been able to work with them in the long run any more than would any other real revolutionary editor with proletarian loyalties. More of that later.

II. The Intended Position of the Paper.

Straightaway, on 24 July, Bernstein informs Hirsch that the prob-

11. *Freiheit* was published by Johann Most from the beginning of 1879, first in London, later in New York. Most was already veering towards anarchism, and was expelled from the SAPD in 1880.

lems which he, as a *'Laterne'* man, has had with individual comrades, would make his position difficult.

Hirsch answers that in his judgement the attitude of the paper will have to be the same, in general, as that of the *'Laterne'*, i.e. such as to avoid legal proceedings in Switzerland and not to cause too much alarm in Germany. He asks who the comrades are and continues:

I know only one and I promise you that in a similar case involving a *violation of discipline* I shall treat him again in just the same way.

Bernstein replies in the dignified spirit befitting his new office of censor:

As far as the attitude of the paper is concerned, however, it is the view of the supervisory commission that it should not take the *'Laterne'* as its model; the paper is, in our opinion, to be less totally taken up with political radicalism and to be kept fundamentally socialist. Cases such as the attack on Kayser, which was disapproved of by all comrades without exception [!], must be avoided at all costs.

Etcetera, etcetera. Liebknecht calls the attack on Kayser 'a blunder' and Schramm considers it so dangerous that he proceeds to impose censorship on Hirsch.

Hirsch writes once again to Höchberg that a case such as that of Kayser

cannot occur if an official party organ exists whose clear explanations and well-meaning hints *cannot* be so boldly disregarded by a deputy.

Viereck, too, writes that the new paper is 'directed to adopt a dispassionate attitude and, as much as possible, to ignore all differences of opinion which have occurred hitherto'; it is not to be an 'expanded *Laterne*' and Bernstein 'could be reproached at most with having too moderate a position, if that is a reproach at a time when, of course, we cannot proceed under full sail'.

Now, what is this Kayser affair, this unforgivable crime which Hirsch is supposed to have committed? Kayser is the only Social-Democratic deputy who speaks and votes in the Reichstag in favour of protective tariffs. Hirsch accuses him of having violated party discipline.

1. By voting for direct taxation, the abolition of which the party programme expressly demands;

2. By voting monies to Bismarck and thus infringing the first basic rule of our party tactics: Not a farthing for this government.

In both points Hirsch is undoubtedly right. And after Kayser had trampled, on the one hand, upon the party programme, to which the deputies, as it were, took an oath in the form of a congress resolution, and, on the other, upon the most imperative, most fundamental rule of party tactics, and had *voted* Bismarck *monies as thanks for the Anti-Socialist Law*, Hirsch was equally right, in our opinion, to attack him as roughly as he did.

We have never been able to understand why people in Germany have become so furious about this attack on Kayser. Now Höchberg tells me the 'parliamentary party' gave Kayser *permission* to act as he did and as a result of this permission Kayser is considered covered.

If this is the case, it is really a bit much. Firstly, Hirsch could not know of this secret resolution any more than could the rest of the world.[12]

Furthermore, the disgrace for the party, which before could have been laid on Kayser alone, becomes even greater as a result of this affair, as does Hirsch's merit, too, in having exposed to all the world these absurd turns of phrase and even more absurd votes of Kayser's and thus in having saved the party's honour. Or has German Social Democracy indeed been infected by the parliamentary disease and does it really believe that with the popular vote the Holy Ghost is poured out over the elect, that meetings of the parliamentary party are transformed into infallible councils and party decisions into inviolable dogmas?

A blunder has indeed been committed, but however not by Hirsch but by the deputies who covered Kayser with their decision. And if those whose task it is above all others to attend to party discipline, violate this party discipline themselves so outrageously, so much the worse. But it is worse still to go so far as to believe that it was not Kayser, with his speech and vote, and the other deputies, with their resolution, who have violated party discipline, but Hirsch, with his attack on Kayser – despite this resolution, which was still unknown to him anyway.

By the way, it is certain that the party has adopted the same unclear and indecisive attitude on the protective tariff system as it

12. Crossed out in the manuscript: 'Supposing, also, two or three other Social-Democratic deputies (for there could hardly have been more there) had been tempted to allow Kayser to produce his bilge in public and to vote monies for Bismarck, they would have been obliged to assume the responsibility in public and to wait and see what Hirsch would say about it.'

has done hitherto on almost all economic questions which have assumed practical importance, e.g. the question of the state railways. This happens because the party organs, in particular *Vorwärts*,[13] instead of discussing this question thoroughly have preferred to apply themselves to the construction of a social order for the future. When the protective tariff question suddenly became a practical problem *after* the Anti-Socialist Law, the views expressed diverged in the most various ways and not one was to be found which possessed the prerequisites for the formation of a clear and correct judgement: knowledge of the condition of German industry and its position on the world market. Groups in favour of protective tariffs could not, then, be avoided here and there among the voters, and the party wanted, of course, to make allowance for these people. They failed to act decisively and take the only way out of this confusion by reaching a purely political understanding of the question (such was offered in the *Laterne*). It was inevitable, therefore, that in this debate the party appeared for the first time hesitant, uncertain and confused, and that it finally thoroughly disgraced itself in the person and in the case of Kayser.

The attack on Kayser is now taken as an excuse to preach to Hirsch in all tones of voice that the new paper is under no circumstances to imitate the excesses of the *Laterne*; it is to be less taken up with political radicalism and rather to be kept fundamentally socialist and dispassionate – by Viereck no less than by Bernstein, who seems to Viereck to be the right man precisely because he is too moderate, because it is not possible to proceed under full sail at the present time.

But why does one go abroad at all if not to proceed under full sail? Abroad nothing stands in the way. In Switzerland the German press laws, laws of association and penal laws do not apply. It is not only possible, therefore, to say the things there that it was not possible to say at home even before the Anti-Socialist Law, on account of the ordinary German laws; one has a *duty* to do so. For one stands here not only before Germany but before Europe; one has the duty, so far as the Swiss laws allow it, to demonstrate to Europe with all frankness the tendencies and aims of the German party. Anyone who wants to bind himself to *German* laws in

13. *Vorwärts* was the central organ of the SAPD after its foundation at Gotha in 1875. In October 1878, after the passage of the Anti-Socialist Law, it was forced to cease publication and did not reappear until 1890.

Switzerland merely proves that he is worthy of these German laws and in fact has nothing to say other than what was allowed in Germany before the emergency law.[14] No regard must be paid either to the possibility of temporarily cutting off the return of the editor to Germany. Anyone who is not prepared to take this risk is not suitable for an honorary office which is so exposed.

Furthermore, the emergency law has outlawed the German party precisely because it was the only serious opposition party in Germany. If in a foreign journal it renders thanks to Bismarck by giving up this role of the only serious opposition party, by behaving nice and tamely, and if it puts up with the kick and shows no passion, it only proves that it has deserved the kick. Of all the German emigrant newspapers which have appeared abroad since 1830, the *Laterne* is certainly one of the most moderate. But if even the *Laterne* was too impudent – then the new organ can only compromise the party in the eyes of the supporters in non-German countries.

III. The Manifesto of the Three Zurichers.
In the meantime Höchberg's *Jahrbuch* has reached us and it contains an article: 'The Socialist Movement in Germany in Retrospect',[15] which, as Höchberg has told me himself, has been written by the three members of this same Zurich commission. We have here their authentic criticism of the movement so far and hence their authentic programme for the position of the new organ in so far as this attitude depends on them.

At the very beginning they say:

The movement, which Lassalle regarded as an eminently political one, to which he summoned not only workers but all honourable democrats and *at whose head* the independent representatives of science and *all men filled with true love of humanity* were to march, was reduced under the presidency of J. B. von Schweitzer to a *one-sided struggle for the interests of the industrial workers.*

I will not investigate whether and to what extent this is historically the case. The special reproach which is directed at Schweitzer here consists in Schweitzer's having *reduced* Lassalleanism, which is understood here as a bourgeois democratic-philanthropic

14. I.e. the Anti-Socialist Law.
15. This article, signed with three asterisks, was the work of Höchberg, Schramm and Bernstein.

movement, to a one-sided struggle for the interests of the workers, whereas he *deepened* its character by making it a class struggle of the industrial workers against the bourgeoisie. He is further reproached with having 'rejected bourgeois democracy'. But what place has bourgeois democracy within the Social-Democratic Party? If it consists of 'honest men' it cannot want to be admitted, and if it nevertheless wishes to be admitted then this is only to cause trouble.

The Lassalle party 'preferred to conduct itself in a most *one-sided* fashion as a *workers' party*'. The gentlemen who wrote this are themselves members of a party which conducts itself in a most one-sided fashion as a workers' party; they now hold office and honour in it. This is an absolute incompatibility. If they mean what they write then they must leave the party, or at least resign from office and dignities. If they do not, then they admit that they intend to use their official position to combat the proletarian character of the party. The party, therefore, will betray itself if it leaves them their office and dignities.

In the view of these gentlemen, then, the Social-Democratic Party is *not* to be a one-sided workers' party but a party open on all sides 'for all men filled with true love of humanity'. It is to prove this, above all, by divesting itself of rough proletarian passions and by placing itself under the leadership of educated, philanthropic bourgeois in order to 'develop good taste' and 'to learn good form'. Then the 'disreputable behaviour' of many of its leaders will give way to an exemplary 'bourgeois behaviour'. (As if the superficially disreputable behaviour of those referred to were not the least they can be reproached with!) Then, too, '*numerous* supporters from the circles of the *educated* and *propertied* classes will join. But *these* must first be won, if the . . . agitation which is conducted is to achieve *tangible* successes'. German socialism has 'attached too much importance to winning the *masses* and has failed to conduct energetic (!) propaganda in the so-called upper strata of society'. For 'the party still lacks men who are fitted to represent it in the Reichstag'. But it is 'desirable and necessary to entrust mandates to men who have had opportunity and time enough to acquaint themselves with the relevant material. The simple worker and small craftsman . . . have the necessary leisure for this only in the most exceptional cases.'

So vote bourgeois!

In short, the working class is incapable of liberating itself by its own efforts. For this purpose it must first accept the leadership of 'educated and propertied' bourgeois, who alone have 'opportunity and time' to acquaint themselves with what is good for the workers. And secondly, the bourgeoisie is on no account to be combated, but to be *won* by energetic propaganda.

But if the upper strata of society, or even only their well-meaning elements are to be won, they must on no account be alarmed. And here the three Zurich people believe they have made a reassuring discovery:

The party is showing precisely at the present time, under the pressure of the Anti-Socialist Law, that it *does not desire* to follow the path of violent, bloody revolution, but is determined . . . to pursue the path of legality, i.e. of *reform*.

Thus, if 500,000–600,000 Social-Democratic voters, one tenth to one eighth of the whole electorate, dispersed, furthermore, far and wide across the whole country, are sensible enough not to run their heads against a wall and to attempt a 'bloody revolution', one against ten, this proves that they for ever exclude the possibility of making use of a tremendous external event, of a sudden revolutionary upsurge which might result from it, indeed of a *victory* gained by the people in a conflict arising from it! If Berlin should be again so uneducated as to have another 18 March,[16] the Social Democrats, instead of taking part in the struggle as 'rabble with a mania for barricades', must rather 'pursue the path of legality', curb the movement, clear away the barricades and, if necessary, march with the splendid army against the rough, one-sided, uneducated masses. If the gentlemen maintain that this is not what they meant, then what did they mean?

It becomes even better. 'Hence, the more calm, objective and deliberate it' (the party) 'is in its criticism of existing conditions and in its proposals for changing them, the less it will be possible to repeat the present successful move' (at the time of the introduction of the Anti-Socialist Law) 'with which the conscious forces of reaction have intimidated the bourgeoisie with their fear of the red bogey' (p. 88).

In order to dissolve the last trace of fear on the part of the bourgeoisie it must be shown clearly and convincingly that the red bogey is really only a phantom and does not exist. But what is the

16. 18 March 1848 saw the erection of barricades, as the German revolution reached Berlin.

secret of the red bogey if not the fear felt by the bourgeoisie of
the inevitable life-and-death struggle between itself and the proletariat? The fear of the inevitable decision in the modern class
struggle? Abolish the class struggle, and the bourgeoisie and 'all
independent men' will 'not hesitate to go hand in hand with the
proletarians'! And who would then be cheated if not precisely the
proletarians?

Let the party demonstrate, therefore, by its humble and sorrowful
demeanour that it has once and for all laid aside the 'improprieties
and excesses' which gave rise to the Anti-Socialist Law. If it promises voluntarily that it intends only to operate within the limits of the
Anti-Socialist Law, Bismarck and the bourgeoisie will then surely
have the goodness to repeal this law, which will then be superfluous!
'Let no one misunderstand us!'

We do not want to give up our party and our programme, but we are of
the opinion that we have enough to do for years to come if we direct our
whole strength, our whole energy to the achievement of certain immediate
goals, which must be achieved in any case before there can be any thought of
fulfilling the more far-reaching aspirations.

Bourgeois, petty bourgeois, and workers who 'are now deterred by
the far-reaching demands', will then join us in masses too.

The programme is not to be *abandoned* but only *postponed* –
for an indefinite period. It is accepted, but not actually for oneself
and for one's own lifetime, but posthumously, as an heirloom for
one's children and one's children's children. In the meantime one
applies 'all one's strength and energy' to all sorts of petty trifles and
to patching up the capitalist social order, so that at least it looks as if
something is happening and so that at the same time the bourgeoisie
is not alarmed. Compared with that I would much prefer the communist Miquel, who proves his unshakeable belief in the inevitable
overthrow of capitalist society in a few hundred years by indulging
in swindles for all he is worth, making an honest contribution to the
crash of 1873 and thus *really* doing something to bring about the
collapse of the existing order.

Another offence against form was evident in the 'exaggerated
attacks on the "founders" ',[17] who, of course, were 'only children

17. The 'founders' (*Gründer*) were the entrepreneurs who enriched themselves
from the boom of the early 1870s, based on French reparations payments and the
stimulus given by German unification. Bethel Strousberg, a railway magnate who was
bankrupted by the 1873 crash, was a typical *Gründer*.

of the age'; 'it would have been better to abstain from the abuse of Strousberg and such people'. Unfortunately all people are 'only children of the age', and if this is an adequate excuse nobody may be attacked anymore and all polemics and all struggle on our part must come to an end; we simply put up with all the kicks from our opponents because we, in our wisdom, know of course that they are 'only children of the age' and cannot act any other way. Instead of repaying their kicks with interest we should rather feel pity for the poor souls.

Similarly, the support for the Commune, of course, had the disadvantage that 'people otherwise well disposed towards us were repelled and in general the *hatred felt by the bourgeoisie* towards us became greater'. And, furthermore, the party is 'not wholly blameless as far as the passing of the October law[18] was concerned, for it increased the *hatred of the bourgeoisie* unnecessarily'.

There you have the programme of the three Zurich censors. In clarity it leaves nothing to be desired. Least of all for us, as we know all these phrases very well from 1848. They are the representatives of the petty bourgeoisie who are making their presence felt, full of fear that the proletariat, under the pressure of its revolutionary position, may 'go too far'. Instead of a determined political opposition – general mediation; instead of the struggle against government and bourgeoisie – the attempt to win them over and persuade them; instead of defiant resistance to mistreatment from above – humble submissiveness and the admission that the punishment is deserved. All historically necessary conflicts are reinterpreted as misunderstandings and all discussions are brought to an end with the protestation that ultimately we are all agreed on the main points. The people who appeared as bourgeois democrats in 1848 can now just as well call themselves Social Democrats. Just as for the former the democratic republic was unattainably remote so, too, is the overthrow of the capitalist order for the latter, and it has therefore absolutely no significance for the political practice of the present day; one can mediate, compromise and philanthropize to one's heart's content. And it is just the same with the class struggle between the proletariat and the bourgeoisie. On paper it is acknowledged because its existence can no longer be denied; but in practice it is hushed up, watered down, attenuated. The Social-Democratic Party *is not* to be a

18. I.e. the Anti-Socialist Law, which had been passed the previous October.

workers' party; it is not to incur the hatred of the bourgeoisie or of anyone; above all it should conduct energetic propaganda among the bourgeoisie; instead of stressing far-reaching goals which deter the bourgeoisie and are unattainable in our generation anyway, it should rather devote its whole strength and energy to those petty-bourgeois patchwork reforms which could provide the old social order with new supports and hence perhaps transform the final catastrophe into a gradual, piecemeal and, as far as possible, peaceful process of dissolution. These are the same people who, under the guise of unflagging activity, not only do nothing but also try to prevent anything happening at all, except – chatter; the same people whose fear of every action in 1848 and 1849 obstructed the movement at every step and finally caused its downfall; the same people who never see reaction and are then quite amazed to find themselves in a blind alley, where neither resistance nor flight is possible, the same people who want to banish history to the confines of their own narrow philistine horizon and over whose heads history always proceeds to the real business on the agenda.

As far as their socialist substance is concerned this has already been adequately criticized in the 'Manifesto', in the section on 'German or "True" Socialism'.[19] When the class struggle is rejected as a disagreeable 'coarse' phenomenon, nothing remains as the basis of socialism other than 'true love of humanity' and empty phrases about 'justice'.

It is an inevitable phenomenon which is rooted in the course of the development that people from the hitherto ruling class join the struggling proletariat and supply it with educative elements. We have already stated this clearly in the Manifesto. But two points must be noted here:

Firstly, in order to be of use to the proletarian movement these people must bring real educative elements with them. But this is not the case with the great majority of the German bourgeois converts. Neither the *Zukunft* nor the *Neue Gesellschaft*[20] have contributed anything which has advanced the movement one step. Here there is an absolute lack of real educative material, factual or theoretical. Instead, attempts to harmonize superficially acquired socialist thoughts with the most varying theoretical stand-

19. See above, pp. 84–7.
20. The *Zukunft* and the *Neue Gesellschaft* were both short-lived journals of the reformist intellectuals who gravitated around the SAPD.

points which the gentlemen have brought with them from the university or elsewhere and of which each is more confused than the one before, thanks to the process of decomposition which the remnants of German philosophy are undergoing today. Instead of first thoroughly studying the new science himself, each of them preferred to trim it according to the standpoint which he had brought with him, made forthwith his own private science, and came forward with the pretension of wanting to teach it. That is why among these gentlemen there are almost as many standpoints as heads; instead of bringing clarity anywhere they have only created dire confusion – fortunately almost exclusively among themselves. Such educative elements, whose first principle it is to teach what they have not learnt, the party can very well do without.

Secondly, when such people from other classes join the proletarian party the first requirement is that they do not bring any remnants of bourgeois, petty-bourgeois etc. prejudices with them, but that they adopt the proletarian outlook without prevarication. These gentlemen, however, as has been demonstrated, are chock full of bourgeois and petty-bourgeois ideas. In such a petty-bourgeois country as Germany these ideas certainly have their justification. But only *outside* the Social-Democratic Workers' Party. If these gentlemen constitute themselves as a social-democratic petty-bourgeois party they have a perfect right to do so; it would be possible, then, to negotiate with them and to form a common front with them under certain circumstances. But in a workers' party they are an adulterating element. If there are reasons for tolerating them in it for the present then it is our duty *only* to tolerate them, to allow them no influence on the party leadership and to remain conscious of the fact that the break with them is only a matter of time. The time, moreover, seems to have come. It seems to us incomprehensible that the party can allow the authors of this article in its midst any longer. But if the party leadership should fall more or less into their hands, then the party will simply be castrated and that would be the end of its proletarian drive.

As far as we are concerned, after our whole past only one way is open to us. For almost forty years we have stressed the class struggle as the most immediate driving power in history and, in particular, the class struggle between the bourgeoisie and the proletariat as the great lever of the modern social upheaval; therefore it is impossible for us to ally ourselves with people who want to eliminate this class struggle from the movement. When the International was formed, we expressly formulated the battlecry: the emancipation of the working class must be the work of the working class itself. We cannot ally ourselves, therefore, with people who openly declare that the workers are too uneducated to free themselves and must first be liberated from above by philanthropic big bourgeois and petty bourgeois. If the new party organ assumes a position which corresponds to the opinions of those gentlemen, which is bourgeois and not proletarian, then nothing remains, much though we should regret it, but to declare publicly our opposition to it and to abandon the solidarity with which we have hitherto represented the German party abroad. We hope, however, that it will not come to *this*.

This letter is intended for communication to all five members of the executive in Germany and to Bracke . . .

As far as we are concerned nothing stands in the way of its communication to the members of the Zurich commission.

Introduction to the Programme of the French Workers' Party[1]

Considering,

That the emancipation of the class of producers is that of all human beings, without distinction of sex or race;

That the producers can only be free when they are in possession of the means of production;

That there are only two forms in which the means of production can belong to them:

1. The individual form, which was never a universal phenomenon and is being ever more superseded by the progress of industry,

2. The collective form, the material and mental elements for which are created by the very development of capitalist society;

Considering,

That collective appropriation can only proceed from the revolutionary action of the class of producers – the proletariat – organized in an independent political party;

That such an organization must be pursued by all means that are available to the proletariat, especially including universal suffrage,

1. The Parti Ouvrier was founded in 1879 at Marseilles. It was federal in structure and contained anarchist and reformist components as well as socialist, and it was not long before the French workers' movement was again fragmented. Jules Guesde, the leading Marxist activist in the French workers' movement, visited London in May 1880 to draw up a programme for the new party in time for the forthcoming elections, in conjunction with Lafargue, Engels and Marx. Marx dictated to Guesde this theoretical introduction. The whole programme was published in *Égalité*, the journal of Guesde's group, on 30 June 1880, and it was adopted, against anarchist opposition, at the 'revolutionary workers' congress' at Le Havre in September 1880, after socialists and anarchists had walked out of the Parti Ouvrier congress at which the reformists were in a majority. It is translated here from the French text reproduced in Marx–Engels *Gesamtausgabe*, I/25, Berlin, 1985, p. 280.

which will thus be transformed from the instrument of fraud that it has been up till now into an instrument of emancipation;

The French socialist workers, who have set themselves in the economic arena the goal of the return of all means of production to collective ownership, have decided, as the means of organization and struggle, to enter the elections with the following minimum programme.[2]

2. This minimum programme demanded an extension of democratic liberties, including the general arming of the people, also economic reforms such as the eight-hour day, progressive income tax, and equal pay for men and women.

On Poland and Russia

WHAT HAVE THE WORKING CLASSES TO DO WITH
POLAND?[1]

Frederick Engels

I *Commonwealth*, 24 March 1866

Wherever the working classes have taken a part of their own in political movements, there, from the very beginning, their foreign policy
was expressed in the few words – restoration of Poland. This was
the case with the Chartist movement so long as it existed; this was
the case with the French working men long before 1848, as well as
during that memorable year, when on 15 May they marched on to the
National Assembly to the cry of *'Vive la Pologne!'* – Poland for ever![2]
This was the case in Germany, when, in 1848 and 1849, the organs
of the working class demanded war with Russia for the restoration of
Poland.[3] It is the case even now; with one exception – of which more
anon – the working men of Europe unanimously proclaim the restoration of Poland as a part and parcel of their political programme, as the
most comprehensive expression of their foreign policy. The middle
class, too, have had, and have still, 'sympathies' with the Poles;
which sympathies have not prevented them from leaving the Poles
in the lurch in 1831, in 1846, in 1863, nay, have not even prevented

1. This series of articles was written by Engels at Marx's explicit request for the
Commonwealth, a London workers' paper. It was directed against the position of the
French and Belgian Proudhonists, as expressed particularly by Hector Denis in *Le
Tribune du Peuple* of Brussels and by the Proudhonist delegates at the 1865 London
Conference of the International.

2. On 15 May 1848 150,000 demonstrators, led by Auguste Blanqui, marched on
the French National Assembly, which was debating Poland, and demanded military
help for the Polish struggle. When this was refused, they attempted to overthrow the
National Assembly, but were defeated by the bourgeois National Guard (see 'The
Class Struggles in France', above, p. 392).

3. This refers in particular to the *Neue Rheinische Zeitung* which Marx and Engels
edited in 1848. See above, pp. 42–6.

them from leaving the worst enemies of Poland, such as Lord Palmerston, to manage matters so as to actually assist Russia while they talked in favour of Poland. But with the working classes it is different. They mean intervention, not non-intervention; they mean war with Russia while Russia meddles with Poland; and they have proved it every time the Poles rose against their oppressors. And recently, the International Working Men's Association has given a fuller expression to this universal instinctive feeling of the body it claims to represent, by inscribing on its banner, 'Resistance to Russian encroachments upon Europe – Restoration of Poland'.[4]

This programme of the foreign policy of the working men of western and central Europe has found a unanimous consent among the class to whom it was addressed, with one exception, as we said before. There are among the working men of France a small minority who belong to the school of the late P. J. Proudhon. This school differs *in toto* from the generality of the advanced and thinking working men: it declares them to be ignorant fools, and maintains on most points opinions quite contrary to theirs. This holds good in their foreign policy also. The Proudhonists, sitting in judgement on oppressed Poland, find the verdict of the Staleybridge jury, 'serves her right'. They admire Russia as the great land of the future, as the most progressive nation upon the face of the earth, at the side of which such a paltry country as the United States is not worthy of being named. They have charged the [General] Council of the International Association with setting up the Bonapartist principle of nationalities, and with declaring that magnanimous Russian people without the pale of civilized Europe, such being a grievous sin against the principles of universal democracy and the fraternity of all nations. These are the charges. Barring the democratic phraseology at the wind-up, they coincide, it will be seen at once, verbally and literally with what the extreme Tories of all countries have to say about Poland and Russia. Such charges are not worth refuting; but, as they come from a fraction of the working classes, be it ever so small a one, they may

4. The London Conference of September 1865 had carried the resolution, 'That it is imperative to annihilate the invading influence of Russia by applying to Poland "the right of every people to dispose of itself", and re-establishing that country on a social and democratic basis' (*IWMA* I, pp. 246–7). However, the resolutions on Poland which the General Council submitted to the Geneva Congress of September 1866 (see 'Instructions for Delegates', above, pp. 777–8) were defeated by the opposition of the Proudhonists.

render it desirable to state again the case of Poland and Russia, and to vindicate what we may henceforth call the foreign policy of the united working men of Europe.

But why do we always name Russia alone in connection with Poland? Have not two German powers, Austria and Prussia, shared in the plunder? Do not they, too, hold parts of Poland in bondage, and, in connection with Russia, do they not work to keep down every national Polish movement?

It is well known how hard Austria has struggled to keep out of the Polish business; how long she resisted the plans of Russia and Prussia for partition. Poland was a natural ally of Austria against Russia. When Russia once became formidable, nothing could be more in the interest of Austria than to keep Poland alive between herself and the newly rising empire. It was only when Austria saw that Poland's fate was settled, that with or without her, the other two powers were determined to annihilate her, it was only then that in self-protection she went in for a share of the territory. But as early as 1815 she held out for the restoration of an independent Poland; in 1831 and in 1863 she was ready to go to war for that object, and give up her own share of Poland provided England and France were prepared to join her. The same during the Crimean War. This is not said in justification of the general policy of the Austrian government. Austria has shown often enough that to oppress a weaker nation is congenial work to her rulers. But in the case of Poland the instinct of self-preservation was stronger than the desire for new territory or the habits of government. And this puts Austria out of court for the present.

As to Prussia, her share of Poland is too trifling to weigh much on the scale. Her friend and ally, Russia, has managed to ease her of nine tenths of what she got during the three partitions.[5] But what little is left to her weighs as an incubus upon her. It has chained her to the triumphal car of Russia, it has been the means of enabling her government, even in 1863–4, to practise unchallenged in Prussian Poland those breaches of the law, those infractions of individual liberty, of the right of meeting, of the liberty of the press, which were so soon afterwards to be applied to

5. The Congress of Vienna of 1814–15 left Prussia with a considerably smaller share of Poland than she had acquired by the earlier partitions, as the greater part of Poland was now constituted into the 'Kingdom of Poland', and placed under tsarist rule. By way of compensation, Prussia received the Rhineland. 'Nine tenths', how-ever, is a bit of an exaggeration.

the rest of the country; it has falsified the whole middle-class liberal movement which, from fear of risking the loss of a few square miles of land on the eastern frontier, allowed the government to set all law aside with regard to the Poles. The working men, not only of Prussia, but of all Germany, have a greater interest than those of any other country in the restoration of Poland, and they have shown in every revolutionary movement that they know it. Restoration of Poland, to them, is emancipation of their own country from Russian vassalage. And this we think puts Prussia out of court too. Whenever the working classes of Russia (if there is such a thing in that country, in the sense it is understood in western Europe) form a political programme, and that programme contains the liberation of Poland – then, but not till then, Russia as a nation will be out of court too, and the government of the tsar will remain alone under indictment.

II *Commonwealth*, 31 March 1866

It is said that to claim independence for Poland is to acknowledge the 'principle of nationalities', and that the principle of nationalities is a Bonapartist invention concocted to prop up the Napoleonic despotism in France. Now what is this 'principle of nationalities'?

By the treaties of 1815 the boundaries of the various states of Europe were drawn merely to suit diplomatic convenience, and especially to suit the convenience of the then strongest continental power – Russia. No account was taken either of the wishes, the interests, or the national diversities of the populations. Thus, Poland was divided, Germany was divided, Italy was divided, not to speak of the many smaller nationalities inhabiting south-eastern Europe, and of which few people at that time knew anything. The consequence was that for Poland, Germany, and Italy, the very first step in every political movement was to attempt the restoration of that national unity without which national life was but a shadow. And when, after the suppression of the revolutionary attempts in Italy and Spain, 1821–3,[6] and again, after the

---

6. In January 1820 a military rising in Madrid forced the Spanish monarchy to revive the democratic constitution of 1812. In the summer of 1820 revolutions inspired by the Spanish example broke out in Naples and Piedmont. In March 1821 Austrian troops moved in to crush the Italian revolutions, and in April 1823 France invaded Spain in order to abolish the constitution and restore King Ferdinand.

revolution of July 1830 in France, the extreme politicians of the greater part of civilized Europe came into contact with each other,[7] and attempted to mark out a kind of common programme, the liberation and unification of the oppressed and subdivided nations became a watchword common to all of them. So it was again in 1848, when the number of oppressed nations was increased by a fresh one, viz., Hungary. There could, indeed, be no two opinions as to the right of every one of the great national subdivisions of Europe to dispose of itself, independently of its neighbours, in all internal matters, so long as it did not encroach upon the liberty of the others. This right was, in fact, one of the fundamental conditions of the internal liberty of all. How could, for instance, Germany aspire to liberty and unity, if at the same time she assisted Austria to keep Italy in bondage, either directly or by her vassals? Why, the total breaking-up of the Austrian monarchy is the very first condition of the unification of Germany!

This right of the great national subdivisions of Europe to political independence, acknowledged as it was by the European democracy, could not but find the same acknowledgement with the working classes especially. It was, in fact, nothing more than to recognize in other large national bodies of undoubted vitality the same right of individual national existence which the working men of each separate country claimed for themselves. But this recognition, and the sympathy with these national aspirations, were restricted to the large and well-defined historical nations of Europe; there was Italy, Poland, Germany, Hungary. France, Spain, England, Scandinavia were neither subdivided nor under foreign control, and therefore but indirectly interested in the matter; and as to Russia, she could only be mentioned as the detainer of an immense amount of stolen property, which would have to be disgorged on the day of reckoning.

After the coup d'état of 1851, Louis Napoleon, the emperor 'by the grace of God and the national will',[8] had to find a democraticized and popular sounding name for his foreign policy. What could be better than to inscribe upon his banners the 'principle

7. Engels is alluding here to Mazzini's secret organization Young Europe, which was formed in 1834 by the federation of Young Italy, Young Germany, and the Polish nationalist organization.

8. This phrase was used to justify the installation of Louis Philippe as the French king in 1830.

of nationalities'? Every nationality to be the arbiter of its own fate – every detached fraction of any nationality to be allowed to annex itself to its great mother-country – what could be more liberal? Only, mark, there was not, now, any more question of *nations*, but of *nationalities*.

There is no country in Europe where there are not different nationalities under the same government. The Highland Gaels and the Welsh are undoubtedly of different nationalities to what the English are, although nobody will give to these remnants of peoples long gone by the title of nations, any more than to the Celtic inhabitants of Brittany in France. Moreover, no state boundary coincides with the natural boundary of nationality, that of language. There are plenty of people out of France whose mother tongue is French, same as there are plenty of people of German language out of Germany; and in all probability it will ever remain so. It is a natural consequence of the confused and slow-working historical development through which Europe has passed during the last thousand years, that almost every great nation has parted with some outlying portions of its own body, which have become separated from the national life, and in most cases participated in the national life of some other people; so much so, that they do not wish to rejoin their own main stock. The Germans in Switzerland and Alsace do not desire to be reunited to Germany, any more than the French in Belgium and Switzerland wish to become attached politically to France. And after all, it is no slight advantage that various nations, as politically constituted, have most of them some foreign elements within themselves, which form connecting links with their neighbours, and vary the otherwise too monotonous uniformity of the national character.

Here, then, we perceive the difference between the 'principle of *nationalities*' and the old democratic and working-class tenet as to the right of the great European *nations* to separate and independent existence. The 'principle of nationalities' leaves entirely untouched the great question of the right of national existence for the historic peoples of Europe; nay, if it touches it, it is merely to disturb it. The principle of nationalities raises two sorts of questions; first of all, questions of boundary between these great historic peoples; and secondly, questions as to the right to independent national existence of those numerous small relics of peoples which, after having figured for a longer or shorter period on the stage of history, were finally absorbed as integral portions into one or the other of those more powerful nations whose greater vitality enabled them to overcome greater obstacles. The European importance, the vitality of a people is as nothing in the eyes of the principle of nationalities; before it, the Roumans of Wallachia, who never had a history[9] nor the energy required to have one, are of equal importance to the Italians who have a history of 2,000 years, and an unimpaired national vitality; the Welsh and Manxmen, if they desired it, would have an equal right to independent political exist-ence, absurd though it would be, with the English. The whole thing is an absurdity, got up in a popular dress in order to throw dust in shallow people's eyes, and to be used as a convenient phrase, or to be laid aside if the occasion requires it.

Shallow as the thing is, it required cleverer brains than Louis Napoleon's to invent it. The principle of nationalities, so far from being a Bonapartist invention to favour a resurrection of Poland, is nothing but a *Russian invention concocted to destroy Poland*. Russia has absorbed the greater part of ancient Poland on the plea of the principle of nationalities, as we shall see here-after. The idea is more than a hundred years old, and Russia uses it now every day. What is pan-Slavism but the application, by Russia and Russian interest, of the principle of nationalities to the Serbians, Croats, Ruthenes, Slovaks, Czechs, and other remnants of bygone Slavonian peoples in Turkey, Hungary, and Germany? Even at this present moment, the Russian government have agents travelling among the Lapponians in northern Norway and Sweden, trying to agitate among these nomadic savages the idea of a 'great Finnic nationality', which is to be restored in the extreme north of Europe, under Russian protection, of course. The 'cry of anguish' of the oppressed Laplanders is raised very loud in the Russian papers – not by those same oppressed nomads, but by the Russian agents – and indeed it is a frightful oppression, to induce these poor Laplanders to learn the civilized Norwegian or Swedish language, instead of confining themselves to their own barbaric, half Eskimo idiom! The principle of nationalities, indeed, could be invented in eastern Europe alone, where the tide of Asiatic invasion, for a thousand years, recurred again and again, and left on the shore those heaps of intermingled ruins of nations which even now the ethnologist can scarcely disentangle,

9. On Engels's mistaken conception that the smaller Slav peoples 'never had a history', see the Introduction to *The Revolutions of 1848*, above p. 45.

and where the Turk, the Finnic Magyar, the Rouman, the Jew, and about a dozen Slavonic tribes, live intermixed in interminable confusion. That was the ground to work the principle of nationalities, and how Russia has worked it there, we shall see by-and-by in the example of Poland.

III *Commonwealth*, 5 May 1866

The doctrine of nationality applied to Poland.

Poland, like almost all other European countries, is inhabited by people of different nationalities. The mass of the population, the nucleus of its strength, is no doubt formed by the Poles proper, who speak the Polish language. But ever since 1390[10] Poland proper has been united to the Grand Duchy of Lithuania, which has formed, up to the last partition in 1795, an integral portion of the Polish republic. This Grand Duchy of Lithuania was inhabited by a great variety of races. The northern provinces, on the Baltic, were in possession of *Lithuanians* proper, people speaking a language distinct from that of their Slavonic neighbours; these Lithuanians had been, to a great extent, conquered by German immigrants, who again found it hard to hold their own against the Lithuanian Grand Dukes. Further south, and east of the present Kingdom of Poland, were the *White Russians*, speaking a language betwixt Polish and Russian, but nearer the latter; and finally the southern provinces were inhabited by the so-called *Little Russians*, whose language is now by best authorities considered as perfectly distinct from the Great Russian (the language we commonly call Russian). Therefore, if people say that to demand the restoration of Poland is to appeal to the principle of nationalities, they merely prove that they do not know what they are talking about, for the restoration of Poland means the re-establishment of a state composed of at least four different nationalities.

When the old Polish state was thus being formed by the union with Lithuania, where was then Russia? Under the heel of the Mongolian conqueror, whom the Poles and Germans combined, 150 years before, had driven back east of the Dnieper. It took a long struggle until the Grand Dukes of Moscow finally shook off the Mongol yoke, and set about combining the many different principalities of Great Russia into one state. But this success seems only to have increased their ambition. No sooner had Constantinople

10. This union in fact dates from 1386, when Jagiello of Lithuania married Jadviga of Poland.

fallen to the Turks, than the Muscovite Grand Duke placed in his coat-of-arms the double-headed eagle of the Byzantine emperors, thereby setting up his claim as successor and future avenger, and ever since, it is well known, the Russians worked to conquer Tsarigrad, the town of the tsar, as they call Constantinople in their language. Then, the rich plains of Little Russia excited their lust of annexation; but the Poles were then a strong, and always a brave people, and not only knew how to fight for their own, but also how to retaliate; in the beginning of the seventeenth century they even held Moscow for a few years.[11]

The gradual demoralization of the ruling aristocracy, the want of power to develop a middle class, and the constant wars devastating the country, at last broke the strength of Poland. A country which persisted in maintaining unimpaired the feudal system of society, while all its neighbours progressed, formed a middle class, developed commerce and industry, and created large towns – such a country was doomed to ruin. No doubt the aristocracy did ruin Poland, and ruin her thoroughly; and after ruining her, they upbraided each other for having done so, and sold themselves and their country to the foreigner. Polish history, from 1700 to 1772, is nothing but a record of Russian usurpation of dominion in Poland, rendered possible by the corruptibility of the nobles. Russian soldiers were almost constantly occupying the country, and the kings of Poland, if not willing traitors themselves, were placed more and more under the thumb of the Russian ambassador. So well had this game succeeded, and so long had it been played, that, when Poland at last was annihilated, there was no outcry at all in Europe, and, indeed, people were astonished at this only, that Russia should have the generosity of giving such a large slice of the territory to Austria and Prussia.

The way in which this partition was brought about is particularly interesting. There was, at that time, already an enlightened 'public opinion' in Europe. Although *The Times* newspaper had not yet begun to manufacture that article, there was that kind of public opinion which had been created by the immense influence of Diderot, Voltaire, Rousseau, and the other French writers of the eighteenth century. Russia always knew that it is important to have public opinion on one's side, if possible, and Russia took care to have it, too. The court of Catherine II was made the

11. In 1605–6, and again in September 1610, the Poles occupied Moscow. The city was finally freed by a popular uprising under Minin and Pozharski.

headquarters of the enlightened men of the day, especially Frenchmen; the most enlightened principles were professed by the empress and her court, and so well did she succeed in deceiving them that Voltaire and many others sang the praise of the 'Semiramis of the North', and proclaimed Russia the most progressive country in the world, the home of liberal principles, the champion of religious toleration.

Religious toleration – that was the word wanted to put down Poland. Poland had always been extremely liberal in religious matters; witness the asylum the Jews found there while they were persecuted in all other parts of Europe. The greater portion of the people in the eastern provinces belonged to the Greek faith, while the Poles proper were Roman Catholics. A considerable portion of these Greek Catholics had been induced, during the sixteenth century, to acknowledge the supremacy of the Pope, and were called United Greeks; but a great many continued true to their old Greek religion in all respects. They were principally the serfs, their noble masters being almost all Roman Catholics; they were Little Russians by nationality. Now, this Russian government, which did not tolerate at home any other religion but the Greek, and punished apostasy as a crime; which was conquering foreign nations and annexing foreign provinces right and left; and which was at that time engaged in riveting still firmer the fetters of the Russian serf – this same Russian government came soon upon Poland in the name of religious toleration, because Poland was said to oppress the Greek Catholics; in the name of the principle of nationalities, because the inhabitants of these eastern provinces were *Little* Russians, and ought, therefore, to be annexed to *Great* Russia; and in the name of the right of revolution arming the serfs against their masters. Russia is not at all scrupulous in the selection of her means. Talk about a war of class against class as something extremely revolutionary; – why, Russia set such a war on foot in Poland nearly 100 years ago, and a fine specimen of a class war it was, when Russian soldiers and Little Russian serfs went in company to burn down the castles of Polish lords, merely to prepare Russian annexation, which being once accomplished the same Russian soldiers put the serfs back again under the yoke of their lords.

All this was done in the cause of religious toleration, because the principle of nationalities was not then fashionable in western Europe. But it was held up before the eyes of the Little Russian peasants at the time, and has played an important part since in Polish affairs. The first and foremost ambition of Russia is the union of all Russian tribes under the tsar, who calls himself the autocrat of all Russias, and among these she includes White and Little Russia. And in order to prove that her ambition went no further, she took very good care, during the three partitions, to annex none but White and Little Russian provinces; leaving the country inhabited by Poles, and even a portion of Little Russia (eastern Galicia) to her accomplices. But how do matters stand now? The greater portion of the provinces annexed in 1793 and 1795 by Austria and Prussia are now under Russian dominion, under the name of the Kingdom of Poland, and from time to time hopes are raised among the Poles, that if they will only submit to Russian supremacy, and renounce all claims to the ancient Lithuanian provinces, they may expect a reunion of all other Polish provinces and a restoration of Poland, with the Russian emperor for a king. And if at the present juncture Prussia and Austria come to blows, it is more than probable that the war will not be, ultimately, for the annexation of Schleswig-Holstein to Prussia, or of Venice to Italy, but rather of Austrian, and at least a portion of Prussian, Poland to Russia.

So much for the principle of nationalities in Polish affairs.

FOR POLAND[12]

Karl Marx and Frederick Engels

Der Volksstaat, 24 March 1875

This year, too, a meeting took place to commemorate the Polish uprising of 22 January 1863. Our German party comrades took part in this commemoration in large numbers; many of them made speeches, among them Engels and Marx.

'We have spoken here,' said Engels, 'of the reasons why the revolutionaries of all countries are bound to sympathize with

12. The following speeches were delivered by Marx and Engels at an international meeting held in London to commemorate the twelfth anniversary of the Polish uprising of 22 January 1863. Engels himself wrote up the report of his and Marx's speeches for *Der Volksstaat*, the organ of the SDAP, and they are translated here from the texts reproduced in *MEW* 18.

and stand up for the cause of Poland. Only one point has been forgotten and it is this: the political situation into which Poland has been brought is a thoroughly revolutionary one, and it leaves Poland with no other choice but to be revolutionary or perish. This was evident even after the First Partition,[13] which was brought about by the efforts of the Polish nobility to preserve a constitution and privileges which had forfeited their right to exist and were detrimental to the country and to general order instead of preserving the peace and securing progress. Even after the First Partition a section of the aristocracy recognized their mistake and became convinced that Poland could only be restored by means of a revolution; – and ten years later we saw Poland fighting for freedom in America. The French revolution of 1789 found an immediate echo in Poland. The constitution of 1791, embodying the rights of man, became the banner of the revolution on the banks of the Vistula and made Poland the vanguard of revolutionary France, and that at a moment when the three powers which had already plundered Poland were uniting to march on Paris and to stifle the revolution there. Could they allow revolution to nestle at the centre of the Coalition? Impossible! Again they threw themselves upon Poland, this time intending to rob it completely of its national existence. The unfurling of the revolutionary banner was one of the main reasons for the subjugation of Poland. A land which has been fragmented and struck off the list of nations because it has been revolutionary can seek its salvation nowhere but in revolution. And thus we find Poland taking part in all revolutionary struggles. Poland understood this in 1863 and during the uprising whose anniversary we are celebrating today it published the most radical revolutionary programme which has ever been laid down in eastern Europe. It would be ridiculous, because of the existence of a Polish aristocratic party, to regard the Polish revolutionaries as aristocrats who want to restore the aristocratic Poland of 1772. The Poland of 1772 is lost for ever. No power on earth will be able to raise it up from the grave. The new Poland to which the revolution will give birth differs, from a social and political point of view, just as fundamentally from the Poland of 1772 as does the new society which we are rapidly approaching from present society.

'Another word. No one can enslave a nation with impunity.

13. Of 1772.

The three powers which murdered Poland have been severely punished. Let us look at my own fatherland, Prussia–Germany. In the name of national unification we have annexed Poles, Danes and Frenchmen – and we now have *a Venice three times over*;[14] we have enemies everywhere, we burden ourselves with debts and taxes in order to pay for countless masses of soldiers, who, at the same time, are used to oppress German workers. Austria – even official Austria – knows all too well what a burden its bit of Poland is. At the time of the Crimean War Austria was ready to march against Prussia on condition that Russian Poland was occupied and liberated. This, however, did not enter into the plans of Louis Napoleon and even less into the plans of Palmerston. And as far as Russia is concerned, we can see that in 1861 the first significant movement broke out among the students, which was all the more dangerous because the people everywhere were in a state of great agitation following the emancipation of the serfs; and what did the Russian government do, seeing, as it did, the danger? – *It provoked the uprising of 1863 in Poland*; for it has been *proved* that this uprising was its work. The movement among the students, the deep agitation among the people disappeared immediately and their place was taken by Russian chauvinism, which poured over Poland once the preservation of Russian rule in Poland was at stake. Thus, the first significant movement in Russia came to an end as a result of the pernicious struggle against Poland. Indeed, the reunification of Poland lies in the interests of revolutionary Russia and it is with pleasure that I learn this evening that this view corresponds with the convictions of the Russian revolutionaries' (who had expressed a similar view at the meeting).[15]

Marx spoke to this effect: 'The workers' party of Europe takes the most decisive interest in the emancipation of Poland and the original programme of the International Working Men's Association expresses the reunification of Poland as a working-class

14. In the province of Venice, under Austrian rule from 1798 to 1805 and from 1814 to 1866, the Italian national movement could only be kept down by a large and expensive military presence.

15. W. Smirnov, the editor of the Russian democratic newspaper *Vperiod (Forward)*, had stressed the common interest of the Russian and Polish workers.

political aim.[16] What are the reasons for this special interest of the workers' party in the fate of Poland?

'First of all, of course, sympathy for a subjugated people which, with its incessant and heroic struggle against its oppressors, has proven its historic right to national autonomy and self-determination. It is not in the least a contradiction that the *international* workers' party strives for the creation of the Polish nation. On the contrary; only after Poland has won its independence again, only after it is able to govern itself again as a free people, only then can its inner development begin again and can it cooperate as an independent force in the social transformation of Europe. As long as the independent life of a nation is suppressed by a foreign conqueror it inevitably directs all its strength, all its efforts and all its energy against the external enemy; during this time, therefore, its inner life remains paralysed; it is incapable of working for social emancipation. Ireland, and Russia under Mongol rule, provide striking proof of this.

'Another reason for the sympathy felt by the workers' party for the Polish uprising is its particular geographic, military and historical position. The partition of Poland is the cement which holds together the three great military despots: Russia, Prussia and Austria. Only the rebirth of Poland can tear these bonds apart and thereby remove the greatest obstacle in the way to the social emancipation of the European peoples.

'The main reason for the sympathy felt by the working class for Poland is, however, this: Poland is not only the only Slav race which has fought and is fighting as a *cosmopolitan soldier of the revolution*. Poland spilt its blood in the American War of Independence; its legions fought under the banner of the first French republic; with its revolution of 1830 it prevented the invasion of France, which had been decided upon by the partitioners of Poland; in 1846 in Cracow it was the first to plant the banner of revolution in Europe, in 1848 it had a glorious share in the revolutionary struggles in Hungary, Germany and Italy; finally, in 1871 it provided the Paris Commune with the best generals and the most heroic soldiers.

'In the brief moments when the popular masses in Europe have been able to move freely they have remembered what they owe to Poland. After the victorious March revolution of 1848 in Berlin

16. See 'Inaugural Address of the International Working Men's Association', above, p. 765.

the first act of the people was to set free the Polish prisoners, Mieroslawski and his fellow sufferers, and to proclaim the restoration of Poland;[17] in Paris in May 1848 Blanqui marched at the head of the workers against the reactionary National Assembly to force it into armed intervention on behalf of Poland; finally in 1871, when the French workers had constituted themselves as a government, they honoured Poland by giving its sons the leadership of its armed forces.[18]

'And at this moment, too, the German workers' party will not in the least be misled by the reactionary behaviour of the Polish deputies in the German Reichstag; it knows that these gentlemen are not acting for Poland but in their private interests; it knows that the Polish peasant, worker, in short, every Pole not blinded by the interests of social status, is bound to recognize that *Poland has and can only have one ally in Europe – the workers' party*.

'*Long live Poland!*'

17. Ludwig Mieroslawski was a leader of the 1846 Cracow uprising.
18. See p. 901, n. 71.

The Curtain Raised[1]

World, 18 JULY 1871

From our Special Correspondent
London, 1 July

... I went straight to my business. The world, I said, seemed to
be in the dark about the International, hating it very much, but not
able to say clearly what thing it hated. Some, who professed to
have peered further into the gloom than their neighbours, declared
that they had made out a sort of Janus figure with a fair, honest
workman's smile on one of the faces, and on the other a murderous conspirator's scowl. Would he light up the case of mystery in
which the theory dwelt?

The professor [*sic*] laughed, chuckled a little I fancied, at the
thought that we were so frightened of him.

'There is no mystery to clear up, dear sir,' he began, in a very
polished form of the Hans Breitmann dialect,[2] 'except perhaps
the mystery of human stupidity in those who perpetually ignore
the fact that our Association is a public one and that the fullest
reports of its proceedings are published for all who care to read
them. You may buy our rules for a penny, and a shilling laid out
in pamphlets will teach you almost as much about us as we know
ourselves.'

REPORTER: Almost – yes, perhaps so: but will not the something
I shall not know constitute the all-important reservation? To be
quite frank with you, and to put the case as it strikes an outside
observer, this general claim of depreciation of yours must mean
something more than the ignorant ill-will of the multitude.

1. This interview was conducted at Marx's home in Hampstead by the New York
World's reporter R. Landor. The reporter's introduction and conclusion have been
omitted.
2. After the 'Breitmann ballads' of Charles Godfrey Leland, which parodied the
speech of the German settlers in America.

1078 *The Curtain Raised*

And it is still pertinent to ask even after what you have told me, what is the International Society?

DR MARX: You have only to look at the individuals of which it is composed – workmen.

REPORTER: Yes, but the soldier need be no exponent of the statecraft that sets him in motion. I know some of your members, and I can believe that they are not the stuff of which conspirators are made. Besides, a secret shared by a million men would be no secret at all. But what if these were only the instruments in the hands of a bold, and I hope you will forgive me for adding, not over scrupulous conclave.

DR MARX: There is nothing to prove it.

REPORTER: The last Paris insurrection?[3]

DR MARX: I demand firstly the proof that there was any plot at all – that anything happened that was not the legitimate effect of the circumstances of the moment; or the plot granted, I demand the proofs of the participation in it of the International Association.

REPORTER: The presence in the Communal body of so many members of the Association.

DR MARX: Then it was a plot of the Freemasons, too, for their share in the work as individuals was by no means a slight one. I should not be surprised, indeed, to find the pope setting down the whole insurrection to their account. But try another explanation. The insurrection in Paris was made by the workmen of Paris. The ablest of the workmen must necessarily have been its leaders and administrators; but the ablest of the workmen happen also to be members of the International Association. Yet the Association as such may be in no way responsible for their action.

REPORTER: It will still seem otherwise to the world. People talk of secret instructions from London, and even grants of money. Can it be affirmed that the alleged openness of the Association's proceed-ings precludes all secrecy of communication?

DR MARX: What association ever formed carried on its work without private as well as public agencies? But to talk of secret instructions from London, as of decrees in the matter of faith and morals from some centre of papal domination and intrigue, is wholly to misconceive the nature of the International. This would imply a centralized form of government for the Inter-

3. I.e. the Paris Commune.

national, whereas the real form is designedly that which gives the greatest play to local energy and independence. In fact, the International is not properly a government for the working class at all. It is a bond of union rather than a controlling force.

REPORTER: And of union to what end?

DR MARX: The economical emancipation of the working class by the conquest of political power. The use of that political power to the attainment of social ends. It is necessary that our aims should be thus comprehensive to include every form of working-class activity. To have made them of a special character would have been to adapt them to the needs of one section – one nation of workmen alone. To have done that the Association must have forfeited its title of International. The Association does not dictate the form of political movements; it only requires a pledge as to their end. It is a network of affiliated societies spreading all over the world of labour. In each part of the world some special aspect of the problem presents itself, and the workmen there address themselves to its consideration in their own way. Combinations among workmen cannot be absolutely identical in Newcastle and in Barcelona, in London and in Berlin. In England, for instance, the way to show political power lies open to the working class. Insurrection would be madness where peaceful agitation would more swiftly and surely do the work. In France a hundred laws of repression and a mortal antagonism between classes seem to necessitate the violent solution of social war. The choice of that solution is the affair of the working classes of that country. The International does not presume to dictate in the matter and hardly to advise. But to every movement it accords its sympathy and its aid within the limits assigned by its own laws.

REPORTER: And what is the nature of that aid?

DR MARX: To give an example, one of the commonest forms of the movement for emancipation is that of strikes. Formerly, when a strike took place in one country it was defeated by the importation of workers from another. The International has nearly stopped all that. It receives information of the intended strike, it spreads that information among its members, who at once see that for them the seat of the struggle must be forbidden ground. The masters are thus left alone to reckon with their men. In most cases the men require no other aid than that. Their own subscriptions or those of the societies to which they are more immediately affiliated supply them with funds, but should the pressure upon them become too heavy and the strike be one of which the Association approves, their necessities are supplied out of the common purse. By these means a strike of the cigar-makers of Barcelona was brought to a victorious issue the other day.[4] But the society has no interest in strikes, though it supports them under certain conditions. It cannot possibly gain by them in a pecuniary point of view, but it may easily lose. Let us sum it all up in a word. The working classes remain poor amid the increase of wealth, wretched amid the increase of luxury. Their material privation dwarfs their moral as well as their physical stature. They cannot rely on others for a remedy. It has become then with them an imperative necessity to take their own case in hand. They must revise the relations between themselves and the capitalists and landlords, and that means they must transform society. This is the general end of every known workmen's organization; land and labour leagues,[5] trade and friendly societies, cooperative stores and cooperative production are but means towards it. To establish a perfect solidarity between these organizations is the business of the International Association. Its influence is beginning to be felt everywhere. Two papers spread its views in Spain, three in Germany, the same number in Austria and in Holland, six in Belgium, and six in Switzerland. And now that I have told you what the International is, you may, perhaps, be in a position to form your own opinion as to its pretended plots.

REPORTER: I do not quite understand you.

DR MARX: Do you not see that the old society, wanting the strength to meet it with its own weapons of discussion and combination, is obliged to resort to the fraud of fixing upon it the imputation of conspiracy?

REPORTER: But the French police declare that they are in a position to prove its complicity in the late affair, to say nothing of preceding attempts.

DR MARX: But we will say something of those attempts, if you please, because they best serve to test the gravity of all the

4. Either Marx or the reporter is in error here. The spring 1871 strike in Barcelona was of textile workers, while the strike of cigar workers in which the International intervened was in Belgium.

5. On the Land and Labour League, see the Introduction to this volume, p. 29, n. 47.

charges of conspiracy brought against the International. You remember the last 'plot' but one.[6] A plebiscite had been announced. Many of the electors were known to be wavering. They had no longer a keen sense of the value of the Imperial rule, having come to disbelieve in those threatened dangers from which it was supposed to have saved them. A new bugbear was wanted. The police undertook to find one. All combinations of workmen being hateful to them, they naturally owed to the International an ill turn. A happy thought inspired them. What if they should select the International for their bugbear, and thus at one stroke discredit that society and curry favour for the Imperial cause? Out of that happy thought came the ridiculous 'plot' against the emperor's life – as if we wanted to kill the wretched old fellow. They seized the leading members of the International. They manufactured evidence. They prepared their case for trial, and in the meantime they had their plebiscite. But the intended comedy was too obviously but a broad, coarse farce. Intelligent Europe, which witnessed the spectacle, was not deceived for a moment as to its character, and only the French peasant elector was befooled. Your English papers reported the beginnings of the miserable affair; they forgot to notice the end. The French judges, admitting the existence of the plot by official courtesy, were obliged to declare that there was nothing to show the complicity of the International. Believe me, the second plot is like the first. The French functionary is again in business. He is called in to account for the biggest civil movement the world has ever seen. A hundred signs of the times ought to suggest the right explanation – the growth of intelligence among the workmen, of luxury and incompetence among their rulers, the historical process now going on of that final transfer of power from a class to the people, the apparent fitness of time, place and circumstance for the great movement of emancipation. But to have seen these the functionary must have been a philosopher, and he is only a *mouchard*.[7] By the law of his being, therefore, he has fallen back upon the *mouchard*'s explanation – a 'conspiracy'. His old portfolio of forged documents will supply him with the proofs, and this time Europe in its scare will believe the tale.

6. On the summer 1870 trial of the Paris Internationalists, see p. 857, n. 3.
7. Police spy.

REPORTER: Europe can scarcely help itself, seeing that every French newspaper spreads the report.

DR MARX: Every French newspaper! See, here is one of them [taking up *La Situation*], and judge for yourself of the value of its evidence as to a matter of fact, [reads:] 'Dr Karl Marx, of the International, has been arrested in Belgium, trying to make his way to France. The police of London have long had their eye on the society with which he is connected, and are now taking active measures for its suppression.' Two sentences and two lies. You can test the truth of one story by the evidence of your own senses. You see that instead of being in prison in Belgium I am at home in England. You must also know that the police in England are as powerless to interfere with the International society as the society with them. Yet what is most regular in all this is that the report will go the round of the continental press without a contradiction, and could con-tinue to do so if I were to circularize every journal in Europe from this place.

REPORTER: Have you attempted to contradict many of these false reports?

DR MARX: I have done so till I have grown weary of the labour. To show the gross curiousness with which they are concocted I may mention that in one of them I saw Félix Pyat set down as a member of the International.

REPORTER: And he is not so?

DR MARX: The Association could hardly have room for such a wild man. He was once presumptuous enough to issue a rash proclamation in our name, but it was instantly disavowed, though to do them justice, the press of course ignored the disavowal.[8]

REPORTER: And Mazzini, is he a member of your body?

DR MARX [laughing]: Ah, no. We should have made but little progress if we had not got beyond the range of his ideas.

REPORTER: You surprise me. I should certainly have thought that he represented the most advanced views.

DR MARX: He represents nothing better than the old idea of a midd-le-class republic. We seek no part with the middle class. He has fallen as far to the rear of the modern movement as the

8. Félix Pyat, who dominated the London French branch of the International, compromised the Association by calling for the assassination of Louis Napoleon. See *IWMA* II, p. 224.

German professors, who, nevertheless, are still considered in Europe as the apostles of the cultured democratism of the future. They were so at one time – before '48, perhaps, when the German middle class, in the English sense, had scarcely attained its proper development. But now they have gone over bodily to the reaction, and the proletariat knows them no more.

REPORTER: Some people have thought they saw signs of a Positivist[9] element in your organization.

DR MARX: No such thing. We have Positivists among us, and others not of our body who work as well. But this is not by virtue of their philosophy, which will have nothing to do with popular government, as we understand it, and which seeks only to put a new hierarchy in place of the old one.

REPORTER: It seems to me, then, that the leaders of the new international movement have had to form a philosophy as well as an association for themselves.

DR MARX: Precisely. It is hardly likely, for instance, that we could hope to prosper in our way against capital if we derived our tactics, say, from the political economy of Mill. He has traced one kind of relationship between labour and capital. We hope to show that it is possible to establish another.

REPORTER: And as to religion?

DR MARX: On that point I cannot speak in the name of the society. I myself am an atheist. It is startling, no doubt, to hear such an avowal in England, but there is some comfort in the thought that it need not be made in a whisper in either Germany or France.

REPORTER: And yet you make your headquarters in this country?

DR MARX: For obvious reasons: the right of association is here an established thing. It exists, indeed, in Germany, but it is beset with innumerable difficulties: in France for many years it has not existed at all.

REPORTER: And the United States?

DR MARX: The chief centres of our activity are for the present among the old societies of Europe. Many circumstances have hitherto tended to prevent the labour problem from assuming an all-absorbing importance in the United States. But they are

9. The disciples of Auguste Comte. Edward Beesly, a London University professor and a leading figure of English Positivism, collaborated with Marx at this time in defending the Paris Commune. In this he was virtually unique among the British intelligentsia.

rapidly disappearing, and it is rapidly coming to the front there with the growth as in Europe of a labouring class distinct from the rest of the community and divorced from capital.

REPORTER: It would seem that in this country the hoped-for solution, whatever it may be, will be attained without the violent means of revolution. The English system of agitating by platform and press until minorities become converted into majorities is a hopeful sign.

DR MARX: I am not so sanguine on that point as you. The English middle class has always shown itself willing enough to accept the verdict of the majority so long as it enjoyed the monopoly of the voting power. But mark me, as soon as it finds itself outvoted on what it considers vital questions we shall see here a new slave-owners' war . . .[10]

R. LANDOR

10. Marx's reference here is to the North American civil war.

Index